WORKERS' COMPENSATION

CASES AND MATERIALS

Seventh Edition

■ ■ ■

by

Joseph W. Little
Professor of Law Emeritus
University of Florida

Thomas A. Eaton
J. Alton Hosch Professor of Law
University of Georgia

Gary R. Smith
Professor of Law Emeritus
Emory University

AMERICAN CASEBOOK SERIES®

WEST ACADEMIC PUBLISHING

Mat #41277998

444 Cedar Street, Suite 700
St. Paul, MN 55101
1-877-888-1330

Printed in the United States of America

ISBN: 978-0-314-28149-4

Gary R. Smith makes his dedication to the love of his life, his dear wife, Dr. Elizabeth Jane Wooten Smith

Thomas Eaton makes his dedication to Joanna, Amanda, Andy, Rice, Lynn, Connor and Kennedy

Joseph W. Little makes his dedication to the memory of the original editors of this book, Marcus L. Plant and Wex S. Malone

PREFACE

This book originates in the workers' compensation portion of Workers' Compensation and Employment Rights book by the late Wex S. Malone, the late Marcus L. Plant, and Joseph W. Little. That book itself sprang from an earlier workers' compensation text authored by Malone and Plant. Hence, this book returns full circle (except for Chapter 1) to an exclusive and concentrated focus on workers' compensation instead of the more generalized employment rights approach employed for the preceding fifteen or so years.

Two major factors explain the workers' compensation focus. Foremost is that the topic is important and rich enough to receive the full attention of an entire course and an entire book. The place of compensation for industrial injuries in our culture and law is not waning and neither is the need for lawyers who are educated to cope with the legal issues. Many, if not most, law schools offer courses in the subject. Workers' compensation also remains this country's longest standing, most comprehensive and most successful "tort reform." Moreover, a study of the workers' compensation system may yield valuable insights into contemporary tort reform proposals pertaining to other fields.

The second major reason for exclusive attention to workers' compensation is almost the mirror image of the first. Developments in other employment areas, e.g., OSHA, anti-discrimination, and social security, continue to produce new volumes of materials that collectively justify separate treatment independent of workers' compensation. Indeed, it has almost become too much of a task to press workers' compensation and the other employment rights topics into a single two or three hour course. Hence, we have opted for separation.

The basic structure of this book is generally modelled after the workers' compensation portion of its immediate predecessor. Nevertheless, each chapter has been thoroughly revised, adding new case and text materials and eliminating those portions that are superseded or outdated.

We know that we are bound to have made some mistakes in editing, in case selection, and in textual materials and urge the readers of the book to contact any of us with corrections, comments, and suggestions.

JOSEPH W. LITTLE
THOMAS A. EATON
GARY R. SMITH

February 2014

SUMMARY OF CONTENTS

TABLE OF CONTENTS

TABLE OF CASES

The principal cases are in bold type.

WORKERS' COMPENSATION

CASES AND MATERIALS

Seventh Edition

CHAPTER 1

EMPLOYEES' REMEDIES PRIOR TO AND APART FROM WORKERS' COMPENSATION

■ ■ ■

1. THE NEED FOR A WORKERS' COMPENSATION SYSTEM

A beginning student of workers' compensation might sensibly inquire, "What is the need for a special compensation system for work injuries?" Although a full answer requires a detailed examination of the history and interrelationship among the rate of production of injuries and death suffered by workers in industry, the law of torts as applied to work injuries, and the social structure for treating otherwise uncompensated injuries suffered by individuals, essential facts as they existed at the time the initial British workers' compensation act was enacted in 1906 can be succinctly put.

1. Industrial injuries were a virtual scourge of working people in the nineteenth and early twentieth centuries. This point is amplified below.
2. The law of torts was not a compensation system, but instead, was a means of making wrongdoers accountable for wrongful acts that caused harm. Hence, injuries that did not fit within the confines of tort law went uncompensated under it.
3. The notion of the welfare state was ill developed. Hence, unfortunate victims of injuries of any sort often had recourse only to uncertain and parsimonious charity.

This section elaborates the first point and the next the second. The third will be left to stand on its own, save as it is supported inferentially by the examination of the other two.

In modern times we know a lot about how many work injuries occur, why they occur, and what they cost. The data in Table 1 lend an inference that industry at large remains a dangerous and costly enterprise for the workers that make it go. These are consequences of an economy employing more than 140 million workers to produce a gross domestic product approaching $14 trillion.

Table 1: Work Injury Data*—2010

Numbers of Workers, Injuries, and Deaths**	
Total No. Workers	140,288,000
Total unintentional-injury-related deaths***	3,783
Medically Consulted Injuries****	5,100,000
Time Lost	
Time Lost in 2010 from 2010 injuries	60 million days
Time Lost in 2010 from pre-2010 injuries	40 million days
Estimated future time loss from 2009 injuries	50 million days
Financial Costs	
Total Costs 2010 work injuries	$ 176.9 billion
Wage and Productivity Losses 2010 work injuries	$ 86.8 billion
Medical Costs 2010 work injuries	$ 43.2 billion
Administrative Expenses 2010 work injuries	$ 32.0 billion
Cost per worker	$ 1,300
Cost per death	$ 1,350,000
Cost per medically consulted injury	$ 37,000
Workers' Compensation Payments (estimated) 2010*****	
Total payments	$ 57.5 billion
Medical and hospital	$ 28.1 billion
Wages	$ 29.5 billion

* Source: *Injury Facts*, 2012 Edition, National Safety Council, pages 58, and 62.

** The data in this table were extracted from *Injury Facts* 2012 Edition, National Safety Council, p. 52.

*** Bureau of Labor Statistics data from the Census of Fatal Occupational Injuries indicates an additional 780 deaths in 2011 due to intentional injuries (homicide and suicide).

**** A medically consulted injury is one that was serious enough that a medical professional was consulted.

***** Source: National Academy of Social Insurance, Worker's Compensation, Benefits, Coverage 2010 and Costs, August 2012.

These modern data, grim as the picture they depict may be, do not convey the danger inherent in nineteenth century industry in which machinery was more primitive and dangerous and the institutional concern for safety was much lower. Whereas empirical accounts of those days are imperfect, current observers captured them in dramatically descriptive accounts. One of the most telling is summed up in this 1893 statement of the first Secretary of the Interstate Commerce Commission:

> There is something appalling in the statement that more hardworking and faithful railway employees in the United States went down in sudden death last year than the entire number of Union men who died at the Battle of the Wilderness; nearly as many as those who died the bitter death at Spotsylvania; more than three times the number of the Union dead at Lookout Mountain, Missionary Ridge and Orchard Knob combined, and that more of the grand army of railway men of this country were cut and bruised and maimed and mangled last year than all the Union wounded and missing on the bloody field of Gettysburg; (and) nearly equal in number to the wounded and missing in the reign of death and devastation of Shiloh, first and second Bull Run and Antietam combined. . . .[1]

The probability of death or injury in certain occupations, particularly railroading, was fearful. For example, one commentator assessed "a brakeman's chances of dying a natural death in 1888 [as] 1 to 47" and the "average life expectancy of a switchman in 1893 [as] seven years."[2] Worse, many of the victims were children, especially in textile industries in which many women and children were employed. An 1888 account of the situation in England reported:

> Formerly accidents were a frequent source of mischief to the children employed in Cotton Mills, owing to the machinery not being sufficiently guarded; their fingers and hands were often crushed and lacerated, the skin and muscles being in some instances stripped off to the bone; and I have reason to believe . . . that this great evil still exists to a considerable extent.[3]

The same reporter made a "survey of a Manchester Sunday School that revealed that 45 per cent of the boys present 'were found to have been . . . injured in a greater or lesser degree,' " which was thought to understate the true injury rate among working children "since only the best conditioned part of them [factory children] attend Sunday Schools."[4]

---

[1] Melvin L. Griffith, "The Vindication of a National Public Policy Under the Federal Employers' Liability Act," 18 Law and Contemp. Prob. 160, 163 (1953), quoting Edward A. Moseley.

[2] Id., at 162, 163.

[3] P. Bartrip's, Workmen's Compensation in Twentieth Century Britain (1987), 3, quoting N. Gould.

These data and accounts of the physical risks are only a part of the story so far as injured workers are concerned. The other part, and often the larger part, was the consequences of industrial injuries and death to the economic and emotional well being of the victims. Again adverting to the nineteenth century, one observer concluded:

> Probably the most important requirement for a Victorian workman, in a largely full-employment but still relatively low-welfare society, was for a fit and healthy body. Only with such could he undertake the full-time work necessary to keep himself and his family in food, clothing and shelter without recourse to the dreaded Poor Law, private charity, or other forms of non-wage financial support. One of the greatest threats to bodily and material sufficiency, particularly for miners, railwaymen, merchant seamen and others in dangerous occupations, was provided by industrial injury without compensation.[4]

The remainder of this book deals primarily with the plan that is intended to minimize the threat of "industrial injury without compensation."

The modern reader will have concluded by now that society ought to spend at least as much energy in preventing injuries as in compensating them. Many people believe, quite wrongly, that nineteenth century tort law was deliberately shaped to remove the costs of industrial injuries from industry.[5] The truer view is that the industrial revolution imposed a hierarchy of remote institutional activity upon a common law legal system that was premised upon individual human accountability and that was unable to adjust to the peculiar demands of institutionalized risks.[6] For whatever reason nineteenth century industry lacked an industrial ethic to promote safety and to provide benefits when injuries did occur. As

---

4 Id. at 1.

5 There is an orthodox view of the negligence concept to which I believe most legal scholars and historians would subscribe that runs as follows: Until the nineteenth century a man was liable for harm caused by his accidents whether or not he was at fault; he acted at his peril. The no-fault standard of liability was relaxed in the nineteenth century under the pressure of industrial expansion and an individualistic philosophy that could conceive of no justification for shifting losses from the victim of an accident unless the injurer was blameworthy (negligent) and the victim blameless (not contributorily negligent). The result, however, was that accident costs were "externalized" from the enterprises that caused them to workers and other individuals injured as a byproduct of their activities.

R. Posner, "A Theory of Negligence," 1 J.Legal Studies 29 (1972).

6 After extensive examination of late nineteenth century and early twentieth century appellate decisions, Posner concluded, "I discern no systematic bias in the law of negligence as it was applied between 1875 and 1905 in favor of industrial growth and expansion. . . ." Id., at 73. This conclusion, while probably correct, neglects the historic fact that the law of negligence had been mainly fixed in its primary features before 1875. Better proof of the point that the makers of the law were not in some sort of sub silentio conspiracy with the captains of industry is obtained by textual examination of the facts of the precedential decisions almost all of which arose in pre-industrial revolution contexts.

a result the cost of industrial injuries was borne primarily by workers and their families. A major factor in this was that the law pertaining to liability for industrial injuries created no incentive for the captains of industry to prefer safety over injuries. Despite this, some judges were aware that broad economic consequences of tort law had the power to induce safer workplaces. This was adverted to in Justice O'Neall's dissenting opinion in Murray v. South Carolina Railroad Company [see Section 2] wherein he said:

> But, it is said, it would be impolitic to make the defendants liable for any injury accruing to a fireman, from the neglect of the engineer. This would be worth inquiring into with great care in the Legislature; but, in a Court, I think we have nothing to do with the policy of a case; the law of it is our guide. But if we are to look to the policy, then I should argue that the more liability imposed on the railroad company, the more care and prudence would be thereby elicited. This result is what the community desires. For it secures life and property, committed to their care.

The remainder of this chapter provides a brief overview of various strategies that have been employed in efforts to alleviate the hardships created by workplace injury and diseases. Any comprehensive approach to this goal must strive both to prevent injuries and to compensate those that occur. In the United States, positive regulation of workplace safety was left primarily to the individual states until Congress enacted the Occupational Safety and Health Act (OSHA) in 1970. That Act and its state counterparts constitute the current central regulatory mechanism to avoid workplace injuries. Section 4 describes the basic structure, operation, and limitations of OSHA.

The compensation objective is to alleviate the economic consequences of injury to the individual worker.[7] While workers' compensation laws constitute the current legally mandated mechanism to provide economic assistance to disabled workers, it is but one of many possible approaches. Section 2 of this chapter examines the application of tort law to workplace injuries with particular emphasis on the doctrinal limitations on liability that existed at the time most workers' compensation laws were initially adopted. Section 3 briefly explores statutory schemes other than workers' compensation, with special emphasis on the Federal Employers' Liability Act (FELA) and social security.

---

[7] Of course, the goals of injury prevention and compensation are not entirely separate. The central insight of the law and economics movement is that liability for payment of compensation may create an incentive to reduce risk. See G. Calabresi, The Cost of Accidents (1970). One critical factor in evaluating various compensation systems is their impact on safety incentives. See R. Victor, Workers' Compensation and Workplace Safety: The Nature of Employer Financial Incentives (1982).

2. THE COMMON LAW AS APPLIED TO EMPLOYEES' WORKPLACE INJURIES

The story of industrial accidents and the law is filled with striking incongruities. Nearly everywhere today, two radically different methods exist side by side for determining the claims of injured employees against their employers. These methods stand in sharp opposition to each other both in theory and in practical effect; yet the choice between them may be determined by seemingly trivial considerations. Even today, some employments are not covered by workers' compensation statutes, injured employees will be obliged to prove that their employers were negligent to obtain a tort recovery, and some may be required to prove that they, the employees, were not aware of the danger created by that negligence. Furthermore, in some jurisdictions employees may not be permitted to recover if the injuries suffered were caused by the negligence of a fellow employee. Like other plaintiffs in negligence suits these employees may see their recoveries diminished (or even barred in a few jurisdictions) as a result of their own contributory negligence.

In contrast, other injured employees, whose situations are indistinguishable except for their being employed in employments covered by workers' compensation statutes, will succeed in establishing claims for compensation. They will recover by merely showing that, while working, they were hurt by a cause that arose out of work. Neither their own negligence nor that of their employers or fellow employees will bar or diminish their entitlement to benefits. But, although their chances of recovery are thus immeasurably enhanced, they will often recover benefits in amounts less commensurate with the losses suffered as measured by principles of tort damages. Rather than recover an amount that covers all economic and non-economic losses, they will be granted a sum fixed by statute that represents only a part of lost wages. This award is called compensation. They will also receive reimbursement for some or all of the medical and rehabilitation costs of curing the injuries and coping with their effects.

In making comparisons between these two systems, the reader should bear in mind that the vast majority of American workers is now covered by workers' compensation laws. Hence, as to most work injuries, the discussion of antecedent tort doctrines provides historical setting rather than the current legal basis for recovering against employers for work place injuries and deaths. In contrast, the rules of tort apply to non-employment injuries.

How tort law failed to satisfy the need for a general work injury compensation scheme is briefly summarized in succeeding paragraphs.

A. THE FELLOW SERVANT DEFENSE

Negligence law was in its earliest stages when the English courts were first called upon to fix the rights of an injured employee against his employer in Priestley v. Fowler (1837) 3 M & W 1, 150 Eng.Rep. 1030. The plaintiff was injured when a van, negligently overloaded by a fellow servant, broke down and threw him violently to the ground. The plaintiff sued his employer, claiming that the employer was vicariously liable to him for the negligent acts of his co-worker. Lord Abinger, C.B., denied recovery in a judgment that dwelt at length upon the consequences (regarded by him as absurd) which could follow if a master were made responsible to one servant for harm inflicted through the negligence of his fellow servants. Abinger's attention was focused upon simple accidents occurring within a typical master-servant relationship in which masters and servants often worked side by side in workshops.

At that time servants, even those in commercial rather than purely domestic pursuits, were often members of the master's household. Consequently, they were thought to be entitled to no more care than were the master himself and members of his household. The appreciation of how advanced industrial and transportation employments institutionalized risks and separated employees physically from employers still lay ahead at the time of the decision. Nevertheless, Priestley v. Fowler fixed common law precedents that later were applied in the new and different contexts. That decision is regarded as the fountainhead of two distinct, but related, propositions: first, the principle of respondeat superior making the master vicariously liable for the torts of the servant does not apply where the suit is by one servant against the master for the negligence of a fellow servant; and, second, a worker, by accepting employment, assumes the risk of being injured or killed by reason of dangerous working conditions that an alert worker would discover. For these the master is therefore not responsible.

The introduction at this particular time in history of the fellow-servant rule and the doctrine of implied assumption of risk was disastrous for worker safety. It came immediately on the development of the steam propelled railroad and the emergence of the factory age. The coming of the industrial revolution brought a profound change in the relationship of employers to employees. Enterprise came to be conducted through the agency of corporations which were incapable of any personal fault and could act only through agents or employees. The owners of capital and even the factory bosses no longer worked side by side with the general employees, as in the pre-industrial era, but became physically separated. The idea that employers and employees were equally exposed to all the risks of the employment was no longer true. But cases like Priestley v. Fowler, coupled with a rigid view of *stare decisis,* disabled the courts from taking a fresh look at what care the general principles of the evolving law of negligence should demand from employers to protect employees in the drastically different industrial setting. For this reason the fellow-servant rule as applied in cases such as the one that follows, threatened to extinguish any prospect of employers' tort liability for negligent injuries suffered by transportation and industrial workers.

JAMES MURRAY V. SOUTH CAROLINA RAILROAD COMPANY

26 S.C.L. 385, 36 Am.Dec. 268.
(Charleston. Feb., 1841).

Before O'NEALL, J., BARNWELL, July Extra Term, 1838.

This was an action on the case, against the defendants, for an injury sustained in their service.

The plaintiff is a tailor by trade. He resided at Aiken, and applied to Capt. Robertson, the agent of the company, for employment. He declined employing him, on account of his intemperate habits and consequent rashness. He, however, went on to Charleston, and was employed as a second fireman, on the 18th of May. He selected the engine and engineer to which he was to be attached and under whom he was to serve. William E. Perry was the engineer.

About the 27th of May, 1837, the plaintiff's second or third trip, as the engine was ascending the road from Charleston, near the Four Hole Swamp, just before entering an excavation, and within about three hundred yards of it, one of the witnesses (Johnson, the first fireman) said he saw a horse standing near the commencement of the excavation, within ten steps of the road, feeding slowly towards it: he touched the engineer on the back, and asked him if he saw the horse; he made no reply: the engine ran on: the plaintiff said to the engineer, "stop we are in danger:" the engine still proceeded, until within fifty or sixty yards of the horse: this witness said he then put his hand on the "escape steam valve," and told the engineer again to stop, for there was danger of running over the horse, and pointed towards him: he, the engineer, then shut off the steam: by this time the horse stepped upon the road, and there stood: the engine with the steam shut off, ran within six or eight feet of the horse: the engineer gave her all the steam she could carry, to carry her as quick as possible, and with the least danger, over the horse. At this moment, this witness took hold of the awning post, and swung himself outside the engine, for the purpose of jumping off on the left hand side of it: in this position he could see under the engine which struck and ran over the horse: as it left the road on the right hand side, the witness jumped off on the left. His post was on the left, and the plaintiff's on the right, of the engine: the brake to stop the engine was on the right, and nearer the plaintiff than the witness: when the engineer shut off the steam, the brake was not let down: (he said he was too much agitated by fear to think of the brake:) had it been let down, the engine might have been stopped.

As the engine left the road, the plaintiff's leg dropped between the foot board of the engine and tender, and as these two came violently together, when the engine stopped, his leg was crushed, and his thigh was afterwards amputated midway. This witness gave it as his opinion, very distinctly, that the accident might have been avoided, and resulted from the carelessness of the engineer, in not stopping the engine as soon as cautioned: he thought that as the engine was running only at the rate of ten or twelve miles per hour, it might have been stopped before they reached the horse. He said it was not the fireman's duty to let down the brake, unless ordered by the engineer.

Meredith, the conductor of the train, said, just as they emerged from an excavation, he saw the horse about fifteen yards from the road, moving from behind some bushes, and running in an oblique direction towards the road, and in the direction the engine was pursuing; he ran thus about twenty yards, when he leaped upon the road between the rails, just at the entrance of another excavation: as he did so, the engine struck him, and passed over him, and was thrown off the track. The engine was running from sixteen to twenty miles an hour. From the time this witness saw the horse, he said that he thought the only way to avoid him was to outrun him. He said, that to stop the engine, it is the duty of the engineer to shut off the steam, and the firemen to let down the "brake;" it is, however, the engineer's duty to order the fireman to let down the brake.

Perry was proved to be a skillful professional engineer. The witnesses, Robertson and Ross, concurred in saying, that it was the duty of the engineer to shut off the steam, and the fireman to let down the brake (and that was the particular duty of the second fireman) whether ordered by the engineer or not to stop the engine and prevent any accident. About three hundred feet is as short a space as within which the engine can be stopped, when running at the average rate of fifteen miles an hour.

The jury were instructed that the plaintiff's service subjected him to all the ordinary risks and perils of the employment. Each officer of the company, as to strangers and inferiors, was to be considered as the company; and every command or act given or done by him, must be regarded as given or done by the company themselves. If a superior officer had given an order to an inferior, to do an act not necessary to be done, and not within the duty of the inferior, and in doing it, injury resulted to the inferior, then the company would be responsible. If, in running the road, a superior officer (the engineer) did his duty so carelessly as to subject a servant of the company to unnecessary danger, and which the servant could not avoid, then the company would be liable. But if the peril, from which the injury resulted, was unavoidable, or if the engineer did every thing ordinary prudence suggested, to avoid it—and, notwithstanding, a servant sustained injury, it would be one of the risks to which his contract of service subjected him, and he could not recover. So, too, if the servant (the second fireman,) did not do his duty, and to its neglect (as not letting down the brake) the injury might be fairly ascribed, then, in that case, his injury would be attributable to himself and he could have no redress against the company.

The facts under these instructions, were submitted to the jury. I thought, and still think, there was very little proof to justify a verdict, but still that little may sustain the verdict, $1500, found by the jury for the plaintiff.

The defendants appeal, on the annexed grounds.

Grounds of Appeal

1. Because the plaintiff, being a fireman actually employed on the car to which the accident occurred, cannot recover against the company in whose service he was.

2. Because the ordinary risks of the occupation of the plaintiff are to be sustained by himself, and the accident was the result of such risks.

3. Because the plaintiff himself was partly in charge of the car to which the accident occurred, and might have prevented it himself, by the timely discharge of his own duty.

4. Because the plaintiff, being a tailor by trade, imposed himself upon the company as fireman, and the accident is attributable to his own negligence and want of skill.

5. Because it was clearly proved, that there was no want of skill or diligence on the part of the engineer, or other servants of the company.

6. Because the accident itself was unavoidable, and the verdict is contrary to the evidence in all these particulars.

Curia, per EVANS, J.

In the consideration of the question involved in this case, I shall assume that the verdict establishes the fact that the plaintiff's injury was the effect of the negligence of the engineer, and then the question arises whether the railroad company is liable to one servant for an injury arising from the negligence of another servant. The business of the company is the transportation of goods and passengers. Its liability in these respects, is, in general, well defined and understood by the profession; and if the plaintiff's case came within any of the principles applicable to these cases, we should have no difficulty in deciding it. The application of steam power to transportation on railroads, is of recent origin, but the principle by which the liability of a carrier is fixed and ascertained, is as old as the law itself. There is nothing in the fact, that the defendant is a corporation, except that of necessity it must act altogether by agents. The liability is precisely the same as if the defendant was an individual acting by the agency of others.

The principle is the same, whether you apply it to a railroad, a steamboat, a wagon, a stage coach, or a ship. If this plaintiff is entitled to recover, I can see no reason why the owner of any of the above modes of conveyance, should not be liable under the same circumstances. If the owner of a wagon should employ two men, one to drive and the other to load, and either of them should so negligently perform his work as to injure the other, the owner of the wagon would be liable. The principle will extend to all the vocations of life wherein more than one person is employed to effect a single object; and a new class of liabilities would arise, which I do not think has ever heretofore been supposed to exist. It is admitted, no case like the present has been found, nor is there any precedent suited to the plaintiff's case, unless he stands in the relation of a passenger to the company. In this point of view, his counsel has chosen to regard him, for I understand the declaration alleges he was a passenger. Now, a passenger is every where spoken of as one who pays for transportation. In all the operations necessary for this, he is passive. The moment he becomes an operator, for then his character is changed, he becomes the servant of the company, and not its passenger. It would be a confusion of terms so to regard him. He is no more a passenger than a sailor or a stage driver. There is nothing in the definition of bailment, or the classification of the different kinds of liability growing out of that relation, which applies to the plaintiff's case, and if he is entitled to recover, it must be on principles which apply equally to all operations of life in which agents are employed. There is no question that, in general, the principal is liable for the acts of the agent, performed in the execution of his agency, or in and about the business of his principal. Thus, the owners of a railroad would be liable to passengers for an injury sustained by the negligence of any of its servants, superior or subordinate, because it is implied in the undertaking to carry, not only that the road and cars are good, but that the servants employed are competent and will perform their duty.

For the loss of goods, the law annexes a still greater responsibility. So, also, if one employ an agent to execute any work whereby an injury may result to a stranger, the law requires it to be done with care, and if a stranger sustain an injury, his principal is liable, as was decided in O'Connell v. Strong (Dud.Rep. 265.)

But the plaintiff is neither a passenger nor a stranger, and if he can recover, it must be in his hermaphrodite character as a passenger fireman. In the cases above enumerated, the principal is represented by the agent, and unless he is liable, the great operations of life cannot be carried on—no man would have adequate security for his person or his property. The owner of goods would not trust them on a railroad, or a steamboat, if his only security was the liability of the mere servants employed. No passenger would commit his safety to a railroad, steamboat, or stage coach, if, in case of injury, he could look to none but the agents usually employed about these modes of transportation. So, also, no man would have any guarantee for the security of his property, if his only remedy for negligence was the irresponsible or insolvent agents which another might employ. In all these, and similar cases, the reasons of the liability of the principal are clear, and the law books are full of cases or precedents which apply to them; but it is not so with the plaintiff's case; there is neither authority nor precedent for it.

It was said, in the argument, that if the engineer had been the owner of the road, he would have been liable. Of this I apprehend there would have been no doubt, but then his liability would have arisen, not from his being the owner, but because the injury arose from his own act. That he is now liable, seems to me to admit of no doubt. But it by no means follows as a consequence, that because he is liable, those who employ him are liable also. One acting as agent may subject himself to liability in a variety of cases, for which his principal would not be liable; and this may be as well in cases of contract as in cases of tort. The extent of the liability of the principal, for the acts of the agent, can, in general, be readily ascertained from the object of the contract, and the relative position of the parties. A passenger desires to be transported from one place to another; the carrier undertakes to do this, and is liable if he fails. It is wholly immaterial by whose default the injury resulted. There has been a breach of the contract, and he has a right to look to him with whom his contract was made.

With the plaintiff, the defendants contracted to pay hire for his services. Is it incident to this contract that the company should guarantee him against the negligence of his co-servants? It is admitted he takes upon himself the ordinary risks of his vocation; why not the extraordinary ones? Neither are within his contract—and I can see no reason for adding this to the already known and acknowledged liability of a carrier, without a single case or precedent to sustain it. The engineer no more represents the company than the plaintiff. Each in his several department represents his principal. The regular movement of the train of cars to its destination, is the result of the ordinary performance, by each, of his several duties. If the fireman neglects his part, the engine stands still for want of steam; if the engineer neglects his, everything runs to riot and disaster. It seems to me, it is, on the part of the several agents, a joint undertaking, where each one stipulates for the performance of his several part. They are not liable to the company for the conduct of each other, nor is the company liable to one for the misconduct of another; and, as a general rule, I would say, that where there was no fault in the owner, he would be liable only for wages to his servants; and so far has this doctrine been carried, that in the case of seamen, even wages are forfeited if the vessel be lost, and no freight earned.

In the above observations, I have endeavored to confine myself strictly to the case before the Court. It is not intended to prejudge other questions, which may arise between the company and its servants; nor do I mean to say, that a case may not occur where the owner, whether an individual or company, will be liable for the acts of one agent to another; but then it must be in such cases as where the owner employs unfit and improper persons as agents, by whose ignorance or folly another is injured. Upon such a case it will be time enough to express an opinion when it arises. The present is not such a case. The engineer, according to the evidence, was competent, though he may have been rash in the particular instance in which the plaintiff's injury was sustained. He was known to the plaintiff as well as to the company, for it appears by the report that he selected the engineer under whom he was willing or prepared to serve. It seems to me the plaintiff is not, therefore, entitled to retain his verdict, and a motion for a new trial is granted.

RICHARDSON, EARLE, BUTLER, HARPER, DUNKIN, JJ. and CC., concurred.

JOHNSON, CHANCELLOR.

I concur in this opinion, and will only add a word in illustration of my own views of the question.

The foundation of all legal liability, is the omission to do some act which the law commands, the commission of some act which the law prohibits, or the violation of some contract by which the party is injured. There is no law regulating the relative duties of the owners of a steam car, and the persons employed by them to conduct it. The liability, if any attaches, must therefore arise out of contract. What was the contract between these parties? The plaintiff, in consideration that the defendants would pay him so much money, undertook to perform the service of fireman on the train. This is all that is expressed. Is there anything more implied? Assuming that the injury done, was in consequence of the negligence of the engineer, the defendants would not be liable, unless they undertook to answer for his diligence and skill. Is that implied? I think not. The law never implies an obligation in relation to a matter about which the parties are or may, with proper diligence, be equally informed. No one will ever be presumed to undertake for that which a common observer would at once know was not true. The common case of the warranty of the soundness of a horse, notoriously blind, may be put in illustration. The warranty does not extend to the goodness of the eyes, because the purchaser knew or might have known, with proper care, that they were defective.

Now the plaintiff knew that he was not to conduct the train alone. He knew that he was to be placed under the control of the engineer. He knew that the employment in which he was engaged was perilous, and that its success was dependent on the common efforts of all the hands; and, with proper diligence and prudence, he might have been as well, and it does not follow that he might not have been better informed than the defendants, about the fitness and security of all the appointments connected with the train. If he was not, is it was his own want of prudence, for which defendants are not responsible. If he was, he will be presumed to have undertaken to meet all the perils incident to the employment.

There is not the least analogy between this case and that of common carriers of goods or transporters of persons. They are liable in respect to the price paid. Not so here. The plaintiff paid nothing for his transportation; on the contrary, he was to be paid for his labor, and for the perils to which he was exposed, as incident to his employment. No prudent man would engage in any perilous employment, unless seduced by greater wages than he could earn in a pursuit unattended by any unusual danger.

O'NEALL, J., dissenting.

This case was tried by myself, and although, had I been on the jury, I should have found for the defendants, yet there were certainly facts in the evidence, which might have led another to a different conclusion; and, therefore, I am not disposed to disturb the verdict. This makes it necessary to consider the legal doctrine which I laid down to the jury.

In substance, I held, that if the injury to the plaintiff resulted from the negligence of the engineer, then the plaintiff was entitled to recover. This doctrine, a large majority of my brethren think erroneous, and however much deference is due to their opinions, yet, as I consider them to be wrong, I think it my duty to state my own views.

This case is one of the first arising out of the conveyance of human beings by locomotives on railroads. It goes beyond the ordinary case of a passenger, and presents a claim on the part of a hired servant, against his employers, for an injury sustained in their service. If it arose out of any of the old-fashioned modes of conveyance, managed by the defendants themselves, could there be a doubt that they would be liable, if the injury resulted from negligence? Take the case of a stage coach, driven by the owner, and let it be supposed that the plaintiff was hired as a guard, and that he was injured in that employment, by the careless driving of the defendant, who would hesitate to say that he was entitled to recover? No one who had a proper regard to legal principles.

Is there any distinction in law as to the effect which the employment of the plaintiff is to have, in the different kinds of service in which he may engage? I think there is none. If Mr. Tupper, the able and efficient officer of the company, had, in person, managed the engine, and the plaintiff had been injured by his carelessness, I would most respectfully ask, how could it be pretended that the company was not liable?

I admit here, once and for all, that the plaintiff, like any other servant, took, as consequence of his contract, the usual and ordinary risks of his employment. What is meant by this? No more than that he could not claim for an injury, against which the ordinary prudence of his employers, their agents or himself, could provide. Whenever negligence is made out as the cause of injury, it does not result from the ordinary risks of employment.

How far are the defendants liable for the acts of the engineer? In the language used in Bacon's Abridgment, Tit. Master and Servant, letter R., "it is highly reasonable that they should answer for such substitute, at least civiliter; and that his acts, being pursuant to the authority given him, should be deemed the acts of the master." Now, to this authority, it will not do to say the defendants did not authorize the engineer to run his engine so carelessly as to injure the plaintiff. They put him in command of it, and authorized him with it to run the road. If, in the doing of this act, which is according to their authority, he acts negligently, then they are liable for the consequences, for they result from the doing of their business, by one then employed by them. The cases of Drayton ads. Moore, and Parker & Co. v. Gordon (Dudley's Rep. 268 [270].) and of O'Connell v. Strong (Ib. 265.) are full to this point. In ordinary cases, this would not be questioned. But it is supposed that this case is not governed by the ordinary rules applicable to cases of liability, arising out of the relation of master and servant. I am at a loss to conceive any just reason for this notion. The law, it seems to me, is to be regarded as a general science, applicable to every case coming within the letter or the reason of the rule. Where it is within neither, it becomes an exception to it.

It is only necessary to state this case, to see that it is within both the letter and reason of the rule; for the defendants employ the plaintiff to act under the command of another of their servants. In such a case, the servant in command is in the place of the employers. When they hire another to engage in a service, where neither his own care nor prudence can shield him from injury, which may arise from the act of another of their agents, having the control of him, the question of their liability depends upon the care used by such superior agent. The ordinary rule in cases of hiring goods, is, that the hirer should use that degree of care which a prudent man would take of his own goods. If this degree of care is shown, then the hirer is not liable for any injury which may result to the goods hired. This rule, it seems to me, must, necessarily, be that which applies to this case. Is more favor to be bestowed on a man's goods than on his person? It would be strange that this should be so.

* * *

But, it is said, it would be impolitic to make the defendants liable for any injury accruing to a fireman, from the neglect of the engineer. This would be worth inquiring into with great care in the Legislature; but, in a Court, I think we have nothing to do with the policy of a case; the law of it is our guide. But if we are to look to the policy, then I should argue that the more liability imposed on the railroad company, the more care and prudence would be thereby elicited. This result is what the community desires. For it secures life and property, committed to their care.

I think the motion ought to be dismissed.

GANTT, J., concurred.

J. JOHNSTON, CH., also dissenting.

It may not diminish the force of the observations made by MR. JUSTICE O'NEALL, if I state very briefly the reasons which induce me to concur in his dissent.

It is admitted that the duties and liabilities between masters and hired servants result only from the nature and terms of the contract which forms the relation; and that neither party is allowed to extend or abridge the contract. That the master cannot exact other services than those stipulated for; nor, by any indirection, subject the servant to any other than the ordinary perils incident to the employment; and that if he does, by any agency whatever, or by any means, whether of design or negligence, accumulate upon the servant, while in the performance of his duty, any dangers beyond these inherent in the service itself, they fall upon the latter, not as a servant (for his contract does not bind him to endure them,) but as a man, and the law entitles him to redress.

* * *

The elements of the contract between him and the defendants are these: On their part, so far as they were to contribute to the propelling of the cars, that they would carry him safely; and, on his part, that on the trip he would perform certain offices. With respect to the last, he was their servant; with regard to the first, he was their passenger; and as their passenger they have crippled him. The distinction is plain, and the propriety of applying it would be as plain, if instead of being stationed where he was, he had only been a clerk, hired by the company to travel up and down in the cars, and take a minute of their operations. Yet, on principle, no discrimination can be drawn against him on account of his being a fireman, and not travelling clerk; because he had as little connection with, or control over, the department from which his injury sprang, or the agent to whom it was exclusively committed by the defendants, as if he had been assigned any imaginable duty in the remotest part of the train.

NOTES

1. Underlying the fellow-servant immunity were the notions of assumption of risk and mutuality of risk. In the formative era, the servant was as likely to expose the master to danger as vice versa and was equally able to look out for his own safety as was the master. Hence, servants and masters were under mutual obligations and had more or less equal capacities to look out for themselves and each other. That being so, the courts thought it natural to conclude that a servant had bargained away any claim to hold the employer responsible for any of the dangers normally incident to his employment. At first this even included dangers created by the master's direct negligence. An employee, recognizing that there was danger involved, by remaining at work was deemed to have accepted the situation. The fact that few servants had any prospect of alternative employment and thus had no real option to staying on the job except to surrender their livelihoods was never considered to be a compelling factor in the development of this body of law. The prospect of the carelessness of a fellow worker was merely one of the risks assumed. Bartonshill Coal Co. v. Reid (1858) 3 Macq. 266 (H.L.). Farwell v. The Boston and Worcester Rail Road Corporation, 45 Mass. 49 (1842). (Holding that when entering employment contracts, employees accept the proposition that fellow employees are better able to avoid injuring each other than are employers).

2. As evidence by the two powerful dissents in the South Carolina decision, the unfairness of the unbridled fellow servant rule as applied to injured workers in the industrial setting was not without its critics even at the very beginning. Moreover, nineteenth century doctrine evolved devices to soften the rigors of the rule. One was to acknowledge limitations as to who was a fellow servant for whose carelessness the employer was not responsible, and another was to treat certain activities as nondelegable duties of the master, whose breach, even by the direct negligence of a fellow servant, was chargeable to the master even as to an injured co-worker.

3. Because most work injuries to employees are now compensated under workers' compensation laws, the fellow servant defense is now rarely litigated. These facts have lead some courts to abolish the rule as serving no useful purpose. Buckley v. City of New York, 56 N.Y.2d 300, 452 N.Y.S.2d 331, 437 N.E.2d 1088 (1982) and Glass v. City of Chattanooga, 858 S.W.2d 312 (Tenn. 1993). Nevertheless, the defense could arise in employments not covered by workers' compensation in states where the defense has not been abrogated.

4. In England, the application of the fellow servant defense was first limited by the Employers' Liability Act, 1880. Section 1 of that Act provided:

Amendment of law.—Where personal injury is caused to a workman,

(1) By reason of any defect in the condition of the ways, works, machinery, or plant connected with or used in the business of the employer; or

(2) By reason of the negligence of any person in the service of the employer who has any superintendence entrusted to him whilst in the exercise of such superintendence; or

(3) By reason of the negligence of any person in the service of the employer whose orders or directions the workman at the time of the injury was bound to conform, and did conform, where such injury resulted from this having so conformed; or

(4) By reason of the act or omission of any person in the service of the employer, done or made in obedience to the rules or bylaws of the employer, or in obedience to particular instructions given by any person delegated with the authority of the employer in that behalf; or

(5) By reason of the negligence of any person in the service of the employer who has the charge or control of any signal, points, locomotive engine, or train upon a railway.

The workman, or in case the injury results in death, the legal personal representatives of the workman, and any persons entitled in case of death, shall have the same right of compensation and remedies against the employer as if the workman had not been a workman of nor in the service of the employer, not engaged in his work.

Did this Act entirely abrogate the rule? The Act also affected the assumption of risk defense, examined in the next section.

B. ASSUMPTION OF RISK

Individual accountability is deeply embedded in common law principles that provide the core of tort doctrines. Among these is the doctrine that courts will provide no relief to an injured person for a harm whose infliction the plaintiff consented to accept. In common law vernacular, particularly as employed in English courts, *"volenti non fit injuria."* This is, "He who consents cannot receive an injury."[8] In American jurisprudence the doctrine is more commonly referred to as *assumption of risk.*

Whether expressed as *volenti* or as assumption of risk an affirmative defense based upon consent evolved within the theory of negligence liability during the nineteenth century. The operative effect of the

[8] Black's Law Dictionary (4th Ed.)

consent-based defense was to defeat a plaintiff's action based upon negligence. Indeed, in the limited circumstances where still applicable, assumption of risk still defeats a negligence action.[9]

In its orthodox rigorous form, the consent-based defense is distinctively different from contributory negligence. It requires the defendant to prove:

1. The plaintiff *subjectively knew* of the exact risk involved;
2. The plaintiff *subjectively* appreciated the risk; and,
3. The plaintiff *voluntarily*, without compulsion, consented to accept the risk.

Each of these elements requires proof with the burden being upon the defendant.

Despite the rigor of the orthodox defense, application of *volenti non fit injuria* took on a curious expanded application in the employment sphere during the nineteenth century both in England and the United States. As expressed by Cockburn, C.J. in *Woodley v. The Metropolitan District Railway Company* (1876–77) LR 2 Ex. D. 384, 388 (CA 1877), "A man who enters on a necessarily dangerous employment with his eyes open takes it with all accompanying risks." Put another way, upon entering into employment, an employee assumes all the ordinary risks of a well regulated work place.[10]

Courts differed as to the correct conceptual meaning of this. Some took the view that the employer owed no duty of care to an employee as to risks that were readily observable to one "with his eyes open." Others, took the view that the employee *impliedly consented* to accept those risks; i.e., he impliedly *assumed the risks* inherent in the employment. Whatever its conceptual basis, the doctrine insulated employers from liability to workers who were hurt by employment risks that were in some sense observable or knowable, even if the risks were negligently created and the injured workers had not actually known of or observed them. Quite plainly, application of *volens* in this fashion ignored the strict

---

[9] Lambert v. Will Bros., 596 F.2d 799 (8th Cir. 1979); Kuehner v. Green, 436 So.2d 78 (Fla. 1983).

[10] As summarized by Lord Watson in Smith v. Baker & Sons (1891) A.C. 325, 354: "The maxim ('*Volenti non fit injuria*,') originally borrowed from the civil law, has lost much of its literal significance. A free citizen of Rome who, in concert with another, permitted himself to be sold as a slave, in order that he might share in the price, suffered a serious injury; but he was in the strictest sense of the terms *volens*. The same can hardly be said of a slater who is injured by a fall from the roof of a house; although he too may be *volens* in the sense of English law. In its application to questions between the employer and the employed, the maxim as now used generally imports that the workman had either expressly or by implication agreed to take upon himself the risks attendant upon the particular work which he was engaged to perform, and from which he has suffered injury. The question which has most frequently to be considered is not whether he voluntarily and rashly exposed himself to injury, but whether he agreed that, if injury should befall him, the risk was to be his and not his masters."

elements of *volenti non fit injuria*. It also virtually insulated employers from liability for work place injuries. Even worse, having little risk of being required to compensate injured workers, employers had equally little incentive to invest in work place safety. In consequence, nineteenth century work places were dangerous and few of the resulting injuries were compensable in the law of torts. Nevertheless, even in this stringent environment, the common law would not deem an employee to have been *volens* to a risk that an employer had actively concealed.

To provide workers some relief from the expansive *volens* doctrine, Parliament enacted the Employer Liability Act 1880.[11] Although it may be debatable as to whether the Act improved the plight of injured workers, it did modify the law of *volens* as applied to the employment sphere by placing employees injured on an employer's premises on the same legal footing as occupied by invited strangers there. As stated by Fry, L.J., in *Thomas v. Quartermaine* (1887) L.R. 18 Q. B. D. 685, 703 (CA 1887); "In a word then, my opinion is that the statute was intended to place the workman in the same position as stranger lawfully on the property by the invitation of the occupier, but in no higher or better position; that the maxim non fit *injuria* would apply in apposite circumstances to such a person; and that consequently it applies under the like circumstances to a servant suing under the statute."[12]

In the closing decades of the nineteenth century, some American jurisdictions also adopted statutes modifying the assumption of risk and fellow servant defenses. The provisions of the Federal Employer's Liability Act, which is still applicable in its sphere, are exemplary. See Appendix B.

The British Parliament adopted a workers' compensation act early in the twentieth century and thus aborted this line of development in English jurisprudence. States of the United States immediately commenced to enact workers' compensation statutes based upon the English model, and the movement extended itself to all the states when Mississippi enacted its first workers' compensation statute in 1948. As is demonstrated in later chapters of this text, these statutes have rendered the old common law defenses virtually without application within the employment sphere. Moreover, even in non-employment cases,[13] most common law jurisdictions now apply the *volens* doctrine only in its

---

[11] 2.43 § 44 Vic. C. 42. See note 4, pp. 16–17.

[12] Another section of the Act dealt with the fellow servant defense. As stated by Lord Watson in Smith v. Baker & Sons (1891) A.C. 325, 353: "The main, although not the sole, object of the Act of 1880, was to place masters who do not upon the same footing of responsibility with those who do personally superintend their works and workmen, by making them answerable for the negligence of those persons to whom they intrust the duty of superintendence, as if were there own."

[13] See e.g., Meistrich v. Casino Arena Attractions, 31 N.J. 44, 155 A.2d 90 (1959), and Kuehner v. Green, 436 So.2d 78 (Fla. 1983).

rigorous form and only to a small category of cases involving actual consent.

C. CONTRIBUTORY NEGLIGENCE

Contributory negligence was perhaps the least formidable of the employer defenses and remains so in the relatively few cases now invoking tort liability. In application to employment injuries the common law defense that an injured party who was contributorily negligent cannot recover from a negligent defendant is subject to the exceptions that a negligent employee may recover if the employer had the last clear chance, or was guilty of gross, wilful, or wanton negligence. Nevertheless, because industrial workers are regularly exposed to risks of injury through momentary forgetfulness or lack of caution, the defense, where it exists, often imposes a genuine obstacle to recovery. The following commentary briefly sums up many workplace contributory negligence decisions.

Where the alleged negligence of the employer is failure to provide a reasonably safe place to work or to furnish suitable tools or equipment, an employee who should have been aware of the danger and failed to take reasonable precautions to avoid it may be barred from recourse (or have recovery diminished under a modern comparative negligence rule). Nevertheless, the worker is not obliged to inquire as to latent defects, and may assume that the employer has made a reasonable inspection of the premises or equipment and has provided all necessary protection. Furthermore, an employee's knowledge of the existence of a defect does not necessarily compel a finding of contributory negligence if it appears that the worker was unaware of the threat to safety, and some courts refuse to apply contributory negligence to known and understood risks unless the apparent risk was imminent. Forgetfulness of a specific danger is not necessarily contributory negligence, particularly where the scene of the employee's operations is shifting constantly or where duties demand undivided attention. Some decisions hold that an employee who is ordered by a superior to encounter a known and understood risk or is assured that there is no danger, is not guilty of contributory negligence.

Employers' duties to correct dangerous conditions must normally be performed by the employees. Ordinarily, if the workers assigned to do these tasks are properly instructed and equipped for that work, they cannot recover if by chance they are injured by the defective conditions they are repairing. Similarly, if they neglect to do the job assigned them and the danger remains, they cannot recover if injured thereby.

The common law bar of recovery to a plaintiff whose own negligence was a cause of the injury has now been supplanted by diminished recovery under some variant of the comparative negligence doctrine in almost all common law jurisdictions. See, e.g., Hoffman v. Jones, 280 So.2d 431 (Fla.1973).

3. LEGISLATIVE REFORMS APART FROM WORKERS' COMPENSATION

Judicial decisions that expanded the common law duties of employers were only a reflection of the growing public concern for the financial insecurity of the working classes. This concern found an expression in the legislative halls as well. The chief target for action was the fellow-servant rule. In 1877 a committee of the House of Commons urged that the rule be substantially modified by statute. In response, the Parliament enacted the English Employer's Liability Act of 1880. Stats. 43 & 44. Vict.C. 42. This act, however, left contributory negligence and assumption of risk defenses unaffected. Its chief advantage for workers was to establish for England the vice principal doctrine, which was already in effect by virtue of judicial decisions in many United States jurisdictions. Finally, Parliament abolished the fellow-servant defense in 1948. Personal Injuries Act, 1948, 11 & 12, Geo. VI.C. 41, § 1. In addition, a multiplication of statutory duties (chiefly the Factories Acts of 1937, 1948, 1959, and 1961) substantially improved prospects that injured workers would be compensated for work injuries. Samuels, Factory Law (8th Ed.1969).

Although a few American states had enacted statutes for the benefit of workers prior to the enactment of the English Employer's Liability Act, these pertained mainly to railroad employees. The great tide of legislative reform did not swell until after 1880. The statutes varied considerably both in scope of coverage and in scope of the substantive changes. See 5 Labatt, Master and Servant (2d Ed.1913). Colorado was the first state to abolish the fellow-servant rule for all employments. Colo.Stat.Ann. (1911) § 2060. Most states were content to follow the English model and most confined even this reform to railway employees. Often, the acts amounted to no more than statutory recognition of earlier judicial modifications of the fellow-servant rule. See, e.g., Shohoney v. Quincy, O. & K.C.R. Co., 231 Mo. 131, 132 S.W. 1059 (1910).

A. VIOLATION OF STATUTE

Under general negligence doctrine a court may treat a penal statute or regulation pertaining to safety of employees as particularizing the standard of care employers owe employees, thereby making a violation negligence per se. Bayne v. Todd Shipyards Corp., 88 Wash.2d 917, 568 P.2d 771 (1977). The statute or regulation must be intended to protect employees of the claimant's class against the particular risk encountered. Restatement, Second, Torts § 288. In addition, courts are inclined to treat violations of statutes with more general purposes as evidence of negligence rather than as negligence per se. Restatement, Second, Torts § 288(B)2.

The Federal Occupational Safety and Health Act of 1970 (OSHA), examined in more detail hereafter, was designed to avoid workplace injuries by imposing positive obligations upon employers to comply with workplace safety standards and regulations. Nevertheless, OSHA creates no new basis to compensate injuries but is wholly preventive in approach. The measure contains the following provision to minimize its effect in civil proceedings for damages:

> Nothing in this Chapter shall be construed to supersede or in any manner affect workmen's compensation law or to enlarge or diminish or affect in any other manner the common law statutory rights, duties, or liabilities of employers and employees under any law with respect to injuries, diseases, or death of employees arising out of, or in the course of employment. 29 U.S.C.A. § 653(B)(4).

Accordingly, the courts have generally held that a violation of OSHA or of regulations promulgated thereunder cannot serve as the independent basis for a civil suit for damages. See, e.g., Pedraza v. Shell Oil Co., 942 F.2d 48, 52 (1st Cir.1991). Nevertheless, this restriction against a new basis of liability does not prevent a court from instructing a jury in a proper case that an employer's violation of OSHA can be considered as evidence of negligence or even as negligence per se. Id. at 264. A state-by-state summary of the evidentiary impact of OSHA standards can be found in M. Rothstein, Occupational Safety and Health Law § 513.

B. FEDERAL RAILROAD SAFETY ACTS

The first federal employee safety legislation was the Safety Appliance Act of 1893, 27 Stat. 531 (1893), which related to braking systems and car couplers for rail carriers in interstate commerce. The Act prescribed penalties for violations but provided no express right of action by injured persons. It did, however, limit the operation of common law defenses as follows:

> Any employee of any such common carrier who may be injured by any locomotive, car, or train in use contrary to the provision of this act shall not be deemed thereby to have assumed the risk thereby occasioned, although continuing in the employment of such carrier after the unlawful use of such locomotive, car, or train has been brought to his knowledge.

A companion statute, the Boiler Inspection Act, was enacted in 1911.

Although neither of these statutes created a new basis of liability, both had the effect of extending the reach of negligence liability under the theories discussed above. See, e.g., San Antonio & Aransas Pass Ry. Co. v. Wagner, 241 U.S. 476, 36 S.Ct. 626, 60 L.Ed. 1110 (1916) (liability for violation constitutes "negligence" under FELA) and Brady v. Terminal R.R. Ass'n, 303 U.S. 10, 58 S.Ct. 426, 82 L.Ed. 614 (1938) (liability is established in a claim similar to a common law suit for negligence.) Recovery under the safety statutes is not restricted to employees of the offending carrier. Brady permitted an employee of one railroad to recover against a connecting carrier that delivered a defective car to plaintiff's employer. Because the claimant was a railroad employee, the safety statute's abolition of assumption of risk applied.

C. FEDERAL EMPLOYERS' LIABILITY ACT

In the early twentieth century, the railroad industry was both the largest and most dangerous source of employment. In 1907, 11,839 of an estimated one million railroad workers were killed in occupationally-related incidents. Elkind, Should the Federal Employers' Liability Act Be Abolished?, 17 The Forum 415, 418 (1981). It is not surprising, then, that the railroad industry became the focal point of reform when Congress enacted the Federal Employers' Liability Act (FELA) in 1906. The Supreme Court quickly invalidated the statute under the commerce clause jurisprudence of the day as an unconstitutional regulation of *intrastate commerce,* Employers' Liability Cases, 207 U.S. 463, 28 S.Ct. 141, 52 L.Ed. 297 (1908), but Congress reenacted it in 1908 in a constitutional form that regulated only interstate railroad activities.

FELA is not a no-fault compensation system and retains many of the basic characteristics of tort litigation. [Organized labor did not support the passage of the FELA, but favored the creation of a federal no fault compensation system for injured railroad workers. Elkind, Should the Federal Employers' Liability Act Be Abolished?, 17 The Forum 415 (1981).] Under it, the obligation to compensate an injured worker is conditioned upon proof of employer fault and the measure of recovery is full compensatory damages. Nevertheless, FELA modifies common law tort doctrine in several important respects. The 1908 Act adopted a pure comparative negligence standard, except that the employee's negligence would not reduce recovery where the injury was caused by the employer's violation of a federal safety statute or regulation. Moreover, the defense of assumption of risk was eliminated in cases involving violations of safety statutes.

In 1939, Congress substantially expanded FELA's its scope to include "any employee . . . whose duties . . . shall be the furtherance of interstate or foreign commerce . . . or shall, in any way directly or closely and substantially, affect such commerce. . . ." This language brought clerical employees and others not directly involved in the more dangerous aspects of railroading under FELA's protection. This aspect of the 1939 amendments played a major role in the Supreme Court's post-New Deal expansion of the reach of the commerce clause. See, Reed v. Pennsylvania Railroad Co., 351 U.S. 502, 76 S.Ct. 958, 100 L.Ed. 1366 (1956). The 1939 amendments also abolished the assumption of risk defense in all cases. See, Tiller v. Atlantic Coast Line R.R. Co., 318 U.S. 54, 63 S.Ct. 444, 87 L.Ed. 610 (1943).

FELA doctrine has continued to evolve primarily through judicial interpretation. In reading the following case, the student should consider the similarities and differences between a claim brought under FELA and one pursued under traditional principles of state tort law.

ARMSTRONG V. KANSAS CITY SOUTHERN RAILWAY COMPANY

United States Court of Appeals, Fifth Circuit, 1985.
752 F.2d 1110.

ROBERT MADDEN HILL, CIRCUIT JUDGE:

The Louisiana & Arkansas Railway Co. (L & A) appeals from a jury verdict holding it liable under § 1 of the Federal Employers' Liability Act (the Act or FELA)[1] for injuries incurred by one of its brakemen in an automobile accident. L & A challenges the sufficiency of the evidence to support the jury verdict. In addition, L & A appeals from the district court's dismissal of its third party indemnity action against Miller Cab Company (Miller).[2] L & A contends that the jury's implicit finding of negligence on the part of Miller in the FELA action entitled L & A to indemnity under Louisiana law. For the reasons that follow, we affirm the judgment of the district court.

I. Case History

Armstrong brought this action against Kansas City Southern Railway Company (KCS) and L & A, under the Act, for injuries he sustained in an automobile accident during the course of his employment with L & A as a brakeman.[3] KCS and L & A filed a third-party complaint against Miller and its insurer, New Hampshire Insurance Company, seeking indemnity should judgment in Armstrong's action be rendered

[1] This FELA suit is grounded solely upon the negligence provisions of § 1 of the Act, 45 U.S.C. § 51, which provide in pertinent part that a common carrier by railroad shall be liable for "injury or death resulting in whole or in part from the negligence of any of the officers, agents, or employees of such carrier, or by reason of any defect or insufficiency, due to its negligence, in its cars, engines, appliances, machinery, track roadbed . . . or other equipment."

[2] The parties do not dispute that Miller, the third party defendant that was transporting Armstrong at the time of the accident, was L & A's agent for the purposes of the Act.

[3] KCS is the parent corporation of L & A.

against them. After the jury rendered a verdict in favor of Armstrong and against KCS and L & A, the third-party indemnity claim, which was tried concomitantly by the district court, was dismissed.

The testimony and exhibits established the following facts. On the evening of September 22, 1978, Armstrong was travelling as a brakeman on a freight run from New Orleans to Alexandria, Louisiana. The freight train approached Alexandria during the early hours of September 23, in the vicinity of Willow Glen River Road. Armstrong, pursuant to orders from L & A, disembarked from the train to assist in placing a cut of cars on a side track and to allow another crew to board and complete the train's journey to Shreveport. In accordance with its custom, L & A summoned a taxicab, owned and operated by Miller, to the railroad crossing at Willow Glen River Road to transport Armstrong and his co-worker Murphy Batiste to the railroad's yard office. . . .

[Armstrong was injured when an eastbound motorist struck the cab from the rear. The cab then rolled forward approximately thirty yards. As a result of this collision Armstrong suffered neck injuries.]

Upon the district court's entry of judgment in favor of Armstrong, the railroads moved for judgment notwithstanding the verdict or alternatively for a new trial. The railroads also filed a motion to delete KCS from the judgment as the parties had agreed that L & A was the proper party. After a hearing, the district court denied the motion for judgment notwithstanding the verdict and/or new trial and granted the motion to delete KCS from the judgment. L & A then duly perfected this appeal.

II. Sufficiency of Evidence

The jury found that the driver of the cab owned by Miller was negligent and that such negligence was a legal cause of damage to Armstrong. L & A contends, however, that the evidence was insufficient to justify a jury verdict of negligence in Armstrong's favor. More specifically, L & A asserts that the driver of the cab could not have reasonably foreseen that another motorist would strike the cab from the rear. As we believe sufficient evidence supports the jury verdict, we decline to hold that the district court's denial of L & A's motion for judgment notwithstanding the verdict constitutes reversible error.

The Act allows recovery of damages for personal injuries to an employee of a railroad if the injuries resulted "in whole or in part from the negligence of any of the officers, agents, or employees of such carrier." 45 U.S.C. § 51. Under the Act, a railroad will be liable if its negligence or its agent's negligence played any part, even the slightest, in producing the employee's injury. *Richardson v. Missouri Pacific Railroad Co.*, 677 F.2d 663, 665 (8th Cir.1982) (citing *Rogers v. Missouri Pacific R.R.*, 352 U.S. 500, 506, 77 S.Ct. 443, 448, 1 L.Ed.2d 493 (1957)). "Since the act explicitly makes an employer liable if an injury results only in part from his negligence, the common-law proximate cause standard is modified, and the employee has a less demanding burden of proving causal relationship." *Nivens v. St. Louis Southwestern Railway Co.*, 425 F.2d 114, 118 (5th Cir.1970). Nevertheless, we note that L & A is correct in asserting that Armstrong's prima facie case under the Act must include all the same elements as are found in a common law negligence action. Specifically, he still has the burden of proving that the "employer, with the exercise of due care, could have reasonably foreseen that a particular condition could cause injury; foreseeability is 'an essential ingredient' of negligence under the Act." Id. (quoting *Gallick v. Baltimore & Ohio Railroad Co.*, 372 U.S. 108, 117, 83 S.Ct. 659, 665, 9 L.Ed.2d 618 (1963)).

Addressing the function of this Court in reviewing a jury finding of negligence under the Act, the Supreme Court has stated:

> Only when there is a complete absence of probative facts to support the conclusion reached does a reversible error appear. But where, as here, there is an evidentiary basis for the jury's verdict, the jury is free to discard or disbelieve whatever facts are inconsistent with its conclusion. And the appellate court's function is exhausted when the evidentiary basis becomes apparent, it being immaterial that the court might draw a contrary inference or feel that another conclusion is more reasonable.

Lavender v. Kurn, 327 U.S. 645, 653, 66 S.Ct. 740, 744, 90 L.Ed. 916 (1946), quoted in *Lang v. Texas & Pacific Railway Co.*, 624 F.2d 1275, 1278 (5th Cir.1980).

In the instant case, there exists a sufficient evidentiary basis for the jury to infer negligence on the part of the cab driver. It was dark; nevertheless, the cab driver stopped on Willow Glen River Road in the eastbound lane approximately four or five feet from the elevated railroad crossing and failed to turn on his emergency flashing lights. Further, the cab driver could have parked on the adjacent shoulder of the road or in a nearby parking lot. From this evidence, it was reasonable for the jury to infer negligence; more specifically, this evidence sufficiently supports the inference that the cab driver, with the exercise of due care, could have reasonably foreseen that parking his cab in such a position and manner at that time in the morning could result in a rear-end accident.

The testimony of Murphy Batiste, the passenger in the cab, does cast some doubt on the evidence supporting the jury's conclusion. Batiste testified that the shoulder of the road was too narrow for the cab to safely pull off the road; he also testified that the crossing was not elevated thus establishing uninhibited vision on the part of oncoming motorists. The jury was free, however, to give more credence to Armstrong's testimony than to Batiste's and to infer that the cab driver was negligent in stopping the cab at that time and location and in that manner. Similarly, evidence tending to establish the negligence of the motorist who ran into the rear of the cab does not preclude the jury's finding that the cab driver's negligence played at least *some part* in Armstrong's injuries. Because there is not a complete absence of probative facts to support the finding of negligence, we reject [the] contention that there was insufficient evidence to support the jury verdict.

III. Indemnity

L & A next contends that the district court erred in finding that L & A is not entitled to indemnity under Louisiana law in its third-party action against Miller and its insurer. In considering L & A's indemnity action against Miller and its insurer, the district court stated it was not bound by the fact finding of the jury as to the negligence of the cab driver. The court, after making credibility choices, found that the cab driver was not negligent. The court went on to state that even if he had been found negligent, the cab driver's negligence must have been a "substantial producing cause to the accident" under Louisiana law in order for L & A to prevail on its third-party indemnity claim. The district court then found that the cab driver's assumed negligence was not a substantial producing cause of the accident and that the sole cause of the accident was the negligence of the motorist who ran into the rear of Miller's taxi cab.

While L & A's negligence under the Act is determined as a matter of federal law interpreting and implementing the Act, L & A's right to indemnity is determined by state law. To succeed in his FELA action against L & A, Armstrong was required to show that Miller's cab driver was negligent in the manner and place in which he stopped his cab and that such negligence played some part, however slight, in producing Armstrong's injury. See *Rogers*, 352 U.S. at 506, 77 S.Ct. at 448. To succeed in its third party indemnity action against Miller, however, L & A was required to show under Louisiana law that Miller's fault or negligence was the proximate cause of Armstrong's injury. See *Dupree v. Pechinay Saint Gobain Co.*, 369 So.2d 1075, 1081–82 (La.App.), *cert. denied*, 371 So.2d 1341 (La.1979) (citing *Appalachian Corp. v. Brooklyn Cooperage Co.*, 151 La. 41, 91 So. 539, 541 (1922)). . . .

L & A asserts that even though it is without fault, it is nevertheless statutorily required under FELA to pay for the acts or omissions of Miller. It argues that because the jury found Miller negligent in Armstrong's FELA action, L & A is entitled to indemnification for the damages it was required to pay as the result of Miller's negligence. This argument ignores the different causation standards of these two actions: the FELA action is governed by federal law while the indemnity action is governed by state law. In *Nivens v. St. Louis Southwestern Railway Co.*, 425 F.2d 114 (5th Cir.1970), we stated:

> The standards of liability for negligence under § 1 of the Act are significantly broader than in ordinary common-law negligence actions. The Supreme Court has succinctly stated the now settled principle that in these cases,
>
> > "the test of a jury case is simply whether the proofs justify with reason the conclusion that employer negligence played any part, even the slightest, in producing the injury * * *. It does not matter that, from the evidence, the jury may also with reason, on grounds of probability, attribute the result to other causes * * *. The employer is stripped of his common-law defenses and for practical purposes the inquiry in these cases today rarely presents more than the single question whether negligence of the employer played any part, however small, in the injury or death which is the subject of the suit." *Rogers v. Missouri Pac. Ry.*, 352 U.S. 500, 506–508, 77 S.Ct. 443, 449, 1 L.Ed.2d 493 (1957).
>
> Since the Act explicitly makes an employer liable if an injury results only in part from his negligence, the common-law proximate cause standard is modified, and the employee has a less demanding burden of proving causal relationship.

Id. at 118.

The district court found that even if the cab driver was negligent, his negligence was not the proximate cause of Armstrong's injuries; rather, the court determined the sole cause of the accident was the negligence of the motorist who rear-ended the taxi cab. The district court's finding is reviewed on appeal under the clearly erroneous standard. * * *

The record adequately supports the district court's finding. Batiste, Armstrong's co-worker, testified that there was insufficient room on the shoulder of the road to allow the taxi cab to completely pull off the road and that the railroad crossing was not elevated. He also testified that there were no cars in the area and no cars in the lane opposite to the taxi cab, that the night was clear and that an oncoming motorist would have been able to see the flashing lights on the track as well as the parking lights of the stopped taxi cab. While the testimony of Armstrong to a certain extent contradicts Batiste's testimony, an appellate court is in a particularly poor position to second guess the district court's credibility choices among differing pieces of testimony. *Ayers v. United States*, 750 F.2d 449 at 456 (5th Cir.1985). Because we believe that there was sufficient evidence to support the district court's finding that the cab driver's negligence did not proximately cause Armstrong's injury, we decline to hold that the district court erred in dismissing L & A's indemnity action against Miller. The district court's denial of L & A's motion for judgment notwithstanding the verdict was proper.

Accordingly, the judgment of the district court is AFFIRMED.

NOTES

1. Are Armstrong's injuries fairly considered to be costs of running a railroad? *Thornberry v. Grant Trunk Western Railroad*, 776 F.Supp. 2d 453 (E.D. Mich. 2011) is a similar case. There, a railroad employee recovered in a FELA action against his employer for injury from a defective switch but the employer's state law indemnity claim against the contractor that had been hired to maintain the switch failed.

2. *Armstrong* illustrates several of the tort-like qualities of FELA litigation. The claim is filed in a state or federal court with a jury serving as the fact finder in many instances. Liability hinges on a finding that the railroad or its agent was negligent. Moreover, compensation in both a traditional tort or FELA case is measured in terms of the actual loss to the particular claimant. The individualized damage remedy means that two workers suffering what seem to be similar injuries may recover vastly different sums of money. Compare *Kelly v. Illinois Cen. Gulf R.R.*, 552 F.Supp. 399 (W.D.Mo.1982) (employee who lost a leg awarded $2,000,000) with *Flanigan v. Burlington N. Inc.*, 632 F.2d 880 (8th Cir.1980) (employee who lost a leg awarded $500,000). Although not an issue in *Armstrong*, FELA retains conduct-based defenses applied through the principles of pure comparative negligence. See, e.g., *Gish v. CSX Transp. Inc.*, 890 F.2d 989 (7th Cir.1989) (damage award reduced by percentage of employee's negligence in attempting to lift a 175 lb. manhole cover without assistance); and *Plambeck v. Union Pacific R.R. Co.*, 232 Neb. 590, 441 N.W.2d 614 (1989) (damage award reduced by percentage of employee negligence in failing to obey workplace safety rules).

3. While *Armstrong* highlights similarities between FELA and tort law, it also illustrates some important differences. Evidence sufficient to support Armstrong's claim against the railroad under FELA does not support the railroad's claim for indemnity under traditional tort principles. The differences between a FELA action and a conventional tort action were described by the Supreme Court as follows:

> Under this statute the test of a jury case is simply whether the proofs justify with reason the conclusion that employer negligence played *any part, even the slightest*, in producing the injury or death for which damages are sought. . . .

Rogers v. Missouri Pacific R.R. Co., 352 U.S. 500, 506–510, 77 S.Ct. 443, 1 L.Ed.2d 493 (1957) (emphasis added and footnotes omitted).

It seems fair to say that courts require less proof of negligence in FELA cases than in ordinary tort actions. See, e.g., Ringhiser v. Chesapeake & Ohio Ry. Co., 354 U.S. 901, 77 S.Ct. 1093, 1 L.Ed.2d 1268 (1957) (engineer answering call of nature while hidden inside gondola car, injured when cars were switched without knowledge of his presence); Gallick v. Baltimore & Ohio Railroad Co., 372 U.S. 108, 83 S.Ct. 659, 9 L.Ed.2d 618 (1963) (insect bite possibly attributable to stagnant pond near right of way); Pehowic v. Erie Lackawanna R.R. Co., 430 F.2d 697 (3d Cir.1970) (employee stung by bee in undergrowth accumulated near right of way); and, Ybarra v. Burlington Northern, Inc., 689 F.2d 147 (8th Cir.1982) (employee was injured while lifting a 40–50 lb. bucket of oil in violation of employer safety rule; jury could award damages based on employer's negligence in failing to enforce the safety rule). Moreover, courts appear to apply less stringent standards of causation in FELA actions. See, e.g., Kernan v. American Dredging Co., 355 U.S. 426, 78 S.Ct. 394, 2 L.Ed.2d 382 (1958) (lamp on boat carried at lower than eight feet above water level in violation of Coast Guard visibility regulation, ignited oil on surface of water, resulting in injury from burn); and, Mitchell v. Missouri–Kansas–Texas Railroad Co., 786 S.W.2d 659 (Tex.1990) (error to instruct jury in terms of common law proximate cause; the proper standard under FELA was whether the employer's negligence played "any part, even the slightest" in producing the injury or death). Nevertheless, even under FELA's generous standards of proof a claimant's mere speculation about what an employer "should have done" is not sufficient to support a claim. McCarty v. Canadian National/Illinois Central Railroad, 3:06–CV–177–HTW–LRA, 2008 WL 872327 (S.D. Miss. 2008).

4. A wide variety of injuries and forms of misconduct come within the coverage of the FELA. "Negligence" under the statute embraces assault by one worker upon another in the course of employment, Jamison v. Encarnacion, 281 U.S. 635, 50 S.Ct. 440, 74 L.Ed. 1082 (1930); false imprisonment and detention overnight, no physical consequences alleged, Slaughter v. Atlantic Coast Line R.R., 302 F.2d 912 (D.C.Cir.1962), declined to follow, Teague v. National R.R. Passenger Corp., 708 F.Supp. 1344 (D.Mass.1989); and, failure to provide medical attention for ill worker in emergency, Rival v. Atchison, Topeka & Santa Fe Ry., 62 N.M. 159, 306 P.2d 648 (1957). The Act has been interpreted to cover an occupational disease (silicosis) arising from employment, Urie v. Thompson, 337 U.S. 163, 69 S.Ct. 1018, 93 L.Ed. 1282 (1949), and nervous breakdown caused by unreasonably heavy work, McMillan v. Western Pacific R.R. Co., 54 Cal.2d 841, 9 Cal.Rptr. 361, 357 P.2d 449 (1960).

5. A railroad employer may be liable on principles of imputed negligence. For example, a railroad that procured a public taxi for an employee who was injured while being transported in the cab that lacked seat belts was held liable under FELA for its "negligent" selection of the vehicle even though the taxicab proprietors were exonerated of liability. Benson v. Penn Central Transportation Co., 463 Pa. 37, 342 A.2d 393 (1975). Similarly, in Sinkler v. Missouri Pacific R.R. Co., 356 U.S. 326, 78 S.Ct. 758, 2 L.Ed.2d

799 (1958), the Supreme Court held a railway employer liable for injury caused to its employee by the negligence of an independent contractor hired by the railway. The court observed:

> In interpreting the FELA, we need not depend upon common law principles of liability. This statute, an avowed departure from the rules of the common law * * * was a response to the special needs of railroad workers who are daily exposed to the risks inherent in railroad work and are helpless to provide adequately for their own safety * * * The cost of human injury, an inescapable expense of railroading, must be borne by someone, and the FELA seeks to adjust that expense equitably between the worker and the carrier. 356 U.S. 326, 329, 78 S.Ct. 758, 762, 2 L.Ed.2d 799.

6. FELA critics maintain that it has become, in effect, a "no-fault" system of compensation without any corresponding reduction in administrative costs. Coupling relaxed standards of negligence and causation with tort damages is said to unfairly subject railroads to a competitive disadvantage with other modes of transportation. Schwartz and Mahshigian, The Federal Employers' Liability Act, A Bane for Workers, A Bust for Railroads, A Boon for Lawyers, 23 San Diego L.Rev. 1 (1986); Haynes and Anderson, The Federal Employers' Liability Act: A Compensation System in Urgent Need of Reform, 34 Fed.Bar News & J. 310 (1987). FELA defenders assert that it serves as a real and valuable incentive to promote workplace safety and operates at a cost comparable to workers' compensation systems. See, Phillips, An Evaluation of the Federal Employers' Liability Act, 25 San Diego L.Rev. 49 (1988).

7. The Jones Act, 41 Stat. 1007, 46 U.S.C.A. § 688, extended FELA principles to employment of seamen. See, O'Donnell v. Great Lakes Dredge & Dock Co., 318 U.S. 36, 63 S.Ct. 488, 87 L.Ed. 596 (1943); Yehia v. Rouge Steel Corp., 898 F.2d 1178 (6th Cir.1990).

D. SOCIAL SECURITY DISABILITY BENEFITS

The federal social security acts provide benefits to disabled workers under a plan that is at the same time broader in scope and more limited in specific application than the typical workers' compensation plan as described in succeeding portions of this text. Federal disability benefits are broader in scope because they are payable without regard to what caused the disability; that is, the act imposes no requirement that the disability have any connection to the disabled worker's employment. By contrast, the disability plan is more limited in specific application because it provides only earnings loss benefits—no medical benefits—and applies only to workers who are totally injured for extended periods of time.

The disability benefits plan is one element of the federal Old Age Survivors and Disability Insurance scheme (OASDI) that was part of President Franklin D. Roosevelt's new deal legislative package of the mid-

1930s. This part of the social security plan is funded by employment and excise taxes imposed upon both employees and employers and is known as an insurance system because it creates benefit entitlements as a matter of right. These social security taxes are paid in respect of wages paid and self-employment income earned. They are collected from employees by withholding them from the wages paid by employers. The employers periodically submit the withheld income taxes paid by employees and an equal amount payable by them as excise taxes to the United States Treasury where the funds are ultimately deposited to the exclusive credit of social security trust funds from which benefits are paid.

The original social security act did not include the disability benefits element. The history of that element has been described as follows:

"The original American OASI program, adopted in the depression days of 1935, provided for the two groups most obviously and urgently in need of protection, the unemployed and the aged. Widows and dependent children were soon added to the beneficiaries.

"World War II interrupted the progress of social security legislation, but in 1948 the Advisory Council on Social Security recommended that benefits be provided also for the disabled. A series of bitter debates followed, reminiscent of [later] battles over Medicare, with sharply divided camps warning of the dire consequences of passage or failure of the legislation. Protection for disabled workers came only in 1956 after a long and bitter struggle, and then only for the permanently and totally disabled. The legislation provided that insured persons who were so disabled could retire at 50 or older and receive the OASI benefits to which they would have been entitled at normal retirement age. There were no benefits for dependents. In contrast to the pattern in other countries, the adopted definition of disability was unusually strict; and there was no provision for higher benefits where constant attendance was needed. * * * Benefits for the wives and children of the disabled were added in 1958, and the age 50 requirement was dropped in 1960. Work requirements for eligibility were also liberalized."[15]

Both the scope and the limits of the disability benefits plan are revealed by the structure of the statutory plan as follows:

Disability insurance benefits are payable to a worker who:

(A) is insured for disability insurance benefits * * *,

(B) has not attained the retirement age [historically 65, but now variable],

(C) omitted

---

[15] Cheit, "Workmen's Compensation, OASDI: The Overlap, 3 Industrial Relations" 63, 65 (1964).

(D) has filed an application for disability insurance benefits, and

(E) is under a disability * * *.[16]

Unless the worker has had prior qualifying disabilities under specified conditions, monthly disability payments begin the month after the expiration of a waiting period of five consecutive calendar months of disability.[17] (What is the purpose for imposing such a requirement? Does it tell anything about the philosophy of the disability benefits?)

In order to be "insured for disability insurance benefits" in any month, a person must have had a history of employment that satisfies the criteria prescribed by the statute. Although the requirements are detailed, a simplified test is whether the worker had 10 full years of employment in insured work.[18] Satisfying that test always satisfies the "insured" criterion and meeting lesser periods of coverage sometimes qualifies young workers and others in special circumstances.

In addition to satisfying the foregoing requirements, a worker must also be "disabled." The statutory definition of that term bears stating in full:

> (d)(1) The term "disability" means—
>
> (A) inability to engage in any substantial gainful activity by reason of any medically determinable physical or mental impairment which can be expected to result in death or which has lasted or can be expected to last for a continuous period of not less than 12 months; or
>
> (B) in the case of an individual who has attained the age of 55 and is blind * * * inability by reason of such blindness to engage in substantial gainful activity requiring skills or abilities comparable to those of any gainful activity in which he has previously engaged with some regularity and over a substantial period of time.
>
> (2) For purposes of paragraph (1)(A)—
>
> (A) an individual * * * shall be determined to be under a disability only if his physical or mental impairment or impairments are of such severity that he is not only unable to do his previous work but cannot, considering his age, education, and work experience, engage in any other kind of substantial gainful work which exists in the national

[16] 42 U.S.C.A. § 423(a).

[17] 42 U.S.C.A. § 423(c); prior to 1972 amendments (Pub.L. 92–603) the waiting period was six months.

[18] 42 U.S.C.A. § 423(c).

> economy, regardless of whether such work exists in the immediate area in which he lives, or whether a specific job vacancy exists for him, or whether he would be hired if he applied for work. * * * "[w]ork which exists in the national economy" means work which exists in significant numbers either in the region where such individual lives or in several regions of the country.
>
> * * *
>
> (3) For purposes of this subsection, a "physical or mental impairment" is an impairment that results from anatomical, physiological, or psychological abnormalities which are demonstrable by medically acceptable clinical and laboratory diagnostic techniques.[19]

To re-emphasize how limited the application of the federal disability benefits plan truly is, a student might refer back to this provision after examining the requirements of a compensable injury under workers' compensation laws.

A qualified disabled worker is entitled to a "primary insurance amount" determined by formula on the basis of the amount of time employed in insured employment and the rate of earnings during that time.[20] In addition, if the conditions of the statute are satisfied[21] spouses and children of qualified disabled workers are entitled to a benefit equal to one-half the primary insurance amount.[22]

Although the criteria for what is a disability are set by the Social Security Act, the program administrator may authorize designated state agencies to make the medical determinations.[23]

Because the federal disability program imposes no causal nexus between the claimant's employment and the disability, many disabled workers receive social security disability benefits but no workers' compensation benefits. Nevertheless, a worker who is disabled by a work injury might be entitled to benefits from both sources, thus permitting some disabled workers to receive combined benefits in amounts that exceed pre-injury earnings. The initial federal disability benefits law made no deduction to prevent this, which proved to be a source employer of discontent. In 1972 the National Commission on State Workmen's Compensation Laws recommended that social security benefits be reduced in the presence of workers' compensation benefits (R. 3.18).

---

[19] 42 U.S.C.A. § 423(c).

[20] 42 U.S.C.A. § 415.

[21] 42 U.S.C.A. § 1402(b), (c), (d); 20 CFR §§ 404.333, 404.353.

[22] 42 U.S.C.A. § 1402(b), (c), (d); 20 CFR §§ 404.333, 404.353.

[23] 42 U.S.C.A. § 421(a).

Thereafter, Congress enacted the following provision:[24]

> If for any month prior to the month in which an individual attains the age of 65—
>
> (1) such individual is entitled to [disability benefits] . . . and
>
> (2) such individual is entitled for such month to—
>
> (A) periodic benefits on account of his or her total or partial disability (whether or not permanent) under a workmen's compensation law or plan of the United States or a State, or
>
> (B) omitted
>
> the total of his [disability] benefits shall be reduced (but not below zero) by the amount by which the sum of—
>
> (1) such total of [disability] benefits for such month, and
>
> (2) such periodic benefits payable (and actually paid) for such month to such individual under such laws or plans, exceeds the higher of—
>
> (3) 80 per centum of his "average current earnings." * * *

Does this "overlap" deduction provide a systematic cost savings to the combined workers' compensation and social security disability benefits system? Does it make any difference as to how the savings is allocated?

DEPARTMENT OF PUBLIC HEALTH, DIVISION OF RISK MANAGEMENT V. WILCOX

Supreme Court of Florida, 1989.
543 So.2d 1253.

PER CURIAM.

* * *

In a worker's compensation proceeding, the respondent, Muriel Wilcox, was awarded temporary total and permanent total disability benefits, costs, interests, and medical expenses. Her employer, the State of Florida, Department of Public Health, Division of Risk Management, subsequently determined that Wilcox was also receiving federal social security benefits, and reduced the amount of her workers' compensation award pursuant to the offset provision in section 440.15(9), Florida Statutes (1985).

Wilcox contends that the setoff provision in section 440.15(9) cannot be taken by her employer on its own accord, but rather must be

[24] 42 U.S.C.A. § 421(a).

authorized by the deputy commissioner. The Third District Court of Appeal agreed with Wilcox and held that her employer could not take the setoff unilaterally. The court held that the compensation award could only be reduced by the deputy commissioner in a modification proceeding. Wilcox, 504 So.2d at 444 (Fla.1987).

The state, as the employer, argues that the offset provision is self-executing and can be taken unilaterally. Thus, the issue presented is whether Wilcox's employer (the state) may unilaterally take the setoff authorized by section 440.15(9). We hold that it may.

Section 440.15(9)(a), Florida Statutes (1985), requires that weekly workers' compensation benefits be reduced by the amount that they and social security benefits, in the aggregate, exceed eighty percent of the injured worker's average weekly wage.[1] The language is unequivocal. The offset is mandatory if the combined benefits exceed eighty percent of the worker's salary. Correspondingly, at the federal level, 42 United States Code section 424a (1935), requires that the Social Security Administration take the setoff if it is not taken under a state workers' compensation program.

We note at the outset that section 424a was enacted to prevent injured workers from receiving "windfall" benefits from the combination of social security disability benefits and workers' compensation benefits.[2] Congress feared that the duplication of benefits would reduce a worker's incentive to return to work impeding rehabilitative efforts.[3] Several states, including Florida, enacted similar statutes requiring state employers to take the setoffs first, thereby saving money. Although section 440.15(9) does not expressly address whether an employer may take the setoff unilaterally, section 424a clearly allows the Social Security Administration to do so.[4]

---

1 Section 440.15(9)(a), Florida Statutes (1985), states:

> Weekly compensation benefits payable under this chapter for disability resulting from injuries to an employee who becomes eligible for benefits under 42 U.S.C. § 423 shall be reduced to an amount whereby the sum of such compensation benefits payable under this chapter and such total benefits otherwise payable for such period to the employee and his dependents, had such employee not been entitled to benefits under this chapter, under 42 U.S.C. §§ 423 and 402, does not exceed 80 percent of the employee's average weekly wage. However, this provision shall not operate to reduce an injured worker's benefits under this chapter to a greater extent than such benefits would have otherwise been reduced under 42 U.S.C. § 424(a) [sic]. This reduction of compensation benefits is not applicable to any compensation benefits payable for any week subsequent to the week in which the injured worker reaches the age of 62 years.

2 Kristal, *Social security disability benefits: Benefit or burden to the severely injured workers' compensation claimant?*, 61 Fla. B.J. 65 (July/Aug. 1987).

3 *Id.*

4 42 U.S.C. § 424a(h)(2) states:

> The Secretary [of the Department of Health and Human Services] is authorizes to enter into agreements with States, political subdivisions, and other organizations

The rationale underlying the federal statutory scheme is sound. The Social Security Administration has knowledge of the amount of social security benefits an employee receives. It must then obtain information regarding the amount of workers' compensation benefits from the state that is administering the plan.[5] When the Social Security Administration has this information, the amount of the setoff can be quickly and easily determined by using a simple mathematical calculation. The federal statute recognizes this and thus allows the setoff to be taken administratively. We find the federal scheme persuasive.[6]

Similarly, section 440.15(9)(c) imposes no obligation on the employee to inform his employer that he has begun receiving social security disability benefits, nor does it require the employee to calculate the requisite eighty percent limit and remit the excess. Rather, the employer must take the initiative in determining the applicability of the reduction. No deduction can be taken until the employer receives the worker's social security disability information from the Social Security Administration. Then, the setoff only can be taken prospectively. *Department of Transportation v. Lindsey*, 383 So.2d 956 (Fla. 1st DCA 1980).

Thus, section 440.15(9) requires a Florida employer to obtain the same reliable information that the federal statute demands. Since both the Florida employer and the Social Security Administration rely upon the same information in determining the applicability of the setoff, we see no reason why the state setoff should not also be self-executing. Therefore, we hold that the setoff provision in section 440.15(9) may be taken administratively by an employer/carrier.

We reject the respondent's contention that the setoff can be made only by the deputy commissioner in a modification proceeding. This proceeding would insure against an employer miscalculating the amount of the setoff. We fail to see how this possible benefit to the employee outweighs the additional expense and delay it imposes on the employer. The employer has little incentive to miscalculate the amount of the setoff because review by the deputy commissioner is always available to the employee. The First District Court of Appeal has consistently held that the offset provision in section 440.15(9) is self-executing. See *Colonel's Table v. Malena*, 412 So.2d 64 (Fla. 1st DCA 1982); *Florida Power &*

---

that administer a law or plan subject to the provisions of this section, in order to obtain such information as he may require to carry out the provisions of this section.

5 Id.

6 Our statutes recognize the persuasiveness of federal laws in the worker's compensation area. Section 440.44(1), Florida Statutes (1985), states:

> (1) INTERPRETATION OF LAW.—As a guide to the interpretation of this chapter, the Legislature takes due notice of federal social and labor acts and hereby creates an agency to administer such acts passed for the benefit of employees and employers in Florida industry, and desires to meet the requirements of such federal acts wherever not inconsistent with the Constitution and laws of Florida.

Light Co. v. Adkins, 377 So.2d 57 (Fla. 1st DCA 1979); *Borden, Inc. v. Butler*, 377 So.2d 795 (Fla. 1st DCA 1979); *Sherrod Dry Wall v. Reeves*, 378 So.2d 301 (Fla. 1st DCA 1979).

Accordingly, we hold that the setoff provision in section 440.15(9) is self-executing in nature and therefore, can be taken unilaterally by the employer. We quash the decision of the Third District Court of Appeal and remand the case for further proceedings consistent with this opinion.

It is so ordered.

E. NON-INJURY COMPENSATING LABOR ACTS

During the course of the twentieth century Congress and many state legislatures enacted numerous statutes prescribing rights and duties of employees and employers in the employment relationship apart from compensating injuries or directly enhancing job safety. At the federal level these include the seminal Railway Labor Act of 1923[25] and the Wagner Act of 1935 (the National Labor Relations Act).[26] These acts provide what may be regarded as "bills of rights" and require employers to bargain with employees (or, more specifically, the employees' chosen bargaining representatives—typically unions) about wages, hours of work and working conditions, but of themselves prescribe no particular benefits.

In time Congress enacted specific statutes to provide guaranteed substantive employment benefits that can be augmented by bargaining but in generally cannot be bargained away. These include:

- The Fair Labor Standards of Act of 1938, [27] prescribing minimum wages, maximum hours, and child labor standards in covered employments.
- The Age Discrimination Act of 1963[28] providing anti-discrimination job protection for older workers in covered employments.
- Title VII of the Civil Rights Act of 1964[29] making it an unlawful employment practice to discriminate against persons based upon race, color, religion, sex, or national origin in covered employments.

---

[25] 45 U.S.C.A. Ch. 8. Railway Labor Act. Originally, the Railway Labor Act covered only to railroad workers but has been extended to cover workers in the airline industry.

[26] 29 U.S.C.A. Ch. 7. National Labor Relations Act. Among the most important adjuncts to the NLRA is the Labor Management Relations (Taft-Hartley) Act of 1947, 29 U.S.C. § 185.

[27] 29 U.S.C.A. Ch. 8. Fair Labor Standards Act.

[28] 29 U.S.C.A. §§ 621 et seq.

[29] 42 U.S.C.A. Ch. 21. Title VII of the Civil Rights Act of 1964.

- The Rehabilitation Act of 1973[30] providing rehabilitation services to handicapped people in order to enhance employment opportunities.
- The Employee Retirement Income Security Act of 1974[31] ("ERISA") providing protection to employee pension plans in covered employments.
- The Americans with Disabilities Act of 1990[32] making it illegal to "discriminate against a qualified individual with a disability because of the disability of such individual in regard to job application procedures, the hiring, advancement, or discharge of employees, employee compensation, job training, and other terms, conditions, and privileges of employment" in covered employments.
- The Family Medical Leave Act of 1993[33] requiring covered employments in commerce to provide medical leave for employees who experience child birth, adoption of a child, need to care for a family member with a serious health condition, or serious medical condition.

None of these federal non-compensatory statutes possesses much potential to conflict directly with a state's workers' compensation statute even to the limited extent that social security disability benefits pose the conflict referred to in the preceding section. Nevertheless, some injured workers have attacked particular workers' compensation provisions as being in conflict with ADA. As is exemplified by the opinion below, most of these efforts have failed.

BREEN V. CARLSBAD MUNICIPAL SCHOOLS

New Mexico Court of Appeals, 2003.
133 N.M. 618, 67 P.3d 908,
reversed on equal protection grounds, 120 P.3d 413 (N.M. 2005).

Opinion

PICKARD, JUDGE.

This is a consolidated appeal from orders of the Workers' Compensation Judge (WCJ) denying Workers' applications for

---

30 PL 93–112, 87 Stat 355. In part, the preamble states: Sec. 2. The purpose of this act is to provide a statutory basis for the rehabilitation services administration, and to authorize programs to—(1) develop and implement comprehensive and continuing state plans for meeting the current and future needs for providing vocational rehabilitation services to handicapped individuals and to provide such services for the benefit of such individuals, serving first those with the most severe handicaps, so that they may prepare for and engage in gainful employment.

31 29 U.S.C.A. Ch. 18. ERISA.

32 42 U.S.C.A. § 12101. Americans with Disabilities Act.

33 PL 103–3, 29 U.S.C.A. § 2601 *et. seq.*

supplementary compensation orders. In it, we consider whether provisions in the Workers' Compensation Act (WCA), NMSA 1978, §§ 52–1–41 (1999) and –42 (1990), that limit the duration of benefit payments for those workers disabled due to mental impairment, violate the equal protection clauses of the United States Constitution and the New Mexico Constitution. We also consider whether the same provisions violate the mandate of the Americans With Disabilities Act (ADA), 42 U.S.C. §§ 12101 through 12213 (2000). We hold that there is neither a constitutional nor a statutory violation.

I. Facts and Background

In August 1999, the WCJ entered compensation orders awarding temporary total disability benefits to Workers Breen and Carrasco (Workers) for injuries that resulted in temporary total disability due to a conditioned psychological response to odors and dust. Employer Carlsbad Municipal Schools and Insurer New Mexico Public School Insurance Authority (Employer/Insurer) appealed these compensation orders to this Court, which upheld the orders in a memorandum opinion filed on May 29, 2001. Following the mandate from this Court to the district court, Employer/Insurer submitted payment to Workers that totaled 100 weeks of compensation pursuant to the WCA. See §§ 52–1–41(B);–42(A)(3).

Workers then moved for supplementary compensation orders, arguing that since this Court upheld the award of temporary total disability benefits and did not limit them, Workers were due more than the 100 weeks of benefits because the WCJ's original order was "ongoing." After a hearing, the WCJ found that Workers suffered from a primary mental impairment and were due only 100 weeks of compensation under the WCA. See id. Workers now appeal the WCJ's order of 100 weeks of compensation. They raise three issues on appeal: (1) the WCJ erred in refusing to enforce his original compensation orders that were upheld on appeal (2) the provisions in the WCA that limit benefits of workers disabled due to mental impairments violate the equal protection clauses of the United States Constitution and the New Mexico Constitution, and (3) the provisions in the WCA that limit benefits of workers disabled due to mental impairments violate the ADA. We affirm the orders of the WCJ.

II. Discussion

A. Enforcement of Original Order

Workers argue that the WCJ erred in awarding only 100 weeks of benefits after this Court affirmed the WCJ's original findings of compensability and temporary total disability. They claim that because the WCJ's compensation orders provided for benefits that were "ongoing" and because those orders were upheld by this Court on appeal, the WCJ's subsequent denial of benefits beyond 100 weeks pursuant to Section 52–1–41(B) contravenes this Court's order on remand.

* * *

Workers rely on a decision from a Missouri Court of Appeals for the general rule that "after affirmance of a lower court judgment any subsequent orders or adjudications in the cause must be confined to those necessary to execute the judgment." McPherson Redevelopment Corp. v. Shelton, 807 S.W.2d 203, 205 (Mo.Ct.App.1991) (internal quotation marks and citations omitted). Rather than support Workers' argument, we find that this general rule supports our conclusion that the WCJ necessarily relied on the appropriate statute to execute our judgment that the Workers suffered from a primary mental impairment. Accordingly, we hold that the WCJ did not err in its award of 100 weeks of benefits to Workers.

B. Equal Protection

Workers argue that Sections 52–1–41(B) and 52–1–42(A)(3) treat similarly situated individuals differently: those who are temporarily totally disabled due to physical impairment and those who are temporarily totally disabled due to primary mental impairment. Because workers with physical impairments can receive up to 500 or 700 weeks of benefits and workers with primary mental impairments are capped at 100 weeks of benefits, Workers assert that Section 52–1–41(B), capping their benefits at 100 weeks, violates the equal protection rights guaranteed by the United States and New Mexico Constitutions.

* * *

[Equal protection analysis omitted, except for this conclusion]: Having decided that this statute is rationally related to legitimate government purposes, we will not question further the wisdom of what is the legislature's clear intent. . . .

Accordingly, we hold that Sections 52–1–41(B) and 52–1–42(A)(3), which result in dissimilar treatment of similarly situated workers, do not violate the equal protection clauses of the United States Constitution or the New Mexico Constitution because they are rationally related to legitimate government purposes.

[Note: The equal protection portion of the opinion was rejected by the New Mexico Supreme Court. Breen v. Carlsbad Municipal Schools, 120 P.3d 413 (N.M. 2005). The supreme court held that disparate treatment of physical and mental disabilities violated the New Mexico equal protection clause. The supreme court did not address the following ADA analysis.]

C. Americans With Disabilities Act

Workers claim that Sections 52–1–41(B) and 52–1–42(A)(3) establish disparate treatment that violates the ADA. They essentially make a Title I claim, citing 42 U.S.C. § 12112(a) of the ADA. They argue that Workers'

Compensation is a privilege of employment, and as such, New Mexico's scheme that treats persons temporarily totally disabled due to a mental impairment differently from persons temporarily totally disabled due to a physical impairment is discriminatory in regard to a privilege of employment and violative of the ADA. *See id.*; see also *Harding v. Winn–Dixie Stores, Inc.*, 907 F.Supp. 386, 390 (M.D.Fla.1995) ("[A]n entitlement to workers' compensation benefits is a privilege of employment subject to the antidiscrimination provisions of the ADA.").

Employer/Insurer essentially argues that Workers do not have standing to bring an ADA claim. To establish a prima facie case under the ADA, a plaintiff must demonstrate (1) that she is disabled within the meaning of the ADA (2) that she is qualified—with or without reasonable accommodation, and (3) that she was discriminated against because of her disability. *Aldrich v. Boeing Co.*, 146 F.3d 1265, 1269 (10th Cir.1998). Employer/Insurer further argues that even if Workers did have standing, they have introduced no evidence to prove that Employer/Insurer had discriminatory intent or that the Workers' Compensation scheme resulted in disparate impact, the two theories under which an ADA claim must fall. See § 12112(a) and (b)(3); 29 C.F.R. § 1630.7 (2001).

We understand Workers' argument to be that they are not bringing a claim under the ADA per se, but are seeking to have its provisions enforced so as to preempt Sections 52–1–41 and –42 of New Mexico's Workers' Compensation statute. Under the preemption doctrine, rooted in the supremacy clause of Article VI of the United States Constitution, states "may not frustrate either through legislation or judicial interpretation" federal law. *Self v. United Parcel Serv., Inc.*, 1998–NMSC–046, ¶ 7, 126 N.M. 396, 970 P.2d 582 (internal citations omitted). Statutory interpretation is a question of law which this Court reviews de novo. . . .

1. Purposes of WCA and ADA

The purpose of the WCA is "to provide a workers' benefit system . . . to assure the quick and efficient delivery of indemnity and medical benefits to injured and disabled workers at a reasonable cost to the employers." NMSA 1978, § 52–5–1 (1990). "The workers' benefit system in New Mexico is based on a mutual renunciation of common law rights and defenses by employers and employees alike." Id. In short, the act is a legislative balance of an employer's assumption of liability without fault and a worker's exclusive but efficient remedy. *See id.*; *Sanchez*, 103 N.M. at 296–97, 706 P.2d at 160–61. In order to be eligible for benefits an employee must show total disability, partial disability, permanent partial disability, injury to specific body members, facial disfigurement, hernia, or death. NMSA 1978, §§ 52–1–41 through –46 (1987, as amended through 1999). The amount and duration of benefits paid are determined according to the statutory scheme that outlines the degree of the impairment, loss of use, and ability to work. Id. Thus, the WCA provides an exclusive and efficient remedy for injured employees by using an objective standard to determine levels and duration of disability benefits. . . .

The purpose of the ADA is to eliminate discrimination against individuals with disabilities. 42 U.S.C. § 12101. It provides that:

> No covered entity shall discriminate against a qualified individual with a disability because of the disability of such individual in regard to job application procedures, the hiring, advancement, or discharge of employees, employee compensation, job training, and other terms, conditions and privileges of employment.

42 U.S.C. § 12112(a). A "qualified individual with a disability" is an "individual with a disability who, with or without reasonable accommodation, can perform the essential functions of the employment position that such individual holds or desires." 42 U.S.C. § 12111(8). Thus, the ADA provides a remedy for disabled workers who can work but have somehow been discriminated against because of a disability.

The ADA does not abrogate or invalidate or limit remedies, rights, and procedures of any other federal or state laws that provide "greater or equal protection for the rights of individuals with disabilities than are afforded by this chapter." 42 U.S.C. § 12201(b). New Mexico's WCA and the ADA do not conflict with each other, but rather they have different purposes and provide remedies for different grievances. *See e.g., Harding*, 907 F.Supp. at 391–92 (finding that ADA does not require Florida Workers' Compensation Act to provide equal eligibility in benefits); *Hensley v. Punta Gorda*, 686 So.2d 724, 728 (Fla.Dist.Ct.App.1997) (finding no inconsistency between the goals of the ADA and Florida's Workers' Compensation Act); *Bailey v. Reynolds Metals*, 153 Or.App. 498, 959 P.2d 84, 89 (1998) (finding that Oregon's Workers' Compensation benefits protect workers precisely when the workers are not protected by the ADA); see also EEOC Compliance Manual, Vol. II, § 138, No. 915.002 (Sept. 3, 1996) (stating that the purposes of the ADA and Workers' Compensation Laws are not in conflict).

2. Analysis of Workers' Claim

Workers do not provide, nor can we find, any authority that directly addresses their argument that in a workers' compensation scheme, persons with disabilities due to mental impairment cannot be treated differently under the ADA than persons with disabilities due to physical impairments. However, many courts have found, in similar contexts, that the ADA does not require equal benefits be given to all disabled persons equally. As a starting point, we look to the United States Supreme

Court's interpretation of the Rehabilitation Act of 1973, which standards are applied to ADA provisions. *See* 42 U.S.C. § 12201(a); *McPherson v. Mich. High Sch. Athletic Ass'n, Inc.*, 119 F.3d 453, 459–60 (6th Cir.1997) (determining that because the standards under both statutes are largely the same, cases construing Rehabilitation Act are instructive in construing ADA); *Doe v. Univ. of Md. Med. Sys. Corp.*, 50 F.3d 1261, 1264–65 n. 9 (4th Cir.1995) (applying the same analysis of ADA as of Rehabilitation Act because the language is the same). The United States Supreme Court analyzed Tennessee's Medicaid Program and found that a reduction in hospital services did create a disparate impact on handicapped individuals, but that the Rehabilitation Act required only that handicapped individuals have meaningful access to services. *Alexander v. Choate*, 469 U.S. 287, 304, 105 S.Ct. 712, 83 L.Ed.2d 661 (1985). The Act does not guarantee the handicapped equal results from state Medicaid provisions even if some measure of equality could be constructed. Id. The Supreme Court later reiterated this interpretation in finding that "[t]here is nothing in the Rehabilitation Act that requires that any benefit extended to one category of handicapped persons also be extended to all other categories of handicapped persons." *Traynor v. Turnage*, 485 U.S. 535, 549, 108 S.Ct. 1372, 99 L.Ed.2d 618 (1988).

a. Decisions Regarding Distinctions in Workers' Compensation Schemes

Several federal and state courts have relied on the Unites States Supreme Court's guidance in *Alexander* and *Traynor* to find that the ADA does not require that all disabled persons, regardless of the differences in each person's disabilities, receive equal eligibility for workers' compensation benefits. Workers in Florida challenged the Florida's workers' compensation scheme that awards benefits based on levels of physical impairment as violative of the ADA, arguing that persons with lesser impairment ratings and lesser benefits may be more disabled than persons with higher impairment ratings. *Cramer v. State of Fla.*, 885 F.Supp. 1545, 1550 (M.D.Fla.1995),*aff'd*, 117 F.3d 1258 (11th Cir.1997). The United States District Court found that the ADA "applies only to discrimination against disabled persons compared to non-disabled persons," *id.* at 1551, and held that the Florida Workers' Compensation Act (FWCA) did not violate the ADA even if disabled workers were treated differently. *Id.* at 1553. The court determined that disability statutes like the ADA do not ensure evenhanded treatment as compared to other disabled persons. *Id.*; *see also Harding*, 907 F.Supp. at 391–92 (finding, in a similar challenge, that the ADA does not require all disabled persons to receive equal eligibility requirements under FWCA benefits and finding that the FWCA complied with the ADA by providing "meaningful access to benefits to all disabled persons or injured workers").

Florida state courts have reached a similar conclusion. See *Barry v. Burdines*, 675 So.2d 587, 589 (Fla.1996) (finding no discriminatory intent or result in FWCA scheme of impairment ratings and no violation of ADA because ADA does not guarantee equal rights to all disabled workers); *Hensley*, 686 So.2d at 728 (finding that Florida's decision to exclude FWCA compensation for mental or nervous injuries unrelated to compensable physical injury not inconsistent with the goals of the ADA).

The Oregon Court of Appeals also has found that its workers' compensation scheme that treats injured workers with preexisting conditions differently from injured workers with no preexisting condition is not in conflict with the ADA because the ADA does not require that all disabled persons have identical access to benefits of employment. *Bailey*, 959 P.2d at 87.

b. Decisions Regarding Distinctions in Health and Human Services

[omitted.]

The only court that has concluded differently from the courts noted above, and the only case Workers rely on, is the United States Court of Appeals for the 11th Circuit in its decision in *Johnson v. K Mart Corp.*, 273 F.3d 1035, 1054 (11th Cir.2001) (finding that ADA prohibits a distinction in benefit payments between mental and physical disabilities). However, we note that the opinion was vacated and was then stayed until K Mart emerges from bankruptcy proceedings. *Johnson v. K Mart Corp.*, 281 F.3d 1368 (11th Cir.2002). Thus, this case has no binding effect on this or any other court, and we do not find it persuasive in any event.

3. New Mexico's WCA Does Not Violate ADA

We come to the inescapable conclusion, as have the many federal and state courts discussed above, that the ADA does not require that the state or an employer confer the same benefits to people with different disabilities. New Mexico's WCA applies equally to all workers employed by employers who come within the Act. *See* NMSA 1978, § 52–1–2 (1987). It provides meaningful access to benefits for all workers, whether they are disabled due to mental or physical impairments. See §§ 52–1–41 and –42; *Alexander*, 469 U.S. at 304, 105 S.Ct. 712. Workers Breen and Carrasco received the same benefits as any other covered worker would receive. They do not claim that they were denied benefits by reason of their disability as is prohibited by 42 U.S.C. § 12112(a) of the ADA. Rather, they claim that, because of their disabilities, they are due benefits that have not been provided. However, as determined by the many other courts discussed in this opinion, this is not a cognizable claim under the ADA because the ADA does not mandate equal treatment between disabled persons. Rather, the ADA mandates equal treatment of disabled persons with non-disabled persons. Accordingly, we hold that

New Mexico's WCA, which treats persons with mental impairments differently from persons with physical impairments, does not violate the ADA.

III. Conclusion

We affirm the order of the Workers' Compensation Judge.

4. PREVENTING WORK INJURIES: THE OCCUPATIONAL SAFETY AND HEALTH ACT

Prior to 1970 Congress left the regulation of industrial safety standards, practices and procedures primarily to the states. In that year, responding to an annual toll of approximately 14,000 industrial deaths and millions of injuries, Congress assumed a new role of preventing industrial accidents through the enactment of the Occupational Safety and Health Act of 1970 (OSHA). Although OSHA requirements can be expensive for many employers to meet and their violation can result in substantial penalties, it does not set up the potential adversarial relationship between a claiming employee and a defending employer (or benefits agency) as do tort law and various compensation programs. No court has ruled that OSHA creates private compensatory rights for employees. Because of that, the conflicts under OSHA arise primarily between employers and the agencies charged with administering the law; namely, the Secretary of Labor and the Occupational Safety and Health Review Commission. Accordingly, legal disputes under OSHA usually arise in the processes for setting and enforcing safety standards. The following is a brief overview of the Act, highlighting those processes.

OSHA applies to employers "engaged in a business affecting commerce."[34] As written, its application apparently extends to the furthest reaches of Congress' commerce clause power without being foreshortened by any limits on the size of covered employers such as is are seen in the Fair Labor Standards Act of 1938 and in Title VII of the Civil Rights Act of 1964. For example, OSHA has been applied to cover workers who were clearing land that would later grow grapes to be used to make wine for sale in commerce. Godwin v. OSAHRC, 540 F.2d 1013 (9th Cir.1976).

OSHA imposes a basic duty on employers under the so-called general duty clause:

> [Each employer] shall furnish to each of his employees employment and a place of employment which are free from recognized hazards that are causing or are likely to cause death or serious physical harm to employees; [and] shall comply with

[34] Occupational Safety and Health Act of 1970, Pub.L. 91–596, § 3(5), 29 U.S.C.A. § 651 et seq.

occupational safety and health standards promulgated under [OSHA].[35]

The correlative duties of employees are to "comply with occupational safety and health standards and all rules, regulations, and orders * * * which are applicable to their own actions and conduct."[36] In addition to the basic duties, employers are obliged to comply with specific occupational safety and health standards that are promulgated by the Secretary of Labor.[37] The Secretary may have the assistance of a National Advisory Committee on Occupational Safety and Health, composed of representatives of management, labor, occupational safety and occupational health professions, and the public;[38] an advisory standard setting committee;[39] the Secretary of Health and Human Services;[40] and the specially created National Institute for Occupational Safety and Health.[41]

The stringency tone of OSHA standards is set by the criterion that standards dealing with "toxic materials or harmful physical agents" are to assure that "to the extent feasible * * * no employees will suffer material impairment of health or functional capacity even if such employee has regular exposure to the hazard * * * for the period of his working life."[42]

OSHA standards are promulgated by rule[43] under rulemaking procedures prescribed by the Act.[45] The process includes publishing the proposed rule in the Federal Register and affording an opportunity for comment.[43] If requested, the Secretary must hold a public hearing.[44] Any person adversely affected by an OSHA standard may seek judicial review of the promulgating process in a United States Court of Appeals at any time before the expiration of 60 days from the date the Secretary promulgates it.[45] The Secretary's administrative determination of the factual predicate for any standard will be conclusively upheld in the courts if supported by "substantial evidence considered in the record as a

[35] Id., § 654(a).

[36] Id., § 654(b).

[37] Id., § 654(b)(2).

[38] Id., § 656(a)(2). The Committee is charged to "advise, consult with and make recommendations * * * on matters relating to the administration of the Act."

[39] Id., § 656(b).

[40] Id., § 669(2).

[41] Id., § 671.

[42] Id., § 655(b)(5).

[43] Id., § 655(a)

[45] Id., § 655(a).

[43] Id., § 655(b)(2).

[44] Id., § 655(b)(3).

[45] Id., § 655(f).

whole,"[46] but the reviewing courts exercise plenary review of questions of law.

Employers may seek temporary variances[47] while they are attempting to comply with standards, or permanent variances issued where the employer has demonstrated by a preponderance of evidence that the variant conditions would be "as safe and healthful as those which would prevail if he complied with the standard."[48]

The Secretary's primary enforcement tools are the authority to enter work places, inspect working conditions, question employees and employers, and inspect records kept by employers concerning occupational deaths and injuries as required by regulations issued under the Act.[49] The Secretary, upon presenting "appropriate credentials", may enter a work place "without delay and at reasonable times"[50] * * * "to inspect and investigate during regular working hours and at other reasonable times, and within reasonable limits and in a reasonable manner"[51] working conditions, machinery and so forth.

Initially, over the objection of employers, the Secretary took the position that the law authorized inspectors to make warrantless searches without notice. The Supreme Court rejected that argument in *Marshall v. Barlow's Inc.*, 436 U.S. 307, 98 S.Ct. 1816, 56 L.Ed.2d 305 (1978), and held that a search warrant is required. Nevertheless, the criteria for the Secretary's getting a warrant are less stringent than probable cause. It will be enough for the Secretary to present the judicial officer with "an administrative plan containing specific neutral criteria." Then the warrant will issue.

Once within a work place the OSHA investigator has the authority to make a walk-around inspection while accompanied by a representative of the employer and one designated by the employees.[37] Acknowledging that the Secretary will not be able to inspect all work places within a reasonable period of time, the Act provides for employees or their representatives to make written requests that the Secretary make inspections under circumstances where a violation of a standard "threatens physical harm or * * * an imminent danger exists."[38] The Secretary must have procedures of informal review, including written explanation, of refusals to issue citations in situations where employees

---

[46] Id., § 655(f).

[47] Id., § 655(b).

[48] Id., § 655(d).

[49] Id., § 657.

[50] Id., § 657(a)(1).

[51] Id., § 657(a).

[37] Id., § 657 (e).

[38] Id., § 657(f)(1).

or their representatives have given written notice of an alleged violation and no citation is issued thereafter.[39]

Obviously, the foregoing investigatory scheme will generate disputes between employers and the Secretary and also between employees and the Secretary. In some instances, the process becomes entangled in general labor-management disputes, but it more often leads to enforcement actions under the Act.

Upon finding a violation of the Act, the Secretary must issue a written citation to the employer, fixing a reasonable time for abatement.[40] Thereafter, the Secretary may propose a penalty[41] in an amount that varies according to whether the violation is "wilful and repeated," "serious"[42] or only "nonserious,"[43] or is a failure to correct a violation within the period permitted.[44] Within 15 working days from receipt of notice of the proposed penalty, the employer must notify the Secretary of the intention to contest either the citation or the proposed penalty. If this is not done, the citation and proposed penalty become final and "*not subject to review by any court or agency*."[45] If the employer contests the citation or proposed penalty, or if an employee or employee's representative contests the time period fixed for abatement, the Occupational and Safety Health Review Commission must review the matter and give an opportunity for a hearing.[46] The Commission may modify, affirm or vacate the Secretary's citation or proposed penalty or give other appropriate relief.[47]

Despite the fact that the Commission's order can impose a civil fine, the employer is not entitled to a trial by jury in a court on the question of whether or not the Act was violated. According to *Atlas Roofing Co., Inc. v. Occupational Safety, Etc.*, 430 U.S. 442, 97 S.Ct. 1261, 51 L.Ed.2d 464 (1977), new statutory rights created by Congress, such as those in OSHA, do not fall under the injunction of the Seventh Amendment. Although the Commission's order becomes final 30 days after issuance, any person "*adversely affected or aggrieved*" may obtain appellate review in an appropriate United States court of appeals by filing a petition seeking to have the order modified or set aside within 60 days of its issuance.[48] Although fact findings of the Commission are binding if supported by

---

[39] Id., § 658(a).

[40] Id., § 658(a).

[41] Id., § 666(a). Civil penalty not more than $70,000 but not less than $5,000 per violation.

[42] Id., § 666(b). Civil penalty of up to $7,000 per violation.

[43] Id., § 666(b). Civil penalty of up to $7,000 per violation.

[44] Id., § 666(d). Civil penalty of up to $7,000 per violation.

[45] Id., § 659(a).

[46] Id., § 659(c)

[47] Id., § 659(c).

[48] Id., § 660(a).

"substantial evidence on the record considered as a whole," the appellate court may order the Commission to hear additional evidence in appropriate situations.[49] United States courts of appeal also enforce Commission orders through the contempt powers.[50]

In addition to civil penalties, the Act imposes criminal penalties for wilful violations of standards and orders that cause the death of an employee;[51] provides remedies in Federal district courts for employees who are discharged or discriminated against by employers because of activities authorized by the Act;[52] outlaws giving an employer advance notice of an inspection;[53] outlaws making false statements[54] by any person; and, outlaws failure to correct violations.[55]

OSHA relates to accident prevention and does not "supersede or in any manner affect" the reparation functions of state workers' compensation laws.[56] Moreover, courts are apparently unanimous in holding that OSHA creates no private cause of action for injured workers, either against an employer, see, e.g., Knight v. Burns, Kirkley & Williams Constr. Co., Inc., 331 So.2d 651 (Ala.1976), or the federal government for failure to enforce OSHA rigorously. See e.g., Davis v. United States, 536 F.2d 758 (8th Cir.1976). Nevertheless, state courts may admit an OSHA standard as evidence to particularize an employer's standard of care in a negligence action. DiSabatino Brothers, Inc. v. Baio, 366 A.2d 508 (Del.1976).

To the extent that OSHA standards do not relate to a given "occupational safety or health issue" the states may assert regulatory jurisdiction.[57] Moreover, states may assume responsibility for developing and enforcing standards in areas preempted by OSHA upon approval of a state plan by the Secretary of Labor.[58] Federal agencies are not governed by OSHA enforcement procedures[59] but are directed to establish programs for federal employments consistent with OSHA standards.[60]

---

[49] Id., § 666(a).

[50] Id., § 660(b).

[51] Id., § 666(e). Fine not more than $10,000; or 6 months imprisonment; or both for first conviction.

[52] Id., § 660(c)(2). Federal district courts may issue restraining orders and order appropriate relief, including rehiring and back pay.

[53] Id., § 666(f). Fine not more than $1,000; or not more than 6 months imprisonment; or both.

[54] Id., § 666(g). Fine not more than $10,000; or not more than 6 months imprisonment; or both.

[55] Id., § 666(d). Fine of not more than $7,000 for each day.

[56] Id., § 653(b)(4).

[57] Id., § 667(a).

[58] Id., § 667(b).

[59] Id., § 653(a)(1).

[60] Id., § 667(c)(6).

Moreover, an approved state enforcement plan must provide state employees job safety protection "to the extent permitted by its law."[61]

A. COMMENTARY

Not all theorists believe that direct regulation internalizes the costs of work injuries better than tort litigation does. The following extract (footnotes omitted) from Pierce, "Encouraging Safety: The Limits of Tort Law and Government Regulation," 33 Vanderbilt Law Rev. 1281, 1308–1319 (1980) discusses some of the limitations.

> "IV. Direct Regulation as a Substitute for, or a Supplement to, the Market and Tort Law
>
> *"A. Advantages of Direct Regulation*
>
> "Direct regulation is usually justified on the theory that, in some areas at least, the combination of the market and tort law has proven ineffective as a mechanism for encouraging safety. Thus, it is the failure of other parts of the legal system to internalize accident costs that forces reliance upon direct safety regulation. Once the inadequacies of the operation of the market and tort law are recognized in a particular context, direct regulation appears to be the only available option for reducing accident costs. As demonstrated in the prior parts of this Article, the market and tort law are increasingly less effective (and more costly). Hence, the growth of direct regulation and its rapid spread to new areas is both understandable and seemingly justified.
>
> "The theory underlying direct regulation is relatively simple; if an activity is producing too many accident costs, prohibit the activity or require that it be carried on in a different manner. There is no reason in theory why direct regulation cannot produce an optimal level and pattern of spending on safety. As with the market and tort law, however, direct regulation in practice falls well short of its theoretically attainable goals.
>
> *"B. Limits of Direct Regulation*
>
> "1. Setting Appropriate Standards
>
> "A major problem inherent in direct regulation is the difficulty of determining which safety standards or rules will produce the optimum level of spending on safety. The current debate focuses on the extent to which explicit quantification and comparison of the costs and benefits of various standards should be relied upon in lieu of purely subjective balancing of safety

[61] Id., § 668(a).

against costs. If cost-benefit analysis (CBA) can be applied to the process of establishing safety standards with acceptable results, direct regulation provides a promising alternative means of encouraging safety. Thus, to evaluate the efficacy of safety regulation, it is first necessary to explore the major impediments to the use of CBA as a means of determining optimal safety standards.

"Determining causal relationships is, of course, indispensable to calculating the benefits of a proposed safety standard. Yet, this determination is often difficult, and the result is invariably imprecise. Carcinogenicity determinations provide a particularly apt illustration of the problem. With respect to most suspected carcinogens, it is impossible even to be certain that the agent causes cancer in humans, though animal test results provide reasonably reliable indications. Determining with a high degree of confidence the number of cases of cancer that the particular agent will cause at particular exposure levels is beyond the state of the art. . . . In determining carcinogenicity, as in many other areas of accident causation, the state of the art and data availability limit regulators to a crude approximation of causal relationships.

"It must be recognized, however, that regulatory agencies are probably institutionally better suited to determine causation than are courts. The regulatory agency can deal with statistical and probabilistic causation with all the data gathering and calculational advantages of a centralized decisionmaker. By contrast, courts have great difficulty dealing with probabilistic and joint causation, have limited access to relevant data, and have virtually no ability to make sophisticated calculations. Moreover, curing these deficiencies would be prohibitively expensive because of the large number of courts and the institutional characteristics of courts as decisionmakers.

"A second advantage enjoyed by a centralized regulatory decisionmaker is the ability to determine the 'cause' of accidents by identification of the entity that can avoid accident costs most effectively and at least cost. As Professor Calabresi has demonstrated, the party causally responsible for a particular type of accident in this sense often is not even before the court in a tort action. [G. Calabresi, The Costs of Accidents (1970), at 256.] Again, trying to cure this defect in the tort system would vastly increase its already staggering administrative costs by transforming every tort case into a polycentric dispute of the type the judicial system simply has not been able to accommodate. Thus, while causation remains a major problem in the centralized decisionmaking of regulatory agencies, those agencies are better able to deal with the problem than courts.

"Determining causal relationships, however, is only one of many problems with the use of CBA. After causal relationships have been approximated, it is necessary to calculate the magnitude of costs and benefits using a common denominator, usually dollars. CBA has been subject to considerable criticism on the basis that it is much easier to calculate costs of regulation than to calculate benefits. In fact, calculating either side of the equation is very difficult, and significant costs of regulation often are omitted.

[Discussion of difficulties of putting a price on a human life is omitted.]

"There are other costs that flow from the use of CBA as well. Use of CBA to set safety standards necessarily produces high transaction costs in the regulatory process. A thorough CBA for a proposed safety standard requires hundreds of highly skilled man-hours. Even assuming that efficient decisionmaking procedures are used, the regulatory system permits (and often, as a practical matter, demands) that several CBAs be conducted for any proposed standard which is subject to dispute. The regulatory transaction costs become staggering when the quite rational requirement of incremental CBAs and CBAs for proposed alternatives are added.

"The final major difficulty in establishing safety standards based on CBA is the tremendous potential for manipulation of the numerical ratio. As Amory Lovins has persuasively demonstrated, result-oriented technicians can use a variety of techniques in calculating the CBA to mask what otherwise would be recognized as blatant biases and analytical errors. The often symbiotic relationship between regulators and a narrow constituency causes this potential abuse of CBA to take on considerable importance.

"Throughout the foregoing discussion, I have assumed that a quantitative decisionmaking aid should be employed to determine appropriate safety standards for use in direct regulation. There is, of course, the alternative, supported by many, of relying entirely upon a combination of subjective decisionmaking and absolute pursuit of safety. Congress often eschews use of CBA in favor of subjective absolutism in determining safety standards. Four significant problems with this approach are apparent. First, if the agency actually follows the absolute safety mandate, the result is likely to be overspending on some aspects of safety and underspending on others, with a significant net reduction in accident costs avoided per dollar spent on safety. Second, subjective decisionmaking is as likely to mask biases, errors, and result-oriented regulation as is decisionmaking aided by CBA. Third, regulators confronted with a mandate to obtain absolute safety still use some form of *sub rosa* quantified balancing. Fourth, when agencies use a combination of official subjective absolutism and *sub rosa* quantified balancing, irrational patterns of spending on safety inevitably evolve.

"Actual adherence to an absolute standard of safety in a particular area necessarily produces badly skewed safety spending patterns. It is impossible for society to pursue an absolutist philosophy in all contexts or even to do so with respect to a broad category of risks, such as involuntary exposure risks. Given this basic premise, it necessarily follows that total accident costs always can be reduced by shifting safety spending from an activity in which absolutism has prevailed to virtually any other activity. This proposition is very simple to prove using the marginal analysis that is central to microeconomics.

"Subjective decisionmaking has been used effectively for years as a means of disguising biases and analytical flaws in order to reach a predetermined result dictated by factors never alluded to in the decision itself. Just as the good numbers mechanic can engage in mathematical subterfuge, the good verbal mechanic can use semantic tricks to hide political favoritism, vindictiveness, and incomplete analysis. Indeed, because there is more precision and uniform terminology in the language of mathematics, it is easier to demonstrate the flaws in a decision reached with the aid of a quantification tool such as CBA than to pierce the artful prose of a poorly reasoned but cleverly written subjective decision. Thus, the manipulation of decisionmaking tools by result-oriented regulators and technicians must be attacked through more basic changes in institutional decisionmaking.

"It is highly unlikely that any agency with an absolutist mandate actually follows that mandate consistently and eschews all efforts to balance the costs and benefits of safety standards. Rather, agencies make at least rough calculations covertly and disguise the quantitative basis for their decision through the use of ambiguous subjective terminology. As a result, the actual basis for the decision is never publicly revealed, the decisionmaking pattern is grossly distorted by sub rosa calculations in which implicit values are irrationally determined, and the potential for politically motivated, result-oriented decisions is even greater than in a system relying explicitly on quantification aids.

"OSHA's approach to determining safety standards for toxic chemicals provides a good example of how the process can work. OSHA disavows all reliance upon CBA in establishing safety standards. Based upon a reasonably well-supported interpretation of its organic act, OSHA takes the position that safety standards for workers are required to provide as much safety as is "feasible," and that the concept of feasibility negates any inference that costs should be balanced against benefits. Of course, OSHA is still required to apply the term "feasible" in determining standards. With some assistance from the courts, OSHA has defined "feasible" as any standard that will not place a substantial number of affected employers out of business. In other words, what began as an absolutist basis for standards was transformed into a basis dependent upon determinations of the financial viability of each affected industry and the major firms within that industry. As a result, OSHA's interpretation still requires use of mathematical aids in decisionmaking. Only the nature of the calculations and the values inherent in the results differ from a traditional CBA calculation.

* * *

"2. Other Costs and Limits of Direct Regulation

"There are problems associated with direct safety regulation in addition to those encountered in determining safety standards. In a dynamic economy, significant technological and economic changes occur rapidly. Yet recalculating CBAs for every conceivable alternative standard in response to changes in economic or technologic factors is prohibitively expensive. As a result, safety standards rapidly become obsolete.

"Enforcement too is a major problem of direct regulation. Some studies have shown that safety standards in the occupational safety area have no effect whatsoever on the actual level of accident costs. There undoubtedly are circumstances in which some safety standards have some beneficial effect, but the empirical data on the relationship between safety standards and accident costs are not encouraging.

"There is also considerable evidence that direct safety regulation increases the concentration of market power in an industry. Some of this effect probably is attributable to economies of scale in providing safety and, to that extent, it must

> be accepted as a consequence of any method of inducing greater safety. Much of the concentration effect of safety regulation, however, is attributable to economies of scale in conducting tests, filing reports, and otherwise complying with the administrative burdens attendant to direct regulation.
>
> "Perhaps the most important disadvantage of direct safety regulation is its effect upon individual freedom. Substitution of direct safety regulation for market-determined levels of safety has significant implications for freedom and the ability of individuals to choose the mixture of comfort, pleasure, and risk they prefer. Safety decisions made in the context of direct regulation necessarily are based upon some measure of average or median tastes and preferences. The individual with a strong aversion to risk or a strong taste for risk must simply accept that level of risk determined collectively to be acceptable to society. The Pareto optimality and accommodation of individual tastes theoretically attainable through the market (were it not for externalities and transaction costs) is impossible to achieve through direct regulation. Some degree of constraint upon individual tastes and freedom is absolutely essential in any society, but complete abandonment of the market and internalization of accident costs in all areas of safety would force reliance upon direct regulation so pervasive as to undermine totally the individual freedom so highly prized in our society. . . ."

See also, Shavell, "Liability for Harm Versus Regulation for Safety," 13 J. of Legal Studies 357 (1984).

A more pragmatic limitation on a regulatory strategy for improving workplace safety is the availability of resources to enforce standards. Consider the following assessment of OSHA's performance:

> Enforcement of the statutory duties through workplace inspections by compliance officers and issuance of citations has been glaringly inadequate "to assure so far as possible every working man and women in the Nation safe and healthful working conditions." The reasons are not difficult to discern.
>
> First, the resources devoted to the effort are not equal to the task. The statute covers some 5 million workplaces with 85 million employees. At its peak, OSHA had less than 3,000 inspectors, and in 1987 had less than 1200 federal inspectors. Even with scheduled inspections limited to more hazardous industries, establishments cannot be inspected once in five years.

> The inadequacy of inspections is indicated by the fact that Sweden, with a working population of 4 million makes as many health and safety inspections each year as the United States with a working population of more than 100 million.
>
> * * *
>
> The second source of enforcement inadequacy has been the puniness of penalties. With the remote likelihood of being inspected, recalcitrant employers will be induced to comply only by penalties sufficient to make violations unprofitable. The statutory schedule of penalties is plainly inadequate, with the maximum for a serious violation being $1,000, and the maximum for a repeated or willful violation of $10,000. OSHA, however, seldom imposes these meager maximums, as the cases studied have shown, with serious violations typically resulting in penalties of a few hundred dollars. Penalties in 1985 averaged only $77.68 per violation. (85 Colum.L.Rev. at 138, n. 138). As the Second Circuit said in Olin Construction Co. v. OSHRC, 525 F.2d 464, 467 (2d Cir.1975), "As for the penalties, we are amazed at their paucity, reflecting more of a license than a penalty."
>
> The real puniness of the penalty is frequently somewhat disguised by settlements for substantially less than those proposed in the citation. To obtain a settlement, monetary penalties may be completely eliminated, even where serious violations have been cited. See, Donovan v. OCAW, 718 F.2d 1341, 1343 n. 5 (5th Cir.1983); and "serious" violations may be recharacterized as "non-serious," see Donovan v. International Union, Allied Industrial Workers, 722 F.2d 1415, 1416 (8th Cir.1983).
>
> * * *

M. Franklin, A. Goldman and C. Summers, Legal Protection For the Individual Employee 461–463 (1989). See also, Office of Technology Assessment, U.S. Congress, Preventing Illness and Injury in the Workplace (1985) ("OSHA and the State programs have been able to inspect * * * at most, 4 percent of all establishments and less than 20 percent of manufacturing establishments each year. In addition, the penalties for violations are, on average, very low, and in most cases, much smaller than the potential costs of controls.").

Despite criticisms of OSHA, the death rate in all industries in the United States fell from 18 deaths per 100,000 workers in 1969, the year preceding OSHA's enactment, to 3.0 deaths per 100,000 workers in 2010 (Injury Facts 2012, p. 58). This correlation tends to support the value of OSHA. Nevertheless, the difficulty in attributing cause and effect is shown by the fact that without OSHA the death rate fell from 38 deaths per 100,000 workers in 1938 to 18 deaths per 100,000 workers in 1969. Perhaps this suggests that as industry becomes safer ever more costly new measures will be required to make additional gains. Whether new money spent in the work safety field could be allocated to other fields (i.e. highway and home safety) with greater overall savings in lives, suffering and dollars is a legitimate economic and political question, but not a legal question as such.

CHAPTER 2

THE COMPENSATION PRINCIPLE

■ ■ ■

1. HISTORICAL AND CONSTITUTIONAL BACKGROUND

The reader can only conjecture as to what the law of employment injuries would be like if state legislatures had taken the course of FELA to enlarge the common law duties of employers and emasculate the fellow servant, assumption of risk and contributory negligence defenses. Perhaps the outcomes would have varied immensely from state to state, depending upon differing political pressures, but the answer will never be known because of the pervasive emergence of workers' compensation, which substituted a different method of compensating employment injuries and deaths.

The compensation movement originated on the European continent and was first adopted in the German Compensation Act of 1884 after two years of legislative consideration in that country. Under the German Act, the first thirteen weeks of a worker's disability caused by either sickness or accident was compensated from a Sickness Fund supported by the compulsory contributions of both employers and employees. Payments for more extended disabilities were made from an Accident Fund which employers alone financed. The German Act was initially restricted to hazardous occupations, such as mining, manufacturing, and transportation, but was extended several times until, finally, in 1911 it embraced all employments. For a full account of the history and development of the German Act see Twenty-fourth Annual Report of the Commissioner of Labor, 1909, Vol. 1, pp. 975–1493.

In Great Britain, following several unsuccessful legislative attempts to rectify the shortcomings of the common law, Parliament adopted the Workmen's Compensation Act of 1897. The initial British bill was also confined to hazardous employments. It differed from the German Act by placing the funding responsibility exclusively on the shoulders of employers, who were permitted to secure the benefits by purchasing insurance from private companies. Various amendments broadened the scope of the Act until in 1906 it applied to almost all employments. During this same period the compensation scheme spread throughout continental Europe, and by 1908 workers' compensation laws existed in almost all western industrial countries except the United States. The

Compendium on Workmen's Compensation of the National Commission on State Workmen's Compensation Laws (1973), pp. 61–98, provides a study of comparative approaches to work injury compensation in international perspective.

Shortly after the turn of the twentieth century Maryland and Montana adopted statutes that applied to limited groups of industries. Both statutes were declared unconstitutional. See, e.g., Cunningham v. Northwestern Improvement Co., 44 Mont. 180, 119 P. 554 (1911). (The Maryland statute was held unconstitutional by a lower court and no appeal was taken.) Many other states appointed commissions to investigate the need to compensate industrial injuries and to recommend specific measures. The influential New York commission concluded: the existing common law system provided woefully insufficient compensation by way of damages for injured workers and their families; common law litigation imposed substantial court costs and attorneys' fees upon employers and produced little corresponding benefit for workers; and the extended amount of time required to take a case to trial forced many needy employees into a Hobson's choice—either to forego money needed immediately for support and cure or to accept a disadvantageous settlement in order to secure ready cash. New York Employers' Liability Commission, First Report (1910) Vol. 1. The report is summarized in Dodd, Administration of Workmen's Compensation (1936) pp. 19–26. This report was a primary impetus in the enactment of the New York workers' compensation statute that was closely modeled after the 1906 British Act. Students may compare that act as described in the next case with any modern workers' constitution statute to adjudge how influential it has been down to the present.

NEW YORK CENTRAL R.R. CO. V. WHITE

Supreme Court of United States, 1917.
243 U.S. 188, 37 S.Ct. 247, 61 L.Ed. 667.

MR. JUSTICE PITNEY delivered the opinion of the court:

A proceeding was commenced by defendant in error before the Workmen's Compensation Commission of the State of New York, established by the Workmen's Compensation Law of that state, to recover compensation from the New York Central & Hudson River Railroad Company for the death of her husband, Jacob White, who lost his life September 2, 1914, through an accidental injury arising out of and in the course of his employment under that company. The Commission awarded compensation in accordance with the terms of the law; its award was affirmed, without opinion, by the appellate division of the supreme court for the third judicial department, whose order was affirmed by the court of appeals, without opinion. 169 App.Div. 903, 152 N.Y.S. 1149, 216 N.Y. 653, 110 N.E. 1051. Federal questions having been saved, the present writ of error was sued out by the New York Central Railroad Company, successor, through a consolidation of corporations, to the rights and liabilities of the employing company. * * *

The errors specified are based upon these contentions: (1) that the liability, if any, of the railroad company for the death of Jacob White, is defined and limited exclusively by the provisions of the Federal Employers' Liability Act of April 22, 1908, chap. 149, 35 Stat. at L. 65, Comp.Stat.1913, § 8657, and (2) that to award compensation to defendant in error under the provisions of the Workmen's Compensation Law would deprive plaintiff in error of its property without due process of law, and deny to it the equal protection of the laws, in contravention of the 14th Amendment.

* * * [The court disposed of the contention that the controversy was controlled by FELA by pointing out that decedent's work bore no direct relation to interstate commerce. According to the Court, White "was a night watchman, charged with the duty of guarding tools and materials intended to be used in building a new station," and thus was not in commerce. The conclusion on this point, though no longer valid under later constructions of the commerce clause, permitted the Court to reach the critical workers' compensation issues.]

We turn to the constitutional question. The Workmen's Compensation Law of New York establishes forty-two groups of hazardous employments, defines "employee" as a person engaged in one of these employments upon the premises, or at the plant, or in the course of his employment away from the plant of his employer, but excluding farm laborers and domestic servants; defines "employment" as including employment only in a trade, business, or occupation carried on by the employer for pecuniary gain, "injury" and "personal injury" as meaning only accidental injuries arising out of and in the course of employment, and such disease or infection as naturally and unavoidably may result therefrom; and requires every employer subject to its provisions to pay or provide compensation according to a prescribed schedule for the disability or death of his employee resulting from an accidental personal injury arising out of and in the course of the employment, without regard to fault as a cause, except where the injury is occasioned by the wilful intention of the injured employee to bring about the injury or death of himself or of another, or where it results solely from the intoxication of the injured employee while on duty, in which cases neither the injured employee nor any dependent shall receive compensation.

By § 11 the prescribed liability is made exclusive, except that, if an employer fail to secure the payment of compensation as provided in § 50, an injured employee, or his legal representative, in case death results from the injury, may, at his option, elect to claim compensation under the act, or to maintain an action in the courts for damages, and in such an action it shall not be necessary to plead or prove freedom from contributory negligence, nor may the defendant plead as a defense that the injury was caused by the negligence of a fellow servant, that the employee assumed the risk of his employment, or that the injury was due to contributory negligence.

Compensation under the act is not regulated by the measure of damages applied in negligence suits, but in addition to providing medical, surgical, or other like treatment, it is based solely on loss of earning power, being graduated according to the average weekly wages of the injured employee and the character and duration of the disability, whether partial or total, temporary or permanent; while in case the injury causes death, the compensation is known as a death benefit, and includes funeral expenses, not exceeding $100, payments to the surviving wife (or dependent husband) during widowhood (or dependent widowerhood) of a percentage of the average wages of the deceased, and if there be a surviving child or children under the age of eighteen years an additional percentage of such wages for each child until that age is reached.

There are provisions invalidating agreements by employees to waive the right to compensation, prohibiting any assignment, release, or commutation of claims for compensation or benefits except as provided by the act, exempting them from the claims of creditors, and requiring that the compensation and benefits shall be paid only to employees or their dependents. Provision is made for the establishment of a Workmen's Compensation Commission with administrative and judicial functions, including authority to pass upon claims to compensation on notice to the parties interested. The award or decision of the Commission is made subject to an appeal, on questions of law only, to the appellate division of the supreme court for the third department, with an ultimate appeal to the court of appeals in cases where such an appeal would lie in civil actions.

A fund is created, known as "the state insurance fund," for the purpose of insuring employers against liability under the law, and assuring to the persons entitled the compensation thereby provided. The fund is made up primarily of premiums received from employers, at rates fixed by the Commission in view of the hazards of the different classes of employment, and the premiums are to be based upon the total pay roll and number of employees in each class at the lowest rate consistent with the maintenance of a solvent state insurance fund and the creation of a reasonable surplus and reserve. Elaborate provisions are laid down for the administration of this fund. By § 50, each employer is required to secure compensation to his employees in one of the following ways: (1) By insuring and keeping insured the payment of such compensation in the state fund; or (2) through any stock corporation or mutual association authorized to transact the business of workmen's compensation insurance in the state; or (3) "by furnishing satisfactory proof to the Commission of his financial ability to pay such compensation for himself, in which case the Commission may, in its discretion, require the deposit with the Commission of securities of the kind prescribed in § 13 of the Insurance Law, in an amount to be determined by the Commission, to secure his liability to pay the compensation provided in this chapter." If an employer fails to comply with this section, he is made liable to a penalty in an amount equal to the pro rata premium that would have been payable for insurance in the state fund during the period of noncompliance; besides which, his injured employees or their dependents are at liberty to maintain an action for damages in the courts, as prescribed by § 11. * * *

The scheme of the act is so wide a departure from common-law standards respecting the responsibility of employer to employee that doubts naturally have been raised respecting its constitutional validity. The adverse considerations urged or suggested in this case and in kindred cases submitted at the same time are: (a) That the employer's property is taken without due process of law, because he is subjected to a liability for compensation without regard to any neglect or default on his part or on the part of any other person for whom he is responsible, and in spite of the fact that the injury may be solely attributable to the fault of the employee; (b) that the employee's rights are interfered with, in that he is prevented from having compensation for injuries arising from the employer's fault commensurate with the damages actually sustained, and is limited to the measure of compensation prescribed by the act; and (c) that both employer and employee are deprived of their liberty to acquire property by being prevented from making such agreement as they choose respecting the terms of the employment.

In support of the legislation, it is said that the whole common-law doctrine of employer's liability for negligence, with its defenses of contributory negligence, fellow servant's negligence, and assumption of risk, is based upon fictions, and is inapplicable to modern conditions of employment; that in the highly organized and hazardous industries of the present day the causes of accident are often so obscure and complex that in a material proportion of cases it is impossible by any method correctly to ascertain the facts necessary to form an accurate judgment, and in a still larger proportion the expense and delay required for such ascertainment amount in effect to a defeat of justice; that, under the present system, the injured workman is left to bear the greater part of industrial accident loss, which, because of his limited income, he is unable to sustain, so that he and those dependent upon him are overcome by poverty and frequently become a burden upon public or private charity; and that litigation is unduly costly and tedious, encouraging corrupt practices and arousing antagonisms between employers and employees.

In considering the constitutional question, it is necessary to view the matter from the standpoint of the employee as well as from that of the employer. For, while plaintiff in error is an employer, and cannot succeed without showing that its rights as such are infringed * * *, yet, as pointed out by the court of appeals in the Jensen Case (215 N.Y. 526), the exemption from further liability is an essential part of the scheme, so that the statute, if invalid as against the employee, is invalid as against the employer.

The close relation of the rules governing responsibility as between employer and employee to the fundamental rights of liberty and property is, of course, recognized. But those rules, as guides of conduct, are not beyond alteration by legislation in the public interest. No person has a vested interest in any rule of law, entitling him to insist that it shall remain unchanged for his benefit. * * * The common law bases the employer's liability for injuries to the employee upon the ground of negligence; but negligence is merely the disregard of some duty imposed by law; and the nature and extent of the duty may be modified by legislation, with corresponding change in the test of negligence. Indeed, liability may be imposed for the consequences of a failure to comply with a statutory duty, irrespective of negligence in the ordinary sense; safety appliance acts being a familiar instance. * * *

The fault may be that of the employer himself, or—most frequently—that of another for whose conduct he is made responsible according to the maxim respondeat superior. In the latter case the employer may be entirely blameless, may have exercised the utmost human foresight to safeguard the employee; yet, if the alter ego, while acting within the scope of his duties, be negligent,—in disobedience, it may be, of the employer's positive and specific command,—the employer is answerable for the consequences. It cannot be that the rule embodied in the maxim is unalterable by legislation.

The immunity of the employer from responsibility to an employee for the negligence of a fellow employee is of comparatively recent origin, it being the product of the judicial conception that the probability of a fellow workman's negligence is one of the natural and ordinary risks of the occupation, assumed by the employee and presumably taken into account in the fixing of his wages. * * * The doctrine has prevailed generally throughout the United States, but with material differences in different jurisdictions respecting who should be deemed a fellow servant and who a vice principal or alter ego of the master, turning sometimes upon refined distinctions as to grades and departments in the employment. * * * It needs no argument to show that such a rule is subject to modification or abrogation by a state upon proper occasion.

The same may be said with respect to the general doctrine of assumption of risk. By the common law the employee assumes the risks normally incident to the occupation in which he voluntarily engages; other and extraordinary risks and those due to the employer's negligence he does not assume until made aware of them, or until they become so obvious that an ordinarily prudent man would observe and appreciate them; in either of which cases he does assume them, if he continues in the employment without obtaining from the employer an assurance that the matter will be remedied; but if he receive such an assurance, then, pending performance of the promise, the employee does not, in ordinary cases, assume the special risk. * * * Plainly, these rules, as guides of conduct and tests of liability, are subject to change in the exercise of the sovereign authority of the state.

So, also, with respect to contributory negligence. Aside from injuries intentionally self-inflicted, for which the statute under consideration affords no compensation, it is plain that the rules of law upon the subject, in their bearing upon the employer's responsibility, are subject to legislative change; for contributory negligence, again, involves a default in some duty resting on the employee, and his duties are subject to modification.

It may be added, by way of reminder, that the entire matter of liability for death caused by wrongful act, both within and without the relation of employer and employee, is a modern statutory innovation, in which the states differ as to who may sue, for whose benefit, and the measure of damages.

But it is not necessary to extend the discussion. This court repeatedly has upheld the authority of the states to establish by legislation departures from the fellow-servant rule and other common-law rules affecting the employer's liability for personal injuries to the employee. * * *

It is true that in the case of the statutes thus sustained there were reasons rendering the particular departures appropriate. Nor is it necessary, for the purposes of the present case, to say that a state might, without violence to the constitutional guaranty of "due process of law," suddenly set aside all common-law rules respecting liability as between employer and employee, without providing a reasonably just substitute. Considering the vast industrial organization of the state of New York, for instance, with hundreds of thousands of plants and millions of wage earners, each employer, on the one hand, having embarked his capital, and each employee, on the other, having taken up his particular mode of earning a livelihood, in reliance upon the probable permanence of an established body of law governing the relation, it perhaps may be doubted whether the state could abolish all rights of action, on the one hand, or all defenses, on the other, without setting up something adequate in their stead. No such question is here presented, and we intimate no opinion upon it.

The statute under consideration sets aside one body of rules only to establish another system in its place. If the employee is no longer able to recover as much as before in case of being injured through the employer's negligence, he is entitled to moderate compensation in all cases of injury, and has a certain and speedy remedy without the difficulty and expense of establishing negligence or proving the amount of the damages. Instead of assuming the entire consequences of all ordinary risks of the occupation, he assumes the consequences, in excess of the scheduled compensation, of risks ordinary and extraordinary. On the other hand, if the employer is left without defense respecting the question of fault, he at the same time is assured that the recovery is limited, and that it goes directly to the relief of the designated beneficiary. And just as the employee's assumption of ordinary risks at common law presumably was taken into account in fixing the rate of wages, so the fixed responsibility of the employer, and the modified assumption of risk by the employee under the new system, presumably will be reflected in the wage scale.

The act evidently is intended as a just settlement of a difficult problem, affecting one of the most important of social relations, and it is to be judged in its entirety. We have said enough to demonstrate that, in such an adjustment, the particular rules of the common law affecting the subject matter are not placed by the 14th Amendment beyond the reach of the lawmaking power of the state; and thus we are brought to the question whether the method of compensation that is established as a substitute transcends the limits of permissible state action.

We will consider, first, the scheme of compensation, deferring for the present the question of the manner in which the employer is required to secure payment.

Briefly, the statute imposes liability upon the employer to make compensation for disability or death of the employee resulting from accidental personal injury arising out of and in the course of the employment, without regard to fault as a cause except where the injury or death is occasioned by the employee's wilful intention to produce it, or where the injury results solely from his intoxication while on duty; it graduates the compensation for disability according to a prescribed scale based upon the loss of earning power, having regard to the previous wage and the character and duration of the disability; and measures the death benefits according to the dependency of the surviving wife, husband, or infant children. Perhaps we should add that it has no retrospective effect, and applies only to cases arising some months after its passage.

Of course, we cannot ignore the question whether the new arrangement is arbitrary and unreasonable, from the standpoint of natural justice. Respecting this, it is important to be observed that the act applies only to disabling or fatal personal injuries received in the course of hazardous employment in gainful occupation. Reduced to its elements, the situation to be dealt with is this: Employer and employee, by mutual consent, engage in a common operation intended to be advantageous to both; the employee is to contribute his personal services, and for these is to receive wages, and, ordinarily, nothing more; the employer is to furnish plant facilities, organization, capital, credit, is to control and manage the operation, paying the wages and other expenses, disposing of the product at such prices as he can obtain, taking all the profits, if any there be, and, of necessity, bearing the entire losses. In the nature of things, there is more or less of a probability that the employee may lose his life through some accidental injury arising out of the employment, leaving his widow or children deprived of their natural support; or that he may sustain an injury not mortal, but resulting in his total or partial disablement, temporary or permanent, with corresponding impairment of earning capacity.

The physical suffering must be borne by the employee alone; the laws of nature prevent this from being evaded or shifted to another, and the statute makes no attempt to afford an equivalent in compensation. But, besides, there is the loss of earning power,—a loss of that which stands to the employee as his capital in trade. This is a loss arising out of the business, and, however it may be charged up, is an expense of the operation, as truly as the cost of repairing broken machinery or any other expense that ordinarily is paid by the employer.

Who is to bear the charge? It is plain that, on grounds of natural justice, it is not unreasonable for the state, while relieving the employer from responsibility for damages measured by common-law standards and payable in cases where he or those for whose conduct he is answerable are found to be at fault, to require him to contribute a reasonable amount, and according to a reasonable and definite scale, by way of compensation for the loss of earning power incurred in the common enterprise, irrespective of the question of negligence, instead of leaving the entire loss to rest where it may chance to fall,—that is, upon the injured employee or his dependents. Nor can it be deemed arbitrary and unreasonable, from the standpoint of the employee's interest, to supplant a system under which he assumed the entire risk of injury in ordinary cases, and in others had a right to recover an amount more or less speculative upon proving facts of negligence that often were difficult to prove, and substitute a system under which, in all ordinary cases of accidental injury, he is sure of a definite and easily ascertained compensation, not being obliged to assume the entire loss in any case, but in all cases assuming any loss beyond the prescribed scale.

Much emphasis is laid upon the criticism that the act creates liability without fault. This is sufficiently answered by what has been said, but we may add that liability without fault is not a novelty in the law. The common-law liability of the carrier, of the innkeeper, or him who employed fire or other dangerous agency or harbored a mischievous animal, was not dependent altogether upon questions of fault or negligence. Statutes imposing liability without fault have been sustained. St. Louis & S.F.R. Co. v. Mathews, 165 U.S. 1, 22, 41 L.Ed. 611, 619, 17 Sup.Ct.Rep. 243. . . .

We have referred to the maxim, respondeat superior. In a well-known English case, Hall v. Smith, 2 Bing. 156, 160, 130 Eng.Reprint, 265, 9 J.B. Moore, 226, 2 L.J.C.P. 113, this maxim was said by Best, Ch. J., to be "bottomed on this principle, that he who expects to derive advantage from an act which is done by another for him, must answer for any injury which a third person may sustain from it." And this view has been adopted in New York. Cardot v. Barney, 63 N.Y. 281, 287, 20 Am.Rep. 533. The provision for compulsory compensation, in the act under consideration, cannot be deemed to be an arbitrary and unreasonable application of the principle, so as to amount to a deprivation of the employer's property without due process of law. The pecuniary loss resulting from the employee's death or disablement must fall somewhere. It results from something done in the course of an operation from which the employer expects to derive a profit. In excluding the question of fault as a cause of the injury, the act in effect disregards the proximate cause and looks to one more remote,—the primary cause, as it may be deemed,—and that is, the employment itself. For this, both parties are responsible, since they voluntarily engage in it as coadventurers, with personal injury to the employee as a probable and foreseen result. In ignoring any possible negligence of the employee producing or contributing to the injury, the lawmaker reasonably may have been influenced by the belief that, in modern industry, the utmost diligence in the employer's service is in some degree inconsistent with adequate care on the part of the employee for his own safety; that the more intently he devotes himself to the work, the less he can take precautions for his own security. And it is evident that the consequences of a disabling or fatal injury are precisely the same to the parties immediately affected, and to the community, whether the proximate cause be culpable or innocent. Viewing the entire matter, it cannot be pronounced arbitrary and unreasonable for the state to impose upon the employer the absolute duty of making a moderate and definite compensation in money to every disabled employee, or, in case of his death, to those who were entitled to look to him for support, in lieu of the common-law liability confined to cases of negligence.

This, of course, is not to say that any scale of compensation, however insignificant, on the one hand, or onerous, on the other, would be supportable. In this case, no criticism is made on the ground that the compensation prescribed by the statute in question is unreasonable in amount, either in general or in the particular case. Any question of that kind may be met when it arises. * * * We recognize that the legislation under review does measurably limit the freedom of employer and employee to agree respecting the terms of employment, and that it cannot be supported except on the ground that it is a reasonable exercise of the police power of the state. In our opinion it is fairly supportable upon that ground. And for this reason: The subject matter in respect of which freedom of contract is restricted is the matter of compensation for human life or limb lost or disability incurred in the course of hazardous employment, and the public has a direct interest in this as affecting the common welfare. * * *

We conclude that the prescribed scheme of compulsory compensation is not repugnant to the provisions of the 14th Amendment, and are brought to consider, next, the manner in which the employer is required to secure payment of the compensation. By § 50, this may be done in one of three ways: (a) State insurance; (b) insurance with an authorized insurance corporation or association; or (c) by a deposit of securities. * * *

The system of compulsory compensation having been found to be within the power of the state, it is within the limits of permissible regulation, in aid of the system, to require the employer to furnish satisfactory proof of his financial ability to pay the compensation, and to deposit a reasonable amount of securities for that purpose. * * *

Judgment affirmed.

NOTES

1. Six years before *White* was decided, the New York Court of Errors and Appeals had invalidated the New York compulsory compensation statute of 1910 on the ground that it denied due process of law to both employers and employees by imposing liability without fault upon employers and by arbitrarily restricting the amount to be recovered by employees. *Ives v. South Buffalo Ry. Co.*, 201 N.Y. 271, 94 N.E. 431 (1911). During the period between the *Ives* and *White* decisions most states adopted initial compensation statutes. Of thirty-three states, only *eight* imposed compulsory compensation laws, and of these eight, *four* did so only after the state constitutions were amended. Consequently, under these early statutes, a choice was made available to employers and employees as to whether the compensation principle or the common law should apply.

2. Because of initial concerns about the constitutionality of the workers' compensation principle, see e.g., Ives v. South Buffalo R. Co., 201 N.Y. 271, 94 N.E. 431 (1911), the legislatures of many states (e.g., California, Illinois, Kansas, Massachusetts, New Hampshire, New Jersey, and Wisconsin) applied the statutes only to those employers and employees who elected to accept their provisions. In time, the threat of unconstitutionality largely disappeared and most statutes now prescribe compulsory coverage (perhaps excepting Texas.)[1] Even the remaining "elective" statutes strongly encourage employers to elect coverage by amending the common law to exclude or modify the three common law defenses in actions brought by employees against employers as to work injuries. The Report of the National Commission on State Workmen's Compensation Laws (1972) recommends (R.2.1) that workers' compensation be made compulsory in all respects. What choices, if any, does your state's current statute afford?

3. *White* allayed fears of fundamental constitutional impediments and the compensation scheme thereafter proliferated rapidly. See also Mountain Timber Co. v. State of Washington, 243 U.S. 219, 37 S.Ct. 260, 61 L.Ed. 685 (1917) upholding the constitutionality of the Washington exclusive state fund law (i.e., benefits are secured by a state fund financed by employers rather than by private insurance.) Nevertheless, specific provisions of statutes that arbitrarily excluded certain activities or workers from general schemes were thereafter occasionally declared unconstitutional as violative of equal protection or due process. Gallegos v. Glaser Crandell Co., 388 Mich. 654, 202 N.W.2d 786 (1972) (exclusion of agricultural workers paid on a piecework basis and agricultural workers who do not work 35 or more hours per week held invalid), partially overruled by Eastway v. Eisenga, 420 Mich. 410, 362 N.W.2d 684 (1984); De Monaco by Giacobe v. Renton, 18 N.J. 352, 113 A.2d 782 (1955) (exclusion of newsboys; similar); and De Ayala v. Florida Farm Bureau Cas. Ins., 543 So.2d 204 (Fla.1989) (statute providing lesser death benefit for alien workers than non aliens denies equal protection). Cf., Price v. All American Engineering Co., 320 A.2d 336 (Del.1974) (statute retroactively increasing compensation benefits held constitutional). By 1920 all but eight states had adopted workers' compensation statutes, and the system became universal when Mississippi adopted a statute in 1948. As indicated in the next chapter, however, this does not mean that all employees are covered by compensation. For example, most statutes do not apply to employments with a small number of employees. As to those employments, the common law of torts, as amended if at all, continues to apply. For a summary of the historical development of Workers' Compensation, see Compendium on Workmen's Compensation, National Commission on State Workmen's Compensation Laws (1973), pp. 11–19.

4. *White* upheld the constitutionality of the most extensive "tort reform" legislation that had ever been enacted. Does the quid pro quo

---

[1] In Texas, employees have the option to submit to the workers' compensation act by electing to obtain insurance coverage. Tex. Lab. Code §406.002. Similarly, an employee may elect to waive coverage and retain rights under the common law. Tex. Lab. Code §406.034.

analysis employed therein suggest that the legislature must, as a matter of due process, provide some alternative remedy or commensurate benefit before taking away a person's common law tort remedy? In a 1978 decision that upheld the constitutionality of a statutory limitation on damages for nuclear accidents, the Supreme Court expressed doubt that a quid pro quo is always required. Duke Power Co. v. Carolina Environmental Study Group, Inc., 438 U.S. 59, 98 S.Ct. 2620, 57 L.Ed.2d 595 (1978). Therein, the Court stated: "Initially, it is not at all clear that the Due Process Clause in fact requires that a legislatively enacted compensation scheme either duplicate the recovery at common law or provide a reasonable substitute remedy. However, we need not resolve this question here since the Price–Anderson Act does, in our view, provide a reasonably just substitute for the common-law or state tort law remedies it replaces." Id. at 88, 98 S.Ct. at 2638.

5. Despite *Duke Power*, the constitutional dimension of *White's* quid pro quo analysis resurfaced as a central feature of late twentieth century challenges to tort reform legislation. Compare Fein v. Permanente Medical Group, 38 Cal.3d 137, 211 Cal.Rptr. 368, 385 n. 18, 695 P.2d 665, 681 n. 18 (1985), appeal dism'd for want of a substantial federal question, 474 U.S. 892, 106 S.Ct. 214, 88 L.Ed.2d 215 (1985) (upholding the constitutionality of a $250,000 cap on noneconomic damages for medical malpractice and noting that "even if due process principles required some 'quid pro quo' to support [the cap] . . . the preservation of a viable medical malpractice insurance industry in this state . . . [is] an adequate benefit. . . .") and Smith v. Department of Insurance, 507 So.2d 1080, 1088 (Fla.1987) (striking down under the Florida constitution a $450,000 cap on noneconomic damages, in part, because the legislation did not provide "an alternative remedy and commensurate benefit" to individuals suffering greater injury). The same court has applied the *quid pro quo* analysis to statutes that deprive defendants of common law defenses. Agency for Health Care Admin. & Associated Insurers of Florida, Inc., 670 So.2d 1239 (Fla. 1996). See also Samsel v. Wheeler Transport Services, Inc., 246 Kan. 336, 789 P.2d 541 (1990) (collecting cases), and Bair v. Peck, 248 Kan. 824, 811 P.2d 1176 (Kan. 1991), examining the limits of how far a legislature may go in limiting the rights of employees in an amendment to an existing remedial statute before the initial quid pro quo is invalidated.

6. Most states require employers to secure the payment of workers' compensation benefits in one of two ways: either to purchase insurance from a private insurance company or to qualify as self-insurers. Various means have been adopted to compel the securing of insurance, including criminal penalties and enhancing the amount of compensation the employer must pay (e.g. California, Colorado, and Georgia). See § 54, Workmens' Compensation and Rehabilitation Law, App. B. A few states (e.g. Nevada, North Dakota, Oregon, Puerto Rico, and Wyoming) have established state insurance funds as the exclusive source for the payment of compensation claims. The funds are supported by assessments against employers and exclude the participation of private insurance companies. In a few other states employers

are permitted either to participate in the state fund, to secure protection from a private insurer, or to establish themselves as self-insurers. See §§ 46–56, Workmens' Compensation and Rehabilitation Law, App. B. What choices have been made in the statute of your state?

7. At one time private insurers were commonly thought to have enjoyed a 40 percent profit factor on rates charged employers. More recent studies, however, suggest that when all relevant factors are taken into account, the true loading factor is probably less than 25 percent. It is also true that insurance rates tend to fluctuate in inverse relationship to prevailing interest rates in the economy. Although private insurers incur costs of sales and taxes that are avoided by compulsory state funds, this approach is often opposed as an inappropriate governmental usurpation of a function that should be performed in the private sector. The Report of the National Commission on State Workmen's Compensation Laws (R.6.20) recommends leaving the choice of insuring method to each state.

8. In 1916 Congress enacted the Federal Employee's Compensation Act, see 5 U.S.C.A §§8101 et. seq., to provide medical and disability benefits to federal employees injured on the job without regard to fault. The Act also provides a death gratuity for eligible survivors of federal workers killed on the job. 5 U.S.C.A. §8102a. This federal law is structured similarly to a typical state workers' compensation law.

2. THE THEORY OF WORKERS' COMPENSATION

Workers' compensation rests upon the principle that employers and entrepreneurs who enjoy the economic benefits of businesses should ultimately bear the cost of the injuries and deaths that are incident to the manufacture, preparation and distribution of goods and services. This principle always applied to the accidental destruction of capital structures, machinery and equipment used to produce and distribute industrial goods and services. Fixing up and replacing these losses has always been treated as a cost of doing business without consideration of whether the losses resulted from someone's fault or from an unavoidable source. Workers' compensation applies the same principle, irrespective of fault, to injuries and deaths of the employees. The projected cost of these injuries and deaths can be secured in advance through the medium of insurance.

Under workers' compensation the element of personal fault loses all significance except in extreme cases. In theory, the employer initially absorbs the cost of work injuries and ultimately passes it down the stream of commerce in the prices of products until it is spread in dilution among the consuming public. So long as all competing employment units in a given industry are uniformly affected, no producer gains any substantial competitive advantage or suffers any appreciable loss by the uniform application of the compensation principle. On a more specific level, however, some employers are less able to pass on the costs than others. For example, an American producer of a good may not be able to raise the price to pay for added workers' compensation expenses if in direct competition with producers of similar goods manufactured in jurisdictions with lower workers' compensation costs. Nevertheless, these micro-economic imperfections have not defeated the universal adoption of workers' compensation laws and their economic consequences are outside the scope of this book's treatment of the legal aspects of the law in application.

If the compensation principle is to operate effectively, the costs of industrial injuries and deaths must be predictable and fixable in an amount that will not disrupt the exchange of goods and services. Thus, reasonable predictability and moderate cost are necessary from the broad economic viewpoint. They are also desirable from the personal point of view of employers and, apart from specific injuries, from the point of view of workers at large. Frequently, an injured employee's greatest need is for immediate cash to ameliorate the initial shock of the injury. If the amount of a compensation claim is so high as to encourage disputation, the delays of the old system and disputes about the validity of the compensation law compromise will be resurrected, perhaps undermining the humane purposes of compensation plan. Hence, the plan must compensate most injuries without dispute. It should also establish a moderate compensation rate that does not invite malingering and feigned injury. Also, from a general economic point of view, if the overall cost of compensation constitutes a relatively small part of the total cost of production, more room is left for free play of competition among producers.

On the other hand compensation levels must be high enough to provide adequate income to replace lost earnings of injured workers and to create an incentive for employers to adopt injury prevention measures. Otherwise employers would be tempted to take the risk of paying workers' compensation claims on the cheap instead of making more costly expenditures to avoid injuries.

Compensation differs from the conventional damage liability in two important respects: fault on the part of either employers or employees is made irrelevant; and compensation is made payable according to a prescribed and limited scheme. No matter how much they may differ in details, all modern workers' compensation statutes accept these two foundational premises.

As noted in *White*, workers' compensation represents a compromise in which both employers and employees surrender certain advantages in order to gain others deemed to be more important. Employers give up the immunity that would otherwise apply in cases where they were not at fault, and employees surrender their former right to full damages in the few instances when they could recover under tort law and accept more modest assured benefits for all injuries and deaths. Although importance of the *compromise* cannot be overemphasized, the states vary greatly with reference to the proper point of balance. Variables include: the amount of weekly compensation payments; the duration of the period in which compensation is to be paid; the amount of the death benefits; and, the amount of payable medical costs.

The constitutionality of any compensation statute will be influenced by a court's evaluation of the basic point of compromise established in it. If a court believes that the statutory compromise unduly favors employers, it is tempted to restrike the balance by adopting an interpretation that favors workers. This ameliorating power is embodied in the oft-repeated maxim that remedial statutes are to be liberally construed to accomplish their intended purposes. Using it, a sympathetic court may transform a compensation act drawn in a spirit of extreme conservatism into a fairly liberal instrument. Conversely, courts may narrowly interpret an act that greatly favors workers, leaving employers little reason to complain. Much of the apparent unevenness and conflict in compensation decisions among the various jurisdictions may be attributed to the different point of balance established in different statutes. See, 1973 Compendium on Workmen's Compensation, pp. 21–26.

3. COMPENSATION AS SOCIAL INSURANCE

Workers' compensation bears the imprint of social legislation in many important respects. The scheme contemplates that compensation is to be measured in terms of basic support rather than in terms of the true value of all aspects of a worker's personal loss. To this end, workers' compensation benefits are usually paid weekly in amounts proportioned to the amount of lost wages, rather than in a single lump sum. These payments are usually exempt from the claims of creditors. Nevertheless, some compensation statutes and cases tend to treat workers' compensation as merely a modified form of tort liability. As later chapters reveal, many statutes exclude (or limit) the payment of benefits to employees who at the time of accident are engaged in unlawful conduct, or who violate safety statutes, or who are intoxicated, or who intend to injure themselves or another worker. Moreover, courts sometimes avoid compensating an "undeserving" worker by administering the requirement that the accident "arise out of" the employment in a manner that excludes a particular injury. On the other hand, some statutes enhance the amount of compensation paid in respect of injuries caused by serious and willful misconduct of employers. All these adjustments based upon the content of behavior are plainly derogatory of the pure compensation principle, which would ignore the element of blameworthiness and allocate all costs of industrial injuries and deaths to employers and, ultimately, to the consumers of goods and services. Nevertheless, they reflect the fact that compensation statutes, like all others, must be applied by human decision makers who are apt to take into account extremely aberrant behavior in construing the balances and compromises embodied within them.

Some courts manifest an almost irresistible urge to assimilate the compensation statutes into tort law. This is partially explained by the fact that employees in many jurisdictions obtain compensation by making a claim against the employer or the latter's insurer. In some jurisdictions (e.g., Alabama and Tennessee) compensation claims are asserted in court just like any other litigated matter, and nearly all the laws permit compromises between employers and employees. Furthermore, the scheme is somewhat adversarial in nature even though fault is immaterial; that is, the injured worker attempts to extract money directly from the employer. This adversarial context can be highlighted by contrasting it to a general social welfare system in which the injured worker's claim is made against a benefits agency and does not directly involve the employer. This mode is epitomized in the New Zealand plan that completely assimilates workers' compensation into a national comprehensive social security scheme that is financed by general taxation rather than by private insurance. Similarly, the British workers' compensation system is now administered within the social security system of Great Britain. Social Security Act of 1975 (c. 14); Chapter IV. An English worker who is hurt on the job is eligible for more compensation benefits than if hurt while unemployed or injured outside employment, but the benefits are obtained from the national insurance fund. The additional money is provided through a separate Industrial Injuries Fund financed by contributions from employers, employees, and the general treasury. It is also true, however, that the current British plan apparently poses no bar to tort suits against employers who are negligent in causing work injuries. Does your state's statute permit this? A comparison among objectives and methods in American, British and New Zealand plans is found in 1 A. Larson, The Law of Workmen's Compensation (1990) §§ 3.10–3.40.

Although some statutes employ courts as the administering agencies, workers' compensation claims are more often adjudicated by administrative tribunal. The goal is to provide a more expert forum for the resolution of compensation disputes than is afforded by courts of general trial jurisdiction. This specialization permits the proof of facts without resort to technical rules of evidence and the evaluation of technical evidence particularly on medical questions by expert fact-finders (the hearing officers) who possess more training and experience in dealing with them than lay juries would. Moreover, unlike court adjudication, administrative determination of compensation awards provides a mechanism to oversee the payment of continuing awards and an administrative system for reporting accidents, rehabilitating injured workers, administering the insurance features of the act, studying the overall performance of the plan, and issuing periodic reports and recommendations for legislative attention.

— In the United States the interrelationship between workers' compensation systems that are largely privately financed and the ever-expanding social security system has become complex. The difficulty was enhanced in 1956 by the enactment of the federal social security disability benefits plan referred to in Chapter 1. The same National Commission on State Workmen's Compensation Laws that in 1972 recommended that social security disability benefits be reduced in the presence of workers' compensation benefits also recommended that workers' compensation death benefits be reduced by the amount of social security benefits paid to the deceased worker's family (R.3.27). The Commission rejected a proposal to disassemble workers' compensation and to assign the components to other programs and also rejected proposals to assign permanent total disability claims exclusively to the federal social security system, to assign temporary disability cases exclusively to state temporary disability insurance programs, to administer the medical component under an expanded Medicare program, and to assign rehabilitation programs to state departments of vocational rehabilitation. This package was deemed to be too complex for resolving current conflicts. Report of the National Commission on State Workmen's Compensation Laws (1972), page 120. Although a variety of public and private programs offer income and medical protection to disabled workers, the extent of overlap between workers' compensation and other benefits programs such as federal disability and old-age insurance benefits, unemployment compensation insurance benefits, veterans' benefits, FELA, Jones Act, and no fault automobile compensation plans, is not believed to be large. 1973 Compendium on Workmen's Compensation, page 58.

Despite the economic and administrative advantages of workers' compensation, the scheme has its limitations and is far from uniform in detail among the states. The Report of the National Commission summarizes five objectives against which specific programs should be evaluated: broad coverage; protection against interruption of income; sufficient medical care and rehabilitative services; encouragement of safety; and prompt and efficient delivery of benefits. (Report, at 117.) The Commission deemed many state plans to be inadequate by these measures and the general failure of state legislatures to rectify shortcomings led to the introduction of federal legislation (Senate Bill 420, 96th Congress, 1st Session) to prescribe minimum standards for state workers' compensation plans. This bill, which would have constituted a partial federal take-over of a traditionally state-controlled program, was not enacted. Opinions differ as to the desirability and propriety of federal intervention. See Workmen's Compensation: National Commission on State Workmen's Compensation Laws: Import for Oklahoma (1973) 26 Okla.L.R. 453; Potential Federalization of State Workmen's Compensation Laws—The Kansas Response (1976) 15 Washburn L.J. 251. So far, Congress has not adopted legislation of this sort.

4. THE ACCEPTANCE OF WORKERS' COMPENSATION

Workers' compensation is now a stable part of the legal and economic employment enterprise throughout the United States. Although the details of the laws are being constantly adjusted, no proposal to repeal them or to replace them with drastically different plans is likely to receive generous attention anywhere. Hence, workers' compensation is a given, and the basic compromise, discussed above, is accepted. For these reasons, little writing is to be found about what would be a better way for dealing with industrial injuries and death.

Curiously enough, the current level of acceptance does not reflect the initial lack of enthusiasm for the advent of workers' compensation laws. The following excerpt describes the reaction in England, which was not unlike the reaction in the United States. Particularly noteworthy is the lukewarm reception given workers' compensation by organized labor:

"The Significance of Workmen's Compensation[2]

"The Workmen's Compensation Act was greeted in emotional terms by its supporters and opponents. The latter anticipated rising unemployment, deteriorating industrial relations, destruction of self-reliance and ruination for the friendly societies. Some felt it would cripple the international competitiveness of British industry, despite the fact that other countries, notably Germany, already had similar or more comprehensive legislation. On the other hand, its champions considered it to be 'a great boon' to workers and 'one of the leading enactments of the century'. One historian, echoing a [union] president, terms the Act 'revolutionary' and has even gone so far as to claim: 'There can be no doubt that the Workmen's Compensation Act was one of the most important ever passed by Parliament'. In 1897 the significance of the Act was only imperfectly understood. * * * It may be noted here however that in terms of achievements on the factory floor, as opposed to the principles it enshrined, the word 'revolutionary' is an inappropriate description of

[2] P. Bartrip, Workmen's Compensation in Twentieth Century Britain, Law, History and Social Policy (1987), pp. 11–12.

the 1897 Act. At first it applied to only a minority of workers; except for coal miners after 1934 it provided no guarantee of compensation. The coming of workmen's compensation certainly did not place accident victims in the 'circumstances of independence and luxury' anticipated by some. Nevertheless, it was a great step forward. In comparison with the position in the 1830s the injured worker, relieved of the necessity to prove fault, enjoyed an immeasurably improved position.

"According to William Beveridge, workmen's compensation was 'the pioneer system of social security'. In one sense this was an accurate characterisation, for the Act established a working class entitlement or right, that is, to a measure of financial security in the event of work injury, which corresponded to other rights won in the course of the nineteenth century such as the vote, freedom to form trade unions and to work in reasonable conditions. Moreover, by recognising that there should be public solutions to social problems the Act furthered the idea that the beneficiaries of a worker's labour owed him support in such circumstances as illness and old-age. As a speaker at the 1898 [union] conference put it: 'if . . . the national prosperity depends on the well-being of the worker, the necessary corollary is that the state should care for him in times of sickness . . . [and] old age'. Thus, although passed by a Conservative Government, the Workmen's Compensation Act can, in some ways, be viewed as a forerunner of the Liberal Welfare Reforms (which included the Workmen's Compensation Act, 1906) of the Edwardian era. In other respects, however, the Act was decidedly different, particularly in that it provided no public funds and a very limited administrative function for government. Furthermore, the terms of the 1897 Act, whereby claims were to be against individual employers who would be entitled to oppose claimants in the courts, meant that the workmen's compensation system would, in many respects, be similar to the tort system.

"Finally, it is worth asking why a Workmen's Compensation Act became law in 1897. The question is particularly intriguing in that the groups one might expect to have pressed for it, the [coalition of union] and the individual unions, were, * * * no more than lukewarm towards the reform. They claimed to be uninterested in compensation as opposed to industrial safety. But if trades unionists were not behind the Act, who was? In general terms the Act reflected, as some later welfare legislation did, the growing influence of the enfranchised working classes and the competition among the political parties for their support. More specifically, emphasis needs to be given to the role of individuals such as Ashley, Chadwick and Chamberlain. But their views gained legislative acceptance only because they found support elsewhere. In fact, paradoxically, Chamberlain's compensation ideas were received with enthusiasm by few parties. They were influential because they represented an acceptable compromise to an intractable problem.

Lawyers, who first raised the insurance solution, liked it because it did not interfere with the sanctity of the common law as employers' liability reform threatened to do. Business interests came to accept workmen's compensation as a necessary evil, better at least than the alternative of a tough liability law. The Conservative Party saw it as a means of outmanoeuvring the Liberals and attracting working class support. Labour leaders grudgingly supported it as a benefit which was on offer whereas their favoured outcome was not practical politics. Workmen's compensation was, therefore, the solution which least divided the various interest groups.

"That it came about in 1897 can only be explained by reference to the reform process over more than two decades, to the example set by other nations, especially Germany, and to a growing realisation that if Britain were to compete with its international rivals more would have to be done to promote national efficiency. Part of the answer to this was greater investment in welfare."

American states gradually adopted workers' compensation laws patterned on the English model until Mississippi made it universal in 1948. Although this removal of work place injuries from the tort system may be seen as a victory for social reformers, modern economic investigations have suggested that it was a cooperative endeavor. Some employers may have favored workers' compensation to reduce labor unrest and others may have supported—or at least not opposed—it, believing they could pass on the costs of the plan to the workers in lower wages. P. V. Fishback and S.E. Kantor, "The Adoption of Workers' Compensation in the United States, 1900–1930," 41 J.L. & Econ. 305 (1998).

5. POLICY AND POLITICS

The general theory and objectives of a workers' compensation system are not disputed They are to (1) provide broad coverage of employees and work-related injuries and diseases; (2) provide substantial protection against interruption of income; (3) provide sufficient medical care and rehabilitation services; (4) encourage workplace safety; and (5) deliver benefits in an efficient and effective manner. (National Commission Report of 1972 at 117–18).

The initial prevailing view was that workers' compensation statutes are remedial in character and, accordingly, are to be liberally construed in favor of providing benefits to injured workers. See, e.g., Alvarez v. Liberty House, Inc., 85 Hawai'i 275, 942 P.2d 539, 542 (Haw.1997). The politics in much social legislation in the late twentieth century turned away from remedies and toward cost cutting. In some states this movement resulted in statutory abrogation of pro-compensation liberality in favor of a statement of neutrality. This excerpt from the New Mexico statute is illustrative:

> It is the intent of the legislature in creating the workers' compensation administration that the laws administered by it to provide a workers' benefit system be interpreted to assure the quick and efficient delivery of indemnity and medical benefits to injured and disabled workers at a reasonable cost to the employers who are subject to the provisions of the Workers' Compensation Act . . . and the New Mexico Occupational Disease Disablement Law. It is the specific intent of the legislature that benefit claims cases be decided on their merits and that the common law rule of "liberal construction" based on the supposed "remedial" basis of workers' benefits legislation shall not apply in these cases. The workers' benefit system in New Mexico is based on a mutual renunciation of common law rights and defenses by employers and employees alike. Accordingly, the legislature declares that the Workers' Compensation Act and the New Mexico Occupational Disease Disablement Law are not remedial in any sense and are not to be given a broad liberal construction in favor of the claimant or employee on the one hand, nor are the rights and interests of the employer to be favored over those of the employee on the other hand.

N.M.S.A. § 52–5–1 (1998). Florida adopted a similar provision, § 440.015 Fla. Stat. (1997), as did Colorado, but the Colorado measure was quickly repealed. See, Co. St. 8–40–102 (1994) (Historical and Statutory Notes).

At the time workers' compensation was invented the power of labor vis-a-vis capital was puny. Hence, the so-called workers' compensation bargain was initially seen as a victory for reformers whose goal was general betterment of living condition for the mass of ordinary working people. By the latter decades of the twentieth century living standards had changed beyond recognition when contrasted by the standard of the rank and file of a century earlier. If not caused by it, this advance was certainly accompanied by the adoption of the worker friendly statutes outlined in Chapter 1.

Consistent with the liberal remedial purposes of the original movement,workers' compensation laws were gradually amended to extend coverage to additional categories of employees, to expand the scope of compensable injuries and to enlarge the generosity of benefits. The most recent stages of this development came along about the same time that law and economic analysts began to evaluate everything in terms of economic efficiencies and cost transfers. See, e.g., R. Butler and J. Worrall, "Wage and Injury Response to Shifts in Workplace Liability," 61 Ind. Lab. Rel. Rev. 181 (2008). One body of work suggests that some employments have funded the increased costs by paying lower wages. P. Fishback and S. Kantor, "Did Workers Pay for the Passage of Workers' Compensation Laws?," 11 Quarterly J. of Econ. 713 (1995). Should it be a surprise that these studies found that passing-on the costs by paying lower wages is more effective in non-union employments? Some believe the accepting lower wages as a trade-off may be tolerable to most workers as long as parity is maintained among all the members of the protected class. C. Sunstein, "Switching the Default Rule", 77 N.Y.U.C. L. Rev. 106 (2002). By contrast, doing away with workers' compensation would place the burden of many workplace injuries on the shoulders of the injured alone. Hence, distributing the costs to all though lowered wages may be a tolerable alternative.

The late twentieth century employer movement to trim coverage and benefits argues against the claim that added workers' compensation benefits are ultimately paid by workers. The early demand that the "price of the product bear the blood of the worker" has been smothered by the claim that work place injuries can be prevented only if workers are more careful on the job. The validity of this proposition and the movement to pare down workers' compensation benefits have themselves been strongly attacked. D. Haas, "Falling Down of the Job: Workers' Compensation Shifts from a No-Fault to a Worker-Fault Paradigm," 79 N. Dak. L. Rev. 203 (2003) and M. McClusky, "The Illusion of Efficiency in Workers' Compensation 'Reform'," 50 Rutgers L. Rev. 657 (1998).

Whatever the cause, the working place is remarkably safer now then it was in pre-workers' compensation days. The frequency of work place deaths is one measure. Consider this report.

> Between 1912 and 2006, unintentional work deaths per 100,000 population were reduced 92%, from 21 to 1.7. In 1912, an estimated 18,000 to 21,000 workers' lives were lost. In 2005, in a work force nearly quadrupled in size and producing ten times the good and services, there were only 4,988[3] accidental work deaths.

Injury Facts (2008), National Safety Council, p. 48.

In the meantime courts continue to apply their workers' compensation laws as they find them, but on the whole with the same general spirit of liberality that has always imbued the subject.

The remainder of this book focuses on the subject of greatest concern for most attorneys—workers' compensation doctrine. The student, however, should evaluate the cases and the statutes by reference to compensation theory and the underlying social policies.

---

[3] The number of deaths fell to 3783 in 2010. *Injury Facts* (2012), National Safety Council, p. 60.

CHAPTER 3

THE EMPLOYER-EMPLOYEE RELATIONSHIP

■ ■ ■

1. INTRODUCTION

Because workers' compensation is designed to provide benefits only to employees and their survivors, the student must understand what employment means as contemplated under the statutes. Because employment is a particular kind of contractual relationship, whether or not one person is an employee of another ultimately depends upon whether a contract of employment was entered into by them. In most instances, the employment relation is not disputed. Often a written application and acceptance will memorialize it. Nevertheless, many injuries occur under circumstances in which one person appears to be working for another in some capacity but no contract has ever been overtly executed or even discussed by the parties. Under these circumstances the courts are left to interpret the factual context of what transpired and whether it satisfies the legal criteria of an employment contract as opposed to some other relationship.

In the days before the industrial revolution, employment was referred to as the master-servant relationship, reflecting the close personal relationship and propinquity between the employer and employee. The elements of that relationship were well known to judges and lawyers before the inception of the compensation movement and were inevitably imported into it. A leading factor has always been whether the purported master had the legal right to control the details of how the purported servant did assigned work. If so, the master-servant relationship existed, if not, some other relationship existed, such as principal-independent contractor. The outcome of this test often determined whether the master was legally liable to some third person for harm done by the negligent act of someone else in performing the master's work. If the actor was a servant, then the master was vicariously liable under the *respondeat superior* doctrine. If an independent contractor, then the independent contractor, but not the master, was liable.

As would be expected, rules applicable to contract formation, torts and agency were transplanted into compensation law without much debate as to the appropriateness of application in the new scheme. This was particularly true of the "control" test of *respondeat superior*, whose use in compensation cases produced much confusion in early decisions. The courts were slow to accept the truth that the relatively narrow scope of the common law master-servant relationship did not conform to the broad workers' compensation goal of distributing the cost of employment injuries through the economic system. In more recent years, the ramifications of the employment relationship have been expanded by the emergence of other pieces of social legislation, such as unemployment compensation, wage and hour legislation, social security, and anti-discrimination legislation, all of which tend to broaden to some extent the meaning of the employment relationship. The social welfare goals of these statutes have lead many courts to reach beyond the strict tests of the master-servant relationship to determine who is an employee. One court, for example, applied a "totality of the circumstances" test, including especially "the extent of the economic dependence of the worker upon the business he serves and the relationship of his work to the operation of that business," to award workers' compensation benefits to a claimant who would hardly have been a servant under the common law. Biger v. Erwin, 108 N.J.Super. 293, 261 A.2d 151, 154 (1970) (jockey for only one race held to be employee of owner who was in the business of racing horses). This broadening of the reach of the employment relationship, even under statutes that purport to apply common law tests, is common.

The social welfare character of workers' compensation becomes more understandable as the student tackles questions pertaining to which employments are included within the coverage of the statutes. Some employments readily lend themselves to transmitting the cost of employment injuries and deaths down the channels of commerce to the consuming public; while other employments, such as domestic service, hirings by charitable and religious undertakings, and perhaps some agricultural employments, do not fit the theory. Furthermore, some employments such as small firms, charitable organizations, transitory businesses and the like find it to be too costly or burdensome to be included. Legislatures do not want the imposition of workers' compensation to be an engine for destroying employments of these kinds and have often exempted them by classification schemes. These exemptions create many specific disputes as to whether coverage applies to a particular injury.

In addition, considerable legislative and judicial ingenuity has been expended in fixing the boundary between employment and other similar relationships that fall outside the coverage of the statutes. These include principal and independent contractor, buyer and seller, lessor and lessee, and even debtor and creditor. Furthermore, mixed relationships sometimes present themselves. For example, an employee may participate in the profits (and possibly losses) of the employing enterprise either as a stockholder, a corporate officer, or a partner. Should these special factors affect whether or not worker's compensation is payable to the worker? Should the worker's personal capacity to purchase personal health and accident insurance have a bearing on whether workers' compensation applies?

2. THE CONTRACT OF EMPLOYMENT

JOHNSON V. CITY OF ALBIA

Supreme Court of Iowa, 1927.
203 Iowa 1171, 212 N.W. 419.

FAVILLE, J.

On November 15, 1923, the plaintiff was in the employ of the defendant, as the engineer in charge of its pumping plant. He had been engaged in such employment for the seven years preceding. On the morning of November 15, he notified the chairman of the waterworks committee that he would terminate his services that evening. Pursuant to such notice, the committee immediately made arrangements with one Seibert to take the job thus to be vacated by the plaintiff. The plaintiff operated the engine and pumps until 7:15 p.m., at which time he had the tanks filled. At that hour he left the plant for home. On the way home he met Seibert and advised him where he would find the key. Under plaintiff's contract of employment, he was furnished with a residence near the plant and with a place to keep his cow and his portable garage. He had vacated the residence on November 15, and had moved his family into another house down town. This latter was the residence to which he came after leaving the plant at 7:15 p.m. There still remained upon his employer's premises his cow, his portable garage and a car therein, and his tools, consisting of a sledge, a screwdriver, and three wrenches. * * *

Upon the testimony of the plaintiff himself, the defendant predicates its contention that the relation of employer and employee between plaintiff and defendant was fully terminated on the evening of November 15. The accident under consideration occurred on the morning of November 16. The plaintiff returned to the plant at 8 o'clock that morning, solely for the purpose of getting his tools. He found Seibert there, and found him in trouble with the machinery. He was unable to start one of the pumps. This pump had a defective valve, which required a peculiar manipulation in order to start it. This defect was explained by the plaintiff to Seibert. Seibert requesting the assistance of the plaintiff to start the pump, he went into the pumphouse and into the pit where the pumps were located for the purpose of rendering such assistance. While engaged in such attempt, he was accidently caught in some gearing and lost his left arm as a result.

The tools which plaintiff left at the pumphouse on the evening of November 15 were his personal property and the necessary tools which he used in the operation of the plant. He testified that he left them there on that evening that they might be used in case of necessity. So far as appears, they were the only tools at the plant which were available for use at the time the accident occurred on the morning of November 16. The purpose of the plaintiff in going to the plant on the morning of November 16, was solely to get his tools and to make preparations for removing the rest of his property, and incidentally to milk his cow. [The Industrial Commissioner found that Johnson was a covered employee and awarded benefits. The employer appealed to a trial court, which affirmed. The employer then appealed to the Indiana Supreme Court.]

The trial court decided the case solely on the ground that a fact question was involved, and that the order of the Industrial Commissioner was conclusive on the court. If there is a disputed question of fact, the decision of the commissioner is binding on the court. The conclusions of law of the commissioner on undisputed facts are, however, proper questions for the determination of the court. Three questions appear to be involved: (1) Was the employe still within the scope of his employment at the time of the injury when he returned to get his tools? (2) Did an emergency arise at the time which called for assistance to the new engineer and clothed him with sufficient authority to bind the city in employing the workman at that time? (3) Is there evidence of such a custom among engineers that the outgoing engineer shall assist the incoming one as made the workman an employe at the time?

I. Was appellee still an employe under his original employment?

At the time the injury occurred, Code Supplement of 1913 was in force, and section 2477m16, par. (b) is as follows:

> "'Workman' is used synonymously with 'employe' and means any person who has entered into the employment of or works under contract of service express or implied or apprenticeship for an employer."

In Knudson v. Jackson, 191 Iowa 947, 183 N.W. 391, we considered this paragraph of the statute in considering the meaning of the word "employe," and in said case reviewed the authorities at length, and held that we cannot enlarge the provisions of the statute and that an employe within the meaning of this act, "in order to come under this statute, must have a contract of service, express or implied, with the employer who is sought to be charged with liability." The question at once, then, in the case, is whether or not the appellee at the time of the injury, to wit, on November 16, had a contract of employment, express or implied, with the appellant. According to his own testimony he had quit on the 15th of November. He had notified the waterworks committee of the city council in the forenoon of that day that he would quit, and he turned in his key. There is no claim that he was ever employed by the city council thereafter. He came to the place of his employment for a purely personal reason, namely, to secure his tools that were located on the premises. He did not come there to assist the new engineer or to do any work. At the request of the new employe, he attempted to assist him in the operation of the machinery on the place. This was purely voluntary on his part. There is no intimation in the record that any person authorized to engage employes for the city even so much as knew that the appellee was on the premises, and there is no suggestion that any one in behalf of the appellant requested, or in any manner authorized, the appellee to assist the regular employe of the appellant who was then in charge of the work.[1]

The appellee places great reliance upon the following quotation from 1 Honnold on Workmen's Compensation, p. 353, where the rule is stated as follows:

> "An employe is under the protection of the Compensation Act even after his *discharge*, providing he be injured upon the premises of the employer while remaining there for reasons connected with his former employment."

This quotation from Honnold is supported by a single case in the footnote, to wit, Goering v. Brooklyn Mining Company, 2 Cal.I.A.C.Dec. 124. In that case an employe a few minutes after being discharged, was cleaning up his work preparing to leave the premises. He was injured by an accident, and it was held that such accident occurred in the course of his employment, and that he was entitled to compensation.[2] Neither the text nor the authority sustaining it are broad enough to support the appellee's contention in the instant case. It is obvious that a different situation is presented where, without the knowledge of the former employer, a discharged employe, the next day or later, after he has left the premises and terminated his contract of employment, re-enters the premises for purposes of his own, and voluntarily assists the new employe in performing his work. * * *

---

1 Editor's Note: Generally an ordinary employee has no authority to hire. Roach v. J.S. Bryan & Sons Corp. (1938) 184 Okl. 211, 86 P.2d 304; Board of Com'rs of Wells County v. Merritt (1924) 81 Ind.App. 488, 143 N.E. 711 (workman injured several hours after undertaking his indisposed brother's job, but before any representative of the employer had knowledge of the substitution). Conversely, an employee cannot be transferred to the employ of another without his consent. Holloway v. G.O. Cooley & Sons (1946) 208 S.C. 234, 37 S.E.2d 666 (employer sold his business without knowledge of his employee).

2 Editor's Note: Accord, Peterson v. Moran (1952) 111 Cal. App. 2d 766, 245 P.2d 540. Cf. Nash v. Longville Lbr. Co. (1921) 148 La. 943, 88 So. 226 (suit in tort by employee who quit job due to reckless action of foreman and subsequently was attacked by him with an axe).

III. The appellee claims that at the time of his employment and service there was a general custom in that locality between engineers and their employers that upon the termination of the service of the employed engineer it was his duty to impart reasonable instruction and extend reasonable aid to his successor in the operation of the plant. The Industrial Commissioner made no finding that there was such a rule and custom prevailing in that locality. His decision does not rest upon any proof of custom. In fact he does not refer to the question in his award, so we have no decision whatever upon this question, and hence nothing to review. In any event, he could not have found that such was established under the record in this case. Furthermore, there is no contention that, if a custom existed as claimed, it was known to the appellant, or that it was so general that appellant was bound to know of it. In the Mitchell case[3] the discharged workman had certain duties to perform in direct connection with finishing or cleaning up his work, under specific orders. His employment and orders included this very work and while engaged in it he was injured. It was also shown to be the custom that he should do this work. Not so in the case at bar. The appellee had quit the employment the day before the injury. He had surrendered his key to the premises. He was not there to complete any unfinished work. He did not go there at all for the purpose of aiding the new engineer. He went there *solely* for his own private purpose—to get his tools. While there the new engineer asked him to assist him in starting the pump. This he tried to do and was injured.

However deplorable the accident, the claimant cannot recover unless he comes within the class provided for by the statute.

There is no disputed fact question in the case. Upon the facts as found by the Industrial Commissioner the claimant was not within the coverage of the statute.

The judgment must be reversed.

EVANS, C.J. (dissenting).

I am not able to concur in the majority opinion. In my judgment it presents a too restricted view of the operation of the Workmen's Compensation Act, and emphasizes the letter in violation of the spirit thereof. * * *

The plaintiff pleaded, and the evidence tended to prove, that at the time of plaintiff's employment and service there prevailed a general custom or rule in that locality as between engineers and their employers, that upon the termination of the services of the employed engineer, it was his duty to impart reasonable instruction and extend reasonable aid to his successor in the operation of the plant. It is the contention of the plaintiff

[3] Editor's Note: Mitchell v. Consolidated Coal Co., 192 N.W. 145 (Ia. 1923).

that he was fulfilling his obligation in obedience to this rule at the time of his injury, and that, for the purpose of such service and within its scope, he was still an employee of the defendant within the meaning of the Compensation Act, notwithstanding that he had already quit the general service of the employer. Here is the pivot of the case. If the contract of employment had been in writing, and if such writing had imposed such obligation upon the employee, it would hardly be claimed but that the obligation to perform such duty rested upon him, notwithstanding he had terminated his general service. The contract, however, was oral. Even an oral agreement to such effect would have been equally binding upon him. But no such express agreement was made. Nor is there any evidence of *any* express agreement in the oral contract of employment. It appears to have been informal and to rest upon legal implication. If there was a general custom, as contended by the plaintiff, and as found by the Industrial Commissioner, it would become a part of the contract of employment by legal implication. If the rule established by the prevailing custom became a part of the contract of employment, then it has an important bearing upon the question whether the relation of employer and employee was terminated on the evening of November 15.

The termination of the relation of employer and employee, within the meaning of the Compensation Act, is often, if not usually, a mixed question of law and fact. It is not necessarily accomplished by mere words, however direct and positive they may be. A discharge may be peremptory and a resignation may be immediate and abrupt, and yet for certain purposes that are incidental to the termination of the employment, and for a reasonable time the relation may continue; that is to say, there may be duties owing by one to the other, or privileges due to one or the other, which are incidental to the termination of the employment. The law allows a reasonable time for the performance of such duties, or the exercise of such privileges. In the performance of such duties or the exercise of such privileges within such reasonable time, the relation of employer and employee is deemed to continue within the meaning of the Compensation Act. For instance it is quite universally held that a discharged employee has a right, after his discharge, to enter upon the premises of his employer for the purpose of removing his tools. While so engaged within a reasonable time, he is deemed an employee and not a trespasser, nor a licensee, and is under the protection of the Compensation Act. Not only so, but he is bound by the limitations of the Compensation Act, and may not resort to a common-law remedy for injuries, which he may suffer at such time. * * *

* * * When he got to the pumphouse, he found Seibert in trouble and apparently helpless to furnish the necessary amount of water to supply the town. Seibert, as a witness for the defendant, described his own state of mind as follows: "When Johnson came up and inquired how everything

was, I swore." It is clear that Johnson at this juncture found Seibert in need of instruction and help, even though he had not expected to find him in such state. It was his clear duty under the implications of his contract of employment to render such reasonable assistance as he could. In responding in good faith to that duty, he was to that extent an employee and within the protection of the Compensation Act. Such was our holding in the Mitchell case. In that case the duties, which the employee was performing were not imposed by any express provisions of his contract, but were imposed by a general custom, which prevailed in that locality, and which became a part of his contract by legal implication only. Such is the situation in the case at bar. So far as the facts of this case are concerned, I have taken no account of conflicting evidence. The facts which I have assumed, all have the support of evidence and I would give effect to the finding of the Commissioner accordingly.

I would affirm.

NOTES

1. In contrast, Nails v. Market Tire Co., Inc., 29 Md.App. 154, 347 A.2d 564 (1975), permitted recovery in a similar case based upon custom in the industry and the fact that the employee's tools were useful to employer. Similarly, Mitchell v. Consolidated Coal Co., 195 Iowa 415, 192 N.W. 145 (1923), distinguished in the Albia, awarded compensation because the discharging supervisor had said, "square up your place and take out your tools." Similarly, Reed v. Yackett, 473 Mich. 520, 703 N.W.2d 1 (2005) deemed a "fired" worker to be an employee when he was subsequently injured while assisting another employee, but the facts differed in three ways. First, the assisted worker had authority to pay a helper and was doing so. Second, the action was a tort claim for damages against the former employer. Third, finding the plaintiff to be an "employee" would have defeated the former employer's tort action against the former employer. Should these facts require a different outcome from City of Albia?

See also, Roush v. Town of Esmond, 73 S.D. 406, 43 N.W.2d 547 (1950) (failure to follow the statutory procedure for executing a municipal contract of hire resulted in a denial of compensation to person informally employed by officials to remove abandoned electric poles and wires; dissent); State v. Industrial Com'n, 250 Wis. 140, 26 N.W.2d 273 (1947) (student nurse who failed to comply with civil service regulations was not an employee of state, even though working in state hospital). Can these situations be distinguished from illegal employments, discussed infra?

2. Courts sometimes rely on other aspects of the law of contracts to resolve workers' compensation disputes. Compensation may be denied, for example, when a contract of hire exists but is voidable because of the employee's fraudulent misrepresentations in the employment application. See, e.g., Georgia Electric Co. v. Rycroft, 259 Ga. 155, 378 S.E.2d 111 (1989)

(misrepresented prior injuries). Compensation will be allowed, however, if the fraudulent misrepresentations are unconnected to the injury. See, e.g., Byrd's Electric & Plumbing, Inc. v. Johnson, 199 Ga.App. 621, 405 S.E.2d 548 (1991).

3. At one time, many states closely restricted or prohibited contracts between spouses. Bendler v. Bendler, 3 N.J. 161, 69 A.2d 302 (1949), overruled by Romeo v. Romeo, 84 N.J. 289, 418 A.2d 258 (1980), examined the effect of these restrictions upon compensation rights. These restrictions are now largely or wholly repudiated. See, e.g., Flynn v. State Compensation Com'r, 141 W.Va. 445, 91 S.E.2d 156 (1956).

ASPEN HIGHLANDS SKIING CORPORATION V. APOSTOLOU

Supreme Court of Colorado, *en banc*, 1994.
866 P.2d 1384.

JUSTICE LOHR delivered the Opinion of the Court.

We granted certiorari to review the decision of the Colorado Court of Appeals in Aspen Highlands Skiing Corporation v. Apostolou, 854 P.2d 1357 (Colo.App.1992), which sustained an award of workers' compensation benefits to John J. Apostolou. The issue on appeal was whether under the facts of this case, Apostolou was an "employee" of Aspen Highlands Skiing Corporation (Highlands), and therefore entitled to such benefits, when he was injured while working for Highlands on the ski patrol. We affirm the judgment of the court of appeals.

I. John J. Apostolou was employed by Highlands as a part-time ski instructor during the 1989–1990 ski season. As part of his compensation for this work, he was given a photographic identification card (photo ID) that enabled him to ski free at any time at Aspen Highlands.

In January 1990, Highlands told its ski instructors that it needed persons with CPR qualifications [Ed., "cardiopulmonary resuscitation"] and first aid training to work on ski patrol. The ski patrol consisted of two categories of workers: professionals, who worked full-time and were paid a salary, and other workers, who worked part-time, received no monetary compensation, but were given photo IDs that enabled them to ski free at any time at Aspen Highlands.

Apostolou mentioned that he had the requisite qualifications and was referred to the ski patrol director. Because he already had a photo ID, Apostolou negotiated an agreement with the ski patrol director to receive daily ski passes for his girlfriend in exchange for his ski patrol work. The agreement entitled the girlfriend to as many daily ski passes as she was able to use during the period that Apostolou performed ski patrol duties. Each pass had a retail value of $36.00, and Apostolou would not have agreed to work on the ski patrol if the arrangement had not been made.

On February 20, 1990, Apostolou fell while on ski patrol duty, injuring his knees. A week later he underwent surgery on his right knee. As a result of his injuries, Apostolou was unable to continue working as either a ski instructor or a ski patrol person. Apostolou filed a workers' compensation claim. Highlands and its workers' compensation insurer, Colorado Compensation Insurance Authority (CCIA), contested the claim, asserting that Apostolou was not an employee at the time of his injuries, but was a volunteer, and as such, not entitled to workers' compensation benefits. After a hearing, an administrative law judge (ALJ) concluded that Apostolou was working as an employee of Highlands at the time he was injured and ordered Highlands and CCIA to provide compensation. The Industrial Claim Appeals Panel affirmed the ALJ's order, and the Colorado Court of Appeals, with one judge dissenting, in turn affirmed the order of the Panel. See Aspen Highlands Skiing Corp. v. Apostolou, 854 P.2d 1357 (Colo.App.1992). We granted certiorari to determine whether the ALJ erred in determining that Apostolou was an employee of Highlands at the time he was injured and therefore was entitled to workers' compensation benefits.

II. In Colorado, workers' compensation legislation "provides exclusive remedies for compensation of an employee by an employer for work-related injury." Triad Painting Co. v. Blair, 812 P.2d 638, 641 (Colo.1991). Under the Workmen's Compensation Act of Colorado (the Act), an employee is entitled to receive compensation for an injury incurred while "performing service arising out of and in the course of his employment," s 8–52–102(1)(b), 3B C.R.S. (1986), and "proximately caused by an injury . . . arising out of and in the course of his employment . . . ." An employee, as relevant here, is defined as "[e]very person in the service of any . . . private corporation . . . under any contract of hire, express or implied . . . but not including any persons who are expressly excluded from [the Act]. . . ." s 8–41–106(1)(b), 3B C.R.S. (1986) (now appearing at s 8–40–202(1)(b), 3B C.R.S. (1993 Supp.)). In 1989, the Colorado legislature amended the Act to exclude a class of persons from the definition of "employee" by adding the following provision: " '[E]mployee' excludes any person who volunteers his time or services as a ski patrol person, a ski instructor. . . ."

We first consider whether Apostolou was an "employee" of Highlands under the basic definition of that term. We then address Highlands' argument that Apostolou was not an employee because he was not paid "wages" as that term is defined in the Act. Finally, we address Highlands' contention that Apostolou volunteered his services and therefore was among the persons specifically excluded from the definition of "employee" by the 1989 amendment.

A. The initial question is whether Apostolou satisfied the basic definition of "employee" as a person "in the service of" Highlands "under any contract of hire, express or implied." See s 8–41–106(1)(b). In Denver Truck Exchange v. Perryman, 134 Colo. 586, 307 P.2d 805 (1957), we noted that "[a] contract of hire is subject to the same rules as other contracts even though workmen's compensation laws are liberally construed in our state." Id. at 593, 307 P.2d at 810. We also stated: "'A contract is an agreement which creates an obligation. Its essentials are competent parties, subject matter, a legal consideration, mutuality of agreement, and mutuality of obligation.'" Id. at 592, 307 P.2d at 810 (quoting 17 C.J.S. 310, s 1a). A contract of hire may be formed even though not every formality attending commercial contractual arrangements is observed as long as the fundamental elements of contract formation are present. . . .

In Hall v. State Compensation Ins. Fund, 154 Colo. 47, 387 P.2d 899 (1963), a hospital provided free lunches to a person working with a volunteer service unit at the hospital. In holding that the person was not working under a contract of hire, we noted: "She was not under contract—at no time did she expressly or by implication obligate herself to the hospital, nor did the hospital at any time obligate itself to her." Id. at 50, 387 P.2d at 901.

Under the facts as found by the ALJ, a contract of hire existed between Aspen and Apostolou. Apostolou negotiated with his employer and agreed to work only in exchange for the benefit of daily passes for his girlfriend. He worked under Highlands' direction, with the expectation of compensation in the form of the daily passes. The ALJ determined that "[i]n essence, [Apostolou] obligated himself to perform ski patrol services for [Highlands] and in return, [Highlands] obligated itself to provide free daily ski passes to [Apostolou] or his designee." Under those circumstances, we conclude that Apostolou worked under a contract of hire and fell within the basic definition of "employee" for the purposes of the Act.

B. Highlands, however, urges us to construe the term "employee" as defined in section 8–41–106(1)(b) to include the requirement that a "contract of hire," which is an essential part of the definition, must provide for the payment of "wages," and that for this purpose we should employ the definition of "wages" found [in the Colorado statute]. Highlands asserts that such a construction would provide a desirable measure of clarity in distinguishing between employees and persons who volunteer time and services as ski patrol persons and thus are excluded from the definition of employee under . . . the Act. . . . A ski pass is not included in the definition of "wages," so the adoption of Highlands' proposed statutory construction would result in the conclusion that Apostolou was not an employee of Highlands. [Ed., the statutory definition of "wages" included: "reportable tips, the amount of the employee's cost of continuing the employer's group health insurance plan and, upon termination of the continuation, the employee's cost of conversion to a similar or lesser insurance plan, and the reasonable value of board, rent, housing, and lodging received from the employer, the reasonable value of which shall be fixed and determined from the facts * * * in each particular case, but shall not include any similar advantage or fringe benefit not specifically enumerated above."].

Highlands' proposed construction finds no support in the statutes. Section 8–47–101(2) appears in a section of the Act providing rules for determining the average weekly wage of an injured employee for the purpose of computing compensation payments. See s 8–47–101(1), 3B C.R.S. (1986). There is no suggestion that it was intended to have any application to the determination of employee status. Moreover, the term "wages" is not used in the definition of "employee" applicable here. See s 8–41–106(1)(b), 3B C.R.S. (1986) (an "employee" is "[e]very person in the service of any . . . private corporation . . . under any contract of hire, express or implied"). Therefore, there is no basis to utilize the definition of "wages" in determining the meaning of the term "employee."

In deciding whether a person is an employee for purposes of workers' compensation laws, other jurisdictions have not found the form of compensation determinative of the existence of an employer-employee relationship. . . . Betts v. Ann Arbor Public Schools, 403 Mich. 507, 271 N.W.2d 498 (1978) (claimant paid in form of training, college credits, and the meeting of prerequisites for the state teaching requirements was an "employee"). Accordingly, we reject the argument that an employment contract must provide for the payment of "wages" in order that one employed under such a contract may qualify as an "employee" under the Act.

C. We now turn to Highlands' principal argument for reversal: that Apostolou was expressly excluded from the definition of "employee" by legislative amendment in 1989 as a "person who volunteers his time or services as a ski patrol person . . . for a passenger tramway operator. . . ." See ch. 67, sec. 2, s 8–41–106(5), 1989 Colo.Sess.Laws 409, 410. As the ALJ noted, it is undisputed that Highlands is a passenger tramway operator. The crucial question is whether Apostolou volunteered his time or services within the meaning of the statutory exclusion.

Familiar principles guide us in construing a statute. Foremost among them is that our task is to determine and give effect to the intent of the legislature. . . . This intention is to be determined primarily from the statutory language, giving effect to the statutory terms in accordance with their commonly accepted and understood meanings. . . . Words or phrases that have acquired a technical or particular meaning, however, whether by legislative definition or otherwise, must be construed in accordance with the acquired meaning. . . . Statutes susceptible to more than one interpretation are ambiguous and must be construed in light of the legislative intent and purpose. . . . If statutory language is ambiguous, a court may consider the legislative history in determining the intent of the legislature. . . .

The common definition of "volunteer" is "[a] person who gives his services without any express or implied promise of remuneration." Black's Law Dictionary 1576 (6th ed. rev. 1990). Highlands contends, however, that the legislature intended "any person who volunteers his time or services as a ski patrol person," within the context of section 8–41–106(5), to include all those persons who work on ski patrol duty without monetary compensation but who receive ski passes entitling them to ski free at any time. It asserts that a ski pass is not remuneration, but a fringe benefit regularly given to "volunteers" within the ski industry, that this practice was recognized by the legislature when it adopted section 8–41–106(5), and that the legislature did not intend the receipt of a ski pass to preclude application of the exclusion.

We find it unnecessary to determine whether ski patrol workers who receive ski passes for personal use as a gratuity consistent with an allegedly standard practice of a passenger tramway operator are excluded from the definition of employee by section 8–41–106(5), for the facts do not correspond to any such practice. Apostolou did not receive a ski pass for himself as a standard fringe benefit provided to persons whose services are otherwise uncompensated. Instead, he specifically bargained for daily passes to be issued to his girlfriend, would not have worked on the Highlands ski patrol absent an agreement by Highlands to issue such passes, and entered into an agreement with Highlands involving mutual obligations. Apostolou obligated himself to perform ski patrol services, and Highlands obligated itself to provide the ski passes.

The ALJ specifically addressed the issue of whether Apostolou volunteered his time and services and made the following findings and conclusions: The respondent-employer [Highlands] approached its workers, including the claimant [Apostolou], seeking persons with CPR and first aid knowledge. The claimant, possessing such a background, was sent to interview with Mr. Smith, the director of the ski patrol. During the interview, the claimant expressed his reluctance to perform ski patrol duties if he was to receive only another photo ID ski pass since he already possessed one. As Mr. Smith was unwilling or unable to issue a photo ID ski pass to the claimant's girlfriend, it was agreed between the claimant and Mr. Smith that the claimant would receive unlimited free daily ski passes in return for performing duties as a ski patrolman. In essence, the claimant obligated himself to perform ski patrol services for the respondent-employer and in return, the respondent-employer obligated itself to provide free daily ski passes to the claimant or his designee. If such an arrangement had not been made available to the claimant, he would not have performed duties as a ski patrolman. The daily ski pass is valued at $36.00. If the claimant worked eight hours per day and obtained a ski pass for each day that he worked, the financial return for his performance of ski patrol duties would be $4.50 per hour. Under these circumstances, it cannot be concluded that the claimant volunteered his services to the respondent-employer. Rather, it is concluded that the claimant was an employee of the respondent-employer when he injured his knees on February 20, 1990, while performing duties as a ski patrolman. The factual findings in the ALJ's order are fully supported by substantial evidence in the record and are therefore binding on this court. See Fulton v. King Soopers, 823 P.2d 709, 712–13 (Colo.1992). Based on these facts, we conclude that Apostolou did not volunteer his services within the common meaning of that phrase and that the special meaning urged by Highlands even if accepted is not applicable. Accordingly, we agree with the conclusion of the ALJ, as did the court of appeals, that under the facts as found in the ALJ's ruling, it cannot be concluded that Apostolou volunteered his services to Highlands within the meaning of section 8–41–106(5).

III. We hold that the ALJ correctly concluded that Apostolou was an employee of Highlands at the time he was injured based on the facts as he found them. We find it unnecessary and inappropriate to go beyond the facts of this case in delineating the scope of the exclusion in section 8–41–106(5).

We affirm the judgment of the Colorado Court of Appeals.

JUSTICE VOLLACK, dissenting:

The majority holds that, because the claimant, John Apostolou, bargained for his position as a member of the ski patrol in exchange for ski passes for his girlfriend, he is not a "volunteer" under section 8–40–301(4), 3B C.R.S. (1993 Supp.), and is thus not excluded from receiving workers' compensation benefits. The majority affirms the decision of the administrative law judge that Apostolou was an employee of Aspen Highlands for purposes of receiving benefits under the Workers' Compensation Act, and was not a volunteer under the statute. Because I believe that, by the language of the statute, the legislature clearly intended to exclude someone in Apostolou's position from benefits, and because I do not believe an employment relationship was created between the parties, I dissent.

* * *

Apostolou is a sympathetic claimant. His injury prevented him from working for eight months. At the time of the hearing he had accumulated over $15,000 in medical bills, and it was possible that he needed additional surgery. The majority, however, should not create a legal fiction that Apostolou was an employee of Aspen Highlands so that he may collect workers' compensation benefits. The statutory language is clear: volunteer ski patrol members are not "employees" under the Workers' Compensation Act. The majority circumvents section 8–40–301(4) and, through judicial fiat, creates a new class of employees to receive workers' compensation benefits: those who have "bargained" for some condition of their volunteer position. In my opinion, the legislature clearly intended, by the language of the statute, that someone in Apostolou's circumstances was not entitled to workers' compensation benefits. I dissent.

I am authorized to say that CHIEF JUSTICE ROVIRA and JUSTICE SCOTT join in this dissent.

NOTES

1. On similar facts Hoste v. Shanty Creek Management, Inc., 459 Mich. 561, 592 N.W.2d 360 (1999) held that an injured ski patrol member was not an employee and not entitled to workers' compensation benefits. According to the Michigan court, "Quite simply, plaintiff was a 'gratuitous worker,' who was not an 'employee,' but rather an individual assisting another with a view toward furthering his own interests." *Id.*, 592 N.W.2d at 578. The court noted that Hoste did not depend upon ski patrolling as the source of his income and viewed the relationship as an exchange of gratuities rather than a contract of hire. Nordic Hills, Inc. v. Labor and Industry Review Commission, 242 Wis. 2d 473, 125 N.W. 2d 360 (Ct. App. 2001), rejected Hoste and upheld a holding that employment existed under similar facts. The court also noted Wisconsin's statute "has its own set of policy values unassociated with other states' workers' compensation statutes." *Id.*

The California definition of "Employee" explicitly *excludes* "Any person performing voluntary service as a ski patrolman who receives no compensation for those services other than meals or lodging or the use of ski tow or ski lift facilities." Cal. Labor Code § 3352(c).

2. Grant v. Blazer Coordinating Council of Youth Development, 111 N.J.Super. 125, 267 A.2d 568 (1970) found that an unpaid welfare-recipient trainee in a public work training program was an employee for the purposes of the New Jersey workers' compensation law. The court acknowledged that payment of wages is a factor to be considered in making an employment determination but explicitly concluded that "it is not a controlling factor." The court also held that the fact that the so-called employer was a nonprofit organization was not determinative. Upon appeal the appellate court affirmed, stating: "the County Court's determination of the existence of an employer-employee relationship and the modification of the award was reasonably reached on sufficient credible evidence present in the record considering the proofs as a whole, with due regard to the expertise of the Judge of Compensation and his opportunity to appraise the credibility of witnesses." Grant v. Blazer Coordinating Council of Youth Development, 116

N.J.Super. 460, 282 A.2d 769, 770 (1971). Accord, Tommy Nobis Center v. Barfield, 187 Ga.App. 394, 370 S.E.2d 517 (1988) (trainee who received $100 per week in federally funded job training program is an "employee"), and Wright v. Wilson Memorial Hospital, Inc., 30 N.C.App. 91, 226 S.E.2d 225 (1976) (student in laboratory assistantship program received room and board). See also Scissons v. City of Rapid City, 251 N.W.2d 681 (S.D.1977) (poor "relief worker" who was compensated with voucher coupons redeemable at area stores was held to be an employee of the county). In contrast, Dyess v. Meagher County, 315 Mont. 35, 67 P.3d 281 (2003) held that an EMT trainee who was suing the county for damages for an injury suffered while in training was not an employee under the workers' compensation statute.

3. Are "student teachers" employees? If so, are they employees of the school districts where they train or the colleges where they receive academic credit? Compare, Betts v. Ann Arbor Public Schools, 403 Mich. 507, 271 N.W.2d 498 (1978) (student teacher is an employee of the school district; course credit and experience are "value received"), cited in the principal case, with School Dist. No. 60, Pueblo County v. Industrial Commission, 43 Colo.App. 38, 601 P.2d 651 (1979) (student teacher is an employee of the university that paid the school district to accept its students). See also Ryles v. Durham County Hospital Corporation, Inc., 107 N.C.App. 455, 420 S.E.2d 487 (N.C.App.1992) (technical institute respiratory therapy student became an "apprentice" under the workers' compensation statute while delivering respiratory therapy treatments in a hospital; as a consequence, workers' compensation immunity barred a tort suit against the hospital). See also Rensing v. Indiana State University Board of Trustees, 444 N.E.2d 1170 (Ind. 1983), holding that an injured scholarship inter-collegiate football player was not an employee of the university.)

4. A defendant's truck transporting lethal gases in an area remote from its headquarters wrecked and imperiled the surrounding countryside. The chief of police called on plaintiff, an off-duty employee of an unrelated employer for assistance. The plaintiff, who was an expert in toxic gases, was injured. Is he entitled to compensation? If so, who is the employer, the police agency or the trucking company or someone else? See Tipper v. Great Lakes Chemical Co., 281 So.2d 10 (Fla.1973).

5. Are citizens called on by officials to perform a public service regarded as employees under workers' compensation laws? Compare Metropolitan Dade County v. Glassman, 341 So.2d 995 (Fla.1976) (claimant ordered to report for jury duty injured at the courthouse, not employee of county) with Yount v. Boundary County, 118 Idaho 307, 796 P.2d 516 (1990) (opposite result). Where the public service is performed in emergencies, the cases often turn on customary practices and the legal authority of the requesting officer to enlist assistance. Compare, Conley v. Industrial Commission, 43 Colo.App. 10, 601 P.2d 648 (1979) (compensation awarded dependents of an "off duty" but "on call" police officer who was killed while directing traffic during a flood in a neighboring county; informal practice of law enforcement agencies to assist others in emergencies) and Moore v. State,

200 N.C. 300, 156 S.E. 806 (1931) (claimant deputized by forest warden to assist in putting out a fire was entitled to compensation), with Morley v. Workmen's Compensation Appeal Bd., 49 Pa.Cmwlth. 98, 410 A.2d 110 (1980) (former mayor injured while assisting chief of police in directing traffic at scene of an accident was not an "auxiliary policeman"; compensation denied) and Leon County v. Sauls, 151 Fla. 171, 9 So.2d 461 (1942) (constable requested that Sauls assist him in making an arrest; compensation denied).

6. Questions of employment status also arise in cases involving mutual assistance arrangements. In Gant v. Industrial Com'n, 263 Wis. 64, 56 N.W.2d 525 (1953), a claimant farmer was denied recovery for an injury received while returning work on a neighbor's farm in accordance with local custom, and in Alexander v. J.E. Hixson & Sons Funeral Home, 44 So.2d 487 (La.App.1950) a florist injured while lifting a casket lid pursuant to a mutual assistance agreement between him and an undertaker in their respective endeavors was not an employee of the undertaker. But compare, Debold v. H.P. Martell & Sons, 300 Minn. 296, 219 N.W.2d 623 (1974) (claimant who often exchanged equipment and services with subcontractor held to be employee of the latter).

7. If money is paid an apparent employee, must it be paid in return for work performed? In Smith v. Valentine Estates, Inc., 45 A.D.2d 789, 357 N.Y.S.2d 150 (1974), a youngster was given an odd job on a construction site to keep him busy and deter him from damaging the property. The court found that no employer-employee relationship existed. Similarly, no employment was found where a father, in order to stop his minor son's excessive demands for money, ordered his company to pay the son a weekly salary of $35.00. The court regarded this an "allowance", despite the fact that the son, who lived with the father, did some work in the father's plant. Caldwell v. Caldwell, 55 So.2d 258 (La.App.1950). A contrary result was reached under similar facts in Denius v. North Dakota Workmen's Compensation Bureau, 68 N.D. 506, 281 N.W. 361 (1938). The Idaho statute excludes from the definition of "employee" members of the employer's family "dwelling in his house." Idaho Code § 72–213.

8. One person may be held to be the employer of another, even though an independent third person actually pays the employee for the service rendered. Claremont Country Club v. Industrial Accident Com'n, 174 Cal. 395, 163 P. 209 (1917) (caddy was employee of country club although paid by individual players); Board of Educ. of the City of Chicago v. Industrial Com'n, 57 Ill.2d 339, 312 N.E.2d 244 (1974) (claimant held to be an employee of the Board of Education despite the fact that P.T.A. paid salary); and Workmen's Comp. Appeal Bd. v. American Mut. Liability Ins. Co., 19 Pa.Cmwlth. 502, 339 A.2d 183 (1975) (paper company salesman with bad eyesight hired a driver; driver held to be employee of paper company).

9. People who volunteer services temporarily or in emergencies have been variously treated: Edwards v. Hollywood Canteen, 27 Cal.2d 802, 167 P.2d 729 (1946) (volunteer hostess "jitterbugged" with over-zealous Marine;

not an employment relationship); Armitage v. Trustees of Mt. Fern Methodist Episcopal Church, 33 N.J.Super. 367, 110 A.2d 154 (1954) (church member injured while doing work on church building to discharge his pledge at stipulated hourly rate, not an employment relationship); Glamm v. City of Amsterdam Fire Dept., 54 A.D.2d 996, 388 N.Y.S.2d 55 (1976) (volunteer assisting fireman held not to be employee, arrangement ambiguous); Charlottesville Music Center, Inc. v. McCray, 215 Va. 31, 205 S.E.2d 674 (1974) (fifteen-year-old boy who did not expect compensation for helping his friend erect shelves is not an employee). Many statutes explicitly address coverage of "volunteers" and often mandate coverage of persons assisting in delivery of emergency public services. Should it make a difference in cases such as these whether the injured worker is claiming benefits the employer denies or whether an employer is claiming workers' compensatuion immunity to an employee's tort action?

3. EMPLOYMENTS DISTINGUISHED FROM OTHER RELATIONS

HANSON v. TRANSPORTATION GENERAL, INC.

Supreme Court of Connecticut, 1998.
245 Conn. 613, 716 A.2d 857.

PETERS, ASSOCIATE JUSTICE.

The Workers' Compensation Act (act), General Statutes § 31–275 et seq., provides benefits only for those workers who have the status of "employees" at the time of their injury. The principal issue in this certified appeal is whether an owner-operator of a taxicab qualifies as an employee of the taxicab company with which he contracted to provide taxicab service. The plaintiff, Janet Hanson, the surviving spouse of Allen Hanson (decedent), filed a workers' compensation claim to recover survivor benefits for the death of the decedent while he was driving a taxicab in accordance with his written agreement with the defendants, Transportation General, Inc. doing business as Metro Taxi Service (Metro), and Hartford Insurance Company. The compensation commissioner for the third district (commissioner) dismissed Hanson's claim as a result of his finding that, on the date of the decedent's death, he had been an independent contractor and not an employee of Metro. Hanson appealed to the compensation review board (board), which affirmed the decision of the commissioner. That decision was then affirmed by the Appellate Court. Hanson v. Transportation General, Inc., 45 Conn.App. 441, 447, 696 A.2d 1026 (1997).

We granted Hanson's petition for certification to consider the merits of her claim for compensation, either under a proposed "relative nature of the work" test or under the existing "right to control" test. Hanson v. Transportation General, Inc., 243 Conn. 914, 914–15, 701 A.2d 329

(1997). We also agreed to determine Hanson's ancillary evidentiary claim.[2] We affirm the judgment of the Appellate Court.

The opinion of the Appellate Court outlines the basic facts. "[Metro] . . . operated a fleet of taxicabs through the use of both owner-operator and lease agreements. Drivers could either lease or purchase cabs from [Metro]. The decedent, under an owner-operator agreement, drove a Metro [cab] from 1987 until he was murdered while operating a Metro [taxicab] on April 16, 1990. Under the terms of [Metro's] standard owner-operator agreement, [Metro] held legal title to the [taxicab] and the owner-operator maintained a beneficial ownership. Upon the termination of the relationship, which could be done by either party after forty-eight hours notice, legal title [to the taxicab] would be transferred back to the owner-operator. In return for the weekly payment by the owner-operator of 'stand dues'[4] in the approximate amount of $425, plus an additional $100 per week if a second driver was used, [Metro], under a certificate issued to it by the department of transportation, allowed the owner-operator the right to operate a taxicab. [Metro] required the owner-operator to be properly licensed, to use a taxicab meter and radio approved by the department of transportation and to obey its regulations and to adhere to all federal, state and local laws. The owner-operators also were required to maintain insurance in the minimum amount required by law at their own expense and to pay for the use and operation of the [taxicab] including repairs, maintenance, fines, tickets, towing and all taxes or other assessments imposed by governmental agencies. Under the agreement, the owner-operator could set the hours of operation, hire a driver for the taxicab, use the vehicle for personal use and keep all fares derived from the operation of the [taxicab]. [Metro] did not pay the owner-operator, provide benefits, request income records or collect payroll or social security taxes." Hanson v. Transportation General, Inc., supra, 45 Conn.App. at 442–43, 696 A.2d 1026.

I.

The first issue presented by Hanson's appeal is whether, in deciding whether a worker is an employee under the act, we should adopt the "relative nature of the work" test as an alternative to the "right to

---

[2] Our grant of certification was limited to the following issues:

"Should the relative nature of the work test be adopted as an alternative to the right to control test in concluding whether the plaintiff's decedent, a cab driver, was an independent contractor and not an employee of the defendant taxi cab company?

"Did the Appellate Court properly affirm the finding of dismissal pursuant to the right to control test in light of the department of transportation regulations?

"Did the Appellate Court properly affirm the compensation review board's refusal to correct the finding of dismissal as requested by the plaintiff?" Hanson v. Transportation General, Inc., supra, 243 Conn. 914–15, 701 A.2d 329.

[4] " 'Stand dues' are a combination of leasing, taxes and insurance costs." Hanson v. Transportation General, Inc., supra, 45 Conn.App.at 442 n. 3, 696 A.2d 1026.

control" test. The Appellate Court declined to address this issue on its merits because it felt bound by this court's decision in Ross v. Post Publishing Co., 129 Conn. 564, 29 A.2d 768 (1943). In that case, we held that "[t]here is no dispute about the ultimate test. It is the right of general control of the means and methods used by the person whose status is involved." Id., at 567, 29 A.2d 768. Although the issue of the propriety of recourse to the "relative nature of the work" test raises serious questions that warrant plenary exploration by this court; Doe v. Stamford, 241 Conn. 692, 696–97, 699 A.2d 52 (1997); we are not persuaded that we should engraft this test onto our longstanding workers' compensation law.

A

The issue that Hanson has raised must be decided in the context of two jurisprudential principles that limit our authority to afford her the relief that she seeks. First, because this is a workers' compensation case, it is governed by the special rules of construction that we have long held applicable in such cases.[5] Second, because this is a case in which Hanson asks us to overrule a line of judicial precedents that the legislature has left intact for eighty years, it must be reconciled with the principles of stare decisis. It is true that the right to control test, in its present form, was embedded into the act by early cases relying on similar rules in tort cases. Nonetheless, that construction of the act has been ratified by legislative acquiescence.

Connecticut first adopted a statutory scheme of workers' compensation in 1913. Dodd v. Middlesex Mutual Assurance Co., 242 Conn. 375, 381, 698 A.2d 859 (1997). Although some statutes have common-law roots that may enlighten their construction, the act is not such a statute. "[T]he workers' compensation system in Connecticut is derived exclusively from statute. . . . A commissioner may exercise jurisdiction to hear a claim only under the precise circumstances and in the manner particularly prescribed by the enabling legislation." (Citations omitted; internal quotation marks omitted.) Discuillo v. Stone & Webster, 242 Conn. 570, 576, 698 A.2d 873 (1997); . . . ; Gagnon v. United Aircraft Corp., 159 Conn. 302, 305, 268 A.2d 660 (1970). "Because of the statutory nature of our workers' compensation system, policy determinations as to what injuries are compensable and what jurisdictional limitations apply thereto are for the legislature, not the judiciary or the board, to make." Discuillo v. Stone & Webster, supra, at

[5] This appeal does not involve the rights of a third party tort victim to recover against Metro for the misconduct of one of its drivers on the basis of the principles of actual, implied, or apparent authority. See, e.g., Beckenstein v. Potter & Carrier, Inc., 191 Conn. 120, 132–41, 464 A.2d 6 (1983) (discussing agency principles in contract case); Fireman's Fund Indemnity Co. v. Longshore Beach & Country Club, Inc., 127 Conn. 493, 496–97, 18 A.2d 347 (1941) (applying similar agency principles in tort action). The issue, rather, is what the decedent driver knew or should have known of his own status under the act.

577, 698 A.2d 873. Whatever the policy implications of this case may be, "the issue presented is, at bottom, a matter of statutory construction." Doe v. Stamford, supra, 241 Conn. at 697, 699 A.2d 52.

As a matter of statutory construction, to overrule our long-standing invocation of the "right to control" test, we would have to reconcile such a ruling with the presumption of legislative acquiescence in judicial interpretations that the legislature has not overturned. We have long acted on the hypothesis that the legislature is aware of the interpretation that the courts have placed upon one of its legislative enactments. Once an appropriate interval to permit legislative reconsideration has passed without corrective legislative action, the inference of legislative acquiescence limits judicial authority to reconsider the merits of its earlier decision . . . In this context, only "the most cogent reasons and inescapable logic" . . . ; can justify judicial abandonment of judicial precedents dating back more than eighty years. See Thompson v. Twiss, 90 Conn. 444, 447, 97 A. 328 (1916). We can perceive no such cogent reasons or inescapable logic to justify altering our long-standing judicial interpretation of one of the fundamental premises of our workers' compensation statute. This is particularly true for this statute, which has been the subject of extensive legislative amendment over its entire life, without any legislative indication of disagreement with the right to control test. Furthermore, it is fair to assume that employers and insurers have relied justifiably on that interpretation in ordering their business affairs. For us to abandon that interpretation would upset their legitimate expectations.

B

Recognizing that these principles create obstacles to judicial reconsideration of our long-standing "right to control" test, Hanson attempts a bypass, arguing that the "relative nature of the work" test can coexist with the "right to control" test. We disagree.

The "relative nature of the work" test determines the relationship between a worker and a putative employer by asking whether the worker's performance is an integral part of the regular business of the putative employer. 3 A. Larson & L. Larson, Workmen's Compensation (1997) § 45.00, p. 8–193. The "right to control" test determines the same relationship by asking whether the putative employer has "the right to control the means and methods" used by the worker in the performance of his or her job. . . .

Dual standards for determining whether a worker is an employee or an independent contractor would complicate the administration of our workers' compensation system. Although there well may be circumstances under which the results reached by application of the two tests will be identical, more often than not the results will differ. In all probability, a workers' compensation commissioner applying the "relative nature of the work" test would be required to broaden the class of "employees" to include workers who currently are characterized as independent contractors. See, e.g., Harger v. Structural Services, Inc., 121 N.M. 657, 916 P.2d 1324, 1329–31 (1996). Indeed, unless differing results were contemplated, there would be little to gain from adopting a new test. Hanson has proffered no criteria to define the underlying circumstances under which one or the other test would be the more appropriate. If a workers' compensation commissioner had undefined and hence unlimited authority to invoke either test, the scope of the term "employee" would be left in confusion. We are persuaded, therefore, that we must evaluate Hanson's argument in favor of the "relative nature of the work" test as an outright alternative to the "right to control" test.[6]

C

We turn now to the merits of replacing the "right to control" test with the "relative nature of the work" test. As advocated by Hanson, the "relative nature of the work" test would require a two part analysis, each part requiring consideration of three separate factors. With respect to the character of the work performed, the claimant would be required to show: (1) the degree of skill involved; (2) the degree to which the work is a separate calling or business; and (3) the extent to which a worker so situated reasonably can be expected to carry the burden of accident. With respect to the relationship of the work to the putative employer's business, the claimant would have to establish: (1) the extent to which the work is a regular part of the putative employer's regular business; (2) the extent to which the work is being performed continuously or intermittently; and (3) the extent to which the work is of sufficient duration to constitute continuing services rather than a particular assignment. See 3 A. Larson & L. Larson, supra, § 43.51, p. 8–23, and § 45.10, p. 8–193.[7]

---

[6] Hanson's argument relies on four out-of-state cases that we find unpersuasive. See Stampados v. Colorado D & S. Enterprises, 833 P.2d 815, 817 (Colo.App.1992); Kertesz v. Korsh, 296 N.J.Super. 146, 152–55, 686 A.2d 368 (App.Div.1996); Kaiel v. Cultural Homestay Institute, 129 Or.App. 471, 477, 879 P.2d 1319, rev. denied, 320 Or. 453, 887 P.2d 792 (1994); Claim of Griffin, 466 N.W.2d 148, 150 (N.D.1991).

[7] As Metro observes, although Professor Larson's treatise describes the "relative nature of the work" test as a new test currently superseding the "right to control" test, that statement no longer reflects the totality of the relevant case law. Earlier editions of his celebrated work demonstrate that, for almost thirty years, Professor Larson has been a staunch advocate of the, "relative nature of the work" test. During this time period, however, only a few state courts have adopted this test in substitution for the "right to control" test . . . Connecticut has not done so, either by way of legislation or by way of judicial opinion. See DaSilva v. Danbury Publishing Co., 39 Conn.App. 653, 656, 666 A.2d 440, cert. denied, 235 Conn. 936, 668 A.2d 374 (1995). Connecticut is not alone. See, e.g., Kirkwood v. Industrial Commission, 84 Ill.2d 14, 23–24, 48 Ill.Dec. 556, 416 N.E.2d 1078 (1981); Youngblood v. North State Ford Truck Sales, 87 N.C.App. 35, 37–38, 359 S.E.2d 256 (1987), aff'd, 321 N.C. 380, 364 S.E.2d 433 (1988). A contrary decision by the Supreme Court of Maine; Timberlake v. Frigon & Frigon, 438 A.2d 1294, 1297–98

Hanson advances four arguments in favor of adoption of the "relative nature of the work" test. She derives three of these arguments from the unchallenged proposition that workers' compensation is social legislation. In that light, she argues that, in preference to the "right to control" test, the proposed test: (1) more effectively implements the objectives of this social legislation; (2) more accurately depicts the employer-employee relationship by precluding employer reliance on contracts drafted to avoid the costs of this social legislation; (3) more directly advances the remedial purposes of social legislation. In addition, she argues that the "right to control" test is too vague to be applied fairly. We are not persuaded. Evaluation of Hanson's first three arguments cannot be undertaken by this forum; their resolution is grist only for the legislative mill. Hanson's final argument is unpersuasive on its merits.

In the absence of any claim of constitutional vagueness in the "right to control" test, Hanson must demonstrate that fact-finding under this test exceeds the discretionary authority normally afforded to any trier of fact. Undeniably, whenever the parties disagree, a determination of fact has elements of uncertainty. Hanson has not shown that, in application, the "right to control" test has created more uncertainty than factual disputes about, for example, contractual intent or tortious misbehavior. Indeed, as is illustrated by the Alaska case upon which Hanson relies, close questions of fact are also likely to arise in the application of the "relative nature of the work" test. Grothe v. Olafson, 659 P.2d 602, 606 (Alaska 1983).[8]

II

The second issue raised by Hanson's appeal is whether, if the "right to control" test applies, the trier of fact improperly determined that the decedent was not an employee at the time of his death. She claims that Metro retained enough authority over the taxicab fleet bearing its name to demonstrate a right to general control that made the decedent its employee rather than an independent contractor. We disagree.

"The determination of whether an injury arose out of and in the course of employment is a question of fact for the commissioner." Spatafore v. Yale University, 239 Conn. 408, 418, 684 A.2d 1155 (1996).

(Me.1982); was overturned five years later by that state's legislature. See West v. C.A.M. Logging, 670 A.2d 934, 937 n. 2 (Me.1996).

8 The relationship between the parties in this case illustrates the factual uncertainties that may arise in the application of the "relative nature of the work" test. Concededly, the decedent was free to use his taxicab for private engagements entirely unrelated to the business of Metro. Would the decedent's status depend on whether, when he was killed, he was engage in business obtained through Metro's dispatcher or through his own enterprise? Would the status of other taxi drivers who were accidently injured depend solely, or principally, on the percentage of the time that they used the taxicab for Metro business? We do not suggest that these questions are unanswerable. They illustrate, however, that there will be close issues of fact, whichever test is applied.

Accordingly, we apply the same deferential standard of review that we accord to findings of fact by a trial judge or jury. Id., at 419, 684 A.2d 1155. Keeping these principles in mind, we turn to Hanson's claim that Metro retained sufficient control to render her decedent an employee. For Connecticut authority, Hanson relies principally on Lassen v. Stamford Transit Co., 102 Conn. 76, 128 A. 117 (1925), a case which, like this one, involved the "right to control" test for taxicab drivers, and which held that the drivers were employees. That case, however, is distinguishable on its facts. For example, the taxicab company in that case required drivers to turn over their fares to the company and paid the drivers 75 percent of that amount. Id., at 79, 128 A. 117. Furthermore, company dispatchers designated the driver who was to transport any particular passenger. Id., at 78–79,128 A. 117. In this case, Metro took care to avoid such indicia of control, leaving it to taxicab drivers like the decedent to decide, in the exercise of their own discretion, when and where they would take the taxicabs on the road.

As a more general matter, Hanson cites the fact that Metro required cabdrivers to conform to department of transportation regulations with respect to such matters as licenses, meters, fares, records, dispatch and safety. The argument that such state regulatory requirements automatically satisfy the right to control test would make irrelevant the contractual terms of the relationship between the parties. It is axiomatic that every taxicab company must comply with state regulations. We are not persuaded, therefore, that Metro's requirement that owner-operators comply with government regulations definitively demonstrates an employer-employee relationship. See, e.g., La Grande v. B & L Services, Inc., 432 So.2d 1364, 1366 (Fla.App.1983).

Contrary to Hanson's argument, we agree with the Appellate Court, the board and the commissioner that the totality of the evidence did not demonstrate that Metro had retained sufficient control to require a finding of an employer-employee relationship between Metro and the decedent. True, the commissioner made some subordinate factual findings that, if viewed in isolation, might have supported a different determination. For example, Metro required its drivers to: (1) report all traffic violations to Metro; and (2) obtain Metro's approval of any outside insurance. Metro also held legal title to the vehicles, and painted and marked the cars as Metro cabs. Other subordinate findings by the commissioner, however, paint a clearer picture of the contractual relationship between Metro and its drivers. In the daily use of their cabs, drivers could set their own hours, work anywhere in the Metro service area, refuse to accept dispatch calls, and hire a second driver for the cab. Drivers had sole responsibility for all expenses related to operation of their cabs and had the right, to regain total ownership rights to their cabs upon the termination of their relationship with Metro. Administratively, moreover, Metro did not pay any salary or fringe benefits to the drivers and did not require the drivers to report their fares to Metro. We conclude that the commissioner reasonably found that the totality of factors in this case indicates that Metro taxi drivers were not employees as that term is used under the act.[10]

In sum, the Appellate Court properly reviewed the commissioner's determination under the terms of the "right to control" test. We concur in the Appellate Court's conclusion that, under the circumstances of this case, Hanson's decedent was not an employee, but, rather, an independent contractor.

* * *

The judgment of the Appellate Court is affirmed.

BERDON, ASSOCIATE JUSTICE, dissenting.

* * *

I

Reversal is required in this case because the compensation commissioner for the third district (commissioner) did not properly review all the circumstances of the decedent's work relationship to determine whether he was an employee or an independent contractor. . . .

The Restatement (Second) of Agency, § 220 (1958) (hereinafter referred to as § 220), . . . defines the relationship of master and servant as follows:

(1) "A servant is a person employed to perform services in the affairs of another and who with respect to the physical conduct in the performance of the services is subject to the other's control or right to control.

(2) In determining whether one acting for another is a servant or an independent contractor, the following matters of fact, among others, are considered:

(a) the extent of control which, by the agreement, the master may exercise over the details of the work;

[10] The principal issue was the propriety of a motion to correct to add a finding that, on the date of his death, the decedent was on the road in response to a call that he had received from Metro's radio dispatcher. There was, however, neither a finding, nor a request to add a finding, to the effect that the decedent had used his taxicab exclusively or even predominantly in response to calls from the dispatcher. Significantly, the commissioner found that the decedent had used his own cellular phone for servicing customers and that he had shared the use of his cab with a second driver. Furthermore, in one of the requests for correction of the finding, Hanson herself asked for inclusion of a finding that: "The work performed by [the decedent] was not for the completion of a particular job but consisted of an ongoing relationship between [the decedent] and [Metro]."

(b) whether or not the one employed is engaged in a distinct occupation or business;

(c) the kind of occupation, with reference to whether, in the locality, the work is usually done under the direction of the employer or by a specialist without supervision;

(d) the skill required in the particular occupation;

(e) whether the employer of the workman supplies the instrumentalities, tools, and the place of work for the person doing the work;

(f) the length of time for which the person is employed;

(g) the method of payment, whether by the time or by the job;

(h) whether or not the work is a part of the regular business of the employer;

(i) whether or not the parties believe they are creating the relation of master and servant;

and

(j) whether the principal is or is not in business."

When the claimant proves, pursuant to § 220(1), that the purported employer had a right to control the person's work, the analysis stops there and the employment relationship for purposes of the act has been satisfied. . . .

On the basis of the undisputed findings by the commissioner in this case, I conclude that Metro's right to control the decedent was not so attenuated as to mandate a finding, under subsection (1) of § 220, that the decedent was an independent contractor. Therefore, consideration of all the factors in subsection (2) of § 220 is required to determine the true status of the decedent at the time of his fatal injury. The majority, like the commissioner, however, limits its review of the decedent's relationship to a summary analysis of some, but not all, of the factors set forth in § 220(2).

In general, the "inquiry [into all the factors of subsection (2) of § 220] turns to the economic and functional relationship between the nature of the work and the operation of the business served." Ceradsky v. Mid-America Dairymen, Inc., supra, 583 S.W.2d at 199. . . .

Most importantly, the Restatement directs this court to consider whether the decedent's work was "a part of the regular business of the employer." 1 Restatement (Second), supra, § 220(2)(h). In this case, Metro's sole business was to supply taxi service, precisely what the decedent was doing as a result of his employment by Metro. Indeed, pursuant to Metro's owner-operator agreement, the decedent was hired to perform a continual service of carrying passengers to and from points in Metro's area of operations in order to ensure fulfillment of Metro's obligations to the department of transportation to provide a quality taxicab service meeting certain standards. Although Metro argued before the commissioner that it was in the business of "leasing cars to drivers," Metro was obligated to provide taxi service in accordance with its franchise with the department of transportation. In doing so, Metro received telephone calls from customers for taxi service and dispatched drivers, including the decedent, to these customers. While Metro adopted an ingenious method of fixing the decedent's compensation and permitted him to exercise much discretion over the use of his taxicab, there was, still, "a continuous, essential connection between [Metro's] work and that of the [decedent] . . . making the [decedent's] labor a critical part of the regular business of [Metro]." (Citations omitted; internal quotation marks omitted.) Petition of City Cab of Manchester, supra, 139 N.H. at 222, 652 A.2d 1202; Aisenberg v. C.F. Adams Co., 95 Conn. 419, 422, 111 A. 591 (1920) ("[t]he means and method of conducting this business, as we have in part detailed, comprise the essence of this business").

This last factor, § 220(2)(h), is closely related to the "relative nature of the work" test that the plaintiff urges this court to adopt and that has been embraced by other jurisdictions. See, e.g., Stampados v. Colorado D. & S. Enterprises, 833 P.2d 815, 817 (Colo.App.1992); . . . It is unnecessary for this court to consider the issue of adopting the relative nature of the work test in order to decide this case because, according to our precedent, most of the factors of this test have relevance in the application of the right to control test. . . . For example, in Higley v. Woodford, 106 Conn. 284, 285 86, 137 A. 755 (1927), this court specifically relied on the following factor—the degree to which the claimant's work is a separate calling or business—to conclude that the claimant woodcutter was not an employee of the defendant. The court in Higley emphasized that because the claimant was " 'exercising an independent employment . . . was doing his own business . . . in his own way and under his own will' " he was an independent contractor. Id. Most importantly, in at least two cases this court has relied on the extent to which the work is a regular part of the purported employer's regular business to determine whether a claimant was an employee or an independent contractor. See, e.g., Robert C. Buell & Co. v. Danaher, supra, 127 Conn. at 612, 18 A.2d 697 (claimant was employee because " '[o]n the whole the work which the salesmen are doing is the business of the plaintiff [and t]he advancement of that business depends very largely upon the method and manner of the doing of their work by the salesmen' "); Lassen v. Stamford Transit Co., 102 Conn. 76, 81, 128 A. 117 (1925) (negligent operator of taxicab was employee of defendant who had concession for operating taxi service, in part, because defendant had no "other means of performing this service").[10]

The plaintiff's decedent took a regular and continuous part in the defendant's economic activity of providing taxi service to residents and visitors to the New Haven metropolitan area. Like many of Metro's other drivers, the decedent and his family could not be expected to bear the cost of a serious traffic accident, nor was his place in the overall transportation business such that he could distribute the risk of injury on his own. In every respect then, he is the kind of workers for whose benefit the compensation act was thought necessary. Shinuald v. Mound City Yellow Cab Co., 666 S.W.2d 846, 849 (Mo.App.1984) ("It is a business of the [company] to supply taxicab service to the customers. . . . There is substantial evidence that claimant's work was a regular and continuous part of that business and not an independent business through which it would be feasible to channel the cost of work-connected injury. . . . Therefore, [the] claimant is a fortiori an employee for purposes of the Workers Compensation Law." [Internal quotation marks omitted.])

* * *

Accordingly I dissent.

NOTES

1. Historically, most courts relied primarily if not exclusively on the common law "right to control" test. Many still do. For example, Harger v. Structural Services, Inc., 121 N.M. 657, 916 P.2d 1324 (1996) confirmed: (1) workers' compensation in that state does not cover a broader class of employee or workers' compensation benefits than for other purposes; (2) the test is the approach of Restatement Agency (Second) § 220; (3) no factor is to be given greater weight than any other; (4) and the decision is to be made on the totality of the circumstances. Courts generally agree that "right to control" does not require the employer to be in actual control at the time an injury occurs. Avanti Press, Inc. v. Employment Dept. Tax Section 248 Or.App. 450, 274 P.3d 190 (Or. App. 2012).

The Harger court also noted that the "right to control" the details of an employee's work is different from the right to control the timing and sequencing of when independent contractors perform their independent tasks. Most courts follow the guidelines of Restatement (Second) of Agency, § 220, as employed by dissenting Justice Berdon in Hanseon, to distinguish employment contracts from independent contractor agreements.

---

[10] By implication, if the defendant in Lassen did not have any other means of providing taxi service to its customers, the taxicab operator's work was a regular part of the defendant's business, and consequently, was a good indication that the defendant was the operator's employer.

Not all courts agree with the Harger statement that the Restatement § 220 factors are of equal weight. Nelson v. Yellow Cab Company, 349 S.C. 589, 564 S.E.2d 110 (2002) applied the right of control test to the claim of survivors of a murdered taxi cab driver. The facts were similar to those in Hanson. The court individually considered whether these four factors weighed for or against employment: right to control "the method and manner in which he drove;" furnishing equipment; right to fire; and method of payment. The court found two factors favoring employment, one neutral (furnishing equipment) and one favoring independent contract (method of payment). Applying the "states' policy in favor of inclusion of employees under the Workers' Compensation Act," the court approved a finding that the decedent had been a covered employee. GKN Co. v. Magness, 744 N.E.2d 397 (Ind. 2001) applied a similar analysis to determine whether an injured truck driver was an employee of a general contractor or of a subcontractor. The court applied the four Nelson factors plus three others: Belief of the Parties in the Existence of an Employer-Employee Relationship; Length of Employment; and Establishment of Work Boundaries. Balancing the factors, the court approved a finding that the employer-employee relationship did not exist. While "not dispositive," the court held the right to control the manner and means by which the work is to be accomplished is the single most important factor in determining the existence of an employer-employee relationship.

2. Do you agree with the proposition that the "right to control" test may be used to determine whether an employer is to be held vicariously liable for harm caused to a third person by a particular worker's act while simultaneously the "relative nature of the work" test is applied to determine whether the same employer would be liable to provide workers' compensation benefits to the same worker for injuries arising out of the same accident? It is possible that a worker could be an employee of a particular employer as to a particular act for one purpose and not the other?

3. In determining employment status, many decisions look to the economic and social objectives that underlie the workers' compensation legislation. Laurel Daily Leader, Inc. v. James, 224 Miss. 654, 80 So.2d 770 (1955) (newsboy held to be an employee for purposes of compensation although court conceded he would not be a servant for the purposes of *respondeat superior* liability); N.L.R.B. v. Hearst Publications, 322 U.S. 111, 64 S.Ct. 851, 88 L.Ed. 1170 (1944) (newsboys treated as employees under National Labor Relations Act). These decisions fit with the general view that remedial statutes should be liberally construed to satisfy their purposes. Do they also fit with the economic assumptions about how best to distribute the costs of work injuries?

4. As Hanson demonstrates, many courts have incorporated the functional view of employment into a broader "relative nature of the work" test. Contrary to the unwillingness of the Hanson majority opinion, several courts have openly applied the traditional "right of control" and the "relative nature of the work" tests concurrently. For example, Arkansas Transit

Homes, Inc. v. Aetna Life and Casualty, 341 Ark. 317, 16 S.W.3d 545 (2000), applied both Restatement § 220 and the "relative nature of the work" tests. As to the latter test, the court identified two decisive factors: (1) whether and how much the workers' occupation is a separate calling or profession; and (2) what relationship it bears to the regular business of the employer. The Arkansas court concluded that certain truck drivers who were under contract to haul mobile homes were covered by the employer's workers' compensation policy. ConAgra Foods, Inc. v. Draper, 372 Ark. 361, 276 S.W.3d 244 (2008), added: "The more the worker's occupation resembles the business of the employer the more likely the worker is to be an employee." Other courts also authorize use of both tests. *See* Sang Hwan Park v. Lee, 53 A.D.3d 936, 862 N.Y.S.2d 199 (2008) and Pollack v. Pino's Formal Wear & Tailoring, 253 N.J.Super. 397, 407 (App.Div.1992), certif. denied, 130 N.J. 6 (1992).

The Benefits Review Board of the United States Department of Labor is said to employ the right to control control test, the relative nature of the work test and the Restatement (Second) of Agency, Section 220 factors in assessing employment status under the Longshore and Harbor Workers' Compensation Act as appropriate under the circumstances. Am. Stevedoring Ltd. v. Marinelli, 248 F.3d 54 (2d Cir.2001). In contrast, the District of Columbia is said to apply the relative nature of the work test. USA Waste of Maryland, Inc. v. Love, 954 A.2d 1027 (D.C.2008).

Rubalcaba v. Nagaki Farms, Inc., 333 Or. 614, 43 P.3d 1106 (2002) also authorized considering "nature of work" factors in "situations in which there is some evidence suggesting that an employer retained the right to control the method and details of the claimant's work." *Id.*, 43 P.3d at 1112. Hence, in Oregon if some "right to control" evidence exists, the court may also consider "nature of work" evidence in determining a claimant's status.

5. In the latter decades of the twentieth century some legislatures retreated from judicial decisions that had applied statutes liberally to protect the interests of employees. See, e.g., N.L.R.B. v. Town & Country Electric, Inc., 516 U.S. 85, 91, 116 S.Ct. 450, 454, 133 L.Ed.2d 371 (1995), noting that the holding in N.L.R.B. v. Hearst, which had held newsboys to be employees rather than independent contractors, had been statutorily overruled. Running somewhat counter to that trend is this modification to the Colorado workers' compensation statute:

> (2)(a) Notwithstanding any other provision of this section, any individual who performs services for pay for another shall be deemed to be an employee, irrespective of whether the common-law relationship of master and servant exists, unless such individual is free from control and direction in the performance of the service, both under the contract for performance of service and in fact and such individual is customarily engaged in an independent trade, occupation, profession, or business related to the service performed.
> * * *

> (b)(I) * * *
>
> (II) To prove independence it must be shown that the person for whom services are performed does not:
>
> (A) Require the individual to work exclusively for the person for whom services are performed; except that the individual may choose to work exclusively for such person for a finite period of time specified in the document;
>
> (B) Establish a quality standard for the individual; except that the person may provide plans and specifications regarding the work but cannot oversee the actual work or instruct the individual as to how the work will be performed;
>
> (C) Pay a salary or at an hourly rate instead of at a fixed or contract rate;
>
> (D) Terminate the work of the service provider during the contract period unless such service provider violates the terms of the contract or fails to produce a result that meets the specifications of the contract;
>
> (E) Provide more than minimal training for the individual;
>
> (F) Provide tools or benefits to the individual; except that materials and equipment may be supplied;
>
> (G) Dictate the time of performance; except that a completion schedule and a range of negotiated and mutually agreeable work hours may be established;
>
> (H) Pay the service provider personally instead of making checks payable to the trade or business name of such service provider; and
>
> (I) Combine the business operations of the person for whom service is provided in any way with the business operations of the service provider instead of maintaining all such operations separately and distinctly. * * *

Co. St. § 8–40–202 (2008). Is a provision such as this better or worse for workers as a whole? The Ohio statute broadly includes within the definition of "Employees" every person "who performs labor or provides services pursuant to a construction contract" if at least ten of 20 prescribed criteria apply. Ohio R. C. § 4123.01(A)(1)(b).

6. In a few states some independent contractors may be entitled to compensation from the entity for whom the contracted work is being done. See, e.g., Wisconsin Statutes § 102.07(8)(a): "[With omitted exceptions] every independent contractor is, for the purpose of this chapter an employee of any employer under this chapter for whom he or she is performing service in the course of the trade, business, profession or occupation of such employer at the time of the injury." See also LSA–R.S. 23:1021 (7). which extends

compensation to all contractors who do a substantial amount of manual labor. The broadest provision is in the Colorado statute which authorizes an award to any contractor doing work which is part of the business of the principal or employer. Colo.Rev.Stats. section 8–41–401. Do these provisions unnecessarily go beyond what is needed to satisfy the remedial and economic premises of the workers' compensation scheme?

7. Nurses and interne physicians in regular employment of hospitals are usually regarded as employees. Matter of Bernstein v. Beth Israel Hospital, 236 N.Y. 268, 140 N.E. 694 (1923) (compensation awarded even though under New York vicarious liability rule hospital would *not* be liable to third persons for interne's negligence); Nordland v. Poor Sisters of St. Francis, 4 Ill.App.2d 48, 123 N.E.2d 121 (1954) (interne was employee of hospital, not of surgeon whom he was assisting at time of injury); State Compensation Ins. Fund v. Industrial Accident Comm., 124 Cal.App.2d 1, 268 P.2d 40 (1954) (special registered nurse for charity patient paid by polio fund, held to be employee of hospital); Industrial Com'n v. Navajo County, 64 Ariz. 172, 167 P.2d 113 (1946) (county physician treated as employee although he performed duties in his office and apparently carried on private practice); West Virginia Coal & Coke Corp. v. State Comp. Com'r, 116 W.Va. 701, 182 S.E. 826 (1935) (physician devoting full time to single industrial concern is covered, but a physician employed only for specific instances is not).

8. Attorneys employed on retainers for extensive services over an indefinite period have occasionally been held to be employees. Industrial Comm. v. Moynihan, 94 Colo. 438, 32 P.2d 802 (1934). Contra, Associated Indem. Corp. v. Industrial Acc. Comm., 56 Cal.App.2d 804, 133 P.2d 698 (1943). Cf. Egan v. N.Y. State Joint Legislative Committee, 2 A.D.2d 418, 158 N.Y.S.2d 47 (1956) (attorney for legislative committee held to be employee). New Independent Tobacco Warehouse, No. 3 v. Latham, 282 S.W.2d 846 (Ky.1955) (architect hired for single project; gave full time and paid on hourly basis; held to be contractor and not employee). Ministers have been regarded as employees of their churches despite the personal and religious character of the services. Meyers v. Southwest Region Conference Ass'n of Seventh Day Adventists, 230 La. 310, 88 So.2d 381 (1956); Potash v. Bonaccurso, 179 Pa.Super. 582, 117 A.2d 803 (1955) (ritual slaughterer of cattle, held employee of packer). Cf. New York Workmen's Compensation Law Ann. (McKinney 1990) § 3 (18) (ministers excluded from coverage of act). Other persons performing highly skilled services who have been regarded as employees include: a licensed pilot, Murray v. Industrial Acc. Commission, 216 Cal. 340, 14 P.2d 301 (1932); a singer in a nightclub who was designated as an "artist" or "principal" in the contract of hire, Russell v. Torch Club, 26 N.J.Super. 75, 97 A.2d 196 (1953); and a professional model, Reyes v. Cowles Magazine, Inc., 5 A.D.2d 708, 168 N.Y.S.2d 660 (1957). But cf. Fisher v. J.F.G. Coffee Co., 221 Tenn. 333, 426 S.W.2d 502 (1967) (decedent devoted part of time to piloting aircraft for several firms, held to be contractor despite payment on per hour basis).

9. Buyers and sellers sometimes exercise such a high degree of control over the other's activities that one may be deemed the employee of the other at a particular point in time. A buyer, for example, may direct the seller to process goods before passing title and exercise considerable control over the seller's conduct in so doing. Myers v. Newport Co., 17 La.App. 227, 135 So. 767 (1931) (complainant injured while cutting timber he had contracted to sell to defendant; held to be employee). Conversely, a vendor may sometimes take such a direct interest in a purchaser's conduct in reselling the commodity, that the vendee for resale may hardly be distinguishable from the ordinary commission salesman. This issue arises most frequently in connection with newspaper sellers. Balinski v. Press Pub. Co., 118 Pa.Super. 89, 179 A. 897 (1935) (newsboy regarded as non-employee independent purchaser for resale); Laurel Daily Leader, Inc. v. James, 224 Miss. 654, 80 So.2d 770 (1955) (newsboy regarded as employee even though he did not have privilege of returning unsold papers; court was not impressed by defendant's contention that newsboy was "little merchant".) Similarly, milk deliverers and cart peddlers of commodities such as ice cream who work on defined routes and maintain a perpetual inventory of products purchased for resale are frequently regarded as employees. Glielmi v. Netherland Dairy Co., 254 N.Y. 60, 171 N.E. 906 (1930) (milkman). In contrast and on different facts, State Ins. Fund v. Circus Man Ice Cream Corp., 185 Misc.2d 507, 721 N.Y.S.2d 712 (N.Y. Sup. 2001) held that ice cream street vendors who leased trucks from the Circus Man Ice Cream Corp. were not employees of the lessor.

10. Numerous courts have awarded compensation to insurance sales agents despite the absence of control over the details of the work and despite overt attempts to exclude the employment status by the terms of the contract. See, e.g., Gordon v. New York Life Ins. Co., 300 N.Y. 652, 90 N.E.2d 898 (1950), and Davis v. Home Ins. Co., 291 So.2d 455 (La.App.1974). Compare Burton v. Crawford & Co., 89 N.M. 436, 553 P.2d 716 (1976) (claims adjuster regarded as independent contractor); Hackler v. Swisher Mower & Machine Co., 284 S.W.2d 55 (Mo.App.1955) (part time salesman of lawn mowers regarded as independent contractor), and Huebner v. Industrial Com'n, 234 Wis. 239, 290 N.W. 145 (1940) (soliciting agent for newspaper was assigned a territory and required to check in at end of each day's work, but was free to work or not as he saw fit; held independent contractor).

4. STATUTORY TREATMENT OF PARTICULAR EMPLOYMENTS

SANDBURN V. HALL

Appellate Court of Indiana, *en banc*, 1951.
121 Ind.App. 428, 96 N.E.2d 912.

WILTROUT, CHIEF JUDGE.

Appellant filed his application for workmen's compensation. The Industrial Board entered an award that he take nothing thereby, and he seeks a review of that award.

The board, with one member not concurring, found: "That on the 25th day of July 1949, plaintiff was performing services both casual and not in the course of employers' regular business for the defendant herein. That on said date plaintiff sustained accidental injuries while performing such services when a piece of plaster fell into plaintiff's left eye resulting in the loss of the industrial vision thereof."

Appellant points out that the burden of establishing that appellant's employment was casual was upon the employer, Meek v. Julian, 1941, 219 Ind. 83, 36 N.E.2d 854, and argues that the evidence, which was substantially uncontradicted, does not sustain the finding that the employment was casual. We must therefore consider the evidence most favorable to appellees. Scott v. Rhoads, 1943, 114 Ind.App. 150, 51 N.E.2d 89.

Appellee John Hall operates the Hall Sales Company, characterized in the evidence as a hardware and machinery business and also as a farm equipment and sales service. The business is owned by Hall and his wife. Appellant never performed any service for this business.

Hall purchased a lot upon which was located a dwelling house and a barn or garage. The house was purchased for his own residence and for no other purpose. He decided to make the house more modern. It did not have a bathroom or a modern kitchen, and needed repairs. To install the bathroom upstairs some changes were required in the general outline of the building.

Appellant and his father were carpenters. Hall engaged appellant and his father to do the work except the electrical wiring and plumbing. They started the work three or four days after the hiring. Neither party contends that the appellant was an independent contractor. They worked steadily, going to work each morning at about the same time and quitting at about the same time, unless lack of material caused them to quit earlier. The plumbing work caused some interruption. Appellant had no other employment while working on this job.

Appellant started working on the house during the first part of July, 1949, and was injured on July 25, 1949. On that date he was plastering a ceiling when plaster fell in his eye.

The work was completed by others after appellant's injury, it being completed somewhere between six and eight weeks after the work was begun.

The questions of whether appellant's employment was casual and whether it was in the usual course of the trade, business, occupation or profession of the employer are questions of fact for the determination of the Industrial Board. If there is any evidence of probative value to sustain the finding of the board, including legitimate inferences which may be drawn from the evidence, such finding is conclusive, and we may not disturb it. J.P.O. Sandwich Shop, Inc. v. Papadopoulos, 1938, 105 Ind.App. 165, 13 N.E.2d 869.

The compensation acts of most American jurisdictions contain provisions regarding casual employments. The statutes of a few states have provided a specific and arbitrary definition of casual employment. In the states, including Indiana, where no statutory definition has been adopted, the usual and ordinary definitions of the word "casual" as given by the lexicographers find acceptance. Mason v. Wampler, 1929, 89 Ind.App. 483, 166 N.E. 885; Coffin v. Hook, 1942, 112 Ind.App. 549, 45 N.E.2d 369; Lasch v. Corns, Ind.App.1950, 89 N.E.2d 553, 555. While these definitions are helpful, as we said in the last above-cited case: "There is no hard and fast rule by which it can clearly and unfailingly be determined where to draw the line between employments which are casual and those which are not. Each case must rest, in the final analysis, upon its own facts and circumstances."

Here the employment was for a single job which would last for a considerable period of time, and the work to be done was substantial in its nature.

Appellant's employment cannot be said to have been fortuitous, uncertain, occasional, haphazard, unsystematic, irregular, happening by chance or accident or without design. Neither was it casual.

It is stated in 58 Am.Jur., Workmen's Compensation, § 94, p. 645: "Whether an employment for a single job or piece of work is or is not to be regarded as causal depends upon the circumstances. The determination of the question may be governed by the length of time contemplated, or by the nature of the contract of employment. While the mere fact that an employment is for a single job does not necessarily make it casual, an employment for one job which occurs by chance or with the intention and understanding on the part of both the employer or employee that it shall not be continuous, cannot be characterized as permanent or periodically regular, and the great majority of the cases hold that such an employment, which is to last but a short time, not more than three or four days or a week, and is for a limited and temporary purpose, is casual. But an employment, though for a single piece or job of work, which lasts for several weeks or months, or for an indefinite period, is usually regarded as regular and not casual employment."

Again it is stated by 2 Schneider, Workmen's Compensation Law 108, § 279(i) (Perm. ed. 1942): "If there is a single employment which lasts for several weeks or months, or for an indefinite period, it is not considered as casual."

It is said in 71 C.J., Workmen's Compensation Acts, § 179, p. 436: "An employment on a building or in repairing a structure will not be regarded as casual where the work for which claimant was engaged will extend for an indefinite period, or will require a considerable length of time for its completion." * * *

Award reversed, with instructions for further proceedings not inconsistent with this opinion.

NOTES

Casual Employments

Few compensation schemes contemplate that every employer is always obliged to pay compensation to every employee who is injured at work. Some statutes restrict coverage to workers of employers that are engaged in a business enterprise of some kind and many require additionally that the worker be employed in furtherance of the employer's business. See, e.g., Lackey v. Industrial Commission of Colorado, 80 Colo. 112, 249 P. 662 (1926).

Many statutes also exclude coverage of "casual workers" whose employment is fortuitous and those who are hired for an isolated job of a temporary nature. Despite the fact that these two restrictions on coverage are different and do not rest upon the same policy considerations, most statutes entangle the two. The provisions fall into several general categories:

(A) Statutes that exclude all "casual" employments.

(B) Statutes that exclude all employments not in the course of the employer's trade, business or occupation, but that make no distinction between the "casual" and noncasual nature of the employment.

(C) Statutes (probably representing the majority) that exclude employments only if they are both "casual" and not in the course of the employer's trade, business or occupation.

(D) Statutes that exclude employment if they are either "casual" or are not in the course of the employer's trade, business or occupation.

(E) Statutes that cover all employees (not otherwise excluded) without reference to casualness or business character of the employment.

(F) Statutes that exclude casual employments unless employers elect to cover them.

This diversity is further complicated by inconsistent court interpretations of the various provisions. Some states treat the term "casual" as referring exclusively to the unstable duration of the employment in point of time as defined by the contract of hire. See, e.g., Moore v. Clarke, 171 Md. 39, 187 A. 887 (1936) (Jockey hired by professional race horse owner to ride in a single race denied compensation). Other courts have found that the term "casual" relates, not to the contract of hire, but to the nature of the work to be done and the relationship of this work to the business of the employer. Courts employ several different interpretive treatments. See, e.g., Dillard v. Jones, 58 Idaho 273, 72 P.2d 705 (1937), Privette v. South Carolina State Forestry Comm., 265 S.C. 117, 217 S.E.2d 25 (1975), Stephens v. Industrial Comm., 26 Ariz.App. 192, 547 P.2d 44 (1976), and McFall v. Barton–Mansfield Co., 333 Mo. 110, 61 S.W.2d 911 (1933).

Even where the term "casual" refers to the irregular or temporary character of the employment, statutes seldom provide guidelines as to when work is sufficiently transitory or temporary to deny coverage. Moreover, statutes that require a connection of some sort between the work done by the employee and the business of the employer seldom define the connection with precision. Sometimes the statute excludes activities "not for pecuniary gain," as in New York and Maryland; others exclude casual employment where the worker is employed "otherwise than for the purpose of the employer's trade;" and, still others exclude casual employments that are "not in the usual course" of the employer's trade or business. Under the Indiana statute in Sandburn, no inquiry into the "casual" character of the employment is pertinent if the work being done is part of the business or trade of the employer, but even this is not always easy to determine. See, e.g., Nelson v. Stukey, 89 Mont. 277, 300 P. 287 (1931) (dentist, who was also owner of an apartment house with fifteen dwelling units, hired claimant to erect an addition thereto; claimant entitled to compensation under statute similar to one in principal case).

Most jurisdictions include essential maintenance and repair work as being within the course of the business even where the work is not routine and requires the services of an expert. See, e.g., Tuscaloosa Compress Co. v. Hagood, 229 Ala. 284, 156 So. 633 (1934). The same is usually true of remodeling and even new construction work in connection with an established business. See, e.g., Mashburn v. Ne–Hi Bottling Co., 191 Tenn. 135, 229 S.W.2d 520 (1950) (construction of new driveway to bottling plant).

Employment of only a few hours, or even days, is often regarded as casual. Nevertheless, employments that are only periodic in occurrence and in duration are usually covered if they recur regularly. The decisions tend to treat one-time employments necessitated by an unexpected emergency as casual. Compare Ludwig v. Kirby, 13 N.J.Super. 116, 80 A.2d 239 (1951), with Tipper v. Great Lakes Chemical Company, 281 So.2d 10 (Fla.1973). Employments that result from an advance plan of the employer are usually treated as non-casual. See, e.g., Graham v. Green, 31 N.J. 207, 156 A.2d 241 (1959).

Minimum Number of Employees

Workers' compensation statutes commonly exclude employers having fewer than a designated number of employees. This reflects a balance between assuring coverage for every employee and relieving small employments from the fixed costs of injuries suffered by workers without any fault on the part of the employer. This is particularly important to many new business ventures as they start up, often on financial shoe strings. Not wishing to make it too difficult for people to start new economic enterprises, legislatures strike a public policy balance by exempting small employments from the expense of workers' compensation until they reach a level of success signified by the minimum number of employees required for coverage. Is this justified? What is the potential tort liability of the exempted employers?

Provisions of this kind appear in about one-third of the states. The most commonly designated minimum employment sizes are three, four, or five. Most numerical minimum provisions, like the one in the principal case, refer to "regular" employment, but the terms "regular" and "continuous" are not synonymous, as demonstrated by employments that vary by season or demand. Mobile Liners v. McConnell, 220 Ala. 562, 126 So. 626 (1930) (employer hired minimum number of employees only when vessels were in port; held injured stevedore employee was covered). Nevertheless, the minimum number must be regularly employed together for some reasonable duration at a point in time not too much in advance of the time of the injury. When this occurs, the courts interpret the numerical minimum liberally in favor of coverage. Typically, only covered employees are included in determining compliance with the minimum provisions. See, e.g. Bettman v. Christen, 128 Ohio St. 56, 190 N.E. 233 (1934). Thus independent contractors, partners, casual workers and other excluded employees are not counted in satisfying the minimum number. Brook's, Inc. v. Claywell, 215 Ark. 913, 224 S.W.2d 37 (1949).

Statutes differ in the treatment accorded employees of employers who conduct several different businesses. In counting the minimum number of employees, most courts include only the employees in the particular business in which the injured employee was engaged. Nevertheless, multiple for-profit operations that are conducted simultaneously are sometimes deemed to constitute a single business and all employees are added together for the purposes of the statute. Chaney v. Industrial Comm., 120 Colo. 111, 207 P.2d 816 (1949) (poultry raising operation and retail outlet for cooked chicken combined for purpose of determining conformity with numerical minimum). Contra., Cohenour v. Papet, 72 So.2d 915 (Fla.1954) (sandwich shop and rental residential property on same lot of land did not constitute a single business).

The Report of the National Commission on State Workmen's Compensation Laws (1972) recommends (R2.2) that all employments be covered without regard to the number of employees. Do you agree? What is the rule in your state?

Illegal Employments

In most states minors employed in violation of child labor statutes are provided compensation by workers' compensation statutes either by express statutory provision or, where silent, by judicial interpretation. See, e.g., Fanion v. McNeal, 577 A.2d 2 (Me.1990). In nearly half of these states illegally employed minors are entitled to additional compensation, frequently double the standard amount (e.g., Alabama, Florida, Indiana, Massachusetts, New York, and Wisconsin). See, Robles v. Mossgood Theatre–Saunders Realty, 53 A.D.2d 972, 385 N.Y.S.2d 822 (1976) (a minor's misrepresentation of his age did not preclude recovery of double compensation). In a few states (e.g., Illinois, and New Jersey) an illegally employed minor has the option to claim compensation or to sue for tort damages, and in some jurisdictions illegally employed minors who suffer work injuries may recover damages in tort litigation solely because of having been unlawfully employed. These decisions exclude from the minor's tort cause of action the requirement that the minor prove that the employer was actually negligent and that the injury was caused by the employer's negligence. Restatement, Second, Torts § 286, comment (e); (1965); Whitney–Fidalgo Seafoods, Inc. v. Beukers, 554 P.2d 250 (Alaska 1976) (illegally employed child may proceed in tort against an employer who has knowingly entered into an illegal contract with him); and, Sloan v. Coit International, Inc., 292 So.2d 15 (Fla.1974) (employing a minor without obtaining the statutory permits was negligence per se without regard to whether the factors that required obtaining the permits caused the injury.)

As to other varieties of illegal employments, a number of jurisdictions distinguish between employments in prohibited businesses, Snyder v. Morgan, 9 N.J.Misc. 293, 154 A. 525 (1931) (employee hired as bartender during prohibition denied compensation), and employments under contracts that are illegal for other reasons, Massachusetts Bonding & Ins. Co. v. Industrial Acc. Comm., 19 Cal.App.2d 583, 65 P.2d 1349 (1937) (night club hostess compensated for injuries received during employment of a type prohibited by California statute) and Commonwealth ex rel. Carter v. Myers, 205 Pa.Super. 478, 211 A.2d 46 (1965) (councilman unlawfully employed by city as street supervisor, held to be an employee although law prohibited his being paid by the city.)

In the absence of a specific statutory exclusion, such as in Wyoming (W.S.1977 § 27–14–102) and Idaho (I.C. § 72–1366), courts may be expected to approve workers' compensation awards to injured workers who happen to be illegal aliens. *Delaware Valley Field Services v. Ramirez*, 2012 WL 8261599 (Del.Super. 2012), aff'd *Delaware Valley Field Services v.*

Melgar-Ramirez, 61 A.3d 617 (Del. 2013) ("The Court holds that his use of false information to become an employee does not remove him from coverage for job related injuries, nor does his illegal status effect his eligibility for benefits.")

Several courts have considered whether the federal Immigration Reform and Control Act, 8 USCS §§ 1324a, preempts state laws and deprives illegal aliens of the status of "employee." See, e.g., *Correa v. Waymouth Farms*, 664 N.W.2d 324, 329 (Minn.2003) ("Immigration Reform and Control does not preempt state laws that otherwise pay workers compensation benefits to injured employees who are illegal aliens."); *Dowling v. Slotnik*, 244 Conn. 781, 712 A.2d 396, 410–411 (Conn.1998) ("The primary purpose of the Immigration Reform Act was to establish procedures that inhibit the employment of undocumented workers and to punish employers who knowingly offer jobs to those workers."); and *Earth First Grading & Builders Ins. Group/Ass'n Services, Inc. v. Gutierrez*, 270 Ga.App. 328, 606 S.E.2d 332 (Ga.App. 2004) (Status as illegal alien did not render worker incapable of accepting employment under workers' compensation law.).

Would it violate the Fourteenth Amendment to deny illegal alien employees benefits that are available to citizens and legal aliens?

Agricultural and Farm Employments

Most compensation statutes expressly exclude some or all agricultural and farm laborers from coverage, but a few extend coverage to agricultural or dairy laborers while engaged in the operation of designated farm machinery (See, e.g., South Dakota).

What is and what is not a farming or agricultural pursuit is often disputed. Manning v. Win Her Stables, Inc., 91 Idaho 549, 428 P.2d 55 (1967) (training race horses not agricultural), overruled by Tuma v. Kosterman, 106 Idaho 728, 682 P.2d 1275 (1984). Coverage is usually determined by the nature of the employee's work, rather than the type of business conducted by the employer. Dost v. Pevely Dairy Co., 273 S.W.2d 242 (Mo.1954) (janitor maintaining heat for greenhouses awarded compensation; describes distinction between agricultural pursuit and farm labor). Cf. Fidelity Union Cas. Co. v. Carey, 55 S.W.2d 795 (Tex.Com.App.1932) (employee in covered non-agricultural pursuit of an employer, who also raised hogs, was injured while in a pursuit that benefitted both the covered and exempted aspects of the operation; compensation awarded.) Similarly, where the employer is engaged in two coordinated businesses, e.g. one cultivates farm products and the other processes them for market, the worker's right to compensation is determined by the work being done at the time of accident. Pestlin v. Haxton Canning Co., 299 N.Y. 477, 87 N.E.2d 522 (1949) (employee injured while topping beets in the field using topping machinery and crates provided by the cannery; held to be engaged in excluded farming operation.) Quaere, suppose topping operations had been conducted in the cannery building? See Goodson v. L.W. Hult Produce Co., 97 Idaho 264, 543 P.2d 167 (1975) (employer engaged in both raising and marketing potatoes; employer hurt while washing seed potatoes for sale was employed in covered non-agricultural business.)

Agricultural workers are covered on the same basis as other workers in only a few states (e.g., California and Ohio). Noting this, the Report of the National Commission on State Workmen's Compensation Laws (1972) observed:

> The plight of the injured farm worker is no less serious than that of a worker in a manufacturing plant or a retail store. Indeed, the farm worker is the least likely to have personal insurance or savings. Administrative problems, however, make universal coverage for farm workers more difficult to achieve than coverage for most other employees. The predominance of part-time help on farms, their geographical dispersion, and the fact that migrant farm workers may work for many different employers during the course of the year present difficulties in reporting, rating, medical care, rehabilitation, and auditing * * *.

The Commission recommended that agricultural workers be treated as any other workers after a transitional period of some sort. Do you agree? What does your state's statute provide in this respect?

Does excluding agricultural employees from coverage violate equal protection or due process clauses of state or federal constitutions? See Gallegos v. Glaser Crandell Co., 388 Mich. 654, 202 N.W.2d 786 (1972) (exclusion of agricultural workers paid on a piecework basis and agricultural workers who do not work 35 or more hours per week held to be invalid), overruled by Eastway v. Eisenga, 420 Mich. 410, 362 N.W.2d 684 (1984).

Domestic Employments

Although most workers' compensation statutes initially excluded coverage of domestic employees in private homes, some now do cover regularly employed domestics and others employed under prescribed circumstances. Coverage factors may include amount of payroll, number of employees and hours worked. Other statutes implicitly exclude domestic service and all other non-business employments by exempting coverage of activities that are "not for pecuniary gain" and those not in the course of the employer's trade, business or occupation. See, Aetna Cas. & Sur. Co. v. Estate of Thomas, 547 S.W.2d 694 (Tex.Civ.App.1977) (claimant worked part time as household employee and part time as business employee; accident while he was household employee, compensation denied). The Massachusetts statute was of this variety but was amended to provide explicit coverage for some full-time domestic household employees. Murphy's Case, 63 Mass.App.Ct. 774, 829 N.E.2d 1156 (2005).

Most statutes do not exclude coverage of employees who work in the employers' home in some capacity other than domestic service. Nevertheless, coverage of these workers is hindered by two considerations. First, some provisions exempt all employments having fewer than a designated number of employees, and, second, most exempt "casual" employments as referred to above.

The Report of the National Commission on State Workmen's Compensation Laws (1972), recommends (R2.5) that household workers and all casual workers be covered under workers' compensation at least to the extent that they are covered by the federal social security insurance laws. Do you agree?

Charitable and Non-Profit Employments

Organizations that conduct non-profit pursuits, such as charities, churches and many hospitals, present a workers' compensation quandary. These organizations usually produce no profitable goods and services whose prices would serve to distribute the costs of injuries. Still, work injuries occur in charitable employments and their employees need assistance as much as injured employees of commercial employments do. Some statutes expressly include charitable employers and others include only employments carried on "for pecuniary gain." Compensation is usually denied under statutes of the latter category unless the business has a profit element. See, e.g., Ponca City Welfare Ass'n v. Ludwigson, 882 P.2d 1062 (Okl. 1994).

The Report of the National Commission on State Workmen's Compensation Laws (1972) recommends (R2.7) that employees of charitable employments be covered.

Public Employments and Officers

Although employees of a state, its political subdivisions and other public bodies are afforded at least limited coverage by most acts, the statutes vary in details. In some states coverage of public employees is compulsory and as comprehensive as in other employments. In others coverage is elective. Distinction is sometimes made between coverage of employees of state government and those of local governments. Many statutes cover "employees" and exclude "officers" or "officials" but increasing numbers expressly cover public officials sometimes subject to limitations. Some statutes make what seem to be arbitrary distinctions between elected and appointed officials. What policy, if any, does this advance?

Whether police officers are covered once proved to be particularly disputatious. Some decisions excluded them on the ground that, as officers, they do not serve under a contract of hire. Mitchell v. James, 182 So.2d 144 (La.App.1966). The same rational has also been applied to exclude firefighters. Jackson v. Wilde, 52 Cal.App. 259, 198 P. 822 (1921). Nevertheless, many decisions hold that even in the absence of an express provision police officers and firefighters are covered employees. Fahler v. City of Minot, 49 N.D. 960, 194 N.W. 695 (1923) (police officer); City of Huntington v. Fisher, 220 Ind. 83, 40 N.E.2d 699 (1942) (firefighters). Many statutes expressly cover them. What does your statute provide on this score?

Is a juror hurt while serving on jury duty covered by workers' compensation? Conceding that the number of jurisdictions that denies coverage exceeds the number that grants coverage by a factor of nine-to-one, the Idaho Supreme Court held that the Idaho statute that applies to "all public employments" does cover jurors. Yount v. Boundary County, 118 Idaho 307, 796 P.2d 516 (1990).

Hazardous Businesses and Employments

Early fears that workers' compensation statutes would violate constitutional due process clauses prompted many legislatures to restrict coverage to hazardous or ultra-hazardous employments. This apprehension proved to be unfounded as did a once-popular contention that statutes could not mandate employers to provide insurance to secure benefits for employees who were not regularly exposed to risk of serious injury. Presently, few states (e.g. Wyoming and North Dakota) restrict compulsory coverage to "hazardous" businesses. The restricted statutes pose a range of issues not existing under the more common statutes of universal coverage. For example, are all workers of a hazardous business covered, or only those who face the characteristic danger of the employment? Is coverage controlled by the nature of the business, or by the nature of the injured employee's duties? The Report of the Commission on State Workmen's Compensation Laws (1972) recommends (R2.3) that coverage be extended without regard to hazardousness of business. Do you agree?

5. STATUTORY EMPLOYMENTS

OAKWOOD HEBREW CEMETERY ASSOCIATION V. SPURLOCK

Court of Appeals of Virginia, 1992.
1992 WL 441851 (Va.App.).

COLEMAN, JUDGE.

Oakwood Hebrew Cemetery Association (Association) appeals the Workers' Compensation Commission award of temporary total and permanent partial disability benefits to Massie Charles Spurlock. The Association contends that the commission erred in making an award of compensation because (1) the Association does not have the requisite number of employees to come within the jurisdiction of the Act, Code § 65.1–28 (now Code § 65.2–101); (2) Spurlock was an independent contractor, not an employee of the Association, and, thus, the Association is not liable to him under the Workers' Compensation Act; and (3) mowing and maintenance that the Association contracted to be performed by Charles Lineberry, Spurlock's immediate employer, is not part of the "trade, business or occupation" of operating a cemetery and, thus, Spurlock was not a statutory employee of the Association within the meaning of Code § 65.1–29 (now Code § 65.2–302).

We hold that because the Association has four executive corporate officers who are deemed employees by Code § 65.1–4 (now Code § 65.2–

101), the Association did [. . .] come within the purview of the Act. Thus, the commission had jurisdiction to hear Spurlock's claim. We also hold that the Association did not raise the defense before the commission that Spurlock was an independent contractor. Thus, the Association is procedurally barred from raising that claim as a defense for the first time on appeal. Finally, because mowing and grounds-maintenance is part of the "trade, business or occupation" of operating a cemetery, we uphold the commission's decision that the Association was the statutory employer of Spurlock when he was injured.

The Association is incorporated. It has four executive officers. It is engaged in the business of operating a cemetery. Jerome Meyer is president and chief operating officer of the Association. He handles the routine business of running the cemetery, which includes selling cemetery lots. The Association has no other regular employees. Instead, it contracts with others to perform the services it offers. It contracts with Burruss's Vault Company for the opening of graves. It contracts with Chester W. Lineberry for the maintenance work on the cemetery grounds. Additionally, the financial aspects of the Association's business are handled by the Trust Department of Southern Bank and Trust Company.

Massie Charles Spurlock was employed by Chester Lineberry. Lineberry regularly sent Spurlock to do the maintenance work at the Association's Oakwood Cemetery. Spurlock's job entailed maintenance of headstones, keeping flowers in place on the graves, and mowing the grass. He worked each Friday, after completing his shift at his regular job as a maintenance worker for Forest Lawn Cemetery. He was paid $20 per week for the services he performed on Friday for Oakwood Cemetery.

On Friday, October 20, 1989, while starting his lawn mower, Spurlock's right foot slipped under the mower, and he suffered the traumatic amputation of four toes. Spurlock filed a Workers' Compensation claim against Chester Lineberry and the Association, seeking temporary total and permanent partial disability benefits.

After a hearing, the deputy commissioner dismissed Spurlock's claim, concluding that neither Lineberry nor the Association had the number of employees required by Code § 65.1–28 (now Code § 65.2–101) to come within the purview of the Act. On review, the commission affirmed the deputy commissioner's decision as to Lineberry, but reversed with regard to the Association. The commission concluded that the Association came within the Act because it has four executive officers who are deemed employees by Code § 65.1–4 (now Code § 65.2–101) and, thus, the Association did not fall within the exemption of Code § 65.1–28 (now Code § 65.2–101) for a business with "less than three employees." Additionally, the commission ruled that the Association was the statutory employer of Spurlock because it contracted with Lineberry, Spurlock's immediate employer, to perform work that is part of the "trade, business or occupation" of the Association. Thus, the commission held that the Association was liable to Spurlock for workers' compensation benefits. The Association appealed from this decision.

We hold that the commission had jurisdiction over Spurlock's claim against the Association. Code § 65.1–28 (now Code § 65.2–101) exempted certain employers from the coverage of the Workers' Compensation Act. Code § 65.1–28 provided: "This Act shall not apply to . . . any person, firm or private corporation, including any public service corporation, that has regularly in service less than three employees in the same business within the Commonwealth." (emphasis added). The Association contends that it had no "employees" and, thus, by virtue of Code § 65.1–28, the commission had no jurisdiction to hear Spurlock's claim. The Association acknowledges that because the corporation has four officers, the commission concluded that it had three or more employees. Code § 65.1–4 includes "[e]very executive officer" within the definition of an "employee." [Ed. Code § 65.2–101 provides: " 'Executive officer' means the president, vice president, secretary, treasurer or other officer, elected or appointed in accordance with the charter and bylaws of a corporation."] The Association argues, however, that the Association was composed of "trustees," rather than "officers" and that "trustees" are not deemed employees by Code § 65.1–4. The uncontradicted evidence proves that the corporation had four executive officers who are deemed "employees" within the meaning of Code § 65.1–4. Thus, we reject the Association's argument.

Code § 65.1–4 defines "employee." It provides: "Every executive officer elected or appointed and empowered in accordance with the charter and bylaws of a corporation, municipal or otherwise, shall be an employee of such corporation under this Act." The plain language of the statute, by which we are bound, . . . , provides that executive officers of a corporation are deemed to be employees within the Act. Moreover, the commission has consistently held that corporate officers are employees of the corporation, even when they are not compensated for their services. See Polozzi v. Custom Travel & Designs, Inc., 68 O.I.C. 100, 102 (1989). . . . "[T]he construction accorded a statute by public officials charged with its administration . . . is entitled to be given weight by the court." Baskerville v. Saunders Oil Co., 1 Va.App. 188, 193, 336 S.E.2d 512, 514 (1985) (citation omitted). Where an agency's construction of a statute has been consistent and long continued, it is entitled to great deference because in such a case, the "legislature will be presumed to have acquiesced therein." Id.

Jerome Meyer, president of the Association, testified that the Association is incorporated and has four corporate officers. Code § 65.1–4 clearly states that the corporate officers are "employees" of the corporation. Consequently, because the Association does not have less than three employees regularly in service, it does not come within the exemption provided by Code § 65.1–28. Thus, the commission had jurisdiction over Spurlock's claim against the Association.

The Association next argues that Spurlock was an independent contractor, rather than an employee and, thus, the Association is not liable to pay workers' compensation benefits to him. Spurlock contends that the Association did not raise this issue before the commission, and, therefore, it is procedurally barred from raising it for the first time on appeal. We agree with Spurlock. An issue that is not disputed before the commission will not be considered on appeal. Green v. Warwick Plumbing & Heating Corp., 5 Va.App. 409, 412–13, 364 S.E.2d 4, 6 (1988). . . . The record shows that the Association never contended before the commission that Spurlock was an independent contractor. Consequently, the Association is procedurally barred from interposing the defense for the first time on appeal.

Finally, the Association contends that the commission erred in concluding that mowing and maintenance was part of its "trade, business or occupation" of operating a cemetery. Thus, the Association argues that the commission erred in holding that the Association was the statutory employer of Spurlock. In response, Spurlock argues that we should not reach the merits of this issue because the Association also did not raise this issue before the commission. The issue was raised before the deputy commissioner by the Assistant Attorney General representing the Uninsured Employers' Fund. The issue was raised by a party adverse to Spurlock and was considered and decided by the deputy commissioner and by the commission. Consequently, we reject Spurlock's contention that the issue is procedurally barred.

Code § 65.1–29 provides: § 65.1–29. Liability of owner to workmen of subcontractors.—When any person (in this section and §§ 65.1–31 and 65.1–32 referred to as "owner") undertakes to perform or execute any work which is a part of his trade, business or occupation and contracts with any other person (in this section and §§ 65.1–31 to 65.1–34 referred to as "subcontractor") for the execution or performance by or under such subcontractor of the whole or any part of the work undertaken by such owner, the owner shall be liable to pay to any workman employed in the work any compensation under this Act which he would have been liable to pay if the workman had been immediately employed by him. (Code 1950, § 65–26; 1968, c. 660.) The primary purpose of this statute "is to 'protect the employees of subcontractors who are not financially responsible and to prevent employers from relieving themselves of liability (for compensation) by doing through independent contractors what they would otherwise do through direct employees.'" Bassett Furniture Indust., Inc. v. McReynolds, 216 Va. 897, 902, 224 S.E.2d 323, 326 (1976).

If mowing and maintenance, which the Association contracted to be performed by Chester Lineberry, Spurlock's immediate employer, is part of its "trade, business or occupation" of operating a cemetery, then, pursuant to Code § 65.1–29 (now Code § 65.2–302), it is liable to pay compensation benefits to Spurlock as his statutory employer, just as if Spurlock had been directly employed by the Association.

Deciding what is the "trade, business or occupation" of an entity is a "mixed question of law and fact." Henderson v. Central Telephone Co., 233 Va. 377, 382, 355 S.E.2d 596, 599 (1987). The test for determining whether the activity engaged in by a subcontractor is part of the "trade, business or occupation" of the "owner" varies depending on whether the "owner" is engaged in private business or is a public utility or governmental entity. Id. at 382–83, 355 S.E.2d at 599–600. If the "owner" is a public utility or governmental entity, a court must consider "the laws under which they were created and under which they functioned in determining their trade, business, or occupation." Ford v. City of Richmond, 239 Va. 664, 667, 391 S.E.2d 270, 272 (1990). . . . If the entity is private in nature, however, the test is not one of whether the subcontractor's activity is useful, necessary, or even absolutely indispensable to the statutory employer's business, since, after all, this could be said of practically any repair, construction, or transportation service. The test . . . is whether this indispensable activity is, in the business, normally carried on through employees rather than independent contractors. Henderson, 233 Va. at 382–83, 355 S.E.2d at 599 (quoting Shell Oil Co. v. Leftwich, 212 Va. 715, 722, 187 S.E.2d 162, 167 (1972) (citation omitted) (emphasis in original)).

The Association is engaged in the private enterprise of operating a cemetery. The dispositive issue is whether mowing and maintenance of a cemetery, the activity which Lineberry contracted to perform, is "normally" performed by employees of those in the business of operating a cemetery, rather than independent contractors. Jerome Meyer testified that maintenance is a normal part of the business of running a cemetery. Spurlock, himself, was a regular, full-time employee of Forest Lawn Cemetery, another cemetery enterprise, where he mowed and maintained the cemetery as the regular duties of his employment. In fact, Chester Lineberry, who performed the contracted services for the Association on a part-time basis, was also a regular, full-time employee of Forest Lawn Cemetery. Additionally, Lineberry testified that his two brothers were employees of Mount Calvary Cemetery, doing maintenance work, and the work which he did is typical of what is done in mowing and maintaining cemeteries. Lineberry testified that people in his position could generally be found in any cemetery. The evidence established that mowing and maintenance of cemeteries are activities normally performed by employees of those in the business of operating a cemetery, rather than by independent contractors. Moreover, while the commission may have erroneously alluded to Code § 57–24 defining the powers and duties of trustees who have been appointed by the court as the basis for its holding that mowing and maintenance were part of the Association's "trade, business, or occupation," even though the trustees of the Association were not appointed pursuant to Code § 57–23, the statute recognizes and incorporates the customary and generally recognized duties of operating and maintaining a cemetery. It is apparent that mowing and maintenance are part of the "trade, business, or occupation" of operating a cemetery, and the evidence establishes that cemeteries usually have employees who perform that function. The Association may not escape liability for workers' compensation benefits by contracting for the performance of the mowing and maintenance services it provides, rather than by hiring regular employees. Consequently, we hold that the mowing and maintenance activity that Lineberry contracted to perform for the Association is part of the Association's "trade, business or occupation" within the meaning of Code § 65.1–29, and, thus, the Association was Spurlock's statutory employer when he was injured.

For the foregoing reasons, we affirm the commission's decision awarding workers' compensation benefits to Spurlock. Affirmed.

NOTES

1. Uninsured Employer's Fund v. Gabriel, 272 Va. 659, 636 S.E.2d 408 (2006), applied an exclusion of an employer "that has *regularly in service* less than three employees in the same business *within this Commonwealth*" (italics added) to deny coverage to survivors of a Virginia employee who died in the crash of one of the airplanes hijacked on September 11, 2001. The foregoing criterion excluded a company officer who lived and worked in another state and seldom came to Virginia. Without that officer, the employer had only two employees "regularly in service" in Virginia.

2. All states (except perhaps California, Delaware, Iowa, Maine, Rhode Island and West Virginia) include a "Statutory Employment" or "Contracting Under" provision of some sort. See § 1(b), Workmen's Compensation and Rehabilitation Law, Appendix B. The purpose is to assure that workers on large projects and enterprises are not excluded from workers' compensation coverage by virtue of a fractionation of the employment activities among a number of independent employers, some of which may be too small to be covered under the statutes or financially irresponsible in securing benefits. The statutes specify a statutory employer who must assume workers' compensation liability for all employees within the statutory employment. Under these provisions, the statutory employer is liable to pay workers' compensation benefits to statutory employees who are the actual employees of some other employer. Usually statutory employment liability is not restricted to a technical "contractor" who has subcontracted some part of a

major project to subcontracting employers, but extends to any person who seeks to perform business through a contractor.

The South Carolina statutory employment statute prescribes:

> When any person, in this section . . . undertakes to perform or execute any work which is a part of his trade, business or occupation and contracts with any other person [to perform] the whole or any part of the work undertaken by such owner, the owner shall be liable to pay to any workman employed in the work any compensation under this Title which he would have been liable to pay if the workman had been immediately employed by him.

S.C.Code Ann. § 42–1–400 (2013). South Carolina courts have held that employers may not avoid this provision by artful contract drafting and that no rule or regulation shall relieve an employer of its obligations. Instead:

> To determine whether the work performed by a subcontractor is a part of the owner's business, this [c]ourt must consider whether (1) the activity of the subcontractor is an important part of the owner's trade or business; (2) the activity performed by the subcontractor is a necessary, essential, and integral part of the owner's business; or (3) the identical activity performed by the subcontractor has been performed by employees of the owner.

Fortner v. Thomas M. Evans Const. and Development, LLC, 741 S.E.2d 538 (S.C.App. 2013).

Statutory employment provisions do not necessarily apply to all contractual arrangements that result in leaving some employees without adequate workers' compensation coverage. The business arrangements between large buyers of raw materials from small sellers, which is fairly common in the lumbering industry, may have this effect. Hart v. Richardson, 272 So.2d 316 (La.1973) (employee of independent buyer of timber for corporation held to be covered under corporation's workers' compensation policy that covered independent contractors). Similarly, a so-called lessor may enter a leasing arrangement in order to avoid workers' compensation liability to the so-called lessee's employees. See, e.g., Washel v. Tankar Gas, Inc., 211 Minn. 403, 2 N.W.2d 43 (1941) (employee of filling station leased from distributor held entitled to compensation from latter).

3. As in Spurlock, a frequently disputed matter under statutory employment provisions is whether the work of the injured employee is as part of the regular business of the statutory employer. A single job of erecting, demolishing or repairing a capital structure of the principal will usually be regarded as outside the statutory employer's regular business, unless the principal is in the business of construction for others or for its own business purposes, as is often true of power companies and oil producing concerns. See, e.g., Ray v. Monsanto Co., 420 F.2d 915 (9th Cir.1970) (installation of furnace for phosphate producer was not regular business of producer; producer not liable for benefits for employee of installing contractor); Burroughs v.

Walmont, Inc., 210 Va. 98, 168 S.E.2d 107 (1969) (employee of supplier held not to be the employee of a general contractor to whom claimant was delivering supplies when injured); Cinnamon v. International Business Machines Corp., 238 Va. 471, 384 S.E.2d 618 (Va. 1989) (injured employee of subcontractor of building contractor possessed no tort cause of action against the contracting property owner who was not in the contracting business). Johnson v. Jefferson National Bank, 244 Va. 482, 422 S.E.2d 778, 780 (1992) confirmed that the test of whether a worker's efforts are part of a firm's "trade, business or occupation" is whether an indispensable activity in the business is "*normally* carried on through employees rather than independent contractors." Cf. Weaver v. Mutual Building & Homestead Ass'n, 195 So. 384 (La.App.1940) (mortgage loan company liable to employees of contractor who repaired dwellings on which company held mortgages); and, MacMullen v. South Carolina Electric & Gas Co., 312 F.2d 662 (4th Cir.1963) (construction of power generator part of the business of power company; power company liable to employees of contractor.)

Recurrent minor repairs, redecorating, window washing and similar ancillary operations are usually regarded as part of the business of the principal. Bailey v. Mosby Hotel Co., 160 Kan. 258, 160 P.2d 701 (1945) (floor waxing in hotel). Cf. American Radiator Co. v. Franzen, 81 Colo. 161, 254 P. 160 (1927) (window washing in industrial establishment not part of business). Factors commonly considered are: the past and present practices in the principal's and similar businesses; whether the activity is customarily carried out by the principal's own workers; the regularity or irregularity of the occurrence of the work; and, the specialized or non-specialized character of the work. In making this determination, Finlay v. Storage Technology Corporation, 764 P.2d 62, 67 (Colo. *en banc* 1988) ruled that "courts should consider the elements of routineness, regularity, and the importance of the contracted service to the regular business of the employer."

4. In some states the statutory employer is "primarily" liable to pay the compensation benefits to the injured statutory employee. This means the employee can claim benefits first from the statutory employer and the statutory employer can seek indemnity from the true employer. In other states the statutory employer is secondarily liable and pays the compensation only if the actual employee of the injured worker is uninsured, insolvent, or not covered under the law. Under either view, a statutory employer who is compelled to pay benefits to a statutory employee is entitled to seek indemnity over from an actual employer that is covered by the law (e.g., New York Workmen's Compensation Law (McKinney's) § 56.) Under some statutes, however, a statutory employer that expressly undertakes to assume direct responsibility for compensating statutory employees may forego the indemnity right. Andrews v. Spearsville Timber Co., Inc., 343 So.2d 1008 (La.1977). The distinction between primary and secondary liability of the statutory employer may be important in determining whether the latter is exempt from a tort claim by the statutory employee. See Eger v. E.I. Du Pont DeNemours Company, 110 N.J. 133, 539 A.2d 1213 (1988) (contrasting the

laws of New Jersey under which statutory employers are immune to tort suits from employees of subcontractors and the laws of South Carolina under which they are not immune).

Frank M. Hall & Co. v. Newsom, 125 P.3d 444 (Co. 2005), examined the evolution of the statutory employer provision in the Colorado statutes. The court found that the legislature had consistently attempted to achieve complementary goals: first, to assure that some entity would be responsible to secure workers' compensation benefits for all workers on a construction site no matter how the work was allocated among the general contractor, sub-contractors and sub-sub contractors; and, second, the entity that was ultimately responsible to secure workers' compensation benefits—i.e., the statutory employer—would be immune from tort liability no matter who actually paid the workers' compensation benefits for a particular worker.

5. In the absence of a provision such as that referred to in the principal case, decisions differ on whether employees of intermediate contractors should be added in computing the numerical minimum of employees required for statutory employment coverage. Several states have held that a statutory employer is liable to pay compensation to statutory employees if the sum of all statutory employees and the regular employees of the statutory employer satisfies the minimum. Compare Withers v. Black, 230 N.C. 428, 53 S.E.2d 668 (1949) (principal contractor hired fewer direct employees than the required minimum but employees of subcontractors were added to reach the minimum), Bradshaw v. Glass, 252 Ga. 429, 314 S.E.2d 233 (1984) (general contractor who did not employ the minimum number of employees is not responsible for payment of workers' compensation benefits under a statutory employer provision), and Jackson v. Fly, 215 Miss. 303, 60 So.2d 782 (Miss. 1952) (statutory employer liable for workers' compensation payments to employees of a subcontractor only if the subcontractor has the minimum number of employees required for coverage). Does the *Spurlock* opinion of itself permit a determination of what would have been the outcome of the case under Virginia law if the court had deemed the corporate offices *not* to have been employees?

6. MULTIPLE EMPLOYERS

YBARRA V. JOHN BEAN TECHNOLOGIES CORP.

853 F.Supp.2d 997 (E.D.Cal., 2012.)

SANDRA M. SNYDER, United States Magistrate Judge.

Defendant John Bean Technologies Corporation ("JBT") moves for summary judgment on Plaintiffs' first cause of action for negligence, contending that Plaintiff's negligence claim is subject to and precluded by the exclusive remedy provision of California Labor Code §§ 3600 and 3602. Claiming that he is an independent contractor, Plaintiff argues that the exclusive remedy provision does not apply to him. Having reviewed the parties' briefs and applicable law, this Court now grants Defendant's motion for summary judgment.

I. Undisputed Facts

[Labor broker Placement Pros assigned Plaintiff Pedro Ybarra to JBT in a temporary job as a laborer. JBT supplied training for the assignment. Plaintiff used both his own tools and those PBT provided. Plaintiff was injured while working on PBT's job.] At JBT, Plaintiff worked as a general laborer, which he described being a general helper who went where he was needed. He was initially assigned to the machine shop to deburr machine parts, and later worked in assembly and installation. Plaintiff's work, helping assemble JBT cookers, was part of JBT's regular business. Various JBT employees assigned Plaintiff work and directed his activities; other regular JBT employees could ask Plaintiff for help. Plaintiff testified that JBT controlled and directed his activities while he worked there.

* * *

B. Is Workers' Compensation the Exclusive Remedy Available to Plaintiff?

"Workers' compensation provides the exclusive remedy against an employer for an injury sustained by an employee in the course of employment and compensable under the workers' compensation code." Angelotti v. Walt Disney Co., 192 Cal.App.4th 1394, 1403, 121 Cal.Rptr.3d 863 (2011). See Cal. Labor Code §§ 3600 and 3602. This means that an injured employee may not bring a tort action against the employer if the conditions for workers' compensation are present. . . .

1. Who Is a Special Employee?

Under California's workers' compensation code, an employee is "every person in the service of an employer under any appointment or contract of hire or apprenticeship, express or implied, oral or written, whether lawfully or unlawfully employed. . . ." Cal. Labor Code § 3351. An individual rendering service to another is presumed to be an employee for workers' compensation purposes unless he or she is an independent contractor or is otherwise expressly excluded by the workers' compensation code.

"An employee may have two employers for purposes of workers' compensation." Angelotti, 192 Cal.App.4th at 1403, 121 Cal.Rptr.3d 863. When an employer sends an employee to perform work for another person or entity, and both have certain powers of control over the employee's work, the employee is said to have an original or general employer and a special employer. Kowalski v. Shell Oil Co., 23 Cal.3d 168, 174, 151 Cal.Rptr. 671, 588 P.2d 811 (1979). Both employers must provide workers' compensation benefits, and both are protected by the exclusivity rule. . . .

a. Primary Factor: Control

"The principal test of an employment relationship is whether the person to whom service is rendered has the right to control the manner and means of accomplishing the desired result." Angelotti, 192 Cal.App.4th at 1404, 121 Cal.Rptr.3d 863. See also Kowalski, 23 Cal.3d at 176, 151 Cal.Rptr. 671, 588 P.2d 811. This distinction arose at common law to limit an employer's vicarious liability for the misconduct of those who rendered services to him. . . . In workers' compensation law, the degree of the employer's control over the worker remains the decisive test of employee status.

b. Secondary Factor: Right to Discharge

[Sometimes] the control test alone is insufficient to sort out the many variations in working arrangements. A strong secondary factor supporting the finding of an employment relationship is the employer's right to discharge at will without cause. Borello, 48 Cal.3d at 350, 256 Cal.Rptr. 543, 769 P.2d 399. . . . Additional secondary factors are drawn from the Restatement Second of Agency, § 220. . . . Certain factors tend to negate the existence of a special employment relationship: "the worker is skilled and has substantial control over operational details, the worker is not engaged in the borrower's usual business, the worker works only for a brief period of time, does not use the tools or equipment of the borrowing employer but uses his own tools or the tools of the lending employer and the borrower employer neither pays the worker nor has the right to discharge him." Riley v. Southwest Marine, Inc., 203 Cal.App.3d 1242, 1250, 250 Cal.Rptr. 718 (1988).

d. Analyses in Prior Cases

For example, Angelotti, a movie stuntman, was injured while rehearsing a stunt for a movie production company called Second Mate. Angelotti, 192 Cal.App.4th at 1400, 121 Cal.Rptr.3d 863. Second Mate secured Angelotti's services through his "loan-out company," Skidaddle. . . . Angelotti executed an "inducement" acknowledging that Second Mate was his special employer and that any claims falling within the scope of workers' compensation would be governed by workers' compensation law. . . . Second Mate contracted with a third company, Cast & Crew, to provide payroll services. . . . Cast & Crew agreed to serve as employer of record and to obtain workers' compensation insurance naming Second Mate as an additional insured. . . . After he was injured, Angelotti collected workers' compensation benefits from Cast & Crew, then sued Second Mate and several other persons and entities associated with the film for negligence. . . . The California Appellate Court concluded that because Angelotti was an employee of Second Mate, the exclusivity rule barred his negligence action against it. . . .

In its analysis, the court found compelling, but not conclusive, evidence of an employment relationship in Second Mate's right to control the method and manner of Angelotti's work through its stunt coordinator's determination of Angelotti's daily work schedule and tasks. . . . It found Second Mate's employment of Angelotti through week-long contracts with Skidaddle, which Second Mate was not compelled to renew, to be tantamount to a right to discharge at will. With regard to the other secondary factors the court found that despite the particular skills required of a stunt man, Angelotti had no substantial control over the operational details of his work, which was directed by the stunt coordinator; although Angelotti used some of his own equipment, Second Mate provided the workplace and all essential equipment; Angelotti was paid a set weekly wage with no opportunity for profit or loss based on his managerial expertise; Second Mate paid Angelotti for his time not by the job; the seven-month duration of the work was substantial; film production, including the stunts, was part of Second Mate's regular business as a film producer; and finally, Angelotti himself signed the inducement acknowledging the creation of an employment relationship between him and Second Mate.

[Wedeck v. Unocal Corp., 59 Cal.App.4th 848, 69 Cal.Rptr.2d 501 (1997)] also found a temporary worker to be a special employee. . . . In May 1992, Wedeck, who had a Bachelor of Science degree in Chemistry, began working for Lab Support, an agency that placed temporary employees in companies requiring technical workers. . . . In August 1992, Lab Support assigned Wedeck to work as a full-time chemist at the defendant's refinery. Unocal paid Lab Support for Wedeck's services on an hourly basis, and Lab Support paid Wedeck based on the time reports that she submitted to it. . . . Unocal initially trained Wedeck and provided her with procedural manual to which she periodically referred as she performed her work. Unocal provided equipment and tools needed for the work as well as all necessary safety equipment. It periodically provided Wedeck with a schedule of specific chemical testing and analysis to be performed within a designated period. Wedeck was required to perform weekly quality assurance tests which were periodically reviewed by her Unocal supervisor.

[Wedeck sustained personal injuries attributable to the chemicals she was exposed to at Unocal and filed suit against it for damages.] The court rejected Wedeck's claims that her self-supervision and technical expertise rendered her an independent contractor. . . . The relevant factor was not that the employer exercised control but that the employer had the right to direct the details of the work. The majority of the secondary factors also supported a conclusion that Wedeck was an employee. . . .

[In Riley, Manpower, Inc., a labor broker, assigned Riley to work as a general laborer for Southwest Marine. Riley was injured on the job, obtained workers' compensation benefits from Manpower, and then sued Southwest Marine in tort. A trial court granted Southwest's motion for summary judgment and Riley appealed.] The appellate court held that summary judgment was appropriate, noting that the facts "unequivocally establish[ed]" a special employment relationship as a matter of law:

> [Riley] was an unskilled general laborer who was working exclusively at Southwest Marine's job site. Southwest Marine personnel trained Riley, provided daily job instructions and supervised his work. Southwest Marine provided all safety equipment and work tools. Riley worked for Southwest more than briefly; he had been on the job for more than seven months at the time of his injury. Riley believed Southwest Marine had the power to discharge him. In sum Southwest Marine had the right to control and direct Riley's activities and the manner in which he performed the work; Southwest Marine did not merely make suggestions of details or cooperation.

Id. at 1250, 250 Cal.Rptr. 718.

* * *

In contrast, [in Kowalski] the California Supreme Court held that the trial court erred in entering a judgment notwithstanding the verdict in favor of the defendant when substantial evidence supported the jury's finding that the injured worker was not the defendant's special employee. Kowalski, 23 Cal.3d at 171, 151 Cal.Rptr. 671, 588 P.2d 811. [Kowalski was employed by a maintenance company, Peterson, which contracted with Shell to perform its required maintenance work.]. The [maintenance contract] provided, in part, that: "It is Shell's intent to establish a 'general and special employment relationship' whereby the contractor (Peterson) remains the general employer of its employees and Shell becomes their special employer." Id. . . . During the course of the maintenance, while Kowalski was operating a radial saw provided by Shell, Kowalski's hand was amputated. . . . Shell prepared detailed lists of tasks for Peterson to perform in the area to be . . . maintained. . . . [T]he Shell foremen could stop any Peterson employee doing something of which Shell disapproved and redirect their work. . . .

Nonetheless, all Peterson employees were directly supervised by Peterson foremen. Peterson provided its employees with tools and equipment, and hard hats and badges with Peterson's logo. The saw which injured Kowalski was the only tool provided by Shell. Peterson employees could enter through only one of the many entrances available to Shell employees. Kowalski . . . was on Peterson's payroll and directly supervised by Peterson's carpentry foreman. . . . Shells' direction was limited to informing Peterson of the location and necessary size of scaffolds and occasionally responding to questions from Peterson's carpenters. . . . Shell exercised no control over Kowalski's work; only Peterson's carpentry foreman directed Kowalski. Kowalski was paid by Peterson and had worked for it elsewhere at other times. Peterson provided tools and safety equipment, with the exception of the saw. Although Shell could have asked Peterson to remove Kowalski from the job for unsatisfactory work, Shell could not fire Kowalski. Accordingly, substantial evidence supported the jury's finding that Kowalski was not Shell's special employee.

Just as Shell's [contract failed *ipsa dixit* to make Peterson's employees] its special employees, labeling a worker an independent contractor does not magically transform him or her into an independent contractor. In Borello, a cucumber grower sought to characterize its harvesters, which it called "sharefarmers," as independent contractors, arguing that they managed their own labor, shared the profit or loss from the crop, and agreed in writing that they were not employees. . . . The California Supreme Court rejected the grower's arguments finding that the grower controlled all of the agricultural operations from the crop's planting to its sale. Even though the grower elected to accomplish harvest, a single step in an integrated process, by using worker incentives rather than direct supervision, the court concluded that the grower retained "all necessary control over a job which can only be done only one way." Id. The sharefarmers' work followed the usual patterns of a seasonal employee. "In no practical sense," said the court, "[were] the 'sharefarmers' entrepreneurs operating businesses for their own accounts." Id. Instead, the court concluded that the harvesters were obviously members of the broad class of employees to which workers' compensation law applied.

* * *

The Act accomplishes its goal of comprehensive coverage of employment injuries by generally defining employment to include all those in service to an employer and by presuming that any person serving an employer is a covered employee. California Labor Code § 2750.5. By expressly including an exception for independent contractors, the Act seeks to impose the risk of no-fault injuries directly on the provider of compensated service "when the provider of service has the primary power over work safety, is best situated to distribute the risk and cost of injury as an expense of his own business, and has independently chosen the burdens and benefits of self-employment." Id. Unlike a special employee, a true independent contractor is in a position to insure him- or herself against accidents occurring in the course of work.

2. Who is an Independent Contractor? . . . .

The importance of careful analysis in determining whether a worker is a special employee or an independent contractor is well illustrated by

Marsh v. Tilley Steel Co., 26 Cal.3d 486, 162 Cal.Rptr. 320, 606 P.2d 355 (1980). Plaintiff Marsh was a truck driver for Maxwell Construction, the general contractor in the construction of a freeway. . . . Defendant Tilley Steel was a subcontractor responsible for installing reinforced steel in Maxwell's concrete work. Wynglarz, a skilled crane operator, worked for Tilley Steel. To efficiently complete the project, Maxwell and Tilley Steel closely coordinated supplies and labor. . . . [T]he two companies agreed that when one company needed to use a specific type of crane but did not have one available, it would temporarily borrow the necessary crane and operator from the other company. Neither party would compensate the other if it became necessary to borrow a crane; any borrowed worker would continue to report to his own supervisor and would not be administratively shifted to the other company; borrowed personnel would remain on the payrolls of their regular employers; and the borrowed equipment would retain the insignia and remain wholly the property of its owner. . . .

[in the incident] in which Marsh was injured, Wynglarz's supervisor directed Wynglarz to take his crane to Maxwell's work site to assist in moving equipment, including concrete forms, each of which weighed 1400 pounds. After Wynglarz had loaded the concrete forms onto Marsh's truck, Marsh drove them to their destination and Wynglarz positioned the crane and boom to unload them. Marsh attached the forms to the boom and jumped to the ground to signal their placement. Before Marsh could signal, however, the forms broke free of the boom. Marsh was struck and severely injured. . . .

In Marsh's ensuing negligence action against Tilley Steel, the trial judge granted Tilley Steel's motion for a nonsuit, holding that because Maxwell exercised control over Wynglarz, Wynglarz had become a special employee of Maxwell. As a result, said the trial court, Marsh was limited to his workers' compensation remedy. The California Supreme Court reversed. Reciting the factors relevant to determining a tortfeasor's employment status, the court observed, "[W]here the servants of two employers are jointly engaged in a project of mutual interest, each employee ordinarily remains the servant of his own master and does not thereby become the special employee of the other." Id. at 493,162 Cal.Rptr. 320, 606 P.2d 355.

3. Analysis of Facts in This Case

. . . . First, there is no question regarding the principal factor, JBT's right to control Plaintiff's work. The Temporary Services Agreement between JBT and Placement Pros required Placement Pros to furnish "contingent staff" for "temporary placements" in various job positions at JBT. It provided that JBT would "furnish supervision" and "provide job specific training," and that Placement Pros would "direct placements to perform their duties under the supervision and control of JBT's designated supervisors." In addition, as specified in the undisputed facts, JBT had "full responsibility for the safety of its work, including supervision and performance of all its employees engaged therein."

* * *

Defendant supervised Plaintiff to the extent necessary to enable him to perform his work as a general laborer. Defendant's supervision included daily meetings, supervision by management and the lead man, and immediate supervision and evaluation by his work buddy. . . .

Plaintiff contends that because "[t]ypically [JBT] only spoke with Ybarra for approximately five to seven minutes regarding job assignments and then left Ybarra to do his work for the day," JBT did not supervise him sufficiently to create a special employee relationship. This Court disagrees. Just as in Wedeck, neither party here disputes that Plaintiff was expected to carry out his duties in accordance with the training and direction that JBT provided to him. Plaintiff's ability to perform his job without constant supervisor intervention did not mean that he was not subject to JBT's control and direction. . . . The relevant factor was JBT's right to control and direct the details of Plaintiff's work. Further, at JBT, Plaintiff was regularly supervised by his work buddy, who inspected Plaintiff's work and either confirmed it or directed Plaintiff to do it over. . . . The undisputed facts indicate that Defendant had the right to supervise and control Plaintiff's work and that Defendant actually did supervise and control Plaintiff's work. [Whether Defendant could discharge plaintiff at will was disputed and not controlling.]

* * *

The remaining secondary factors support a finding that Plaintiff was Defendant's special employee. Plaintiff was not engaged in a distinct occupation or business but worked as a general laborer . . . ; general laborers need not possess any special skill; general labor is not typically done by a specialist without supervision; with the exception of safety shoes, Defendant provided the instrumentalities, tools, and work place; Plaintiff was paid on an hourly basis without an opportunity to increase or decrease remuneration by means of his managerial skills; Plaintiff worked for Defendant for limited time periods, when Defendant's work load required additional laborers; Plaintiff was paid hourly; Plaintiff's work for Defendant was part of Defendant's regular business. [The] Agreement between Placement Pros and Defendant contemplated special employment status in that it provided for Placement Pros' securing workers' compensation insurance covering both Placement Pros and Defendant. Although Defendant did not prepare Plaintiff's paychecks, it paid the amount due for Plaintiff's labor to Placement Pros, to which it had delegated payroll responsibilities. . . .

Plaintiff had no opportunity for profit or loss based on his managerial skill; he had no investment in equipment or materials to perform his task and did not employ other workers; his job responsibilities did not require a special skill; although his work for Defendant was temporary, it was an integral part of Defendant's regular business. . . .

Although the trier of fact must generally determine the existence of an employment relationship, the court may determine the issue as a matter of law when the evidence supports only a single conclusion. . . . When the facts of this case are evaluated in light of the applicable statutes and case law, the only possible conclusion is that Plaintiff was Defendant's special employee. Accordingly, Plaintiff's lawsuit is barred under the exclusive remedy provision of California's workers' compensation law. . . .

NOTES

1. Numerous statutes expressly treat the lent employee issue. See Il. St. Ch. 820 § 305/1(4) Conn.Gen.Stat.Ann. § 31–292; and Mass.G.L.A. c. 152 § 18. These measures usually retain the compensation liability of the lending employer in addition to that of the borrower and provide for the adjustment of the two employers' liabilities as between themselves. Chicago's Finest Workers Co. v. Industrial Comm., 61 Ill.2d 340, 335 N.E.2d 434 (1975) (lending employer liable only if borrowing employer does not pay benefits; lender is entitled to indemnity). Liability of both lender and borrower is recognized by judicial decision in several states. See Leggette v. J.D. McCotter, Inc., 265 N.C. 617, 144 S.E.2d 849 (1965) (citing other supporting jurisdictions).

2. Disputes about who is liable to pay compensation to a borrowed employee frequently involve employees who assist each other in carrying out common work, as for example employees of two subcontractors or of one subcontractor and the principal contractor. See Dupre v. Sterling Plate Glass & Paint Co., Inc., 344 So.2d 1060 (La.App.1977) (employee of subcontractor stopped on way back from coffee break to help employee of another subcontractor, held not borrowed).

3. Labor broker cases such as Ybarra frequently raise the question, "In workers' compensation cases, who is the employer, the labor broker or the customer company?" Should worker injuries be considered a cost of the business of supplying labor or a cost of the business of the customer company? The prevailing view treats the labor broker as the "general employer" and the customer company as a "special employer". See, e.g., Lindsey v. Bucyrus–Erie, 161 Ariz. 457, 778 P.2d 1353 (1989); Santa Cruz Poultry, Inc. v. Superior Court (Stier), 194 Cal.App.3d 575, 239 Cal.Rptr. 578 (1987); Sheets v. J.H. Heath Tree Service Inc., 193 Ga.App. 278, 387 S.E.2d

155 (1989); and Goodman v. Sioux Steel Co., 475 N.W.2d 563 (S.D.1991) (collecting cases). United States Fidelity & Guaranty Company v. Technical Minerals, Inc., 934 S.W.2d 266 (Ky.1996), applied the Kentucky statute to treat the employer who hired temporary workers to be a contractor and the company supplying the temporary workers to be a subcontractor. Under this analysis, the "contractor" hiring employer was both immune to tort suits by a temporary worker and liable to pay workers' compensation benefits for injuries sustained, subject to indemnification from the "subcontractor" who had supplied the temporary worker. In some instances whether the employee consented to having been "lent" to the customer company is disputed. See, e.g., Pato v. Sweeney Steel Service Corp., 117 A.D.2d 984, 499 N.Y.S.2d 286 (1986).

4. As in *Kowalski*, which was cited extensively in the principal case, the actual determination of what employment status exits is typically assigned to the finder of fact when facts are in dispute and determined as a matter of law when facts are undisputed. According to Ybarra, what are the important factors? Should the same analysis apply to in cases in which the worker is attempting to avoid being found to be an "employee," as in Ybarra, and those in which the worker is claiming workers' compensation benefits against an "employer's" denial of responsibility? See, e.g., Appeal of Longchamps Electric, Inc., 137 N.H. 731, 634 A.2d 994 (1993) (factual determination of compensation appeal board sustained).

5. Should the "employer" that is not liable for payment of workers' compensation be immune from tort suit? See section 3, Chapter 11.

NATIONAL AUTOMOBILE & CAS. INS. CO. v. INDUSTRIAL ACC. COMM.

District Court of Appeal, California, 1947.
80 Cal.App.2d 769, 182 P.2d 634.

SHINN, ACTING PRESIDING JUSTICE.

Petitioner, the insurance carrier of Glenn Growers Cooperative, Inc., hereinafter called Cooperative, seeks annulment of an award made against it by respondent commission on the two grounds that (1) the claimant, Frank Pitt, was not at the time of his injury acting within the course of his employment by the Cooperative, and (2) was not covered by petitioner's policy of compensation insurance. In support of the first ground petitioner contends that Pitt at the time of his injury was either working solely in the course of his employment by Eibe and Huffman Warehouse Company, Inc., hereinafter called Warehouse Company, in which event petitioner should wholly escape liability, or working in the course of a joint employment by the Cooperative and the Warehouse Company, in which event petitioner's liability should be reduced proportionately. Respondent commission found, in effect, that Pitt was injured solely in the course of his employment by the Cooperative. The initial issue therefore is whether Pitt was solely employed by the Cooperative or employed both by the Cooperative and the Warehouse Company. The facts of the employment relationship between Pitt, the Cooperative, and the Warehouse Company existing at the time of the injury are not in dispute. * * *

The Cooperative operated a rice drier which adjoined the buildings of the Warehouse Company. Pitt served as the manager of both concerns, but his salary and the compensation insurance premiums thereon were paid entirely by the Cooperative, pursuant to an oral arrangement it had with the Warehouse Company during the entire period of Pitt's dual employment. The arrangement was that solely in return for Pitt's services as manager of the Warehouse Company, it made available its scales and a portion of its premises, including part of its warehouse, to the Cooperative. Pitt's injury occurred in the part of the warehouse used by the Warehouse Company, and at that time he was engaged in the supervision of a shipment of rice by the Warehouse Company. However, Pitt divided his working time between the two concerns and when engaged in the work of the one, he was always on call by the other. * * *

* * * The only inference that may properly be drawn from the facts of the instant case is the one of dual employment of Pitt by the Cooperative and the Warehouse Company. Petitioner is therefore entitled to object to the erroneous discharge by the commission of the insurance carrier of the Warehouse Company. Hartford Accident & Indemnity Co. v. Industrial Accident Comm., 8 Cal.2d 589, 591, 67 P.2d 105.

The commission's legal conclusion of sole employment by the Cooperative cannot be sustained. As will be developed more fully, its referee's holding to that effect involved a patent misconstruction of the purpose and effect of the arrangement between the Cooperative and the Warehouse Company as to Pitt's employment. Moreover, the holding was based upon the erroneous conception that the employers could by agreement between themselves control the matter of their liability. This conception runs counter to the now well-established principle in workmen's compensation cases in this state that no apportionment of liability between employers or their insurance carriers can affect a claimant's rights against them. . . . Finally, as will be amplified, the facts of the employment relationship before us, when analyzed, point clearly to the conclusion of dual employment rather than single employment.

The fact that Pitt received his entire salary from the Cooperative does not establish that concern to be his sole employer. . . . The fact that the Cooperative alone paid the compensation insurance premiums upon Pitt's salary is likewise inconclusive. American Motorists Ins. Co. v. Industrial Accident Comm., supra.

Similarly, the fact that no part of Pitt's salary was paid to him directly by the Warehouse Company does not prevent the existence of an employment relationship between them. * * * The terms of the arrangement between the Cooperative and the Warehouse Company as to Pitt's employment show that no part of the services rendered by him to either concern was gratuitous and that the Warehouse Company in reality bore its share of the cost of his services by furnishing to the Cooperative, in return for Pitt's services to the Warehouse Company, the use of certain of its property rent free. The right to control and direct Pitt's work in detail, whether exercised or not, was possessed by both concerns and gave rise to an employment relationship between Pitt and both of them. Industrial Indemnity Exchange v. Industrial Accident Comm., 26 Cal.2d 130, 135, 156 P.2d 926. . . . The commission's finding to the effect that the Cooperative was Pitt's sole employer is contrary to and unsupported by the evidence.

The dual employment of Pitt being established, there remains the question whether as a matter of law such employment was concurrent or joint. The Cooperative claims that Pitt's dual employment was concurrent and therefore that at the time of his injury he was acting only within the course of his employment by the Warehouse Company. It is true that at the time of his injury Pitt was in the portion of the warehouse used by the Warehouse Company rather than the Cooperative and was engaged in supervising a shipment of rice by the Warehouse Company in which the Cooperative had no interest. Consequently his work at the moment of injury was directly for and under the immediate control of the Warehouse Company.[4] Moreover, the more usual bases for the holding of joint employment do not exist here. So far as the record shows there was no joint hiring. Cf. Page Engineering Co. v. Industrial Comm., 322 Ill. 60, 152 N.E. 483, 485. These two employers were not engaged in some species of joint enterprise for their mutual benefit.[5] * * * Pitt was not engaged at

---

[4] Editor's Note: Wood v. Market–Arlington Co., 15 N.J.Misc. 272, 190 A. 785 (1937) (Claimant worked indiscriminately under mutual arrangement for service station operator and car repairman who occupied same premises; injured while changing tire for service station; only latter liable for compensation); Murphy Supply Co. v. Fredrickson, 206 Wis. 210, 239 N.W. 420 (1931) (Watchman hired to watch two buildings; owner of one paid wage and was partially reimbursed by other; injury while watchman was in one building; owner of other building was not liable for compensation). * * * Two different problems may be involved in cases of this type: (1) Are all employers subject to compensation liability?; (2) if only one is liable, should compensation be computed on the basis of the amount contributed by the employer so liable, or on the total wage received from all? Cases collected in Annotation (1924) 30 A.L.R. 1000, supplemented at 58 A.L.R. 1395.

[5] Editor's Note: Ragos v. Industrial Accident Comm., 83 Cal.App. 313, 256 P. 487 (1927) (Lessor and lessee of apartment house undertook cooperatively to clean it and make minor repairs with lessor assuming responsibility for repairs, and lessee for cleaning; plaintiff hired by lessee, injured while cleaning; both parties jointly and severally liable for compensation); * * * United States Fidelity & Guaranty Co. v. R.H. Macy & Co., 156 F.2d 204 (2d Cir.1946) (manufacturer's demonstrator held jointly employed by store), noted (1947) 47 Col.L.Rev. 316.

the moment of his injury in the common work of both.[6] * * * [citations of authorities omitted]. On the other hand, the elements of concurrent employment do not exist here. Pitt's employers did not act independently of each other in their employment of him. Cf. Western Metal Supply Co. v. Pillsbury, 172 Cal. 407, 418, 156 P. 491, Ann.Cas.1917E, 390. There was not a separate and individual employment of him by each.

The answer to the legal question whether the dual employment of Pitt was concurrent or joint turns upon the correct construction of the purpose and effect of the arrangement between Pitt's two employers concerning his employment. The fact that Pitt, under the arrangement, was carried only on the payroll of the Cooperative does not militate against the conclusion of joint employment.... As previously indicated, under the arrangement the Warehouse Company in reality bore the cost of Pitt's services to it. It is true that Pitt's services to his two employers was several in the sense that he did not do the particular work of both simultaneously. But just as the burden of his salary was shared between them, so were his services likewise shared between them. He did not give a specific portion of his working time to each but all of it to both. Cf. Sargent v. A.B. Knowlson Co., 224 Mich. 686, 195 N.W. 810, 811, 30 A.L.R. 993. This is shown by Pitt's testimony that when working for the one, he was always on call by the other. McGowan, the common president of the two employers and apparently Pitt's immediate superior, also understood the purpose and effect of the arrangement to be one of joint employment of Pitt. That is the plain purport of his testimony to the effect that when injured Pitt was performing not only his duties as manager of the Warehouse Company but also his duties as manager of the Cooperative, pursuant to the arrangement between the two concerns. That arrangement was such that his employment for each corporation required him also to work for the other. It is a reasonable inference from the testimony of these two men regarding Pitt's employment relationship to the two concerns that had his services to the one been unsatisfactory, the other would have terminated its end of the dual employment as well—in short, that his employment by them was joint . . . [t]he service Pitt was performing at the time of his injury was in furtherance of the

[6] Editor's Note: Even though one of two employers has no interest in the work to be done for the other by an employee concurrently employed by both, one may be jointly liable for compensation if its work and the work for the other are being discharged simultaneously at the time of the accident. Perry Canning Co. v. Industrial Comm., 75 Utah 1, 281 P. 467 (1929) (Salesman authorized to purchase fruit by two competing packing companies injured while on trip to visit prospective seller, even though chances favored the prospect that one of the companies would be benefited to the exclusion of the other); Vance v. Hut Neckwear, Co., 281 App. Div. 151, 118 N.Y.S. 2d 327 (1952) (Similar outcome for salesman traveling for two concerns injured during off season trip for sale of goods of one them); and Standard Accident Ins. Co. v. Industrial Accident Comm., 123 Cal.App. 443, 11 P.2d 401 (1932) (Salesman representing two manufacturers injured on trip to serve both; joint and several liability applied despite fact that monthly salary from one employer was four times the salary from the other; liability was not apportioned in terms of respective wages paid). Note (1938), 51 Harv. L. Rev. 941.

arrangement made for the mutual benefit of his joint employers and was incidental thereto. The service being joint, the employment was joint. Where employment is joint, it is not the rule in this state to impose liability solely on the employer whose particular work was being done at the moment of injury.

* * *

The award is annulled and the case is returned to the commission for such further proceedings as may be necessary for a proper apportionment of liability between these employers and their insurance carriers.

NOTES

1. Employee E was employed by Company A. Company A sold its business to Company B. Company B agreed to hire E and other Company A employees. E was hurt while attending a Company B orientation session before the transfer was concluded. At that time E was being paid by Company A. Integrated Electric and Datacom v. Hussey, 2008 WL 5051632 (Ky. 2008), held that Company A and Company B were both liable for workers' compensation benefits as concurrent employers.

2. Suppose a worker E's concurrent employment is with employer A covered by a state workers' compensation statute and railroad employer B covered by FELA. See section 3, Chapter 1. Suppose E recovers workers' compensation benefits from A and then sues B in tort under FELA. Is the suit against B barred by immunity? If not, how does E's workers' compensation recovery affect any recovery in the FELA action or vice versa? See Collins v. Union Pacific Railroad Company, 207 Cal.App. 4th 867, 143 Cal.Rptr.3d 849 (2012). See also section 3, Chapter 11.

7. EMPLOYEE PARTICIPATION IN EMPLOYER'S ENTERPRISE

HARRIS V. CASUALTY RECIPROCAL EXCHANGE

Supreme Court of Texas, 1982.
632 S.W.2d 714.

POPE, JUSTICE.

This is a workers' compensation case arising out of the death of Paul C. Stone, Jr., who received a fatal gunshot wound on December 26, 1978, while working at an Austin, Texas, discotheque called "The Green House." Stone was a vice-president and director of Marju Enterprises, Inc., which was doing business as "The Green House." On the night of the shooting, he was acting as the night manager of the club, replacing another manager who had ended his employment several months earlier.

The present suit for workers' compensation benefits was brought by John R. Harris and Paul C. Stone, Sr., executors of the deceased Stone's estate, and by the deceased's ex-wife and two minor children. The suit was filed against Marju Enterprises' compensation insurance carrier, Casualty Reciprocal Exchange, hereafter referred to as Casualty. The jury found that Stone was employed in two capacities and that he was performing the duties of a substitute manager when he was shot. The trial court rendered judgment in accordance with the verdict, but the court of appeals reversed that judgment and rendered judgment that the plaintiffs take nothing. 623 S.W.2d 154. The sole issue on appeal to this court is whether Stone's status as an officer in the corporation precluded recovery of benefits accruing under the corporation's workers' compensation policy. We reverse the judgment of the court of appeals and affirm the judgment of the trial court.

Marju Enterprises, Inc. was incorporated on October 21, 1975, by Gerald Hickson, John Pruitt, and Paul Stone. Hickson and Stone were named vice-presidents of the organization. Pruitt became the secretary-treasurer, and Hickson's wife became the corporation's president. All of the officers received a salary for performance of their duties. Besides the four officers, Marju Enterprises, doing business as "The Green House," employed bartenders, bar "backers," waitresses, doormen, a disc jockey, a gardener, a janitor, and a night manager. The last position mentioned, that of the night manager, was left open as of October 1978 by the departure of the acting manager, Frank Beck. From the time of Beck's termination until the shooting in December 1978, Paul Stone assumed managerial duties at the club. Those duties included hiring and firing workers, scheduling work shifts, and overseeing operations of the club during business hours.

Paul Stone was working as the night manager at The Green House on the evening of December 26, 1978. During a confrontation with two patrons who had been asked to leave the club at closing time but had refused to surrender their drinks, a gun was drawn and Paul Stone was shot. He died of the wounds on January 11, 1979.

The record shows that the compensation insurance premium that was paid by Marju Enterprises during the latter part of 1978 was calculated upon a wage base that included the salary of the night manager. The premium was collected during the time Stone served as substitute manager.

Casualty contends that there is no liability for benefits in this case because Paul Stone was never brought within the coverage of Marju Enterprises' compensation policy, as coverage is defined by this state's workers' compensation statute. Tex.Civ.Stat.Ann. arts. 8306–09h. That statute was clearly written for the coverage and protection of "employees" working within the state. Section 1 of article 8309 of the act provides that the term "employee" as used in the context of workers' compensation "shall mean every person in the service of another under any contract of hire, expressed or implied, oral or written. . . ." Tex.Civ.Stat.Ann. art. 8309, § 1. This general definition is followed by section 1a of the same article, which provides more specifically:

> (a) Notwithstanding any other provision of this law, a subscriber may cover in its insurance contract a partner, a sole proprietor, or a corporate executive officer, except an officer of a state educational institution. The insurance contract shall specifically include the partner, sole proprietor, or corporate executive officer; and the elected coverage shall continue while the policy is in effect and while the named individual is endorsed thereon by a subscriber.

Tex.Civ.Stat.Ann. art. 8309, § 1a (emphasis added). Since it is undisputed in this case that there was no endorsement on Marju Enterprises' policy electing coverage for Paul Stone or any other officer in the corporation, Casualty contends that Stone was not covered by the policy at the time of his death. In response, Stone's survivors point to the jury finding that Stone was hired to work in two capacities. They conclude from this finding that, while Stone was not covered for injuries sustained while acting as an executive officer, he was covered while serving the corporation as an employee/manager.

The position asserted by claimants is frequently referred to as the "dual capacity" doctrine. This rule provides that an executive officer may be considered to be in an employer-employee relationship for workers' compensation purposes if, at the time of an injury, he is performing the tasks of an ordinary employee, as distinguished from his usual executive activities. Bolnick v. Industrial Commission, 81 Ill.2d 22, 405 N.E.2d 771 (1980). Section 54.21 of Larson's Workmen's Compensation Law explains the rule in greater detail:

> As long as an officer's or director's duties are confined to the executive functions associated with the office, such as policy making, hiring and firing, negotiating of important contracts, and the like, the compensation act does not apply. It could be argued, of course, that since technically the only true employer is the corporate entity the officers should be ranged on the employee rather than the employer side. This reasoning overlooks the practical fact that some human beings must exert the powers that belong to the employer-corporation, and those persons, the officers and directors, must therefore for compensation purposes be identified with the employer while exercising those powers.

> It is quite common, however, especially in small corporations whose demands upon their officers take only a small fraction of their time, to find that the officers also discharge duties which, if performed by anyone else, would unquestionably confer employee status. In such cases, when the normal incidents of employment attend the performance of the non-executive work, it is uniformly held that the compensation act applies. The clearest instances are those in which the officer engages in manual or non-supervisory tasks, as in the case of a corporation president working in a coal yard at two dollars a day under the orders of the general manager, * * * a president and principal stockholder doing selling, manual work, and the like, a secretary-treasurer-director-stockholder doing collection work, or an officer doing sales work on the road or behind a counter. In addition, the vast majority of the cases have awarded compensation even when the employment duties were of a supervisory character, such as those of a general manager, superintendent of a department, foreman, or superintendent of construction, since these are all jobs that, in ordinary circumstances, would make the holder an employee.

Id., quoted in M. E. Badon Refrigeration Co. v. Badon, 231 Miss. 113, 95 So.2d 114, 117 (1957). See also 99 C.J.S., Workmen's Compensation, s 82(b) (1958).

Examination of decisions in various jurisdictions reveals a widespread adherence to the "dual capacity" doctrine. Although the precise version of the rule adopted in a particular state varies according to the wording of the applicable compensation statute,[1] the effect in almost all instances is the same-an officer is not precluded from recovering compensation benefits merely because of his title as an officer, provided he is required to perform some functions in the company similar to work performed by the company's ordinary employees, and provided the claimant is injured while acting in that nonexecutive role. . . .

---

[1] Workers' compensation statutes deal with officers in a variety of ways. Some statutes expressly extend coverage to executives. See, e.g., Kan.Stat.Ann. s 44–508(b) (1981); La.Rev.Stat.Ann. s 23:1044 (1964). Some states that extend automatic coverage to officers provide that such coverage may be waived by the employer. See Fla.Stat.Ann. ss 440.02, 440.05 (1981). Some states, like Texas, provide that employers may expressly elect coverage of their officers. See Miss.Code Ann. s 71–3–79 (1972); W.Va.Code § 23–2–1 (1981). Other states specifically except officers from the provisions of their respective acts, although several of these states also allow an express election of coverage. See Idaho Code §§ 72–102(9), –212(6), –213 (1973); Or.Rev.Stat. ss 656.027(7), 656.039 (1979). Most state statutes simply contain a general definition of the term "employee" and extend coverage to those persons meeting the broad definition. Judicial determinations are necessary in such instances to decide whether injured officers fall within the act's general provisions. See Ariz.Rev.Stat.Ann. s 23–901(4)(b) (1956), construed in Williams v. Williams Insulation Materials, Inc., 91 Ariz. 89, 370 P.2d 59 (1962); Ill.Rev.Stat. ch. 48, para. 138.1, s 1(b)(2) (1980), construed in Bolnick v. Industrial Commission, supra.

The "dual capacity" doctrine was first recognized in Texas in Millers' Mutual Casualty Co. v. Hoover, 235 S.W. 863 (Tex.Comm'n App.1921, judgmt adopted). In that case, the court awarded compensation benefits for the accidental death of Hoover, an officer of a corporation who was engaged in the work of an employee at the time of his death. The compensation statute applicable at the time of the injury defined the term "employee" as

> every person in the service of another under any contract of hire, expressed or implied, oral or written, except masters of or seamen on vessels engaged in interstate or foreign commerce, and except one whose employment is not in the usual course of trade, business, profession or occupation of his employer.

1917 Tex.Gen.Laws, ch. 103, part 4, § 1 at 291. Section 1a of article 8309 then provided:

> The president, vice president or vice presidents, secretary or other officers thereof provided in its charter or by-laws and the directors of any corporation which is a subscriber to this Act shall not be deemed or held to be an employe within the meaning of that term as defined in the preceding section hereof.

1917 Tex.Gen.Laws, ch. 103, part 4, § 1a at 292.

The court in Millers' Mutual held that the language of section 1a was not so clear and unambiguous as to preclude judicial construction and inquiry as to legislative intent. Instead, the court construed what it felt to be an ambiguous statute to provide that only officers and directors who acted in their executive capacities were precluded from the benefits of the act. On the other hand, those officers who, like Hoover, acted in a dual capacity, could recover compensation benefits. The court explained its holding:

> The underlying reason for excluding the officers and directors or a corporation as such from the provisions of the act is apparent. The officers and directors of a corporation do not come within the ordinarily accepted meaning of the terms "workmen" and "employes," for whose benefit the legislation is primarily enacted. Their duties toward the corporation and its business are those of managing and directing heads, and they do not, as a rule, perform the ordinary tasks, nor are they subjected to the ordinary risks, of employes or workmen engaged in the service of the corporation. Nor, as a general rule, is their compensation affected by their temporary disability caused by injury while engaged in their employment. On the other hand, where, although occupying an official position with the corporation, they are employed as workmen or employes in the ordinary sense of those terms, and come clearly within the

> provisions of the act, there would appear to be no substantial reason for excluding them from those benefits merely because they also hold official positions with the corporation; and the Legislature should not be presumed to have intended so to exclude them unless the language employed be clearly not susceptible of any other construction.

Millers' Mutual Casualty Co. v. Hoover, supra at 865.

The "dual capacity" doctrine was again applied in Texas in Cook v. Millers' Indemnity Underwriters, 240 S.W. 535 (Tex.Comm'n App.1922, judgmt adopted). In Cook, the claimant served as director, secretary, treasurer, and general manager (supervisor) of the subscribing corporation. He was injured while discharging his duties as a manager. The court, relying upon Millers' Mutual and the "dual capacity" doctrine, held that Cook was not excluded from the benefits of the compensation act merely because he also served as a director and officer of the company.

In an apparent response to Millers' Mutual and Cook, the Texas Legislature in 1923 amended section 1a to prohibit application of the "dual capacity" doctrine in Texas. The new section provided:

> The president, vice-president or vice-presidents, secretary or other officers thereof provided in its charter or by-laws and the directors of any corporation which is a subscriber to this Act shall not be deemed or held to be an employe within the meaning of that term as defined in the preceding section hereof, and this notwithstanding they may hold other offices in the corporation and may perform other duties and render other services for which they receive a salary.

1923 Tex.Gen.Laws, ch. 177, § B1 at 388 (emphasis added). The new wording left little doubt of an intent that all officers, even those also working as "employees" for a company, could not be covered by the company's compensation policy. . . .

The exclusion of "dual capacity" in section 1a remained in effect for over thirty years. Then, in 1965, the legislature reversed its position and extended coverage of the act to all officers of a subscribing company, including those officers performing purely executive functions. After the revision, section 1a declared: "Every executive officer elected or appointed and empowered in accordance with the charter and bylaws of a corporation which is a subscriber to this law . . . shall be an employee of such corporation under this law." 1965 Tex.Gen.Laws, ch. 695, § 1 at 1625. The language in the 1923 act precluding application of the "dual capacity" doctrine was deleted.

The blanket coverage provided by the 1965 version of section 1a was short-lived, however. Two years after amendment, article 8309 was again revised, this time to replace automatic coverage of executive officers with an elective system, whereby employers could choose to cover their officers by way of specific endorsements on the company policy. 1967 Tex.Gen.Laws, ch. 192, § 1 at 426. The current version of section 1a, enacted in 1975, retains this provision for optional executive coverage.

(1) The court of appeals held in the instant case that the present "unambiguous" wording of section 1a of article 8309 indicates an intention on the part of the legislature to preclude application of the "dual capacity" doctrine in Texas. We do not adopt this construction. Rather, we believe that section 1a more likely manifests an intention to make available by way of a specific endorsement optional coverage of officers who are hired only in an executive capacity or who are injured while performing purely executive duties. Under this interpretation, persons who are hired to fill both executive and "employee" positions, and who are injured while performing the latter type of activity, fall squarely within the "employee" definition in section 1 and are thereby covered by the provisions of the act without a specific endorsement. Section 1a has no application in such situations. We adopt this construction because it is consistent with the general purpose of the workers' compensation statute. In short, persons who are "employees" as defined by the act should be allowed to recover employee benefits.

(2) We have repeatedly held that the workers' compensation act should be given a liberal construction to carry out the legislative plan of compensating injured workers and their dependents. . . . In the present case, Paul Stone was killed while acting as a manager for the subscribing corporation. Had the corporation hired another person to perform the work being done by Stone at the time he was killed, and such person had met the same fate as Stone, without question the worker's statutory beneficiaries would have been entitled to recover under the act. Likewise, had Paul Stone been only a night manager, and not also a vice-president of the company, his position would have brought him indisputably within the coverage of the act.

The evidence in the present case showed that Paul Stone was a substitute night manager for the subscribing corporation, that he was hired to serve in this capacity, that the performance of his managerial duties resulted in the loss of his life, and that he was not acting as an officer of the corporation at the time he was killed. Given these facts, we hold that Stone was an "employee" at the time of his death and thereby came within the provisions of the workers' compensation act, and that the benefits sought by his survivors should have been awarded.

The judgment of the court of appeals is reversed, and the judgment of the trial court is affirmed.

NOTES

1. Most statutes draw no distinction between the coverage of highly salaried administrative employees and the ordinary manual wage earners. Most commonly, coverage is universal but some states explicitly exclude corporate officers, e.g. Iowa and Oregon, while others explicitly include them, e.g., Minnesota, New Jersey, New York, and California. In some states corporate officers may elect coverage, e.g., Wash.Rev.Stat. section 51.12.020(8), and in others they may reject it, e.g., Miss.Code Ann. section 71–3–79. Does your statute provide any election to corporate officers?

E was an administrative employee in the office of Corporation C. C made E a vice-president of the corporation for convenience in dealing with corporate filings with governmental agencies. C elected to exclude coverage for all corporate officers. E suffered an injury while doing ordinary administrative work. The Workers Compensation Bureau denied E's claim for benefits. On appeal, Schumacher v. The North Dakota Workers Compensation Bureau, 536 N.W.2d 355 (N.D. 1995), examined the statutes, found that the term "employee" did not "specifically exclude corporate officers," and concluded: "The Legislature did not intend to exclude from mandatory workers compensation insurance coverage a person like Schumacher, who, although invested with a corporate officer's title, was a wage earner engaged in covered employment with no ownership interest in the corporation."

2. In the absence of a special statutory provision the dual capacity doctrine enunciated in the principal case is widely recognized, and the claimant will generally be regarded as engaged in a non-executive activity. Meca Magnetics, Inc. v. Industrial Comm., 40 Ill.2d 103, 237 N.E.2d 707 (1968) (president of corporation injured in auto accident while driving with papers to a consultant held to be employee under the circumstances). Cf. Mine Service Co. v. Green, 265 S.W.2d 944 (Ky.App.1954) (president killed while attending executive's meeting; dual capacity doctrine repudiated and compensation allowed).

Despite the dual capacity doctrine, some decisions treat corporate executives with extensive stock holdings as employers and deny compensation irrespective of the nature of the work being done. Martines v. Terminal Methods, Inc., 101 R.I. 599, 225 A.2d 790 (1967) (claimant was sole employee and also sole stockholder); Ben–Jay Food Distributors v. Warshaw, 70 So.2d 564 (Fla.1954) (all stock owned by claimant and wife). Cf. Claude H. Wolfe, Inc. v. Wolfe, 154 Fla. 633, 18 So.2d 535 (1944) (president held 92 out of 100 shares, held to be an employee); and Industrial Comm. v. Lavach, 165 Colo. 433, 439 P.2d 359 (1968) (president of one man corporation entitled to compensation).

3. An employee whose pay is contingent upon the profits of the employer but who does not share losses is a covered employee. Brewer v. Central Constr. Co., 241 Iowa 799, 43 N.W.2d 131 (1950) (engineer to receive twenty percent of profits of construction firm). In the absence of a specific statutory basis for coverage, however, a partner is generally denied compensation even though a contract wage is paid in addition to a share in profits. Metro Constr., Inc. v. Industrial Comm., 39 Ill.2d 424, 235 N.E.2d 817 (1968). Contra, Trappey v. Lumbermen's Mut. Cas. Co., 229 La. 632, 86 So.2d 515 (1956); and Ohio Drilling Co. v. State Industrial Comm., 86 Okl. 139, 207 P. 314, 25 A.L.R. 367 (1922). Nevertheless, many statutes permit elective coverage for partners in a partnership and many also permit sole proprietors to elect coverage. What does your statute provide in this regard?

8. RETALIATORY DISCHARGE EXCEPTION TO EMPLOYMENT AT WILL

Freedom of contract is one of the strongest tenets of the common law. Moreover, as is indicated by the reasoning of New York Central R.R. v. White, supra, Chapter 2, and many other decisions, the concept has been given constitutional status in the United States. See, e.g., Pierce v. Ortho Pharmaceutical Corp., 84 N.J. 58, 417 A.2d 505, 509 (1980). The common law applied this doctrine to employment contracts in a specific and concrete manner: contracts of employment-at-will—that is, those that are indefinite in duration of the period of service and those that reserve the discretion in either party to terminate at any time for any reason—may be terminated by any party for any reason or for no reason at all without constituting a breach of contract. See, Smith v. Piezo Technology and Prof. Adm'rs, 427 So.2d 182 (Fla.1983). In application to workers' compensation, the employment-at-will doctrine raises the question of whether an employer may discharge an at-will employee in retaliation for the employee's having made a claim for workers' compensation benefits. The common law at will doctrine holds that the employer may do so with impunity beyond paying the underlying workers' compensation claim.

FRAMPTON V. CENTRAL INDIANA GAS COMPANY

Supreme Court of Indiana, 1973.
260 Ind. 249, 297 N.E.2d 425.

HUNTER, JUSTICE.

Plaintiff-employee brought an action against her former employer seeking actual and punitive damages for retaliatory discharge. The Henry Circuit Court dismissed the complaint pursuant to TR. 12(B)(6) IC 1971, 34–5–1–1 (failure to state a claim upon which relief can be granted). The plaintiff appealed. The First District Court of Appeals, in an opinion by Presiding Judge Robertson, affirmed the trial court's dismissal.

The complaint sets out the following facts:

> Plaintiff, an employee of defendant injured her arm while working. Defendant and their insurer paid her hospital and medical expenses, as well as her full salary, during the four months she was unable to work. However, they did not inform her of further benefits that might have been available. When she did return to the job she performed capably. Approximately 19 months after the injury, defendant and its insured were notified of a 30 per cent loss in the use of her arm. Although hesitant to file a claim for fear of losing her job she did so, and received a settlement for her injury. About one month later she was discharged from her employment without reason being given.

Plaintiff prayed for $45,000 in actual damages, and:

> " . . . punitive or exemplary damages in the amount of $135,000.00 which is triple the amount of her actual damages because of the Defendant's intentional acts in defiance of the legislative intent of the Workmen's Compensation Laws which if allowed to persist would effectively thwart the public policy of the State of Indiana."

Workmen's compensation acts are designed to afford injured workers "an expeditious remedy both adequate and certain, and independent of any negligence on their part or on the part of the employer." Prior to workmen's compensation, workers were faced with the harshness of the common law. The employee's only remedy was an action in tort against the employer—actions which were rarely successful. This lack of success is attributed to the common law defenses of assumption of risk, contributory negligence and the fellow servant rule which were accorded inordinate deference.

Workmen's compensation statutes are in derogation of the common law and provide, for those covered, an exclusive remedy for injuries sustained "in the course of" and "arising out of" one's employment. The basic policy behind such legislation is to shift the economic burden for employment connected injuries from the employee to the employer.

> "One of the purposes of the Workmen's Compensation Act is to transfer from the worker to the industry in which he is employed and ultimately to the consuming public a greater portion of economic loss due to industrial accidents and injuries." (authorities omitted)

Mann et al. v. Schnarr (1950), 228 Ind. 654, 667, 95 N.E.2d 138, 143. * * *

Workmen's compensation is for the benefit of the employee. Hoffman v. Brooks Const. Co. (1942), 220 Ind. 150, 41 N.E.2d 613. Accordingly, it is well-established that the Act be liberally construed in favor of the employee so as to not negate the Act's humane purposes. . . .

The Act creates a *duty* in the employer to compensate employees for work-related injuries (through insurance) and a *right* in the employee to receive such compensation. But in order for the goals of the Act to be realized and for public policy to be effectuated, the employee must be able to exercise his right in an unfettered fashion without being subject to reprisal. If employers are permitted to penalize employees for filing workmen's compensation claims, a most important public policy will be undermined. The fear of being discharged would have a deleterious effect on the exercise of a statutory right. Employees will not file claims for justly deserved compensation—opting, instead, to continue their employment without incident. The end result, of course, is that the employer is effectively relieved of his obligation.

Since the Act embraces such a fundamental, well-defined and well-established policy, strict employer adherence is required. IC 1971, 22–3–2–15 (Ind.Ann.Stat. § 40–1215 [1965 Repl.]) states:

> "No contract or agreement, written or implied, no rule, regulation or *other device* shall, in any manner, operate to relieve any employer in whole or in part of any obligation created by this act." (our emphasis)

We believe the threat of discharge to be a "device" within the framework of 22–3–2–15, and hence, in clear contravention of public policy. By denying transfer and allowing the trial court's dismissal to stand we would be arming unethical employers with common law authority. Once an employee knows he is remediless if retaliatorily discharged, he is unlikely to file a claim. What then is to prevent an employer from coercing an employee? Upholding retaliatory discharge opens the door to coercion and other duress-provoking acts.

Retaliatory discharge for filing a workmen's compensation claim is a wrongful, unconscionable act and should be actionable in a court of law. Although, we know of no other cases in this or in any other jurisdiction holding that such a discharge is actionable, there has been a parallel development in landlord and tenant law. Courts in several jurisdictions have held that "retaliatory evictions" offend public policy.[4] "Retaliatory evictions" usually result from a tenant's reporting health or safety code violations to an appropriate administrative body. The tenant, quite often unable to motivate the landlord to make necessary repairs and improvements, reports the violations. The landlord, angered by the

[4] Edwards v. Habib (1968), 130 U.S.App.D.C. 126, 397 F.2d 687; Schweiger v. Superior Court (1970), 3 Cal.3d 507, 90 Cal.Rptr. 729, 476 P.2d 97; Portnoy v. Hill (1968), 57 Misc.2d 1097, 294 N.Y.S.2d 278; Dickhut v. Norton (1970), 45 Wis.2d 389, 173 N.W.2d 297; Wilkins v. Tebbetts (Fla.App.1968), 216 So.2d 477 cert. dis. 222 So.2d 753 (Fla. 1969), are just a few examples. Edwards is considered to be the landmark case in the area.

tenant's temerity, either gives the tenant notice to quit or effectively evicts the tenant by raising the rent to an unreasonable level. The cases hold that retaliatory eviction may be raised as an affirmative defense in an action by the landlord for possession. Going one step further, a recent California decision holds that a landlord's retaliation is the basis of an affirmative cause of action. It should be noted that the California Court of Appeal based its holding on a public policy embodied in a particular section of the Civil Code and not upon any statutorily created cause of action.

Retaliatory discharge and retaliatory eviction are clearly analogous. Housing codes are promulgated to improve the quality of housing. The fear of retaliation for reporting violations inhibits reporting and like the fear of retaliation for filing a claim, ultimately undermines a critically important public policy.

In summary, we hold that an employee who alleges he or she was retaliatorily discharged for filing a claim pursuant to the Indiana Workmen's Compensation Act (IC 1971, 22–3–2–1 et seq. (Ind.Ann.Stat. § 10–1201 et seq. [1965 Repl.])) or the Indiana Workmen's Occupational Diseases Act (IC 1971, 22–3–7–1 et seq. (Ind.Ann.Stat. § 10–2201 et seq. [1965 Repl.])) has stated a claim upon which relief can be granted. We further hold that such a discharge would constitute an intentional, wrongful act on the part of the employer for which the injured employee is entitled to be fully compensated in damages. Of course, the issue of retaliation should be a question for the trier of fact.

We agree with the Court of Appeals that, under ordinary circumstances, an employee at will may be discharged without cause. However, when an employee is discharged solely for exercising a statutorily conferred right an exception to the general rule must be recognized.

For all the foregoing reasons, the petition for transfer is hereby granted and the order of dismissal by the trial court pursuant to TR. 12(B)(6) is hereby reversed. This cause is remanded to the Henry Circuit Court for further proceedings not inconsistent with our opinion.

PRENTICE, J., dissents.

NOTES

1. How important in the Frampton decision is the statutory language outlawing the use of "devices" by employers to relieve themselves of workers' compensation obligations? The Florida supreme court applied the following provision to reach the same conclusion:

> No employer shall discharge, threaten to discharge, intimidate or coerce any employee by reason of such employee's valid claim for

> compensation or attempt to claim compensation under the Workers' Compensation Law.

Smith v. Piezo Technology and Prof. Adm'rs, 427 So.2d 182 (Fla.1983). A Texas statute that prohibits an employer from firing an employee "because an employee has in good faith" filed a workers' compensation claim has been applied in like manner, Azar Nut Company v. Caille, 734 S.W.2d 667 (Tex.1987). Similarly Wiley v. Missouri Pacific Railroad Company, 430 So.2d 1016 (La.App.1982), held that the retaliatory discharge of a workers' compensation claimant violates this statute:

> Art. 2749. If, without any serious ground of complaint, a man should send away a laborer whose services he has hired for a certain time, before that time has expired, he shall be bound to pay to such laborer the whole of the salaries which he would have been entitled to receive, had the full term of his services arrived.

2. Several decisions hold the exceptions to the employment-at-will doctrine in tight rein. See, e.g., Clifford v. Cactus Drilling Corporation, 419 Mich. 356, 353 N.W.2d 469 (1984) (retaliatory discharge exception does not apply to discharge based upon absences from work caused by work related injury as opposed to discharge for making a claim); Daniel v. Magma Copper Company, 127 Ariz. 320, 620 P.2d 699 (1980) (retaliatory discharge exception does not apply to discharge based upon employee's threat to sue employer for nonjob related injury); Burrow v. Westinghouse Electric Corp., 88 N.C.App. 347, 363 S.E.2d 215 (1988) (retaliatory discharge exception does not apply to discharge based upon employee's refusal to drive under dangerous conditions); Rozier v. St. Mary's Hospital, 88 Ill.App.3d 994, 44 Ill.Dec. 144, 411 N.E.2d 50 (1980) (retaliatory discharge exception does not apply to discharge of employee who had lied to employer about job-related matters); and, Rowland v. Val–Agri, Inc., 13 Kan.App.2d 149, 766 P.2d 819 (1988) (retaliatory discharge exception does not apply to discharge based upon employee's having taken six months' consecutive leave.)

3. Can an employer be restrained from firing an employee-at-will claimant in the absence of specific statutory authority? See, e.g., Kelsay v. Motorola, Inc., 74 Ill.2d 172, 23 Ill.Dec. 559, 384 N.E.2d 353, 357 (1978), where the court stated:

> The Workmen's Compensation Act, in light of its beneficent purpose, is a humane law of a remedial nature. . . . It provides for efficient remedies for and protection of employees and, as such, promotes the general welfare of this State. Consequently, its enactment by the legislature was in furtherance of sound public policy. . . . We are convinced that to uphold and implement this public policy a cause of action should exist for retaliatory discharge.
>
> * * *
>
> We are not convinced that an employer's otherwise absolute power to terminate an employee at will should prevail when that

> power is exercised to prevent the employee from asserting his statutory rights under the Workmen's Compensation Act. As we have noted, the legislature enacted the workmen's compensation law as a comprehensive scheme to provide for efficient and expeditious remedies for injured employees. This scheme would be seriously undermined if employers were permitted to abuse their power to terminate by threatening to discharge employees for seeking compensation under the Act. We cannot ignore the fact that when faced with such a dilemma many employees, whose common law rights have been supplanted by the Act, would choose to retain their jobs, and thus, in effect, would be left without a remedy either common law or statutory. This result, which effectively relieves the employer of the responsibility expressly placed upon him by the legislature, is untenable and is contrary to the public policy as expressed in the Workmen's Compensation Act. We cannot believe that the legislature, even in the absence of an explicit proscription against retaliatory discharge, intended such a result.

See also Sventko v. The Kroger Company, 69 Mich.App. 644, 245 N.W.2d 151 (1976), and Rowland v. Val–Agri, Inc., 13 Kan.App.2d 149, 766 P.2d 819 (1988).

4. The public policy exception to the employment at will doctrine originated in non-workers' compensation cases. For example, the plaintiff in Monge v. Beebe Rubber Company, 114 N.H. 130, 316 A.2d 549 (1974), had been fired from her at-will job for refusing to submit to unwanted sexual advances. In the course of a decision that awarded the former employee breach of contract damages, the court stated:

> In all employment contracts, whether at will or for a definite term, the employer's interest in running his business as he sees fit must be balanced against the interest of the employee in maintaining his employment, and the public's interest in maintaining a proper balance between the two. See Note, California's Controls On Employer Abuse of Employee Rights, 22 Stanford L.Rev. 1015 (1970). We hold that a termination by the employer of a contract of employment at will which is motivated by bad faith or malice or based on retaliation is not the best interest of the economic system or the public good and constitutes a breach of the employment contract.

316 A.2d at 551. See also, Cerracchio v. Alden Leeds, Inc., 223 N.J.Super. 435, 538 A.2d 1292 (1988) (retaliatory discharge of employee who reported OSHA violation gives rise to private tort action). Cf. Pierce v. Ortho Pharmaceutical Corporation, 84 N.J. 58, 417 A.2d 505 (1980) (although retaliatory discharge is wrongful if contrary to a public policy, claimant failed to establish that Hippocratic oath contained a clear mandate to justify fired employee's refusal to work.)

In an extremely limited exception to the employment at will doctrine, Haddle v. Garrison, 525 U.S. 121, 119 S.Ct. 489, 142 L.Ed.2d 502 (1998), held that an employer's conspiracy to fire an employee for having answered a federal grand jury subpoena to testify against the employer's interests created a cause of action for injury to "person or property" under 42 U.S.C. Sec.1985(2).

5. May the discharged employee seek a tort remedy for the underlying work injury in a retaliatory claim? Cornejo v. Polycon Industries, Inc., 109 Wis.2d 649, 327 N.W.2d 183 (App.1982), held that worker's compensation is the exclusive remedy.

TOUCHARD V. LA–Z–BOY INC.

Supreme Court of Utah, 2006.
148 P.3d 945.

DURHAM, CHIEF JUSTICE:

INTRODUCTION

[The court accepted three certified questions from the United States District Court for the District of Utah:

1. "Whether the termination of an employee in retaliation for the exercise of rights under the Utah Workers' Compensation Act . . . implicates a 'clear and substantial public policy' of the State of Utah that would provide a basis for a claim of wrongful termination in violation of public policy."
2. Whether such a cause of action applies when "the employee is not fired but resigns under circumstances that constitute a 'constructive discharge' ";
3. Whether such a cause of action applies when "the employee who has filed for benefits under the [Workers' Compensation Act] is neither fired nor constructively discharged, but experiences other discriminatory treatment or harassment from an employer"; and
4. Whether such a cause of action applies when "the employee has not filed for benefits under the [Workers' Compensation Act] but is retaliated against for opposing an employer's treatment of other injured employees who are entitled to file for benefits under the [Act]."]

ANALYSIS

* * *

I. AN EMPLOYEE WHO HAS BEEN TERMINATED FOR EXERCISING RIGHTS UNDER THE WORKERS' COMPENSATION ACT HAS A WRONGFUL DISCHARGE CAUSE OF ACTION

[The court agreed with Frampton that a wrongful discharge cause of action existed. The court considered three primary factors:

A. Does Receipt of Workers' Compensation Benefits Constitute a Clear and Substantial Public Policy? The court answered "Yes."

B. Does the Clear and Substantial Public Policy Underlying Workers' Compensation Outweighs La–Z–Boy's Interests? The court acknowledged that La–Z–Boy did have a substantial interest in the employment-at-will doctrine but held that the workers' compensation interest outweighed it.

C. Does the Workers' Compensation Act Preempt Our Holding that Employees Terminated for Exercising Their Workers' Compensation Rights Have a Wrongful Discharge Cause of Action? The court held that the exclusivity provision of the Act did not constitute a preemption of the wrongful discharge cause of action.]

II. THE WRONGFUL DISCHARGE CAUSE OF ACTION EXTENDS TO CONSTRUCTIVE DISCHARGE

. . . We . . . hold that a resignation under working conditions that a reasonable employee would consider intolerable is equivalent to a termination. Thus, an employee's cause of action for wrongful discharge as a result of the exercise of workers' compensation rights extends to constructive discharge. Holding otherwise would make it possible for employers both to escape their obligations to provide compensation by retaliating against injured employees with intolerable working conditions and to avoid a wrongful discharge cause of action by never actually terminating the employee. Just as allowing an employer to terminate an injured employee seeking compensation undermines the purpose of the Act, so too does allowing an employer to make conditions so intolerable that an employee has no choice but to resign. Therefore, we believe that recognizing constructive discharge as actual termination is necessary to give effect to the purposes of the Act.

III. THE WRONGFUL DISCHARGE CAUSE OF ACTION DOES NOT EXTEND TO RETALIATORY HARASSMENT OR DISCRIMINATION

Having concluded that the public policy exception applies to both actual and constructive discharge, we now address the district court's question regarding whether the wrongful discharge cause of action extends to retaliatory harassment or discrimination. To answer this question, we look to the elements of wrongful discharge. "To make out a prima facie case of wrongful discharge, an employee must show (I) that his employer *terminated* him; (ii) that a clear and substantial public policy existed; (iii) that the employee's conduct brought the policy into play; and (iv) that the discharge and the conduct bringing the policy into play are causally connected." *Ryan v. Dan's Food Stores, Inc.*, 972 P.2d 395, 404 (Utah 1998) (emphasis added) (footnotes omitted). When an employee alleges only retaliatory harassment or discrimination, that employee has failed to satisfy the first element and the wrongful discharge tort does not apply.

Moreover, we decline the invitation to create a new cause of action for retaliatory harassment or discrimination. While retaliatory discrimination or harassment is deplorable, it does not implicate a clear and substantial public policy to the same extent as a discharge. When an employee is discharged in retaliation for pursuing a workers' compensation claim, that employee is placed in the untenable position of choosing between receiving compensation or maintaining employment. Because most employees would choose to retain their jobs, this would in turn relieve employers of their obligations under the Act. *See Frampton v. Cent. Indiana Gas Co.*, 260 Ind. 249, 297 N.E.2d 425, 427 (1973) (recognizing that when employees are forced to choose between their job and compensation, they will generally choose their job, the end result of which relieves the employer of his workers' compensation obligation). We do not think this policy applies to the same extent when the employee suffers unpleasantness, not amounting to constructive discharge, and does not have the fear of losing his or her employment.

In addition, we are concerned that creating a new cause of action for harassment would expand the public policy exception to the at-will rule beyond its intended narrow scope and encourage myriad claims against employers. The concept of discharge is fairly concrete-either the employer actually terminated the employee or the employee resigned under circumstances so unbearable that no reasonable employee could tolerate them. However, discrimination and harassment have the potential to implicate a much broader range of behavior, including demotions, salary reductions, job transfers, or disciplinary actions. See *Zimmerman v. Buchheit of Sparta, Inc.*, 164 Ill.2d 29, 206 Ill.Dec. 625, 645 N.E.2d 877, 882 (1994) (stating the adoption of a cause of action short of termination would "replace the well-developed element of discharge with a new, ill-defined, and potentially all-encompassing concept of retaliatory conduct or discrimination"). . . .

Much as we might lament the suffering of an employee who has been harassed for exercising his or her statutory rights, it is not our prerogative to remedy the situation in the absence of a clear and substantial public policy. Employees under these circumstances should look to the legislature to define their recourse against employers who discriminate against them in retaliation for claiming the compensation to which they are entitled. Indeed, many states have enacted such legislation. *See, e.g.*, Conn. Gen.Stat. § 31–290a (2005) (prohibiting the discharge of or discrimination against an employee who has exercised workers' compensation rights and granting employees a private cause of action against employers who violate the statute); Mo.Rev.Stat. § 287.780 (2000) (same); N.C. Gen.Stat. § 95–241 (2005) (prohibiting retaliatory discrimination against employees who have filed workers' compensation claims). Until our legislature joins these states, employees who have suffered retaliatory discrimination as a result of claiming workers' compensation benefits do not have a cause of action against their employers.

IV. THE WRONGFUL DISCHARGE CAUSE OF ACTION DOES NOT EXTEND TO AN EMPLOYEE WHO OPPOSES HER EMPLOYER'S TREATMENT OF OTHER EMPLOYEES WHO ARE ENTITLED TO WORKERS' COMPENSATION BENEFITS

The final question the federal court has asked us to address is whether an employee who opposes her employer's treatment of injured employees has a wrongful discharge cause of action under the public policy exception to the at-will rule. To fully respond to this inquiry, however, we must recite the relevant facts.

La–Z–Boy hired Marilyn Touchard to serve as an "environmental/assistant safety manager." Her job responsibilities included investigating the cause of La–Z–Boy's high workers' compensation costs. After conducting her investigation, Ms. Touchard wrote La–Z–Boy a memorandum concluding that the company had a high injury rate and that employees were "waiting for extensive periods of time to receive treatment, diagnostic testing, and/or resolution of their claims, due to the intentional mismanagement of their claims." Ms. Touchard also informed La–Z–Boy that its claims adjuster was "hostile" toward employees who filed workers' compensation claims and "documented that [the claims adjuster] attempted to deny benefits to . . . an employee with a documented work-related injury and extensive work history with the company."

In addition to her job investigating La–Z–Boy's workers' compensation costs, Ms. Touchard was the head of the ergonomics team. In this capacity, Ms. Touchard conducted a study and submitted a memorandum concluding that the practices employed on the upholstery production line could cause shoulder injuries.

The allegations of the complaint are that after submitting the memorandum detailing the problems in La–Z–Boy's production line, Ms. Touchard met with Mr. Smith, the Human Resources Director, and informed him of her belief that the "alternate duty assignments" given to injured employees were demeaning. Moreover, she informed him that employees were deciding not to report injuries to avoid being harassed by management. She alleges that, as a result of her complaint, Mr. Smith began criticizing her, recommending that she be "written up," and delaying the implementation of programs she had recommended.

Several months after meeting with Mr. Smith, Ms. Touchard met with Mr. Garren, La–Z–Boy's vice president. At this time, Mr. Garren "falsely accused Ms. Touchard of coaching employees on how they could sue La–Z–Boy and told her that she could not tell employees they had a legal right to contact Utah's Labor Commission (emphasis added)." A few months after this incident, Ms. Touchard voiced her objections to the proposed adoption of a "120-day return to work rule." She alleges that at this time Mr. Garren "got angry with [her] and told her she was never to discuss employees' rights with the employees."

The final incident alleged by Ms. Touchard is that she reported to Mr. Garren that an employee had been injured and that his benefits were being improperly denied. At this time, she was allegedly told "that she would be fired if she ever talked to any employees about their Workers' Compensation issues or their injuries." Several months after this final meeting, Ms. Touchard took maternity leave, during which she was informed she had been terminated and her position had been filled. Ms. Touchard's complaint alleges that La–Z–Boy terminated her "because she opposed its practices of abusing employees who applied for [workers' compensation benefits] and maintaining an unsafe workplace." The employees' brief asserts that Ms. Touchard was fired for "inform[ing] injured workers of their rights to workers' compensation." While the complaint does allege that Ms. Touchard was warned not to discuss workers' compensation claims with La–Z–Boy employees and was accused of "coaching employees on how they could sue La–Z–Boy," an accusation her brief claims was false, she has not pled that she actually discussed workers' compensation benefits with La–Z–Boy employees or assisted them in pursuing claims.

We hold that Ms. Touchard's opposition to her employer's workers' compensation practices does not implicate a clear and substantial public policy of this state. This is not the first time this court has addressed whether an employee terminated for reporting to her employer potential policy or criminal violations has a cause of action under the public policy exception to the at-will rule. In *Heslop v. Bank of Utah*, 839 P.2d 828 (Utah 1992), we were asked whether Mr. Heslop, a senior vice president and manager of the bank's Salt Lake Division, had a cause of action for wrongful discharge. *Id.* at 831. Specifically, Mr. Heslop alleged that he had been terminated for reporting to a bank officer and the bank president that the bank had misstated its income and assets, thereby creating a deficiency between the bank's stated capital and its actual capital. *Id.* While Mr. Heslop eventually reported the deficiency to federal and state bank regulators, *id.* at 832, this court recognized that Mr. Heslop's reporting furthered a substantial public policy because "he pursued all internal methods for resolving the problem." *Id.* at 838. This court did not require him to go "outside the Bank to try to correct the policy violation." *Id.* at 838.

Several years later, we returned to the reporting question in *Fox v. MCI Commc'ns Corp.*, 931 P.2d 857 (Utah 1997). In Fox, a sales representative reported to her employer that her coworkers were "making existing customer accounts appear new on the corporate records so that they could meet sales quotas and earn higher commissions." *Id.* at 858–59. She was terminated shortly after reporting her coworkers' practices. *Id.* The employee claimed she had been terminated in violation of public policy because her internal reporting furthered the public policy found in the sections of the Utah Code that criminalized computer-assisted fraud, Utah Code Ann. § 76–6–703 (1995), and "acts of fraud or embezzlement," Utah Code Ann. §§ 76–6–403, 405 (1995), as well as a statute regulating corporate responsibility, Utah Code Ann. § 76–2–204 (1995). *Fox*, 931 P.2d at 859. This court disagreed. *Id.* at 861. While we recognized that the criminal code implicated a clear and substantial public policy, id. at 860, we held that "if an employee reports a criminal violation to an employer, rather than to public authorities, and is fired for making such reports, that does not, in our view, contravene a clear and substantial public policy." *Id.* In so holding, we explained that "[a]lthough employees may have a duty to disclose information concerning the employer's business to their employer, that duty ordinarily serves the private interest of the employer, not the public interest." *Id.* at 861.

Despite its holding, *Fox* did not eliminate a cause of action for internal reporting in all cases. We recognized as much in *Ryan v. Dan's Food Stores, Inc.*, 972 P.2d 395, 408 n. 7 (Utah 1998). While internal reporting was not at issue in *Ryan*, we discussed both *Heslop* and *Fox* in a footnote to illustrate that "determining what employee conduct . . . furthers a clear and substantial public policy is a still-developing inquiry." *Id.* at 408 & n. 7. The footnote suggests that *Fox* held only that internal reporting does not automatically further a clear and substantial public policy. *See id.* at 408 n. 7. Specifically, we stated, "Although *Heslop* suggests that any internal reporting will support a wrongful discharge claim, we emphasize that only internal reporting that furthers a clear and substantial public policy will satisfy the third element of a wrongful discharge claim." *Id.* We now endorse this conclusion anew and hold that internal reporting can give rise to a wrongful discharge cause of action where it furthers a clear and substantial public policy.

Thus, the inquiry in this case is whether Ms. Touchard's complaints to La–Z–Boy management about La–Z–Boy's workers' compensation and ergonomic practices furthered a clear and substantial public policy. As we have previously stated, we " 'narrowly construe the public policies' which might be used to support a public policy claim." *Ryan*, 972 P.2d at 405 (quoting *Peterson v. Browning*, 832 P.2d 1280, 1282 (Utah 1992)). Although we rely on the Workers' Compensation Act to conclude that an employee who is terminated for exercising his or her workers' compensation rights has a wrongful discharge cause of action, it does not follow that all employee complaints relating to workers' compensation also further the same clear and substantial public policy.

We first discuss Ms. Touchard's objections to the menial tasks being assigned to injured employees. Reporting employee harassment in retaliation for the employees' exercise of workers' compensation rights does not further a clear and substantial public policy. . . . Because the La–Z–Boy employees who have been assigned demeaning tasks do not have a cause of action, it follows that Ms. Touchard also does not have a cause of action for complaining about the way in which the employees were being treated.

Likewise, Ms. Touchard's complaints about La–Z–Boy's management of claims did not further a clear and substantial public policy. Ms. Touchard told La–Z–Boy that she believed claims were being "intentionally mismanaged," that La–Z–Boy's claims adjuster had a hostile attitude toward injured employees who sought workers' compensation benefits, and that the claims adjuster had, in the past, attempted to deny a claim to an employee with a documented injury. Ms. Touchard reported her findings as a result of an investigation, which she was hired to conduct, regarding La–Z–Boy's workers' compensation costs. Thus, it appears she conducted her study and reported her findings to further her employer's interests, to wit: to determine the cause of high workers' compensation costs. However, even if her reported findings furthered a public interest, we do not think it was sufficiently clear and substantial. Reporting the attempted denial of a past claim, however valid, does little to prevent an employer from avoiding its current or future obligations under the Act. Further, we think we would be construing public policy too broadly if we were to hold that an employee's complaint about a hostile claims adjuster or mismanagement of claims further a clear and substantial public policy. We fear that such a construction would render any complaint about an employer's workers' compensation practices actionable.

Moreover, Ms. Touchard's objections to the production line and the proposed 120–day rule did not invoke the actual policies furthered by the Workers' Compensation Act. For example, her claim that the production line had the potential to cause shoulder injuries did not directly implicate her employer's obligation to compensate employees for injuries incurred in the scope of employment; rather, it appears that Ms. Touchard's report regarding the ergonomics of the production line furthered the private interests of La–Z–Boy and its employees. Indeed, one reason to have an ergonomics team is to minimize employee injuries, thereby preventing a decrease in work productivity and an increase in workers' compensation claims. Likewise, while Ms. Touchard was opposed to the 120–day return-to-work rule, there is no indication that an employer may not implement such a rule under the Act. Ms. Touchard has not provided us with any evidence suggesting that her opposition to this rule furthered a clear and substantial public policy.

We note that Ms. Touchard's complaints about La–Z–Boy policies were all made in furtherance of her job duties. La–Z–Boy hired her to conduct investigations regarding both workers' compensation and ergonomics. Ms. Touchard did so, and as part of these duties, reported her concerns and recommendations to La–Z–Boy. . . . Just as employers are free to create such positions, they likewise are free to disagree with the findings made by such employees and terminate employees who make findings with which the employer does not agree.

Finally, we hold that Ms. Touchard's allegation that she challenged La–Z–Boy's purported unfair treatment of an employee's claim also did not further a clear and substantial public policy. In this case, there is no evidence that Ms. Touchard was responsible for processing or overseeing claims or that she had any personal knowledge regarding the employee's claim. The public policy exception would be expanded beyond its intended narrow scope if we were to hold that an employee with no authority over or personal knowledge of an individual workers' compensation claim has a cause of action for expressing her beliefs about the propriety of the employer's treatment of that claim. We fear that if we were to so hold, employers could be held hostage by employees who complain about matters of which they had no personal knowledge.

We commend Ms. Touchard's willingness to express her objections to her employer's practices that she believed were unfair, but her complaints cannot be viewed to further a clear and substantial public policy. We therefore hold that Ms. Touchard does not have a wrongful discharge cause of action for complaining about La–Z–Boy's treatment of injured employees.[4]

CONCLUSION

Based on the foregoing, we hold that retaliatory discharge for filing workers' compensation violates this state's clear and substantial public policy as pronounced by the Workers' Compensation Act. Thus, an

[4] We note that our holding is limited to the question certified to us-whether an employee who *opposes* an employer's treatment of employees who are entitled to workers' compensation has a wrongful discharge cause of action. Our opinion in this case does not address whether a wrongful discharge cause of action exists for an employee who goes beyond opposing employer practices and actually assists injured employees to file workers' compensation claims. . . .

employee who has been terminated or constructively discharged from his or her job in retaliation for the exercise of workers' compensation rights has a wrongful discharge cause of action against his or her employer under the public policy exception to the at-will rule. However, we do not believe the same policy is implicated when an employee suffers retaliatory harassment or discrimination, or when an employer discharges an employee who opposes the employer's treatment of employees who are entitled to benefits.

NOTES

1. McClanahan v. Remington Freight Lines, Inc., 517 N.E.2d 390 (Ind. 1988) extended Frampton to permit a public policy action for retaliatory discharge when an employee refused to commit an illegal act which could have created liability for the employee. Tony v. Elkhart County, 918 N.E.2d 363 (Ind. App. 2009) held that a discharged employee need not necessarily file a discrimination claim before commencing a retaliatory discharge action.

2. Hurst v. IHC Health Services, Inc., 817 F.Supp.2d 1202 (D.Idaho, 2011) concluded that "a majority" of courts were reluctant to involve themselves in workplace disputes and declined to recognize a public policy cause of action for retaliatory employment punishments "just short of actual discharge." The court cited White v. State, 131 Wash.2d 1, 929 P.2d 396 (1997) which denied a cause of action based upon a punitive transfer in retaliation for having reported patient abuse in a state-owned nursing home. Even so, Hurst opined that the Idaho Supreme Court would deem an employer's conduct amounting to constructive discharge based upon an employee's unwillingness to perform medical procedures beyond the scope of her practice to be actionable.

CHAPTER 4

INJURIES OCCURRING WITHIN THE COURSE OF EMPLOYMENT

■ ■ ■

1. INTRODUCTION—THE CLASSIFICATION OF RISKS COVERED BY THE COMPENSATION ACT

Determining whether the workers' compensation statute applies to a particular issue is frequently disputed in compensation claims. Whenever an employee has been exposed to a risk in employment that resulted in injury or death, a court must determine whether the risk falls within the protection of the statute. If it does, the employer must pay benefits and is immune to tort liability. If it does not, the worker receives no compensation benefits but is not statutorily barred from bringing a tort action.

Employment risks can be classified in several different ways, but any system of classification is useful only to the extent that it enables the decision maker to fix attention on some particular facet of the issue. Risks are frequently classified as to *character* or *source*. What *kind* of risk brought about the accident? Is it a type of risk covered by the statute? From this viewpoint the easiest risks to deal with are those that arise from a hazard that is peculiar to an employer's dangerous business—as where an electrician is killed by a lethal charge or a mechanic catches a hand in dangerous machinery. The coverage of injuries that are inherent risks of dangerous jobs was uppermost in the minds of the legislatures when the compensation statutes were enacted.

Nevertheless, under most modern compensation statutes, recovery is not confined to the peculiar risks of the employer's business or to risks posed by inherently dangerous endeavors. The acts protect against all risks of employment, even if they are not of the special type that initially caused the legislature to include the employer's business within the compensation statute. Hence, an employee who is hired to operate dangerous machinery can claim compensation not only if injured by the machinery, but also if burned in a campfire built to provide warmth to the workers. Modern statutes do not require that the worker be doing hazardous work at the time of the injury. If the injury or death was caused by a risk that is normal or usual in the type of work being done by the employee, recovery is routinely obtained.

Courts must often probe deeper. Even if it is admitted that employees are protected against all the normal risks of employment, what is and what is not such a normal risk must still be determined. The compensation acts invented a new term, i.e., did the injury *arise out of the employment*? This test concentrates upon the character and source of the harmful risk to determine whether the injuries it causes are properly charged to the employment. For example, although the operator of dangerous machinery who slips on the oily floor at the work place and breaks an arm in the fall is plainly entitled to compensation, the same employee may be denied recovery if struck by lightening while at work at the same spot. Whether the risk of death by lightening *arose out of* the employment would be a prominent feature of the dispute.

Even though a risk is of such a character and source as to clearly fall within the protection of the compensation act, questions may still arise as to *when* and *where* the risk was encountered. What was this employee doing at the time of the injury? And where was it being done? For example, compensation acts protect truck drivers against risk of collision. But when? Suppose the collision occurred while the driver was riding in a private vehicle on the way home after work? Is the relationship of time and place between accident and employment sufficiently close to bring the situation within the statute? Does the compensation principle justify requiring the employer to be burdened with the costs of the employee's injury or death? In short, did the accident occur while the employee was *within the course of employment*?

Often both the "arising out of" and "within the course of" employment issues arise in a single case. For example, suppose an employee is struck by lightning or injured by a tornado during lunch hour, or while resting, or while going home at the close of the day's work? For coverage to apply, the decision must be that both limbs of the test are satisfied. Nevertheless, the fact that one limb is plainly satisfied may influence a court's decision on the other. For example, the fact that the accident was a type closely associated with the nature of the employment may persuade a court to favor the employee where the time-place relation between accident and job is fairly in doubt. Similarly, an employee who was injured while directly engaged in the employer's work may be compensated for risks that would be excluded from coverage if they had been encountered while the worker was loitering or temporarily attending to personal affairs. The close affinity of the two inquiries is demonstrated throughout the pages that follow.

The materials in this chapter deal principally with questions of what effect to give to the time that the injury occurred and the place where it happened. These inquiries naturally include a consideration of the activity the employee was engaged in when injured or killed—was it working, or eating lunch, or standing by, or attending to personal affairs, or what?

2. INJURIES SUFFERED DURING SOCIAL, RECREATIONAL, AND SIMILAR ACTIVITIES

JOCQUELYN H. SHUNK V. GULF AMERICAN LAND CORP.

Supreme Court of Florida, 1969.
224 So.2d 269.

ERVIN, CHIEF JUSTICE.

We review an order of the Florida Industrial Commission reversing an order of the Judge of Industrial Claims in this case.

In order to reflect the factual situation involved herein, it is necessary to set forth the same at some length, as follows:

Claimant, Mrs. Jocquelyn H. Shunk, testified she has a real estate license; that her employment with Gulf American Land Corporation was to find prospective lot purchasers and to solicit them to travel in a plane provided by employer from the points where the prospects were assembled and emplaned to her employer's real estate development near Naples, Florida.

In Daytona Beach, Florida, claimant solicited one Luther Carrol Tanly, with the knowledge of her immediate supervisor, Howard Keller, to make the plane trip. In the course of persuading Tanly to make the trip, Mrs. Shunk had dinner with Tanly and Keller, and a Mrs. Catherine W. Morris, her fellow employee. After a late dinner (completed about 12:30 A.M.) the night of the claimant's accident, according to claimant's version of the affair, she accompanied Tanly to the Ritz Apartments in Daytona Beach where he was stopping. She said she went to his apartment for the purpose of ascertaining where he stayed so that she could awaken him in time the next morning to see that he got on board the plane along with other prospective customers for the trip to Naples.

It is uncontradicted that it was her duty to assist in seeing that sufficient prospective customers, necessary to fill the required quota for a plane load, were on board in time for scheduled flights to Naples. In this instance, the plane was scheduled to depart from the airport at Daytona Beach at 7:00 A.M., with Tanly included in the quota leaving on the plane that morning.

Claimant testified that upon arriving at the Ritz Apartments she had an altercation with Tanly; that he made improper advances toward her; that in attempting to elude him, she fell 25 feet from a window of the apartment building, injuring herself. The injury occurred at about 2:30 A.M.

Mrs. Shunk testified she had only had two cocktails, one before dinner and one afterwards; that she became nauseated after eating shrimp at the dinner, and that upon arriving at Tanly's apartment she asked him if she could use his bathroom to relieve her nausea. She testified that upon leaving the bathroom and attempting to leave the apartment Tanly's advances and the altercation ensued.

Her unusual hours of employment, sometimes lasting into the early morning hours, and the method of soliciting prospects for plane trips and land sales, were corroborated by the testimony of Mrs. Morris. * * * (other testimony corroborating or contradicting claimant's version omitted).

Mr. Howard Keller, the immediate supervisor of the claimant, testified by deposition that the duties of the solicitors employed by Gulf American Land Corporation included the following: Finding prospects anywhere, any time, any place they could do so (including restaurants, beaches, motels); obtaining from the prospects their hotel or motel room numbers, telephone numbers, and the responsibility for getting the prospects up early in the mornings to catch the 7:00 A.M. plane for the real estate development located near Naples. Mr. Keller stated in this case it was definitely Mrs. Shunk's responsibility and a part of her job to get Mr. Tanly on the plane the morning following the dinner. He testified that to the best of his knowledge all of them, including Mrs. Shunk, were sober when they returned to the San Marina Motel (headquarters of the prospect solicitors) from the late dinner, conversation, cocktails, etc. Mr. Keller testified in his deposition that almost anything Mrs. Shunk or any of the other lady solicitors did in securing prospective customers was part of their jobs, for which they were paid. He stated they had no regular working hours, but worked all the time getting people to go on the plane trips, and then seeing that they woke up and got on the planes.

In his compensation order, the Judge of Industrial Claims found on the "evidence presented * * * as well as the candor and demeanor of the witnesses who testified * * * ," that in the course and scope of her employment Mrs. Shunk accompanied Mr. Tanly to his apartment to ascertain his room number. The Judge of Industrial Claims accepted the testimony of the claimant as corroborated by Mr. Keller and other witnesses for the claimant, including Mrs. Catherine Morris, and found that the accident and injury arose out of and in the course of her employment and are compensable.

However, the Full Commission reversed, holding:

> "We believe that the judge of industrial claims has erred in finding this claim compensable. We feel that the facts clearly show that the claimant had deviated from her employment prior

to the accident. Surely it cannot be said that merely because the claimant was working in an area other than her home area, that she must be considered to be in her employment during an evening involving a late dinner and visits to cocktail lounges. Whatever motivation the claimant may have had for jumping from the window, we feel that the injury cannot be considered to have arisen out of and in the course of her employment."

It is quite true that the particular circumstances related above present a suspicious inference that claimant was not acting in the course of her employment at the time of her injury; that there may have been a deviation by claimant from her employment, and that her presence in the apartment at the late hour may have been a social engagement of her own, rather than one required for the discharge of her employment duties. However, a suspicious inference in these particular circumstances is not necessarily conclusive. The nature of claimant's employment, according to the testimony, involved solicitation, salesmanship and persuasion, and follow-up action to see that prospective customers were on scheduled flights to the development site, not dischargeable only during working hours normal to most employees. Consequently, it seems fairly well established that promotion of real estate sales to prospective customers of the kind here considered involves techniques and methods in a special class that have been found to be necessary in persuading prospective customers to agree to make the related plane trips.

In a debatable situation, such as this one, we conclude we should rest our judgment with the trier of the facts and lay aside our skepticism and natural inclination to be cynically suspicious. * * *

The writ is granted; the Commission's order of reversal is quashed with direction that the order of the Judge of Industrial Claims be reinstated.

It is so ordered.

NOTES

1. Injuries that occur while employees are actively performing assigned work when and where they are supposed to do it are always within the course of employment. Nevertheless, whether the employee is "at work" is often disputed, especially when social relations and business get mixed as in Shunk. The question of whether social activities are "part of the job" arises often in sales work and compensation is frequently granted. See, e.g., Green v. Heard Motor Co., 224 La. 1078, 71 So.2d 849 (1954) (car salesman took airplane ride with intoxicated pilot; compensation was awarded although there was no immediate prospect of sale). Moreover, recovery is not restricted to salesmen. In Harrison v. Stanton, 26 N.J.Super. 194, 97 A.2d 687 (1953), an undertaker persuaded his assistant to join the Optimists' Club. In

preparing to attend the Optimists' Annual Party, the assistant suffered a traffic injury in driving his car to procure a baby sitter. The injury was held to be in the course of employment with undertaker. Cf. University of Denver v. Nemeth, 127 Colo. 385, 257 P.2d 423 (1953) (student employed by university to clean up grounds, injured while playing football; evidence indicated that continuance of his job depended on his participation in organized athletics; held to be compensable). But compare State Comp. Ins. Fund v. Industrial Comm., 135 Colo. 570, 314 P.2d 288 (1957) (no recovery under almost identical facts).

2. Whether or not injuries suffered by employees who participate on company sponsored athletic teams outside regular work hours are within the course of employment engenders much dispute. If the athletic contest takes place on the working premises during the lunch hour or a regular rest or recreation period, recovery is usually allowed. If, however, the contest is held at some place of the employees' own choosing and takes place after working hours, compensation is less frequently awarded. Compare Burnett v. INA, 810 S.W.2d 833 (Tex.App.1991) (compensation denied to employee injured in softball game at company-sponsored picnic; employer received no benefit apart from general improvement of health and morale of employees) with Maycheck v. Tibbets Water & Waste, Inc., 61 A.D.2d 862, 401 N.Y.S.2d 916 (1978) (compensation awarded to employee injured in city-league softball game; team was organized by supervisory personnel). The following factors, inter alia, seem to affect the outcome: the extent of advertising of and public relations benefit from the event enjoyed by the employer; the employer's power to control the activity; the extent to which the event is part of an organized recreational scheme; and, the extent the employer supports the activity—such as allowance of paid time for participation, provision of uniforms, payment of fees, and rent. The greater the benefit to the employer, the more likely these injuries are to be compensable. On the other hand, if the employer seems merely to be accommodating the desires of the employees, compensation is less likely. Wisconsin has supplied a statutory rule on this point: "An employee is not performing service growing out of and incidental to employment while engaging in a program designed to improve the physical well-being of the employee, whether or not the program is located on the employer's premises, if participation in the program is voluntary and the employee receives no compensation for participation." Wis.Stat.Ann. § 102.03(3).

3. Similarly, courts differ sharply in the compensability of injuries suffered at employer-sponsored outings, dinners and other social events. Considerations similar to those above influence the outcomes. Compare Hanks v. Grey Wolf Drilling Company, 574 So.2d 531 (La.App.1991) (compensation awarded to worker hurt at company awards dinner; encouragement of company loyalty provides mutual benefit to employer) with Brown v. W.C.A.B., 138 Pa.Cmwlth. 560, 588 A.2d 1014 (1991) (compensation denied to employee who suffered accident while crossing public road after leaving employer sponsored, voluntary, after hours Christmas party for all

employees); and Chorley v. Koerner Ford, Inc., 19 N.Y.2d 242, 279 N.Y.S.2d 4, 225 N.E.2d 737 (1967) (similar; compensation awarded employee who suffered heart attack while attempting to follow up strenuous jitterbug with intercourse; dissent observed this was not an industrial accident from the "common sense viewpoint of the average man.")

Lozano v. Frank Deluca Construction, 178 N.J. 513, 842 A.2d 156 (2004) involved the claim of a worker who was injured after hours when he crashed a go-car that his employer "forced" him to drive as a recreational venture. The court acknowledged that the legislature had "tightened up" coverage to exclude voluntary social and recreational activities from the scope of the Workers' Compensation Act. Construing that provision, the court held:

> [W]hen an employer compels an employee to participate in an activity that ordinarily would be considered recreational or social in nature, the employer renders that activity work related as a matter of law. . . . Our holding recognizes that an employer always retains the power to expand the scope of employment by directing the employee to engage in tasks outside of the employees' general job duties.

Id., 842 A.d at 167. The court also held, "the employee must demonstrate an objectively reasonable basis in fact for believing that the employer had compelled participation in the activity." *Id.*, 842 A.2d at 168. Who should pay the benefits, the employer or the employer's worker's compensation insurance carrier? In contrast, Michalak v. Liberty Northwest Insurance Corporation, 342 Mont. 63, 175 P.3d 893 (2008) approved an award of benefits to a worker injured while riding a "wave runner" device during a company picnic. The court also reaffirmed application of a four part test: "(1) whether the activity was undertaken at the employer's request; (2) whether the employer, directly or indirectly, compelled the employee's attendance at the activity; (3) whether the employer controlled or participated in the activity; and (4) whether the employer and the employee mutually benefitted from the activity."

Brown v. United Technologies Corporation, 112 Conn. App. 492, 963 A.2d 1027 (2009) denied coverage for an injury suffered by an employee while "power walking" on the premises during a lunch break.

4. The treatment to be accorded to injuries sustained by employees conducting patriotic or civic acts outside regular work hours at the employer's request has not been uniform. Compare Burton v. Board of Educ. of Verona, 21 N.J.Misc. 108, 31 A.2d 337 (Dept. of Labor, 1943) (school teacher assisting in issuance of war ration books at the school house, compensation denied) with Casson v. Industrial Comm., 24 Ariz.App. 385, 539 P.2d 189 (1975) (employer requested that employee serve as member of volunteer fire department, compensation granted). See also Egan's Case, 331 Mass. 11, 116 N.E.2d 844 (1954) (compensation awarded to taxi driver injured while responding to police officer's call; held that answering police officer's call is a compensable street risk). Are these injuries properly chargeable to the employment under the compensation principle?

5. Frequently employers request or encourage employees to engage in non-work activities that are intended to improve the employees' health, education or general well being. Injuries suffered in the course of these activities are usually compensable. See, e.g., Lampkin v. Harzfeld's, 407 S.W.2d 894 (Mo.1966) (saleswoman suffered allergic reaction to flu shots encouraged by employer; compensation allowed. List of authorities in accord); McDaniel v. Sage, 174 Ind.App. 71, 366 N.E.2d 202 (1977) (harm from injection administered for relief of headache unrelated to employment; compensable); Jones v. Hartford Acc. & Indem. Co., 811 S.W.2d 516 (Tenn.1991) (compensation awarded employee injured while acting as union agent on union's time; because employee was taking a message to union president at the direction of the employer, the activity met the "mutual benefit" test); Mikkelsen v. N.L. Industries, 72 N.J. 209, 370 A.2d 5 (1977) (compensation awarded worker injured off duty while returning from union hall where he had attended collective bargaining meeting); Dallas County Pulpwood Co. v. Strange, 257 Ark. 799, 520 S.W.2d 247 (1975) (compensation awarded claimant injured while transporting equipment just purchased as his own property to work site); Sandmeyer v. City of Bemidji, 281 Minn. 217, 161 N.W.2d 318 (1968) (compensation awarded police officer shot while engaged in target practice off-duty); Evans v. Valley Diesel, 111 N.M. 556, 807 P.2d 740 (1991) (compensation awarded to an employee who was fixing his own car after completing the employer's work and before driving off the work premises through a door he was required to lock as a part of his job); Watson v. Nassau Inn, 74 N.J. 155, 376 A.2d 1215 (1977) (employee injured during off hours while taking work clothes from his room off premises to his home for cleaning; compensation awarded).

Nevertheless, when the relationship to employment grows remote, compensation is often denied. See, e.g., Dunavin v. Monarch Recreation Corporation, 812 P.2d 719 (Colo.App.1991) (compensation denied ski instructor hurt while skiing on free time; hearing officer found no benefit to employer); Costa v. New York State Workmen's Compensation Bd., 34 A.D.2d 585, 308 N.Y.S.2d 93 (1970) (employee injured while en route to take promotional examination suggested by employer in view of new opening; compensation denied); Fantasia v. Hess Oil & Chemical Corp., 110 N.J.Super. 360, 265 A.2d 565 (1970) (picketing employee run over in traffic during lockout; compensation denied); and, Miller v. Greene County, 171 Pa.Super. 494, 90 A.2d 262 (1952) (employee dissatisfied with tools provided by his employer, furnished his own; injured while sharpening them at home after hours; compensation denied); and Nichols v. Jay Truck Driver Training Center, 815 S.W.2d 450 (Mo.App.1991) (compensation denied survivors of employee killed when crushed by falling car when jacks collapsed while decedent was repairing his personal vehicle on employer's premises after working hours; no mutual benefit).

TAYLOR V. EWING

Superior Court of Pennsylvania, 1950.
166 Pa.Super. 21, 70 A.2d 456.

RHODES, PRESIDENT JUDGE.

This is a workmen's compensation case in which the compensation authorities made an award to claimant. The court of common pleas affirmed the award and entered judgment for claimant. Defendant's insurance carrier has appealed.

The facts are not in dispute. The question is whether claimant sustained his injury as a result of an accident within or outside the course of his employment with defendant.

Defendant was an automobile dealer in Beaver, Pennsylvania, and in his business he maintained a garage, showroom, and used car lot. Claimant had been employed by defendant for some time as a general utility man at a weekly wage of $35. Claimant's customary duties consisted of cleaning the offices, showroom, and garage, and servicing cars. On the morning of July 10, 1947, claimant having no other duties to perform at that time at the garage or showroom, defendant directed him to proceed to defendant's home and cut some grass with a power lawn mower which defendant owned. While attempting to adjust the belt on the power mower, to which defendant called claimant's attention, claimant accidentally sustained an injury to the index finger of his right hand, which necessitated amputation of a portion of the finger.

Appellant at the time the accident occurred had issued to defendant a "Standard Workmen's Compensation and Employers' Liability Policy." The premises of defendant were described as located at Wayne and Fourth Streets, and Third and Sassafras Lane, Beaver, Pennsylvania. The policy described the business of the insured as follows: "Garages and Automobile Dealers, including accessories, service stations—all employees except office" * * *

In Krchmar v. Oakland Beach Company, 155 Pa.Super. 430, at page 433, 38 A.2d 710, at page 712, we said: "In general, where the accident occurs off the premises of the employer, the proofs must establish that the employee was actually engaged in furthering the business of the employer at the time of the injury. Palko v. Taylor–McCoy Coal & Coke Co. et al., 289 Pa. 401, 137 A. 625. Otherwise, if the act in which the employee was engaged when injured off the premises, was not connected with the employer's business, it must appear that the employer ordered or directed the act. Merely permitting the employee to do the act without directing or ordering its performance will not support an award. Gibson v. Blowers Paint Service et al., 140 Pa.Super. 216, 14 A.2d 154."

Defendant is in no position to say that the services performed for his benefit and at his direction by claimant were not in the course of claimant's employment. Matis v. Schaeffer, 270 Pa. 141, 113 A. 64; Geary v. Martin, 101 Pa.Super. 311. If it had not been for claimant's employment in defendant's business, he would not have been in the place where he was injured, at which time he was working under the direction and control of defendant and in consequence of the relationship of employer and employe.

The Workmen's Compensation Act, 77 P.S. § 1 et seq., was passed for the purpose of protecting employes. An employe does not step in and out of his regular employment with every changing task ordered to be done by his employer. His general employment, not such particular act, ordinarily controls. See Zapos v. Demas, 106 Pa.Super. 183, 161 A. 753 * * * [further citations omitted].

If claimant had been engaged in regular work of a dual nature, appellant's argument would be applicable. But claimant did not become a domestic employe or servant by performing the incidental task which defendant directed him to do when injured, and there was no contract of hiring for domestic service. This work did not terminate the existing status of claimant as an employe in the regular course of defendant's business; he was still working in the sphere of activity in which he was employed and paid. There was no severance of the relationship covered by the insurance policy of appellant, and it is immaterial that defendant and his wife had a liability policy relating to domestic employes. Claimant was engaged in executing a positive command of his employer merely incidental to the business in which claimant was employed by defendant, and the act did not take him out of the course of that employment. "We may well surmise what would have happened to his job had he refused to do this work without any other excuse than that he was not hired for that purpose." Nugent Sand Co. v. Hargesheimer, 254 Ky. 358, 71 S.W.2d 647, 649. See 172 A.L.R. 387. * * *

Judgment is affirmed.

NOTES

1. Accord: Alvarez v. Sem–Chi Rice Products Corp., 861 So.2d 513 (Fla. 1st DCA 2003), Echo Enterprises Inc. v. Aspinwall, 194 Ga.App. 444, 390 S.E.2d 867 (1990), and Harry Fleming Washer Service v. Industrial Comm., 36 Ill.2d 272, 222 N.E.2d 490 (1966).

How closely is the issue in the principal case related to the issue of the borrowed employee and dual employment? See Chapter 3. See, also, Keasey v. Mitzel Bros., 135 Pa.Super. 460, 5 A.2d 631 (1939) (compensation awarded worker employed by partnership engaged in supply business who was directed by a partner to paint his house). Most of the decisions hold that employees are to be compensated while carrying out an order that has nothing to do with the business of the employer only if the order was expressly given by the employer. See, e.g., Sellers v. Reice Constr. Co., 124 Kan. 550, 262 P. 19 (1927). Should it be important that the employee knows that the person giving non-job related orders has no authority to do so? See, e.g., Liberty Mut. Ins. Co. v. Neal, 55 Ga.App. 790, 191 S.E. 393 (1937) (compensation awarded cotton mill worker who was directed by overseer to cut wood which the overseer then sold to the employer at a profit; the overseer was deemed to be a vice principal).

2. An employee who renders personal assistance to a third person at the employer's request is in the course of his employment while so doing. Even in the absence of specific orders, the employee who is injured while performing an act of courtesy for a patron or customer is usually regarded as acting within the course of employment because of the good will garnered to the employer. See, e.g., Olsen v. State Acc. Ins. Fund, 29 Or.App. 235, 562 P.2d 1234 (1977) (compensation awarded worker injured during lunch break while repairing bicycle for coworker; superior observed and did not object). See also Riley v. Perkins, 282 Ala. 629, 213 So.2d 796 (1968). Nevertheless, some courts reject the general good will benefit argument and deny recovery where the assisted person is a stranger to the business. Contrast Rowley v. Industrial Comm., 15 Utah 2d 330, 392 P.2d 1016 (1964) (denying recovery) and Ace Pest Control, Inc. v. Industrial Comm., 32 Ill.2d 386, 205 N.E.2d 453 (1965) (awarding recovery).

3. An employee who without orders from the employer renders assistance for the personal benefit of a co-worker may act outside the course of employment in so doing. Compare Olson Rug Co. v. Industrial Comm., 215 Wis. 344, 254 N.W. 519 (1934) (compensation denied employee injured while driving ill co-worker home in another town; employer had no duty to transport the ill worker home) with Continental Casualty Co. v. Industrial Comm., 28 Wis.2d 89, 135 N.W.2d 803 (1965) (compensation awarded survivors of an employee accidentally killed on the work premises during working hours while helping a superior with a purely personal task; Olson distinguished on the basis of time and place of occurrence). Injuries suffered by employees who undertake jobs assigned to other laborers are more difficult. If the undertaking is merely for the personal convenience of the claimant or the person assisted, or if the task is undertaken to satisfy the claimant's curiosity or desire to experiment, compensation is sometimes denied. See, e.g., Utah Copper Co. v. Industrial Comm., 62 Utah 33, 217 P. 1105 (1923) (fireman and brakeman on train exchanged jobs on successive runs of train in order to equalize their respective exposures to inclement weather; compensation denied). Where, however, the claimant is acting primarily to further the employer's interests by assisting another worker, compensation may be allowed. See, e.g., Groves v. Marvel, 59 Del. 73, 213 A.2d 853 (1965) (compensation awarded to off duty employee who was hurt while helping co-employee with his work; activity created good will for customers).

3. INJURIES SUFFERED BY EMPLOYEES MINISTERING TO PERSONAL NEEDS OR PLEASURE

LECKIE V. H.D. FOOTE LUMBER CO.

Court of Appeals of Louisiana, Second Circuit, 1948.
40 So.2d 249.

KENNON, JUDGE.

This is a suit for 400 weeks compensation, less 70 weeks previously paid. The petition alleges that plaintiff was employed as a saw filer and scaler; that, while in the course of his employment, and, while attempting to trim a piece of lumber by the use of a power driven cut off saw, he received an injury which resulted in the loss of a substantial portion of his left hand, * * *

The District Court found for plaintiff and the case is before us on appeal from that judgment.

Plaintiff was second in charge to a Mr. Baum in the operation of defendant's sawmill. His specific tasks were to scale such logs as were received at the mill and to file crosscut saws. In addition, he performed general tasks around the mill and was free to do whatever seemed necessary in facilitating the mill's operation.

The injury occurred on a Saturday afternoon while only plaintiff and defendant's manager, Mr. Baum, were present at the mill. They were performing the customary Saturday task of preparing the small mill for its weekend shutdown. Part of this weekly shutdown work consisted of burning out the slab pile so as to reduce the fire hazard. Mr. Baum went to the burning pit, leaving plaintiff to attend to the operation of the two engines, which operated the mill machinery, including a blower which accelerated the burning of the slabs and waste. Plaintiff was being paid for this Saturday afternoon work. In addition to being on duty with the engines, he was available—and used when occasion required—to scale any logs that might arrive on Saturday afternoon.

The mechanical set-up of the mill was such that when it was desired to operate the blower which accelerated the burning of waste, all the other machinery connected to the engines was also automatically put in operation. Included in the machinery which was necessarily—though idly—operating on the Saturday afternoon in question, was a circular cut off saw situated about ten feet from the motors which plaintiff was attending. Plaintiff's injury occurred when he picked up a short piece of scrap lumber and proceeded to run it through the cut off saw. Plaintiff's petition alleged that his purpose in using the saw at the time was "to trim a piece of lumber." Defendants introduced evidence at the trial that the material was only a piece of slab, less than 30 inches long, incapable of being used for lumber and that plaintiff's purpose was to cut it in two pieces for his own use as stove wood. The District Court found—and the record amply sustains this finding—that the board being trimmed by plaintiff at the time of his injury was not fit for sale and was usable only as fire wood.

After 70 weeks, defendants discontinued paying compensation and the defense in the present suit is that plaintiff at the time of his injury had turned aside from his employment and was engaged in a task which served his own interest exclusively and had not sufficient relationship to his employment to entitle him to benefits under the compensation law.

Plaintiff's contention is that he was simply taking advantage of the fact that the nature of the duty he was performing—namely, that of watching the engines and being available for the scaling of such logs as might be brought to the mill—permitted him to cut some stove wood for himself, that, when he was injured, he had not left the place of his employment or ceased to perform the duties required of him at the time.

The record discloses that the defendant lumber company permitted its employees to carry away for fuel slabs which otherwise would have been burned as waste and had permitted employees at convenient times while on duty to cut such slabs into convenient lengths for wood. The alternative method of disposing of waste slabs was to place them in the conveyer trough (situated some four feet from the cut off saw) to be carried to the burning pit.

The case turns upon a question of law. Is compensation due an employee who is injured, while at his place of duty, while watching machinery as required by his employer, while available on the premises for his other duty of scaling any logs that might arrive, but whose injury occurs when the employee is also performing some other act for his own benefit? * * *

In an earlier Supreme Court case, Kern v. Southport Mill, Ltd., 174 La. 432, 141 So. 19, the Court laid down the rule that in determining whether an accident arises out of the employment, it is necessary to consider only two questions. First, was the employee then engaged about his employer's business and not merely pursuing his own business or pleasure and second, did the necessity of the employer's business reasonably require that the employee be at the place of the accident at the time the accident occurred.

In the case before us, plaintiff's injury "arose out of his employment" according to the test set forth in the Kern case. Certainly the necessities of the employer's business reasonably required him to be at the place of the accident at the time the accident occurred and, while he was incidentally pursuing his own business in that he was trimming stove wood for himself, he was also satisfactorily performing the required duty of attending to the operation of the motors. He was also about his employer's business to the extent that he was available at the mill site in the event logs should arrive for scaling. The fact that he was at the time, and without ceasing to attend to his employer's business, using the cut off saw, which otherwise would have been idle, for his own benefit did not alter the inescapable fact that he was also at the time performing the duties required of him by his employment. * * *

To sum up, we find as a matter of fact that at the time plaintiff Leckie was injured, he was not engaged in trimming lumber for the benefit of his employer, nor was he engaged in the picking up of boards as a part of any clean-up duty which might have benefited his employer. We find that Mr. Leckie's duty at the time of his injury, as assigned to him by defendant's foreman, was to attend to the running of the engines and machinery, including the blower, and to keep himself available to scale any logs that might arrive at the mill. We find that his injury resulted when he, taking advantage of the fact that his duties did not require the use of his hands for any purpose at the minute, picked up a small board and proceeded to cut some stove wood for his own personal use.

We think that under the Louisiana authorities plaintiff is entitled to compensation. * * *

The judgment is affirmed, with costs.

(Dissenting opinion of HARDY, J. omitted.)

ON REHEARING.

TALIAFERRO, JUDGE.

The facts of this case are clearly set out in our former opinion. They will not be at length iterated herein. The members of this Court are unanimous in the opinion that plaintiff when injured had turned aside from his over-hour duties to his employer and was engaged in the performance of an act purely for his own interest and benefit; that is, to convert a discarded and non-commercial piece of timber into stovewood for his own use; that in so doing he unnecessarily exposed himself to the dangerous instrumentality that caused the injury but for which the accident would not have happened.

The accident happened in the course of plaintiff's employment, but to entitle him to recover compensation, of course, it must be found and held that it arose out of and/or was incidental to such employment. In other words, did the turning aside to engage in a purely personal, dangerous act, several feet from where he was required to be to perform his duties, for the moment, deprive plaintiff of the benefits of the Workmen's Compensation Law, as regards an accident that occurred while he was so engaged? On this question a majority of this court takes the affirmative.

The question is one of law arising from the factual findings of the Court's entire membership.

In cases of this character the courts of this state have frequently held that whether or not an injury arises out of the employment depends necessarily upon the facts and circumstances of each case. No hard and fast rule in such cases is possible of intelligent adoption. If it should be held that the facts of this case warrant recovery by plaintiff, it is difficult to perceive to what extent the rule might be carried. Can it logically be said that had the accident occurred fifty feet farther from the exact locus of his duties, it would not be compensable, whereas since it happened only ten feet therefrom, it is compensable? We believe the factor of distance is not entirely controlling. To the nature of the act of deviation or turning aside should be accredited controlling influence.

The testimony shows that about the immediate locus of the accident plaintiff had assembled a goodly quantity of discarded pieces of lumber he evidently intended to carry home for stovewood. And, it is shown that plaintiff's superiors did not offer objection to this being done, nor to the use of the saws, when not otherwise engaged, to cut the pieces into appropriate lengths, but in so doing in each instance, the employee acted for himself and not for his employer. He was subserving his own personal interest. * * *

For the reasons herein assigned, the judgment from which appeal was taken is reversed, and plaintiff's suit is hereby dismissed at his cost.

KENNON, J., dissents for the reasons assigned in the original opinion, contained herein.

NOTES

1. Decisions differ as to whether injuries suffered on work premises by employees while performing non-prohibited acts for their personal benefit during spare time are compensable. Compare Bell v. Dewey Bros., Inc., 236 N.C. 280, 72 S.E.2d 680 (1952) (watchman washing his own car; practice not prohibited and was known to employer; compensation denied) and Ranger Ins. Co. v. Valerio, 553 S.W.2d 682 (Tex.Civ.App.1977) (during idle moment deliveryman attempted to dislodge a rabbit from a culvert, compensation denied) with Chrisman v. Farmers Cooperative Ass'n, 179 Neb. 891, 140 N.W.2d 809 (1966) (service station operator repairing his own car; compensable) and Lee v. Middleton Logging Co., 198 Ga.App. 585, 402 S.E.2d 536 (1991) (compensation denied to off-duty employee who came to work site on day off and was hurt after his offer to help an onsite subcontractor was rejected). The outcome may be influenced by the time at which the accident occurred. An injury suffered during a stand-by period of enforced idleness caused by the nature of the employer's work is often compensable, and the fact that the employee devotes free time to personal purposes does not arbitrarily serve to deny compensation. See, e.g., Parker v. Travelers Ins. Co.,

142 Ga.App. 711, 236 S.E.2d 915 (1977) (compensation awarded mechanic working on his own car in garage during slack period with knowledge of employer); and Spencer v. Chesapeake Paperboard Co., 186 Md. 522, 47 A.2d 385 (1946) (compensation awarded worker hired to fill heater in papermill; suffered burns when pants caught on fire while taking a nap beside operating machine). But, if the employee converts a stand-by period to personal purposes by abandoning the job or engaging in prohibited conduct or in conduct that is inconsistent with the satisfactory performance of assigned duties, compensation is often denied. See, e.g., Como v. Union Sulphur Co., 182 So. 155 (La.App.1938) (foreman of construction crew left his post to dynamite fish downstream); and Hills v. Servicemaster of Conn. River Valley, Inc., 155 Conn. 214, 230 A.2d 604 (1967) (floor cleaner injured tampering with elevator contrary to orders).

2. Compensability of injuries suffered by employees while standing by for possible call to work may be influenced by the imminence of an expected call to return to duty. The messenger who is merely told to remain on the premises for the afternoon and the employee who is subject to occasional call while at home will be less likely to be awarded compensation than a worker who faces a temporary lull in his work while waiting for a tool. Compare Blackley v. City of Niagara Falls, 284 App.Div. 51, 130 N.Y.S.2d 77 (1954) (policeman subject to call at all times; not within course of employment when going home) and Johnson v. Employee Benefits Ins. Co., 25 Or.App. 215, 548 P.2d 519 (1976) (compensation denied range rider subject to call by two-way radio; injured while beyond range of radio on personal errand on day off) with Paige v. City of Rahway, 74 N.J. 177, 376 A.2d 1226 (1977) (compensation awarded water works supervisor on call, who was assaulted and robbed at home during period), and Meo v. Commercial Can Corp., 76 N.J.Super. 484, 184 A.2d 891 (1962) (compensation awarded management employee battered by striking employees while entering his car at home preparing to go to work.)

3. The argument for recovery in the stand-by or on-call cases is strengthened if the activity in which the employee was engaged at the time of injury, although personal to the employee, nevertheless can be related to the conditions of employment. Compare Clapham v. David, 232 App.Div. 458, 251 N.Y.S. 245 (1931) (compensation awarded nurse of obstreperous child, on twenty-four hours duty, injured while taking short bicycle ride at employer's suggestion to calm her nerves); Fidelity & Cas. Co. of New York v. Industrial Acc. Comm., 176 Cal.App.2d 541, 1 Cal.Rptr. 567 (1959) (compensation awarded survivors of employee subject to call in employment in Indonesia who drowned while swimming in order to get relief from humidity); Miller v. F.A. Bartlett Tree Expert Co., 3 N.Y.2d 654, 171 N.Y.S.2d 77, 148 N.E.2d 296 (1958) (compensation awarded worker injured at tree surgery conference while taking shower in preparation for indoor session after a day in the field), with Yates v. Naylor Industrial Services, Inc., 569 So.2d 616 (La.App.1990) (compensation denied on-call employee who received call to report to assignment in distant town while on personal hunting trip and was injured

suffered injury on way to his home to pick up clothing; claimant was "simply too far removed from employment").

4. Employees who suffer injuries while occupying housing the employers requires them to live in either expressly or by absence of any reasonable alternative are usually deemed to be within the course of employment and compensable. This result, sometimes referred to as the "bunkhouse rule," applies even though the employee is not engaged in actual work at the time and may even be sleeping or administering to personal needs. See, e.g., Wood v. Kings Park State Hospital, 266 App.Div. 804, 41 N.Y.S.2d 391 (1943) (compensation awarded to clerical hospital employee for injury sustained after working hours while dressing in own room; employee was subject to general on-call regulation to perform "usual or special tasks" on holidays and at other times). For the rule to apply, however, the injury must be occasioned by a "risk distinctly associated with the conditions under which the claimant lived." See, e.g., Littles v. Osceola Farms Co., 577 So.2d 657 (Fla.App.1991) (employee killed in "bunkhouse" by disgruntled fellow employee lover not within rule).

Even resident employees who are not subject to call are occasionally regarded as within the course of employment when injured on the premises. See, e.g., Feliciano v. Woodlea Nursery, 57 A.D.2d 979, 394 N.Y.S.2d 109 (1977) (compensation awarded migrant worker who fell downstairs in employer-provided housing on day off) and Kilcoyne's Case, 352 Mass. 572, 227 N.E.2d 324 (1967) (compensation awarded non-on-call employee because the employer was benefitted by the employee's presence). Decisions are often influenced by the character of the activity in which the employee was engaged at the time of the accident. Thus, in Gowan v. Harry Butler and Sons Funeral Home, 204 Kan. 210, 460 P.2d 606 (1969), compensation was awarded a resident domestic employee who broke a leg while changing her dress. Although she was not subject to call, care of her clothing was deemed to be sufficiently related to the discharge of her duties to assure coverage. Contrast Reed v. Loon Lake Hotel, 283 App.Div. 763, 128 N.Y.S.2d 112 (1954) (compensation denied non-on-call domestic employee injured from unknown cause while asleep on premises).

The compensability of an injury suffered by a resident employee who is not subject to call may also be influenced by the nature of the hazard that brought about the injury. Compare Finnegan v. Biehn, 276 N.Y. 50, 11 N.E.2d 348 (1937) (compensation awarded dependents of resident janitor who burned to death in a fire caused by overturning of oil heater in apartment without central heating system) and John H. Kaiser Lumber Co. v. Industrial Comm. of Wisconsin, 181 Wis. 513, 195 N.W. 329 (1923) (compensation awarded mill employee attacked by crazed fellow worker while sleeping in bunkhouse with sixty others) with Pisko v. Mintz, 262 N.Y. 176, 186 N.E. 434 (1933) (compensation denied janitor injured in apartment house fire caused by his smoking in bed) and Fireman's Fund Indem. Co. v. Industrial Accident Comm., 39 Cal.2d 529, 247 P.2d 707 (1952) (compensation denied resident employee injured fifty feet from premises while taking a walk at end of work day).

PACHECO'S DEPENDENTS V. ORCHIDS OF HAWAII

Supreme Court of Hawai'i, 1972.
54 Hawai'i 66, 502 P.2d 1399.

RICHARDSON, CHIEF JUSTICE.

This appeal, pursuant to HRS § 386–88 (Supp.1971) arises out of a workmen's compensation claim by the dependents of Wilma P. Pacheco, deceased, against her employer, Orchids of Hawaii. The claim was denied by the Director of the Department of Labor and Industrial Relations. On appeal, the Labor and Industrial Relations Appeals Board made an award of compensation.

The facts are not in dispute having been stipulated by the parties.

Mrs. Pacheco was employed by Orchids of Hawaii (hereinafter "Employer") on and prior to July 7, 1967. She worked as a member of a production team in an "assembly line" operation.

It was employer's policy to allow a 15-minute coffee break each morning and afternoon during regular working hours. Employees customarily used refreshment facilities on the premises, however, they were free to leave the premises during coffee breaks.

On July 7, 1967 Mrs. Pacheco was given her paycheck after lunch and before the afternoon coffee break. Since it was anticipated that she would work late, the afternoon coffee break afforded Mrs. Pacheco the only opportunity to cash her check before the banks closed. Once previously during her coffee break, Mrs. Pacheco had gone to a bank to cash her paycheck.

At 2:48 P.M. on July 7th, Mrs. Pacheco punched out on her time card to take her afternoon break. With one of three other women employees driving, Mrs. Pacheco left employer's premises intending to cash her paycheck at the nearest bank. Mrs. Yamamoto, Mrs. Pacheco's supervisor, observed the departure and cautioned the group to hurry back.

While the ladies were on their way to the Waiakea branch of the Bank of Hawaii, some three blocks away, their automobile was struck broadside resulting in Mrs. Pacheco's death.

The major issue in this case is whether Mrs. Pacheco's death is compensable under section 386–3 of the Hawaii Revised Statutes. The relevant provision of that section reads "[i]f an employee suffers personal injury . . . *by accident arising out of and in the course of the employment*" he or his dependents are entitled to recover under workmen's compensation. (Emphasis added.)

This court has not fully considered the extent of that critical phrase in our workmen's compensation plan, but we are not inclined to unduly restrict its scope.

The stipulated facts present a borderline case which is not adequately covered by existing law. Professor Larson states:

> Now that the coffee break has become a fixture of many kinds of employment, close questions continue to arise on the compensability of injuries occurring off the premises during rest periods or coffee breaks of various durations. It is clear that one cannot announce an all-purpose "coffee break rule," since there are too many variables that could affect the result.[2]

Compensation for off-premises, rest period injuries is appropriate in Professor Larson's view when the employer "can be deemed to have retained authority over the employee."[3] Authority is said to be retained where, measured by the duration of the break and the distance from the employee's desk, the employment itself was not interrupted.[4]

Bodensky v. Royaltone, Inc., 5 A.D.2d 733, 168 N.Y.S.2d 908 (1957) relies on the reasoning in Caporale and is persuasive on the issue of whether off-premises, "coffee-break" injuries should be compensable. Royaltone permitted its employees a 15-minute coffee break each day. Claimant's practice of leaving the building during this time was known to her employer and allowed. On returning from a coffee shop about a block away, claimant injured herself. The court based its award of compensation on a finding that the employment was not interrupted because the break was an approved one of limited duration and restricted in scope.

We reject appellant's notion that Balsam v. New York State Division of Employment, 24 A.D.2d 802, 263 N.Y.S.2d 849 (1965) is controlling in the present case.

In *Balsam* claimant was injured when she went to a bank to cash a personal check prior to having coffee, but during her rest period. Since employees were free to leave the premises only for coffee at a designated shop, claimant's injury occurred during the course of a "purely personal

---

2 *See* Jordan v. Western Electric Co., Inc., 1 Or.App. 441, 463 P.2d 598, 600 (1970) n. 1 for a representative listing of those cases which allow and those which disallow recovery for injuries occasioned during break time.

3 1 Larson, Workmen's Compensation Law 245, § 15.54 (1968).

4 *Id.*, p. 247.

mission."[5] This deviation from a "prescribed sphere of recreational endeavor"[6] resulted in the dismissal of the claim.

The case at hand does not involve an employee who strayed from an authorized activity, therefore, we find *Balsam* inapposite.

We adopt as a general rule the proposition that an employee, who is allowed to venture off-premises during an authorized work break, and who is injured in the course of reasonable and necessary activity incidental to such break, should be compensated.

A scheduled coffee break serves the dual function of providing an employee a brief respite from his job as well as affording him an opportunity to tend to matters of a personal nature. The former objective has been viewed as a benefit to the employer, because a refreshed employee is often a more productive one. The latter type of activity may or may not directly benefit the employer, but is allowed as a convenience to the employee. An employer may derive substantial benefits from an employee who is allowed time away from the job to accomplish pressing personal business. Injuries occasioned by employees pursuing necessary personal matters off employer's premises are compensable in our view as work-connected, especially if the employer acquiesces in such practices.

Applying the above principles to the present case we find that there is substantial evidence to support a claim for compensation.

Deceased was observing her regular afternoon coffee break when the fatal accident occurred. It was her employer's policy to allow *ex premises* departures during the break for the convenience of the employees. Once previously, deceased had ventured out to cash her paycheck without censure. On the day of the accident, deceased was among a group of employees which was observed departing for the bank by a supervisor. Since late work beyond banking hours was anticipated, it was necessary for deceased to use her free time to cash her paycheck. A substantial benefit accrued to the employer because his production line closed down simultaneously rather than sporadically throughout the workday. The regularly scheduled break promoted a smooth-running, efficient operation.

Based on the foregoing, we affirm the award of the Labor and Industrial Relations Appeals Board * * * .

LEVINSON, JUSTICE (dissenting).

This case is before us upon stipulated facts and presents a question of first impression under Hawaii's Workmen's Compensation Law.[7] The

[5] Caporale v. Department of Taxation and Finance, 2 A.D.2d 91, 153 N.Y.S.2d 738 (1956), aff'd., 2 N.Y.2d 946, 162 N.Y.S.2d 40, 142 N.E.2d 213 (1957).

[6] Balsam v. New York State Division of Employment, 24 A.D.2d 802, 263 N.Y.S.2d 849, 850 (1965).

question is whether an employee who is injured off the employer's premises during an unpaid coffee break but while en route to a bank to cash a paycheck has suffered an injury "arising out of and in the course of the employment." A majority of this court is of the opinion that compensation should be awarded. It reasons that "an employee who is allowed to venture off-premises during an authorized work break, and who is injured in the course of reasonable and necessary activity incidental to such break, should be compensated." In my view, neither the result reached nor the reasoning adopted to support it can be justified under present authority or sound public policy. I dissent.

* * *

I.

In order to focus on the precise issue presented by this record, it is useful first to canvass those matters which this case does not involve.

At the time of the accident, Mrs. Pacheco was quite clearly neither on the premises nor under the control of her employer. She was, instead, on her own time in the company of three other employees, each having no managerial responsibilities, * * * in an automobile four-tenths of a mile away from her employer's premises, * * *. Nor was Mrs. Pacheco, in my view, under the constructive control of her employer. * * * When she left her employer's premises, the only restriction placed upon her was time. She could go wherever she pleased and do whatever she wanted as long as she returned to work in 15 minutes. If Mrs. Pacheco is deemed to have been under the constructive control of the employer merely because her time was restricted, then any activity in which she might have engaged while off premises during the period of the coffee break also must be deemed to have been under the employer's control. In none of the reported cases has the element of control ever been stretched so far.

There is nothing in the facts, all of which were stipulated, indicating that the employer had any knowledge, either actual or constructive, of Mrs. Pacheco's intent to cash her paycheck during the coffee break. Absent such knowledge, it cannot be said that the employer acquiesced in her activity, * * *. Under the stipulation, there is no indication that the employer was aware of the fact that Mrs. Pacheco left the premises for the purpose of cashing her paycheck or that she had ever done so previously. She did, in fact, do so on one previous occasion, but we cannot assume that her employer had knowledge of it. Mrs. Pacheco's supervisor may have guessed at the purpose of the off-premises jaunt, but that is mere speculation.

---

7 Id.

Although Mrs. Pacheco was required to work later than usual, her trip to the bank was at most convenient to her personally and had nothing to do with her ability to work late. Check cashing was certainly not one of her duties as an employee, ...

Nor can it be said that the employer derived a benefit from the activity. . . . The paycheck could have been cashed at some other time and place. Since Mrs. Pacheco anticipated working late, it may have been more convenient for her to cash it during her coffee break. But this was merely a matter of personal convenience unrelated to her work. At most it was intended to save her some inconvenience after work. Cf. Comment, "Workmen's Compensation: The Personal Comfort Doctrine," 1960 Wis.L.Rev. 91. Mrs. Pacheco, for example, did not attempt to go to the bank so that she could pay for a meal while at work, or purchase some article essential to her employment.

The answer to the argument that cashing a check for her personal convenience only is sufficient to render an employer responsible for compensation is that it then would follow that injuries arising out of any activity that might conceivably make employment more convenient for the employee also would be compensable. The connection between an employee's personal convenience and the employment is too tenuous to justify compensation. There is a logical distinction, I believe, between the circumstances under which an employee takes a breath of fresh air, smokes a cigarette, uses the bathroom or talks to another employee, see 1 Larson, The Law of Workmen's Compensation § 21 (1965), and those circumstances under which he goes to a bank to cash his paycheck, . . . takes an airplane ride, . . . or goes shopping at a grocery store for his family. . . .

If Mrs. Pacheco had not engaged in the activity that led to her accident, she might have been anxious about having cash with which to purchase commodities or entertainment for her family. No doubt her anxiety would in some sense affect her while she was at work. But if the avoidance of such anxiety is considered, apart from mere personal convenience, to be of such benefit to the employer so as to render the latter responsible for injuries resulting from employee activities which relieve such anxiety, then with equal force practically any activity engaged in by an employee benefits the employer, whether engaged in during working or leisure hours. Compensation based on anxiety is even more tenuous than compensation based on personal convenience unrelated to work. It is unheard of in the reported cases.

Finally, the check cashing activity was not in accordance with custom, . . . pursuant to any special arrangement between the employer and the bank, . . . or engaged in by Mrs. Pacheco while she was subject to call. . . . The stipulation is silent with respect to any custom or special

relaxation. In pondering the various fact situations that will arise following this case, the majority would do well to consider the following oft-quoted passage from *The Voyages of Sinbad the Sailor*:

> And, lo, the master of the ship vociferated and called out, threw down his turban, slapped his face, plucked his beard, and fell down in the hold of the ship by reason of the violence of his grief and rage. So all the merchants and other passengers came together to him and said to him, "O master, what is the matter?" and he answered them: "Know, O Company, that we have wandered from our course, having passed forth from the sea in which we were, and entered a sea of which we know not the routes."

I would reverse the Decision and Order of the Labor and Industrial Relations Appeals Board and dismiss the claim.

NOTES

1. In M-K Rivers v. Schleifman, 599 P.2d 132 (Alaska 1979), a worker suffered a motorcycle crash while driving to a distant city to cash his pay check. The court affirmed an award of benefits, finding that paying by check benefitted the employer and the off-worksite trip to cash the check was incidental to the employment. Two justices dissented.

Contrary to the principal case, most courts hold that employees who leave the employer's premises on short personal errands are outside the course of employment, even if the employer permits or acquiesces in the activity. Hinkle v. W.C.A.B., 175 Cal.App.3d 587, 221 Cal.Rptr. 40, 43 (1985) denied recovery in a similar check cashing incident, stating, "The essential rule is that an off-duty personal activity, transpiring in an area beyond the employer's dominion and control and yielding neither advantage nor benefit to the employer, is not within the course of employment." See also, McClure v. General Motors, Corp., 408 Mich. 191, 289 N.W.2d 631 (1980), and Corraro's Case, 380 Mass. 357, 403 N.E.2d 388 (1980), denying recovery. Although acknowledging the validity of the "essential rule" of *Hinkle*, a Florida court permitted recovery in a similar case because of an extraordinary risk posed by hazards in the general locality in which the employment was located. Toyota of Pensacola v. Maines, 558 So.2d 1072 (Fla.App.1990). See also St. Anthony Hospital v. James, 889 P.2d 1279 (Okla. App. 1994) (off duty nurse who slipped and fell while entering the hospital where she worked to pick up her pay check on her day off held to be covered by workers' compensation). Hoffmann v. Workers' Compensation Appeal Board, 559 Pa. 655, 741 A.2d 1286 (1999) (Similar facts: benefits approved.) As to other decisions, compare Holditch v. Standard Accident Ins. Co., 208 F.2d 721 (5th Cir.1953) (compensation denied one of several employees taking lunch on premises who was injured while going next door to secure chewing gum for the group) with Prater v. Indiana Briquetting Corp., 253 Ind. 83, 251 N.E.2d 810 (1969) (similar; compensation awarded) and Lanham

v. Department of Environmental Protection, 868 So.2d 561 (Fla. 1st DCA 2004) (compensation awarded to claimant who fell while on a permitted off-premises walk while on short work break).

New Jersey's statute expressly excludes off-work place injuries as follows:

> Employment shall be deemed to commence when an employee arrives at the employer's place of employment to report for work and shall terminate when the employee leaves the employer's place of employment, excluding areas not under the control of the employer; provided, however, when the employee is required by the employer to be away from the employer's place of employment, the employee shall be deemed to be in the course of employment when the employee is engaged in the direct performance of duties assigned or directed by the employer. . . .

[N.J.S.A. 34:15–36.]

Notwithstanding that statute, Sager v. O.A. Peterson Const., Co., 182 N.J. 156, 862 A.2d 1119 (2004), awarded compensation to a worker injured in a vehicle crash returning to the work place from a meal at a local diner. It was September 11, 2001 and the workers were unable to return to their homes because of bridge and tunnel closures in the New York City vicinity. The worker's supervisor had ordered to the workers to take an early supper and return to work.

Similarly, Cooper v. Barnickel Enterprises, Inc., 411 N.J.Super. 343, 986 A.2d 38 (N.J.Super.A.A., 2010), approved an award for an employee who was injured in a car crash driving to a coffee shop during "an extended wait to consult with an expert concerning a work-related issue" at a site where coffee was not available.

2. Most courts also deem employees who take meals off premises on unpaid lunch breaks to be outside the course of employment, both while eating and while proceeding to and from the eating place. The mealtime journey is usually treated like the trip to and from work generally, discussed hereafter. See, e.g., Wallace v. Copiah County Lumber Co., 223 Miss. 90, 77 So.2d 316 (1955). Similarly, if the employee injured off premises during lunch hour can claim one of the exceptions to the general going and coming rule, discussed infra, he will be entitled to compensation.

More generally, if the nature of the employee's duties require substantial adjustment of personal eating habits, as where only a hurried lunch can be taken at varied times and places, off premises injuries have been regarded as within the course of employment. See, e.g., Relkin v. National Transp. Co., 18 A.D.2d 137, 238 N.Y.S.2d 575 (1963) (taxi driver ate in cafeterias); Western Greyhound Lines v. Industrial Accident Comm., 225 Cal.App.2d 517, 37 Cal.Rptr. 580 (1964) (female bus driver assaulted in restaurant); and Pettit v. Keller, 9 Ohio App.2d 91, 223 N.E.2d 67 (1967) (claimant obliged to grab a snack whenever time permitted).

3. The courts are in virtual uniform agreement that an accident occurring on the premises during a lunch hour or recreation or rest period is compensable if it can be attributable to some recognizable hazard in the employment environment and if it happened near the authorized place for eating or recreation. See, e.g., Nicholson v. Industrial Comm., 76 Ariz. 105, 259 P.2d 547 (1953) (compensation awarded to survivors of an employee who had been discharged for the day and was killed by a collapsing platform while eating lunch); and Texas Employers' Ins. Ass'n v. Davidson, 295 S.W.2d 482 (Tex.Civ.App.1956) (compensation awarded employee who slipped on piece of material used in factory while going to garbage can in order to deposit lunch wrappings). It may be immaterial whether the worker is required to eat on the premises or does so by choice. See, e.g., Kennecott Corp., Kennecott Minerals Company Div. v. Industrial Comm., 675 P.2d 1187 (Utah 1983) (compensation awarded survivors of an employee killed while getting a drink of water on employer's premises out of his work area during lunch break; personal comfort doctrine permits recovery for incident that was not so unusual or unreasonable that it could not be considered an incident of employment).

4. The decisions as to lunchtime accidents resulting in part from an employee's desire to satisfy curiosity or for entertainment are also not harmonious. Compare Coates v. J.M. Bucheimer Co., 242 Md. 198, 218 A.2d 191 (1966) (compensation denied employee who explored premises during lunch hour) and McKim v. Commercial Standard Ins. Co., 179 S.W.2d 357 (Tex.Civ.App.1944) (compensation denied hatmaker who was injured when he went downstairs to sales department to purchase a hat) with Dyer v. Sears, Roebuck & Co., 350 Mich. 92, 85 N.W.2d 152 (1957) (compensation awarded employee injured while descending stairs on premises following lunch intending to go to nearby building to pay a bill) and Moore v. Superior Stone Co., 242 N.C. 647, 89 S.E.2d 253 (1955) (compensation awarded employee who experimented with blasting machine during lunch hour and set off three hundred dynamite caps). When compensation is awarded, courts are likely to stress that the employee's mission was in some way beneficial to the employer or that the risk of injury was enhanced by the employment environment. See, e.g., Flamholtz v. Byrde, Richards & Pound, Inc., 37 A.D.2d 645, 322 N.Y.S.2d 382 (1971) (compensation awarded employee injured on way to bank to cash paycheck; mode of payment preferred by employer); Scheffler Greenhouses, Inc. v. Industrial Comm., 66 Ill.2d 361, 5 Ill.Dec. 854, 362 N.E.2d 325 (1977) (compensation awarded employee who swam in pool on premises as relief from humidity); and Turner v. United States Fidelity & Guar. Co., 339 So.2d 917 (La.App.1976) (compensation awarded employee who shot himself playing with coworker's pistol while waiting on premises for lunch whistle; employer had not forbidden or disapproved practice of bringing pistols to premises).

5. Employees who are injured on the employer's premises before and after work while washing, changing clothes, warming themselves and otherwise preparing for beginning or leaving work are often deemed to be

within the course of employment. See, e.g., Montanaro v. Guild Metal Products, 108 R.I. 362, 275 A.2d 634 (1971) (compensation awarded employee who customarily arrived an hour early because of transportation difficulties) and Hill v. Terrazzo Mach. & Supply Co., 279 Minn. 428, 157 N.W.2d 374 (1968) (compensation awarded employee who arrived a few minutes early and fell on premises while leaving to mail letter).

Employees are often deemed to be within the course of employment for a reasonable amount of time needed to leave the premises even after quitting the job or being fired, and some courts have held that terminated employees are within the course of employment when returning to collect unpaid wages. Compare Carter v. Lanzetta, 249 La. 1098, 193 So.2d 259 (1966) (compensation awarded employee who was injured while leaving work premises twenty to thirty minutes after having been fully paid for one-day employment) and Parrott v. Industrial Comm., 145 Ohio St. 66, 60 N.E.2d 660 (1945) (compensation awarded to former employee who was injured on premises when he returned to pick up his final pay check two days after pay day) with Olson v. Hurlbert–Sherman Hotel Co., 210 App.Div. 537, 206 N.Y.S. 427 (1924) (compensation denied employee who returned for pay five days after quitting). Suppose the employee returns for clothes or tools after termination of the contract of hire? See, Johnson v. City of Albia, supra.

4. INJURIES CAUSED BY HORSEPLAY AMONG CO-WORKERS

XENIA RURAL WATER DIST. V. VEGORS

Supreme Court of Iowa, 2010.
786 N.W.2d 250.

STREIT, JUSTICE.

* * *

I. Background Facts and Prior Proceedings.

Norman Vegors worked as a machine inspector for Xenia Rural Water District, a company that installs rural water lines. Vegors was injured at work after a coworker, Casey Byrd, hit him with a pickup truck. Vegors had his hands full and "wiggled [his] butt" at Byrd. Vegors testified that he did so to acknowledge or say hi to Byrd. Vegors then leaned over the bed of his own truck. After this, Byrd attempted to bump Vegors with the mirror of his truck but instead hit Vegors with the truck bed.

Vegors testified that he and Byrd commonly acknowledged each other even when their hands were full, including, for example, waving the boom of the track hoe at the other. Xenia employees testified that Vegors had been involved in a prior incident for which he was disciplined and that he admitted to his supervisor that he and Byrd had just been goofing around.

Vegors sought workers' compensation benefits, and Xenia contested benefits, arguing Vegors was barred from recovering because he engaged in horseplay and asserting the affirmative defense of willful injury. The deputy commissioner held that Xenia, as the employer, had the burden to prove the defense of horseplay. The deputy commissioner found Vegors intended to shake his hind end as a means of communication and not to initiate, instigate, or participate in the horseplay which led to the injury, and, therefore, recovery of workers' compensation benefits was not barred. The commissioner affirmed the decision to award benefits and, although the deputy had not discussed it, separately addressed the affirmative defense found in section 85.16(3) barring compensation when injury is caused by the "willful act of a third party directed against the employee for reasons personal to such employee." The commissioner held the defense did not apply because a coworker is not a third party.

Xenia sought judicial review. The district court addressed the question of whether "the agency erred in finding that petitioners did not meet their burden of proof that the claimant's alleged injury was the result of horseplay, and that the petitioners did not prove an affirmative defense pursuant to Iowa Code § 85.16(3)." The district court reversed and held Vegors was barred from receipt of benefits. Vegors appealed.

* * *

Merits.

A. Burden to Establish Horseplay or Lack Thereof. Xenia, Vegors's employer, argued Vegors cannot be compensated because he engaged in horseplay. The deputy commissioner held that Xenia had the burden to demonstrate horseplay because it is a defense. The deputy commissioner then determined Vegors had not engaged in horseplay. The commissioner affirmed the deputy commissioner but did not address the proper burden. Upon judicial review, the district court reversed the agency and held the claimant bears the burden to demonstrate that the injury arose out of and in the course of employment and therefore, to demonstrate the injury was not the result of horseplay. It appears the district court did not reach an ultimate conclusion on the merits of whether Vegors's alleged horseplay bars recovery because the court went on to hold Vegors's recovery was barred under a separate affirmative defense, which we will address below.

* * *

Prior cases of this court suggest the injured employee must show he or she was not engaged in horseplay as part of the burden to demonstrate the injury arose out of and in the course of employment. See Ford v.

Barcus, 261 Iowa 616, 623, 155 N.W.2d 507, 511 (1968) ("Horseplay which an employee voluntarily instigates and aggressively participates in does not arise out of and in the course of his employment and therefore is not compensable."); Wittmer v. Dexter Mfg. Co., 204 Iowa 180, 185, 214 N.W. 700, 702 (1927) ("We conclude there was evidence supporting the finding of the commissioner that the appellee voluntarily participated in the play—the jostling—that caused his fall and injury, and that the injury did not arise out of his employment.").

These opinions are consistent with treatment of the horseplay issue in other jurisdictions. Some jurisdictions bar compensation for certain types of horseplay based on the "arising out of employment" language. See Lincoln v. Whirlpool Corp., 151 Ind.App. 190, 279 N.E.2d 596, 601 (1972) ("[W]here the 'horseplay' was not acquiesced in by the employer, not a natural condition of the employment, and where, in fact; the employee participated in the 'horseplay,' and was not, therefore, an innocent victim . . . we have consistently denied compensation in such cases for the reason that such activity does not arise out of the employment."); 2 Arthur Larson & Lex K. Larson, Larson's Workers' Compensation Law § 23.07, at 23–13 (2009) [hereinafter Larson's]. Larson's suggests the proper analysis is to look at horseplay as potentially outside the "course" of employment because of a deviation. 2 Larson's § 23.07, at 23–13. We agree the proper analysis is whether the claimant substantially deviated from the course of employment, as will be explored more fully below. Regardless, it is clear that the prohibition on recovery where an injury resulted from the claimant's horseplay stems from the requirement that injuries arise out of and in the course of employment.

Vegors argues that placing the burden upon the claimant to demonstrate that the injury was not the result of horseplay is inconsistent with general legal principles because it requires the claimant to prove a negative. Vegors points to Iowa Rule of Appellate Procedure 6.904(3)(e) which states, "[o]rdinarily, the burden of proof on an issue is upon the party who would suffer the loss if the issue were not established." Vegors contends that if horseplay is not established, the employer will suffer the loss and therefore should bear the burden.

We disagree. The horseplay exception stems from the requirement that the injury arise out of and in the course of employment, and Vegors will bear the loss here if he cannot meet this requirement. Employers may raise any number of arguments to contest an employee's assertion that an injury arose out of and in the course of employment. For example, in Quaker Oats, the employee was injured in a traffic accident after being paged to the plant on a Sunday to fix a mechanical problem. Quaker Oats, 552 N.W.2d at 147. The employer argued that the employee's travel home from the plant was not in the course of employment and that the employee deviated from his employment by taking the more scenic route home. Id. at 150, 153. The employer's arguments were meant to contest whether the injury arose out of and in the course of employment. The burden, however, remained on the employee and did not shift to the employer. Id. at 150.

Similarly, Vegors retains the burden to show his injury arose out of and in the course of employment. His employer, Xenia, argues that he has not met that burden because the injury was the result of horseplay. This argument does not shift the burden to Xenia. . . .

This court has held that horseplay which an employee "voluntarily instigates and aggressively participates in does not arise out of and in the course of his employment." Ford, 261 Iowa at 623, 155 N.W.2d at 511. Not all acts of horseplay or levity will preclude an injured employee from recovery. Instead, a claimant's actions—including horseplay—will bar recovery under the workers' compensation scheme when the claimant substantially deviates from the employment. See Quaker Oats, 552 N.W.2d at 153–54 (noting "injury is not compensable if [claimant] is found to have 'deviated sufficiently from the line of duty so that his or her actions are foreign to the employer's work'" and affirming agency determination of no "substantial deviation from or abandonment of the employment" (quoting Sheerin v. Holin Co., 380 N.W.2d 415, 417 (Iowa 1986)); Eagle–Picher Co. v. McGuire, 307 P.2d 145, 147 (Okla.1957)) ("'This doctrine, that a deviation in a certain limited measure does not take the employee out of the course of employment, is applicable not only to curiosity cases, horseplay and assaults, but also to foolhardy acts.'" (quoting Secor v. Penn Serv. Garage, 35 N.J.Super. 59, 113 A.2d 177, 181 (1955)))

Innocent employees who are injured as the result of another's horseplay may recover. It is "clearly established that the non-participating victim of horseplay may recover compensation." 2 Larson's § 23.02, at 23–2; see also Coleman v. Armour Swift–Eckrich, 281 Kan. 381, 130 P.3d 111, 114–16 (2006) (adopting rule that non-participating victim of horseplay may recover based on "overwhelming weight of . . . authority in our sister states and current legal commentary").

For those employees who have initiated or are participating in horseplay, courts and commentators have suggested four considerations for determining whether the horseplay is a deviation from the course of employment that bars recovery:

> "(1) the extent and seriousness of the deviation (2) the completeness of the deviation (i.e., whether it was commingled with the performance of duty or involved an abandonment of duty) (3) the extent to which the practice of horseplay had become an accepted part of the employment, and (4) the extent to

which the nature of the employment may be expected to include some such horseplay."

Phillips v. John Morrell & Co., 484 N.W.2d 527, 530–31 (S.D.1992) (quoting 1A Larson's Workers' Compensation Law § 23.00 (1990) (now 2 Larson's § 23.01, at 23–2)) (holding slaughterhouse assembly line worker who threw hog sperm cords at a coworker could recover for a serious stabbing injury sustained from the coworker). Courts have also held that the causal connection between a claimant's own conduct and an injury may be severed where there is a passage of time and the employee has returned to the course of employment. See Baird v. Travelers Ins. Co., 98 Ga.App. 882, 107 S.E.2d 579, 583 (1959) (upholding determination that claimant was entitled to compensation after being injured by supervisor's horseplay where claimant's own horseplay had taken place an hour earlier in a separate location); Rex–Pyramid Oil Co. v. Magan, 287 Ky. 459, 153 S.W.2d 895, 899 (1941) (upholding award of benefits to claimant who engaged in a waterfight on employer's property and was afterwards hit by a car while crossing a highway to perform work at another site).

The inquiry should focus on the actions of the claimant.

The substantial character of a horseplay deviation should not be judged by the seriousness of its consequences in the light of hindsight, but by the extent of the work-departure in itself. This is not always easy to do, especially when a trifling incident escalates or explodes into a major tragedy. 2 Larson's § 23.07[3], at 23–23. The character of Vegors's action of shaking his rear end—and not the serious injury resulting from being hit with a truck—must be analyzed to determine whether it is a deviation sufficient to bar recovery.

It cannot be determined as a matter of law that Vegors voluntarily instigated or aggressively participated in horseplay to an extent that prevents compensation. There is evidence in the record that the horseplay was initiated only by Byrd or that any action by Vegors was an insubstantial deviation from his employment. Vegors testified that he acknowledged Byrd with his hind end and that he did not intend to dare Byrd to hit him with a truck, otherwise he would not have turned around and focused his attention on his work prior to being hit. The commissioner made a determination that Vegors meant to shake his posterior as a method of acknowledging his coworker. Vegors's butt wiggle considered in isolation could be thought a "harmless act of levity." Baltimore & Ohio R.R. v. Taylor, 589 N.E.2d 267, 274 (Ind.Ct.App.1992) (affirming trial court determination that "[t]he fact that he was relieving the tedium of his job by a harmless act of levity does not take him outside the scope of his employment"). Additionally, it is claimed the action of Vegors's coworker Byrd was grossly disproportionate to Vegors's own action and the proper focus is on Vegors's action. See Liberty Nw. Ins.

Corp. v. Johnson, 142 Or.App. 21, 919 P.2d 529, 530, 533 (1996) (holding claimant who made a joking comment to a coworker and was injured when coworker twisted him to the ground in a spirit of fun was entitled to compensation); Mustard v. Indus. Comm'n, 164 Ariz. 320, 792 P.2d 783, 784–85 (1990) (holding compensation was not barred because the claimant did not substantially deviate from her employment when the claimant joked that a coworker had dropped his teeth, ran when he good-naturedly chased her, and was hit in the back with a hammer when the two collided).

Because we reverse the agency determination regarding the proper allocation of the burden of proof, we remand to the agency to allow the agency to apply the proper burden to the evidence. Cf. Kohlhaas v. Hog Slat, Inc., 777 N.W.2d 387, 393 (Iowa 2009) ("Although it could be argued there is substantial evidence in the record that Kohlhaas's current condition does not warrant an increase in compensation, it is fair to conclude the commissioner's determination may have been influenced by the language in Acuity we have just disavowed. In that we have clarified the requirements for a review-reopening petition, we reverse and remand. . . ."). The commissioner should evaluate whether Vegors's action was a substantial deviation from his work based on the four factors identified above and applying the proper burden.

NOTES

1. Horseplay decisions tend to fall into two categories: those in which the claimant was an innocent victim who did not participate in the prank; and those in which the victim instigated the horseplay or actively participated in it. Claimants in the first category are almost always compensated unless the employee is deemed to be outside the course of employment for some independent reason. See, e.g., Leonbruno v. Champlain Silk Mills, 229 N.Y. 470, 128 N.E. 711 (1920) and Sizemore v. State Workmen's Compensation Com'r, 160 W.Va. 407, 235 S.E.2d 473 (1977) (employee waiting to leave work premises sustained a playful wallop on the head). Some decisions seem to deny recovery for all horseplay injuries regardless of who instigated it. See, e.g., Kight v. Liberty Mut. Ins. Co., 141 Ga.App. 409, 233 S.E.2d 453 (1977) (compensation denied to worker hurt when co-worker pulled a chair from under him) and Walsh Construction Co. v. Hamilton, 185 Ga.App. 105, 363 S.E.2d 301 (1987) (compensation denied to worker hurt in fight with co-worker who had accused claimant of begging food).

Was Burns v. Merritt Engineering, 302 N.Y. 131, 96 N.E2d 739 (1951) correctly decided? There, a worker checking out from work was handed a bottle labeled "Barclay's Gin" and invited to take a drink. Consuming alcohol on the job violated company policy. The worker stepped out of sight and drank from the bottle. The bottle contained carbon tetrachloride, not gin, which the offering worker knew, and the substance severely injured Burns' internal organs. Benefits were awarded and a Court of Appeals majority affirmed on the grounds that the "claimant here is in very much the same position as the victim of an unprovoked assault." One justice dissented, saying, "It impresses me as a principle turned topsy-turvy to sanction payment of compensation to an employee who performs—or believes he is performing—an act that calls for summary dismissal."

2. Some courts brand instigating claimants as "aggressors," similar to fight situations, and deny them compensation unless one of several conflicting and ill-defined exceptions applies. Compare Jones v. Hampton Pontiac, 304 S.C. 440, 405 S.E.2d 395 (1991) (compensation denied to worker hurt while demonstrating a karate kick to a co-worker) with Industrial Com'r v. McCarthy, 295 N.Y. 443, 68 N.E.2d 434, 435 (1946), which announced an exception that permits a horseplay instigator or participant to recover if the practice has "long been part and parcel, an incident, of the employment." This was applied to award compensation in Montpetit v. Standard Shade Roller Corp., 277 App.Div. 1066, 100 N.Y.S.2d 640 (1950) (practice of throwing water was known to the employer, although workers had been warned not to engage therein; compensation allowed). This so-called "New York" exception merges into an even more liberal view many courts apply to relatively minor horseplay episodes. As one court said:

> For the purposes of the compensation act the concept of course of employment is more comprehensive than the assigned work at the lathe. It includes an employee's ministrations to his own human needs: he must eat; concessions to his own human frailties: he must rest, must now and then have a break, and he sometimes, even on the job, plays practical jokes on his fellows. Course of employment is not scope of employment. The former, as the cases so clearly reveal, is a way of life in a working environment. If the injury results from the work itself, or from the stresses, the tensions, the associations of the working environments, human as well as material, it is compensable. Why? Because those are the ingredients of the product itself. It carries to the market with it, on its price tag stained and scarred, its human as well as its material costs. So says the statute. It does not become us to ignore its plain commands. * * *

Crilly v. Ballou, 353 Mich. 303, 326, 91 N.W.2d 493, 505 (1958). Compare Carvalho v. Decorative Fabrics Co., 117 R.I. 231, 366 A.2d 157 (1976) (airhose playfully inserted in worker's rectum; compensation awarded; immaterial whether victim was or was not a participant) with City of Miami v. Granlund, 153 So.2d 830 (Fla.1963) (police officer shot himself in the head with a pistol he belived to be unloaded: compensation denied; deviation from job too flagrant). As the doctrine has matured, courts are inclined to apply the four-part test approved in Vegors. See, e.g., Petrie v. General Motors Corp., 187 Mich.App. 198, 466 N.W.2d 714 (1991) (compensation denied with regard to worker who left his work area, climbed onto overhead hoist where he had no business, and was electrocuted).

3. Should an injury be regarded as arising out of the employment if it resulted from a practice unknown to the employer but that might have been expected under the circumstance of the employment? See Johnson v. Loew's, Inc., 7 A.D.2d 795, 180 N.Y.S.2d 826 (1958), affirmed 8 N.Y.2d 757, 201 N.Y.S.2d 775, 168 N.E.2d 111 (1960) (employee injured while attempting to shoot paper clip with rubber band; employer charged with knowledge that messenger boys engaged in the practice; compensation awarded). Compare Hayes Freight Lines, Inc. v. Burns, 290 S.W.2d 836 (Ky.1956) (worker injured by horseplay with fire crackers; compensation to be awarded if employer knew of and acquiesced in the practice), and Lubrano v. Malinet, 65 N.Y.2d 616, 491 N.Y.S.2d 148, 480 N.E.2d 737 (1985) (Teenage gas station attendant awarded compensation for burns he suffered when he intentionally threw a lighted match into a bucket that had gasoline residue in it. The bucket exploded. This was a "trick" that he had seen other attendants accomplish without causing an explosion.)

In Jones v. Dougherty, 412 S.W. 3d 188 (Ky. App. 2012) a school principal brought a snake to school to show to a science class. Before going to class, the principal entered the plaintiff's room to show her the snake. Unknown to the principal, the plaintiff had a morbid fear of snakes and suffered severe injuries from the encounter. The plaintiff brought a tort action and alleged the defendants had committed a malicious intentional act of aggression, thus taking the principal out of the course and scope of employment and removing workers' compensation immunity. The trial court granted defendants' summary judgment motion on the ground that the principal's act was merely horseplay and within the principal's course and scope of employment. The appellate court affirmed and added that the actor must have acted with hostile intent to constitute aggression.

5. INJURIES CAUSED BY EMPLOYEES' WILFUL MISCONDUCT AND VIOLATIONS OF RULES AND INSTRUCTIONS

DANIEL V. DEPARTMENT OF CORRECTIONS

Supreme Court of Michigan, 2003.
468 Mich. 34, 658 N.W.2d 144.

WEAVER, J.

In this case we address whether plaintiff, who was disciplined by the Department of Corrections (his employer) for sexually harassing female attorneys, and who suffered depression as a result of the disciplinary proceedings, is barred from worker's compensation benefits pursuant to M.C.L. § 418.305. MCL 418.305 provides, "If the employee is injured by reason of his intentional and wilful misconduct, he shall not receive compensation under the provisions of this act." We hold that M.C.L. § 418.305 precludes benefits in this case and, therefore, we reverse the judgment of the Court of Appeals and reinstate the Worker's Compensation Appellate Commission's (WCAC's) order denying plaintiff benefits.

I

Plaintiff worked as a probation officer with defendant Department of Corrections beginning in 1984. His employment required him to attend probation violation hearings held in circuit court several times a month to interact with defense attorneys representing probationers.

In February 1995, a female defense attorney filed a complaint with plaintiff's immediate supervisor alleging that plaintiff sexually harassed her in August 1994 and February 1995. The attorney testified that it was plaintiff's failure to take her rejection of his advances seriously that prompted her to file her complaint.[1] The attorney's complaint was soon followed by allegations of sexual harassment by plaintiff from three other female defense attorneys.

Plaintiff's supervisor initiated an investigation into the complaints. Over the following months, she interviewed the attorneys and other witnesses. When questioned, plaintiff denied all the allegations. At the close of her investigation, plaintiff's supervisor recommended that a disciplinary conference be held regarding five separate counts of sexual harassment.

. . . Ultimately, plaintiff was disciplined for the two counts of sexual harassment arising from the August 1994 and February 1995 incidents. He was suspended for ten days without pay.

After his return to work in August 1995, plaintiff testified that he felt harassed by both his immediate supervisor and the defense attorneys who had accused him of sexual harassment. He felt "out of control," and, on January 27, 1996, began being treated by psychologist Daniel DeWitt. Dr. DeWitt diagnosed plaintiff as suffering from depression caused by the disciplinary investigation and proceedings as well as the subsequent stresses at work. . . . In June 1996, plaintiff filed a claim for worker's compensation benefits premised on a mental disability arising from the disciplinary proceedings. During the time leading to the trial, plaintiff saw three other doctors at the state's request.

After four days of trial between March and September of 1998, the magistrate concluded that the "discipline, and post-discipline employment events up to February 2, 1996, contributed in a significant manner to [plaintiff's] development of a disabling condition of depression, anxiety, and uncontrolled anger." The magistrate did not address M.C.L. § 418.305

[1] The attorney alleged that in August 1994 plaintiff obscenely propositioned her. She testified that when she rejected plaintiff's advances, he told her that they would have to be "discreet" since he was married with children. . . .

or make specific findings regarding whether plaintiff's conduct was intentional and wilful or otherwise not compensable under that section. Rather, the magistrate's conclusion that plaintiff was entitled to benefits was based on the finding that plaintiff's injury arose out of his employment pursuant. . . . However, the magistrate commented:

> It is clear to me that Plaintiff's problems started with his discipline for the improprieties of which he was accused. It is difficult to have much sympathy for this claimant, since he brought these troubles on himself by his own misconduct. But compensation, like the rain, falls on the just and the unjust alike.

The magistrate awarded plaintiff a closed award of worker's compensation benefits.

Defendant appealed, raising M.C.L. § 418.305 as an affirmative defense. The WCAC agreed with the essence of the magistrate's finding that the plaintiff's injury was self-inflicted, but concluded that M.C.L. § 418.305, "puts up an umbrella to prevent compensation from falling on this particular 'unjust' claimant." The WCAC found that plaintiff was on notice of the rules that prohibited the conduct for which he was ultimately accused and disciplined, but had done "it anyway, in a consistent and repeated pattern over a long period of time." The WCAC concluded that plaintiff's injury arose from his own intentional and wilful misconduct and, therefore, that M.C.L. § 418.305 precluded an award of benefits.

Plaintiff appealed and, as will be discussed below, the Court of Appeals reversed the WCAC decision in a two-to-one decision. The Court of Appeals majority concluded that plaintiff's acts did not rise to the level of intentional and wilful misconduct contemplated by M.C.L. § 418.305. 248 Mich.App. 95, 638 N.W.2d 175 (2001).

* * *

We granted defendant's application for leave to appeal. 466 Mich. 889, 649 N.W.2d 71 (2002).

II

We review de novo questions of law. . . .

III

The focus of our inquiry is solely on the proper application of M.C.L. § 418.305 As quoted above, M.C.L. § 418.305 provides, "If the employee is injured by reason of his intentional and wilful misconduct, he shall not receive compensation under the provisions of this act." This provision has remained essentially unchanged since it was first adopted by the

Legislature in 1912 as part of the original worker's compensation legislation. See 1912 (1st Ex Sess) PA 10, part 2, § 2.

The Court of Appeals majority below divided its analysis of M.C.L. § 418.305 into two parts. It focused first on whether plaintiff's mental injury arose "by reason of" his misconduct, and, second, on whether plaintiff's misconduct was "intentional and wilful". We address and reject the panel majority's analysis of each of these questions.

A

"By reason of"

The panel majority first focused on what it termed the question of causation, i.e., whether plaintiff was injured "by reason of" his intentional and wilful misconduct. The majority rejected the WCAC's finding that plaintiff's injury was "the direct result of his intentional and wilful misconduct," by concluding that the question of "who started it?" was inapposite to the intention of the WDCAWDCA. 248 Mich.App. at 103, 638 N.W.2d 175. The majority concluded that plaintiff's injury was "too attenuated for [it] to have occurred 'by reason of' his acts," *id.*, p. 102, 638 N.W.2d 175, and that plaintiff "was not injured at the time of his act," but was "injured solely because of his status as an employee. . . ." *Id.*, p. 103, 638 N.W.2d 175.

To support its conclusion, the majority analogized to two cases in which fighting or horseplay between employees escalated and resulted in physical injuries. See, e.g., *Crilly v. Ballou*, 353 Mich. 303, 91 N.W.2d 493 (1958), and *Andrews v. Gen. Motors Corp.*, 98 Mich.App. 556, 296 N.W.2d 309 (1980).[8] Our review of those cases reveals that they do not support the panel majority's causation analysis. Indeed, neither case, nor any other we have found, addressed whether the injuries were "by reason of" misconduct pursuant to M.C.L. § 418.305. Rather, the causation inquiry in those cases, and our case law, pertains to the question whether such misconduct can be said to have *arisen out of the course of the employment* as required by M.C.L. § 418.301. . . .[9]

---

[8] Crilly involved an injury caused by employees throwing shingles and nails at one another. The Court conducted an exhaustive review of cases involving on-the-job "sportive assaults" and concluded that injuries received are not outside the realm of the course of employment and were compensable as long as they did not rise to the level of intentional and wilful misconduct. Crilly, *supra*, pp. 326–327, 91 N.W.2d 493. Andrews involved injuries sustained during a fight between employees. The Court of Appeals affirmed the Worker's Compensation Appeal Board's award of benefits, concluding that the conduct did not involve "such a degree of 'moral turpitude' . . . so as to preclude" benefits. Andrews, *supra*, p. 561, 296 N.W.2d 309.

[9] Whether misconduct that causes an injury arose out of and in the course of employment under M.C.L. § 418.301(1) is a *preliminary* question that must be answered affirmatively before the issue whether that misconduct was "intentional and wilful" in light of M.C.L. § 418.305 is reached. . . .

Significantly, defendant no longer disputes, and the magistrate, the WCAC, and the Court of Appeals agreed, that plaintiff's mental disability arose out of and in the course of his employment pursuant to M.C.L. § 418.301(1). Thus, the majority's reliance on *Crilly* and *Andrews* was misplaced.

Moreover, we decline to impose a more direct causation requirement than that plainly expressed by the statute. "By reason of" is defined as "[b]y means, acts, or instrumentality of." Black's Law Dictionary (6th ed). As noted by the Court of Appeals dissenter, the phrase does not require that an injury arise contemporaneously with the misconduct. Rather, as stated by Judge O'Connell:

> [I]t cannot be disputed that [plaintiff's] misconduct was the starting point for the resultant disciplinary proceedings that ultimately caused his injury. Had plaintiff not engaged in sexual harassment, he would not have been subjected to the disciplinary proceedings, and he would not have been suspended from his job.... [T]he disciplinary proceedings, from which plaintiff's mental disability arose, flowed directly and predictably from plaintiff's misconduct as surely as night follows day. [248 Mich.App. at 115–116, 638 N.W.2d 175.]

We agree ... that the record amply supports the WCAC's finding that plaintiff was injured "by reason of" his intentional and wilful misconduct. Because the magistrate failed to address the applicability of § 305 to plaintiff's claim, the WCAC acted within its authority in engaging in supplemental fact-finding and in concluding that plaintiff's injury—although it may well have arisen out of employment events—was nevertheless barred because it occurred by reason of his intentional and wilful misconduct. Therefore, as constrained by our limited judicial appellate review, we abide by the findings of fact by the WCAC. *Mudel, supra*, p. 700, 614 N.W.2d 607.

B

"Intentional and Wilful"

[The Court of Appeals majority] reasoned that plaintiff's conduct, though "voluntary, crude, and unprofessional," did not rise to "intentional and wilful misconduct" as it has been interpreted in this state. 248 Mich.App. at 104, 638 N.W.2d 175.

Our case law has consistently distinguished "intentional and wilful misconduct" from acts of negligence and gross negligence. Benefits are awarded despite M.C.L. § 418.305 where an employee is injured by his own negligence.... However, this Court has held that benefits are precluded under the statute where an employee was injured by conduct of a quasi-criminal nature. *Fortin v. Beaver Coal Co.*, 217 Mich. 508, 510,

187 N.W. 352 (1922). *Fortin* described "quasi-criminal" conduct as "involving the intentional doing of something with knowledge that it is dangerous and with wanton disregard of consequences. . . ." *Id.*

Although plaintiff denies that he made the comments of which he is accused, his denials were not believed at any level reflected in the record. At the disciplinary conference, "a strong basis" was found to support the allegations. The magistrate found that plaintiff had "brought these troubles on himself by his own misconduct." The WCAC found that "[p]laintiff knew what he was doing was wrong" and yet he persisted. Even the Court of Appeals majority called the plaintiff's behavior "voluntary, crude, and unprofessional." 248 Mich.App. at 104, 638 N.W.2d 175. Nevertheless, the majority decided that plaintiff's behavior did not rise to a level of moral turpitude that could be called "intentional and wilful." *Id.*

In our view, the WCAC's conclusion that plaintiff's misconduct was voluntary is amply supported by the record. His repeated acts of sexual harassment were well beyond the realm of mere negligence or gross negligence. That said, it has long been understood that the question whether misconduct is "intentional and wilful" is one of fact. . . .[11] Thus, the Court of Appeals panel majority's rejection of the WCAC's findings regarding whether plaintiff's misconduct was "intentional and wilful" and its substitution of its own fact-finding on the issue does not comport with its limited judicial appellate review. We, therefore, reverse the judgment of the Court of Appeals.

C

We note one final disagreement with the panel majority's reasoning. Regarding whether the plaintiff knew his conduct was prohibited, the panel majority found persuasive the fact that, although plaintiff's comments were alleged to have been made over several years, he "suffered no adverse consequences from his behavior" until 1995. 248 Mich.App. at 103, 638 N.W.2d 175. It reasoned that "[p]laintiff's history of conduct in this case indicates that the rule was not strictly enforced and there are no facts in the record indicating otherwise." *Id.*, p. 105, 638 N.W.2d 175. While this Court has concluded that M.C.L. § 418.305 does not operate to preclude benefits where an employee was injured while violating a work rule that had not been enforced by the employer, . . . the record in this case reflects that plaintiff's immediate supervisor had conducted several investigations into other alleged violations of work

---

[11] In Crilly, *supra*, p. 327, 91 N.W.2d 493, we noted:

> [T]his exclusion of acts of a degree of moral turpitude, it will be observed, is by the legislature itself, not a judicial retrogression to principles of tort. *Further than this in definition we do not attempt to go.* The precise future line of demarcation will be marked out, in the traditional manner, *by the case-to-case decision.* [Emphasis supplied.]

rules by other employees during her supervisory tenure. More critically, that plaintiff's accusers did not file formal complaints triggering the enforcement process is not demonstrative of the defendant's enforcement, or lack thereof, of workplace rules.

IV

For the reasons stated, we reverse the judgment of the Court of Appeals and reinstate the WCAC order denying benefits to this plaintiff.

MICHAEL F. CAVANAGH, J., dissenting.

. . . I agree with the Court of Appeals majority that the connection between plaintiff's acts and his injury is too attenuated for the injury to have occurred "by reason of" his acts. The majority rejects this position, fearing it would impose a requirement that the injury arise contemporaneously with the employee's misconduct. However, saying that plaintiff's acts of sexual harassment and his injury are "too attenuated," does not necessarily impose a requirement that the injury arise contemporaneously with the misconduct.

In this case, plaintiff's injury followed not only plaintiff's own conduct, but also action taken by defendant. One must consider not only the amount of time that elapsed between the employee's conduct and the injury, but also the events that occurred during that time. The disciplinary proceedings conducted by defendant in this case occurred after plaintiff's misconduct, but before his mental injury. Therefore, one could conclude, as the magistrate did, that the discipline was the cause of plaintiff's mental injury.

* * *

Because I would affirm the judgment of the Court of Appeals and reinstate plaintiff's benefits, I, respectfully, dissent.

NOTES

1. A number of compensation statutes expressly deny compensation of injuries caused by the "willful misconduct" of an employee. These provisions usually create affirmative defenses, imposing the burden of proof on the employer, and, under the liberal construction of the statutes in favor of their remedial purposes, seldom defeat claims unless the employee violated an established safety rule. For example, courts frequently hold that even gross negligence does not amount to willful misconduct. Allen v. Columbus Mining Co., 207 Ky. 183, 268 S.W. 1073 (1925) (employee lay down for nap very near a fire on an operating forge; compensation awarded), and Lumbermens Mut. Cas. Co. v. Amerine, 139 Ga.App. 702, 229 S.E.2d 516 (1976) (worker injured while playfully riding on the rear wheel of bicycle; compensation awarded). Neither do courts treat inexcusable ignorance or bad judgment as willful misconduct. See, e.g., Tyree v. Commonwealth, 164 Va. 218, 179 S.E. 297

(1935) (willful misconduct "involves the idea of premeditation and determination to do the act, though known to be forbidden"). The Georgia Supreme Court summed up the requirements of this defense as follows:

> 1. (a) The general rule is that mere violations of instructions, orders, rules, ordinances, and statutes, and the doing of hazardous acts where the danger is obvious, do not, without more, as a matter of law, constitute wilful misconduct.
>
> (b) Such violations or failures or refusals generally constitute mere negligence, and such negligence, however great, does not constitute wilful misconduct or wilful failure or refusal to perform a duty required by statute, and will not defeat recovery of compensation by the employee or his dependents.
>
> (c) Wilful misconduct, or wilful failure or refusal to perform a duty required by statute, is more than negligence or even gross negligence; it involves conduct of a criminal or quasi-criminal nature, the intentional doing of something, either with the knowledge that it is likely to result in serious injury, or with the wanton and reckless disregard of its probable consequences.
>
> (d) Wilful misconduct includes all conscious or intentional violations of definite law or rules of conduct, as distinguished from inadvertent, unconscious, or involuntary violations.
>
> 2. (a) Whether the employee was guilty of wilful misconduct, or was guilty of wilful failure or refusal to perform a duty imposed on him by statute, [are] questions of fact for the [Board of Worker's Compensation], and the findings of the [Board] upon these questions are final, and will not be disturbed where there is evidence to support them.

Roy v. Norman, 261 Ga. 303, 404 S.E.2d 117, 118 (1991) (worker burned while making up fire with gasoline in paper cup not disqualified for willful misconduct).

2. Nevertheless, a deliberate violation of a reasonable safety rule that causes an injury of the type the rule was designed to prevent is frequently held to be willful misconduct. Consequently, some decisions deny compensation to a disobedient employee even though the violation related to the method of doing assigned work and the employee was plainly within the course of employment at the time. See, e.g., Mills v. Virginia Electric Co., 197 Va. 547, 90 S.E.2d 124 (1955) (injury resulted from employee's failure to use rubber gloves when handling high tension wire; compensation denied). Do these decisions comport with the basic premises of the compensation laws?

3. A recurring fact pattern involves workers who misrepresent their physical condition in order to secure employment and later suffer an injury on the job. A typical case involves a worker who failed to disclose prior back injuries on the employment application and then re-injured the back while lifting a heavy object. Professor Larson advocates denying compensation if

three factors exist: (1) the employee must have knowingly and wilfully made a false representation as to physical condition; (2) the employer must have relied upon the false representation and this reliance must have been a substantial factor in the hiring; and (3) there must have been a causal connection between the false representation and the injury. 1C A. Larson, Workmen's Compensation § 47.53 (1991). Some courts have incorporated this defense under the general "wilful misconduct" workers' compensation provisions. See, e.g., Shaw's Supermarkets, Inc. v. Delgiacco, 410 Mass. 840, 575 N.E.2d 1115 (1991) (collecting cases). Other courts treat the fraud as rendering the "contract of hire" voidable. See, e.g., Georgia Electric Co. v. Rycroft, 259 Ga. 155, 378 S.E.2d 111 (1989). Still others refuse to recognize this defense in the absence of a more specific statutory provision. See, e.g., Kraus v. Artcraft Sign Co., 710 P.2d 480 (Colo.1985).

Florida has enacted a statute that deprives an injured worker of all benefits for an otherwise compensable injury if the worker has been found to have committed fraud to obtain one specific unjustified benefit. § 440.09(4) Fla. Stat. The statute has been upheld against constitutional challenge. Medina v. Gulf Coast Linen Services, 825 So.2d 1018 (Fla. 1st DCA 2002), rev. den., 842 So.2d 845 (Fla.2003).

4. Some statutes deny or limit compensation to employees who willfully refuse to obey a safety regulation or willfully fail to use a safety device furnished by the employer. Some of these provisions augment a willful misconduct provision (e.g., Alabama, Delaware, Georgia, South Dakota, Tennessee, Virginia, West Virginia), and others serve as a partial substitute for it (e.g., Florida, Indiana, Kansas, Louisiana, Oklahoma, South Carolina). Under some statutes, both safety rule violations and failures to use safety devices are employer defenses (e.g., Alabama, Florida, Georgia, Indiana, Louisiana, Virginia, and West Virginia), and under others only failure to use a safety device is a defense (e.g., Delaware, Kansas, Oklahoma, South Dakota, and Tennessee). Another group of statutes does not deny compensation because of employees' misconduct, but reduces the amount of compensation awarded (e.g., ten percent in North Carolina and South Carolina; fifteen percent in Kentucky, Missouri, Utah, and Wisconsin; fifty percent in Colorado). Failure of an employee to comply with or report violations of OSHA standards will not be deemed to be willful misconduct if the employer has not enforced the standard as a specific employment rule. See, e.g., Wyle v. Professional Services Industries, Inc., 12 Va.App. 684, 406 S.E.2d 410 (1991).

Mitchell v. Fayetteville Public Utilities, 368 S.W.3d 442 (Tenn. 2012) made a decision against the liberal trend. There the Tennessee Supreme Court applied the statute to disqualify a worker who had intentionally removed his gloves because they encumbered his work. The court applied a four part test: " (1) the employee's actual, as opposed to constructive, notice of the rule, . . . (2) the employee's understanding of the danger involved in violating the rule . . . (3) the employer's bona fide enforcement of the rule . . . and (4) the employee's lack of a valid excuse for violating the rule." Id., 368

S.W.3d at 453. The court referred to Guico v. Excel Corp., 260 Neb. 712, 619 N.W.2d 470, 476–77 (2000); Holscher v. Valley Queen Cheese Factory, 2006 SD 35, ¶ 49, 713 N.W.2d 555, 568–69 (S.D.2006); Saunders v. Indus. Comm'n, 301 Ill.App.3d 643, 235 Ill.Dec. 490, 705 N.E.2d 103, 106 (1998) and Spaulding v. Alliant Foodservice, Inc., 13 Neb.App. 99, 689 N.W.2d 593, 603 (2004) in support of its position.

5. Many statutes couple the willful misconduct disqualification with disqualifications based upon intoxication. Ordinarily, the employer's proof of mere intoxication at the time of the injury will not suffice to invoke this disqualification unless the employer also proves that the intoxication was a cause of the injury. See, e.g., Dobbs v. Liberty Mutual Insurance Company, 811 S.W.2d 75 (Tenn.1991) and Wyle v. Professional Services Industries, Inc., 12 Va.App. 684, 406 S.E.2d 410 (1991). The same requirement has been applied to proven drug use under general willful misconduct standard. See, e.g., Thomas v. Helen's Roofing Company, Inc., 199 Ga.App. 161, 404 S.E.2d 331 (1991) (presence of cocaine in worker's urine not of itself sufficient to prove fall from roof was caused by willful misconduct).

6. Under statutes that have no "willful misconduct" provisions, courts rarely, if ever, deny compensation merely because an employee violated an employer's safety rule. 1 A. Larson, Workmen's Compensation Law (1990) § 33.10. Moreover, an employee's violation of a rule that is frequently disregarded and not diligently enforced by employers will not be deemed to be "willful." See, e.g., Sloss–Sheffield Steel & Iron Co. v. Nations, 236 Ala. 571, 183 So. 871 (1938). In short, the decisions that treat failure to use a safety device as disqualifying "willful misconduct" are rare. Often, even intentional avoidance of the use of such a device is not deemed to be "willful" in this sense. For example, courts will not regard the failure to use a defective device as willful, nor the non-use of one the employee believes to be defective. See, e.g., Herring v. Hercules Powder Co., 222 La. 162, 62 So.2d 260 (1952) (the claimant disconnected airbrakes because they frequently became loose over rough terrain). Nor will the employee's non-use of a device under particular circumstances that would create new perils or interpose a serious obstacle to the effective discharge of duties be deemed to be disqualifying behaviour. See, e.g., American Steel Foundries v. Fisher, 106 Ind.App. 25, 17 N.E.2d 840 (1938). Courts also limit the reach of this defense by treating equipment such as a vehicle's horn, brakes or even its sides as something other than safety devices. See, e.g., Cole v. List and Weatherly Construction Co., 156 So. 88 (La.App.1934) (a ladder was a device for ascending and descending and not primarily for safety). The cases that do deny compensation under this defense require the employer to show that the failure to use the device bore a clear causal relation to the injury or death, e.g., Herring v. Hercules Powder Co., supra, and that the employer furnished the device and made its availability known to the employee. See, e.g., Armour & Co. v. Little, 83 Ga.App. 762, 64 S.E.2d 707 (1951) (failure to give express warning that a rake was a safety device defeated the defense) and Nashville, Chicago & St. Louis Ry. v. Wright, 147 Tenn. 619, 250 S.W. 903 (1923) (posting notice pertaining to use

of goggles was not enough to deny compensation if the employee had not read it).

7. Under statutes that have no "willful disregard" and violation of safety act provisions, an employee's violation of a safety statute has no effect upon the compensability of an injury. Should it? Even if the statute contains an express provision as indicated in the principal case, the *willful* violation requirement often makes the defense unavailable. Accord with principal case: Philbrick Ambulance Service v. Buff, 73 So.2d 273 (Fla.1954) (driver of ambulance injured while running red light; compensation awarded). Nevertheless, an egregious violation may defeat compensation. See, e.g., Young v. American Ins. Co., 110 Ga.App. 269, 138 S.E.2d 385 (1964) (employee injured in collision while driving in excess of 100 m.p.h. in a 70 m.p.h. speed zone, compensation denied because of willful violation).

8. Willful misconduct disqualifications do not usually deny recovery in the absence of proof that the misconduct was a specific cause of the injury. For example, although New York disqualifies injuries suffered while "performing an illegal act," a claimant who was injured while driving without a license was awarded benefits because there was no proof that the unlicensed status resulted from a lack of driving skill that caused the accident. Anderson v. William Cohen Iron Works, 38 N.Y.2d 511, 381 N.Y.S.2d 457, 344 N.E.2d 389 (1976). Similarly, a Massachusetts statute that disqualifies a worker injured by reason of "wilful misconduct" does not apply unless the misconduct is a cause of the injury. See, e.g., Shaw's Supermarkets, Inc. v. Delgiacco, 410 Mass. 840, 575 N.E.2d 1115 (1991) (worker who misrepresented physical condition on job application will be disqualified under the provision only if the worker knowingly and wilfully made a false statement, the employer relied on the false statement in the hiring, and there is a causal connection between the false statement and the injury).

9. Some states require employers to pay greater benefits when a worker's injury resulted from an employer's intentional failure to comply with safety standards. In Ohio, such a provision has been afforded constitutional status, as follows:

> Such board shall have full power and authority to hear and determine whether or not an injury, disease or death resulted because of the failure of the employer to comply with any specific requirement for the protection of the lives, health or safety of employees, enacted by the general assembly or in the form of an order adopted by such board, and its decision shall be final; and for the purpose of such investigations and inquiries it may appoint referees. When it is found, upon hearing, that an injury, disease or death resulted because of such failure by the employer, such amount as shall be found to be just, not greater than fifty nor less than fifteen per centum of the maximum award established by law,

shall be added by the board, to the amount of the compensation that may be awarded on account of such injury, disease, or death, ...

OH Const. Art. II, §35. Applied, Hewitt v. L.E. Myers Co., 134 Ohio St.3d 199, 981 N.E.2d 795 (2012).

6. INJURIES SUFFERED BY EMPLOYEES WHILE COMING TO AND GOING FROM WORK

JUMPP V. CITY OF VENTNOR

Supreme Court of New Jersey, 2003.
177 N.J. 470, 828 A.2d 905.

PORITZ, C.J.

In this case, the Court must determine whether a city worker, whose daily duties required him to visit various sites within the city's boundaries, is eligible for workers' compensation benefits when he was accidentally injured during the workday but while on a personal errand. We hold that generally there must be a finding that the off-premises employee is performing his or her work responsibilities at the time of the injury in order for the injury to be compensable. We also hold that minor deviations from the employee's prescribed responsibilities survive the 1979 amendments to the workers' compensation statute. On the undisputed facts in this record, however, we conclude that petitioner cannot obtain benefits under the statute. We therefore affirm the rulings of the courts below.

I

Petitioner Robert Jumpp, Jr., was employed by the City of Ventnor (City) as a pumping station operator. His job was to monitor twice daily the electrical, chlorination and other systems at each of the six water wells, towers and sewerage pumping stations owned and operated by his employer. Because those facilities were dispersed throughout the City, Jumpp used a City-owned vehicle when traveling to each worksite to perform his duties. On a typical day, petitioner arrived at the municipal public works office at 7:00 a.m. and by 8:30 a.m., after completing some paperwork and answering telephones, proceeded to his first location. Ordinarily, he completed his initial inspection of all six sites by mid-morning and then repeated his rounds during the afternoon. As he was continually in transit, petitioner had no set time for lunch or a coffee break, and therefore, without objection from his direct supervisor Thomas Klein, he was permitted to make brief stops at local establishments for food and beverages or to use the restroom. Petitioner also stopped each day to retrieve his personal mail from a local post office located on the route to one of his job sites, a habit that Klein knew about and allowed. The day of his accident, May 5, 1998, Jumpp followed his usual routine.

On the way to his fourth scheduled inspection, he parked his municipal vehicle around the corner from the post office and left it running while he went in to check his personal mail. As he was returning to the vehicle, however, petitioner slipped and fell on a nearby driveway, suffering a fractured pelvis and severe leg injuries that required hospitalization and the insertion of a pin into his left fibula.

At trial, Jumpp testified that he frequented the post office on a daily basis with the knowledge and permission of his supervisor. Klein agreed, stating that it was an unwritten policy to allow employees "who are coming and going continually" to make brief stops at local establishments in the City to attend to personal business. Despite that testimony, on April 9, 2001, Judge Terry Dailey issued an order and written opinion dismissing petitioner's claim. Although Judge Dailey found that Jumpp was "authorized" to make the post office stop, and that the stop was only a "minor deviation from his responsibilities," the judge concluded that petitioner's injuries were not compensable because he was engaged in a personal errand and not the "direct performance of duties assigned or required by [his] employer." N.J.S.A. 34:15–36.The Appellate Division affirmed Judge Dailey's ruling and rejected petitioner's contention that he is eligible for workers' compensation because his brief visit to the post office constituted but an " 'incidental deviation' " from his duties. *Jumpp v. City of Ventnor*, 351 N.J.Super. 44, 49, 796 A.2d 945, 948 (2002) (citation omitted). The court explained "that by requiring [an] employee [to] be engaged in the 'direct performance' of work-related duties, the Legislature intended to 'sharply curtail' compensation for off-premises accidents." In light of that objective, and based on consistent precedent of the Appellate Division, the court held that "an employee who deviates from the temporal and spacial limits of his . . . employment tasks for the sole purpose of engaging in a personal errand or activity is simply not 'engaged in the *direct* performance of duties' " as required by the statute. Id. at 52,796 A.2d at 950 (emphasis in original). Because Jumpp sustained injuries while attending to a personal errand "neither incidental to his . . . employment, . . . nor beneficial to the employer," the court concluded that he was not entitled to compensation. Id. at 52–53, 796 A.2d at 950.We granted certification.

. . . We now affirm.

II

The Workers' Compensation Act (hereinafter Act) requires employers to compensate employees for accidental injuries "arising out of and in the course of employment." *N.J.S.A.* 34:15–7. The Act describes employment as commenc[ing] when an employee arrives at the employer's place of employment to report for work and terminat[ing] when the employee leaves the employer's place of employment, excluding areas not under the control of the employer; provided, however, when the employee is required by the employer to be away from the employer's place of employment, the employee shall be deemed to be in the course of employment when the employee is engaged in the direct performance of duties assigned or directed by the employer; but the employment of employee paid travel time by an employer for time spent traveling to and from a job site or of any employee who utilizes an employer authorized vehicle shall commence and terminate with the time spent traveling to and from a job site or the authorized operation of a vehicle on business authorized by the employer. Travel by a policeman, fireman, or a member of a first aid or rescue squad, in responding to and returning from an emergency, shall be deemed to be in the course of employment.

[*N.J.S.A.* 34:15–36.]

That definition of employment was part of a package of amendments passed in 1979 and signed into law in 1980. Those amendments were designed to "provid[e] genuine reform and meaningful cost containment for New Jersey employers from unjustified workers' compensation costs that [in the late 1970s were] among the highest in the nation." . . . As the Appellate Division observed below, *Jumpp*, . . . the Legislature sought to reduce costs by, among other things, "sharply curtail[ing compensability for] off-premises accidents." . . . Specifically, that language . . . removed from compensability certain cases heretofore held compensable where special hazard existed *en route* to the employer's premises, off-premises injuries sustained during lunch hour and injuries sustained while traveling at the employer's direction but deviating from a direct line of travel to pursue a purely personal activity.

The legislative history of the Act in respect of compensability for off-premises accidents is instructive. Prior to the 1979 amendments, the Act did not define employment but "simply provided for compensation when employees were injured or killed in accidents 'arising out of and in the course of employment.'" *Livingstone v. Abraham & Straus, Inc.*, 111 N.J. 89, 95, 543 A.2d 45, 49 (1988) (quoting L. 1911, c. 95, § 7, now codified at N.J.S.A. 34:15–7). As a result, "it devolved on the courts to develop principles capable of distinguishing between" compensable and noncompensable injuries. *Id.* at 95,543 A.2d at 49. In *Livingstone, supra*, Justice Stein discussed the development of bases for decision making during that period as follows:

> [I]t was decided that an accident arises in the course of employment "if it occurs while the employe[e] is doing what a man so employed may reasonably do within a time during which he is employed, and at a place where he may reasonably be during that time." Further, . . . an accident arises out of

> employment "when it results from risks reasonably incidental to employment," meaning risks that either "belong to" or are "connected with what a workman has to do in fulfilling his contract of service."

[*Id.* at 95–96, 543 A.2d at 49 (citations omitted).]

Those principles led to the adoption of the "going and coming" or "premises" rule, "which ordinarily precluded benefits for 'injuries sustained during routine travel to and from an employee's regular place of work.' " . . . Under that rule, an employee who had not yet arrived on the employer's premises, or who had departed the premises at the conclusion of a scheduled work period, was not deemed to be "in the course of employment" for the purposes of *N.J.S.A.* 34:15–7. *Ibid.* (citation omitted).

Over time, however, rigid application of the going and coming rule "produced many harsh results" inconsistent with the Act's remedial purpose, leading our "courts to carve out numerous exceptions to it." *Hammond v. The Great Atl. & Pac. Tea Co.*, 56 N.J. 7, 11, 264 A.2d 204, 206 (1970). . . . Thus, we brought within the scope of the Act off-premises injuries sustained by employees who were "directly involved in completing employer related tasks," *Livingstone, supra*, 111 N.J. at 97, 543 A.2d at 50, or engaged in activities approved by their employers and reasonably "incidental to the employment," *Strzelecki v. Johns–Manville Prod. Corp.*, 65 N.J. 314, 320, 322 A.2d 168, 171 (1974). *See, e.g., Watson, supra*, 74 N.J. at 161–63, 376 A.2d at 1218–19 (holding that employee injured on errand to retrieve required uniform was entitled to compensation); *Levine v. Haddon Hall Hotel*, 66 N.J. 415, 420, 332 A.2d 193, 195 (1975) (holding that employee, whose employer diverged from normal practice of providing parking facilities for employees, was entitled to compensation for injuries suffered while crossing street to workplace).

Also during that period, the Court recognized that an on-premises employee might not be "actually working" at the time he or she was injured but that in certain circumstances compensation nonetheless should be available. *Secor v. Penn Serv. Garage*, 19 N.J. 315, 321, 117 A.2d 12, 15 (1955). Under the minor deviation rule, an employee does not become ineligible for workers' compensation simply because he or she stopped work to have a smoke, or to get some fresh air, or to use the telephone, or to satisfy other human needs incidental to his being at his place of employment[. I]t is clear that injuries which occur during such minor deviations are generally sufficiently related to the employment to call for compensation. Similarly employees may stop work to satisfy their interest in a passing parade or in a strange object or their curiosity generally[. S]o long as the deviation is minor it should be disregarded.

[*Ibid.* (citations omitted).]

As broadly formulated, the minor deviation rule in effect considered personal habits or errands, such as smoking or making a phone call, to be in the "course of employment" even though, unlike the indispensable human functions of eating and using the lavatory, employees need not engage in such activities to perform their work duties adequately. A body of case law developed in which injuries suffered by employees engaged in personal activities were found to be compensable when they occurred both on and off the employer's premises, even though the injury was unconnected or only tenuously related to the employee's job duties. . . .

As noted above, in 1979, the Legislature for the first time defined on-premises and off-premises employment. On-premises employment (as its terminology directly implies), begins when the employee gets to the place where he or she works (to the premises), and ends when the employee leaves that place; off-premises employment, however, relates to the doing of the work "assigned or directed by the employer." *N.J.S.A.* 34:15–36. The employee who is "required by the employer to be away from the employer's place of employment [is] in the course of employment," *ibid.*, when he or she is actually carrying out the work assignment and is therefore eligible for benefits if injured at the point. Consonant with that language, and aware of the Legislature's desire to limit the availability of benefits for off-premises injuries, *Napier, supra*, 96 *New Jersey Lawyer* at 18, our courts have since interpreted the statute to bar compensation for injuries sustained in certain activities that prior to the 1979 amendments were deemed within the scope of employment.

Thus, in *Ward v. Davidowitz*, 191 N.J.Super. 518, 468 A.2d 250 (App.Div.1983), an employee was injured in an automobile accident that occurred while she was returning to work from her lunch break. *Id.* at 520, 468 A.2d at 251. Although acknowledging that prior decisions of this Court had considered midday lunch breaks part of the workday, and thus an exception to the going and coming rule, *id.* at 522–23, 468 A.2d at 252–53 (contrasting *Hornyak, supra*, and *Wyatt v. Metro. Maint. Co.*, 74 N.J. 167, 376 A.2d 1222 (1977), with *N.J.S.A.* 34:15–36), the Appellate Division nonetheless held that, after the passage of *N.J.S.A.* 34:15–36, off-premises "lunch break accidents" are no longer compensable "as a matter of law." *Id.* at 524, 468 A.2d at 253. Examining the language and history of Section 36, the court concluded that it was that "specific type of claim which the Legislature intended to eliminate or curtail by enacting a specific definition of employment." *Id.* at 523, 468 A.2d at 252. In the court's view, the statutory definition of employment is keyed to the elimination of an employer's responsibility for accidents occurring in areas not under his control *unless* the employee is required by the employer to be away from the employer's place of employment. In that event the determining element of compensability rests upon the direct performance of duties assigned or directed by the employer rather than the place of employment.

[*Id.* at 523–24, 468 A.2d at 252–53 (emphasis in original).]

Similarly, in *Mangigian, supra*, the Appellate Division upheld the denial of compensation to an employee who was struck by an automobile when she came back at 10:00 p.m. to her motel room after purchasing supper for herself and her supervisor. 205 N.J.Super. at 423–24, 501 A.2d at 179–80. At the time, the employee was responsible for investigating and testing security systems in various retail stores in Rahway, New Jersey. *Id.* at 424, 501 A.2d at 180. When performing their duties, she and her supervisor resided in a motel to which they usually returned at about 8:00 p.m. each evening. *Ibid.* Upholding the denial of compensation, the court observed that the employee had "fully completed her work assignment and was safely ensconced in the motel before she decided to embark upon a purely personal errand." *Id.* at 428, 501 A.2d at 182. The court concluded that she was not in " 'the direct performance . . . of duties assigned [to her] or directed by [her] employer' " for the purposes of N.J.S.A. 34:15–36. *Id.* at 427, 501 A.2d at 181–82. . . .

III

We hold that when an employee is assigned to work at locations away from "the employer's place of employment," eligibility for workers' compensation benefits generally should be based on a finding that the employee is performing his or her prescribed job duties at the time of the injury. Case law subsequent to the 1979 amendments has recognized the legislative intent to focus on the performance of the work, thereby limiting the reach of the workers' compensation statute. In furtherance of that "clear legislative mandate sharply curtailing compensability for off-premises accidents," *Jumpp*, supra, 351 N.J.Super. at 52, 796 A.2d at 949, the Appellate Division held in each of the cases we have reviewed that Section 36 barred recovery because the activities were personal in nature and concerned neither "duties assigned nor directed," nor "business authorized," by the employer. . . . As recognized by the panel here, *Jumpp*, supra, 351 N.J.Super. at 51, 796 A.2d at 949, the rationale of those cases represents a significant departure from our pre-1979 jurisprudence wherein the minor deviation rule was applied broadly in off-premises cases as a means of enlarging the scope of the statute. . . .

That is not to say that off-premises employees are to be treated differently from on-premises employees. Simply put, on-premises employees are not within the scope of employment until they arrive at the employer's place of business, and they shed that status when they depart. Because off-premises employees may not report to a single "premises," the statute provides that they are to be compensated only for accidents occurring in the direct performance of their duties. Those are *not* different standards but only descriptors of the same standard in different contexts. Employees who are where they are supposed to be, doing what they are supposed to be doing, are within the course of employment whether on-or off-premises, except when they are commuting. . . . Nothing in *N.J.S.A.* 34:15–36 suggests that the Legislature intended to create a higher bar for determining scope of employment for off-premises employees than for those whose regular work location is at the employer's place of business.

Nor do we suggest that the minor deviation rule was eliminated by the 1979 amendments. Off-premises employees enjoy the same ability to deal with certain basic needs enjoyed by on-premises employees such as phone calls to babysitters and physicians as well as coffee and lunch breaks. Although the line is difficult to draw, those minor deviations are different in kind from shopping excursions during lunch hour or a visit to a travel agent to plan a vacation, even when the agent works in the same building as the employee seeking benefits. Whether the employer allowed the employee to perform a personal errand during his or her workday does not alter the analysis. In cases involving an alleged minor deviation, the question is not whether the off-premises employee was "satisfying a personal need, the completion of which is neither incidental to his . . . employment . . . nor beneficial to the employer," *ibid.*, but rather, whether that employee has embarked on a personal errand that would have been compensable if carried out by an on-premises employee.

We agree with the Appellate Division, then, that whether "petitioner . . . worked on the road . . . [or] from a specified site [ ] is not significant." *Jumpp, supra*, 351 N.J.Super. at 52, 796 A.2d at 950. We also agree that petitioner's "deviation was no different from the office worker who takes an afternoon break and crosses the street to pick up his personal mail at the local post office." Ibid. Neither deviation would be compensable.

IV

For the foregoing reasons, the decision of the Appellate Division is affirmed.

LONG AND ZAZZALI, JJ., dissenting.

We agree with the majority that:

> [O]n-premises employees are not within the scope of employment until they arrive at the employer's place of business, and they shed that status when they depart. Because off-premises employees may not report to a single "premises," the statute provides that they are to be compensated only for accidents occurring in the direct performance of their duties. Those are *not* different standards but only descriptors of the same standard in different contexts. Employees who are where they are supposed to be, doing what they are supposed to be doing, are within the

course of employment whether on-or off-premises, except when they are commuting. Nothing in *N.J.S.A.* 34:15–36 suggests that the Legislature intended to create a higher bar for determining scope of employment for off-premises employees than for those whose regular work location is at the employer's place of business.

No one, including the majority, would argue that an on-premises employee who walks across the room to the mail basket, retrieves a personal letter addressed to him at work, and is injured on the way back to his desk, should be denied coverage. That fact pattern is analogous to what occurred here. Jumpp had permission from his employer to routinely stop to retrieve his mail from a post office located on his route. On the day in question, he exited his employer's vehicle, which he left running, and entered the post office to get his mail. As he returned to the vehicle, he slipped and fell on the ground, fracturing his pelvis. *Ante* at 474, 828 A.2d at 907.

[The dissenters would award benefits under the "minor deviation" doctrine.]

NOTES

1. Jumpp applied a revised statute designed to supplant decisions that had awarded compensation under a liberal construction of the earlier version. Contrast Kolomiets v. Syncor International Corporation, 252 Conn. 261, 746 A.2d 743 (2000), which compensated injuries suffered by a delivery man who departed from his route to fetch his driving license which he had inadvertently left at home. The Connecticut court held the "minor deviation" did not defeat coverage.

2. As indicated in the principal case, injuries suffered while the employee is going to or coming from work are generally regarded as outside the course of the employment. Within the course is commonly held to begin and end at the threshold of the employer's establishment. See, e.g., Wausau Underwriters Ins. Co. v. Potter, 807 S.W.2d 419 (Tex.App.1991) (injuries sustained on public streets when going to or coming from work are not compensable); Constantineau v. First Nat. Bank in Albuquerque, 112 N.M. 38, 810 P.2d 1258 (App.1991) (compensation denied to employee injured while walking to place of work from city public parking facility not provided especially for employer's workers); and Tate v. Bruno's Inc./Food Max, 200 Ga.App. 395, 408 S.E.2d 456 (1991) (compensation denied employee injured after leaving work from shopping mall store while driving out of shopping mall parking lot where both shoppers and store employees parked). With these compare Arrington v. Goldstein, 23 N.J.Super. 103, 92 A.2d 630 (1952) (compensation awarded employee who reached employer's premises and was

blown back into street by eighty mile per hour gust of wind), Owens v. Southeast Arkansas Transportation Co., 216 Ark. 950, 228 S.W.2d 646 (1950) (compensation awarded employee struck while dashing across the street to catch bus), and Husted v. Seneca Steel Service, 50 A.D.2d 76, 375 N.Y.S.2d 911 (1975) (compensation awarded employee preparing to enter employer's parking lot, who was impelled into the lot and injured there by a collision in public way).

Many decisions extend the "threshold" of the employer's premises concept to permit recovery in situations far removed from the employee's work premises. See, e.g., Board of Trustees v. Novik, 87 Md.App. 308, 589 A.2d 976 (1991) (compensation awarded to employee injured while walking on public street toward work place from parking lot provided by her employer); Briggs v. Passaic Bd. of Educ., 23 N.J.Super. 79, 92 A.2d 513 (1952) (closed public street adjacent to school regarded as school premises); and Smith v. Industrial Accident Comm., 18 Cal.2d 843, 118 P.2d 6 (1941) (entire island road system under control of employer, regarded as premises for employee who worked at various places on roads). In line with extending the meaning of where the threshold is, some decisions hold that an employee who is on private premises near the place of employment at the time of injury is entitled to compensation. See, e.g., Cerria v. Union News Co., 31 N.J.Super. 369, 106 A.2d 745 (1954), awarding compensation to an employee who was injured in a railroad terminal building where his employer leased space and operated a concession and Simkins v. General Motors Corporation, 453 Mich. 703, 556 N.W.2d 839 (1996) awarded compensation for an injury suffered when a worker fell near the employer's premises. The court stated this rule: "an employee is injured in the course of his employment while traveling to or from work when either (1) the injury occurred on property owned, leased, or maintained by the employer, or (2) the injury occurred while the employee was traveling on a reasonably direct path between the worksite and an employee parking lot owned, leased, maintained by the employer." The particular case was remanded for additional fact findings.

3. The doctrine most commonly employed to permit recovery for coming and going injuries is to treat risks of travel as risks of the employment if the risk exposes the worker to a threat of danger greater than that to which the general traveling public is exposed. See, e.g., Cudahy Packing Co. of Nebraska v. Parramore, 263 U.S. 418, 44 S.Ct. 153, 68 L.Ed. 366 (1923); Jaynes v. Potlatch, 75 Idaho 297, 271 P.2d 1016 (1954), and Toyota of Pensacola v. Maines, 558 So.2d 1072 (Fla.App.1990). These decisions award compensation to employees injured by some abnormal risk in the public road or public transportation system that the employees of the particular employer must confront more frequently than most members of the general travelling public, usually because of location.

Many decisions pinpoint some specific hazardous highway condition such as a railway crossing or an area of highly congested traffic. Moreover, when the exposure of the worker to some particular travel danger is dramatic and obvious, courts tend to ignore the fact that the place of accident was some distance removed from the premises. Compare Diffendaffer v. Clifton, 91 Idaho 751, 430 P.2d 497 (1967) (compensation awarded reforestation project worker injured while proceeding to work on isolated and dangerous narrow mountain road several miles from place of work) and Bechtel Corp. v. Winther, 262 Ark. 361, 556 S.W.2d 882 (1977) (compensation awarded employee drowned in lake while attempting to cross causeway one quarter mile from premises), and Kramer v. Palm Beach County, 978 So.2d 836 (Fla. 1st DCA 2008) (worker who tripped on a pile of hurricane debris while walking to work from a temporary parking site in a mall was entitled to the special hazard exception to the going and coming rule) with Quarant v. Industrial Comm., 38 Ill.2d 490, 231 N.E.2d 397 (1967) (compensation denied teacher injured in congested traffic on way to work) and Eisenberg v. Industrial Comm., 65 Ill.2d 232, 2 Ill.Dec. 366, 357 N.E.2d 533 (1976) (compensation denied welfare worker assaulted near entrance of work premises in dangerous neighborhood). Nevertheless, many courts insist that the place of injury or the source of danger, although not necessarily on the employer's premises proper, must be immediately adjacent to them, and many announce that workers' compensation does not protect coming-and-going workers on the entire journey merely because it is dangerous. See, e.g., Boone v. Industrial Comm., 12 Ariz.App. 521, 472 P.2d 490 (1970) (compensation denied elevator man obliged to pass through dangerous neighborhood on way to work; assaulted eleven blocks from building where employed).

Conversely, unless the predicament of the worker can in some way be carved out from the general hazards of travel, compensation will be denied even though the place of accident is immediately adjacent to the premises. See, e.g., Ocean Pavilion v. Betancourt, 578 So.2d 467 (Fla.App.1991) (compensation denied worker hurt at place of special danger by causative force having nothing to do with special danger); and Templet v. Intracoastal Truck Line, Inc., 255 La. 193, 230 So.2d 74 (1969) (compensation denied worker for injury suffered in collision on public street while making left turn into employer's premises where there was no special hazard). Contrast Greydanus v. Industrial Accident Comm., 63 Cal.2d 490, 47 Cal.Rptr. 384, 407 P.2d 296 (1965) (identical facts, compensation awarded). The decisions disagree as to whether the danger must lie on the only available route to the employer's premises, whether it must lie on the most conveniently and frequently used route, or whether it is sufficient that the employee uses the dangerous route with the tacit consent of the employer. Compare Collier v. B.F. Goodrich Co., 90 Ohio App. 181, 104 N.E.2d 600 (1950) (safe route provided by employer; employees, however, regularly used railroad right of way as approach; compensation denied), with Sokolowski v. Best Western, 813 P.2d 286 (Alaska 1991) (compensation awarded employee for injury suffered while jaywalking at dangerous place, but only because of the absence of any reasonably safe and convenient alternative route to work) and Doyle v. Penton Lumber Co., 56 So.2d 774 (La.App.1952) (compensation awarded employee who took seldom used short cut along railroad right of way).

4. A number of statutes embody one of several variations of "going and coming" rules. For example, the Wisconsin statute provides:

> 2. Any employee going to and from his or her employment in the ordinary and usual way, while on the premises of the employer, or while in the immediate vicinity thereof if the injury results from an occurrence on the premises, any employee going between an employer's designated parking lot and the employer's work premises while on a direct route and in the ordinary and usual way, or any fire fighter or municipal utility employee responding to a call for assistance outside the limits of his or her city or village, unless that response is in violation of law, is performing service growing out of and incidental to employment.
>
> 3. An employee is not performing service growing out of and incidental to his or her employment while going to or from employment in a private or group or employer-sponsored car pool, van pool, commuter bus service or other ride-sharing program in which the employee participates voluntarily and the sole purpose of which is the mass transportation of employees to and from employment.

Wis.Stat.Ann. 102.03. A provision added to the Kansas statute during the time legislatures were "tightening up" workers' compensation statutes in the final decade of twentieth century provides:

> The words "arising out of and in the course of employment" as used in the workers compensation act shall not be construed to include injuries to the employee occurring while the employee is on the way to assume the duties of employment or after leaving such duties, the proximate cause of which injury is not the employer's negligence. An employee shall not be construed as being on the way to assume the duties of employment, if the employee is a provider of emergency services responding to an emergency.

K.S.A. 44–508(f) The final sentence of this provision was enacted as an amendment to the first. Despite the fact that the accident in Estate of Soupene v. Lignitz, 265 Kan. 217, 960 P.2d 205 (1998) occurred after the first portion of the statute was enacted but before the final portion was, the Kansas supreme court held that the final sentence merely clarified but did not change underlying law and, thus, upheld a decision that the highway crash death of an unpaid voluntary firefighter who was on the way to a fire was compensable under the statute.

Does your statute have a provision such as these? Do the approaches of these statutes lessen the scope of dispute?

5. Colorado applies a "quasi-course of employment doctrine" that covers new injuries suffered by an employee while traveling to and from medical visits required by a covered injury. Turner v. Industrial Claim Appeals Office of the State of Colorado, 111 P.3d 534 (Colo.App.2005),

discusses the cases applying this doctrine and extends it to include an injury suffered by an employee while traveling to receive a vocational rehabilitation evaluation the employer was not required to supply. Nevertheless, *Kelly v. Industrial Claim Appeals Office*, 214 P.3d 516 (Colo. App. 2009) held that a substantial deviation for another purpose from the expected route took the employee out of the "quasi-course" and denied recover. The Colorado supreme court declined to review the decision. Kelly v. Western Eagle County Hospital District, 2009 WL 2357736 (Co. 2009).

COMMENTARY

The decisions have widely acknowledged four general exceptions to the coming and going rule.

1. *Going to and Coming from Work, Off Premises, Special Errand.* Once an employee enters employment at one site, subsequent trips between separated work sites during the work day are usually deemed to be within the course. See, e.g., Hinkle v. Lexington, 239 N.C. 105, 79 S.E.2d 220 (1953) (cemetery caretaker on way to funeral establishment to determine whether there were any graves to be dug); and Wilson v. Rowan Drilling Co., 55 N.M. 81, 227 P.2d 365 (1950) (head driller had duty to secure transportation for other drillers from nearby town to drill site; injured while going from town to drill site; no payment for transportation and no payment for travel time; compensation awarded).

Similarly, the trip from home to work or return may in some cases be regarded as a substantial part of the duties to be performed by the worker, especially when the worker has no fixed first work site. See, e.g., Guest v. Workmen's Comp. Appeals Bd., 2 Cal.3d 670, 87 Cal.Rptr. 193, 470 P.2d 1 (1970) (police officer injured on trip from home to place of special assignment rather than to usual duty station); Le Vasseur v. Allen Electric Co., 338 Mich. 121, 61 N.W.2d 93 (1953) (electrician temporarily laid off, received call from employer to do a special job at a school; injured en route from home); Bengston v. Greening, 230 Minn. 139, 41 N.W.2d 185 (1950) (bookkeeper with regular hours called by employer for emergency on Saturday, which was not ordinarily a work day; injured returning home after alighting from car in front of her home); and Briggs v. American Biltrite, 74 N.J. 185, 376 A.2d 1231 (1977) (employee injured en route to work pursuant to overtime call, where such calls were infrequent). Contrast Moosebrugger v. Prospect Presbyterian Church of Maplewood, 12 N.J. 212, 96 A.2d 401 (1953) (sexton injured on way to open church at night for group meeting; compensation denied); Phillips v. Fitzhugh Motor Co., 330 Mich. 183, 46 N.W.2d 922 (1951) (employee, with no regular hours, injured on way home from visit to office initiated because of pressing work; compensation denied); Lyons v. Ford Motor Co., 330 Mich. 684, 48 N.W.2d 154 (1951) (employee killed on way home after working overtime; compensation denied); and Foster v. Brown Transport

Corp., 143 Ga.App. 371, 238 S.E.2d 738 (1977) (on-call employee injured while en route to answer a call to duty; compensation denied).

Employees who are regularly engaged in travelling or have no fixed place for the performance of their duties are sometimes regarded as within the course of their employment from the moment they leave home for work until the moment they return. Compare Bickley v. South Carolina Elec. & Gas Co., 259 S.C. 463, 192 S.E.2d 866 (1972) (lineman called out to make emergency repairs wherever needed; awarded compensation); and Sentara Leigh Hosp. v. Nichols, 12 Va.App. 841, 407 S.E.2d 334 (1991) (compensation denied to homecare nurse injured while en route to patient's home on ground that mere absence of regular workplace did not create exception to going and coming rule); and, Matter of Glickman v. Greater New York Taxpayers, 305 N.Y. 431, 113 N.E.2d 548 (1953) (compensation denied claims investigator, whose duties were performed in various neighboring areas, who was killed while returning to work area from vacation home to resume duties).

2. *Riding in Vehicle Supplied by Employer.* Where the employer undertakes to transport the employee to and from work the journey is usually deemed to be within the course of employment. See, e.g., Hansen v. Estate of Harvey, 119 Idaho 333, 806 P.2d 426 (1991) (compensation awarded when employee was killed when employer's truck taking him to work site ran off highway); Neyland v. Maryland Cas. Co., 28 So.2d 351 (La.App.1946) (employer provided bus and charged employees fare; could have discontinued at any time; compensation awarded for accident while riding in vehicle); and Katz v. Katz, 137 Conn. 134, 75 A.2d 57 (1950) (employer regularly transported employee home in company vehicle; employee was injured while attempting to ride public bus on one occasion company vehicle was not available; compensation awarded). Contrast, White v. State, 338 Mich. 282, 61 N.W.2d 31 (1953) (employer furnished employee car for duties and permitted employee to drive it to and from home; compensation denied for injury suffered on trip home); and Gwin v. Liberty Northwest Ins. Corp., 105 Or.App. 171, 803 P.2d 1228 (1991) (compensation denied to worker injured while travelling in company truck for a weekend at home from a distant worksite where the worker was on a six month assignment; worker was free to bring his own car on the assignment and used employer's truck with permission for personal convenience only).

Occasional casual transportation may not come within the exception to the coming and going rule. Compare Makal v. Industrial Comm., 262 Wis. 215, 54 N.W.2d 905 (1952) (employee injured while in his own car proceeding to secure employer's car which he was obliged to drive to work; compensation denied), and Thompson v. Bradford Motor Freight Line, 148 So. 79 (La.App.1933) (implied understanding that employee could ride home on any of employer's trucks that might happen to be going in his direction, but no undertaking to provide regular transportation; compensation awarded).

3. *Payment by Employer for Time of Travel or Travel Expense.* When the employer pays the employee for the time consumed by travel to and from work or pays the travel expenses, the journey is ordinarily regarded as within the course of employment. See, e.g., Provident Life & Accident Ins. Co. v. Barnard, 236 Va. 41, 372 S.E.2d 369 (1988) (compensation paid to worker in travelling to first work site when employer paid mileage expenses); Cardillo v. Liberty Mut. Ins. Co., 330 U.S. 469, 67 S.Ct. 801, 91 L.Ed. 1028 (1947) (car pool arrangement; fact that wages were not being paid the decedent at time of accident immaterial); In re Jensen, 63 Wyo. 88, 178 P.2d 897 (1947) (employer paid one employee a daily amount to bring fellow employees to work in his car; employee being so transported entitled to compensation); O'Reilly v. Roberto Homes, 31 N.J.Super. 387, 107 A.2d 9 (1954) (employee paid six dollars for extra night job; actual work consumed only fifteen to thirty minutes, but travel time consumed an hour; no specific agreement as to payment for travel; compensation awarded); Griffith Const. Co. v. Workmen's Compensation Appeals Bd., 9 Cal.App.3d 606, 88 Cal.Rptr. 346 (1970) (workers in remote desert area were allowed subsistence pay; justified conclusion that pay contemplated expense of travel to and from work even though accommodations were available at work site; compensation awarded); and Scott v. Foodarama Supermarkets, 398 N.J.Super. 441, 942 A.2d 107 (2008) (Employee who received payment for gasoline but no wages for coming-and-going travel denied compensation.)

The decisions vary on compensation for injuries suffered during deviations from paid travel to or from work. Compare Dooley v. Smith's Transfer Co., 26 N.J.Misc. 129, 57 A.2d 554 (1948) (employee injured on highway leading to home ten hours after leaving premises and after having engaged in many personal activities; compensation denied) with Reading & Bates, Inc. v. Whittington, 208 So.2d 437 (Miss.1968) (employee drinking while driving home; stopped, went behind car to relieve himself; stepped into hole; compensation awarded).

KAPLAN V. ALPHA EPSILON PHI SORORITY

Supreme Court of Minnesota, 1950.
230 Minn. 547, 42 N.W.2d 342.

MATSON, JUSTICE.

Certiorari to review an order of the industrial commission denying compensation on the ground that relator's injury did not arise out of and in the course of her employment.

Relator, Dora Kaplan, was employed as house mother for the respondent Alpha Epsilon Phi Sorority. She lived in the sorority house, which is located near the University of Minnesota campus in Minneapolis. Girls who come from homes outside the city live and regularly take their meals in the sorority house. Other members from the Twin Cities area eat occasional meals at the house. Relator, who was subject to call 24 hours a day, performed duties akin to those of a mother in looking after her home and family. She ordered the food, supervised the preparation of meals and household cleaning, acted as a chaperon, hostess, confidante and adviser for the girls, and was responsible for the observance of reasonable hours.

Relator sustained her injury on the evening of October 31, 1947, after she had left the sorority house, which is located on Tenth avenue southeast and Fifth street. She walked on the west side of Tenth avenue until she reached Fourth street, where she proceeded to cross to the east side of Tenth avenue. As she was about to step up on the opposite Tenth avenue curb, which had been greased by Halloween pranksters, she slipped, fell, and broke her hip. Relator testified that at the time she was on her way to Grays Drug Store located about four blocks to the east at the corner of Fourteenth avenue southeast and Fourth street to purchase bandages to replenish the supply which she maintained as part of the sorority house first-aid kit, and that she intended, after making such purchase, to take a streetcar to attend religious services at Temple Israel, where she had been a communicant for 20 years.

1. Although the evidence will reasonably sustain a finding that relator's intended trip to Temple Israel was a personal mission and not a mission undertaken as part of her duties as spiritual supervisor for the girls or for the benefit of the sorority generally in cultivating favorable public relations with the parents of present and future sorority members, the decision of the industrial commission must be reversed and the matter remanded for a rehearing, in that the findings, taken as a whole, were made under an erroneous application of the law. Where an award or denial of compensation has been made through a misapprehension or misapplication of a controlling principle of law, the case may be remanded to the commission for rehearing. Hogan v. Twin City Amusement Trust Estate, 155 Minn. 199, 193 N.W. 122; Klika v. Independent School Dist. No. 79, 161 Minn. 461, 202 N.W. 30; 6 Dunnell, Dig. & Supp., § 10426.

The commission's majority opinion, in reversal of the referee's findings, after determining that relator's dominant purpose in leaving the sorority house was to go on a personal mission to Temple Israel, held that the accident did not arise out of and in the course of her employment, although at the time of her injury she may have been on her way to the drugstore to buy bandages for her employer. Apparently, the commission assumed that, if the trip to the drugstore was but an incidental part of her personal activities that evening, it necessarily followed that any injury sustained on that trip did not arise out of her employment. The application of the dominant-motive or dominant-purpose rule does not call for a construction which arbitrarily holds the entire journey of an employe to be wholly "fish or fowl" without regard to whether a deviation or detour is involved. An errand or movement of an employe, the purpose of which is dominantly personal, *may* involve a deviation or detour which is made *necessary* by the employer's business; and, if an injury occurs during such deviation or detour, it arises out of and in the course of the employment. In a number of cases we have so held. Confusion has apparently resulted from the application of the dominant-purpose test in Olson v. Trinity Lodge, 226 Minn. 141, 146, 32 N.W.2d 255, 258, wherein we said: "If a movement on the part of an employe is undertaken from a mixture of motives, the major motive or dominant purpose thereof, as a general rule, controls in determining whether an injury sustained in the course of such movement arises out of and in the course of his employment."

The authoritative scope of the dominant-purpose rule becomes clear if we keep in mind the controlling facts to which it was applied in the Olson decision. In that case, the employe had but a *single destination, namely, the lodge building*, to which he was en route for the two distinct or dual purposes of (1) personally enjoying the comforts of his private rent-free room, and (2) tending the employer's furnace. If either purpose had been eliminated, the trip to the lodge building would, nevertheless, have been made because of the remaining purpose. It therefore became pertinent to ascertain which purpose was dominant. Obviously, the dominant purpose was the employment, in that the cold January weather created an immediate and compelling necessity for tending the furnace, which had not been taken care of since morning. No deviation or detour was involved, and therefore the dominant-purpose test, without qualification, was both sufficient and decisive. Cf. Erickson v. Erickson & Co., 212 Minn. 119, 2 N.W.2d 824.

2–3. In keeping with our former decisions, where a principal movement or errand of an employe is accompanied by a deviation or detour therefrom, the dominant-purpose test should be used for the limited function of determining, when the principal movement or errand is undertaken from a mixture of motives, whether such principal movement or errand belongs to the employer or to the employe personally.

Of course, if the employment creates the necessity for the principal errand in the sense that it would not have been made in the absence of such necessity, the principal errand unquestionably belongs to the employer, although the employe is serving at the same time some purpose of his own. If, however, the personal business or activities of the employe create the necessity for the principal errand in the sense that it would not have been made if such employe's personal business or activities had been abandoned, the principal errand belongs to the employe, although he is serving at the same time some purpose of the employment. Where the necessity which gives birth to an errand may be ascribed exclusively to either the employment or to the employe's personal affairs—that is, the necessity of one to the exclusion of the other—there is no need to consider or give weight to the dominant purpose as a separate and distinct element. We may have a situation, however, such as in the Trinity Lodge case, where a dual-purpose errand would have been made even though one of the purposes, whether it was that of the employment or that of the employe personally, might have been absent, and in that event the element of dominant motive or purpose would become of primary importance in determining to whom the principal errand belonged. When the character of the principal movement has thus once been determined, accidental injuries sustained during a detour or deviation are to be ascribed to the employment or to the employe personally, as the case may be, in compliance with the following rule—which is in accord with our decisions—as stated in Barragar v. Industrial Comm., 205 Wis. 550, 553, 238 N.W. 368, 369, 78 A.L.R. 679: " * * * it is essential * * * to determine whether, *at the outset*, the trip in question was that of the employer, or that of the employee. Having determined that it was the employer's trip, the employee is engaged in his employer's business and acting within the scope of his employment while going to and returning from the terminus of the trip. If it is the employee's trip, he is not within the scope of his employment while en route to, or returning from, the terminus of his trip. In case it is the employer's trip, and there are any detours for purely personal objectives, such detours must be separated from the main trip and the employee held to be outside the scope of his employment during such detour. *If it is his own trip, then such detours as are made for the purpose of dispatching business for his employer must be held to be within the scope of his employment.*" (Italics supplied.) * * *

The rule as above stated clarifies the controlling principles applicable to the instant case. Assuming that relator here left the sorority house for the dominant purpose of attending religious services at Temple Israel for her own personal reasons, her accidental injuries, nevertheless, arose out of and in the course of her employment *if at the time of the accident, as a deviation from her own personal mission, she was in the act of going to the drugstore to obtain bandages for her employer*. In the absence of a specific finding as to whether she was on her way to the drugstore for the purpose of her employment, it becomes necessary to remand the case to the commission for rehearing.

4. Although we have observed that the evidence sustains a finding that relator's intended trip to Temple Israel was for her own individual purpose and not for her employer, we do not say that a finding to the contrary might not possibly be sustained. Upon rehearing, new findings

should also be made as to the purpose of her trip to the synagogue, in that the findings heretofore made *may* have been controlled by the erroneous assumption that her contemplated attendance at the synagogue could not be attributed to her employment unless such attendance would be of "material benefit" to the employer. If the employment creates the necessity for an employe's errand, it is wholly immaterial whether such errand is beneficial or detrimental to the employer. Although the term "benefit" may have been used in an entirely different sense, nevertheless, in view of the resulting uncertainty, new findings are necessary.

The matter is remanded to the commission for rehearing and decision in accordance with this opinion. Relator is allowed $250 attorney's fees upon this appeal.

Reversed and remanded with directions.

NOTES

1. Marks' Dependents v. Gray, 251 N.Y. 90, 93, 167 N.E. 181 (1929), the lead dual-purpose decision, laid down this rule: "[i]f the work of the employee creates a necessity for travel, he is in the course of his employment, though he is serving at the same time some purpose of his own. * * * If, however, the work has had no part in creating the necessity for travel, if the journey would have gone forward though the business errand had been dropped, and would have been cancelled upon failure of the private purpose, though the business errand was undone, the travel is then personal, and personal the risk." Id., at 182–183. This is frequently termed the "dominant purpose" rule. In Marks' Dependents a plumber's helper was injured on a trip to a neighboring city to meet his wife. His employer had requested him to do a minor repair job while there—a task which presumably would not have been undertaken otherwise. The court denied compensation saying, "[w]e hold that Marks was not placed upon the highway by force of any duty owing to his employer, and that the risk of travel was his own." Id., at 183. Similarly, in Miller v. Bill Miller's Riviera, Inc., 21 N.J.Super. 112, 90 A.2d 889 (1952), the steward of a New Jersey restaurant, while on an extended vacation motoring trip in Florida, purchased six boxes of grapefruit to be shipped home to his employer. Later he was killed on the return trip north. Compensation was denied. See also Clover v. Snowbird Ski Resort, 808 P.2d 1037 (Utah 1991), acknowledging that the employee is not within the course if the primary motivation is personal despite the performance of some incidental employment errand.

If the trip for personal purposes would not have been made if the business had not required a similar trip, compensation is almost always awarded. See, e.g., Matthews v. Naylor, 42 Cal.App.2d 729, 109 P.2d 978 (1941). The most difficult situations are those where the trip would have been made anyway and the employer's business would also have required the same or a similar trip irrespective of the personal motivation for the particular dual purpose journey. See, e.g., Rosencrantz v. Insurance Service Co., 2

Or.App. 225, 467 P.2d 664 (1970) (employee killed on trip to a single site for the dual purposes of paying personal debts and collecting on debts owed to employer; compensation awarded for "concurrent cause" injury); and Standard Oil Co. v. Smith, 56 Wyo. 537, 111 P.2d 132 (1941) (compensation awarded to employee returning from vacation trip who picked up two barrels of oil for employer at intermediate point on route home and was killed before reaching final destination; special trip would not have been made for two barrels alone, but a trip would be required eventually for a larger quantity of oil). If these cases are correct, does "dominant purpose" mean anything more than that the business required that the same or a similar mission be performed irrespective of the personal motive that also inspired the trip?

The Nebraska Supreme Court applies a rule that awards compensation if the employer's needs required the trip to be made at some time even though it need not have been coincidental with the employee's personal journey. Jacobs v. Consolidated Telephone, 237 Neb. 772, 467 N.W.2d 864 (1991). A few statutes apply the dual purpose rule to exclude only those trips that would have been made even though there were no business purposes. See, for example, Vernon's Texas Labor Code § 401.011(2), which provides:

> Course and scope of employment" means an activity of any kind or character that has to do with and originates in the work, business, trade, or profession of the employer and that is performed by an employee while engaged in or about the furtherance of the affairs or business of the employer. The term includes an activity conducted on the premises of the employer or at other locations. The term does not include:
>
> (A) transportation to and from the place of employment unless:
>
> (i) the transportation is furnished as a part of the contract of employment or is paid for by the employer;
>
> (ii) the means of the transportation are under the control of the employer; or
>
> (iii) the employee is directed in the employee's employment to proceed from one place to another place; or
>
> (B) travel by the employee in the furtherance of the affairs or business of the employer if the travel is also in furtherance of personal or private affairs of the employee unless:
>
> (i) the travel to the place of occurrence of the injury would have been made even had there been no personal or private affairs of the employee to be furthered by the travel; and
>
> (ii) the travel would not have been made had there been no affairs or business of the employer to be furthered by the travel.

Leordeanu v. American Protection Ins. Co., 330 S.W.3d 239 (Tex. 2010) held that subsection (A) codified the coming and going rule and subsection (B) applied to other forms of "dual purpose" travel. The majority rejected the dissenting justice's view that both (A) and (B) applied to "coming and going" trips on the grounds that (B)(ii) would deny recovery in every case. Texas courts have also held that this statute must be applied to the entirety of a dual-purpose trip (i.e., an entire weekend) and not merely to the specific segment in which the accident occurred. See, e.g., Employers Casualty Company v. Hutchinson, 814 S.W.2d 539 (Tex. App,. 1991).

2. Injuries suffered by employees who are directed by employers to perform errands while en route to home from work or vice versa are often compensated. Compare Knipe v. Texas Employer's Ins. Ass'n, 234 S.W.2d 274 (Tex.Civ.App.1950), affirmed 150 Tex. 313, 239 S.W.2d 1006 (1951) (compensation awarded oil driller injured while returning home from isolated area under instruction to report progress to central office when returning home); Hall v. Aetna Life Ins. Co., 158 So. 658 (La.App.1935) (compensation awarded to survivors of an employee assigned to deliver work cards to laborers at a job site on his way home and who was killed at railroad crossing before delivering the cards) with Mims v. Nehi Bottling Co., 218 S.C. 513, 63 S.E.2d 305 (1951) (compensation denied employee who regularly dropped letters in mailbox on way home and who was injured while making a personal stop in a laundry before reaching the mailbox).

What constitutes an employment errand? Compare Blackman v. Great American First Sav. Bank, 233 Cal.App.3d 598, 284 Cal.Rptr. 491 (1991) (employee who had car crash after leaving work on way to attend college course provided as an employment fringe benefit not within the course) and Industrial Comm. v. Harkrader, 52 Ohio App. 76, 3 N.E.2d 61 (1935) (compensation denied teacher who required a kettle for a school pageant, retraced her steps home after having started to school, procured the kettle and was injured while leaving her home), with Gelbart v. New Jersey Federated Egg Producers Ass'n, 17 N.J.Misc. 185, 7 A.2d 636 (1939) (compensation awarded employee who was charged with duty of opening establishment, forgot key, retraced steps home and was thereafter injured).

3. After the overall trip is determined to be personal or business, the issue of whether an injury suffered on a deviation from the principal purpose can still arise. Is a detour from a business trip for a personal mission covered? A detour from a personal trip for a business purpose?

(A) If the trip is essentially a business trip with a business destination and a separate personal destination ahead on the same route and an accident occurs before reaching either destination, the accident is within the course of employment. See, e.g., Brenneisen v. Leach's Standard Service Station, 806 S.W.2d 443 (Mo.App.1991) (compensation awarded for death of off-duty employee who was driving to place of employment on day off to drop off soiled work uniforms for laundering before continuing personal affairs) and Levy v. Levy's Bazaar, 257 App.Div. 885, 12 N.Y.S.2d 131 (1939) (compensation awarded employee injured while on an employment errand while also transporting his mother to a more distant site).

(B) If the trip is essentially a business trip and the employee reaches the employment destination first and then proceeds onward to personal destination, injuries suffered after leaving the business destination are not within the course. Compare State v. Russo, 155 Ohio St. 341, 98 N.E.2d 830 (1951) (compensation denied) with Avila v. Pleasuretime Soda, Inc., 90 N.M. 707, 568 P.2d 233 (1977) (compensation awarded employee who detoured from route home in order to perform a personal errand and was injured after leaving the errand destination but before reaching the route home).

(C) If the trip is essentially a business trip and the employee detours from the route for a personal errand, injuries suffered by the employee after completing the personal errand but before reaching the business route from which he had departed are not within the course. See, e.g., Public Service Co. v. Industrial Comm., 395 Ill. 238, 69 N.E.2d 875 (1946) (compensation denied employee who had reached business destination and proceeded farther for personal errand; injured on return toward business destination but prior to reaching it) and Warren v. Globe Indem. Co., 217 La. 142, 46 So.2d 66 (1950) (travelling employee who was killed on purely personal journey after completing work activities was not within the course of employment).

(D) If the trip is essentially a business trip and the employee detours from the shortest route for a personal errand, the decisions divide as to whether to compensate injuries suffered by employees while angling back from the errand site toward the ultimate business destination on a direct route, although longer than without the detour. Compare Federal Mut. Liability Ins. Co. v. Industrial Accident Comm., 94 Cal.App. 251, 270 P. 992 (1928) (compensation awarded), with Red Arrow Bonded Messenger Corp. v. Industrial Accident Comm., 39 Cal.App.2d 559, 103 P.2d 1004 (1940) (compensation denied).

(E) If the trip is essentially a personal trip or an extension beyond a personal destination for an employment purpose, an injury suffered while making the employment detour at any time before returning to the route selected for a continuation of the personal trip is within the course of employment. See, e.g., Sater v. Home Lumber & Coal Co., 63 Idaho 776, 126 P.2d 810 (1942).

4. In line with the tendency to expand the exceptions to the going-to-and-coming-from rule, some decisions compensate injuries that occur during deviations for entirely personal errands if the deviations are not "extensive." See, e.g., Thomas v. Certified Refrigeration, Inc., 392 Mich. 623, 221 N.W.2d 378 (1974), awarding compensation to a refrigeration serviceman who was injured while driving his child to school in a company truck kept at his home at night, even though the school was in the opposite direction from the work site and the injury occurred an hour before work was to begin. In describing the trip as for a "dual purpose," the court suggested that whenever an employee drives an employer's truck in public, bearing the employer's name and business address and with the employer's consent, any injury

suffered will be considered within the course of employment. Do the underlying economic premises support this conclusion?

5. The "dual purpose" issue also arises when an employee takes work home to be done at night. Does the mere fact that the employee is taking papers home in a briefcase remove the trip from the coming and going rule? Ordinarily not. Compare Sylvan v. Sylvan Bros., 225 S.C. 429, 82 S.E.2d 794 (1954) (compensation denied with the observation, "[a] member of this court who takes a brief home with him to read is not in the course of his employment when on the way to or from his office") with Levi v. Interstate Photo Supply, 46 A.D.2d 951, 362 N.Y.S.2d 70 (1974) (compensation awarded employee who frequently worked at home but was not required to; assaulted while returning to home with work papers which he intended to use there). By contrast, compensation may be awarded if the home is made the work site because of some particular need, or if the home is a usual place of employment. See, e.g., Berry's Coffee Shop, Inc. v. Palomba, 161 Colo. 369, 423 P.2d 2 (1967) (delicacy of subject of conference made office an unsuitable place; employee and manager went to employee's home) and Kaycee Coal Co. v. Short, 450 S.W.2d 262 (Ky.1970) (equipment had been installed in the home to permit work there).

Swartz v. McDonald's Corp., 788 So.2d 937 (Fla. 2001) and Gilbert v. Publix Supermarkets, Inc. 790 So.2d 1057 (Fla. 2001) show how small factual distinctions produce different outcomes. In Swartz a worker injured returning home while transporting materials to be used in her attendance at an employment function the next day was covered for compensation; in Gilbert a worker injured while traveling to work from home with a newsletter she had prepared at home the previous evening was not covered because the accident did not occur "while the claimant was pursuing both work-related and personal travel." Gilbert. 790 So.2d at 1060. Similarly, Stewart v. Lakeland Funeral Home, 86 So.3d 1205 (Fla. App. 1st DCA 2012) denied recovery to a funeral director who suffered a motorcycle crash on the way to direct a funeral on his day off.(which was customary) because "he had not yet undertaken any business of the employer . . . was simply going to work . . . [and] there was no business purpose." Stewart, 86 So.3d at 1207.

Injuries that employees suffer while actively working at an in-home business situs are compensable, but injuries caused by general premises risks are disputable. Compare Joe Ready's Shell Station and Cafe v. Ready, 218 Miss. 80, 65 So.2d 268 (1953) (employee who did bookkeeping work at home accidentally shot herself while removing husband's shotgun from couch in preparing to sit down to perform her duties, compensation awarded) and Glasser v. Youth Shop, 54 So.2d 686 (Fla.1951) (employee who took books home to prepare a report was injured after completing work in upstairs room while descending stairs with books in his hands to breakfast; compensation denied).

7. TRAVELING EMPLOYEES

BALL–FOSTER GLASS CONTAINER CO. V. GIOVANELLI

Supreme Court of Washington (*en banc*), 2008.
163 Wash.2d 133, 177 P.3d 692.

C. JOHNSON, J.

This case asks us to determine whether, under the traveling employee doctrine, a worker from out-of-state, injured while working in Washington, is entitled to workers' compensation benefits under the Industrial Insurance Act (IIA), Title 51 RCW. The Department of Labor and Industries, an industrial appeals judge, the Board of Industrial Insurance Appeals, the superior court, and the Court of Appeals all relied on the traveling employee doctrine to find the injured worker in this case entitled to workers' compensation benefits. We affirm.

FACTUAL AND PROCEDURAL HISTORY

Alfred Giovanelli is a highly skilled and experienced firebrick mason. Although he resides in Pennsylvania, he regularly travels around the country to work on glass furnace rebuilds. Petitioner Ball–Foster Glass Container Company (currently known as Saint–Gobain Corporation) owns and operates 18 glass container manufacturing plants around the country, including one in Seattle. Saint–Gobain Corporation (St. Gobain) scheduled a rebuild of one of its glass furnaces at its Seattle plant in 2001.

Under the union contract, St. Gobain paid for travel to and from the work location for all of the out-of-state masons, including Giovanelli. Giovanelli was also paid his hourly wage for eight hours while traveling to Seattle and an additional eight hours for traveling home. St. Gobain paid the out-of-state masons a per diem of $78 for every day they were employed during the project, regardless of whether the mason was required to work that day. St. Gobain also provided Giovanelli with a rental car. St. Gobain points out that, unlike a typical St. Gobain employee, Giovanelli and the other out-of-state masons did not receive medical, dental, life insurance, or 401K benefits, nor were they reimbursed for the actual cost of hotel and meal expenses, over the per diem payment. The day Giovanelli was injured he was with the superintendent of St. Gobain's Seattle project, Royce A. (Sonny) Champ. Both men were staying at the same hotel. . . .

While Giovanelli was expected to be available to work on Sundays, he was not scheduled to work on Sunday, August 12, 2001, the day of the accident. When the accident occurred, he and Champ had started to walk across the street directly in front of their hotel-and were headed to the nearby park-when Giovanelli was hit and injured by a moving car. [Ed., the evidence suggested that a music concert was to take place in the park. The majority deemed this to be of no relevance.] . . . Giovanelli sustained serious injuries, including multiple fractures, degloving of his skin, and a head injury that resulted in permanent blindness. Giovanelli applied for workers' compensation benefits and the Department of Labor and Industries (Department) ordered St. Gobain to allow the claim. [This order was affirmed in proceedings up through the Washington Court of Appeal. The Supreme Court accepted review.]

ISSUE

Does Giovanelli qualify for workers' compensation benefits under the traveling employee doctrine?

ANALYSIS

Washington, like most other states, adopted a workers' compensation act nearly a century ago. . . .

Workers' compensation is a particularly dynamic field of legislative activity, as the forces of labor and industry assert their interests at each legislative session. However, while specific criteria vary from state to state and change over time, the general standard governing compensability of an injury is remarkably uniform and unchanging. The general coverage provision in the workers' compensation acts of 43 states as well as the Longshore and Harbor Workers' Compensation Act, 33 U.S.C. § 901, all share the language first used in the "British Compensation Act formula: injury 'arising out of and in the course of employment.' " 1 Larson & Larson, supra, § 3.01.

Washington is one of the few states that depart from the formula. . . . Under Washington law, there is no requirement that an injury "arise out of" employment, only that the worker was within "the course of employment" when injured. RCW 51.32.010. The language of the statute shows the intent of the Washington Legislature to adopt a broader and more comprehensive statute than other states.

Although new to this court, the traveling employee doctrine is not a novel concept. The traveling employee doctrine, also known as the "commercial traveler rule," or the "continuous coverage rule," is the prevailing view throughout the United States. *See Buczynski v. Indus. Comm'n*, 934 P.2d 1169, 1173 (Utah Ct.App.1997). A traveling employee is generally considered to be in the course of employment continuously during the entire trip, except during a distinct departure on a personal errand. 2 ARTHUR LARSON & LEX K. LARSON, LARSON'S WORKERS' COMPENSATION LAW § 25.01 (2006). The rationale for this extended coverage is that when travel is an essential part of employment, the risks associated with the necessity of eating, sleeping, and ministering to personal needs away from home are an incident of the employment even though the employee is not actually working at the time of injury. . . . The rule recognizes that a traveling employee is subjected to " 'hazards [he or] she would otherwise have the option of avoiding,' " and that the hazards of travel become the hazards of the employment. *Chavez v. ABF Freight Sys. Inc.*, 2001–NMCA–39, 130 N.M. 524, 528, 27 P.3d 1011 (internal quotation marks omitted) (quoting *Ramirez v. Dawson Prod. Partners, Inc.*, 2000–NMCA–011, 128 N.M. 601, ¶ 12, 995 P.2d 1043).

In *Shelton*, the Court of Appeals adopted the traveling employee doctrine, stating the general rule as: "When employees are required by their employers to travel to distant jobsites, courts generally hold that they are within the course of their employment throughout the trip, unless they are *pursuing a distinctly personal activity*." *Shelton v. Azar, Inc.*, 90 Wash.App. at 933, 954 P.2d 352 (1998) (emphasis added).

Consistent with our decisions recognizing the exceptions to the coming and going rule, we now recognize that traveling employees are entitled to expanded coverage for travel-related injuries. Of course, the traveling employee doctrine does not require coverage for every injury. A traveling employee may depart on a personal errand just like any other type of employee, thus losing the right to compensation benefits during such departures. *Silver Eng'g Works, Inc. v. Simmons*, 180 Colo. 309, 505 P.2d 966 (1973). Both the nature of the activity and the manner in which the employee performs it must be reasonable. *See Ray Bell Const. Co. v. King*, 281 Ga. 853, 642 S.E.2d 841 (2007).

In evaluating whether a worker has left the course of employment, we believe the proper inquiry is whether the employee was pursuing normal creature comforts and reasonably comprehended necessities or strictly personal amusement ventures. Although distinguishing between reasonable personal ministrations and purely personal amusement ventures may be difficult, courts have had little difficulty denying compensation for unusual or unreasonable activities. *See, e.g., E. Airlines v. Rigdon*, 543 So.2d 822 (Fla.Dist.Ct.App.1989) (denying compensation for employee injured during skiing trip at resort over 50 miles from hotel); *Buczynski*, 934 P.2d 1169 (hot tub injury occurring in hotel 150 miles away from convention center and days before convention not compensable).

There will, of course, be difficult cases where reasonable minds may differ. Therefore, in order to provide guidance to the courts of this state we believe the approach followed in Texas, which has a workers' compensation act similar to ours, strikes the proper balance. *See Shelton v. Standard Ins. Co.*, 389 S.W.2d 290 (Tex.1965). The test used by Texas courts is whether the injury " 'has its origin in a risk created by the necessity of sleeping or eating away from home. . . .' " *No. River Ins. Co. v. Purdy*, 733 S.W.2d 630, 632–33 (Tex.Ct.App.1987) (alterations in original) (quoting Shelton, 389 S.W.2d at 293). This test focuses the court's inquiry upon whether the injury relates to a risk incidental to employment or from an entirely independent act.

. . . [I]n evaluating the compensability of injuries occurring off-duty, the focus should be whether the injury is fairly attributable to the increased risks of travel. Thus, we believe the standard for determining whether an activity is a "distinct departure" should be consistent with the standard applicable to injuries that occur on the jobsite, while the employee is not actually engaged in work, such as during a rest break or lunch period. This is consistent with the reasoning of decisions by this court, the Court of Appeals, and the Board.

The Board has recognized that an injury resulting from a wholly independent act of the employee for his own benefit or gain, particularly where the employee's act has no connection with the employee's work, is generally not compensable. . . . The Board has observed, "[w]e believe the Legislature by enacting RCW 51.32.015 [extending coverage to lunch period injuries on the jobsite] intended to give the same coverage during the lunch hour as that applicable during the work period." *In re Morrill*, No. 29,704, Bd. of Indus. Ins. Appeals (Wash. Dec. 7, 1970). The Board's analysis is sound and applies as well to the traveling employee doctrine.

The relevant inquiry for purposes of workers' compensation is whether the injury is related to a risk of employment. A general reasonableness standard without a finding of a connection to the employee's work would go too far in covering the social and recreational activities of traveling employees. The injury must have its origin in a travel related risk. A rule allowing coverage for all reasonable activities untethers the concept of employment risk from the "course of employment" analysis. Since the traveling employee doctrine is an exception to the general rule that injury is not compensable when it occurs off the employer's premises, when the worker is not actually engaging in work activity, coverage should be limited to injuries fairly attributable to the risks of travel.

Application

Giovanelli Is a Traveling Employee

Applying the traveling employee doctrine to the facts of this case, we must first determine whether Giovanelli falls within the category of "traveling employee." There are two widely recognized definitions of a traveling employee. Under Larson's formulation of the rule, a traveling employee is one "whose work entails travel away from the employer's premises." 2 LARSON & LARSON, *supra*, § 25.01. An alternate definition provides: "A traveling employee is one whose job requires travel from place to place or to a place away from a permanent residence or the employee's place of business." 2 JOHN P. LUDINGTON, MODERN WORKERS COMPENSATION § 111:15 (Matthew J. Canavan ed., 1993).

The traveling salesperson and the long-haul truck driver are prototypical examples of traveling employees. However, workers who have no fixed site of employment or whose business is travel are not the only categories of employees who fall within the definition. Traveling employees also include those on temporary assignment at a fixed location.

Courts routinely apply the traveling employee doctrine to hourly wage workers who travel to a fixed site to perform a job assignment of temporary duration. This scenario frequently arises in the context of construction workers sent to work on a discrete project. . . . Courts have little difficulty treating itinerant construction workers as traveling employees when the worker is required, as a condition of the employment, to travel to a distant jobsite, away from home, and find overnight lodging, particularly when the employer provides compensation for the worker's travel expenses.

For example, in *Olinger Construction Co. v. Mosbey*, 427 N.E.2d 910 (Ind.App.1981), a construction worker was assigned to a jobsite 150 miles from his home. He lived in a motel while working on the project where, one night, a former co-worker entered his room and stabbed him. The Indiana court held that his death was compensable. The court rejected the employer's argument that the traveling employee rule was inapplicable to a worker assigned to a fixed jobsite for a job of temporary duration, stating, "because of his job . . . his activities, such as eating and sleeping in a distant location, are done for the benefit of the employer." *Olinger*, 427 N.E.2d at 915.

St. Gobain contends that Giovanelli should be treated as a "local hire" rather than as a traveling employee. They contrast his situation with that of Ernie Peters, a permanent St. Gobain employee who traveled from the corporate headquarters in Muncie, Indiana to oversee the furnace rebuild. Unlike Peters, St. Gobain argues, Giovanelli was not "required" to accept the work assignment in Seattle, but could have elected to stay home.

A distinction based on whether an employee had the option to decline a work assignment that entails travel would resurrect the assumption of risk doctrine, a tort concept that is inapt in evaluating the compensability of a work-related injury. Workers' compensation acts were in great part necessitated by the judicial foreclosure of common law remedies for injured workers through application of the assumption of risk doctrine.

The adoption of the IIA represents the rejection of the assumption of risk doctrine in favor of no fault insurance for work-related injuries. No distinction may be drawn between an employee who volunteers for a job that entails travel and one who is "required" by the employer to do so. The question is whether the job assignment entails travel such that the risks of travel become part of the risks of employment.

A more difficult issue is whether a worker who accepts a series of temporary assignments, with breaks in between, can be viewed as a "traveling employee." As noted, there are two definitions of a traveling employee. Giovanelli clearly qualifies under the first definition, as "one whose job requires travel from place to place or to a place away from a permanent residence or the employee's place of business." 2 MODERN WORKERS COMPENSATION, *supra*, § 111:15. Giovanelli's job assignment to Seattle required him to travel to a place away from his permanent residence. In recognition of that fact, St. Gobain agreed not only to reimburse him for his travel expenses, but also to compensate him for making the journey itself. It paid him for his travel time to and from Seattle and a per diem during his entire stay in Seattle, including his days off.

Under Larson's formulation, which is more widely relied upon by courts, a traveling employee is one who travels "away from" an employer's premises. 2 LARSON & LARSON, *supra*, § 25.01. Viewing Giovanelli's Seattle-based job assignment in isolation, he was hired to travel to, not away from, the employer's premises, and thus falls outside the definition. However, considering the nature and history of Giovanelli's employment relationship with St. Gobain, he qualifies as a traveling employee even under Larson's more restrictive test.

[I]n the context of determining an injured worker's eligibility for workers' compensation, courts should examine the nature of the employment relationship with a wide angle lens, rather than narrowly focusing on a discrete job assignment or period of employment.

Accordingly, in evaluating whether Giovanelli is a traveling employee, the proper focus is not Giovanelli's particular job assignment to St. Gobain's Seattle plant, but his ongoing employment relationship with St. Gobain, the multinational corporation, which has 18 glass manufacturing plants nationwide. . . . Giovanelli had an ongoing and exclusive employment relationship with his employer. Giovanelli worked for St. Gobain more than 15 years, exclusively for the previous five years. His job assignments were coordinated and travel expenses were authorized and reimbursed through St. Gobain's headquarters in Muncie, Indiana. St. Gobain contemplated that Giovanelli would return home after the Seattle job was finished, until it was time to travel to the next scheduled furnace rebuild. For all of its furnace rebuilds, St. Gobain relied on Giovanelli's skill and expertise to help ensure the expeditious completion of each project. Failing to recognize Giovanelli as a traveling employee under the facts of this case would be to elevate form over substance, contrary to the remedial purpose of our IIA.

The record is clear: Giovanelli did not merely leave home to seek out better employment. Rather, St. Gobain, through its agent, Sonny Champ, sought him out at his Pennsylvania home and offered him a temporary assignment in Seattle just as it had done numerous times over many years. The terms of the offer were that Giovanelli would fly to Seattle on a specified date, after arranging his flight through the corporate office in Indiana, receive travel pay as well as reimbursement of travel expenses, enjoy the use of a company paid rental car, and receive a per diem to defray the costs of food and lodging during his stay in Seattle.

St. Gobain contends that Giovanelli is not a traveling employee because it did not compensate him for his travel expenses but merely offered "premium pay" as an incentive to accept the Seattle job. It argues that treating Giovanelli as a traveling employee dramatically expands liability every time an employer offers relocation expenses or a housing subsidy. But this is not a case where Giovanelli was relocating for a job; both St. Gobain and Giovanelli expected he would fly home at the end of his assignment.

Giovanelli's willingness to travel from state to state to work on St. Gobain's furnace rebuilds clearly benefited St. Gobain and furthered its business. St. Gobain relied on Giovanelli, along with a small group of firebrick specialists, which it designated "travelers," to provide the expertise necessary to allow it to expeditiously complete a furnace rebuild. It is fair and proper to provide expanded coverage commensurate with the expanded risks of employment faced by Giovanelli and similarly situated "travelers" and to hold St. Gobain liable for injuries related to the expanded risks of employment.

As a traveling employee, Giovanelli was "in the course of employment" continuously during his trip. The next question is whether he "distinctly departed" from the course of employment at the time of his injury.

Giovanelli Did Not Distinctly Depart on a Personal Errand

Although Giovanelli was not required to accompany his supervisor, Sonny Champ, on a Sunday stroll, that does not mean he took himself outside the course of employment by doing so. In determining whether there has been a "distinct departure" that takes one outside the course of employment, courts analogize to the "personal comfort" doctrine. *Bergmann Precision, Inc. v. Indus. Comm'n*, 199 Ariz. 164, 15 P.3d 276 (Ct.App.2000). Compensation in such areas is predicated on the premise that these acts do not take the employee out of the scope of employment because they are necessary to his health and comfort. *N. & L. Auto Parts Co. v. Doman*, 111 So.2d 270, 272 (Fla.Dist.Ct.App.1959).

The scope of activities covered by the personal comfort doctrine depends on the particular circumstances of employment. A traveling employee is entitled to broader coverage than a nontraveling employee because a traveling employee is in a significantly different position of risk than a nontraveling employee. The nontraveling employee may satisfy his personal needs without leaving the comfort of home. In contrast, the traveling employee must face the perils of the street in order to satisfy basic needs, including sleeping, eating, and seeking fresh air and exercise.

The risk of getting injured while negotiating unfamiliar streets is among the classic "street risks" covered by the traveling employee doctrine, along with hotel fires and mishaps at restaurants. Under the street risk doctrine, injuries to employees whose duties increase their exposure to the hazards of the street arise out of employment. 1 LARSON & LARSON, *supra*, § 6.01. If the employment occasions the worker's use of the street, the risks of the street become part of the risks of employment. Accordingly, "when a traveling employee slips in the street, *or is struck by an automobile when traveling on foot* or is involved in an accident while driving between the hotel and a restaurant, the injury has been held compensable." 2 LARSON & LARSON, *supra*, § 25.03[1] (emphasis added) (footnotes omitted).

St. Gobain asserts that Giovanelli is not entitled to coverage because he was not en route to a restaurant. Rather, St. Gobain contends that Giovanelli was engaged in a "purely recreational activity" at the time of his injury, which has "no business purpose." Yet the rationale of the personal comfort doctrine is that ministering to one's personal comforts is not a "purely personal" activity because attending to one's personal health and comfort furthers the employer's interest by ensuring that an employee is healthy, well rested, and comfortable, and thus able to perform his or her job functions more efficiently. Giovanelli worked 14 hours per day, six days per week. Going for a Sunday stroll on his single day off was a reasonable activity that falls well within the personal comfort doctrine. As one court observed:

> To restrict [a traveling employee] to the confines of his room or place of transacting business in his lodging place and hold that he is not covered except when either actually, directly conducting his employer's business or engaged in some activity which is strictly a *necessity* of life, would unduly limit the intended

beneficial purpose of this remedial social insurance, which is to be liberally construed."

McDonald v. State Highway Dep't, 127 Ga.App. 171, 176, 192 S.E.2d 919 (1972).

In taking a Sunday stroll to the park on his single day off, Giovanelli did not "distinctly depart" from the course of employment on a "personal errand." Neither the nature of his activity nor the manner in which he engaged in it was unreasonable or unusual. The risk of getting injured while crossing the street in front of his hotel during a walk to the park was a risk of his employment. Accordingly, he is entitled to compensation.

Providing coverage to St. Gobain's traveling employees is entirely appropriate under our IIA. St. Gobain made the economic decision to use "travelers" presumably because the value they bring to the project, in terms of greater efficiency and quality of work product, more than offsets the increased costs associated with their use. To the extent our decision increases St. Gobain's costs of production by increasing its insurance premiums for the workers engaged in the manufacture of glass containers at its plants, our IIA will operate as the legislature intended.

. . . We affirm the Court of Appeals.

J.M. JOHNSON, J. (dissenting).

Washington law imposes limited employer liability for employees injured while in travel status and does not collect premium for or compensate for any injury unrelated to employment. In this case, a brick worker's attendance at a music concert on a day off is not employment related and does not meet the "course of employment" test for employer liability as defined in RCW 51.08.013(1). Alfred Giovanelli was injured while wandering toward a Sunday concert, which does not qualify his expedition as "employment related"-even for a travel status employee. I would reverse the Court of Appeals and remand this case. Because the majority reaches a contrary conclusion and will burden the State of Washington system with claims unrelated to employment, I dissent.

* * *

NOTES

1. Would you deem the injury Giovanelli suffered to be one the employer should be required to compensate? As noted in Ball–Foster, employees, such as sales agents who are paid to travel are within the course while actually traveling, and many decisions also compensate injuries suffered while these employees are eating, sleeping, or enjoying recreation. See, e.g., Ridgway v. Combined Ins. Companies of America, 98 Idaho 410, 565 P.2d 1367 (1977) (employee on two weeks training program injured while proceeding from hotel to restaurant; compensation awarded); David Wexler &

Co. v. Industrial Comm., 52 Ill.2d 506, 288 N.E.2d 420 (1972) (salesman "on the road" on Memorial Day; went fishing and was killed while returning to motel; compensation awarded); McKay v. Republic Vanguard Ins. Co., 27 A.D.2d 607, 275 N.Y.S.2d 742 (1966) (traveler died of carbon monoxide poisoning while highly intoxicated and asleep in motel; compensation awarded); and, Financial Institute Insurance Serv. v. Hoy, 770 So.2d 994 (Miss. App. 2000) (Traveling employee fell on wet floor when she arose from her motel bed to visit the bathroom; compensation awarded.)

2. In Duplechain v. Bell Office Supply, 926 So.2d 149 (La.App. 3 Cir. 2006), a worker made a delivery to a town 20 miles from his workplace. After making the delivery, the worker ate supper with family members in a restaurant in the delivery town. Thereafter, he headed back to his place of employment and was injured in a crash within a mile of reaching it. The court affirmed a holding that the deviation for supper was over and the claimant was back within the course and scope of employment when the injury occurred. The court found it unnecessary to address whether the worker would have been entitled to benefits if the injury had occurred at the restaurant.

3. The High Court of Australia has attempted to provide a general test to determine when an injury suffered while not doing actual work—denoted as an "interval" between working periods—occurred "within the course of employment." These intervals between periods of actual work may occur at a regular workplace and also when an employee is assigned to work at a place remote from the regular workplace. The former would apply to injuries suffered on lunch and coffee breaks and the latter to injuries suffered in hotels and restaurants or in recreational activities after a work day had concluded at a remote site.

In *Comcare v. PVYW* [2013] HCA 41 an employer assigned a female employee to a two-day out of town work assignment. The employer arranged and paid for hotel accommodations. After a day of work, the employee invited a friend to supper in her hotel. After dining, the two adjourned to the employee's hotel room. While having sexual intercourse one of the two pulled a light fixture into the employee's face, causing severe injuries. The case arrived in the High Court of Australia with a ruling that the injury was compensable because it occurred in a work interval at a place the employer "induced or encouraged" the worker to be. The High Court reversed, and held that a work interval injury would be compensable in a place the employer "induced or encouraged" the worker to be (such as the hotel) only if the injury was consequent to something about the place (i.e., a defective bed or slippery tub). Moreover, an injury consequent to an activity would be compensable only if the employer "induced or encouraged" the employee to engage in that activity (such as an approved recreational activity). Hence, even though PVYW was injured at a place the employer "induced or encouraged" her to be, the injury was not compensable because the employer had not "induced or encouraged" the sexual activity. Dissenting justices favored a rule that would permit recovery if either one or other of the conditions was satisfied: at a place the employer "induced or encouraged" the employee to be, or from an activity the employer "induced or encouraged" the employee to undertake.

8. SYNTHESIS: RELATIONSHIP OF "WITHIN THE COURSE" AND "ARISING OUT OF" TESTS

STROTHER V. MORRISON CAFETERIA

Supreme Court of Florida, 1980.
383 So.2d 623.

ALDERMAN, JUSTICE.

We have for review by petition for writ of certiorari an order of the Industrial Relations Commission reversing the order of the judge of industrial claims and denying claimant Blanche Strother workers' compensation on the basis that while her injuries did arise out of her employment, they were not sustained in the course of her employment. The commission rendered a contrary decision in *Sixty-Seven Liquors v. Gamel*, IRC No. 265–25–3664 (IRC Jan. 1979), *cert. denied*, 383 So.2d 628 (Fla.1980), and awarded compensation to a doorman-bouncer who had been injured away from the employer's premises and outside his working hours on the ground that his injury was clearly shown to have arisen out of his employment.

The sole issue in this case of first impression is whether Strother sustained a compensable accident when she was assaulted outside the time and space limits of her employment. We hold that Strother's injuries, which had their origin and cause entirely within the course of her employment and which arose out of her employment, are compensable.

Strother, a cashier at Morrison's Cafeteria, was charged with the responsibility of handling the payment of food bills from customers from mid-afternoon to closing at nine each night. Although not a part of her regular employment, on two occasions she drove the cafeteria's manager to the bank to deposit the day's receipts. On the two days preceding the incident which resulted in the injury for which she now seeks workers' compensation, Strother observed two men in the cafeteria who were not customers or employees. On the evening of the incident, she noticed the same two men enter the cafeteria in the same manner as they had entered on the two previous days. This evening, she left work and drove directly home (some fifteen or twenty minutes' drive from the cafeteria) where she was assaulted by and her purse was taken by one of the men whom she had observed in the cafeteria.

The judge of industrial claims determined that Strother was injured in a compensable accident since the circumstances of her employment exposed her to a greater risk than that of a regular cashier and that the assault arose out of and in the course of her employment. The judge accepted Strother's testimony that she was followed and attacked by the same men who were at the cafeteria, and he concluded that they thought she was carrying the cafeteria's money since they demanded "the money or deposits."

Relying on *Hill v. Gregg, Gibson & Gregg, Inc.*, 260 So.2d 193 (Fla.1972), Strother argues that her injuries are compensable because they "arose out of and in the course of employment" as this language is defined by *Hill*. She submits that her injuries arose out of and solely because of conditions connected with her employment.

Respondents, on the other hand, rely on *Bituminous Casualty Corp. v. Richardson*, 148 Fla. 323, 4 So.2d 378 (1941), and *Southern Bell Telephone and Telegraph Co. v. McCook*, 355 So.2d 1166 (Fla.1977), and recite that to be compensable, the assault must not only have arisen out of Strother's employment but also must have occurred within the time and space limits of her employment. Respondents further contend that this case does not fall within the special hazard exception to the going and coming rule.

Section 440.02(6), Florida Statutes (1977), defines injury, for purposes of the workers' compensation act, as "personal injury or death by accident arising out of and in the course of employment, and such diseases or infection as naturally or unavoidably result from such injury." Our early decision of *Bituminous Casualty Corp. v. Richardson* construed this language as requiring a showing that the injury both arose out of employment *and* occurred in the course of employment. "Arising out of" was defined to mean the origin or cause of the accident. "In the course of" employment was defined as the time, place, and circumstances under which the accident occurs. We stated as a general rule that the accident must occur while the employee is acting within the duties of his employment or in some act incidental thereto. *See also Foxworth v. Florida Industrial Commission*, 86 So.2d 147 (Fla.1955), wherein we stated that compensation coverage is confined to an injury arising out of and in the course and scope of employment and both circumstances must appear before compensation can be awarded; *Travelers Ins. Co. v. Taylor*, 147 Fla. 210, 3 So.2d 381 (1941), wherein we held that arising out of and in the course of employment are used conjunctively, and it is indispensable to recovery that both of them be established; *Fidelity & Casualty Co. of New York v. Moore*, 143 Fla. 103, 196 So. 495 (1940), wherein it was held that to arise out of and in the course of employment, an injury must occur within the period of employment at a place where the injured employee may reasonably be and while he is reasonably fulfilling duties of his employment or is engaged in something incidental thereto.

More recently, in *Southern Bell Telephone and Telegraph v. McCook*, we reaffirmed our decision of *Bituminous Casualty Corp. v. Richardson* and explained that "arising out of" and "in the course of" were separate elements which must be proved to establish a compensable accident. In McCook, we were concerned with the "arising out of" element rather than "in the course of." Relying on *Suniland Toys & Juvenile Furniture, Inc. v. Karns*, 148 So.2d 523 (Fla.1963), we defined "arising out of" to mean originating in some risk connected with employment or flowing as a natural consequence from the employment.

Although in several decisions, we have referred to the distinct and separate nature of the two elements of "arising out of" and "in the course of," we have also, in other decisions, tended to merge these two factors together into a test of work connectedness. In *Fidelity & Casualty Co. of New York v. Moore*, we said:

> The cases generally hold that for an injury to arise out of and in the course of one's employment, there must be some causal connection between the injury and the employment *or* it must have had its origin in some risk incident to or connected with the employment *or* that it flowed from it as a natural consequence. *Another definition* widely approved is that the injury must occur within the period of the employment, at a place where the employee may reasonably be, and while he is reasonably fulfilling the duties of his employment or engaged in doing something incidental to it.

196 So. at 496 (emphasis added).

Then in *Sweat v. Allen*, 145 Fla. 733, 200 So. 348 (1941), we allowed recovery to a deputy sheriff who, while on his way to work, was struck by a delivery truck and sustained injury to his leg which ultimately resulted in its amputation. We determined that by the nature of his employment, the deputy was continuously under a duty to protect the peace and safety of the community and to apprehend those guilty of its violation. In explanation of our result, we declared that an injury must both arise out of and be in the course of employment and proceeded to recite the alternative definitions for arising out of and in the course of one's employment which we had earlier enunciated in *Fidelity & Casualty Co. of New York v. Moore*.

Again, in *Suniland Toys & Juvenile Furniture, Inc. v. Karns*, we relied on the alternative definitions established by *Fidelity & Casualty Co. of New York v. Moore* to award compensation to an employee who had sustained an allergic reaction to a typhoid inoculation administered at a physician's office. We said: "[T]o be compensable, an injury must have originated in some risk connected with the employment or flowing as a natural consequence from the employment." 148 So.2d at 524.

In our 1972 decision of *Hill v. Gregg, Gibson & Gregg, Inc.*, we again emphasized the alternative nature of the definitions established in *Fidelity & Casualty Co. of New York v. Moore*. We quashed the commission's order which denied compensation and held that an assault which arose out of Hill's employment was compensable even though it did not occur on the employer's premises or during working hours, and we said:

> From their orders, it appears the Judge of Industrial Claims and the Industrial Relations Commission looked only to the last definition [*i.e.*, the injury must occur within the period of employment, at a place where the employee may reasonably be, and while he is reasonably fulfilling the duties of his employment or engaged in doing something incidental to it] and concluded Petitioner could not recover because he was not injured while at his job site working and benefiting his employer. While such a conclusion is proper under the fourth *Moore* definition, it is not determinative of the issue. It is necessary to also consider the first three definitions. All are alternatives. *Sweat v. Allen*, 1941, 145 Fla. 733, 200 So. 348.

260 So.2d at 195.

It is apparent that our prior decisions have developed inconsistent interpretations of the statutory language "arising out of and in the course of employment." One line of cases establishes a two-prong test of work connectedness where both prongs must be separately proven. The other line of cases effectually develops an arising out of and an originating in the course of employment test where either element may suffice. The present case has spotlighted the uncertainty created by the conflicting lines of cases. A resolution of this conflict must be made before we can determine whether Strother's injury is compensable.

Larson, in his treatise *Workmen's Compensation Law*, volume 1A, section 29.00, discusses this problem area of workers' compensation law and analyzes numerous decisions from other jurisdictions involving fact situations somewhat similar to the present case where indisputably the injury arose out of the employment and where the originating cause of the injury occurred entirely within the time and space limits of employment, but where the actual injury occurred while the employee was not acting within the duties of his employment. He asserts that grave injustice occurs when courts insist on the separateness of "arising out of" and "in the course of" when the latter denotes occurrence within the period of employment at a place where the injured employee may reasonably be and while he is reasonably fulfilling duties of employment or is engaged in doing something incidental thereto. He suggests that the more reasoned approach, consistent with the goals of workers' compensation acts, is not to apply these concepts entirely independent of each other but rather to view them as parts of a single test of work connectedness where deficiencies in the strength of one factor may, in some cases, be made up by the strength in the other. He proposes that the term "arising" in the statutory phrase "arising out of and in the course of employment" be employed not only to modify "out of" but also to modify "in the course of" and then declares that arising connotes origin, not completion or manifestation. Summarizing his analysis, Larson concludes that in the cases allowing compensation for the type of injury with which we are presently concerned, the common element is the fact that the originating cause of injury arose out of and in the course of employment:

> The time bomb, so to speak, is constructed and started ticking during working hours; but it happens to go off at a time and place remote from the employment. The hazards of the employment, whether the animosity of a fired employee, a needle-like shaving in the eyebrow, or dynamite cap in the pocket, follow the claimant beyond the time and space limits of his work, and there injure him.

Larson, *Workmen's Compensation Law*, volume 1A, section 29.22 at 5–376–77.

The early case of *Matter of Field v. Charmette Knitted Fabric Co.*, 245 N.Y. 139, 156 N.E. 642 (1927), authored by Justice Cardozo laid the groundwork in these types of cases for utilizing the originating in the course of employment test. There recovery of workmen's compensation was allowed to a general manager and superintendent of a mill who was assaulted outside working hours and off employment premises by an employee he had discharged. On the work premises, the employee had moved threateningly toward the superintendent but had been pulled away. Justice Cardozo said: "[C]ontinuity of cause has been so combined with contiguity in time and space that the quarrel from origin to ending must be taken as one." 156 N.E. at 643. He explained that this assault was engendered on the work premises.

In cases analogous to the present one, other jurisdictions, whose workers' compensation acts speak in terms of an injury by accident "arising out of and in the course of employment," have seen fit to adopt Larson's originating rationale to avoid the inequity and illogic of denying compensation to one whose injuries indisputably arose out of employment and where the originating cause of the injury occurred during working hours and on the employment premises. For example, in *Thornton v. Chamberlain Manufacturing Corp.*, 62 N.J. 235, 300 A.2d 146 (1973), while on the job, Thornton, a production foreman, reprimanded an employee for repeated failure to wear safety glasses and several times reported these failures to the employer. One of these times, the employee threatened Thornton by saying he would take care of Thornton's eyes later. The employee was terminated from his employment and nine days thereafter attacked Thornton and said, "Remember me, remember me." As a result of this attack, Thornton sustained total loss of vision in his right eye. Thornton was denied compensation by the commission because his injuries did not occur in the course of employment, and the county court affirmed. The New Jersey Supreme Court reversed and found that, unquestionably, the attack had its genesis in Thornton's employment. He incurred his attacker's wrath and enmity because he had performed his assigned employment duty. Had he been at work when the attack occurred, there would have been no question as to the compensability of his injuries. The New Jersey court found Larson's construction of "arising out of and in the course of" reasonable and conducive to the advancement of the basic purpose of the workmen's compensation act and concluded:

> Here the injuries were caused in every realistic sense by petitioner's exposure at work. We can think of no reason why the Legislature would want to deny relief because the work-generated force overtook petitioner at one moment rather than another.

300 A.2d at 149. See also *Daniello v. Machise Express Co.*, 119 N.J.Super. 20, 289 A.2d 558 (1972), *aff'd*, 122 N.J.Super. 144, 299 A.2d 423 (App.Div.1973).

In *Graybeal v. Board of Supervisors of Montgomery County*, 216 Va. 77, 216 S.E.2d 52 (1975), claimant, a county prosecutor, was injured by a bomb explosion at his home. The bomb was placed by an individual whom he had successfully prosecuted for second-degree murder and who, after conviction, vowed revenge on everyone who had anything to do with his conviction. The Supreme Court of Virginia acknowledged its earlier rulings that an accident occurs in the course of employment when it takes place within the specified time, space, and circumstance of the employment but modified the rule for the particular facts of the case before it where the accident arose in the course of employment. The court explained that a modified rule is permitted by the statutory language "arising . . . in the course of the employment." It then proceeded to give arising its ordinary meaning of originating but further explained:

> Upon first examination, this rule might appear to constitute a blending into one single test of the dual "arising out of" and "in the course of" requirements. But *the "arising out of" requirement refers to causation*, only incidentally related to considerations of time and space, and must be satisfied by a showing of causal connection between work and injury. *The "course of" requirement, on the other hand, refers to continuity of time, space and circumstances*, only incidentally related to causation. *This*

> *requirement must be satisfied by a showing of an unbroken course beginning with work and ending with injury under such circumstances that the beginning and the end are connected parts of a single work-related incident.*

216 S.E.2d at 54 (emphasis added).

This originating in the course of employment test has been carefully limited to those situations where the fact that originated the cause of injury occurred entirely within the time and space limits of employment. The Court of Appeals of New York, in *Malacarne v. City of Yonkers Parking Authority*, 41 N.Y.2d 189, 391 N.Y.S.2d 402, 359 N.E.2d 992 (1976), denied compensation to a parking lot employee who was shot in the back and killed while outside his sister's home by an assailant who had demanded the money bag containing parking lot receipts which the employee usually deposited in the bank across the street from his employment. The court determined that there was no evidence to indicate that an event ultimately culminating in the employee's death occurred within working hours and at the business premises and reasoned:

> Consequently, if, in the case before us, there had been substantial evidence rather than mere conjecture to support a finding that an attempted robbery had begun at the deceased's point of departure from the parking lot itself, the board might have been entitled to consider whether that event and the subsequent shooting were but two parts of a whole. The reality, however, is that there was not a scintilla of evidence of any earlier event related to the shooting. The "money bag" statement attributed to the decedent during the testimony before the referee does not supply it. That bare statement did not include, for instance, anything to indicate that suspicious persons had been lurking in the vicinity of the parking lot, or that anyone had been seen to follow the decedent from there or, for that matter, that he had observed anyone following him at any time during his half hour's drive to his sister's house until he had already arrived on her street. Even assuming that the decedent had in fact made the "money bag" statement and, in doing so, had accurately quoted his assailant, on the record here we are left then with nothing but speculation on which to base a choice from among the countless number of possibilities of where, how or why the assailant came to the erroneous belief that Malacarne would have a money bag on him when he arrived at his sister's house.

391 N.Y.S.2d at 407–8, 359 N.E.2d at 995–996.

We find the construction of "arising out of and in the course of employment," proposed by Larson and adopted by several jurisdictions to be reasonable and conducive to the basic purposes of the workers' compensation act. Essentially, the preliminary predicate for the two-pronged work connectedness test was laid in *Fidelity & Casualty Co. of New York v. Moore* and *Hill v. Gregg, Gibson & Gregg, Inc.*

We hold that to be compensable, an injury must arise out of employment in the sense of causation and be in the course of employment in the sense of continuity of time, space, and circumstances. This latter factor may be proved by showing that the causative factors occurred during the time and space limits of employment.

Thus, employing this test, we hold that Strother's injury is compensable. There is no issue that the injury sustained as a result of the assault arose out of employment. Furthermore, it had its genesis at the place of employment since the assailants were actually on the business premises, casing it so to speak, and, then when Strother left, they followed her home and there assaulted her and robbed her of her purse which they thought contained the cafeteria's cash-receipts. The time bomb began ticking while she was on the business premises and during working hours.

Accordingly, the order of the Industrial Relations Commission is quashed, and the order of the judge of industrial claims is reinstated.

It is so ordered.

NOTES

1. See Technical Tape Corp. v. Industrial Comm., 58 Ill.2d 226, 317 N.E.2d 515 (1974) for a similar holding. Can the Florida court's conclusion that Strother's injury is compensable be justified on the basis of any of the approaches noted heretofore? Was there any special errand? Did the accident occur on or near the work premises? Was the spot where the accident happened one of peculiar peril? Was the risk an ordinary incident of Strother's employment? Are you satisfied with the outcome? Why?

2. In Lane v. Industrial Commission of Arizona, 218 Ariz. 44, 178 P.3d 516 (Ariz. App. 2008), an off duty police officer and companion were on a biking venture. The police officer's employment duties included responding to public safety threats at any time. The two heard gunshots and the officer rode his bike to where his vehicle was park, intending to respond if needed. A vehicle drove up, Lane heard a voice say, "We got her five times," and the occupants began firing guns at Lane and his companion. Lane found safety behind his vehicle and then saw that his companion was "frozen" in the open. Lane left his protected spot to bring the companion to safety and suffered a gunshot wound. An administrative law judge denied Lane's workers' compensation claim on the ground that the injury did not arise out of the course and scope of employment. The appellate court reversed, finding that "Lane's employment as a police officer caused him to face both an increased

and distinctly work-related risk of injury from gunfire" and holding that the injury arose out of employment. The appellate court also found that under the circumstances Lane's response to the emergency placed him within the course of his employment and that his act taken to rescue his companion was not a deviation but the kind of action his employment required.

3. Does the mere fact that a risk arises out of employment satisfy the within the course of employment requirement? Can we surmise that an accident is compensable whenever it either arises out of the employment or occurs during the course of it, and that it need not satisfy both requirements? Or is it enough to note that the two requirements interact upon each other? That is, will a strong showing of "arise-out-of" serve to compensate for a weak showing of "during-course-of"? Arabie Bros. Trucking Co. v. Gautreaux, 880 So.2d 932 (La. App. 1 Cir. 2004) stated:

> The terms "arising out of" and "in the course of" . . . are dual requirements that cannot be considered in isolation from each other. In a close case, a strong showing with reference to one requirement may compensate for a weak showing with reference to the other requirement. When there is a weak showing with respect to both requirements, the employee is not entitled to compensation benefits.
>
> To evaluate the "course of employment" requirement, the court focuses on whether the employee sustains an injury while actively engaged in the performance of his duties during working hours, either on the employer's premises or at a place contemplated by employment activities. This inquiry focuses upon the time and place relationship between the injury and the employment. When considering the "arising out of employment" requirement, the court inquires into the character or origin of the risk suffered by the employee and determines whether this risk was incidental to the employment. An injury arises out of employment if the risk from which the injury resulted was . . . greater for the employee than for a person not engaged in the employment.

4. The next chapter permits consideration of the converse situation; that is, can a strong showing of "within the course of" compensate for a weak showing of "arising-out-of"? See, e.g., Mitchell v. Employers Mut. Liability Ins. Co., 341 So.2d 35 (La.App.1976).

CHAPTER 5

INJURIES ARISING OUT OF THE EMPLOYMENT

■ ■ ■

1. THE JOB AS THE SOURCE OF THE HARMFUL AGENCY

To effectuate the workers' compensation goals of carving out "employment risks" from the general body of perils that beset all mankind and making them a cost of doing business, compensation statutes prescribe standards to distinguish compensable employment injuries from those that are not compensable. The approach devised in the original British workers' compensation act has been adopted virtually universally: namely, an employment injury must "arise out of" and be suffered "within the course" of the employment. If the "within the course" criterion is satisfied, the "arising out of" criterion is undisputed in most actions; that is, if a boiler explodes, or a worker slips and falls while involved in strenuous employment effort, this issue is rarely contested. No one can sensibly argue that these injuries ought not be treated as a cost of doing business. By contrast some injuries are plainly not the responsibility of the employer, as for example, an injury caused entirely by a genetic deficiency.

Between the classes of indisputably compensable and indisputably non-compensable injuries falls a wide, gray area of dispute. Suppose, for example, a lightning bolt strikes a highway worker hard at work on the roadway. Does it comport with the underlying workers' compensation economic premises to burden the employer with the costs of the resulting injury any more so than to require the employer to pay for the same injuries had the lightning struck the same employee while walking at the same spot on the road on a day off? Or, suppose a worker suffers a heart attack at work caused by a combination of work stress and a congenitally weak heart. Can a principled argument be made to treat the so-called "neutral" source injuries (i.e., lightning strike) different from what might be called "mixed" sources injuries (i.e., a heart attack)? To what extent may this issue be resolved by attempting to isolate the "source" of the causative force of the injury?

In examining the following materials the student should consider whether isolating the source of the injury was important to the courts' resolutions of the "arising out of" issues. The student should also be mindful that a few states have added causative criteria to the traditional "arising out of and within the course of employment" formulation to limit the ambit of compensability under the statutes. Oregon initiated this development by including this criterion in its statute:

> (7)(a). . . .
>
> (A) No injury or disease is compensable as a consequence of a compensable injury unless the compensable injury is the *major contributing cause* of the consequential condition.

OR ST § 656.005. (e.s.) Oregon backs up this additional compensability requirement by permitting an injured employee to bring a civil action against an employer "only after an order determining that the claim is not compensable has become final." OR ST § 656.019.

South Dakota has a provision modeled closely upon the Oregon statute, as follows:

> (7)(a) No injury is compensable unless the employment or employment related activities are a *major contributing cause of the condition complained* of. . . .

SD ST § 62–1–1. Florida has further extended this notion by re-defining "arising out of" as follows:

> (36) "Arising out of" pertains to occupational causation. An accidental injury or death arises out of employment if work performed in the course and scope of employment is the *major contributing cause* of the injury or death.

F.A.S. 440.02(36) (e.s.) The Florida courts initially held that the *major contributing cause* must be the one that is greater than any other as opposed to predominating over all others. Closet Maid v. Sykes, 763 So.2d 377 (Fla. 1st DCA 2000) (*en banc*) (for the work to be the "major contributing cause" among two or more causes requires that the "workplace accident contributes more to the disability or need for treatment than any other single cause."). The statute was quickly amended to require predominance. South Dakota has also added the "major" contributing cause requirement, SD St. § 62–1–1(7). Montana and Utah, employ the criterion to exclude coverage of injuries caused by use of illegal drugs or alcohol.

DAVIS V. HOUSTON GENERAL INS. CO.

Court of Appeals of Georgia, 1977.
141 Ga.App. 385, 233 S.E.2d 479.

MARSHALL, JUDGE.

This appeal arises out of an award denying compensation to a claimant for workmen's compensation. Appellant Mrs. Davis, claimant below enumerates as error the denial of compensation as affirmed by the Georgia Board of Workmen's Compensation and the superior court.

As relevant to these proceedings, the facts show that Mrs. Davis was employed as a nurse's aide at the Shoreham Convalescent Center, Inc. She had been so employed for about four or five months. On December 18, 1974, after completing her normal day's work, Mrs. Davis was putting on her outer coat preparatory to going home. Apparently she had placed her right arm in the coat and reached behind to place her left arm into the coat sleeve. At that time she felt a "pop." She reported this incident to her supervisor, but experienced no immediate pain, discomfort or other physical limitation. Several weeks later Mrs. Davis experienced a second episode involving the lifting of a patient, but that episode is not a part of this litigation. Following the second episode, Mrs. Davis was required to undergo two back operations and apparently is unable to perform her duties as before. In her own testimony, Mrs. Davis admitted that she had never experienced any back pain or limitation nor had she ever experienced any back trouble of any kind prior to the "pop" which occurred on December 18, 1974. On the basis of this evidence, the administrative law judge concluded that Mrs. Davis was injured in the course of her employment but that the injury did not arise out of her employment. Mrs. Davis enumerates as error this conclusion. *Held*:

The appellees, insurer and employer, admit that the injury occurred in the course of employment but continue to deny that the injury arose out of employment. The terms "in the course of" and "out of" are not synonymous. Both must occur to render the case a compensable one. Maryland Cas. Co. v. Peek, 36 Ga.App. 557, 559, 137 S.E. 121. The words "arising out of" mean that there must be some causal connection between the conditions under which the employee worked and the injury which she received. The causative danger must be incidental to the character of the employment, and not independent of the relation of master and servant. The accident must be one resulting from a risk reasonably incident to the employment. Thornton v. Hartford Accident etc. Co., 198 Ga. 786, 792, 32 S.E.2d 816.

An accident "arises out of" employment when there is apparent to the rational mind, upon consideration of all the circumstances, a causal connection between the conditions under which the work is required to be performed and the resulting injury. Under this test, if the injury can be seen to have followed as a natural incident of the work, and to have been contemplated by a reasonable person familiar with the whole situation as a result of the exposure occasioned by the nature of the employment, then it arises "out of" the employment. But it excludes an injury which can not fairly be traced to the employment as a contributing proximate cause and which comes from a hazard to which the workman would have been equally exposed apart from the employment. The causative danger must be peculiar to the work. It must be incidental to the character of the business, and not independent of the relation of master and servant.

In this case the administrative law judge, acting as the "reasonable person" heard testimony that for four or five months Mrs. Davis had worked as a hospital aide without any difficulty. She had never had any back trouble. On the day of the alleged injury she was engaged in an effort (putting on her coat) which logically was a hazard to which she was equally exposed apart from her employment. There was absolutely no evidence that the "pop" which occurred while putting on her outer coat was related in any way to or caused by the peculiar nature of her duties. In the absence of any evidence showing a connection between the strain of reaching behind to pull on a coat and the duties of a nurse's aide or that the duties of a nurse's aide were incidental to or the probable causation of the "pop," it was not unreasonable for the "rational mind" of the administrative law judge, upon a consideration of all the evidence to fail to find a causal connection between the conditions under which the work was required to be performed and the resulting injury.

A finding of fact by an administrative law judge or the State Board of Workmen's Compensation, when supported by any evidence, is conclusive and binding upon both the superior court and this court. Speight v. Container Corp., 138 Ga.App. 45, 46–47, 225 S.E.2d 496. The finding of the administrative law judge in this case is fully supported by the evidence before him.

Judgment affirmed.

NOTE

Compare, Strategic Marketing Systems v. Soranno, 559 So.2d 353 (Fla.App. 1st DCA 1990) (claimant, a computer operator, "popped" his knee when arising to change position in his chair; no impact was suffered and claimant had no history of knee trouble; compensation denied on ground that "mere occurrence of an injury at work, without more, is not compensable").

2. EMERGENCE OF THE POSITIONAL RISK DOCTRINE—STREET RISKS

In an effort to confer meaning on the spare "arising out of" phrase the courts in the earliest decisions adopted an approach which came to be known as the "increased risk" test; namely, "Was the risk of the particular injury greater for the worker than for someone not so employed?" Another way of expressing this was to ask whether the harmful agency was or not "peculiar" to the employment. Later experience, however, showed that this inquiry did not resolve all issues appropriately. For example, suppose the cause of harm was not a lightning flash, but merely an ordinary traffic crash that the general travelling public must confront? Is this a stronger or weaker case for imposing liability on the employer? The following case and those in succeeding sections demonstrate the evolution and varieties of theories the courts have developed to deal with them.

DONAHUE V. MARYLAND CAS. CO.

Supreme Judicial Court of Massachusetts, 1917.
226 Mass. 595, 116 N.E. 226.

Application by Patrick M. Donahue for compensation for injuries under the Workmen's Compensation Act, resisted by Thomas J. Flynn & Co., employer, and the Maryland Casualty Company, insurer. From the judgment on the decision of the Industrial Accident Board awarding compensation, the insurer appeals. Reversed, and decree entered for insurer.

CROSBY, J.

The evidence presented to the committee of arbitration was in substance as follows: The claimant, who was employed by the insured in the sale of church goods, on February 21, 1916, left his employer's place of business in Boston, and proceeded by train to Lowell and thence by electric cars to the village of Collinsville in Lowell. Upon leaving the electric cars, he went to the house of a clergyman, which was distant about ten minutes' walk from the car line, and after completing his business there left and started to walk back. He had proceeded about thirty-five or forty feet when he slipped on the ice and fell, sustaining a broken ankle. When injured he was walking in the middle of the street, the sidewalk being impassable on account of ice. He was employed principally as a traveling salesman, but worked in the store during the Christmas and Easter seasons. More than half of the time he was outside his employer's store visiting different places throughout New England for the purpose of selling church goods. He traveled by steam railroads, electric cars, and on foot,—using cars when available. When he left the house of the clergyman he intended to take a car to Lexington to sell some goods there. The committee found that the employee received an injury in the course of and arising out of his employment.

At the hearing before the Industrial Accident Board in addition to the evidence before the committee above recited, the employee testified:

> "I was going to get a car to Lexington when I fell. The street was a mass of ice. I never saw anything like it before or since."

The finding that the injury was received in the course of the employment was warranted. The question remains whether there was any evidence that the injury arose out of the employment. An injury arises out of the employment when there is a causal connection between the conditions under which the work is to be performed and the resulting injury. An injury cannot be found to have arisen out of the employment unless the employment was a contributing, proximate cause. If the risk of injury to the employee was one to which he would have been equally exposed apart from his employment, then the injury does not arise out of it. As was said by this court in McNicols' Case, 215 Mass. 497, at page 499, 102 N.E. 697, L.R.A.1916A, 306:

> "The causative danger must be peculiar to the work and not common to the neighborhood. It must be incidental to the character of the business and not independent of the relation of master and servant."

The undisputed evidence shows that while the employee was walking along the street in the course of his employment on his way to the electric car line, he slipped upon the ice and received the injury for which he seeks compensation. Manifestly the injury so received did not result in any proper sense from a risk incidental to the employment. It seems plain that the danger of the employee's slipping upon the ice in a public street was not peculiar to his work, but was a hazard common to persons engaged in any employment who had occasion to travel along the streets. The risk of slipping upon the icy pavement was common to the public who had occasion to pass over it on foot. It was a danger due to climatic conditions to which persons in that locality, however employed or if not employed at all, were equally exposed. * * *

As the hazard of slipping on the ice in the street was not a causative danger peculiar to the claimant's employment, the injury received could not properly be found to have arisen out of the employment.

The decree of the superior court must be reversed, and a decree entered in favor of the insurer.

So ordered.

KATZ V. A. KADANS & CO.

Court of Appeals of New York, 1922.
232 N.Y. 420, 134 N.E. 330.

POUND, J.

This is a workmen's compensation case. Louis Katz, the claimant, was a dairyman's chauffeur. On May 7, 1920, when he was driving his employer's car west on Canal street after delivering some cheese, an insane man stabbed him. A lot of people were running after the insane man and he stabbed any one near him. The question is whether claimant's injuries arose out of his employment.

If the work itself involves exposure to perils of the street, strange, unanticipated, and infrequent though they may be, the employee passes along the streets when on his master's occasions under the protection of the statute. This is the rule unequivocally laid down by the House of Lords in England:

> "When a workman is sent into the street on his master's business, * * * his employment necessarily involves exposure to the risks of the streets and injury from such a cause [necessarily] arises out of his employment." Finlay, L.C., in Dennis v. White, [1917] L.R.App.Cas. 479.

So we have to concern ourselves only with the question whether claimant's accident arose out of a street risk.

Cases may arise where one is hurt in the street, but where the risk is of a general nature, not peculiar to the street. Lightning strikes fortuitously in the street; bombs dropped by enemy aircraft do not expose to special danger persons in a street as distinguished from those in houses.[1] Allcock v. Rogers, [1918] House of Lords, 11 B.W.C.C. 149. The danger must result from the place to make it a street risk, but that is enough if the workman is in the place by reason of his employment, and in the discharge of his duty to his employer. The street becomes a dangerous place when street brawlers, highwaymen, escaping criminals, or violent madmen are afoot therein as they sometimes are. The danger of being struck by them by accident is a street risk because it is incident to passing through or being on the street when dangerous characters are abroad.

Particularly on the crowded streets of a great city, not only do vehicles collide, pavements become out of repair, and crowds jostle, but mad or biting dogs may run wild, gunmen may discharge their weapons, police officers may shoot at fugitives fleeing from justice, or other things may happen from which accidental injuries result to people on the streets

[1] Editor's Note: Horovitz notes that there are at least 19 exceptions and that Larson adds many more which are supported by cases throughout the country. 41 Neb.L.Rev., supra at 51.

which are peculiar to the use of the streets and do not commonly happen indoors.

The risk of being stabbed by an insane man running amuck seems in a peculiar sense a risk incidental to the streets to which claimant was exposed by his employment. Matter of Heidemann v. Am. Dist. Tel. Co., 230 N.Y. 305, 130 N.E. 302, does not hold that where the street risk is one shared equally by all who pass or repass, whether in or out of employment, it should be shown that the employment involves some special exposure; that the night watchman is exposed by his employment to the risk of being shot by accident as he nears a sudden brawl which it is his duty to investigate, while the night clerk whose business brings him on the street, but whose duty is not to seek danger, is not so exposed. We decided the case before us and no other, dwelling naturally upon those features of the situation which emphasized the connection between the risk and the employment. But the fact that the risk is one to which every one on the street is exposed does not itself defeat compensation. Members of the public may face the same risk every day. The question is whether the employment exposed the workman to the risks by sending him on to the street, common though such risks were to all on the street. Moran's Case, 234 Mass. 566, 125 N.E. 591; Dennis v. White, supra.

The order should be affirmed, with costs.

HOGAN, CARDOZO, AND CRANE, JJ., concur.

HISCOCK, C.J., and MCLAUGHLIN and ANDREWS, JJ., dissent.

Order affirmed.

NOTES

1. In addition to street risk injuries, courts have awarded compensation for injuries caused by numerous risks that are not inherent and peculiar to travel on highways. Examples include, Scandrett v. Industrial Comm., 235 Wis. 1, 291 N.W. 845 (1940) (portions of a building thrown into the street by a windstorm); Friel v. Industrial Comm., 398 Ill. 361, 75 N.E.2d 859 (1947) (a football kicked into the street shattered glass in the worker's vehicle); Everard v. Woman's Home Companion Reading Club, 234 Mo.App. 760, 122 S.W.2d 51 (1938) (a worker jammed a splinter into his foot on the highway); and City of Chicago v. Industrial Comm., 389 Ill. 592, 60 N.E.2d 212 (1945) (a worker stubbed a toe on a curb). Decisions such as these eliminate any requirement that the agency that caused the harm be an ordinary risk of the highway, such as a negligently driven vehicle, blowout, or defective pavement. The proposition applied by these cases was expressed by United Service Ins. Co. v. Donaldson, 254 Ala. 204, 48 So.2d 3, 6, 7 (1950), as follows:

> As to 'street accidents,' or 'perils of the street or highway,' this Court has adopted the more liberal view that in case of workmen whose

duties require them to be continually or frequently in or upon the street or highway and who are injured as a result thereof, the injury is one arising out of their employment.

2. All courts are not so generous in what is a street risk. See, e.g., Gooch v. Industrial Comm., 322 Ill. 586, 153 N.E. 624 (1926) (iceman injured in street by toy bomb discharged in Fourth of July celebration; compensation denied); and Morrow v. Orscheln Bros. Truck Lines, 235 Mo.App. 1166, 151 S.W.2d 138 (1941) (dust blown into claimant's eye while in the street; would have been a street risk if stirred up by traffic, but not because merely carried by wind), and Liebman v. Colonial Baking Co., 391 S.W.2d 948 (Mo.App.1965) (employee was assaulted in street for no apparent reason, compensation denied).

3. INJURIES CAUSED BY ACTS OF NATURE AND FORTUITOUS FORCES FROM OUTSIDE THE EMPLOYMENT

WHETRO V. AWKERMAN

Supreme Court of Michigan, 1970.
383 Mich. 235, 174 N.W.2d 783.

T.G. KAVANAGH, J.

These cases were consolidated pursuant to our order. * * *

They turn on the same question, for the damages for which workmen's compensation was awarded in each case were caused by the Palm Sunday, 1965, tornadoes which devastated parts of southern Michigan.

Carl Whetro was injured when the tornado destroyed the residence wherein he was working for his employer and seeks reimbursement for his medical expenses. Henry E. Emery was killed when the motel in which he was staying while on a business trip for his employer was destroyed by the tornado, and his widow seeks compensation for his death.

In each case the hearing referee found that the employee's injury arose out of and in the course of his employment. The award was affirmed by the appeal board in each case and by the Court of Appeals in the Whetro case.

The defendant-appellants in both cases base their defense on the assertion that tornadoes are "acts of God" or acts of nature and injuries which are caused by them do not arise "out of" the employment and hence are not compensable under the workman's compensation act. * * * For this reason they maintain that the cases were erroneously decided as a matter of law and the awards should be set aside.

The appellants in each case maintain that the injury did not arise "out of" the employment because that phrase, as it is used in the act, refers to a causal connection between the event which put in motion the forces which caused the injury and the work itself or the conditions under which it is required to be performed.

Employment as a caretaker-gardener or salesman, they argue, does not include tornadoes as incidents or conditions of the work, and the path of injury is determined by the tornado, not the employment.

Appellants cite a series of Michigan decisions involving injury by lightning: Klawinski v. Lake Shore & M.S.R. Co. (1915), 185 Mich. 643, 152 N.W. 213; Thier v. Widdifield (1920), 210 Mich. 355, 178 N.W. 16; Nelson v. Country Club of Detroit (1951), 329 Mich. 479, 45 N.W.2d 362; Kroon v. Kalamazoo County Road Commission (1954) 339 Mich. 1, 62 N.W.2d 641, in which compensation was denied, and assert that a tornado is like lightning in that it acts capriciously, leaving its victims and the untouched side by side. The decisions in all of these "lightning cases" denied compensation on the ground that the injury did not arise "out of" the employment because the employment did not expose the workman to any increased risk or to a more hazardous situation than faced by others in the area.

The Court of Appeals was able to distinguish between a tornado and a bolt of lightning as a causative force of injury and base its decision affirming the award for Carl Whetro on the reasoning of the Massachusetts supreme court in Caswell's case (1940), 305 Mass. 500, 26 N.E.2d 328, wherein recovery was allowed for injuries received when a brick wall of the employer's factory was blown down on workmen during a hurricane. This "contact with the premises" met the requirement that the injury arise "out of" the employment in the mind of the Court of Appeals.

We are unable to accept the distinction drawn between a tornado and bolt of lightning when viewed as the cause of an injury. As we see it, a tornado, no less than a bolt of lightning or an earthquake or flood is an "act of God" and if the phrase "out of" the employment in the workmen's compensation act necessarily entails the notion of proximate causality, no injury received because of an "act of God" should be compensable.

But we are satisfied that it is no longer necessary to establish a relationship of proximate causality between employment and an injury in order to establish compensability. Accordingly we no longer regard an "act of God" whether it be a tornado, lightning, earthquake, or flood as a defense to a claim for a work-connected injury. Such a defense retains too much of the idea that an employer should not pay compensation unless he is somehow at fault. This concept from the law of tort is inconsistent with the law of workmen's compensation.

The purpose of the compensation act as set forth in its title is to promote the welfare of the people of Michigan relating to the liability of employers for injuries or death sustained by their employees. The legislative policy is to provide financial and medical benefits to the victims of work-connected injuries in an efficient, dignified, and certain form. The act allocates the burden of such payments to the most appropriate source of payment, the consumer of the product. * * *

Fault has nothing to do with whether or not compensation is payable. The economic impact on an injured workman and his family is the same whether the injury was caused by the employer's fault or otherwise.

We hold that the law in Michigan today no longer requires the establishment of a proximately causal connection between the employment and the injury to entitle a claimant to compensation. The cases which have allowed recovery for street risks, * * * increased risks, * * * and on-the-premises accidents * * * were made without consideration of the proximate causal connection between the nature of the employment and the injury. They have brought the law in Michigan to the point where it can be said today that if the employment is the occasion of the injury, even though not the proximate cause, compensation should be paid. * * *

Accordingly, we hold that the employment of Carl Whetro and Henry E. Emery in each case was the occasion of the injury which they suffered and therefore the injuries arose "out of" and in the course of their employment.

The award in each case is affirmed.

[Omitted is an appendix listing chronologically Michigan cases demonstrating the evolutionary trend in Michigan leading to this decision. Omitted also is the special concurring opinion of Black, J.]

T.E. BRENNAN, C.J. (dissenting).

The function of the workmen's compensation act is to place the financial burden of industrial injuries upon the industries themselves, and spread that cost ultimately among the consumers.

This humane legislation was developed because the industrialization of our civilization had left in its wake a trail of broken bodies.

Employers were absolved from general liability for negligence, in exchange for the imposition of more certain liability under the act.

But it is a mistake to say that employers were absolved from fault. Liability is the basis of legal remedy. Fault is the basis of moral responsibility.

The workmen's compensation law is society's expression of the moral responsibility of employers and consumers to the workmen whose health and whose lives are sacrificed to industrial and commercial progress and production.

Fault is not the same thing as proximate cause. The compensation law does not use the word *cause*. Rather, it expresses the concept of employer and consumer responsibility in the phrase "arising out of and in the course of" the employment.

The terms "arising out of" and "in the course of" are not redundant. They mean two different things. An adulterous cobbler shot at his last by his jealous wife may be "in the course of" his employment. But the injury does not "arise out of" his job. On what basis of moral responsibility should his injuries be paid for by his employer? By what logic would society decree that his disability should add a farthing to the price of shoes?

The workmen's compensation law is not a utopian attempt to put a price tag on all human suffering and incorporate it into the cost of living.

Lightning, flood, tornadoes and estranged wives will always be with us, in this vale of tears. They were the occasion of human injury when our forebears were tilling the soil with sharp sticks. They are not a by-product of the industrial revolution, nor are they in any sense the moral responsibility of those who profit by, or enjoy the fruits of, our modern industrialized society.

I would reverse without apology for the precedents.

DETHMERS and KELLY, JJ., concurred with T.E. BRENNAN, C.J.

NOTES

1. The decisions pertaining to injuries and deaths caused by lightning, windstorm, earthquake and other acts of nature can generally be placed in one of four categories as follows:

(a) The increase in risk caused by the employment must have been a cause in fact of the injury or death. See, e.g., Campbell 66 Express, Inc. v. Industrial Comm., 83 Ill.2d 353, 47 Ill.Dec. 730, 415 N.E.2d 1043 (1980) (travel requirement of truck driver's employment increased risk to injury from inclement weather). This approach formerly prevailed in Michigan, but is now generally rejected. Kroon v. Kalamazoo County Road Comm., 339 Mich. 1, 62 N.W.2d 641 (1954) (compensation denied to survivors of worker killed when lightning struck metal shovel he held).

(b) The working environment at the time must have exposed the worker to a greater risk of injury or death by an act of nature than "one not so employed" would have been exposed to. Hill v. St. Paul Fire & Marine Ins. Co., 512 S.W.2d 560 (Tenn.1974).

The increase in risk may be created by a variety of factors. Parrish Esso Service Center v. Adams, 237 Ark. 560, 374 S.W.2d 468 (1964) (worker obliged to go out in storm to protect employer's property); State Highway Dept. v. Kloppenberg, 371 S.W.2d 793 (Tex.Civ.App.1963) (employee worked on high ground close to bridge; struck by lightning); and Arrington v. Goldstein, 23 N.J.Super. 103, 92 A.2d 630 (1952) (worker thrown into street by hurricane; proximity of ten story building contributed to erratic gusts of wind). Contrast J.I. Case Co. v. Industrial Comm., 36 Ill.2d 386, 223 N.E.2d 847 (1966) (employee paralyzed by lightning; compensation denied); and Crow v. Americana Crop Hail Pool, Inc., 176 Neb. 260, 125 N.W.2d 691 (1964) (worker struck by tornado while driving a truck on employment mission; compensation denied; employment did not cause increase of risk).

(c) Although not enhancing the likelihood of a natural disaster, the work environment makes the consequences more severe for the worker when it occurs. This approach is sometimes referred to as the "contact with the premises doctrine." See, e.g., Inland Steel Co. v. Industrial Comm., 41 Ill.2d 70, 241 N.E.2d 450 (1968) (worker struck by falling tile dislodged by tornado; heavy tile roof tended to fall into building rather than be thrown out and away; compensation awarded) and Ingram v. Bradley, 183 Neb. 692, 163 N.W.2d 875 (1969) (unstable ticket booth blown down upon employee, compensation awarded).

(d) The work required the employee to be at the place where the injury occurred. This is positional risk test applied in the principal case. Other cases include Harvey v. Caddo De Soto Cotton Oil Co., 199 La. 720, 6 So.2d 747 (1942) (employee at work when tornado struck, compensation awarded) and Wiggins v. Knox Glass, Inc., 219 So.2d 154 (Miss.1969) (same).

Would you draw a distinction between permitting recovery under the positional risk test in the many cases in which the injured worker was actively working at the spot where the natural disaster struck, and in cases where the employee was then doing no work, such as the employee Emery in the principal decision who was asleep in a motel when it was fortuitously struck by a tornado? Is it sufficient to say that if he had not been employed as he was, he would have been safely sleeping at a place of less actual risk? If so, does anything remain of the "arising out of" requirement? The positional risk test was rejected by Brady v. Louis Ruffolo & Sons Construction Company, 143 Ill.2d 542, 161 Ill.Dec. 275, 578 N.E.2d 921 (1991) (worker injured when truck slid off abutting icy public street and crashed through building where employee was working; compensation denied in absence of proof that construction of building increased risk of harm). See also Gayler v. North American Van Lines, 566 N.E.2d 84 (Ind.App.1991) (worker injured in car crash while en route to employer-authorized treatment for work related injuries; causal connection to work severed by aberrant driving of third person whose car caused the crash).

2. Many decisions permit recovery for injuries caused by fortuitous forces having no connection with either the injured employee or the employer that come onto the work site and injure or kill an employee. See, e.g., Industrial Indem. Co. v. Industrial Accident Comm., 95 Cal.App.2d 804, 214 P.2d 41 (1950) (while working in a bar, the employee was killed by a bullet fired at a customer by the customer's irate spouse; compensation awarded); Gargiulo v. Gargiulo, 24 N.J.Super. 129, 93 A.2d 598 (1952), affirmed 11 N.J. 611, 95 A.2d 646 (1953) (while at work, a butcher's helper was accidentally struck by an arrow shot by small boy next door: "But for the employment, the appellant would not have been in the back yard and in the path of the arrow," Id. at 132, 93 A.2d at 600); and Powell v. Great Western Ry. Co. 1 [1940] All Eng.Rep. 87 (a locomotive fireman was hit by pellet from air gun: "The accident happened to the workman because the workman's duties required him to be on the engine. Thus, it seems to me to follow that the accident arose out of the employment." Id. at 90). Other decisions permitting recovery for harm done by random risks that are extraneous to the employment include: Baran's Case, 336 Mass. 342, 145 N.E.2d 726 (1957) (stray bullet); Kitchens v. Department of Labor & Employment, Division of Labor, 29 Colo.App. 374, 486 P.2d 474 (1971) (accidental shooting while waiting for employer's vehicle); and, Avis v. Electrolux Corp., 2 A.D.2d 717, 151 N.Y.S.2d 542 (1956) (salesman's eye injured by talon of roving owl).

3. New York decisions generally allow compensation without referring to the positional risk doctrine. Instead the courts stress the New York statutory presumption that the accident arose out of the employment. See e.g., DeAngelis v. Garfinkel Painting Co., 20 A.D.2d 162, 245 N.Y.S.2d 485 (1963).

4. Some courts have expressly refused to extend the positional risk doctrine to places other than streets unless the employment environment created an "increased risk" of harm. In addition to the decisions referred to in the principal case, see Lathrop v. Tobin–Hamilton Shoe Mfg. Co., 402 S.W.2d 16 (Mo.App.1966) (runaway automobile crashed through window of factory where claimant worked; compensation denied; positional risk doctrine rejected); and, Christiansen v. Hill Reproduction Co., 262 App.Div. 379, 29 N.Y.S.2d 24 (1941) (salesman killed while waiting for customer at a bar; compensation denied).

5. A few states reject positional risk in favor of an "actual risk" test. The Virginia Supreme Court explained this doctrine as follows:

> Under this test, if the injury can be seen to have followed as a natural incident of the work and to have been contemplated by a reasonable person familiar with the whole situation as a result of the exposure occasioned by the nature of the employment, then it arises "out of" the employment. *But it excludes an injury which cannot fairly be traced to the employment as a contributing*

> *proximate cause and which comes from a hazard to which the workman would have been equally exposed apart from the employment.* The causative danger must be peculiar to the work and not common to the neighborhood. It must be incidental to the character of the business and not independent of the relation of master and servant. It need not have been foreseen or expected, but after the event it must appear to have had its origin in a risk connected with the employment, and to have flowed from that source as a rational consequence.

Baggett Transp. Co. v. Dillon, 219 Va. 633, 638, 248 S.E.2d 819, 822 (1978). Applied, Hill City Trucking, Inc. v. Christian, 238 Va. 735, 385 S.E.2d 377 (1989) (long distance truck driver shot after being stopped by robbers while on the road; compensation denied). See also In re McNicol, 215 Mass. 497, 102 N.E. 697 (1913), and Hughes v. St. Patrick's Cathedral, 245 N.Y. 201, 156 N.E. 665 (1927) ("actual risk" test adopted in heat exposure case).

6. Most of the decisions in which the positional risk theory is arguably applicable involve what are often referred to as "neutral" risks. That is, they are neither distinctly employment nor distinctly personal in character. Another modality is that the cause of an injury is simply unknown, making it impossible to attribute a cause and effect relationship between the harmful agency and either the employment or to an act or characteristic personal to the injured employee. Where an employee falls for no explainable reason, compensation is generally awarded if the activity in which the worker was engaged at the time was being done in the line of duty. See, e.g., Burroughs Adding Machine Co. v. Dehn, 110 Ind.App. 483, 39 N.E.2d 499 (1942); Ball v. Workmen's Compensation Appeal Bd., 19 Pa.Cmwlth. 157, 340 A.2d 610 (1975); and, Circle K Store No. 1131 v. Industrial Comm., 165 Ariz. 91, 796 P.2d 893 (1990) (claimant fell after depositing employer's trash bag in garbage dumpster while on her journey home. Compensation granted on basis that claimant would not have been at dumpster "but for" her assigned employment duty, thereby raising a presumption of "arising out of" that employer had not rebutted). The decisions, however, are not uniform. See, e.g., Finn v. Industrial Comm., 165 Colo. 106, 437 P.2d 542 (1968).

7. What if an unimpaired worker stumbles and falls on the job for no apparent reason while ascending well maintained normal steps? Is the resulting injury compensable? A Plus Home Health Care Incorporated v. Miecznikowski, 983 N.E. 2d (Ind. App. 2012), transfer denied, 985 N.E.2d 338 (Ind. 2013)(treating the unexplained fall as a "neutral risk) and Dawson v. State, 262 P.3d 358 (Kan. App. 2011) (treating a fall on a wet step a "normal risk of traveling") approved recoveries. In contrast County of Chesterfield v. Johnson, 237 Va. 180, 376 S.E.2d 73 (Va.1989) denied recovery when "there was nothing unusual about or wrong with the steps at Johnson's workplace." Johnson distinguished an earlier decision that had awarded compensation when a fall had occurred on a "slightly unusual series of steps.

4. INJURIES CAUSED BY IMPORTED AND PERSONAL RISKS

HILL–LUTHY CO. V. INDUSTRIAL COMM.

Supreme Court of Illinois, 1952.
411 Ill. 201, 103 N.E.2d 605.

CRAMPTON, JUSTICE.

Arthur L. Rumple filed an application with the Industrial Commission for adjustment of compensation, charging that he lost the sight of an eye as the result of an accident arising out of, and in the course of, his employment. An arbitrator's award of compensation was sustained by the commission. Upon *certiorari* to the circuit court of Peoria County the decision of the commission was set aside. We have granted a petition for writ of error, and the record is submitted for further review.

The facts are not in dispute. Claimant was the only witness who testified. He was employed to drive a truck carrying soft water tanks, and to deliver the tanks to customers' homes, where he installed them. On the morning of July 31, 1947, after having delivered and installed one of the tanks, he entered the truck and started the motor. Before moving on to the next stop, however, he proceeded to light a cigarette. When he struck the match the head of it flew off, hitting him directly in the left eye and inflicting the injury in question. After receiving medical treatment and hospitalization he returned to work on November 17, 1947. It was stipulated herein that the loss of the left eye was the direct result of the burning by the match head on July 31, 1947.

Since the facts are uncontroverted the question whether claimant's injuries arose out of, and in the course of, his employment is one of law. Math Igler's Casino, Inc. v. Industrial Comm., 394 Ill. 330, 68 N.E.2d 773. The Workmen's Compensation Act requires that an accidental injury, to be compensable, must not only be sustained in the course of the employment but must also arise out of it. It is clear plaintiff in error's injury was received in the course of his employment, for the accident occurred within the period of the employment at a place where he reasonably may have been in the performance of his duties and while he was fulfilling those duties or engaged in something incidental thereto. But it is equally clear that the injury did not arise out of his employment. It arose from a cause having no relation to the nature of the employment. To entitle a claimant to obtain workmen's compensation benefits under the statute, his injury must be of such character that it may be seen to have had its origin in the nature of, or have been incidental to, the employment, or it must have been the result of a risk to which, by reason of the employment, the injured employee was exposed to a greater degree than if he had not been so employed. Loyola University v. Industrial Comm., 408 Ill. 139, 96 N.E.2d 509.

In the case at bar, the injury was caused by the defective match head, which flew off as plaintiff in error attempted to light a cigarette. The use of matches or the act of smoking was in no way incidental to the employment. The risk encountered was entirely divorced from it, and was one to which the general public is equally exposed while performing such acts in homes or elsewhere for personal enjoyment and comfort. The moving cause of the injury was not peculiar to the work but was common to the public. It was not incidental to the character of the employer's business but was entirely independent of the relationship of employment. In short, there was no causal connection between Rumple's employment and his injury.

Plaintiff in error has called our attention to a number of cases from foreign jurisdictions wherein injuries suffered while attempting to smoke or perform other acts of personal comfort were held to be compensable. No purpose would be served, however, by distinguishing each such case herein. Examination of their facts discloses direct connections between the injuries and conditions relating to the employment. Where clothing becomes oily, greasy, or otherwise inflammable from the nature of the work, the risk of igniting it in the act of smoking is obviously greater than it would be under ordinary conditions. Where an injury is incurred from a fall, or from breaking the glass in a door, or from being struck by an automobile or other object, or from an explosion of some substance on the employer's premises, any of which may occur while the employee has stopped for a smoke or is in the act of lighting a pipe or cigarette, its origin in the nature or conditions of the employment is not by virtue of the act of smoking but by virtue of the other factors involved.

Plaintiff in error contends that an employee may do those things which are necessary for his own health and comfort, such as smoking, warming himself, seeking shelter, or leaving work to answer a call of nature, procure a drink, food, or fresh air, and that such acts will be considered incidental to his employment. Several cases are cited upholding awards where the injuries were sustained in the course of such activities. But plaintiff in error fails to distinguish between the requirement that the injury arise out of the employment and the requirement that it be sustained in the course of the employment. Cases holding that no break in the employment is caused by the mere fact that the employee is engaging in the incidental activities referred to can be of no aid to him. The issue here concerns the origin or cause of the accident. The rule is well settled that an injury arises out of the employment when there is apparent to the rational mind a causal connection between the conditions under which the work is to be performed and the resulting injury. Under this test, if the injury can be seen to have followed as a natural incident to the work and as a result of the exposure occasioned by the nature of the employment, then it arises out of the employment. But the rule excludes an injury which cannot fairly be traced to the employment as a contributing proximate cause, and which comes from a hazard to which the workman would have been equally exposed apart from the employment. Risks of injury from defective matches used in the act of smoking are clearly those to which the general public is exposed. They are not within the contemplation of workmen's compensation acts, even though the injured person, at the time he suffered his injury, may have been performing duties incident to, and in the course of, his employment. See Ceisel v. Industrial Comm., 400 Ill. 574, 81 N.E.2d 506.

Given its logical effect, the contention of plaintiff in error would have the employer liable for any injury sustained by his employee, provided only that it occur while the latter is engaged in his employment. But the Workmen's Compensation Act does not make the employer an insurer of the safety of his employees while engaged in his service. Its intention is to protect the employee against the risks and hazards taken in order to perform the tasks assigned to him, and if no such risk or hazard caused, or contributed to cause the injury, the employee is not entitled to compensation.

We conclude that the judgment of the circuit court of Peoria County was correct, and it is affirmed, accordingly.

Judgment affirmed.

— *NOTES* —

1. But apparently contra, Puffin v. General Electric Co., 132 Conn. 279, 43 A.2d 746 (1945) (employee smoking during rest period; cigarette ignited angora sweater; compensation awarded).

2. Even a personal risk, such as smoking, eating, or drinking, may be compensable if causally enhanced in some way by the duties of the employment or the work environment. Cases that have awarded compensation include Burton v. Broadcast Music Inc., 31 A.D.2d 557, 294 N.Y.S.2d 406 (1968) (corporation president on travel killed by fire started in hotel suite; asleep for several hours following business conference in which there was smoking and drinking); Snyder v. General Paper Corp., 277 Minn. 376, 152 N.W.2d 743 (1967) (travelling employee choked to death on large piece of steak at hotel dinner where he was entertaining a prospective customer); Steel Sales Corp. v. Industrial Comm., 293 Ill. 435, 127 N.E. 698 (1920) (employee burned when matches carried in his pocket for personal use were ignited through friction contact with a work locker); Boullier v. Samsan Co., 100 R.I. 676, 219 A.2d 133 (1966) (intense fumes in factory obliged worker to go to rest room to smoke; fumes ignited by flame); and Bletter v. Harcourt, Brace & World, Inc., 30 A.D.2d 601, 290 N.Y.S.2d 59 (1968) (young editor fell while attempting to execute a dance step in a self-operated

elevator, because, as he testified, "I was in good spirits because I was enjoying the job. * * *;" compensation awarded). Perhaps the most lenient decision on this point is Wiseman v. Industrial Accident Comm., 46 Cal.2d 570, 297 P.2d 649 (1956) (corporation officer on trip spent leisure time with woman in hotel for romantic purposes; both burned to death in fire started by careless smoking in bed; compensation awarded). Contra, Kaplan v. Zodiac Watch Co., 20 N.Y.2d 537, 285 N.Y.S.2d 585, 232 N.E.2d 625 (1967) (travelling employee who had spent the night at a motel, entangled his leg in his trousers; fell and sustained a back injury; compensation denied because the risk was exclusively personal).

3. Injuries caused by risks imported into the employment for the employee's personal convenience and pleasure have been variously treated. Compare Hatfill v. Industrial Comm., 202 Ill.App.3d 547, 148 Ill.Dec. 67, 560 N.E.2d 369 (1990) (compensation denied employee injured while jumping over ditch in employer's parking lot as a short cut to his car; personal risk doctrine precludes recovery), and Ward v. Halliburton Co., 76 N.M. 463, 415 P.2d 847 (1966) (employee was killed when his hunting gun accidentally discharged while he was fetching his work uniform from his car; compensation denied); and Loveless v. Industrial Comm., 6 Ariz.App. 345, 432 P.2d 600 (1967) (claimant, an overseer whose job required him to carry a gun was shot as result of handing it to his son for examination; compensation denied), with Joe Ready's Shell Station and Cafe v. Ready, 218 Miss. 80, 65 So.2d 268 (1953) (employee of service station preparing to do bookkeeping work at home was shot while removing her husband's hunting gun from sofa; compensation allowed).

4. Suppose the employee is injured while attempting to start or maintain a private automobile on the employer's premises during work hours? The decisions vary. Fisher Body Division, General Motors Corp. v. Industrial Comm., 40 Ill.2d 514, 240 N.E.2d 694 (1968) (claimant was injured when his car battery blew up while he was trying to start his car in employer's lot on cold day; compensation denied). Compare Buerkle v. United Parcel Service, 26 N.J.Super. 404, 98 A.2d 327 (1953) (employee slipped on ice while taking a battery booster to his stalled vehicle on the employer's parking lot; compensation awarded); and California Cas. Indem. Exchange v. Industrial Acc. Comm., 21 Cal.2d 751, 135 P.2d 158 (1943) (employee tripped on hem of her skirt while alighting from vehicle after a personal errand; compensation awarded).

5. Suppose the employee brings contaminated or otherwise harmful food to work and is injured while consuming it during a lunch break? Goodyear Aircraft Corp. v. Industrial Comm., 62 Ariz. 398, 158 P.2d 511 (1945) (employee injured when defective soft drink bottle that he had brought to work broke while he was opening it; compensation awarded). Contrast Williams v. Industrial Comm., 38 Ill.2d 593, 232 N.E.2d 744 (1967) (clerk choked on doughnut bought at employer's store and eaten on premises; risk was regarded as personal and compensation denied).

FETZER V. NORTH DAKOTA WORKFORCE SAFETY AND INSURANCE

Supreme Court of North Dakota, 2012.
815 N.W.2d 539.

KAPSNER, JUSTICE.

Beverly Fetzer appeals from a district court judgment affirming a Workforce Safety and Insurance ("WSI") order denying her request for benefits. Because we conclude claimants must prove a causal connection between their employment and injury, and because Fetzer was unable to prove such a connection, we affirm.

I

While walking down a hallway on her employer's premises and during work hours, Fetzer thought she heard someone call her name. Turning in response, Fetzer caught her foot and fell, fracturing her left hip and wrist. No cause of the fall was apparent. Fetzer filed a claim for workers' compensation benefits with WSI, and WSI denied her claim. Fetzer submitted a request for reconsideration. WSI issued an order consistent with its prior decision, determining Fetzer's injury "occurred in the course of, but did not arise out of" her employment. WSI added, "Mere walking, without more, is not an activity that is sufficiently linked to Claimant's employment so that the injury can be deemed to have arisen from employment."

Fetzer requested a hearing. Because the parties did not dispute the facts, they waived hearing and entered into a stipulation of facts. The stipulation noted the floor on which Fetzer fell "was even with no obstruction, slippery spills, fraying or rips in the carpet." The stipulation also provided, "The fall is unexplained and not attributable to a risk personal to Fetzer." An Administrative Law Judge ("ALJ") issued findings, conclusions, and an order, stating, "The fact that the fall is unexplained causes a problem of proof for the claimant. If the fall is unexplained, the claimant cannot show the requisite causation entitling her to benefits." The ALJ summarized Fetzer's argument that with unexplained falls, "the risk should be borne by the employer, rather than the employee. [Fetzer] urges the application of the 'positional risk' doctrine. That is, if the employee was at work or performing some work-related function when the unexplained fall occurred, the fall is compensable." Affirming WSI's order denying Fetzer's claim, the ALJ determined that accepting Fetzer's argument would negate North Dakota's requirement that claimants prove their work injuries arose out of their employment. Fetzer appealed the ALJ decision to the district court. The court affirmed, noting "the ALJ concluded that North Dakota law requires a claimant to prove that her injury arose from her employment and that Fetzer did not do so. [The ALJ's] conclusions are in accordance with the law, not with what Fetzer would like it to be."

— II —

On appeal, Fetzer argues her injury is compensable under the positional risk doctrine, which requires the employer to bear the risk of loss when an employee sustains an unexplained fall at work. Fetzer contends we previously recognized the positional risk doctrine in a case involving horseplay at work, and she claims our earlier holding should be extended to award compensation to an employee who falls at work without explanation.

* * *

Claimants have a burden of proving by a preponderance of the evidence that they suffered a compensable injury, entitling them to workers' compensation benefits. N.D.C.C. § 65–01–11; Swenson v. Workforce Safety & Ins. Fund, 2007 ND 149, ¶ 24, 738 N.W.2d 892. "Compensable injury" is defined as "an injury by accident arising out of and in the course of hazardous employment which must be established by medical evidence supported by objective medical findings." N.D.C.C. § 65–01–02(10) (emphasis added). Generally, "course of employment" refers to the time, place, and circumstances of the accident resulting in the injury, and "arising out of" refers to a causal connection between the injury and the employment. Choukalos v. N.D. Workers' Comp. Bureau, 427 N.W.2d 344, 345–46 (N.D.1988). "[A] claimant must prove by a preponderance of the evidence that the medical condition for which benefits are sought is causally related to a work injury." Bergum v. N.D. Workforce Safety & Ins., 2009 ND 52, ¶ 11, 764 N.W.2d 178. In this case, the parties dispute whether the "arising out of" element is satisfied.

Fetzer claims a majority of states "conclude that the positional risk doctrine supports compensation award[s] to employees injured as a result of a neutral risk—that is, a risk not personal to the claimant." To support her position, Fetzer relies heavily on a treatise by Professor Larson, a prominent scholar on workers' compensation, who describes the positional risk doctrine with the following:

> An important and growing number of courts are accepting the full implications of the positional-risk test: An injury arises out of the employment if it would not have occurred but for the fact that the conditions and obligations of the employment placed claimant in the position where he was injured. It is even more common for the test to be approved and used in particular situations. This theory supports compensation, for example, in . . . situations in which the only connection of the employment with the injury is that its obligations placed the employee in the

> particular place at the particular time when he or she was injured by some neutral force, meaning by "neutral" neither personal to the claimant nor distinctly associated with the employment.

1 Larson, Workers' Compensation Law § 3.05 (2011). Larson adds, "In a pure unexplained-fall case, there is no way in which an award can be justified as a matter of causation theory except by a recognition that this but-for reasoning satisfies the 'arising' requirement." 1 id. § 7.04[1][a]. Fetzer notes unexplained falls are positional risk cases, arguing "[b]ut for the employment, the claimant would not have been injured at that time and place." Fetzer states the "arising out of" element is satisfied under the positional risk doctrine, and she contends "North Dakota law . . . is perfectly consistent with the positional risk principle." WSI counters that an employee who endures an unexplained fall at work has not automatically satisfied the "arising out of" element merely because the fall occurred on work premises, arguing "[t]here can and should be an analysis of the causal connection between the employment and the injury." WSI claims that adoption of the positional risk doctrine would change existing North Dakota law, which is a matter for legislative, rather than judicial, determination.

Because we have not previously discussed the "arising out of" element in the context of unexplained falls, we first turn our attention to the legislative history of N.D.C.C. § 65–01–02. In 1977, the Legislature added the "arising out of" language to the definition of a compensable injury. 1977 N.D. Sess. Laws ch. 579, § 2. The drafter's note to the 1977 amendment explained:

> Presently the law only requires that an injury arise in the course of employment. Our courts have interpreted that to mean that if an employee is at the place he is supposed to be at the time he is supposed to be there, and engaged in an activity whose purpose is related to employment, any injury he receives is compensable.
>
> . . . It is hoped—and it is the intent of the Bureau—that the addition of "[arising] out of and" would change that interpretation.

Hearing on S.B. 2158 Before the Senate Indus., Bus., and Labor Comm., 45th N.D. Legis. Sess. (Jan. 19, 1977) (testimony of Richard Gross, Counsel for Workmen's Compensation Bureau). The legislative history demonstrates that, by amending the statute to define a compensable injury with conjunctive language as one "arising out of and in the course of" employment, the Legislature and WSI—then referred to as "the Bureau"—intended for claimants to prove more than that they merely suffered an injury on work premises and during work hours to receive compensation for the injury.

* * *

While the positional risk doctrine may be consistent with a liberal construction of workers' compensation law, our Workforce Safety and Insurance Act specifically provides, "This title may not be construed liberally on behalf of any party to the action or claim." N.D.C.C. § 65–01–01. A state with a similar law is Nevada, which provides "the provisions of chapters [governing workers' compensation claims] must not be interpreted or construed broadly or liberally in favor of an employee . . . or the dependents of the employee, or . . . an employer[.]" Nev.Rev.Stat. § 616A.010(4). Nevada likewise requires claimants to prove their injury "arose out of and in the course of" employment, Nev.Rev.Stat. § 616C.150(1), and the Nevada Supreme Court has considered an unexplained fall case involving a claimant who urged the adoption of the positional risk doctrine. Mitchell v. Clark Cnty. Sch. Dist., 121 Nev. 179, 111 P.3d 1104, 1106 (2005). In declining to adopt the positional risk doctrine, the Nevada Supreme Court stated the doctrine "reduces the claimant's burden and requires only a showing that the claimant sustained an injury on the job," in circumvention of Nevada's statutory requirements. Id. at 1107.

Similarly, we conclude that the but-for reasoning of the positional risk doctrine is incompatible with the North Dakota Workforce Safety and Insurance Act. Because the positional risk doctrine requires a claimant only to show that an injury was sustained while at work, the doctrine directly contravenes both the language of N.D.C.C. § 65–01–02(10) and the Legislature's stated intent in adding the "arising out of" element. As noted by the ALJ in this case, "Accepting the 'but-for' reasoning as satisfying the 'arising out of' requirement would negate the necessity of showing the 'arising out of' prong altogether. . . . If merely being at work was sufficient to show causation, the legislature need not have required the 'arising out of' test." We have often noted the presumption that the Legislature acts with purpose and does not perform idle acts. See, e.g., Wheeler v. Gardner, 2006 ND 24, ¶ 15, 708 N.W.2d 908; see also N.D.C.C. § 1–02–38(2) ("In enacting a statute, it is presumed that . . . [t]he entire statute is intended to be effective."). In light of this presumption and the pertinent legislative history, we hold the but-for reasoning of the positional risk doctrine is inconsistent with our statute that requires claimants to prove a causal connection between their employment and injury. We have consistently stated our function is to interpret the law, not to legislate, noting "[i]f the rule is wrong, the legislature has ample power to change it[.]" Olson v. Workforce Safety & Ins., 2008 ND 59, ¶ 23, 747 N.W.2d 71 (quoting CybrCollect, Inc. v. N.D. Dep't of Fin. Inst., 2005 ND 146, ¶ 23, 703 N.W.2d 285). If the Legislature intends for WSI to award compensation to claimants who suffer unexplained falls at work, the Legislature has the power to amend the plain language of N.D.C.C.

§ 65–01–02(10) to reflect that intent. Because Fetzer was unable to show a causal connection between her fall and her employment, the ALJ properly denied Fetzer's request for compensation.

III

We affirm the district court judgment affirming WSI's order to deny Fetzer's request for benefits.

MARING, JUSTICE, dissenting.

I respectfully dissent. I would adopt the positional-risk doctrine and reverse the district court judgment affirming the Administrative Order. . . .

MILLEDGE V. THE OAKS

Supreme Court of Indiana, 2003.
784 N.E.2d 926.

RUCKER, JUSTICE.

Case Summary

This case presents the question of when and to what extent an injury resulting from an unexplained accident occurring in the workplace is compensable under Indiana's Worker's Compensation Act. We conclude that an unexplained accident represents a "neutral risk" and that the "positional-risk" doctrine applies. Under which, an injury is compensable if it would not have occurred but for the fact that the condition or obligation of the employment put the employee in the position at the time of injury.

Facts and Procedural History

In 1983 Phyllis Milledge began working as a housekeeper at a nursing home known as "The Oaks, A Living Center." On October 21, 1994, she arrived at work shortly before 7 a.m. to begin her usual shift and parked her car in the nursing home parking lot. After closing the door upon exiting the car Milledge twisted her ankle. She proceeded to her job and completed the majority of her shift but the pain in her ankle prevented Milledge from finishing her duties. Leaving work early, Milledge went to the emergency room of a local hospital where x-rays revealed a sprained ankle. However, her ankle still bothered her a week after the injury. Among other things she suffered swelling in her right leg, and her right foot was severely discolored. In addition, a large blister had developed on her ankle, which her husband lanced on two occasions. Milledge returned to the hospital on November 6, 1994, where she was treated with antibiotics. On November 14, 1994, after surgical procedures failed to control the infection that had developed, Milledge's right leg was amputated below the knee. Subsequently, she was fitted with a prosthesis.

When The Oaks' worker's compensation insurance carrier denied her claim for benefits on March 3, 1995, Milledge filed an Application for Adjustment of Claim before the Worker's Compensation Board. On July 21, 1999, a hearing was conducted before a single-member hearing officer who denied the claim concluding in part:

> The record shows [Milledge's] injury may have occurred in the course of her employment, but fails to show any causal connection between her ankle sprain and her work duties for [The Oaks]. Thus, [Milledge's] injury did not arise out of and in the course of her employment with [The Oaks] for the purposes of the [Indiana Worker's Compensation] Act.

Appellant's App. at 9. In a vote of five to two, the Full Board adopted the single hearing officer's decision. The Court of Appeals affirmed in a published opinion. *See Milledge v. The Oaks*, 764 N.E.2d 230 (Ind.Ct.App.2002). Having previously granted transfer, we now reverse the decision of the Worker's Compensation Board and remand this cause for further proceedings.

Discussion

There is no question that the injury Milledge sustained in this case occurred in the course of her employment. She sprained her ankle on the parking lot of her employer while arriving for work at her regularly scheduled time. *See, e.g., Lawhead v. Brown*, 653 N.E.2d 527, 529 (Ind.Ct.App.1995) (employee entitled to compensation where injury occurred immediately after employee "clocked-out" but while present on employer-controlled parking lot); *Ward v. Tillman*, 179 Ind.App. 626, 386 N.E.2d 1003, 1005 (1979) ("[L]iability of employers has been extended beyond the immediate job site.... Accidents resulting from the ingress-egress of employees to a plant within workmen's compensation coverage [are] an employment-related risk."). Rather, the question is whether Milledge's injury arose out of her employment. Highlighting the Board's finding that the parking lot was "clean, dry, level and clear of debris" the Court of Appeals concluded the injury Milledge sustained did not arise out of her employment. *Milledge*, 764 N.E.2d at 234. This was so because the facts of this case lacked the requisite causal connection between the injury and the employment. Id.

Commenting on the causal connection necessary to show that an accidental injury arises out of employment, this Court has said "[the] nexus is established when a reasonably prudent person considers the injury to be born out of a risk incidental to the employment, or when the facts indicate a connection between the injury and the circumstances under which the employment occurs." *Wine–Settergren v. Lamey*, 716 N.E.2d 381, 389 (Ind.1999); *see also Blaw–Knox Foundry & Mill Machinery, Inc. v. Dacus*, 505 N.E.2d 101, 102–03 (Ind.Ct.App.1987) ("[A] connection is established when the accident arises out of a risk which a reasonably prudent person might comprehend as incidental to the work. It is not necessary that the injury should have been expected or foreseen."), trans. denied.

The "risk[s] incidental to employment" fall into three categories: (1) risks distinctly associated with employment (2) risks personal to the claimant, and (3) risks of neither distinctly employment nor distinctly personal in character. *Roush*, 706 N.E.2d at 1114; *see also* 1 Arthur Larson & Lex K. Larson, *Larson's Workers' Compensation Law* 4–1 (2002). Risks that fall within categories numbered one and three are generally covered under the Indiana Worker's Compensation Act. However risks personal to the claimant, those "caused by a pre-existing illness or condition unrelated to employment," are not compensable. *Kovatch v. A.M. Gen.*, 679 N.E.2d 940, 943 (Ind.Ct.App.1997), *trans. denied.*

Risks in category number one are those we intuitively think of as work connected. As Professor Larson explains, this category includes: "[a]ll the things that can go wrong around a modern factory, mill, mine, transportation system, or construction project . . . and constitute the bulk of what not only the public but perhaps also the original drafters of compensation acts had in mind as their proper concern." Larson, *supra*, § 4.01, at 4–1–4–2. See, e.g., *Control Techniques, Inc. v. Johnson*, 762 N.E.2d 104, 106 (Ind.2002) (electrician severely burned while measuring the voltage in a circuit breaker at a factory); *Mid–West Box Co. v. Hazzard*, 195 Ind. 608, 146 N.E. 420, 420–21 (1925) (employee's finger severed while operating machinery); *Turner v. Richmond Power & Light Co.*, 756 N.E.2d 547, 550 (Ind.Ct.App.2001) (employee electrocuted when excavating a sewer line after co-worker hit a buried power line), *trans. denied.* The underlying theme uniting these cases is that the injury sustained by the claimant was the result of conditions inherent in the work environment. In this case there was nothing inherent in The Oaks' parking lot that either caused or contributed to Milledge's injury. As such her injury was not born out of a risk categorized as distinctly associated with employment.

As for category number two, the record does not show that Milledge's injury to her ankle was the result of a pre-existing illness or condition. To the contrary, although the Board made no finding on this point, uncontroverted evidence of record reveals that prior to the accident of October 21, 1994, Milledge experienced no problems with her right leg in general or to her ankle in particular. R. at 21, 32–33. The record also shows, that although Milledge suffered from diabetes for thirty years, at the time of the accident she was taking medication for her diabetes and she reported having no trouble with the illness; additionally, she noted that diabetes had never prevented her from fulfilling her job responsibilities. R. at 13, 24. In this case Milledge simply has no explanation of what caused her to twist her ankle; nor does the record give any indication of causation. The facts here are thus analogous to those cases involving injuries suffered by an employee as the result of an "unexplained" fall. As the Court of Appeals has observed:

> Workplace falls can result from either an employment, personal or neutral risk, or from a combination thereof. Some falls clearly result from risks personal to the employee; that is, they are caused by a pre-existing illness or condition, unrelated to employment. As a general matter, these "idiopathic" falls are not compensable. In contrast, some falls are "unexplained" in that there is no indication of causation. Most jurisdictions compensate such falls, classifying them as neutral risks.

Kovatch, 679 N.E.2d at 943 (citations omitted).[2]

Courts have taken three approaches in addressing the "arising out of" element in unexplained fall cases. One approach requires the worker to rule out idiopathic causes for the fall. If the worker carries that burden, then an inference arises that the fall arose out of employment. Using this approach the Oregon Supreme Court has applied a "work-connection" test to determine whether an injury arises out of and in the course of employment. *Phil A. Livesley Co. v. Russ*, 296 Or. 25, 672 P.2d 337, 339, 340 (1983). The "work-connection" test focuses on whether the relationship between the injury and the employment is sufficient for the injury to be compensable. *Id.* at 339. If the "in the course of" element is fully met, then it will satisfy the "arising out of" element, provided the employee rules out idiopathic causes. *Id.* at 342. *See also Waller v. Mayfield*, 37 Ohio St.3d 118, 524 N.E.2d 458, 464–65 (1988) ("Where the course of employment test is fully met, where cause-in-fact cannot be directly established, and where the claimant has met his burden of eliminating idiopathic causes, we interpret the Workers' Compensation Act to allow the inference that the unexplained fall arose out of employment."). Although this is an attractive approach, it nonetheless places the employee in the position of attempting to prove a negative. This is not a burden we believe the employee should have to bear. *See, e.g., Town of Montezuma v. Downs*, 685 N.E.2d 108, 116 n. 9 (Ind.Ct.App.1997) ("To require the Downs to affirmatively prove that the pipeline was not inspected would require them to prove a negative, something which we refuse to do."), *trans. denied*; *Jackson v. Warrum*,

[2] "[M]eaning by 'neutral' neither personal to the claimant nor distinctly associated with the employment." Larson, *supra*, § 3.05, at 3–6.

535 N.E.2d 1207, 1218 (Ind.Ct.App.1989) (describing as "impossible" the "burden of proving a negative fact"). We therefore decline to adopt this view.

A second approach leaves the burden on the employee to show a causal connection between the injury and the employment. This is the most difficult burden to meet when an injury occurs without explanation. And although it is especially well suited for injuries that result from risks distinctly associated with employment, as discussed in more detail below, it is problematic for risks that are neither distinctly employment related nor distinctly personal in character. This is essentially the approach adopted by the Court of Appeals in this case.

A third approach involves applying the "positional risk test" also referred to as the "positional risk doctrine." *See Smith v. Bob Evans Farms, Inc.*, 754 N.E.2d 18, 26 n. 1 (Ind.Ct.App.2001) (observing that under Indiana law "the positional risk doctrine is generally applied to neutral risks"), *trans. denied*; *accord K–Mart Corp. v. Novak*, 521 N.E.2d 1346, 1348–49 (Ind.Ct.App.1988), *trans. denied*. Under this doctrine "[a]n injury arises out of the employment if it would not have occurred *but for* the fact that the conditions and obligations of the employment placed claimant in the position where he was injured." Larson, *supra*, § 3.05, at 3–6. This but for reasoning is the foundation of the positional risk doctrine, under which if the "in the course of" employment element is met, then there is a rebuttable presumption that the injury "arises out of" employment. Although similar to the "work connection" test mentioned above, here the burden is on the employer to demonstrate that the injury was actually the result of a cause personal to the claimant.

The positional risk doctrine is generally applied in those instances where injuries result from risks that are categorized as neutral. *See, e.g., Logsdon v. ISCO Co.*, 260 Neb. 624, 618 N.W.2d 667, 673–74, 675 (2000) (noting that Nebraska applies the positional risk doctrine when faced with a neutral risk such as an unexplained fall and under the doctrine a claimant is not required to rule out idiopathic causes, but where there is at least some evidence of a possibility of a personal or idiopathic factor contributing to the fall, the fall is not properly categorized as a purely unexplained fall); *Cartwright v. Onondaga News Agency*, 283 A.D.2d 837, 728 N.Y.S.2d 105, 106 (N.Y.App.Div.2001) (explaining that an unexplained fall that occurs in the course of employment is presumed to arise out of employment in the absence of substantial evidence to the contrary).

We acknowledge, as has the Court of Appeals, that neutral risks present risk of loss problems. See *Milledge*, 764 N.E.2d at 235 (citing *K–Mart*, 521 N.E.2d at 1349 n. 1). This is so because the risk does not fall clearly upon the employer or the employee. *Id.* Responding to the question of who should bear this risk, Professor Larson observes:

> [T]he usual answer in the past has been to leave this loss on the employee, on the theory that he or she must meet the burden of proof of establishing affirmatively a clear causal connection between the conditions under which the employee worked and the occurrence of the injury. More recently, some courts have reasoned in the following vein: Either the employer or the employee must bear the loss; to show connection with the employment, there is at least the fact that the injury occurred while the employee was working; to show connection with the employee there is nothing; therefore, although the work connection is slender, it is at least stronger than any connection with the claimant's personal life.

Larson, *supra*, § 4.03, at 4–3.

We believe the positional risk doctrine is the appropriate analytical tool for resolving questions concerning injuries that result from neutral risks. It has been adopted by a majority of jurisdictions that have spoken on the subject.[3] And it is consistent with the underlying purpose of the Worker's Compensation Act: to provide compensation to workers suffering from work-related injuries without meeting the liability requirements of tort law. Worker's compensation is for the benefit of the employee, and the Act should "be liberally construed . . . so as not to negate the Act's humane purposes." *Frampton v. Cent. Ind. Gas Co.*, 260 Ind. 249, 297 N.E.2d 425, 427 (1973).

In this case the injury to Milledge's ankle is without explanation. It is thus classified as a neutral risk in that the cause of the injury is neither personal to Milledge nor distinctly associated with her employment. The injury would not have occurred but for the fact that the conditions and obligations of her employment placed Milledge in the parking lot where she was injured. In turn, The Oaks has not carried its burden of demonstrating that this unexplained accident, which precipitated the ankle injury, was the result of idiopathic causes. Milledge is thus entitled to compensation under the Indiana Worker's Compensation Act.

This does not however end our analysis. Milledge sought worker's compensation not for her ankle injury alone, but also, and primarily, for the disability arising from the injury including the surgery that led to the amputation of her leg. Whether Milledge was entitled to such compensation was fiercely contested before the single-member hearing officer. However, determining that Milledge failed to show any causal connection between her ankle injury and her employment, neither the

---

3 Editor's Note: The court provided a footnote with citations to decisions from numerous jurisdictions.

hearing officer nor the full Board ever reached the question of whether Milledge's infection and subsequent amputation were causally connected to her ankle injury. Therefore this cause is remanded to the Board for consideration of this issue.

Conclusion

We conclude that an injury resulting from an unexplained accident falls under the category of a neutral risk, one neither distinctly personal to the claimant nor distinctly associated with the employment. We conclude also that in the case of a neutral risk, the positional risk doctrine applies. As applied in this case, Milledge would not have been at the place where she injured her ankle injury but for the duties of her employment. Consequently, a presumption arises that her injury "arose out of" employment. Because The Oaks presented no evidence that the injury was the result of idiopathic causes, it has not rebutted this presumption. On this issue, we reverse the judgment of the Worker's Compensation Board. However, issues still remain as to whether Milledge's other medical problems including the amputation of her leg were causally connected to the ankle injury. Accordingly, on this issue we remand this cause to Worker's Compensation Board for further proceedings.

Judgment reversed and cause remanded.

NOTES

1. How do you explain the different outcomes in Fetzer and Milledge? Is it due to factual, judicial policy, or statutory distinctions?

2. In workers' compensation disputes, an idiopathic fall injury is one that is caused by the fall itself rather than the personal physical condition or attribute that caused the fall. The ideopathic condition itself is not chargeable to the employment and not compensable. Nevertheless, even in the case of a truly ideopathic fall (i.e., one caused by a personal condition not related to the employment), if the injury can be attributed to the falling body's collision with a dangerous work condition, and sometimes even a "neutral risk" such as a hard factory floor, compensation is often awarded. George v. Great Eastern Food Products, Inc., 207 A.2d 161 (N.J. 1965) treated an idiopathic fall as an unexplained fall, and thus compensable. This is probably a minority position. But, see, Nowlin v. Industrial Commission, 167 Ariz. 291, 806 P.2d 880 (1990) (compensation awarded receptionist whose unexplained back injury occurred as she was sitting down in her receptionist's chair; the injury resulted from an actual risk of the job activity).

3. In most jurisdictions the victim of an idiopathic fall must show that the employment or its environment enhanced the risk of injury in some way, either in having accentuated the weakness of the personal condition, thereby contributing to the cause of the fall, or by having exposed the falling person

to the risk of suffering a more dangerous collision than would be expected in a non-work setting. The latter situation is sometimes referred to as the "increased risk hazard." Contrast Leon County School Bd. v. Grimes, 548 So.2d 205 (Fla.1989) (an employee's leg brace, required because of weakness caused by polio, gave way causing him to fall to a carpeted floor; compensation denied), and Protectu Awning Shutter Co. v. Cline, 154 Fla. 30, 16 So.2d 342 (1944) (worker fainted from idiopathic cause and fractured skull on concrete floor; compensation awarded on basis of increased hazard). See, also, Ledbetter v. Michigan Carton Co., 74 Mich.App. 330, 253 N.W.2d 753 (1977).

4. How should this case be decided? An ideopathic condition caused a worker to become delusional who was working on a bridge 60 feet high. At the end of the work day the worker walked around protective obstacles, climbed over a high barrier, and fell to his death. Other workers followed a clear and safe route off the bridge. The hearing officer found that the decedent did not commit suicide. The Kentucky Supreme Court concluded that the bizarre behavior was induced by an idiopathic condition. Should workers' compensation benefits be paid survivors? See Hampton v. Intech Contracting, LLC, 2013 WL 1188040 (Ky.).

5. Consider Zemis v. SCI Contractors, Inc./E.E. Black, Inc., 80 Hawai'i, 911 P.2d 77 (1996) in connection with the cases in Section 5. There, while at work the claimant was injured in an altercation with a non-employee who came into the claimant's workplace to dispute a car crash that was not job related. Although the Hawai'i court ordinarily applies the positional "but-for" risk test, it declined to apply it to an imported "purely private and personal" risk and denied recovery.

5. INJURIES CAUSED BY FIGHTS AND ASSAULTS AMONG CO-WORKERS

HARTFORD ACCIDENT & INDEM. CO. v. CARDILLO

United States Court of Appeals for the District of Columbia, 1940.
72 App.D.C. 52, 112 F.2d 11.

RUTLEDGE, ASSOCIATE JUSTICE.

The appeal is from an order of the District Court dismissing the complaint of the Hartford Accident and Indemnity Company, employer's insurance carrier, against Frank A. Cardillo, deputy commissioner of the United States Employees' Compensation Commission, and Ray Bridges, to enjoin enforcement of a compensation order favoring Bridges. The findings of fact, insofar as they are pertinent to the appeal are as follows:

On October 10, 1938, the claimant Bridges, "while employed as a helper in the employer's [Sanitary Grocery Company, Inc.] produce warehouse and engaged in loading vegetables on the employer's truck, sustained personal injury resulting in his disability when a co-worker assaulted him suffering a laceration of the right eyebrow and a fracture of the right maxilla; * * * that the work performed by the claimant was supervised by a checker, Roy Downey; that in directing the claimant in the performance of his duties Downey addressed the claimant as 'Shorty'; that the claimant resented being called 'Shorty' and when Downey continued to so address the claimant, the latter called Downey a vile name; that Downey thereupon struck the claimant a blow on the right side of the face with his fist, inflicting the injuries above described; that the claimant did not strike or attempt to strike his superior, Downey; that Downey was the aggressor in the assault * * *." From these facts the deputy commissioner concluded "that the injury had its origin in the employment and that it arose out of and in the course of the said employment."

It is not contended that the injury did not occur "in the course of the employment," since it took place at the very time that Bridges was loading the truck for the employer. But the arguments of the plaintiff are directed against the finding that it "arose out of" the employment. Plaintiff asserts that the assault by Downey upon Bridges was caused by a purely personal quarrel, which had no relation to their work and, therefore, that the injury is not compensable. This is predicated on the facts as found and on other evidence not mentioned in the findings. That was to the effect that for about two months Downey and Bridges, while at work, had engaged in friendly banter concerning the respective merits of their watches, which was renewed on the morning of the injury. It is claimed that this led to the altercation and made it an entirely personal quarrel, unrelated to the work. * * *

[There follows an excellent but lengthy discussion of the shift by courts away from the increased risk notion whenever the employee was injured or killed at a time when and at a place where he was securely within the course of his employment. The court notes the emergence of the positional risk approach, which, the opinion observes, is in recognition of the fact that the work brings the employee within its peril and makes it, for purposes of compensation, "part of the work".] The opinion continues:

Recognition that this is so came more easily as to physical than as to human forces. As with street risks, the early disposition in cases of human action was to emphasize the particular act and its nature, except anomalously when it involved merely negligence of the claimant or fellow employees. The statutory abolition of common law defenses made easy recognition of the accidental character of negligent acts by the claimant and fellow servants. The extension to their accidental (i.e., nonculpable, but injurious) behavior was not difficult. So with that of strangers, including assault by deranged persons, and their negligence intruding into the working environment. But these extensions required a shift in the emphasis from the particular act and its tendency to forward the work to its part as a factor in the general working environment. The shift involved recognition that the environment includes associations as well as conditions, and that associations include the faults and derelictions of human beings as well as their virtues and obediences. Men do not discard their personal qualities when they go to work. Into the job they carry their intelligence, skill, habits of care and rectitude. Just as inevitably they take along also their tendencies to carelessness and camaraderie, as well as emotional make-up. In bringing men together work brings these qualities together, causes frictions between them, creates occasions for lapses into carelessness, and for fun making and emotional flare-up. Work could not go on if men became automatons repressed in every natural expression. "Old Man River" is a part of loading steamboats. These expressions of human nature are incidents inseparable from working together. They involve risks of injury and these risks are inherent in the working environment. * * * This view recognizes that work places men under strains and fatigue from human and mechanical impacts, creating frictions which explode in myriads of ways, only some of which are immediately relevant to their tasks. Personal animosities are created by working together on the assembly line or in traffic. Others initiated outside the job are magnified to the breaking point by its compelled contacts. No worker is immune to these pressures and impacts upon temperament. They accumulate and explode over incidents trivial and important, personal and official. But the explosion point is merely the culmination of the antecedent pressures. That it is not relevant to the immediate task, involves a lapse from duty, or contains an element of volition or illegality does not disconnect it from them nor nullify their causal effect in producing its injurious consequences. Any other view would reintroduce the conceptions of contributory fault, action in the line of duty, nonaccidental character of voluntary conduct, and independent, intervening cause as applied in tort law, which it was the purpose of the statute to discard. It would require the application of different basic tests of liability for injuries caused by volitional conduct of the claimant and those resulting from negligent action, mechanical causes and the volitional activities of others.

The limitation, of course, is that the accumulated pressures must be attributable in substantial part to the working environment. This implies that their causal effect shall not be overpowered and nullified by influences originating entirely outside the working relation and not substantially magnified by it. Whether such influences have annulling effect upon those of the environment ordinarily is the crucial issue. * * *

It follows that the judgment must be affirmed. Taking full account not only of the findings but of all the evidence, it is clear that the entire sequence of incidents occurred not only while the claimant and his assailant were at work, but as a natural and normal product of working together. The record shows no private or personal relations between them. The discussion about watches, if that were material as contended by appellant, was carried on in the normal intercourse of employee with employee. It was not relevant to any particular duty; neither was it an interruption or a departure from the work, much less an "independent, intervening agency." If "personal," it was one of those personal things which employees constantly do, not only while, but because they are working together. All this may be said also concerning the use of the respective appellations of "Shorty" and "Skinny," both in the banter and in the official acts of giving and receiving orders. The claimant may have been at fault in resenting his superior's ridicule, expressed perhaps as much in tone as in language, by repeated use of the diminutive nickname, both personally and officially. His remonstrance should have ended the practice. When it did not, the fighting word sprang to the lips, and the superior employee responded with his fist. Claimant may have been at fault, but he was the aggressor neither in the banter nor in the physical encounter.

We do not put the case on the narrow ground that Downey was Bridges' superior and as such owed him the duty not to belittle him or ridicule his physical stature. Fault there was on both sides, the graver perhaps in Downey for the fact that he was the superior and knew not when to stop. But compensability in these circumstances is not a matter of comparative fault. The entire sequence of events arose out of the fact that the work of the participants brought them together and created the relations and conditions which resulted in the clash. Nothing in the record shows that Bridges was intoxicated or had any intention to injure himself or another. He was guilty at most of contributory fault. But it was not sufficient, within either the statutory language or the principle of our previous decisions, to constitute a departure from the work, a matter purely personal, or a disconnecting intervening agency. * * *

The judgment is affirmed.

NOTES

1. Where an assault arises out of a dispute among co-workers concerning the performance of the employer's work, the working tools, the protection of the employer's property, the collection of money owed the employer, or some other aspect of the employment, compensation is generally awarded. See, e.g., Lyons v. Bechtel Corporation, 788 So.2d 34 (La.App. 3 Cir.2000) (injury suffered in after-hours fight with supervisor over employment matters; compensable); State v. Purmort, 143 Ga.App. 269, 238 S.E.2d 268 (1977) (fight arose out of a dispute as to method of doing work); and Alpine Roofing Co. v. Dalton, 36 Colo.App. 315, 539 P.2d 487 (1975)

(following a dispute over his paycheck, claimant was dismissed immediately; while still on the premises he was assaulted following a heated exchange with his foreman; compensation awarded). In Pennsylvania the law raises a presumption that an injury suffered in a work-place altercation is compensable but an employer may rebut it with evidence to show a non-work cause. Helms v. W.C.A.B., 654 A.2d 106 (Pa.Cmwlth.1995), app. denied, 541 Pa. 645, 663 A.2d 696 (1995).

2. Many decisions also award compensation for injuries suffered by workers in fights among themselves arising from disputes over non-work matters. See, Hanhan v. Worker's Compensation Appeals Board, 67 Cal. Comp. Cases 1551 (Cal. App. 4 Dist. 2002) (compensation is to be denied only if "events in the employee's private life were the sole cause of the attack.") Mutual Implement & Hardware Ins. Co. v. Pittman, 214 Miss. 823, 59 So.2d 547 (1952) (assault resulted from horseplay between employees; compensation awarded); Chanin v. Western Union Telegraph Co., 271 App.Div. 763, 64 N.Y.S.2d 670 (1946) (fight resulted from bragging of pugilistic ability); Townsend Paneling, Inc. v. Butler, 247 Ark. 818, 448 S.W.2d 347 (1969) (worker assaulted for refusal to make a bet with co-worker); De Nardis v. Stevens Const. Co., 72 N.J.Super. 395, 178 A.2d 354 (1962) (worker injured in fight in dispute over an umbrella); and Keyhea v. Woodard–Walker Lumber Co., 147 So. 830 (La.App.1933) (families of two workers resided in employer's mill quarters; one worker killed another over attentions the decedent had paid the assailant's wife; compensation awarded on the ground that the employees' being constantly thrown together in employment aggravated personal enmity).

3. Many courts deny compensation for injuries caused by a "personal" dispute even though the claimant's employment brought the disputatious parties into contact. See, e.g., Malco, Inc. v. Industrial Comm., 65 Ill.2d 426, 3 Ill.Dec. 448, 358 N.E.2d 1133 (1976) (assault arose out of dispute over paycheck "pool" or "poker"; compensation denied although the plaintiff was actively at work when assaulted); Nash–Kelvinator Corp. v. Industrial Comm., 266 Wis. 81, 62 N.W.2d 567 (1954) (claimant who signed what was believed to be a communist inspired peace petition was battered by fellow workers; compensation denied); Birchett v. Tuf–Nut Garment Mfg. Co., 205 Ark. 483, 169 S.W.2d 574 (1943) (employee assaulted when she seized newspaper belonging to co-worker; court conceded plausibility of reasoning in *Cardillo*, but denied its application to the facts involved and denied compensation); Texas Indem. Ins. Co. v. Cheely, 232 S.W.2d 124 (Tex.Civ.App.1950) (false report on one worker of insults allegedly made by another worker led to assault; compensation denied on ground that attack was "personally" motivated), and, Scholtzhauer v. C. & L. Lunch Co., 233 N.Y. 12, 134 N.E. 701 (1922) (waitress shot when she sharply declined a co-worker's request for a date; compensation denied).

4. Initially, most courts denied compensation to any claimant who was the "aggressor" in a fight among employees even in the absence of any special statutory provision. Horvath v. La Fond, 305 Mich. 69, 8 N.W.2d 915 (1943)

(decedent attacked fellow worker in an altercation related solely to employer's business; aggression made the fight personal and severed any causal relation with employment; compensation denied); and Staten v. Long Turner Const. Co., 185 S.W.2d 375 (Mo.App.1945) (aggressive act regarded as conduct outside the course of employment; compensation denied). These decisions have been criticized as improperly re-injecting employee fault into compensation disputes and later decisions tend to reject the aggressor doctrine and permit compensation. See, e.g., State Compensation Ins. Fund v. Industrial Accident Comm., 38 Cal.2d 659, 242 P.2d 311 (1952), Southern Cotton Oil Division v. Childress, 237 Ark. 909, 377 S.W.2d 167 (1964) (compensation paid in regard to worker killed in horseplay accident when an air hose thrust into his mouth burst his lungs; who was instigator held to be irrelevant), and Jolly v. Jesco, Inc., 271 Minn. 333, 135 N.W.2d 746 (1965) (dispute over method of doing work; compensation awarded). See also Ringier America v. Combs, 41 Ark.App. 47, 849 S.W.2d 1, 2 (1993) (noting a trend toward abolishing the aggressor doctrine and also noting that "an injury to a non-participating victim of horseplay is compensable."). 1 A. Larson, Workmen's Compensation (1991) § 11.15(c), observes that the abolition of the aggressor doctrine is "one of the most rapid * * * reversals in the volatile history of compensation law." Nevertheless, a few jurisdictions continue to deny benefits to aggressors in work-related fights. See, e.g., Johnson v. Nanias (Bridal Originals), 738 S.W.2d 164 (Mo.App.1987) and Rorie v. Holly Farms Poultry Co., 306 N.C. 706, 295 S.E.2d 458 (1982).

5. The statutes of many states, the Longshore and Harbor Workers' Act, and the United States Employees Compensation Act exclude injuries resulting from "willful intention to injure another" or from "willful misconduct." As commonly applied, these provisions require more aggression than mere verbal abuse, an impulsive punch, simply "being to blame," and other forms of minor misconduct by the injured employee. One court justified awarding compensation, saying: "Arguments, altercations and assaults are as inevitable as they are undesirable. Where they arise out of the employment, they may properly be regarded as an employment hazard. Such actions are misconduct but are not serious misconduct unless of a grave and aggravated character. Such actions are not willful misconduct unless deliberate or premeditated." Newell v. Moreau, 94 N.H. 439, 445, 55 A.2d 476, 481 (1947). See also Youmans v. Coastal Petroleum Co., 333 S.C. 195, 508 S.E.2d 43 (App.1998) (a finding that claimant spontaneously struck a supervisor who addressed him angrily with a racial slur did not barred claimant's recovery for injuries suffered in ensuing fight); In re Tripp's Case, 355 Mass. 515, 246 N.E.2d 449 (1969) (victim struck first blow in fight related to employment; held not to be disqualifying "serious and willful misconduct"); and Velotta v. Liberty Mut. Ins. Co., 241 La. 814, 132 So.2d 51 (1961) (claimant hurled a pair of trousers at co-worker; took a serious beating in return; "aggressor doctrine" repudiated).

6. Grabowski v. Mangler, 956 A.2d 1217 (Del.Supr. 2008), held that the test applied to determine that a horseplay injury to one worker was

compensable also applied to determine that the workers who engaged in the horseplay were entitled to co-worker tort immunity under the Delaware statute. Progressive Halcyon Insurance Co. v. Philippi, 754 N.W.2d 646 (S.D. 2008).

7. In In Re Question Submitted by the United States Court of Appeals for the Tenth Circuit v. Martin Marietta Corporation, 759 P.2ssd 17 (Colo. *en banc* 1988), a worker was attached and raped while walking to have lunch in the employer's cafeteria. The attacker was unknown to the victim and was never identified. The parties agreed that the victim was on duty at the time and the attack was not personal to her. Finding the attack to be "'neutral' in the sense that it was not specific" to the victim, the court concluded that the attack arose out of employment.

6. INJURIES CAUSED BY ON THE JOB ASSAULTS BY NON CO-WORKERS

WEISS V. CITY OF MILWAUKEE

Supreme Court of Wisconsin, 1997.
208 Wis.2d 95, 559 N.W.2d 588.

ANN WALSH BRADLEY, JUSTICE.

Holly Lynn Weiss seeks review of an unpublished court of appeals decision which affirmed a summary judgment dismissal of her complaint against the defendants, the City of Milwaukee and its employee, Yvette Marchan (together, "the City"). Weiss argues that the court of appeals erred in determining that the Workers' Compensation Act (WCA) provides the exclusive remedy for her claim of emotional distress resulting from the City's disclosure of her home address and telephone number to her abusive former spouse. Because we conclude that Weiss has alleged injuries covered by the Worker's Compensation Act, and that the exclusive remedy provision of the WCA precludes her common law action against the defendants for negligent infliction of emotional distress, we affirm the decision of the court of appeals.

The relevant facts are not in dispute. On July 31, 1990, Weiss obtained a temporary restraining order against her abusive husband, Osama Abughanim. Shortly thereafter, she commenced a divorce action. Abughanim, forced to vacate the marital residence, began a campaign of harassing telephone calls and personal visits during which he would threaten the lives of Weiss and their two children. In October 1990, Weiss vacated the residence and moved in with her parents in order to escape her husband's harassment. Abughanim persisted in making threatening telephone calls, both to Weiss's parents' residence and to her place of employment. The calls to Weiss's employer were of such frequency that they resulted in her termination in December 1990.

In February 1991, Weiss obtained employment with the City of Milwaukee as an engineering technician. As an employee, she was required to establish residence in Milwaukee within one month of hiring. She therefore moved from her parents' residence in Waukesha County to an apartment located in Milwaukee. At that time, Abughanim did not know Weiss's Milwaukee address or telephone number.

Weiss was instructed by her supervisor to provide her address and telephone number to the City's payroll department. She contacted the payroll department, explained that she had an abusive former husband, and expressed her desire that her residential information remain confidential. A City payroll clerk assured Weiss that the City had a policy prohibiting the disclosure of such employee information to private individuals. Relying on the clerk's assurance, Weiss provided her address and telephone number to the payroll department.

On July 10, 1991, Abughanim contacted the City's Department of Employee Relations and spoke with Sheila Bowle, an employee of the department. Abughanim falsely represented to Bowle that he was calling on behalf of a bank and needed to confirm Weiss's address and telephone number for credit purposes. Bowle relayed the bogus inquiry to her supervisor, Yvette Marchan, who, without attempting to verify Abughanim's claimed credentials, authorized Bowle to disclose Weiss's residential information.

By this ruse, Abughanim obtained Weiss's home address and telephone number. Thereafter, Abughanim regularly telephoned Weiss at work to inform her that he now knew her home address and telephone number, and that he would kill her and their two children. Her awareness that Abughanim knew her address, and her then existing financial inability to change her residence, caused Weiss severe emotional distress arising from fear for her safety and that of their two children.

Weiss commenced a common law action in the circuit court against the City to recover damages for negligent infliction of emotional distress arising from the City's unwitting disclosure to Abughanim. The City filed a motion for summary judgment, asserting that the WCA covered Weiss's injuries, and the statute's exclusive remedy provision therefore barred Weiss's suit. The City also maintained that it had no duty to keep confidential Weiss's home address and telephone number, because such information was available to the public pursuant to Wisconsin's open records law.

The circuit court granted the City's motion for summary judgment, dismissing Weiss's complaint. . . . The court of appeals affirmed [Ed., on grounds that Weiss's] common law negligence action against the City was barred by the statute's exclusive remedy provision, Wis.Stat. s 102.03(2). . . .

We have repeatedly stated that the provisions of Chapter 102 must be liberally construed to effectuate the WCA's goal of compensating injured workers. * * * However, courts must also exercise care to avoid upsetting the balance of interests achieved by the WCA. . . .

Generally, an employer's obligation to pay worker's compensation accrues under Chapter 102 when all of the following conditions are present: 1) the employee sustains an injury; 2) at the time of the injury, both the employer and the employee are subject to the provisions of the WCA; 3) at the time of the injury, the employee is performing service growing out of and incidental to his or her employment; 4) the injury is not intentionally self-inflicted; and 5) the accident or disease causing injury arises out of the employment. Wis.Stat. §§ 102.03(1)(a)–(e). For purposes of our review of summary judgment in this case, our inquiry is limited to determining whether, at the time of her injury, Weiss was performing service growing out of and incidental to her employment, and whether the accident causing injury arose out of her employment.

It is well settled that when the § 102.03(1) conditions of liability for worker's compensation are satisfied, the exclusive remedy provision, § 102.03(2), precludes an injured employee from maintaining a negligence action against his or her employer and fellow employees. . . . Jenson, 161 Wis.2d at 263, 468 N.W.2d 1 (plaintiff's "common law action is barred by the exclusivity provisions if she in all other respects is entitled to recovery under the Act"). Thus, Weiss's common law action against the City is barred if her alleged injuries are covered by Chapter 102.

The City asserts that Weiss meets each of the five criteria set out in §§ 102.03(1)(a)–(e), and that the remedy for her injuries is therefore solely that which is provided under the WCA. [Ed., material from an omitted footnote states: "The legal positions of the employer and employee in this instance are the reverse of those found in many worker's compensation cases. Often it is the employer who resists coverage under the WCA, and the employee who desires such coverage. As Weiss candidly admits, she has filed a common law action because she feels that a recovery under the WCA would be inadequate compared to a jury award on her tort claim. Conversely, the City invokes the WCA in this instance in order to limit Weiss's potential recovery for its allegedly wrongful disclosure of her residential information."] In attempting to establish that her injury is not covered by Chapter 102, Weiss contends that at the time she was injured, she was not performing service growing out of and incidental to her employment. She also argues that the court of appeals erred when it determined that "the incident causing the injury arose out of Weiss's employment." Weiss, slip op. at 6–7.

We deal first with Weiss's claim that her injury is not encompassed within the WCA because at the time of the injury, she was not "performing service growing out of and incidental to . . . her employment," as required by § 102.03(1)(c). In essence, Weiss's argument is that an employee cannot satisfy § 102.03(1)(c) when receiving a personal telephone call at work. We disagree.

The statutory clause "performing service growing out of and incidental to his or her employment" is used interchangeably with the phrase "course of employment." . . . Both phrases refer to the "time, place, and circumstances" under which the injury occurred. Goranson v. DILHR, 94 Wis.2d 537, 549, 289 N.W.2d 270 (1980).

An injury is said to arise in the course of the employment when it takes place within the period of the employment, at a place where the employee reasonably may be, and while he [or she] is fulfilling his [or her] duties or engaged in doing something incidental thereto. 1 The Law of Workmen's Compensation § 14.00.

There is no dispute that Weiss's alleged injury occurred within the time and place of her employment. The question is whether receiving a personal phone call at work constitutes a "circumstance" of employment. We conclude that it does. Under the liberal construction given to Chapter 102, an employee acts within the course of employment when he or she is otherwise within the time and space limits of employment, and briefly turns away from his or her work to tend to matters "necessary or convenient to his [or her] own personal health or comfort." American Motors Corp. v. Industrial Comm., 1 Wis.2d 261, 265, 83 N.W.2d 714 (1957) (citations omitted). The personal comfort doctrine does not apply, and an employee is not within the course of employment, if the "extent of the departure is so great that an intent to abandon the job temporarily may be inferred, or . . . the method chosen is so unusual and unreasonable that the conduct cannot be considered an incident of the employment." Id. Applying the doctrine to the facts of this case, we conclude that regardless of the contents of a brief personal telephone call, the act of taking such a call at work constitutes a momentary departure from work duties to attend to a matter of personal comfort. Thus, when Weiss answered the personal telephone call from Abughanim, she was engaged in an activity incidental to employment, and was therefore within the course of employment.

Weiss next contends that the accident causing her injury did not arise out of her employment. § 102.03(1)(e). Citing Goranson and cases from other jurisdictions, Weiss asserts that where, as here, an employee is injured at work by a non-employee for purely personal reasons, the injury is noncompensable under the WCA.

We agree with Weiss that Goranson stands for the proposition that injuries sustained in an assault occurring in the course of employment are generally noncompensable under the WCA when the assailant is motivated purely by personal animus, and the employment in no way contributes to the incident. We also agree that Weiss's employment did not create the initial threat posed to her by Abughanim. We nevertheless conclude that the accident did arise out of Weiss's employment with the City, because the conditions of Weiss's employment facilitated her eventual injury.

The "arising out of" language of § 102.03(1)(e) refers to the causal origin of an employee's injury. Goranson, 94 Wis.2d at 549, 289 N.W.2d 270. However, "arising out of his or her employment" is not synonymous with the phrase "caused by the employment." Id. at 555, 289 N.W.2d 270. In interpreting § 102.03(1)(e), we have adopted the "positional risk" doctrine: [A]ccidents arise out of employment if the conditions or obligations of the employment create a zone of special danger out of which the accident causing the injury arose. Stated another way, an accident arises out of employment when by reason of employment the employee is present at a place where he is injured through the agency of a third person, an outside force, or the conditions of special danger. Id. at 555, 289 N.W.2d 270. However, when the origin of the assault is purely private and personal, and the employment in no way contributes to the incident, the positional risk doctrine does not apply. Id. at 556–57, 289 N.W.2d 270 The Law of Workmen's Compensation § 11.21(c).

For example, in Goranson, a charter bus driver was injured after he drove a group of people to Green Bay. Upon arriving in Green Bay, the driver checked into a hotel along with his passengers. Later in the evening, he leaped from his third floor hotel room onto the roof of another section of the hotel two floors below, sustaining a broken hip and other injuries. There was evidence that the driver had been drinking throughout the evening with a woman, and that he had quarreled in his hotel room with the woman just prior to jumping from the hotel window.

This court upheld a denial of worker's compensation benefits. While there was no dispute that the driver was in the course of employment at the time of injury, the court determined that the accident did not arise out of the driver's employment, because the injuring force was purely personal to him. Goranson, 94 Wis.2d at 557, 289 N.W.2d 270.

The facts of this case are distinguishable from those in Goranson. In Goranson, the bus driver's employment did not contribute to or facilitate the accident causing the injury he suffered jumping from the hotel window. In this case, however, Weiss was required to provide her residential address and telephone number to the City as a condition of employment. If Weiss had never been required to provide the information to the City, the accident would not have occurred. The City's unwitting disclosure of that information to a private individual, Weiss's abusive former husband, was an accident that led to her injury. Because a condition of her employment facilitated the accident which caused her injury, we conclude that the accident arose out of her employment. See 1 The Law of Workmen's Compensation § 11.21(c) (privately motivated assaults generally do not arise out of employment, except where the employment facilitates the assault).

Weiss cites several cases from foreign jurisdictions for the proposition that when purely private animosity manifests itself in a workplace attack, the employment connection to the injury is so minimal that worker's compensation should be denied. Monahan v. United States Check Book Co., 4 Neb.App. 227, 540 N.W.2d 380 (1995); Ross v. Mark's, Inc., 120 N.C.App. 607, 463 S.E.2d 302 (1995). In both Monahan and Ross, a non-employee attacked and killed an ex-spouse at the ex-spouse's place of employment. Worker's compensation was denied in both cases, on the ground that assaults do not arise out of employment when they involve private quarrels imported into the workplace. In neither case did the court find evidence that the employment contributed to or facilitated the attacks.

We find unpersuasive the examples of worker's compensation denials cited by Weiss. Consistent with Goranson, we are of the view that in certain situations, "an injury from an admittedly private source should be compensable because it [is] facilitated or contributed to by the employment environment." 1 The Law of Workmen's Compensation § 11.23. For example, in Carter v. Penney Tire & Recapping Co., 261 S.C. 341, 200 S.E.2d 64 (1973), the claimant had previously quarreled with Crosby, a non-employee. On the date of the assault, Crosby threatened the claimant while the latter was engaged in repairing his employer's roof. Before returning to the roof, the claimant reported the threats to his employer, who responded that the claimant would be protected and should proceed with his work. Crosby later returned and shot the claimant, inflicting grievous injuries. The South Carolina Supreme Court determined that the claimant's injuries arose out of his employment, because: the employee was required to perform his duties under circumstances where he was endangered by a peril from a source outside of and unrelated to his actual work, which peril was known to the employer and against which the employer afforded no protection or relief. Id. 200 S.E.2d at 67.

Similarly, in Raybol v. Louisiana State University, 520 So.2d 724 (La.1988), superseded by statute as stated in Guillory v. Interstate Gas Station, 653 So.2d 1152 (La.1995), the Supreme Court of Louisiana awarded worker's compensation to a dormitory worker who was assaulted at work by her estranged former boyfriend. The court concluded that the worker's injuries arose out of her employment, based in part on its determination that "the employer's custodial workers contributed to the danger of the assault by informing the assailant of the plaintiff's work location in the building and by assisting him in gaining access to her by unlocking a door to the dormitory." Id. at 727.

In California Compensation & Fire Co. v. Workmen's Compensation Appeals Bd., 68 Cal.2d 157, 65 Cal.Rptr. 155, 436 P.2d 67 (1968), a worker at a table pad manufacturer was shot and killed by her ex-husband. The worker's employment required her to visit the homes of customers in order to measure the dimensions of tables. Upon learning that the worker intended to remarry, her ex-husband rented an apartment, ordered a table pad, and requested that someone be sent to measure the table. When his ex-wife arrived at the apartment, he murdered her and then committed suicide. The supreme court of California affirmed an award of death benefits in part on the grounds that the husband's elaborate plot was facilitated by the conditions of the worker's employment. Id. at 157, 436 P.2d at 69.

Finally, in Epperson v. Industrial Commission, 26 Ariz.App. 467, 549 P.2d 247 (1976), the claimant informed a security guard at her place of employment that she was having personal difficulties with her husband and did not wish to speak to him. Her husband later appeared at the building, observed the claimant, and proceeded unimpeded past the security guard's desk to confront the plaintiff. During the course of his ensuing conversation with the claimant, the husband shot her. The Arizona court of appeals concluded that the assault did not arise out of the course of her employment. However, it intimated that a different result would have been reached had the claimant informed the security guard of her fears and the dangers posed by her husband in a manner sufficient to justify reliance on the guard's protection. Id. 549 P.2d at 250.

None of the cited cases is on all fours with the one presently before us. However, each stands for the proposition that when an attack occurs during the course of employment and arises from personal animus imported from a private relationship, the incident arises out of the claimant's employment if employment conditions have contributed to or facilitated the attack. Weiss was required to provide her residential information to the City as a condition of employment. That condition of employment facilitated the City's subsequent accidental release of the information to a private individual, Weiss's abusive former spouse. The disclosure of the residential information in turn enabled Abughanim to threaten Weiss. We therefore conclude that the accident causing Weiss's injury arose out of her employment with the City.

In summary, Weiss has alleged an emotional injury which occurred in the course of employment and was caused by an accident arising out of that employment. Accordingly, we conclude that Weiss's complaint states a claim covered under § 102.03(1) of the WCA. Because the exclusive remedy provision of the WCA, § 102.03(2), bars Weiss's common law tort action against the City, the circuit court properly granted summary judgment dismissing the complaint, and the court of appeals correctly upheld the circuit court's decision.

The decision of the court of appeals is affirmed.

NOTES

1. As noted in *Weiss*, in Raybol v. Louisiana State University, 520 So.2d 724 (La.1988) the Louisiana Supreme Court held that a former boyfriend's physical attack upon a maintenance employee at the employee's job site caused a compensable injury arising out of the employment. The rationale of the decision was that the worker was "squarely in the course of employment when the attack occurred and she had not invited the attack through any willful intention to injure another." Id. at 727. Thereafter, the Louisiana legislature amended the workers' compensation statute to include this provision:

> An injury by accident should not be considered as having arisen out of the employment and thereby not covered by the provisions of this Chapter if the employer can establish that the injury arose out of a dispute with another person or employee over matters unrelated to the injured employee's employment.

La.R.S. 23:1031(D). The Louisiana supreme court applied this provision in Guillory v. Interstate Gas Station, 653 So.2d 1152 (La.1995) to deny coverage to a worker who was shot by her estranged husband while she was on the job in a retail gasoline station. The post-*Raybol* statutory change illustrates the ultimate control legislatures possess over workers' compensation policies.

2. In Bear v. Honeywell, Inc., 468 N.W.2d 546 (Minn.1991), an employee was raped by a man to whom she had given a ride from the company parking lot. She had mistakenly believed the rapist to be a co-worker whose car would not start. The employee brought a tort action against her employer alleging negligent security. The employer raised workers' compensation exclusivity as a defense. The Minnesota supreme court categorized the cases as follows:

> Compensation cases arising from assault fall mostly into three groups. Non-compensable are cases where the assailant was motivated by personal animosity toward his victim, arising from circumstances wholly unconnected with the employment.
>
> In contrast and compensable are injuries resulting from assault where provocation or motivation arises solely out of the activity of the victim as an employee.
>
> In a middle ground are cases * * * where the assault was directed against the victim, neither "as an employee" nor for "reasons personal to him." Injuries so arising are ordinarily compensable.

Id., at 547. Into which category does *Bear* fit?

3. Where the nature of the job or the working environment increases the risk of assault by a stranger to the employment, compensation is usually awarded. See, e.g., Bryan v. Best Western/Coachman's Inn, 47 Ark.App. 75, 885 S.W.2d 28 (1994) ("Assaults arise out of the employment either if the risk of this sort of assault is increased by the nature of the work, or if the reason for the assault was a quarrel having its origin in the work.") Williams v. Duplex Metal Corp., 60 A.D.2d 741, 400 N.Y.S.2d 905 (1977) (corporation president who frequently carried home large amounts of cash due to fear of theft in work premises was shot during robbery in driveway of his home); Town of Granite v. Kidwell, 263 P.2d 184 (Okl.1953) (Town Marshall shot during discharge of duties); Vivier v. Lumbermen's Indemnity Exchange, 250 S.W. 417 (Tex.Com.App.1923) (watchman killed at night in course of robbery in which only his personal property was taken; not necessary that assault be directed at victim in his capacity as employee); California Compensation & Fire Co. v. Workmen's Comp. Appeals Bd., 68 Cal.2d 157, 65 Cal.Rptr. 155, 436 P.2d 67 (1968) (deceased employee was directed by her employer to do work at a residence which had been leased by the employee's estranged husband as part of the husband's scheme to get her alone in isolation; she was shot; compensation awarded); Associated Vendors, Inc. v. Industrial Comm., 45 Ill.2d 203, 258 N.E.2d 354 (1970) (worker installing vending machines in tavern assaulted); Torosian v. Nash Cab, 27 A.D.2d 767, 277 N.Y.S.2d 112 (1967) (taxi driver assaulted in dispute over fare), and Walters v. American States Insurance Company, 654 S.W.2d 423 (Tex.1983) (death benefits paid to employee who was murdered along with his employer while the two were on an trip to the airport to pick up a client). Contrast Gallimore v. Marilyn's Shoes, 292 N.C. 399, 233 S.E.2d 529 (1977) (shoe store employee kidnapped and murdered in course of robbery of her store; unknown to assailant she carried bank deposits for employer; compensation denied).

4. Where the employment merely happens to be the place where an assailant, who is not a co-worker, makes a non-employment, personally motivated attack upon an employee, compensation is commonly denied. Rice v. Revere Copper & Brass, Inc., 186 Md. 561, 48 A.2d 166 (1946) (assailant resented deceased's alleged misconduct with women in a dwelling occupied by both); Epperson v. Industrial Comm., 26 Ariz.App. 467, 549 P.2d 247 (1976) (marital difficulties led assailant to assault his wife while she was at work; compensation denied); and Ellis v. Rose Oil Co. of Dixie, 190 So.2d 450 (Miss.1966) (employee shot by jealous husband of employee's mistress). Contrast Livingston v. Henry & Hall, 59 So.2d 892 (La.App.1952) (worker assaulted by irate husband (not fellow worker) over love affair; compensation awarded under positional risk theory). Nevertheless, if the working environment enhances the opportunity or otherwise plays a causal part in what is otherwise an entirely personal, non-employment matter, compensation is more likely to be awarded. Brookhaven Steam Laundry v. Watts, 214 Miss. 569, 59 So.2d 294 (1952) (employee formed an alleged liaison with the wife of a customer; she placed laundry on her front porch as a signal that the coast was clear; employee was killed by irate husband when the signalling system went wrong; compensation initially awarded but

reversed in reconsideration) and Todd v. Easton Furniture Mfg. Co., 147 Md. 352, 128 A. 42 (1925) (night watchman murdered for personal reasons while making his rounds; compensation awarded). Contrast Andrews v. Hoss, 286 Minn. 514, 174 N.W.2d 134 (1970) (use of gun supplied by employer as instrument of personally motivated assault did not cause it to arise out of employment).

5. Injuries suffered by employees as a result of disputes with non co-workers arising out of traffic incidents and collisions are commonly compensable, if the injured employees were within the course of employment. See, e.g., Augelli v. Rolans Credit Clothing Store, 33 N.J.Super. 146, 109 A.2d 439 (1954) (anger aroused on recalling traffic dispute of four weeks earlier prompted assault) and John Hancock Trucking Co. v. Walker, 243 Miss. 487, 138 So.2d 478 (1962).

6. If the motive for the assault can be attributed in substantial part to the employment, compensation is generally awarded despite any exacerbation by personal animosity. See, e.g., Brewster Motor Co. v. Industrial Comm., 36 Ill.2d 443, 223 N.E.2d 131 (1967) (auto salesman directed by sales prospect to bring truck to prospect's residence as excuse for opportunity to kill him over imagined romance with wife) and Crowder v. State Comp. Com'r, 115 W.Va. 12, 174 S.E. 480 (1934) (filling station worker left open the door to a job site toilet in a manner offensive to a neighboring property owner; neighbor shot and killed worker; compensation awarded).

7. Occasionally, an employee is battered by a still inflamed adversary sometime after the initial work connected dispute occurred. The mere intervention of a cooling off period does not break the causal relationship (i.e. "arising out of") with the employment, if it actually existed. See, e.g., Ward v. Typhoon Air Conditioning Co., 27 A.D.2d 785, 277 N.Y.S.2d 315 (1967); and Augelli v. Rolans Credit Clothing Store, 33 N.J.Super. 146, 109 A.2d 439 (1954) (claimant had traffic dispute with apparent stranger on the highway; in chance encounter five weeks later in the employer's plant the stranger gave employee a sound thrashing; compensation awarded).

8. Attacks by strangers, children, and insane co-workers, mistaken attacks, and other neutral risks associated neither with the employer's business nor with the employee's personal life are often treated in line with the prevailing positional risk or street risk doctrine. Compare Belden Hotel Co. v. Industrial Comm., 44 Ill.2d 253, 255 N.E.2d 439 (1970) (shot by insanely jealous husband of co-employee; no basis for jealousy; compensation denied) with Mayo v. Safeway Stores, Inc., 93 Idaho 161, 457 P.2d 400 (1969) (attack by an apparently sane man but for no rational reason; positional risk doctrine applied to award compensation). Finally, what about completely unexplained attacks? Should these be regarded as arising out of the employment just as unexplained falls are usually so regarded? See, e.g., C.A. Dunham Co. v. Industrial Comm., 16 Ill.2d 102, 156 N.E.2d 560 (1959) (traveling employee on business trip killed when bomb planted in plane exploded, compensation awarded).

9. The statutes of several states contain special assault provisions that commonly *exclude* "injuries caused by the act of a third person or fellow employee intended to injure the employee for reasons personal to him, and not directed against him as an employee or because of his employment." See, e.g., Ga.Code Ann. § 34–9–1(4) (injury "shall not include injury caused by the willful act of a third person directed on employee for reasons personal to such employee") and Kessen v. Boise Cascade Corp., 71 Or.App. 545, 693 P.2d 52 (1984) (applying Oregon statute). In contrast, other statutes expressly *include* "an injury caused by the willful act of a third person directed against the employee *because of his employment*." (Italics added.) See, e.g., Lippmann v. North Dakota Workmen's Comp. Bureau, 79 N.D. 248, 55 N.W.2d 453 (1952) and Longshore and Harbor Workers Act. A Maryland statute goes further to cover "an injury caused by a willful or negligent act of a third person directed against a covered employee in the course of the employment of the covered employee." LE § 9–101(b)(2). When this provision is satisfied, an employee need prove only that the injury occurred in the course of employment regardless of who injured the employee and regardless of why. Doe v. Buccini Pollin Group, Inc. 201 Md. App. 409, 29 A.3d 999 (2011.)

7. INJURIES SUFFERED BY EMPLOYEES WHILE ATTEMPTING RESCUES

BLAKESLEE V. PLATT BROS. AND CO.

Supreme Court of Connecticut, 2006.
279 Conn. 239, 902 A.2d 620.

BORDEN, J.

The plaintiff, Michael G. Blakeslee, Jr., appeals from the decision of the workers' compensation review board (board) affirming the decision of the workers' compensation commissioner for the fifth district (commissioner). The commissioner had dismissed the plaintiff's application for benefits for injuries the plaintiff sustained when his coworkers physically had restrained him after he suffered a noncompensable seizure. The plaintiff claims that the board improperly concluded that his injuries resulting from the restraint were not compensable under the Workers' Compensation Act (act), General Statutes § 31–275 et seq., because they did not arise out of his employment. We agree with the plaintiff and reverse the board's decision.

The plaintiff filed a workers' compensation claim, which the commissioner dismissed. The plaintiff appealed to the board, which affirmed the commissioner's decision. This appeal followed.

The commissioner found the following facts, which are undisputed. On February 13, 2002, the plaintiff suffered a grand mal seizure while he was at work for the named defendant, Platt Brothers and Company. The seizure itself was not a compensable injury. As a result of the seizure, the plaintiff fell to the ground, unconscious, near a large steel scale in his workplace. As the plaintiff regained consciousness, he began flailing around, swinging his arms and kicking his legs. Mike Noel, a coworker, witnessed this incident and summoned two other coworkers, Bob Grenick, whom Noel referred to in his testimony as a paramedic, and Emo Bimmler, a factory foreman. The three men, in an attempt to prevent the plaintiff from injuring himself, as well as others, restrained the plaintiff. They held the plaintiff's arms down to the floor while the plaintiff attempted to break free from the restraint. As a result, the plaintiff suffered dislocations of both of his shoulders. The plaintiff initially sought treatment and ultimately surgery from Michael Sermer, an orthopedic surgeon. Sermer thereafter reported that he had concluded, on the basis of a reasonable medical certainty, that the plaintiff's shoulder dislocations were a result of the restraint, not the seizure.

The commissioner identified as the sole issue regarding the plaintiff's entitlement to workers' compensation benefits whether the plaintiff's injuries arose out of his employment. The commissioner made the following determinations based on his factual findings: (1) "The chain of causation which resulted in the [plaintiff's] shoulder injuries was set in motion by the [plaintiff's] grand mal seizure;" (2) "The seizure did not arise out of the [plaintiff's] employment"; and (3) "The [plaintiff's] injuries were caused by the intervention of other employees in his workplace who were trying to assist the [plaintiff]." In light of these determinations, the commissioner concluded that the injuries did not arise out of the plaintiff's employment and dismissed his claim for benefits.

The plaintiff then appealed from that decision to the board, which affirmed the commissioner's decision. . . .

The plaintiff claims that the board improperly concluded that his injuries did not arise out of his employment. We agree with the plaintiff that his injuries arose out of his employment and, therefore, are compensable.

"It long has been a fundamental tenet of workers' compensation law . . . that an employer takes the employee in the state of health in which it finds the employee." (Internal quotation marks omitted.) *Id.*, at 40, 787 A.2d 541. Thus, "an injury received in the course of the employment does not cease to be one arising out of the employment merely because some infirmity due to disease has originally set in action the final and proximate cause of the injury. The employer of labor takes his workman as he finds him and compensation does not depend upon his freedom from liability to injury through a constitutional weakness or latent tendency. Whatever predisposing physical condition may exist, if the employment is the immediate occasion of the injury, it arises out of the employment because it develops within it." (Internal quotation marks omitted.) *Savage v. St. Aeden's Church*, 122 Conn. 343, 346–47, 189 A. 599 (1937). . . .

Compensability also may not be denied simply because the plaintiff could have been exposed to a similar risk of injury from the administration of aid had he suffered the seizure outside of work. "[A]n injury may arise out of an employment although the risk of injury from that employment is no different in degree or kind [from that] to which [the employee] may be exposed outside of his employment. The injury is compensable, not because of the extent or particular character of the hazard, but because it exists as one of the conditions of the employment." (Internal quotation marks omitted.) *Triano v. United States Rubber Co.*, 144 Conn. 393, 397, 132 A.2d 570 (1957).

It is axiomatic, however, that "[t]he conditions of employment are not confined to those which the employer creates. . . . In determining whether the injury does result from the conditions of the employment, the normal reactions of men to those conditions are to be considered. . . . [Thus] the right of an employee to recover compensation is not nullified by the fact that his injury is augmented by natural human reactions to the danger or injury threatened or done. . . . The question is whether taking all the facts into consideration the conditions of the employment are the legal cause of the injury." (Citations omitted; internal quotation marks omitted.) *Stulginski v. Waterbury Rolling Mills Co.*, 124 Conn. 355, 360–61, 199 A. 653 (1938). In assessing such natural human reactions, we have stated that, "[w]henever an employer puts his employees at work with fellow servants, the conditions actually existing-apart from the possibility of wilful assaults by a fellow servant independent of the employment-which result in injury to a fellow employee, are a basis for compensation under the implied contract of th[e] [a]ct." *Anderson v. Security Building Co.*, 100 Conn. 373, 377, 123 A. 843 (1924).

It seriously cannot be questioned that a risk exists in the workplace that an employee might fall stricken to the ground, thereby prompting the natural, foreseeable reaction of coworkers to render aid. With respect to the employer's liability for injuries arising from such actions, in his treatise, Professor Arthur Larson sets forth the general proposition that, "the scope of an employee's employment is impliedly extended in an emergency to include the performance of any act designed to save life or property in which the employer has an interest." 2 A. Larson & L. Larson, *Workers' Compensation Law* (2006) § 28.01[1], p. 28–2. "The most common type of rescue case is the rescue of coemployees, and compensation is clearly payable for injuries so sustained, on the theory that the employer has a duty to aid its own employees in peril and that any employee is impliedly authorized to discharge this duty in an emergency." *Id.*, at p. 28–4. Courts have recognized under similar statutory schemes that, "[a] reasonable rescue attempt . . . may be one of the risks of employment, an incident of the service, foreseeable, if not foreseen, and so covered by the statute." (Internal quotation marks omitted.) *O'Leary v. Brown–Pacific–Maxon, Inc.*, 340 U.S. 504, 507, 71 S.Ct. 470, 95 L.Ed. 483 (1951).[5]

Under these principles, it is clear that, had the plaintiff's coworkers themselves *sustained* injuries while tending to the plaintiff, their injuries would have been compensable. It would be anomalous, therefore, to conclude that injuries that these same coworkers, while acting in the course of their employment, *inflicted* on the plaintiff in attempting to prevent him from injuring himself and other workers would *not* be compensable. In other words, whether the rescue attempt at issue is characterized as a risk of, or a condition incident to, employment for those engaged in the conduct, the essential character of the act does not change when viewed from the perspective of the coworker injured by that same conduct. Cf. *Mascika v. Connecticut Tool & Engineering Co.*, 109 Conn. 473, 481, 147 A. 11 (1929) (Explaining, in a case in which the plaintiff, while on his way into work, was struck by a stick thrown by his coworkers who were engaging in horseplay: "So far as the plaintiff was concerned the legal situation was the same as if he had been struck while actually engaged in the operation of his press. The risk of being injured by reason of the skylarking of his fellow employees while he himself was a passive actor was one of the risks of his employment, being incident to the conditions under which his work was performed."). Indeed, this uniform treatment of the conduct and injuries arising therefrom is compelled in the present case, given that the commissioner found that the plaintiff's coworkers had acted to prevent injury both to the plaintiff, "*as well as others. . . .*"[6] (Emphasis added.)

We have recognized that, "[i]f the act is one for the benefit of the employer or for the mutual benefit of both an injury arising out of it will

---

5 In O'Leary, the court emphasized that the commissioner's conclusions that the claimant had acted reasonably in attempting the rescue and that his death fairly may be attributable to the risks of the employment were based on permissible, but not compelled, inferences from the evidence. O'Leary v. Brown–Pacific–Maxon, Inc., supra, 340 U.S. at 508, 71 S.Ct. 470. The rescue at issue in that case, however, was of a third person not employed by the defendant employer. Our survey of the case law in which an employee came to the aid of a coworker does not reveal any case in which a court concluded that the rescue was not a foreseeable risk or condition of the employment. To the extent that O'Leary suggests that the reasonableness of the rescue effort is a prerequisite to compensability, we note that, in the present case, the reasonableness of the efforts of the plaintiff's coworkers is not at issue.

6 The dissent recognizes that there "may be cases where the provision of aid increases the risk of injury," and suggests that, consistent with case law from some other jurisdictions, such an injury could "arise out of the employment" if the aid were rendered negligently. Our statutory scheme, however, eschews any proof of fault or degree of culpability as a prerequisite for compensation. Bergeson v. New London, 269 Conn. 763, 768, 850 A.2d 184 (2004) ("[a]ct was enacted to provide compensation for any injury arising out of and in the course of employment, without regard to fault, by imposing a form of strict liability on the employer" [internal quotation marks omitted]). Thus, we disagree that the degree or presence of culpable conduct determines whether that conduct is a condition of employment.

usually be compensable; on the other hand, if the act being performed is for the exclusive benefit of the employee so that it is a personal privilege or is one which the employer permits the employee to undertake for the benefit of some other person or for some cause apart from his own interests, an injury arising out of it will not be compensable." *Smith v. Seamless Rubber Co.*, 111 Conn. 365, 368–69, 150 A. 110 (1930).[7] Thus, when the action giving rise to injury provides some benefit to the employer, the claimant need not prove the employer acquiesced to the action in order to establish compensability. See *McNamara v. Hamden*, 176 Conn. 547, 553–54, 398 A.2d 1161 (1979) (concluding that meaning of activity deemed "incidental to" employment and hence compensable is not limited to "compulsion by or benefit to the employer" but also includes "customary activity sanctioned by the employer through approval or acquiescence" [internal quotation marks omitted]). Such acquiescence, or constructive knowledge, is implicit by virtue of the benefit. See *Kish v. Nursing & Home Care, Inc.*, 248 Conn. 379, 389–90 n. 14, 727 A.2d 1253 (1999) (noting that, under our case law, constructive knowledge may be imputed as matter of law).

In light of the commissioner's finding that the plaintiff's coworkers had rendered aid to prevent injury not only to the plaintiff, but also to other workers, the *only* reasonable inference from this fact is that, contrary to the board's conclusion, the coworkers' actions were undertaken to benefit both the plaintiff *and* the defendant. Given this mutual benefit, the injuries sustained as a result thereof must fall within the scope of the general rule that an injury sustained in the course of employment also arises out of the employment. See *Labadie v. Norwalk Rehabilitation Services, Inc.*, supra, 274 Conn. at 237, 875 A.2d 485 ("[a]n injury which occurs in the course of the employment will ordinarily [also] arise out of the employment; but not necessarily so, for the injury might occur out of an act or omission for the exclusive benefit of the employee, or of another than the master, while the employee is engaged in the course of his employment" [internal quotation marks omitted]); see also *Ryerson v. A.E. Bounty Co.*, 107 Conn. 370, 379, 140 A. 728 (1928) (plaintiff's action for his own safety, although ultimately causing injury, "was as important an act for the employer as for the employee, so that the master's work could be done" and thus gave rise to compensable injury).

---

[7] Smith v. Seamless Rubber Co., supra, 111 Conn. at 368–69, 150 A. 110, is instructive in that this court suggested therein that, when there is evidence of a mutual benefit from an employer's action in tendering medical aid to an employee, injury resulting from such aid would be compensable. In that case, the court affirmed the commissioner's decision that the plaintiff's infection resulting from a smallpox vaccination administered at his workplace did not arise from the plaintiff's employment. *Id.*, at 367, 150 A. 110. [Smith found that the purpose of the vaccinations was for "the general good of the community and not the 'working conditions in the company's factory.' "] In present case, however, the necessary inference from the commissioner's finding that the plaintiff's coworkers intervened "in an attempt to prevent the [plaintiff] from injuring himself, as well as others" is that a mutual benefit inured to both the employer and employee.

Indeed, although it is not a prerequisite to compensability that the risk of injury be greater to the employee than to a member of the public; *Triano v. United States Rubber Co.*, supra, 144 Conn. at 397, 132 A.2d 570; it cannot be questioned that the plaintiff was more likely to be physically restrained by his coworkers than by strangers had he suffered the seizure in some neutral, public forum. The incentive to act in the employer's interest, the community of purpose among coworkers and the relationships engendered by that purpose would make intervention, and hence injury therefrom, more likely.

———

The defendant contends, however, that public policy counsels against the compensability of the injury in the present case because such a result would have a chilling effect on coworkers and employers rendering aid to a stricken employee. We disagree that such a consequence is likely. Employers have a vested interest in the welfare of their employees and an even greater interest in preventing and minimizing compensable injuries. Employees witnessing a coworker in distress generally will not know whether the distress results from, or will lead to, a compensable or noncompensable injury. Moreover, it seems doubtful that an employer would risk possible liability for an employee's injuries that were sustained as a result of the employer's categorical bar on direct aid to an injured employee.

Therefore, we conclude that the defendant's public policy argument is unpersuasive.

The decision of the board is reversed and the case is remanded to the board with direction to sustain the plaintiff's appeal.

SULLIVAN, C.J., with whom ZARELLA, J., joins, dissenting.

———

Because the record in the present case establishes unequivocally that the initial causal factor of the plaintiff's injuries was an idiopathic medical condition, and because there is no evidence that his coworkers' provision of assistance increased the risk of injury from that condition, I would conclude that the evidence amply supports the commissioner's finding that the injuries did not arise out of employment. Accordingly, I would conclude that the commissioner properly dismissed the plaintiff's application for workers' compensation benefits.

NOTES

1. Injuries suffered by an employee in attempting to rescue a fellow worker, a customer, or a passenger, or to preserve the employer's property are routinely compensated. Moreover, an injury suffered in an employee's

attempt to rescue a stranger is compensable if the employer would be subjected to possible liability if the stranger were injured. Ocean Accident & Guarantee Corp., Ltd. v. Industrial Acc. Comm., 180 Cal. 389, 182 P. 35 (1919); Reilly v. Weber Engineering Co., 107 N.J.Super. 254, 258 A.2d 36 (1969) (death from attempt to rescue a stranger was held to be compensable under the positional risk theory where the duties brought the worker to the spot where the attempted rescue occurred); Matter of Babington v. Yellow Taxi Corp., 250 N.Y. 14, 164 N.E. 726 (1928) (policeman leaped on taxi driven by the decedent and directed him to pursue another car; driver killed in resulting collision; compensation awarded from taxi company); and O'Leary v. Brown–Pacific–Maxon, Inc., 340 U.S. 504, 71 S.Ct. 470, 95 L.Ed. 483 (1951) (employer maintained recreation center on island of Guam; employee drowned while attempting to rescue a swimmer in difficulty; compensation awarded).

2. Some decisions compensate injuries incurred in a rescue attempt on the basis that rescues are expectable human responses to the perception that someone needs help. See, e.g., D.L. Cullifer and Son, Inc. v. Martinez, 572 So.2d 1360 (Fla.1990) (compensation awarded fruitpickers injured while helping push disabled vehicle of passing motorist from its position of imminent hazard to motoring public; response to emergency is incidental to employment), Edwards v. Louisiana Forestry Comm., 221 La. 818, 60 So.2d 449 (1952) (observer in a fire tower attempted to rescue a child attacked by dog): and Puttkammer v. Industrial Com., 371 Ill. 497, 21 N.E.2d 575 (1939). Other decisions compensate the rescuer on the ground that the rescue accrues good will to the employer. Compare Carey v. Stadther, 300 Minn. 88, 219 N.W.2d 76 (1974) (feed salesman met death attempting to rescue a stranger from a cesspool; compensation awarded) with Weidenbach v. Miller, 237 Minn. 278, 55 N.W.2d 289 (1952) (employer riding with employee in truck urged the latter to stop when a drowning man was seen; employee was injured in rescue attempt; compensation denied). How can the latter decision be justified?

3. In Re D'Angeli's Case, 369 Mass. 812, 343 N.E.2d 368 (1976) illustrates decisions that tend to enlarge coverage of rescue attempts. There, a travelling employee was struck by a passing car while he was gratuitously attempting to remove dangerous debris from the highway. In awarding compensation the court observed:

> It is our present view that when a conscientious citizen is in the course of his employment and perceives an imminent danger to the public, as would appear to have been the case this instance, his endeavor to alleviate the danger should be considered incidental to his employment. In holding that emergency public service may be warranted in the course of employment we are following good precedent. 369 Mass. 812, 343 N.E.2d 368, 371.

4. Pennsylvania has addressed the rescue issue in its statutory definition of "employees:"

(10) An employe who, while in the course and scope of his employment, goes to the aid of a person and suffers injury or death as a direct result of any of the following:

(i) Preventing the commission of a crime, lawfully apprehending a person reasonably suspected of having committed a crime or aiding the victim of a crime. . . .

(ii) Rendering emergency care, first aid or rescue at the scene of an emergency.

Pa. St. 77 P.S. § 1031(10).

8. UNEXPLAINED DEATHS

HYPL V. INDUSTRIAL COM'N OF ARIZONA

Court of Appeals of Arizona, 2005.
210 Ariz. 381, 111 P.3d 423.

HOWARD, PRESIDING J.

In this statutory special action, petitioner/employee Jaroslav Hypl challenges the administrative law judge's (ALJ) decision concluding that Hypl had failed to show that his injury occurred in the course of and arose out of his employment with Corexpress. The ALJ made this determination based, in part, on his conclusion that Hypl was not entitled to the benefit of a presumption. Because we conclude that Hypl may be entitled to a presumption if he can show his injuries occurred during the time and space limitations of his employment, we set aside the award.

The facts relevant to this special action are undisputed. On May 2, 2002, Hypl accepted a job with Corexpress to transport several barrels of wire from Nogales, Arizona, to El Paso, Texas, a distance of approximately 350 miles. Hypl began the trip at approximately 6:00 p.m. that evening and was instructed to deliver the wire by 6:00 a.m. the next morning. At 6:30 a.m., a half hour past the required delivery time, Hypl was arrested on Interstate 10 near Deming, New Mexico, after a police officer witnessed him driving erratically. At the time of his arrest, Hypl was traveling westbound, i.e., away from El Paso, but had not yet delivered the wire to its destination.

Presuming Hypl was intoxicated, the officer took him to a police station for booking. After closer examination, the officer realized Hypl was injured and sought medical attention for him. Hypl was taken to a nearby hospital where physicians determined that he had a skull fracture on the top of his head, blood clots in the frontal and temporal lobes of his brain, and blood in the surface of his brain. He was transported by helicopter to University Medical Center in Tucson, Arizona, for emergency surgery and remained in a coma for over eight hours after the surgery.

Hypl filed a claim for workers' compensation benefits, which was denied. Hypl requested a hearing and testified at the hearing that he had no memory of the events that had caused his injury. Although he remembered loading the wire onto the truck in Nogales and driving toward Interstate 10, he recalled nothing else until he awoke from the coma after his surgery. The ALJ determined that Hypl had not met his burden of proving the injury had occurred within the course and scope of his employment. The ALJ further concluded that the "unexplained death presumption" had not been extended in Arizona to an applicant who was alive and declined to extend it in this case. Ultimately, the ALJ found the injury noncompensable. The award was affirmed upon administrative review, and this statutory special action followed.

Hypl argues on review that the ALJ's award is not reasonably supported by the evidence, claiming he was entitled to a presumption that the injury occurred within the course and scope of his employment. On review of an award, we deferentially review an ALJ's factual findings reasonably supported by the record but review the ALJ's legal conclusions de novo. . . .

A compensable injury must both arise out of and occur in the course of employment. A.R.S. § 23–1021(A). The "arising out of" requirement refers to the origin or cause of the injury and is met when the claimant shows a causal relationship between the employment and the injury. . . . The "in the course of" requirement is satisfied if the claimant shows the injury occurred during the time, place, and circumstances of the claimant's employment. . . . As the claimant, Hypl had the burden of establishing both of these elements. . . . It is not the employer's burden to disprove the statutory requirements.

The unexplained death presumption, however, can shift the burden of producing evidence. See *Martin v. Indus. Comm'n*, 73 Ariz. 401, 404, 242 P.2d 286, 288 (1952). . . . But the exact factual predicate for and the effect of the unexplained death presumption have not always been clearly stated. In *Martin*, the issue was whether a ranch foreman, who had died in a car accident after leaving a bar while taking care of either business or personal concerns, was covered by workers' compensation. In that case, our supreme court adopted the unexplained death presumption without so labeling it, saying:

> "It is generally held that when it is shown that an employee was found dead at a place where his duties required him to be, or where he might properly have been in the performance of his duties during the hours of his work, in the absence of evidence that he was not engaged in his master's business, there is a

> presumption that the accident arose out of and in the course of the employment within the meaning of the compensation acts."

Ariz. at 404, 242 P.2d at 288 (emphasis deleted), *quoting* 120 A.L.R. 683. Thus, Arizona's first supreme court case on this issue indicated that the presumption could apply to both "the arising out of" and "in the course of" requirements, after a claimant has shown that he or she meets the place and time restrictions of the employment. After finding the claimant had produced sufficient facts to raise the presumption, the court set aside the award denying Martin's survivors death benefits. *Id.* at 405, 242 P.2d at 289.

The following year, in an unrelated case that coincidentally involved the same name, our supreme court considered the issue again in *Martin v. Industrial Commission*, 75 Ariz. 403, 257 P.2d 596 (1953). There, a worker died of carbon monoxide poisoning after business hours while in a company truck on the employer's premises; it was unclear why the employee was there. The court stated the sole question was whether the employee had been in the course of his employment because, if so, the poisoning would clearly arise from his employment. The court cited Arthur Larson, *The Law of Workman's Compensation* (1989) as the "correct statement of the law" concerning the death presumption:

> "When an employee is found dead under circumstances indicating that death took place within the time and space limits of the employment, in the absence of any evidence of what caused the death most courts will indulge a presumption or inference that the death arose out of the employment."

Martin, 75 Ariz. at 411, 257 P.2d at 601, *quoting* 1 Larson, *supra*, § 10.32, at 3–101. Therefore, the second supreme court case, which concerned only the in the course of employment requirement, stated that the death presumption applies to the "arising out of" requirement after the claimant demonstrates that the time and space requirements are met. In that case, however, the court found that the presumption did not apply because sufficient facts concerning the cause of death were known and the commission was entitled to infer from the facts that the claimant had not yet entered into the course of his employment. *Martin*, 75 Ariz. at 411, 257 P.2d at 601.

In *Downes v. Industrial Commission*, 113 Ariz. 90, 546 P.2d 826 (1976), an employee was killed when the company vehicle he was driving was run over by a 150-ton ore truck. Because the cause of the injury was apparent, the supreme court only needed to decide whether the employee had been within the course of his employment at the time of the accident. Without mentioning the term "death presumption," but citing the first *Martin* case, our supreme court found that certain presumptions applied to the course of employment requirement:

> There is a presumption that if an employee is injured while on company property during working hours, he is injured while within the scope and course of his employment. . . .
>
> * * *
>
> There is a further presumption that when a workm[a]n is killed on the job he was, at the time of the fatal accident, within the scope and course of his employment. . . .

Downes, 113 Ariz. at 92–93, 546 P.2d at 828–29. The court determined that the employee's heirs had raised a rebuttable presumption that he had died in the course of his employment and set aside the award denying them death benefits. *Id.* at 94, 546 P.2d at 830.

In *Bennett v. Industrial Commission*, 163 Ariz. 534, 536, 789 P.2d 401, 403 (App.1990), Division One of this court stated that the presumption may apply to both the course of employment and the arising out of employment requirements: "The unexplained death presumption relaxes a claimant's ordinary burden to prove that death or injury arose out of and in the course of employment." The *Bennett* court then stated that the "presumption arises when a worker's unexplained death occurs within the time and space limits of employment" and quoted Larson's statement that the presumption applies to the arising out of requirement. *Id.* The court followed this analysis by quoting another passage from Larson that discussed applying the unexplained death presumption when a claimant satisfies the in the course of employment requirement:

> "The occurrence of the death within the course [i.e., the time and space limits] of employment at least indicates that the employment brought deceased within range of the harm, and the cause of harm, being unknown, is neutral and not personal. The practical justification lies in the realization that, when the death itself has removed the only possible witness who could prove causal connection, fairness to the dependents suggests some softening of the rule requiring claimant to provide affirmative proof of each requisite element of compensability."

Id. at 536, 789 P.2d at 403, *quoting* 1 Larson, *supra*, § 10.32, at 3–101 to 3–110.

Finally, in *Konichek v. Industrial Commission*, 167 Ariz. 296, 806 P.2d 885 (App.1990), this court did not distinguish between the in the course of employment and the arising out of employment requirements:

> The presumption operates to relax a claimant's burden to prove that death occurred *in the course of employment*. Larson explains the rule as follows:

> When an employee is found dead under circumstances indicating that death took place within the time and space limits of the employment, in the absence of any evidence of what caused the death, most courts will indulge a presumption or inference that the death *arose out of* the employment.

Id. at 298, 806 P.2d at 887 (emphasis added), *quoting* 1 Larson, *supra*, § 10.32, at 3–100.

Larson has recognized the difficulty that occurs when doubt exists on whether the employee was in the course of employment at the time of death. After stating that the death presumption applies to the arising out of requirement in the absence of proof of a cause of death, Larson acknowledges that applying the presumption to that requirement "becomes less clear when there is some room for doubt whether the injury even took place in the course of employment." 1 Arthur Larson & Lex K. Larson, *Larson's Workers' Compensation Law* § 7.04(2)(c), at 7–29 (2004). Larson further states: "When . . . the evidence leaves a wide area of uncertainty about the decedent's movements between the last time he or she was seen and the discovery of his or her death, denials have been issued because of the failure to bring the episode within the course of employment in the first place." Larson & Larson, *supra*, § 7.04(2)(c), at 7–30. Larson then cites cases in which sufficient connection to employment has been found and cases in which such a connection has not been found. In each case, at least circumstantial evidence of relation to the course of employment was required in order to invoke the presumption. Larson & Larson, *supra*, § 7.04(2)(c), at 7–30 to 7–35.

Based on the case law, we conclude that the unexplained death presumption softens both the in the course of employment element and the arising out of employment element. Therefore, in the absence of any contrary evidence, if a claimant proves by a preponderance of the evidence that the decedent was within the time and space limitations of employment when injured, we presume that the injury occurred in the course of employment, *i.e.*, the employee was injured while doing the employer's work and not while on a personal deviation, and that the unexplained injury arose out of the employment.

In this case, the ALJ correctly noted that the death presumption has never been applied in Arizona to a living claimant. But this presumption developed out of fairness to claimants "when the death itself has removed the only possible witness who could prove causal connection." Larson & Larson, *supra*, § 7.04(2), at 7–22. Hypl's injury has left him unable to remember anything about how he was injured and, thus, has effectively removed the only possible witness who could prove his injury was causally related to his employment. We must therefore determine whether the unexplained death presumption, or a similar type of presumption, should apply in the case of a living claimant who, by reason of the injury, is unable to testify about how he or she was injured.

———

Although this issue is one of first impression in Arizona, other states have considered similar issues with differing results. One state has applied this presumption in cases comparable to the present one in which the claimant is comatose or otherwise unable to explain the injury. *See Sena v. Cont'l Cas. Co.*, 97 N.M. 753, 643 P.2d 622 (N.M.Ct.App.1982). And several states have extended this presumption to an employee who became ill or comatose at the place of employment but died at a hospital several days later. *See Gen. Accident Fire & Life Ins. Co. v. Sturgis*, 136 Ga.App. 260, 221 S.E.2d 51 (1975); *Nettles v. Gulf City Fisheries, Inc.*, 629 So.2d 554 (Miss.1993). But other states have rejected applying the unexplained death presumption to a living claimant as an unwarranted extension of the doctrine. *See, e.g., Salyers v. G. & P. Coal Co.*, 467 S.W.2d 115 (Ky.Ct.App.1971); see also *A.H. Angerstein, Inc. v. Jankowski*, 187 A.2d 81, 85 n. 8 (Del.Super.Ct.1962) ("[O]ur statute does not permit the adoption and utilization of the '[unexplained death] presumption.' . . . It cannot be reconciled with our decided cases. . . ."); *Pinkerton's, Inc. v. Helmes*, 242 Va. 378, 410 S.E.2d 646, 648 (1991) ("Broadening the use of the [unexplained death] presumption to such an extent [would] significantly alter [ ] the jurisprudence of workers' compensation law.").

———

In order to effectuate the principle that the workers' compensation statutes shall be liberally construed in favor of payment of compensation benefits, see *Bennett*, 163 Ariz. at 536, 789 P.2d at 403, we conclude that a presumption similar to the unexplained death presumption should apply to an injury to a living worker who, due to the injury, is unable to testify about how the injury happened. Thus, an injured worker who proves by a preponderance of the evidence that he or she is unable to remember or to communicate the circumstances and cause of an injury due to the injury and who proves by a preponderance of the evidence that the injury occurred during the time and space limitations of the employment is presumed to have been injured while doing the employer's work, *i.e.*, in the course of the employment, and the injury is presumed to have arisen from the employment in the absence of evidence that the worker was not within the course of the employment or that the injury did not arise from the employment.

In this case, the ALJ found that Hypl has no memory of the cause of or the events leading to his injury. And neither the employer nor the insurer disputed below that Hypl had suffered amnesia as a result of the injury and cannot remember the events. Therefore, if Hypl can provide a sufficient factual basis to allow an inference that he was injured in the time and space limitations of his employment, he is entitled to a presumption that his injury occurred in the course of and arose out of his employment.

The ALJ [also] found that "the preponderance of the evidence presented does not establish [Hypl] was in the course and scope of his employment or that the 'injury' arose out of the employment." But the ALJ then stated: "There [fore], [Hypl] has not met his burden and the claim must be found non-compensable unless there is a presumption in favor of [Hypl] in view of his lack of memory that would soften the requirement of affirmative proof of an injury arising out of and in the course and scope of his employment." We have now adopted that presumption. And, although the ALJ made findings of fact that could indicate he found Hypl had failed to satisfy the time and space limitations necessary to invoke the presumption, neither the exact requirements to invoke the presumption nor the presumption had been defined previously. Accordingly, we cannot say that the ALJ had them in mind when making his findings. Therefore, we set aside the award.

NOTES

1. In Taylor v. Industrial Commission of Arizona, 2011 WL 5387599 (Ariz. App. Div 2, 2011) and Sanderson v. Industrial Commission of Arizona, 2011 WL 5866929 (Ariz. App. Div 1, 2011) clarified the Hypl presumption of compensability. Taylor held that the presumption did not apply when a living claimant did not establish by preponderance of evidence that "his injuries impaired his consciousness, memory, or ability to communicate" and Sanderson held that evidence that an unexplained fall resulted from an idiopathic condition defeated the presumption. Taylor also failed to prove that the particular injury he suffered occurred at work. Both claims were rejected.

2. The statutes of several states prescribe presumptions "that in the absence of substantial evidence to the contrary, that the claim comes within the provisions" of the worker's compensation law. The New York statute is exemplary:

McKinney's Workers' Compensation Law § 21. Presumptions

In any proceeding for the enforcement of a claim for compensation under this chapter, it shall be presumed in the absence of substantial evidence to the contrary;

1. That the claim comes within the provision of this chapter;
2. That sufficient notice thereof was given;
3. That the injury was not occasioned by the willful intention of the injured employee to bring about the injury or death of himself or of another;

4. That the injury did not result solely from the intoxication of the injured employee while on duty.

5. That the contents of medical and surgical reports introduced in evidence by claimants for compensation shall constitute prima facie evidence of fact as to the matter contained therein.

Florida had such a provision but it was repealed and replaced with a provision that states the workers' compensation statute is not to be construed "liberally in favor of either employee or employer." F.S.A. 440.015. Does it occur to you that these presumptions, if interpreted broadly, would do away with the statutory tests of compensability in many instances? The courts do not always read them that liberally. See, e.g. Pridgen v. International Cushion Co., 88 So.2d 286 (Fla.1956) (employee suddenly dropped dead from unexplained cause while at work; the court held that the statutory presumption is not a substitute for evidence of a causal connection between the employment and the death and stated that the purpose of the provision is to raise a presumption where the physical cause has been established and the remaining question is whether death occurred during course of employment); and McCormack v. National City Bank of New York, 303 N.Y. 5, 99 N.E.2d 887 (1951) (same outcome in divided decision). Similarly, in Leblanc's Case, 332 Mass. 334, 125 N.E.2d 129 (1955), refused to apply that presumption to an unexplained death claim "which occurs at the place of his employment and during his working hours, and which there is substantial evidence tending to show is disconnected from and unrelated to his employment."

One court has stated:

> When substantial evidence is introduced by the party against whom a presumption operates controverting the presumed fact, then its existence or non existence is to be determined from the evidence, exactly as if no presumption had been operative in the case. In other words, such presumptions are procedural (placing the burden upon the party denying their truth to produce evidence) and not for consideration of the trier of the facts who has the function of determining what facts are proved by the evidence produced.

Duff v. St. Louis Mining & Milling Corp., 363 Mo. 944, 948, 255 S.W.2d 792, 793 (1953). Other cases denying compensation include: Hunter v. American Steel & Wire Co., 293 Pa. 103, 141 A. 635 (1928) (body of worker found in river at place one hundred and twenty-five feet from toilet; compensation denied); Pinkerton's, Inc. v. Holmes, 242 Va. 378, 410 S.E.2d 646 (1991) (injuries to employee found unconscious in her wrecked car shortly after her shift as night security guard ended: held; in the absence of death, the court refused to presume injuries arose out of and within course of employment and denied benefits); and Green v. Simpson & Brown Constr. Co., 14 N.J. 66, 101 A.2d 10 (1953) (a night watchman on barge last seen at a gate leading to waterfront and place of work but was not missed until several days later; body found in water where it had floated downstream, but with no proof as to when or how it came to be in the water; compensation denied). Noted (1954) 8 Rutgers L.Rev. 100.

Nevertheless, other decisions award compensation in equally problematic situations. See, e.g., Downes v. Industrial Comm., 113 Ariz. 90, 546 P.2d 826 (1976); Slotnick v. Howard Stores Corp., 58 A.D.2d 959, 397 N.Y.S.2d 179 (1977) (store manager, whose duties compelled his presence on streets was discovered nude and unconscious with a two inch cut on his head and a beer can in his hand; compensation awarded because the statutory presumption that he was in the course of employment was not rebutted).

3. A similar but distinguishable issue arises when the evidence supports inferences of two competing possible causes of death, one of which would be definitely attributable to the employment, and the other not. Many decisions award compensation. See, e.g., Southwest Forest Industries v. Industrial Comm., 96 Ariz. 91, 392 P.2d 506 (1964) (the body of a worker who was hired to divert coal onto conveyor belt was found buried under four feet of coal at the end of the belt; did he die of heart attack and fall onto belt, or did the coal slide and bury him?; evidence supported award of compensation); American Sugar Refining Co. v. Ned, 209 F.2d 636, 638 (5th Cir.1954) (a worker on a barge fell into river; did he die of heart attack or drowning?; compensation awarded; "The death was accidental even though the man might have died a few minutes later from natural causes if he had not met with the accident"); and Southern Motor Lines Co. v. Alvis, 200 Va. 168, 104 S.E.2d 735 (1958) (unexplained death of worker found dead at place and at time work required his presence presumed to be compensable). Compare Henry v. Schenk Mechanical Contractors, Inc., 169 Ind.App. 178, 346 N.E.2d 616 (1976) (an employee's death was caused by the puncture of his temple with a Ram Set tool; was it an accident or suicide?; compensation denied because circumstantial evidence supported finding of suicide).

Not all courts are so liberal. Jennings v. Chambers Development Company, 335 S.C. 249, 516 S.E.2d 453 (Ct. App. 1999) held that death by aneurysm does not raise a presumption of compensability. In such a case the claimant must first prove the aneurysm occurred while the worker was engaged in work that created unusual stress. Wilkinson County Board of Education v. Johnson, 732 S.E.2d 765 (Ga. App. 2012) held that application of the presumption was not defeated by the fact that death from an unexplained injury suffered on the job did not result until the worker was hospitalized. Nevertheless, Wilkinson affirmed that the participating cause of the job injury must be unexplained and the initial fact-finder must make that factual determination.

Metcalf v. A.M. Express Moving Systems, Inc., 230 Va. 464, 339 S.E.2d 177 (1986) held that the presumption of compensability applies only if something about the employment is the only rational inference arising from the evidence. There, a traveling employee was shot while sleeping in a company truck. The attack was an apparent random act committed against an easy target. Benefits were denied because no evidence showed that the employment somehow enhanced the probability that the attack would occur. Is this too narrow a view? Similarly, Parrish v. Kansas City Security Service, 682 S.W.2d 20 (Mo. App. 1985) denied recovery to survivors of a worker found dead at his place and time of work because other evidence gave rise to a presumption that he was killed while attempting to repair his personal car.

CHAPTER 6

ACCIDENT AND OCCUPATIONAL DISEASE

■ ■ ■

1. INTRODUCTION TO THIS CHAPTER

In the early days of the workers' compensation movement in England and most of the American states, it was the policy not to cover loss of wages caused by occupational disease. The goal of the new program was limited to providing an effective remedy for disability resulting from industrial accident. Occupational disease was not initially considered to be within the ambit of the workers' compensation statutes. This general limitation of purpose was reflected in the original statutes by terms restricting compensation to cases of "injury by accident" or "accidental injury," which as shown below, were not originally interpreted by the courts to include diseases.

As time passed, a variety of influences brought about a modification of the original approach. Occupational diseases did occur and no alternative means to compensate affected workers materialized. Problems of interpretation arose as to what constituted an "injury by accident" and it became difficult to determine where the outer boundaries of the limitation were to be fixed. It was found that accident and disease blend into each other by minute gradations. Furthermore, it became obvious that the exclusion of occupational disease left many disabled workers without assistance under circumstances economically identical to those of fellow workers disabled by accident, bringing into focus the arbitrariness of the restriction. For these and other reasons, England and almost all the American states amended their laws or passed new ones to provide compensation for losses caused by occupational disease.

In this chapter the student is directed to the legal issues surrounding the concept of "accident" and the application of the different types of occupational disease laws. The reader will recognize that these problems constitute another phase of the familiar general policy issue that underlies so many areas of workers' compensation law, namely, to what risks ought workers' compensation coverage be extended?

2. THE CONCEPT OF "ACCIDENT"

MATTHEWS v. R.T. ALLEN & SONS, INC.

Supreme Court of Maine, 1970.
266 A.2d 240.

WEATHERBEE, JUSTICE.

On May 1, 1969 an Industrial Accident Commissioner rendered a decree denying an award of compensation to the Petitioner.

[The opinion first discussed certain alleged irregularities in the post-decree procedure. After concluding that the case was reviewable as to questions of substantive law, it continued].

We must decide the single issue of whether the Petitioner suffered a personal injury arising out of and in the course of his employment.

The Petitioner, a 43 year old woodsworker, testified that on November 13, 1967 he was employed loading pulpwood onto trucks by hand. He had worked at this since 7:00 A.M. and the lifting evidently involved bending and straightening the back. The sticks were four feet long and from four inches to two feet in diameter. At about 10:30 or 11:00 A.M. he felt pain in his back but he continued to work. During his noon lunch period while he ate his lunch in the truck, the pain became worse. He worked one to one and a half hours after lunch at which time the pain was so great that he reported to his employer that he was unable to continue and went home. During the next four days the back pain continued to increase in severity and he could not go to work. On November 18 he was admitted to the Maine Coast Memorial Hospital in Ellsworth and on December 10 he was transferred to the Maine Medical Center in Portland where a herniated disc was removed. He returned to work the first of May, 1968.

On cross-examination he testified that the pain began that morning gradually and was not associated with any "specific lifting, slipping or tripping". He admitted he had told an insurance company investigator that the pain came on while he was sitting in the truck at noon but he testified that he had noticed the pain while working that morning " * * * [B]ut when I first noticed it why it didn't bother me to lift or anything. It was after when I started to straighten up to pull myself back." At noon it had become worse. He agreed that he told the doctors that the pain came on gradually and "got worse and worse and worse" as he worked. He also said that on previous occasions while doing woods work he had had low back pains but they were never disabling.

The doctors' reports and hospital discharge summaries add only that the Petitioner had been admitted to the Ellsworth hospital suffering such severe pain that he "could hardly move". During the next four days the pain increased in severity and also radiated down into his left leg and foot. After two weeks of conservative treatment his condition had only worsened. A myelogram showed a defect in the L4–5 interspace on the left and surgery disclosed an acutely herniated disc in that area, which was removed.

The doctors' reports expressed no opinion as to the precipitating cause of the injury, whether it may have developed prior to November 13, 1967 or, if so, whether the exertion of November 13 may have aggravated the condition except for one significant comment to be discussed later.

The Commissioner found:

> "The evidence, we find, is insufficient to support a finding that Mr. Matthews sustained a personal injury by accident arising out of and in the course of his employment. We cannot conclude from the testimony that the disc condition which disabled him on November 13, 1967, resulted from any single episode, or traumatic incident. The medical history given by Mr. Matthews and his testimony on cross examination, indicate that the symptoms of the underlying disc condition became disabling on November 13, 1967, but that the herniated disc had developed prior to that time—probably gradually. It is our decision that the petition must be dismissed."

Our own findings lead us to an opposite conclusion.

The Petitioner has the burden of proving that he suffered a personal injury by accident arising out of and in the course of his employment. 39 M.R.S.A. § 52.

The Workmen's Compensation Law represents a relatively recent concept of responsibility without negligence. While the early cases usually concerned accidental injuries where an external force was applied to an external portion of the body, our own Court decided early in the development of our law that the term injury by accident includes incidents where internal parts of the physical structure break down under external force, including the stress of labor. While this may more dramatically occur as a result of a slip, a fall or a single unusual strained effort, we have found other such internal breakdowns to have resulted from the usual work which the workman was performing in his usual, normal way. In short, we have construed the term "accident" to include not only injuries which are the results of accidents but also injuries which are themselves accidents. 58 Am.Jur., Workmen's Compensation, § 195. In Brown's Case, 123 Me. 424, 123 A. 421 (1924) a fatal heart dilation resulted from the exertion of shoveling snow. In Patrick v. J.B. Ham Co., 119 Me. 510, 111 A. 912 (1921) the Petitioner's husband suffered a cerebral hemorrhage while performing his regular duties of lifting sacks of grain. In Taylor's Case, 127 Me. 207, 142 A. 730 (1928) the Petitioner's husband had been lifting heavy objects in the course of his usual work and a particularly vigorous straining caused a pulmonary embolism.

This position is in agreement with that taken by the great majority of American jurisdictions and follows the rule recognized in England which in many respects furnished the model for our own Act. Brzozowski's Case, 328 Mass. 113, 102 N.E.2d 399 (1951); Kacavisti v. Sprague Electric Co., 102 N.H. 266, 155 A.2d 183 (1959); Bryant Stave & Heading Co. v. White, 227 Ark. 147, 296 S.W.2d 436 (1956); Larson's Workmen's Compensation Law, Vol. 1A, 38.20. In England the Courts soon came to hold that an unexpected, unforeseen or unintended result from usual or customary exertion constitutes an injury by accident even though there is no unexpected or fortuitous cause. Fenton v. Thorley Co., Ltd., A.C. 443 (House of Lords) (1903); Clover, Clayton & Co. v. Hughes, A.C. 242, 3 B.W.C.C. 775 (1910); A Problem in the Drafting of Workmen's Compensation Acts by Francis H. Bohlen, 25 Harvard Law Review, 328 at page 337.

In some of the earlier decisions holding that the breaking down of internal parts might be accidents under the statute, the death or incapacity occurred suddenly as the internal part dramatically gave way. This furnished another similarity to the usual concept of accident occurring when an external force is applied violently to an external part and assisted this Court in arriving at its conclusion that the Legislature intended both situations to be considered industrial accidents.

> "If a laborer performing his usual task, in his wonted way, by reason of strain, breaks his wrist, nobody would question the accidental nature of the injury. If instead of the wrist it is an artery that breaks, the occurrence is just as clearly an accident." Brown's Case, supra, 123 Me. at 425, 123 A. at 422.

Certainly the sudden quality of a mishap often makes it more clearly distinguishable from the mere malfunctioning of an organ which develops through natural progression, unrelated to the employment.

This thinking led our Court in early decisions to describe an accidental injury as being "unusual, undesigned, unexpected, sudden" (Brown's Case, supra, where the employee "suddenly became dizzy, faint and short of breath" while shoveling snow). As recently as in Bernier v. Coca–Cola Bottling Plants, Inc., Me., 250 A.2d 820 (1969) in pointing out that the Petitioner need not prove that his back strain resulted from "any unusual slip, fall, etc., in other words, external injury" we quoted Brown's Case to hold that "an internal injury that is itself sudden, unusual, and unexpected is none the less accidental because its external cause is a part of the victim's ordinary work."

* * *

We find no significant dispute in the testimony. It reveals a 43 year old woodsworker who had had low back pains in the past, usually associated with his work, but never to the extent of being disabling. On this occasion the pain began while he was loading sticks of pulpwood, some very heavy. He continued to work several hours while the pain got "worse and worse and worse". After he stopped working the pain continued to increase in severity and to extend in area until relieved by surgery. Surgery disclosed that an extruding mass from the ruptured disc was pressing against the nerve and obviously bowing it outward and upward.

* * *

We are called upon to decide whether Petitioner's disability, hospitalization and surgery were causally connected with his activities while loading pulpwood that November 13. Whether Petitioner's disc ruptured abruptly the morning of November 13 or whether the defective condition developed gradually during his previous episodes of low back pain is not controlling here. The scanty facts presented to us lead us to the conclusion that in either case the heavy labor of November 13 constituted the critical episode which completely incapacitated the man with increasing and unrelieved crippling pain until surgery removed the ruptured part.

While we do not know the moment when the actual herniation occurred its causal connection with the labor of November 13 seems apparent. In other words the personal injury appears either to have been caused by the exertions of November 13 or aggravated by them. We have repeatedly held that if stress of labor aggravates or accelerates the development of a preexisting infirmity causing an internal breakdown of that part of the structure a personal injury by accident occurs. *Hull*'s Case, supra; *Swett*'s Case, supra. The point is dramatized by the language of the Court in Lachance's Case, 121 Me. 506 at page 510, 118 A. 370 at page 372 (1922):

> "If Lachance, but for the hurt, would not have died at the time at which, and in the way in which, he did die, then, within the meaning of the Workmen's Act the unfortunate occurrence, though it merely hastened a deep-seated disorder to destiny, must be held to have resulted in an injury causing death."

Although neither the Ellsworth orthopedic surgeon who originally treated Petitioner nor the Portland neuro-surgeon who performed the surgery was called to testify, the orthopedic surgeon (who also assisted in the operation) commented tersely in his written report:

> "Unfortunately, after the pain had developed he continued to work until the job was completed."

We infer from this that it was his opinion that Petitioner's exertion in loading the trucks at least contributed to his disability and to his need for surgery.

We find that Petitioner sustained a personal injury by accident arising out of and in the course of his employment on November 13, 1967.

* * *

Appeal sustained. Case remanded to the Industrial Accident Commission for determination of compensation. * * *

NOTES

1. The issue presented in the foregoing case was perceived to be a potential source of difficulty at an early date in the development of workers' compensation in the United States. It constitutes one branch of a two-pronged problem that resulted from the use in workers' compensation statutes of the term "personal injury by accident" or "accidental injury" or some similar expression.

The nature of the problem was outlined by Professor Francis H. Bohlen in 1912. (25 Harv.L.Rev. 328) He wrote:

> "The term 'by accident' has been consistently construed to include two different ideas: the first is that of unexpectedness; the second, that of an injury sustained on some definite occasion, the date of which can be fixed with reasonable certainty. The first idea would be as well conveyed by the word 'accidentally' or by any phrase or phrases in which unforeseen harm is sharply contrasted with harm intended or expected to result. The latter idea, it is submitted, is not necessarily included in the term 'accidental' or 'accidentally'; such words, especially if the phrases employed in such legislation are to be construed in accordance with the popular meaning of the terms used, do not appear necessarily to indicate the existence of an accident, but would seem to relate solely to the injury being neither intended nor expected."

The *Matthews* case involves the first aspect of the term "accident", namely, unexpectedness. What unexpected event will satisfy that requirement? Is it necessary that, in addition to the unexpected injury, there be some contemporaneous occurrence of a causal nature such as a fall, a slip, a blow or similar incident? Or is the unexpected injury standing alone sufficient to constitute the "accident"?

The problem had been identified and solved in England long before any statute had come into effect in the United States. In 1903 it was held by the House of Lords in Fenton v. Thorley & Co., Ltd, [1903] A.C. 443, that the unexpected injury itself could constitute the accident, reversing the position originally taken on this question by an English court in Hensey v. White, [1900] 1 Q.B. 481. In the United States, however, the early holdings in many states having statutes containing the term "accident" or "accidental" required that there must be some external event other than the injury itself in order to bring the case within the purview of the statute. Some jurisdictions demanded that something unusual or out of the ordinary course of the employee's work must be shown to have occurred contemporaneously with the injury in order to comply with the requirement of "accidental personal injury". E.g., Kelly–Springfield Tire Co. v. Daniels, 199 Md. 156, 85 A.2d 795 (1952) (compensation denied for injury to intervertebral disc when lifting air bag and hooking it on a machine while in a stooping position). The majority of jurisdictions in the United States at the present time are in accord with the view expressed in Matthews and do not require an unusual event in addition to the unexpected injury. See, 2 A. Larson & L. Larson, Larson's Workers' Compensation § 43.01(2013).

2. Some jurisdictions distinguish between usual and unusual exertion in construing the term "accident" or "accidental." If the injury occurs while the employee is engaged in the usual exertion called for by the job, there is no "injury by accident"; but if the injury results from some special activity culminating in extraordinary strain, the injury is considered an accident. E.g., Virginia Electric and Power Co. v. Cogbill, 223 Va. 354, 288 S.E.2d 485 (1982) (gradual back injury is not an industrial accident since it was not caused by an employment-related activity requiring different or unusual exertion); Satrom v. North Dakota Workmen's Comp. Bureau, 328 N.W.2d 824 (N.D.1982) (hairdresser's acute disc syndrome held compensable under finding that it was caused by unusual exertion); Harrison v. Lucent Technologies, 156 N.C.App. 147, 575 S.E.2d 825 (2003) (benefits denied when claimant failed to prove that her shoulder injury was caused by unusual exertion). Today, most courts will award compensation when usual exertion leads to some sort of "breakage" in the body, such as a herniated disc. E.g., Builders & Managers, Inc. v. Cortilesso, 608 A.2d 725 (Del.1992) (injuries to foot and ankle resulting from usual exertion are compensable); Wolfgeher v. Wagner Cartage Serv., Inc., 646 S.W.2d 781 (Mo.1983) (back injury is a compensable accident when caused by routine exertion of carrying a refrigerator at work); Village v. General Motors Corp., 15 Ohio St.3d 129, 472 N.E.2d 1079 (1984) (a back "injury caused by the performance of an employee's job duties, which develop gradually over a period of time, is a compensable injury. . . ."); Allen v. Industrial Comm., 729 P.2d 15 (Utah 1986) (low back injury sustained while lifting milk crates is an "injury by accident" even if not the result of any unusual stress). Moreover, courts that adhere to the "unusual exertion" requirement often find that the exertion that produced the injury was "unusual." E.g., Ogden Allied Aviation Services v. Shuck, 18 Va.App. 756, 446 S.E.2d 898 (Va.App.1994) (airplane refueller whose neck "popped" while he looked at a fuel gauge under the wing of a plane was allowed to recover; incident was sufficiently unusual).

The Maryland Court of Appeals abandoned its prior requirement that an injury be caused by some unusual work activity to be compensable. Harris v. Board of Education, 375 Md. 21, 825 A.2d 365 (2003). After exhaustively reviewing decisions from Maryland and throughout the states, the court concluded that the "judicially invented 'unusual activity' requirement" had been applied in a haphazard manner that was inconsistent with the benevolent purposes of the workers' compensation laws. 825 A.2d at 387–88.

3. The National Commission of State Workmen's Compensation Laws recommended that the accident requirement be dropped as a test of compensability. See the Commission's Report, July 1972, page 49. Several states have since deleted the words "accident" or "accidental" from their workers' compensation statutes. Maine, the jurisdiction of the principal case, did so in 1973. 1973 Me.Laws Ch. 389. States that do not define coverage in terms of "injury by accident" include California, Colorado, Iowa, Maine, Massachusetts, Minnesota, Pennsylvania, Rhode Island, and South Dakota. See 2 A. Larson & L. Larson, Larson's Workers' Compensation Law § 42.01 (2013).

4. The *Matthews* court recognized that the real issue presented in these cases is one of factual causation. Did the occupational activity of the employee have any substantial causal relation in a medical sense to the injury suffered? An example of this type of approach may be seen in Barrett v. Herbert Engineering, Inc., 371 A.2d 633 (Me.1977) in which claimant in the course of his employment was walking along to fetch some tools when one of his fellow employees yelled at him. He turned around to ask what was wanted and was requested to bring a special tool. Resuming his walk he "quickened his pace and while walking along at his normal gait he felt a sharp pain in the lower lumbar region of his back." The pain caused him to drop to his knees. He had had a long intermittent history of low back discomfort. Compensation was denied, the Supreme Court writing ". . . the petitioner's lumbar-sacral strain did not spring into activity by reason of any work he was doing, but occurred while he was walking at his normal gait to fetch some tools." The injury ". . . was not legally causally related to the employment." See also Caldwell v. John Morrell & Co., 489 N.W.2d 353 (S.D.1992) (claimant who sustained a herniated disc only needs to prove that employment was a contributing factor to his back injury rather than the existence of a specific accident).

PEORIA COUNTY BELWOOD NURSING HOME V. THE INDUSTRIAL COMMISSION

Illinois Court of Appeals, 1985.
138 Ill.App.3d 880, 93 Ill.Dec. 689, 487 N.E.2d 356 (1985),
aff'd 115 Ill.2d 524, 106 Ill.Dec. 235, 505 N.E.2d 1026 (1987).

BARRY, PRESIDING JUSTICE.

The critical issue in this appeal is whether an injury sustained as the result of work-related repetitive trauma is compensable under the Workers' compensation Act absent one precise, identifiable incident which a court may label an "accident." Based upon the purpose of the Workers' Compensation Act (Ill. Rev. Stat. 1983, ch. 48, par. 138.1 et seq.)

(hereafter the Act) and recognizing the new and changing nature of the employment environment, we hold that such injuries, when the claimant's burden of proof has been met, are compensable under the Act.

* * *

This appeal is brought by the claimant's employer, Peoria County Belwood Nursing Home (hereafter Belwood). The claimant, Wanda Cagle, filed a claim for compensation under the Act on August 24, 1979. The claimant alleged that she developed carpal tunnel syndrome in her left wrist in the course of her job in the laundry room of Belwood. She had been employed by Belwood for 12 years. She worked in the laundry room for the six years prior to her injury. Her duties in the laundry room consisted of sorting laundry and loading the laundry into two 200-pound capacity washing machines. Each machine was operated six times a day and was loaded by operating a spring-loaded door into each of three compartments. She was also required to carry laundry bags weighing from 25 to 50 pounds.

The claimant initially identified the date of her injury as October 5, 1976. At trial, she testified that she noticed pain, numbness and tingling for a substantial period of time prior to October 5. Her testimony was confused as to exactly how long she experienced symptoms, but she did experience symptoms on October 5, 1976. On October 5, 1976, she consulted Dr. McLean, a neurologist, regarding her symptoms. She continued to work until August 23, 1977, when she underwent outpatient surgery for carpal tunnel syndrome.

Based on this evidence, the arbitrator amended the application for benefits to reflect a date of injury of October 4, 1976. The arbitrator awarded benefits for temporary total disability and for 25% permanent total disability. The Industrial Commission affirmed the award. The circuit court of Peoria County confirmed the Commission's decision. Belwood brings the instant appeal.

Belwood raises two interrelated issues. It asserts, first, that the Industrial Commission's finding that the claimant sustained an accidental injury is contrary to the manifest weight of the evidence. In a related argument, the employer asserts that the claim for benefits is barred by the statute of limitations.

The arbitrator and Commission found that the claimant had sustained an accidental injury as a result of repeated trauma to her wrist in operating the two large washing machines. The employer argues that because there was no specific incident by which the claimant's injury could be traced to a definite time, place and cause, the injury was not an "accidental injury" under the Act. The Commission's finding that the claimant suffered an "accidental injury" is, according to Belwood, contrary to the manifest weight of the evidence.

The crux of this issue, then, is what constitutes an "accidental injury" under the Act. The Illinois Supreme Court has held that an injury is "accidental" within the meaning of the Act if it is traceable to a definite time, place and cause. (International Harvester Co. v. Industrial Com. (1973), 56 Ill.2d 84, 305 N.E.2d 529). The employee in *International Harvester* developed emphysema as a result of his employment. Barred from recovery under the Workmen's Occupational Diseases Act, the employee sought recovery under the Workmen's Compensation Act. The Illinois Supreme court noted that aggravation of a pre-existing disease was compensable under the Act where the "employee's existing physical structure, whatever it may be, gives way under the stress of his usual labor and he is suddenly disabled." . . . The court thus reasoned that either the cause or the effect of the aggravation of disease must be traceable to a specific time, place and cause in order for an employee to recover under the Act.

* * *

The requirement that an accidental injury be traceable to a definite time, place and cause was reiterated in General Electric Co. v. Industrial Com. (1982), 89 Ill. 2d 432, 433 N.E.2d 671. The claimant in *General Electric* sought compensation for carpal tunnel syndrome sustained as the result of work-related repetitive trauma. General Electric argued that there was no accidental injury because the claimant's injury was not traceable to a definite time, place and cause. The supreme court held that the claimant sustained an accidental injury despite the fact that the injury was the result of repeated trauma because there was a precise identifiable incident in which her physical structure gave way under the stress of her usual work tasks.

Thus, the rule has evolved that in order to demonstrate an "accidental injury," a claimant must trace the injury either to a specific accident identifiable as to time and place or to the specific moment of collapse of one's physical structure, identifiable as to time and place. Under the present interpretation of the Act, it is not sufficient for a claimant to show that a bodily structure eroded over time to the point of uselessness as a result of employment. Instead, a claimant must demonstrate a precise moment of collapse and dysfunction.

We consider the implication of this rule for all of the employees, factory workers, supervisors, managers, secretaries, salesperson and others, working in Illinois in this technological age. In real life, the erosion of a bodily structure to the point of uselessness translates into arms that cannot lift, legs that cannot walk, knees that cannot bend, lungs that cannot breathe, and eyes chronically irritated or worse. But evidence of such work-related injuries alone is not sufficient under the prior interpretations of "accidental injury." Instead, useless limbs, damaged organs and disabled bodies must be pushed to a precise moment of collapse and dysfunction. Then, and only then, according to these interpretations, may a court of this State find an employee eligible for compensation under the Act.

The time has come to abandon an interpretation of "accidental" which fails to address documentable and medically recognizable risks faced by the individuals in connection with their employment. The risk of injury from repeated trauma and exposure endured by truck drivers, CRT operators, chemists and others must be recognized. The judicial interpretation of "accident" must be refined to reflect the purpose of the Act and the reality of employees obligated to perform repetitive tasks.

The purpose of the Act is that the burdens of caring for the casualties of industry be borne by industry and not the employees or the public. . . . The primary objective of the Act is to afford employees and their dependents a measure of financial protection while eliminating the vast costs of tens of thousands of potential common law actions filed against employers. . . . The Act represents the exchange of previously existing common law rights and remedies between employers and employee. . . . In construing the Act, courts must give its provisions the practical and liberal interpretation intended by the legislature. . . . [T]he Act is a humane law of remedial nature.

* * *

We concede that . . . issues of law and fact will arise because we today recognize gradual injury due to repetitive trauma as compensable under the Act. However . . . a claimant must fulfill his obligation of proof and show that his injury is work-related and not the product of the aging process.

An employee alleging injury based on repetitive trauma must meet the same standard of proof as claimants alleging a single, definable accident. The difficulty in proving that injury resulting from repeated trauma arose out of and in the course of employment will pose a serious burden for a claimant. The difficulty of resolving any such issues should not prevent this court, like Ohio, from considering just compensation for all employees so injured.

* * *

[T]his court finds that an employee may be "accidentally injured" under the Act as the result of repetitive, work-related trauma even absent a final, identifiable episode of collapse. We reject an interpretation of "accidental" which forces injured employees needing the protection of the Act to choose between foregoing that protection, "creating" one identifiable incident, or pushing their now-injured bodies to the point of collapse or dysfunction. The elimination of this too narrow definition of "accidental injury" will effectuate the purpose of the Act and provide equal protection for all manner of employees of this State.

Absent the narrow construction of "accident" in the case at bar, the evidence was sufficient to prove that the claimant sustained an accidental injury arising out of and in the course of her employment. Although the date of injury alleged by the claimant differed from the date of injury assigned by the arbitrator, the claimant established by her testimony that she was injured during her employment. The claimant testified that she experienced pain and tingling in her left arm. While she worked a regular work schedule on October 4, on October 5, she informed her physician that she experienced extreme difficulty in gripping the washer doors due to the severity of her symptoms. Both the claimant and Dr. Rivero related the symptoms to her employment. The medical testimony as to the claimant's conditions was uncontroverted. We find that the claimant proved that she sustained an "accidental injury" under the Act.

Because we so find, we must now consider whether the claim was timely filed. Belwood argues that the claim is barred by the statute of limitations.

Section 6(c)(2) of the Act provides, in relevant part, that a claim for compensation must be filed within three years after the date of the accident. (Ill. Rev. Stat. 1975, ch. 48, par. 138.6(c)(2).) To determine whether the filing of the claim was timely, we must first determine the date of the claimant's accident.

Professor Larson suggests that the date of an "accident" in cases of repetitive trauma be defined as "the date on which the disability, manifests itself." (1B Larson, Workmen's Compensation sec. 39.50 (1985.))* * *

Two alternative criteria are set forth by Larson for fixing the date when the injury manifests itself. The first is the time at which the employee can no longer perform his job. * * *

The alternate criteria set forth by Larson is the onset of pain which necessitates medical attention. * * *

We adopt the rule propounded by Larson and find that where an employee in Illinois suffers a work-related injury due to repeated trauma, the date of the accidental injury is the date on which the injury "manifests" itself. Manifest means to show plainly or make palpably evident. (Webster's Third New International Dictionary 1375 (1971).) We further find that an injury has manifested itself when both the fact of the injury and the causal relationship between the injury and the employment are plainly evident.

The time at which both the fact of the injury and the causal relationship became plainly evident will be a question of fact. The claimant may demonstrate the manifestation of the injury with divers facts. The criteria suggested by Larson, the onset of pain and the inability to perform one's job, are among the facts which may be introduced to establish the date of injury.

In sum, in the instant case the claimant experienced symptoms on October 4, 1976. On October 5, 1976, she sought medical attention, at which time the doctor confirmed that her injury was caused by the conditions of her employment. Thus, the arbitrator correctly set forth the date of claimant's injury as October 4, 1976, the last day on which she worked before the fact of the injury and the causal connection became apparent. On that date, both the fact of her injury and the causal relationship were plainly evident. The claimant filed her application of claim on August 24, 1979. The claim for benefits under the Act was, therefore, filed within the three-year statute of limitations.

The claimant was awarded benefits by the arbitrator and the Commission. The award of benefits was confirmed by the circuit court. We affirm the judgment of the circuit court of Peoria County.

Affirmed.

PRESIDING JUSTICE WEBBER, dissenting:

I respectfully dissent from the principal opinion and suggest that it represents a usurpation of the legislative prerogative and purports to overrule many holdings of our supreme court while at the same time paying lip service to them.

* * *

[a lengthy discussion of Illinois cases is omitted]

All of this authority reiterates and reemphasizes the rule of *International Harvester*: to be compensable under the Workers' Compensation Act, an injury must be accidental; to be accidental, an injury must be traceable to a definite time, place, and cause. The term "accidental injury" subsumes and encompasses a cause-and-effect analysis; the accident is viewed as the cause and the injury as the result. Therefore, most cases may be analyzed in terms of causation. This appeared to be the basis of decision in the three carpal tunnel syndrome cases described above. In General Electric the sudden sharp pain coupled with the medical evidence supported the Commission's determination of accident; the opposite situation obtained in *Johnson* and *Caterpillar*; there was insufficient evidence to support a finding of accident. Thus, the cause of the injury is much narrower in scope than that posited by the repeated-trauma theory. It is not impossible for repeated trauma to lead up to an accident, but the accident, itself, the cause of the injury, must be pinpointed by clear evidence; it is not sufficient that a bodily structure eroded to the point of uselessness; there must be a precise moment of collapse and dysfunction.

There are a number of practical reasons for the rule. An exact time, place, and cause may be necessary to determine which employer and which compensation insurance carrier are on the risk; whether any statutory amendments are applicable; and, as in the case at bar, whether any limitations problem exists.

In the instant case, there was insufficient evidence of accidental injury within the meaning of the rule discussed above. There was no evidence of any unusual happening on October 4, 1976. Claimant testified that she worked a regular day on that date. She continued to work following her visit to Dr. McLean up to the time of her surgery in August 1977. Dr. McLean in his deposition described the surgery as elective, claimant's condition not having deteriorated to the point at which it might be described otherwise.

* * *

I would reverse the order of the circuit court of Peoria County.

NOTES

1. The foregoing case and many like it in the United States involve the second aspect of the term "accident" mentioned in the notes to the *Matthews* case, i.e., the idea of an injury sustained on some definite occasion, the time of which can be ascertained with reasonable certainty. As noted in the dissenting opinion, there are practical reasons why it is important to be able to specify the time when the injury was sustained. On that fact may turn various decisions, such as which of several employers should be held responsible for compensation, what wage rates were in effect at the time of injury, what other statutory provisions were then operative, what pertinent court decisions applied at that date, whether notice of injury and claim for compensation were timely, and similar matters.

2. Wanda Cagle's injury was a type of cumulative trauma disorder (CTD). "CTDs are musculoskeletal disorders that result from tissue damage accumulating over time. . . . Common CTDs include localized muscle fatigue, tendon-related disorders such as tendinitis, nerve entrapment syndromes, carpal tunnel syndrome, and hand-arm vibration syndrome." David M. Repel et. al., Work-Related Cumulative Trauma Disorders of the Upper Extremity, 267 JAMA 838 (1992). CTDs are thought to be caused by the performance of repetitive tasks that over time injure soft tissue, ligaments, nerves and tendons. Certain occupations are thought to be especially susceptible to CTDs, including cashiers, secretaries, electricians, butchers, data entry clerks, textile sewing machine operators and construction workers. Id., 267 JAMA at 839.

CTD is a growing type of workers' compensation claim. The Bureau of Labor Statistics estimates that the occurrence of CTDs increased 1,000% between 1982 and 1991. Theresa A. Cortese, Comment, Cumulative Trauma Disorders: A Hidden Downside to Technological Advancement, 11 J. Contemp. Health L. & P. 479 n. 2 (1995). OSHA reports that nearly one of every three dollars that employers spend on workers' compensation are due to repetitive motion injuries and injuries due to overexertion. Charles N. Jeffress, Protecting the Lives of Working Americans (April 15, 1998) https://www.osha.gov/pls/oshaweb/owadisp.show_document?p_table=SPEECHES&p_id=211. Aetna Life and Casualty found that 45% of its claim payments were for CTDs. Emily A. Spieler, Perpetuating Risk? Workers' Compensation and the Persistence of Occupational Injures, 31 Hou. L. Rev. 119, 148 (1994). "Even with the large number and size of compensation claims currently associated with repetitive trauma, these claims are probably vastly under reported in the compensation systems." Id., at 149. The cost of an average CTD workers' compensation claim is twice that of an average non-CTD claim. "CTDs tend to be the most frequently litigated of all workers' compensation claims, often leading to significant delays for the injured employee in receiving medical care." Jason M. Solomon, Note, "Fulfilling The Bargain: How the Science of Ergonomics Can Inform the Laws of Workers' Compensation," 101 Colum. L. Rev. 1140, 1141 (2001). Robert B. Reich, Preventing Repetitive Stress Injuries (December 10, 1996), https://www.osha.gov/pls/oshaweb/owadisp.show_document?p_table=SPEECHES&p_id=206.

See generally, Denise Paul Juge, et. al., Cumulative Trauma Disorders—"The Disease of the 90s": An Interdisciplinary Analysis, 55 La.L.Rev. 895 (1995); H. Douglas Jones and Cathy Jackson, Cumulative Trauma Disorders: A Repetitive Strain on the Workers' Compensation System, 20 N. Ky. L. Rev. 765 (1993); Theresa A. Cortese, Comment, Cumulative Trauma Disorders: A Hidden Downside to Technological Advancement, 11 J. Contemp. Health L. & Pol'y 479 (1995).

3. The states are divided on how to properly characterize CTD claims. Many states, perhaps a majority, are consistent with *Belwood* and classify CTD claims as accidents. E.g., Kildow v. Baldwin Piano & Organ, 333 Ark. 335, 969 S.W.2d 190(1998); Satilla Regional Medical Center v. Corbett, 254 Ga.App. 576, 562 S.E.2d 751 (2002); Meyer v. IBP, Inc., 710 N.W.2d 213 (Iowa 2006); Kraft v. Flathead Valley Labor & Contractors, 243 Mont. 363, 792 P.2d 1094, 1096 (Mont. 1990); In re Musick, 143 N.J. 206, 670 A.2d 11, 14–15 (1996); Barker v. Home–Crest Corp., 805 S.W.2d 373, 376 (Tenn.1991). A number of cases conclude that CTD is not an accident due to the absence of a specific time of injury and consider it an occupational disease. E.g., Kinney v. Tupperware Co., 117 Idaho 765, 792 P.2d 330, 333 (1990); Lettering Unltd. v. Guy, 321 Md. 305, 582 A.2d 996, 998–99 (1990). A Kansas court declared that CTD claims were "neither fish nor foul," falling somewhere between the definitions of disease and injury by accident, but concluded that they were compensable in any event. Berry v. Boeing Military Airplanes, 20 Kan.App.2d 220, 885 P.2d 1261, 1267 (Kan.App.1994). Subsequent decisions established

that a CTD claim should be treated as an accidental injury with the date of the accident being the last day the employee was able to work. Kimbrough v. University of Kansas Medical Center, 276 Kan. 853, 79 P.3d 1289 (2003). Virginia courts concluded that CTD disabilities are not compensable under either the injury by accident provisions or as an occupation disease. Stenrich Group v. Jemmott, 251 Va. 186, 467 S.E.2d 795 (1996). For citations to cases from various jurisdictions see Allied Fibers v. Rhodes, 23 Va.App. 101, 474 S.E.2d 829, 833–835 (1996); Subsequent legislation classified carpal tunnel syndrome as an occupational disease that is compensable under certain circumstances. Lee County School Bd. v. Miller, 38 Va.App. 253, 563 S.E.2d 374 (2002). For citations to cases from various states, see Scott Green, Note, Carpal Tunnel Workers' Compensation Claims in Iowa, 45 Drake L. Rev. 233, 237 n. 31 (1997).

4. Does it matter whether a claim is labeled an accident or an occupational disease? As will be seen in Section 3 of this chapter, most states have separate occupational disease provisions that often incorporate more rigorous standards of proof regarding work-relatedness than govern accidental injury claims. Thus, a claimant's attorney will generally try to pursue a claim as an accidental injury if possible. A relatively recent series of cases illustrate this point. Some workers complain that occupational exposure to various chemicals produces a disabling condition known as Multiple Chemical Sensitivity Syndrome (MCS) and seek compensation benefits under the occupational disease provisions. Virtually every court to consider the issue has concluded that MCS does not meet the requirements of the statutory definition of occupational disease. E.g., Canavan's Case, 432 Mass. 304, 733 N.E.2d 1042 (2000); Valentine v. Conrad, 110 Ohio St.3d 42, 850 N.E.2d 683 (2006). See generally. Kelly Corbett, Comment, Multiple Chemical Sensitivity Syndrome: Occupational Disease or Work-Related Accident? 24 B.C. Envir. Aff. L.Rev. 395, 406 n. 94 (1997). Some commentators argue that the prospects for recovery would be greater if these claims were cast in terms of an "accident," using CTD cases like *Belwood* as analogous authority. Id. at 414–23.

5. Even if a CTD is theoretically compensable as an accidental injury, the plaintiff must prove that the injury is sufficiently work-related. Courts deny benefits to workers who fail to present persuasive medical evidence linking the disability to the conditions of employment. In Stoner v. City of Lawton, 934 P.2d 340 (Ok.1997) a police officer presented testimony of a medical expert linking the carpal tunnel syndrome in his left hand and wrist to writing traffic citations. The employer countered with evidence of the claimant's hobbies of fishing, woodworking, building models, and working on a home computer. The employer's medical expert opined that the claimant's carpal tunnel syndrome was neither caused nor aggravated nor accelerated by his employment as a police officer. In the face of conflicting expert opinion, the lower court's denial of benefits was upheld. See also, Johnson v. Industrial Comm'n, 89 Ill.2d 438, 60 Ill.Dec. 607, 433 N.E.2d 649 (1982) (denying claim for bilateral carpal tunnel syndrome when there was no

medical evidence that her condition could have been caused by her work); Dioguardi v. Holiday Inn, 833 So.2d 380 (La. App. 2002) (affirming denial of benefits citing the absence of physician testimony on causation); Satilla Regional Medical Center v. Corbett, 254 Ga.App. 576, 562 S.E.2d 751 (2002) (Board finding of no compensable injury, affirmed).

6. A problem similar to that presented by CTDs arises in cases where an employee inhales a chemical or other substance on the job and later develops a disabling respiratory condition. Some courts will treat the disability as an accidental injury, at least if the occupational exposure occurred in a relatively short period of time. Campbell v. Heinrich Savelberg, Inc., 139 Vt. 31, 421 A.2d 1291 (1980) (four to six weeks exposure to varnish and paint fumes was a sufficiently specific trauma to constitute an accident); Texas Employers' Ins. Ass'n v. Murphy, 506 S.W.2d 312 (Tex.Civ.App.1974) (claimant inhaled fumes containing lead and zinc over a three day period aggravating a pre-existing emphysema and bronchitis condition which ultimately proved disabling; compensation granted); English v. Industrial Comm., 73 Ariz. 86, 237 P.2d 815 (1951) (inhalation of nitric acid and sulfur dioxide fumes for a period of less than one month caused injury of which claimant became aware some five years later; dismissal of claim reversed); Murch–Jarvis Co. v. Townsend, 209 Ark., 956, 193 S.W.2d 310 (1946) (employee's exposure to dust and fumes for a period of several days culminated in total disability from asthma five or six weeks later, held compensable); Industrial Comm. v. Ule, 97 Colo. 253, 48 P.2d 803 (1935) (unusual exposure for three days to "dope" spray used on airplane bodies caused death seven months later; held compensable). In this class of cases the brevity of the period during which the causal circumstances function enables the court to fix the time of injury with satisfactory certainty.

When the exposure is long term and the disabling condition develops gradually, courts may be more reluctant to find an injury by accident. E.g., Tegels v. Western Chevrolet Co., 81 S.D. 592, 139 N.W.2d 281 (S.D. 1965) (two years exposure to paint fumes produced headaches, instability, eye trouble, and hair loss; because his condition "developed gradually and progressively over a relatively long period of time" the injury was not compensable). On the other hand, some courts have found an injury by accident even under these circumstances. E.g., Jenkins v. Ogletree Farm Supply, 291 So.2d 560 (Miss.1974) (occupational exposure to fertilizer dust over a six year period aggravated Jenkins' asthma and eventually produced a total disability; disability was characterized as "an accidental injury").

3. INFECTIOUS DISEASE AS AN ACCIDENTAL INJURY

CONNELLY V. HUNT FURNITURE CO.

Supreme Court of New York, 1925.
240 N.Y. 83, 147 N.E. 366.

CARDOZO, J.

Claimant's son, Harry Connelly, was employed by an undertaker as an embalmer's helper. In the line of his duty, he handled a corpse, which by reason of the amputation of a leg had become greatly decayed and was full of gangrenous matter. Some of this matter entered a little cut in his hand, and later spread to his neck, when he scratched a pimple with the infected finger. General blood poisoning set in, and caused his death. His dependent mother obtained an award for death benefits. The Appellate Division reversed, and dismissed the claim.

" 'Injury' and 'personal injury' mean only accidental injuries arising out of and in the course of employment and such disease or infection as may naturally and unavoidably result therefrom." Workmen's Compensation Law (Consol.Laws, c. 67) § 2, subd. 7. A trifling scratch was turned into a deadly wound by contact with a poisonous substance. We think the injection of the poison was itself an accidental injury within the meaning of the statute. More than this, the contact had its occasion in the performance of the servant's duties. There was thus not merely an accident, but one due to the employment. We attempt no scientifically exact discrimination between accident and disease, or between disease and injury. None perhaps is possible, for the two concepts are not always exclusive, the one of the other, but often overlap. The tests to be applied are those of common understanding as revealed in common speech. Lewis v. Ocean Accident & Guarantee Corporation, 224 N.Y. 18, 21, 120 N.E. 56, 7 A.L.R. 1129; cf. Van Vechten v. Am. E.F. Ins. Co., 239 N.Y. 303, 307, 146 N.E. 432.

We have little doubt that common understanding would envisage this mishap as an accident, and that common speech would so describe it. Germs may indeed be inhaled through the nose or mouth, or absorbed into the system through normal channels of entry. In such cases their inroads will seldom, if ever, be assignable to a determinate or single act, identified in space or time. Matter of Jeffreyes v. Sager Co., 198 App.Div. 446; Id., 233 N.Y. 535, 135 N.E. 907. For this as well as for the reason that the absorption is incidental to a bodily process both natural and normal, their action presents itself to the mind as a disease and not an accident. Our mental attitude is different when the channel of infection is abnormal or traumatic, a lesion or a cut. If these become dangerous or deadly by contact with infected matter, we think and speak of what has happened as something catastrophic or extraordinary, a mishap or an accident (cf. Lewis v. Ocean A. & G. Corp., supra, at page 21, 120 N.E. 56), though very likely a disease also. "A common-sense appraisement of everyday forms of speech and modes of thought must tell us when to stop." Bird v. St. Paul F. & M. Ins. Co., 224 N.Y. 47, 51, 120 N.E. 86, 87, 13 A.L.R. 875.

If Connelly's death was the outcome of an accident, as we think indisputably it was, only a strained and artificial terminology would refuse to identify the accident with the pernicious contact and its incidents, and confine that description to the scratch or the abrasion, which had an origin unknown. On the contrary, when a scratch or abrasion is of itself trivial or innocent, the average thought, if driven to a choice between the successive phases of the casualty, would find the larger measure of misadventure in the poisonous infection. The choice, however is one that is needless and misleading. The whole group of events, beginning with the cut and ending with death, was an accident, not in one of its phases, but in all of them. If any of those phases had its origin in causes engendered by the employment, the act supplies a remedy. * * *

An argument is built upon the wording of the statute. Workmen's Compensation Law, § 2, subd. 7. The statute speaks, as we have seen of "accidental injuries arising out of and in the course of the employment," and also of "such disease or infection as may naturally and unavoidably result therefrom." The point is made that infection is here coupled with disease as something other than an accident or an injury, though a possible concomitant. We think the intention was by the addition of these words to enlarge and not to narrow. Infection, like disease, may be gradual and insidious, or sudden and catastrophic. It may be an aggravation of injuries sustained in the course of the employment and arising therefrom, in which event it enters into the award, though its own immediate cause was unrelated to the service. It may be an aggravation of injuries which in their origin or primary form were apart from the employment, in which event, if sudden and catastrophic and an incident of service, it will supply a new point of departure, a new starting point in the chain of causes, and be reckoned in measuring the award as an injury itself.

The order of the Appellate Division should be reversed and the award of the State Industrial Board affirmed, with costs in this court and the Appellate Division.

POUND, CRANE, and LEHMAN, JJ., concur.

HISCOCK, C.J., and MCLAUGHLIN and ANDREWS, JJ., dissent, and vote to affirm the order of the Appellate Division on opinions of KELLOGG and VAN KIRK, JJ., below.

CITY OF NICHOLS HILLS v. HILL

Supreme Court of Oklahoma, 1975.
534 P.2d 931.

BARNES, JUSTICE:

This proceeding for review seeks to vacate an order awarding compensation for accidental injury from exposure to contaminated dust, which caused or aggravated histoplasmosis resulting in permanent partial disability.

Original claim for compensation alleged accidental injury by inhalation of dust July 1, 1970, causing illness and disability.

Petitioners, respondents herein, answered denying fact of injury in covered employment, and alleged claimant suffered from disease neither caused nor aggravated by employment. Further, claimant never requested medical treatment, or gave notice he suffered from condition within provisions of 85 O.S.1971, § 1, prior to filing claim, and failure to give notice prejudiced respondents.

At a hearing January 17, 1973, claimant was permitted to amend his claim to show injury occurred May 25, 1970, and that injury was to throat, lungs, and respiratory injury to body as a whole.

Respondents stipulated as to employment and compensation rate, but denied notice of injury, or that illness resulted from employment. Respondents also moved to amend answer by denial of jurisdiction of the court to adjudicate the claim, upon the ground claim was for an illness not enumerated in Section 3 of the Act, supra. This motion was denied.

Two extended hearings were held, which included both oral and deposition testimony from medical experts, hereafter summarized. The trial judge excused failure to give statutory written notice because respondents had knowledge of the occurrence and were not prejudiced by failure. The court found claimant sustained accidental personal injury during performance of work, from exposure to contaminated dust which caused or aggravated histoplasmosis and resulted in 50% permanent partial disability to the body as a whole. On appeal to State Industrial Court *en banc*, this order was affirmed by divided [3–2] vote.

Stedman's Medical Dictionary, [3rd L.Ed.], p. 581, defines histoplasmosis as a human infection acquired by inhalation of spores of the fungus in dust, particularly from soils contaminated by dejecta of fowls, birds, or bats.

Testimony of two physicians, and a doctor of veterinary medicine with doctorate in public health, reflects matters hereafter summarized. Histoplasmosis is a widely occurring common infection, but relatively uncommon as a clinical illness recognizable as causing disability. The disease was recognized in 1905 and first was cultured in 1934. Scope of the disease was recognized following development of a serum test in 1946, and it is estimated fifty million persons within the Mississippi Valley area presently are infected.

Causative organisms are located in soil contaminated by droppings of various animals, and particularly fowls and birds. The disease enters the human body by inhalation of dust which contains spores of fungi into the lungs, and remains associated with defensive [phagocytic] cells throughout the body. In a majority of cases the person is unaware of inhalation and suffers no debilitating illness. After a short incubation period following heavier inhalation, a mild flu-like or pneumonia-like illness may result. Ordinarily, even severe infections heal spontaneously with nothing more than supportive treatment required.

Although infection ordinarily is expelled from the body, the organisms can remain viable and capable of dissemination for years, when bodily resistance declines from other causes; i.e., leukemia, administration of drugs, or processes which interfere with physical resistance. When heavy exposure occurs the patient may suffer cyanosis, tightness of the chest, unproductive cough, fever, and shortness of breath for weeks or months. The disease attacks the lungs, but causes trouble in other parts of the body [brain, bones] as infection grows. Although chronic histoplasmosis may result in mild illnesses mentioned, the infection remains, and, in an acute or disseminated state incited by interference with bodily resistance, histoplasmosis can be fatal. The disease is treated by controlled intravenous injection of a highly toxic drug.

Respondent, hereinafter the claimant, was a 63-year-old maintenance worker, employed by petitioners, herein the respondents. Employment duties included operation of a Ford tractor [brush hog] mower, and on May 25, 1970, claimant was directed by the supervisor to mow specified lots which were overgrown with grass, sunflowers and high weeds. The weather was dry and windy, mowing created a great deal of dust, and there were many birds and bird nests in the area being mowed.

Prior to this occurrence, claimant never had difficulty with nose, throat, or lungs, and had not suffered breathing problems. During the afternoon, claimant began experiencing extreme thirst, drank excessive amounts of water, and suffered dryness and burning in his nose, throat and lungs, and difficulty in breathing. These difficulties continued through the night and necessitated claimant seeing a physician before reporting for work. Claimant told the foreman of his difficulty after the mowing episode and was advised to go in and see a doctor if feeling too bad. Claimant worked the following day with same complaints, but did not return to work thereafter. Treatment continued from this doctor for a week, during which injections for a cold were administered without relief.

Claimant has never been able to work since the third day following this occurrence.

On July 1, 1970, claimant saw Dr. R.F.R., related history of occurrence on job, illness and treatment by other doctors, continuing complaints of sore throat and tongue, and general debility with progressively severe symptoms. Examination revealed lesions of tongue extending into posterior pharynx. Succeeding treatments were unsuccessful, cultures attempted to identify any organisms in area were unsuccessful, and by July 22nd claimant's deteriorating condition resulted in Dr. R.F.R. referring claimant to a specialist [Dr. R.M.]. Claimant was hospitalized for laryngoscopy and biopsy of nodules on right vocal cord and tongue lesions.

Claimant was discharged after three days and removed to another hospital for treatment. A specialist, Dr. H.G.M., was called into consultation following biopsy of tongue, which revealed presence of histoplasmosis. From tests and X-rays, this physician ascertained presence of calcification in the lungs, indicating existence of infection for six months. Upon this basis the physician testified it was possible, but considered improbable, claimant contracted the disease at the time and in the manner alleged.

Claimant introduced deposition testimony given February 14, 1972, by Dr. R.F.R., who first saw claimant July 1, 1970, and initiated consultation and research which established presence of this disease. This doctor continued to attend and treat claimant over entire period. Based upon history of exposure, subsequent diagnostic findings and ensuing treatment, this physician testified there was little doubt exposure and infection occurred as claimed. Subsequent course of illness, and eventual findings based upon diagnosis and biopsies from different sites, indicated dissemination of the disease was compatible with date of exposure, normal incubation period, and illness. As a result of exposure and disease, claimant was permanently totally disabled.

The only real conflict in the medical evidence concerning cause of illness results from evidence related to finding calcification in claimant's lungs. In the opinion of two experts, it would be unusual to find this condition in less than six months following infection. However, on cross-examination, one doctor stated the incubation period for acute histoplasmosis ranged between five to twenty days, and lung congestion should indicate something was wrong. The doctor also fixed two months minimum for calcification of the lungs. Neither expert evaluated extent of claimant's resulting disability.

Respondent also introduced a medical report of Dr. C.A.G., based upon physical examination and X-ray studies. This physician agreed both with diagnosis and treatment, but was of the opinion claimant had recovered, and had suffered no permanent partial disability as a result of this "rather remarkable disease."

Respondents first contend the Act, supra, was intended to provide compensation only for accidental injury in hazardous employment and occupational diseases enumerated in § 3(16), which cannot include diseases contracted in course of ordinary living. Thus, since claimant was afflicted by disease not mentioned in the statute, State Industrial Court had no jurisdiction to adjudicate this claim.

This argument need not be noted, other than to observe there was no claim of occupational disease, nor medical evidence supporting this theory. Medical testimony only suggested possible sources of infection. And, when viewed in proper context, particularly in view of wide-spread, infectious nature of histoplasmosis, the evidence negates consideration of the disease as an occupational hazard.

* * *

Under the Act [§ 11], and settled decisional law, compensation is allowable for accidental injury which results from accidental means which are unexpected or undesigned, or which result from miscalculation or mischance concerning effect of voluntary action. In determining whether accidental injury has occurred, the Act is not given a narrow, restricted meaning, but must receive a broad and liberal interpretation to effect intent of the Act. Armour & Co. v. Worden, 189 Okl. 106, 114 P.2d 173. Any reasonable doubt whether injury arose out of and in course of employment should be resolved in favor of an injured workman. In Re Martin [Okl.], 452 P.2d 785.

What constitutes accidental injury within meaning of the Act has been stated many times. An oft-quoted definition appears in Andrews Mining & Milling Co. v. Atkinson, 192 Okl. 322, 135 P.2d 960:

> "An 'accident' is an event happening without any human agency, or if happening through human agency, an event which, under the circumstances, is unusual and not expected to the person to whom it happens. In the term 'accidental injuries', the substantive 'injuries' expresses the notion of a thing or event, that is, the wrong or damage done to the person, while 'accidental' qualifies and describes the noun by ascribing to 'injuries' a quality or condition of happening, or coming by chance or without design, taking place unexpectedly or unintentionally."

* * *

Medical findings, ascertained from examination of claimant on July 1, 1970, were consistent with history of exposure to contamination and ensuing debilitating effects. This was basis of the physician's conclusion that there was little doubt exposure to histoplasmatic material was compatible with history of dust exposure, with the mouth and throat the likely site for entry of infection.

We have noted evidentiary matters concerning claimant's duties and working conditions, absence of prior physical difficulties, facts of exposure and immediate onset of difficulty, with ensuing progression of diagnostically established, disseminated histoplasmosis. This injury was not a designed or expected consequence of the work in which claimant was engaged, and was not categorized as an occupational disease by experts who testified. To the contrary, competent evidence established this injury resulted from unexpected exposure, which occurred at a definite time and caused infection and disability. This evidence measured by factors declared to constitute accidental injury under Atkinson, supra, clearly establishes correctness of the finding claimant sustained accidental injury within meaning and intent of the Act, supra.

See Victory Sparkler & Specialty Co. v. Francks, 147 Md. 368, 128 A. 635, 44 A.L.R. 363, at 371, which differentiates between occupational disease and accidental disease or injury.

Evidence which established disability resulted from histoplasmosis was sufficient to support an award based upon finding of accidental injury from exposure to contamination at a definite time. Respondents' evidence indicated claimant had been infected at least six months, but infection could remain dormant a long period before being triggered into activity by a variety of circumstances. The State Industrial Court resolved this conflicting evidence in claimant's favor. Weight and credibility of expert testimony is exclusively for determination of the trier of facts. Blue Bell, Inc. v. Owens [Okl.], 463 P.2d 969. Probative value of medical evidence is for State Industrial Court, which may accept all or part of such evidence, or reject this evidence entirely. Arnold v. J.F. Pritchard & Co. [Okl.], 399 P.2d 481.

We have determined the trial court was correct in finding occurrence of accidental injury. Under our decisions, the fact claimant suffered prior infection of the disease as reflected by respondents' evidence would not be decisive. Where accidental injury aggravates or lights up a pre-existing condition, the resulting disability is compensable. National Zinc Co. v. Cichon [Okl.], 364 P.2d 699, and cases cited. Under either hypothesis, the trial court's finding of accidental injury, which resulted in disability, is sustained by competent evidence.

* * *

Award sustained.

NOTES

1. The question whether disability resulting from infectious disease is compensable has caused difficulty throughout the history of workers' compensation. It has been assumed from the beginning that workers' compensation laws are not intended to provide general health insurance. For this reason, courts were inclined originally to deny compensation in disease cases. As time went on, however, it has become clear that certain diseases are so closely related to the claimant's employment and are so similar to personal "injury" that they merit compensation. Yet in many states in which the statute contains the term "personal injury" and has no express provision on the subject of disease, there is a substantial question whether an infectious disease constitutes a "personal injury" within the contemplation of the law. If the statute also uses terms suggesting that the injury must be accidental, there may be problems on the two aspects of the concept of accident discussed above, namely the requirement of unexpectedness and that of definiteness in time of occurrence.

2. Some statutes specifically define "personal injury" in terms allowing compensation for a disease that *follows* an accidental injury but excluding all other diseases from the definition. E.g., Arizona Rev.Stats.Ann. § 23–901(12) (" 'personal injury by accident arising out of and in the course of employment' . . . does not include a disease unless resulting from the injury."); Georgia Code Ann. § 34–9–1(4) (" 'Injury' and 'personal injury' . . . shall not, except as hereinafter provided, include a disease in any form except where it results naturally and unavoidably from the accident . . . "); S.C.Code Ann. § 42–1–160 (" 'Injury' and 'personal injury' . . . shall not include a disease in any form, except when it results naturally and unavoidably from the accident. . . ."). States with statutes of the foregoing type have separate provisions in their acts for "occupational diseases" as discussed later in this chapter. Other statutes expressly require violence to or a change in the physical structure of the body, e.g., Neb.Rev.Stat. § 48–151(4); or "traumatic" injury, e.g., Wash.Rev.Code Ann. 51.08.100. Such provisions present special obstacles to recovery for infectious disease as an accidental injury.

3. The *Connelly* case represents one of the first points of breakthrough in the disease field in holding that if the disease is caused by the entrance of germs into the body at a definite time through an abnormal channel, there is a personal injury and an accident. The decision has been widely approved and a number of state courts have followed it in awarding compensation for disabling infectious disease when it appeared that the disease-causing germs entered claimant's body through a cut or wound or were injected by the bite of an insect. Montgomery v. Industrial Comm'n, 173 Ariz. 106, 840 P.2d 282 (Ariz.App.1992) (Lyme Disease contracted through a tick bite); Baldwin v. Jensen–Salsbery Laboratories, 10 Kan.App.2d 673, 708 P.2d 556 (1985) (brucellosis contracted through cut on hand is compensable as an accidental injury); Okemah Pub. Co. v. Aaron, 285 P.2d 410 (Okl.1955) (death caused by tetanus contracted through a scratch on the finger); Roe v. Boise Grocery Co., 53 Idaho 82, 21 P.2d 910 (1933) and Smith v. McHan Hardware Co., 56 Idaho

43, 48 P.2d 1102 (1935) (Rocky Mountain spotted fever incurred through tick bites); Great Atlantic & Pacific Tea Co. v. Sexton, 242 Ky. 266, 46 S.W.2d 87 (1932) (tularemia or rabbit fever contracted while skinning and dressing a shipment of rabbits); Chicago Rawhide Mfg. Co. v. Industrial Comm., 291 Ill. 616, 126 N.E. 616 (1920) (anthrax contracted by foreman in hide tanning department when he scratched a pimple on his neck). See 3 A. Larson and L. Larson, Larson's Workers' Compensation Laws § 51.02 (2013).

4. In the years that followed *Connelly*, the entrance of disease germs into the body through normal channels came to be recognized by many courts as an accidental injury. This result is frequently reached where claimant experienced some unusual occupational exposure to the disease. E.g., Arkansas Dept. of Correction v. Holybee, 46 Ark.App. 232, 878 S.W.2d 420 (1994) (employee bitten by HIV infected inmate suffered an injury by accident). Jackson Township Volunteer Fire Co. v. Workmen's Comp. App. Bd., 140 Pa.Cmwlth. 620, 594 A.2d 826 (1991) (volunteer ambulance worker's exposure to blood infected with hepatitis B and HIV was an "accident"); Olson v. Executive Travel MSP, Inc., 437 N.W.2d 645 (Minn.1989) (claimant was infected with an Influenza Type B virus while traveling in the Orient for her employer; the virus led to pneumonia which resulted in chronic bronchiectasis; award of benefits under "personal injury" provision of compensation act affirmed); Middleton v. Coxsackie Correctional Facility, 38 N.Y.2d 130, 379 N.Y.S.2d 3, 341 N.E.2d 527 (1975) (a corrections officer who was in repeated and close contact with an inmate who coughed persistently and was later found to be tubercular was awarded compensation for tuberculosis as an "accident"); Cook County v. Industrial Comm., 54 Ill.2d 79, 295 N.E.2d 465 (1973) (claimant contracted tuberculosis working as a pathologist's assistant in hospital autopsy room); Industrial Comm. v. Corwin Hospital, 126 Colo. 358, 250 P.2d 135 (1952) (claimant contracted polio working in polio ward of hospital during epidemic).

5. In states that have separate occupational disease provisions in their statutes, a question may arise as to whether a given disability is compensable as a personal injury or as an occupational disease. In some instances it may be both, and in some neither. The former could be true in a state having a broad definition of occupational disease and court decisions that are not restrictive in delineating the concept of accidental injury. E.g., Bremer v. Buerkle, 223 Mont. 495, 727 P.2d 529 (1986) (contact dermatitis constituted both an injury and occupational disease). But in Stenrich Group v. Jemmott, 251 Va. 186, 467 S.E.2d 795 (Va. 1996) the court declared that cumulative trauma disorders are not compensable as an accident or as a disease. Similarly in Masterson v. Rutland Hospital, Inc., 129 Vt. 91, 271 A.2d 848 (1970) pulmonary tuberculosis contracted during work in a hospital was held not compensable either as an accident or occupational disease.

The possibilities of overlap on the one hand, and incomplete coverage on the other, under such state laws must always be kept in mind by the practicing lawyer. As to some aspects of the case it may make a great deal of difference whether the disabling condition is held to be an accident or an occupational disease; for example, the applicable statute of limitations, time of notice of injury, required period of employment prior to injury and similar requirements and limitations.

4. OCCUPATIONAL DISEASE

A. INTRODUCTION

As it became apparent that the limitations associated with the concept of accidental injury left substantial gaps in the protection afforded disabled workers, states began to adopt statutes providing compensation for occupational disease. It was a slow process but ultimately all states afforded such coverage. Some do it by separate statutes. Some incorporate occupational disease provisions into their workers' compensation law by various devices such as expanding the definition of "injury."

In earlier years, some of the laws confined the protection to a specified list or schedule of diseases named in the statute and in some instances even described how the disease must be contracted. Difficult problems of interpretation were thereby created and sometimes anomalous decisions resulted. For example, in Ridley Packing Co. v. Holliday, 467 P.2d 480 (Okl.1970), claimant, a butcher, contracted brucellosis from killing and skinning cattle in the course of his employment. The occupational disease statute provided for compensation for "glanders and other diseased conditions caused by handling any equine animal or the carcass of any such animal." Compensation was denied because the disease was not contracted by handling a horse or its carcass but from cattle.

Following World War II, a trend developed toward general coverage. Some statutes retained a schedule of diseases but added a general clause affording coverage for any occupational disease. For example, at one time the Ohio statute listed twenty-eight specific occupational diseases and then added the following general clause: "All other occupational diseases: a disease peculiar to a particular industrial process, trade, or occupation and to which an employee is not ordinarily subjected or exposed outside or away from his employment." Ohio Rev.Code Ann. § 4123.68. Today, all states provide general compensation coverage for occupational disease.

There is reason to believe that occupational disease poses special challenges for the workers' compensation system. The number of potential occupational disease claims is quite large. One controversial but frequently cited report estimates that 100,000 workers die each year from occupational disease and an additional 390,000 workers contract some form of work related illness. The President's Report on Occupational Safety and Health 111 (1972). In one article reviewing available studies the authors stated: "[w]e estimated that 817,000 to 907,400 new cases of occupational illnesses and 46,900 to 73,700 deaths resulted from occupational disease in the United States in 1992." J. Paul Leigh et. al., Occupational Injury and Illness in the United States, 267 Arch. Intern. Med. 1157, 1562 (1997). The workplace is thought to be responsible for 6–10% of all cancers, 5–10% of all coronary heart disease, 5–10% of all cerebrovascular disease, and 10% of all chronic obstructive pulmonary disease in the United States. Id. A more recent study by the same author estimates that in 2007 there were 53,445 fatal and 462,704 nonfatal occupational diseases in the United States. J. Paul Leigh, Economic Burden of Occupational Injury and Illness in the United States, 89 The Milbank Quarterly 728, 739 Table 2 (December 2011).

While the number of potential occupational disease claims is quite large, the percentage of potential claimants who receive compensation benefits is quite small. Only 2–3% of the total benefits paid under workers' compensation are for occupational disease claims and only about 5% of all occupational disease victims receive compensation. Thomas O. McGarity & Sidney A. Shapiro, OSHA's Critics and Regulatory Reform, 31 Wake Forest L. Rev. 587, 599–600 (1996). See also, George Freidman–Jimenez, Achieving Environmental Justice: The Role of Occupational Health, 21 Fordham Urban L. J. 605, 606 (1994) ("only three to five percent of occupational disease deaths and eleven to thirty-eight percent of new cases of occupational disease are actually reported as occupational.").

What explains the tremendous gap between the high estimates of incidences of occupational disease and the low number of claims in which compensation benefits are paid? Commentators offer two reasons. First, many workers and their physicians may fail to recognize that an illness is work related, so that no claim is made. Second, claims that are filed must overcome restrictive standards of recovery. Thomas O. McGarity & Sidney A. Shapiro, OSHA's Critics and Regulatory Reform, 31 Wake Forest L. Rev. 587, 600 (1996); Elinor P. Schroeder & Sidney A. Shapiro, Responses to Occupational Disease: The Role of Markets, Regulation, and Information, 72 Geo.L.Rev. 1231, 1246 (1984). Even for well recognized occupational diseases, such as those caused by exposure to asbestos, fewer than half of the potential beneficiaries file a claim for workers' compensation. R. Field & R. Victor, Workers' Compensation Research Institute, Asbestos Claims: The Decision to Use Workers' Compensation and Tort 12 (1988). The few occupational disease claims that enter the system are contested more frequently and take longer to resolve than claims involving accidental injuries. Schroeder, Legislative and Judicial Responses to the Inadequacy of Compensation for Occupational Disease, 49 Law & Contemp. Prob. (no. 4) 151, 157–58 (1986).

The following materials illustrate some of the practical and conceptual problems in processing occupational disease claims within the workers' compensation system. The first case addresses the definition of occupational disease, distinguishing it from ordinary diseases of life. The second set of cases address issues that arise when occupational and nonoccupational factors combine to produce a disabling disease.

B. OCCUPATIONAL DISEASE AND ORDINARY DISEASES OF LIFE

BOOKER V. DUKE MEDICAL CENTER

Supreme Court of North Carolina, 1979.
297 N.C. 458, 256 S.E.2d 189.

Stipulations and plaintiffs' evidence show the following facts:

Booker began working for Duke Medical Center on 24 October 1966. From that date until the first part of July 1971 he worked as a laboratory technician in the Clinical Chemistry Laboratory, where he performed various chemical determinations on serum blood, blood serum, whole blood, and other body fluids. In the process he manually tested blood samples and, although he was a careful and experienced employee, he routinely spilled blood upon his fingers. Each day one or more of the blood samples he tested was infected with serum hepatitis. These samples bore no diagnostic label when they came in or went out, and the lab technicians never knew whether the patient's blood was diseased. The blood samples tested were divided about equally between Duke's in-patients and out-patients. The first of July 1971 Duke began to label all diagnosed hepatic patients' blood which came to the lab, but not all infected blood had been diagnosed.

On 3 July 1971 Booker, who had been totally asymptomatic up until 3 or 4 days prior to that date, developed symptoms which caused him to consult Dr. Joe B. Currin, a specialist in internal medicine. Dr. Currin ascertained that Booker was suffering from serum hepatitis and hospitalized him for ten days. Thereafter Booker, who had worked continually with blood samples, ceased handling blood and worked in the lab as an "electronical engineer."

In July 1972 Dr. Michael E. McLeod of the Department of Medicine at Duke Hospital, Duke Medical Center, took Booker as a patient and treated him for serum hepatitis until Booker's death on 3 January 1974. During this interim Booker was "in and out" of the hospital on sick leave. About 1 October 1973 he became unable "to sustain his performance" at the lab, and on 15 October 1973 Dr. McLeod certified that Booker was no longer able to work. The autopsy, performed 3 January 1974 at Duke

Medical Center, showed that Booker "died of a disease due to serum hepatitis." * * *

[Booker's dependents filed a claim for death benefits. Evidence presented at the hearing established that serum hepatitis is a virus disease of the liver which can be transmitted by contact with even microscopic amounts of infected blood.]

Serum hepatitis is not a disease limited to persons who handle blood. Members of the general public are from time to time afflicted with this disease. Thus, it was not possible for Booker himself or the medical experts and chemist who testified for plaintiffs to state with absolute certainty the time or place at which Booker became infected.

* * *

Mr. Robert F. Wilderman, the chemist in charge of the laboratory where Booker worked, testified that as far as he knew Booker was not exposed to hepatitis other than in his work at Duke; that in the performance of his work there he did know that Booker handled many samples of blood and that he came in contact with blood cells from hepatic patients.

In the opinion of Doctors Currin and McLeod there is a much greater likelihood that laboratory technicians in clinical labs at major medical centers will contract serum hepatitis than that persons working in other places will do so, for "the public is generally not nearly so exposed to the hazard." Booker's situation, Dr. Currin said, was such "that in all likelihood he contracted it through his employment." Dr. McLeod's testimony was that the conditions under which Booker worked put him "at a much, much higher risk to contract the disease serum hepatitis than other employees in the hospital and people who are not employed in the hospital." Public health surveys, he said, supported this conclusion. Further, "all the evidence [Dr. McLeod] could gather did not indicate any other contacts" by Booker "with anybody with hepatitis, jaundice or liver disease."

* * *

SHARP, CHIEF JUSTICE.

For an injury or death to be compensable under our Workmen's Compensation Act it must be either the result of an "accident arising out of and in the course of the employment" or an "occupational disease." The Court of Appeals concluded that Booker's injury was not the result of an "accident" because no specific incident could be identified which led to his contracting the disease. *Booker v. Medical Center*, 32 N.C.App. 185, 231 S.E.2d 187 (1977). None of the parties to this appeal assigned that conclusion as error. The question before us therefore is whether or not his death was the result of an "occupational disease." Because serum hepatitis is not expressly mentioned in the schedule of diseases contained in G.S. 97–53, it is a compensable injury only if it falls within the general definition set out in G.S. 97–53(13) [which provides as follows:]

* * *

> "Any disease, other than hearing loss covered in another subdivision of this section, which is proven to be due to causes and conditions which are characteristic of and peculiar to a particular trade, occupation or employment, but excluding all ordinary diseases of life to which the general public is equally exposed outside of the employment."

* * *

Because serum hepatitis is not a disease which develops gradually through prolonged exposure to harmful conditions but instead is an illness caused by a single exposure to a virus, the Court of Appeals concluded that it was not compensable as an occupational disease. For the reasons which follow we disagree.

We begin by noting Professor Larson's admonition that "[d]efinitions of 'occupational disease' should always be checked against the purpose for which they were uttered." 1B A. Larson, Workmen's Compensation Law § 41.31 (1978). Because the first workmen's compensation acts usually provided coverage for accidental injuries while denying or limiting it for victims of occupational disease, the tendency in early court decisions construing these acts was to expansively define the term "accident" while narrowly construing the term "occupational disease." As jurisdictions amended their laws to provide coverage for all occupationally related illnesses, these older definitions became less viable * * *

* * *

In all of the North Carolina cases cited earlier, the term "occupational disease" was defined solely for the purpose of distinguishing it from an "injury by accident." In *Watkins v. Murrow*, supra, for example, claimant was a truck driver who was permanently disabled by carbon monoxide poisoning when he parked his truck and went to sleep with the motor running. The carbon monoxide entered the cab from a faulty exhaust pipe. Noting that an occupational disease is one which "develops gradually over a long period of time," the Court agreed with the Industrial Commission that claimant had suffered an accidental injury. 253 N.C. at 661, 118 S.E.2d at 11–12. In none of these cases was any attempt made to inclusively define the term "occupational disease." To use the definitions for that purpose is to carry them beyond their intended scope.

The Court of Appeals' construction, moreover, would work a judicial repeal of a portion of the statute. In holding that an illness is compensable only if it falls within prior judicial definitions of the term "occupational disease," the Court noted that even a disease listed by name in G.S. 97–53 would be noncompensable under that statute if it were the result of "a single event" as opposed to being the "cumulative effect of [a] series of events." 32 N.C.App. at 192–93, 231 S.E.2d at 192–93. Of the occupational diseases listed by name in the statute, however, at least three—anthrax, psittacosis, and undulant fever—are infectious diseases which are contracted, like serum hepatitis, by a single exposure under optimum conditions to the virus or bacteria causing the disease. Stedman's Medical Dictionary (22nd ed. 1972); G.S. 97–53(1) (26) (27). The Court of Appeals' construction would in effect read these diseases out of the statute.

Finally, the Court of Appeals' interpretation must be rejected as inconsistent with the overriding legislative goal of providing comprehensive coverage for occupational diseases. Except for those diseases specifically named in the statute, it is our view that the legislature intended the present version of G.S. 97–53(13) to define the term "occupational disease." To the extent that this statute conflicts with prior judicial definitions of the term "occupational disease," the older definitions must give way.

As Professor Larson points out, the "element of gradualness, so heavily stressed in definitions contrived to distinguish accident, loses its importance when the sole question is the inclusiveness of an occupational disease statute. If the inherent conditions of employment produce outright infection, . . . it may be treated as an occupational disease although the process is much more sudden than that described in the older definitions." 1B A. Larson, Workmen's Compensation Law § 41–40 (1978).

If an employee contracts an infectious disease as a result of his employment and it falls within either the schedule of diseases set out in the statute or the general definition of "occupational disease" in G.S. 97–53(13), it should be treated as a compensable event regardless of the fact that it might also qualify as an "injury by accident" under G.S. 97–2(6).

* * *

Having concluded that G.S. 97–53(13) is to be interpreted independently of any prior definitions of "occupational disease," we turn now to its construction. To be compensable under subsection (13) a disease must, *inter alia*, be "characteristic of and peculiar to a particular trade, occupation or employment."

A disease is "characteristic" of a profession when there is a recognizable link between the nature of the job and an increased risk of contracting the disease in question. *See Harman v. Republic Aviation Corp.*, 298 N.Y. 285, 82 N.E.2d 785 (1948). Appellees argue, however, that serum hepatitis is not "peculiar to" the occupation of laboratory technician since employees in other occupations and members of the general public may also contract the disease.

Statutes similar to G.S. 97–53 have been examined by the courts of many states. Conn.Gen.Stat. § 5223, for example, defined an occupational disease as "a disease peculiar to the occupation in which the employee was engaged and due to causes in excess of the ordinary hazards of employment as such." (Current version at Conn.Gen.Stat.Ann. 31–275 (West 1972)). In *LeLenko v. Wilson H. Lee Co.*, 128 Conn. 499, 503, 24 A.2d 253, 255 (1942) that statute was construed as follows:

> "The phrase, 'peculiar to the occupation', is not here used in the sense that the disease must be one which originates exclusively from the particular kind of employment in which the employee is engaged, but rather in the sense that the conditions of that employment must result in a hazard which distinguishes it in character from the general run of occupations (see Oxford Dictionary; Funk & Wagnalls Dictionary). . . . To come within the definition, an occupational disease must be a disease which is a natural incident of a particular occupation, and must attach to that occupation a hazard which distinguishes it from the usual run of occupations and is in excess of that attending employment in general. *Glodenis v. American Brass Co.*, 118 Conn. 29, 40, 170 A. 146, 150."

In *Ritter v. Hawkeye–Security Insurance Co.*, 178 Neb. 792, 795, 135 N.W.2d 470, 472 (1965) the Nebraska Supreme Court examined a statute almost identical to our own. See Neb.Rev.Stat. § 48–151 (1974). In upholding a disability award to a dishwasher who developed contact dermatitis as a result of the use of cleansing chemicals in his work, the court made the following remark:

> "'The statute does not require that the disease be one which originates exclusively from the employment. The statute means that the conditions of the employment must result in a hazard which distinguishes it in character from employment generally."

Similarly, in allowing an award to a nurse's aide who contracted tuberculosis from her patients, the Supreme Court of Maine in *Russell v. Camden Community Hospital*, 359 A.2d 607, 611–12 (Me.1976) said:

> "The requirement that the disease be 'characteristic of or peculiar to' the occupation of the claimant precludes coverage of diseases contracted merely because the employee was on the job.

For example, it is clear that the Law was not intended to extend to an employee in a shoe factory who contracts pneumonia simply by standing next to an infected co-worker. In that example, the employee's exposure to the disease would have occurred regardless of the nature of the occupation in which he was employed. To be within the purview of the Law, the disease must be so distinctively associated with the employee's occupation that there is a direct causal connection between the duties of the employment and the disease contracted."

* * *

It is clear from this evidence that a distinctive relation exists between Mr. Booker's occupation and the disease serum hepatitis. The evidence amply supports the Commission's determination that Booker's job exposed him to a greater risk of contracting the disease than members of the public or employees in general. This finding of fact supports its legal conclusion that serum hepatitis is a disease "characteristic of and peculiar to his occupation of lab technician." We note that many other states have similarly recognized that hospital employees may face an increased risk of contracting communicable diseases. See Note, *Occupational Diseases and the Hospital Employee—A Survey*, 5 Mem.St.U.L.Rev. 368 (1975) and cases cited therein.

Appellees also argue that serum hepatitis is an "ordinary disease of life" and is therefore noncompensable. They cite in particular Dr. Michael McLeod's statement on cross-examination that "[s]erum hepatitis is not a disease which is limited to persons who handle blood. Members of the general public from time to time are [also] afflicted with this disease." Clearly, serum hepatitis is an "ordinary disease of life" in the sense that members of the general public may contract the disease, as opposed to a disease like silicosis or asbestosis which is confined to certain trades and occupations. Our statute, however, does not preclude coverage for all ordinary diseases of life but instead only those "to which the general public is *equally exposed* outside of the employment." G.S. 97–53(13) (Emphasis added). The testimony of Dr. McLeod and Dr. Currin cited earlier supports the Commission's conclusion that the public is exposed to the risk of contracting serum hepatitis to a far lesser extent than was Mr. Booker.

As the Michigan Supreme Court observed when faced with a similar argument in *Mills v. Detroit Tuberculosis Sanitarium*, 323 Mich. 200, 209, 35 N.W.2d 239, 242 (1948): "[T]he statute does not place all ordinary diseases in a non-compensable class, but, rather those 'to which the public is generally exposed outside of the employment.' The evidence in this case indicates that the plaintiff was exposed in his employment to the risk of contracting tuberculosis in a far greater degree and in a wholly different manner than is the public generally." The greater risk in such cases provides the nexus between the disease and the employment which makes them an appropriate subject for workmen's compensation.

The final requirement in establishing a compensable claim under subsection (13) is proof of causation. It is this limitation which protects our Workmen's Compensation Act from being converted into a general health and insurance benefit act. *Bryan v. Church*, 267 N.C. 111, 115, 147 S.E.2d 633, 635 (1966).

* * *

In the case of occupational diseases proof of a causal connection between the disease and the employee's occupation must of necessity be based on circumstantial evidence. Among the circumstances which may be considered are the following: (1) the extent of exposure to the disease or disease-causing agents during employment (2) the extent of exposure outside employment, and (3) absence of the disease prior to the work-related exposure as shown by the employee's medical history.

Evidence on each of the foregoing three points was presented at the hearing before the Commissioner and may be summarized as follows: Serum hepatitis is a liver disease transmitted most often through injections, blood transfusions, by nicks and scratches on the skin, or by handling fecal materials. A person cannot contract serum hepatitis unless he comes in direct contact with the virus, which must enter his blood stream in one of the manners set out above. Only one contact is necessary to produce the disease. The maximum incubation period is six months.

During the four years he worked at the laboratory, Booker handled and tested blood samples, some of which would routinely spill on his fingers. Each day one or more of these samples showed a positive diagnosis of serum hepatitis. Booker's hobby was gardening and from time to time he would nick or cut his fingers. It was not unusual for him to work in the laboratory with unhealed nicks or scratches on his hands.

For more than six months prior to diagnosis of his disease Booker had no injections of any type and no illnesses. The only time a needle was inserted in his body during this period was when he donated blood at the Duke Blood Bank. All such donations were obtained by disposable needles; that is, the needles were used once and then destroyed. So far as Booker and his wife knew and as far as his physicians could ascertain, at no time or place outside of the Duke Medical Center lab where he worked had Booker ever come into contact with any person, blood or blood product infected with serum hepatitis.

The Commission's findings of fact based on the foregoing evidence substantially exclude the possibility that Booker contracted the disease outside of his employment. It is also perfectly obvious that his occupation exposed him to a greatly increased risk of contracting serum hepatitis for each day he handled unmarked vials of blood infected with the disease. These findings are sufficient to sustain the Commission's conclusion that Booker's disease was caused by his employment.

* * *

For the reasons stated, the decision of the Court of Appeals is reversed and the case is returned to the Court of Appeals with directions that it be remanded to the North Carolina Industrial Commission for the implementation of its award.

Reversed and Remanded.

BRITT and BROCK, JJ., took no part in the consideration or decision of this case.

NOTES

1. The *Booker* case illustrates the central problem of distinguishing occupational from nonoccupational disease. Why is it considered both theoretically and practically necessary to maintain a distinction between occupational and nonoccupational diseases? Do any of the assumptions underlying the compensation principle discussed in Chapter 2 provide guidance on how to make this distinction?

2. The starting point for analysis is the statutory definition of occupational disease, which often provides specific criteria for inclusion and exclusion. Many statutes, such as that construed in *Booker*, define occupational disease to exclude "ordinary disease of life." E.g., N.D.Cent.Code § 65–01–02(9)(a) S.C.Code Ann. § 42–11–10(4); Va.Code Ann. § 56.2–101. Others include only those diseases caused by conditions "characteristic of and peculiar to" the employment. E.g., Ala.Code § 25–5–110(1); Mich.Comp.Laws Ann. § 418.401(2)(b); Okla.Stat.Ann. tit. 85, § 3(10). As was the case in *Booker*, the definition often will include several standards. Consider the definition contained in Ga.Code Ann. § 34–9–280(2) which provides:

> " 'Occupational disease' means those diseases which arise out of and in the course of a particular trade . . . provided the employee . . . first proves . . . all the following:
>
> (A) A direct causal connection between the conditions under which the work is performed and the disease;
>
> (B) That the disease followed as a natural incident of exposure by reason of the employment;
>
> (C) That the disease is not of a character to which the employee may have had substantial exposure outside of the employment;

(D) That the disease is not an ordinary disease of life to which the general public is exposed;

(E) That the disease must appear to have had its origin in a risk connected with the employment and to have flowed from that source as a natural consequence."

Is this five-part definition any improvement over the "arising out of and in the course of" test of work connectedness used in accident cases?

3. In determining whether a particular illness is a non-compensable ordinary disease of life or is a covered occupational disease, courts often compare the level of risk created by the work environment with that existing outside the job. If a worker is exposed to a known dangerous substance primarily encountered during employment, the resulting illness is most likely to be covered. Robbins v. Wake County Bd. of Educ., 151 N.C.App. 518, 566 S.E.2d 139 (2002) (occupational exposure to asbestos); Reynolds Metals Co. v. Stults, 532 So.2d 1035 (Ala.Civ.App.1988) (occupational exposure to asbestos); United Electrical Coal Co. v. Industrial Comm., 74 Ill.2d 198, 23 Ill.Dec. 535, 384 N.E.2d 329 (1978) (evidence of claimant's exposure to coal dust for 28 years supported finding that pneumoconiosis is an occupational disease); Al's Radiator Service v. Workmen's Comp. App. Bd., 157 Pa.Cmwlth. 432, 630 A.2d 485 (1993) (auto repair worker exposed to lead fumes; lead poisoning); Service Adhesive Co. v. Industrial Comm'n, 226 Ill.App.3d 356, 168 Ill.Dec. 366, 589 N.E.2d 766 (1992) (leukemia caused by exposure to benzene).

Other conditions, such as contagious diseases and various respiratory ailments, may appear to be work related but also could be contracted by the general public. These diseases lie at the borderline separating occupational from ordinary diseases of life. As reflected in *Booker*, coverage frequently hinges on whether the work conditions increased the employee's chances of contracting the particular illness. Accordingly, tuberculosis and emphysema have been considered occupational diseases where the incidence of those diseases was greater among workers than in the general population. Nathan v. Presbyterian Hospital, 66 A.D.2d 933, 411 N.Y.S.2d 419 (1978) (tuberculosis as an occupational disease); Borovich v. Colt Industries, 492 Pa. 372, 424 A.2d 1237 (1981) (emphysema). Conversely, where evidence of increased risk was lacking, these same diseases have been labeled ordinary diseases of life. Lindenfeld v. City of Richmond, 25 Va.App. 775, 492 S.E.2d 506 (1997) (deputy sheriff denied compensation for tuberculosis; ordinary disease of life); Brawn v. St. Regis Paper Co., 430 A.2d 843 (Me.1981) (emphysema). See also, Fairfax County Fire & Rescue Dept. v. Mottram, 263 Va. 365, 559 S.E.2d 698 (2002) (post traumatic stress disorder is a compensable occupational disease when employee was exposed to a series of work-related stressful events and there was no evidence of stress outside the workplace). See generally 3 A. Larson and L. Larson, Larson's Workers' Compensation Law § 52.03[3] (2013).

4. As a threshold matter, the employee bears the burden of proof in establishing that he contracted the disease on the job. How did Booker's attorney build the case for an occupational origin of the disease? See also, Flor v. Holguin, 94 Hawai'i 70, 9 P.3d 382 (2000) (dental hygenist met her burden of proving that she contracted hepatitis C as a result of her employment); Fairfax County v. Espinola, 396 S.E.2d 856 (Va. App. 1990) (hepatitis C was an occupational disease for a police technician exposed to blood products through blood and breathalyzer tests); SCI Waymart v. Workers' Compensation Appeal Bd., 766 A.2d 900 (Pa.Commw.2000) (claimant met his burden of proving that he contracted Hepatitis C at work). The claim will fail, however, if the employee does not carry this threshold burden. E.g., Carroll v. Town of Ayden, 160 N.C.App. 637, 586 S.E.2d 822 (2003) (municipal sewer worker who was in regular contact with raw sewage and contracted Hepatitis C was denied benefits under occupational disease law; while the claimant's treating physician testified that he believed the disease was attributable to work-related contact with sewage, the Commission's findings to the contrary were supported by expert testimony that exposure to sewer water had not been linked to the transmission of Hepatitis C); Flamily v. City of Orlando, 924 So.2d 78 (Fla App. 2006) (denial of claim is affirmed on strength of expert testimony that firefighters, police officers and corrections officers were no more likely to contract Hepatitis (than a control group of blood donors)); Fulton–DeKalb Hosp. Authority v. Bishop, 185 Ga.App. 771, 365 S.E.2d 549 (1988) (emergency medical technician who contracted Hepatitis B was denied compensation where the evidence indicated that the general public was exposed to the disease and the record was silent on whether the claimant had substantial exposure to the disease outside employment). The strength of the evidentiary record and the discretion of the fact finder are often determinative of such claims.

For an interesting comparison with *Booker*, see Kashino v. Carolina Veterinary Specialists Medical Services, 186 N.C.App. 418, 650 S.E.2d 839 (2007). Kashino was a technician in an animal hospital who had long term exposure to animals, many of which were infected with fleas and ticks. She developed Lyme disease, which is commonly transmitted by ticks. The Commission denied benefits despite the claimant's physician's testimony that "more likely than not" Kashimo contracted the disease from a tick bite at work and that people who work with dogs and cats are at an increased risk for contracting the disease. The Commission reasoned that additional evidence was needed regarding the type of ticks involved and the duration of the claimant's exposure. The Court of Appeals affirmed. Is *Kashino* consistent with *Booker*?

5. A determination that the claimant has an occupational disease will support an award for medical benefits, and perhaps preventative care, even if the employee is not entitled to income benefits because he has not suffered any wage loss. E.g., City of Philadelphia v. Workers' Compensation Appeal Board (Cosepelich), 893 A.2d 171 (Pa. Comm. 2006) (firefighter who was exposed to blood and other bodily fluids during his 15 years on the job, was

diagnosed with hepatitis C; awarded medical benefits for an occupational disease even though he had no loss of earnings); Frey v. Gunston Animal Hospital, 39 Va.App. 414, 573 S.E.2d 307 (2002) (veterinarian technician bit by potentially rabid cat entitled to preventative rabies injections).

6. An increased risk analysis will lead to the denial of compensation in cases where there is only a fortuitous causal relationship between the workplace and the disease. E.g., Paider v. Park East Movers, 19 N.Y.2d 373, 280 N.Y.S.2d 140, 227 N.E.2d 40 (1967) (truck driver contracted tuberculosis from a co-worker; compensation denied); Young v. City of Huntsville, 342 So.2d 918 (Ala.Civ.App.1976) (compensation denied when claimant's employment as a nurse did not expose her to a danger of developing thrombophlebitis materially in excess of that to which people not so employed); Snir v. J.W. Mays, Inc., 19 N.Y.2d 373, 280 N.Y.S.2d 140, 227 N.E.2d 40 (1967) (a cashier claiming her myositis of the neck and shoulder was caused by a cold draft from the air conditioning at work was denied compensation). If a jurisdiction has adopted positional risk analysis for determining whether accidents are sufficiently work related, what is the justification for applying an increased risk standard for disease claims? See, Crossett School District v. Gourley, 50 Ark.App. 1, 899 S.W.2d 482 (1995) (awarding benefits to a school teacher whose sinus surgery was rendered necessary by mold in her employer's heating and air conditioning system.).

7. What is the proper geographic reference point in determining whether a disease is "ordinary"? In McCarty v. Delta Pride, 247 Ga.App. 734, 545 S.E.2d 117 (2001), an employee contracted malaria while working in Belize. The evidence established that malaria was a common disease in Belize but not in Georgia. In affirming an award of compensation, the court deferred to the Board in ruling that malaria was not an ordinary disease of life which the public in Georgia was exposed. See also Pressley v. Southwestern Freight Lines, 144 N.C.App. 342, 551 S.E.2d 118 (2001) (long haul truck driver who contracts coccidioidomycosis from a fungus indigenous to the southwest United States but not found east of the Mississippi River can recover under North Carolina occupational disease law; not an ordinary disease of life in North Carolina).

8. Some diseases might satisfy the increased risk test of *Booker*, yet coverage is still disputed. The controversy often centers around nonoccupational factors in the diseases' etiology. The next two cases explore the issues presented by diseases having multiple causal factors.

C. DUAL CAUSATION

OLSON V. FEDERAL AMERICAN PARTNERS

Supreme Court of Wyoming, 1977.
567 P.2d 710.

RAPER, JUSTICE.

From a judgment of the district court denying claimant-appellant's claims for herself as a widow and on behalf of the dependent child of an employee covered by Wyoming's Occupational Disease Law, § 27–288, et seq., as amended (repealed, § 4, Ch. 149, S.L.Wyo.1975), arising out of the death of her husband, allegedly by malignancy caused by radiation, she appeals. We will affirm.

Section 27–290, of the Occupational Disease Law, stated in pertinent part:

> "(a) The list of authorized compensable occupational diseases shall include:
>
> * * *
>
> "(xxii) ionizing radiation, radiation poisoning or malignancy caused thereby. . . ."

* * *

Section 27–293 provided:

> "When an employee has suffered a compensable occupational disease covered by this act, the employer's account in whose employment said employee was last injuriously exposed to the hazards of the disease at the time of exposure shall alone be liable therefore, without right to contribution from any prior employer."

Section 27–297(a) covered burden of proof:

> "The burden in contested cases shall be upon the employee to make proper proof of his claim by a preponderance of the evidence, and to likewise prove by competent medical authority that this claim arose out of and in the course of his employment by showing by a preponderance of such evidence that:
>
> "(i) there is a direct causal connection between the condition under which the work is performed and the occupational disease,
>
> "(ii) the disease can be seen to have followed as a natural incident of the work as a result of the exposure occasioned by the nature of the employment,

"(iii) the disease can be fairly traced to the employment as the proximate cause,

"(iv) the disease does not come from a hazard to which workmen would have been equally exposed outside of the employment,

"(v) and the disease is incidental to the character of the business and not independent of the relation of employer and employee."

The claimant's husband had been employed as an underground uranium miner, as follows:

Jan. 3, 1958–Feb. 27, 1970	Continental Uranium Co.
Mar. 4, 1970–Sept. 10, 1970	Federal American Partners
Oct. 11, 1970–Jan. 15, 1971	Continental Uranium Co.
Jan. 18, 1971–Dec. 29, 1971	Federal American Partners

The appellee-employer was Olson's last employer. While in that employment, he became ill and on May 23, 1973, died of lung cancer. The claimant at the trial asserted that her husband died of a lung cancer induced by occupational radiation exposure arising out of his last employment. The last employer denied liability, claiming that Olson had not been subjected to injurious radiation exposure during his employment by it, so there was no causal connection between the employment with it and the lung cancer and, additionally, that there was no certainty that his cancer developed in his employment as a uranium miner. It was admitted that the deceased was an habitual cigarette smoker, having smoked daily at least a package to a package and a half from 1949 until 1971. The record evidence indicates he may have smoked even more.

The court's findings were:

"1. That it is unable to find that the Claimant has established by competent medical authority by a preponderance of the evidence that the disease of the decedent, Ralph R. Olson, did not come from a hazard to which the workman would have been equally exposed outside of his employment.

"2. That it is unable to find on the evidence in this case that the Claimant has established by the prescribed burden of proof that the disease in this case is not independent of the relation of Employer and employee.

"3. That it is unable to find that the Claimant has established that the disease is not independent of the relation of this particular Employer and this particular employee involved in these proceedings.

> "4. That it is unable to find from the evidence that this Employer is the one in which the last injurious exposure occurred, neither is it able to make a contrary finding, and so that portion of the resolution of this case against the Claimant is made on the failure of the Claimant to carry the burden of proof prescribed by statute."

We see the only issue to be whether the trial judge erred in holding that the claimant failed in her statutory burden of proof.

Since the case is fact-oriented for disposition, the case has been predominantly studied and decided, having in mind the appellate rule that we will examine the evidence in the light most favorable to the prevailing party. *P & M Cattle Company v. Holler*, Wyo.1977, 559 P.2d 1019. Strangely enough here, the evidence most persuasive in support of the trial court's position came from the claimant's own expert witness. The employer's expert witness, a medical doctor, with a considerable experience in the study and treatment of cancer in uranium miners, was not in substantial disagreement. * * *

Dr. Victor E. Archer, a nationally recognized expert in the field of cancer induced by radiation, associated with the mining of uranium, testified for the claimant. He was commendably frank in his appraisal of the dead miner's disease and its connotations.

It was Dr. Archer's testimony that there is a high incidence of lung cancer amongst uranium miners. In order to determine the amount of radiation to which decedent had been exposed in his lifetime, his body was disinterred and parts, particularly bones, removed for testing. The results of inhaling air laden with an inert gas, radon, a decay product of radiation, ends up as a further radiation decay product in the bones of a human being as lead-210. The amount of that end product in the bones can be measured and with adjustments for periods of nonexposure or noninjurious exposure will reveal with accuracy the amount of radon gas taken into the lungs during a lifetime of uranium mining.

As previously indicated, Olson had been employed by Continental Uranium Company upon his entry into his occupation as a miner in 1958 and worked for that company continuously until 1970, a period of about 12 years. He was with his last employer here intermittently for a total period of about 18 months. Clinical appearance of the cancer developed after 13 years of uranium mining. There is what is known as an induction-latent period, a length of time between when a man first starts uranium mining, and the advent of cancer. This period is usually around 15 years though the cancer may appear at any time after five years, here 13 years.

According to Dr. Archer, tobacco use to the extent engaged in by Olson can either be the cause of the cancer here involved or it may promote the development of cancer induced by radiation. The latter is referred to as a synergizing effect. Tobacco use also leaves lead-210 in the body. Dr. Archer explained that the incidence of lung cancer amongst uranium miners is greater to a definite extent among smoking miners than nonsmoking miners.

While the trial judge may have been able, at the most, to find that the cancer of which decedent died might have been induced by radiation from uranium mining in the first employer, the proof completely breaks down as far as "injurious exposure" with the last employer, with whom we are concerned, is involved. There was no proof that the working level of radiation in the Federal American Partners mine was not within practical prescribed limits of safety.[2] The evidence in that regard fails also to show that Olson was even working in areas of the mine where radiation at any level was present. There was no proof that Olson was "injuriously exposed" to the hazards of radiation-induced cancer with the employer here.

The clincher, however, was when the following question and answer by Dr. Archer went into the record:

> "Q. Can you tell from your records with medical certainty that the death of Mr. Olson occurred or was caused solely by radiation exposure?
>
> "A. No. I don't think we could be that certain about it."[3]

Dr. Archer specifically testified that if the working level exposure of Olson was within the United States Government permissible limits, there would not be injurious exposure; it would not contribute to or promote a cancer induced several years earlier with a different company but not discovered until later. The proof of the employer was that the exposure was within the safe limits. The claimant furnished no acceptable proof to the contrary.

If there is any reasonable basis for the findings of the trial judge as the fact finder, we must affirm. The outline we have just undertaken demonstrates the correctness of the district court and we likewise, as did

---

2 The standard of measurement is "Working Level Months" (abbreviated "WLM"), a term incorporating a particular fixed quantity of radiation exposure over a work period of one month. The federal government standard of maximum exposure at the time in issue was four "Working Level Months" per year. The only acceptable proof of exposure with the employer party here was a total of around three WLM (.76 in 1970 and 2.31 in 1971) over a period of 18 months, not regarded an injurious exposure. The government-established standard, if followed during a working life as a uranium miner, would not induce cancer by radiation.

3 There must be a direct causal connection between the causal conditions under which the work is performed and the occupational disease. Section 27–297(a)(I). While statistically the risk of a uranium miner is increased, that does not rise to the standard of reasonable medical certainty to establish causal connection. O'Connor v. Industrial Commission, 19 Ariz.App. 43, 504 P.2d 966 (1972).

the district court, hold there to have been a failure of proof under the applicable statutes, §§ 27–293 and 27–297, then in effect. * * *

Affirmed.

ROSE, JUSTICE, dissenting.

* * *

The majority opinion, as I read it, seems to treat the instant case as purely fact-oriented. I, on the other hand, would view the appeal as representing a misunderstanding or, if you will, a misapplication of the law as it relates to the facts presented. Once the proper legal standards are applied, it would have been my holding that the appellant did in fact satisfy her statutory burden of proof. This being so, I would direct that she should have been awarded appropriate compensation for the death of her husband, out of the fund established by his last employer, the appellee.

* * *

In a contested occupational-disease case, I see the claimant's burden as twofold: (1) He or she must show by competent medical evidence that his or her claim arose out of and in the course of the worker's employment—this burden is discharged if the five factors set forth in § 27–297(a) [Section 10(a)], supra, are satisfied; and (2) the claimant must show for which employer the worker was working when he received his last injurious exposure.

Connection to Employment

In satisfying the burdens of the first step, as they relate to § 27–297(a) [Section 10(a)], supra, the meaning of the word "employment" becomes critical. It is here that I would hold the trial court to have first erred in delineating or construing the appropriate legal standards. * * *

* * * Where there is a direct causal connection between the worker's several employments and his disability or death, the occupational disease is compensable as "arising out of and in the course of the employment." This test in no way detracts from the express language set forth by the legislature—it merely places that language in its proper perspective. There seems to be no question but that a malignancy caused by radiation poisoning and exposure is a compensable occupational disease. § 27–290(a)(xxii) [Section 3(a)(xxii)] of the Occupational Disease Law, supra. The problem during the first stage of proof is to show that the malignancy had a direct causal connection with the worker's several employments.

The hazard with which the instant case is concerned is radiation exposure. The claimant's husband worked as an underground uranium miner from January 3, 1958 to December 29, 1971—a period of some 13 years. The record discloses that during the course of such employment his exposure to radiation was equivalent to at least 926 Working Level Months. After the worker's body was disinterred, a radiometric analysis of his bone specimens revealed an adjusted concentration of lead-210 of 1.63 picocuries lead per gram of tissue. The normal concentration of lead-210 in the dead bone tissue of the general non-mining public ranges from .01 to .05 picocuries lead-210 per gram of tissue, according to studies disclosed by expert witness Dr. Archer's testimony. These studies also disclosed that among the general non-mining public, extremely heavy smoking would only raise the concentration to about .06 to .08 picocuries lead-210 per gram of tissue. Dr. Archer, as pointed out in the majority opinion, testified under cross-examination that he could not be certain that the worker's death "occurred or was caused solely by radiation exposure." [Emphasis supplied]. But Dr. Archer later went on, under cross-examination, to state:

> "One cannot be absolutely sure in a situation like this, but I would say most probably his [Mr. Olson's] lung cancer resulted from his occupational exposure to radiation."

* * *

The burden of the claimant, under § 27–297(a) [Section 10(a)], supra, is to prove his or her claim by a preponderance of the evidence. This can be taken to mean that there must be proof which leads the trier-of-fact to find that the existence of a contested fact is more probable than its nonexistence, as distinguished from proof which is clear and convincing. In my judgment, the medical evidence here is sufficient to show that the claimant's husband "most probably" (Dr. Archer, supra) died as a result of radiation exposure which occurred during his several employments. The existence of heavy cigarette smoking cannot be discounted, but in this case the appellee has offered no reason to believe that the likelihood of contracting lung cancer from smoking was more than a mere possibility. See *McAllister v. Workmen's Compensation Appeals Board*, 69 Cal.2d 408, 71 Cal.Rptr. 697, 702–703, 445 P.2d 313, 318–319 (1968). I think a claimant has proven his or her claim according to the statute's burden-of-proof requirements when a medical expert states without direct contradiction that the worker "most probably" died of an occupational exposure to radiation—as opposed to testimony to the effect that there is a "possibility" that death was otherwise causally connected. See *McAllister v. Workmen's Compensation Appeals Board*, supra, 71 Cal.Rptr. at 701, 445 P.2d at 317. We cannot demand that experts be more certain, since the industrial causation itself need only be more probable than not.

* * *

I would have held, therefore, that the claimant sustained her burden of proof under § 27–297(a) [Section 10(a)], supra.

Last Injurious Exposure

During the second stage of proof, the claimant need not prove that the worker's occupational disease was contracted or induced while he was working for a particular employee, but the proof-burden will be deemed satisfied when it is established by a fair preponderance of evidence in whose employ he was "last injuriously exposed." * * *

The Occupational Disease Law defines "injurious exposure" as:

> " . . . an exposure to such disease which is reasonably calculated to *bring on* the disease in question." § 27–289(d) [Section 2(d)], supra. [Emphasis supplied].

Virginia's definition of "last injuriously exposed" is substantially identical to our definition. In *Pocahontas Fuel Co. v. Godbey*, supra, at 864, the court observed that

> " . . . the phrase 'last injuriously exposed', as used in the statute, means an exposure or contact with the dangers of the disease which proximately causes the malady, or *augments or aggravates the pre-existing disease. Haynes v. Feldspar Producing Co.*, 222 N.C. 163, 22 S.E.2d 275, *Bye v. Interstate Granite Co.*, supra. . . ." [Emphasis supplied].

Since the claimant need not necessarily show that the disease was caused while in the employment of the party from whom he seeks compensation, emphasis should properly be placed on *aggravation* of the disease in cases such as the one at Bar. . . . Where the occupational disease is characterized as being gradual in development, and where several employers have been involved, it is incumbent upon the claimant to show that the disease was promoted or accelerated during his employment with the particular employer from whom compensation is sought. We are not concerned with an exposure which would cause the disease, only one which would be reasonably calculated to *aggravate, promote or accelerate* the disease.[7] Once some such contributing exposure is shown, the employer making that contribution is charged with full liability for the condition, even though it may have developed over a number of years. 4 Larson's Workmen's Compensation Law, § 95.21, at 77–87 (1976); and § 27–293 [Section 6] of the Occupational Disease Law.

* * *

[7] This is not a case, therefore, like Climax Uranium Company v. Death of Smith, 33 Colo.App. 337, 522 P.2d 134, where the claimant must show an exposure to a concentration of toxic material which would eventually cause an occupational disease. See also Mathis v. State Accident Insurance Fund, 10 Or.App. 139, 499 P.2d 1331; and White v. Scullin Steel Company, Mo.App. 435 S.W.2d 711—where a claimant must show conditions which are conclusive to the development of the disease, as opposed to aggravation of the disease.

The record is replete with testimony as to the promoting or accelerating effect of any radiation exposure. Dr. Archer explained this effect in the following discourse:

> "Q. (By Mr. Zollinger) Taking the one unit or one measure of radiation, which we'll call Working Level, each unit that the human being receives is not greater nor less injurious than any other unit that person has received; is that correct?
>
> "A. Yes. That's probably true on a theoretical basis; but in actual practice there, the effects might well be different because of the time element. The time element for the first unit received might be compatible with the development of cancer, whereas the last one received might not be.
>
> "Q. Could you elaborate on that or explain that?
>
> "A. The length of time for the induction, induction-latent period between when the man first started mining and when he developed cancer, among uranium miners is usually around 15, 16 or 17 years average time. The minimum time of this period, it's been noted in uranium miners, is somewhere around four or five years. So that the unit of radiation which the man received, say, 15 or 20 years earlier would be more likely to be associated with his present cancer than a comparable unit received one year before cancer developed. But even this isn't completely true because even though the last units of radiation received—even though it might not be held responsible for initiating his cancer, it still might be of help in promoting or speeding up the cancer, because there are many things which act as promoting agents for tumors. Sometimes the same agent which induces them may also promote them.
>
> * * *
>
> "Q. So that referring now to our hypothetical case, if the miner's disease, which is diagnosed as small-cell carcinoma, is diagnosed within two or three years of employment from mining company 'B' then would you say that would be circumstantial evidence that the cause of the carcinoma was not the exposure received from employment with mining company 'B'?
>
> "A. Yes. I would say that most probably. However, one could not completely dismiss that last radiation because, although it's pretty certain it did not induce the cancer, it still might have had some sort of promoting effect to cause it to appear a little sooner.
>
> * * *

"Q. Your statement that the period in which the claimant received the greatest amount of exposure is the probable cause of the induction of cancer, does that statement preclude the possibility of further injurious exposure subsequent to the induction of cancer?

"A. No, because it can't exclude the possibility that the later radiation acts as a promoting agent for the tumor which was induced at an earlier date.

* * *

"Q. Could exposure to radiation subsequent to the induction of a tumor be described as injurious?

"A. Under some circumstances, it could, yes.

"Q. Could that exposure promote or accelerate a clinical tumor?

"A. I think the answer to that depends somewhat on the amount of that exposure. I would say it's—if it was a substantial amount, then yes."

The only response to this testimony came in an exchange to which Dr. Connell responded as follows:

"Q. So in all cases, and I assume your testimony to be about latency—in all cases in which the carcinoma is found in a uranium miner, it would be your testimony that the carcinoma was essentially developed several years prior to that?

"A. Essentially developed, yes.

"Q. And that all of the exposure that occurred subsequent to the beginning of the initiation of that latent period is just kind of water over the dam, it doesn't have any effect whatever on the carcinoma?

"A. Yes, I think that's right."

I do not view Dr. Connell's observation as a direct contradiction of the testimony of Dr. Archer, but rather as a statement which indicates that once the carcinoma is induced, then further exposure to radiation will not have a *causative* effect. This is not to say that some subsequent radiation exposures will not have a *promoting* effect. The subsequent exposures need not have a *substantial* effect—only *some* effect is required. 4 Larson's Workmen's Compensation Law, § 95.21, supra. I am convinced by a reading of the entire record that there was sufficient evidence presented which would indicate that the radiation exposure received at the appellee's mine promoted or accelerated the cancer which killed the claimant's husband. * * *

Had I been writing for the majority, I would have reversed the trial court's judgment.

RUTLEDGE v. TULTEX CORP./KINGS YARN

Supreme Court of North Carolina, 1983.
308 N.C. 85, 301 S.E.2d 359.

EXUM, JUSTICE.

The questions for decision are whether the Industrial Commission applied the wrong legal standard in its order denying benefits to claimant and whether there is evidence from which the Commission could have made findings, using the correct legal standard, that would support a conclusion that claimant contracted an occupational disease. We answer both questions affirmatively.

After hearing evidence for claimant and defendants, Deputy Commissioner Denson concluded that claimant had not contracted an occupational disease. This conclusion was based in part on the following factual findings, which are summarized unless quoted, to which no exception has been taken: Plaintiff, born 8 August 1935, has a tenth grade education and now lives in Georgia. She has smoked cigarettes from about age fifteen until February 1979 at the rate of approximately one pack per day. She has worked for four textile mills: (1) United Merchants in Buffalo, South Carolina, from 1953 until 1971 as a weaver; (2) Milliken at Union, South Carolina, from 1971 to 1973 as a "dry cleaner"; (3) Aleo Manufacturing, Rockingham, North Carolina, from 1975 to 1976 as a weaver; and (4) for defendant from 25 October 1976 until 12 January 1979 as a winder and then as a spinner. She was absent "for bronchitis" from 28 January 1977 until 13 May 1977. She "retired" on 12 January 1979.

All the plants where plaintiff worked "had a lot of cotton dust and lint" but defendant's premises, both in the weaving and spinning areas, were "relatively clean." Defendant's mill processed essentially 50 percent cotton blend materials and occasionally blends made of even a smaller percentage of cotton. "Although there was respirable cotton dust in [defendant's] weave room, there was much less than . . . in other premises." Plaintiff began developing a cough at work in 1969 or 1970. "[H]er cough was associated with her presence at work. Her shortness of breath became severe in December of 1976 and she has had various bouts with it since that time having to be out of work. . . . Plaintiff suffers from chronic obstructive pulmonary disease [with elements] of pulmonary emphysema and chronic bronchitis. . . . Plaintiff is disabled, because of her pulmonary impairment from all but sedentary . . . work which must be in a clean environment because of her reaction to cotton dust and other such irritants."

Deputy Commissioner Denson also made certain findings to which claimant excepted. The first was that in 1971 claimant "began developing a shortness of breath." Second was the following which the Deputy Commissioner included in the findings of fact:

> 6. . . . Cigarette smoking and recurrent infection have played prominent roles in the pulmonary impairment. Cotton dust may aggravate it, but since plaintiff was showing her symptomatology in problems prior to her employment with defendant employer, *exposure at defendant employer has neither caused nor significantly contributed to plaintiff's chronic obstructive pulmonary disease.*
>
> * * *
>
> 8. Plaintiff has not contracted chronic obstructive lung disease *as a result of any exposure while working with defendant employer*. [Emphasis added.]

The Full Commission, with one commissioner dissenting, adopted Deputy Commissioner Denson's findings, conclusions, opinion and award as its own.

The Court of Appeals concluded that although the Commission erred "in requiring plaintiff to prove that her last employment was the cause of her occupational disease," the error was harmless since there was insufficient evidence before the Commission to show that plaintiff had ever contracted an occupational disease during her working life. *Rutledge v. Tultex Corp./Kings Yarn*, 56 N.C.App. 345, 350, 289 S.E.2d 72, 74 (1982).

Because of the italicized portions of findings 6 and 8, it does appear that the Commission thought that in order successfully to claim against defendant, claimant's last employer, claimant must establish that her exposure there either caused or significantly contributed to her chronic obstructive pulmonary disease. This is not the law. That part of G.S. 97–57 pertinent to this case provides:

> In any case where compensation is payable for an occupational disease, the employer in whose employment the employee was last injuriously exposed to the hazards of such disease, and the insurance carrier, if any, which was on the risk when the employee was so last exposed under such employer, shall be liable.

Under this statute, consequently, it is not necessary that claimant show that the conditions of her employment with defendant caused or significantly contributed to her occupational disease. She need only show: (1) that she has a compensable occupational disease and (2) that she was "last injuriously exposed to the hazards of such disease" in defendant's employment. The statutory terms "last injuriously exposed" mean "an exposure which proximately augmented the disease to any extent, however slight." *Haynes v. Feldspar Producing Company*, 222 N.C. 163, 166, 169, 22 S.E.2d 275, 277, 278 (1942).

* * *

The Court of Appeals correctly concluded, therefore, that the Industrial Commission applied the wrong legal standards to this claim.

We hold that the Court of Appeals erred, however, in concluding that there is no evidence that plaintiff had contracted an occupational disease. We think there is evidence from which the Industrial Commission could have made findings which in turn would have supported a conclusion that claimant's chronic obstructive lung disease was an occupational disease. Dr. Williams, after a lengthy recitation of certain assumed facts, was asked the following question:

> Now, based upon these facts and upon your examination and testing of Ms. Rutledge, do you have an opinion satisfactory to yourself to a reasonable medical certainty as to whether Ms. Rutledge's exposure to cotton dust for in excess of 25 years in her employment was probably a cause of her chronic obstructive lung disease which you diagnosed in your report?

When he replied, "Yes," the following colloquy occurred:

> Q. What is that opinion?
>
> A. Yes. That it probably was a cause. Based upon the same facts and upon my examination and testing of Mrs. Rutledge, I have an opinion as to whether her impairment with respect to her ability to perform labor is related to her pulmonary disease. That opinion is that it is.

* * *

[The defendants argued that Dr. Williams' opinion was not competent evidence since the hypothetical question posed by claimant's counsel did not expressly refer to claimant's history of cigarette smoking. The court rejected this argument noting that (1) the defendants did not object to the question nor move to strike the answer; (2) Dr. Williams based his opinion, in part, on his examination of the claimant which included taking a history that revealed claimant's smoking; and (3) the effect of claimant's smoking on Dr. Williams' opinion was explored by defendants' counsel on cross-examination.]

The thrust of Dr. Williams' entire testimony, then, seems to be that both her exposure to cotton dust over her working life and her cigarette smoking were causative factors in claimant's chronic obstructive lung disease. He also said other components of the lung disease were "pulmonary emphysema" and "chronic bronchitis" and that "chronic obstructive lung disease includes pulmonary emphysema, chronic bronchitis, and possibly asthma."

After relating his considerable experience in the treatment and study of respiratory diseases among textile workers, such as claimant here, Dr. Williams testified that these workers are "at an increased risk of contracting chronic obstructive pulmonary disease." Dr. Williams also testified that when claimant began such work in October 1976 "she was suffering from pulmonary emphysema, chronic bronchitis and chronic obstructive pulmonary disease . . . caused by circumstances which existed prior to her employment by Kings Yarn." Although testifying that claimant's exposure to cotton dust at Kings Yarn's plant would have "minimal" effect on her condition and that she would not have had there a "very substantial exposure" to cotton dust, Dr. Williams did say that such exposure as she had at Kings Yarn "could have some aggravating effect on [her] underlying condition" and that removal from the Kings Yarn "environment would probably improve her symptoms . . . primarily, her symptoms of cough." Dr. Williams testified flatly that claimant's exposure to respirable cotton and synthetic dust at Kings Yarn "would have aggravated her condition." Medical records offered in evidence tended to show that claimant's lung function had decreased some 25 to 30 percent during the period from January 1977 to March 1979, while she worked for defendant employer.

Claimant, herself, described in some detail the dusty conditions under which she had worked for twenty-five years in various textile mills. She said she developed a breathing difficulty in 1971 which by 1977 had begun "affecting my ability to do my job" because it caused her to be too fatigued to work. She said she stopped work in January 1979 "because I was unable to perform my duties on my job. From tiredness, short of breath, cold sweats, headaches and I felt I was not being fair to myself or the company. I did not just quit, I was advised by my doctor . . . to quit." Claimant testified that when she quit work "my symptoms were difficulty breathing, wheezing, tiredness, cold sweats, [and] stiffness in my neck. I coughed so hard until the [neck] muscle, you know, it's ruptured in the left side." By January 1979 claimant said that she did not have the "strength or ability to do my housework, my shopping or any of those things. I am able to do my daily routine, I can make a bed, at which time I have to rest. . . . I help [my mother] watch dinner and the rest of my day consists of soap operas and rest. I crochet, anything to pass time. I just cannot be exerted because if I do I just don't have the breath. I do drive. I don't have any training for jobs besides working in the mill."

For a disease to be occupational under G.S. 97–53(13) it must be (1) characteristic of persons engaged in the particular trade or occupation in which the claimant is engaged; (2) not an ordinary disease of life to which the public generally is equally exposed with those engaged in that particular trade or occupation; and (3) there must be "a causal connection between the disease and the [claimant's] employment." *Hansel v. Sherman Textiles*, 304 N.C. 44, 52, 283 S.E.2d 101, 105–06 (1981); *Booker v. Duke Medical Center*, 297 N.C. 458, 468, 475, 256 S.E.2d 189, 196, 200 (1979). To satisfy the first and second elements it is not necessary that the disease originate exclusively from or be unique to the particular trade or occupation in question. All ordinary diseases of life are not excluded from the statute's coverage. Only such ordinary diseases of life to which the general public is exposed equally with workers in the particular trade or occupation are excluded. *Booker v. Duke Medical Center*, supra, 297 N.C. at 472–75, 256 S.E.2d at 198–200. Thus, the first two elements are satisfied if, as a matter of fact, the employment exposed the worker to a greater risk of contracting the disease than the public generally. *Id.* "The greater risk in such cases provides the nexus between the disease and the employment which makes them an appropriate subject for workmen's compensation." *Id.* at 475, 256 S.E.2d at 200.

This Court has had little difficulty either articulating or applying the first two standards in occupational disease cases generally. They were articulated and properly applied in *Booker*, a hepatitis case, and reiterated and properly applied in *Hansel*, a lung disease case. We have had some difficulty in the lung disease cases, however, in both articulating and applying a factual standard for determining whether there is an appropriate causal connection between the employment and the disease. . . .

This difficulty in the lung disease cases stems largely from the complex medical picture often presented by chronic obstructive lung disease and chronicled in the medical testimony in *Walston*, *Hansel* and *Morrison*. This disease, as we understand it from the medical testimony presented in these cases and the literature to which we have been referred * * * has several components. Some of these components are seemingly not, in their incipience at least, work related, for example, bronchitis, emphysema and asthma; while at least one component, i.e., Byssinosis, is work related. Byssinosis may be understood as the adverse effect on the lungs resulting from the inhalation of cotton dust, a substance generally present in the work environment of textile mill employees. Other complicating factors are that chronic obstructive lung disease may apparently be brought on by just the continuous inhalation of cotton dust, just the continuous inhalation of other substances, such as cigarette smoke, or by the inhalation of both kinds of substances together. It is apparently medically impossible even on autopsy objectively to distinguish the effect on the lungs of cigarette smoke inhalation and the inhalation of cotton dust, or between the effects of bronchitis and the inhalation of these substances. Thus when a textile worker who is also a habitual cigarette smoker and who suffers from bronchitis, emphysema, or asthma, contracts disabling, chronic obstructive lung disease, the medical experts and, in turn, the Commission and the courts are presented with a difficult factual question on the causation issue. Since courts generally develop principles of law to deal as justly as possible with the facts of given cases, complex facts which the experts themselves have difficulty unraveling make the articulation of appropriate legal principles correspondingly difficult for the courts.

* * *

Our answer to the question posed is that chronic obstructive lung disease may be an occupational disease provided the occupation in question exposed the worker to a greater risk of contracting this disease than members of the public generally, and provided the worker's exposure to cotton dust significantly contributed to, or was a significant causal factor in, the disease's development. This is so even if other non-work-related factors also make significant contributions, or were significant causal factors.

Significant means "having or likely to have influence or effect: deserving to be considered: important, weighty, notable." Webster's Third New International Dictionary (1971). *Significant* is to be contrasted with *negligible, unimportant, present but not worthy of note, minuscule, or of little moment.* The factual inquiry, in other words, should be whether the occupational exposure was such a significant factor in the disease's development that without it the disease would not have developed to such an extent that it caused the physical disability which resulted in claimant's incapacity for work.

* * *

[T]he significant contribution principle which we adopt puts upon the claimant in these lung disease cases a somewhat heavier burden than our sister states seem to require or that we require in industrial accident cases. Our purpose in adopting this principle is to strike a fair balance between the worker and the employer in the administration of our Workers' Compensation Act as it is applied to the difficult lung disease cases. To hold that the inhalation of cotton dust must be the sole cause of chronic obstructive lung disease before this disease can be considered occupational establishes too harsh a principle from the standpoint of the worker and the purposes and policies of our Workers' Compensation Act. This Act "should be liberally construed so that the benefits under the Act will not be denied by narrow, technical or strict interpretation." *Stevenson v. City of Durham*, 281 N.C. 300, 303, 188 S.E.2d 281, 283 (1972). On the other hand, to hold the causation requirement is satisfied if cotton dust exposure contributes to the slightest extent, however minuscule or insignificant, to the etiology of chronic obstructive lung disease, places too heavy a burden on industry. This holding would compromise the valid principle that our Workers' Compensation Act should not be transformed into a general accident and health insurance law.

In determining whether a claimant's exposure to cotton dust has significantly contributed to, or been a significant causative factor in, chronic obstructive lung disease, the Commission may, of course, consider medical testimony, but its consideration is not limited to such testimony. It may consider other factual circumstances in the case, among which are (1) the extent of the worker's exposure to cotton dust during employment (2) the extent of other non-work-related, but contributing, exposures and components, and (3) the manner in which the disease developed with reference to the claimant's work history. See *Booker v. Duke Medical Center*, supra, 297 N.C. at 476, 256 S.E.2d at 200.

* * *

From [the] evidence the Commission could have found as facts, although it would not have been compelled to find, that: (1) claimant has chronic obstructive lung disease; (2) the two primary causes of this disease are the inhalation of cotton dust for twenty-five years while claimant was a textile worker and the inhalation of cigarette smoke over a similar period of time; (3) the disease also has components of chronic bronchitis and emphysema; (4) the disease developed gradually over the period of claimant's working life until by 1971 claimant had developed a breathing difficulty; (5) by 1977 her breathing difficulty began to affect her ability to do her job because it caused her to be too fatigued to work; (6) by January 1979 claimant's disease had rendered her physically unable to work in the textile industry; (7) the disease would not have developed to this extent had it not been for her exposure to cotton dust and her inhalation of cigarette smoke, both of which significantly contributed to, or were significant causative factors in, the development of the disease; (8) because of her age, limited education, and her lifetime of employment in the textile industry, claimant is neither trained nor qualified to do other kinds of work and, at this time, is not able to be gainfully employed; (9) claimant's chronic obstructive lung disease was aggravated to some extent by her exposure to cotton dust at Kings Yarn; and (10) claimant's job in the textile industry exposed her to a greater risk of contracting chronic obstructive lung disease than members of the public generally.

These findings of fact, if made by the Commission, would support the following legal conclusions: (1) claimant's chronic obstructive lung disease is due to causes and conditions characteristic of and peculiar to the textile industry under G.S. 97–53(13); (2) claimant's chronic obstructive lung disease is not an ordinary disease of life to which the general public not employed in the textile industry is equally exposed under G.S. 97–53(13); (3) claimant's chronic obstructive lung disease is, therefore, an occupational disease under G.S. 97–53(13); (4) claimant is totally incapacitated for work under G.S. 97–29, 97–54, and 97–2(9); (5) claimant's total incapacity for work results from her occupational disease under G.S. 97–52; and (6) claimant's last injurious exposure to the hazards of her occupational disease were in the employment of defendant Kings Yarn under G.S. 97–57. These conclusions of law would, in turn, support an award against defendants and in favor of claimant for workers' compensation benefits for total incapacity for work by reason of an occupational disease.

On the other hand there is some testimony from Dr. Williams which would have supported a finding that claimant's exposure to cotton dust played an insignificant causal role in, or did not significantly contribute to, the development of Ms. Rutledge's lung disease. If the Commission so finds, it would have to conclude that the disease is not an occupational disease in this case.

* * *

* * * The only question for reconsideration by the Commission is whether the pulmonary disease is an occupational disease when the legal principles set out in this opinion are applied to the facts.

Affirmed in part; reversed in part and remanded.

MEYER, JUSTICE, dissenting.

I respectfully dissent.

* * * The majority obviously believes that the testimony of Dr. Williams to the effect that the mere exposure to cotton dust creates an increased risk of lung disease somehow establishes that all of Mrs. Rutledge's diseases (including, we must assume, her many non-lung related diseases) are "occupational diseases" provided any "significant contribution" to those diseases by the cotton dust can be established. This position was rejected by the majority opinion in *Morrison [v. Burlington Industries*, 304 N.C. 1, 282 S.E. 2d 458 (1981)]. I find it shocking that a disability from this range of diseases and conditions, most of which are ordinary diseases of life, would be fully compensable because of the "significant contribution" to only the lung conditions by the inhalation of cotton dust. While her non-lung related conditions did not contribute to her pulmonary conditions, it is inescapable that they contributed to her disability.

Nor do I find it unusually significant, as does the majority, that Dr. Williams was of the opinion that textile workers are "at an increased risk of contracting chronic obstructive pulmonary disease," which according to

Dr. Williams includes "pulmonary emphysema, chronic bronchitis and possibly asthma" as well as byssinosis. We are repeatedly told by expert medical witnesses that the same is true of cigarette smokers and others who may be in no way connected with the textile industry. We are even told that the same is true of those exposed to concentrations of ordinary household or yard dust. It is interesting that in this very case Dr. Williams testified: "I think that exposure to *any type of dust* in someone with pre-existing chronic bronchitis could have some aggravating effect on the underlying condition." He also said "I stated that exposure to any kind of dust in an individual with underlying lung disease would have an aggravating effect." (Emphasis added). It is indeed on the basis of the last quoted sentence that the majority opinion characterizes Dr. Williams as saying "that such exposure as she had at Kings Yarn 'could have some aggravating effect on [her] underlying condition.'" As is obvious, this characterization of that testimony is completely misleading.

* * *

The case should *not* be remanded for the purpose of applying the new "substantial contribution" principle—if it is to be remanded at all it should be for the purpose of apportionment of Mrs. Rutledge's disability to work-related and non-work-related causes.

I agree with the majority's conclusion that it is not necessary that Mrs. Rutledge show that the conditions of her last employer's workplace were the *sole* causes of her disability and that it is only necessary for her to show that the conditions of her last employer's workplace "augmented the disease to any extent, however slight."[2] I vote to affirm the opinion of the Court of Appeals and to modify it to the extent necessary to correct this error.

BRANCH, C.J., and COPELAND, J., join in this dissent.

NOTES

1. Are the different outcomes reached in *Olson* and *Rutledge* best explained in terms of differences in facts, statutory language, or policy? Can you identify precisely where the majority and dissent disagree in both cases?

2. Establishing a causal connection between employment and disease is especially difficult in cases like *Olson* and *Rutledge* where the employee's life style or personal habits are suspected to be a significant contributing factor. The term "dual causation" is often used to describe such cases. *See* 3 A.

---

[2] I must point out, however, what I consider to be a significant omission in the majority's statement that "She need only show: (1) that she has a compensable occupational disease and (2) that she was 'last injuriously exposed to the hazards of such disease' in defendant's employment." The omission from (1) that the occupational disease be the cause of her disability is fatal and will come back to haunt us. The first requirement should be accurately stated as follows: "that she has an occupational disease which caused her disability."

Larson & L. Larson, Larson's Workers' Compensation Law § 52.06[4](2013). Workers who smoke and are exposed to industrial irritants present the paradigm dual causation problem. These workers may develop lung cancer, emphysema, bronchitis or other respiratory ailments. As one might expect, the evidence of industrial causation presented by the claimant and employer is frequently conflicting. This is an especially fact-sensitive inquiry and the record often contains testimony that could support either the grant or denial of compensation benefits. The finder of fact enjoys substantial discretion in such cases. Compare Dunn v. Vic Mfg. Co., 327 N.W.2d 572 (Minn.1982) (claimant was a pack-a-day smoker for twenty-five years who was employed as a sandblaster for nine or ten years. He died of respiratory problems. In light of conflicting medical testimony, referee's finding that the death was caused by work-related exposure to dust was affirmed) with Howard v. Johns–Manville Sales Corp., 420 So.2d 1190 (La.App.1982) (claimant was a heavy smoker who was exposed to asbestos fibers during his twenty-one years of employment. The denial of benefits was affirmed where medical testimony was divided on whether the claimant's respiratory ailment was asbestosis or cigarette induced emphysema). Occasionally, however, an appellate court will reverse findings on the basis that they are not supported by the evidence. E.g., Home Insurance Co. v. Davis, 642 S.W.2d 268 (Tex.App.1982). The more common ground for appeal, as reflected in *Olson* and *Rutledge*, is that the lower court or administrative agency applied an incorrect legal standard. In this regard, what are the practical effects of the "significant causal factor" test approved by the majority opinion in *Rutledge* as compared to the standard applied in *Olson*? One student commentator argues that Rutledge "radically simplified the legal landscape" of occupational disease and led to a tremendous increase in the number of such claims in North Carolina. Veronica D. Higgs, "Revisiting *Rutledge*, A Survey of Recent Developments in Occupational Disease Law Under the North Carolina Workers' Compensation Act," 78 N.C.L. Rev. 2083 (2000).

Some states employ formal presumptions to bolster the occupations disease claims of certain workers. For example, New Jersey has a presumption of work-relatedness for professional firefighters who develop lung diseases. This presumption can support an award for permanent partial disability for a firefighter with 25 years of work experience and a 28 year history of smoking more than a pack of cigarettes a day. Culbert v. City of Jersey City, 175 N.J. 286, 814 A.2d 1094 (2003). The court extended this presumption to volunteer firefighters. Lindquist v. City of Jersey City, 175 N.J. 244, 814 A.2d 1069 (2003).

3. The detail with which both the *Olson* and *Rutledge* courts analyzed the medical testimony emphasizes its central importance in resolving occupational disease claims. The expert witnesses for the respective sides are called upon to give their opinions as to the cause of the claimant's condition. This opinion, moreover, often must be expressed in terms of a "reasonable medical certainty." See note 6 following *Lancaster v. Gilbert Development* in the next section. Unfortunately little is "certain" regarding the cause of most

diseases. The etiology of many diseases is simply unknown. The long latency period between industrial exposure and the onset of symptoms hinders efforts to isolate and identify particular occupational hazards. Even when there is a suspected linkage between occupational exposure to a particular substance and disease, proving causation in specific cases remains a formidable task. A great deal of the current scientific knowledge about occupational diseases is based on aggregate statistical data. Workers' compensation claims, however, are adjudicated on a case by case basis. Data indicating that the cancer rate for workers in a particular industry is higher than the national norm, for example, does not tell us which individual cancers are work induced. A large number of suspected carcinogens are plentiful in our nonindustrial environment and can cause illness and death of persons who are out of the work force. The dilemma facing the workers' compensation system was summed up by one expert as follows: "Workers' compensation judges may be asked to extrapolate causes in specific claims based on animal experiments or on isolated and often ambiguous epidemiological studies. Aside from the lack of competence that such hearing officers often have to reach decisions that as yet have no definitive answers, the record is replete with inconsistencies and capriciousness." Barth, A Proposal for Dealing with the Compensation of Occupational Diseases, 13 J.Legal Stud. 569, 572 (1984). For a more technical discussion of the etiological and diagnostic issues in occupational disease claims, see P. Barth & H. Hunt, Workers' Compensation and Work-Related Illnesses and Diseases 61–89 (1980).

4. In cases involving both occupational and nonoccupational causal factors there are several possible ways to allocate the cost of diseases. One option, reflected in *Olson*, is to deny compensation and thereby allocate such costs in the first instance to the worker. It should be obvious, however, that many workers will not be capable of shouldering those costs without assistance. A likely source of support is the Social Security system. Indeed, more workers disabled by occupational disease receive income benefits from Social Security than from workers' compensation. A. Packer, Assistant Secretary for Policy, Evaluation, and Research, Department of Labor, An Interim Report to Congress on Occupational Diseases 85 (1980). *Rutledge*, with its more relaxed "significant causal factor" test, effectively lumps many of these costs within the workers' compensation system. A third option is to apportion the costs between the worker and employer. States are divided on whether compensation awards should be reduced to reflect the nonoccupational contributions to the illness. Compare Fry's Food Stores v. Industrial Comm'n, 177 Ariz. 264, 866 P.2d 1350 (1994) (claimant who was exposed to flour dust on the job for seven years and smoked two packs of cigarettes a day for thirty seven years developed chronic obstructive pulmonary disease; apportionment was not allowed because the smoking did not disable the claimant prior to his occupational exposure to the flour dust; discussing cases) and Askew v. Industrial Claim Appeals Office, 927 P.2d 1333 (Colo.1996) (apportionment is appropriate only when a prior impairment has been sufficiently identified, treated or evaluated to be rated as contributing factor in the subsequent disability) with Bolivar County

Gravel Co. v. Dial, 634 So.2d 99 (Miss.1994) (claimant smoked between one and one-half and two packs of cigarettes a day for 25–28 years and was exposed to welding fumes on the job; permanent total disability benefits were reduced by 90% to account for preexisting obstructive lung disease) and Colorado Mental Health Inst. v. Austill, 940 P.2d 1125 (Colo.App.1997) (award for permanent total disability should be apportioned to account for claimant's preexisting pulmonary condition). Where apportionment is permitted, the burden rests with the employer to prove what percentage of the disability is attributable to nonoccupational factors. e.g., Fiore v. Consolidated Freightways, 140 N.J. 452, 659 A.2d 436 (1995); Watkins Engineers and Constructors v. Wise, 698 So.2d 294 (Fla.App.1997). Some decisions appear to reject apportionment even when it is authorized by law and fact. E.g., Brown v. Greenwood Mills, 366 S.C. 379, 622 S.E.2d 546 (2005) (worker who was exposed to cotton dust for 30 years and smoked a pack of cigarettes a day for 45 years; one expert attributed 70% of her disability to smoking and 30% to occupational exposure to cotton dust; award of full benefits, affirmed). What is the ideal allocation of costs when employment and nonoccupational factors combine to produce a disabling disease? What practical, theoretical or doctrinal problems do you see in achieving such an allocation?

5. Is the problem of allocating disease costs significantly different when work conditions aggravate a preexisting allergy? The problem of allergies and their disabling consequences has been treated in several different ways by the courts. At a time when there was little coverage of occupational disease, several courts treated allergic reactions to workplace chemicals as compensable accidents. E.g., Webb v. New Mexico Pub. Co., 47 N.M. 279, 141 P.2d 333 (1943) (allergy to soap causing disabling skin disorder); Hardin's Bakeries, Inc. v. Ranager, 217 Miss. 463, 64 So.2d 705 (1953) (contact dermatitis caused by allergy to baker's mitten); Vogt v. Ford Motor Co. 138 S.W.2d 684 (Mo.App.1940) (asthma and other ailments brought on by inhalation of chemicals and paint fumes).

A majority of states today compensate for disabling allergic reactions to workplace substances under the occupational disease statute if the causation and other required elements are present. E.g., Aleutian Homes v. Fischer, 418 P.2d 769 (Alaska 1966) (allergic reaction to paper and other office supplies); Ross v. Baldwin Filters, 5 Neb.App. 194, 557 N.W.2d 368 (1996) (same); A New Leaf, Inc. v. Webb, 26 Va.App. 460, 495 S.E.2d 510 (1998) (contact dermatitis is compensable as an occupational disease); Revere Copper & Brass, Inc. v. Industrial Comm., 97 Ill.2d 388, 73 Ill.Dec. 560, 454 N.E.2d 657 (1983) (allergic reaction to nickel); Greger v. United Prestress, Inc., 180 Mont. 348, 590 P.2d 1121 (1979) (contact dermatitis due to allergic reaction to chromate and nickel ions present in cement additive). *Cf.* St. Luke's Hospital v. Gray, 604 N.W.2d 646 (Iowa 2000) (nurse who developed allergy to latex could recover under "injury" provision of statute). A minority of courts hold that an allergic reaction is not a compensable occupational disease. E.g., Pearce v. Reintjes Co., 493 So.2d 892 (La.App.1986) (allergic condition aggravated by work environment but producing no permanent disability); Thompson v. Burlington Industries, 59 N.C.App. 539, 297 S.E.2d 122 (1982) (asthma exacerbated by work conditions but no permanent functional impairment).

6. Another type of apportionment issue is raised in cases where a worker is exposed to disease producing conditions in several employments over many years. Recall, for example, that Mr. Olson worked in two different uranium mines and Ms. Rutledge was employed in four textile mills before becoming disabled. Where disability benefits are awarded, should responsibility be divided among the prior employers? A variation of this problem presents itself when a single employer was insured by several different carriers during the time the disabled worker was exposed to the harmful substance. Which insurance carrier is responsible for payment of benefits? A majority of jurisdictions apply what is known as the "last injurious exposure" rule in these situations. Under this rule, the employer and insurance carrier at the time the claimant was last injuriously exposed to the disease producing substance are responsible for payment of the benefits. E.g., CES Card Establishment Services v. Doub., 104 Md.App. 301, 656 A.2d 332 (1995); McSpadden v. Big Ben Coal Co., 288 N.W.2d 181 (Iowa 1980), Carter v. Avondale Shipyards, Inc., 415 So.2d 174 (La.1981); Bertrand v. API, Inc., 365 N.W.2d 222 (Minn.1985). The responsible employer/insurer is determined by fixing the date of disability and the last time the claimant was injuriously exposed to the disease-producing substance. Hull v. Aetna Ins. Co., 247 Neb. 713, 529 N.W.2d 783 (1995). The last injurious exposure rule is justified primarily on the basis of administrative efficiency. It allows agencies or courts to award benefits quickly without becoming bogged down in efforts to identify and assess all the exposures to toxic substances a claimant might have had during a work life.

Although the rule generally facilitates the processing of disease claims, problems in administration do arise. The last injurious exposure may have been with an out of state employer against whom the claimant cannot proceed. In such cases, several courts have applied the rule to the last in-state employer. E.g., Wolfer v. Veco, Inc., 852 P.2d 1171 (Alaska 1993); Garner v. Vanadium Corp., 194 Colo. 358, 572 P.2d 1205 (1977); Hamilton v. S.A. Healy Co., 14 A.D.2d 364, 221 N.Y.S.2d 325 (1961). Other states, however, will deny benefits when the last injurious exposure occurred outside the court's jurisdiction. e.g., Grice v. Graniteville Co., 278 S.C. 461, 298 S.E.2d 446 (1982). Cf. Williams v. Port Authority of New York and New Jersey, 175 N.J. 82, 813 A.2d 531 (2003) (employee was exposed to chemical fumes over a four month period in New Jersey and for almost twenty-one years in New York; limited exposure in New Jersey cannot satisfy the "injury" requirement for the exercise of extraterritorial jurisdiction).

Problems may also arise in determining whether the last exposure was "injurious." Most courts assign liability to the last employer so long as there was some exposure of a kind that could have caused, aggravated, or promoted the disease. E.g., Liberty Northwest Insurance Corp. v. Montana State Fund,

353 Mont. 299, 219 P.3d 1267 (2009) (the last injurious exposure is one that "was of a kind which could have caused the" occupational disease). See generally 9 A. Larson & L. Larson, Larson's Workers' Compensation Law § 153.02 (2013). This standard can result in one employer being charged with full liability for diseases that most probably developed in prior employments. E.g., Union Carbide Corp. v. Industrial Comm., 196 Colo. 56, 581 P.2d 734 (1978) (claimant worked for Union Carbide eight days before becoming disabled. During that time he was exposed to radiation which amounted to 1/10,000 of his total exposure during his entire mining career. Union Carbide was held solely responsible for death benefits under the last injurious exposure rule); Caudle–Hyatt, Inc. v. Mixon, 220 Va. 495, 260 S.E.2d 193 (1979) (claimant's husband died of asbestos-induced cancer after having worked with insulation for many years, including four months with his last employer. The last employer was liable for the entire claim). Some decisions require that the last exposure be a "substantial contributing cause" of the disease. In these cases, it may be the next to last or some earlier employer who ultimately must provide compensation. E.g., Scott Co. v. Workers Comp. App. Bd., 139 Cal.App.3d 98, 188 Cal.Rptr. 537 (1983) (claimant was exposed to asbestos while working for various employers from 1938–1970. An award of benefits against the employer for the period 1959–66 was affirmed where there was medical testimony that exposures after 1963 did not cause or aggravate the tumor); Halverson v. Larrivy Plumbing & Heating Co., 322 N.W.2d 203 (Minn.1982) (second to last employer was held solely liable for compensation benefits when medical testimony indicated that subsequent exposures to asbestos would not result in any measurable injury for another five years or more). Only a few states, either by statute or judicial opinion, allow apportionment between two or more employers. Me.Rev.Stat.Ann. tit. 39, § 104 B; R.I.Gen.Laws § 28–34–8; Cooper v. Chrysler Corp., 125 Mich.App. 811, 336 N.W.2d 877 (1983) (benefits awarded an auto worker exposed to fumes and dust were apportioned between General Motors and Chrysler). Where apportionment is allowed, the shares of each employer are usually based on the employee's length of time in each employer's service.

The last injurious exposure rule does not generally apply to "accidents". Cowlitz Stud Co. v. Clevenger, 157 Wash.2d 569, 141 P.3d 1 (2006). The responsibility for "accidents" when multiple employers are implicated is addressed in Chapter 7, Section 4.

See Russell G. Donaldson, Annot., Workers' Compensation: Liable of Successive Employers for Disease or Condition Allegedly Attributable to Successive Employment, 34 A.L.R. 4th 958 (1984).

7. Several occupational disease statutes contain time-based restrictions on coverage. Some states impose minimum exposure limitations as a condition of coverage. A disease will not be compensable under these statutes unless the employee proves he was exposed to a particular substance on the job for the specified period of time. E.g., S.C.Code Ann. § 42–11–60 (worker must be exposed to organic or inorganic dust for seven years to recover for byssinosis); Nev.Rev.Stat. § 617.460(4) (no compensation for

disease related to asbestos or silicosis unless the worker was exposed to the harmful substance at least one year while working in state for the employer against whom recovery is sought). A different type of time-based restriction is in the nature of a statute of repose. Compensation benefits for occupational disease may be awarded under these statutes only if the death or disability occur within a specified period after the last day of work or the last injurious exposure. E.g., Ind. Code Ann. § 22–3–7–9 (f) (Three years from last exposure for silica, coal, and asbestos dust cases, and two years for other occupational diseases).

These time-based restrictions on coverage are intended to guarantee that a particular death or disability is genuinely work related. In practice, however, they often serve to deny compensation claims even when the disabling disease was clearly caused by job conditions. The problem is that occupational diseases rarely develop according to a legislatively prescribed time table. In Magma Copper Co. v. Gonzales, 62 Ariz. 9, 152 P.2d 618 (1944), for example, the claimant indisputably became disabled by silicosis as a result of his four and one-half year employment in the defendant's mine. The employee was denied workers' compensation benefits, however, because he became disabled too soon. The Arizona statute then in effect conditioned coverage of silicosis on a minimum five year exposure to silicon dioxide dust. Conversely, statutes of repose may bar the compensation claims of employees who die or become disabled too slowly. The widow of a Texas worker who died from occupationally induced cancer was denied benefits because her husband's death occurred more than three years after his last day of employment. Legate v. Bituminous Fire & Marine Ins. Co., 483 S.W.2d 488 (Tex.Civ.App.1972).

Such time-based restrictions can produce harsh results in individuals cases. For example, in Ganske v. Spahn & Rose Lumber Co., 580 N.W.2d 812 (Iowa 1998), the three year repose provision barred the employees's occupational disease claim for asbestos-related cancer. He then sued his employer in tort. The court held that his tort claim was banned by the exclusive remedy doctrine. See Chapter 11. Even though there was no serious dispute regarding the work-relatedness of the cancer, Ganske was left without a remedy in tort or workers' compensation. This decision is criticized in Kevin R. Sander, Comment, "The Cold Shoulder of Occupational Disease Recovery: Ganske v. Spahn & Rose Lumber Co.," 25 Iowa J. Corp. L. 407 (2000). Not surprisingly, other commentators also roundly criticize rigid time restrictions on filing occupational disease claims. See, 3 A. Larson & L. Larson, Larson's Workers' Compensation Law § 53.03–53.04(2013); Schroeder, Legislative and Judicial Responses to the Inadequacy of Compensation for Occupational Disease, 49 Law & Contemp.Probs. (No. 4) 151 (1986); Locke, Adapting Workers' Compensation to the Special Problems of Occupational Disease, 9 Harv.Envtl.L.Rev. 349 (1985).

Legislatures in several states have repealed or modified time based restrictions to give greater coverage for occupational disease. Courts in many of these states have given retroactive effect to such legislation. E.g., Puckett

v. Johns–Manville Corp., 169 Cal.App.3d 1010, 215 Cal.Rptr. 726 (1985) (retroactive application given to statute extending time period in which to file claims for asbestosis); Long v. North Carolina Finishing Co., 82 N.C.App. 568, 346 S.E.2d 669 (1986) (statute extending limitation period for asbestos claims applied to pending cases). Other courts have invalidated repose type restrictions under provisions of the state constitution. E.g., Walters v. Blair, 120 N.C.App. 398, 462 S.E.2d 232 (1995) aff'd 344 N.C. 628, 476 S.E.2d 105 (1996) (minimum exposure provision for silicosis and asbestosis violate state and federal equal protection clauses); Alvarado v. Industrial Comm., 148 Ariz. 561, 716 P.2d 18 (1986) (statutory provision that barred the claim of the widow of a miner who died of silicosis more than five years from his last day of employment was held to deny the claimant the right to a remedy for work related injuries guaranteed by Arizona constitution); Caruso v. Aluminum Co. of America, 15 Ohio St.3d 306, 473 N.E.2d 818 (1984) (denial of death benefits to the widow of an employee who died more than eight years after last injurious exposure to silica dust was held to be an unconstitutional denial of equal protection under both federal and state constitutions); Wrolstad v. Industrial Comm'n, 786 P.2d 243 (Utah App.1990) (one year statute of repose as applied to a worker disabled ten years after his occupational exposure to asbestos was found to violate the open courts provision of the Utah constitution). But see, Bunker v. National Gypsum Co., 441 N.E.2d 8 (Ind.1982) (upholding the constitutionality of a statute that barred occupational disease claims unless brought within three years of the claimant's last exposure to asbestos).

5. HEART CONDITIONS, MENTAL AND NERVOUS INJURY, AND OTHER SPECIAL CASES

LANCASTER V. GILBERT DEVELOPMENT

Supreme Court of Utah, 1987.
736 P.2d 237.

DURHAM, JUSTICE:

The claimant, James Lancaster, seeks review of the denial of workers' compensation benefits by the State Industrial Commission for injuries from a heart attack that occurred while he was clearing snow with a backhoe at Brian Head Ski Resort. We examine the evidence on this writ of review to determine if the claimant's heart attack is the result of an injury "by accident arising out of or in the course of his employment." U.C.A., 1953, § 35–1–45 (Supp.1986). We recently established the analytical framework for internal injury cases such as this in *Allen v. Industrial Commission*, 729 P.2d 15 (Utah 1986). Using the analysis in *Allen*, we affirm the decision of the Industrial Commission.

On February 17, 1984, the claimant, aged 43, arrived for work at Brian Head Resort at his usual hour of 7:00 a.m. The elevation at Brian Head Resort is approximately ten thousand feet. Claimant's first task was to clear snow using a backhoe. Although the temperature outside was cold, the cab of the backhoe was heated. All of the backhoe controls were hydraulically operated and required no unusual effort to operate. During the morning's work, the claimant climbed in and out of the backhoe two or three times.

The claimant experienced chest pains, which became more severe as the day progressed. These pains were more severe than similar pains he had experienced four days earlier. When the pains became debilitating, he informed his supervisor, who then called paramedics; the claimant was transported to a hospital in Cedar City, Utah. The treating physician determined that the claimant was suffering from acute anterior myocardial infarction. After one week at the hospital, the claimant was released to the care of his personal physician, Dr. Chanderraj. Although this was the claimant's first heart attack, he had several preexisting risk factors that predisposed him to heart attacks: a twenty-year smoking history, an elevated serum cholesterol level, an elevated uric acid level, and borderline diabetes.

On August 10, 1984, the Industrial Commission held a hearing in which one doctor, Dr. Perry, was appointed to a medical panel. A hearing on the medical panel finding was held on March 24, 1985. On April 5, 1985, the administrative law judge issued his findings of fact, conclusions of law, and order. The administrative law judge reviewed the conflicting medical evidence and then adopted the medical findings of the medical panel as his own. The administrative law judge found:

> [T]he Applicant's work activities and the myocardial infarction of [February 17, 1984] do not constitute an injury by accident. The Applicant's heart attack was unexpected, but there was nothing about his work activities that could constitute an unanticipated, unintended occurrence different from what would normally be expected to occur in the usual course of events. His heart attack appears to have been a mere coincidence, and his work activities did not contribute significantly to its occurrence. At best, it is conjectural as to whether it even precipitated his heart attack, but it clearly was not a significant precipitating cause. There was no evidence that the Applicant's work activities on February 17, 1984 were particularly different from the activities he had been performing for many weeks prior thereto.

The administrative law judge ultimately denied the claim on the ground that the claimant failed to show that the heart attack was "by accident" and that the heart attack was medically caused by an exertion in the workplace.

Our scope of review of factual findings in Industrial Commission cases is limited. We have explained in prior cases:

> The reviewing court's inquiry is whether the Commission's findings are "arbitrary and capricious" or "wholly without cause" or contrary to the "one [inevitable] conclusion from the evidence" or without "any substantial evidence" to support them. Only then should the Commission's findings be displaced.

Kaiser Steel Corp. v. Monfredi, 631 P.2d 888, 890 (Utah 1981). * * * At the time of his decision, the administrative law judge did not have the benefit of our analytical framework for accident cases involving internal failures set forth in *Allen v. Industrial Commission*, 729 P.2d 15 (Utah 1986). Nevertheless, the record is sufficiently developed for us to apply *Allen* to the facts and conclusions in the case before us.

In *Allen v. Industrial Commission*, we explained that the Utah Workers' Compensation Act, section 35–1–45, requires proof that an injury occurred "by accident" and proof of a causal connection between the accident and the activities or exertions required in the workplace. 729 P.2d at 18. The administrative law judge's ruling shows that he found the evidence insufficient to meet both the accident and the causation elements.

In *Allen*, we embraced the definition of "by accident" first formulated in *Purity Biscuit Co. v. Industrial Commission*, 115 Utah 1, 201 P.2d 961 (1949). We rejected the position that an accident requires an unusual event or occurrence. 729 P.2d at 20. An ordinary or usual exertion is sufficient to meet the "by accident" definition if "the result of an exertion was different from what would normally be expected to occur, the occurrence was unplanned, unforeseen, unintended and therefore by accident." 729 P.2d at 22. The critical factor when determining whether an incident is by accident is unexpectedness. 729 P.2d at 22.

Despite a finding that the heart attack was unexpected, the administrative law judge concluded there was no accident primarily because the claimant was undertaking his usual work duties. That conclusion cannot stand in light of the standard set forth in *Allen*. Although the claimant had experienced similar pains four days earlier, he had not been advised of the etiology of those pains and he had no forewarning that they would occur again on February 17. Moreover, there is nothing in the claimant's job duties to suggest that he would suffer a heart attack. There is overwhelming evidence that the claimant did not intend to have a heart attack, nor did he anticipate one. These factors, taken together with the finding that the myocardial infarction was the "unexpected" result of an exertion in the workplace, require the conclusion that the heart attack was "by accident."

The next step requires us to analyze the causal connection between the heart attack and the working conditions. See *Hone v. Shea*, 728 P.2d 1008, 1011 (Utah 1986). We adopted Professor Larson's two-step causation analysis in *Allen v. Industrial Commission*, 729 P.2d at 25. In order to meet the causation requirement, there must be sufficient evidence of legal cause and medical cause. Under the legal cause test, "a claimant with a preexisting condition must show that the employment contributed something substantial to increase the risk he already faced in everyday life because of his condition." 729 P.2d at 25. When a claimant has no preexisting risk factors, any exertion connected with the employment and causally connected with the injury as a matter of medical fact will satisfy the legal causation test. 729 P.2d at 26.

In addition to proving legal causation, the claimant must also prove medical causation. "Under the medical cause test, the claimant must show . . . that the stress, strain or exertion required by his or her occupation led to the resulting injury or disability." 729 P.2d at 27.

In this case, the administrative law judge did not distinguish in his causation analysis between legal and medical causation. However, it is clear from the medical testimony and other evidence presented to the administrative law judge that his decision was based on the failure to prove medical causation. Because the result in this case turns on the issue of medical causation, we will not examine the issue of legal causation.

The claimant argues that his work activities in cold weather and at a high altitude precipitated the myocardial infarction. The medical evidence before the administrative law judge was less than conclusive. The claimant's physician, Dr. Chanderraj, was the doctor most certain that the working conditions at Brian Head contributed to the injury. His opinion, however, was not unequivocal. He stated that the altitude, cold, and working conditions "probably" precipitated the heart attack. Dr. Chanderraj answered questions by the claimant's counsel as follows:

> Q. Let me ask you, Doctor, during all of the time that Mr. Lancaster has been your patient, have you had an opportunity to form an opinion as to whether or not the elevation, the cold, and the working conditions at the time of Mr. Lancaster's myocardial infarction precipitated that heart attack?
>
> A. This is a very difficult question to answer because it's a gray area in the field of cardiology; the exact role of precipitating factors in producing the event, but it is well known that high altitude, where the oxygen content of the air is low, especially in cold weather, can induce a myocardial event * * *.

> Q. Would it be your opinion that the cold, exposure, and the altitude, and the work conditions played a significant role or would be the trigger or the lighting up process of the myocardial infarction?
>
> A. I think we did go over this. I do feel it triggered—let me put it another way. If he had not been working up on that particular day in the cold atmosphere, operating the heavy equipment, in spite of having—in spite of five days history of chest pain, he probably would not have sustained a myocardial infarction.

Dr. Perry, the chairman of the medical panel and a cardiologist, testified it was "likely" that the conditions under which Mr. Lancaster was working aggravated his preexisting heart condition. However, Dr. Perry also was less than certain about the causal connection between the work conditions and the myocardial infarction. In his report to the administrative law judge, Dr. Perry identified and ranked the role of various risk factors, including those associated with work, in precipitating the claimant's myocardial infarction. He stated in his report:

> Mr. Lancaster has mild diabetes mellitus, smokes cigarettes, has an elevated uric acid and an elevated serum cholesterol level, all of which increase risk of coronary artery disease. In very rough terms the cigarette smoking, diabetes and high cholesterol approximately each double the risk of coronary artery disease such that with these three plus the uric acid elevation, his risk for coronary artery disease is 8–10 times higher than another male of his same age. From information gleaned from the records, summary of testimony and talking to Mr. Lancaster himself, I did not view his work as a risk factor for a myocardial infarction. While it was apparently cold, he was not involved in any unusual exertion, neither was he subjected to any unusual stress.
>
> * * *
>
> * * * While it is possible the cold exposure and his exertion had a role in precipitating the myocardial infarction, it is my opinion that it is unlikely they played a significant role. His 5 days of unstable angina lead me to believe that the patient was about to have a myocardial infarction, and the rather moderate amount of exertion and the length of time spent working simply offered an appropriate time and place for this event.

When asked to quantify the contribution of preexisting risk factors and work factors to the claimant's myocardial infarction, Dr. Perry assigned a value of 90 percent to preexisting conditions and 10 percent to work conditions. Dr. Perry explained, however, that his assessment of the factors was "a fairly random guess."

In addition, the State Insurance Fund had its doctor, Frank Dituri, review the claimant's medical records. Dr. Dituri opined that there was no evidence to indicate that the claimant's myocardial infarction was caused by his work or the altitude and cold at his place of work. Dr. Dituri concluded, "The type of work activities described could not precipitate any acute myocardial infarction." According to Dr. Dituri, the claimant's injury was "due to the normal progression of arteriosclerotic coronary artery disease that had been present for several years and was due to such factors as his smoking, his hypercholesterolemia, his poorly controlled diabetes and his prior history of alcohol abuse."

Thus, although there may have been some connection between the heart attack and the cold weather and high altitude, the evidence of any such connection is inconclusive. Not one of the doctors was willing to state with medical certainty that the claimant's injury was caused by work-related factors. Thus, there is competent and comprehensive medical evidence in the record upon which the administrative law judge could rely in concluding that medical causation was lacking. Although the medical evidence was conflicting, it is the responsibility of the administrative law judge to resolve factual conflicts.

We hold that the Industrial Commission's conclusion that there was no medical causal connection between work conditions and the claimant's heart attack is neither "arbitrary or capricious" nor "without any substantial evidence to support it." We therefore affirm the order of the Industrial Commission.

HALL, C.J., and HOWE and ZIMMERMAN, JJ., concur.

STEWART, ASSOCIATE C.J., concurs in the result.

NOTES

1. The compensability of death or disability from diseases of the heart or blood vessels has been described as "probably the most prolific and troublesome problem in workers' compensation law." Larson, The "Heart Cases" in Workmen's Compensation: An Analysis and Suggested Solution, 65 Mich.L.Rev. 441 (1965). The problem exists because diseases of the heart and blood vessels are capable in their normal course of causing incapacity or death without any work connected activity whatsoever. Almost everyone has known someone who suffered a heart attack while asleep or while physically inactive. On the other hand, heart attacks may be precipitated by the physical and emotional stress of the job. Thus, the "heart" cases present another variation of the now familiar question of how to allocate injury costs when occupational and nonoccupational causal factors are difficult to separate.

2. Many courts, perhaps a majority, award compensation for heart attacks caused by ordinary job stress. E.g., Grainger v. Alaska Workers' Compensation Bd., 805 P.2d 976 (Alaska 1991) (awarding benefits to obese workers whose heart disease was triggered by ordinary stress); Bush v. Industrial Comm., 136 Ariz. 522, 667 P.2d 222 (1983) (compensation awarded to an accountant whose heart attack was triggered by the stress of an increased work load without regard to whether the stress was labeled unusual); Twice Over Clean, Inc. v. Industrial Commissioner, 214 Ill.2d 403, 877 N.E.2d 409 (2005) (laborer whose ordinary exertion contributed to a heart attack awarded benefits); Wynn v. Navajo Freight Lines, Inc., 654 S.W.2d 87 (Mo.1983) (benefits awarded to the family of a truck driver who died from a heart attack while driving a normal run); Kirnan v. Dakota Midland Hospital, 331 N.W.2d 72 (S.D.1983) (awarding compensation to an employee whose heart attack was triggered while performing ordinary housekeeping duties). Cf. Chesler v. City of Derby, 96 Conn.App. 207, 899 A.2d 624 (2006) (affirming an award of benefits to the widow of a school superintendent who suffered a fatal heart attack following a contentious school board meeting; no mention of stress being "unusual").

3. A substantial number of courts require a showing of "unusual" physical exertion or emotional stress to support an award for a job related heart attack. E.g., Family Dollar Stores, Inc. v. Edwards, 97 Ark.App. 156, 245 S.W.3d 181 (2006) (cashier suffers heart attack during armed robbery; "unusual and extraordinary exertion"); State Industrial Ins. System v. Foster, 110 Nev. 521, 874 P.2d 766 (1994) (heart attacks triggered by ordinary stress are not compensable); Landis Office Center v. Barefield, 73 Md.App. 315, 533 A.2d 1332 (1987) (awarding compensation to a typewriter salesman whose heart attack was triggered by the unusual strain of removing old typewriters from client's office in 85-degree heat and pushing them up a 150 foot 30 degree incline); Grace v. North Dakota Workmen's Comp. Bureau, 395 N.W.2d 576 (N.D.1986) (denying compensation to masonry foreman with history of heart disease who suffered heart attack while working in 120-degree heat; no unusual stress). Cf. Fiore v. Consolidated Freightways, 140 N.J. 452, 659 A.2d 436 (1995) (claimant must show that heart disease is due in "material degree" to work conditions that "substantially" contributed to the development of the disease); Roberts v. Waldburns, 98 A.D.3d 1211, 951 N.Y.S.2d 590 (2012) (grocery store manager suffered a fatal heart attack hours after having an altercation with an irate customer on Super Bowl Sunday; award of death benefits affirmed; the combination of the altercation and the demands of Super Bowl Sunday created "significant work-related stress").

An implicit question lurking within the "unusual" exertion or stress standard is: unusual as compared to what? Some jurisdictions compare the occupational emotional or physical strain that triggered the heart attack with that encountered by other employees in similar jobs. E.g., Matter of Desotell, 767 P.2d 998 (Wyo.1989) (denying compensation to widow of truck driver whose heart attack was triggered by stress of having to reload improperly balanced trailer); Moore v. Motel Six Operations, LP, 741 N.W.2d 822 (Iowa App. 2007) ("unusual" as compared to the same or similar jobs is the appropriate standard). Occasionally the comparison is made between the claimant's job stress and that of workers generally. e.g., Baggett v. Industrial Comm'n, 201 Ill.2d 187, 266 Ill.Dec. 836, 775 N.E.2d 908 (2002) (claimant must prove that workplace stress is greater than the stress experienced by the general population); Ryan v. Connor, 28 Ohio St.3d 406, 503 N.E.2d 1379 (1986) (heart attack induced by job related emotional distress is compensable only if the emotional strain is greater than that to which all workers are occasionally subjected). Other courts look to whether the heart attack was caused by stress that was unusual for that particular employee, e.g., Mudd v. Neosho Mem. Regional Med. Ctr., 275 Kan. 187, 62 P.3d 236 (2003) (claimant must prove that stroke was triggered by more than the employee's usual work stress); Matter of Carr v. Industrial Comm., 709 P.2d 52 (Colo.App.1985) (awarding compensation to the widow of a water commissioner whose heart attack was precipitated by the physical strain of turning water control equipment; this was seasonal activity, but more strenuous than his ordinary duties). Which comparison is the most appropriate?

Once the proper point of comparison is selected, there remains the formidable task of measuring relative levels of physical and emotional stress. Which is the more "unusual" stress for a police officer, forcibly removing from a public bar the disorderly date of the officer's daughter, or responding to a major fire? Compare Creek v. Town of Hulett, 657 P.2d 353 (Wyo.1983) with Town of Kaycee v. Van Buskirk, 721 P.2d 570 (Wyo.1986).

4. A third approach, favored by Professor Larson and illustrated in *Lancaster*, distinguishes between claimants with preexisting heart conditions and those with no such preexisting risk factors. The latter may receive compensation for heart attacks caused by ordinary occupational exertion or stress, while the former must prove that the heart attack was caused by unusual stress or exertion. What policy considerations might support such a distinction? A number of jurisdictions have adopted this approach. E.g., Trinity Industries Inc. v. Cunningham, 680 So.2d 262 (Ala.1996); Wilson v. Good Will Publishers, 671 N.W.2d 479 (Iowa 2003); Guidry v. Sline Indust. Painters, 418 So.2d 626 (La.1982); Cheshire Toyota/Volvo, Inc. v. O'Sullivan, 129 N.H. 698, 531 A.2d 714 (1987).

5. Some states have statutes that specifically address the issue, often making recovery more difficult. Oregon, for example, requires that employment conditions be "the major contributing cause" of a stress-induced heart attack. In Estacada Rural Fire District v. Hull, 303 P. 3d 969 (Ore. App. 2013), the claimant was a fire chief who, at the request of the Sheriff, acted as an undercover witness to gather evidence of embezzlement within the department. While talking to his wife about the stress created by his involvement in the embezzlement investigation, the claimant suffered a heart attack. Five medical experts agreed that the claimant had an underlying coronary artery disease (arteriosclerosis) unrelated to his employment.

Several of these experts agreed that the stress of the embezzlement investigation contributed to some extent to the heart attack—one saying the stress was a "causative factor"; another testifying that the stress and the arteriosclerosis "contributed equally"; one labeling it "at most a trigger or precipitating factor"; and two experts testified that any contribution by the work stress was "minor." The court held that this claim was governed by "the heightened compensability standards" for mental disorders imposed by an Oregon statute. Under Ore. Rev. Stat. § 656.802(2)(a), the claimant must prove that "employment conditions were the major contributing cause of the disease." Would the expert testimony summarized here meet this standard?

6. Allocation of injury costs under any of the aforementioned approaches is on an all-or-nothing basis. Either the employer or the employee bears the entire cost of the heart attack. Would it be theoretically preferable to apportion injury costs in cases where occupational and nonoccupational factors combine to produce a disabling condition? How should the loss be apportioned? Is such a division practical? See Rootenberg & Getz v. Workers' Compensation Appeals Bd., 94 Cal.App.3d 265, 156 Cal.Rptr. 314 (1979) (discussing the potential apportionment of disability benefits for a heart attack under Cal.Labor Code § 4663); Road Maintenance Supply, Inc. v. Dependents of Maxwell, 493 So.2d 318 (Miss.1986) (employee with a history of heart disease suffered a fatal heart attack on the job; compensation to be reduced by the proportion which the preexisting heart disease contributed to the heart attack pursuant to Miss.Code Ann. § 71–3–7 (1972)). Are there ways to provide complete compensation to the disabled worker and still limit the employer's liability to the occupational share of causal responsibility? See Yocom v. Loy, 573 S.W.2d 645 (Ky.1978) (apportioning compensation benefits for a heart attack between employer and statutory Special Fund). The use of special funds is explored in more detail in Chapter 8.

7. Regardless of which measure of comparative stress controls, the claimant must always prove a causal connection between that stress and the heart attack. Even when ordinary occupational stress is sufficient to support coverage, compensation will be denied if the claimant fails to prove medical causation. e.g., Pitts v. City of Rome, 256 Ga.App. 278, 568 S.E.2d 167 (2002); Deuschle v. Bak Construction Co., 443 N.W.2d 5 (S.D.1989) (both upholding findings that the claimant's heart attack was not caused by occupational factors). Causation is most often established through the opinion testimony of expert witnesses who must express their opinions in terms of probabilities or reasonable medical certainty. Equivocal expert testimony may not support an award of benefits. E.g., Wiedmaier v. Robert A. McNeil Corp., 718 S.W.2d 174 (Mo.App.1986) (expert opinion that physical and emotional strain of work "could or might have caused" the heart attack does not discharge the claimant's burden of proof). Would the testimony of Dr. Perry and Dr. Chanderraj regarding causation have been sufficient to uphold an award of benefits in *Lancaster* if the Commission had ruled for the claimant? *Lancaster* suggests that there are significant differences between legal and medical standards of causation. What are they? See, Danner and Sagall,

Medicolegal Causation: A Source of Professional Misunderstanding, 3 Am.J.L. & M. 303 (1977); Small, Gaffing at a Thing Called Cause: Medicolegal Conflicts in the Concept of Causation, 31 Tex.L.Rev. 630 (1953). How far can or should an attorney go ethically in preparing a prospective expert witness to testify on the issue of causation? See, Piorkowski, Professional Conduct and the Preparation of Witnesses for Trial: Defining the Acceptable Limitations of "Coaching," 1 Geo.J. Legal Ethics 389 (1987).

SPARKS V. TULANE MEDICAL CENTER HOSPITAL & CLINIC

Supreme Court of Louisiana, 1989.
546 So.2d 138.

CALOGERO, JUSTICE.

The Louisiana Worker's Compensation Act provides coverage to any employee who suffers "*personal injury* by accident arising out of and in the course of his employment." La.R.S. 23:1031 (emphasis added). We have previously determined that mental injury induced by physical trauma and physical injury induced by mental stress are compensable "personal injuries" under the Act.

The primary issue presented in this case, heretofore not addressed by this Court, is whether a mental injury induced by mental stress is compensable when it is caused by a significant employment incident and is not accompanied by any apparent signs of physical trauma * * *.

[Claimant Sparks worked in a supervisory capacity for Tulane Medical Center. In 1982, she incurred the resentment of her co-workers by initiating a program to eliminate illegal drug use by employees on the hospital premises. Sparks soon thereafter became the victim of a series of thefts and vandalism, including urination into her coffee pot and waste basket. The court stated that many of these incidents appeared to be intentional and designed to harass or intimidate the claimant. No one was ever apprehended in connection with these incidents.

On April 6, 1987, Sparks suspended two employees who failed to stock the supply room. That same day, Sparks was informed that "a lot of people round here want to kick your butt." She became upset at the threat and left work. On April 7, 1987, Sparks was examined by an internist who diagnosed her as suffering from "tension headaches, which were probably related to . . . stress she was encountering at work." When Sparks' condition did not improve, the internist referred her to a psychiatrist. The psychiatrist diagnosed Sparks as suffering from an "adjustment disorder" that was "definitely job related". Over the course of several months Sparks received counseling from a clinical social worker who also found that Sparks' condition was both disabling and work related.

Defendant, while presenting no medical witnesses, produced evidence that plaintiff was diagnosed with depression in 1970, and that she was treated for sinus headaches in 1985. The plaintiff's medical records also revealed a one-time doctor's visit in 1986 for headaches she suffered after a blow to the head.]

* * * The trial court denied the plaintiff's claims for benefits. The trial judge concluded that the plaintiff had been temporarily mentally disabled, but that she had not suffered the requisite "accident" under La.R.S. 23:1031. The court of appeals reversed and awarded plaintiff benefits for a five month period of disability. 537 So.2d 276 (La.App.1988). * * *

In summary, then, we have a plaintiff who was diagnosed with a psychological adjustment disorder, depression and tension headaches, and who also complained of anxiety, loss of appetite, insomnia and nightmares. Three experts, an internist, a psychiatrist and a clinical social worker, related these problems to plaintiff's employment. Defendant presented no medical testimony but attempted to establish that plaintiff had pre-existing medical problems.

(II) Law and Analysis

Defendant argues that there are a number of reasons why the events described above do not provide a basis for recovery under the Louisiana Worker's Compensation Act. First, defendant argues that plaintiff did not prove that her injury resulted from an "accident" as that term is defined in the Act, because there was no "unexpected or unforeseen event happening suddenly or violently . . . and producing at the time objective symptoms of an injury." La.R.S. 23:102(1). Secondly, defendant argues that because any injury suffered by plaintiff was not induced by physical trauma, there was not a compensable injury under the Act which involved "violence to the physical structure of the body." La.R.S. 23:1021(7). As a third and alternative contention, defendant argues that even if injuries are compensable absent evidence of physical trauma, this plaintiff failed to show that her medical problems were causally related to her employment.

* * *

(A) The Accidental "Event" Requirement

La.R.S. 23:1021(1) defines "accident" as "an unexpected or unforeseen event happening suddenly or violently, with or without human fault, and producing at the time objective symptoms of an injury."

The "event" which qualifies as an accident can be and often is a forceful and readily identifiable occurrence which *causes injury* to the employee, e.g., an automobile collision, a fall, an explosion, an assault, etc. However, under the jurisprudence, the sudden and unexpected appearance of a *physical injury*, such as a heart attack or stroke, is also viewed as an "accident." *See, e.g., Ferguson v. HDE, Inc.*, 270 So.2d 867, 869–70 (La.1972) (stroke). In such cases, the onset of the illness or injury is viewed as the accident because, from the employee's perspective, the injury was an unforeseen event which occurred suddenly or violently. *Ferguson v. HDE, Inc., supra*, 270 So.2d at 870.

The "event" which triggers coverage, then, may be an unexpected and sudden or violent occurrence which *causes injury*, or it may be an unexpected change in the employee's *physical condition*, which renders him incapable of working, a change caused at least in part by an employment incident. See Malone & Johnson, 13 Louisiana Civil Law Treatise, Worker's Compensation, § 214 (1980 & 1989 Supp.).

(B) The "Injury" Requirement

The terms "injury" and "personal injuries" are defined by the Act as "injuries by violence to the physical structure of the body and such disease or infections as naturally result therefrom." La.R.S. 23:1021(7). "These terms shall in no case be construed to include any other form of disease or derangement, however caused or contracted." *Id.*

The definition of "injury" contains a requirement of "violence to the physical structure of the body," but the statutory definition does not use the terms "physical injury" or "mental injury." Nor does the statutory definition attempt to provide any basis or method for distinguishing between "physical" and "mental" injuries.

Nevertheless, in attempting to determine the types of injuries covered by the Act, Louisiana courts have often drawn distinctions between physical and mental injuries. In Louisiana, as well as in other jurisdictions, worker's compensation cases involving mental injury or trauma have been grouped by courts and commentators into three general categories: (1) cases in which observable physical trauma causes mental injury ("physical-mental" injury cases); (2) cases in which mental stress or stimulus causes observable physical trauma ("mental-physical" injury cases); and (3) cases in which mental stress or stimulus causes so-called "purely mental" injuries, that is, injuries unaccompanied by any observable or apparent physical trauma ("mental-mental" injury cases). *See* Larson, 1B Workmen's Compensation Law, § 42.20 (1986 & 1988 Supp.). *See also Jordan v. Southern Natural Gas Co.*, 455 So.2d 1217, 1223–26 (La.App. 2d Cir.1984). While the distinction between these categories may often be less than precise,[2] the categories provide a

[2] "It must be understood that this use of such words as mental, nervous, emotional, stress, stimulus, psychic, and the like is only a rough expedient adopted in order to sort out an almost infinite variety of subtle conditions and relationships for compensation law purposes, and especially in order to narrow down the range of situations where controversy seems to persist." Larson, 1B Workmen's Compensation, *supra*, § 42.20 at 7–586.

helpful basis for reviewing the jurisprudence pertinent to mental injuries and for resolving the issues presented by this case.

In so-called "physical-mental" injury cases, where a mental injury or illness develops secondary to an ascertainable physical injury, Louisiana courts have uniformly found that the employee is entitled to compensation benefits for any disability resulting from the mental injury and to reimbursement for medical expenses incurred in the treatment of that condition. *See, e.g., Westley v. Land & Offshore*, 523 So.2d 812 (La.1988) (employee suffered post traumatic stress syndrome secondary to physical injury caused by fall); *Droddy v. Cliff's Drilling, Inc.*, 471 So.2d 223 (La.1985) (employee suffered depressive neurosis as "emotional overlay" to physical injury caused by fall). *See also Jordan v. Southern Natural Gas Co.*, supra, 455 So.2d at 1222 ("[W]hen a plaintiff develops a disabling anxiety syndrome, traumatic neurosis, or other mental disorder as a result of a work related physical injury, he can recover compensation benefits even if he has recovered physically from the injury."). Allowance of coverage in these "physical-mental" injury cases seems clearly appropriate under the Act's definition of "injury," which covers not only the initial injury suffered by the employee but also "such disease or infections as naturally result therefrom."

We have also recognized that coverage is appropriate where mental stress or strain related to employment causes physical trauma ("mental-physical" injury cases). The leading Louisiana case in this area is *Ferguson v. HDE, Inc.*, 270 So.2d 867 (La.1972), wherein coverage was allowed for an employee who suffered a stroke while arguing with his supervisor. Noting that the claimant unquestionably would have been entitled to compensation if the stroke had been brought on by physical stress, however minimal, we found no basis for denying recovery when the injury was precipitated by mental stress.

* * *

In the third category are the "mental-mental" injury cases, in which there is no indication of apparent physical trauma but the claimant sustains disability due to mental illness precipitated by work-related mental stress. We have never considered whether such injuries are compensable, and our courts of appeal are divided on the issue.[3] This case, which concerns an injury that was not precipitated by any observable physical trauma, squarely presents that issue.

The Louisiana court of appeal decisions which have denied coverage in this area have done so primarily on the ground that the statutory

[3] Courts throughout the country are also divided on this issue. While the majority of jurisdictions permit recovery in "mental-mental" injury cases, a substantial minority do not. *See* Larson, *supra* § 42.23. On the other hand, almost all jurisdictions permit recovery in "physical-mental" injury and "mental-physical" injury cases. *Id.* §§ 42.21–22.

requirement of an injury "by violence to the physical structure of the body" is not satisfied unless the injury was caused by some blow or physical force which causes observable physical injury. For example, in *Sutherland v. Time Saver Stores, Inc.*, 428 So.2d 972 (La.App. 1st Cir.1983), the employee, a convenience store clerk, suffered mental complications after she was robbed at gunpoint. The robber ordered the plaintiff to disrobe, and as she was doing so the police arrived and arrested the perpetrator. Although plaintiff was not physically assaulted in any way, expert testimony established that she suffered from a disabling anxiety syndrome as a result of the incident. The court of appeal affirmed summary judgment in favor of the employer, holding that the employee was not entitled to compensation because "in order to recover in workmen's compensation for a mental disability there must first exist a physical detriment as a causative or contributory factor." 428 So.2d at 972.

* * *

On the other hand, Louisiana court of appeal decisions which have permitted recovery for these types of injuries have concluded that when an employee suffers from a mental disability which is serious enough to render that employee unable to work, then the injury has done "violence to the physical structure of the body." For example, in *Jones v. City of New Orleans*, 514 So.2d 611 (La.App. 4th Cir.1987) *writ denied*, 515 So.2d 1111 (La.1987), compensation benefits were awarded to an employee who suffered from post traumatic stress syndrome as a result of threats to her safety that were made during the course of her employment. In allowing coverage, the court of appeal stated that "[w]e cannot ignore the scientific fact that mental disorders constitute an injury to the physical capabilities of a worker." 514 So.2d at 814.

* * *

Thus, the essential issue over which our courts of appeal are divided, and which we are called upon to resolve here, is whether the statutory requirement of injury "by violence to the physical structure of the body" is satisfied when the employee suffers a mental disability that is not accompanied by apparent physical trauma or physiological damage. In resolving this issue, we will consider both the requirement of "violence," as interpreted by well-established jurisprudence, and the meaning and scope of the phrase "physical structure of the body."

The statutory requirement of violence is satisfied when the injury has a violent or harmful *effect* on the employee's physical condition, even if the cause of that change was not in itself violent. Under the jurisprudence, there need not be a blow or visible application of force in order for the "violence" aspect of the statutory definition to be satisfied.

See, e.g., Parks v. Insurance Co. of North America, 340 So.2d 276 (La.1976) (inhalation of fumes and lint caused chronic bronchitis, which in turn caused "violence" to the employee's body); *Cannella v. Gulf Refining Co.*, 154 So. 406, 413 (La.App.Orl.1934) (lead poisoning from fumes caused "violence . . . to both the blood and the intestines"); *Rochell v. Shreveport Grain & Elevator Co.*, 188 So. 429 (La.App. 2d Cir.1939) (small particle lodged in employee's eye and caused blindness); *Smith v. Brown Paper Mill Co.*, 152 So. 700 (La.App. 2d Cir.1934) (infection resulting from hypodermic injection); *Woodward v. Kansas City Bridge Co.*, 3 So.2d 221 (La.App. 1st Cir.1941) (inflammation of skin by creosote and poison ivy).

Thus, there is an "injury" when there is "violence," i.e., a harmful effect, to the "physical structure of the body." One possible interpretation of the phrase "physical structure of the body" is that it refers only to those physical component parts which make up the body, e.g., bones, tissues, organs, etc. We note, however, that the Texas Supreme Court, when interpreting a statutory definition in the Texas worker's compensation act that is similar to our own, rejected this interpretation and held that the "physical structure of the body" refers to:

> the *entire* body, not simply to the skeletal structure or to the circulatory system or to the digestive system. It refers to the *whole*, to the complex of perfectly integrated and interdependent bones, tissues and organs which function together by means of electrical, chemical and mechanical processes in a living, breathing, functioning individual. To determine what is meant by "physical structure of the body," the structure should be considered that of a living person—not as a static inanimate thing. *Bailey v. American General Ins. Co.*, 154 Tex. 430, 279 S.W.2d 315, 318 (1955) (emphasis by the court).

In *Bailey*, the claimant was working on a high-level scaffold with another worker. The scaffold collapsed and plaintiff, who was able to avoid injury to himself because he was caught in a cable, watched his co-employee plunge to this death. Afterward plaintiff claimed inability to work because of a disabling neurosis. The Texas court determined that plaintiff was entitled to benefits because the medical testimony established that as a result of his disabling neurosis, "plaintiff's body no longer functions properly." *Id.* 279 S.W.2d at 318. The court found itself unable to conclude that "though a 'physical structure' no longer functions properly, it has suffered no 'harm.' " *Bailey*, 279 S.W.2d at 318.

We agree with the analysis employed by the Texas Supreme Court in *Bailey*, while interpreting a statutory definition of injury similar to our own, as well as the reasoning used by the Louisiana Fourth Circuit Court of Appeal in *Jones*, *supra*, and *Taquino*, *supra*. An individual's mental health is an essential component to the overall operation of the physical structure of his body. If an injury so disables the mental machinery of a worker that "his body no longer functions properly," *Bailey, supra*, and he is unable to perform his employment duties, then the statutory requirement of violence (harm) to the physical structure of the body is satisfied. This is true regardless of whether the injury was prompted by observable physical trauma and regardless of whether the injury might be characterized as more "mental" in nature than "physical."

* * *

Furthermore, it has been persuasively argued that there is no bright-line distinction between "physical" and "mental" injuries, either in medicine or in law, which provides a reliable basis for awarding or denying workmen's compensation benefits. Many injuries which appear essentially mental in nature may actually be caused or accompanied by physiological change.[6]

* * *

Finally, we note that by rejecting the "nineteenth century approach" of making the availability of benefits dependent upon a rigid and absolute distinction between physical and mental injuries, Larson, *supra* at 7–651 n. 82, we reach a result that has been approved by a majority of the jurisdictions in this country. *Id.* at 7–639.

We emphasize, however, that a mere showing that a mental injury was related to *general conditions* of employment, or to incidents occurring over an extended period of time, is not enough to entitle the claimant to compensation. The mental injury must be precipitated by an accident, i.e., an unexpected and unforeseen event that occurs suddenly or violently.[7]

---

6 That the distinction between physical and mental injury is often obscure is demonstrated by two recent worker's compensation cases, Davis v. Oilfield Scrap & Equipment Co., 482 So.2d 970 (La.App. 3d Cir.1986) and Guillot v. Sentry Insurance Co., 472 So.2d 197 (La.App. 5th Cir.1985). Seemingly, the facts of Davis present a classic "mental-mental" injury case. The plaintiff suffered a mental disability after her supervisor shot himself at work and died in her arms. While plaintiff suffered from no apparent physical injury or trauma, medical evidence established that plaintiff's mental disability was accompanied by a physiological change in her body that could be measured by electroencephalograms (EEG) and chemical analysis. Because of this evidence, the court of appeal was satisfied that an "injury" had been proven, and allowed compensation. In Guillot, *supra,* the claimant alleged that he suffered a nervous breakdown as the result of job related stress. There was no evidence of injury by physical trauma, but medical testimony established that the "breakdown" was accompanied by "physiological changes in brain cells along with biochemical changes that could be measured chemically," and recovery of benefits was allowed.

7 While the sudden onset of physical injury may qualify as the compensable "accident" in some cases, *see* Ferguson v. HDE, Inc., *supra* (stroke), an employee's subjective assertion that he had a sudden onset of symptoms of mental injury, such as depression or anxiety, is not alone sufficient to show that an accident occurred. The employee must be able to point to a discernible employment-related event which caused the mental injury, an event separate and apart from the onset of the symptoms of that mental injury.

Among the cases involving work-related disabilities which appear to be essentially mental in nature, there are a number of examples of the type of sudden and unusual event which can truly be considered an "accident." *See, e.g., Bailey v. American General Ins. Co., supra* (plaintiff watched co-employee fall to death after collapse of scaffold); *Sutherland v. Time Saver Stores, Inc., supra* (robbery and fear of imminent sexual abuse); *Davis v. Oilfield Scrap & Equipment Co.*, 482 So.2d 970 (La.App. 3d Cir.1986) (co-employee suicide, see discussion in note six, *supra*). In cases involving such readily identifiable, unusual and dramatic events, compensation is appropriate when there is sufficient evidence that the sudden event caused the disabling mental condition. On the other hand, absent an identifiable accident of this type, an employee's general allegation that he is unable to work due to stress or tension caused by working conditions would not give rise to a compensable claim.

* * *

(C) Application of the Accidental Event and Injury Requirements to This Case; Causation

Defendant argues that there was no "accident" under the Act because "plaintiff never alleged a single, unexpected, unforeseen and catastrophic event which gave rise to her injuries," but rather alleged "a series of events which took place over the course of six and one-half years. . . ." Under the Act, defendant argues, there must be a single, identifiable "event" which produces injury, and separate events which occurred over a six year period cannot constitute an accident.

We find, however, that the communication of the threats to plaintiff on April 6, 1987 was the event which produced injury in this case, not the incidents which occurred in the years prior to the threats. The accident thus occurred on April 6, 1987, and the events prior to that date are relevant simply to the extent that they reinforce the seriousness of the threats and lend credibility to plaintiff's assertion that the threats caused her severe anxiety and distress.

It is evident from the record that plaintiff suffered a temporarily disabling mental injury as a result of learning of the threats that had been made against her. Prior to April 6, 1987, plaintiff had an excellent seven-year work record at the medical center, a record which included a promotion to a supervisory position of substantial responsibility and highly favorable annual evaluations. Prior to April 6, 1987, plaintiff had missed some work due to illness but never for any significant period of time. And prior to April 6, 1987, plaintiff had been able to perform her employment duties in an able and competent manner. Yet after the events on the morning of April 6, 1987, when plaintiff learned of a physical threat to her safety, she experienced an unexpected and sudden inability to perform her normal employment duties. The breakdown or adjustment disorder which she experienced was accompanied by the immediate onset of headaches, tension and loss of appetite. The record evidences that the threats of harm precipitated a change in plaintiff from an able and competent worker to a person who was unable to engage in any meaningful activity, including employment, for almost five months.

All three of the experts called by plaintiff agreed that she was unable to work during the period that they treated her, because of her mental injury, and also because of the related headaches, insomnia and loss of appetite. All three of the experts also expressed the view that the disabling mental condition was caused by the fear and anxiety plaintiff had regarding returning to her job. The defendant presented no medical testimony to the contrary. In fact, the defendant presented no expert testimony at all regarding plaintiff's condition after April 6, 1987.

* * *

Finally, while there was evidence that plaintiff had some prior medical problems, including sinus headaches in 1985 or 1986 and depression in 1970, there is no indication in the record that whatever problems she experienced prior to April 6, 1987 were related to the disability which she suffered after that date.

In summary, since three experts affirmatively testified that plaintiff's disability was related to her employment, since defendant produced no testimony to the contrary, and since whatever previous medical problems plaintiff experienced were clearly not of the same severity and scope as those brought on by the events of April 6, 1987, we find that plaintiff established by a preponderance of the evidence that her injury was precipitated by the threats to her safety.

Decree

For the foregoing reasons, we agree with the court of appeal that this plaintiff suffered a compensable "injury by accident" under the Louisiana Worker's Compensation Act. Therefore, we affirm the court of appeal's judgment, ordering defendant to pay plaintiff $7,303.24 in benefits and medical expenses, plus legal interest and court costs.

AFFIRMED.

[Three justices dissented in two opinions that argued that Sparks was not entitled to compensation because: (1) the events leading to Sparks' disability could not be characterized as an "accident"; (2) Sparks had not suffered any damage to the "physical structures of the body"; (3) the statute excluded coverage of any "disease" other than "that naturally resulting from injuries by violence to the physical structure of the body"; and (4) any expansion of coverage for mental disabilities should come from the legislature.]

NOTES

1. Medical science has identified a broad spectrum of mental disorders, each with its own diagnostic nomenclature and characteristic symptoms. The primary source for standard psychiatric diagnosis is the American Psychiatric Association, Diagnostic and Statistical Manual of Mental Disorders (4th ed. 2000) (DSM–IV revised). Three types of psychological disorders appear with some frequency in workers' compensation cases. The first is commonly referred to as post traumatic stress disorder. This condition is marked by symptoms of stress exhibited more than a month following an especially traumatic event, such as a serious workplace accident. A second type of common psychological injury is known as psychogenic pain disorder. A person experiencing psychogenic pain disorder expresses genuine sensations of pain for which no organic explanation can be found. The third common claim involves a conversion disorder in which the patient suffers a loss of physical function unconsciously caused by a psychological conflict or need rather than any physical injury.

2. Workers seeking compensation for such psychological disorders face two recurring questions: is the injury genuine and, if so, is it sufficiently work related? The fundamental problem was succinctly described by one commentator as follows:

> The precise etiology of most mental disorders is inexplicable. Mental disorders result from an extraordinarily complex interrelation between an individual's internal or subjective reality and his external or environmental reality. . . . The precise psychogenesis of an individual's subjective reality is impossible to determine. . . . When mental disorder symptoms appear in parts of the body other than the brain, medical science is able, in most cases, to attach a quantitative or qualitative etiological probability. Scientists cannot make this determination, however, when the symptoms manifest themselves subjectively. An individual who suffers a mental disorder has an a priori personal subjective vulnerability or predisposition to the disorder. . . . Although mental injuries medically are as genuine as physical disorders, their subjective quality creates the possibility that the individual may feign a mental disorder. The specter of fraud has influenced judicial attitudes toward mental injuries.

Joseph, The Causation Issue in Workers' Compensation Mental Disability Cases: An Analysis, Solutions, and a Perspective, 36 Vand.L.Rev. 263, 271–273 (1983).

The potential number of claims for stress-related disabilities is enormous. A study conducted by the California Workers' Compensation Institute (CWCI) documented a 700% increase in the number of pure mental stress claims between 1979 and 1988. The benefit costs of such claims filed in California in 1987 alone was estimated to be $383 million. Peter S Barth, Workers' Compensation for Mental Stress Cases, 8 Behavioral Sci. & L. 349,

358 (1990). Other states have experienced similar increases in stress claims. See Nugent, Workers' Compensation and Stress, 14 Employee Rel.L.J. 239, 240 (1988). Cf. Aya V. Matsumoto, Comment, Reforming the Reform: Mental Stress Claims Under California's Workers' Compensation System, 27 Loy.L.A. L. Rev. 1328, 1335 (1994) (mental disorders currently rank among the top ten work-related injuries and illnesses in the nation); Natalie D. Riley, Employment Law: Mental–Mental Claims—Placing Limitations on Recovery Under Workers' Compensation Laws for Day-to-Day Frustrations, 65 Mo. L. Rev. 1023 (2000) (asserting that the dramatic rise in mental stress claims has placed pressures on courts and legislatures to place restrictions on coverage).

3. Professor Larson organizes his analysis of the cases by characterizing the cause and effect of disability as either physical or mental. 3 A. Larson and L. Larson, Larson's Workers' Compensation Laws § 56.01 (2013). This framework was utilized by the court in *Sparks* and is followed in many jurisdictions. Courts and administrative agencies are most likely to award compensation for mental injuries in cases in which the disabling mental disturbance is caused by some work related physical injury (so-called physical-mental cases). e.g., Shivel v. Wexford Health Sources, 66 P.3d 414 (Ok.2003) (compensation awarded for mental distress following work-related stabbing); Southwire Co. v. George, 266 Ga. 739, 470 S.E.2d 865 (1996) (benefits awarded truck driver for post-traumatic stress disorder following an accident in which the claimant observed a person crushed to death on the grill of the truck; the driver also suffered physical injury to his knee, hip and chest; physical injury need not be the "precipitating cause" of the psychic trauma so long as it "contributes" to its continuation); Hollar Oil Co. v. Bryant, 644 So.2d 951 (Ala.1994) (compensation awarded for mental disorder caused by industrial accident in which the claimant lost a testicle); Harrison v. Osco Drug, Inc., 116 Idaho 470, 776 P.2d 1189 (1989) (employee awarded compensation for "foot drop" caused by "conversion hysteria" following work related slip and fall). Similarly, compensation is generally awarded for disabling pain following a physical work injury even if the pain is linked to psychological factors. e.g., Ex Parte Vongsouvanh, 795 So.2d 625 (Ala.2000) (physical injury was a "contributing cause" to mental impairment along with other factors; compensation allowed); Bruce v. Clear Springs Trout Farm, 109 Idaho 311, 707 P.2d 422 (1985) (psychogenic pain syndrome following on-the-job slip and fall); Gutierrez v. Amity Leather Products Co., 107 N.M. 26, 751 P.2d 710 (App.1988) (upholding award for psychogenic pain disorder following work related shoulder injury).

Should compensation be awarded an employee who comes in contact with blood and develops a disabling psychological condition from the fear of becoming infected with the HIV virus? Does it matter whether the blood is actually infected with the virus? Compare Guess v. Sharp Mfg. Co., 114 S.W.3d 480 (Tenn.2003) (compensation should be awarded only when the worker proves actual exposure to infected blood through a medically recognized channel of transmission.) with Richard E. Jacobs Group v. White,

202 S.W.3d 24 (Ky. 2006) (security guard who shot a suspect was exposed to the victim's blood and developed a fear of contracting a disease was awarded benefits despite the fact that the victim's blood tested negative for HIV or hepatitis.). See also Norfolk & Western Ry. Co. v. Freeman, 538 U.S. 135, 123 S.Ct. 1210, 155 L.Ed.2d 261 (2003) (allowing railroad workers who were exposed to asbestos to recover for their fear of developing cancer under FELA).

In many of the cases describe above, coverage may turn on the strength of the evidence connecting the psychological disability to the physical injury. Compare Armstrong v. John R. Jurgensen Co., 136 Ohio St. 3d 58, 990 N.E.2d 568 (2013) (credible evidence supported the trial court's finding that the employee's physical injuries suffered in a truck-automobile collision did not cause his PTSD; the PTSD was caused by witnessing the death of the driver of the other vehicle; compensation denied) with Southwire Co. v. George, 266 Ga. 739, 470 S.E.2d 865 (1996) (employee suffered from PTSD after witnessing the death of another person involved in a traffic accident; employee suffered a knee injury; the knee injury was not the "precipitating cause" of the PTSD, but it did "contribute" to it; compensation awarded).

4. Courts and agencies also generally award compensation when nervous shock brings about a disabling physical reaction (so-called mental-physical cases). e.g., McCowan v. Matsushita Appliance Co., 95 S.W.3d 30 (Ky.2002) (heart attack following heated argument with supervisor; compensation awarded); Reeser v. Yellow Freight System, 938 S.W.2d 690 (Tenn.1997) (stroke precipitated by unusual stress of driving through an ice storm; compensation awarded); Snyder v. San Francisco Feed & Grain, 230 Mont. 16, 748 P.2d 924 (1987) (reversing the denial of compensation to employee who suffered a ruptured aneurysm following a period of unusual stress in her job); Ferguson v. HDE, Inc., 270 So.2d 867 (1972) (claimant engaged in angry altercation with superiors over his pay and suffered either cerebral thrombosis or cerebral hemorrhage which disabled him; compensation awarded). This type of fact pattern frequently arises in the context of heart conditions, such as those reflected in *Lancaster* and ensuing notes.

Of course, such mental-physical claims will be denied if the evidence fails to establish the requisite causal connection. E.g., Wilson v. Catoosa Public Schools, 157 P.3d 1149 (Okla. 2007) (evidence failed to prove that stroke was caused by occupational stress in excess of ordinary living); Mudd v. Neosho Memorial Regional Medical Center, 275 Kan. 187, 62 P.3d 236 (2003) (evidence failed to prove that fatal stroke was caused by unusual occupational exertion); Lee–Hoofkin v. Advantage Nursing Services, Inc, 865 So.2d 85 (La. 2004) (evidence failed to prove that slip and fall on the job caused a stroke). Cf., Estacada Rural Fire District v. Hull, 2013 Ore.App. Lexis 560 (2013) (unusual work-related stress was not proven to be the "major contributing cause" of a heart attack; claimant had pre-existing arteriolsclerosis).

5. The most difficult cases involve workers who suffer psychological disabilities as a result of some work related nervous shock or protracted stress (so-called mental-mental cases). A substantial majority of states now compensate employees for this type of claim under some circumstances. There is considerable variation, however, in how far courts will go in awarding compensation for a mental disability produced by a mental stimulus. Perhaps the fact pattern in which compensation is most frequently awarded involves a psychological disability brought about by a specific and sudden precipitating event. E.g., Pathfinder Co. v. Industrial Comm., 62 Ill.2d 556, 343 N.E.2d 913 (1976) (employee suffered emotional disorder after rescuing fellow worker whose hand was amputated by punch press); Belcher v. T. Rowe Price, 329 Md. 709, 621 A.2d 872 (1993) (compensation awarded to an office worker who suffered post traumatic stress disorder after a three ton steel beam crashed through the office wall); RAG (Cyprus) Emerald Resources LP v. Workers' Compensation Appeal Bd., 590 Pa. 413, 912 A.2d 1278 (2007) (Vietnam war veteran who suffered flashbacks and recurrence of Vietnam related PTSD following work-related sexual harassment; benefits awarded); Wolfe v. Sibley Lindsay & Curr Co., 36 N.Y.2d 505, 369 N.Y.S.2d 637, 330 N.E.2d 603 (1975) (employee psychologically disabled after discovering the body of her supervisor who had committed suicide). Some states limit compensation to this type of fact pattern. E.g., Henley v. Roadway Express, 699 S.W.2d 150 (Tenn.1985) (refusing to compensate injuries caused by chronic stress or emotional strain and instead requiring fright, shock or excessive unexpected anxiety); Transportation Insurance Co. v. Maksyn, 580 S.W.2d 334 (Tex.1979) (newspaper production manager disabled by anxiety depression triggered by years of stress was not entitled to compensation because he could not pinpoint a definite time, place and cause of mental trauma).

Should it matter whether the stress was brought on, at least in part, by the employee's own misconduct? In 2011, a University of California policeman casually doused students participating in a peaceful demonstration with pepper spray. A photograph of the officer spraying the protesters was widely distributed in the national media and internet. A state-level investigation produced a report finding that the university police used poor judgment and excessive force in the confrontation. The officer featured in the photograph became the focal point of public criticism. A lawsuit brought by twenty-one students who were doused with pepper spray was settled for $1 million. The officer appearing in the photograph was suspended and ultimately left the campus police force. In 2013 the officer filed a workers' compensation claim alleging that he was disabled by the psychologically stress he endured as a result of this incident and its aftermath. The workers' compensation claim was resolved with the officer receiving a payment of $38,055. Steve Gorman, University of California Cop Who Pepper-Sprayed Student Protesters Awarded $38,000 (Reuters) (October 23, 2013) http://www.reuters.com/article/2013/10/24/us-usa-pepperspray-california-idUSBRE99N02M20131024.

The most controversial cases involve psychological disabilities brought on by gradual stress. The trend is to award compensation in such cases. Courts disagree, however, whether the disabling stress must be "unusual" in some manner. Some decisions limit coverage to disabilities brought about by gradual stress that is greater than that normally encountered by similarly situated employees. e. g., Davis v. Workers' Compensation Appeal Bd., 561 Pa. 462, 751 A.2d 168 (2000) (compensation denied to police officer when evidence failed to establish that his post-tramatic stress disorder was caused by abnormal working conditions); Dunlavey v. Economy Fire & Casualty Co., 526 N.W.2d 845 (Iowa 1995) (adopting an "unusual stress" standard; excellent discussion of cases); Bedini v. Frost, 165 Vt. 167, 678 A.2d 893 (1996) (stress caused by increased job responsibilities is not "unusual"; benefits denied).

The most liberal position is to award compensation to those disabled by the effects of ordinary occupational stress. E.g., Ann Marie Robinson's Case, 416 Mass. 454, 623 N.E.2d 478 (1993) (stress occasioned by reduction in workforce can support a disability claim under an "ordinary stress" standard); Hansen v. Von Duprin, Inc., 507 N.E.2d 573 (Ind.1987) (stress related disability caused by "horseplay" is compensable; proof of unusual stress is not required).

6. A significant minority of states deny benefits to workers who suffer a psychological disability caused by stress or nervous shock. E.g., Abernathy v. City of Albany, 269 Ga. 88, 495 S.E.2d 13 (1998) (park maintenance supervisor disabled by psychic trauma caused by having to retrieve caskets and cadavers lifted from a cemetery by a flood; mental-mental claims are not covered); Frantz v. Campbell County Memorial Hospital, 932 P.2d 750 (Wyo.1997) (worker disabled by protracted stress related to job security is not entitled to compensation; mental injuries are not compensable unless they are the result of physical injuries); Stratemeyer v. Lincoln County, 259 Mont. 147, 855 P.2d 506 (1993) (sheriff who suffered psychological disability after responding to a suicide and witnessing the aftermath is denied compensation; mental disability must be caused by a physical injury).

Sometimes even a sympathetic court finds its hands tied by restrictive statutes. In Wheeler v. Wyoming Workers' Safety and Compensation Division, 245 P.3d 811 (Wyo. 2010), a volunteer fireman developed post traumatic stress disorder (PTSD) and major depressive disorder (MDD) after seeing other firemen burned beyond recognition in fire occuring in an apartment in which his family resided. The Wyoming statute excluded from coverage any "mental injury unless it is caused by a compensable physical injury." Despite the uncontroverted expert testimony that PTSF and MDD involve physical changes to the brain, the court concluded that the legislature intended to exclude coverage for PTSD and MDD unless they were caused by some physical injury "outside the biological changes in the brain associated with mental disorders. While we respect that [medical experts] disagree the legislature's policy choice to disallow mental injuries, we cannot overlook the clear language of the statute." To the same effect, see Bentley v. Spartanburg County, 398 S.C. 418, 703 S.E.2d 296 (2012).

7. Increasingly, states are amending their workers' compensation statutes to explicitly address the compensability of psychological disabilities. Legislation of this type generally limits the circumstances where compensation can be awarded, often in response to a more liberal judicial decision. E.g., Alaska Stat. § 23.30.395.17 (adopting a "extraordinary and unusual" stress standard in mental-mental cases); Ark. Code Ann. § 11–9–113(a) (excluding coverage of mental injury unless diagnosed by a licensed psychiatrist or psychologist using criteria contained in the DMS); Fla. Stat. Ann. § 440.093 (2) (restricting coverage for mental-mental claims and imposing a clear and convincing burden of proof for physical-mental claims); Mont. Code Ann. § 39–71–119 (limiting coverage of mental disabilities to those caused by physical injury); W. Va. Code § 23–4–1f (limiting coverage of mental disability; "the purpose of this section is to clarify that so-called mental-mental claims are not compensable").

Legislation that went into effect after *Sparks* was decided limits coverage to mental injuries caused by "unexpected and extraordinary stress." Partin v. Merchants & Farmers Bank, 810 So.2d 1118 (La.2002). Would *Sparks* be decided differently under this standard? South Carolina limits coverage of stress-related claims to situations in which the "conditions of employment causing the stress . . . were extraordinary and unusual in comparison to the particular employment." S.C. Code § 42–1–160. In Bentley v. Spartanburg County, 398 S.C. 418, 703 S.E.2d 296 (2012) a deputy sheriff became disabled due to psychological symptoms after fatally shooting man at the scene of a neighborhood disturbance. The shooting was not deemed to be an "extraordinary and unusual" condition of employment as a deputy sheriff, so compensation was denied. While the Court explained that, in its view, the elimination of the "heightened requirement" for coverage of mental-mental claims would not lead to a flood of litigation, only the legislature can change the statutory standard.

Should such legislation apply retroactively? See Ann Marie Robinson's Case, 416 Mass. 454, 623 N.E.2d 478 (1993) (amendment increasing plaintiff's burden of proof in mental-mental cases does not apply to claims arising prior to the effective date of the legislation); Conley v. Workers' Compensation Division, 199 W.Va. 196, 483 S.E.2d 542 (1997) (amendments intended to exclude mental-mental claims from coverage are not retroactive).

Constitutional challenges to statutes that erect greater barriers to coverage for mental disabilities than for physical disabilities have been largely unsuccessful. Courts tend to find that the distinction between physical and mental injuries is rational given the greater uncertainty in verifying the genuineness and work-relatedness of mental injuries. E.g., Williams v. Department of Revenue, 895 P.2d 99 (Alaska 1995); Stratemeyer v. Lincoln County, 259 Mont. 147, 855 P.2d 506 (1993); Frantz v. Campbell County Memorial Hospital, 932 P.2d 750 (Wyo.1997).

8. A worker's predisposition to emotional or psychological disorders will not lessen the compensability of a mental injury if the evidence otherwise satisfies the standard for compensability. As in instances of preexisting physical weaknesses, the employer is said to take the employee as "he finds him." e.g., RAG (Cyprus) Emerald Resources LP v. Workers' Compensation Appeal Bd., 590 Pa. 413, 912 A.2d 1278 (2007) (Vietnam war veteran who suffered flashbacks and recurrence of Vietnam-related PTSD following work-related sexual harassment; benefits awarded); Gartrell v. Dept. of Correction, 259 Conn. 29, 787 A.2d 541 (2002) (compensation awarded when the claimant's pre-existing psychiatric condition was aggravated by work-related cardio-vascular disorder); Amoco Oil Co. v. Industrial Comm'n, 218 Ill.App.3d 737, 161 Ill.Dec. 397, 578 N.E.2d 1043 (1991) (affirming an award of benefits to a worker whose preexisting emotional instability was aggravated by compensable physical injury); Federal Mogul Corp. v. Campbell, 494 So.2d 443 (Ala. App. 1986) (awarding compensation to a borderline mentally retarded worker who suffered a mental breakdown following a serious fall). Cf. Bedini v. Frost, 165 Vt. 167, 678 A.2d 893 (1996) (reaffirming the principle that the employer takes his employees as he finds them, but upholding the denial of benefits because the Commissioner found no "unusual" stress); Shealy v. Aiken County, 341 S.C. 448, 535 S.E.2d 438 (2000) (same).

When the legal standard allows compensation for mental injures, the claim will be denied if the worker fails to convince the finder of fact that the mental disability was caused by the work environment. Sometimes a claimant's predisposition to mental illness may be relevant to the determination of causation. In Kuklok v. North Dakota Workers' Compensation Bureau, 492 N.W.2d 572 (N.D.1992), a worker with history of mental illness sought benefits for psychological disability allegedly related to compensable physical injury. The Bureau's denial of benefits was affirmed on the strength of expert testimony that the claimant's current psychological problems were not related to the compensable physical injuries. Cf., Branscum v. RNR Construction Co., 60 Ark.App. 116, 959 S.W.2d 429 (1998) (affirming the denial of benefits for post traumatic stress disorder following a 35 foot fall on strength of Commission's findings that diagnosis did not meet standards set forth in the DSM IV).

Of course, compensation will not be awarded to a claimant whose alleged traumatic neurosis is found to be nothing more than malingering. E.g., Sinegal v. Louisiana Blasters, Inc., 546 So.2d 308 (La.App.1989) (claimant alleged to be disabled by pain in the lower back was observed "moving freely" at a local night club and described by five physicians as exhibiting some kind of "inappropriate illness response," "malingering," or "exaggeration;" compensation denied).

9. Regardless of the controlling legal standard, the two most basic problems with cases like *Sparks* are determining the genuineness of the disability and its causal relationship with the employment. In this and most of the cases examined in this chapter, courts and administrative agencies are

invariably thrust into a classic battle of experts. How is the fact finder to resolve the conflict among expert witnesses? Consider the testimony in Ladner v. Higgins, 71 So.2d 242, 244 (La.App.1954). In response to the question "Is [it] your conclusion that this man is a malingerer?", the expert responded, "I wouldn't be testifying if I didn't think so, unless I was on the other side, then it would be a post traumatic condition."

10. What is the relationship between the psychological disability cases discussed in this section and the "accident v. disease" materials discussed in section 1 of this Chapter? The Supreme Court of New Jersey recently held that post traumatic stress disorder may be compensable as an "accident" if caused by a single event. The same condition should be evaluated as an "occupational disease" if caused by recurrent traumatic events. Brunell v. Wildwood Crest Police Dept., 176 N.J. 225, 822 A.2d 576 (2003).

11. Claims for "heart" and psychological disabilities are considered difficult because of the uncertainty of their underlying work relatedness. Other disabling conditions that present similar difficulties are sometimes addressed by specific statutory provisions. Several states have enacted statutes containing criteria for establishing the compensability of a hernia alleged to have arisen in the course of employment. The Wyoming statute is fairly representative. It provides:

> (c) If an employee suffers a hernia, he is entitled to compensation if he clearly proves that:
>
> (i) The hernia is of recent origin;
>
> (ii) Its appearance was accompanied by pain;
>
> (iii) It was immediately preceded by some accidental strain suffered in the course of employment; and
>
> (iv) It did not exist prior to the date of the alleged injury. Wyo.Stat. § 27–14–603.

See also, Ga.Code Ann. § 34–9–266; Mo.Ann.Stat. § 287.195; N.C.Gen.Stat. § 97–2(18). Under such statutes "the character and quantum of evidence necessary in hernia claims is perhaps somewhat stricter than is required in other claims" for compensation. Hagan v. Mayflower Transit Co., 483 S.W.2d 119 (Ky.1972). For a compilation of special hernia statutes see, 3 A. Larson & L. Larson, Larson's Workers' Compensation § 50.07(2013).

Another special problem area is occupational loss of hearing. There are divergent views whether hearing loss should be treated as an "accidental injury" or occupational disease. Compare, Peabody Galion Corp. v. Workman, 643 P.2d 312 (Okl.1982) (hearing loss is not an occupational disease, but is compensable as an accidental injury under the "repeated-impact" theory) with Clinchfield Coal Co. v. Barton, 6 Va.App. 576, 371 S.E.2d 39 (1988) (hearing loss compensable under the recently amended occupational disease statute). Many states have specific statutory provisions addressing occupational hearing loss. This legislation often establishes minimum levels of noise exposure necessary to support compensation. The threshold exposure is commonly expressed in terms of decibels and time. E.g., Ill.Ann.Stat. ch. 820.310/7(c); Wis.Stat.Ann. 102.555. These provisions are designed to ensure that the hearing loss is sufficiently work related to justify coverage under workers' compensation. See, 3 A. Larson & L. Larson, Larson's Workers' Compensation § 52.05(20013). In this respect, these hearing loss provisions are similar to minimum exposure requirements that sometime govern claims for silicosis related disabilities. See Manalapan Mining Co., Inc. v. Lunsford, 204 S.W.3d 601 (Ky. 2006) (statute of repose barred hearing loss claim); Hamilton v. Industrial Comm'n., 203 Ill.2d 250, 271 Ill.Dec. 645, 785 N.E.2d 839 (2003) (applying last injurious exposure rule to hearing loss claim).

6. EVIDENTIARY ISSUES

Throughout this Chapter, the causal relationship between work and disability has been the central contested issue. In order to prevail, the claimant must offer evidence that his back injury was caused by loading wood; or that he contracted serum hepatitis due to his occupational exposure to infected blood; or that her pulmonary impairment was caused by occupational exposure to cotton dust; or that her nervous breakdown was triggered by occupational stress; or that work exertion caused a heart attack. In each of these cases, the claimant offered evidence from expert witnesses regarding the causal connection between work and the contested accident or disease. The qualifications of such expert witnesses and the basis for their opinions has come under heightened scrutiny. Prior to the early 1990s, the primary test of the reliability of expert testimony was the so-called *Frye* test, named after Frye v. United States, 293 F. 1013 (App.D.C. 1923). Under *Frye*, expert testimony was admissible if it was "generally accepted" within the relevant scientific community. A significant shift occurred with the Supreme Court's decision in Daubert v. Merrell Dow Pharmaceuticals, Inc., 509 U.S. 579, 113 S.Ct. 2786, 125 L.Ed.2d 469 (1993). In *Daubert*, the Court held that under Federal Rules of Evidence, Rule 702, the trial judge had to independently assess a variety of factors to determine whether expert testimony was both reliable and relevant. These factors included such things as testing, peer review, error rates, as well as the acceptability within the relevant scientific community. The upshot of *Daubert* was to thrust the trial judge into the role of "gatekeeper" to make sure the jury was not exposed to "junk science." The following case and notes explore the extent to which this development has spilled over into the workers' compensation system.

CITY OF OWENSBORO V. ADAMS

Supreme Court of Kentucky, 2004.
136 S.W.3d 446.

OPINION OF THE COURT BY JUSTICE COOPER

Upon reopening a previously settled award in this workers' compensation case, the administrative law judge (ALJ) found that Gary Dewayne Adams was totally disabled as a result of a work-related injury, and awarded benefits. Both the Workers' Compensation Board and the Court of Appeals affirmed. The primary issue on appeal is not the extent and duration of Adams's disability, but its cause. The employer asserts here as it did below that the ALJ based his decision that Adams's disability was work-related on expert medical evidence that was unreliable and thus inadmissible under *KRE 702*, and the principles enunciated in *Daubert v. Merrell Dow Pharmaceuticals, Inc.*, 509 U.S. 579 (1993). We affirm.

I. FACTS.

On May 15, 1987, Adams, then age twenty-one, and a co-worker were cleaning a section of sewer line for their employer, the City of Owensboro. Adams's co-worker descended into the manhole and almost immediately collapsed, overcome by methane gas. After radioing for help, Adams attempted a rescue but was also overcome by the gas and fell, striking his head. Rescuers eventually arrived and began pumping oxygen into the manhole. Although Adams later regained consciousness and was taken to safety, his co-worker died from methane inhalation. At the time of his initial application for benefits, Adams had returned to work but still suffered from a sore neck and intermittent pain above his right eye and along the right side of his face. In July 1989, he settled his claim for $6,125.00, representing a lump sum payment for a 9.5% occupational disability.

Although Adams's neck pain abated, episodes of facial pain persisted. He testified upon reopening that he first experienced intermittent episodes of sharp pain that began over his right eye and spread to his face. In 1994, the episodes became more frequent and severe, and he was diagnosed with bilateral trigeminal neuralgia. Eventually, even morphine failed to control it. He underwent fourteen facial surgeries in an attempt to treat the condition but had obtained only temporary relief. Since the May 17, 1987, injury, he had also been treated for meningitis, an abscessed tooth, and shingles. He quit working in September 2000 due to the severity of his facial symptoms. He filed his motion to reopen on December 12, 2000.

II. MEDICAL EVIDENCE.

The record contains medical reports and records prepared by numerous physicians, only a few of whom rendered opinions as to the causation of Adams's bilateral trigeminal neuralgia. The only medical expert who actually testified was Dr. Harry R. van Loveren, a neurosurgeon affiliated with the Mayfield Clinic and the University of Cincinnati. Dr. van Loveren, who began treating Adams in 1994 and was the first physician to diagnose his condition as trigeminal neuralgia, testified that he had treated approximately 1,000 trigeminal neuralgia patients. According to Dr. van Loveren, the ailment is a very rare and specific condition that is typically sudden in onset. It affects the areas of the face controlled by the trigeminal nerve and its three branches, and is characterized by intermittent episodes of very sharp facial pain, followed by remissions and exacerbations. It is also typically undetectable by X-ray and laboratory studies. The immediate cause of the condition is a deterioration of the myelin sheath that encases the trigeminal nerve, which can result from a number of factors, including abnormal blood vessel growth around a nerve, a tumor, multiple sclerosis, trauma, and exposure to toxic chemicals. Dr. van Loveren ultimately opined that Adams's condition was caused by his 1987 exposure to toxic methane gas.

* * *

[The court's discussion of the testimony of four other expert witnesses is omitted. In short, these witnesses concluded that either the claimant's condition was most likely caused by a relapse of multiple sclerosis or that there was insufficient evidence to link his condition to the 1987 incident.]

Dr. van Loveren testified that the onset of Adams's condition was gradual rather than dramatic. When he failed to respond typically to treatment and when the condition became bilateral, also atypical, Dr. van Loveren attempted to determine causation by a process of elimination. The surgeries revealed no tumor or blood vessel abnormality, and seven years of repeated radiographic studies and spinal fluid analyses had failed to confirm the presence of multiple sclerosis. Although acknowledging that multiple sclerosis was the only well-documented cause of trigeminal nerve dysfunction, Dr. van Loveren stated that the repeated diagnostic studies and the lack of any neurological deficits outside the facial area led him to conclude that Adams did not suffer from multiple sclerosis. According to Dr. van Loveren, approximately one in 4,000 persons suffers from trigeminal neuralgia but only approximately one person in 400,000 suffers from the bilateral form; and in perhaps only four or five cases per year is the onset gradual. He admitted that he had seen only one other such case, and there, the patient was diagnosed with multiple sclerosis. He acknowledged that the medical literature contained no documented case associating a specific toxin with trigeminal neuralgia but pointed out that exposure to toxins was a known cause of nerve damage. Convinced that the claimant did not suffer from multiple sclerosis or any of the other known causes of trigeminal neuralgia, and emphasizing that the symptoms began within a year of Adams's exposure to toxic methane gas, Dr. van Loveren was steadfast in his opinion that the exposure caused Adams's condition.

* * *

The ALJ relied almost entirely on Dr. van Loveren's opinion in determining that Adams's 1987 work-related exposure to sewer gas was the cause of his disability. Appellant asserts that the ALJ erred in relying on Dr. van Loveren's opinion, arguing that it did not satisfy the Daubert test for reliability with respect to the admissibility of scientific, technical or other specialized knowledge. We disagree.

III. *DAUBERT.*

We start with the proposition that the principles established in *Daubert, supra*, apply to the consideration of Dr. van Loveren's opinion as to causation in this case. The Kentucky Rules of Evidence govern workers' compensation proceedings, 803 KAR 25:010E § 14, and *Daubert* governs the admissibility of expert testimony under KRE 702. Virtually every state that applies the rules of evidence to workers' compensation proceedings holds that either *Daubert* or *Frye v. United States*, 293 F. 1013 (D.C. Cir. 1923), whichever it has adopted, governs the admissibility of expert opinion testimony in workers' compensation proceedings.

The ALJ's function as both "gatekeeper" and fact-finder is irrelevant to this inquiry, and does not preclude the application of *Daubert* to workers' compensation proceedings. It is uniformly held that *Daubert* applies to bench trials as well as jury trials.

* * *

Like a trial judge in a bench trial, an ALJ in a workers' compensation case is no more authorized to consider inadmissible evidence than is a jury.

The difference between the application of *Daubert* in a jury trial and its application in a bench trial or a workers' compensation proceeding is only procedural. In a jury trial, a *Daubert* hearing, is usually required "to protect juries from being bamboozled by technical evidence of dubious merit." . . . However, in a bench trial, the trial court, without a *Daubert* hearing, will often admit the evidence first and then disregard it upon deciding that it is unreliable.

"The trial court's broad latitude to make the reliability determination does *not* include the discretion to abdicate completely its responsibility to do so." . . . A trial court must, at least, state on the record its *Daubert* conclusion with respect to reliability. In doing so, however, the court need not recite any of the *Daubert* factors, so long as the record is clear that the court effectively conducted a *Daubert* inquiry.

* * *

Daubert does not require exclusion of Dr. van Loveren's opinion as to causation in the case *sub judice*. The fact that other experts disagree with his opinion is not conclusive. *Daubert* specifically held that the "general acceptance" test enunciated in *Frye v. United States*, had been superseded by *FRE 702*. A theory's general acceptance in the relevant scientific community is now but one factor to be considered. Furthermore, even though *Daubert* suggests other relevant factors, *i.e.*, whether the theory has been tested, whether it has been subjected to peer review, and the known or potential rate of error "the inquiry envisioned by *Rule 702* is, we emphasize, a flexible one."

As such, the fact that this is the first known case where trigeminal neuralgia was deemed caused by exposure to toxic gas does not render Dr. van Loveren's opinion *per se* inadmissible. The issue is not whether anyone else has ever espoused Dr. van Loveren's opinion that trigeminal neuralgia can be caused by exposure to toxic gas, but whether his opinion was reached by a valid scientific method or process, according it a sufficient measure of scientific validity, or whether it is the product of only subjective belief or unsupported speculation, *i.e.*, "junk science."

Because Dr. van Loveren used sound scientific methodology in reaching his conclusions, we find that the ALJ correctly exercised his discretion in considering them. While the ALJ did not hold a "*Daubert* hearing" (none was requested), it is clear that he properly conducted the required *Daubert* analysis. Acknowledging *Daubert* and its application to workers' compensation proceedings, the ALJ wrote:

> In this instance, the vitae of Dr. Van Loveren [sic] was introduced through his testimony. His qualification leaves no doubt that he is an experienced and recognized expert in the treatment of trigeminal neuralgia. Additionally, he testified that he had treated over 1000 cases in his career. He further explained that the situation presented by Mr. Adams was indeed unique. By reviewing diagnostic testing, he eliminated other potential causes, including the most common, multiple sclerosis, as a cause of Mr. Adams' condition. He further testified that Mr. Adams was exposed to a toxic substance, methane, which was also toxic to nerves. Having eliminated other potential causes of the condition and noting the onset of the preliminary stages of the condition following the 1987 injury and exposure, Dr. Van Loveren [sic] concluded that it was a probable cause of the

> Plaintiffs condition. *I am persuaded by his exoertise* [sic] *and analysis, in conjunction with the scientific testing done to eliminate other potential causes*, that the exposure to methane in 1987 was the cause of the Plaintiff's trigeminal neuralgia *and that Dr. Van Loveren's [sic] opinion comports with the requirements of KRE 702.*

(Emphasis added.)

Accordingly, we affirm.

NOTES

1. As explained in Chapter 10, Section 5(d), disputed workers' compensation hearings are often governed by the same rules of evidence as would apply in civil bench trials. *City of Owensboro* illustrates that this principle may lead to the application of the *Daubert* standards to contested workers' compensation claims. However, it is also common for states to relax some rules of evidence in the workers' compensation setting to facilitate the admission of routine medical evidence. For example, medical records and physician statements are often admissible without strict compliance with traditional evidentiary rules regarding hearsay. The policies underlying *Daubert* and the policies underlying the relaxation of some traditional rules of evidence lie in tension with one another. The policy underlying *Daubert* is to require a more rigorous screening of expert testimony to protect against the fact finder being "bamboozled" by "junk science." The policy underlying the relaxing of some rules of evidence is to allow workers' compensation claims to be resolved in an expeditious and less costly manner. *City of Owensboro* illustrates one court's effort to balance these competing policy objectives. Does *City of Owensboro* strike the right balance?

2. A number of states apply *Daubert* to workers' compensation claims. E.g., Canavan's Case, 432 Mass. 304, 733 N.E.2d 1042 (2000); Scruggs v. Edwards, 154 P.3d 1257 (Okla. 2007); Wells v. Howe Heating & Plumbing, Inc., 677 N.W.2d 586 (S.D. 2004); Standard Distributing Inc. v. Hall, 897 A.2d 155 (Del. Supr. 2006); Arceneaux v. The Shaw Group, Inc., 103 So.3d 1086 (La.App. 2012). An important factor in each of these cases is that the *Daubert* standards had been incorporated into the state's rules of evidence either by statute or judicial decision.

In civil trials, the question of whether the contested scientific evidence meets the *Daubert* test (and, hence, is admissible) is determined in an independent pre-trial hearing. Causation, of course, is an indispensable element of most civil claims. If the scientific evidence of causation is excluded under *Daubert*, the plaintiff's claim is often summarily disposed without the necessity of a trial. In the workers' compensation setting, the administrative law judge serves as both the gatekeeper and the finder of fact. This confluence of functions lessens the danger of the fact finder being "bamboozled" by unreliable evidence. For this reason, the court in *City of*

Owensboro allowed the ALJ to dispense with a separate *Daubert* hearing. The ALJ can hear the contested evidence at the full hearing on the merits and later decide whether the evidence is reliable and relevant. This practice provides for some flexibility and eliminates the time and expense of conducting a separate pre-hearing hearing. However, if the contested evidence is deemed admissible, the order issued by the ALJ must demonstrate that he or she did evaluate the evidence under the *Daubert* standards. E.g., Corkern v. T.K. Valve & Manufacturing Inc., 934 So.2d 102 (La. App. 2006) (reversing the award of benefits when the ALJ's order did not demonstrate that he evaluated the admissibility of the contested evidence under the *Daubert* standards).

Appellate review of the decision to admit or exclude evidence is generally governed by the abuse of discretion standard. While this standard gives considerable deference to the decision of the ALJ, that deference is not unlimited. E.g., Canavan's Case, 432 Mass. 304, 733 N.E.2d 1042 (2000) (agency abused its discretion in admitting claimant's evidence that his disability was caused by occupational exposure to certain chemicals (multiple chemical sensitivities)); Valentine v. Conrad, 110 Ohio St.3d 42, 850 N.E.2d 683 (2006) (abuse of discretion found in admitting evidence that brain cancer was caused by occupational exposure to chemicals).

3. Should the *Daubert* standards apply to the opinions of treating physicians? In Canavan's Case, 432 Mass. 304, 733 N.E.2d 1042 (2000), the court held it was an abuse of discretion to admit the testimony of the claimant's treating physician regarding the diagnosis and cause of multiple chemical sensitivities. The physician's opinions were based on the claimant's medical history, the physician's clinical observations, and the doctor's review of the medical literature. In the court's view, this did not adequately demonstrate that the testimony was scientifically reliable. If the treating physician's opinions are not admissible, who else could provide the essential testimony? What is likely impact of such a ruling on the cost of processing claims? For a different view see Armstrong v. City of Wichita, 21 Kan.App.2d 750, 907 P.2d 923 (1995) (treating physician opinions are always admissible). Cf., Sanderson Farms, Inc. v. Johnson, 68 So.3d 67 (Miss. App. 2010) (Workers' Compensation Commission is not required to strictly adhere to *Daubert* standards when evaluating the admissibility of the testimony of the claimant's treating physician).

The application of the *Daubert* standards may also lead to the exclusion of the employer's expert's testimony. In Wells v. Howe Heating & Plumbing, Inc., 677 N.W.2d 586 (S.D. 2004) the employer offered the testimony of his service manager that the cause of an electrical fire was the claimant's failure to use a safety device (and hence the claim would be denied under the state's wilful misconduct provision). The court held that this testimony was properly excluded because the employer failed to establish that it was based on sound scientific methodology under *Daubert*.

4. A number of other courts have held that the *Daubert* standards do not apply to workers' compensation claims. Some of these opinions rest on the fact that the state had not adopted the *Daubert* standards as part of their general rules of evidence. E.g., United States Sugar Corp. v. Henson, 787 So.2d 3 (Fla. 2000); Veatch v. American Tool, 267 Neb. 711, 676 N.W.2d 730 (2004); Lane v. American National Can Co., 181 N.C.App. 527, 640 S.E.2d 732 (2007); Armstrong v. City of Wichita, 21 Kan.App.2d 750, 907 P.2d 923 (1995).

A few courts have ruled that the *Daubert* standards should not apply in workers' compensation cases despite the fact that the state has adopted *Daubert* for civil cases generally. E.g., Banks v. IMC Kalium Carlsbad Potash Co., 134 N.M. 421, 77 P.3d 1014 (2003); Mulroy v. Becton Dickenson Co., 48 Conn.App. 774, 712 A.2d 436 (1998). Two points are central to the reasoning of these decisions. First, "[a] determination of whether the health care provider's testimony meets [*Daubert*] would be overly burdensome for workers as well as the process the Legislature created and is inconsistent with the Legislature's intent." Banks v. IMC Kalium Carlsbad Potash Co., 77 P.3d at 1021. Second, "rigorous exclusionary rules for the administration of evidence make little sense in hearings before an administrative agency where the [ALJ] acts as both judge and factfinder. When the judge is also the factfinder, he [or she] is equally exposed to evidence whether he [or she] admits it or excludes it." Banks v. IMC Kalium Carlsbad Potash Co., 77 P.3d at 1022 quoting United States Steel Mining Co. v. Dir., Office of Workers' Comp. Programs, 187 F.3d 384, 388 (4th Cir. 1999).

CHAPTER 7

EFFECT OF CAUSES AND CONDITIONS INDEPENDENT OF THE WORK RELATION

■ ■ ■

1. INTRODUCTION TO THIS CHAPTER

This chapter considers the extent to which compensation is or should be awarded for injuries enhanced by the employee's preexisting condition and injuries brought about by some incident or force which comes into operation after the original compensable accident has been sustained. The employee who has suffered a work injury that is covered by the workers' compensation law may have the injury aggravated or may suffer a new injury as a result in part of antecedent or subsequent conditions or events for which the employer is not responsible but which bring about an increase or prolongation of disability or even cause death. For example, the original injury may become infected and the infection may lead to an amputation, or some third party may treat the injury negligently and make the condition worse, or a weakened bodily member may cause a fall, or the employee's mind may give way leading to self-inflicted injury or suicide. Should compensation be awarded for such additional disability or death?

The question is reminiscent of the problem of "proximate cause" or "legal cause" in tort law, and the workers' compensation tribunals quite often employ terminology such as "proximate cause," "direct or natural cause," "intervening cause," or "superseding cause" in disposing of the cases in this category. The reader should recognize that, as in the common law area of proximate cause, the issues could be resolved by resorting to fundamental policy considerations underlying compensation law in order to enlighten the decision as to how far and to what kinds of risks compensation liability ought to extend.

Courts and administrators sometimes fail to differentiate between cases presenting the question of whether or not the injury "arose out of the employment" and those presenting the issue considered in this chapter. An example may be found in the cases of Saenger v. Locke, 220 N.Y. 556, 116 N.E. 367 (1917) (employee fainted following dispute with her superior and was injured when a well-meaning co-worker mistakenly threw ammonia in her face, compensation denied) and Fishman v. S.W. Layton, Inc., 284 App.Div. 165, 130 N.Y.S.2d 656 (1954) (employee became drowsy from working in dark place, co-worker advised her to take mixture of Coca-Cola and benzedrine, resulting in rupture of blood vessels; held compensable). Neither of the foregoing cases actually involved aggravation of a previous work-connected injury. By contrast, a true post-accident risk situation is found in Mackin & Assoc. v. Harris, 342 Md. 1, 672 A.2d 1110 (1996) (former employee fell on ice while traveling to physical therapist's office for treatment of a prior compensable injury; held compensation denied). A clear understanding of the basic issue requires differentiation between the two types of cases.

In addition, no subsequent injury or exacerbation is properly compensable if the claimant fails to establish a cause-in-fact relationship between the initial work injury and the antecedent condition or the second injury. See, e.g., Dutton v. Industrial Commission of Arizona, 140 Ariz. 448, 682 P.2d 453 (1984); Schulle v. Texas Employers' Insurance Association, 787 S.W.2d 608 (Tex.App.1990). If the cause-in-fact relationship exists, the question becomes how and where to establish the outer limits of workers' compensation coverage.

2. RESULTS OF PRE-EXISTING WEAKNESS OR DISEASE

BRAEWOOD CONVALESCENT HOSPITAL V. WORKERS' COMPENSATION APPEALS BOARD

Supreme Court of California, 1983.
34 Cal.3d 159, 193 Cal.Rptr. 157, 666 P.2d 14.

RICHARDSON, JUSTICE.

Braewood Convalescent Hospital and its workers' compensation carrier, Cypress Insurance Company (hereinafter collectively referred to as employer), seek annulment of a decision of the Workers' Compensation Appeals Board (WCAB) awarding Eugene Bolton (applicant) compensation for (1) the cost of a self-procured, out-of-state weight reduction program (2) temporary disability during his participation in that program and (3) expenses for his future participation therein. We conclude that the WCAB acted within its authority in making the challenged awards and will affirm its decision.

Statement of the Case

On January 6, 1978, applicant, while employed as a cook for employer, slipped and sustained injuries to his back and right elbow. At that time applicant, who had been chronically overweight since childhood, weighed approximately 422 pounds. Employer provided temporary disability benefits while applicant undertook treatment for his back injury.

Dr. Wells, applicant's personal treating physician, and two of employer's physicians joined in recommending that applicant lose weight in order to facilitate his recovery from his injuries. Applicant unsuccessfully had undertaken numerous weight reduction programs throughout his life, and at the time of the accident, was participating in a weight loss program; he claimed, however, not improbably, that this latest program "had not been too successful." None of the physicians recommended a specific weight reduction program, nor had the employer offered to pay for any such program. Upon the recommendation of a close friend, who had participated successfully in a regimen of the Duke University Medical Center obesity clinic in Durham, North Carolina (hereinafter Clinic), applicant enrolled in the Clinic in February 1979. Applicant described the Clinic, which provides closely supervised, live-in treatment, as the "number one obesity clinic in the world." With the consent and support of Dr. Wells, applicant participated in the Clinic until November 1979. During that period he lost approximately 175 pounds. Dr. Wells, in a letter dated June 29, 1979, reiterated that it is "imperative [applicant] lose weight to obtain relief from his industrial injury . . . [and that Dr. Wells] is in total agreement with the program and believes it is an integral part of his treatment."

By November 1979, applicant could no longer afford to continue with the Clinic. He returned to California and commenced work as a part-time security guard, continuing with a modified version of the Clinic program under local medical supervision. During the two month period from November 10, 1979, to January 8, 1980, he regained 16 pounds.

Applicant filed a claim for reimbursement of his Clinic's expenses, including requests for medical, lodging, special diet and transportation costs. The workers' compensation judge (WCJ) made awards, inter alia, for applicant's temporary disability prior to his enrollment in the Clinic, for the cost of the Clinic and for future participation therein, observing that reimbursement for the Clinic costs was justified by the employer's failure to provide applicant with any alternative weight reduction program.

Employer sought reconsideration, challenging the award for past and future self-procured medical treatment. On its own motion, the WCAB granted reconsideration of the WCJ's failure to award temporary disability benefits during the time of applicant's treatment at the Clinic. (See Lab.Code § 5906; all further statutory references are to this code.) After reconsideration, the WCAB affirmed the WCJ's award for self-procured past and future medical treatment and extended the temporary disability award to include the period of treatment outside California.

On appeal employer contends that the WCAB erred in awarding (1) reimbursement for the expenses of any self-procured weight reduction program (2) temporary disability for the time that applicant spent in the Clinic, and (3) compensation for future medical treatment in the form of a continuing weight reduction program.

* * *

We turn to the merits: * * *

1. Reimbursement for Self-procured Treatment

* * *

It is a long accepted workers' compensation rule that the employer takes the employee as he finds him. (Lamb v. Workmen's Comp. Appeals Bd. (1974) 11 Cal.3d 274, 282, 113 Cal.Rptr. 162, 520 P.2d 978; Ballard v. Workmen's Comp.App.Bd. (1971) 3 Cal.3d 832, 837, 92 Cal.Rptr. 1, 478 P.2d 937.) Thus, an employee who suffers from a pre-existing condition and is thereafter disabled by an industrial injury is entitled to compensation and reimbursement of medical expense, even though a healthy person would not have been injured by the event (Ibid.) This is so even though the specific treatment is for a nonindustrial condition which must be treated in order to cure or relieve the effects of the industrial injury. (Granado v. Workmen's Comp. App. Bd. (1968) 69 Cal.2d 399, 405B406, 71 Cal.Rptr. 678, 445 P.2d 294; Dorman v. Workers' Comp. Appeals Bd. (1978) 78 Cal.App.3d 1009, 1020, 144 Cal.Rptr. 573; McGlinn v. Workers' Comp. Appeals Bd. (1977) 68 Cal.App.3d 527, 535, 137 Cal.Rptr. 326; 2 Hanna, Cal.Law of Employee Injuries and Workmen's Compensation, § 16.03[1], [2].) While such expenses, in order to be compensable, must be reasonably necessary to cure or relieve the effects of an industrial injury, the statutes do not require any finding of disability, temporary or permanent, as a condition to such recovery. (Cedillo v. Workmen's Comp. Appeals Bd. (1971) 5 Cal.3d 450, 454, 96 Cal.Rptr. 471, 487 P.2d 1039.) Here, applicant was injured on the job and employer was fully aware of the injury. Applicant was directed by three physicians, including two of employer's physicians, to lose weight in order to obtain relief from, and to aid in the cure of, his industrial injury. He was advised to participate in a careful program of weight reduction. All three physicians acknowledged that applicant had been extremely overweight all his life, had unsuccessfully participated in many weight loss programs and was, at that time, involved in such a program with only limited success. At no time did any of the physicians recommend a specific weight reduction program, nor did the employer ever offer to reimburse applicant for the expenses incurred in such program. Thus, while employer initially had the right to direct applicant to a specific program, that right was lost as a result of employer's failure to act by identifying and offering such an alternative program. At that point applicant acquired the right to choose for himself which program he reasonably might undertake. The right to appropriate reimbursement was a part and parcel of the proper exercise of applicant's right to choose.

* * *

Consistent with section 4600 applicant presented evidence which demonstrated that his cost of attending the Clinic itemizing his expenses for medical treatment, food, shelter and transportation, was in the aggregate sum of $7,725.91 for 10 months' treatment. Employer, in response presented neither evidence that the cost of the Clinic was unreasonable nor testimony as to the reasonable cost for such treatment. Thus, no comparative costs were introduced and the board was justified in relying entirely on the testimony and documentation presented by applicant. * * *

While section 4600 requires that the applicant's medical treatment choice be located within a reasonable geographic area, as defined by the Administrative Code, in the present case employer has produced no comparative evidence contradicting applicant's claim that the Clinic's location is geographically reasonable in light of his needs. Applicant testified that he had a life-long obesity problem which he had been unsuccessful in treating with traditional weight loss methods. He further testified that to his knowledge, the Clinic was a unique facility. The record establishes that, in fact, the Clinic achieved remarkable results in his case.

We have consistently held that the Workers' Compensation Act is to be construed liberally for the purpose of extending its benefits for the protection of persons injured in the course of their employment (McCoy, supra, 64 Cal.2d at p. 86, 48 Cal.Rptr. 858, 410 P.2d 362). Because applicant's evidence has not been impeached, we conclude that the WCAB's award for reimbursement of Clinic expenses is based upon substantial evidence and, therefore, was proper.

2. Temporary Disability During Participation in the Program

Employer urges that applicant is not entitled to an award of temporary disability for the period during which he participated in the program because such participation was not reasonably necessary to facilitate applicant's recovery. An employer is under a statutorily imposed duty to pay temporary disability compensation for the period during which an injured employee who, while unable to work, is undergoing medical diagnostic procedure and treatment for an industrial injury. (§ 4600; Granado, supra, 69 Cal.2d at p. 403, 71 Cal.Rptr. 678, 445 P.2d 294.) The primary purpose of a temporary disability award being to compensate for wage loss (ibid.; Allied Compensation Ins. Co. v. Industrial Acc. Com. (1963) 211 Cal.App.2d 821, 831, 27 Cal.Rptr. 918) that purpose was served by the award here. Employer presented no evidence demonstrating that applicant should not be considered to be temporarily disabled during his participation in the Clinic. On the other hand, applicant did present evidence demonstrating that he was unable to work while being treated at the Clinic. He also submitted a letter from Dr. Wells, dated December 13, 1979, commenting on his "remarkable progress," but noting that applicant still was experiencing limited motion of the lumbosacral spine, concluding that he should be considered temporarily disabled until the completion of the weight reduction program. While this letter reflects the conclusion of only one physician, it is well established that the relevant and considered opinion of one physician may constitute substantial evidence in support of a factual determination of the WCAB. [citing cases] We uphold WCAB's award of temporary disability.

3. Future Medical Treatment

We are also unable to accept employer's final contention that applicant is not entitled to future medical treatment because his industrial injury has become permanent and also because his weight problem is incurable. Employer essentially argues that the purpose of section 4600 is to provide benefits until the employee's ailment is cured, and that if such ailment is not curable, then the disability should be deemed permanent and medical treatment benefits should cease.

Employer, however, overlooks the wording of section 600, which authorizes treatment required to "cure or relieve from the effects of the injury. . . ." (see Fidelity etc. Co. v. Dept. of Indus. Relations (1929) 207 Cal. 144, 150, 277 P. 492.) Applicant presented the recommendations from both Dr. Wells and Dr. Compton that he continue losing weight in order to relieve him from the effects of the industrial injury. Such evidence is sufficient to support the board's award of future medical treatment. (LeVesque, supra, 1 Cal.3d at p. 639, 83 Cal.Rptr. 208, 463 P.2d 432.) The present treatment aimed at affording applicant relief from the effects of an industrial injury represents a compensable expense under Section 4600.

On the evidentiary record before us, we affirm the WCAB's award in its entirety.

BIRD, C.J., MOSK, BROUSSARD, REYNOSO, GRODIN and RICKLES, JJ., concur.

NOTES

1. Other cases involving pre-existing obesity have reached results similar to *Braewood.* See, e.g., Van Blokland v. Oregon Health Sciences University, 87 Or.App. 694, 743 P.2d 1136 (1987) (claimant 5′6″ tall weighed 234–300 pounds; following knee injuries, doctor advised weight loss; employer offered to pay for Weight Watchers program; when that failed,

doctor recommended another program; court approved because treatment of preexisting obesity necessary to treat compensable knee injury); Mellon Sec. & Sound v. Custer, 687 So.2d 1372 (Fla.App.1 Dist.1997) (employer held responsible for treatment of claimant's pre-existing obesity and hypertension because this was medically necessary to the treatment of the compensable injuries to back and neck); Saif Corp. v. Sprague, 345 Or. 661, 217 P.3d 644 (2009) (claimant weighed 225 pounds at time of knee injury in 1976; in 2001, when claimant weighed 350 pounds he had gastric bypass surgery to treat obesity; court held employer responsible for the gastric surgery because that was necessary to knee replacement surgery even though compensable knee injury had not contributed to obesity); Boston's Gourmet Pizza v. Childers, 910 N.E.2d 809 (Ind.App. 2009) (employer liable for lap band surgery designed to help claimant lose weight prior to back fusion surgery for work related injury); Amerisure Ins. Co. v. Jones, ___ So.3d ___, 2013 WL 7117395 (La. App. 1 Cir. 2013) (claimant whose weight fluctuated at or over 600 pounds injured back while lifting pallets; he requested and Board agreed to a prescription for Weight Watchers weight reduction program). An easier case for compensation arises when the weight gain is attributed to the sedentary lifestyle necessitated by the work related injury. See, e.g., Krier v. John Morrell & Co., 473 N.W.2d 496 (S.D.1991) (employee weighed 195 pounds at time of injury to knee; after injury, employee forced to become more sedentary and weight went to 260 pounds; doctor ordered Opti–Fast weight loss program; held employer responsible for $1,873 cost of weight reduction program); Matter of Laezzo v. N.Y. State Thruway Auth., 71 A.D. 3d 1252, 896 N.Y.S. 2d 257 (2010) (claimant gained a substantial amount of weight due to sedentary lifestyle imposed by his compensable injuries; employer held responsible for cost of gastric by-pass surgery).

2. The central problem in *Braewood* and the cases cited in note 1 is, of course, related to the claimant's pre-existing obesity. Do you see any problem in adding the costs associated with treatment of non-work related obesity to the costs already borne by the workers' compensation system? As you think about this question, keep the following points in mind. There is continuing evidence that Americans are getting heavier. In 2003, the Federal Aviation Administration adjusted upward by 10 pounds its estimated weight for air passengers, a figure which is used to determine whether a plane is overloaded. FAA Estimates Fatten People, Luggage, The Atlanta Journal and Constitution, at page A3, May 13, 2003. Reuters reported in 2012 that hospitals are removing wall toilets and replacing them with floor models to better support obese patients and that the Federal Transit Administration wants buses to be tested for the effect of heavier riders on steering and braking. The same article estimated that cars are burning nearly a billion more gallons of gasoline a year than would be the case if passengers weighed what they did in 1960. http://www.reuters.com/article/2012/04/30/obesity-idUSL2E8FO3MV201204 30; (last visited October 31, 2013). In 2012, the National Centers for Health Statistics of the U. S. Centers for Disease Control reported that a survey conducted for the years 2009–2010 indicated that an estimated 69.2% of the U.S. population was either overweight (33.3%)

or obese (35.9%). See http://www.cdc.gov/nchs/fastats/overwt.htm (last visited October 31, 2013).

The classification of obesity as a serious disease is well supported in the professional literature. The disease meets all of the accepted criteria which define a chronic illness (1. gradual, not acute, onset; 2. long duration with frequent recurrence; 3. definite morbid process which affects the entire body; and 4. identifiable pathology and prognosis). Sachiko St. Jeor, New Trends in Weight Management, 97 Journal of the American Dietetic Assoc. 1096 (1997). One study reported that nationally obesity costs $190.2 billion a year in additional medical spending. Cawley J, Meyerhofer C. The Medical Care Costs of Obesity: an instrumental variables approach, 31 Journal of Health Economics 219–230 (2012). And, while estimates have varied widely, the U.S. Surgeon General reported in 2013 that obesity (defined as a BMI greater than 30) may be responsible annually for about 300,000 deaths and that obese individuals have a 50–100% increased risk of premature death. http://www.surgeongeneral.gov/library/calls/obesity/fact_consequences.html (last visited October 31, 2013).

Obesity is a complex phenomenon which has its roots in biological, behavioral, and environmental components. A 2007 study, published in the International Journal of Bioinformatics Research and Applications, considered the genetics of the modern Pima Indian. That study points to new evidence that genetics plays a key role in obesity. http://www.sciencedaily.com/releases/2007/10/071016074958.htm (last visited October 31, 2013). So persistent is the problem that even treatment modalities which are targeted directly at the sources of obesity have extremely high recidivism rates. The majority of people who participate in lifestyle modification programs regain all of the weight lost within three to five years. Most pharmacotherapy patients return to their original weight within one year of completing their course of medication. Gary Egger, et.al. An Ecological Approach to the Obesity Pandemic, 315 British Medical Journal 477 (1997). And while gastric surgery has demonstrated significant efficacy, access to that approach will usually be limited to individuals at the very highest risk and those who can afford the procedure. It is also a procedure accompanied by potential adverse effects. See Walls H, Peeters A, Proietto J, McNeil J., Public Health Campaigns and Obesity—A Critique, 11 BMC Public Health 136 (2011).

The following notes outline the typical judicial analysis of the relationship between pre-existing conditions and work related injuries. Consider the decision in *Braewood* against this backdrop. Is there something inherent in the condition of obesity which would call for courts to approach it differently than they do other types of pre-existing diseases?

3. The general principle of compensation law that the employer "takes the employee as he finds the employee," i.e., with the employee's weaknesses, predispositions and personal susceptibilities is well established. See, e.g., Colonial Ins. Co. v. Industrial Accident Comm., 29 Cal.2d 79, 172 P.2d 884, 887 (1946); Patterson v. Clarke County Motors, Inc., 551 So.2d 412

(Ala.Civ.App.1989); Swartz v. Ill. Indus. Com'n, 359 Ill.App.3d 1083, 297 Ill.Dec. 486, 837 N.E.2d 937 (2005) ("A claimant with a pre-existing condition that makes him more vulnerable to injury may obtain compensation under the Act so long as employment was a causative factor of his accidental injury"); Harris v. Peach County Board of Commissioners, 296 Ga. App. 225, 674 S.E.2d 36 (2009) (claimant weighed a little less than 300 pounds; bending over to pick up an object, she injured her knee; court held fact that obesity helped produce injury is irrelevant because an employee need not be in perfect health or free from disease; the "employer takes the employee as it finds him...."); and Judd v. State of Wyoming, 2010 Wyo. 85, 233 P.2d 956 (2010) (claimant suffering from preexisting arthritis and obesity injured knee necessitating knee replacement surgery; held surgery compensable). This is acknowledged not only in those cases in which the pre-existing condition makes the employee peculiarly susceptible to injury, such as in the *Harris* case, supra, and in cases involving idiopathic falls discussed in the *Fetzer* and *Milledge* cases in Chapter 5, *supra*, but also in instances where the employee, having sustained a compensable injury that was not due to any special personal condition or weakness, suffers disabling consequences that are greater or more extensive than would have been suffered normally by a person who did not labor under the pre-existing weakness or peculiarity. Workers in this category are at abnormally high risk of disability from the accident. See, e.g., Sisbro, Inc. v. Industrial Com'n, 207 Ill.2d 193, 278 Ill.Dec. 70, 797 N.E.2d 665 (2003) (claimant suffering from a diabetes related degenerative bone condition twisted ankle while working causing onset of charcot osteoarthropathy; compensation awarded; "It is axiomatic that employers take their employees as they find them."). This issue is often addressed in the lexicon of tort law as involving the plaintiff with the "eggshell skull." See Prosser & Keeton, The Law of Torts' 43 (5th Ed.1984).

4. Although an employee is generally taken by the employer "as is," such employee must always prove the existence of a causal relationship between the ultimate disability and the workplace. See, e.g., Hardin's Bakeries v. Harrell, 566 So.2d 1261 (Miss.1990) (In a workers' compensation case the claimant bears the burden of proving by a preponderance of the evidence (1) an accidental injury (2) arising out of and in the course of employment, and (3) a causal connection between the injury and the death or claimed disability). Among the states, the causal connection requirement is cast in different forms. Statutes such as the one in Oregon mandate that the workplace injury be the "major contributing cause" of the disability. O.R.S. § 656.005(7)(a)(B) (2012). The Massachusetts statute allows compensation so long as the workplace injury is a major but not necessarily predominate cause of the combined disability. Ma. St. 152 § 1 (7A) (2011). Mississippi provides the condition must be aggravated or accelerated by the employment in a "significant manner." Miss. Code Ann. Section 71–3–3(b) (2013). Some states address the problem by restricting the employee's recovery to that portion of the disability attributed solely to the workplace. See, e.g., Ballard v. Workmen's Compensation Appeals Board, 3 Cal.3d 832, 92 Cal.Rptr. 1, 478 P.2d 937 (1971); Escambia County Council on Aging v. Goldsmith, 500 So.2d

626 (Fla.App.1 Dist.1986); and see West F.S.A. § 440.02(1) and 440.15(5) (2013); and see Georgia's statute allowing compensation only as long as the employment aggravation of the pre-existing condition causes the disability, O.C.G.A. 34–9–1 (4) (2012).

5. A number of issues are implicated when the claimant suffers from a pre-existing condition. See, e.g., Bailey v. Reynolds Metals, 153 Or.App. 498, 959 P.2d 84 (1998) (requirement that claimant prove that job-related factors were the major contributing elements of her injury held not to violate the Americans with Disabilities Act); Reaching the same conclusion regarding the Americans with Disabilities Act is the decision in Horsley v. North Dakota Workers' Compensation Bureau, 2000 WL 35444941 (Dist.Ct. N.D. 2000); Caldwell v. Aarlin/Holcombe Armature Co., 267 Ga. 613, 481 S.E.2d 196 (1997) (employee provided, false information in his employment application regarding his pre-existing back condition; employer defended claim for disability based on the false representation; even if application questions violated Americans with Disabilities Act provisions prohibiting pre-offer inquiries, employer could still rely on false representation defense; held compensation denied). In regard to the effect of claimant's misrepresentation of health or physical condition, see, generally, 12 A.L.R.5th 658 (2013); and see Brown v. A–Dec, Inc., 154 Or.App. 244, 961 P.2d 280 (1998) (the natural effects of the aging process can be considered a pre-existing weakness or condition thus placing the burden of satisfying the predominate cause hurdle upon the claimant; and this does not violate the constitution or the American's with Disabilities Act). For a general discussion of the connections between workers' compensation acts and the Americans with Disabilities Act, see Breen v. Carlsbad Mun. Schools, 133 N.M. 618, 67 P.3d 908 (2003). Of course, as was seen in Chapter 5, *supra,* risks which are purely personal to the employee and not enhanced by the employment generally are not compensable. This is typically the result in idiopathic fall cases. See, e.g., Svehla v. Beverly Enterprises, 5 Neb.App. 765, 567 N.W.2d 582 (1997) (employee had pre-existing gait imbalance; employee fell on employer's sidewalk; neither the positional risk nor idiopathic fall doctrines allowed death benefits where claimant failed to prove employment enhancement or contribution); Lucas v. Anderson Ford, 13 Neb.App. 133, 689 N.W.2d 354 (2004) (employee fell at desk; recovery denied because fall due to personal risk with no demonstrated employment contribution); Burdette v. Perlman-Rocque Company, 954 N.E.2d 925 (Ind. Ct. App. 2011) (claimant died after falling at work hitting his head; evidence indicated preexisting vertigo; held, recovery denied; employee's fatal head injury caused by personal condition and employment did not increase the risk); but see, Hampton v. Intech Contracting, LLC, 2013 WL 1188040 (Ky. Supreme Ct. 2013) (claimant an insulin dependent diabetic suffering from low blood sugar became confused, climbed over a guardrail and fell sixty feet to ground; board disallowed compensation; court reversed finding claimant's idiopathic fall was contributed to and enhanced by a dangerous work place).

6. Should compensation be awarded for the abnormal consequences (even death) of an admittedly compensable injury, assuming, of course, that factual cause is established? The answer is frequently in the affirmative, at least in the absence of statutory provisions to the contrary. Where a latent or weakened but not disabling condition resulting from disease or prior injury is activated or accelerated by a compensable injury and the result is death or prolonged or disproportional disability, compensation is often awarded. See, e.g., Chicago, Wilmington & Franklin Coal Co. v. Industrial Comm., 400 Ill. 60, 78 N.E.2d 104 (1948) (miner suffered injury to tip of index finger, infection followed ultimately causing amputation of finger, which weakened him so that tuberculosis germs latent in his body became active and he died of tuberculosis; held death compensable); Storie v. Taylor Supply Co., 190 Tenn. 149, 228 S.W.2d 94 (1950) (injuries in work-related automobile accident activated a pre-existing "mild form of syphilis" which ultimately caused decedent's death, held death compensable); Pettit v. Austin Logging Co., 9 Or.App. 347, 497 P.2d 207 (1972) (back strain masked existence of multiple sclerosis thereby delaying treatment and aggravating the disease; results held compensable); Champion Home Builders v. Industrial Commission, 703 P.2d 306 (Ut.1985) (pre-existing ulcer perforated while claimant was lifting heavy beam; held compensable); Jameson v. SAIF, 63 Or.App. 553, 665 P.2d 379 (1983) (a work injury to the shoulder and back followed by back surgery caused a pre-existing lipoma to become larger leading to disabling pain in back, held compensable); Jackson v. True Temper Corp., 151 Vt. 592, 563 A.2d 621 (1989) (pre-existing encephalopathy due to malnourishment and alcohol abuse was aggravated by a rip saw injury at work; resulting disability due to periodic seizures, held compensable); Conway v. Blackfeet Indian Developers, Inc., 205 Mont. 459, 669 P.2d 225 (1983) (pre-existing multiple sclerosis aggravated by work related fall became symptomatic; held compensable). But, cf. Giles v. Bozeman Public Schools, 257 Mont. 289, 849 P.2d 180 (1993) (unlike Conway, *supra*, medical testimony indicated no connection between trauma and onset of multiple sclerosis symptoms; held not compensable). See generally, Workers' Compensation: Compensability of Multiple Sclerosis, 36 Am. Jur. Trials 573 (Originally published 1988, updated August 2013).

7. In cases in which the employee was suffering from a fatal disease that would have caused death eventually and where it appears that the work connected injury weakened the employee's resistance or otherwise hastened the time of death, compensation is often awarded. See, e.g., Murphy's Case, 328 Mass. 301, 103 N.E.2d 267 (1952) (worker with carcinoma of the bladder that "would be fatal in any event, that was certain death" suffered coronary thrombosis at work that shortened the employee's life; held compensable); McCann Steel Co. v. Carney, 192 Tenn. 94, 237 S.W.2d 942 (1951) (employee suffering from leukemia injured his hand and contracted "blood poisoning;" medical testimony was that his inevitable death from leukemia was hastened; held death compensable); Oswald v. Connor, 16 Ohio St.3d 38, 476 N.E.2d 658 (1985) (pre-existing heart disease which would eventually cause death was hastened by avian tuberculosis, an occupational disease, which

caused unusual stress and fatal heart attack; held death compensable); Bradford v. Workers' Compensation Commissioner, 185 W.Va. 434, 408 S.E.2d 13 (1991) (worker died of metastatic cancer; his severe occupational pneumoconiosis had prevented surgical treatment for the cancer; the occupational pneumoconiosis was found to have been a major contributing factor of his death; held widow entitled to death benefits); But see Schulle v. Texas Employers' Insurance Association, 787 S.W.2d 608 (Ct.App.Tx.1990) (employee was in pain and confined to bed following a compensable back injury; employee was subsequently diagnosed with lung cancer; his doctor stated that the back pain led to employee's loss of will to live and to rejection of aggressive cancer treatment; doctor concluded while cancer would have been terminal in any event, the refusal of aggressive treatment hastened the death; court found connections between back injury and death too weak to support award; held death benefits denied).

8. The general rule in this area applies as well to cases in which a claimant's mental, emotional or other personality traits at time of injury cause consequences from a work injury that would not ordinarily be expected. In Bullington v. Aetna Cas. & Sur. Co., 122 Ga.App. 842, 178 S.E.2d 901 (1970) decedent had a "moderate drinking problem" prior to injury; thereafter pain and enforced idleness aggravated his drinking until it finally caused death which was held compensable. Reversed for procedural irregularities, 227 Ga. 485, 181 S.E.2d 495 (1971), vacated 123 Ga.App. 781, 182 S.E.2d 487 (1971). In Ballard v. Workmen's Compensation Appeals Board, 3 Cal.3d 832, 92 Cal.Rptr. 1, 478 P.2d 937 (1971), the claimant with a preexisting psychological susceptibility to drug dependency became addicted to various drugs following a work related back injury. The aggravation of the previously asymptomatic condition was held to be compensable. In Globe Machine v. Yock, 79 Or.App. 9, 717 P.2d 1235 (1986), the claimant who suffered from preexisting alcoholism had apparently stopped drinking for two years prior to his disability, but, as a result of job related stress, began drinking again. The worsening of his preexisting condition caused total disability which was held to be compensable. In Matter of Compensation of Gygi, 55 Or.App. 570, 639 P.2d 655 (1982), claimant, an attorney, who suffered from preexisting mental health problems became depressed and alcoholic as a result of stress in his law practice. The court held that the aggravation of the preexisting condition was compensable. See also Jackson v. True Temper Corp. *supra*, note 6. Some jurisdictions address by statute the compensability of alcoholism and drug addiction following a work related injury. See, e.g., O.C.G.A. 34–9–1(4) (2012).

9. Issues in *Braewood* related to the reasonableness and necessity of medical benefits are treated in Chapter 8, Section 2, *infra*. The "second injury" problem is considered in Chapter 8, Section 4, *infra*, with observations that are instructive in resolving some of the apportionment issues raised in this chapter. Various options include apportioning the pre-existing condition (1) to the employer (2) to the employee or (3) to a "second

injury" fund. See 5–90 Larson's Workers' Compensation Law §§ 90.01 *et seq.* (2013).

3. FALLS AND SIMILAR MISHAPS

WILLIAMS CONSTR. CO., INC. V. GARRISON

Court of Special Appeals of Maryland, 1979.
42 Md.App. 340, 400 A.2d 22.

LISS, JUDGE.

Williams Construction Company, Inc., employer and American Automobile Insurance Company, insurer (hereinafter jointly designated as appellants), have filed this appeal from an order of the Circuit Court for Baltimore County which granted a summary judgment in favor of the claimant, Jesse R. Garrison, Jr. (hereinafter designated as appellee).

Appellants contend that the trial court erred in affirming an order of the Workmen's Compensation Commission dated August 9, 1977 by which the Commission found that the appellee was entitled to additional temporary total disability and was permanently totally disabled as a result of an accidental injury sustained by the appellee on July 25, 1974, which arose out of, and in the course of, his employment.

Appellants raise the following issues in support of their contention that the trial judge should not have granted appellee's motion for summary judgment:

(1) That the injuries and disability suffered by the appellee were caused by the claimant's own reckless and unreasonable conduct; and (2) that the initial compensable injury of July 25, 1974 was not the proximate cause of the injuries sustained by the appellee on December 28, 1974, and that the appellee's permanent total disability occurred by reason of appellee's own intervening unreasonable conduct.

The facts in the case are virtually undisputed. On August 13, 1974, appellee filed a claim for compensation with the Workmen's Compensation Commission in which he stated that on July 25, 1974, while in the employ of Williams Construction Company as a bulldozer operator, he fell from the tracks of a pusher-tractor and sustained injuries to his back. The appellants did not contest the claim and the Commission found the claim to be compensable. The insurer paid temporary total benefits for the period the appellee did not attend work and for the medical expenses incurred. No claim for permanent partial benefits was filed by the appellee. Appellee returned to his same employment with Williams Construction Company on August 13, 1974 and worked for an additional four months as a bulldozer operator until December 6, 1974, when he was laid off. Appellee then began to work for himself as a tree trimmer. On December 28, 1974, the appellee, while carrying a chain saw, ascended a forty-foot ladder and was engaged in trimming a tree when he fell from the ladder, struck the ground and sustained extremely serious injuries. In the latter part of 1976, after extensive medical treatment, the appellee requested that the claim involving his accident of July 25, 1974 be reopened on the theory that the injuries sustained by the claimant in his fall from the ladder on December 28, 1974, were caused by the disability which resulted from his accident of July 25, 1974. Appellants raised issues before the Commission as to whether the appellee sustained an accidental personal injury arising out of, and in the course of, employment with Williams Construction Co. on December 28, 1974. They also raised the issue of whether the disability of the employee was the result of an accidental personal injury arising out of, and in the course of, employment on July 25, 1974. The Commission held that the appellee was entitled to additional temporary total benefits and was permanently totally disabled as a result of the accident of December 28, 1974, and that that accident was attributable to the disabilities he sustained as a result of his injury on July 25, 1974. An award of benefits was made reflecting the Commission's decision, and the appellants appealed from the award to the Circuit Court for Baltimore County. Depositions were taken and filed with appropriate affidavits by the parties, and after a hearing, the trial judge granted appellee's motion for summary judgment affirming the decision of the Workmen's Compensation Commission. It is from this action that this appeal was taken.

The depositions and affidavits submitted in support of the several motions for summary judgment filed respectively by the appellants and appellees established that shortly after the original fall by the appellee in the accident of July 25, 1974, the claimant began to experience dizzy spells intermittently which required him to take medication prescribed by the treating physician, but which were not so severe as to prevent claimant from working. Although the claimant complained of dizziness to the attending physician on three separate visits, the doctor allowed him to return to work and placed no restrictions on the appellee. The claimant testified that when he returned to work for Williams Construction he noticed that he would from time to time suffer dizzy spells in which everything would "go round and round" and during which he would hang on to something until the dizzy spell subsided.

Appellants admit they have no evidence to contradict the appellee's contention that the dizzy spells which ultimately resulted in his fall from the ladder were related to the dizzy spells he experienced as a result of the original fall in July. They urge, however, that the appellee was aware of his condition; that he acted in a reckless and unreasonable manner in climbing the ladder knowing that he was having dizzy spells; and that if, in fact, the dizzy spells did cause his fall, then his reckless and unreasonable conduct in climbing the ladder amounted to a break in the direct causal relationship between the accident of July 1974 and the injuries sustained in the fall in December of 1974.

Appellants rely for legal sustenance on Watts v. Young Co., 245 Md. 277, 225 A.2d 865 (1967), a case which is factually distinguishable from the case *sub judice*. In *Watts,* the Court of Appeals had before it the case of a claimant who had sustained injuries and who refused to undergo corrective surgery. The Court, in holding that the refusal to undergo surgery justified the withholding of an award for permanent partial disability, gave as one of its reasons the conclusion that the claimant's intentional and unreasonable conduct broke the chain of causation between his employment and his injury. It held that to the extent the claimant's disability was found to relate to his arbitrary refusal to assent to treatment, such disability did not arise out of his employment. In support of this holding, the Court cited 2 Larson, Workmen's Compensation Law sec. 13.22 (1952).

In a discussion of the range of compensable consequences, Larson suggests the rule should be that when the primary injury is shown to have arisen out of, and in the course of, employment every natural consequence that flows from the injury likewise arises out of the employment, unless the injury is the result of an independent intervening cause attributable to claimant's own intentional conduct. The employee's own contributory negligence with regard to the primary injury is ordinarily not an intervening cause preventing initial compensability. But when the question is whether compensability should be extended to a subsequent injury or aggravation related in some way to the primary injury, Larson suggests the basic rule should be that a subsequent injury, whether an aggravation of the original injury or a new and distinct injury, is compensable if it is the direct and natural result of a compensable primary injury. He then suggests that when a subsequent injury arises out of what he designates a "quasi-course" activity, such as a trip to the doctor's office, the chain of causation should not be deemed broken by mere negligence in the performance of that activity, but only by intentional conduct which may be regarded as expressly or impliedly prohibited by the employer. Larson further develops his legal theory by stating that when the injury following the initial compensable injury does not arise out of a "quasi-course" activity, as when the claimant with an injured hand engages in a boxing match, the chain of causation may be deemed broken by either intentional or negligent claimant misconduct. 2 Larson, *supra*, sec. 13.11.

Although our courts have not expressly adopted the proposition that Larson posits, the law in Maryland, by statute and case law has considered the effect of the conduct of a claimant on his right to compensation benefits.

The Court of Appeals, in Dayton v. Davis, 218 Md. 614, 618, 147 A.2d 699, 701 (1959), speaking through Chief Judge Brune, said: "There are very few unavoidable accidents; negligence produces most of them and an employee's non-wilful negligence—his lapse from care—does not keep an injury-producing occurrence from being an accident nor bar his right to compensation."

Pursuant to the Workmen's Compensation Law, the right to compensation exists without reference to the care of the employee, and compensation is not denied by reason of contributory negligence on his part.

The Legislature of Maryland has explicitly stated the circumstances under which an employee otherwise eligible for compensation benefits will be denied those benefits in Article 10, Section 45 of the Annotated Code of Maryland (1957, 1979 Repl.Vol.):

> Notwithstanding anything hereinbefore or hereinafter contained, no employee or dependent of any employee shall be entitled to receive any compensation or benefits under this article on account of any injury to or death of an employee caused by self-inflicted injury, the willful misconduct, or where the injury or death resulted solely from the intoxication of the injured employee or solely from the effect upon him of any narcotic, depressant, stimulant, hallucinogenic or hypnotic drug or from the effect upon him of any other drug which renders him incapable of satisfactorily performing his job, except when such drug has been administered or taken in accordance with a physician's prescription.

The only portion of this section which might even remotely be applicable in this case is the segment involving the willful misconduct of an employee. 99 C.J.S. Workmen's Compensation § 258 (1958) defines willful misconduct as the intentional doing of something either with the knowledge that it is likely to result in serious injury or with a wanton and reckless disregard of its probable consequences.

* * *

In Karns v. Liquid Carbonic Corporation, 275 Md. 1, 338 A.2d 251 (1975), the Court of Appeals said willful misconduct may be found where the employee intended to place himself in a position whereby he might expect to meet with injury or death, and in carrying out his intention meets his death as a result of the injuries sustained. The actions of the employee must be such as to show that he intended thereby to place himself in such a hazardous position that injury or death might result as the reasonable consequence of his act.

We do not reach the conclusion that the appellee's conduct in this case amounted to such willful misconduct as to create an intervening superseding cause which was sufficient to break the chain of causation between the original injury and the subsequent injury so as to preclude the claimant from being entitled to compensation benefits flowing from the original accident.

We note from the testimony of the various witnesses included in the record extract that there is no evidence that the employer imposed any restrictions on the appellee's performance of his duties for the employer subsequent to the claimant being able to return to work. The appellee performed essentially the same climbing duties in the operation of the tractor bulldozer during the four months he remained employed by the appellant after the initial injury. The attending physician had knowledge of the appellee's complaint of giddy spells and dizziness. He was also aware of the circumstances of the fall from the bulldozer and that the claimant had struck his head in the fall. In addition, the doctor had made a notation in his records that several days after the accident the appellee had attempted to return to work but was too dizzy to continue to perform his duties. Although the complaints of giddiness continued on three separate visits to the doctor, the doctor, nevertheless, felt the appellee was ready to return to work by August 13, 1974. The doctor did not place any restrictions on the claimant's activities. And although the doctor felt that the dizzy spells were caused by a cerebral contusion, he did not feel it was warranted to send the appellee to anyone for additional tests. The attending physician indicated that he felt the appellee was capable of performing his functions when he discharged him. Not only were there no work restrictions placed on the appellee by the doctor, but the doctor's advice was also devoid of any restrictions whatsoever regarding any other activities in which the claimant might engage. In the light of this factual situation, the conduct of the employer and paucity of instructions by the physician, we think it totally unreasonable to hold that the actions of the appellee were of such a reckless and unreasonable nature as to amount to conduct which would break the chain of causation between the initial injury and the subsequent injury.

Thus it is clear that in the case *sub judice*, as there were no restrictions placed on the employee's activities either by the prior employer or the attending physician, the appellee's conduct in ascending the ladder in view of his prior episodes of dizziness was, at the most, poor judgment rather than willful misconduct.

The trial judge in his consideration of the depositions and exhibits filed in support of the motion for summary judgment by the appellee concluded that there was no disputed issue of fact as to whether the accident of December 28, 1974 was the direct result of the injuries sustained by the appellee, and that as a matter of law and of fact that the appellee's conduct in climbing the ladder, in view of his prior episodes of dizziness, was not sufficient to be an intervening cause so as to destroy the chain of causation between the original injury and the subsequent fall which resulted in the appellee's paralysis.

As a reviewing body, we are bound by our own Maryland Rule 1086 which states that this Court will review the case upon both the law and the evidence, but the judgment will not be set aside unless clearly erroneous. We find that the conclusions of fact by the trial judge are not erroneous and are correct as to the law.

Judgment affirmed; costs to be paid by appellants.

SULLIVAN V. B & A CONSTR., INC.

Court of Appeals of New York, 1954.
307 N.Y. 161, 120 N.E.2d 694.

FULD, JUDGE.

Claimant, a painter by trade, sustained, in the course of two different employments, compensable injuries to his right knee. In March of 1948, while in the employ of appellant B & A Construction, Inc., he slipped on a paint brush and caught his right leg on a step; again, in June, 1949, while employed by appellant A.L. Turner, a ladder which he was climbing broke and he struck and twisted the same leg. As a result of these injuries, his right knee, previously sound, acquired a pronounced tendency to "lock," so that claimant, until he could "shake" it back into place, found himself—as he put it—"paralyzed * * * from my knee to my hip," and deprived of all use and control of his right leg. From the report of a doctor, made after the second accident, it appears that "even mild trauma such as that caused by stepping over a small stone on the road or a high place in the sidewalk * * * [created] the sensation of the 'knee giving away.' "

Claimant suffered this locking, and the accompanying pain and paralysis, frequently, not only while walking but, indeed, whenever he put pressure on his knee. Driving an automobile became particularly hazardous; claimant himself testified that "once or twice a week," in applying pressure to the brake, his knee slipped into such a position that "he would have to stop and unlock it." Nevertheless, he continued to operate his car.

On June 30, 1950, a year after the second injury, claimant was hurt in an automobile accident, and it is solely from that accident that the present award stems. He was driving in the state of Maryland, at a speed of between forty and forty-five miles an hour, when "something [went] haywire with" the steering wheel; the tie rod, by which the front wheels are controlled, had, it subsequently appeared, broken. Although in the past claimant had always succeeded in stopping his car, on this occasion, when he tried to press down on the brake, nothing happened. His knee "locked," it was "paralyzed" and useless, and the car, out of control, careened off the highway, into the woods, and struck a tree. Claimant lay unconscious for some time and, when taken to a local hospital, was found to have suffered a comminuted fracture of the right femur.

Having previously received an award for his earlier injuries, claimant now seeks compensation for the injuries sustained in the automobile accident. This latest mishap did not arise in the course of his employment, for, concededly, claimant was driving on his own personal business. An award is, therefore, warranted only if the automobile accident and the consequent injuries resulted directly and naturally from claimant's prior injuries and the disability thereby produced. * * * If such injuries only remotely caused or contributed to the accident on the road, then claimant is not entitled to compensation; or, to express it somewhat differently, if claimant is to recover, the disability occasioned by the earlier accidents must have been a proximate not simply a "but for," cause of his latest mishap.

Here, quite obviously, it was claimant's own temerity, not the physical handicap resulting from the industrial accidents, that was primarily responsible for the later, 1950, accident. Despite his serious infirmity and despite the obvious risk involved—to innocent passers-by as well as to himself—he persisted in operating a car, indeed, in driving at what was, for him, the immoderate speed of over forty miles an hour. Even the simple precaution of adding an auxiliary hand or left-foot brake, such as those used by others who are disabled, was omitted. Eventually, the inevitable accident occurred. While the earlier injuries may have been a "but for" cause of the accident, they certainly did not constitute the requisite legal or proximate cause. When claimant ignored his locking knee and, without justification, continued to drive, responsibility for the accident and its consequences could no longer be ascribed to his employment-created disability.

Had claimant been ignorant of the extent of his disability, had his knee not previously locked while driving, the case might conceivably have been different. In the light of the record before us, however, it is indisputable that claimant's own act of driving, supervening between the industrial accidents and the car crash, broke the essential chain of causation.

The order of the Appellate Division should be reversed, the award of the Workmen's Compensation Board annulled and the claim dismissed, with costs in this court and in the Appellate Division against respondent Workmen's Compensation Board.

LEWIS, C.J., and CONWAY, DESMOND, DYE, FROESSEL and VAN VOORHIS, JJ., concur.

NOTES

1. As the foregoing cases suggest, subsequent injuries caused by falls or other mishaps due to the handicapped physical condition resulting from the original work accident are compensable consequences of the original injury; at least where the employee's unreasonable conduct is not the primary cause. Many cases have awarded compensation. See, e.g., Randolph v. E.I. Du Pont De Nemours & Co., 130 N.J.L. 353, 33 A.2d 301 (1943) (original injury to eyes required claimant to wear dark glasses as a result of which he lost his footing and fell down stairs; held injury from fall compensable); Mondillo v. Ward Baking Co., 73 R.I. 473, 57 A.2d 447 (1948) (claimant suffered injury to right leg and foot causing weakness, was inducted into army where marching caused development of club foot; held compensable); Great Atlantic & Pacific Tea Co. v. Hill, 201 Md. 630, 95 A.2d 84 (1953) (fracture of lower leg caused weakness which caused another fall three years later; held second fall compensable); Carabetta v. Industrial Comm., 12 Ariz.App. 239, 469 P.2d 473 (1970) (injury to claimant's knee caused it to give way or "buckle" at irregular intervals; injury suffered from fall at a funeral; held compensable); Barre v. Roofing and Flooring, Inc., 83 A.D.2d 681, 442 N.Y.S.2d 246 (1981) (first injury caused residual dizziness; dizziness caused claimant to fall causing second injury; held second injury compensable); Erwin v. Harris, 474 So.2d 1125 (Ala.Civ.App.1985) (work related knee injury; while on vacation, claimant fell due to weakened knee; held compensable); Pellerin v. New York State Dept. of Correction, 215 A.D.2d 943, 627 N.Y.S.2d 147 (1995) (work related injury in 1980 caused claimant's leg to buckle periodically; in 1990, claimant's leg buckled and he fell from a hunter's tree stand; court concluded employee's conduct was not too rash or irresponsible and thus did not break the chain of causation; held compensable); Wallace v. Oswego Wire, Inc., 29 A.D.3d 1057, 814 N.Y.S.2d 380 (N.Y.A.D.3 Dept.2006) (work related knee injury; while at home cutting wood with table saw, knee gave out resulting in cut hand; held claimant's conduct not unreasonable and hand injury compensable); Moorehead Elec. Co., Inc. v. Payne, 962 N.E.2d 657 (Ind. App. 2011) (after surgery for work-related shoulder injury, claimant was ordered to wear a bulky shoulder brace 24 hours a day; while later attending a wedding reception, shoulder brace obstructed claimant's view causing fall which reinjured shoulder; held, last injury compensable); and, see Killam's Case, 83 Mass. App. Ct. 1102, 979 N.E.2d 237 (2012) (claimant injured back at work, and later painted brother's kitchen causing injury which may have contributed to ultimate disability; held, compensation awarded; "non-work-related activity which is normal and reasonable, and not performed negligently in light of the . . . impairment, does not constitute an intervening cause. . . .").

2. As the *Sullivan* case demonstrates, however, if a claimant's subsequent injury results from intentional involvement in behavior of a kind that is inappropriate for a person with such an injury, compensation may be denied. See, e.g., Yarbrough v. Polar Ice & Fuel Co., 118 Ind.App. 321, 79 N.E.2d 422 (1948) (claimant had a weak knee caused by compensable work

injury; while negligently attempting to carry a load of trash down stairs at home, his knee gave way and he fell fracturing his jaw; held fractured jaw not compensable); Johnnie's Produce Co. v. Benedict & Jordan, 120 So.2d 12 (Fla.1960) (claimant who suffered broken right ankle in a compensable accident later negligently jumped from a truck; due to the weakened condition of the ankle employee fell sustaining a back injury; held back injury not compensable); Brown v. State Industrial Insurance System, 106 Nev. 878, 803 P.2d 223 (1990) (employment related carpal tunnel syndrome to both wrists was treated surgically; two months after the last surgery while claimant's hands were still weak, claimant fell and broke both wrists while riding a horse through a barrel racing course; the fall occurred due to insufficient strength in hands to hold on to saddle horn; held claimant's negligent conduct was a superceding cause of the second injury and compensation denied).

3. Contrast State Comp. Ins. Fund v. Industrial Acc. Comm., 176 Cal.App.2d 10, 1 Cal.Rptr. 73 (1959), in which an employee suffering "double vision," due to a work related accident, decided to cut some "junk lumber" at his home for use in his fireplace. While the off duty worker did this with an electric power handsaw, the saw "jumped and kicked" amputating one of his fingers. An award of compensation for the loss of the finger was affirmed in an opinion that warns "against atavistic attempts to retain common law concepts for tort and negligence in the compensation field." The cases are reviewed and disagreement expressed with the approach taken in the *Sullivan* case, *supra*. According to the court, "the employee's negligence actually is irrelevant in the second injury as it admittedly is in the first." The California Supreme Court declined to review the decision. On the topic of the relationship of the employee's negligence in the second injury, see also the *Hallisey* case *infra*, note 5. The *Hallisey* court agrees that the negligence of the employee does not break the causal chain.

Larson concluded the California decision went too far and, as noted in the *Williams* case, *supra*, suggested a distinction along the following lines: if the employee is engaged in what he called a "quasi-course (of employment) activity," e.g. going to the doctor or taking medication for the work related injury, the employee's negligence should have no significance; but if the employee is not engaged in a quasi-course activity, e.g. taking part in an after work boxing match, then the negligence should bar compensation. Interestingly, however, Larson suggests the California court may have gotten it right, after all. He reasoned that because, apparently, the claimant's doctor had ordered him to exercise his eye and rehabilitate himself, the claimant's activity of cutting lumber could have been found to be a "quasi-course of activity" in which case negligence should not defeat recovery. 1–10 Larson's Workers' Compensation Law §§ 10.06(3) (2013).

4. In response to judicial precedents such as those summarized in notes 1 and 3, *supra*, the state of Florida enacted legislation in 1991 apparently seeking to restrict recovery in the "subsequent injury" cases. F.S.A. § 440.092(5) provides: "Injuries caused by a subsequent intervening

accident arising from an outside agency which are the direct and natural consequence of the original injury are not compensable unless suffered while traveling to or from a health care provider for the purpose of receiving remedial treatment for the compensable injury." Nevertheless, one Florida appellate court opinion has interpreted the statute narrowly. See U–Haul of South Florida v. March, 645 So.2d 581 (Fla.App.1994) (claimant wearing a short leg cast and using crutches following a compensable fracture of his right foot, fell injuring his shoulder while descending a flight of stairs at his home; employee testified he lost his balance and his left foot slipped out from under him due to the cast and crutches and his resulting awkward effort to descend the stairs; court concluded the claimant's own left foot could not be considered an "outside agency;" held compensable).

5. In a related but factually distinguishable context, the original work injury in no way causes or contributes to the happening of the subsequent non-work accident but the original injury is aggravated by or implicated in the subsequent occurrence. See, e.g., In Re Fisher, 189 P.3d 866 (Wyo.2008) (employee was rendered paraplegic due to compensable work injury; twelve years later, fire occurred at employee's home; smoke inhalation led to pneumonia and death; doctor testified the paraplegia rendered him unable to cough so as to relieve mucus congestion; held death compensable). Results, in terms of compensability, vary depending upon one or more of the following: (1) policy considerations; (2) the nature of the employee's conduct in relation to the subsequent accident; (3) the jurisdiction's apportionment statute; or (4) the applicable burden of proof. See, e.g., Kill v. Industrial Comm., 160 Wis. 549, 152 N.W. 148 (1915) (employee who suffered work related wrist injury later engaged in a boxing match against physician's advice and suffered a bacterial infection at the site of the original injury; resulting loss of use of hand found not compensable due to employee's conduct); Amick v. National Bottle, 507 A.2d 1352 (Sup. Ct. R.I. 1986) (over three year period, employee suffered two work related back injuries and two non-work related back injuries; after the fourth injury, which was non-work related, claimant became severely depressed and sought benefits for psychiatric care; court concluded, under Rhode Island law, claimant had burden of proving emotional disability resulted solely from work injuries; held compensation denied); Schaefer v. Williamston Community Schools, 117 Mich.App. 26, 323 N.W.2d 577 (1982) (work related injury to claimant's back was exacerbated when he lifted boxes at his home, "something I shouldn't have done;" court held this could be a compensable aggravation if the board concluded the activity of moving the household goods was not negligent in light of employee's knowledge of his pre-existing condition); Amey v. Friendly Ice Cream Shop, 231 N.J.Super. 278, 555 A.2d 677 (1989) (work related injury to flexor tendon of claimant's right hand; hand re-injured while employee was working on his car at home; doctor had warned claimant not to put pressure on the hand; held compensation denied); Webb v. Industrial Commission of Ohio, 76 Ohio App.3d 701, 602 N.E.2d 1265 (1991) (employee had work related knee injury surgically repaired; two years later, employee injured the same knee while playing touch football; doctor testified the knee was prone to

such later injury due to the earlier work injury; court held employee must show a direct and substantial causal relationship between the first and second injuries but that the work injury need not be the sole cause of the ultimate disability); Aragon v. State of New Mexico Corrections Dept., 113 N.M. 176, 824 P.2d 316 (1991) (employee suffered work related back injury in 1983; in 1988 employee aggravated the back injury while repairing his personal truck at home; court reasoned an employee is entitled to benefits for disability arising immediately from a work related accident and for disability which develops later as a result of the normal activities of life; but the worker is not provided an insurance policy of indefinite duration to cover every non-work related accident that magnifies the original injury; held compensation denied); Kroh v. American Family Insurance, 487 N.W.2d 306 (N.D.1992) (employee suffered work related back injury; two months later claimant injured back again in non-work related vehicle accident; court applied North Dakota's aggravation apportionment statute and concluded that benefits are to be awarded only for work injuries and not for aggravation thereof by a non-work injury); Rogers v. Cascade Pacific, 152 Or.App. 624, 955 P.2d 307 (1998) (employee who suffered work related back injuries later suffered a neck injury while doing exercises as part of his preventative physical therapy regimen; court found the work injuries were not a "major contributing cause" of the neck injury as required by O.R.S. § 656.05(7)(a)(A); held compensation denied); Addington Resources v. Perkins, 947 S.W.2d 421 (Ct.App.Ky.1997) (employee suffered work related injury at the C5–C6 level of the spine; five years later employee suffered a non-work injury at the C6–C7 level; court concluded the work related injury caused the part of the back which was subsequently injured to be more susceptible to injury; held second injury compensable); Benton v. Winn–Dixie Montgomery, Inc., 705 So.2d 495 (Ala.Civ.App.1997) (work related back injury required surgical fusion of several vertebrae; five years later claimant was involved in non-work related vehicle accident; after car accident, fractures were detected in the previously fused vertebrae; held compensable); and Hallisey v. Fort Howard Paper Co., 268 Ga. 57, 484 S.E.2d 653 (1997) (employee suffered work related back injury; two days later during a day off from work after his tee shot on the twenty-fourth hole of golf, his back pain became so severe that he had to quit and seek medical treatment; ALJ awarded compensation but Court of Appeals reversed due to claimant's negligence in playing golf; Supreme Court reinstated the award holding that Georgia's Workers' Compensation Act does not treat an employee's negligence in aggravating an injury as an intervening cause). How would the *Hallisey* case be resolved if Larson's "quasi-course of activity" analysis were to be applied? See note 3, *supra*.

6. In 1998, Georgia passed legislation which purported to codify existing case law in the "subsequent injury" case. See O.C.G.A. § 34–9–204(a) which provides: "No compensation shall be payable for the death or disability of an employee if his or her death is caused by or, insofar as his or her disability may be aggravated, caused or continued by a subsequent non-work related injury which breaks the chain of causation between the compensable

injury and the employee's disability." How, if at all, should this statute affect the outcome in the *Hallisey* case, *supra?*

4. COMPLICATIONS AND ACCIDENTS DURING MEDICAL TREATMENT

NOTES

1. Is disability or death compensable if not a normal effect of the original compensable injury but rather a consequence of adverse medical developments that follow it or transpire during its treatment? Most decisions award compensation. The development of an infection following an injury that delays recovery or even causes death is compensable as part of the original injury. Magnus v. Krug Electric Co., Inc., 271 App.Div. 761, 64 N.Y.S.2d 624 (1946) (trauma to thumb in November, subsequent infection necessitating amputation in January; held compensable); Allen v. Industrial Commission, 110 Utah 328, 172 P.2d 669 (1946) (bruise on leg, resulting in septicemia and pulmonary embolism and death; held compensable); Herre Bros., Inc. v. W.C.A.B. ex rel. Mumma, 75 Pa.Cmwlth. 499, 462 A.2d 907 (1983) (broken ribs in employment related truck accident; employee died at home seven days later of pneumonia; held compensable); American Smelting & Refining Co. v. Industrial Comm., 25 Ariz.App. 532, 544 P.2d 1133 (1976) (compensation awarded for death resulting from an infection that developed 30 years after the original injury); Johnson Controls, Inc. v. Russell, 95 S.W.3d 921 (Ky.App.2002) (decedent severely strained arm muscle at work; hematoma developed; bacterial infection led to septic shock, multi-system organ failure and death; held death compensable); Matusko v. Kennedy Valve Mfg. Co., 296 A.D.2d 726, 745 N.Y.S.2d 302 (3 Dept.2002) (decedent suffered work related injuries to hand and shoulder in 1981; these injuries rendered symptomatic a pre-existing cranio-cervical abnormality which progressed causing multiple complications resulting in death in 1995; held death compensable); Archer v. MDS Bldg., Inc., 841 A.2d 801(Me.2004) (claimant suffered amputation of left thumb and index finger; doctors amputated great toe and reattached it to hand to replace thumb; "it is well established in Maine that employers are liable for consequences of reasonable and proper medical treatment related to workers' compensation injuries;" held specific loss benefits payable for toe amputation); Droogan v. Raymark Industries, Inc., 59 A.D.3d 803, 872 N.Y.S.2d 752 (2009) (claimant received workers' compensation benefits due to contraction of asbestosis in 1987; death occurred in 2005 due to complications, including pneumonia, following a stroke; held compensation awarded for death; court concluded, "decedent's work related illness need not be the sole or even the most direct cause of death, provided the claimant demonstrates that the compensable illness was a contributing factor in the decedent's demise").

2. Further injury resulting from both the normal and unusual hazards of medical treatment required by a compensable injury are almost always

compensable. In Beech Creek Coal Co. v. Cox, 314 Ky. 743, 237 S.W.2d 56 (1951), an employee, convalescing at home from a compensable leg fracture, fell breaking the same leg in a different place. Death suffered during surgery required by the second injury was held compensable. Many other cases have awarded compensation. See, e.g., Paul Constr. Co. v. Powell, 200 Md. 168, 88 A.2d 837 (1952) (injury to back required operation which precipitated attack of acute toxic hallucinations; held death compensable); Abney and Eaves, Inc. v. Redeker, 303 P.2d 417 (Okl.1956) (as treatment for compensable work injury, claimant was injected with medicine that caused her to faint and fall; held injuries from fall compensable); Royal Palm Market v. Lutz, 126 So.2d 881 (Fla.1961) (operation for work connected hernia caused stroke; held compensable); Elmore's Variety Store v. White, 553 S.W.2d 350 (Tenn.1977) (claimant was being treated for a compensable puncture wound when a brain aneurysm ruptured; held both injuries compensable); Elizabethtown Sportswear v. Stice, 720 S.W.2d 732 (Ky.App.1986) (employee injured back and suffered death from allergic reaction to dye used in myelogram; held death compensable); City of Buford v. Thomas, 179 Ga.App. 769, 347 S.E.2d 713 (1986) (employee, hospitalized due to compensable work injury, fell while out of bed against doctor's orders; held, getting out of bed was not an independent intervening cause and death due to fall compensable); Eagle v. State of Nebraska, 237 Neb. 961, 468 N.W.2d 382 (1991) (a screw, implanted as part of surgery for a compensable injury, became loose and caused damage to the claimant's hip, held additional award granted for hip trauma); American Filtrona Co. v. Hanford, 16 Va.App. 159, 428 S.E.2d 511 (1993) (employee contracted hepatitis C from blood transfusion given during treatment of work related knee surgery; held compensation awarded for hepatitis C infection); Barrett v. Hames, 130 Or.App. 190, 881 P.2d 816 (1994) (worker suffered compensable shoulder injury; aggressive physical therapy injured ulnar nerve; held additional compensation awarded for the injury to the nerve); Smith v. Goodyear Tire and Rubber Co., 10 Neb.App. 666, 636 N.W.2d 884 (2001) (employee suffered separate work related injuries to knee, back and elbow; physical therapy for all conditions caused additional injury to knee; held additional knee injury compensable); Spacal v. Marietta, 642 So.2d 46 (Fla.App.1994) (even where the connection between the original compensable injury and the subsequent surgery is unclear, the employer will be liable for any complications that arise from that surgery if the employer has authorized it); Transport Associates v. Butler, 892 S.W.2d 296 (Sup.Ct.Ky.1995) (employee consulted physicians for treatment of compensable back injury; one recommended surgery while other did not; employer held responsible for additional injury caused by unnecessary surgery due to employer's failure to exercise its statutory right to request that claimant be treated by another physician); Heesch v. Swimtastic Swim School, 20 Neb. App. 260, 823 N.W.2d 211 (2012) (claimant suffered work-related back injury; allergic reaction to epidural cortisone injection treatment also compensable); ABS Global, Inc. v. Draper, 2012 WL 6652825 (Ky. App. 2012) (claimant suffered work-related neck and arm pain; physical therapy regimen caused a herniated cervical disc; held, therapy induced injury was a compensable work related event). See generally, 1–10 Larson's Workers' Compensation Law, Matthew Bender, 10.09[1] (2013).

3. If the claimant fails to establish a cause-in-fact connection between the original injury or its treatment and the subsequent injury, compensation for the subsequent injury will be disallowed. See, e.g., Sicker v. Karl Schroll & Associates, Inc., 19 A.D.2d 925, 244 N.Y.S.2d 20 (1963) (death caused by cancer unrelated to employment, held compensation denied); Bauman v. Lord Electric Co., 79 A.D.2d 806, 435 N.Y.S.2d 98 (1980) (auto accident injured knee, buttock and thigh; frustration and inactivity arguably led to obesity; intestinal bypass surgery to ameliorate obesity resulted in surgical complications and death; held obesity not shown to be caused by accident and compensation denied); Matter of Injury to Loveday, 711 P.2d 396 (Wyo.1985) (compensable back injury treated surgically; back pain continued so a second surgery was performed; heart attack occurred two days after second surgery; held not compensable because of failure in proof of causation); Rogers v. Cascade, 152 Or.App. 624, 955 P.2d 307 (1998) (claimant completed course of treatment for a compensable back injury and was instructed to perform exercises in order to avoid future injury; injury to back occurred while performing exercises; held, exercises were not part of treatment of compensable injury and compensation denied); Farmington Country Club, Inc. v. Marshall, 47 Va.App. 15, 622 S.E.2d 233 (2005) (claimant suffered compensable spinal cord injury after fall from ladder; recovery sought for subsequent gastro-esophageal reflux disease (gerd) claiming it was due to stress associated with spinal injury; held causal link too attenuated; compensation for treatment of gerd denied).

To the contrary is Vanecek v. Greeley Square Bldg. Co., 278 App.Div. 869, 104 N.Y.S.2d 214 (1951) which permitted compensation under extended circumstances. The employee suffered a compensable scalp laceration which resulted in headaches and dizziness. Because of possible post-traumatic bleeding, two exploratory operations of the cranium were performed. No bleeding was found, but the second operation revealed a tumor that was not a result of the work accident. The tumor was removed and as a result of the surgery the patient died. An award of compensation was affirmed on the theory that the purpose of the operation was to determine the effect of the original injury.

4. The cause in fact issue also appears in cases which involve a distinction between medical care for a compensable injury and medical care for a condition which, although not work related, must be addressed before the work injury can be safely or effectively treated. The analyses in these cases are often very fact sensitive, and, because minor variations in fact may yield different outcomes, results within a jurisdiction sometimes appear to conflict. See Public Service Co. of Colorado v. Industrial Claim Appeals Office of State of Colo., 979 P.2d 584, at 585 (Colo.App.1999) (different outcomes within same jurisdiction serve only to underscore the factual nature of the determination). For a sampling of the cases, see, e.g. Rank v. Lindblom, 459 N.W.2d 247 (S.D.1990) (claimant, a ranch hand, suffered knee injury by

stampeding calves; during pre-operative workup, doctors discovered pulmonary disorder which required surgical correction before knee surgery could be safely done; Board awarded compensation for lung surgery; Supreme Court reversed holding that the pulmonary surgery would have been needed even in absence of the knee surgery); State of Wyoming v. Girardot, 807 P.2d 926 (Wyo.1991) (claimant hospitalized for surgical repair of compensable hernia; during pre-operative examination severe arterial blockage of the heart was diagnosed; heart by-pass surgery was required before hernia repair; held, compensation awarded ($3,790) for hernia repair but denied ($35,000) for heart by-pass). Similarly, see Haftsavar v. All Am. Carpet & Rugs, Inc., 59 Va. App. 593, 721 S.E.2d 804 (2012) (claimant suffered work-related inguinal hernia; during pre-operative physical examination need for cardiac by-pass surgery was determined; held, compensation denied because cardiac condition and by-pass surgery not work related); and see Beasley v. Industrial Commission of Arizona 175 Ariz. 521, 858 P.2d 666 (1993) (holding where an unrelated condition would require treatment irrespective of the compensable injury, treatment of that condition is not covered by workers' compensation; and the unrelated condition does not become compensable even when treatment for it is a pre-requisite to treatment for a compensable injury, or when left alone, the unrelated condition would cause a worsening of the covered injury). Compare Forni v. Pathfinder Mines, 834 P.2d 688 (Wyo.1992) (claimant who suffered from work related back injury had preexisting diabetes and depression; doctors concluded the preexisting conditions needed treatment before the back surgery could be accomplished; both preexisting conditions required post-surgery treatment as well; held compensation awarded for treatment of the preexisting conditions); And, to the same effect, see Palmer v. State ex rel. Wyoming Workers' Safety and Compensation Div., 192 P.3d 125 (Wyo.2008) (employee suffered injury to spine necessitating fusion at L4–L5; additional fusions at other discs approved even though those were non-compensable but necessary to treat the compensable injury). And see SAIF Corp. v. Sprague, 345 Or. 661, 217 P.3d 644 (2009) (employee who suffered from pre-existing obesity suffered work related knee injury; employer liable for gastric bypass surgery to relieve obesity even though knee injury did not cause obesity). And see *Braewood, supra,* and the other cases cited in Note 1 following that opinion at pp. 424–425 all of which held the employer liable for medical expenses associated with treating the employee's pre-existing obesity.

5. Should an accident which happens while the employee is visiting a health care provider for treatment of a compensable injury be compensable? Larson considers this a compensable "quasi-course of employment activity" injury unless the claimant's conduct leading to the injury is characterized as intentional rather than merely negligent; see summary of Larson's position in *Garrison* supra at page 433, and see 1–10 Larson's Workers' Compensation Law, Matthew Bender § 10.07 (2013). Suppose an ambulance, hastening from the scene of an industrial accident, crashes into a tree and kills the injured worker. Would the result be different if there were no haste? Contrast Kiger v. Idaho Corp., 85 Idaho 424, 380 P.2d 208 (1963) (compensation denied) with

Immer and Co. v. Brosnahan, 207 Va. 720, 152 S.E.2d 254 (1967) (automobile accident while going to doctor's office; held compensation awarded). See also, Case of McElroy, 397 Mass. 743, 494 N.E.2d 1 (1986) (back injury on assembly line; additional injuries in a car crash while driving for treatment; held compensable; street risk rule applied); and, see D.O.T. v. King, 554 So.2d 1192 (Fla.App.1989) (claimant suffered work related injuries to her leg; doctor told claimant to walk for physical therapy; while walking, claimant was struck by auto; held compensable); Green v. Coca–Cola Bottling Co., 329 Ark. 345, 948 S.W.2d 92 (1997) (employee was driving to the doctor for treatment of work related injury when he stopped to assist an elderly driver whose car had broken down; claimant's car was struck by another motorist injuring claimant; applying Larson's prohibited conduct test, the court held that the claimant had not deviated from his journey; such conduct could not be classified as expressly or impliedly prohibited by the employer); IMC Phosphates Co. v. Prater, 895 So.2d 1263 (Fla.App.1 Dist.2005) (driven by wife, claimant was traveling to doctor for treatment of previous work related knee injury; travel included intermediate stop at auto dealership; auto accident occurred before arrival at dealership; held compensation awarded because ultimate purpose of travel was treatment for work related injury); but, see Flores v. Dependable Tire Co., Inc., 315 Ga. App. 311, 726 S.E.2d 776 (2012) (claimant suffered injuries in auto accident when leaving doctor's office after treatment of work-related injuries; held, no recovery for injuries solely related to auto accident if: (a) trip was voluntary and not a prerequisite to returning to work, (b) the employer did not set up the appointment or provide the transportation, and (c) the employee was free to use his time for his own affairs). And, if the claimant terminates the employment relationship prior to the auto accident, compensation might be denied. In this regard, contrast Bankers Investment Co. v. Boyd, 560 P.2d 958 (Okl.1977) with Telcon, Inc. v. Williams, 500 So.2d 266 (Fla.App.1 Dist.1986). See also, Barrett Business Services v. Hames, 130 Or.App. 190, 881 P.2d 816 (1994) in which the court discussed changes to the Oregon statute which replaced the but-for causation standard with a "major contributing cause" test. The court quoted from the legislative debate which preceded this statutory change ". . . you have a broken arm [from a compensable accident] . . . and you're crossing the street on the way to see your doctor, and the doctor's office is right over there . . . and a car runs you down . . . you got hurt on the way to the doctor. Requiring major contributing cause means that no, being run down crossing the street on the way to the doctor is not covered."

6. Exacerbation of the consequences of a compensable injury caused by subsequent acts of third persons are frequently compensable, particularly exacerbation caused by bad medical treatment of the original injury. See, e.g., Flanagan v. Charles E. Green & Son, 122 N.J.L. 424, 5 A.2d 742 (1939) (claimant hospitalized with a compensable injury broke arm while cooperating with nurses in changing the bed clothes; broken arm held compensable); McAvoy v. Roberts & Mander Stove Co., 173 Pa.Super. 516, 98 A.2d 231 (1953) (claimant underwent surgery as a result of a work injury; while still under anesthesia she was dropped from a litter and sustained a

concussion; held disabling post-concussion syndrome compensable); Mallette v. Mercury Outboard Supply Co., Inc., 204 Tenn. 438, 321 S.W.2d 816 (1959) (claimant, hospitalized due to work injury, was paralyzed when a nurse "threw him around and twisted him" while bathing him; held, compensation awarded); Heumphreus v. State, 334 N.W.2d 757 (Ia.1983) (claimant, a prisoner, suffered possible work related heart attack; jailor negligently delayed transport to hospital causing death; held death compensable); Sutherland v. Illinois Employers Ins. Co., 696 S.W.2d 139 (Tex.App.1985) (claimant fell at work injuring neck and back; in preparation for myelogram, medical staff negligently strapped claimant to the examination table; claimant fell to floor causing further injury; held compensable). When the claimant renders non-prescribed post work-injury medical care to himself, the result may be different. See, e.g., City of Atlanta v. Roach, 297 Ga.App. 408, 677 S.E.2d 426 (2009) (claimant, police officer, broke hip in work related traffic accident; two years later, hip became sore; employee fell asleep on heating pad suffering third degree burns; held heating pad treatment had not been prescribed for hip and did not arise from medical treatment; compensation denied). How would this case be resolved using Larson's "quasi-course of activity" analysis? See *note 3*, following the *Sullivan* case, *supra*.

7. The foregoing principle has been applied to award compensation for the consequences of a physician's negligent treatment of a compensable injury if the claimant used a properly chosen physician. The medical negligence may be in prescribing medication, in setting fractures and in performing other types of medical and surgical procedures. See, e.g., City of Lakeland v. Burton, 147 Fla. 412, 2 So.2d 731 (1941) (negligent prescription of narcotic caused death; held death compensable); Mitchell v. Peaslee, 143 Me. 372, 63 A.2d 302 (1948) (negligence by properly chosen physician in setting fracture; held compensable); Houston General v. Campbell, 964 S.W.2d 691 (Tex.App.1998) (claimant's compensable injury aggravated by doctor's malpractice; employer paid claimant additional compensation due to malpractice and would have subrogation interest in employee's common law malpractice action against doctor).

If the employee negligently selects an incompetent physician, compensation for the doctor's aggravation of the work injury may be denied. See, e.g., Cross v. Hermanson Bros., 235 Iowa 739, 16 N.W.2d 616 (1944) (Chiropractor broke claimant's vertebra during treatment of work related injury; no negligence found in selection of chiropractor); and Spencer v. Department of Industry, Labor and Hum. Rel., 55 Wis.2d 525, 200 N.W.2d 611 (1972) (claimant is not to be faulted for following erroneous medical advice, as long as he did so in good faith). Under Larson's "quasi-course" approach how would the employee's conduct in selecting a physician be assessed? See 1–10 Larson's Workers' Compensation Law, Matthew Bender §§ 10.01 and 10.09[4] (2013).

The method of selecting a physician or other health care provider is usually dictated by the state's workers' compensation act. See Chapter 8, *infra.* Failure to follow the statute may cause a loss of medical benefits including, it would seem, loss of any compensation due to malpractice by the improperly selected health care provider. See, e.g., Johnson Drug Co. v. Thaxton, 121 So.2d 158 (Fla.1960) first holding the employer not liable for the malpractice and, on rehearing, reversing itself by a closely divided vote. In Armstrong v. Stearns–Roger Electrical Contractors, Inc., 99 N.M. 275, 657 P.2d 131 (App.1982), cert. denied 99 N.M. 226, 656 P.2d 889 (1983), the employee did not resort to the employer's list of approved physicians but rather sought care from his family doctor who employed treatment that interfered with the decedent's heart pacemaker causing cardiac arrest and death. Death benefits were denied because of the decedent's failure to follow the employer's procedures. In Crews v. WCAB, 123 Pa.Cmwlth. 610, 554 A.2d 190 (1989), claimant's recovery was apparently slowed because claimant followed his personal physician's prescribed exercise program at the YMCA rather than physical therapy at a rehab center as prescribed by the employer provided physician. This choice was held to be unreasonable.

8. Many statutes include an express statutory provision that damages resulting from medical malpractice shall be deemed part of the injury resulting from the accident. See, e.g. Ga. Code Ann. § 34–9–203 (b) (2013). And see Bennett v. St. Elizabeth Health Systems, 273 Neb. 300, 729 N.W.2d 80 (2007) (employee sued hospital, her employer, in tort, alleging physical therapy which she received at hospital for work related injury was negligently performed; held summary judgment granted; tort action against hospital barred by exclusive remedy provision of workers' compensation act; employee's remedy against employer for negligent medical treatment of work related injury is to be pursued under the workers' compensation act).

Common law suit against the physician as a "third party" for damages for the tortious treatment of the claimant is considered in Chapter 11, *infra.*

5. NEW INJURY OR RECURRENCE OF OLD INJURY

When a work related injury is followed by a subsequent work related injury, the most recent injury may be considered either as a new injury or a recurrence of the old injury. The classification may be important in determining, among other things, which of two or more successive employers or insurance carriers is liable to the employee for the resulting disability; the relevant date of the injury so as to determine the appropriate rate of compensation to which the employee is entitled; whether the claimant is time barred from seeking additional compensation for a "change in condition"; and, perhaps, even whether or not the same tribunal has jurisdiction to resolve the successive claims. The following case and note materials are illustrative.

LOCKHEED MISSILES & SPACE COMPANY, INC. v. BOBCHAK

Court of Appeals of Georgia, 1990.
194 Ga.App. 156, 390 S.E.2d 82.

BANKE, PRESIDING JUDGE.

The claimant in this workers' compensation case sustained an osteochondral fracture to his left knee on August 10, 1987, while employed as a laborer for W.H. Gross Construction Company. He underwent arthroscopic surgery as treatment for this injury and was paid disability benefits until October 12, 1987, when he began working for Lockheed Missiles & Space Company. On February 25, 1988, he noticed a "tired and weak feeling" in the knee after climbing and descending a ladder at Lockheed. By that evening the knee had become painful and swollen, resulting in further disability and, eventually, the need for additional surgery.

At issue in this appeal is whether the knee impairment which the claimant experienced at Lockheed must, as a matter of law, be considered the result of a new accident, with the result that Lockheed would be required to provide compensation for it, or whether it may instead be treated as a change in condition for which Gross Construction Company would be responsible. Based on findings that the claimant's "employment duties at Lockheed were not more strenuous as compared to the heavy labor type work he engaged in with W.H. Gross" and that "[n]o incident occurred that aggravated claimant's prior injured knee," the administrative law judge concluded that the claimant had experienced a change in condition. The full board affirmed; however, the superior court reversed, concluding that the record was "totally devoid of any evidence of a gradual worsening of claimant's condition as a result of the activity connected with his normal duties for the four and one-half month period immediately prior to the ladder incident," and further concluding that there was "no evidence whatever . . . to support the board's conclusion that no specific incident occurred aggravating the claimant's previous injury." The case is before us pursuant to our grant of Lockheed's application for discretionary appeal. See generally OCGA § 5–6–35. Held:

1. "[W]here there is no actual new accident, ordinarily the distinguishing feature that will characterize the disability as either a 'change of condition' or a 'new accident' is the intervention of new circumstances. If the claimant leaves the old employer and goes to work in a different environment with a new employer, there are new circumstances with a new employer; and this is particularly true when the activity performed for the new employer exceeds the limits of the light duty offered by the old employer." Certain v. U.S. Fidelity & Guaranty Co., 153 Ga.App. 571, 573, 266 S.E.2d 263 (1980). The claimant in *Certain* had been injured while performing strenuous work for his original

employer. He was later given a light-duty job assignment by that employer but left that assignment almost immediately to begin working for a new employer. "For [the next] five months, he worked at the same type strenuous work which he had been medically forbidden to do at the first employer's, and from which he had been relieved to perform light work duties. After five months, although he did not have an actual new accident, his condition worsened so that he again became totally disabled. . . ." *Id.* at 572, 266 S.E.2d 263. We held that under these circumstances his disability must, as a matter of law, be considered the result of a fictitious "new accident" rather than a change in condition.

Subsequently, in Beers Constr. Co. v. Stephens, 162 Ga.App. 87, 90, 290 S.E.2d 181 (1982), we emphasized that "[t]he decision in *Certain* that the claimant had suffered a new accident and not a change of condition was not controlled by the mere fact that the claimant was employed by a new employer in a different environment but by the additional new circumstances that the work performed for the second employer exceeded the limits of light work duties offered by the previous employer." We also emphasized in *Beers* that "a 'specific incident' is not [a] prerequisite to a finding of new accident. . . ." *Id.* at 91, 290 S.E.2d 181, citing Blackwell v. Liberty Mut. Ins. Co., 230 Ga. 174, 175, 196 S.E.2d 129 (1973). By the same token, we do not believe that in all cases where the worsening of a pre-existing condition can be traced to a "specific incident" occurring on the new job, that incident must necessarily be considered a "new accident." Rather, the determinative inquiry is whether the circumstances associated with the incident and with the new employment in general were "such as to independently aggravate the condition" or whether the renewed impairment instead resulted from the "wear and tear of ordinary life in connection with performance of normal duties. . . ." *Beers*, *supra*, 162 Ga.App. at 90–91, 290 S.E.2d 181. As previously indicated, the administrative law judge in this case found that "[c]laimant's employment duties at Lockheed were not more strenuous as compared to the heavy labor type work he had performed for W.H. Gross." Furthermore, although the claimant stated that his knee had been improving prior to the ladder incident, he acknowledged that he had continued to experience pain and stiffness in it; and one of the physicians who examined him subsequent to the incident testified: "My experience with those people who have sustained large osteochondral fractures is that they never return to their steady state and may periodically need an arthroscopic debridement every two to five years." As for the ladder-climbing incident itself, it appears to have been completely uneventful. There is no suggestion that the claimant was carrying a heavy object at the time, nor is there any indication that he twisted the knee or otherwise sustained any unusual trauma to it as a result of the climbing. We hold that even though the administrative law judge may have been authorized under these circumstances to conclude that the claimant had experienced a "new accident," he was also authorized to conclude that the claimant had undergone a change in condition, with the result that the superior court erred in substituting its judgment on this issue for that of the board. See generally Atkinson v. Home Indem. Co., 141 Ga.App. 687, 234 S.E.2d 359 (1977).

2. The appellees urge that in the event the judgment of the superior court is reversed, the case should be remanded for a determination of whether or not the administrative law judge made a misstatement of significant testimony when he found as a fact that "[t]he ladder climbing was a part of claimant's ordinary work." It is contended that this finding conflicts with the claimant's undisputed testimony that he had not previously climbed any ladders in connection with his work at Lockheed but had climbed only stairs. However, we do not interpret this statement by the administrative law judge as a finding that the claimant was routinely required to climb ladders at Lockheed; rather, we interpret it to mean simply that the incident occurred while he was engaged in the performance of his ordinary and usual duties there. In any event, regardless of how many ladders the claimant had climbed at Lockheed, there was no indication that the demands placed on his weakened knee by his job responsibilities at Lockheed exceeded those which would have been placed on the knee had he returned to work for his prior employer, where he had also been required to climb ladders. Consequently, we do not believe the administrative law judge's finding in this regard can be considered unfavorable to the appellees, regardless of how it is interpreted.

Judgement reversed.

SOGNIER and POPE, JJ., concur.

NOTES

1. In Cypress Companies v. Brown, 246 Ga.App. 804, 542 S.E.2d 544 (2000), the court characterized the inquiry as whether the "underlying facts . . . establish[ed] an accident, a change in condition or a fictional new accident." Referencing a prior decision in Central State Hospital v. James, 147 Ga.App. 308, 248 S.E.2d 678 (1978), the court said, "When a claimant sustains an injury, is awarded compensation, returns to his normal and ordinary job duties, but then as a result of 'the wear and tear of ordinary life and the activity connected with performing his normal duties,' his condition gradually deteriorates . . . such facts constitute a change in condition . . . On the other hand, when a claimant is injured on the job but continues, without an agreement or award, to perform duties of his employment until forced to cease work because of a gradual worsening of his condition that is at least partly attributable to his physical activity in continuing to work, such facts constitute a 'new accident.' " And, see Oconee Area Home Care Services, Inc. v. Burton, 275 Ga.App. 784, 621 S.E.2d 859 (2005) (" . . . when a

claimant sustains a second accident as the result of a specific job related incident, which aggravates a pre-existing condition arising from a prior accident, then the second accident is a new injury if it at least partially precipitated the claimant's disability."); Trucks, Inc. v. Trowell, 302 Ga. App. 488, 690 S.E.2d 880 (2010) (claimant was injured while working for Employer 1 and received medical benefits but not disability benefits; medical treatment continued after claimant began working for Employer 2; eventually claimant ceased working and sought disability benefits from Employer 1; Employer 1 argued claimant suffered new injury while employed by Employer 2; held, compensation awarded against Employer 1 neither on basis of change of condition (for that requires a previous award of disability benefits which had not occurred in this case) nor on basis of a new injury but rather on basis that initial injury suffered while working for Employer 1 persisted and ultimately caused the claimed disability).

2. In Gonzales v. Stanke–Brown and Associates, Inc., 98 N.M. 379, 648 P.2d 1192 (1982), the claimant suffered a 1976 work related back injury which was found to cause a 45 percent permanent partial disability. The claimant suffered a 1979 injury to the same area of the back adding an additional 10 percent disability, or a total of 55 percent. The court held the compensation insurance carrier at the time of the second incident was liable for 55 percent partial disability benefits at the 1979 wage rate while the carrier at the time of the first injury was liable for 45 percent benefits at the 1976 wage rate. The court further held that pursuant to a statutory provision, N.M.S.A. Sec. 52–1–47 (D), the second carrier's liability would be reduced by the amount of benefits paid or payable by the first carrier. Regarding apportionment of costs and attorney fees, the court held that each carrier would be responsible in proportion to its share of compensation payable to the claimant. And see, Tom Growney Equipment Co. v. Jouett, 137 N.M. 497, 113 P.3d 320 (2005) (" . . . the question is which employer is liable when the worker suffered an initial non-disabling injury, aggravated the injury through later employment, and became disabled while working for a successive employer. The employer and compensation carrier at the time of the second accidental injury are initially liable for disability resulting from the second accidental injury, to the full extent of the disability . . . this liability on the part of the successive employer may be reduced under [N.M.S.A.] Section 52–1–47 (D) if the initial injury resulted in disability prior to the subsequent injury.").

3. In Fisher v. K Mart Corp., 174 Mich.App. 669, 436 N.W.2d 434 (1989), a claimant who suffered an initial injury to his foot in 1976 re-injured the foot and fractured his wrist in 1977. In 1978, the claimant's foot pain became so severe he left work, underwent surgery and remained disabled. The ensuing workers' compensation claim raised the issue of whether he was entitled to compensation at the rate provided for in the 1976 statute or at the rate provided by 1978 legislation. The workers' compensation appeal board, in a split decision, held the 1978 disability to be a recurrence of the 1976 injury not a "new injury" and applied the 1976 rate. The Michigan Court of

Appeals reversed and applied the 1978 rate on the ground that the 1978 disability constituted a "new injury." The new injury was held to have occurred on the date that the pain from the 1976 accident became so great that the claimant was no longer able to work.

4. In Harris v. District of Columbia Office of Worker's Compensation, 660 A.2d 404 (D.C.Ct.App.1995), the employee's first injury occurred before the effective date of the workers' compensation statute. The second event took place after the law was in force. The hearing officer found the second event was a re-occurrence of the first injury and, thus, non compensable. The court reversed finding that the second event was an aggravation of the prior injury and that the employee was entitled to an award for the aggravation. The employee eventually failed to prevail on other grounds in Harris v. District of Columbia Department of Employment Services, 746 A.2d 297 (D.C. 2000).

5. Andras v. Donovan, 414 F.2d 241 (5th Cir.1969) raised a dispute as to whether compensation should be paid under the Longshore and Harbor Workers' Compensation Act or under a state workers' compensation law. The claimant suffered the first injury, a traumatic neurosis, and was compensated under the Longshore Act. As part of the treatment for his psychiatric injuries, his physician directed him to return to work in the shipyards. Claimant subsequently injured his back in the course of his land-based employment duties. The deputy commissioner refused jurisdiction under the Longshore Act for the second injury because, being a land-based injury, it was beyond the jurisdiction of the statute. The fifth circuit reversed and remanded for the deputy to determine whether there was any causal connection between the two injuries. If such connection was found, the deputy could properly award compensation for both injuries.

6. In Insurance Co. of N.A. v. U.S. Department of Labor, Office of Workers' Compensation Programs, 969 F.2d 1400 (2d Cir.1992), The employee died of lung cancer after on-the-job exposure to asbestos. The question of compensation hinged on whether the version of the Longshore and Harbor Workers' Compensation Act in effect on the date of last exposure or the amended version in place on the date of first manifestation of illness controlled. The answer would determine whether the employee had met the situs requirement of the statute and, thus, whether his widow would receive death benefits.

7. Sometimes it makes a difference whether a disability is labeled a new injury or a change of condition due to the applicable statutory time frame within which the claim or a re-opening of a previous claim must be filed. In this regard see Shaw Industries, Inc. v. Scott, 310 Ga. App. 750, 713 S.E.2d 917 (2012) (because claimant's disability was a change of condition not a new injury, claim was barred because the two-year time frame for re-opening the award due to a change of condition had elapsed); Evergreen Packaging, Inc. v. Prather, 318 Ga. App. 440, 734 S.E.2d 209 (2012) (here the board and court determined that claimant suffered a new injury not a change

of condition and thus the claim was not barred by the two-year change of condition time limitation).

8. Regarding many of these issues, and for a discussion of the variations of the "last injurious exposure" rule, which Larson describes as a frequently applied apportionment approach in the successive injury cases, see generally 9–153 Larson's Workers' Compensation Law § 153.01 *et seq.* (2013). In the context of occupational disease, the "last injurious exposure" rule, as a basis for apportionment in successive disability cases, is addressed in Chapter 6, Section 4 (C), *supra*. For additional discussion regarding the "change of condition" issue, see Chapter 10, Section 7, *infra*.

6. REFUSAL TO ACCEPT MEDICAL TREATMENT

COMMONWEALTH, DEPT. OF HIGHWAYS V. LINDON

Court of Appeals of Kentucky, 1964.
380 S.W.2d 247.

DAVIS, COMMISSIONER.

Following an accident in the course of his employment with the Kentucky Department of Highways in which he sustained a minor, temporary injury to his left foot, William A. Lindon, Jr., developed a condition described by one doctor as a "psychoneurosis conversion hysteria which was superimposed on a minor foot injury." Lindon became convinced in his mind that he had constant pain in his foot and leg and as a result he was unable to work. The Workmen's Compensation Board gave him an open-end award for total permanent disability, based on a finding that he was suffering from "compensation neurosis" (a medically recognized mental aberration distinguished from conscious malingering). On appeal to the circuit court judgment was entered upholding the award. The Department of Highways has appealed here from that judgment.

We find merit in the appellant's contention that the compensation board erred in holding that Lindon's refusal to submit to certain psychiatric treatment was not unreasonable. (KRS 342.035 provides that no compensation shall be payable for disability of an employee "in so far as his disability is aggravated, caused or continued, by an unreasonable failure to submit to or follow any competent surgical treatment or medical aid or advice.")

A psychiatrist who treated Lindon recommended that he submit to a sodium amytal interview, which would involve administering a sedative similar to "truth serum," would make the patient drowsy and less resistant and more amenable to suggestion. The purpose would be to overcome the neurosis by suggestion. The psychiatrist stated that if the treatment were successful a cure could be effected in two or three sessions. Lindon refused to take the treatment. His personal physician stated that he did not believe the psychiatric treatment alone would effect a cure.

The compensation board expressed the views that the proposed treatment might further deter Lindon's improvement, and that the treatment would be of no good effect if Lindon resisted its purpose. There is no evidence in the record to sustain these views. No doctor testified that the treatment might be harmful, or that Lindon's resistance would make the treatment completely ineffectual.

The appellee argues that the board's ruling should be upheld under the rule that if there is a difference of expert opinion as to the danger *or efficacy* of medical or surgical treatment the employee's refusal to submit is not unreasonable. * * * However, the cases stating that rule all involved *operations,* where there was some degree of physical suffering involved from the operation. Here there is nothing to indicate that the treatment would involve any suffering or even material discomfort. Under such circumstances, in our opinion, the mere fact that there is a difference of expert opinion as to the possible success of the treatment is not sufficient to support a refusal to take the treatment. We think this is particularly so in the case of mental disturbances, where the methods of treatment have not yet reached the stage of development where successful results can accurately be predicted.

It is our conclusion that the compensation board erred in finding that Lindon's refusal to submit to the proposed treatment was not unreasonable. Upon remand of the case the board will enter an order withholding compensation payments until Lindon submits to the treatment.

The appellant makes a further contention that the evidence does not support the board's finding that there was a causal connection between the traumatic injury and the disability. We believe there was adequate proof of causal connection. Dr. Maddox stated in a written report that the accident was the only cause of Lindon's condition. Dr. Wiesel testified that the injury precipitated the condition. It no doubt is true, as stated by Dr. Maddox, that Lindon's psychoneurotic tendencies existed before the injury; however, he had no disability until the tendencies were activated by the injury. We agree with the authorities holding that the injury is the cause of the compensation neurosis disability in such circumstances. See Larson, Workmen's Compensation, Volume I, sec. 42.24.

* * *

The judgment is reversed with directions to enter judgment remanding the case to the Workmen's Compensation Board for further proceedings in conformity with this opinion.

NOTES

1. The Kentucky statute set out in the principal case is similar to that in many other states. See, e.g., Ariz. Rev. Stats. Ann. § 23–1027 (2012); 77 Pa. Stats. Ann. 531(8) (2012); 9A Tenn. Code Ann. § 50–6–204(8) (2012); and Va. Code Ann. § 65.2–603(B) (2011).

2. In the absence of specific statutes, courts commonly apply the same general principle on the theory that an injury caused by an employee's unreasonable refusal of needed treatment "is not proximately caused by the accident, but is the direct result of such unreasonable refusal." Lesh v. Illinois Steel Co., 163 Wis. 124, 157 N.W. 539 (1916). Larson suggests that because the employee's conduct in accepting or rejecting medical treatment for a work related injury involves a "quasi-course-of-employment" activity, compensation should be suspended only if the employee's conduct is intentional and clearly unreasonable and not merely negligent. 1–10 Larson's Workers' Compensation Law § 10.10 (2013).

3. Applying this principle is sometimes troublesome particularly because of a convention that forfeiture statutes, such as these, must be "strictly construed." See, e.g., Wood v. Wagner Electric Corp., 192 S.W.2d 579 (Mo.App.1946), opinion modified 355 Mo. 670, 197 S.W.2d 647 (1946) (claimant over sixty years of age with high blood pressure, refused to undergo hernia operation; held not unreasonable); Amerisure Ins. Co. v. Jones, ___ So.3d ___, 2013 WL 7117395 (La.App. 1 Cir. 2013) (because reduction of benefits under the Louisiana statute is penal in nature, it is to be strictly construed). Once compensation is awarded, the award ordinarily will not be terminated in the absence of strong justification. See, e.g. Stump v. Norfolk Shipbuilding & Dry Dock Corp., 187 Va. 932, 48 S.E.2d 209 (1948) (employee refused medication for infected abrasion of skin, ultimate loss of leg; held not compensable); Skidmore v. Drumon Fine Foods, Inc., 119 So.2d 523 (La.App.1960) (claimant with persistent pain following amputation of a finger was required to submit to simple, minor surgery or lose his compensation); Sanderson v. Secrest Pipe Coating Co., 465 S.W.2d 65 (Ky.1971) (failure to follow a course of exercises); Byrd v. WCAB, 81 Pa.Cmwlth. 325, 473 A.2d 723 (1984) (claimant cancelled eight of twelve physical therapy sessions and suffered second injury because of failure to complete therapy; held unreasonable); Menges v. WCAB, 93 Pa.Cmwlth. 395, 501 A.2d 347 (1985) (leg surgery was refused by claimant because "some people told [him] it wouldn't help any;" evidence showed surgery would reduce disability by one half, would reduce pain and had a 80 percent success rate; held refusal unreasonable); Dabney v. Boh Brothers Construction Co., 710 So.2d 1106 (La.App.1998) (Court found the statute to be mandatory, clear and unambiguous in its call for a fifty percent reduction in benefits when a claimant refuses to participate fully in a vocational rehabilitation program).

4. What criteria should courts invoke in determining whether the medical procedure is "reasonably required" so that the employee's refusal to undergo the treatment is "unreasonable" or "unjustifiable?" The principal

considerations seem to be: the prospect of success of the surgical procedure or medical treatment; the amount of pain and suffering it entails; and, the danger to the claimant's health or life. Where the prospects for success are poor or uncertain, courts commonly hold that the claimant's refusal to accept the treatment is not unreasonable. The Kentucky court has upheld claimant's refusal where "the result of his operation would be speculative." Melcher v. Drummond Mfg. Co., 312 Ky. 588, 229 S.W.2d 52 (1950) (hernia); and see Couch v. Saginaw Malleable Iron Plant, 42 Mich.App. 223, 201 N.W.2d 681 (1972) (50% chance of success; held refusal not unreasonable). In Martinez v. Excel Corp., 32 Kan.App.2d 139, 79 P.3d 230 (2003) the employee refused carpal tunnel surgery. The court affirmed the Board's determination that the refusal was reasonable because some patients experience no relief and some get worse after surgery. One Doctor testified that only about 50% of patients regain normal strength. And, see Alltel, Inc. v. W.C.A.B., 829 A.2d 739 (Pa. Cmwlth.2003) (court held employee's refusal of cervical disc surgery was reasonable; while proposed surgeries were low risk and had 80% probability of reducing some symptoms, they had only 50% chance of improving claimant so he could resume employment). And see LiSanti Painting Co. v. W.C.A.B., 973 A.2d 464 (Pa.Cmwlth.2009). Contrast the following cases: Joyce Western Corp. v. WCAB, 518 Pa. 191, 542 A.2d 990 (1988) (in case involving a proposed corneal implant; held, what constitutes reasonable surgery in a particular case will be determined by the fact-finder; and if "the evidence establishes that the recommended surgery involves minimal risk to the patient and offers a high probability of success, the proposed surgery is reasonable"; benefits will be properly denied if the claimant rejects such a procedure); and, Sanchez, Inc. v. W.C.A.B., 209 WL 9101160 (Pa. Cmwlth., 2009) (doctor recommended claimant undergo discectomy and spinal fusion; doctor testified procedure would benefit claimant significantly, that surgery entailed no unreasonable risk, and that 85% of patients do well; claimant offered insufficient counter-evidence; held, compensation properly suspended).

5. An employee's age, general physical condition, and specific medical circumstances, such as high blood pressure, are all taken into account. In Parker v. Mead Corp., 91 F.Supp. 960 (E.D.Tenn.1949), affirmed 183 F.2d 952 (6th Cir.1950), a sixty-two year old claimant who suffered from "smothering spells," tortuosity and enlargement of descending aorta, enlargement of the liver, calcification in the left lung and near spleen, arthritic lipping in the spine, and arthritic spurs in the lumbar region was held justified in refusing a herniotomy. In Waldroup v. J.C. Penney Co., 30 Or.App. 443, 567 P.2d 576 (1977), a claimant, suffering from a low back injury, refused myelography and surgery because she was receiving treatment from a chiropractor who reported she was "responding very satisfactorily." The court held that the refusal was reasonable. Reef v. Willamette Industries, 65 Or.App. 366, 671 P.2d 1197 (1983) (held, reasonableness is a question of fact and the determination must be based upon all relevant factors including the worker's present physical and psychological condition).

In Flaherty v. Industrial Comm., 73 Ariz. 74, 237 P.2d 806 (1951), the court, in upholding an award of benefits, took into account the immediate economic necessity of the claimant who refused treatment, in part, because he believed that the application of a cast would prevent him from working and earning an income. The court also considered evidence that the doctors delayed casting claimant's fractured wrist because of a missed diagnosis and that the delay might cause the treatment to be ineffectual.

6. Courts are unlikely to require an employee to submit to repeated tests where the first one proves negative. See, e.g., Zanotti v. New York Telephone Co., 61 A.D.2d 861, 401 N.Y.S.2d 911 (1978).

Where an operation has been performed previously and has not been successful, courts are not likely to require claimant to endure a second one. See, e.g., City of Olive Hill v. Parsons, 306 Ky. 83, 206 S.W.2d 41 (1947) (hernia; and citing cases from other jurisdictions holding similarly); and Dudansky v. L.H. Sault Const. Co., 244 Minn. 369, 70 N.W.2d 114 (1955) (disc). Contrast, Muse v. W.C.A.B., 514 Pa. 1, 522 A.2d 533 (1987) (first surgery to repair hernia resulted in complications and need for second corrective surgery which offered high probability of success and little risk; held second surgery reasonable and refusal thereof unreasonable).

7. An employee's fear of the operation may be a sufficient ground to hold the refusal reasonable. See, e.g., Morgan v. Sholom Drilling Co., 199 Kan. 156, 427 P.2d 448 (1967) (85 to 90% chance of success but fear present; held refusal reasonable); American Asbestos Textile Corp. v. Ryder, 111 N.H. 282, 281 A.2d 53 (1971) (fear of laminectomy); Fluor Alaska, Inc. v. Mendoza, 616 P.2d 25 (Ak.1980) (fear of dying during laminectomy); Small v. Combustion Engineering, 209 Mont. 387, 681 P.2d 1081 (1984) (manic-depressive claimant refused knee surgery due to fear of detrimental consequences; held refusal not unreasonable because of mental disorder) and Grandinetti v. Syracuse University, 134 A.D.2d 683, 521 N.Y.S.2d 343 (1987) (claimant refused myelogram and back surgery because of attendant serious dangers and because claimant's wife and brother-in-law had experienced adverse results from myelogram; held refusal reasonable); Dorris v. Mississippi Regional Housing Authority, 695 So.2d 567 (Miss.1997) (included in the court's reasons for finding the refusal to undergo surgery justifiable was claimant's subjective fear).

8. Should the reasonableness of an employee's refusal of treatment be examined objectively or subjectively? States differ in their approach. See, e.g., Genuardi Supermarkets v. WCAB, 674 A.2d 1194 (Pa.Cmwlth.1996) (the standard for determining whether a claimant's refusal to accept medical services is reasonable is whether the services themselves are reasonable, not whether the claimant's refusal is reasonable). To the same effect, see Lisanti Painting Co. v. W.C.A.B. 973 A.2d 464 (Pa.Cmwlth.2009); Schwab Construction v. McCarter, 25 Va.App. 104, 486 S.E.2d 562 (1997) ("the test employed ... [in an unjustified refusal of treatment case] is a subjective one—whether the claimant acted reasonably in refusing the medical

treatment"); Johnson v. Jones, 123 N.C.App. 219, 472 S.E.2d 587 (1996) (test is whether a reasonable person who is motivated to improve his or her health would accept the proffered treatment).

9. Sometimes an employee's refusal of medical services may be less direct but will nevertheless raise similar problems. Suppose, for example, that in the *Braewood* case, in Section 1 of this chapter, *supra*, the doctors had ordered the claimant to lose weight before proceeding with rehabilitative therapy. Would the claimant's refusal or failure to lose weight be tantamount to a refusal of medical services? See Amerisure Ins. Co. v. Jones, ___ So.3d ___, 2013 WL 7117395 (La. App. 1 Cir. 2013) (claimant who weighed at or over 600 pounds, suffered a work-related back injury; claimant received medication and physical therapy for his injury and asked for and received a prescription for the Weight Watchers program; employer sought to reduce payments arguing claimant was not complying with the weight reduction program; held evidence supported finding that claimant was compliant; court further discussed Louisiana precedent which noted the persistence of obesity and the difficulty of treating failure to lose weight as willful failure to cooperate with medical treatment). See the discussion and cases cited in 1–10 Larson's Workers' Compensation Law Section, Matthew Bender § 10.10[4] (2013) (suggesting courts are apparently reluctant to treat as willful refusal matters involving addictions related to food; after all, we all know someone who has tried but failed to lose weight). What if a claimant needs surgery but is ordered to stop smoking in order for surgery to be safely performed. Should claimant's inability or refusal to cease smoking be deemed an unreasonable refusal of medical care? In this context, should addiction to tobacco be treated differently than traditional refusal of medical care? Is addiction solely a matter of will power? If the claimant makes a good faith effort, achieves substantial progress but is not completely successful in the attempt to break the addiction, should this still be treated as refusal of medical care? Does it matter whether or not the addiction exists prior to the accident in question. See Shawnee Management Corp. v. Hamilton, 24 Va.App. 151, 480 S.E.2d 773 (1997) (claimant's continued smoking was refusal of treatment precluding right to compensation); reversed on rehearing 25 Va.App. 672, 492 S.E.2d 456 (1997) (evidence was sufficient to support Commission's finding that claimant's unsuccessful attempt to quit smoking was not wilful refusal of medical services). And see Naumann v. Foreway Transportation, Inc., 477 Mich. 970, 724 N.W.2d 476 (2006) (claimant suffered work-related neck injury; as precondition to neck surgery, Dr. Ordered cessation of smoking for six months; after three months, she resumed smoking; hearing officer held failure to stop smoking was unreasonable refusal of medical care; Workers' Compensation Appeals Court reversed; Supreme court refused to hear appeal; very strong dissent to effect that failure to cease smoking effectively constituted refusal of medical treatment, but question of unreasonableness needed further fact finding).

10. Should a refusal to accept medical treatment because of religious convictions be a basis for terminating or denying compensation? In the

following excerpts, compare the ways in which the courts in *Martin* and *Montgomery* address the intersection of: (1) the First Amendment; (2) the financial needs of the employee; and (3) the increased monetary burden that may be imposed upon both the employer and the state compensation funds as the result of the employee's continuing disability or death:

Martin v. Industrial Accident Commission
147 Cal.App.2d 137, 304 P.2d 828 (1956).

* * *

"Section 4056 of the Labor Code is a part of the statutory plan or scheme for workmen's compensation which imposes liability upon the employer for an industrial injury without regard to fault, and the Legislature clearly had the right to make it a condition of the right to receive compensation and of the imposition of liability on the employer that the employee should not unreasonably refuse to accept medical care."

"Petitioner's entirely overlook the fact that not only are Martin's rights to compensation involved but the employer's liability for the payment of compensation is also involved. Certainly it was not unreasonable for the Legislature to fix as a condition to the employer's liability that the death of an employee must arise out of his employment and that it should not exist where death is the result of the voluntary act of the employee in refusing medical attention. Here the commission not only found that Martin's refusal of medical care was unreasonable but that his death was due not to the injury received in the scope and course of his employment but by his refusal of transfusions of whole blood. Martin was not obligated to work in an employment that rendered him subject to the Workmen's Compensation Act, and if he accepted such employment he accepted it, insofar as his right to compensation is concerned, subject to the conditions imposed by the Legislature upon the right to such compensation."

"It is Petitioners' contention, however, that if the statute is construed as permitting the commission to hold that an employee's refusal to accept medical aid is unreasonable where the acceptance of such aid is contrary to his religious beliefs, the statute denies him his constitutional right of religious freedom and to the equal protection of the laws."

"There is no merit in this contention, for '[a]lthough freedom of conscience and the freedom to believe are absolute, the freedom to act is not.' Pencovic v. Pencovic, 45 Cal.2d 97, 103, 287 P.2d 501, 504; Prince v. Massachusetts, 321 U.S. 158, 169–170, 64 S.Ct. 438, 88 L.Ed. 645; Jacobson v. Massachusetts, 197 U.S. 11, 29, 25 S.Ct.

358, 49 L.Ed. 643; Adler v. Board of Education, 342 U.S. 485, 72 S.Ct. 380, 96 L.Ed. 517. Under the statute here Martin was free to believe and worship as he chose, and he was further free, if he so chose, to practice his belief; but if he exercised that choice and his death resulted from his choice, petitioners were not entitled, as a matter of right, to the benefits of the workmen's compensation laws."

"Petitioners cite, in support of their proposition that the statute is unconstitutional, West Virginia State Board of Education v. Barnette, 319 U.S. 624, 63 S.Ct. 1178, 87 L.Ed. 1628, and Hardwick v. Board of School Trustees, 54 Cal.App. 696, 205 P. 49. These cases, however, are clearly distinguishable. In each of them the statute made the performance of an act contrary to the religious belief of the petitioner compulsory, and the refusal to conform subjected the one so refusing to penal action. There is nothing in the present statute that compels an employee to accept medical treatment of any kind, and he is free to make his choice between the practice of his religion and the acceptance of treatment that may be contrary thereto; but if he refuses, the commission is bound, as a court or jury would be in a tort action, to look at all of the facts and to determine therefrom whether his refusal was reasonable."

* * *

Montgomery v. Board of Retirement

33 Cal.App.3d 447, 109 Cal.Rptr. 181 (1973).

* * *

"The denial of disability retirement forces appellant to choose between following the precepts of her religion and forfeiting the disability retirement benefits on the one hand and abandoning one of the precepts of her religion in order to cease to be permanently disabled and return to work on the other hand. In effect, the appellant may not practice her religion and receive benefits. . . ."

* * *

" . . . [W]e perceive no compelling state or county interest enforced in the eligibility provisions of the disability retirement statute justifying the substantial infringement of appellant's First Amendment right to the free exercise of her religion. We glean from respondent's brief three such interests: (1) The preservation of the life and health of citizens; (2) the preservation of an active and capable and productive county work force; (3) the preservation of the financial integrity of the fund upon which the members rely through the preservation of a reasonably objective medical standard for determining what type of condition constitutes a permanent incapacity."

"There is no factual showing and reason does not support a conclusion that any of these interests would be substantially threatened by a rule permitting employees to reject medical treatment because the treatment conflicts with their religious beliefs. In the absence of some factual showing, we are unwilling to speculate that the number of employees who fit appellant's mold is so large as to have other than a minimal impact upon the health of public employees, disrupt the public service, or substantially affect the financial integrity of the fund."

* * *

"The preservation of the financial integrity of the retirement fund is a legitimate governmental interest. However, there is no showing nor any finding that the integrity of the fund will be threatened by permitting appellant to receive retirement benefits. Moreover, as was said in Sherbert v. Verner, *supra*, 374 U.S. at page 407, 83 S.Ct. at p. 1796: 'For even if the possibility of spurious claims did threaten to dilute the fund and disrupt the scheduling of work, it would plainly be incumbent upon the appellees to demonstrate that no alternative forms of regulation would combat such abuses without infringing First Amendment rights. . . .' Furthermore, in a constitutional context involving basic rights, the preservation of moneys is not of primary significance. (Goldberg v. Kelly, 397 U.S. 254, 90 S.Ct. 1011, 25 L.Ed.2d 287.)"

* * *

"Martin has not been cited in any subsequent case. . . . The conclusion is un-avoidable that the principles set forth in Martin . . . no longer represent the law in this field."

* * *

---

11. In Wilcut v. Innovative Warehousing, 247 S.W.3d 1 (Mo.App. E.D.2008), the employee truck driver sustained severe injuries in a road accident. He refused a blood transfusion due to religious beliefs and death followed. Doctors testified that he would have lived had he received blood. The hearing officer awarded compensation. The Commission reversed. The Missouri Court of Appeals reversed and allowed compensation. In its opinion the Court discussed the California cases of *Martin* and *Montgomery, supra,* suggesting *Montgomery* had overruled *Martin.* It reasoned that invoking strong and sincerely held religious beliefs did not constitute an unreasonable refusal of medical care. Judge Romines issued a strong dissent; and, see Williams v. State ex rel. Wyo. Workers' Safety and Compensation Division,

209 Wy. 57, 205 P.3d 1024 (Wyo. 2009) (employee suffered serious injury in a work-related auto accident; he refused blood transfusion due to religious beliefs and ultimately died; in their testimony, doctors were less than certain regarding the medical effect of the refusal; board denied recovery for employee's death; court reversed finding insufficient evidence that refusal of blood products caused death).

12. In Walter Nashert and Sons v. McCann, 460 P.2d 941 (Okl.1969) the court held that an employee who suffered multiple work related heart attacks and then refused, because of his religious beliefs, to take doctor prescribed medicines was entitled to compensation for his heart injury attributable to the work but not for the disability attributed to his refusal of medication.

13. If a religious based refusal of medical treatment is permitted, an accompanying issue may be whether all religions, faiths and equivalent belief systems must be treated similarly. The court, in Kemp v. Workers' Compensation Dept., 65 Or.App. 659, 672 P.2d 1343 (1983); review denied 296 Or. 638, 678 P.2d 739 (1984), held that a Workers' Compensation Department rule and a virtually identical provision in the workers' compensation statute which authorized compensation for workers who chose to be treated by "a duly accredited practitioner of a well-recognized church" violated the First Amendment to the U.S. Constitution as well as Article I sections 2 and 3 of the Oregon constitution. The court held that the state cannot extend a benefit to one person and withhold it from another because the former belongs to an established religious denomination while the latter does not. The court further reasoned that in deciding whether a principled refusal of medical treatment will work a forfeiture of workers' compensation coverage, the State must treat people equally regardless of whether they belong to recognized churches, are members of little known denominations, or are individuals "whose personal conscience without the dictates of a formal religious belief mandate no medical treatment." Compare the 1984 amendment to the Longshore and Harbor Workers' Compensation Act, 33 U.S.C.A. § 907(K)(*l*), "nothing in this chapter prevents an employee whose injury or disability has been established under this chapter from relying in good faith on treatment by prayer or spiritual means alone, in accordance with the tenets and practice of a recognized church or religious denomination. . . ." How does this statute fare in the light of a *Kemp* type analysis?

14. A number of states have legislation that either allows, or requires, the awarding of benefits to an employee who chooses to have a work related injury treated exclusively by religious methods. These statutes differ from one another in terms of the scope of coverage that they provide. The principal variables are: (1) Whether coverage is conditioned upon an agreement between employer and employee (See, e.g., Vernon's Ann. Missouri Stat. Sec. 287.140(9) (2013); Ark. Code Ann. Sec. 11–9–515 (2013); Kan. Stat. Ann. Sec. 44–510h(c) (2011); Ind. Stat. Ann. Sec. 22–3–3–4(c) (2013)); (2) must the church or denomination in question be a "recognized" or "well recognized" one

(See, e.g., O.R.S. 656.010 (2013); Me. R.S.A. 39–A Sec. 207 (2001); D.C. Code Sec. 32–1507(h) (2007)); and (3) is payment for the costs of the spiritual treatment at the employer's discretion? (See, e.g., O.R.S. 656.010 (2013); R.I. Gen. Laws Sec. 28–33–41(B)(I)–(II) (2000)).

7. SUICIDE AS AN INTERVENING ACT OR CAUSE

VREDENBURG V. SEDGWICK CMS

Supreme Court of Nevada, 2008.
188 P.3d 1084.

OPINION

By the Court, PARRAGUIRRE, J.:

In this appeal, we address a single issue of first impression: whether and under what circumstances surviving family members may recover workers' compensation death benefits if an injured employee commits suicide as the result of an industrial injury. While workers' compensation benefits are generally available for accidental employee deaths, under N.R.S. 616C.230(1), Nevada's willful self-injury exclusion, the employee's surviving family members are precluded from recovering benefits if the employee's death results from a "willful intention to injure himself." Although we have not previously addressed the scope of this exclusion, we now conclude that suicides are not willful for purposes of N.R.S. 616C.230(1) if a sufficient chain of causation has been established. Under this construct, a claimant must demonstrate that (1) the employee suffered an industrial injury (2) the industrial injury caused some psychological condition severe enough to override the employee's rational judgment, and (3) the psychological condition caused the employee to commit suicide. In light of this newly announced standard, we reverse the district court's order denying judicial review and remand this matter so that the appeals officer may conduct further proceedings.[1]

FACTS AND PROCEDURAL HISTORY

After undergoing extensive treatment for pain related to a back injury that he incurred when he slipped on a flight of stairs while working as a bartender for respondent Flamingo Hilton–Laughlin, Danny Vredenburg committed suicide. Before ending his own life, Danny recovered industrial insurance benefits for his back injury. The compensability of that injury is, therefore, undisputed.

Following his accident on the stairway, Danny began to experience neck and lower back pain and was diagnosed with internal disc derangement at several locations along his spine. Danny then underwent

1 Editor's note: Some footnotes have been omitted, and others have been renumbered.

a 360-degree anterior-posterior fusion surgery. Despite his fusion surgery, Danny continued to experience pain.

When advised that additional surgical procedures could not offer him any further relief, Danny consulted a series of pain management specialists who prescribed him pain medication and muscle relaxants. Still experiencing pain, however, Danny consulted Dr. Daniel Kim and was diagnosed with "failed back syndrome." In his medical evaluation, Dr. Kim noted that Danny's current regimen of care, consisting mainly of pain medication and pain management therapy, could not effectively address Danny's clinical condition.

Pursuing a more aggressive approach, Dr. Kim recommended an anti-inflammatory agent, stronger pain medication, and an antidepressant to counteract Danny's paradoxical reaction to his muscle relaxants, which kept him awake. Later, when the pain did not subside, Danny elected to surgically implant a morphine infusion pump in his spine and undergo a round of epidural steroid injections.

According to Dr. Kim, however, even with these additional procedures, Danny's lower back pain was "intractable." Moreover, because of the chronic nature of this pain, in Dr. Kim's view, Danny had become "psychologically de-stabilized." Recognizing that, as a result, Danny was unfit to return to work, Dr. Kim recommended that Danny claim permanent disability status, and he informed the Flamingo of Danny's condition. In the month that followed, Danny committed suicide by a self-inflicted gunshot wound to the head.

Before ending his own life, Danny composed several suicide notes expressing his need to be at peace, and he called a longtime friend, telling him that "he could no longer take the pain and all of his pain medications." According to the friend, Danny had become dependent on his pain medication, which tended to increase his mobility but "made [Danny] think funny."

According to others who knew him, until his fusion surgery, Danny was sociable and extroverted. After his surgery, by contrast, Danny was a "different person," as his life had become "dominated by the pain from his injury." Furthermore, as recorded in the affidavits of coworkers and friends, Danny became increasingly humorless and withdrawn. He was unable to eat and lost weight, his self-esteem decreased, and his physical appearance deteriorated. Walking became difficult and painful, one coworker observed, and with each movement Danny noticeably suffered.

In Dr. Donovan Anderson's medical opinion, Danny "committed suicide as a result of [ongoing] intractable pain that was unrelenting." Based on Dr. Anderson's opinion, appellant Sharon Vredenburg, Danny's surviving spouse, filed a claim for death benefits, asserting that Danny "took his own life because he was in so much pain from his industrial injury." Noting that Dr. Anderson's opinion lacked a medical rationale linking Danny's suicide to his industrial injury, the Flamingo's insurance administrator denied the claim.

After a hearing officer affirmed the claim denial, Vredenburg appealed to an appeals officer, and the parties were directed to address the compensability of industrially related suicides in Nevada. Although at the time no controlling test existed, Vredenburg argued that Danny's suicide was compensable under the chain-of-causation test outlined by the Arizona Supreme Court in Graver Tank & Manufacturing Co. v. Industrial Commission, 97 Ariz. 256, 399 P.2d 664, 668 (1965).

Disagreeing with Vredenburg, the appeals officer affirmed the claim denial, concluding that (1) the chain-of-causation test was not binding in Nevada; (2) even if it was, *Graver Tank* was distinguishable because Danny's suicide was deliberate instead of the product of insanity; and (3) Vredenburg failed to present conclusive evidence that Danny was devoid of normal judgment and dominated by a disturbance of mind directly caused by his industrial injury. Vredenburg unsuccessfully petitioned for judicial review in the district court. This appeal followed.

DISCUSSION

In this appeal, we consider whether N.R.S. 616C.230(1), Nevada's willful self-injury exclusion, precludes surviving family members from recovering death benefits for employee suicides that are causally connected to an industrial industry. Answering this question in the negative, we next consider how to determine when a suicide is sufficiently causally connected to an industrial injury to qualify an employee's survivors for death benefits. For the reasons set forth below, we adopt the chain-of-causation test and thereby join the majority of states that have considered the compensability of suicides under willful self-injury exclusions analogous to our own.

Standard of review

Like the district court, we review an appeals officer's decision in a workers' compensation matter for clear error or an abuse of discretion. Manwill v. Clark County, 123 Nev. 28, 162 P.3d 876, 879 (2007). An appeals officer's fact-based conclusions of law are entitled to deference and will not be disturbed if supported by substantial evidence. *Id* at 879. In conducting this review, we are confined to the record before the appeals officer, and we may not substitute our judgment for that of the appeals officer as to the weight of the evidence on a question of fact. *Id* at 879. Pure questions of law, however, like the one considered below, we review de novo. *Id.*

N.R.S. 616C.230(1)—Nevada's willful self-injury exclusion

In Nevada, workers' compensation death benefits are payable to eligible survivors for the death of an employee caused by any "injury by accident arising out of and in the course of employment." N.R.S. 616C.505. This rule, however, is not without limitation. Under N.R.S. 616C.230(1), Nevada's willful self-injury exclusion, an employee's death is not compensable if, instead of resulting from an original industrial accident, it results from a "willful intention" to inflict self-injury.

Notably, we have not had occasion to consider whether and under what circumstances suicides can be deemed to be caused by an industrial accident and considered nonwillful under N.R.S. 616C.230(1), thus qualifying the employee's survivors for death benefits. Despite this lack of guidance, the parties here acknowledge that certain suicides may not be willful within the meaning of N.R.S. 616C.230(1) if they are sufficiently causally connected to an industrial injury, a conclusion with which we agree. Our jurisprudence in the area of workers' compensation has always viewed the compensability of a consequential injury, physical or mental, relative to its causal connection to the original industrial accident.* * * The parties disagree, however, with respect to whether we should adopt the more restrictive, minority approach for determining causation, known as the "voluntary willful choice" test, or the modern majority position, referred to as the chain-of-causation test.

The voluntary willful choice test

The more restrictive, minority test governing the compensability of suicides originated with the Massachusetts Supreme Court decision, In re Sponatski, 220 Mass. 526, 108 N.E. 466, 468 (1915), and contains two basic prongs. Under this voluntary willful choice test, a suicide is compensable only if it (1) resulted from an uncontrollable impulse or delirium of frenzy, and (2) occurred without the employee's knowledge of the physical consequences of his or her actions. 2 Arthur Larson & Lex Larson, Larson's Workers' Compensation Law Section 38.02[2], 38–5 (2007) [hereinafter *Workers' Compensation Law*]. These two prongs were distilled from *Sponatski* by later commentators and courts. See, e.g. Saunders v. Texas Employers' Ins. Ass'n, 526 S.W.2d 515, 517 (Tex.1975) (citing this distillation with approval).

While the first prong of this test addresses an employee's volition, the second prong relates to an employee's understanding. *Workers' Compensation Law,* Sec. 38.02[1], at 38–6. If either prong is not met, the suicide acts as an independent intervening cause severing the relationship between the employee's death and the industrial injury. See *Saunders*, 526 S.W.2d at 517. For the reasons discussed below, however, both prongs are problematic in the modern workers' compensation context and have been modified or abandoned in recent years as jurisdictions have gradually converged on some version of the chain-of-causation test.

Because the first prong of the voluntary willful choice test requires a complete absence of volition, courts applying this test traditionally were certain about compensating only suicides whose spontaneity and violence demonstrated that the employee was afflicted with a psychological condition approximating insanity at the time the suicidal act was performed. *Workers' Compensation Law* Section 38.02[1], at 38–4. However, by relying on spontaneity and the method of self-destruction as aids in determining volition, this test excludes suicides that might otherwise be causally connected to an industrial injury simply because the method used was undramatic or because the two events were separated by a significant period of time.

In addition to recognizing the first prong's underinclusiveness, we also note the common criticism of this test's second prong. Specifically, by requiring a claimant to demonstrate that an employee did not understand the consequences of the suicidal act, the second prong imports an overly restrictive criminal law standard of insanity into a remedial context. See, *Workers' Compensation Law* Sec. 38.02[2], at 38–6 and 15 A.L.R.3d at 621 Sec. 3(a). Since, however, concepts of fault are alien to workers' compensation laws, Hansen v. Harrah's, 100 Nev. 60, 64, 675 P.2d 394, 397 (1984), the only legal issue in suicide compensation cases is causation. Whether an employee understood the consequences of committing suicide is irrelevant to whether the act was caused by an original industrial injury.

Based on these and other concerns, the voluntary willful choice test has been either modified or abandoned by a majority of states that have considered the compensability of suicides under their respective willful self-injury exclusions. *Workers' Compensation Law* § 38.02[2], at 38–7; *Saunders*, 526 S.W.2d at 517; and Schwab v. Department of Labor and Industries, 76 Wash.2d 784, 459 P.2d 1, 6 (1969). In states where the test has been modified, the first prong is relaxed and the second prong is practically eliminated. *Workers' Compensation Law* § 38.02[2], at 38–7. By eliminating the second prong, and relaxing the first, these states adhere to the functional equivalent of the chain-of-causation test. Joining this trend, we reject the voluntary willful choice test and instead embrace the chain-of-causation test set forth below.

The chain-of-causation test

The chain-of-causation test requires the claimant to establish an unbroken chain of causation between an industrial injury and the employee's eventual suicide. *Workers' Compensation Law* 38.02[1], at 38–

5. Although the test varies slightly across the states that employ it,[2] Vredenburg urges us to adopt its most common formulation, which is outlined in Graver Tank & Manufacturing Co. v. Industrial Commission, 97 Ariz. 256, 399 P.2d 664, 668 (1965).

In Graver Tank, the Arizona Supreme Court criticized the voluntary willful choice test for failing to recognize "the role which pain or despair may play in breaking down a rational mental process." *Id* at 667–68. The court then renounced that test in favor of a "better rule" that would compensate suicides if "the original work connected injuries suffered by the employee result in his becoming devoid of normal judgment and dominated by a disturbance of mind directly caused by his injury and its consequences, such as severe pain and despair." *Id* at 668.

This formulation of the test requires the claimant to demonstrate that (1) the employee suffered an industrial injury (2) the industrial injury caused some psychological condition severe enough to override the employee's rational judgment,[3] and (3) the psychological condition caused the employee to commit suicide* * *.

For the following reasons, we adopt this formulation of the chain-of-causation test. First, unlike the voluntary willful choice test, volition and knowledge problems under the chain-of-causation test are largely eliminated. Since an industrial injury and its consequences may suppress an employee's will to resist the impulse to commit suicide, a claimant may recover under this test even if the employee's choice to commit suicide was deliberate. Delaware Tire Center, 411 A.2d at 607. In acknowledging human psychology's role in causation, this test is widely recognized to accord with principles of modern medicine. See *Saunders*, 526 S.W.2d at 517.

Second, the test closely aligns with the remedial purpose of Nevada's workers' compensation scheme. See, e.g., Gallagher v. City of Las Vegas, 114 Nev. 595, 600, 959 P.2d 519, 521 (1998); In re Dube's Case, 70 Mass.App.Ct. 121, 872 N.E.2d 1171, 1176 (2007); and Globe Sec. Systems Co. v. W.C.A.B., 518 Pa. 544, 544 A.2d 953, 957 (1988). Under the voluntary willful choice test, work-related suicides are analyzed as potential independent intervening causes, and thus are viewed through

[2] States' versions of the chain-of-causation test differ, most notably, regarding the severity of the psychological condition required to establish the intermediate link between an industrial injury and a suicide. This difference is expressed in the use of varying terms to describe this psychological condition, ranging, for example, from a "disturbance," to a "derangement," to an "unsoundness" of mind. See Workers' Compensation Law § 38.02[1], at 38–3.

[3] Notably, although Graver Tank mentioned only pain and despair, later courts have explicitly concluded that an employee's rational judgment may be overridden by depression, as well as a psychoactive reaction to prescription medication. See, e.g., Delaware Tire Center v. Fox, 411 A.2d 606, 607 (Del.1980); Kahle v. Plochman, Inc., 85 N.J. 539, 428 A.2d 913, 916 (1981); Saunders v. Texas Employers' Ins. Ass'n, 526 S.W.2d 515, 517 (Tex.1975); Schwab v. Department of Labor and Industries, 76 Wash.2d 784, 459 P.2d 1, 6 (1969).

the conceptual lens of tort liability. See Leslie A. Bradshaw, Annotation, Suicide as Compensable Under Workmen's Compensation Act, 15 A.L.R.3d 616, at 621 § 3(a) (electronically updated as of 2008, originally published in 1967). However, in recognizing the role which pain and despair can play in breaking down the rational mental processes, the chain-of-causation test accords with the basic policy of this state's workers' compensation scheme: to deliver "economic assistance to persons who suffer disability or death as a result of their employment," Gallagher, 959 P.2d at 521, regardless of fault, in exchange for limiting the tort liability of employers. Hansen v. Harrah's, 100 Nev. 60, 64, 675 P.2d 394, 397; see also In re Dube's Case, 872 N.E.2d at 1176; Globe Sec. Systems Co., 544 A.2d at 957.

Third, the chain-of-causation test neatly harmonizes with our doctrine of compensable consequences, which permits claimants to recover for an employee's subsequent health conditions, physical or mental, caused by the employee's original industrial accident. Roberts v. SIIS, 114 Nev. 364, 368–69, 956 P.2d 790, 792–93 (1998); Imperial Palace v. Dawson, 102 Nev. 88, 91, 715 P.2d 1318, 1320 (1986). Thus, by requiring a causal connection between an industrial injury, a resulting psychological condition, and an employee's eventual suicide, this test is a logical extension of our workers' compensation jurisprudence regarding the compensability of subsequent employee injuries. In this, we conclude that our adoption of the chain-of-causation test is in harmony with the requirement of a neutral, rather than a liberal, construction of the Nevada Industrial Insurance Act. See N.R.S. 616A.010(2).

For these reasons, we conclude that the chain-of-causation test, as articulated above, most accurately reflects the compensability of work-related suicides in Nevada, and we hereby adopt that test. In accord with the evidentiary burdens under this state's workers' compensation scheme, N.R.S. 616C.150(1), the claimant must satisfy this test's three-part showing by a preponderance of the evidence.

Appeals officer's decision

Having concluded that workers' compensation death benefits are available for suicides sufficiently connected to an industrial injury, and having adopted the chain-of-causation test for determining whether a sufficient work connection exists, we next consider the appeals officer's denial of Vredenburg's claim for death benefits. The appeals officer purported to base her decision on the same chain-of-causation test we have adopted today. Nevertheless, Vredenburg asserts that the appeals officer's application of the test was clearly erroneous and that her fact-based conclusions were not supported by substantial evidence. We agree.

While purporting to analyze Vredenburg's claim under the chain-of-causation test and attempting to distinguish this case from *Graver Tank*, the appeals officer, in effect, applied the stricter voluntary willful choice test. The appeals officer concluded that Vredenburg failed to establish a sufficient work connection under the chain-of-causation test because Danny's "suicide was the result of a deliberate decision on his part and not an act of insanity." As we explained above, however, whether an employee acts deliberately is irrelevant under the chain-of-causation test. Moreover, the psychological condition linking a suicide and an industrial injury under this test may be significantly less severe, clinically, than insanity.

Apparently relying on this distorted version of the chain-of-causation test, the appeals officer then imposed a spurious evidentiary requirement on Vredenburg. Specifically, the appeals officer concluded that Vredenburg failed to present "conclusive evidence establishing that [Danny] was devoid of normal judgement and dominated by a disturbance of mind directly caused by his industrial injury as required by the *Graver Tank* standard." However, nothing in *Graver Tank* supports the requirement of "conclusive" evidence. Indeed, under NRS 616C.150(1), so long as the preponderance of the evidence would lead a reasonable mind to conclude that a causal nexus exists, the evidence supporting an appeals officer's decision in Nevada need not be conclusive, and may even be conflicting.[4] For these reasons, the appeals officer clearly erred by misapplying the chain of causation test in this case.

Similarly, we conclude that substantial evidence does not support the appeals officer's finding of fact that Danny's "suicide constituted a deliberate decision on his part," which suggests that the appeals officer concluded that Danny's suicide must have stemmed from a source other than his industrial injury. Notably, the record before the appeals officer contained Dr. Kim's medical evaluations, the medical opinion of Dr. Anderson, and the affidavits of multiple friends and coworkers, which together implicate many of the hallmarks of a compensable suicide under the chain-of-causation test: an irreversible injury, unrelenting pain, a possible psychoactive reaction to prescribed medication, and extreme depression.

Although we are restrained from reweighing this evidence on appeal, Manwill v. Clark County, 162 P.3d 876, 879 (2007), we discuss it only for

---

[4] See McClanahan v. Raley's, Inc., 117 Nev. 921, 925–26, 34 P.3d 573, 576 (2001) ("'[P]reponderance of the evidence' merely refers to '[t]he greater weight of the evidence.'") (quoting Black's Law Dictionary 1201 (7th ed.1999)). Furthermore, to the extent the appeals officer's decision suggests that Graver Tank requires expert medical testimony to succeed under the chain-of-causation test, we disagree. As one recent Arizona appellate court noted when applying Graver Tank, expert medical testimony is not necessary where causation is clearly apparent without it. T.W.M. Custom Framing v. Industrial Com'n, 198 Ariz. 41, 6 P.3d 745, 749 (App.2000); see United Exposition Service Co. v. SIIS, 109 Nev. 421, 424–25, 851 P.2d 423, 425 (1993) (requiring medical testimony or sufficient facts to demonstrate the causal connection between an industrial injury and a subsequent injury); see also *Workers' Compensation Law* § 38.05, at 38–18.

contrastive purposes. In contrast to Vredenburg, the Flamingo presented little, if any, evidence to counter the causal narrative displayed by Vredenburg's evidence. The Flamingo failed, for example, to present evidence suggesting that Danny had preexisting health conditions, physical or mental, which could have supported an alternative theory for taking his own life. Instead, the Flamingo contends that Vredenburg failed to make out a prima facie case under the chain-of-causation test by failing to present expert medical testimony regarding Danny's psychological condition. However, since expert medical testimony is not necessarily required to succeed under the chain-of-causation test if causation is apparent from other evidence, Vredenburg's failure in this regard was not fatal to her claim. See T.W.M. Custom Framing, 6 P.3d at 749; United Exposition Service Co., 109 Nev. at 424–25, 851 P.2d at 425; *Workers' Compensation Law* § 38.05, at 38–18. Since the Flamingo failed to present evidence of this type, the appeals officer's finding, which suggested that Danny's suicide was attributable to a source other than his industrial injury and its aftermath, is unsupported in the record.

CONCLUSION

We conclude that suicides may be nonwillful deaths under Nevada's workers' compensation law if they are sufficiently causally connected to an industrial injury. In reaching this conclusion, we adopt the chain-of-causation test to determine whether a sufficient causal connection exists. With respect to the appeals officer's decision in this case, we conclude that it was based on a clearly erroneous application of the chain-of-causation test and is unsupported in the record. Accordingly, we reverse the district court's order denying Vredenburg's petition for judicial review and remand this matter with instructions to the district court to, in turn, remand the matter to the appeals officer for proceedings consistent with the standard announced in this opinion.

We concur: GIBBONS, C.J., MAUPIN, HARDESTY, DOUGLAS and CHERRY, JJ.

NOTES

1. In Food Distributors v. Estate of Ball, 24 Va.App. 692, 485 S.E.2d 155 (1997) the court traced the historical development in employee suicide cases and described the four approaches taken by the courts: (1) the "voluntary willful choice rule" developed in *Sponatski's Case*, described as the minority rule; (2) the "chain of causation rule" discussed in *Vrendenburg* as the majority rule; (3) the "New York rule," essentially a chain of causation rule with the possible added requirement of physical damage to the brain itself; and (4) the "English rule" which provides that the insanity must be a direct result of the injury itself or the shock produced by it, and not an indirect result caused by brooding over the injury and its consequences.

As *Vrendenburg* illustrates, the issue of suicide raises difficult questions regarding the proper relationship between causation (as developed in the criminal law and tort law contexts) and the goals of the workers' compensation system. When the employee is the victim, not of an outside agent, but of his own self destructive act, can logic support the claim that "the act causing death [is] an intervening act but not an intervening cause." See State v. Ramsey, 839 P.2d 936, 940 (Wyo.1992). Would it be better to recognize that the traditional understanding of legal causation is not as relevant because of the humane objectives of workers' compensation which favor payment of death benefits when an employee chooses to end life rather than live with the consequences of work related injuries? See, e.g., Globe Security Systems Co. v. WCAB, 518 Pa. 544, 553, 544 A.2d 953, 957 (1988) in which the court found the chain of causation test consistent with the humanitarian purposes of the workers' compensation system. And, see Kealoha v. Director, Office of Workers' Compensation Programs, 713 F.3d 521 (9th Cir. 2013) (court concluded suicide or injuries from a suicide attempt are compensable under the Longshore Act "when there is a direct and unbroken chain of causation between a compensable work-related injury and the suicide attempt. The claimant need not demonstrate that the suicide or attempt stemmed from an irresistible suicidal impulse. The chain of causation rule accords with our modern understanding of psychiatry. It also better reflects the Longshore Act's focus on causation, rather than fault.").

2. While usually, as in the *Vrendenburg* case, the suicide occurs as a consequence of a compensable physical injury, compensation is also awarded on occasion where the original work injury is a mental or emotional disturbance attributed to the stress or demands of the job. See, e.g., Wilder v. Russell Library Co., 107 Conn. 56, 139 A. 644 (1927) (a temperamentally over conscientious librarian whose work was demanding and highly frustrating committed suicide; held compensation awarded); Anderson v. Armour & Co., 257 Minn. 281, 101 N.W.2d 435 (1960) (truck driver with a 25 year record of safe driving, while in the course of employment, ran into a pedestrian; after six weeks of brooding he took his life; held death compensable); Fitzgibbons' Case, 374 Mass. 633, 373 N.E.2d 1174 (1978) (employee suffered severe mental shock when fellow worker whom he had ordered to quell an inmate disturbance was killed by inmates; employee's mental condition deteriorated for three weeks at which time he killed himself; held death compensable); Globe Security Systems Co. v. WCAB, 518 Pa. 544, 544 A.2d 953 (1988) (employee, security guard at a liquor store, thwarted a store robbery but in process accidentally shot one of the would be robbers; apparently upset by this, the employee then turned the gun on himself taking his own life; held death compensable); Chu v. WCAB, 49 Cal.App.4th 1176, 57 Cal.Rptr.2d 221 (1996) (employee, a police sergeant, suffered from severe work related stress which lead to depression and eventual suicide; held death compensable); Indiana State Police v. Wiessing, 836 N.E.2d 1038 (Ind.App.2005) (decedent, a state trooper, during a routine traffic stop, shot and killed motorist who tried to grab his gun; six years later the trooper, suffering from chronic post-traumatic stress disorder attributed to the shooting, took his own life;

compensation awarded under chain of causation test); but, see Thomas v. City of Springfield, 88 S.W.3d 155 (Mo.App.S.D.2002) (claimant, 18 year veteran of the Springfield police department, requested but was denied a transfer from "an unbearably stressful workload"; failed suicide attempt led to serious injuries; court applied the voluntary willful choice test; held compensation denied).

CHAPTER 8

COMPENSATION FOR NON-FATAL INJURY

■ ■ ■

1. INTRODUCTION TO THIS CHAPTER

At the outset, the student must bear in mind that the intent of a workers' compensation law is not to furnish damages for physical injury in the common law sense. The ultimate purpose is to provide for payments of money to, or for the benefit of, an injured employee, which payments are intended to mitigate the disastrous economic effects of a work injury. These payments are usually called "benefits". If the injury does not cause death, they fall into two general categories: (1) medical and rehabilitation benefits; and (2) disability benefits.

Provisions pertaining to medical and rehabilitation benefits involve fewer legal disputes than do disability benefits provisions. Section 1 highlights judicial efforts to define the scope of the employer's obligation to provide medical care and rehabilitation for the injured worker. Section 2 surveys a variety of issues pertaining to disability benefits. Specifically, the student's attention is directed to kinds of disability, the general concept of disability, disputes that arise in applying that general concept, the amount of and method of determining compensation, and proof of disability. It is in this area that the states have met some of the most difficult practical problems in the administration of the workers' compensation system. The third section of this chapter considers possible ways to apportion responsibility for the cumulative effect of successive injuries. Section 4 concludes this chapter with a discussion of how to coordinate an award of workers' compensation benefits with other payments that may be available from public or private sources.

2. MEDICAL AND REHABILITATION BENEFITS

SQUEO v. COMFORT CONTROL CORP.

Supreme Court of New Jersey, 1985.
99 N.J. 588, 494 A.2d 313.

GARIBALDI, J.

The primary issue in this workers' compensation case is whether the construction of a self-contained apartment attached to the home of an injured worker's parents may constitute "medical, surgical or other treatment . . . necessary to cure and relieve" or "other appliance" under N.J.S.A. 34:15–15 of the Workers' Compensation Act (Act); and if so, whether there is sufficient credible evidence in the record to support the finding that the construction of the apartment addition was necessary and that its cost was reasonable.

The petitioner, Eugene M. Squeo (Squeo), is a quadriplegic. He was injured in 1978 when he fell from a roof while working for respondent, Comfort Control Corp. (Comfort Control). He is totally and permanently disabled. In 1979, a judgment ordering disability payments was entered by a judge of the Division of Workers' Compensation.

In February, 1982, Squeo filed an Application for Review or Modification of Formal Award seeking, *inter alia*, an order requiring Comfort Control to construct a self-contained apartment attached to the home of his parents. [Instead of the usual addition of a room and bath, with ingress to and egress from the home, the plan contemplated a separate apartment attached to the home. The apartment would contain a bedroom, kitchen, living room, bathroom, carport, basement, and hydraulic lift, and would require its own electricity, plumbing and heating. The architect estimated the cost to be in excess of $65,000.] The compensation court ordered that such construction be undertaken. [It ordered that Squeo be charged with the cost of constructing any additions to the standard apartment and with the care, maintenance, capital repairs, insurance, and any taxation to be associated with the construction.] The Appellate Division affirmed the Order of the compensation court 194 N.J.Super. 366, 476 A.2d 1265. [The Appellate Division instructed that the "cost of the apartment not go beyond providing for petitioner's basic need for independent living quarters." It ordered that the employer be secured by a mortgage executed by Squeo's parents so that if Squeo should no longer use the apartment, the employer would be compensated for any significant value the apartment may add to the property in the event it is sold, rented, or mortgaged.] We granted Comfort Control's petition for certification. 99 N.J. 148, 491 A.2d 664 (1984).

N.J.S.A. 34:15–15 in pertinent part provides:

> The employer shall furnish to the injured worker such medical, surgical and *other treatment*, and hospital service *as shall be necessary to cure and relieve the worker of the effects of the injury* and to restore the functions of the injured member or organ where such restoration is possible; . . . the Division of Workers' Compensation after investigating the need of the same and giving the employer an opportunity to be heard, shall determine that such physicians' and surgeons' treatment and hospital

> services *are or were necessary and that the fees for the same are reasonable* and shall make an order requiring the employer to pay for or furnish the same.
>
> * * *
>
> When an injured employee may be partially or wholly relieved of the effects of a permanent injury, by use of an artificial limb or *other appliance*, which phrase shall also include artificial teeth or glass eye, the Division of Workers' Compensation, *acting under competent medical advice, is empowered to determine the character and nature of such limb or appliance, and to require the employer or the employer's insurance carrier to furnish the same.* [Emphasis added.]

Pursuant to N.J.S.A. 34:15–15, it is evident that an employer must provide an injured worker with "other treatment" or "other appliance" that serves to cure and relieve a worker of the effects of his work-connected injury. The employer contends, however, that "other treatment" or "appliance" under N.J.S.A. 34:15–15 is not intended to encompass the construction of a self-contained apartment.

There is no express legislative or judicial definition of these terms in New Jersey. However, it has long been recognized that the Act is remedial social legislation and as such is to be liberally construed so that its beneficent purposes may be accomplished. * * *

The expansion in coverage since the Act's inception, as evidenced by the legislative history of N.J.S.A. 34:15–15, supports a liberal interpretation of the Act.

When N.J.S.A. 34:15–15 was first enacted in 1911 it simply provided:

> During the first two weeks after the injury the employer shall furnish reasonable medical and hospital services and medicines, as and when needed, not to exceed one hundred dollars in value, unless the employee refuses to allow them to be furnished by the employer. [L.1911, c. 95, § 14.]

> The Act was amended in 1918, and again in 1919. The latter amendment extended recovery under the Act beyond medical and hospital services and medicines.

> [I]n severe cases requiring unusual medical or surgical treatment or calling for artificial limb or other mechanical appliances, the employee or his representative shall be authorized to present a petition to the Workmen's Compensation Bureau, and the Commissioner, deputy commissioner or referee thereof is hereby empowered, when warranted by the evidence produced, to order additional services, artificial limbs or other

> appliances not to exceed in total the sum of two hundred dollars, or to extend over a period not to exceed in total seventeen weeks. This paragraph shall apply only to nonfatal cases. [L.1919, c. 93, § 4].

In 1922, the statute was amended again and its coverage expanded. The 1922 amended statute, virtually identical to the present version, is especially pertinent to our analysis. The 1922 amendment removed the monetary limitation on benefits to be paid by the employer and authorized the Workmen's Compensation Bureau to allow such treatment or services as it found to be "necessary." Moreover, the words "unusual medical surgical treatment" were omitted and in lieu thereof appeared the words "medical, surgical and *other treatment*, and hospital services as shall be necessary to cure and relieve the workman of the effects of the injury." (Emphasis added).

* * *

Although this Court has liberally construed the Act to promote its beneficent purposes, we have always imposed the limitation that no expense incurred may be recovered that is not shown to be reasonable and necessary by sufficient competent medical evidence. . . .

We have also emphasized that claimant bears the burden thus to establish his claim. *Kahle v. Plochman, supra,* 85 N.J. at 548, 428 A.2d 913.

II

Other jurisdictions have also liberally construed the terms "treatment" and "appliance" so as to allow such expenses as may be said to be reasonable and necessary for the cure of an ailment or relief of its symptoms. Courts have been generous in allowing recovery as "treatment" not only the cost of medical and hospital services, but also of necessary incidentals such as transportation, apparatus, and even nursing care furnished by a member of claimant's own family. 2 A. Larson, *Workmen's Compensation Law* § 61.00 (1983).

For instance, under the Florida Workmen's Compensation Statute, an act similar to ours, an employer was required to reimburse claimant for expenses incurred for child care. Claimant's inability to care for her child due to a work-connected injury resulted in the development of a severe depressive neurosis. In light of the extreme circumstances, the court held it medically necessary for treatment of her psychiatric condition and hence for claimant's recovery, that her daughter be placed in a nursery school. *Doctors Hosp. of Lake Worth v. Robinson,* 411 So.2d 958 (Dist.Ct.App.1982).

In *Talas v. Correct Piping Co., Inc.,* 435 N.E.2d 22, 27 (Ind.1982), the Supreme Court of Indiana awarded benefits for the palliative care of claimant, a quadriplegic, provided through nonprofessional nursing services while claimant's wife was working. The Court found that the nursing care was required to prevent the development of life-threatening disease, such as pneumonia; therefore the care could be said to be within the statutory requirement of being "necessary to limit or reduce the amount and extent of such impairment." * * *

[I]n *Haga v. Clay Hyder Trucking Lines*, 397 So.2d 428 (Fla.Dist.Ct.App.), review denied, 402 So.2d 609 (Fla.1981), the employer of a double amputee who had suffered numerous complications after his injury was ordered to assume the reasonable costs for installation and maintenance of an in-ground pool with access facilities for the handicapped, or, in the alternative, to provide the claimant with daily access, along with reimbursement expenses, to a pool within a reasonable distance from claimant's home. In reliance upon the testimony of claimant's treating physicians and because of the claimant's severe and unusual injuries, the court held that the installation of a swimming pool was medically necessary to provide him with needed cardiovascular exercise as part of his rehabilitation program and to control his weight. * * *

In *Peace River Elec. Corp. v. Choate*, 417 So.2d 831 (Fla.Dist.Ct.App.1982), petition for review dismissed, 429 So.2d 7 (Fla.1983), the court ordered that claimant be awarded rent-free use of a wheelchair-accessible modular home to replace the dilapidated wood shed he had been occupying. All title and right of ownership would remain in the employer, as would the responsibility to provide adequate maintenance. The claimant would assume responsibility for real estate taxes and assessments. The court there rejected the employer's suggested alternative of remodeling claimant's existing dwelling since "nothing short of bulldozing the dwelling would serve to remedy the situation." *Id.* at 832.

In *Pine Bluff Parks and Recreation v. Porter*, 6 Ark.App. 154, 639 S.W.2d 363 (1982), although the relevant statute made no express provision for rental payments, the court ordered the employer of a paraplegic to assume liability for part of the rental cost of living in a project designed for paraplegics. The Workers' Compensation Commission, after hearing testimony from claimant's treating physician and from a hospital administrator, who himself was a quadriplegic, determined that the requested program in the special facility for the claimant was reasonable and necessary under the Arkansas Compensation Law. That law requires that an employer supply an employee with "services and apparatus" as necessitated by an employee's injuries. *Id.* at 366. Accordingly, the court held that the Commission should determine what portion of the total cost to the claimant of living in the special facility was attributable to those services and apparatus required to be furnished by the employer under the compensation law and what portion was noncompensable under that statute;[3] . . . *Contra, Low Splint Coal Co., Inc. v. Bolling*, 224 Va. 400, 297 S.E.2d 665 (1982) (court's decision to disallow claimant's request for an improved entrance ramp at rear of residence and modifications to bathroom turned on language of particular statute. Court found that such structural improvements could not be considered to be either "other necessary medical attention" or "reasonable and necessary vocational rehabilitation training services" within purview of Virginia Compensation Statute).

It is important to note that in those cases in which courts have allowed recovery for unusual requests, for example, the construction of a swimming pool or use of a modular home, they have premised their decision on the unique circumstances of the particular case. . . .

In view of the remedial nature of the New Jersey Workers' Compensation Act and the liberal construction accorded to it, we conclude that under certain unique circumstances, when there is sufficient and competent medical evidence to establish that the requested "other treatment" or "appliance" is reasonable and necessary to relieve the injured worker of the effect of his injuries, the construction of an apartment addition may be within the ambit of N.J.S.A. 34:15–15. We caution however that it is only the unusual case that may warrant such extraordinary relief.

III

We find this to be such an "unusual case," and, consequently, the apartment addition is to be considered "other treatment" within the intendment of N.J.S.A. 34:15–15. The facts before us support this conclusion.

Dr. Sullivan testified that instead of the usual eight weeks required by most quadriplegics to recover, Squeo was unwell for about two and one-half years. He had "just about every complication that God ever put on earth for him." Squeo's living arrangements were further complicated by the fact that he had been living independently of his parents prior to his accident. As Dr. Sullivan testified, this "*is an unusual case* where the individual is twenty-five years old when he sustains the injury and he is already out on his own and now he has to be reintroduced into the family picture." (Emphasis added).

---

[3] The court recognized that the employer had a statutory obligation to furnish ramps, rails, wheelchairs, widened doors, special commodes, and shower facilities and other *apparatus* required by claimant. However, it questioned whether there existed any liability for custodial care, lodging, or other non-medical services such as housekeeping. Pine Bluff Parks, *supra,* 639 S.W.2d at 366.

Apart from his quadriplegia, which cannot be reversed, and physical complications, which are treated as they arise, Squeo has suffered serious psychological setbacks. No one disputes that these emotional problems are a result of his work-connected injury and its consequences. Nor is it disputed that Squeo's depression is so aggravated by living in the nursing home that he has tried to kill himself on three occasions. We find these three factors—Squeo's unremitting physical ailments, his age and his having lived independently of his parents for several years prior to the accident, and his psychological dread of institutional living, culminating in three suicide attempts—are sufficient to consider this an unusual case calling for unusual relief.

Moreover, we find that competent medical testimony exists on this record to hold that the construction of the apartment addition was reasonable and necessary treatment to relieve Squeo of his severe mental depression. See *Howard v. Harwood's Restaurant Co., supra*, 25 N.J. at 93, 135 A.2d 161.

It is undisputed that the nursing home is the worst place in the world for Squeo. Dr. Crain testified that Squeo's depression was rooted in the resentment and frustration he experienced while living in the nursing home, where he felt his life was neglected. He stated that continuous living in that nursing home environment would certainly lead to yet another suicide attempt, and perhaps a successful one. Other witnesses, Anthony and Davis, testified that it was extremely important to the functional well-being of a disabled person that he be permitted to choose his own living environment. Anthony testified that lack of options makes the disabled "angry, frustrated and depressed." Davis opined that confining Squeo to a nursing home would condemn him "to a fate worse, worse than death." Further, the witnesses' testimony indicates that relegating Squeo to a state-sponsored facility would neither fulfill Squeo's psychological need for independent living, nor assuage his fear of institutional living, nor lessen his suicidal inclinations. . . .

We stress that in determining what is reasonable and necessary, the touchstone is not the injured worker's desires or what he thinks to be most beneficial. Rather, it is what is shown by sufficient competent evidence to be reasonable and necessary to cure and relieve him. Here, that relief is of a psychological nature. The source of Squeo's severe mental depression is his fear of institutionalization. The testimony of all witnesses substantiates that this psychological disturbance can be relieved only by Squeo's living in an independent setting. Thus, we find sufficient credible evidence on the record to establish that construction of the apartment addition is necessary to cure and relieve the mental depression caused by Squeo's work-related injury.

There is also sufficient credible evidence to establish that the cost of the addition is reasonable. While there are no monetary limitations on the cost of treatment set forth in the statute, the cost must be reasonable. Both the compensation court and the Appellate Division were careful to restrict the cost of the proposed construction. Further, the Appellate Division provided the employer with protection against Squeo's failure to use the apartment by ordering Squeo's parents to execute a mortgage in the employer's favor. 194 N.J.Super. at 371, 476 A.2d 1265.

We agree with the restrictions on the cost of the construction of the apartment imposed by both the compensation judge and the Appellate Division. We find that within the limits of such restrictions the cost of the construction of the apartment will be reasonable.

The award also appears reasonable when viewed in comparison to the cost of the available alternatives which the employer was willing to pay. Although the employer indicates that the cost of the apartment would be greater than that of the other alternatives, no such evidence was submitted. In fact, while the cost of the proposed addition initially may be greater, in the long run it is likely to be far less than the expense of maintaining a young man in a nursing home or rental unit for the rest of his life.

We affirm the judgment of the Appellate Division. At oral argument we learned that the Squeos have constructed the apartment. Accordingly, we remand to the Division of Workers' Compensation for a determination as to the portion of the cost of the construction of the apartment for which the employer will be liable, within the restrictions set forth by the Division and the Appellate Division.

NOTES

1. The most immediate need of an injured worker is medical attention and in many cases hospitalization. In recognition of this, all workers' compensation statutes require medical aid to be furnished to injured employees. In earlier days this class of benefits was closely circumscribed and limited as to time and amount. All states but a few now provide for medical aid on an "unlimited" basis or authorize the administrative body to extend the time of medical aid indefinitely. See, Workers' Compensation Research institute (WCRI), Workers' Compensation Laws 2012, Table 3 (2012) [hereinafter WCRI, Workers' Compensation Laws 2012]. Beginning July 1, 2013, medical benefits in Georgia will be limited to 400 weeks except in cases of "catastrophic" injuries as defined by statute. O.C.G.A. § 34–9–200(a)(2).

2. Medical benefits cover the reasonable cost of physicians, hospitalization, medication and other necessary treatment. As illustrated by *Squeo*, a variety of incidental care and equipment may also be covered by workers' compensation. e.g., All Clear Locating Services v. Shurrum, 855 So.2d 1208 (Fla.App.2003) (employer ordered to provide employee with

wheelchair accessible and barrier-free housing). See 5 A. Larson & L. Larson, Larson's Law of Workers' Compensation § 94.03[1] (2013) (collecting cases). Professional nursing services are routinely covered. See, Hopson v. Hickman, 182 Ga.App. 865, 357 S.E.2d 280 (1987); Currier v. Hruska, 228 Neb. 38, 421 N.W.2d 25 (1988). Though once a point of controversy, a majority of states today require employers to pay family members who provide medically necessary nursing services. See, Close v. Superior Excavating Co., 166 Vt. 318, 693 A.2d 729 (1997) (collecting cases). But see, Sullivan v. Edwards Oil Co., 141 S.W.3d 544 (Tenn. 2004) (denying payments to mother who provided nursing care for injured son; statute authorized payments only for professional nursing). Transportation costs incurred in connection with medical treatment are generally compensable. Sigman Meat Co. v. Industrial Claim Appeals Office, 761 P.2d 265 (Colo.App.1988) (taxi fare to and from doctor's office); Miceli v. Industrial Comm., 135 Ariz. 71, 659 P.2d 30 (1983) (out of town travel to consult a specialist). Child care expenses may be compensable if incidental to needed medical treatment. Bellone v. Industrial Claim Appeals Office, 940 P.2d 1116 (Colo.App.1997). However an employee cannot recover the cost of an airline ticket to fly in her sister to take care of her children during a one week hospitalization. Kuziel v. Pet Fair, Inc., 931 P.2d 521 (Colo.App.1996). A weight loss program was approved as part of a medical/rehabilitation plan, but the court denied approval of compensation for a stomach-stapling procedure when the claimant failed to maintain weight loss. Shepherd v. Van Ohlen Trucking, 49 Ark.App. 36, 895 S.W.2d 945 (1995). In *Mace v. Industrial Comm'n.*, 204 Ariz. 207, 62 P.3d 133 (2003) the Court held that marriage counseling was "treatment" and could be awarded if such counseling was reasonably necessary to ameliorate the effects of a compensable injury. An employer may be required to pay for nutritional supplements deemed medically necessary by the treating physician. Tiznado v. Orlando Regional Healthcare Systems,, 773 So.2d 584 (Fla. App. 2000).

Courts are divided on whether employers are obligated to modify automobiles for physically disabled workers. Compare, McDonald v. Brunswick Elec. Membership Corp., 77 N.C.App. 753, 336 S.E.2d 407 (1985) (statutory authorization of "other treatment or care" or "rehabilitative services" did not include "tangible, non-medically related items such as a van") with Griffiths v. W.C.A.B., 596 Pa. 317, 943 A.2d 242 (2008) (employer must pay for a quadriplegic worker's wheel-chair accessible van under its duty to pay for "orthopedic appliances" of disabled workers). See also Weakland v. Toledo Engineering Co., Inc., 467 Mich. 344, 656 N.W.2d 175 (2003); Petrilla v. Workmen's Compensation Appeal Bd., 692 A.2d 623 (Pa.Cmwlth.1997) (employer is not responsible for cost of vehicle, but must pay for modifications to make it wheelchair accessible). See also, Stone Container Corp. v. Castle, 657 N.W.2d 485 (Iowa 2003) (employer must replace laptop computer for severely injured worker; computer was analogous a van which provided the injured worker with access to the outside word).

3. Universal limitations on coverage are the medical necessity and reasonableness of the cost of the treatment or apparatus. An employer is not required to pay for treatment or equipment that might be medically appropriate in some instances if the medical need in the particular case is attenuated. E.g., R & T Construction Co. v. Judge, 323 Md. 514, 594 A.2d 99 (1991) (refusing to order the remodeling of the quadriplegic employee's house when the requested changes would give the claimant "a sense of increased independence and self-worth", but were not needed to provide medical "necessities"); Glinka v. Workmen's Compensation Appeal Board, 104 Pa.Cmwlth. 175, 521 A.2d 503 (1987) (disapproving medical expenses of $1,080 for weekly rubdowns when employer's physician testified that such treatment was no longer necessary); Boleratz v. W.C.A.B., 932 A.2d 1014 (Pa. Comm. 2007) (employer does not have to pay for massage therapy even when prescribed by a physician; covered medical services must be provided by a "licensed medical practitioner"); Hisler v. Dist. of Columbia Dept. Of Employment Services, 950 A.2d 738 (D.C. App. 2008) (employer does not have to pay for IV megavitamin infusions for treatment of chronic fatigue syndrome in the absence of an explicit finding that such infusions were reasonable and necessary).

EX PARTE BROOKWOOD MEDICAL CENTER, INC. (IN RE JANICE NIXON V. BROOKWOOD MEDICAL CENTER, INC.)

Court of Civil Appeals of Alabama, 2004.
895 So.2d 1000.

Brookwood Medical Center, Inc. ("the employer"), the defendant in a pending action brought by Janice Nixon ("the employee") pursuant to the Alabama Workers' Compensation Act, petitions for a writ of mandamus directing the Jefferson Circuit Court to rescind an order compelling the employer to provide the employee with a list of four pain-management physicians. For the reasons stated herein, we grant the petition and issue the writ.

Among other things, the Act provides that an employer of an employee suffering a work-related injury shall pay for "reasonably necessary medical and surgical treatment and attention, physical rehabilitation, medicine, [and] medical and surgical supplies." In that regard, the Act substantially mirrors medical-benefit provisions present in workers' compensation laws in all states. See 5 Arthur Larson & Lex K. Larson, *Larson's Workers' Compensation Law* § 94.01[1] (2003). However, all states do not allocate the power to choose who will provide medical and/or surgical services in the same way; while some states permit an employee to choose his or her own physician, either freely or from an approved panel, other states vest that power in employers. Larson at § 94.02[1].

From the original adoption of the Act in 1919 until 1973, Alabama allocated employers the exclusive power to designate a physician or a surgeon to render medical or surgical treatment for which the employer was financially responsible under the Act. Although the Act did provide an exception for "emergency" care, the prevailing rule was that "[o]nly if the employer did not promptly assert its right to furnish medical treatment could the employee select his or her own health care provider."

Between 1973 and 1985, the Legislature amended the Act on three pertinent occasions. The Act was first amended in 1973.

* * *

[T]he 1973 amendment indicated that "the employer has the right to select the medical or surgical attendant who will treat the employee" and that "if the employee is dissatisfied with the physician selected by the employer, he should advise the employer of this fact so that the employer can select another physician." We also indicated that "the unjustified obtainment by an employee of medical care from sources other than those selected by the employer without the latter's knowledge or consent may, in appropriate instances, excuse the employer from liability for the costs incurred by the employee.

The Act was again amended in 1975. . . .

> "[I]f the employee is dissatisfied with the second physician selected by the employer, the employee may so advise the employer and in such [event] the employee shall be referred to a third physician selected by the employer. In the event surgery is required, if the employee is dissatisfied with the designated surgeon, he may so advise the employer, and in such event the employee shall be referred to a second surgeon selected by the employer; if the employee is dissatisfied with the second surgeon designated by the employer to perform surgery, the employee may so advise the employer and in such event the employee shall be referred to a third surgeon selected by the employer."

Although the Legislature, in adopting the 1975 amendment to the Act, had given injured employees, in effect, two "rights of refusal" with respect to employer-selected treating physicians and surgeons, we did not construe that amendment as having substantially altered the physician-selection process:

"Section 25–5–77(a)[, Ala.Code 1975,] provides in pertinent part that the 'employer shall pay the cost of reasonably necessary' medical expenses arising out of a work-related accident. As provided in that section, the employer is to select the physician, but '[i]f the employee is dissatisfied with the initial treating physician, selected by the employer and if further treatment is required, the employee shall be referred to a second physician selected by the employer.' If the employee is dissatisfied with the second physician, he may notify his employer who will select another physician. . . . Thus, it is clear from the statute that *the selection of the initial physician and of other physicians in the event of employee dissatisfaction is a decision for the employer.* It is also clear from the statute that the employee must notify the employer before consulting a physician or before changing physicians except in the case of an emergency. *United States v. Bear Brothers, Inc.*, 355 So.2d 1133 (Ala.Civ.App.1978)."

In 1985, the Legislature again amended the Act with respect to physician selection, but it utilized a different approach. Under Ala.Code 1975, § 25–5–77(a), Ala. Acts 1984, and as currently in force, an employee's former right to dissent to two employer-selected physicians or surgeons rather than one was replaced by a single right of dissent however, employees were, for the first time, afforded a limited right of selection:

> "If the employee is dissatisfied with the initial treating physician selected by the employer and if further treatment is required, the employee may so advise the employer, and the employee shall be entitled to select a second physician from a panel or list of four physicians selected by the employer. If surgery is required and if the employee is dissatisfied with the designated surgeon, he or she may so advise the employer, and the employee shall be entitled to select a second surgeon from a panel or list of four surgeons selected by the employer. If four physicians or surgeons are not available to be listed, the employer shall include on the list as many as are available. The four physicians or surgeons selected by the employer hereunder shall not be from or members of the same firm, partnership, or professional corporation."

[W]e summarized the current state of the law with respect to an employer's rights and duties concerning medical care due employees arising from work-related injuries:

> "Section 25–5–77(a), Ala.Code 1975, provides, among other things, that an employer of an injured worker shall timely pay for that worker's 'reasonably necessary medical and surgical treatment and attention, physical rehabilitation, medicine, [and] medical and surgical supplies . . . as the result of an accident arising out of and in the course of the employment.' That duty to pay is accompanied under the Act by a corresponding power in the employer to exercise considerable control over the medical care for which it must pay, including the right to choose the employee's physician in the first instance and the right to compel

> the injured employee to submit to an examination by that physician at all reasonable times. . . . Although the Act provides that the employee may advise the employer if he or she is dissatisfied with the physician designated by the employer, the employee's remedy in such a circumstance is to select another physician from a panel or list of available physicians (usually four) specified by the employer. Whether designated in the first instance by the employer or chosen by the employee from a so-called 'panel of four' provided by the employer, the selected physician becomes the employee's authorized treating physician under the Act."

Having set forth the legal background, we now turn to the dispute between the parties that implicates the foregoing statutes. In July 2002, the employee suffered a work-related injury to her back, which resulted in, among other things, a herniation of one of the employee's vertebral disks. The employee initially underwent treatment for that injury provided by Dr. Carter Morris, a physician chosen by the employer; among other things, Dr. Morris recommended, and later performed, a surgical procedure known as a "microdiskectomy" on the employee's lumbar spine in March 2003, and he referred the employee to physical therapy.

In August 2003, Dr. Morris referred the employee (apparently with the employer's consent) to Dr. Matthew Berke for further treatment with respect to "pain management" and released the employee to return to light-duty work. A few days after Dr. Morris indicated that the employee could return to work, the employee notified the employer of her dissatisfaction with Dr. Morris as her authorized treating physician, whereupon the employer supplied the employee with a panel of four physicians from which the employee selected Dr. Martin Jones to be her authorized treating physician. Dr. Jones, like Dr. Morris had done, referred the employee to Dr. Berke for further treatment. Dr. Berke, in turn, referred the employee in October 2003 to Dr. Ronald Moon for further pain-management treatment. However, the employee failed to keep a scheduled appointment with Dr. Moon and, through counsel, requested that a *second* panel of four physicians be provided. Although counsel for the employer notified the employee's counsel that it did not believe the employee was entitled to a second panel of physicians, the employer nominated another physician in lieu of Dr. Moon; however, the employee, through counsel, rejected that alternate physician as well.

On October 27, 2003, the employee filed a motion seeking to compel the employer to provide a second panel of four physicians. Specifically, the employee contended that she was "entitled to a panel of pain management doctors from whom to choose one to treat her at [the employer's] expense." The employer opposed the employee's motion, arguing that requiring it to provide a panel of four physicians after one had already been provided to the employee would "exceed[ ] the delineated scope of § 25–5–77(a)." On December 9, 2003, the trial court entered an order granting the employee's request. Invoking the doctrine that "workers' compensation laws are to be liberally construed to effectuate the beneficent purposes of the Act," the trial court opined that a second panel was warranted because "the practice of medicine has evolved from the days of the traveling family doctor . . . into a highly specialized team approach," and it averred that the "beneficent purposes of the Act are best served by permitting the injured worker as much flexibility as is fair within the strictures of the law." The trial court expressly held that "as an injured worker progresses with medical treatment for an injury through different areas of medical specialty, the worker is entitled to a panel of doctors from which to choose a replacement *from each medical specialty*" (emphasis added). As a final note, the trial court added that "[i]f the intention of the Legislature is to restrict the choice of the injured worker otherwise, this Court invites that body to clarify its intent."

On January 13, 2004, the employer filed a petition for a writ of mandamus seeking an order compelling the trial court to vacate its December 9, 2003, order. . . .

As we have detailed, at no point has the Legislature, as a component of the Act's remedial scheme, afforded employees complete freedom to select a physician who will provide medical services at the employer's ultimate expense. That said, § 25–5–77(a), as currently in force, reflects the current sense of the Alabama Legislature that there should be some sort of "compromise between the employer's desire to completely control the physical rehabilitation process and the employee's desire for complete freedom of choice as to his or her physician." The history of the Act, as we have set forth, indicates that the Legislature, in 1973, first acknowledged the possibility that an injured employee may have valid reasons for objecting to a particular employer-selected physician and that, in that event, that employee should be able to reject that particular physician and have another selected by the employer. In doing so, the Legislature first attempted to balance two seemingly desirable, yet somewhat conflicting, values:

> "The first is the value of allowing an employee, as far as possible, to choose his or her own doctor. This value stems from the confidential nature of the doctor-patient relation, from the desirability of the patient's trusting the doctor, and from various other considerations. The other desirable value is that of achieving the maximum standards of rehabilitation by permitting the compensation system to exercise continuous control of the nature and quality of medical services from the

> moment of injury. If the injured employee has completely unlimited free choice of [a] doctor, in some cases he or she may select a doctor, because of personal relationship or acquaintance, who is not qualified to deal with the particular kind of case, or who at any rate is incapable of providing service of the quality required for the optimum rehabilitation process."

5 Arthur Larson & Lex K. Larson, *Larson's Workers' Compensation Law* § 94.02[2] (2003) (footnote omitted).

* * *

We recognize, like the trial court, that the practice of medicine has changed, in many respects, since the Act was first passed by the Legislature in 1919. We further acknowledge the abstract force of the employee's contentions that the trial court's ordering a second panel of four in this case might represent a "logical evolution" in the law, that it might further the "beneficent purposes" of the Act, and that affording employees greater choice in who provides them medical services might be "fair." However, it is not the role of the judiciary to "improve upon" legislation such as the Act, even upon such grounds as necessity based upon the passage of time. In this specific context, the Alabama Supreme Court has emphasized that while we must liberally construe the Act to effectuate its beneficent purposes, "such a construction must be one that the *language of the statute* 'fairly and reasonably' supports."

The employee contends on rehearing that to allow only one panel of four "surely is not consistent with legislative intent"; she posits that in some instances, such as where an employee suffers multiple injuries, it is possible that an employer could assign, or a designated treating physician could refer, an employee who has previously exhausted his or her panel rights to an incompetent physician. Even were an employer or a treating physician to undermine that understanding by selecting an incompetent physician, however, our law recognizes that there are certain instances in which an employee's obtaining treatment other than that offered by the employer may properly be deemed justified, including where the employer has "neglected or refused" to provide necessary medical care.

In this case, the employer was wrongly compelled, in contravention of § 25–5–77(a), to provide a second panel of four physicians after the employee had already expressed dissatisfaction with a former treating physician and had already been allowed to choose another physician from an employer-nominated panel of four. Because we conclude that the order under review deprives the employer of its rights regarding the selection of a treating physician, we grant the employer's petition for a writ of mandamus. The trial court is hereby directed to rescind its December 9, 2003, order.

[dissenting opinion is omitted]

NOTES

1. One of the most controversial issues in the medical benefits area involves the selection of the treating physician. Several considerations bear on this controversy. Employees, like other patients, have an interest in choosing their own physicians. The intimate and fiduciary nature of the doctor-patient relationship suggests that a patient should be free to choose a greatly trusted doctor. This interest transcends the personal compatibility of doctor and patient. The selection of a physician may also affect the range of treatment options as well. A patient with a back injury, for example, may prefer chiropractic care to that offered by an orthopedist. These interests are advanced by giving employees great latitude in selecting their physicians. A patient's ability to select his or her physician has eroded with the rise of managed care. Managed care is also an important feature of the workers' compensation system. Employers and their insurers have an interest in controlling costs. This objective can be accomplished most effectively if the party that pays the bills also selects the health care provider. Both the employer and employee have an interest in ensuring that the treating physician is competent and qualified to treat the underlying injury or illness. Yet, they may honestly disagree whether the orthopedist or the chiropractor is best qualified to treat the employee's back injury. Finally, but perhaps most importantly, each party may seek a tactical advantage in the compensation claim by selecting a physician who tends to sympathize with its side in evaluating the extent of the worker's injury.

2. States have found various ways to balance the competing interests of employers and employees in selecting the treating physician. The most prevalent approach is to allow the employee to make the initial selection. E.g., 820 Ill.Comp.Stat.Ann. 305/8(a); Or.Rev.Stat. § 656.245; R.I.Gen.Laws § 28–33–8. Some states require that the employee select a physician from a list prepared by a state agency or maintained by the employer. E.g., N.Y. Work.Comp. Law § 13–a (state agency); Ga.Code Ann. § 34–9–201 (employer list). A significant number of states give the employer the right to select the physician. E.g., Fla.Stat.Ann. § 440.13; N.J.Stat.Ann. § 34:15–15; N.M.Stat.Ann. § 52–1–49. In states where the employer controls the initial selection, the employee may petition the agency for a change in physicians. E.g., Colo.Rev.Stat. § 8–43–501. See also, Cal.Labor Code § 4600 (employee may change physician after a specified period of time); Ga.Code Ann. §§ 34–9–200, 34–9–201 (employee may select another physician from among those listed on the employer's list, but must petition the Board for permission to make a second change or select a physician not listed); Vt.Stat.Ann. tit. 21, § 640 (if the employee is dissatisfied with the physician selected by the employer, the employee shall have the right to select his own physician upon giving written notice to his employer). For a listing of positions of the states, see WCRI, Workers' Compensation Laws 2012,Table 3 (2012).

3. Employers are not responsible for medical expenses incurred through unauthorized treatment. This issue often arises in jurisdictions that give employers the initial control over the selection of physicians and the

employee obtains treatment from an unapproved physician. E.g., Zheng v. New Grand Buffet, Inc., 740 S.E.2d 302 (Ga. App. 2013) (employer is not responsible for medical expenses when employee unilaterally elected to see a physician who was not part of the employer panel of physicians); and Lavine v. SAIF Corp., 79 Or.App. 511, 718 P.2d 1391 (1986) (claimant is not entitled to payment for cost of unauthorized thermogram test). While an employer does not have to pay for unauthorized treatment or examination, the results still may be relevant in determining whether an employee is entitled to indemnity benefits. E.g., Dramis v. Palm Beach County School Board, 829 So.2d 346 (Fla. App. 2002) (ALJ erred in refusing to consider the testimony of unauthorized physician in assessing the extent of the employee's disability even though the employer's compensation insurer did not have to pay for those medical services); Valdez v. Workers' Compensation Appeals Bd., 143 Cal. Rptr. 3d 11 (Cal. App. 2012) (same).

4. The cost of medical benefits has increased dramatically. In 2010, approximately $27 billion were expended for workers' compensation medical benefits. National Academy of Social Insurance, Workers Compensation: Benefits, Coverage, and Costs, 2010, Table 9 (2012). While medical benefits once accounted for less than 25% of the total workers' compensation benefits package, they accounted for slightly more than 50% of all workers' compensation payments in 2010. Id. Medical costs have risen at a faster rate for workers' compensation than in the general health care system. Between 1985 and 1990 the annual average percentage increase for workers' compensation medical costs was 15.1% while the comparable figure for non-workers' compensation medical costs was 9.9%. Stacey M. Eccleston, Managed Care and Medical Cost Containment in Workers' Compensation 4 (Workers' Compensation Research Institute 1995). Some researchers attribute the faster rise of workers' compensation medical costs to two factors. First, unlike conventional medical insurance, workers' compensation does not utilize deductibles or coinsurance that might deter patients from over-utilizing medical services. Second, historically, employers and their insurers have had little bargaining power regarding physician and hospital fees. Leslie I. Bodon and Charles A. Fleishman, Medical Costs in Workers' Compensation: Trends and Comparisons 18–19 (Workers' Compensation Research Institute 1989).

Beginning in the late 1980s, states began experimenting with various cost containment strategies. Among the common strategies in place by the mid-1990s were: limiting employee choice of medical providers; limiting changes in physicians; use of physician fee schedules; hospital payment regulation; development of treatment guidelines for common injuries; and facilitating, or in some cases mandating, the use of managed care. See Stacey M. Eccleston, Managed Care and Medical Cost Containment in Workers' Compensation 13–14 (Workers' Compensation Research Institute 1995). A few states have imposed deductibles or co-payment requirements on the employee. See WCRI, Workers' Compensation Laws 2012, Table 3 (2012). More than half the states now regulate or mandate managed care in workers' compensation. Stacey M. Eccleston, Managed Care and Medical Cost Containment in Workers' Compensation 67 (Workers' Compensation Research Institute 1995). For a detailed discussion of how a "public health" model of managed care might be structured to optimize a reduction in workplace accident costs, see Dean M. Hashimoto, The Future Role of Managed Care and Capitation in Workers' Compensation, 22 Am. J. L. & Med. 233 (1996). Many states have intensified their efforts to combat fraud as a means of containing workers' compensation costs, including medical costs. E.g. Fla. Stat. Ann. § 440.105. This development is discussed in Chapter 10. For a comprehensive listing of various cost containment strategies, see Ramona P. Tanabe, Workers' Compensation Medical Cost Containment—A National Inventory, 2013 (Workers' Compensation Research Institute 2013).

Pennsylvania purports to control medical costs by authorizing insurers to suspend payments for medical treatment pending an independent review of whether the treatment is "reasonable and necessary". Payments can be suspended without prior notice to the worker or a hearing. The Supreme Court held that private compensation carriers who invoke these procedures are not "state actors" under the Fourteenth Amendment and that the Pennsylvania regime does not deprive injured workers of "property" within the meaning of that amendment. American Manufacturers Mutual Insurance Co. v. Sullivan, 526 U.S. 40, 119 S.Ct. 977, 143 L.Ed.2d 130 (1999). For a detailed examination of the quality and efficiency of medical care delivered under California's workers' compensation system, see California Commission on Health and Safety and Workers' Compensation, Research Colloquium on Workers' Compensation Medical Benefit Delivery and Return to Work (Rand Institute for Civil Justice 2006). See also, WCRI, How Have Worker Outcomes and Medical Costs Changed in Wisconsin (2010).

There are surprisingly few comprehensive studies of the effectiveness of cost containment efforts in the workers' compensation system. One early effort at such an assessment concluded that "traditional approaches to health care cost containment in workers' compensation programs have not effectively restrained medical cost growth." Silvana Pozzebon, Medical Cost Containment Under Workers' Compensation, 48 Indus. & Labor Rel. Rev. 153 (1994). More specifically, Professor Pozzebon found that states with limits on choice of providers have higher medical benefit expenditures than other states, the effect of fee schedules on medical costs is "less clear," and that regulation of hospital costs is "the only cost containment strategy that appears to effectively decrease medical benefit spending. . . ." Id., 48 Indus. & Labor Rel. Rev. at 164. Some studies suggest that the costs savings resulting from the introduction of managed care produced a one-time change and do not lead to a permanent reduction in the rate of cost growth. Michael E. Chernew et al., Managed Care, Medical Technology, and Health Care Cost Growth: A Review of the Evidence, 55 Medical Care Research and Review 259–288 (1998). A more recent study found that giving the employee the right to select the medical provider was associated with higher costs and worse return to work outcomes. David Neumark, Peter S. Barth, and Richard A.

Victor, The Impact of Provider Choice on Workers' Compensation Costs and Outcomes, 61 Indus. & Lab. Rel. L. Rev. 121 (2007).

5. The Patient Protection and Affordable Care Act (ACA) was enacted in 2010. 26 U.S.C. § 5000A. The Supreme Court upheld most of the ACA over constitutional challenge in National Federation of Business v. Sebelius, 132 S.Ct. 2566 (2012). Since the ACA does not directly speak to state workers' compensation and many of the law's key provisions do not go into effect until 2014, any assessment of the effect of the ACA on workers' compensation is largely conjecture. Some observers have suggested that the ACA may reduce medical benefit costs under workers' compensation. The Rand Institute for Civil Justice conducted a study of impact of health care reform in Massachusetts on the state's workers' compensation medical benefits costs. The ACA was modeled in significant respects on the Massachusetts legislation. This study concluded that workers' compensation hospital billings fell by 5 to 10 percent following the implementation ACA-like health care reform. Paul Heaton, The Impact of Health Care Reform on Workers' Compensation Medical Care: Evidence from Massachusetts (Rand Institute for Civil Justice 2012). The author of the study stated that the decline in workers' compensation costs could be "plausibly attributed to coverage expansions induced by health care reform . . . [which may have] led health insurers to pay for some care that would have been billed to the WC system in the absence of reform. Thus, reform may actually reduce medical costs born by the WC system." Id., at 37. Another respected scholar speculates that if "the Affordable Care Act succeeds, workers' compensation health benefits may be merged over time into the general employment-based health benefits system." Tom Baker, Health Insurance, Risk, and Responsibility After the Patient Protection and Affordable Care Act, 159 U. Pa. L. Rev. 1577, 1594–95 (2011). Professor Baker opines that "[s]uch a measure is likely to be very politically popular in light of (a) the increasing recognition within the business community that workers' compensation has become an expensive form of health insurance and (b) the obvious efficiencies from eliminating the need to determine whether an injury or illness is caused by employment." Id., at 1595 n. 89.

SMITH V. HASTINGS IRRIGATION PIPE CO.

Supreme Court of Nebraska, 1986.
222 Neb. 663, 386 N.W.2d 9.

GRANT, JUSTICE.

This action was brought by appellee, Linda K. Smith, to recover workmen's compensation benefits from the appellant, Hastings Irrigation Pipe Co. (Hastings Pipe). Smith was injured while working for Hastings Pipe on October 10, 1983, and filed a petition with the Nebraska Workmen's Compensation Court on July 12, 1984. After rehearing, a three-judge panel of the Workmen's Compensation Court, with one judge dissenting, modified a single-judge order and found that Smith was entitled to the costs of certain medical treatment by Dr. John L. Greene, together with temporary total disability payments during that treatment, and that Smith was entitled to rehabilitation services. Hastings Pipe appeals from that order, assigning as error the findings set out above.

* * *

[Smith suffered the amputation of several fingers while operating a punch press.]

In its other assignment of error, Hastings Pipe contends the Workmen's Compensation Court erred "In finding that the plaintiff [Smith] was entitled to vocational rehabilitation services." The record shows that Smith has a 12th-grade education and is currently attending Hastings Central Community College and taking classes which will enable her to do managerial-type duties in the retail horticultural field.

In *Evans v. American Community Stores*, 222 Neb. 538, 540, 385 N.W.2d 91, 93 (1986), we held:

> The right of an injured workman to vocational rehabilitation depends upon his inability to perform work for which he has previous training and experience. § 48–162.01; *Behrens v. Ken Corp.*, 191 Neb. 625, 216 N.W.2d 733 (1974). This is ordinarily a question of fact to be determined by the compensation court. *Pollock v. Monfort of Colorado, supra* [221 Neb. 859, 381 N.W.2d 154 (1986)].

Smith testified her arm still is essentially useless. Prior to her employment at Hastings Pipe, Smith held jobs which required two good hands and arms. Most, if not all, of these jobs were minimum-wage-type jobs. Smith's vocational training will allow her to obtain a job which will not require constant use of two good hands and arms. The Workmen's Compensation Court found vocational rehabilitation training was authorized under Neb.Rev.Stat. § 48–162.–01(6) (Reissue 1984).

The dissenting judge of the three-judge panel felt that the "loss of her long and ring fingers . . . is [not] sufficient to entitle her to vocational rehabilitation . . . particularly . . . in view of the plaintiff's work history which shows that she has experience and training in several jobs that she can do." It is true that in her 10 years in the work force, Smith had jobs as a worker in the kitchen and dining room of a retirement home, as a filing clerk with an insurance company, as a waitress in bars and a restaurant, and as a sales clerk in various retail establishments. Smith testified, however, that each of these jobs required the use of both hands and both arms and that, although she had done such jobs in the past, she was unable to do them after her injury. Smith's testimony as to the physical requirements of each of her jobs, and her inability to perform the jobs after her injury, constituted sufficient evidence to support the findings of the majority of the panel, which found that Smith had suffered a reduction in her earning power as a result of her accident and injury and determined that Smith was entitled to rehabilitation in an effort to increase her earning capacity. The evidence before the panel was sufficient to support these findings.

We determine that the evidence before the three-judge panel was sufficient to support the award entered by the court. The judgment of the compensation court is affirmed, and Smith is allowed the sum of $1,000 for the services of her attorney in this court.

AFFIRMED.

NOTES

1. Vocational rehabilitation and its relationship to medical benefits has been described by one expert as follows:

> Operationally, rehabilitation consists of a range of services bracketed by the two mentioned above—medical management and formal education. Among these services are counseling, guidance, evaluation, retraining, and job placement. Rehabilitation may involve job redesign and modifications to the work place or even to the home environment, although, most commonly, rehabilitation services are directed toward improving the individual and his job chances, rather than the environment in which he functions.
>
> Rehabilitation is said to be a team effort involving the physician, allied health professionals, and persons from a host of assorted disciplines—vocational education, social work, work evaluation, etc. The coordinator of the team may be a professional rehabilitation counselor. It is a continuous integrated progress, with one service melding into and flowing from the other. The focus is on the client and the accomplishment of the stated objectives, be they return to the worker's old job, or possibly some more ambitious objective such as restoration of the maximum capabilities of the person given his residual functioning capacities. If the process is truly a continuous one, then there is no real dividing line between medical and vocational rehabilitation. Yet one of the difficulties of bringing rehabilitation into workers' compensation is that the laws of some jurisdictions require such a distinction, since they provide for different payers for the different types of services.

Berkowitz, *Rehabilitation and Workers' Compensation: Incompatible or Inseparable?*, in Benefits, Costs, and Cycles in Workers' Compensation 80–81 (P. Borba and D. Appel eds. 1990).

2. The importance of vocational rehabilitation in a workers' compensation scheme has long been recognized. As early as 1916, the International Association of Industrial Accident Boards and Commissions

(IAIABC) called for greater provision of rehabilitation services to the injured worker. Yet, until recently, workers' compensation statutes guaranteed few rehabilitation benefits. Today, every state has some kind of rehabilitation provision in its statute. These statutes vary widely in terms of the scope of coverage. A survey of twelve states found that awards for rehabilitation benefits are made in approximately 10% of the claims involving permanent partial disability. Variations among states in the frequency of awards are considerable. Rehabilitation benefits were awarded in 50% of the Florida claims surveyed while such benefits were awarded in only 3% of the claims surveyed in New York and Wisconsin. See, Berkowitz, *Rehabilitation and Workers' Compensation: Incompatible or Inseparable*, in Benefits, Costs, and Cycles in Workers' Compensation 79, 87–88 (P. Borba and D. Appel eds. 1990).

3. How far should states go in mandating vocational rehabilitation under workers' compensation laws? Most statutory rehabilitation provisions condition benefits on an administrative finding that rehabilitation would be "feasible," "desirable," or "necessary." See, 5 A. Larson & L. Larson, Larson's Workers' Compensation Law § 95.03 (2013). Some courts apply these terms liberally so that rehabilitation may be considered "necessary" if it will materially assist in restoring the employee's impaired earning capacity. E.g., Norby v. Arctic Enterprises, Inc., 305 Minn. 519, 232 N.W.2d 773 (1975). Other courts adopt more restrictive interpretations and find that rehabilitation is not "necessary" unless the employee's disability rises nearly to the level of total incapacity. E.g., McInnis v. Town of Bar Harbor, 387 A.2d 739 (Me.1978). For a state by state description of rehabilitation practices, see United States, Chamber of Commerce, 2013 Analysis of Workers' Compensation Laws, Chart X (2013).

Whether a specific rehabilitation plan will be found to be feasible or necessary often depends on the facts of the particular case. In evaluating a claim for rehabilitation benefits, courts commonly consider the relative costs and benefits of the program, the employee's worklife expectancy, and the ability and motivation of the employee. See, National Tea Co. v. Industrial Comm., 97 Ill.2d 424, 73 Ill.Dec. 575, 454 N.E.2d 672 (1983). Vocational rehabilitation benefits will not be granted when the plan is too vague, or the employee is untrainable, or the employee is capable of earning pre-injury wages without additional training. E.g., Madonna v. Industrial Comm., 171 Ill.App.3d 301, 121 Ill.Dec. 469, 525 N.E.2d 275 (1988) (rehabilitation not necessary when laborer is able to perform pre-injury work and plans for rehabilitation are vague); Hewson v. Stevenson, 225 Neb. 254, 404 N.W.2d 35 (1987) (66 year old mechanic with severe physical limitations and no other training or skills was not entitled to rehabilitation). See also, Rydwell v. Anchorage School Dist., 864 P.2d 526 (Alaska 1993) (claimant with a 0% impairment rating under the AMA Guides is not entitled to rehabilitation benefits); Ward v. Bonne Idee Aero Service, Inc., 687 So.2d 629 (La.App.1997) (claimant who can perform old job is not entitled to rehabilitation); Bishop v. Town of Barre, 140 Vt. 564, 442 A.2d 50 (1982) (disapproving rehabilitation plan that would cost $2,500 but would produce only $200 in annual income). On the other hand, substantial rehabilitation services will be provided when the anticipated impact on the claimant's earning capacity is great. E.g., Howlett's Tree Service v. Industrial Comm., 160 Ill.App.3d 190, 111 Ill.Dec. 836, 513 N.E.2d 82 (1987) (awarding rehabilitation benefits including a one-year course in agricultural business to a highly motivated worker with a 30 year worklife expectancy); Thom v. Lutheran Medical Center, 226 Neb. 737, 414 N.W.2d 810 (1987) (approving a two-year training course in business and computer studies for a nurse whose physical injury substantially reduced employment potential as a nurse); Held v. North Dakota Workers Compensation Bureau, 540 N.W.2d 166 (N.D.1995) (approving plan to retrain an auto service technician to work as an account clerk). Should it matter whether the proposed rehabilitation plan might give the employee a greater earning capacity than existed before the injury? Is Smith such a case? See Ex Parte Beaver Valley Corp., 477 So.2d 408 (Ala.1985) (reversing award of rehabilitation benefits that included college tuition because this would not merely "restore" the employees' earning capacity, but would "improve his station in life.").

When appropriate, incidental expenses are included as part of the rehabilitation award. E.g., Mosley v. Bank of Delaware, 372 A.2d 178 (Del.1977) (rehabilitation benefits include the costs of travel to and from training center); Grover v. Industrial Comm., 759 P.2d 705 (Colo.1988) (child care expenses of worker undergoing vocational training are compensable).

4. The employer may have a positive interest in vocational rehabilitation as when restoring an employee's pre-injury earning capacity would reduce the employer's liability for disability benefits. Thus, employers may support rehabilitation efforts and press for incentives to encourage employee cooperation. In some states, disability benefits of an employee who unreasonably refuses rehabilitation may be denied or suspended. E.g., Stone v. Industrial Comm., 286 Ill.App.3d 174, 221 Ill.Dec. 373, 675 N.E.2d 280 (1997) (terminating temporary total disability benefits to worker who did not cooperate with rehabilitation); Paris v. J.A. Baldwin Mfg. Co., 216 Neb. 151, 342 N.W.2d 198 (1984) (disability benefits could be terminated when employee failed to cooperate with vocational training); Ga.Code Ann. § 34–9–200.1(d) ("the refusal of the employee without reasonable cause to accept rehabilitation shall entitle the board in its discretion to suspend or reduce the compensation otherwise payable. . . ."). Cf. Fuhrman v. North Dakota Workers Compensation Bureau, 569 N.W.2d 269 (N.D.1997) (expense of commuting between Bismarck and Minneapolis to receive training was "good cause" for not complying with rehabilitation plan).

5. Some states have held that although undocumented workers may recover medical benefits for work-related injuries, they are not eligible for rehabilitation benefits. E.g., Moyera v. Quality Pork Int'l., 284 Neb. 963, 825 N.W.2d 409 (2013) (undocumented worker may recover medical benefits); Ortiz v. Cement Products, 270 Neb. 787, 708 N.W.2d 610 (2005) (undocumented worker is not entitled to rehabilitation benefits); Tarango v.

State Industrial Ins. System, 117 Nev. 444, 25 P.3d 175 (2001) (undocumented worker is entitled to medical benefits but not rehabilitation). The rationale underlying the distinction is that medical care associated with a work-related injury is a cost of production and should be internalized into the price of goods and services offered by the employer. Rehabilitation, on the other hand, is intended to prepare the worker for future employment, something that the undocumented worker is prohibited from doing under federal immigration laws. See generally, Jerry Joe, Defending Against Suits Brought by Illegal Aliens, 76 Def. Counsel J. 319, 326 (2009). For an argument that this position is "shortsighted," "contradicts traditional American notions of justice," and is economically inefficient see Robert I. Correales, Workers' Compensation and Vocational Rehabilitation Benefits for Undocumented Workers: Reconciling the Purported Conflicts Between State Law, Federal Immigration Law, and Equal Protection to Prevent the Creation of a Disposable Workforce, 81 Denv. U. L. Rev. 347, 349 (2003).

3. DISABILITY BENEFITS

A. INTRODUCTION: DURATION AND DEGREE OF DISABILITY

Disability benefits are money payments made directly to injured workers to compensate for earnings lost as a result of compensable injuries. These benefits are sometimes also referred to as "income," "indemnity" or "cash" benefits, and are most commonly calculated as a percentage of the recipient's average weekly wage, subject to a specified dollar limit. In New York, for example, total disability is compensated at the rate of 66 2/3% of the worker's average weekly wage, but no more than $772.96 per week. N.Y. Work.Comp. Law § 15. While the percentage of wages payable as compensation varies among the states, the 66 2/3 % figure is common. In a different approach, Michigan and Iowa define disability benefits in terms of 80% of a worker's "spendable weekly earnings". Iowa Code Ann. § 85.34 (but not more than 184% of the average statewide weekly wage); Mich.Comp.Laws Ann. § 418.351 ("after-tax" average weekly wage). The maximum benefit payable ranges widely among the states. For example, in 2012, a totally disabled worker in New Hampshire could receive as much as $1,276.50 per week, whereas in Georgia, the maximum was $500. For a state-by-state summary of total disability benefits, see United States Chamber of Commerce, 2013 Analysis of Workers' Compensation Laws, Chart VI (2013).

Under section 104(a)(1) of the Internal Revenue Code, workers' compensation benefits are excluded from the definition of "gross income" and hence are not subject to federal income tax.

Some statutes express the maximum weekly payment as a flat dollar amount. E.g., Ga.Code Ann. § 34–9–261. In these states the maximum weekly payment remains constant until the legislature amends the statute. Other states tie the maximum weekly payment to some index, such as the state's "average weekly wage," which allows adjustment in compensation levels without legislative amendment. E.g., 820 Ill.Comp.Stat.Ann. 305/8(b)(4) (maximum weekly compensation payment is 100% of state's average weekly wage as adjusted annually.)

Benefits are often classified according to the degree and duration of disability. The degree of disability refers to its extent. A disability may be total (i.e., the worker is completely unable to work) or partial (i.e., the worker is injured, but is capable of performing some work). The duration of the disability may be temporary or permanent. These variables produce the four common categories of disability benefits: temporary total disability, temporary partial disability, permanent total disability, and permanent partial disability.

The vast majority of compensable work injuries involve a temporary total disability rendering the injured employee unable to work for the time being. Whether in the hospital or healing and recuperating at home, the worker is expected to recover fully. Accordingly, disability benefits are payable until the worker has recovered and returned to work, subject to statutory limitations as to amount and duration. Temporary disability accounts for 61.2% of cases involving cash benefits and 17.3% of the benefits paid. National Academy of Social Insurance, Workers' Compensation: Benefits, Coverage and Costs, 2010, 12 (2012).

Permanently and totally disabled employees are not able to do any substantial work and are not expected ever to do so. Some states limit permanent total disability benefits by amount and duration, e.g., S.C.Code Ann. § 42–9–10 (limiting benefits to a maximum of 100% of state average weekly wage per week for 500 weeks with some limited exceptions) but many pay them for the duration of the disability or life. E.g., 820 Ill.Comp.Stat.Ann. 305/8 (benefits payable for life). Claims for permanent total disability are fewer in number, but greater in average cost. Fewer than 1% of all workers' compensation claims involve permanent total disability, but these claims account for 8.6% of all the disability benefits paid under the system. National Academy of Social Insurance, Workers' Compensation: Benefits, Coverage, and Costs, 2010, 12 (2012).

More dollars are paid out for permanent partial disability benefits than in any other category of disability. In fact, 71.8% of all the disability benefits paid to injured workers are for permanent partial disabilities. National Academy of Social Insurance, Workers' Compensation: Benefits, Coverage, and Costs, 2010, 12 (2012). This class of cases involves employees who are permanently impaired in some manner, but are able to perform some fairly substantial kind of work. In most states, certain types of permanent partial disabilities are compensable according to a statutory "schedule". The statute specifies the amount of benefits for particular injuries, such as the loss of an arm, a leg, or an eye. For example, a worker in Tennessee who loses a hand in an occupational accident is entitled to a maximum payment of $118,350.00 for permanent partial disability. Tenn.Code Ann. § 50–6–207. As the following subsections illustrate, the standards for determining disability and the widespread use of schedules are points of controversy within the workers' compensation system. With this background, the student may now address the issue of determining what constitutes a "disability."

B. DISABILITY AS IMPAIRED EARNING CAPACITY

FLETCHER V. DANA CORPORATION

Court of Appeals of North Carolina, 1995.
119 N.C.App. 491, 459 S.E.2d 31.

JOHN, JUDGE.

Defendants appeal an award to plaintiff by the North Carolina Industrial Commission (the Commission) of temporary total disability accrued during the period between 7 November 1989 and 1 April 1991. Defendants contend the Commission erred by basing its determination of disability upon plaintiff's inability to obtain employment during the period in question.

We find defendants' argument unpersuasive.

Relevant background information includes the following: Plaintiff was injured 27 January 1989 in the course of his employment with defendant Dana Corporation (Dana). He was struck in the left arm by a steel chip buggy, part of a train of carts containing scrap metal moved by a tow motor.

After undergoing surgery on his shoulder, plaintiff returned to work 24 July 1989.

On 8 September 1989, plaintiff was assessed by Dr. Larry G. Anderson, his treating physician, as having 20% permanent partial disability of the left arm.

Plaintiff received temporary total disability compensation until returning to work as well as compensation for the permanent disability rating.

On 17 October 1989, plaintiff reinjured his shoulder while attempting to move a basket containing approximately one dozen 60-pound axle tubes. He thereafter was restricted by Dr. Anderson from lifting more than 40 pounds and from lifting overhead.

However, neither plaintiff's job nor any other position then available at Dana was consistent with the limitations imposed by Dr. Anderson.

Plaintiff consequently was discharged 7 November 1989.

Despite extensive efforts, he was unable to secure employment until 1 April 1991.

On 1 February 1991, plaintiff's claim for disability benefits was heard by Deputy Commissioner Charles Markham who ruled plaintiff was not entitled to temporary total disability benefits for the period subsequent to 7 November 1989.

Plaintiff appealed the decision to the full Commission. In an Opinion and Award filed 28 September 1993, the Commission reversed the Deputy Commissioner and ordered defendants to pay temporary total disability accrued during the period of 7 November 1989 through 1 April 1991. In pertinent part, the Commission specified the following findings and conclusions:

> 10. Dr. Anderson believed that as of October 25, 1989, when he gave plaintiff the written restriction as to the 40 pound weight limitation, plaintiff had essentially reached the maximum point of medical improvement. It was his opinion that as of October 25, 1989, Mr. Fletcher could work with the restrictions given him, that is, not lifting anything above 40 pounds. From a medical point of view, plaintiff would have been able to perform sales work or administrative work as of October 25, 1989.
>
> 11. Dana Corporation had no jobs available which met plaintiff's physical restrictions. Therefore, he was terminated on November 7, 1989. . . .
>
> 12. After his termination November 7, 1989 and until the time of the hearing [before the Deputy Commissioner], plaintiff made extensive but unsuccessful efforts to gain employment. Plaintiff did not limit himself in this search to industrial work but included supervisory positions and jobs in state government. He was involved with the Employment Security Commission. While he was initially somewhat selective in terms of the pay expected, he lowered his sights, and finally was willing to take anything he could find (except selling insurance). Plaintiff had and sought no medical treatment after November, 1989 except that he received pain medications from his family physician. He did not re-apply for a position with [Dana] as far as its personnel director was aware.
>
> * * *

> 17. Despite reasonable efforts, the plaintiff was not able to actually obtain employment from his discharge on November 7, 1989 until returning to work on April 1, 1991.
>
> * * *
>
> CONCLUSION OF LAW
>
> As a result of the compensable injury, the plaintiff was unable to obtain employment, despite reasonable efforts, until April 1, 1991, and plaintiff is entitled to temporary total disability benefits from the time of his discharge from defendants' [sic] employment on November 7, 1989 until obtaining employment on April 1, 1991, and such other and further medical compensation as may effect a cure, give relief or shorten the period of the claimant's disability.
>
> Defendants gave notice of appeal to this Court 8 October 1993.

* * *

Defendants and amicus counsel argue the Commission committed error of law by awarding temporary total disability benefits to plaintiff under circumstances wherein he possessed the capacity to earn wages and thus was not totally disabled. Defendants assert the Commission thereby "stretched [the Workers' Compensation Act] to provide unemployment insurance for workers ready, willing and able to work, who have qualifications to obtain employment, but who are unemployed because of economic conditions." We disagree.

A claimant seeking to recover under the Workers' Compensation Act (the Act) bears the burden of proving both the existence and extent of disability. . . . Under the Act, an employee injured in the course of his employment is "disabled" if the injury results in an "incapacity . . . to earn the wages which the employee was receiving at the time of injury in the same or any other employment." N.C. Gen. Stat. § 97–2(9) (1991). Disability as defined in the Act is thus the impairment of the injured employee's earning capacity rather than physical disablement. . . .

A claimant may meet the burden of proving inability to earn the same wages earned before injury by showing "he is capable of some work, but that he has, after a reasonable effort on his part, been unsuccessful in his effort to obtain employment."

Defendants assert the Commission misinterpreted Russell and "erroneously focused on whether plaintiff was able to actually obtain employment" instead of whether plaintiff was capable of earning the same wages. Amicus counsel maintains an injured employee in the circumstance of plaintiff must demonstrate "he is unable to work and not merely that he unsuccessfully sought work." In addition, counsel reiterates defendants' contention that the holding of the full Commission in reliance upon Russell "in effect converted temporary total disability into unemployment compensation."

However, the Court in Russell did not address the causes of plaintiff's inability to obtain employment, but rather focused upon evidence of plaintiff's reasonable efforts to obtain employment as being one means of meeting his burden of showing incapacity to earn the same wages earned prior to injury.

"The so-called 'work search' test is merely the evidentiary vehicle by which employability, or lack of it, is proven," Flesche v. Interstate Warehouse, 411 So. 2d 919, 922 (Fla. 1st DCA 1982), and "there are a number of criteria by which wage-earning capacity must be measured, and 'no single factor is conclusive.' "

As opposed to Russell, the issue in the case sub judice is whether plaintiff, having met the Russell test with credible (as determined by the Commission) evidence of diligent efforts to find employment, is entitled to receive compensation benefits where his inability to earn the same wages was caused in part by unavailability of area jobs consistent with his physical limitations. Not only this Court, but a leading workers' compensation scholar and courts from other jurisdictions suggest an affirmative response.

In Bridges v. Linn–Corriher Corp., 90 N.C. App. 397, 368 S.E.2d 388, disc. review denied, 323 N.C. 171, 373 S.E.2d 104 (1988), this Court observed:

> the Workers' Compensation Act was enacted to ameliorate the consequences of injuries and illnesses in the workplace and one of those consequences, at least on occasion, is that a recuperated worker capable of holding a job cannot get one. A capable job seeker whom no employer needing workers will hire is not employable.
>
> Additionally, in the opinion of Professor Larson:
>
> Inability to get work, traceable directly and substantially to a compensable injury, may be as effective in establishing disability as inability to perform work. . . . The two essentials [of disability are]: wage loss, and causation of the wage loss by work-connected injury. The fact that the wage loss comes about through . . . unavailability of employment rather than through incapacity to perform the work does not change the result [of disability].

1C Arthur Larson, Larson's Workmen's Compensation Law § 57.61(a), 10–389–397.

Moreover, other jurisdictions support the proposition that compensation is allowable where unavailability of jobs prevents a claimant from earning the same wages received prior to injury. In Regency Inn v. Johnson, 422 So. 2d 870 (Fla. 1st DCA 1982), disc. review denied, 431 So. 2d 989 (Fla.1983), for example, the claimant was injured during the course of her occupation as a housekeeper and consequently was required to seek lighter work. Id. at 872–73. Although she actively pursued other employment in the area, including seeking assistance from the Florida State Employment Office, her efforts were unsuccessful and she was subsequently awarded wage loss benefits for the period of her unemployment. Id. at 873.

As in our jurisdiction, the Florida statute then in effect placed the burden on the employee "to establish that any wage loss claimed is the result of the compensable injury." Fla. Stat. § 440.15(3)(b)(2) (1979).

The Florida Court of Appeals, in the *en banc* portion of the Regency opinion, pointed out that

> whether the nonavailability of jobs due to economic conditions is a factor to be considered or ignored in determining the after-injury wages an employee is 'able to earn,' is not immediately apparent from a literal reading of the statute itself.

422 So. 2d at 875 (citation omitted). Relying on prior case law, the court went on to state that

> in the broadest sense, 'able to earn' takes into account many factors, including the availability of jobs, and such a broad interpretation is consistent . . . with the principle which requires a liberal construction in favor of the injured employee.

Id. The full court upheld the original panel's conclusion that since the claimant would not have suffered wage loss if the injury had not occurred, the statutory requirement of causation was satisfied. 422 So. 2d at 872.

In other words, "but for" the work-related injury she sustained, the Florida claimant, like plaintiff herein, would not have become unemployed and suffered wage loss in consequence of the unavailability of other employment. Her wage loss was thus caused by and resulted from the injury she sustained within the scope and course of her employment.

The employer in Regency Inn had insisted that a work search which is unsuccessful due to unavailability of employment precludes compensation because such evidence does not prove a wage loss due to a compensable disability. Id. The panel disagreed:

> For wage loss the statute provides simply for general causal relation by covering such loss which 'is the result of the . . .

> injury.' If the intent had been to require wage loss from physical incapacity for work (independent of job availability) as an absolute condition to compensation for wage loss, the alternative language would surely have been used.

422 So. 2d at 873. We note again that disability under our Act relates to impairment of the injured employee's earning capacity rather than physical infirmity. Peoples, 316 N.C. at 434–35, 342 S.E.2d at 804 (citations omitted).

In a similar vein, the full Florida court emphasized that

> had the legislature intended 'able to earn' to be further qualified so as to preclude consideration of non-availability of jobs because of economic conditions, it would have been a simple matter for this to have been written into the law.

* * *

The rationale of the *en banc* opinion in Regency Inn also addresses the assertion of defendants and amicus counsel herein that the Commission in effect converted workers' compensation benefits into unemployment benefits.

First, the court observed that the Florida workers' compensation act contained no indication its legislature "devised and enacted a system of reparations for injured workers that would fulfill its purposes in time of relative economic prosperity, but would automatically withhold or suspend such reparations in time of economic depression." 422 So. 2d at 878. We likewise find no such legislative indication in our workers' compensation law. Whatever the health of the economy at any given time, workers' compensation statutes are to be liberally construed to give full effect to their humane purpose and remedial character. See Hartley v. Prison Department, 258 N.C. 287, 290–91, 128 S.E.2d 598, 600–01 (1962) (citations omitted).

Next, the court continued, employees receiving unemployment compensation "do not suffer compensable industrial accidents; only employed workers do." Regency, 422 So. 2d at 878.

> The employed worker is an integral part of the productive machinery of society and he is entitled to be treated as still belonging to that segment of the economy after a compensable accident, rather than categorized as a member of the unfortunate group whose unemployed status is due solely to economic conditions.

Id. Thus, workers who would not be unemployed but for a work-related injury should be compensated by workers' compensation, a system "intended to relieve society of the burden of caring for injured workers and to place the responsibility on the industry served." Id. (citation omitted).

The court concluded by pointing out that unemployment compensation is of "more limited amount and duration than workers' compensation benefits, and these benefits are not provided as an alternative to any other form of legal redress, as is true of workers' compensation." Id. (citation omitted). . . .

In Michigan, moreover, the Supreme Court, in Sobotka v. Chrysler Corporation, 447 Mich. 1, 523 N.W.2d 454 (1994), considered the implications of the circumstance that, as in North Carolina, "worker's compensation benefits in Michigan are payable on the basis of wage loss and not on the basis of physical impairment." The court determined as follows:

> Where, on account of an injury, an employee is, in fact, unemployed, the employee is entitled to [workers' compensation benefits] because the employee is not "able to earn" wages postinjury.
>
> [A] disabled worker does not bear the burden of unfavorable economic conditions that further diminish his ability to find suitable work.
>
> This means that the partially disabled employee's only burden is to show he is unable to earn wages because of his injury, not that he must show that the economy or other factors are not the cause of unemployment.
>
> The court went on to hold that while
>
> it is the employee's burden to show a link between wage loss and the work-related injury . . . , once the employee shows a work-related injury and subsequent wage loss, the factfinder may infer that the employee cannot find a job because of the injury.
>
> Finally, the courts in Maine have adopted a similar approach:
>
> To be entitled to compensation for total incapacity when only partially disabled in the medical sense, the employee must show "that he has engaged in a good faith effort to obtain work within the tolerance of his physical condition, and . . . that he failed in his effort, either because employers in his community would not hire people with such a limited capacity to do the type of work within his tolerance, or because there was no reasonably stable market in his community for that restricted work of which he was capable."

The rationale of the foregoing authorities is sound and consistent with our statements in Russell and Bridges. We therefore hold that an employee who suffers a work-related injury is not precluded from workers' compensation benefits when that employee, while employable within limitations in certain kinds of work, cannot after reasonable efforts obtain employment due to unavailability of jobs.

Based on the foregoing, the Commission's award to plaintiff of temporary total disability is affirmed.

Affirmed.

JUDGES GREENE and MARTIN, JOHN C. concur.

NOTES

1. The principal case reflects the historical view that "disability" in the workers' compensation field means more than the physical impairment sustained by the employee as a result of his injury. The ultimate question is to what extent has the employee lost his or her capacity to earn wages as a result of the injury. Physical condition is an important factor and may be decisive for a particular case, but it is by no means the only consideration.

The earliest workers' compensation cases defined disability in terms of impaired earning capacity. In 1912, the House of Lords decided Ball v. William Hunt & Sons, Ltd., [1912] A.C. 496, in which the claimant lost an eye in a work-related injury and thereafter was unable to obtain employment despite his physical ability to perform his usual type of work. A judgment denying compensation was reversed with Lord Atkinson commenting: "The earning of wages depends as much on the demand for the workman's labor as it does upon his physical ability to work. If because of his apparent physical defects no one will employ him, however efficient he may be in fact, he has lost the power to earn wages as completely as if he were paralyzed in every limb." For an early American case reaching the same result, see Fennell's Case, 289 Mass. 89, 193 N.E. 885 (1935) ("when one is unable to obtain other employment because of visible, physical results of an industrial accident, that person's earning capacity is as much impaired as if he were physically disabled to the extent that he could do no work").

Defining disability in terms of impaired earning capacity allowed the claimants to recover in *Fletcher* and *Fennell's Case*. It can also lead to the denial of benefits to workers who suffer significant physical injury but no wage loss. E.g., City of Philadelphia v. Workmen's Compensation Appeal Board, 695 A.2d 910 (Pa.Cmwlth.1997) (denying benefits to worker whose job related hearing loss did not affect his ability to earn a wage).

2. Defining disability in terms of impaired earning capacity is often referred to as a "wage loss" system. The Michigan Supreme Court explained the philosophy underlying a wage loss system as follows:

> [t]he central idea is that each worker will be treated individually, and will receive, in addition to necessary medical expenses, a percentage of his or her actual wage loss (or more precisely, loss of earning capacity), however short or long that loss may continue. The key advantage of this approach, of course, is that it adapts much more readily to the widely varying circumstances of given cases. The lawyer who has lost the little finger on his left hand will receive little or nothing; the concert pianist with the same injury will be entitled to benefits until reasonable alternative employment is made available. . . .

Sobotka v. Chrysler Corporation, 447 Mich. 1, 523 N.W.2d 454, 459 (1994) (quoting St. Antoine, Workers' Compensation in Michigan, Cost, Benefits, and Fairness 25–26).

3. The issue in *Fletcher* was whether the claimant could be considered totally disabled when he could not find employment consistent with his physical restrictions. Are there explanations other than the claimant's work injury that might explain his inability to secure employment? Who has the burden of proof? See Padgett v. Waffle House, Inc., 269 Ga. 105, 498 S.E.2d 499 (1998) (burden of proof is on the employer to prove that a suitable job is available when the employee was terminated for reasons related to a disability). What sort of evidence is needed to establish or refute a claim of impaired earning capacity? These issues are explored in more detail in the case below.

KARR V. ARMSTRONG TIRE & RUBBER

Supreme Court of Mississippi, 1953.
216 Miss. 132, 61 So.2d 789.

[Claimant suffered a compensable injury by inhaling chemical smoke. It caused painful irritation of his chest, face and throat. He was unable to work for 4 weeks and suffered an 80% loss of his voice. The administrative officer allowed compensation for the 4 weeks. He disallowed any compensation for the voice loss, although he found it was caused by the smoke. Claimant testified that he did not use his voice in his work "too much" but that "You can't work without saying something sometime"; that when he did say something above a hoarse whisper "it'll tire me."]

ROBERDS, PRESIDING JUSTICE. * * *

The Attorney-Referee also had before him the fact that when the injury occurred claimant was earning $45.12 per week working 6 days and at the time of the hearing he was making $60.40 a week working five days at the same employment for the same employer. And that, of course, is strong evidence he had suffered no loss in earning capacity. That comparative actual wage pay, we take it from the arguments, was the test applied at the hearing to determine whether the earning capacity of applicant had been decreased by the eighty percent impairment in his speech. And some of the authorities seemingly hold that such comparative actual wage pay is the correct and only test. The statutes vary. Our statute does not test the earning capacity by the comparative wages received by applicant before and after the injury. It is not a comparison of actual wage with actual wage. The benefits are figured on a percentage of applicant's average weekly wages at the time of the injury as compared to "his wage-earning capacity thereafter in the same employment or otherwise. . . ." Chapter 354, Sec. 8(c)(21) General Laws of Miss. 1948. In determining the wage-earning capacity of claimant after the injury a number of factors are to be considered in addition to the actual pay received by him when injured as compared to his actual earnings thereafter. Larson has a very good discussion of the elements of proof entering into the question. Vol. 2, Sec. 57.21, page 4:

> "Degree of disability is calculated under most acts by comparing actual earnings before the injury with earning capacity after the injury.
>
> "It is at once apparent that the two items in the comparison are not quite the same. Actual earnings are a relatively concrete quantity; rules for their measurement, for this purpose and for the general purpose of fixing claimant's benefit level, are set out in a later section. Earning capacity, however, is a more theoretical concept. It obviously does not mean actual earnings, since the legislature deliberately chose a different phrase for the post-injury earnings factor. Even under those statutes which compare, for example, 'average monthly wages before the accident' with 'the monthly wages he is able to earn thereafter', the test remains one of capacity. If the legislature had spoken of the wages 'he has earned thereafter', or even the wages 'he has been able to earn thereafter', the comparison of actual wage with actual wage would be indicated. But the concept of wages he 'is able' to earn cannot mean definite actual wages alone, especially in the absence of a fixed period of time within which post-injury wages are to be taken as controlling.
>
> "In essence, the problem is one of tying earnings to a period of time. The relevant period of time for prior earnings can be made relatively short and definite, such as the six months preceding the accident. Once an arbitrary past period is specified as setting the basis for computing an average weekly wage, there can be little argument about what wages were in fact earned. But the relevant period for post-injury earnings melts away into the indefinite future. Obviously we cannot take an arbitrary period of, say, six months after the injury as conclusive, since for a multitude of reasons that period might be entirely

nonrepresentative. On the other hand, we cannot wait out the rest of claimant's life to see what his average weekly wage loss ultimately turned out to be, for by then it would be too late for the award to do him any good. An award must be made now and paid now. The only possible solution is to make the best possible estimate of future impairment of earnings, on the strength not only of actual post-injury earnings but of any other available clues.

"It is uniformly held, therefore, without regard to statutory variations in the phrasing of the test, that a finding of disability may stand even where there is evidence of actual post-injury earnings equaling or exceeding those received before the accident. The position may be best summarized by saying that actual post-injury earnings will create a presumption of earning capacity commensurate with them, but the presumption may be rebutted by evidence independently showing incapacity or explaining away the post-injury earnings as an unreliable basis for estimating capacity. Unreliability of post-injury earnings may be due to a number of things: increase in general wage levels since the time of accident; claimant's own greater maturity or training; longer hours worked by claimant after the accident; payment of wages disproportionate to capacity out of sympathy to claimant; and the temporary and unpredictable character of post-injury earnings.

"The ultimate objective of the disability test is, by discounting these variables, to determine the wage that would have been paid in the open labor market under normal employment conditions to claimant as injured, taking wage levels, hours of work, and claimant's age and state of training as of exactly the same period used for calculating actual wages earned before the injury. Only by the elimination of all variables except the injury itself can a reasonably accurate estimate be made of the impairment of earning capacity to be attributed to that injury."

There was no proof on a number of these elements. For instance, it is not shown whether the increase in wages being paid claimant at the time of the hearing, as compared to his wages at the time of the injury, was the result of a general rise in wage scales, or was influenced by sympathy of the employer for the injured employee, or the result of enlarged experience of the applicant. A general discussion of the factors entering into this question, taken from cited cases, will be found in the annotation in 149 A.L.R. beginning at page 413. Everything considered we believe that justice requires that this matter be reconsidered. By this we do not mean to adjudicate, or intimate, what the result of another hearing should be.

Reversed and remanded.

HALL, KYLE, ARRINGTON and ETHRIDGE, J.J., concur.

NOTES

1. *Karr* illustrates the generally accepted principle that a determination of earning capacity involves more than a comparison of post and pre-injury earnings. Such a comparison yields relevant, but not conclusive, evidence of earning capacity. See, Johnson v. Industrial Comm., 40 Ohio St.3d 384, 533 N.E.2d 775 (1988) (evidence of increased or decreased wages may be considered in determining the impact of an injury on earning capacity, but such evidence is not by itself determinative of the issue); Fairbanks North Star Borough School Dist. v. Crider, 736 P.2d 770 (Alaska 1987) (in evaluating the claimant's earning capacity, the Board should consider increases in salary that would have taken place if claimant had not been injured); Mountainside Medical Center v. Tanner, 225 Ga.App. 722, 484 S.E.2d 706 (1997) (Board should consider evidence of what the claimant is *able* to earn, not simply *actual* earnings).

2. Actual earnings, however, serve as an effective presumption of earning capacity. 4 A. Larson and L. Larson, Larson's Workers' Compensation Law § 81.01 (2013). Some states presume a worker has not suffered any impairment of earning capacity when post-injury earnings equal or exceed pre-injury wages. E.g., Jim Walter Resources, Inc. v. Hall, 576 So.2d 673 (Ala.Civ.App.1991) (unrebutted evidence of higher post-injury earnings mandated a reversal of compensation award); Bragg v. Evans–St. Clair, Inc., 15 Ark.App. 53, 688 S.W.2d 956 (1985) (evidence that the employee returned to work at an equal or higher wage creates a presumption of no loss in earning capacity); Ruddy v. I.D. Griffith & Co., 237 A.2d 700 (Del.Supr.1968) (returning to same job at the same pay raised a rebuttable presumption that there was no loss of earning capacity).

Geography may be a relevant consideration in evaluating earning capacity. In Giboo v. Certified Transmission Rebuilders, 275 Neb. 369, 746 N.W.2d 362 (2008), the court held that an injured worker who moves to a rural area may have a greater impairment of earning capacity than a worker with the same injury who resided in a larger city.

A worker may be considered disabled despite earning more after the accident, however, if the higher pay can be explained by other factors. e.g., Warren v. Indust. Comm'n, 202 Ariz. 10, 39 P.3d 534 (App.2002) (higher post-injury salary may be explained by two cost of living raises); Cherokee Electric Coop. v. Lecroy, 587 So.2d 351 (Ala.Civ.App.1991) (evidence that claimant needed help by co-workers to perform job duties supported finding of impaired earning capacity despite evidence of greater post-injury earnings); Twiggs v. Municipality of Anchorage, 938 P.2d 1046 (Alaska 1997) (evidence of greater post-injury earnings not dispositive when the claimant alleged the compensable injury caused him to lose a second promotion); Don Ward & Co. v. Industrial Comm., 722 P.2d 1026 (Colo.App.1986) (claimant who increased post-accident earnings by working longer hours for a lower hourly wage could be considered disabled); Gregg v. Natchez Trace Elec. Power Assoc., 64 So.2d 473 (Miss. 2011) (power company employee who received post-injury wage increases rebutted the presumption of an absence of impaired earning capacity with evidence that his income would have been even higher were it not for post-injury restriction on his ability to climb utility poles).

Similarly, evidence of lower post-accident earnings does not conclusively establish impaired earning capacity. Occasionally, a worker who accepts employment at lower wages will be found not to have suffered any impairment of earning capacity. E.g., Wilde v. Taco Bell Corp., 531 So.2d 918 (Ala.Civ.App.1988) (claimant returned to work at same pay, but was fired for reasons unrelated to his injury; he secured a similar job paying less money; based on the testimony of the vocational expert and its own observations, the court determined that claimant had not suffered any loss of earning capacity). Cf. Mountainside Medical Center v. Tanner, 225 Ga.App. 722, 484 S.E.2d 706 (1997) (claimant with no actual post-injury earnings may not be disabled if the employer proves that suitable jobs were available within the claimant's work restrictions).

3. Evidence that the claimant is able to secure occasional employment does not preclude a finding of total disability. As stated by the Minnesota Supreme Court,

> An employee who is so injured that he can perform no services other than those which are so limited in quality, dependability, or quantity that a reasonably stable market for them does not exist, may well be classified as totally disabled.

Lee v. Minneapolis St. Ry., 230 Minn. 315, 41 N.W.2d 433, 436 (1950). This principle dates back to an early English decision that referred to this type of worker as an "odd lot" in the labor market. Cardiff Corporation v. Hall, [1911] 1 K.B. 1009, 1021. Judge Cardozo quoted from *Cardiff* with approval in describing the "odd lot man" as "nondescript in the labor market. Work, if he gets it, is likely to be casual and intermittent. . . ." Jordan v. Decorative Co., 230 N.Y. 522, 525, 130 N.E. 634, 635 (1921). What has now become known as the "odd lot doctrine" is accepted in virtually all jurisdictions. It instructs agencies and courts to look beyond any intermittent employment the claimant might secure when determining total disability. The court or agency must also consider whether the claimant's residual physical limitations, mental capacity, age, experience, education, skills and training, considered collectively, preclude regular employment. Accordingly, the odd lot doctrine justifies an award of total disability benefits to workers who may be able to secure occasional jobs. e.g., Joslins Dry Goods Co. v. Indust. Claim Appeals Office, 21 P.3d 866 (Colo.App.2001) (permanent total disability benefits may be awarded employee who secures some sort of post-injury employment if the evidence shows that he is unlikely to sustain such employment); Guyton v. Irving Jensen Co., 373 N.W.2d 101 (Iowa 1985) (40 year old, mildly retarded, illiterate manual laborer with residual back injury); Piggly Wiggly v. Houston, 464 So.2d 510 (Miss.1985) (claimant with a fractured kneecap found totally disabled when she lacked the skills or training to obtain a job that would not require lifting and/or standing); Money v. Tyrrell Flowers, 275 Neb. 602, 748 N.W.2d 49 (2008) (combination of residual physical limitations, pain, and cognitive limitations rendered claimant permanently totally disabled under the "Odd Lot" doctrine), Swanson v. Westport Lumber Co., 4 Or.App. 417, 479 P.2d 1005 (1971) (63 year old sawmill worker with an eighth grade education and no specialized skills found to be totally disabled). The critical question is whether suitable work is regularly and continuously available to the claimant. In many jurisdictions, the employer bears the burden of proving that regular and continuous employment is available once the worker is shown to be in the odd-lot category. *Guyton*, supra; *Swanson*, supra. See generally, 4 A. Larson and L. Larson, Larson's Workers' Compensation Law § 83.01 (2013).

4. Certain kinds of physical injuries may be defined or presumed by statute to constitute total and permanent disability. In California, for example, permanent total disability is "conclusively presumed" whenever a worker suffers the loss of both eyes, both hands, practical total paralysis, or incurable mental incapacity or insanity as a result of a compensable injury. Cal. Labor Code § 4662. Such presumptions are quite common. See, e.g., Fla. Stat. Ann. § 440.15 (rebuttable presumption); Ga.Code Ann. § 34–9–263(g) (rebuttable presumption); Mich.Comp.Laws Ann. § 418.361(3) (conclusive presumption). Conclusive presumptions of permanent total disability obviate the need for evidence of impaired earning capacity. In this respect, they are similar to scheduled permanent partial disabilities discussed in the next subsection.

MARTINES V. WORLEY & SONS CONSTRUCTION

Court of Appeals of Georgia, 2006.
278 Ga.App. 26, 628 S.E.2d 113.

SMITH, PRESIDING JUDGE.

We granted the claimant's application for discretionary appeal in this workers' compensation case to consider the scope of a "justified" refusal to accept a "suitable job" within the meaning of OCGA § 34–9–240. We conclude that an injured worker's refusal to accept a suitable job based on a *legal* inability to perform the job resulting from the worker's voluntary conduct, rather than a lack of skill or physical capacity, is not justified as a matter of law. We therefore affirm the judgment of the superior court.

The facts of this case are not in dispute. While working for Worley & Sons Construction, Merced Martines suffered a work-related injury to his left foot. After medical treatment, he was released by his physician to return to work with restrictions. His employer offered him a position as a delivery truck driver, a job falling within the restrictions set by his physician. He agreed to accept the job, and reported to work. Before allowing him to drive a company truck, however, his employer asked him to show a driver's license and documentation that he was in the country legally. At that time, he revealed that he could not produce a Georgia driver's license and could not obtain one because, as all parties concede, he entered this country illegally.

No evidence was presented that he is unable to drive for any physical or health-related reason or that he does not possess the ability to operate the vehicle. In fact, although he testified at the hearing that he did not know how to drive "very well," he acknowledged that he drove in Mexico and also was confronted with his earlier deposition testimony that he knew how to drive and would drive if he could obtain a license. Martines left his employer's office and did not return to work. . . . The ALJ found that the job offered to Martines was not suitable because he does not possess the driver's license required for the job. The Appellate Division of the State Board of Workers' Compensation affirmed the judgment of the ALJ.

In a detailed 11-page order, the superior court carefully analyzed the issues and reversed the Board, finding that it applied the wrong legal standard to determine the suitability of the proffered job. The court went on to conclude that Martines did not meet his burden of demonstrating that his refusal of the work was justified. . . . The court accordingly reversed the award of temporary total disability benefits. . . .

The issues presented on appeal are . . . whether the Board erred as a matter of law in determining that the proffered work was not suitable, and whether the superior court correctly concluded that Martines's refusal of work was not justified.

OCGA § 34–9–240 provides:

> (a) If an injured employee refuses employment procured for him or her and suitable to his or her capacity, such employee shall not be entitled to any compensation, except benefits pursuant to Code Section 34–9–26, at any time during the continuance of such refusal unless in the opinion of the board such refusal was justified.

* * *

The Georgia Supreme Court has directly addressed this Code section in *City of Adel v. Wise*, 261 Ga. 53, 401 S.E.2d 522 (1991):

> The test of OCGA § 34–9–240 is two-pronged. The board must first determine whether the employment offered by the employer

> and refused by the employee is suitable to the capacity of the employee. If the board finds that the proffered employment is suitable within the meaning of the statute, the employee is not entitled to compensation during the continuance of his refusal to work unless in the opinion of the board such refusal was justified. The cases make it clear that the phrase "suitable to his capacity" refers to the employee's capacity or ability to perform the work within his physical limitations or restrictions.

The superior court was therefore correct in its determination that the Board erred in determining that the proffered work was not "suitable to [Martines's] capacity."

We must next address whether Martines's refusal of the work was justified. For a refusal to be justified, it "must relate to the physical capacity of the employee to perform the job; the employee's ability or skill to perform the job; or factors such as geographic relocation or travel conditions which would disrupt the employee's life." An "employee's refusal to accept employment must relate, in some manner, to his physical capacity or his ability to perform the job in order for his refusal to be justified within the meaning of OCGA § 34–9–240."

The Supreme Court gave specific examples in *Wise* of physical capacity or ability to perform the job. The Court noted that an employee is justified in refusing work that aggravates his injury, or work that requires relocation, or work that he lacks the skills to perform, such as typing. But he is not justified in refusing work due to personal choices unrelated to his work, such as the desire to work a particular shift or avoid nonunion work.

The circumstances here do not present an issue of physical ability or skill to perform the proffered job. The only evidence in the record is that Martines can in fact drive a car and has driven in Mexico, but chose to enter this country illegally and apparently chose not to jeopardize his situation by attempting to obtain a driver's license. It is therefore not a question of his inability to drive a car but his inability to acquire a Georgia driver's license because of his illegal status. OCGA § 40–5–1(15) ("[N]o person shall be considered a resident for purposes of this chapter unless such person is either a United States citizen or an alien with legal authorization from the U.S. Immigration and Naturalization Service.").

Martines's situation is analogous to that of the individual whose license has been suspended or revoked for a violation of the law. Such reasons are unrelated to a driver's "physical capacity or his ability to perform the job," but rather arise from his unrelated decision to violate the laws of this state so as to render his license subject to suspension or revocation. Martines's legal status is also analogous to that of the person incarcerated after an adjudication of guilt.

Our decision in *Earth First Grading v. Gutierrez*, 270 Ga.App. 328, 606 S.E.2d 332 (2004), is instructive here. Gutierrez's illegal status was unknown when he was hired, and he worked for approximately one year before being injured. He applied for temporary total disability benefits, and the employer argued that "his undocumented status rendered him ineligible to receive TTD benefits." Although *Earth First* did not involve a proffer of alternative work, the employer argued that illegal alien status was analogous to incarceration and that Gutierrez therefore "could not meaningfully accept" *any* work. We rejected this argument, noting that Gutierrez's immigration status was unknown until long after the period for which he sought benefits and that he actually performed work for the employer despite his immigration status. We concluded that his "illegal immigration status did not render him unable to meaningfully accept employment during the pertinent period." Here, in contrast, Martines's admitted illegal immigration status was revealed at the time he refused an otherwise suitable job due to his legal inability to obtain a Georgia driver's license. His illegal immigration status therefore caused his inability to accept the proffered employment.

* * *

Martines also contends that equity should forbid the employer from asserting his illegal status, because the employer failed to require that Martines complete the U.S. Department of Justice, Immigration and Naturalization Service ("INS") Employment Eligibility Verification Form, commonly known as the "I-9 Form." But Martines does not cite any authority to show that his employer's failure to require an employment form sometime before his injury has any legal effect on whether or not his refusal of proffered light duty work was justified. Moreover, one "who would have equity must do equity," and Martines filled out an employment application and provided his employer with a Social Security number which belonged to someone else. To insist upon such an argument would place Martines in the anomalous position of having to contend that he never should have been allowed to work, or receive benefits, at all.

* * *

In sum, no evidence was presented that Martines had a physical limitation or a lack of ability or skill which prevented him from physically performing the job of delivery driver at the time he reported for work. His inability to perform the job stems rather from his legal inability to acquire the necessary Georgia driver's license. The superior court therefore correctly found that the Board erred as a matter of law and that Martines's refusal to accept the proposed light-duty work was not justified.

Judgment affirmed.

NOTES

1. Impaired earning capacity is often measured in terms of the ability to perform or obtain work "suitable" to claimant's qualifications and training. Accordingly, workers, like the claimant in *Fletcher*, who are unable to secure employment for which they are qualified may be considered disabled. If they cannot find any employment, they may be deemed totally disabled. If the only suitable employment pays less than their former job, they may be deemed partially disabled. The converse, of course, is that workers who can obtain "suitable" employment are not totally disabled. If the suitable employment pays as much or more than their previous position, the employee may not have incurred any impairment of earning capacity. If the suitable employment pays less than the previous position, the employee may have a partial disability. Thus, an important and frequently contested issue is whether a particular job is "suitable."

2. The suitability inquiry in the more conventional cases focus on the physical abilities, job skills, and work experience of the injured worker. E.g., Moore v. RPM Industries, Inc., 144 A.D.2d 135, 534 N.Y.S.2d 463 (1988) (cement worker disabled by asthma may be considered totally disabled if not qualified to perform other work); Reust v. State Accident Insurance Fund, 60 Or.App. 9, 652 P.2d 884 (1982) (back injury prevented claimant from performing any work previously performed; error to reduce award for permanent partial disability); Posey v. State Workmen's Compensation Commissioner, 157 W.Va. 285, 201 S.E.2d 102 (1973) (nearly illiterate manual laborer who suffered knee injury is entitled to permanent total disability benefits since he is unable to perform any work for which he is qualified). Workers who are unable to return to their former jobs may nevertheless be able to secure employment in unrelated areas. Most jurisdictions consider post-injury earnings in unrelated employments in determining whether and to what extent a claimant is disabled. E.g., Lusietto v. Industrial Commission, 174 Ill.App.3d 121, 123 Ill.Dec. 634, 528 N.E.2d 18 (1988) (iron worker who is physically unable to perform manual labor is not entitled to permanent total disability benefits because he had been performing sedentary work at his wife's company); Smith–Gruner v. Yandell, 768 P.2d 388 (Okl.App.1989) (securing employment in a different line of work creates a rebuttable presumption that claimant was not totally disabled).

3. *Martines* illustrates that factors other than physical ability, job skills and work experience may bear on the issue of whether a particular employment is suitable. While Martines' immigration status did not preclude his entitlement to workers' compensation benefits for his initial injury, it had a decisive effect on the duration of those benefits. Can you explain why? See also, Farmers Brothers Coffee v. WCAB, 133 Cal.App.4th 533, 35 Cal. Rptr. 3d 23 (2005) (award of compensation benefits to an undocumented alien under state law is not pre-empted by federal immigration laws); Amoah v. Mallah Management, LLC, 57 A.D.3d 29, 866 N.Y.S.2d 797 (2008) (undocumented worker who use illegally used another person's Social Security card and driver's license to secure employment was entitled to

collect workers' compensation benefits for work-related injury); Matrix Employee Leasing v. Hernandez, 975 So.2d 1217 (Fla. App. 2008) (injured worker is entitled to workers' compensation benefits even though he unlawfully presented a false Social Security card to secure employment). See generally, Katrina Gonzales, Note, Undocumented Workers and Workers' Compensation: Rejecting Federal Preemption of the California Workers' Compensation Act, 41 U.C. Davis 2001 (2008); Jason Schumann, Note, Working in the Shadows: Illegal Aliens Entitlement to Workers' Compensation, 89 Iowa L. Rev. 709 (2004). Recall that immigration status may also affect entitlement to vocational rehabilitation benefits. See Note 5 following Smith v. Hastings Irrigation Pipe Co.

4. Employment has been deemed suitable (and hence its refusal constitutes ground for terminating or reducing compensation benefits) when the injured worker is ineligible due to a criminal conviction, e.g., Sweatt v. Dept. of Corrections, 468 Mich. 172, 661 N.W.2d 201 (2003); Furrer v. Suffolk County Police Dept., 45 A.D.3d 996, 846 N.Y.S.2d 397 (2007); or when a worker declines a position that she deems inconsistent with her professional aspirations, e.g., Matter of Barbuto, 303 A.D.2d 798, 755 N.Y.S.2d 761 (2003) (decision of police academy trainee injured during training to decline reassignment to a dispatcher job is characterized as a voluntary withdrawal from the labor market).

On the other hand, proffered employment may be deemed not suitable (and hence its refusal would not constitute grounds for terminating or reducing compensation benefits) when the available job would expose the employee to a significant risk of sexual harassment, e.g., Cavender v. PIP Printing, Inc., 31 Kan.App.2d 127, 61 P.3d 101 (2003); Noel v. Home Health Care 2000 Inc., 867 So.2d 945 (La. App. 2004); or if the position would require the employee to incur a long commute, e.g., Gajeske v. Integrated Electrical Services, Inc., 859 So.2d 896 (La. App. 2003) (claimant was offered a light duty job at corporate headquarters; position would require a 180 mile commute; fact issue whether this was reasonable).

5. Injured workers sometimes accept new employment at a lower wage rate and seek partial disability benefits from the first employer. Whether the first employer is obligated to pay for the wage loss often depends on whether it was "reasonable" for the employee to accept the lower paying position. In State ex rel. Ameen v. Industrial Commission, 100 Ohio St.3d 161, 797 N.E.2d 78 (2003) a nurse who was injured on the job returned to college and became a school teacher earning less than she did as a nurse. She applied for wage loss benefits. The Commission denied her claim on the grounds that by becoming a school teacher, the claimant chose to earn less than she could earn as a nurse. The Ohio Supreme Court reversed, holding that teaching was a suitable employment even if it paid less than nursing. Does *Ameen* force an employer to subsidize the vocational preferences of the injured worker? Compare Yates v. Abbott Labs, Inc., 766 N.E.2d 956 (Ohio 2002) (employer should not be penalized for what amounted to a "lifestyle choice" on the part of an injured employee who, due to personal preferences, moved

to another town, took a less demanding job, and made insufficient attempts to find suitable employment). See also, Thompson v. Earle W. Noyes & Sons, 935 A.2d 663 (Me. 2007) (injured worker returned to light duty work and later resigned from his job to accept lower paying position that allowed him to care for his ill wife; Board should consider the employee's need to care for his ill wife in deciding whether the new employment was "reasonable").

C. DISABILITY AS PHYSICAL IMPAIRMENT

BISHOP V. TOWN OF BARRE

Supreme Court of Vermont, 1982.
140 Vt. 564, 442 A.2d 50.

OPINION BY: HILL

OPINION: This case concerns the proper standard for computing benefits under the Vermont Workmen's Compensation Act, 21 V.S.A. §§ 601–709. The claimant, Leroy Bishop, challenges the amount of compensation he was awarded by the Commissioner of Labor and Industry. . . .

I.

The facts in this case are straightforward. On October 3, 1973, the claimant suffered an injury to his back while employed as a laborer by the Town of Barre. Although he returned to work for short periods of time, he has not worked since October of 1977. From December 15, 1973, to April 8, 1974, and from October 3, 1977, to January 22, 1979, the claimant received temporary total disability benefits. On January 22, 1979, the defendants discontinued temporary benefits on the ground that the claimant had reached the "end result" of the healing process.

The claimant filed for permanent disability and vocational rehabilitation benefits. At the hearing on these claims, the medical testimony stood uncontradicted: the claimant's back impairment would not improve, resulting in a thirty-five to forty per cent permanent impairment of the spine, and a twenty per cent impairment to the whole man. The claimant also adduced testimony that, taking account of his age, training, and educational background, he would be unable to work again. . . .

The Commissioner found that the claimant was entitled to sixty-six weeks of permanent partial disability benefits, computed on the basis of a twenty per cent impairment to the whole man. The Commissioner based this decision on medical evidence alone, and did not address the claimant's age, education, or training. . . .

The claimant appealed the Commissioner's decision to the Washington Superior Court, which certified the following questions to this Court under V.R.A.P. 5(a):

(1) Did the Commissioner of Labor and Industry err in concluding that claimant was only 20% permanently disabled?

(2) Is the Commissioner of Labor and Industry's conclusion of 20% permanent partial disability in error because it is based only on permanent physical impairment and not permanent economic impairment?

(a) Did the Commissioner of Labor and Industry err in not finding that the claimant has sustained permanent economic impairment?

(3) Was it error for the Commissioner of Labor and Industry to conclude the claimant is only 20% permanently partially disabled in light of Dr. Felix Callan's testimony that claimant sustained a 20% permanent partial disability to the "whole man" and 35–40% permanent partial disability to his spine?

* * *

We answer questions one [and] three . . . in the affirmative, and two [and] two (a) . . . in the negative, for reasons which will be discussed in the remainder of this opinion.

II.

A.

The Vermont Workmen's Compensation Act provides two distinct classes of benefits. Temporary disability benefits are provided for workers who suffer a "disability for work," 21 V.S.A. §§ 642, 646, during the period between their injury and final recovery. Once the recovery process has ended, or the worker has achieved the maximum possible restoration of his earning power, he is no longer entitled to temporary disability benefits. At this point, the worker has reached the "end result" of the healing process. . . . Because the claimant's condition has reached an "end result," claims for benefits are then treated under the permanent disability sections, 21 V.S.A. §§ 644, 648. . . .

Our case law has established different criteria for computing temporary, as opposed to permanent, benefits. Temporary disability benefits are awarded on the basis of an individual's incapacity for work. . . . This involves consideration of not only physical injury, but also of other factors restricting the claimant's capacity to obtain work. . . . In contrast, permanent disability benefits are calculated solely on the basis of physical impairment: "[The permanent disability] statute has arbitrarily fixed the amount of compensation to be paid for scheduled specific injuries regardless of loss of present earning power." Beane v. Vermont Marble Co., 115 Vt. 142, 145, 52 A.2d 784, 786 (1947). . . .

The claimant challenges the validity of these different standards set forth in Vermont case law. He asserts that permanent disability, like temporary disability, should be evaluated by reference to any factor which restricts capacity for work. In support of this position, he advances several arguments. First, he contends that the Act's use of the word "disability" connotes more than physical impairment, thereby requiring evaluation of ability to work. Second, he asserts that by allowing compensation for unscheduled injuries, see 21 V.S.A. §§ 644(b), 648(20), the Act sanctions consideration of factors other than physical injury. Third, he argues that the purpose of the statute is to compensate for lost wages, which requires consideration of capacity for work. Thus, he concludes that the Commissioner erred in failing to consider the claimant's ability to work, and in relying solely on physical impairment in setting compensation.

The claimant's arguments do not persuade us to reject our precedent. Earning capacity is significant to the Workmen's Compensation Act, but it performs a far different function than envisioned by the claimant.

The claimant correctly assigns protection against wage loss as one of the Act's purposes. The Act, however, also seeks to establish an expedient, efficient remedy for injured workers. . . . Simplifying the elements of recovery is the Act's mechanism for achieving efficiency. To be entitled to benefits, a claimant need only establish that he suffered "a personal injury by accident arising out of and in the course of his employment by an employer subject to [the Act]." 21 V.S.A. § 618. The employee need not show that the employer was negligent . . . or that he actually suffered a wage loss. . . . Because resolution of these issues on a case by case basis would impede the process, thereby delaying awards to needy beneficiaries, the legislature has chosen a "scheduled benefits" system. The rate of compensation for listed injuries has been conclusively determined in the Act. See 21 V.S.A. §§ 644, 648. The system still protects against wage loss, but it fulfills this aim by awarding permanent disability benefits on the basis of physical impairment as a means to insure against wage loss. Professor Larson explains how a scheduled benefits system, such as Vermont's, insures against wage loss:

> [Exclusion of individual wage loss evidence] is not, however, to be interpreted as an erratic deviation from the underlying principle of compensation law—that benefits relate to loss of earning capacity and not to physical injury as such. The basic theory remains the same; the only difference is that the effect on earning capacity is a conclusively presumed one, instead of a

specifically proved one based on the individual's actual wage-loss experience.

2 A. Larson, Workmen's Compensation Law § 58.11, at 10–173 to 174 (1981) (footnotes omitted).

The yardstick is general, not particular. The total disability section compensates for injuries which, as a general rule, tend to have the most severe impact on earning capacity. The partial disability section compensates for injuries which generally have a less serious impact, and rates the scheduled impairments accordingly.

The claimant's arguments that the plain meaning of disability and the presence of compensation for unscheduled injuries compel consideration of individual wage loss must be rejected in light of the elaborate and carefully drawn scheme of scheduled benefits. . . . The Act enumerates "partial disabilities" in 21 V.S.A. § 648, and "total disabilities" in 21 V.S.A. § 644. Yet, each of the "partial disabilities" could, depending upon a person's age, occupation, and training, prevent a worker from obtaining employment. Similarly, a worker could suffer a disability listed as "total," yet return to his or her previous job.[1] If we were to inject individual wage loss into this scheme, as urged by the claimant, we would effectively collapse the distinctions between total and partial benefits explicitly drawn by the legislature.

The claimant also points to the statutory definition of "partial disability" as supporting his position. Subsection ten of 21 V.S.A. § 601 states: " 'Partial disability' may be held to include diminished ability to obtain employment owing to disfigurement resulting from an injury." Thus, the claimant argues, individual ability to work is, by definition, a factor in computing benefits. This analysis collapses under careful scrutiny. First, it ignores the theory of a scheduled benefits act and the carefully drawn distinction between partial and total disability, subjects previously discussed in this opinion. Second, there is a more plausible application of the definition: it only addresses the award of temporary benefits under 21 V.S.A. § 646, the temporary disability section. As previously discussed, ability to work is a crucial factor in awarding temporary disability benefits. The section dealing with temporary disability awards compensation "[where] the disability for work resulting from an injury is partial." 21 V.S.A. § 646. The permanent disability section awards compensation on the basis of "sixty-six and two-thirds percent of the average weekly wages . . . for the periods stated against such injuries respectively." 21 V.S.A. § 648. Thus, although the headnote

[1] For example, a typist might be able to work after losing both feet, yet be "totally disabled" under 21 V.S.A. § 644(a)(2). The loss of one hand would prevent the same typist from returning to work, yet, the injury would be a "partial disability" under 21 V.S.A. § 648(4). Indeed, the claimant himself would be unable to resume work as a laborer if he suffered any one of several of the impairments scheduled in 21 V.S.A. § 648.

to the permanent disability section contains the defined term, its text does not. This contrasts with the quoted portion of the temporary disability section.

Given the Act's history and structure, we must reject the claimant's contention that individual wage loss should be considered in computing permanent benefits. The plain meaning of the statute precludes consideration of individual wage loss. We reaffirm the distinction between temporary and permanent benefits.

* * *

III.

Certified questions one and three present the same issue: whether, based on the evidence in the record, the Commissioner's decision, finding the claimant to be twenty per cent permanently partially disabled, correctly computes his physical impairment. The issue can be narrowed considerably. Our holding concerning the effect of an individual's economic impairment on the award of benefits precludes our finding the claimant to be totally disabled. There is no medical evidence that the claimant suffers an impairment approaching the severity of those listed in 21 V.S.A. § 644. Thus, it is clear that the claimant is only entitled to partial disability. Furthermore, there is no dispute concerning the medical evidence, which was uncontradicted. The only remaining question is the legal effect of that evidence.

The medical testimony indicated, and the Commissioner found, that the claimant suffered a thirty-five to forty per cent impairment of the spine, resulting in a twenty per cent impairment of the "whole man." The Commissioner awarded compensation on the basis of the twenty per cent figure, which yielded sixty-six weeks of benefits. The claimant argues that it was error not to use the thirty-five to forty per cent figure, which would yield 115.5 to 132 weeks of benefits.

The issue is whether impairment to the "whole man" or impairment to the affected part of the body is the proper standard. Back injuries are not scheduled under 21 V.S.A. § 648. Rule 10(a)(3) [of the Rules Pertaining to Workmen's Compensation and Occupational Disease] addresses the level of compensation for back injuries:

> The back. In the event an employee receives a personal injury by accident arising out of and in the course of his employment resulting in the permanent and complete loss of the use of his back the employee shall be entitled to 330 weeks of compensation. If the loss of the use of his back is partial he shall be entitled to that percentage of 330 weeks of compensation which is represented by the loss.

In assessing what figure is "the percentage . . . represented by the loss," the Commissioner used the whole man figure. His reasoning was that the maximum recovery allowable for total disability is 330 weeks. See 21 V.S.A. § 645. Therefore, benefits for back impairments are calculated on the basis of the percentage of disability caused to the "whole man." The claimant argues that the percentage of loss to the back is the appropriate standard. We agree with the claimant.

Interpretations of their own regulations by administrative agencies are usually given great weight by this Court. See In re Brooks, 130 Vt. 83, 85–86, 286 A.2d 279, 281 (1971). Yet, in this case, we believe that the Commissioner's interpretation of Rule 10(a)(3) is clearly erroneous. The Act, in providing compensation for unscheduled injuries, focuses solely upon the injuries themselves. The statute allows benefits for "all other cases in this class, or where the *usefulness of a member or any physical function is permanently impaired.*" 21 V.S.A. § 648(18) (emphasis added). Similarly, the rule itself only makes reference to "loss of the use of [the] back." Rule 10(a)(3). Nowhere, in either the rule or the statute, is reference made to any criterion other than impairment to the injured body part. Using 330 weeks as the basis for calculating benefits does not, as the Commissioner apparently held, alter the plain language of the rule. If a claimant completely lost the use of his back, he would be totally disabled within the meaning of 21 V.S.A. § 644(b). The 330-week figure simply reflects the severity of back injuries, and assures that compensation for back impairments will be proportional to the scheduled benefits. See Part II A of this opinion, supra.

Given these factors, the Commissioner erred in interpreting Rule 10(a)(3) by reference to a "whole man" standard. The claimant's benefits should have been calculated on the basis of his back impairment, which is thirty-five to forty per cent. It is axiomatic that an administrative agency must follow its own substantive regulations in deciding contested cases. . . . Thus, the Commissioner's decision must be reversed. On remand, the Commissioner should award benefits on the basis of the claimant's thirty-five to forty per cent back impairment.

* * *

Certified questions one [and] three . . . are answered in the affirmative. Certified questions two [and] two (a) . . . are answered in the negative. The case is remanded for the entry of an award consistent with this opinion.

* * *

NOTES

1. Most workers' compensation acts include provisions similar to sections 644 and 648 of the Vermont statute at issue in *Bishop*. Such statutes specify a precise and uniform measure of benefits for loss of certain mentioned members of the body. These are commonly referred to as "scheduled benefits". Thus, the loss of a leg or a foot or an eye is a "scheduled loss" in most states. The precise amount of the scheduled benefits is commonly expressed in terms of a number of weeks to which the claimant is entitled to receive income benefits. Scheduled benefits are often payable in an immediate lump sum. The number of weeks specified in the statute to calculate the amount of the award varies with the particular loss. In 2012 in Georgia, for example, a worker is entitled to 225 weeks of income benefits for the loss of an arm or leg, 160 weeks of income benefits for the loss of a hand, and 135 weeks of income benefits for the loss of a foot. Ga.Code Ann. § 34–9–263(c). There is considerable variation among states with regard to the number of weeks used in the schedule for the same loss. The loss of an arm entitles the employee to benefits for 225 weeks in Georgia, and 500 weeks in Wisconsin. See Ga. Code Ann. § 34–9–263(c)(1); Wis. Stat. Ann. § 102.52. The combination of variations in the maximum weekly income benefit and the number of weeks to which a claimant is entitled to receive benefits, produces significant differences among the states in the amount of compensation a worker will receive for a particular scheduled injury. For example, the New Hampshire worker who loses an arm will receive a maximum of $281,445 under the schedule, while a worker in Oklahoma would receive a maximum of $88,825. A comprehensive comparison of benefit levels for certain common scheduled losses can be found in United States Chamber of Commerce, Analysis of Workers' Compensation Laws 2013, Chart VII (2013).

2. Scheduled benefits are payable without proof of actual wage loss or impairment of earning capacity. In effect, the schedule provides a conclusive presumption that a worker will sustain wage loss that justifies compensation in the prescribed amount. The Supreme Court explained the rationale underlying the use of schedules as follows: "The lump-sum awards for total and permanent disability under [the Alaska] Compensation Act ignore wage losses. Whatever the employee may have made before, whatever his wages may be after the injury, the award is the same. To that extent it is an arbitrary amount. But it is the expression of a legislative judgment that on the average there has been a degree of impairment, and whatever may be the fact in a particular case, the lump-sum should be paid without more." Alaska Industrial Board v. Chugach Electric Ass'n., Inc., 356 U.S. 320, 323–24, 78 S.Ct. 735, 737–38, 2 L.Ed.2d 795 (1958). Schedules also do not distinguish between different occupations or how the loss of the specific member might effect a particular worker's job. "The schedule . . . awards the same benefit to a piano player as to a night watchman for the loss of a finger, hand, or arm." Hise Construction v. Candelaria, 98 N.M. 759, 652 P.2d 1210, 1211 (1982). Why would the legislature award the same benefits to these two workers

when the effect of the injury on their respective earning capacities is so very different?

3. The use of schedules under the earliest workers' compensation statutes was quite limited. Only a few major appendages, such as arms and legs, were included in the statutory schedule, and the concept of "loss" was strictly construed to require an actual severance or its functional equivalent. Over time, the scheduled injury principle expanded greatly. An increasing number of smaller members, such as portions of fingers and toes, were added to the statutory schedule. The more inclusive "loss of use" concept replaced amputation as the degree of physical impairment necessary to trigger the schedule. Providing scheduled benefits for "partial loss of use" vastly expanded the number of injuries compensable without proof of wage loss. The most recent expansion of the schedule injury principle has been to move beyond specific members to "the body as a whole" or the "whole person". This addition to the list of scheduled injuries allows physicians to express the claimant's non-specific residual physical limitations as a percentage loss of the "body as a whole". Injuries to internal organs and the back, for example, are compensable under the body as a whole provision without proof of wage loss. E.g., Thom v. Callahan, 97 Idaho 151, 540 P.2d 1330 (1975) (restaurant worker with back injury awarded permanent partial disability benefits for 25% impairment of "the whole person"); Bess v. Tyson Foods, Inc., 125 N.C.App. 698, 482 S.E.2d 26 (1997) (loss of sense of taste and smell is compensable as a permanent injury to an "important external or internal organ").

4. The expansion of the scheduled injury principle is discussed and criticized in Larson, *The Wage-Loss Principle in Workers' Compensation*, 6 Wm. Mitchell L.Rev. 501 (1980). Larson states that when lump sum payments are routinely provided under vastly expanded schedules, "all resemblance to a wage-loss system is lost. If a worker is given $20,000 for some internal organ damage that has no conceivable effect, actual or presumptive, on earning capacity, it is no longer possible to pretend that the statute is still somehow only an extrapolation of the wage-loss principle aided by the conclusive presumption of eventual wage loss." 6 Wm. Mitchell L.Rev. at 512.

Professor Larson advocated the abandonment of schedules and a return to wage-loss as the guiding standard for awarding disability benefits. Florida enacted such a system in 1979. The Florida law eliminated the use of schedules for virtually all permanent partial disabilities. Benefits were awarded in most instances exclusively on the basis of wage-loss. Florida's return to a wage-loss approach to compensating permanent partial disability was expected to reduce both the cost of processing and number of claims. These savings, in turn, were supposed to be channeled to workers who suffer actual wage loss by increasing the level of maximum weekly benefits. Reviews of the Florida system were mixed. Professor Larson reported that "on the whole, the Florida reforms are succeeding in achieving the improvements that had been hoped for. Litigation has been reduced; total claims have been sharply cut, and the great majority of these have been disposed of without hearings; legal costs and insurance rates have decreased; and general surveys show that claimants are satisfied with the system." Larson, *Tensions in the Next Decade*, in New Perspectives in Workers' Compensation 34 (Burton ed. 1988). Professor Burton, on the other hand, was less certain that cost reductions are inherent in the wage-loss approach. Burton, *Introduction*, in New Perspectives in Workers' Compensation 5 (Burton ed. 1988). A Florida study concluded that "the current system of paying workers under the wage loss system is not working as originally perceived and intended." Governor's Task Force on Workers' Compensation, *Florida Workers' Compensation System Part III: Recommendations for Solving Problems* 20 (March 1, 1989). In 1990, Florida returned to an impairment schedule. See Timothy A. Watson and Michael J. Valen, A Historic Review of Workers' Compensation Reform in Florida, 21 Fla. St. U. L. Rev. 501 (1993).

5. An important practical issue is the extent to which the schedule provides the exclusive measure of compensation. This issue commonly presents itself in two contexts. The first involves the loss of a smaller member that might also be viewed as a fractional loss of a larger member, as when the loss of a finger might also be considered the partial loss of a hand. The second context involves a worker who claims to suffer a permanent total disability as the result of a scheduled injury. The common question presented by these types of cases is whether the worker is limited to the benefits authorized by the most specific provisions of the schedule.

There is widespread agreement that if the loss of a scheduled member adversely affects another part of the body, benefits are not limited to those prescribed for the scheduled member. If the other part of the body affected by the scheduled injury is not itself a scheduled injury, the schedule does not provide the exclusive measure of benefits. E.g., Ex Parte Hayes, 70 So.3d 1211 (Ala. 2011) (physical injury to right foot combined with pre-existing congenital defects in left foot rendered a custodian unable to work; since the effects of the physical injury to the right foot "extend to and interfere with the effective functioning of the remainder of his body", the claimant is entitled to benefits outside the schedule); Mountain City Meat Co. v. Oqueda, 919 P.2d 246 (Colo.1996) (when an employee suffers a work-related accident that results in both a scheduled and non-scheduled injury, the scheduled injury must be converted to a whole person impairment rating and combined with the non-scheduled injury's whole person rating in calculating permanent disability benefits); Dye v. Industrial Comm., 153 Ariz. 292, 736 P.2d 376 (1987) (injury to the arm bone (a scheduled injury) produced residual impairment of the shoulder (an unscheduled injury); benefits are not limited to the schedule for the arm bone); Harrison v. Animas Valley Auto & Truck Repair, 107 N.M. 373, 758 P.2d 787 (1988) ("implicit" finding that injuries extended beyond the wrist, hand and arm authorized an award of benefits based on 80% permanent partial disability of the "whole man"). If the other part of the body affected by the scheduled injury is also a scheduled injury, the worker may recover the greater of the two. E.g., United Parcel Service v. Outlaw, 190 Ga.App. 840, 380 S.E.2d 310 (1989) (claimant whose three toes were amputated as a result of a work injury was rated as suffering a 100% loss of the three toes, a 25% impairment of the foot, and a 15% impairment of the leg; claimant could recover under whichever calculation produced the greatest recovery, but could not cumulate all three); Onley v. National Union Fire Ins. Co., 785 S.W.2d 348 (Tenn.1990) (worker suffered a broken bone in thumb that resulted in a 60% residual impairment of thumb (60 weeks of benefits) and a 50% residual impairment of hand (150 weeks of benefits); benefits may be awarded under the schedule for impairment of the hand).

The more difficult cases are those in which the only physical injury is to a scheduled member, but when combined with other factors, produces an impairment of earning capacity that exceeds the schedule. Van Dorpel v. Haven–Busch Co., 350 Mich. 135, 85 N.W.2d 97 (1957) was an early and influential decision that upheld an award of benefits that exceed those authorized under the schedule. This position has been adopted by a number of other courts. E.g., McNeely v. Clem Mill & Gin Co., 241 Ark. 498, 409 S.W.2d 502 (1966) (worker who suffered the loss of a leg (a scheduled injury) awarded benefits for total disability); Whitley v. Columbia Lumber Mfg. Co., 318 N.C. 89, 348 S.E.2d 336 (1986) (cabinet maker who suffered a 75% impairment to right hand and 30% impairment to left hand (both scheduled injuries) could be awarded benefits for permanent total disability); Jensen v. Zook Bros. Const. Co., 178 Mont. 59, 582 P.2d 1191 (1978) (left-handed construction worker who had his left hand crushed could be awarded permanent total disability benefits despite having been given only a 5% partial disability rating by an orthopedic surgeon).

When the physical injury is confined to the scheduled member, however, some courts view the schedule as the exclusive basis for the award of benefits. E.g., Potomac Electric Power Co. v. Director, Office of Workers' Compensation Programs, 449 U.S. 268, 101 S.Ct. 509, 66 L.Ed.2d 446 (1980) (clear statutory language and legislative history supports limiting worker to scheduled benefits notwithstanding his greater impairment of earning capacity; the court notes the trend to the contrary); Ratliff v. Alaska Workers' Compensation Bd., 721 P.2d 1138 (Alaska 1986) (claimant is limited to compensation for a scheduled injury to knee in the absence of a finding that the knee injury had an effect on any other portion of the body); Ex parte Drummond Co., 837 So.2d 831 (Ala.2002) (same). See also Insurance Co. of the State of Pa. v. Muro, 347 S.W.3d 268 (Tex. 2011) (an award of permanent total disability benefits is precluded by legislation limiting an award of lifetime benefits to specific injuries notwithstanding the finding that the cumulative effect of non-listed injuries resulted in the claimants inability to work).

6. A work-connected injury that disfigures the victim with scars or distorted appearance may impair wage-earning capacity. In that case an award of compensation is entirely consistent with the principles on which the workers' compensation system is founded. People engaged in certain

occupations, e.g., receptionist, model, television performer, are more likely to be adversely affected by these injuries than others who do not encounter the public in their occupations.

Where there is no evidence that the disfigurement has had an impact on the claimant's ability and opportunity to work and earn, the workers' compensation principle would suggest that no award be made. In the absence of a special statute such is the result reached in the case of the so-called "cosmetic injury". McPherson v. American Mut. Liability Ins. Co., 208 S.C. 76, 37 S.E.2d 136 (1946) (award for injury to hand for disfigurement disallowed because earning capacity not impaired); Wengler v. Grosshans Lumber Co., 173 Neb. 839, 115 N.W.2d 415 (1962) (award refused for scar, loss of teeth and speech defect).

Most states have enacted special statutory provisions governing compensation for disfigurement. Although these statutes differ widely in scope and method of operation, some relate the award directly to loss of earning power. In Jolly v. J.M. Hampton & Sons Lumber Co., 234 Ark. 574, 353 S.W.2d 338 (1962), the statute provided:

> The Commission shall award compensation for serious and permanent facial or head disfigurement in a sum not to exceed two thousand ($2,000.00) dollars, based solely upon the effect such disfigurement shall have on the future earning capacity of the injured employee in similar employment.

Claimant suffered an electrical burn that caused loss of facial tissue which was repaired by plastic surgery leaving permanent scars on his face and ear. Although the claimant testified that he was embarrassed when meeting people, there was no evidence that he could not work or that he had been refused employment. Compensation was denied.

Other statutes authorize the administrative agency to make awards for disfigurement of certain parts of the body such as "serious facial or head disfigurements", but do not expressly condition the disfigurement award on a reduction of earning capacity. These statutes presume that certain disfigurements impair earning capacity. In upholding the validity of such a statute, the New York court said: "But one of the truths of life is that serious facial disfigurement has a tendency to impair the earning power of its victims." Sweeting v. American Knife Co., 226 N.Y. 199, 123 N.E. 82 (1919), affirmed 250 U.S. 596, 40 S.Ct. 44, 63 L.Ed. 1161 (1919). See also, 820 Ill.Comp.Stat.Ann. 305/8(c) (employee is entitled to compensation "for any serious and permanent disfigurement to the hand, head, face, neck, arm, leg below the knee, or chest above the axillary line"); Del.Code Ann. tit. 19 § 2326 (employee may receive compensation for permanent disfigurement that is "visible and offensive when the body is clothed normally"). Under some state laws, disfigurement benefits may be awarded even in the absence of visible scars. E.g., County of Dane v. Labor and Industrial Review Comm'n., 759 N.W.2d 571 (Wis. 2009) (accident left worker with a pronounced foot-dragging limp but no visible scarring, burns or amputations).

If the state allows compensation for disfigurement, benefits may be awarded for the medical expense of cosmetic surgery. Thus in Akers Auto Salvage v. Waddle, 394 P.2d 452 (Okl.1964), in which claimant suffered marked disfigurement of the right ear, compensation was allowed for the medical expense of reconstructive surgery. Conversely, if compensation for the disfigurement is not allowable, the expenses of corrective plastic surgery are not recoverable. Eckert v. Yellow Freight Systems, Inc., 170 Ind.App. 196, 351 N.E.2d 924 (1976).

Should compensation be allowed for both bodily impairment and disfigurement? Compare, Ind.Code Ann. § 22–3–3–10 (no compensation for disfigurement where benefits are payable under other provisions) with Mass.Gen.Laws Ann., ch. 152, § 36 (employee may receive compensation for disfigurement "in addition to all other sums due").

For a summary of state laws providing disfigurement benefits see WCRI, *Workers' Compensation Laws*, 2012 Table 11 (2012).

7. Are the income benefits provided by workers' compensation adequate to meet the financial needs of the injured workers? While the definition of "adequate" is inherently subjective, most students of the workers' compensation systems use two-thirds of the worker's gross wages as the benchmark. That is, income benefits are considered adequate if they replace two-thirds of the injured employee's gross wages. A number of studies suggest that workers' compensation is falling substantially below this standard. For workers who miss significant time from work or have permanent disabilities, workers' compensation income benefits may replace only 25–45% of actual wage loss over time. These studies are summarized in National Academy of Social Insurance, Adequacy of Earning Replacement in Workers' Compensation Programs: A Report of the Study Panel on Benefits Adequacy of the Workers' Compensation Steering Committee (Alan Hunt editor) (2004). See also, Leslie I. Boden et. al, The Adequacy of Workers' Compensation Cash Benefits, in Workplace Injuries and Diseases, Prevention and Compensation, Essays in Honor of Terry Thomason 37 (Roberts, Burton and Bodah eds. 2005). See also Xuguang Guo and John F. Burton, Workers' Compensation: Recent Developments in Moral Hazard and Benefits Payments, 63 Indus. & Lab. Rel. Rev. 340, 353 (2010) (attributing the divergence between expected and incurred benefits over time to a "tightening of compensability rules and greater stringency in providing benefits to injured workers").

SLOVER MASONRY, INC. V. INDUSTRIAL COMMISSION

Supreme Court of Arizona, 1988.
158 Ariz. 131, 761 P.2d 1035.

FELDMAN, VICE CHIEF JUSTICE.

Claimant seeks review of a court of appeals' opinion denying his workers' compensation award. The court vacated the award because the administrative law judge (ALJ) did not strictly adhere to the American Medical Association's *Guides to the Evaluation of Permanent Impairment* (the AMA Guides) when determining the percentage of claimant's permanent impairment. We must decide whether an administrative law judge is bound to follow the AMA Guides as the sole measure of impairment.

Factual and Procedural Summary

The operative facts are undisputed. Thaddeus J. Williamson (claimant) was a hod carrier employed by Slover Masonry (respondent). On December 3, 1984, claimant fell off a scaffold at work, fracturing the tibial condyle of his right knee. James Alway, M.D., a board-certified orthopedic specialist, performed five surgical operations on claimant's leg. The surgeries did not entirely repair the damage, and claimant continued to suffer cramping, pain, loss of balance, foot drop, numbness, tingling, and restricted extension and flexion of both the right leg and right foot.

On January 7, 1986, the Industrial Commission (the Commission) issued a Notice of Permanent Disability Benefits (Scheduled) stating that claimant had suffered a fifty percent loss of function in his right leg. The fifty percent loss entitled claimant to fifty percent of his average monthly wage for twenty-five months. A.R.S. § 23–1044(B)(15) and (21). Claimant requested a hearing to prove that his permanent disability was greater than fifty percent.

The Commission held hearings on July 25 and August 16, 1986 to determine the correct percentage of permanent disability for claimant's injury. * * *

Claimant explained that . . . he could not complete [five of the seven] tasks related to his hod carrier job, which constituted about seventy-eight percent of his job when measured by time allotted each task. A labor market consultant confirmed that claimant's injury disabled him from performing sixty-five percent of a hod carrier's job.

Dr. Alway testified that he evaluated claimant's permanent injuries under the AMA Guides and concluded that claimant had a fifty percent functional loss of his right lower leg. However, Dr. Alway made it clear that the AMA Guides did not actually measure ability to perform a specific job or occupation: . . .

> On August 26, 1986, the ALJ conducting the hearing summarized Dr. Alway's testimony in his decision:
>
> > Dr. Alway opined that the A.M.A. Guidelines do not attempt to take into consideration the applicant's impairment in terms of his job functions. Stated another way, Dr. Alway said that the working disability the applicant suffers is not totally covered by the Guides. Dr. Alway agreed with the

> applicant's assessment of which job functions he can no longer do.

Decision Upon Hearing, August 26, 1986 (Findings), at para. 4.

The ALJ recognized that the "effect [of the injury] on earning capacity is not a factor to be considered," but concluded also that the AMA Guides did "not provide a fair, accurate measure of the degree of impairment." *Id.* at para. 8 and 9. After making an "independent evaluation of the record," the ALJ found that claimant had sustained a seventy-percent permanent impairment of function. *Id.* at para. 9 and 11. He awarded claimant fifty percent of his average monthly wage for a period of thirty-five months, a total of $23,187.50. A.R.S. § 23–1044(B)(15) and (21).

Pursuant to the employer's request, the ALJ reviewed his decision and affirmed the award. See A.R.S. §§ 23–942(D), –943(A) and (B). The employer and compensation carrier then sought special action reviewed by the court of appeals. A.R.S. §§ 23–951(A); 12–120.21(B); Rule 1, Ariz.R.P.Spec.Act., 17B A.R.S.

Court of Appeals

The court of appeals set aside the award, concluding it was "inconsistent" with the medical testimony and with Arizona Supreme Court decisions. The court reasoned that *unless* a medical expert determines that the AMA Guides do not "adequately" rate claimant's impairment, an ALJ cannot consider a claimant's inability to perform his job in determining the correct disability rating.

* * *

The Issues

This case presents two interrelated issues:

> 1. When may an ALJ reject the AMA Guides in determining a claimant's percentage of permanent impairment?
>
> 2. Did the ALJ here abuse his discretion in concluding that the AMA Guides did not accurately reflect the true percentage of claimant's leg impairment?

Discussion

The Arizona workers' compensation program provides benefits to covered employees disabled by industrial accidents. The program attempts to accurately ascertain the worker's disability and promptly distribute his benefits. To streamline procedures, the legislature created standard compensation percentages for specific ("scheduled") injuries. For instance, for the loss of a leg, the state compensation fund will pay fifty-five percent of a covered employee's average monthly wage for fifty months. A.R.S. § 23–1044(B)(15). This sum is in addition to compensation for any temporary total disability. A.R.S. § 23–1044(B). If the impairment is only partial, the fund will pay fifty percent of the worker's average monthly wage for the proportionate number of months that the partial loss bears to the total loss of use. A.R.S. § 23–1044(B)(21). Thus, if a leg is fifty percent impaired, the fund will pay benefits for only twenty-five months (fifty percent x fifty months). If the leg is seventy percent impaired, the payments are for thirty-five months (seventy percent x fifty months).

Normally the Commission determines the percentage of the leg's loss based on the treating physician's rating of the impairment resulting from the injury. When the physician discharges a claimant, the physician rates the percentage of functional impairment in accordance with the AMA Guides, if they apply, with a clinical report sufficiently detailed to support the percentage rating. See A.C.R.R. R4–13–113(D). The AMA Guides measure the clinical or physiological percentage of impairment without regard to how the injury affects a person's ability to perform his job. *See Adams v. Industrial Commission*, 113 Ariz. 294, 295, 552 P.2d 764, 765 (1976).

If a claimant is dissatisfied with the Commission's initial rating, he may seek a hearing before an ALJ. An ALJ determines the correct percentage of a claimant's disability and may consider a wide range of evidence to ensure "substantial justice." A.R.S. § 23–941(F). Although the AMA Guides are important in the disability rating, they are not the philosopher's stone: . . .

Indeed, non-medical factors may be vital when assessing a disability, despite the AMA Guides. See *Jaske v. Murray Ohio Manufacturing Co., Inc.*, 750 S.W.2d 150, 151 (Tenn.1988). In fact, sometimes the AMA Guides do not apply. *See, e.g., Dayron Corp. v. Morehead*, 509 So.2d 930 (Fla.1987) (AMA Guides inadequately gave a rating of zero to five percent permanent impairment for a machinist who could no longer perform his craft because of acute contact dermatitis to cutting oils); *OBS Co., Inc. v. Freeney*, 475 So.2d 947 (Fla.Dist.Ct.App.1985) (AMA Guides gave no ratable permanent impairment for journeyman plasterer who developed severe contact dermatitis to wet plaster and cement); *Kroeplin v. North Dakota Workmen's Compensation Bureau*, 415 N.W.2d 807 (N.D.1987) (employee entitled to industrial award even though the AMA Guides did not substantiate subjective pain symptoms). Therefore, when other evidence requires a different result, a medical expert cannot bind the ALJ to unreasoning adherence to the AMA Guides.

Here, claimant sought a hearing to establish the correct rating of his permanent disability. Using the AMA Guides as his only criterion, Dr. Alway concluded that claimant has a fifty percent impairment in his right leg. However, Dr. Alway also testified that the AMA Guides provided a fair measure of claimant's medical impairment "but not his disability as far as his former occupation." Claimant testified, on the other hand, that he could only perform about twenty-two percent of his duties as a hod carrier. Dr. Alway agreed with this assessment. The labor consultant concurred in the general range, stating that claimant could perform about thirty-five percent of his job.

The ALJ is responsible for determining the percentage of disability, not simply the percentage of physiological impairment in the functioning of limbs and organs. The AMA Guides measure only clinical, physical impairment expressed in percentage of loss of motion. The ALJ, however, must determine the degree of functional loss or impairment, and thus may consider claimant's inability to pursue the specific craft, job, or profession he or she practiced at the time of the incapacitating industrial injury. *Dutra*, 135 Ariz. at 61, 659 P.2d at 20.

Therefore, the individual claimant's occupation, viewed in light of the physical impairment, affects the ALJ's determination of the claimant's "disability." Each craft, calling, or job places unique demands on the body. Thus, a five percent loss of leg movement might slightly disable a lawyer or computer programmer but could markedly disable a laborer or professional dancer. Of course, we leave undisturbed the rule that in no event should the ALJ consider the actual loss of individual earning capacity in establishing the correct percentage of scheduled disability. *See* A.R.S. § 23–1044(H); *Gomez*, 148 Ariz. at 569, 716 P.2d at 26. . . .

The AMA Guides are only a tool adopted by administrative regulation to assist in ascertaining an injured worker's percentage of disability. Thus, when the AMA Guides do not truly reflect a claimant's loss, the ALJ must use his discretion to hear additional evidence and, from the whole record, establish a rating independent of the AMA recommendations. *W.A. Krueger Co.*, 150 Ariz. at 68, 722 P.2d at 236. That is why A.C.R.R. R4–13–113(D) states that the AMA Guides "should" be used to establish a rating of functional impairment "*if applicable*" (emphasis added). If an injury has resulted in a functional impairment not adequately reflected by clinical measurement under the AMA Guides, then an ALJ must consider impact on job performance. *See Gomez*, 148 Ariz. at 569, 716 P.2d at 26.

Conclusion

An ALJ may properly consider the impact of the industrial accident on a claimant's ability to perform his or her job. Here, the AMA Guides gave only a fifty percent rating when the medical expert, the labor consultant, *and* the claimant all agreed that the impact on claimant's ability to perform his job was greater than fifty percent. The ALJ's resulting seventy percent rating reasonably conformed to the testimony. Thus, the award was supported by the evidence.

We vacate the court of appeals' opinion and reinstate the Commission's award.

NOTES

1. The American Medical Association created a committee on the topic of rating permanent impairment in 1956. Over the next fifteen years, the committee developed guides for rating particular impairments. In 1971, the AMA compiled and published the standards that had been developed at that time. This work become known as the American Medical Association *Guides to the Evaluation of Permanent Impairment* (AMA *Guides*). The AMA *Guides* are revised periodically and the sixth edition was published in 2008.

2. Each chapter of the *Guides* prescribes specific means for measuring impairment of particular organs or bodily system and translating such measurements into percentage ratings. The percentage is calculated on both an organ and "whole person" basis. The knee injury involved in *Slover Masonry*, for example, would be covered in Chapter 3. The AMA *Guides* instruct the examining physician to measure the degree of lost flexion in the knee by the use of an instrument called a goniometer; and then provides a chart that translates that measurement into a "percentage impairment of the lower extremity" and "percentage impairment of the whole person". The actual application of the *Guides* can be quite complex. See, e.g., Deschampe v. Arrowhead Tree Service, 428 N.W.2d 795 (Minn.1988) (calculating impairment rating for brain injury); York v. Burgess–Norton Mfg. Co., 803 P.2d 697 (Okl.1990) (calculating impairment rating for injury to lung and respiratory system).

Sometimes it may not be easy to reconcile the statutory mandate to use the AMA *Guides* with the *Guides'* own recognized limitations on their use. For example, in S.L.H. v. State Compensation Mutual Ins. Fund, 303 Mont. 364, 15 P.3d 948 (2000), the claimant had been kidnapped from her job as a bartender and severely beaten and raped. The contested issue was how to factor in her post-traumatic stress disorder and depression in calculating an impairment rating. The Montana statute required that impairment ratings "must" be based on the most recent edition of the AMA *Guides* and "must" be expressed as a percentage of the whole person. But the applicable edition of the AMA *Guides* did not provide for percentage calculations for mental impairment. Instead, the AMA *Guides* evaluated mental impairment under a five-class rating system, ranging from no impairment (Class 1) to extreme impairment (Class 5). The psychiatrist who examined the claimant testified that her post-traumatic stress disorder fell within Class 3 as moderate impairment while her major depressive disorder fell between Class 3 and Class 2, and was, therefore, moderate to mild impairment. The psychiatrist refused to translate the claimant's mental impairment into a percentage. The court held that under these circumstances, the finder of fact could translate the psychiatrist's evaluation of mild-to-moderate mental impairment into a percentage in order to comply with the statute.

3. In 1972, *The Report of the National Commission on State Workmen's Compensation Laws* recommended that states use the AMA Guides as a source of standardized and medically justified criteria for measuring physical impairment. *Id.*, at 69. The Report cautioned, however, that physical "impairment" was a more limited concept than "disability"; and that disability should be the primary basis for awarding permanent partial disability benefits. At first, states were slow to adopt the AMA *Guides* as standards. During the 1980s, a number of states embraced the AMA *Guides.* Today, more than thirty states either mandate or approve the use of the AMA *Guides* in calculating disability benefits. See Steven Babitsky and James J. Mangraviti, Jr., *Understanding The AMA Guides in Workers' Compensation* (2d ed. 1996) (listing jurisdictions). Proponents of the use of the AMA *Guides* maintain that they will "establish more certainty and uniformity" to the rating of permanent impairment. E.g., Tenn. Code Ann. § 50–6–204(d)(3); Kroeplin v. North Dakota Workmen's Compensation Bureau, 415 N.W.2d 807, 808 (N.D.1987).

4. Several commentators have criticized the mechanical reliance on the AMA *Guides* to calculate indemnity benefits for permanent partial disability. These criticisms are summarized as follows:

> Nevertheless, 2 types of serious and legitimate criticisms have been directed as the *Guides.* First, criticisms focus on internal deficiencies, including that it fails to provide a comprehensive, valid, reliable unbiased, and evidence-based systems for the rating of impairments; that the impairment ratings do not reflect perceived and actual loss of function and quality of life; and that the numerical ratings represent legal fiction, not medical reality. . . .
>
> The second set of criticisms focuses on how workers' compensation systems use the *Guides'* ratings. The concern is that the ratings are improperly used as a substituto for a full assessment of the impact of impairment on work and nonwork capabilities, and that therefore workers receive inappropriate compensation.

Emily S. Spieler, Peter S. Barth, John F. Burton, Jr., Jay Himmelstein, and Linda Rudolph, Recommendations to Guide Revision of the *Guides to the Evaluation of Permanent Impairment*, 283 JAMA 519, 520 (2000) (citations omitted). John Burton also criticizes the AMA *Guides* for not taking into account wage-loss studies and quality of life research in calculating impairment ratings. John F. Burton, The AMA Guides and Permanent Partial Disability Benefits, 45 IAIABC Journal 13 (Fall 2008). In the view of Burton and other critics, the limited perspective of the AMA *Guides* leads to a systematic undercompensation for the actual wage loss suffered by the employee.

A 2012 study of the California system conducted by the Center for the Study of Social Insurance concluded that the adoption of the AMA Guides produced an overall reduction in payment of workers' compensation benefits. This study compared permanent disability claims filed before and after the state's adoption of the AMA Guides. It found that the adoption of the AMA Guides (1) reduced the average disability rating by 31.5%; (2) produced a greater apportionment of disability to non-employment causes; and (3) reduced the percentage of indemnity claims with permanent disability ratings above zero percent. Frank Neuhauser, Impact of the Adoption of AMA-based Permanent Disability Rating Schedule in California (January 12, 2012).

For other critiques see Ellen Pryor, Flawed Promises: A Critical Evaluation of the American Medical Association's Guides to the Evaluation of Permanent Impairment, 103 Harv. L. Rev. 964 (1990); S. Babitsky and G. Shapiro, The Use of the AMA Guides to the Evaluation of Permanent Impairment in Workers' Compensation Cases 30–40 (1986); Gene Stephens Connolly, Hidden Illness, Chronic Pain: The Problems of Treatment and Recognition of Fibromyalgia in the Medical Community, 5 DePaul J. Health Care L. 111 (2002). For a series of articles commenting on various aspects of the 6th Edition of the AMA *Guides*, see Responses to the Sixth Edition of the AMA Impairment Guides, 45 IAIABC Journal 13 (Fall 2008).

5. Challenges under federal and state constitutions to the mandated use of the AMA *Guides* have generally failed. E.g., Texas Workers' Compensation Comm'n. v. Garcia, 893 S.W.2d 504 (Tex.1995); Brown v. Campbell Bd. of Educ., 915 S.W.2d 407 (Tenn.1995); Allen v. Natrona County School Dist., 811 P.2d 1 (Wyo.1991). Cf. Adkins v. R & S Body Co., 58 S.W.3d 428 (Ky.2001) (use of the impairment rating derived from the AMA Guides as one factor in a statutory formula for calculating benefits is not arbitrary). But see Repass v. Workers' Compensation Division, 212 W.Va. 86, 569 S.E.2d 162 (2002) (the Commissioners' adoption of the AMA Guides as the exclusive measure of disability conflicted with a number of specific statutory provisions constitutioned an impermissible delegation of legislative authority to the extent that the agency's rule).

6. Many jurisdictions adhere to the approach reflected in *Slover Masonry*, that the AMA *Guides* are not the exclusive measure of disability. In addition to the authorities cited in the principal case, see Cabatbat v. County of Hawaii, 103 Hawai'i 1, 78 P.3d 756 (2003); City of Aurora v. Vaughn, 824 P.2d 825 (Colo.App.1991). Cf. Adkins v. R & S Body Co., 58 S.W.3d 428 (Ky.2001) (AMA Guides are one of three factors considered in calculating award).

7. The court in *Slover Masonry* noted that scheduled benefits for permanent partial disability are payable in addition to whatever benefits have been paid for temporary total disability. The cumulation of temporary total and permanent partial disability benefits is quite common. E.g., Md.Code Ann., Lab. And Emp. § 9–639; Ohio Rev.Code Ann. § 4123.57. A few

states reduce the award for permanent partial disability by the amount paid for temporary total or temporary partial disability. E.g., La.Rev.Stat.Ann. § 23:1223. See generally, WCRI, Workers' Compensation Laws, Table 8 (2012) (describing the practices of various states).

8. The line separating "temporary" from "permanent" is often expressed in terms of the claimant's physical condition. An employee who has not reached "maximum medical improvement" may be eligible for temporary disability benefits (total or partial), but is not entitled to permanent disability benefits (total or partial). E.g., J.A. Riggs Tractor Co. v. Etzkorn, 30 Ark.App. 200, 785 S.W.2d 51 (1990) (payments made during the "healing period" are classified as temporary total disability benefits and are not credited against the maximum permanent total disability benefits to which the employee is entitled; payment of permanent total disability begins only after the "healing period" is completed). Conversely, entitlement to temporary disability benefits (total or partial) ceases upon the claimant's reaching maximum medical improvement. E.g., Coca–Cola Bottling Co. v. Tunson, 534 So.2d 910 (Fla.App.1988) (since all the medical testimony established that the claimant had reached maximum medical improvement, no award could be made for temporary total disability benefits).

The use of maximum medical improvement standard to separate temporary from permanent disability can have a significant impact on the total duration of benefits, and hence, total costs. Consider the following discussion:

> In every workers' compensation system there comes a point when the injured worker is no longer considered to have a "temporary" disability and becomes eligible for "permanent" disability benefits. In a majority of states the line that separates temporary from permanent is called "maximum medical improvement" (MMI). As the name implies, MMI is a measure of physical ability, not job performance. When workers reach MMI, they no longer receive temporary total disability benefits and are evaluated for permanent disability benefits. This evaluation may result in an award of permanent partial disability benefits (PPD).
>
> Georgia does not use the MMI standard. Instead, a Georgia worker is entitled to receive temporary (total or partial) disability benefits until he or she returns to work at or above the pre-injury wage. The "return to work" standard used to end temporary total disability benefits in Georgia is framed in functional terms (i.e., can the worker perform her job?) rather than an abstract measure of physical ability.
>
> [Workers Compensation Research Institute (WCRI)] recently examined PPD claims in six states (California, Connecticut, Georgia, Florida, Texas, and Wisconsin). The purpose of the study was to identify factors associated with the incidence of PPD awards. WCRI found that of these six states, Georgia had the longest

duration of temporary disability benefits and the largest percentage of lump-sum payments. [Workers Compensation Research Institute, Who Obtains Permanent Partial Disability Benefits: A Six State Analysis, 61 (December 2002).] This study concludes that

> The absence of MMI drives the use of lump-sum settlements and lengthens duration of temporary disability in Georgia. In our group of six states, Georgia is an exception. It does not use maximum medical improvement (MMI) as the basis for ending temporary disability benefits and rating workers for permanent disability. It seems evident that the absence of MMI in Georgia has an impact on the duration of claims, the use of lump-sum settlements, and their respective relationship to PPD rates. If policy makers in Georgia wonder why the use of lump sum settlements in their state is high, they need to focus on their unusual practice of not using MMI as a point at which impairment is rated.

However, Georgia's "return to work" standard may have cost-saving effects not measured by the duration of temporary disability benefits. Under a return to work standard, an employer must continue paying temporary disability benefits until the injured employee can return to work at his or her pre-injury wage. This creates an incentive for employers to return injured workers to suitable employment as quickly as possible. This incentive may help explain why Georgia has one of the lowest percentages of claims with seven or more days' lost time. As discussed in Part IV B, the low percentage of claims with more than seven days' lost time is a major reason why Georgia's average total cost per claim on all claims was one of the lowest of the states included in the WCRI study. Thus, while MMI may shorten the average duration of temporary disability claims, a return to work standard may reduce the number of claims with seven or more days' lost time.

Thomas A. Eaton and David D. Mustard, Report of the Governor's Workers' Compensation Review Commission, 38 Ga. L. Rev. 1241, 1301–02 (2004).

Which is more likely to be true: that the MMI standard reduces total costs by shortening the temporary total disability payments, or that it increases total costs by diluting employer incentives to find suitable work for injured employees? How would you go about testing which proposition is more likely to be true?

9. Should vocational rehabilitation influence the classification of a disability as permanent or temporary? Vocational rehabilitation may reduce the long range impact of an injury on earning capacity without improving the worker's physical condition. It is also apparent that a worker's medical condition might stabilize before vocational rehabilitation is complete. Should a worker who has reached maximum medical improvement be eligible for

temporary disability benefits while undergoing vocational rehabilitation? See Allee v. Contractors, Inc., 783 P.2d 273 (Colo.1989) (finding worker is "entitled to receive temporary partial disability benefits between the time when the worker attains maximum medical improvement and the time when the worker commences a vocational rehabilitation program or an administrative determination is made that vocational rehabilitation is unnecessary to render the worker fit for a remunerative occupation"; Wroten v. Lamphere, 147 Vt. 606, 523 A.2d 1236 (1987) (employee who had reached maximum medical improvement is not entitled to receive temporary total disability benefits while completing vocational rehabilitation).

4. THE "SECOND INJURY" PROBLEM

LAWSON V. SUWANEE FRUIT & STEAMSHIP CO.

Supreme Court of the United States, 1949.
336 U.S. 198, 69 S.Ct. 503, 93 L.Ed. 611.

MR. JUSTICE MURPHY delivered the opinion of the Court.

This is a workmen's compensation case, under the Longshoremen's and Harbor Workers' Compensation Act, 44 Stat. 1424, 33 U.S.C. § 901 et seq., 33 U.S.C.A. § 901 et seq. A narrow and difficult question of statutory construction confronts us.

John Davis lost the sight of his right eye in an accident unconnected with industry or his employment. He was later hired by respondent. An injury occurred during this employment, and he is now blind in both eyes. The parties agree that he is totally disabled within the meaning of the Act; they also agree that the employer is liable for compensation for the loss of the left eye. The dispute is narrowed to this question: should the employer or the statutory second injury fund, administered by petitioner, be liable for the balance of payments to equal compensation for total disability?

Petitioner concluded that the employer was liable. The employer secured a reversal of this determination in the District Court for the Southern District of Florida, 68 F.Supp. 616, and the Court of Appeals for the Fifth Circuit affirmed the judgment of the District Court. 166 F.2d 13. Because this decision conflicted with that of the Court of Appeals for the District of Columbia in National Homeopathic Hospital Association of District of Columbia v. Britton, 79 U.S.App.D.C. 309, 147 F.2d 561, certiorari denied 325 U.S. 857, 65 S.Ct. 1185, 89 L.Ed. 1977, we granted certiorari.

Section 8(f)(1) of the Act provides that "If an employee receive an injury which of itself would only cause permanent partial disability but which, *combined with a previous disability*, does in fact cause permanent total disability, the employer shall provide compensation only for the disability caused by the subsequent injury: *Provided, however*, That in addition to compensation for such permanent partial disability, and after the cessation of the payments for the prescribed period of weeks, the employee shall be paid the remainder of the compensation that would be due for permanent total disability. Such additional compensation shall be paid out of the special fund established in section 44." The court below [166 F.2d 13, 14] held that this section is "clear and unambiguous, and therefore needs no construction. When read in its ordinary sense it can have but one meaning": liability for the second injury fund.

But the word "disability" is defined in the statute. Section 2 provides that "when used in this Act . . . (10) 'Disability means incapacity because of *injury*. . . .' " (Emphasis supplied.) The word "injury" is, in turn, defined as "accidental injury or death arising out of and in the course of employment. . . ." § 2(2). If these definitions are read into the second injury provision, then, it read as follows: "If an employee receive an injury which of itself would only cause permanent partial disability but which, combined with a previous *incapacity because of accidental injury or death arising out of and in the course of employment*, does in fact cause permanent total disability, the employer shall provide compensation only for the disability caused by the subsequent injury." Because Davis' previous injury was nonindustrial, this reading points to liability for the employer.

If Congress intended to use the term "disability" as a term of art, a shorthand way of referring to the statutory definition, the employer must pay total compensation. If Congress intended a broader and more usual concept of the word, the judgment below must be affirmed. Statutory definitions control the meaning of statutory words, of course, in the usual case. But this is an unusual case. If we read the definition into § 8(f)(1) in a mechanical fashion, we create obvious incongruities in the language and we destroy one of the major purposes of the second injury provision: the prevention of employer discrimination against handicapped workers. We have concluded that Congress would not have intended such a result.

Chief Justice Groner, dissenting in the National Homeopathic case, supra, 147 F.2d at page 565, noticed that the "interreplacements of words" we have set out above "produces a manifest incongruity, for . . . it would literally result in this: ' . . . a previous *incapacity* because of accidental injury or *death'*—And if to avoid this it be argued that only a portion of the definition of injury should be inserted, the result would be to change or at least to limit the statutory definition only to produce a desired result, which no one would urge or defend. It is evident, therefore," that the definition of disability was "not made with watch-like precision" and should not be so applied in § 8(f)(1). If the intent of Congress had been to limit the applicability of this subsection in the fashion for which petitioner contends, "it could easily have accomplished this by the insertion of the word 'compensable' between the words 'previous' and 'disability'. . . ." And see Atlantic Cleaners & Dyers v. United States, 286 U.S. 427, 52 S.Ct. 607, 76 L.Ed. 1204.

More important, perhaps, is the disservice we would do to the purpose of the second injury provision. We must look to the explanation of congressional intent behind the subsection. A witness at a hearing on the measure outlined his reasons for favoring the provision in the following manner: "The second injury proposition is as much to the advantage of the employer and his interests as it is for the benefit of the employee. It protects the employer who has hired, say, a one-eyed worker who goes and loses his other eye and becomes a total disability. The employer without this sort of thing would have to pay total permanent disability compensation. Then, on the other hand, this also protects the worker with one eye from being denied employment on account of his being an extra risk. Now, by simply taking this up in this way it is possible to protect both the employer and to protect the one-eyed employee also."

Petitioner relies on the statement of another witness before the Senate Committee, who favored inclusion of the second injury provisions because "they have become a commonplace . . . in State compensation legislation and ought to be included in the Act." And petitioner states that "we may appropriately refer, therefore, to the second injury provisions in other statutes and to the evaluations made by administrative experts in the field for guidance with respect to the manner in which opposing policy considerations have been resolved." But our search for guidance in the sources suggested by petitioner convinces us that petitioner's theories are not well-founded.

From the attitude of experts in the field, one would not expect Congress to distinguish between two types of handicapped workers. The annual conventions of the International Association of Industrial Accident Boards and Commissions provide the most helpful considerations of the problem. At the 1931 convention, Mr. Joseph Parks of the Massachusetts Commission spoke as follows of workmen's compensation legislation without a second injury provision: "I little knew that this great piece of legislation . . . would become an instrument of persecution, as I may call it, of men who are physically handicapped, but that is what it has become. Men who are physically handicapped are being discriminated against in our Commonwealth."

This attitude has been echoed by Mr. Charles Sharkey of the United States Bureau of Labor Statistics; Miss Frances Perkins, then Industrial Commissioner in New York; and others. Perhaps the most impressive evidence of the force behind these statements is that offered by Mr. I.K. Huber of Oklahoma. Nease v. Hughes Stone Co., 114 Okl. 170, 244 P. 778, held the employer liable for total compensation for loss of the second eye.

After the decision, Mr. Huber reports, "thousands of one-eyed, one-armed, one-handed men in the State of Oklahoma were let out and can not get employment coming under the workmen's compensation law of Oklahoma. . . . Those . . . court decisions put us in bad shape. . . . The decision displaced between seven and eight thousand men in less than 30 days in Oklahoma."

A distinction between a worker previously injured in industry and one handicapped by a cause outside of industry has no logical foundation if we accept the premise that the purpose of the fund is that of aid to the handicapped. This is the conclusion of Mr. Fred Wilcox, then Chairman of the Wisconsin Commission: "Wisconsin takes no account of where the injured man may have gotten his first injury. It makes no difference where he got it. It is just as serious to him, when he has the second injury, as if he had gotten the first one in industry." We cannot attribute the illogic of petitioner's position to Congress.

Our conclusion is reinforced by the administrative practice under the New York statute. The federal statute is based upon New York law. In New York "the commission holds that if the man loses his second eye in an industrial accident it is immaterial how he lost his first eye. The loss of eyesight in one eye may have been congenital; it may have occurred when the child was two years old, or it may have occurred after he was grown, but not in an industrial accident. Nevertheless, at the time he loses his second eye he has suffered total disability. . . ."

Petitioner's most strenuous argument is that the fund will soon be insolvent if we open liability to a nonindustrial previous injury, and that therefore Congress could not have contemplated the result we reach. Petitioner's worries seem exaggerated in the light of Wisconsin and New York experience. From 1919 to 1933, Wisconsin's fund had only 50 second injury cases charged against it. Second-Injury Funds as Employment Aids to the Handicapped, U.S. Division of Labor Standards (1944) p. 7. From 1919 to 1943, only 99 cases were charged against the New York fund. Id., p. 5. In 1930 Miss Frances Perkins told her associates that the problem is "not so large . . . as it appears."

On the basis of the incongruity involved in applying the definition mechanically, the unmistakable purpose of the second injury fund, and the interpretation of the State statute on which the federal act is based, we conclude that the term "disability" was not used as a term of art in § 8(f)(1), and that the judgment must be affirmed.

Affirmed.

MR. JUSTICE DOUGLAS dissents.

[Footnotes to the opinion have been omitted.]

NOTES

1. How should a worker be compensated when successive injuries produce a total disability greater than the sum of the individual effects of the two or more injuries? There are at least three possible solutions to the problem.

One is to require the last employer to bear the entire compensation burden for the total disability that was brought into existence by the last injury. For example, if the employee had previously lost one eye, and while working for the last employer lost the second eye, the last employer, under this plan, would pay compensation for total blindness. This is the general rule where there is no statute providing for a "second injury" or "subsequent injury" fund, or where the case is not covered by such a statute. Schwab v. Emporium Forestry Co., 216 N.Y. 712, 111 N.E. 1099 (1915) (claimant, who had previously lost his left hand, lost his right hand at the wrist as a result of an industrial injury, held entitled to compensation for permanent total disability); Polston v. Ready Made Homes, 171 Kan. 336, 232 P.2d 446 (1951) (claimant suffered loss of eye in industrial accident but previous injury to other eye did not bring case within second injury statute, employer held liable for permanent total disability).

Another solution is apportionment under statutes that limit the liability of employers in whose employment the last injury was sustained to only the compensation that would normally be payable for that injury standing alone. If there is no second injury fund statute coupled with such an apportionment provision, the worker receives compensation only for the second injury. E.g., Georgia Ins. Service v. Lord, 83 Ga.App. 28, 62 S.E.2d 402 (1950) (employee who was blind in his right eye lost the sight in his left eye in second injury, held compensation limited to loss of one eye).

The third solution, illustrated by *Lawson*, is the so-called second injury or subsequent injury plan which apportions responsibility for compensating the worker between the employer and a fund. A substantial majority of states employ this type of apportionment regime. The second injury fund has been eliminated or is being phased out in approximately fifteen states. For a description of the practices in each state, see United States Chamber of Commerce, 2012 Analysis of Workers' Compensation Laws, Chart XIII (2012).

2. In many states the Fund's contribution to the final award is the difference between the compensation that would be payable for the second injury alone and the compensation payable for the combined injuries. E.g., 820 Ill.Comp.Stat.Ann. 305/8(f); N.J.Stat.Ann. § 34:15–95. Other states utilize a more rigid formula to apportion disability costs between the employer and the Fund. E.g., Haw.Rev.Stat. § 386–33 (employer pays disability benefits for the first 104 weeks of disability and the Fund pays any benefits beyond 104 weeks).

In some states the employer pays only for the disability attributable to the second injury and the employee must apply directly to the Second Injury Fund for additional compensation. E.g., Cal.Labor Code § 4751; Ark. Code Ann. § 11–9–525. In other states the employer compensates the employee for the entire disability and seeks reimbursement from the Fund for a portion of its payments. E.g., Ga.Code Ann. § 34–9–360; N.Y. Work. Comp. Law § 15(8)(d). What difference does it make whether the employer or the employee applies for payment from the Second Injury Fund? Which approach do you think is preferable?

Second Injury Funds commonly are financed by payments from workers' compensation insurance carriers in cases of work-related deaths where there are no dependents to collect death benefits. A portion of the death benefits that would have been payable to dependents is paid to the Fund. See, Colo.Rev.Stat. § 8–46–102. Other common sources of funding include small percentage assessments against all compensation carriers or other special assessments.

3. What type of preexisting injury or condition is necessary to trigger recourse to the Second Injury Fund? The primary issue addressed in *Lawson* concerns the origin of the preexisting condition. A variation of this issue was addressed in McLean's Case, 326 Mass. 72, 93 N.E.2d 233 (1950). McLean had a congenital dislocation of the lens of his right eye, and later suffered a work injury that detached the retina of his left eye. The work injury in combination with the congenital condition left the worker with the industrial loss of both eyes. The employer sought reimbursement from the Second Injury Fund. The specific statutory provision in effect at that time covered employees who had "previously suffered a personal injury." The court interpreted this phrase as excluding congenital conditions. Consequently, the employer was not entitled to reimbursement from the Fund and had to pay full compensation for the loss of both eyes. The Massachusetts second injury fund statute was later amended to include congenital conditions. See, Fireman's Fund Ins. v. Commonwealth, 18 Mass.App.Ct. 129, 463 N.E.2d 582 (1984). Today, most second injury fund provisions cover preexisting congenital conditions. E.g., Second Injury Fund v. Conrad, 947 S.W.2d 278 (Tex.App.1997) (Fund is liable when claimant's work-related injury combined with birth defect to produce permanent total disability); Fierro v. Stanley's Hardware, 104 N.M. 411, 722 P.2d 662 (App.1986) (second injury fund is responsible for a portion of benefits paid to a worker who had a preexisting congenital condition in the right eye and suffered a work injury to the left eye); Whiteside v. Morrison, Inc., 799 S.W.2d 213 (Tenn.1990) (apportioning compensation between employer and Fund for disability resulting from work injury and congenital vascular malformation).

Some states limit the application of the second injury fund to specific preexisting conditions, such as the loss of a hand or eye. If the employee's prior impairment is not included on the list of covered conditions, neither the employer nor the worker may resort to the second injury fund. E.g., Golden Bay Earthquakes v. W.C.A.B., 129 Pa.Cmwlth. 236, 565 A.2d 212 (1989) (claimant had lost the hearing in one ear as a child and lost the hearing in the other ear as the result of being hit in the head while playing professional soccer; since the preexisting hearing loss was not a covered condition under the statute, claimant could not secure additional benefits from second injury fund). Second injury funds in other states are less rigidly limited and usually cover an array of preexisting general injuries. See generally, 5 A. Larson and L. Larson, Larson's Workers' Compensation Law § 91.02[6] (2013).

Two other common limitations based on the nature of the preexisting condition are worth noting. The first limitation is the permanence of the employee's prior condition. Virtually all states require that the preexisting condition have been "permanent" in order to trigger second injury fund liability. If the prior condition was not permanent, the Fund bears no liability and the employer pays for the entire disability. E.g., D.A. Netzel, Inc. v. Special Disability Trust Fund, 681 So.2d 874 (Fla.App.1996) (claimant's obesity was not a permanent physical impairment entitling employer to reimbursement); Todd Shipyards v. Director, Office of Workers' Compensation Programs, 793 F.2d 1012 (9th Cir.1986) (employer is not entitled to reimbursement by Fund when employee's prior back injury produced no permanent impairment). The second limitation is whether the preexisting condition actually or potentially impaired the claimant's earning capacity prior to his second injury. As a general matter, the prior impairment needs to have been of a physical quality that did or reasonably could have interfered with the claimant's securing employment. Compare Hettenhausen v. Gene Jantzen Chevrolet, 499 S.W.2d 785 (Mo.1973) (Second Injury Fund should not provide additional compensation to worker whose preexisting condition (surgical removal of testicle) did not impair his earning capacity) with Archer v. Bonners Ferry Datsun, 117 Idaho 166, 786 P.2d 557 (1990) (Second Injury Fund must contribute to permanent total disability award made to employee whose preexisting knee injury "constituted a hindrance or obstacle to obtaining employment for the particular claimant").

4. It is not enough that the preexisting permanent impairment actually or potentially impaired the worker's ability to secure employment. The preexisting condition must contribute in some significant way to the disability resulting from the second injury. This requirement is defined by Ga.Code Ann. § 34–9–351(1) as follows:

(a) Had the preexisting permanent impairment not been present, the subsequent injury would not have occurred;

(b) The disability resulting from the subsequent injury in conjunction with the preexisting permanent impairment is materially, substantially, and cumulatively greater than that which would have resulted had the preexisting permanent impairment not been present, and the employer has been required to pay and has paid compensation for that greater disability; or

(c) Death would not have been accelerated had the preexisting permanent impairment not been present.

If the preexisting condition did not significantly contribute to the final disability, no claim against the second injury fund can be made. e.g., JPS Carpets v. Troupe, 417 S.E.2d 333 (Ga. App. 1992) (denying second injury fund liability for claimant's work related injuries when preexisting condition (prior knee injury and weakened knee) did not cause nor enhance subsequent injury to arm); Norris v. Iowa Beef Processors, Inc., 224 Neb. 867, 402 N.W.2d 658 (1987) (Second Injury Fund is not liable for any portion of claimant's work related injuries when preexisting conditions (blindness in one eye) neither caused nor enhanced the subsequent injuries to arm, knee, and shoulder).

5. *Lawson* explains that one of the primary purposes of second injury funds is to remove some of the economic disincentives that might discourage employers from hiring persons with permanent disabilities. Because only employers who are aware of a worker's preexisting condition would be so discouraged, most statutes condition the application of the second injury fund upon proof of the employer's awareness of the employee's preexisting permanent disability. The degree of awareness demanded varies among jurisdictions. The most demanding states require written documentation of the employer's knowledge of the employee's preexisting condition. E.g., Sea–Land Services, Inc. v. State, Second Injury Fund, 737 P.2d 793 (Alaska 1987) (employer who had actual knowledge of employee's prior back surgery could not make a claim against the Second Injury Fund when the employer's written record did not clearly reflect that the employee suffered from a permanent impairment). Other states condition second injury fund liability on proof that the employer had "actual knowledge" of the employee's preexisting condition, although proof of actual knowledge may be circumstantial. E.g., Whiteside v. Morrison, Inc., 799 S.W.2d 213 (Tenn.1990) (employer who had actual knowledge of employee's physical limitations may make a claim against the Second Injury Fund despite ignorance of the underlying medical cause of the limitation). Perhaps the most common approach is to require that the prior impairment be "obviously manifested." This standard is met when the preexisting permanent disability would be "obvious and apparent from observation and examination by an ordinary layman." Special Indemnity Fund v. Scott, 652 P.2d 278 (Okl.1982) (preexisting congenital pilonidal cyst was sufficiently manifest to fall within the second injury fund statute). The broadest second injury fund coverage is found under statutes that apportion liability between the employer and the Fund even when the preexisting condition was not known or manifest. E.g., Flores v. Honolulu Dept. of Parks & Recreation, 67 Hawai'i 663, 701 P.2d 1282 (1985) (second injury fund liable for 80% of disability even though worker's preexisting heart condition was not manifest).

6. The second injury fund cases raise questions concerning the apportionment of disability costs that are reminiscent of those explored in Chapter 6 dealing with occupational disease, heart conditions, and

psychological disabilities and in Chapter 7 dealing with the effect of independent causes after the accident. Collectively, these materials have examined several alternative apportionment schemes that might be employed when factors other than the claimant's last employment contributed to producing a disability. What are the most important considerations to take into account in apportioning disability costs? In light of those considerations, what is the ideal method of apportionment when factors other than the claimant's last employment help produce the disability?

7. The Americans With Disabilities Act (ADA), 42 U.S.C.A. § 12101 et. seq., prohibits employment discrimination against physically disabled persons. This federal statute raises a number of issues pertaining to state workers' compensation laws, including second injury funds. As discussed in note 5 above, many state second injury fund statutes require some evidence that the employer was aware of the worker's pre-existing disability as a prerequisite for asserting a claim against the fund. The ADA, however, prohibits employers from asking prospective employees about their workers' compensation history and greatly restricts pre-employment medical examinations. How is an employer to obtain the kind of information needed to assert a claim under the state second injury fund provision without violating the federal ADA? For a reflection on the practical ramifications of the ADA's apparent conflict with second injury funds' general requirement of employer awareness, see William D. Sheldon and Douglas Grimwood, Nobody Wins: Conflicts Between the Apportionment Provisions of the Arizona Workers' Compensation Act and the American with Disabilities Act, Ariz. Atty 34 (April 2000).

A common purpose of both state second injury fund laws and the ADA is to facilitate the employment of workers with pre-existing disabilities. Second injury funds advance this goal by reducing one economic disincentive to hiring the disabled. The ADA acts more directly by prohibiting discrimination. In light of the direct prohibitions of the ADA, are second injury funds needed to make employment opportunities available to those with pre-existing permanent impairments? For an argument that second injury funds are no longer needed, see Catherine M. Doud, Comment, Oklahoma's Special Indemnity Fund: A Fund Without a Function?, 30 Tulsa L. Rev. 745 (1995). The availability of remedies under the ADA was one of the reasons given in support of the prospective repeal of the Colorado and Kansas second injury fund laws. Id., at 765.

The ADA intersects with other provisions of state workers' compensation laws. In some states, an employer may not have to pay compensation benefits to an employee who falsely answers questions about prior injuries on his employment application. Georgia Electric Co. v. Rycroft, 259 Ga. 155, 378 S.E.2d 111 (1989). The ADA now prohibits employers from asking the type of question that gave rise to the misrepresentation defense in *Rycroft*. Is the workers' compensation defense of misrepresentation abrogated by an employer's violation of the ADA? The Georgia Supreme Court answered this question in the negative. Caldwell v. Aarlin/Holcombe Armature Co., 267 Ga.

613, 481 S.E.2d 196 (1997). The court reasoned that state workers' compensation and the federal ADA were separate sets of laws. If the employers' conduct violated the ADA, the employee can pursue remedies under the ADA. See also, Equal Employment Opportunity Commission v. Woodbridge Corp., 263 F.3d 812 (8th Cir.2001) (employer who refused to hire job applicants who failed physical test to determine whether they were susceptible to carpal tunnel syndrome did not violate the ADA because rejected applicants for assembly line positions were considered for other positions at the facility).

Two other sets of issues merit brief mention. Under the "employment-at-will" doctrine, a few states allow employers to terminate employees who file workers' compensation claims. E.g., Evans v. Bibb Co., 178 Ga.App. 139, 342 S.E.2d 484 (1986); Kelly v. Mississippi Valley Gas Co., 397 So.2d 874 (Miss.1981). The ADA obligates employers to accommodate workers with disabilities who are nonetheless able to do their job. How does the duty to accommodate under the ADA affect workers who have been injured on the job? For a discussion of what constitutes "reasonable accommodation" of workers who suffered repetitive stress injuries on the job, see Dalton v. Subaru–Isuzu Automotive, Inc., 141 F.3d 667 (7th Cir.1998). The ADA only protects "qualified" workers with disabilities, i.e., those who can perform the essential job functions with or without reasonable accommodation. 42 U.S.C.A. § 12111(8). Can a worker who claims to be "disabled" for purposes of workers' compensation be considered "qualified" for purposes of the ADA? Some courts have concluded that employees who seek disability benefits under state workers' compensation laws cannot be considered "qualified" workers under the ADA. E.g., Hensley v. City of Punta Gorda, 686 So.2d 724 (Fla.App.1997); Jackson v. County of Los Angeles, 60 Cal.App.4th 171, 70 Cal.Rptr.2d 96 (1997). See Maureen C. Weston, The Road Best Traveled: Removing Judicial Roadblocks that Prevent Workers From Obtaining Both Disability Benefits and ADA Civil Rights Protection, 26 Hofstra L. Rev. 377 (1997).

For a more detailed discussion of the interplay of the ADA and workers' compensation, see Alison Steiner, The Americans With Disabilities Act of 1990 and Workers' Compensation: An Employee's Perspective, 62 Miss. L.J. 631 (1993); Scott A. Carlson, Comment, The ADA and the Illinois Workers' Compensation Act: Can Two "Rights" Make a "Wrong"?, 19 S. Ill. U. L. J. 567 (1995); Catherine M. Doud, Comment, Oklahoma's Special Indemnity Fund: A Fund Without a Function?, 30 Tulsa L. Rev. 745 (1995); 5 A. Larson and L. Larson, Larson's Workers' Compensation Law § 91.03[7](2013).

5. COORDINATING WORKERS' COMPENSATION WITH OTHER SOURCES OF BENEFITS

DEPARTMENT OF PUBLIC HEALTH V. WILCOX

[Reprinted in Chapter 1, Section 3.]

NOTES

1. Should the disabled worker be allowed to recover both social security disability and workers' compensation benefits? If some sort of adjustment is to be made, is it preferable to reduce social security benefits by reason of receipt of workers' compensation benefits, or vice versa?

2. Approximately one-third of the states reduce workers' compensation benefits in some manner when the employee also receives social security disability benefits. These setoff provisions vary widely in their scope and method of operation. For example, some states apply the social security setoff against both permanent and temporary disability benefits while others reduce only permanent total disability benefits. Compare State, Department of Transportation v. Jackson, 379 So.2d 1045 (Fla.App.1980) ("the setoff is applicable to all weekly benefits, whether permanent, temporary, total, or partial") with Huval Baking Co. v. Fontenot, 629 So.2d 431 (La.App.1993) (statute allows setoff for social security benefits only when the employee is permanently and totally disabled). In some states the setoff is limited to one-half the social security benefits received. E.g., Mich.Comp.Laws § 418.354; N.D.Cent.Code § 65–05–09.1. This limitation reflects the fact that employees and employers each contribute half of the payments into the social security system. Some consider it unfair to reduce an employee's workers' compensation benefits because of an "insurance policy" paid for by the employee. The intricacies of coordinating workers' compensation and social security are discussed in 9 A. Larson and L. Larson, Larson's Workers' Compensation Law § 157.03 (2013).

3. Should workers' compensation benefits be reduced if the employee is receiving benefits under some private health, accident or disability insurance plan? Compare Varnell v. Union Carbide, 29 Ark.App. 185, 779 S.W.2d 542 (1989) (employee who injured her back had medical expenses paid by her employer's group health insurer and received income benefits under employer's sick pay plan; the injury was later ruled to be covered under workers' compensation; held that employer is not entitled to "credit" for payments made by group health carrier or sick pay plan) with Scriven v. Industrial Comm., 736 P.2d 414 (Colo.App.1987) (workers' compensation award properly reduced by amounts received under employer-financed pension plan) and Warsocki v. City of Omaha, 1 Neb.App. 874, 510 N.W.2d 446 (1993) (workers' compensation may be offset by employer's proportional share of service-connected disability pension benefits).

4. Should workers' compensation disability benefits be adjusted when the disabled worker reaches the normal retirement age? Some states make adjustments. E.g., Mont.Code Ann. § 39–71–710 (terminating permanent total disability benefits when employee is eligible to receive "full social security retirement benefits"); Mich.Comp.Laws § 418.354(1)(a) (reducing permanent total disability benefits by 50% of old age insurance benefits under social security); Polomski v. Mayor of Baltimore, 344 Md. 70, 684 A.2d 1338 (App.1996) (firefighter's workers' compensation benefits were reduced so that those benefits combined with retirement benefits would not exceed his weekly wage). But see State ex rel. Boan v. Richardson, 198 W.Va. 545, 482 S.E.2d 162 (1996) (statute mandating setoff of permanent total disability benefits when the claimant receives old age benefits under Social Security Act violates equal protection by not treating all social security recipients equally).

Does continuing payment of disability benefits past the age of normal retirement force the workers' compensation system to do more than protect against wage-loss? Does the answer to this question depend on whether there is any legally enforceable mandatory retirement age? See, C. Williams and P. Young, *Workers' Compensation Disability Benefits During Retirement Years: Proper and Present Role*, in Benefits, Costs, and Cycles in Workers' Compensation (Borba and Appel eds. 1990).

CHAPTER 9

DEATH BENEFITS

■ ■ ■

1. INTRODUCTION TO THIS CHAPTER

One of the purposes of workers' compensation law in cases in which the work injury results in death of the employee, is to provide funds to cover burial expenses. This is true in all states. The amount provided for such expense varies from one state to another from $2,500.00 in South Carolina to $16,825.20 in Oregon.[1] Some states also provide additional funds to cover the costs of transporting the employee's body from the place of death to the place of burial. No substantial legal problems arise in connection with these provisions.

The other purpose of providing benefits in cases of death from work injury is to take care of the members of the decedent's family and other individuals who were economically dependent upon the decedent's capacity to earn income. This chapter examines a substantial number of legal problems that arise in this context. Among the subjects considered are the nature of dependency; what persons are included in certain statutory descriptions or terms such as "widow," "widower," and "children"; who are "members of the family"; what is the relationship, if any, between the right of the injured employee to compensation during life and the right of the dependents to compensation after the employee's death; priorities among different dependents or classes of dependents; and the legal status of accrued and unaccrued benefits at the time of the death of the employee.

2. NATURE OF DEPENDENCY

DURBIN V. ARGONAUT INSURANCE CO.

Court of Appeal of Louisiana, 1980.
393 So.2d 385.

LOTTINGER, JUDGE.

The parents of a deceased employee brought this action for death benefits against the employer's workmen's compensation insurance

[1] U.S. Chamber of Commerce, 2013 Analysis of Workers' Compensation Laws, Chart VIII (2013) (updated annually).

carrier. The insurer appeals the trial court judgment awarding the plaintiffs $25.00 per week for 400 weeks. The plaintiffs have not appealed the trial court judgment rejecting their tort suit against the employer's executive officers. That matter is now final.[1]

The sole issue on appeal is whether the plaintiffs proved they were actually dependent upon the deceased at the time of death. La.R.S. 23:1252, 1254. Eddie Durbin suffered a compensable fatal injury in 1976 while in the course and scope of his employment with Dibert Bancroft & Ross, Limited. At the time of death and for the two or three months he was working for the company, Eddie lived at home. Both parents testified that Eddie gave them $10.00 to $20.00 per week, depending upon the size of his check, up to a month before his death. His mother told him he need not continue contributing the money because he was getting married and he needed the money to establish his new apartment. Eddie's mother fixed him two meals a day while he lived at home and she fixed him a lunch to take to work. She washed his clothes and took care of his room. In his spare time, Eddie helped around his family's 110-acre farm by feeding the animals and getting the corn ground for about 100 head of cattle. He also occasionally helped out at a family restaurant. The father claimed the deceased on the father's income tax during the year of death. Both parents testified that the money given to them by Eddie was not in return for his living at the house.

In written reasons for judgment, the trial court found that there was a "partial actual dependency" on the part of the plaintiffs attributable to Eddie's earnings and to his work on the farm. The court explicitly took into account Eddie's contributions through work on the farm in finding under La.R.S. 23:1231 that Eddie contributed 20% of his total weekly wages to the plaintiffs.[2]

The defendants contend on appeal that the plaintiffs failed to prove that they were dependent either partially or fully on contributions from the deceased for their support. They cite the following facts to back up their claim: The parents' testimony regarding the contributions was self serving; The parents instructed the deceased to stop payments one month before the fatality since the son was soon to be married; The father claimed the son on his income tax return; The father occasionally gave Eddie money for work Eddie did on the farm or at the restaurant.

Under La.R.S. 23:1252 the question of legal and actual dependency in cases in which conclusive dependency does not exist shall be determined "in accordance with the facts as they may be at the time of the accident

---

1 Editors's note: Some footnotes have been omitted.

2 Eddie earned $3.26 per hour on the date of death which computes to $130.40 for a 40-hour week. A contribution of $10.00 to $20.00 per week out of that amount would represent 7.5% to 15% of the total weekly wage. The trial court apparently found that the work on the farm accounted for the remainder of the 20% which the deceased contributed to the plaintiffs.

and death." La.R.S. 23:1254 provides that "the relation or dependency must exist at the time of the accident and at the time of death, and the mere expectation or hope of future contribution to support of an alleged dependent by an employee, shall not constitute proof of dependency as a fact."

In its latest discussion of the dependency issue, the Louisiana Supreme Court in Hurks v. Bossier, 367 So.2d 309 (La.1979), cited with approval Larson's definition of dependency.

> "The general test of dependency may be stated as follows: A showing of actual dependency does not require proof that, without decedent's contributions, claimant would have lacked the necessities of life, but only that decedent's contributions were relied on by claimant to maintain claimant's accustomed mode of living." The Law of Workmen's Compensation, Matthew Bender, Volume 2, 1976, § 63.11.

As to partial dependency, Larson states at 63:12:

> "Partial dependency may be found when, although the claimant may have other substantial sources of support in his own work, from property, or from other persons on whom claimant is also dependent, the contributions made by the decedent were looked to by the claimant for the maintenance of his accustomed standard of living."

The court in Hurks held that the contributions by the deceased of $50.00 to $60.00 a week to his mother who lived in poverty with her invalid mother and with the deceased supported a showing of dependency. The Hurks court cited McDermott v. Funel, 258 La. 657, 247 So.2d 567 (1971), where the Supreme Court held that a mother proved dependency by showing that her son contributed $15.00 to $20.00 a week out of a $55.00 paycheck. The mother earned about $40.00 a week as a domestic worker.

The defendants assert that the rule fashioned in Hurks and McDermott, *supra*, requires the plaintiffs to show that Eddie's contributions were relied on by his parents to maintain their accustomed mode of living. They also claim that the fact that the payments had ceased one month before the time of death shows that the Durbin family did not rely on Eddie's contributions to maintain their accustomed mode of living.

In 14 Louisiana Civil Law Treatise, Workers' Compensation, Section 309 (West, 2nd Ed.1980), Professors Wex Malone and H. Alston Johnston, III, comment that: ". . . in all cases (except where the dependency of the spouse and child is conclusively presumed), the claimant must prove dependency by establishing both a need for support and also the fact that contributions to his support were actually made by the deceased during the latter's lifetime. . . .

> "Thus, it is commonly held that neither need for support nor the existence of a moral or legal obligation to support is sufficient proof of dependency if there is not showing that the deceased in fact contributed to the claimant's support. . . .
>
> "The dependency must have existed at the time of the accident and death. Proof of prior dependency is not sufficient, and contributions made by the deceased to a partial dependent more than a year before the death cannot be included in determining the amount of compensation to which a partial dependent is entitled."

We think the law of this state is clear that for a dependency relationship to be shown the relationship must exist at the time of death. Additionally, a decedent's contributions must be relied upon by the claimant to maintain the claimant's accustomed mode of living. The fact that the decedent in this case stopped making the payments to his mother about one month prior to his death and the fact that his parents were adequately supporting themselves without the decedent's contribution leads us to the conclusion that the decision of the trial court must be reversed. See Darrow v. Travelers Ins. Co., 175 So. 98 (La.App. 2d Cir.1937), writ denied, June 21, 1937, wherein termination of contributions more than a year prior to death was used by the court to hold that the decedent was not supporting his parents at the time of death. Therefore, for the above and foregoing reasons, the decision of the trial court is reversed, and plaintiffs' petition is dismissed with prejudice. All costs in both the trial court and this court are assessed against plaintiffs-appellants.

Reversed and rendered.

NOTES

1. Statutes often provide for a conclusive presumption of dependency as to certain relatives of the decedent, usually the surviving spouse, and children under a specified age. See, for example, Code of Laws of S.C. § 42–9–110 (2012); Ky. Rev. Stat. Ann. § 342.750 (2013); and N.D. Century Code § 65–05–17 (2013).

Sometimes the conclusive presumption of dependency is on condition that the relatives named were living with the decedent at the time of the fatal accident or, if living apart from, were doing so because of the decedent's misconduct. See, for example, Ala. Code 1975 § 25–5–61 (2013); 19 De. Code Ann. § 2330 (d) (2013); Mn. St. Ann. § 176.111(a) (2013); Tenn. Code Ann. § 50–6–210(a)(1) (2013). Compare, 77 Pa. St. § 562 (2013) (if a wife was not living with her husband at the time of his death, she must show that she

". . . was then actually dependent upon him and receiving from him a substantial portion of her support."). Does the payment of a mutual debt such as a mortgage qualify as support? The answer depends on several factors which include which spouse is living in the former marital home and which partner, if either, repudiated the marriage. Compare S and S Associates, Inc. v. W.C.A.B., 77 Pa.Cmwlth. 11, 465 A.2d 57 (1983) (decedent, husband, lived in the home after the separation and had instituted divorce proceedings on grounds of desertion; held, benefits from the payment of the mortgage had flowed to the husband and, consequently did not constitute support for the wife); and M.D.S. Laboratories v. W.C.A.B., 111 Pa.Cmwlth. 541, 534 A.2d 844 (1987) (wife left husband because of his alcoholism; neither party disavowed marriage; court affirmed referee's findings that: (1) husband and wife had agreed that payment by husband of mortgage and taxes on marital home, in which he resided, would be in lieu of court-ordered spousal support; (2) payment of the mortgage and taxes protected the interests of the wife and children in the home; and (3) the mortgage payment was a form of a substantial support for the wife).

As to persons who enjoy the conclusive presumption, there is no necessity to analyze the "nature of dependency." In Adkins v. Comcar Industries, 323 S.C. 409, 475 S.E.2d 762 (1996) the statute provided for payment of death benefits to parents, regardless of need, if decedent left no dependents. Even though the father had abandoned his son, the decedent, many years earlier, he was still entitled to death benefits because the statute did not qualify the word "father."

The conclusive presumption of dependency may result sometimes in twice the usual recovery. Thus, in United States Nat. Bank of Denver v. Industrial Comm., 128 Colo. 417, 262 P.2d 731 (1953), the claimants' mother and father, both of whom were employed and contributed their earnings to the support of the family, were killed in the same accident. It was held that in view of the statutory presumption of the dependency of a child on its parents, the claimants were entitled to an award for each death. A similar result was reached in State ex rel. Olsen v. Industrial Comm., 9 Ohio St.2d 47, 223 N.E.2d 362 (1967).

2. It has been held that the statutory creation of a conclusive presumption of dependency of a surviving wife is within the power of the legislature. State ex rel. London & Lancashire Indemnity Co. v. District Ct., 139 Minn. 409, 166 N.W. 772 (1918). The same result has been reached with respect to a conclusive presumption of dependency of children. Shahan v. Beasley Hot Shot Service, Inc., 91 N.M. 462, 575 P.2d 1347 (1978). Prior to 1980, a number of state workers' compensation acts created a conclusive presumption of dependency as to widows but required widowers to prove actual dependency. The U.S. Supreme Court in Wengler v. Druggists Mutual Insurance Co., 446 U.S. 142, 100 S.Ct. 1540, 64 L.Ed.2d 107 (1980), held such a provision of the Missouri Statute to be unconstitutional as prohibited gender-based discrimination under the Equal Protection Clause of the Fourteenth Amendment. The court, in essence, left it to the states to

determine whether the violation should be remedied by extending the conclusive presumption of dependency to widowers or by removing such presumption for widows. Both approaches have been followed by the states.

3. As to persons not presumed to be dependent, questions often arise as to what constitutes dependency. How great must the reliance of the claimant be upon the deceased employee? The principal case reflects the rule in most states that dependency does not mean destitution or poverty in the sense that the survivor would have been on the welfare rolls without the financial help of the decedent. It means the survivor was receiving financial aid from the decedent and relied on that support in maintaining the usual standard of living; see also, Lineal Industries v. W.C.A.B., 542 Pa. 595, 669 A.2d 329 (1995) (the test for dependency of parents is "[I]f contributions of the deceased child were necessary to maintain the parents in an established standard of living"; monthly expenditures must be reasonable given the circumstances as of the date of child's death; whether a particular debt of parent's is reasonable is determined by the life situation at time debt was incurred); Chevron USA, Inc. v. W.C.A.B., 19 Cal.4th 1182, 81 Cal.Rptr.2d 521, 969 P.2d 613 (1999) (question of dependency, for purposes of determining the individual's entitlement to death benefits, does not turn on whether the individual relied on the decedent for life's necessities, but rather, whether the individual looked to the contributions of the decedent for support according to his or her accustomed mode of living; to substantiate partial dependency, the claimant must prove the actual dollar amount annually devoted by the decedent to the community and to the spouse's support); Henley v. Tan Co., 140 S.W.3d 195 (Mo.Ct.App.2004) (decedent and her daughter bought a home together; at the time of purchase, they agreed to a division of the living expenses; as part of the agreement, decedent paid for her granddaughters' orthodontia, school supplies and clothing; held, granddaughters awarded death benefits because they established dependence upon decedent for at least a part of their support and maintenance.); Wyoming Valley Health Care Systems v. W.C.A.B., 921 A.2d 91 (Pa.Cmwlth. 2007) (In the context of a workers' compensation claim, the test of dependency is whether or not the child's earnings were needed to provide the parents with some of the ordinary necessities of life suitable for persons in their class and position and that the parents were, consequently, dependent to some extent upon the child at the time of the accident causing the death); Russell v. House of Raeford Farms of Louisiana, Inc., 968 So.2d 919 (La.App. 2 Cir. 2007) (claimant must prove that the decedent was actually making contributions at the time of his death and that the claimant was either totally or partially dependent on the contributions; the claimant does not have to show that he would have lacked the necessities of life without the support, only that he relied upon it to maintain his accustomed standard of living); Sifford v. Sifford, 58 Va. App. 722, 716 S.E.2d 128 (2011) (claimant and decedent had executed a separation agreement; in lieu of child support, husband paid household expenses; after husband's work-related death, wife sought death benefits; held, she established actual dependence upon her estranged husband's contributions for reasonable necessaries consistent with

her station in life); and see Oil Transport v. Jordan, 22 Va.App. 633, 472 S.E.2d 291 (1996) (parent who has only enough resources for bare survival is "financially vulnerable" and considered destitute by code § 65.2–515(A)(4) and, thus conclusively presumed to be wholly dependent for support upon deceased employee; here, however, claimant failed to establish dependency, either actual or as a result of being financially vulnerable). As to expectation of support, see Maryland House of Correction v. Jenkins, 228 Md. 146, 178 A.2d 892 (1962) (decedent was a prisoner at the time of death; had contributed to claimant's support prior to incarceration and expected to do so after release; death benefits granted); but see, Vice v. Advantage Waste Services, Inc., 298 S.W.3d 145 (Mo. 2009) (decedent had lived away from home for 16 months before his death; he told his mother he would start contributing $100 a month, in two monthly installments, towards her expenses; after making one $50 payment decedent suffered fatal work injury; held, a one-time payment to help with a cell phone bill is not sufficient proof of dependency).

As to the effect of claimant's other means of support, many cases in which the survivor had some income from sources other than the deceased still found a state of dependency had existed. Zelizer v. Prospect Inn, 28 A.D.2d 1034, 283 N.Y.S.2d 736 (1967) (parents of college student held dependent on him though father was employed); Paul Spellman v. Spellman, 103 So.2d 661 (Fla.App.1958) (deceased and two working sisters lived with mother and deceased made regular contributions to the "family pot"). But see, Terrinoni v. Westward Ho!, 418 So.2d 1143 (Fla.App.1982) (mother held dependent upon son at time of death; three months after son's death, mother received $155,000 from a combination of sources; held no longer dependent); Compare Carroll Steel Erectors v. Alderman, 599 So.2d 181 (Fla.App. 1 Dist.1992) (receipt of $70,000 life insurance proceeds did not terminate dependency); but see Federico v. Industrial Comm. of Arizona, 186 Ariz. 382, 923 P.2d 848 (1996) (a parent is entitled to death benefits only during the period of dependency; mother's dependency ceased when she received $200,000 as beneficiary of son's life insurance policy); Miller & Long Co. of Virginia, Inc. v. Frye, 215 Va. 591, 212 S.E.2d 258 (1975) (decedent was one of nine children, lived with his parents, received food, housing and the use of telephone and car; contributed about $67 out of his $110 weekly wages to help pay for food, telephone and entertainment of his sisters; his father's net weekly earnings were $396; benefits denied on the ground that this was "a situation of mutual assistance and not one of unilateral reliance."); and see, Sifford, *supra* (claimant wife earned part-time income of $600 a month, increasing to around $1,000 a month just prior to her estranged husband's death [husband and wife had executed a separation agreement]; decedent supported claimant regularly paying all household expenses including mortgage, property taxes, utilities, and all health and car insurance; held, actual dependency established); and Roanoke Belt v. Mroczkowski, 20 Va.App. 60, 455 S.E.2d 267 (1995) (in determining whether mother was destitute and thus presumptively wholly dependent upon deceased son, court held mother's receipt of unemployment benefits were status based not need based and thus had to be considered as part of mother's income).

4. Adults who are not in the categories of persons presumed to be dependent must offer evidence as to why the claimed dependency exists, Gherardi v. Connecticut Co., 92 Conn. 454, 103 A. 668 (1918), and the explanation cannot be simply that the claimant does not like the work available locally. Ferriter's Case, 269 Mass. 267, 168 N.E. 747 (1929). A justifiable explanation may be incapacity to work because of physical or mental illness or deficiency. See Reilly v. Weber Engineering Co., 107 N.J.Super. 254, 258 A.2d 36 (1969); Columbus Mining Co. v. Pelfrey, 237 S.W.2d 847 (Ky.1951); and Currie v. Workmen's Compensation Appeal Board, 102 Pa.Cmwlth. 398, 518 A.2d 348 (1986). Another acceptable explanation is that the decedent's domestic arrangements were sufficient evidence of the dependency of the adult survivor. Steverson v. Struck Constr. Co., 243 S.W.2d 494 (Ky.1951); Milwaukee Casket Co. v. Kimball, 201 Wis. 516, 230 N.W. 627 (1930) (daughter separated then divorced, resided with her father and kept house for him, held a dependent). Inability to find work because of economic depression was held to be sufficient to support a finding of dependency in Northern Hotel Co. v. Industrial Comm., 223 Wis. 297, 270 N.W. 66 (1936). The Longshore and Harbor Workers' Compensation Act as well as most state workers' compensation statutes permit a child 18 or over who is a student, as defined in the statutes, to be considered dependent. 33 U.S.C.A. § 902, paragraphs 14 and 18 (2009). See Death & Permanent Disability Trust v. Anderson, 83 Ark.App. 230, 125 S.W.3d 819 (2003) (decedent's daughter, a full-time college student over 18 years of age, was entitled to death benefits although she did not attend college during summer vacation). See, generally Age of Child as Affecting Dependency, 99 CJS Workers' Compensation § 314 (2013).

5. What significance attaches to the existence or lack of a legal obligation on the part of decedent to support the claimant? In general, in the absence of a statutory requirement, the basis of beneficial status is determined by dependency in fact and not by legal obligation. Leigh Coal Co., Inc. v. Cantrell, 434 S.W.2d 315 (Ky.1968) (brother supported his siblings). In some states, the statute attaches a conclusive presumption of dependency to the legal obligation to support. See, e.g., Holley v. Mississippi Lime Co. of Missouri, 266 S.W.2d 606 (Mo.1954) (affirming an award of compensation to a child under eighteen even though mother had remarried after divorce and her second husband supported the child); and Rocky Mountain Helicopter v. Carter, 652 P.2d 893 (Utah 1982).

In the converse situation, the courts are divided as to whether an unfulfilled legal obligation to support claimant is enough to base a finding of dependency. See, e.g., Ladner v. Mason Mitchell Trucking Co., 434 A.2d 37 (Me.1981) (employee's legal obligation to support the minor children of a prior marriage was not alone sufficient to make the children "dependents"); C.W. Wright Constr. Co., Inc. v. Brannan, 217 Md. 397, 142 A.2d 574 (1958) (decedent separated from wife and made payments for child support for nine of eleven months but for twenty months thereafter made no payments and disappeared; wife divorced him and remarried; compensation for child denied); and Yanofchick v. State Workmen's Ins. Fund, 174 Pa.Super. 182, 100 A.2d 387 (1953) (decedent and wife separated and wife obtained a court order of support; decedent never complied with the order fully but would occasionally send small sums to her, and for more than ten years claimant wife did not try to enforce the court order; compensation denied). Contrast State ex rel. Wright v. Industrial Comm., 141 Ohio St. 187, 47 N.E.2d 209 (1943) (divorce decree obligated father to support child but he never complied with it during his lifetime; dependency is based on the right to support rather than on actual fact of support; child awarded compensation); Snodgrass v. AMF Bowling Center, 1997 WL 343087 (Oh.App. 10 Dist.1997) ("Under the Workers' Compensation Act, dependency is based upon the right to support rather than the actual fact of support. . . . Thus, the fact that [father] Roy, Jr. had not been ordered to provide support, nor had he actually provided support, does not determine whether [son] Eric is entitled to workers' compensation benefits"); and Menard v. Fairchild, 254 Ga. 275, 328 S.E.2d 721 (1985) (dependency under workers' compensation act was not eliminated by previous judicial termination of parental rights; the termination of parental rights " . . . merely terminates the rights and obligations flowing between a parent and a child. They remain parent and child." The statutory presumption of dependency is a status not a dependency based determination).

6. Whether dependency is established as of the date of the accident or as of the date of death can have an outcome determinative effect. See the *Steven Lee Enterprises* case, *infra*; and see, National Corp. For Housing Partnership Meadowood Townhouse, Inc. v. Keller, 353 Md. 171, 725 A.2d 563 (1999) (dependency is to be determined in accordance with the circumstances existing at the time of the accident); Vice, *supra, note 3* (fact of dependency determined at time of injury); Walmart Stores, Inc. v. Holmes, 416 Md. 346, 7 A.3d 13 (2010) (dependency is determined at time of injury rather than time of death). And see note 7, Section 4, *infra*.

7. To establish dependency, the contributions by the decedent must have been something more than occasional irregular gratuities. American Fuel Co. of Utah v. Industrial Comm., 60 Utah 131, 206 P. 786 (1922) (brother occasionally sent sister cash to purchase clothing and other items for school; held dependency not established); Rhoden v. Smith & Decker Electric Co., 107 Ind.App. 152, 23 N.E.2d 306 (1939) (occasional gifts by brother to sister to enable her to dress as did other students at her school; held dependency not established); Fernwood Industries, Inc. v. Mitchell, 219 Miss. 331, 68 So.2d 830 (1953) (deceased's only contributions over a four-year period for support of his illegitimate son consisted of three pairs of pants, a shirt, and now and then a nickel, dime, or quarter; held dependency not established); Lopez v. Schultz & Lindsay Construction Co., 79 N.M. 485, 444 P.2d 996 (1968) (son living at home made one contribution during 1 1/2 month period he worked for employer; parents held not dependent on him;

dissent; compare with principal case); and see to the same effect, Gallegos v. Homestake Mining Co., 97 N.M. 717, 643 P.2d 281 (1982); and see Vice, *supra note 3* (in 2004, while living at home, decedent gave his mother, the claimant, $5,000 for household expenses; decedent moved out of state for the 16 months prior to his death and made no further contributions; shortly before his death decedent said he would begin contributing $50 twice a month for his mother's phone expenses; after one $50 contribution, decedent suffered a fatal work-related injury; held, facts do not support a finding of dependency).

8. Ordinarily, the evidence to prove regular contributions consists of conventional records such as checks, account books, and similar means; although, in sympathetic cases, appellate courts have permitted the administrative body to find dependency on the basis of testimony of the claimant alone with very little substantiation. Thus, in Bridges v. Merritt–Chapman and Scott Corp., 11 A.D.2d 854, 203 N.Y.S.2d 132 (1960), the claimant testified that her son sent her money from time to time and that it came by check and money order "although she was vague as to the times and amounts." The president of her bank stated that he knew that she received money from her son. The court sustained a finding of dependency. Contrast, *Oil Transport v. Jordan*, *supra*, note 3 (mother "produced no tax returns, no documentation of bills being paid by her son, nor any other tangible objective evidence" and, consequently, failed to prove that she had been dependent upon her son).

A. PARTIAL DEPENDENCY

Although the receipt of income other than the contributions of the decedent may not completely negate the existence of dependency, it may change the case from one of "total dependency" to one of "partial dependency." Partial dependency is said to exist "when the dependent receives less than all of his support from the deceased employee." Schneider, Workmen's Compensation Text, vol. 9, p. 21, sec. 1906(b), Thomas Law Book Co. (1973). Rose v. Paper Mills Trucking Co., 47 Mich.App. 1, 209 N.W.2d 305 (1973) granted only partial dependency to a surviving child who was receiving $105 per month social security benefits at the time his stepfather was killed. His mother was saving these payments for his education. The court held that any substantial and regular income from any source other than the decedent will in most cases bar a finding of total dependency. Similarly, Mario Anello & Sons, Inc. v. Dunn, 217 Md. 177, 141 A.2d 731 (1958) awarded only partial dependency benefits to a widow who was employed and earning about $30 per week at the time of the decedent's death. The decedent had earned $90 per week and the two pooled their money and used it to pay their bills.

The determination that a survivor's dependency is partial rather than total will affect the amount of compensation awarded. The methods by which the different states compute compensation for partial dependency vary. Some states award the part of a total dependency award that is proportional to the percentage that the decedent's contribution bore to the decedent's total earnings; thus if the decedent contributed one-half of earnings, the partial dependent would get one-half of the amount of a total dependency award. West's Ann. Ind. Code § 22–3–3–18(d) (2013). In some states the amount of a partial award is related to the proportion that decedent's contribution bore to the total income of the dependent; thus if the dependent had a total income of $100 per month of which the deceased contributed $25, the claimant would be entitled to one-fourth of the amount of a total dependency award. Minn.Stats.Ann. § 176.111, subd. 17 (2013). Some states delegate broad discretion to workers' compensation administrators in the determination of the amounts of partial dependency awards. See, e.g., West's Wis.Stats.Ann. § 102.48 (2013):

> " . . . (2) In all other cases the death benefit shall be such sum as the department shall determine to represent fairly and justly the aid to support which the dependent might reasonably have anticipated from the deceased employee but for the injury."

3. "WIDOW" "WIDOWER" "CHILD" "MEMBER OF THE FAMILY"

SPALDING COUNTY COMMISSIONERS V. TARVER

Court of Appeals of Georgia, 1983.
167 Ga.App. 661, 307 S.E.2d 58.

CARLEY, JUDGE.

On November 17, 1963, James Tarver married Mary Tarver. This ceremonial marriage ended by divorce on September 17, 1964. Nine days later, on September 26, 1964, James Tarver entered into a ceremonial marriage with Patricia Jo Tarver. On April 3, 1966, while James Tarver was ostensibly married to Patricia Jo Tarver, a child, Barry Tarver, was born to Mary Tarver and James Tarver. James Tarver and Patricia Jo Tarver were divorced in 1968 and remarried in 1969. In April of 1974, Patricia Jo Tarver and James Tarver were again divorced. Subsequently, James Tarver married and divorced again. Thereafter, in January of 1976, James Tarver married Revia Tarver and this marriage also ended in divorce on April 26, 1979.[1]

[James Tarver, a Spalding County Deputy Sheriff, on December 24, 1980, while in the course of his employment with Spalding County, was

[1] Editor's Note: At the time of death, decedent was living with Revia, who claimed their relationship constituted a common law marriage (Brief for Appellant at 2–3, Tarver v. Martin, 175 Ga.App. 689, 334 S.E.2d 18) (1985).

struck and killed by a truck driven by Mark Martin, a third-party tortfeasor. A wrongful death action was brought against Martin and his employer. In that action, the plaintiffs were two of Tarver's sons[2] and two women alleging they were his widow—Mary Tarver and Revia Tarver. The trial court joined all plaintiffs in order to allow the jury to determine the proper party. The plaintiffs sought immediate review. The Georgia Court of Appeals accepted the interlocutory appeal and held that the trial court should have determined the proper party plaintiff(s) by declaratory judgment because if such were left to the jury the decedent's colorful marital history would have a prejudicial effect on their deliberations. Tarver v. Martin, 175 Ga.App. 689, 334 S.E.2d 18 (1985).]

Three separate [workers' compensation] claims were made for dependency benefits pursuant to OCGA § 4–9–13 (Code Ann. § 114–414).

At the time of the hearing, one claimant [Mary Tarver as common law wife of James] was dismissed as a party.[3] The two remaining individuals making claims for dependency benefits were: Revia Tarver, who was claiming entitlement as the alleged common law wife of James Tarver at the time of his death, and Mary Tarver, acting solely as appointed guardian of Barry Tarver, the minor child of James Tarver. The administrative law judge awarded compensation benefits to Barry Tarver and denied the claim of Revia Tarver. The award was premised upon the finding that, prior to James Tarver's ceremonial marriage to Patricia Jo on September 26, 1964, James Tarver and Mary entered into a common law marriage. The administrative law judge further found that because the common law marriage created between James and Mary Tarver was never dissolved by divorce, all subsequent marriages entered into by James Tarver were not valid, including the common law marriage with Revia Tarver. A de novo hearing was held before the full Board and the award of the administrative law judge was adopted and affirmed with minor modifications.

On appeal, the superior court found there was no evidence to support the finding of the existence of a common law marriage between James Tarver and Mary Tarver. The case was remanded for additional findings concerning the existence of such a common law marriage. This court granted a discretionary appeal. * * * [T]he Spalding County Commissioners appeal from the order of the superior court remanding the case to the Board of Workers' Compensation.

---

[2] Editor's Note: James M. Tarver, Jr. and Jeffrey Tarver, were born during James and Patricia Jo Tarver's first marriage of May 27, 1954. Both were over 18 years of age at decedent's death and did not claim workers' compensation dependency benefits. (Brief for Appellant at 2, Spalding County Commissioners v. Tarver, 167 Ga.App. 661, 307 S.E.2d 58) (1983).

[3] Editor's Note: At time of death, decedent was living apart from Mary, who was not actually dependent upon him and thus not entitled to dependency benefits under Georgia's Workers' Compensation Act, O.C.G.A. § 34–9–13 (Brief for Appellant at 2, Spalding County Commissioners v. Tarver, 167 Ga.App. 661, 307 S.E.2d 58) (1983).

* * *

OCGA § 34–9–105(a) (Code Ann. § 114–710) provides, in relevant part, that an award of the State Board of Workers' Compensation "shall be conclusive and binding as to all questions of fact." Neither the superior court nor the Court of Appeals has any authority to substitute itself as the fact-finding body in lieu of the Board of Workers' Compensation. "Even though the evidence is conflicting, or not altogether complete and satisfactory, an award must be affirmed if there is any evidence to support it." Depart. of Public Safety v. Rodgers, 149 Ga.App. 683, 255 S.E.2d 139 (1979). There is evidence in the instant case which would support the finding that a common law marriage was created between James and Mary Tarver subsequent to the entry of their divorce decree on September 17, 1964, and prior to James Tarver's marriage to Patricia Jo Tarver nine days later, on September 26, 1964. There is some evidence that, during this period, the deceased and Mary Tarver mutually agreed to be husband and wife, that they held themselves out as such, and that there was a consummation of that relationship. Askew v. Dupree, 30 Ga. 173, 178 (1860). Prior to the entry of the divorce decree on September 17, 1964, Mary Tarver moved into her sister's apartment. Also prior to September 17, 1964, James Tarver informed Mary that he had stopped the divorce proceedings, and he then moved his clothes and possessions into the apartment with Mary. Mary Tarver testified that subsequent to the entry of the divorce decree, of which she had no knowledge, she and the deceased continued to share a room in her sister's apartment, shared the same bed, and held themselves out as man and wife. Mary Tarver's sister testified that at all times when Mary and the deceased were living in the apartment with her, they held themselves out as man and wife, and, in fact, she did not even know that a divorce had been obtained during that time. When James Tarver did inform Mary of the divorce, he told her that a lawyer had pressed him to complete the case and that he had made the divorce between them final, but told her "that we were still married, it didn't make no difference." Several other witnesses testified that at all times during the period in question Mary Tarver and the deceased held themselves out as man and wife. "While a proven ceremonial marriage will prevail over a presumption of marriage founded on cohabitation and repute, yet such a ceremonial marriage will not prevail over a properly proven previous common-law marriage." Carter v. Graves, 206 Ga. 234, 56 S.E.2d 917 (1949). The evidence was sufficient to support a finding of a common law marriage. See Kickasola v. Jim Wallace Oil Co., 144 Ga.App. 758(1), 242 S.E.2d 483 (1978).

Accordingly, the superior court erred in finding that there was no evidence to support the finding of the Workers' Compensation Board that a common law marriage between Mary and James Tarver had been created but never terminated by divorce, and that, therefore, all subsequent marriages entered into by James Tarver were invalid, including the alleged common law marriage to Revia Tarver.

* * *

Judgment * * * reversed.

NOTES

1. Courts ordinarily interpret the terms "wife," "widow," "husband," and "widower" or "child" as used in the workers' compensation statutes in light of the local domestic relations law. This approach has not escaped criticism. In Albina Engine and Machine Works v. O'Leary, 328 F.2d 877, 879 (9th Cir.1964) the court said, "The application of state domestic relations law, developed in other contexts, to the solution of problems under workmen's compensation statutes, produces results which at best have only a fortuitous relation to the remedial purposes of the compensation acts, and often are in direct conflict with them. When the state law does provide a definition of marital status deliberately shaped to compensation act purposes alone, there is no reason why that definition should not be applied under the federal statute in preference to one drawn from the state's domestic relations law."

Is the Albina Engine court correct? Do the objectives of domestic relations law differ from those of workers' compensation law in such ways as to necessitate distinct definitions for central terms such as "marital status?" Is the same true for statutory terms such as "child," "widow," "widower" and "member of the family?" In Banegas v. State Indus. Ins. System, 117 Nev. 222, 19 P.3d 245 (2001), the court denied death benefits to a woman who was cohabiting but not married to the decedent. The court reasoned that because the legislature repudiated a liberal reading of the Nevada Workers' Compensation Act, the term "wife" or "spouse" cannot be read to include a putative or common law wife.

2. As illustrated by the *Spalding* case, some involved situations have come before the courts where the lives of the decedent and intermittent domestic helpmates have been uninhibited and unconventional. See, for example, Mims v. Hardware Mut. Cas. Co., 82 Ga.App. 210, 60 S.E.2d 501 (1950), in which claimant, at the time she married the decedent, was already married to X, who was already married to A, who was already married to H, no divorce having been previously secured by any of the parties at the time that they married each other. The court found the key to the puzzle in the fact that at the time A married H, she (A) was only twelve years old; hence her marriage to H was invalid and her later marriage to X was valid, thus making X's marriage to claimant invalid and claimant's marriage to the decedent valid, with the result that claimant could be allowed compensation as a widow. See also, Ritchie v. Katy Coal Co., 313 Ky. 310, 231 S.W.2d 57 (1950) (Bertha, wife of decedent, was given dependency benefits as was Lonnie who had entered into a bigamous marriage with decedent).

In cases of alleged bigamous marriages, the courts sometimes resort to the presumption that the last marriage is the legal one. See generally Keefe, Annotation, Presumption as to Validity of Second Marriage, 14 A.L.R.2d 7 (originally published in 1950, electronically updated as of 2011). Denson v. C.R. Fish Grading Co., Inc., 28 N.C.App. 129, 220 S.E.2d 217 (1975) (burden of proof was on the first wife to produce evidence of the invalidity of the second marriage. Mere proof that the first wife had not obtained a divorce and that first wife was never served with papers of divorce proceeding was not sufficient to overcome the presumption of validity of the second marriage); And, to the same effect, see In re Estate of Hanner, 146 N.C.App. 733, 554 S.E.2d 673 (2001); Newburgh v. Arrigo, 88 N.J. 529, 538, 443 A.2d 1031 (1982) (" . . . irrespective of the factual context in which the issue may arise, the last of two or more marriages is presumptively valid. The presumption . . . may be overcome only by clear and convincing evidence that (1) there was a prior marriage (2) the prior marriage was valid, and (3) the prior marriage was not terminated by death or divorce before the latest marriage."); see also, Estate of Allen, 738 P.2d 142 (Okla.1987) (wife left husband and, without divorcing him, established a common law marriage with another man; after first husband died, she filed for death benefits as his widow; held, ". . . appellee is estopped from asserting her continual marital status with the decedent . . . if this court . . . allow[ed] appellee to participate in decedent's estate, this would prejudice those who are rightfully entitled to share in the estate. Because of her previous conduct, appellee should have no right to share in the estate.").

The presumption can be rebutted, however, by appropriate evidence. See, e.g., Metropolitan Life Insurance Co. v. Jackson, 896 F.Supp. 318 (S.D.N.Y.1995) ("Under New York law, the presumption in favor of a second marriage is rebutted when diligent record searches, in the counties where both parties to the first marriage resided, fail to show evidence of the dissolution of the first marriage.") and DeGeorge v. American Airlines, Inc., 338 F. Appx. 15 (C.A. 2 (N.Y.) 2009); See also, Daniels v. The Retirement Board of the Policeman's Annuity and Benefit Fund, 106 Ill.App.3d 412, 62 Ill.Dec. 304, 435 N.E.2d 1276 (1982); and 29 Am. Jur.2d Evidence § 238 Strength and Effect of Presumption and § 239 Rebutting the Presumption (current through August 2013).

3. Where the domestic arrangements in which claimant was involved with the decedent were actually illicit but this aspect of the relationship was not known to claimant, the court may give weight to the claimant's good faith and allow an award to claimant as widow or widower or as a dependent "member of the family." Dawson v. Hatfield Wire & Cable Co., 59 N.J. 190, 280 A.2d 173 (1971) (good discussion of the issue; court noted, "[claimant] entered into relationship with decedent in entire good faith....her bona fides is unquestioned;" the relationship began with a ceremonial marriage and lasted 16 years and was unchallenged during that time; held, compensation awarded); see also Parkinson v. J. & S. Tool Co., 64 N.J. 159, 313 A.2d 609 (1974) (claimant was a de facto spouse and qualified as a dependent); and see

Burton v. Chater, 1996 WL 310299 (E.D.Ark.1996) (state law holds a person who goes through a ceremonial marriage and lives with another in good faith belief that the marriage is valid is "a putative spouse with all the rights of a legal spouse." But if good faith is not found, the individual will not be accorded the status of a putative spouse and will not have the legal rights thereof); and Visconti v. Secretary of Health, Education and Welfare, 374 F.Supp. 1272 (W.D.Pa.1974), affd. 556 F.2d 570 (3d Cir.1977) (benefits will be awarded to a "good faith" widow unless, if at the time of her application, another person has filed for benefits and that other person is (or is deemed to be) the widow of the decedent). See Social Security Act, 42 U.S.C. § 416(h)(1)(A)(i) and (B)(i) (2012).

If the arrangements and conduct of the parties resulted in a valid common law marriage, the survivor's claim as surviving spouse is valid. In addition to the principal case see Parker v. 36 South Oxford St., Inc., 28 A.D.2d 1031, 283 N.Y.S.2d 700 (1967). If, however, it appears that claimant was aware of the unlawful nature of the cohabitation, and no common law marriage is established or recognized, most courts deny compensation to the survivor in any capacity. Powell v. State Compensation Ins. Fund, 496 F.2d 1248 (9th Cir.1974), certiorari denied 419 U.S. 1032, 95 S.Ct. 514, 42 L.Ed.2d 307 (1974); Reichert v. Sunshine Mining Co., 95 Idaho 647, 516 P.2d 704 (1973); Tatum v. Tatum, 736 P.2d 506 (Okl.1982), rehearing denied 736 P.2d 506 (Okl.1982); and In re Bryan, 76 P.3d 653 (Okla.2003); In McDonald v. Kelly Coal Co., 335 Mich. 325, 55 N.W.2d 851 (1952) the Michigan Supreme Court stated: "Public policy does not sanction the payment of compensation arising out of a meretricious cohabitation." Contrast West v. Barton–Malow Co., 394 Mich. 334, 230 N.W.2d 545 (1975) which awarded compensation to a claimant who had lived with decedent for 13 years and held herself out as his wife although during that time she was legally married to another man. The court held "[s]he did bear to Clarence West the relationship of a wife for the 13 years preceding his untimely death. During those years plaintiff was responsible for maintaining their household while the deceased undertook the responsibility for furnishing them both with monetary support." *West* distinguished *McDonald* on the ground that the *McDonald* relationship was "of short duration based on meretricious cohabitation."

West is consistent with the cases that take the position that "dependency" has no moral attributes or requisites but should be found in accordance with the facts. See, e.g., Henderson v. Travelers Ins. Co., 354 So.2d 1031 (La.1978) (the Court cited Professor Wex Malone's authoritative treatise in which he argued that the denial of compensation to the concubine because of moral turpitude "is more moralistic than it is sound. No other claimant need prove his moral worthiness so long as he or she is dependent. . . . The social need for compensation here is as great. . . ."; held, compensation awarded); Winn v. Thompson–Hayward Chemical Co., 522 So.2d 137 (La.App.1988); Kendall v. Housing Authority of Baltimore City, 196 Md. 370, 76 A.2d 767 (1950) ("The Workmen's Compensation Act is not a code of morals, but is a practical device for the economic protection of employees and those dependent upon them."); and Russell v. Johnson, 220 Ind. 649, 46 N.E.2d 219 (1943) (Neither statute nor public policy excludes a woman who has shared an adulterous relationship with a man from receiving compensation as his dependent.) In Burgess Constr. Co. v. Lindley, 504 P.2d 1023 (Ak.1972) the concurring opinion suggests that the distinction between a "legal wife" and one sharing an illicit relationship is an unconstitutional denial of equal protection of law.

RANNEY V. WHITEWATER ENGINEERING

Supreme Court of Alaska, 2005.
122 P.3d 214.

BRYNER, CHIEF JUSTICE.

I. INTRODUCTION

The Alaska Workers' Compensation Act provides that when an employee suffers a work-related death, the employee's surviving widow or widower is eligible for death benefits. When Sharon Ranney sought death benefits after the work-related death of her long-term partner, Gary Stone, the Alaska Workers' Compensation Board ruled that she was not eligible for benefits because she and Stone had never been married. Ranney challenges this ruling, arguing that the board misinterpreted the workers' compensation act and violated her rights to privacy and equal protection under the Alaska Constitution. We affirm the board's decision, holding that the decision correctly interpreted the act and did not deprive Ranney of her constitutional rights, since denying spousal death benefits to Ranney did not substantially burden her freedom to have an unmarried intimate relationship with Stone and was fairly and substantially related to the act's goal of providing quick, efficient, fair, and predictable benefits to families of deceased workers at a reasonable cost to employers.[1]

II. FACTS AND PROCEEDINGS

Sharon Ranney and Gary Stone became romantically involved in the spring of 1995 and moved in together that fall. Although Stone and Ranney were never legally married, they lived together as a couple until Gary Stone's death in April 1999.

While together they shared a joint checking account. They were jointly listed in the Cordova telephone book. And they purchased various kinds of machinery together—a small sawmill, a crane, and a truck. Stone also purchased a life-insurance policy and named Ranney the primary beneficiary. Although Ranney worked off and on throughout their relationship, she depended on Stone's income to maintain her standard of living. Ranney submitted many affidavits from friends

---

1 Editor's Note: Some footnotes have been omitted, and others have been re-numbered.

attesting to the couple's intent to get married. And Ranney testified that Stone bought her a wedding ring in 1997 and that he formally proposed to her in March of 1999.

In April 1999 Stone was killed in a work-related accident while employed by Whitewater Engineering. Ranney then filed a claim for death benefits as Stone's "unmarried spouse." Whitewater and its insurer, Fremont Compensation/Cambridge Integrated Services Group, controverted Ranney's claim on the ground that she was never Stone's wife and that she was therefore not entitled to benefits under the act.

In addressing Ranney's claim, the Alaska Workers' Compensation Board noted that AS 23.30.215 provides for the payment of death benefits to the "widow or widower or a child or children of the deceased." Because the act defines "widow" to include "only the decedent's wife living with or dependent for support upon the decedent at the time of death, or living apart for justifiable cause or by reason of the decedent's desertion at such a time," [AS 23.30.395 (33)] the board reasoned that Ranney would qualify as "the decedent's wife" only if she had actually been married to Stone. Since Ranney had never married Stone, the board concluded that she was ineligible for benefits as his "wife."

After appealing to the superior court, which affirmed the board's decision, Ranney filed this appeal.

III. DISCUSSION

On appeal, Ranney argues that the unmarried partners of deceased employees are eligible to receive death benefits under the workers' compensation act. Moreover, if the act does not cover unmarried but committed relationships like hers and Stone's, Ranney asserts, it violates her rights to privacy and equal protection under the Alaska Constitution.

A. Standard of Review

In an appeal from a decision entered by the superior court as an intermediate court of appeal in a workers' compensation case, "we independently review and directly scrutinize the merits of the board's decision." [Alyeska Pipeline Serv. Co. v. DeShong, 77 P.3d 1227, 1231 (Alaska 2003)]. Determining the proper meaning of the act in this case requires us to interpret the words "widow" and "married"; we review an agency's interpretation of non-technical statutory terms such as these under the substitution of judgment standard. (citation omitted). Whether the act violates the Alaska Constitution presents a legal question and does not involve agency expertise. We use our independent judgment to review constitutional questions. (citation omitted).

B. The Act's Express Language

Ranney argues that, as Stone's "[u]nmarried, [d]ependent [w]idow," she is entitled to death benefits under the Alaska Workers' Compensation Act. Whitewater responds that because Ranney was never married to Stone, she fails to qualify as his "widow," and so cannot properly claim benefits under the act.

When interpreting a statute, "we consider its language, its purpose, and its legislative history, in an attempt to 'give effect to the legislature's intent.'" (citations omitted). Although "[w]e have rejected a mechanical application of the plain meaning rule," we have placed a heavy burden on parties who urge us to adopt an interpretation that appears contrary to a statute's plain language. (citation omitted).

The workers' compensation act specifies that where a work-related injury causes an employee's death, death benefits are payable to "a widow or widower or a child or children of the deceased." [AS 23.30.215(a)(2)]. If there is no widow or widower and there are no children, then benefits must be paid to specified members of the extended family. [AS 23.30.215(a)(4)].

The act defines "widow" as "only the decedent's wife living with or dependent for support upon the decedent at the time of death, or living apart for justifiable cause or by reason of the decedent's desertion at such a time." [AS 23.30.395(33)] The act does not define "wife," but does provide that " 'married' includes a person who is divorced but is required by the decree of divorce to contribute to the support of the former spouse." [AS 23.30.395(19)].

Ranney contends that the act's definition of "wife" could plausibly be read to include unmarried cohabitants, so that they would fall within the definition of "widow."

We disagree. The Alaska legislature has directed that [w]ords and phrases shall be construed . . . according to their common and approved usage. Technical words and phrases and those which have acquired a peculiar and appropriate meaning, whether by legislative definition or otherwise, shall be construed according to the peculiar and appropriate meaning. [AS 01.10.040(a); remainder of citation omitted].

Because "wife" has not been defined statutorily and has no technical meaning in the present context, we look to common usage, where the word ordinarily refers to a married woman. [citations omitted]. "Marriage" has been defined by statute. The Alaska Marriage Code provides:

(a) Marriage is a civil contract entered into by one man and one woman that requires both a license and solemnization.

. . . .

(b) A person may not be joined in marriage in this state until a license has been obtained for that purpose as provided in this chapter. A marriage performed in this state is not valid without solemnization as provided in this chapter. [AS 25.05.011].

We have previously held that this definition of marriage does not recognize common law marriage. [Harrelson v. Harrelson, 932 P.2d 247, 250 (Alaska 1997)]. Thus, neither common usage nor legislative definition suggests that people in Ranney's position—unmarried cohabitants—should be considered "wives" or "husbands" under the workers' compensation act.

Moreover, the detailed benefits scheme set out in the workers' compensation act suggests that the legislature did not intend to include unmarried cohabitants as beneficiaries. Alaska Statute 23.30.215 provides that if there is a widow or widower and/or children, they are entitled to benefits.[2] If there is no widow or widower and no children, death benefits may go to the employee's parents, grandchildren, brothers, and sisters if they were "dependent upon the deceased at the time of injury." [AS 23.30.215(a)(4)].

Where a statute expressly enumerates the things or persons to which it applies, we often invoke the principle of statutory construction *expressio unius est exclusio alterius*. This principle "establishes the inference that, where certain things are designated in a statute, 'all omissions should be understood as exclusions.'" [citations omitted]. We have indicated that "[t]he case for application of *expressio unius est exclusio alterius* is

---

2 AS 23.30.215 provides in relevant part:

(a) If the injury causes death, the compensation is known as a death benefit and is payable in the following amounts to or for the benefit of the following persons:

. . . .

(2) if there is a widow or widower or a child or children of the deceased, the following percentages of the spendable weekly wages of the deceased:

(A) 80 percent for the widow or widower with no children;

(B) 50 percent for the widow or widower with one child and 40 percent for the child;

(C) 30 percent for the widow or widower with two or more children and 70 percent divided equally among the children;

(D) 100 percent for an only child when there is no widow or widower;

(E) 100 percent, divided equally, if there are two or more children and no widow or widower;

. . . .

(4) if there is no widow or widower or child or children, then for the support of father, mother, grandchildren, brothers and sisters, if dependent upon the deceased at the time of injury, 42 percent of the spendable weekly wage of the deceased to such beneficiaries, share and share alike, not to exceed $20,000 in the aggregate;

(5) $5,000 to a surviving widow or widower, or equally divided among surviving children of the deceased if there is no widow or widower.

particularly compelling, where . . . the scheme is purely statutory and without a basis in the common law." [citation omitted]. In the context of the workers' compensation act, which creates a detailed and complicated scheme for requiring employers to provide support to some surviving members of the employee's family, it is appropriate to apply this canon of interpretation. Because the act includes a detailed list of beneficiaries, the failure to include unmarried cohabitants suggests their exclusion.

In addition, as Whitewater points out, the act includes in its definition of "child," a "child in relation to whom the deceased employee stood in loco parentis for at least one year before the time of injury." [AS 23.30.395(6)]. And it defines "married" to include "a person who is divorced but is required by the decree of divorce to contribute to the support of the former spouse." [AS 23.30.395(19)]. The legislature's expansion of these definitions shows that where the legislature intended to expand the meanings of commonly understood words, it did so expressly.

Ranney nonetheless contends that "[t]he concept of 'family' is changing," so that she should be included within the definition of family. She notes that state law in many instances includes unmarried persons within its definition of spouse. She cites Alaska's regulations for adult public assistance, which include within the definition of spouse "unmarried persons who live together and hold themselves out to the community as husband and wife." [7 Alaska Adm. Code (AAC0 40.240(b)(2)]. And she points to similar language in Alaska's childcare assistance program and its disaster relief regulations. [citations omitted]. She argues that these programs are "intended to prevent people from going hungry or homeless." Because "[w]orkers' compensation death benefits serve a very similar purpose," she contends, a similarly broad definition of family should be read into the workers' compensation act.

But as Whitewater correctly observes in response, under the regulations cited by Ranney the non-traditional family members qualify precisely "because the regulations expressly allow them to do so." At most, these regulations illustrate that agencies are capable of expanding the meanings of common terms when they intend to do so. It may be true that the act's purpose is analogous to the purposes of the various public assistance programs cited by Ranney. But where those programs include non-traditional family members, they do so expressly. Here if the legislature had intended to include unmarried cohabitants in its definition of "widow," it similarly could have done so expressly. Accordingly, it appears that the legislature's intent, as manifested in the statutory language, was to limit beneficiaries to those expressly enumerated in the statute. As Stone's unmarried cohabiting partner, Ranney is not eligible for death benefits under the act's language.

Despite the express language of the statute, Ranney contends that she should be deemed eligible for benefits under our ruling in *Burgess Construction Co. v. Lindley*. [citation omitted].

In *Lindley*, the unmarried partner of a construction worker sought workers' compensation benefits when her partner was killed on the job. Jeanne Lindley and the deceased worker, Ronald Lindley, were originally married but had gotten divorced and then later resumed living together. Their divorce decree required Ronald to contribute to Jeanne's support. The construction company argued that because the Lindleys were divorced, Jeanne was not a "surviving wife" entitled to death benefits under the act.

To determine whether Jeanne Lindley was a "surviving wife" we examined the act's language. We observed that it defined "married" to include "a person who is divorced but is required by the decree of divorce to contribute to the support of his former wife." And we noted that "widow" included "the decedent's wife living with or dependent for support upon him at the time of his death." These definitions led us to conclude that the decedent, though divorced, was "married" for the purpose of the Workmen's Compensation Act, for the divorce decree required him to contribute to appellee's support. It follows that under the Act appellee would be regarded as his "surviving wife."

We then determined that because she was his wife for purposes of the statute, and because she was living with him and was dependent upon him for her support, Jeanne Lindley qualified as Ronald Lindley's widow. We therefore held that Jeanne Lindley was entitled to benefits.

Ranney argues that *Lindley* stands for the proposition that an unmarried dependent live-in partner is a spouse for purposes of the act; to hold otherwise, Ranney suggests, would frustrate the "liberal humanitarian purposes" of the act.

But Ranney's reliance on *Lindley* is misplaced. To be sure, we described our holding in Lindley as required by the "liberal humanitarian purposes of the Act." But *Lindley* hardly supports Ranney's further contention that "the goal of the [Workers' Compensation Act] is to compensate dependent people, not to compensate dependent people who went through a formal ceremony." *Lindley* did not hold that Jeanne Lindley's dependency alone sufficed to render her eligible for benefits. Instead, it relied primarily on the statutory definitions. Under those definitions, Jeanne qualified as being "married" to Ronald Lindley when he died. Consequently, she qualified as his "wife." The definition of widow includes wives who were living with the decedent or who were dependent upon him. Jeanne was both. She therefore qualified as his widow. As his widow, she qualified for benefits. In other words, it was Jeanne's formal, legal relation with Ronald, coupled with her dependency upon him, that qualified her for benefits.

By contrast, Ranney was not, and had never been, married to Stone when he died. And Stone was not legally obligated to support her. Under *Lindley*, then, Ranney does not qualify for benefits.

Ranney further argues that the purpose of the act is to compensate dependents for a worker's death. She insists that in light of this purpose, the distinctions created by the statute between married and unmarried "wives" should be ignored. Yet compensating dependents is not the act's singular purpose.[3] The act's broader purpose is to provide a system of compensation that is "quick, efficient, fair and predictable"—and is not unreasonably expensive for employers. [citation omitted].

As Whitewater points out, allowing unmarried partners to receive benefits would require the board to distinguish between relationships that were sufficiently serious to merit the award of benefits and those that were not. Whitewater also notes that requiring such a fact-intensive inquiry could substantially delay the award of benefits and undermine the quick and predictable award of benefits.

The legislature could have adopted a system that required that each relationship be scrutinized on an individual basis to determine whether death benefits should be granted. But it did not. Instead, it engaged in the traditional legislative practice of line drawing. The legislature apparently determined that the potentially increased precision of requiring an ad hoc decision in all cases would be so administratively costly that the system would better be served by using a more formal rule—in this case requiring marriage—for determining which relationships require the payment of benefits.[4] By adopting marriage as the primary criterion for determining when an intimate partner qualifies for benefits, the legislature has determined that legal marriage is an adequate proxy for the more particularized inquiry concerning whether a relationship is serious enough or the partner is sufficiently dependent to justify awarding benefits.

As with all line drawing, particularly where social welfare legislation is involved, the precise point where the line is drawn may seem arbitrary, and there may be "close cases at the margins." [citation omitted]. But this does not mean that line drawing is impermissible. This kind of line

---

[3] Indeed, dependency alone is not enough under the act to render someone eligible for benefits. For example, cousins and friends are never eligible for benefits. The dependent must be a grandchild, a parent, or a sibling. And even those dependents are only eligible if there is neither a surviving spouse nor any children. AS 23.30.215(a)(4).

[4] In Trombley v. Starr–Wood Cardiac Group, PC, 3 P.3d 916, 923 (Alaska 2000), we noted "the difficulty of assessing the emotional, sexual and financial relationship of cohabiting parties to determine whether their arrangement was the equivalent of a marriage. . . ." (quoting Elden v. Sheldon, 46 Cal.3d 267, 250 Cal.Rptr. 254, 758 P.2d 582, 590 (1988)).

drawing—which involves balancing the benefits of greater precision against its costs and determining how the workers' compensation system can best provide support for workers and their families—is within the legislature's competence. We decline Ranney's invitation to substitute our judgment for the legislature's.

C. Right to Privacy

Ranney alternatively argues that the board's determination that she was ineligible for benefits because she was never married to Stone violates her constitutional right to privacy. Ranney posits that she has a fundamental right "to live with Mr. Stone in a marriage-like relationship without the formality of a civil or religious marriage ceremony." And she argues that "the Board's interpretation of [AS 23.30.215] infringes upon Ms. Ranney's right to privacy because she cannot exercise that right in respect to her intimate relationships without losing her right as a dependent to death benefits under [the statute]."

Article I, section 22 of the Alaska Constitution provides that, "[t]he right of the people to privacy is recognized and shall not be infringed." The right of privacy protects "fundamental rights of personal autonomy," [citation omitted], including a person's right to control his appearance, [citation omitted], a patient's "privacy interest in protecting sensitive personal information from public disclosure," [citation omitted], and a woman's reproductive rights. [citation omitted]. Ranney argues that the right to privacy similarly protects her right to have an unmarried intimate relationship with Stone.

When a party argues that a statutory provision violates the party's right to privacy, we ordinarily balance the importance of the individual right allegedly infringed against the interests of the state. [citation omitted]. Where a fundamental right is infringed, we require the state to articulate a compelling interest and to demonstrate the absence of a less restrictive alternative. In contrast, where the state "interferes with an individual's freedom in an area that is not characterized as fundamental," we require the state to "show a legitimate interest and a close and substantial relationship between its interest and its chosen means of advancing that interest." [citations omitted].

Here, we assume for purposes of our decision that Ranney has a fundamental right to have an unmarried intimate relationship with Stone. But even so, her constitutional claim falls short because the workers' compensation act at most imposes only a minimal burden on the relational freedom asserted by Ranney.

Ranney's privacy argument seems to assume that conferring a benefit on persons who marry necessarily burdens liberty interests of persons who freely choose not to. But the state's decision to provide benefits to people who choose to exercise a constitutional right does not invariably require it to provide equal benefits to those who decline to exercise the right. For example, the state provides free public schooling at state expense. [AS 14.03.080]. But providing these benefits to parents does not require the state to provide matching funds to people who choose not to have children. Nor does the state's failure to do so impose any significant burden on their important privacy interest in choosing not to have children. Similarly, in the present case, the state's decision to provide benefits to married people unquestionably benefits couples who choose to marry; but giving this admittedly one-sided benefit to persons who marry does not in itself equate to imposing a significant burden on those who freely choose not to. Yet apart from relying on the one-sided nature of the benefit, Ranney has failed to explain how her relational rights have been burdened. Nor do we perceive any significant burden. To be sure, our substantive due process clause requires that all laws bear a reasonable relation to a legitimate state purpose. [citation omitted]. But as we explain below in discussing Ranney's equal protection complaint, the challenged legislation easily satisfies that standard. Thus, given Ranney's failure to identify any significant burden on the rights of unmarried couples to pursue committed relationships while choosing not to marry, we find no violation of her right to privacy.

D. Equal Protection

Ranney also argues that the workers' compensation act infringes her right to equal protection under the law. She argues that she is similarly situated to legally married wives: "Ms. Ranney was dependent upon Mr. Stone at the time of his death just like legally married wives are dependent upon their husbands." And she contends that because, unlike legally married wives, "dependents in her situation" are not eligible for benefits, AS 23.30.215 violates the equal protection clause.

We apply a sliding scale to equal protection analysis.

To implement Alaska's . . . equal protection standard, we have adopted a three-step, sliding-scale test that places a progressively greater or lesser burden on the state, depending on the importance of the individual right affected by the disputed classification and the nature of the governmental interests at stake: first, we determine the weight of the individual interest impaired by the classification; second, we examine the importance of the purposes underlying the government's action; and third, we evaluate the means employed to further those goals to determine the closeness of the means-to-end fit. [citation omitted].

We have held that "[w]orkers' compensation benefits are merely an economic interest, and therefore, are entitled only to minimum protection under this court's equal protection analysis." [citation omitted]. Under this level of protection, the state's ends need only be legitimate and the statute's classification must "bear a fair and substantial relationship to the purposes of the Act." [citation omitted].

As we noted above, the act's purpose—to "ensure the quick, efficient, fair and predictable delivery of indemnity and medical benefits to injured workers at a reasonable cost to employers"—is certainly legitimate. [citation omitted]. Ranney nonetheless argues that the state cannot show that the challenged provision bears a fair and substantial relation to the act's purpose, because the Act is not intended to do anything except compensate injured workers and their *dependents* for work-related injuries and deaths. The Act is not intended to encourage marriage or to strengthen any traditional concept of marriage or family—its intent under these circumstances is to compensate dependents of a deceased worker. Given this purpose, Ranney maintains, the distinction between legally-married spouses and unmarried cohabitants is untenable.

Yet even if one purpose of the act is to compensate *dependents* rather than families,[5] Ranney's argument overlooks the fact that the act also serves another, even broader purpose: to provide benefits in a manner that is "quick, efficient, fair, and predictable," at a reasonable cost to the employer. [citation omitted]. The act's spousal benefit substantially furthers this overarching purpose, even if it might fall short in compensating all potential "dependents."

Because the act's spousal death benefit provision bears a close and substantial relationship to furthering a legitimate state interest, it does not violate Ranney's constitutional right to equal protection. The legislature also had to devise a system that was quick, efficient, and predictable and that could provide benefits without unduly burdening employers. As already noted, the legislature could have taken an ad hoc approach. But it could just as reasonably have concluded that such an approach would be slower, less efficient, and less predictable for beneficiaries and unduly expensive for employers. The legislature's reliance on marriage as the determining factor for spousal death benefits thus bears a fair and substantial relationship to the goal of ensuring the "quick, efficient, fair and predictable" delivery of benefits at a reasonable cost. The act's balance between perfect fairness on the one hand, and cost, efficiency, speed, and predictability on the other, does not violate the equal protection clause.

---

[5] Compare Taylor v. Southeast–Harrison Western Corp., 694 P.2d 1160, 1162 (Alaska 1985) (characterizing the goal of the Act as being "to secure guaranteed and expeditious compensation for injured workers and their dependents. . . .") (emphasis added) with Wien Air Alaska v. Arant, 592 P.2d 352, 357 (Alaska 1979) (describing the purpose as "to compensate the victims of work-rated injury for a part of their economic loss, measured by the wage loss to the worker or the surviving family) (emphasis added) (overruled on other grounds by Fairbanks N. Star Borough Sch. Dist. v. Crider, 736 P.2d 770, 775 (Alaska 1987)).

IV. CONCLUSION

For the foregoing reasons, we AFFIRM the decision of the board denying death benefits to Ranney.

NOTES

1. The materials in this chapter preceding *Ranney* have shown that the workers' compensation act of each state must be consulted for a description of the persons eligible to recover workers' compensation death benefits. As *Ranney* demonstrates, some jurisdictions require a legally established marriage in order to recover benefits as a husband/wife or widow/widower. See also, Banegas v. State Indus. Ins. System, 117 Nev. 222, 19 P.3d 245 (2001). Other jurisdictions allow less formal arrangements including common law marriages. See, e.g. the relationships in the *Spalding* case and related notes, *supra*, and see Meeks v. W.C.A.B., 720 A.2d 162 (Pa.Cmwlth., 1998). For a listing of the fifty states and whether or not arrangements other than legal marriage are recognized, see http://www.unmarried.org/legal.information-resources-by-state/ (last visited October 31, 2013).

2. Just two weeks after its decision in *Ranney*, the Alaska Supreme Court rendered its decision in Alaska Civil Liberties Union v. State of Alaska and Municipality of Anchorage, 122 P.3d 781 (Alaska 2005). In that case, public employees with same-sex domestic partners filed an action alleging that the defendants were offering health insurance and other valuable benefits to married employees' spouses which were not offered to unmarried employees' domestic partners. The Court held that despite Alaska's "one man, one woman" definition of marriage, the programs involved had violated the aggrieved employees' rights to equal protection under the Alaska Constitution.

3. Eight years after the *Ranney* and *ACLU* decisions, the issues surrounding Alaska's definition of marriage are winding their way back to the Alaska Supreme Court in the case of Harris v. Millennium Hotel. This time the facts involve an individual seeking workers' compensation death benefits as a result of the work-related death of her same-sex partner. The *Ranney* and *ACLU* decisions will likely be central to the Alaska Court's analysis. Harris v. Millennium Hotel, which follows, is the administrative appeal from the Alaska Workers' Compensation Board's denial of benefits in Fadely and Harris v. Millenium Hotel and New Hampshire Ins. Co., 2013 WL 1179272 (AWCB Case NO. 201116890) (2013).

Harris v. Millennium Hotel

Alaska Workers' Compensation Appeals Commission
Decision No. 183. 2013 WL 3367315 (2013)

KEYES, CHAIR.

1. Introduction.

Appellant, Deborah Harris (Harris), was the same-sex domestic partner of Kerry Fadely (Fadely). At all relevant times, Fadely was employed by the appellee, the Millennium Hotel (Millennium) in Anchorage, as a food and beverage manager. On October 29, 2011, while at work, Fadely was fatally shot by a disgruntled former employee of the hotel whom she had terminated a few days earlier.[1]

Harris submitted a workers' compensation claim dated March 27, 2012, seeking death benefits. Millennium filed an Answer and a Controversion Notice dated May 4, 2012, denying that Harris was entitled to death benefits. The parties stipulated to a set of facts on December 19, 2012. Harris's claim was heard on the written record by the Alaska Workers' Compensation Board (board) on February 26, 2013.

The board issued its decision on March 21, 2013. On the basis of certain provisions of the Alaska Workers' Compensation Act (Act) and a decision of the Alaska Supreme Court (supreme court), *Ranney v. Whitewater Engineering,* 122 P.3d 214 (Alaska 2005), the board denied Harris's claim. The board also declined to consider Harris's constitutional challenges to Alaska law that preclude her from obtaining benefits as a same-sex domestic partner, concluding that it lacked jurisdiction to decide constitutional issues.

Harris appealed the board's decision to the Workers' Compensation Appeals Commission (commission). Acknowledging that the commission, like the board, lacks jurisdiction to decide constitutional issues, the parties have appropriately postured this appeal to preserve for appeal to the supreme court 1) the issue whether Harris is entitled to death benefits, and 2) their constitutional arguments in a forum that has jurisdiction to hear them. The commission affirms the board's denial of death benefits to Harris.

2. Factual background and proceedings.

As mentioned, the facts were stipulated to by the parties. Because they are not disputed and have been succinctly stated in the board's decision, we adopt its recitation of the facts.[2] We have omitted those facts that are not significant to the analysis. On

---

[1] Editor's note: Some footnotes have been omitted and others re-numbered.

[2] The board refers to Harris as the Claimant, Fadely as the Employee, and Millennium as the Employer.

October 29, 2011, Employee, a food and beverage manager at the Millennium Hotel in Anchorage, Alaska, died in a work-related injury.

Claimant contends she was in a same-sex relationship with Employee when Employee died, and was her same-sex domestic partner. Claimant's assertions include: if Alaska law allowed her and Employee to marry, or recognized an out-of-state same-sex marriage certificate, they would have married; Claimant and Employee were in an exclusive, committed, financially interdependent relationship for over a decade by the time of Employee's death in 2011; Claimant and Employee lived for the majority of their ten-year relationship together in Anchorage; they wore matching rings to signify their love and commitment for one another and referred to each other as "partner" or "spouse"; they jointly submitted an Affidavit of Domestic Partnership so Claimant could access health insurance Employee received through a prior employer; had joint credit card accounts; jointly leased an apartment and were looking to jointly purchase a home; and on Facebook, a social media website, Employee listed Claimant as her "spouse" and stated Employee and Claimant were in a domestic partnership. Claimant submitted affidavits from herself, her daughter, and a friend attesting to the couple's committed and financially interdependent relationship. Claimant asserts she was financially dependent upon Employee.

Claimant and Employee were not married to one another when Employee died, and had never been married to one another.

Employee's death occurred in the course and scope of employment.

3. Standard of review.

The commission is to uphold the board's findings of fact if they are supported by substantial evidence in light of the whole record. Substantial evidence is such relevant evidence which a reasonable mind might accept as adequate to support a conclusion. [citation omitted]. The question whether the quantum of evidence is substantial enough to support a conclusion in the contemplation of a reasonable mind is a question of law. [citation omitted]. We exercise our independent judgment when reviewing questions of law and procedure. [AS 23.30.128(b)].

4. Discussion.

a. Harris is not entitled to death benefits.

Under AS 23.30.215(a) (footnote omitted) death benefits are payable to the widow or widower and children of the deceased employee. AS 23.30.395(40) defines "widow" as the decedent's wife; AS 23.30.395(41) defines "widower" as the decedent's husband. Furthermore, AS 25.05.013(b) states: "A same-sex relationship may not be recognized by the state as being entitled to the benefits of marriage." In terms of this statutory law, Harris does not qualify as a widow or widower eligible to receive death benefits.

The supreme court has provided additional case law authority for denying Harris death benefits in *Ranney v. Whitewater Engineering*. In that appeal, a surviving unmarried cohabitant of the deceased employee was denied death benefits.

Based on the foregoing law, Harris cannot be considered married to Fadely, nor is she the widow or widower of Fadely. Therefore, Harris is not entitled to death benefits and Millennium is under no obligation to pay them.

b. The commission does not have jurisdiction to decide constitutional issues.

In a relatively recent decision, the supreme court held that "[administrative agencies do not have jurisdiction to decide issues of constitutional law." [citation omitted]. The commission, like the board, is an administrative agency. [citation omitted]. We have acted in conformity with this restriction on our jurisdiction. [citation omitted]. Accordingly, the commission must decline to hear and decide Harris's constitutional challenges to the Act, including any federal constitutional challenge to Art. I, § 25 of the Alaska Constitution, which reads: "To be valid or recognized in this State, a marriage may exist only between one man and one woman."

5. Conclusion.

We AFFIRM the board's decision insofar as it denies death benefits to Harris.

---

4. The notice of appeal in *Harris* was filed by Appellant with the Alaska Supreme Court in July of 2013. The average time-frame for disposition of a case by the Alaska Supreme Court appears to be about one year and eight months from the date of filing of the notice of appeal. The brief of Appellant, Harris, was filed in the Alaska Supreme Court on October 14, 2013 and can be seen at http://www.lambdalegal.org/in-court/cases/harris-v-millennium-hotel (last visited on November 4, 2013). The brief of Appellees is expected to be filed on or before December 16, 2013. The Appellant's brief relied on, *inter alia*, Alaska Civil Liberties Union v. State of Alaska, *supra*, Notes 2 and 3, and U.S. v. Windsor, *infra*, Notes 8 and 9.

5. The two previous editions of this casebook included opinions from the state of New York involving denials of claims filed by same-sex partners for common law wrongful death damages (Raum v. Restaurant Associates, Inc., 252 A.D.2d 369, 675 N.Y.S.2d 343 (1998)) and workers' compensation death benefits (Langan v. State Farm Fire & Cas., 48 A.D.3d 76, 849 N.Y.S. 2d 105 (2007). Other New York decisions had denied benefits in Langan v. St.

Vincent's Hosp. of N.Y., 25 A.D.3d 90, 802 N.Y.S.2d 476 (2005) (denial of common law wrongful death benefits to same-sex partner); and Valentine v. American Airlines, 17 A.D.3d 38, 791 N.Y.S.2d 217 (2005) (denial of workers' compensation death benefits to same-sex partner). While none of these decisions have been directly overruled, they have lost most of their vitality because the New York legislature in 2011, enacted legislation legalizing same-sex marriages. See N.Y. Dom. Rel. Law Ann. § 10–a (1) and (2), which provides, in part, "A marriage that is otherwise valid shall be valid regardless of whether the parties to the marriage are of the same or different sex."

6. Before the enactment of the 2011 legislation, New York had rendered decisions recognizing the rights of same-sex partners who had legally entered into valid marriages in a jurisdiction which sanctioned them. See Martinez v. County of Monroe, 50 A.D.3d 189, 850 N.Y.S.2d 740 (2008) (marriage of same-sex Canadian citizens was recognized in relation to claims for spousal health benefits); and Lewis v. N.Y. State Dept. of Civil Services, 60 A.D.3d 216, 872 N.Y.S.2d 578 (2009) (held, under N.Y.'s "marriage recognition rule" parties to a valid out-of-state, same-sex marriage were viewed as spouses).

7. On the broader national scene, in 1996, during the Clinton Administration, the federal Defense of Marriage Act (DOMA) was enacted by the United States Congress. See 1 U.S.C. § 7 and 28 U.S.C. § 1738C. This legislation declared that (a) a marriage is a union between a man and a woman, and that (b) no state shall be "required to give effect" to a same-sex union legally entered into in another jurisdiction. In response to the enactment of the federal DOMA, many states enacted their own legislative DOMAs and/or amendments to their state constitutions disallowing either same-sex unions, same-sex marriages or both.

8. In U.S. v. Windsor, 133 S.Ct. 2675, 186 L.Ed.2d 808, 81 U.S.L.W. 4633 (2013), a taxpayer, a New York resident, as surviving spouse of a same-sex marriage (the marriage took place in Ontario, Canada in 2007 and was recognized as valid in New York) was denied the benefit of the federal estate tax spousal deduction because of the definitions of "marriage" and "spouse" contained in the federal Defense of Marriage Act. She sued for a refund of the federal estate taxes paid. The United States Supreme Court granted certiorari and affirmed the lower federal courts' decisions which had held in favor of the taxpayer. The Court held that Section 3 of the federal Defense of Marriage Act (which defined "marriage" as between a man and a woman and a "spouse" as only a person of the opposite sex who was a husband or wife) was unconstitutional. Section 2 of DOMA which allows states to refuse to recognize same-sex marriages performed under the laws of other states was not before the Court.

Justice Kennedy, for the majority, wrote at some length about how, "By history and tradition, the definition and regulation of marriage ... has been treated as being within the authority and realm of the separate states." (133 S.Ct. 2675, at 2689–2690). He noted that while "State laws defining and regulating marriage, of course, must respect the constitutional rights of persons... regulation of domestic relations is an area that has long been regarded as a virtually exclusive province of the states." (133 S.Ct. 2675 at 2691). He continued, "Consistent with this allocation of authority, the Federal Government, through our history, has deferred to state-law policy decisions with respect to domestic relations." (133 S.Ct. 2675, at 2691). And while he pointed to discrete examples of limited federal enactments in the domestic relations arena, he concluded that DOMA's reach was much greater, affecting over 1,000 federal statutes and the whole realm of federal regulations. He further noted that the operation of DOMA was directed to a class of persons that the domestic relations law of New York and 11 other states has sought to protect. (133 S.Ct. 2675 at 2690). In announcing the holding of the Court in this 5 to 4 decision, Justice Kennedy stated, in part:

> "The power the Constitution grants it also restrains. And though Congress has great authority to design laws to fit its own conception of sound national policy, it cannot deny the liberty protected by the Due Process Clause of the Fifth Amendment.
>
> " . . . the principal purpose and the necessary effect of this law are to demean those persons who are in a lawful same-sex marriage. This requires the Court to hold, as it now does, that DOMA is unconstitutional as a deprivation of the liberty of the person protected by the Fifth Amendment of the Constitution.
>
> "The liberty protected by the Fifth Amendment's Due Process Clause contains within it the prohibition against denying to any person the equal protection of the laws. . . . While the Fifth Amendment itself withdraws from Government the power to degrade or demean in the way this law does, the equal protection guarantee of the Fourteenth Amendment makes the Fifth Amendment right all the more specific and all the better understood and preserved.
>
> "The class to which DOMA directs its restrictions and restraints are those persons who are joined in same-sex marriages made lawful by the State. DOMA singles out a class of persons deemed by a State entitled to recognition and protection to enhance their own liberty. . . . The federal statute is invalid, for no legitimate purpose overcomes the purpose and effect to disparage and to injure those whom the State, by its marriage laws, sought to protect in personhood and dignity. . . . This opinion and its holding are confined to those lawful marriages." (133 S.Ct. 2675 at 2695–2696).

9. As noted, *Windsor* addressed only Section 3 of the federal DOMA. It did not consider state definitions of marriage. So, at this time, definitions of marriage as seen in Alaska and other states adopting DOMA-like provisions remain unchanged by the Supreme Court's decision. For a listing of the fifty states and an indication of which allow and which do not allow same-sex

marriages or civil unions, see http://www.unmarried.org/legal.information-resources-by-state/ (last visited on October 31, 2013). That source indicates that as of October 2013, thirteen states have given same-sex couples the right to marry.

10. In light of the *Ranney* decision, *supra*, and the above note materials, what do you believe will be the outcome of the Alaska Supreme Court's decision in *Harris v. Millennium Hotel, supra*? Why?

11. Take another look at Note 1 and the last paragraph of Note 3, following the *Spalding* case, *supra*. In the context of unmarried opposite-sex couples and non-sanctioned same-sex unions, where dependency is established, should workers' compensation boards and courts utilize interpretations of terms such as "widow," "widower," "spouse," and "member of the family" which may differ from their traditional "domestic relations" counterparts? Why or why not?

STEVEN LEE ENTERPRISES V. VARNEY

Supreme Court of Kentucky, 2000.
36 S.W.3d 391.

COOPER, JUSTICE.

Danny Varney became disabled by pneumoconiosis on March 5, 1988. He filed his verified application for adjustment of claim in May 1988. His application identified his wife as Ardena Varney and his dependent children as Darrell Varney, Danny Varney and Jason Varney, all residing with him at General Delivery, Kimper, Kentucky. Varney was found to be totally disabled under the 1988 version of KRS 342.732(1)(d) and was awarded workers' compensation benefits, which were apportioned 25% against the employer and 75% against the Special Fund as then required by KRS 342.316(10)(a). The claimant in this case, Samantha Varney, was born of Danny Varney and Tressa Sue Brewster on December 29, 1993. The record does not reflect when Danny divorced Ardena Varney; but he married Brewster in January 1994 and subsequently divorced her in July 1995. Varney died as a result of his pneumoconiosis on December 10, 1996. On January 10, 1997, Tressa Brewster Varney filed this motion to reopen Danny Varney's workers' compensation claim for the purpose of obtaining death benefits for Samantha under KRS 342.730(3). (Since it is undisputed that Varney died as a result of his compensable disease, Samantha's claim for benefits should have been brought under KRS 342.750(1)(d)).

By its own language, KRS 342.750 applies only to deaths caused by work-related injuries. Its provisions are made applicable to deaths caused by occupational diseases by KRS 342.316(4), now (5)(c), and KRS 342.316(7), now (8). At all relevant times, KRS 342.316(7) provided:

> No compensation for death from occupational disease shall be payable to any person whose relationship to the deceased, which, under the provisions of this chapter would give right to compensation, arose, subsequent to the beginning of the first compensable disability, save only to after-born children of a marriage existing at the beginning of such disability.

Relying on this statute, both the Administrative Law Judge (ALJ) and the Workers' Compensation Board denied Samantha's claim for death benefits. The Court of Appeals, however, found that because the statute compensated only after-born children of a marriage existing when the deceased worker's disability began, it impermissibly discriminated against after-born illegitimate children such as Samantha. For that reason, the Court of Appeals declared the statute to be in violation of the Equal Protection Clauses of the United States and Kentucky Constitutions and, thus, invalid. U.S. Const., amend. XIV, Ky. Const. § 3.

KRS 342.316(7), now (8), is but a codification of what we have consistently recognized as a basic principle of workers' compensation law, *i.e.,* entitlement to benefits is determined as of the date of the compensable event, which, with respect to an occupational disease, is the date of the last injurious exposure or the date of actual disability, whichever is later. KRS 342.316(1)(b). *E.g., Newberg v. Davis,* Ky., 867 S.W.2d 193 (1993) (widow's entitlement to death benefits is governed by the law in effect on the date of the worker's last injurious exposure rather than on the date of his death); *Vogt & Conant Co. v. Boelhauf,* Ky., 317 S.W.2d 163 (1958) (relationship of dependency must be determined in accordance with the facts existing at the time of the accident); *Miller v. Elkhorn Coal Corp.,* 284 Ky. 737, 145 S.W.2d 822 (1940) (dependency for purposes of workers' compensation is determined as of the time of the accident); *Franklin Fluorspar Co. v. Bell,* 247 Ky. 507, 57 S.W.2d 481 (1933) (the object of the Workers' Compensation Act is to compensate those who were dependent on the employee at the time of the accident). Unlike the Court of Appeals, we do not view KRS 342.316(7), now (8), as discriminating against after-born children of a marriage which did not exist on the date of the compensable event. Rather, we agree with the ALJ's observation that the statute is, in fact, a saving statute which *extends* benefits to after-born children of a marriage existing on the date of the compensable event. Otherwise, no after-born children would be entitled to benefits. But even if we agreed with the Court of Appeals on that issue, we would still disagree with the equal protection analysis applied by that Court to this statute.

A statute challenged on equal protection grounds is subject to "strict scrutiny," *i.e.,* sustainable only if the statute is suitably tailored to serve a "compelling state interest," if it affects a fundamental right or a suspect classification, such as race, alienage or ancestry. *Massachusetts Bd. of*

Retirement v. Murgia, 427 U.S. 307, 312, 96 S.Ct. 2562, 2566, 49 L.Ed.2d 520 (1976). However, if the statute merely affects social or economic policy, it is subject only to "rational basis" analysis. *City of Cleburne v. Cleburne Living Center, Inc.,* 473 U.S. 432, 440, 105 S.Ct. 3249, 3254, 87 L.Ed.2d 313 (1985). In *Wynn v. Ibold, Inc.,* Ky., 969 S.W.2d 695 (1998), we rejected an equal protection challenge to KRS 342.730(4) (the so-called "tier-down" statute), holding that workers' compensation statutes affect only economic policy and matters of social welfare, as opposed to fundamental rights or suspect classes; thus, the statute did not violate the Equal Protection Clause since it was "*rationally related* to a legitimate state objective." *Wynn v. Ibold, Inc., supra,* at 696 (emphasis added).

The Court of Appeals correctly identified illegitimacy as a "suspect classification," which, like gender, is subject to a higher level of scrutiny than mere "rational basis" analysis. *Lalli v. Lalli,* 439 U.S. 259, 265, 99 S.Ct. 518, 523, 58 L.Ed.2d 503 (1978); *Weber v. Aetna Cas. & Sur. Co.,* 406 U.S. 164, 92 S.Ct. 1400, 31 L.Ed.2d 768 (1972). Under this higher standard, usually referred to as "heightened scrutiny," discriminatory laws survive equal protection analysis only "to the extent they are *substantially related* to a legitimate state interest." *City of Cleburne v. Cleburne Living Center, Inc., supra,* at 441, 105 S.Ct. at 3255 (emphasis added). KRS 342.316(7), now (8), is substantially related to two legitimate state interests: (1) to compensate members of the deceased worker's family as it existed on date of the compensable event, per *Franklin Fluorspar Co. v. Bell, supra,* plus after-born children of that marriage; and (2) "to reduce the overall cost of maintaining the workers' compensation system, thereby improving the economic climate for all the citizens of the state," per *Wynn v. Ibold, Inc., supra,* at 697.

Nevertheless, KRS 342.316(7), now (8), does not discriminate against Samantha Varney because of her illegitimate birth. The statute would deny benefits to her *even if her parents had been married to each other on the date of her birth,* December 29, 1993. The statute denies her benefits *because her parents were not married to each other on the date of the compensable event,* March 5, 1988.[1] On that date, Danny Varney was married to someone else and had three dependent children by that marriage who *would* have been entitled to benefits upon his death if they satisfied any of the criteria listed in KRS 342.750(1)(e), *i.e.,* under the age of eighteen, actually dependent, or a full-time student under the age of twenty-two.

Since Samantha is not being denied benefits because of her illegitimacy, KRS 342.316(7), now (8), is subject only to "rational basis"

---

[1] For the same reason, the statute would have denied death benefits to Samantha's mother, Tressa Brewster Varney, even if she had been married to Danny Varney at the time of his death.

analysis, not to "strict scrutiny" or "heightened scrutiny." It is appropriate, therefore, to revisit the nature of that inquiry. The best summary of what rational basis analysis entails and what it does not entail is that set forth in *Heller v. Doe by Doe,* 509 U.S. 312, 113 S.Ct. 2637, 125 L.Ed.2d 257 (1993), in which the United States Supreme Court analyzed two Kentucky statutes, KRS 202A.076(2) and KRS 202B.160(2), and discerned no violation of the Equal Protection Clause.

> "We many times have said, and but weeks ago repeated, that rational-basis review in equal protection analysis 'is not a license for courts to judge the wisdom, fairness, or logic of legislative choices. . . .' Nor does it authorize 'the judiciary [to] sit as a superlegislature to judge the wisdom or desirability of legislative policy determinations made in areas that neither affect fundamental rights nor proceed along suspect lines. . . .' For these reasons, a classification neither involving fundamental rights nor proceeding along suspect lines is accorded a strong presumption of validity. . . . Such a classification cannot run afoul of the Equal Protection Clause if there is a rational relationship between the disparity of treatment and some legitimate governmental purpose. . . . Further, a legislature that creates these categories need not 'actually articulate at any time the purpose or rationale supporting its classification. . . .' Instead, a classification 'must be upheld against equal protection challenge *if there is any reasonably conceivable state of facts* that could provide a rational basis for the classification. . . .'
>
> "A State, moreover, has no obligation to produce evidence to sustain the rationality of a statutory classification. '[A] legislative choice is not subject to courtroom factfinding and may be based on rational speculation unsupported by evidence or empirical data. . . .' A statute is presumed constitutional, . . . and '[t]he burden is on the one attacking the legislative arrangement *to negative every conceivable basis which might support it,*' . . . whether or not the basis has a foundation in the record. Finally, courts are compelled under rational-basis review to accept a legislature's generalizations even when there is an imperfect fit between means and ends. A classification does not fail rational-basis review because it 'is not made with mathematical nicety or because in practice it results in some inequality. . . .' 'The problems of government are practical ones and may justify, if they do not require, rough accommodations—illogical, it may be, and unscientific.' " *Id.* at 319–21, 113 S.Ct. at 2642–43. (citations omitted) (emphasis added).

Accordingly, if there is any "reasonably conceivable state of facts" supporting the perceived discrimination in KRS 342.316(7), now (8), the statute does not violate the Equal Protection Clause and must be upheld even if it is perceived to be unwise, unfair or illogical. In fact, there are numerous "reasonably conceivable" factual bases supporting the General Assembly's decision to extend death benefits for occupational diseases to after-born children of a marriage existing on the date of the compensable event, but not to after-born children of subsequent marriages (or, for that matter, to after-acquired spouses, new stepbrothers and stepsisters, new brothers and sisters by the half-blood, new stepparents, and the children of newly adopted children or newly acquired stepchildren, all of whom would be entitled to benefits per KRS 342.085 and KRS 342.750(1)(f), (g) if KRS 342.316(7), now (8), is declared invalid).

Unlike deaths from compensable *injuries,* deaths from compensable diseases normally do not occur simultaneously with or shortly after the compensable event. As here, a worker afflicted with an occupational disease may linger for years before finally succumbing to its effects. In the interim, the disabled worker could confer a continuation of his benefits upon literally generations of after-acquired relatives by, *e.g.,* marrying a friend or relative's child or grandchild, marrying a much younger spouse with infant stepchildren, or adopting his or her spouse's nieces, nephews or grandchildren in contemplation of his own death. In this regard, it is appropriate to note that according to official records of the Department of Veterans Affairs, the last dependent of a Revolutionary War veteran died in 1911 and the last dependent of a veteran of the War of 1812 died in 1946; and that as of July 1, 1998, the V.A. was still paying pension benefits to one surviving spouse and fourteen surviving children of Civil War veterans and to 570 surviving spouses and 309 surviving children of Spanish-American War veterans.[2]

By enacting KRS 342.316(7), now (8), the General Assembly limited death benefits for occupational diseases to those persons related to the disabled worker as of the date of the compensable event, plus after-born children of a marriage existing on that date. By excluding all other after-acquired relatives, the General Assembly gave the employer, its insurer and the Special Fund a reasonable basis to anticipate the amount and duration of their potential liability for a particular claim and to establish reasonable monetary reserves to cover that liability. In doing so, the statute reduces the overall cost of maintaining the workers' compensation system and thereby improves the economic climate for all citizens of the Commonwealth. *Wynn v. Ibold, Inc., supra,* at 697. Thus, as in *Wynn,* there is a rational basis for what Samantha Varney perceives as discrimination against after-acquired relatives in KRS 342.316(7), now (8). That being the case, even if the statute did discriminate against after-

---

[2] Department of Veterans Affairs, *America's Wars* (visited Aug. 2, 2000) http://www.va.gov/pressrel/Am–Wars99.htm.

acquired relatives, it would not violate the Equal Protection Clauses of the United States and/or Kentucky Constitutions.

Accordingly, we reverse the Court of Appeals and reinstate the orders of the ALJ and the Workers' Compensation Board dismissing Samantha Varney's claim for death benefits.

GRAVES, JOHNSTONE, and KELLER, JJ., concur.

STUMBO, JUSTICE, dissenting.

Respectfully, I must dissent. I do not believe that KRS 342.316(7) can withstand equal protection scrutiny. I can find no legitimate state interest, substantial or otherwise, for distinguishing between the two classes of after-born children. KRS 342.316(7) discriminates between after-born children born of a marriage in existence at the time the disability commenced, and after-born children who were not born of a marriage in existence at the time the disability commenced. While the statute does not discriminate among after-born children based upon the status of legitimacy, it does so on a far less tangible basis: the timing of the child's birth. Both illegitimacy and the timing of birth are beyond the individual's control and bear "no relation to the individual's ability to participate in and contribute to society." *Mathews v. Lucas,* 427 U.S. 495, 505, 96 S.Ct. 2755, 2762, 49 L.Ed.2d 651, 660 (1976). Consequently, the statutory classification is subject to the heightened scrutiny standard of review.

Steven Lee argues that the limitation on the payment of occupational disease benefits is a legitimate attempt on the part of the legislature to contain the number of persons to whom employers would be liable for payment of continuation benefits. The General Assembly has a legitimate interest in limiting potential claims in order to preserve the integrity of the workers' compensation system. *Mullins v. Manning Coal Corp.,* Ky., 938 S.W.2d 260, 263 (1997). However, KRS 342.316(7) does not further the legitimate interest of limiting the liability of the employer or the Special Fund for payment of continuation benefits. Under KRS 342.750, the employer or the Special Fund may be liable for payment of continuation benefits to children who are not in existence at the time the award was made.

KRS 342.316(7) arbitrarily discriminates between after-born children who are born of a marriage in existence at the time of the worker's disability began and those who were not. The statute cuts off the right of certain after-born children from receiving continuation benefits from a deceased parent. Yet, in doing so, it does not further a legitimate state interest or base this distinction upon any rational or substantial bases. As a result, I would find that KRS 342.316(7) is unconstitutional as a violation of Samantha's right to equal protection of the law.

LAMBERT, C.J., and WINTERSHIMER, J., join this dissent.

NOTES

1. In determining the rights of dependent children, courts are less captive to conventional family law then in determining marital relationships. See, Ryan–Walsh Stevedoring Co., Inc. v. Trainer, 601 F.2d 1306 (5th Cir.1979) (in a Longshore and Harbor Workers' Compensation Act case, "the general state law of domestic relations rather than the Longshore Act is determinative of whether a claimant is decedent's widow"; as to children, where decedent treated another's child as his daughter, he stood in *loco parentis* and such child qualified as decedent's child for Longshore Act purposes); and, see Tidewater Marine Towing, Inc. v. Curran–Houston, Inc., 785 F.2d 1317 (C.A.5 (La.) 1986). Some statutes contain provisions expressly defining "child" or "children" to include a stepchild, an adopted child, and an illegitimate child. Some require acknowledgment of the latter. See, e.g., Longshore Act, 33 U.S.C.A. § 902(14) (2012). One of the most inclusive definitions is in the Wyoming statute which provides: "'child' means any unmarried minor or physically or mentally incapacitated individual receiving court ordered support or substantially all of his financial support from the employee at the time of injury or death of that employee and includes an adopted child, stepchild, posthumous child or acknowledged illegitimate child but does not include a parent or spouse of the employee." West's Wyo. Stat. Ann. § 27–14–102(iii) (2013).

2. The treatment of posthumous children varies. See, e.g., Renard v. Security Protection Services, 692 So.2d 9 (La.App.4th Cir.1997) (posthumous child is not a member of the family " . . . for that term connotes a living person . . . the right to compensation is determined upon the basis of facts existing at the time of death of the employee and not deferred to await the contingency of live birth"). Contrast, West's Ann. Cal. Labor Code § 3503 (2013) (including posthumous child within definition of dependent.)

3. The status of illegitimate children varied widely among the states until Weber v. Aetna Cas. & Sur. Co., 406 U.S. 164, 92 S.Ct. 1400, 31 L.Ed.2d 768 (1972), held that the Louisiana workers' compensation statute which denied coverage to unacknowledged illegitimate children violated the Equal Protection Clause of the Fourteenth Amendment. Post-Weber decisions, however, suggest greater constitutional tolerance. See, e.g., Mathews v. Lucas, 427 U.S. 495, 96 S.Ct. 2755, 49 L.Ed.2d 651 (1976); Wittig v. Shalala, 852 F.Supp. 613 (1994) (child born as a result of an adulterous relationship is not a stepchild of the innocent spouse so as to be eligible for child's benefits under the Social Security Act); Hendrix v. Secretary of Health and Human Services, 156 F.3d 1229 (6th Cir.1998) (42 U.S.C. § 416(h)(2)(A) of the Social Security Act provides that an illegitimate child is entitled to death benefits if he or she would have been deemed to be an intestate heir of the deceased under the law of the state in which the decedent was domiciled. " . . . where state intestacy law provides that a child may take personal property from a father's estate, it may reasonably be thought that the child will more likely be dependent during the parent's life and at his death."); and see Finley v. Astrue, 601 F. Supp.2d 1092 (E.D. Ark.2009). See generally, Ellman, Kurtz &

Scott, *Family Law Cases, Text, Problems*, 4th Edition, 1035–1038 (Lexis Law Publishing, 2004), discussing the Supreme Court's ultimate recognition, in a line of pre-Weber and post-Weber cases, of an intermediate level of scrutiny in the context of classifications based on illegitimacy. And, see generally, 16C C.J.S. Constitutional Law § 1404 (2013). Of course, the task of proving that the decedent was the father of the child remains.

"Member of the Family"

1. Many workers' compensation statutes use the term "member of the family" to describe the persons or classes entitled to death benefits. Distilling the characteristics necessary to raise a relationship to the level of "family" is not a new task for the courts. As early as 1924, the Supreme Court of Utah wrote, "Just what relationship must exist between individuals to constitute a family, or to make each individual a member of the same family, probably cannot be stated in any general or comprehensive definition. . . . It is however, in our judgment, clearly deducible from the weight of authority that the family relationship is a social status and not one necessarily founded upon contract; also that the individuals may be members of the same family without sustaining to each other any blood relationship. There must, however, be some legal or moral obligation for support existing between the individuals composing the family." Utah Fuel Co. v. Industrial Commission of Utah, 64 Utah 328, 230 P. 681 (1924).

2. The usual provision grants compensation only to claimants who prove actual dependency and actual status as a member of the family of the decedent. Applying the statute poses no great difficulty as to such close relatives as parents, or children under the statutory age (if not otherwise expressly covered), as long as the evidence supports actual dependency. Caporoz v. Labor Commission, 945 P.2d 141 (Ut.App.1997) (when statutory presumption does not apply, one prerequisite to a finding of dependency is the existence of "some family or other social relationship giving rise to a legal or moral obligation to support."). In addition, there should be a determination that the claimant relied wholly or partially on the decedent or that the claimant would most likely have received assistance from the decedent but for the death. Other close relatives often brought within the term are brothers. See, e.g., Park Utah Consol. Mines Co. v. Industrial Comm., 84 Utah 481, 36 P.2d 979 (1934); Leigh Coal Co., Inc. v. Cantrell, 434 S.W.2d 315 (Ky.1968), and Sawyer v. Dependents of Head, 510 So.2d 472 (Miss.1987); and sisters. See, e.g., Clark v. White, 197 Wis. 597, 222 N.W. 823 (1929); Reese v. Beshel, 10 La.App. 347, 120 So. 530 (1929); Peterson v. Industrial Acc. Comm., 188 Cal. 15, 204 P. 390 (1922); Mile High Masonry v. Industrial Commission, 718 P.2d 257 (Colo.App.1986); and Corbin v. Industrial Commission, 724 P.2d 677 (Colo.App.1986). Contrast Tisdale v. Wilson & Co., 141 Kan. 885, 43 P.2d 1064 (1935) (married sister whose husband had deserted her, supported by deceased brother but, apparently, not living with him; held, compensation denied). Other relatives that have

been awarded compensation include aunts, Peay v. Fred Kulow & Co., 226 Mich. 512, 197 N.W. 1020 (1924) and Harlan v. Industrial Acc. Comm., 194 Cal. 352, 228 P. 654 (1924); but contrast, Stafford's Case, 238 Mass. 93, 130 N.E. 109 (1921) which denied compensation to the aunt who was the actual head of the household; nephews, A.E. Peterson v. Industrial Acc. Comm., 188 Cal. 15, 204 P. 390 (1922); and Franklin v. Jackson, 231 Miss. 497, 95 So.2d 794 (1957); cousins, Holmberg v. Cleveland–Cliffs Iron Co., 219 Mich. 204, 189 N.W. 26 (1922); and grandparents, Howard v. Lenhart & Bennett, 663 P.2d 386 (Okl.App.1983); and grandchildren, Farmer v. Metro Light and Electrical Services, Inc. 708 So.2d 1251 (La.App.1998).

3. In-laws are frequently included. In Goshorn v. Roger Sherman Transfer Co., 131 Conn. 200, 38 A.2d 585 (1944) claimant was the mother-in-law of decedent. She had lived with decedent for about 20 years after he and his wife (her daughter) separated, had raised his child and managed the household as "the mother of the family." Decedent had taken her as a dependent on his income tax returns and had promised he would maintain a home for her as long as she lived and would provide for her in his will. For 7 years prior to his death she had been wholly dependent on him. It was held that while she was not "next of kin," she was a member of decedent's family and entitled to death benefits. See also Archibald v. Employers' Liability Assur. Corp., 202 La. 89, 11 So.2d 492 (1942) (in absence of blood relatives, father-in-law, mother-in-law and two sisters-in-law who lived with deceased and were actually dependent on him could recover compensation as legal dependents); Larsen v. Industrial Acc. Comm., 34 Cal.2d 772, 215 P.2d 16 (1950) (mother-in-law awarded compensation).

4. Even persons not having any blood or other legal relationship to the decedent may qualify for benefits in the absence of a statutory prohibition. Lumbermen's Underwriting Alliance v. Teague, 521 So.2d 820 (La.App.1988) (despite the lack of blood relations or legal obligation, the woman with whom the decedent lived and her child were awarded death benefits to exclusion of the decedent's natural children); Housley v. Everts' Commercial Transport, Inc., 4 Or.App. 80, 475 P.2d 977 (1970) (stepchildren qualified as dependents); Blair v. Keller, 16 Ohio Misc. 157, 241 N.E.2d 767 (1968) (unadopted children of decedent's widow); Southern Motor Car Co. v. Patterson, 168 Tenn. 252, 77 S.W.2d 446 (1935) (nephew of decedent's wife); and Patin v. T.L. James & Co., Inc., 218 La. 949, 51 So.2d 586 (1951) (child of another couple taken at infancy into home of decedent and reared there).

4. SPECIAL ASPECTS OF CLAIMS OF SURVIVORS

BUCHANAN V. KERR–MCGEE CORPORATION

Court of Appeals of New Mexico, 1995.
121 N.M. 12, 908 P.2d 242.

BUSTAMANTE, JUDGE.

Muriel Buchanan (Claimant), widow of Henry Buchanan (Worker), appeals an order denying her claim for death benefits under the New Mexico Occupational Disease Disablement Law (the Occupational Disease Law). NMSA 1978, § 52–3–13 to 60 (Repl.Pamp.1991 & Cum.Supp.1995). Claimant raises two issues on appeal: (1) is Claimant's claim for death benefits barred by a settlement and release made by Worker during his lifetime, and (2) did the Workers' Compensation Judge (WCJ) err in deciding Worker's lung cancer was noncompensable because of the presence of a non-occupational risk factor? Deciding that there is no bar and that the WCJ applied an incorrect standard of proof to the facts, we reverse and remand.

Facts and Proceedings

Worker was an underground uranium miner employed by Kerr–McGee Corporation d/b/a Quivira Mining Company (Employer) and its subsidiaries for more than twenty years. In 1985, Worker suffered a work-related back injury for which he filed a claim for workers' compensation benefits. In addition, Worker joined a silicosis claim under the Occupational Disease Law to the back injury action. In 1987, the district court awarded Worker compensation benefits for his back injury. Contemporaneously, Worker and Employer entered into a settlement agreement with regard to the silicosis claim which required Employer to pay Worker $15,000 in exchange for a release (the Release) in full of all claims under the Occupational Disease Law. Worker signed the Release in January 1987. The Release included the following language:

> [“]However, if it should develop that I did receive any other injuries or damages or was involved in any other accident or suffered any other exposure which might hereafter lead to another occupational disease disablement while employed by KERR–McGEE CORPORATION or QUIVIRA MINING COMPANY, f/k/a KERR–McGEE NUCLEAR CORPORATION, at any time, then this Release forever releases and discharges KERR–McGEE CORPORATION, QUIVIRA MINING COMPANY, f/k/a KERR–McGEE NUCLEAR CORPORATION, and their subsidiaries, insurers, successors and assigns, and their officers, agents, servants and employees who or which could or might possibly be liable for any such injuries, disablement or damages whether discovered or latent or otherwise.[”]

Worker and Employer stipulated that the settlement would bind Worker and "his dependents." Claimant did not read or sign the Release and she took no part in the negotiation and settlement of Worker's claims under the Occupational Disease Law.

In January 1993, Worker was diagnosed with lung cancer. Worker filed an occupational disease claim against Employer. In September 1993, Worker died of " '[m]etastatic squamous cell carcinoma of the lung' " while his Claim was pending. Claimant eventually filed her own complaint seeking death benefits and medical expenses.

The WCJ ordered the case to be submitted on briefs and stipulated facts. After briefing, the WCJ dismissed Claimant's complaint on two grounds, each independently fatal to Claimant's course of action: (1) the Release bars Claimant's claim; and (2) Worker's disablement and death were not caused by an occupational disease arising out of his employment.

Discussion

With regard to issues of fact, we review this case using the whole record standard of review. See Herman v. Miners' Hosp., 111 N.M. 550, 552, 807 P.2d 734, 736 (1991); Tallman v. ABF (Arkansas Best Freight), 108 N.M. 124, 126–30, 767 P.2d 363, 365–69 (Ct.App.), cert. denied, 109 N.M. 33, 781 P.2d 305 (1988). Whole record review is not an excuse for an appellate court to reweigh the evidence and replace the fact finder's conclusions with its own, although it does allow the reviewing court greater latitude to determine whether a finding of fact was reasonable based on the evidence. Herman, 111 N.M. at 553, 807 P.2d at 737. With regard to issues of law, this Court determines whether the WCJ correctly applied the law to the facts, viewing the facts in the light most favorable to the determination below. See Golden Cone Concepts, Inc. v. Villa Linda Mall Ltd., 113 N.M. 9, 12, 820 P.2d 1323, 1326 (1991); see also Texas Nat'l Theatres, Inc. v. City of Albuquerque, 97 N.M. 282, 287, 639 P.2d 569, 574 (1982).

Issue 1. Does the Release Bar Claimant's Recovery for Death Benefits?

The WCJ determined that the express language of the Release bars Claimant's recovery of death benefits. The WCJ reached her decision by applying broadly accepted concepts of contract interpretation and public policy, with which we have no quarrel in the abstract. For example, the WCJ noted that the courts of New Mexico favor settlement and that settlements will be enforced in accordance with their terms absent an ambiguity in the terms of the settlement agreement or release. See Ratzlaff v. Seven Bar Flying Serv., Inc., 98 N.M. 159, 163, 646 P.2d 586, 590 (Ct.App.), cert. denied, 98 N.M. 336, 648 P.2d 794 (1982). In addition, a settlement agreement or release can be challenged if there is a lack of consideration, fraud, misrepresentation, duress, mistake, undue influence, overreaching, or other factors supporting unenforceability. Id. Hendren v. Allstate Ins. Co., 100 N.M. 506, 508, 672 P.2d 1137, 1139 (Ct.App.1983). Claimant did not assert that there was any ambiguity in the Release, and the WCJ found no evidence of fraud, misrepresentation, duress, or other grounds for challenging the Release. Absent a direct challenge to the facial validity of the Release, the WCJ held that Worker had released Employer from all claims arising under the Occupational Disease Law.

The WCJ's decision presupposes that Worker's valid release is also effective to release Claimant's cause of action as a surviving dependent under the Occupational Disease Law. We disagree with this premise and the conclusion that follows from it. We hold that Claimant, as Worker's widow and dependent, has independent statutory rights to death benefits which arise upon Worker's death, and Claimant is not bound by Release. The claim of a dependent arising from the death of a worker is a new and separate claim and is not derivative of the worker's claim. See Gonzales v. Sharp & Fellows Contracting Co., 48 N.M. 528, 537–38, 153 P.2d 676, 681–82 (1944); 2 Arthur Larson, The Law of Workmen's Compensation § 64.10 (1995). A unilateral settlement or release by a worker of his or her own claims does not bar the surviving dependent's claim even if the release signed by the worker explicitly purports to release the dependent's claim, as was the case here. Brown v. General Aniline & Film Corp., 127 N.J.Super. 93, 316 A.2d 478, 480 (Ct.App.Div.1974), aff'd per curiam, 65 N.J. 555, 325 A.2d 689 (1974); Fossum v. State Accident Ins. Fund, 289 Or. 787, 619 P.2d 233, 237 (*en banc*), reh'g denied and modified, 290 Or. 267, 624 P.2d 1074 (1980); 2 Larson, supra, § 64.12 (1995). Our holding is in accord with the great weight of authority from other jurisdictions. See Kay v. Hillside Mines, Inc., 54 Ariz. 36, 39, 91 P.2d 867, 870 (1939); American Steel Foundries v. Industrial Comm'n, 361 Ill. 582, 198 N.E. 687, 690 (1935); Routh v. List & Weatherly Const. Co., 124 Kan. 222, 257 P. 721, 724 (1927); In re Cripp, 216 Mass. 586, 104 N.E. 565, 566 (1914); Smith v. Kiel, 115 S.W.2d 38, 41 (Mo.Ct.App.1938); Viersen & Cochran Drilling Co. v. Ford, 425 P.2d 965, 967–68 (Okla.1967).

Restated in the language of contract law, Claimant's cause of action under the Occupational Disease Law is a new and separate claim, and it is not barred by the Release because Claimant was not a party to the Release and received no consideration for relinquishment of her dependent's claim for death benefits. See Fleet Mortgage Corp. v. Schuster, 112 N.M. 48, 49, 811 P.2d 81, 82 (1991) (it is a general rule that one who is not a party to a contract cannot maintain suit upon it, nor is bound by it).

The Occupational Disease Law does not directly address the issue before us. That is, there is no specific provision of the Occupational Disease Law which explicitly states that survivor's benefits constitute a claim completely separate and apart from the worker's claim. In addition, there is no provision in the statute which addresses in any fashion the effect of a broadly worded release form executed by a worker but not signed by any of worker's dependents. We can glean, however, the outcome most compatible with the intent and purpose of the Occupational Disease Law by comparing its treatment of the worker's disability benefits with the treatment accorded dependent's death benefits.

Section 52–3–10(A) provides:

A. There is imposed upon every employer a liability for the payment of compensation to every employee of such employer who suffers total disablement by reason of an occupational disease arising out of his employment, subject to the following conditions[.]

In contrast, Section 52–3–10(B) provides:

B. There is imposed upon every employer a liability for the payment of compensation to the dependents of every employee in cases where death results from an occupational disease arising out of his employment, subject to the following conditions[.]

The Occupational Disease Law thus draws a clear distinction between an employer's obligation to its employees for benefits during their lifetime and an employer's obligation to "the dependents" of its employees for death benefits.

Similarly, Section 52–3–14(A), (B), and (G) distinguish between the benefits payable to the worker and those payable to the worker's dependents upon the worker's death. The benefits payable to dependents are: (1) funeral and medical expenses (2) such other sums as the deceased may have been paid for disability, and (3) 700 weeks of death benefit payments. The language of Section 52–3–14(G) itself does not provide for a deduction, credit or setoff against an employer's liability to dependents for death benefits on account of payments to a worker during his lifetime under the Occupational Disease Law. We conclude, therefore, that it was the intent of the legislature to award death benefits to a worker's dependents if death arises or proximately results from an occupational disease notwithstanding what the worker received or was deemed entitled to receive during his lifetime. It follows that surviving dependents are entitled benefits notwithstanding any release worker may execute during his or her lifetime.

Employer argues that Hubbs v. Sandia Corp., 98 N.M. 389, 648 P.2d 1202 (Ct.App.), cert. denied, 98 N.M. 478, 649 P.2d 1391 (1982), undercuts Claimant's position that worker and survivor benefits are independent of each other. Hubbs is distinguishable, however, because it dealt specifically with a statute of limitations issue. In Hubbs, the employer asserted the independence of disablement and death benefits in support of its argument that a disablement claim filed within the ten-year period of NMSA 1978, Section 52–3–10(C), could not be used to make a death claim timely when the death claim was filed after the statutory ten-year period had elapsed. The Court and the parties in Hubbs did not disagree that disablement and death claims are distinct and separate. Id. at 391, 648 P.2d at 1204. The only issue was whether their independence affected the statute of limitations issue presented. We held it did not because of the internal wording of the statute, but we did not compromise the distinction between employee's disablement benefits and the surviving dependent's death benefits.

Accordingly, we reverse the WCJ's determination that the Release acted to bar Claimant's recovery. Claimant's recovery of death benefits is, however, also contingent upon whether Claimant can show that Worker died from an occupational disease. We turn now to that issue.

Issue 2. Did the WCJ Error in Concluding that Worker's Death was Not Caused by an Occupational Disease Arising out of his Employment?

* * *

Based on the foregoing, we conclude that the occupational Disease Law does not require Claimant to prove that Worker's exposure to uranium was the only factor causing Worker's fatal lung cancer or even the major factor, as the WCJ apparently concluded. Rather, the occupational Disease Law only requires Claimant to show that as a matter of medical probability there is a recognizable, non-negligible link between Worker's exposure to radiation as a miner for over twenty years and his risk of contracting lung cancer.

* * *

Accordingly, we reverse the WCJs finding that Claimant failed to prove that Worker suffered total disablement or death by reason of an occupational disease arising out of his employment, and remand for reconsideration in light of our opinion.

* * *

IT IS SO ORDERED.

ALARID and WECHSLER, JJ., concur.

DUNI V. UNITED TECHNOLOGIES CORPORATION/PRATT AND WHITNEY AIRCRAFT DIVISION ET AL.

Supreme Court of Connecticut, 1996.
239 Conn. 19, 682 A.2d 99.

PALMER, JUSTICE

The dispositive issue raised by this appeal is whether a stipulation entered into by an employee and his employer in full and final settlement of the employee's workers' compensation claim can bar a claim for survivor's benefits by the employee's widow after the death of the employee. The employee, William Duni (decedent), filed a workers' compensation claim against his former employer, United Technologies Corporation/Pratt and Whitney Aircraft Division (Pratt & Whitney), the named defendant. The decedent, Pratt & Whitney, the defendant Liberty Mutual Insurance Company (Liberty) and the defendant Second Injury and Compensation Assurance Fund (fund) entered into a stipulated settlement agreement that purported to bind the decedent and anyone else who might ever have a claim against the defendants on account of the decedent's work-related injuries. After the decedent's death, his widow, the plaintiff, Beatrice Duni, filed a claim for survivor's benefits under General Statutes § 31–306. Pratt & Whitney and Liberty sought dismissal of the claim on the ground that it was barred by the settlement agreement. The workers' compensation commissioner (commissioner) denied the motion to dismiss. On appeal, the workers' compensation review board (review board) reversed the decision of the commissioner, concluding that the settlement agreement was binding on the plaintiff. The plaintiff appealed from the decision of the review board to the Appellate Court, and we transferred the appeal to this court pursuant to Practice Book § 4023 and General Statutes § 51–199(c). We affirm the decision of the review board.[1]

The facts relevant to this appeal are undisputed. The decedent was employed by Pratt & Whitney from 1941 to December, 1982. On December 3, 1984, the decedent filed a workers' compensation claim asserting that during the course of his employment with Pratt & Whitney he had been exposed to various substances that had caused injury to his lungs, heart, eyes, nose and other body parts, leaving him disabled.

The decedent and the defendants subsequently agreed to settle the claim and entered into an agreement entitled "Stipulation for Full and Final Settlement" (stipulation). Under the terms of the stipulation, the defendants agreed to make a lump sum payment to the decedent in return for his agreement to release them from any further liability in connection with his claim. The stipulation purported to "constitute a complete satisfaction of all claims due or to become due at any time in

---

1 Editor's note: Some footnotes have been omitted and others renumbered.

favor of anybody on account of the claimed injuries or on account of any condition in any way resulting out of the said injuries."[2] The parties' stipulation was approved by the commissioner on September 15, 1986.

On December 14, 1991, the decedent died. Approximately two months later, the plaintiff submitted to Pratt & Whitney a claim for survivor's benefits pursuant to § 31–306. The plaintiff alleged that the decedent's death was the result of the injuries that he had sustained during the course of his employment with Pratt & Whitney and, consequently, that she was entitled to survivor's benefits.

Pratt & Whitney and Liberty contested the claim and, thereafter, sought its dismissal on the ground that the stipulation barred the plaintiff's recovery. The commissioner denied the motion, concluding that the plaintiff's right to survivor's benefits was independent of the decedent's claim and that the plaintiff was not bound by the stipulation because she was not a signatory to it. The defendants appealed to the review board, which reversed the commissioner's decision on the ground that the plaintiffs application for survivor's benefits was precluded by the stipulation. This appeal followed.

On appeal, the plaintiff contends that the review board improperly concluded that she was not entitled to seek survivor's benefits under § 31–306. Specifically, the plaintiff maintains that her right to compensation under § 31–306 is completely independent of the decedent's rights to compensation for work related injuries under the Workers' Compensation Act (act), and, accordingly, that the decedent lacked the authority to settle any claim for survivor's benefits that she might later have arising from his work-related injuries. Alternatively, the plaintiff argues that the stipulation cannot reasonably be construed to bar her right to make a claim under § 31–306. We disagree with both of these claims.

The plaintiff first contends that the stipulation entered into by the decedent does not bar her claim for workers' compensation benefits because her rights under § 31–306 are entirely independent of the decedent's compensation rights and, consequently, that the decedent had no authority to compromise her right to seek benefits under § 31–306 after his death. We disagree.

---

[2] The stipulation provides in relevant part: "The payment of SEVENTY-TWO THOUSAND DOLLARS ($72,000) of which the respondent employer and insurer shall pay $36,000 and the respondent Second Injury and Compensation Assurance Fund shall pay $36,000, shall be made and accepted as a full and final settlement for all compensation including specific[ally] for said injuries and for all results upon the claimant past, present and future for all claims for medical, surgical, hospital and incidental expenses to the end that the payment of such sum shall constitute a complete satisfaction of all claims due or to become due at anytime in favor of anybody on account of the claimed injuries or on account of any condition in any way resulting out of the said injuries." Neither Pratt & Whitney nor the fund admitted any liability for the decedent's injuries.

Our resolution of this issue is guided by well established principles of statutory construction. "Our fundamental objective is to ascertain and give effect to the apparent intent of the legislature. . . . In seeking to discern that intent, we look to the words of the statute itself, to the legislative history and circumstances surrounding its enactment, to the legislative policy it was designed to implement, and to its relationship to existing legislation and common law principles governing the same general subject matter. . . ." (Citations omitted; internal quotation marks omitted.) State v. Metz, 230 Conn. 400, 409, 645 A.2d 965 (1994); Fleming v. Garnett, 231 Conn. 77, 92, 646 A.2d 1308 (1994). "We have previously recognized that our construction of the Workers' Compensation Act should make every part operative and harmonious with every other part insofar as is possible. . . . In applying these principles, we are mindful that the legislature is presumed to have intended a just and rational result. . . ." (Citations omitted; internal quotation marks omitted.) Dos Santos v. F.D. Rich Construction, Inc., 233 Conn. 14, 20–21, 658 A.2d 83 (1995).

"It is well established that [a]lthough not dispositive, we accord great weight to the construction given to the workers' compensation statutes by the commissioner and review board. . . . A state agency is not entitled, however, to special deference when its determination of a question of law has not previously been subject to judicial scrutiny." (Citation omitted; internal quotation marks omitted.) Davis v. Norwich, 232 Conn. 311, 317, 654 A.2d 1221 (1995).

As is often the case in the context of workers' compensation legislation; see Dos Santos v. F.D. Rich Construction, Inc., supra, 233 Conn. at 20, 658 A.2d 83; the statutory language provides little guidance for our determination of whether the decedent, in settling his own workers' compensation claim, also had the authority to compromise whatever right the plaintiff might have to survivor's benefits. Furthermore, the pertinent legislative history is silent on the question. Several considerations persuade us, however, that, under our statutory scheme, a surviving dependent's right to compensation is subordinate to an employee's right to settle his or her workers' compensation claim.

First, the availability of survivorship benefits under § 31–306 is inextricably linked to, and wholly dependent upon, the existence of a compensable injury or illness suffered by the employee. Thus, in the absence of a work related injury or illness, a surviving dependent of the employee has no claim whatsoever under § 31–306. Moreover, a dependent has no compensation rights unless and until the employee dies as a result of the occupational injury or disease. Further, the calculation of the amount of survivor's benefits to which a dependent may be entitled is determined as of the date of the employee's injury and not as of the date on which the dependent becomes eligible to receive such benefits.

General Statutes § 31–306(a)(2). Similarly, a person who has not attained dependent status until after the date of the employee's injury is not entitled to bring a claim under § 31–306. See General Statutes § 31–275(6). Thus, a surviving dependent's compensation rights under § 31–306 flow directly from the work-related injury or disease suffered by the employee.

Second, our conclusion advances the public policy favoring the pretrial resolution of disputes. As we have long recognized in the context of civil actions, "the pretrial settlement of claims is to be encouraged because, in the vast number of cases, an amicable resolution of the dispute is in the best interests of all concerned. 'The efficient administration of the courts is subserved by the ending of disputes without the delay and expense of a trial, and the philosophy or ideal of justice is served in the amicable solution of controversies.' Krattenstein v. G. Fox & Co., 155 Conn. 609, 614, 236 A.2d 466 (1967).... At a time when our courts confront an unprecedented volume of litigation, we reaffirm our strong support for the implementation of policies and procedures that encourage fair and amicable pretrial settlements." Grayson v. Wofsey, Rosen, Kweskin & Kuriansky, 231 Conn. 168, 174, 646 A.2d 195 (1994). We see no reason to eschew this sound public policy in connection with claims arising under our workers' compensation statutes.

To conclude, as the plaintiff urges, that an employee may not compromise his or her dependent's future rights under § 31–306 would unduly undermine the public interest in the prompt and comprehensive resolution of workers' compensation claims. Under the plaintiff's view, a full, final and global settlement of a workers' compensation claim involving a potentially fatal work-related injury or illness would be impossible without the express authorization of all the employee's dependents. Under such circumstances, it is less likely that a comprehensive settlement would be reached. An employer who is faced with the prospect of litigating additional claims upon the employee's death is less apt to be willing to settle the employee's claim.[3]

Finally, the statutory interpretation advanced by the defendants promotes the public policy in favor of administrative simplicity. As we

---

[3] We also note that stipulations in settlement of workers' compensation claims must be approved by the commissioner, a requirement that serves to protect interested parties against settlements that are not fair and equitable. As we have recently stated regarding such stipulations, "[t]he commissioner decides whether to approve a stipulation only after thoroughly reviewing it, along with all the pertinent medical bills and reports, and after evaluating employment possibilities and any concurrent claims. The commissioner undertakes such exhaustive inquiry in order to judge properly whether the stipulation is fair and comprehensive.... We can therefore assume that a commissioner is well acquainted with the terms generally used in stipulations and the proper authority conferred upon commissioners by the legislature." (Citation omitted) Muldoon v. Homestead Insulation Co., 231 Conn. 469, 480 n. 9, 650 A.2d 1240 (1994).

have noted in a related context, the plaintiffs statutory construction would require employers to maintain records for a considerable period of time after each disability compensation claim had been settled, an interpretation that "would undermine the statutory purpose of administrative simplicity." Davis v. Norwich, supra, 232 Conn. at 323, 654 A.2d 1221. This construction would also frustrate the related public interest in the finality of administrative determinations.

The plaintiff cites Muldoon v. Homestead Insulation Co., 231 Conn. 469, 650 A.2d 1240 (1994), in support of her contention that the act should not be read to permit an employee to settle any possible claim that his or her dependent may have under § 31–306 after the employee's death. In Muldoon, the employee and employer entered into a stipulated settlement of the employee's claim for compensation stemming from injuries suffered as a result of exposure to asbestos. Id., at 472, 650 A.2d 1240. Several years after the stipulation was approved, the employee filed a second workers' compensation claim, alleging that, in the interim, additional exposure to asbestos had caused him further injuries. Id., at 473, 650 A.2d 1240. We concluded that the stipulation's preclusion of " 'future . . . claims . . . resulting out of the said injury . . . ' " did not foreclose a future claim based upon a subsequent, although similar, injury. Id., at 479, 650 A.2d 1240. We did so in part "because to decide otherwise would conflict with public policy and the remedial purpose of the act. Except in very rare instances, the settlement and release of a claim does not cover claims based on events that have not yet occurred. . . . The usual general release, then, is not ordinarily construed to include in its coverage claims based upon occurrences which have their beginning after the instrument is executed. . . . For that reason, language covering 'future claims' and 'unknown claims' in releases is ordinarily construed to cover only inchoate claims that are in being at the time of release but which have not yet manifested themselves." (Citations omitted; internal quotation marks omitted.) Id., at 481–82, 650 A.2d 1240.

Contrary to the plaintiff's contention, Muldoon does not support a conclusion that an injured employee who settles his or her workers' compensation claim is without authority to compromise any claims that his or her surviving dependents might have under § 31–306. In fact, the claim asserted by the plaintiff is much more analogous to an "inchoate [claim] that [is] in being at the time of release but which [has] not yet manifested [itself]" than it is to the unforeseeable subsequent injury that was suffered by the employee in Muldoon. Id., at 481–82, 650 A.2d 1240. Although it is true, of course, that the plaintiff's rights under § 31–306 did not arise until after the stipulation had been signed, the decedent's death was a reasonably foreseeable consequence of the disabling occupational injuries that he had suffered and, accordingly, such a consequence was likely within the contemplation of the parties when they agreed to bar all claims "on account of any condition in any way resulting out of the said injuries."[4]

In light of the derivative nature of the rights created under § 31–306 and the public policy considerations involved, we agree with the review board that, under our workers' compensation scheme, an employee, in settling his or her claim for disability compensation, may also compromise his or her surviving dependents' rights under § 31–306.[5] Having determined that the decedent had the authority to extinguish the plaintiff's rights under § 31–306, we now turn to the question of whether the review board properly concluded that the stipulation accomplished that end.

The plaintiff maintains that even if the decedent had the authority to extinguish her rights under § 31–306, the stipulation was ineffective in doing so. We disagree.

In the context of workers' compensation, "[a] stipulation is a compromise and release type of settlement similar to settlements in civil personal injury cases where a claim is settled with a lump sum payment accompanied by a release of the adverse party from further liability. . . . Although the act does not explicitly provide for this type of settlement, we have consistently upheld the ability to compromise a compensation claim as inherent in the power to make a voluntary agreement regarding compensation. . . ." (Citation omitted; internal quotation marks omitted). Muldoon v. Homestead Insulation Co., supra, 231 Conn. at 479–80, 650 A.2d 1240.[6]

The stipulation entered into by the decedent and the defendants provides that it is in "complete satisfaction of all claims due or to become due at any time in favor of anybody on account of the claimed injuries or on account of any condition in any way resulting out of the said injuries." There is no doubt that the stipulation was intended to be broad in scope

---

4 The plaintiff points to cases from other jurisdictions, cited in 2 A. Larson, Workmen's Compensation (1996) § 64. 11, pp. 11–195–11–203, to support her contention that the stipulation does not bar her claim under § 31–306. Each of the cases relied on by the plaintiff, however, is distinguishable from the present case, because in none of those cases had the employee entered into a full, final and comprehensive settlement of his claim prior to his death.

5 As the review board stated, "[a]ll existing rights to compensation for [the decedent's] compensable injuries were vested in [him] at the time he signed the stipulation. No claim then existed that was not personal to him. Therefore, [the decedent] had the authority at the time the settlement was reached to release the [defendants] from liability for future claims arising out of his allegedly compensable injuries."

6 "There are three types of stipulations [in workers' compensation cases]: (1) a full and final stipulation that closes all aspects of the claim whether they are for past, present or future wages and medical expenses, known and unknown; (2) a stipulation to date that is used to close out only a portion of a claim with the remainder left open or that is used to close out an entire claim but only up to a certain date; and (3) an open medical stipulation that closes all aspects of the claim except for medical expenses that are related to the accident or the disease period." Muldoon v. Homestead Insulation Co., *supra*, 231 Conn. at 480, 650 A.2d 1240.

and, by its plain terms, purported to foreclose any and all workers' compensation claims arising out of the decedent's alleged injuries. On its face, then, the stipulation clearly encompasses a workers' compensation claim filed under § 31–306.

Notwithstanding the unambiguous breadth of the stipulation, the plaintiff argues that the word "anybody" in the stipulation reasonably can be construed to include only the estate of the decedent and his creditors but not his surviving dependents. As the review board stated in reversing the decision of the commissioner, however, " '[a]nybody' is a far more general term that simply refers to any person, and we will not favor a strained interpretation of that term over a straightforward one. We think it evident that the parties to the agreement contemplated the release of all claims that might result from the [decedent's] previous injuries, including those arising in favor of a third party." Because we agree with the conclusion of the review board, we reject the plaintiff's argument regarding the scope of the stipulation.

The decision of the review board is affirmed.

In this opinion the other justices concurred.

NOTES

1. As between *Buchanan* and *Duni*, which result is preferable? In a *Buchanan* type jurisdiction, is it ever possible for an employer to settle an employee's claim so as to preclude later claims by dependents for death benefits?

While *Buchanan* expresses the majority view, a few cases, either by statutory construction or common law analysis, take the approach espoused in *Duni*. See, e.g., Pigeon v. Department of Industry, Labor and Human Relations, 109 Wis.2d 519, 326 N.W.2d 752 (1982) (" . . . subject to the provisions of [Wis. Stats.] Sec. 102.16(1), a compromise of all liability entered into by an employee shall be binding upon his dependents"); Condoll v. Johns–Manville Sale Corp., 448 So.2d 169 (La.App.1984) (a compromise settlement of the worker's disability claim simultaneously compromised and settled the widow's claim); but see Bouy v. Teche Elec., 861 So.2d 712 (La.App. 3 Cir.2003) (questioning the correctness of the conclusion reached in *Condoll, supra*); and Lincoln Packing Co. v. Maude Coe, 120 Neb. 299, 232 N.W. 92 (1930) (employee who recovered workers' compensation award agreed to lump sum settlement of the amount; after worker's death, wife sought death benefits; held settlement extinguished wife's claim). And see generally 5–98 Larson's Workers' Compensation Law, Matthew Bender, § 98.01[2] (2013).

2. The *Buchanan* and *Duni* decisions agree that from one event (the compensable accident or disease) flows two distinct sets of injuries. One is incurred by the employee, the other by the dependents. *Buchanan* and *Duni* come to very different conclusions, however, about the ways in which the two

sets of harm relate to each other and to the core policy objectives of providing economic assistance to the decedent's family.

It may be helpful, when examining these connections, to look at how courts have characterized the bonds between personal injury actions, wrongful death claims, and the goals of the common law tort system. Many of the problems are the same.

As with claims for disability and death benefits under workers' compensation, both personal injury actions and wrongful death claims are intended to address the two separate sets of interests that emerge from the single act of the tortfeasor. Similar tensions between protecting unvested interests, avoiding double recoveries, and promoting the swift resolution of disputes are present. Frequently, it is the emphasis which a particular court gives to one or the other of these factors that determines the outcome of a case. See, e.g., Alfone v. Sarno, 87 N.J. 99, 432 A.2d 857, 870 (1981) ("The policy favoring settlement and finality of claims . . . cannot defeat statutory rights created for the protection of survivors of one wrongfully killed.") overruled on other grounds, La Fage v. Jani, 166 N.J. 412, 766 A.2d 1066 (2001); and Schwarder v. United States 974 F.2d 1118, 1123 (9th Cir.1992) (affirming that "California does not permit a decedent to compromise by contract the survivors' rights to wrongful death recovery"). Contrast, Variety Children's Hospital v. Perkins, 445 So.2d 1010, 1014 (Fla.1983) (The primary purpose of a wrongful death claim is to prevent a tortfeasor from avoiding liability for the consequences of his harmful actions. "The majority of courts have held that a judgement for or against the decedent in an action for his injuries commenced during his lifetime or the compromise and release of such action, will operate as a bar to any subsequent suit founded upon his death.").

3. Generally, in the workers' compensation context, the rights of the injured worker and those of the dependents are regarded as separate and independent. The worker's rights originate in the compensable injury and consequent disability whereas those of the dependents originate in the death of the worker as a result of the compensable injury. This independence is reinforced by workers' compensation statutes in several states which explicitly provide that none of an employee's dependents shall be considered parties in interest to any actions undertaken by the employee for the collection or compromise of a compensation claim. See, e.g., Col. Rev. Stat. Ann. § 8–41–504 (2013), Neb. Rev. Stat. § 48–124 (2012), and Mich. Comp. Laws Ann. § 418.341 (2013).

4. Several consequences follow from this independence, one of which is illustrated in *Buchanan.* A worker's release or compromise of a claim does not bar the dependents from claiming death benefits. See also, Brown v. General Aniline and Film Corp., 127 N.J.Super. 93, 316 A.2d 478, affirmed, 65 N.J. 555, 325 A.2d 689 (1974); and Roberts v. All American Engineering Co., 104 N.J.Super. 1, 248 A.2d 280 (1968). And, see generally, Workmen's Compensation—release or waiver of claim by employee as affecting right of

dependents in event of his death as result of injury, 101 A.L.R. 1410 (1936) (last updated 2012).

5. Another consequence of the independence of the worker's claim and that of the dependents, is that decisions and findings in any proceeding to which the worker was a party during the worker's lifetime are not binding as to dependents who survive the death. Thus in Wolanin v. Chrysler Corp., 304 Mich. 164, 7 N.W.2d 257 (1943) the employee suffered two injuries, one in 1934 and the other in 1935. He filed two claims. Compensation proceedings while he was alive determined that the 1934 injury was compensable but that the 1935 injury was not because it was merely a result of the 1934 incident. No appeal was taken. The claimant received compensation until he died in 1940 and his survivors then claimed death benefits. If the death was attributable to the 1934 injury, the dependents' claim was barred by the then existing statute; if it was attributable to the 1935 injury the claim was valid. The court held, first, that the death could be found to be a result of the 1935 injury and, second, that, pursuant to code section 17.157, the un-appealed finding in the prior proceeding (i.e., that the compensable injury occurred in 1934) was not binding on the survivors. Similarly, in Claimants of Hampton v. Director of Division of Labor, 31 Colo.App. 141, 500 P.2d 1186 (1972), the deceased worker's dependents' rights were held to be independent from the rights of the employee, thus the statute of limitations applicable to the worker's claim could not bar subsequent claims for death benefits. But see Chambers v. Electric Boat Corp., 283 Conn. 840, 930 A.2d 653 (2007) (statute of limitation required the filing of some claim within one year; employee lived beyond the one year without filing a claim or notice of claim; held widow's claim denied); Fredette v. Connecticut Nat. Guard, 283 Conn. 813, 930 A.2d 666 (2007) (widow's claim was subject to a 3 year statute of limitation from first manifestation of husband's occupational disease; some claim by employee or dependent must be filed within this 3 year period; held widow's claim timely filed); Wade & Richey v. Oglesby, 251 Ala. 356, 37 So.2d 596 (1948) (a decree fixing 100 weeks as the period of disability and specifying the amount of compensation did not bind the widow's claim for death benefits. ". . . the causes of action by the workman and his dependents on his death under the workmen's compensation act, are separate and distinct. Final determination of his rights under the statute could not conclude their rights under the statute."). And see, Mikolich v. State Industrial Accident Comm., 212 Or. 36, 316 P.2d 812 (1957) (a prior finding that decedent was temporarily disabled did not preclude a finding of permanent disability in the post death proceeding, thereby making possible a claim by the widow who was entitled to compensation only if the deceased had died during the period of permanent disability); and see, Singleton v. Kenya Corp., 961 P.2d 571 (Colo.App.1998) (while Col. Rev. Stat. § 8–42–116 predicates the recovery of death benefits upon proof that an industrial injury caused the deceased employee to suffer a permanent disability, the statute does not foreclose such posthumous proof when the employee dies of unrelated causes before reaching maximum medical improvement.).

Occasionally this principle works to the disadvantage of the claimant. For example, Chuplis v. Steve Shalamanda Coal Co., 192 Pa.Super. 76, 159 A.2d 520 (1960), denied a widow's claim for death benefits on the ground that the decedent was not an employee of the employer even though benefits had been awarded the decedent before his death. Contrast Card v. Lloyd Mfg. Co., 82 R.I. 182, 107 A.2d 297 (1954), in which the court held that a finding that decedent's injury arose out of and in the course of his employment was binding as to a claim filed by the decedent's widow. See generally 5–98 Larson's Workers' Compensation Law, Matthew Bender, § 98.01[4] (2013). And see Res judicata as regards decisions or awards under workmen's compensation acts, 122 A.L.R. 550 (1939) (last updated 2011).

6. A different case is presented, however, if the statutory conditions for compensation are affected by the employee's actions. See, e.g., Bennett Properties Co. v. Industrial Comm., 165 Colo. 135, 437 P.2d 548 (1968) (where death-causing injury resulted from violation of a safety rule for which the statutory penalty was 50% reduction of benefits, survivors were subject to the same reduction). See to the same effect, Aragon v. Anaconda Mining Co., 98 N.M. 65, 644 P.2d 1054 (1982) (employee's violation of safety rule resulted in 10% reduction of survivor's death benefit); and if during the lifetime of the employee, the employer's compensation obligations are fully discharged by payment and the employee thereafter dies due to the injury, the survivors may be limited to funeral and medical expenses of the last illness. See, e.g., Tidey v. Riverside Foundry and Galvanizing Co., 381 Mich. 551, 164 N.W.2d 3 (1969). Moreover, if the employee rejects the compensation law pursuant to statutory provisions authorizing rejection, the statute may thereafter be inapplicable to the worker and the worker's survivors. Coyner v. Industrial Comm., 77 Ariz. 210, 269 P.2d 712 (1954) (dependents' benefits while distinct from the rights of the employee, are contingent upon the existence of a compensable injury; if employee has elected to forgo coverage under the workers' compensation act, then the employee's dependents cannot receive death benefits under the act); and see Robertson ex rel. Robertson v. Industrial Com'n, 2009 WL 1482592 (Ariz.App. Div. 2 2009). When, however, the employee simply fails to seek injury benefits during his lifetime, his dependents may nevertheless recover death benefits. See, e.g., Conley–Slowinski v. Superior Spinning and Stamping Co., 128 Ohio App.3d 360, 714 N.E.2d 991 (1998). See also, Jones v. Multi–Color, 108 Ohio App.3d 388, 670 N.E.2d 1051 (1995) (pursuant to a provision in the Ohio Workers' Compensation Act, an employee may forgo his right to compensation by signing a pre-activity waiver before engaging in an employer sponsored recreational or fitness activity; the signing of the waiver precludes the employee from receiving a workers' compensation award but the dependents may still maintain an action for death benefits). As to the employee's waiver of rights under the workers' compensation act, see Watts v. Newberg, 920 S.W.2d 59 (Ky.1996) (employee given the option of maintaining his workers' compensation coverage and accepting a 20% reduction of wages or choosing an employer sponsored insurance plan and retaining regular salary; held, freedom of choice and an understanding of the consequences are prerequisites

to a valid waiver of workers' compensation coverage; the choice presented was coercive and against public policy; therefore, compensation was granted for injury which occurred after date invalid waiver was signed). But see, Croucher v. Croucher Excavating, Inc., 2013 WL 4040070 (Ky.App., 2013) (employee's rejection of workers' compensation coverage found to be knowing and voluntary).

7. The law in effect at the time of the decedent's injury may differ from that which existed at the time of death. As a result, courts may have to resolve which law is applicable to the survivor's death benefit claim. In Sizemore v. State Workmen's Compensation Com'r., 159 W.Va. 100, 219 S.E.2d 912 (1975), the statute in effect at the date of the decedent's injury conditioned survivor's benefits upon the occurrence of death within six years. The worker survived for nine years, but in the meantime the law had been changed to allow claims for death occurring within 10 years after injury. The court held that the law at the time of death controlled and allowed the claim. See also, Richards v. Richards and Richards, 664 P.2d 254 (Colo.App.1983) (widow's dependency benefits should have been calculated based on percentage of the state average weekly wage at the time of employee's death rather than at the time of his disablement). To the same effect see, Kisco v. Industrial Commission of Arizona, 190 Ariz. 389, 949 P.2d 49 (App.1997) (where injury causes death, death is the ultimate injury; accordingly, the class of beneficiaries and the amount of death benefits are determined as of the date of death); and, reaching the same conclusion, see Survivors of Young v. Island Feelings, Inc., 109 Hawaii 255, 125 P.3d 476 (2005) (calculation of death benefits based upon the maximum weekly benefit at time of employee's death). Contrast Cogswell v. Max Silverstein & Sons Inc., 488 A.2d 732 (R.I.1985) (determination of employee's rate of compensation was res judicata in the subsequent action for death benefits even though death benefits had been increased by legislature by the time of the employee's death). See generally 99 C.J.S. Workers' Compensation § 80, On death of Employee (updated 2013).

8. Each state's law provides a fixed maximum death benefit, which may be stated in terms of: (1) limited duration; (2) dollars per week; (3) total dollars; or (4) a combination of the three. Many states also provide for a minimum weekly payment. Because the number of eligible beneficiaries varies from one case to another, the statutes prescribe means to fix priorities among beneficiaries and to divide benefits among them. Commonly, if the beneficiaries consist only of a surviving spouse and children, the entire award goes to them and may increase according to the number of children. For examples of varying approaches, see O.C.G.A. § 34–9–13 (2013); Ky. Rev. Stat. § 342.750 (2013); McKinney's N.Y. Workers' Compensation Law, Sec. 16, par. 2 (2013).

Another common priority method provides that persons who were wholly dependent on the decedent take to the exclusion of others, sharing the maximum benefits among themselves. For a good discussion, see Pinecrest Memorial Park v. Miller, 7 Ark.App. 185, 646 S.W.2d 33 (1983). If there is no wholly dependent person, then those partially dependent take the benefits. N.C.Gen.Stats. Sec. 97–38 (2011). A survivor is wholly dependent within the meaning of the statute if conclusively presumed so or if dependency is proved as a fact by appropriate evidence. Shealy v. Associated Transport, Inc., 252 N.C. 738, 114 S.E.2d 702 (1960) (statute gave priority to those wholly dependent over those partially dependent; widower, who enjoyed conclusive presumption of total dependency, stood on equal footing with decedent's mother who was wholly dependent in fact). In Duffy v. Walsh–Kaiser Co., 75 R.I. 170, 64 A.2d 863 (1949), a surviving widow was accorded priority over a son of decedent by a former marriage who was living with his mother but was receiving partial support from decedent under a divorce decree.

Under some statutes, close relatives have priority in varying degrees over others, the closeness of relationship usually being the governing consideration. See, e.g., Robinson v. First Nat. City Bank of New York, 6 N.Y.2d 944, 190 N.Y.S.2d 1010, 161 N.E.2d 221 (1959) (future award to mother approved even though spouse and minor child survived); Johnson v. Johnson, 477 So.2d 21 (Fla.App.1985) (the entire benefit awarded to decedent's three children as members of a preferred class to exclusion of decedent's dependent mother); and Aragon v. Anaconda Mining Co., 98 N.M. 65, 644 P.2d 1054 (1982) (pursuant to statutory priority, apportionment of all benefits to decedent's son and none to partially dependent mother, affirmed on appeal). See generally, 99 C.J.S. Workers' Compensation § 321, Class and priority (updated 2013); and 82 Am. Jur.2d Workers' Compensation § 155, Priorities (updated 2013).

9. Most workers' compensation statutes terminate a surviving spouse's weekly death benefits upon remarriage. Frequently, however, the surviving spouse is entitled to a lump sum payment that is equivalent to the present day value of a prescribed number of weeks' worth of benefits. See, e.g., Utah Stat. § 34A–2–414(6)(a) (2013); S.D. Codified Laws Sec. 62–4–12 (2013). This award is separate from the weekly benefits and the employer may not credit the amounts already paid thereto against it. In Fort Smith v. Tate, 311 Ark. 405, 844 S.W.2d 356, 359 (1993), the statute provided that employer was liable for first $50,000 in weekly benefits and the Death and Permanent Total Disability Trust Fund for amounts in excess of $50,000. In holding the employer liable for the lump sum payment even though employer had already satisfied the $50,000 maximum in weekly benefits, the court reasoned, "The obvious purpose of the lump sum benefit provision upon remarriage is to lessen the disincentive to remarry that would be inherent in a flat cutoff of dependency benefits. This disincentive . . . does not cease to exist when the employer reaches his maximum liability in weekly benefits; it continues indefinitely because the widow continues to receive benefits from the Fund. Therefore, the need for the reduction of the disincentive in the form of a lump sum payment is still needed even after the employer reaches this maximum liability." To the same effect, see Arkansas Elec. Co-op Corp. v. Death & Permanent Disability Trust Fund, 2012 WL 11262 (2012 Ark.App. 13). See also, Self v. Industrial Commission of Arizona, 192 Ariz. 399, 966 P.2d 1003

(App.1998) ("The surviving spouse's periodic benefit terminates upon remarriage and the lump sum benefit is an independent payment rather than an advance on monthly compensation. Therefore, when the surviving spouse's monthly benefits terminate, the dependent children's monthly death benefits should be recalculated immediately without consideration of the lump sum benefit."); Todd v. W.C.A.B., 547 Pa. 687, 692 A.2d 1086 (1997) (statute authorized termination of weekly benefits and the payment of a lump sum when a widow remarried; if the widow entered into a meretricious relationship, she forfeited both her weekly benefits and her future entitlement to the lump sum; claimant lived with her fiancé for two years prior to marrying him; Hearing Officer, Appeals Board, and the Commonwealth Court all held that the widow had forfeited her right to the lump sum; State Supreme Court reversed holding the date on which the employer filed the petition to terminate benefits was the date upon which the widow's status was evaluated; as the widow had remarried one month prior to the employer's petition, she retained her right to the lump sum payment). Reaching a contrary result, see J. H. v. W.C.A.B., 810 A.2d 186 (Pa. Cmwlth., 2002) (if surviving spouse enters into a meretricious relationship, death benefits would terminate on date when such relationship began). And, see generally, 82 Am. Jur.2d Workers' Compensation § 180, Marriage or remarriage; effect of annulment thereof (updated 2013).

10. In the absence of a controlling statute, courts generally hold that *unaccrued* installments of a compensation award do not survive the death of the entitled worker. Rozales v. Peerless Welder, Inc., 311 Minn., 6, 246 N.W.2d 851 (1976) (permanent partial disability benefits are personal to the employee; consequently, they do not survive when the death of the employee is from causes unrelated to the compensable injury.) County of Spotsylvania v. Hart, 218 Va. 565, 238 S.E.2d 813 (1977) (decedent's claim for schedule injury had not accrued because his condition had not reached the point of maximum improvement at time of his death from other cause; thus because permanent partial benefits had not accrued, survivors had no right to receive any unpaid benefits); Contrast, Singleton, *supra*, note 5 (worker suffered work-related permanent disability but died of non- work-related cause before reaching maximum medical improvement; court determined proof may be made posthumously that employee suffered a work-related permanent disability; and such proof can be used to estimate the extent of disability that would have remained if the employee had lived long enough to reach maximum medical improvement; based upon such proof, dependent, widow, entitled to recover unpaid and unaccrued permanent disability benefits); and see Floyd v. C. B. Askins & Co. Contractors, 382 S.C. 84, 675 S.E.2d 450 (2009) (pursuant to statute, dependent survivors shall receive unaccrued installments of decedent's scheduled injury losses while dependents of a person totally disabled for another reason (wage loss disability) should not; thus survivors' rights to unaccrued benefits are determined by whether decedent's loss was "physical loss" or "wage loss."); Estate of Peterson v. J.R. Simplot Co., 83 Idaho 120, 358 P.2d 587 (1961) (acknowledging that compensation for permanent partial disability, according to statutory

schedule, was in the nature of liquidated damages and payable to dependents); Parker v. Walgreen Drug Co., 63 Ariz. 374, 162 P.2d 427 (1945) (schedule award is a vested right and payable to dependents after employee's death); and Pfefer v. Winer & Saroff Comm. Co., 227 Mo.App. 280, 49 S.W.2d 293 (1932) (death benefit award to a dependent child survives dependent child's death and his personal representative is entitled to the unpaid portion of the award). See 4–89 Larson's Workers' Compensation Law, Matthew Bender, § 89.03 (2013).

A number of states have enacted statutes providing that unaccrued installments of an injury award are to be paid after death of the employee (from a cause unrelated to the injury) to named persons, usually dependents who would have received support from the payments if the employee had lived. For example, Snyder v. Wickwire Spencer Steel Co., 277 App.Div. 233, 98 N.Y.S.2d 1006 (1950), applied Mckinney's Workers' Compensation Law Sec.15(4), where worker suffered separate and distinct work-related accidents and allowed surviving widow to maintain two claims after the death of her husband—one for a post mortem scheduled award from an earlier work-related injury and the other for death benefits from a later work-related injury. See also, Ala. Code Sec. 25–5–57(5) (2013).

Payments *accrued* but unpaid prior to the death of the employee usually are payable either to the dependents or to the estate. Breen v. Industrial Acc. Bd., 150 Mont. 463, 436 P.2d 701 (1968) (injured employee died from intoxication; widow entitled to accrued unpaid compensation installments but not death benefits). When an injured worker has filed no claim for a compensable injury suffered prior to death from a cause unrelated to the injury, or an award has been made but is on appeal, some courts permit the survivors to file the claim or pursue the award. See, e.g., Kozielec v. Mack Mfg. Corp., 29 N.J.Super. 272, 102 A.2d 404 (1953) (employee had not filed a claim during his lifetime; held, his surviving widow could file an original claim after his death from cause not related to the compensable accident); Black v. Lofland, 869 So.2d 264 (La.App. 2 Cir.2004) (the right of an employee to enforce the obligation of the employer to pay disability benefits is a heritable property right which is transmitted to his heirs upon his death but here decedent had been paid all accrued benefits to which he was entitled); Falcon Coal Co. v. Sweet, 518 S.W.2d 343 (Ky.1974) (decedent died after filing claim and submitting proof but before case was submitted for decision; held, dependents could continue claim and were entitled to compensation); Brandner v. Myers Funeral Home, 330 Mich. 392, 47 N.W.2d 658 (1951) (employee died while award was on appeal in which it was affirmed; administrator of employee's estate entitled to amounts accrued between date of award and date of employee's death). Others do not permit the post-death claims. See, e.g., State of Wisconsin v. Labor and Industry Review Commission, 136 Wis.2d 281, 401 N.W.2d 585 (1987). And see 4–89 Larson's Workers' compensation Laws, Matthew Bender, § 89.05 (2013).

CHAPTER 10

ADMINISTRATION OF WORKERS' COMPENSATION LAWS

■ ■ ■

1. INTRODUCTION TO THIS CHAPTER

For Forms of Government Let Fools Contest;
Whate'er Is Best Administered Is Best:[1]

It would be impossible to overemphasize the importance of effective administration to the success of any workers' compensation law. No such statute, regardless of the high quality of its substantive content, can accomplish or even approach the objectives of the workers' compensation system, if that statute is poorly administered. Some of the disappointments experienced in the past by those interested in the workers' compensation movement are the results of inept administration.

The main purposes of administration are to insure that the law is understood by workers and employers affected by it, that workers are aware of their rights and obligations, and that those rights and obligations are enforced. The fulfillment of these purposes involves many functions entirely apart from the resolution of disputes between contesting parties. Indeed, most compensation claims are uncontested. Included among the necessary administrative functions are dissemination of information to employees and employers; supervision of benefit payments in uncontested cases; surveillance of compromises in cases in which disputes exist; continuing supervision of awards, sometimes over a long period of time; and the encouragement of and assistance in rehabilitation of injured employees. Good administration also includes keeping accident records and related data, compiling statistics about the law's operation and its defects, and making recommendations to the executive and the legislative branches of the state government. These tasks call for the highest caliber of public service, but unfortunately, many of them have not always received the attention, effort, and legislative support they should have had.

This chapter briefly considers some of the more important aspects of workers' compensation administration. Most workers' compensation systems are administered by special agencies. The manner in which these

---

[1] Alexander Pope, *An Essay on Man*, Epistle III, Lines 303–4, 1733–34.

agencies handle uncontested cases has great practical significance, although often its importance is not realized by lawyers accustomed to thinking in terms of adversary proceedings. In contested cases, a number of procedural matters have considerable substantive significance in the functioning of the law. These include notice of injury, statutes of limitation, rules of evidence, judicial review, compromise of disputed claims, lump-sum settlements, and modification and reopening of awards. In these areas each state's laws, practices, customs and traditions are more peculiarly its own than in any other.[2] Consequently, the brief review in this chapter is limited to pointing up the sources and nature of the most common controversies.

2. ADMINISTRATION BY SPECIAL AGENCY

The administrative arrangements of the state, federal, and territorial workers' compensation laws vary greatly in detail, but fall into patterns of identifiable general categories. In most jurisdictions administrative responsibility and authority are vested in a special state agency, but a few states still rely on substantial court involvement in the administration of the law. Students of workers' compensation generally deem court administration to be inferior to agency administration and to reduce the effectiveness of the law substantially.[3] This view holds that courts are not equipped to handle all aspects of workers' compensation administration effectively. For example, injured workers often need the type of help in the early stages of their distress that the initiative of a properly functioning administrative agency can best provide. A court on the other hand must await the initiative of the parties. Moreover, courts generally do not have facilities or staff for following up initial determinations as to disability, insuring prompt payments, keeping statistics, publishing information needed by both employer and employees, and performing the many other tasks that must be done.

Arrangements for administration of the law by special agency may take any one of several forms. Two specific examples are, first, a single administrative officer responsible directly to a state cabinet officer such

[2] For a state-by-state survey of various aspects of administrative practices, Ramona P. Tanable, Workers' Compensation Laws 2012 (Workers' Compensation Research Institute March 2012) [hereinafter referred to as WCRI, Workers' Compensation Laws 2012]; United States Chamber of Commerce, 2013 Analysis of Workers' Compensation Laws. See also National Academy of Social Insurance, Workers' Compensation Benefits, Coverage and Costs, 2010 (August, 2012) (information about costs).

[3] In 1936 Dodd concluded "Where attempted in the United States, it may safely be said that court administration of workmen's compensation has failed." Dodd, Administration of Workmen's Compensation 98 (1936). See also Somers & Somers, Workmen's Compensation 143–150 (1954); National Commission on State Workmen's Compensation, Compendium on Workmen's Compensation 217 (1973). In 2013, Tennessee and Oklahoma moved from a judicial to an administrative system. This leaves Alabama as the last state with a judicial system. 36 Workers' Compensation Law Bulletin, Issue 11, pp. 6–7 (June 10, 2013).

as the Commissioner of Labor, and, second, a commission or board responsible directly to the governor.

In the early part of the century it was common to create an administrative tribunal with legislative (rule-making), administrative, and adjudicative powers and authority. This concept rested on the premise that the bulk of the work in administering a workers' compensation law was to render decisions of contested claims. In fact, however, the vast majority of cases are not disputed and the primary need is for an administrative structure that insures the system efficiently and speedily gets benefit payments into the hands of injured workers and their medical attendants. In light of this need most states now employ a system in which an executive officer and staff administer the ordinary non-contested bulk of the payments, and in which appeals from the decisions of hearing officers are reviewed by a separate independent appeals board. This system is recommended by the National Commission on State Workmen's Compensation Laws.[4]

In some states, advisory committees composed of groups representing labor, industry and the public meet regularly to consider compensation issues and make recommendations for improvement or reform. These recommendations are often submitted to the legislature as agreed bills and thus are not the subject of dispute and debate on the legislative floor. To the extent that this approach permits non-controversial bills to be enacted without unnecessary political battling it serves a highly useful function of keeping the workers' compensation laws up to date. Nevertheless, matters that affect the cost of the plan to employers, such as coverage and benefits, rarely are enacted without extensive consideration by the legislatures. Despite this, an advisory committee composed of conscientious members of good will interested in improving the effectiveness of the law can accomplish a great deal.

3. WAITING PERIOD

The workers' compensation acts of every state provide that a specified period of time must elapse after an injury occurs before the employee has a right to receive disability benefits to offset lost earnings. What this means is that a work injury is not compensable unless the resulting disability continues longer than the stipulated waiting period. For example, an employee who loses three days of pay as a result of an injury will receive no workers' compensation benefits to make up the lost wages in a state with a five day waiting period. (Of course, nothing keeps the employer from voluntarily maintaining the wages.) A waiting period is not normally required for medical benefits.

---

[4] The Report of the National Commission on State Workmen's Compensation Laws 101–103 (1972).

The purposes of the waiting period are to exclude minor injuries from the compensation scheme, to discourage malingering and to avoid excessive costs and administrative overhead. Initially, the customary length of the period was two weeks, but it has steadily diminished until today waiting periods vary among the states from three to seven days.[5] All states provide that if the disability continues more than a specified length of time, compensation benefits are retroactive to the date of injury. The length of that period varies from five days to six weeks.[6]

Varying the lengths of the waiting and retroactivity periods substantially affects benefits. Consider two workers, each earning $500 a week. Worker A is employed in a state with a three day waiting period and a seven day retroactivity period; worker B is employed in a state with a seven day waiting period and a 21 day retroactivity period. Each state's rate of compensation is 66 percent of the weekly wage. The two suffer identical injuries and are disabled for two weeks. Worker A would receive $660 in income benefits while the worker B would receive $330.

4. UNCONTESTED CASES

Approximately 90 percent of the cases of work-connected injury or disease, liability is not disputed either as to matters of fact or questions of law.[7] With them no adversary proceeding is necessary and the paramount administrative task is to see to it that compensation is promptly paid the injured workers. To achieve this most states prescribe that the claim is made directly to the employer or the employer's insurer. In the few states that employ exclusive state funds to pay benefits the claim is made to the agency administering the fund.[8] In the states that currently employ a competitive state fund the claim is made against either the employer or employer's insurer or the state body administering the fund, depending on which is carrying the risk.[9] Thus, in uncontested cases the prime function of agency administering the workmen's compensation act is to insure that the employers and those required to pay the compensation fulfill their obligations under the law. The states have two kinds of payment systems to accomplish this function.

---

[5] WCRI, Workers' Compensation Laws 2012, supra note 2, at table 13.

[6] For a listing of various state waiting periods on this point see WCRI, Workers' Compensation Laws 2012, supra note 2, at table 13.

[7] 8 A. Larson L. Larson, Larson's Workers' Compensation Law § 132.01 (2013).

[8] WCRI, Workers' Compensation Law 2012, supra note 2 at table 1 (listing North Dakota, Ohio, Washington, and Wyoming; Ohio, Washington and Wyoming also permit self insurance in certain instances.)

[9] Id.

A. THE AGREEMENT SYSTEM

The earliest workers' compensation systems employed what is known as the "agreement system" for handling uncontested cases. It assumed that the administration of workers' compensation would be largely an automatic, self-executing and inexpensive process. Under the agreement system an employer or insurer proposes a settlement to the employee. If the proposal is accepted, the employee signs an agreement and payments begin after a somewhat routine approval by the state administrative body. If no dispute arises, state officials neither investigate nor intervene.

Critics of the agreement system deem it to be unsatisfactory for two reasons; first, workers often are not able to protect their own interests; and, second, initial payments are delayed for substantial periods. As to the first point, critics observe that many workers do not read well or understand complicated documents and explanations of the technicalities of the law. By contrast, employers routinely employ experienced representatives who are able to bargain skillfully. Furthermore, employers gain economically from any delays in the commencement of payments, whereas injured workers usually need money quickly. Thus the bargaining position of workers is relatively poor.[10] Whether or not this bargaining disparity actually results in undue delay is harder to verify because of the lack of data demonstrating the facility or sluggishness of the system. Nevertheless, anecdotal evidence supports the criticism. For example, Michigan employed the agreement system for some thirty years before changing to the direct payment plan. One experienced observer concluded that the change immediately increased the number of workers receiving compensation within two weeks of the date of injury by a considerable margin.[11]

B. THE DIRECT PAYMENT SYSTEM

The second basic method used in administering uncontested cases is known as the "direct payment" system. It was initially developed in Wisconsin to shorten the amount of time elapsing between the occurrence of an injury and the time the first benefit payment is made and to subject workers to the least formal procedure. Most states now employ direct payment systems.

Under the direct payment plan, employers report the occurrences of compensable injuries directly to the state administrative body. The initial report is followed by a second report, filed either by the employer or the

---

[10] Harry J. Burczyk, Commissioner Wisconsin Industrial Commission (1947) Bull. No. 87, p. 129, U.S. Department of Labor, Bureau of Labor Standards.

[11] U.S. Department of Labor, Division of Labor Standards, Bull. No. 80, p. 39 at 44 (1946) (statement of Harry A. Nelson, Director, Workmen's Compensation, Wisconsin Industrial Commission); See also comments by James L. Hill quoted in Somers and Somers "Workmen's Compensation" 155 (1954).

insurer, verifying the commencement of payments or stating why no payment has been made. Finally, another report is filed when payments are discontinued stating why, and describing the nature of any dispute that may exist between the parties. Final settlements are promptly reported with a copy of the final receipt signed by the injured employee.

In many states, the administrative agency informs the injured worker in writing of the rights and duties under the statute as soon as it receives notice of a compensable accident. The agency makes a public record of how promptly insurers make payments and may impose penalties on employers and carriers who are guilty of unreasonable delays.

The agency ordinarily does not pass upon the validity of undisputed final settlements and these cases may be reopened within a specified period after the settlements are filed. When settlement is reached after genuine dispute, the agency does approve it and the right to reopen often is limited to a shorter period.

Experienced observers claim that the direct payment system has speeded up payments and created a cordial atmosphere between employees and employers and carriers. One report concluded that it tends to "eliminate contests which otherwise might arise and to prevent hearings and appeals."

5. CONTESTED CASES

A. GENERAL APPROACH

States that utilize an administrative agency to adjudicate disputed workers' compensation claims generally employ informal and expeditious procedures[12] that avoid the sometimes technical and cumbersome procedures that govern civil litigation.[13] The obvious purpose is to facilitate prompt and inexpensive resolution of claims. Nevertheless, the resolution of a contested compensation claim is essentially a judicial function[14] and adherence to prescribed formalities is necessary to ensure fairness and uniformity in the application of the law. Thus, fact finders

[12] E.g., Mo.Rev.Stat. § 287.550 ("All proceedings before the commission or any commissioner shall be simple, informal and summary, and without regard to the technical rules of evidence. . . .").

[13] See generally, 7 A. Larson and L. Larson, Larson's Workers' Compensation Law §§ 124.01–124.08 (2013).

[14] E.g., Reck v. Whittlesberger, 181 Mich. 463, 148 N.W. 247 (1914) (a compensation commission is a judicial as well as an administrative body and should observe the elementary principles governing judicial inquiry); Fremont Indem. Co. v. Workers' Compensation Appeals Board, 153 Cal.App.3d 965, 200 Cal.Rptr. 762 (1984) (the Board acts "in legal effect" as a court and must observe the constitutional mandates of due process, including the prohibition on receiving unsworn testimony).

must be impartial[15] and must base decisions on appropriate evidence that appears in the record.[16] The following subsections address some of the procedural and evidentiary aspects of a contested workers' compensation claim.

B. NOTICE OF INJURY

As a condition precedent to entitlement to benefits, most workers' compensation statutes require employees to notify employers of work injuries "forthwith" or within a period of time specified in the statute.[17] Notice serves two purposes. One is to afford the employer an opportunity to mitigate the effects of the injury by furnishing medical treatment without delay, and the other is to afford the employer an opportunity to investigate the circumstances under which the injury occurred.[18]

In deciding whether the failure to give notice should defeat the claim, courts regularly take into account both the remedial aims of the law and the purposes of the requirement. Lack of notice is often excused, especially if the employer has not demonstrated prejudice. For example, prompt notice is commonly excused if the employee could not reasonably have realized that the injury was one likely to lead to a compensable disability. In this situation, many courts have adopted something akin to the "discovery rule" in civil litigation, under which the time for giving notice does not begin to run until the employee should reasonably recognize the nature, seriousness, and probable compensatory character of the claim. In Slater v. United Parcel Service,[19] for example, a seasonal employee suffered a back injury on his last day of work. At that time he thought he had suffered only a mild back strain. The full extent of his injury was not known until a CAT-Scan was performed several months later. The court held that the claimant's failure to give notice within 30 days of the accident did not bar the claim because the disabling character of the injury was not reasonably known until the CAT-Scan had been performed. This is but one of innumerable decided cases in which administrative bodies and courts, guided by the foregoing principles, have

---

[15] E.g., Delta Air Lines, Inc. v. McDaniel, 176 Ga.App. 523, 336 S.E.2d 610 (1985) (reversing an award made to employee when one of the directors of the State Board of Workers' Compensation that heard the employer's appeal was the father-in-law of the employee's attorney); Vayiar v. Vic Tanny Int'l., 114 Mich.App. 388, 319 N.W.2d 338 (1982) (the composition of the appeals panel violated employer's due process rights when 2 of its 3 members were representatives of employee interests).

[16] E.g., Crowell v. Benson, 285 U.S. 22, 52 S.Ct. 285, 76 L.Ed. 598 (1932) (award cannot be upheld on the basis of evidence that was not placed in the record).

[17] E.g., Ariz.Rev.Stat.Ann. § 23–908(f) ("forthwith"); Mich.Comp.Laws Ann. 418.381(1) (within 90 days); Utah Code Ann. 34A–2–407(3) (within 180 days).

[18] See generally, Bucuk v. Edward A. Zusi Brass Foundry, 49 N.J.Super. 187, 139 A.2d 436 (1958).

[19] 507 So.2d 1146 (Fla.App.1987).

been willing to overlook technical non-compliance with notice of injury requirements.

Another set of "notice" issues focuses on how and to whom notice is given. Strict compliance with formal procedure is not required.[20] No matter how acquired, actual knowledge of the accident by the employer is sufficient to constitute notice,[21] and, most jurisdictions impute notice to the employer when a supervisor or other representative employee is aware of the accident or injury.[22]

Nevertheless, because the notice of injury requirement is imposed by statute, claims are occasionally denied because of lack of notice. For example, an employer's awareness that a worker has congenital problems that often cause pain is not notice of an alleged work-related aggravation;[23] and simply telling co-workers of an alleged injury does not constitute notice if those co-workers have no supervisory or representative responsibilities.[24]

C. STATUTES OF LIMITATIONS

All workers' compensation statutes require that claims be filed within a specified period of time, usually one or two years from the date of injury or accident. This time-based restriction on filing is in the nature of a statute of limitations and is intended to protect employers against claims too old to be successfully investigated and defended. While noncompliance with notice provisions is sometimes excused when there is no showing of prejudice to the employer, statutes of limitations are not as easily avoided. Courts, in effect, construe statutes of limitations as carrying a conclusive presumption that an employer is prejudiced by a late filing.[25]

---

[20] E.g., Ziegler v. Workmen's Compensation Appeals Board, 101 Pa.Cmwlth. 392, 516 A.2d 128 (1986) (employee did not have to comply with employer's internal reporting procedures; notice to the foreman sufficed).

[21] E.g., Moon v. Auto-Owners Ins. Co., 736 S.W.2d 92 (Tenn.1987) (Notice was given when an officer of the corporate employer witnessed the trench cave-in, even though the officer did not believe the claimant had been injured).

[22] E.g., Williams v. Travelers Ins. Co., 153 Ga.App. 443, 265 S.E.2d 354 (1980) (employer had notice because the foreman was aware of the accident); Ross v. Oxford Paper Co., 363 A.2d 712 (Me.1976) (treatment of workplace injury by company doctor is notice to employer); Thompson v. Monfort of Colo., Inc., 221 Neb. 83, 375 N.W.2d 601 (1985) (notice may be satisfied by informing foreman, plant supervisor, or company nurse of injury).

[23] Reil v. Billings Processors, Inc., 229 Mont. 305, 746 P.2d 617 (1987).

[24] E.g., Wallace v. Gentry, 150 So.2d 66 (La.App.1963) (co-workers). Cf. Masters v. Industrial Garments Mfg. Co., 595 S.W.2d 811 (Tenn.1980) (telling Union president of back pain is not notice to the employer).

[25] E.g., Cecil W. Perry, Inc. v. Lopez, 425 So.2d 180 (Fla.App.1983) (claim filed one day after the expiration of the limitation period must be dismissed); Asato v. Meadow Gold Dairies–Hawaii, 68 Hawaii 111, 706 P.2d 13 (1985) (untimely claims are barred even if the employer does not allege that lateness impaired its ability to investigate and defend).

Disputes pertaining to workers' compensation statutes of limitations are most likely to arise in claims involving latent or progressive conditions in which the key issue is determining when the limitation period began to run. In most states, either by statute or judicial opinion, the time period for filing a claim does not begin to run until the claimant reasonably should recognize the nature, seriousness and probable compensable character of the injury or disease.[26] This approach is often referred to as the "discovery rule" and enables a worker to file a claim even if the disabling condition does not become manifest until several years after the work related "accident." The discovery rule is especially important in occupational disease claims involving a long delay between exposure and manifestation of the disability.[27] Where a discovery rule applies, decisions often turn on the fact-specific question of when this claimant should have recognized the presence of a potentially compensable injury or disease. For example, a worker may not be expected to attribute a stomach rash and infectious bone inflammation to an on-the-job back injury until so advised by a treating physician,[28] but may be expected to see the connection between a convulsion requiring hospitalization and an earlier compensable head injury.[29]

In a few states, the statute of limitations begins to run from the date of the "accident." This may lead to the denial of benefits when there is a substantial gap between the time of the "accident" and the onset of "disability." In Ingram v. Land-Air Transportation Co.,[30] for example, the worker fell off a truck injuring his shoulder. Because his treating physician said the injury was not serious, the employee did not file a workers' compensation claim and continued to work. The employee's shoulder gradually deteriorated, reaching the point of "disability" more than two years later. Although recognizing its distinct minority position and the harshness it produces, the court dismissed the employee's claim because it had not been filed within two years of the "accident." Leading

---

[26] E.g., Ariz.Rev.Stat.Ann. § 23–1061(A); Wis.Stat. § 102.12; Dafermo v. Municipality of Anchorage, 941 P.2d 114 (Alaska 1997).

[27] A majority of states today employ a discovery rule for occupational disease claims. E.g., Cal.Labor Code § 5412, Del.Code Ann. tit. 19, § 2361(d); N.J.Stat.Ann. § 34:15–34. Some states have a separate (and generally longer) limitation period for a few particular diseases, such as asbestosis and silicosis. E.g., Ark.Stat.Ann. § 11–9–601. A state by state summary of occupational disease limitation provisions can be found at 3 A. Larson and L. Larson, Larson's Workers' Compensation Law § 53.04[2](2013). The student is reminded that other aspects of time-based restrictions on occupational disease claims are discussed in Chapter 6 in the notes following Rutledge v. Tultex Corp./Kings Yarn.

[28] Sherman v. Industrial Commission, 158 Ariz. 177, 761 P.2d 1081 (App.1988).

[29] Bowers v. Wayne Lovelady Dodge, Inc., 80 N.M. 475, 457 P.2d 994 (App.1969).

[30] 537 N.E.2d 532 (Ind.App.1989). See also, Latino v. Binswanger Glass Co., 532 So.2d 960 (La.App.1988) (The claimant was injured on the job when metal particles blew and implanted into his eyes. This accident did not produce any permanent or temporary disability at the time and no workers' compensation claim was filed. More than two years later, however, the implanted particles rusted, leading to the loss of one eye. The worker was denied compensation under a statute that required all claims to be filed within two years of the original accident).

commentators[31] criticize as unjust a rule that starts the limitation period at the date of accident regardless of the worker's lack of knowledge that an injury has occurred.

Although some early workers' compensation decisions held that timely commencement of compensation proceedings was "jurisdictional" and could not be waived,[32] only a few states currently give limitations periods that conclusive effect.[33] Instead, most states treat an objection to the timeliness of a claim as a defense that may be forfeited by waiver or estoppel. For example, many courts have held that payments made by an employer under group health or nonoccupational disability insurance policies toll the limitation period for filing a workers' compensation claim,[34] especially in "heart attack" and occupational disease cases where the work-relatedness of the disability is uncertain. These payments are most likely to toll the statute of limitations if they offset compensation liability or are reasonably viewed as remuneration in lieu of compensation.[35] Furthermore, employers are estopped from asserting a limitation defense if their actions mislead or prevent an employee from filing a timely claim.[36] Finally, in most jurisdictions lack of timeliness of filing a claim is waived as a defense if it is not raised in a timely fashion.[37]

---

[31] 7 A. Larson and L. Larson, Larson's Workers' Compensation Law § 126.06[3] (2013).

[32] E.g., American Car and Foundry Co. v. Industrial Commission, 335 Ill. 322, 167 N.E. 80 (1929). But cf. Railway Express Agency v. Industrial Commission, 415 Ill. 294, 114 N.E.2d 353 (1953) (calling into question whether limitation period can be waived).

[33] E.g., Seckman v. Wyo–Ben, Inc., 783 P.2d 161 (Wyo.1989) (since limitation periods pertain to the subject matter jurisdiction, a court may properly dismiss, *sua sponte,* compensation claim filed outside the period even if the issue was not raised by the defendant).

[34] E.g., New Castle County v. Goodman, 461 A.2d 1012 (Del.1983) (payment of two medical bills by employer tolled the limitation period for filing claim); Caterpillar Tractor Co. v. Industrial Comm., 33 Ill.2d 78, 210 N.E.2d 215 (1965) (payments made under group insurance plan covering nonoccupational disabilities effectively tolled the workers' compensation limitations period); Jaeger v. Stauffer Chem. Co., 198 Mont. 263, 645 P.2d 942 (1982) (payment of claimant's salary for a year and a half following injury tolled the statute of limitations).

[35] Compare, Frost v. Anaconda Co., 198 Mont. 216, 645 P.2d 419 (1982) ("Compensation, to toll the statute, must be sufficient to convince the recipient that he is receiving such a large percentage of workers' compensation benefits available to him that to seek further benefits would be a wasted effort.") with Maxey v. Fremont Dept. of Utilities, 220 Neb. 627, 371 N.W.2d 294 (1985) (payments for wages or medical services under an employee benefit plan does not toll the statute unless they clearly indicate that they constitute payment of compensation). See also, Caterpillar Tractor Co. v. Industrial Comm., 33 Ill.2d 78, 210 N.E.2d 215 (1965) (payments received under group nonoccupational disability insurance plan tolled the statute of limitations and the employer was entitled to a credit for the group insurance payments).

[36] E.g., Stines v. Winter Haven Hospital, 548 So.2d 818 (Fla.App.1989) (statute of limitation did not bar claim when employer sent "entitlement of rights" letter to wrong address); Hutcherson v. Dawn Trucking Co., 107 N.M. 358, 758 P.2d 308 (App.1988) (claimant's testimony that insurance adjuster assured him that everything will be taken care of raises a fact issue whether claimant had been lulled into letting the statute of limitations elapse).

[37] E.g., Priedigkeit v. Industrial Comm., 20 Ariz.App. 594, 514 P.2d 1045 (1973) (statute of limitations defense was waived when it was not raised at the first hearing); Maryland Casualty Co. v. Smith, 122 Ga.App. 262, 176 S.E.2d 666 (1970) (statute of limitation defense was waived by failing to raise the issue at the administrative hearing).

The limitation period for compensation claims arising from the death of an employee usually runs from the date of death.[38] The dependent's right to death benefits is not derived from the rights of the deceased employee but is created directly by statute and does not accrue until the death of the employee. Thus, it is no defense to a dependent's claim for death benefits that the deceased employee failed to file a timely claim for injuries resulting from the occupational disease or accident that led to death.[39]

D. EVIDENCE

As a general proposition, the rules of evidence are applied in a relaxed fashion in workers' compensation hearings. Indeed, many statutes expressly provide that the hearing is not governed by the technical rules of evidence that apply in civil litigation.[40] The emphasis on informality undoubtedly reflects both the remedial purposes of workers' compensation and the prevalence of professional administrative factfinders. Administrative law judges are more likely to receive hearsay evidence and give a more generous scope to the exceptions to the hearsay rule than would their counterparts on the trial bench. The most striking example of this may be the routine admission of letters and reports of physicians without the rigorous foundation ordinarily required in civil trials.[41] Rarely is an award or denial of workers' compensation benefits reversed because of the improper admission of evidence, but the exclusion of competent evidence is sometimes reversible error.[42] Consequently, hearing examiners and administrative law judges tend to err on the side of admitting disputed evidence.

Evidentiary disputes most frequently arise regarding proof of medical facts. Many of these medical issues have been discussed in earlier chapters. For example, the extent of disability, and hence the amount of compensation, is often determined by reference to the A.M.A. *Guides to*

---

[38] E.g., N.Y. Work.Comp. Law § 28; Ohio Rev.Code Ann. § 4123.84.

[39] E.g., Berkebile v. Workers' Compensation Appeals Board, 144 Cal.App.3d 940, 193 Cal.Rptr. 12 (1983) (widow could file claim for death benefits even if her husband never filed an occupational disease claim arising from lingering illness); Mentzer v. Westinghouse Corp., 10 Ohio App.3d 198, 461 N.E.2d 24 (1983) (widow's claim for death benefits is timely even if her deceased husband's claim was not). See also notes following Deeni v. United Technologies Corp. reprinted in Chapter 9, Section 3.

[40] E.g., N.Y. Work.Comp. Law § 118; Utah Code Ann. § 34A–2–802.

[41] E.g., Foster v. Continental Casualty Co., 141 Ga.App. 415, 233 S.E.2d 492 (1977) (it was proper for the workers' compensation board to consider a letter from a doctor even though the signature was not authenticated); Forrest v. Industrial Commission, 77 Ill.2d 86, 32 Ill.Dec. 346, 395 N.E.2d 576 (1979) (letter from claimant's chiropractor to claimant's attorney was properly admitted into evidence).

[42] E.g., Gill v. Workers' Compensation Appeals Board, 167 Cal.App.3d 306, 213 Cal.Rptr. 140 (1985) (reversing the board's finding of only a partial disability when the board improperly refused to consider report of vocational counselor); Tradewinds Mfg. Co. v. Cox, 541 So.2d 667 (Fla.App.1989) (reversible error not to permit the employer to prove that it made overpayments by calling the claimant as a witness).

the Evaluation of Permanent Impairment.[43] Under the *Guides*, impairment ratings are generally considered a medical fact. Proof of causation is also a frequently disputed medical issue. Did the claimant's work-related trauma cause the subsequent cancer?[44] Did workplace stress cause the disabling heart attack?[45] Was the claimant's disabling respiratory ailment caused by occupational exposure to cotton dust?[46] In short, because medical evidence may be probative of whether a disability is compensable and, if so, to what extent, its admission is often controversial.

A recurring question is whether medical evidence, often in the form of expert opinion, is indispensable to support an award of benefits. Many workers' compensation awards have been upheld despite the absence of strong supporting medical evidence. Thus, benefits have been awarded for heart attacks and occupational diseases when expert opinions regarding causation were equivocal or even totally lacking.[47] On the other hand, many decisions have denied compensation because of lack of supporting medical evidence proving causation.[48] The cases do not definitively prescribe when expert testimony is essential. Perhaps the most that can be said is that medical evidence is highly desirable in all cases, but is more likely to be indispensable if the issue of causation is thought to lie beyond the expertise of the administrative factfinder.

Historically, courts and agencies did not closely scrutinize the qualifications of expert witnesses in workers' compensation cases. Parties were given considerable latitude with regard to the type of expert witness they presented. Thus, chiropractors are commonly allowed to testify about the nature and extent of back injuries[49] and physicians who are not expert in psychiatric disorders have been allowed to diagnose traumatic

---

[43] See Slover Masonry, Inc. v. Industrial Comm'n, Chapter 8, supra.

[44] E.g., Cox v. Ulysses Cooperative Oil & Supply Co., 218 Kan. 428, 544 P.2d 363 (1975).

[45] See, Lancaster v. Gilbert Development, Chapter 6, supra.

[46] See, Rutledge v. Tultex Corp./Kings Yarn, Chapter 6, supra.

[47] E.g., Guye v. Home Indemnity Co., 241 Ga. 213, 244 S.E.2d 864 (1978) (a "natural inference" of causation based on common experience can support an award of benefits to laborer who suffered a heart attack after digging a ditch and lifting a 250 pound pole); King v. Oregon Steel Mills, Inc., 25 Or.App. 685, 550 P.2d 747 (1976) (occupational causation of pulmonary disease may be inferred when claimant's condition improved after quitting his job in the furnace area of a steel plant).

[48] E.g., Maness v. Industrial Comm., 102 Ariz. 557, 434 P.2d 643 (1967) (claimant fell from a roof and later developed an ulcer; since the causal connection between the fall and the ulcer was not apparent to a layman, compensation for the ulcer could not be made in the absence of medical testimony); Interlake Steel Co. v. Industrial Comm., 136 Ill.App.3d 740, 91 Ill.Dec. 493, 483 N.E.2d 979 (1985) (reversing an award of benefits when there was no expert medical evidence to establish that the disabling tumors were work related).

[49] E.g., Chalupa v. Industrial Comm., 109 Ariz. 340, 509 P.2d 610 (1973); Vallejos v. KNC, Inc., 105 N.M. 613, 735 P.2d 530 (1987). But see, Weis v. Division of Workers' Compensation, 232 Mont. 218, 755 P.2d 1385 (1988) (upholding an administrative rule restricting medical evaluations to licensed physicians, thereby excluding chiropractors from the field).

neuroses.[50] An objection to the qualifications of the opposing party's expert witness was often dismissed with the observation that such matters bear more on the weight to be given an opinion than on its admissibility.

As illustrated by City of Owensboro v. Adams in Chapter 6, Section 6 and the cases cited in the accompanying notes, many courts today are more closely scrutinizing the qualifications of expert witnesses. The spark for this renewed interest in the qualifications of expert witnesses is the Supreme Court's decision in Daubert v. Merrell Dow Pharmaceuticals, Inc., 509 U.S. 579, 113 S.Ct. 2786, 125 L.Ed.2d 469 (1993).

E. ADMINISTRATIVE AND JUDICIAL REVIEW

In the few states in which courts administer the workers' compensation law, an award or denial of compensation is subject to judicial review in the same manner as other court judgments.[51] In the great number of jurisdictions in which the law is administered by an agency or commission, special provisions for judicial review are provided and commonly incorporate a review procedure at the administrative level. The original hearing is usually held before an administrative law judge or hearing officer who makes an initial decision that is binding if unappealed. If appealed, the initial decision is reviewed administratively by the full workers' compensation board, a commission, or a board of appeals within the compensation system.[52] In most jurisdictions, the reviewing administrative body is not bound by the hearing officer's findings of fact, but is free to reconsider evidence and adopt or reject the initial findings or conclusions. The reviewing administrative body may also order additional testimony, but this is rarely done. The full board or commission usually limits its review to the record made before the hearing officer or administrative law judge.[53]

After a final decision is concluded within the administrative system, judicial review is available in one of several forms. In a few states, the case is taken to a court for a trial de novo.[54] In these jurisdictions, the reviewing court has greater power to reexamine and reweigh the evidence than is typically allowed in judicial review of administrative decisions, but the particular scope of de novo review varies widely. Most states that allow de novo review limit the appeal to a review of the administrative

[50] E.g., Guillory v. Travelers Ins. Co., 326 So.2d 914 (La.App.1976); Barrett v. Coast Range Plywood, 294 Or. 641, 661 P.2d 926 (1983).

[51] E.g., Ala.Code § 25–5–81.

[52] E.g., Ga. Code. Ann. § 34–9–103(a).

[53] See, 8 A. Larson and L. Larson, Larson's Workers' Compensation Law § 130.03 (2013).

[54] E.g., For a listing of states that provide for judicial review of the administrative decision with a trial de novo, see United States Chamber of Commerce, 2013 Analysis of Workers' Compensation Laws, Chart XV (2013).

record.[55] The decision resulting from the de novo review may then be appealed through conventional avenues of appellate jurisdiction. In recent years, several states have abandoned or substantially modified the de novo appeal procedure.[56]

In most states, judicial review is limited to an appellate court's examination of the record to ensure that the agency correctly applied the law and that its findings of fact are supported by sufficient evidence.[57] This more limited scope of judicial review pays great deference to the discretion of the final administrative factfinder. The administrative body is entrusted to make findings of fact that appellate courts may review only under the "substantial evidence"[58] rule. If sufficient evidence exists, the appellate court must accept the board's findings of fact. Thus, courts will generally defer to the administrative agency's resolution of the "battle of experts" regarding medical causation, the extent of the claimant's disability, and any other disputed issue of fact.

In some states judicial review of the agency's decision is first made by a trial court with any additional appeals proceeding as a matter of discretion by writ of certiorari.[59] As a practical matter, this process usually makes the trial court the tribunal of last resort. Furthermore, because most states do not publish trial court decisions, this procedure produces a body of significant but unreported case law. By contrast, the many jurisdictions that employ appellate court review as the final stage of the process accumulate a mass of published decisions explicating the law.

F. EFFORTS TO REDUCE LITIGATION COSTS AND FRAUD

Although the workers' compensation system processes contested claims more efficiently than does the tort system, many critics maintain that litigation costs are too high. Reduction of the litigation costs has

---

[55] U.S. Chamber of Commerce, 2013 Analysis of Workers' Compensation Laws, chart XV.

[56] E.g., McAlear v. Arthur G. McKee & Co., 171 Mont. 462, 558 P.2d 1134 (1976) (after the repeal of Mont.Code Ann. §§ 92–834 and 92–835 Montana adopted the substantial evidence review standard); Ore. Rev.Stat. § 656.298 (amended in 1987 to not allow any new evidence to be admitted at the court of appeals); Tex.Lab.Code Ann. § 410–306 (amended in 1990 to limit the issues and evidence to be considered by review).

[57] See, 8 A. Larson and L. Larson's, Larson's Workers' Compensation Law § 130.01 (2013).

[58] The most common articulation of the standard of review is in terms of "substantial evidence". E.g., Armstrong v. Iowa Bldgs. & Grounds, 382 N.W.2d 161 (Iowa 1986); Hess Bros. v. Workmen's Compensation Appeal Board, 128 Pa.Cmwlth. 240, 563 A.2d 236 (1989). Other jurisdictions invoke different terminology. E.g., Skelton v. Department of Transportation, 191 Ga.App. 835, 383 S.E.2d 162 (1989) ("any evidence"). The common substantive thrust of these variously phrased standards is to prevent the reviewing court from substituting its judgment for that of the administrative factfinder on contested issues of fact. Variations on the "substantial evidence" standard are discussed in 8 A. Larson and L. Larson, Larson's Workers' Compensation Law § 130.01[3]-(2013).

[59] E.g., Ga.Code Ann. §§ 34–9–105(e) and 5–6–35.

been a primary objective of recent workers' compensation reform efforts. Proponents of such reforms argue that a reduction of litigation costs will reduce insurers' and employers' costs and make more money available for benefits. Two common types of reforms are restriction on claimants' attorneys' fees and mandatory informal claims processing.

In the 1990s many states imposed limits on claimants' attorneys' fees.[60] Some reform measures shifted payment of claimants' attorneys' fees from insurers to injured workers.[61] The impact of some of these reforms on attorneys' fees can be dramatic. In Florida, for example, reforms of this type were reported to result in cuts in attorneys' fees from $15,750 to $10,750 in cases where the benefits were $100,000. For a claim involving benefits of $20,000 a claimant's attorney would have been paid $3,750 before the reform and $2,750 after.[62] This reduction in fees is reportedly making it more difficult for some claimants to secure representation.[63]

A second type of reform involves increased use of informal dispute resolution processes. Several states require mediation or some other informal dispute resolution process prior to a hearing.[64] While such processes can facilitate the resolution of contested claims in many instances, in others it can add delay and cost. In Florida, a worker who has been denied benefits by an employer/insurer may apply to a state ombudsman for informal assistance in resolving the dispute before becoming eligible to file a formal claim.[65] If the worker's claim is not resolved by the ombudsman, the worker may then file a formal claim but it will not be resolved by hearing and legally binding decision until after the disputed claim has been submitted to mediation before a professional state mediator.[66] The parties may be represented by lawyers in the mediation except that an employer may not be represented by legal counsel if the worker is unrepresented. Only if the mediation is unsuccessful will the claim be resolved in formal proceedings conducted by an administrative hearing officer. Does it appear to you that this system systematically favors either employees as a class or employers as a class?

---

[60] Me. Rev. Stat. Ann. tit. 39–A § 325(3) (capping attorney fees at 30%); S.D. Codified Laws § 62–7–36 (capping fees at 25% of settlements, 30% for benefits awarded after a hearing, and 35% in cases appealed to the highest state court).

[61] E.g., Me. Rev. Stat. Ann. tit. 39–A § 325(1).

[62] Martha T. McCluskey, The Illusion of Efficiency in Workers' Compensation "Reform," 50 Rutgers L. Rev. 657, 863 n. 874 (1998).

[63] Id., at 864.

[64] E.g., Me. Rev. Stat. Ann. tit. 39–A § 313 (mandatory mediation); New York Work. Comp. Law § 25(2–b) (claims for benefits of 52 weeks or less to be submitted to informal conciliation process); Tex. Labor Code Ann. § 410.024 (no hearing until informal benefit review conference is conducted).

[65] Fla. Stat. Ann. § 440.191(2).

[66] Fla. Stat. Ann. § 440.25(1).

Several states have created an office of Ombudsman to help injured workers process workers' compensation claims.[67] The services of the Ombudsman are free, thus creating a financially attractive alternative to hiring private counsel. Oregon reports that its Office of the Ombudsman for Injured Workers received about 11,500 inquiries from injured workers in 2007.[68] A commentator who reviewed the Texas system concluded that Ombudsmen have succeeded in reducing the level of attorney involvement in resolving claims, thus reducing transaction costs of processing claims.[69] This study also concluded that the social price for these savings has been high because "[u]nlike attorneys, ombudsmen face severe limitations in the type of assistance they can render on behalf of injured workers. For example, ombudsmen cannot hire an investigator on behalf of the injured worker, assist the worker during judicial review of the case, or provide a letter of protection to a worker's medical providers."[70]

Another popular target for reform is fraud. Since 1989, a majority of states have enacted new laws designed to combat claims of fraud. Such legislation often provides for stronger penalties for fraud, create fraud investigative units vested with enforcement authority, and provides protection for persons reporting fraud.[71]

The types of fraud that can lead to the termination or forfeiture of benefits include making knowingly false statements about one's physical condition, employment, or both. For example, in Retz v. Surpass Chemical Co., 39 A.D. 1037, 834 N.Y.S.2d 389 (2007), the claimant arrived at his doctor's office wearing a full length leg brace and used both a cane and a walker. He told the doctor that lower back pain interrupted his sleep and prevented him from sitting up more than twenty minutes at a time. A surveillance videotape, however, showed the claimant playing catch with his son and walking with a normal gait without the assistance of a cane, walker or leg brace. The tape also show him working on a truck in his garage, bending, squatting, lifting, setting up a campsite, all without any apparent pain or difficulty. An administrative order disqualifying the claimant from receiving wage replacement benefits was affirmed. In Forbes v. Workforce Safety and Insurance Fund, 722 N.W.2d 536 (N.D.

---

67 E.g., Fla. Stat. Ann. § 440.191; Ore. Rev. Stat. 656.709; Tex. Lab. Code Ann. § 404.151.

68 Oregon Department of Consumer & Business Services, Biennial Report on the Oregon Workers' Compensation System 6 (9th Ed. December 2008).

69 Phil Hardberger, Texas Workers' Compensation: A Ten-Year Survey—Strengths, Weaknesses, and Recommendations, 32 St. Mary's L. J. 1, 50 (2000).

70 Id., at 49.

71 E.g., Ark. Code Ann. § 11–9–106 (making willful false statements or representations with respect to workers' compensation claims a felony; creating a fraud investigation unit; granting immunity from employers or employees to an employee who has reported fraud). For a description of other state laws, see Martha T. McCluskey, The Illusion of Efficiency in Workers' Compensation "Reform," 50 Rutgers L. Rev. 657, 873–74 (1998). For a survey of fraud investigation units, their powers and results, see Brian Zaidman & David Berry, State Workers' Compensation Anti-Fraud Activity: Survey Results, Workers' Compensation Year Book 1996, at I–172–I–176.

2006) a nurse who claimed to be unable to work due to back and neck injuries was observed participating in a fitness program that included yoga and weightlifting. She also launched an independent business conducting physical exams and selling cosmetics despite claiming that she was not working. The claimant was ordered to forfeit any future benefits and to repay $20,000 in past income benefits paid by her former employer. See also McDaniel v. Industrial Commission, 118 Ohio St.3d 319, 889 N.E.2d 93 (2008) (terminating benefits of claimant who ran his own lawn service company while collecting permanent total disability benefits). In rare instances workers' compensation fraud may lead to criminal prosecution. E.g., State v. Coulter, 255 S.W.3d 552 (Mo. App. 2008) (conviction for workers' compensation fraud based on knowingly false testimony given in a deposition that she was unable to bend at the waist since her injury); State v. Maynard, 139 Idaho 117, 73 P.3d 731 (2003) (conviction for insurance fraud when claimant falsely denied under oath that he secured employment after undergoing surgery).

Employer conduct that might be characterized as fraud is often subject to fines or penalties under the compensation code. E.g., McCarthy's Case, 66 Mass.App.Ct. 541, 849 N.E.2d 228 (2006) (employer fined $10,000 for paying injured worker out of sick leave and vacation days instead of from workers' compensation); Associated Business Products v. Industrial Claim Appeals Office, 126 P.3d 323 (Colo. App. 2005) (employer penalized $24,900 for failing to pay claimant's cell phone bills on time as ordered by the agency; employer's actions characterized as part of a pattern of "wilful and wanton misconduct").

For a comprehensive description and critique of these and other recent reform efforts, see Martha T. McCluskey, The Illusion of Efficiency in Workers' Compensation "Reform," 50 Rutgers L. Rev. 657 (1998).

6. COMPROMISE (SETTLEMENTS) AND COMMUTATION (LUMP SUM PAYMENTS)

Should an employer and employee be permitted to settle a workers' compensation claim for less than the worker might be entitled to under the law? Just as in tort litigation, uncertainties regarding coverage and the extent of disability often set the stage for compromise. Yet the social insurance aspect of workers' compensation is thought by some to be inconsistent with tort-like settlement practices.

Many workers' compensation acts expressly prohibit contractual waivers or compromises of entitlements under workers' compensation laws.[72] Such provisions reflect a concern that employers would exploit their superior economic position to extract waivers or compromises of

[72] E.g., N.Y. Work.Comp. Law § 33 ("Compensation or benefits due under this chapter shall not be assigned, released or commuted except as provided by this chapter * * * ").

statutory rights from employees. Decisions under these statutes are mixed: some invalidate compromises for less than full benefits and some decisions uphold the compromises.

The argument for restricting settlement of workers' compensation claims was expressed by the New Jersey Supreme Court as follows: "[t]he fulfillment of the statutory policy is of concern to the State. The parties themselves are not free to bargain for the surrender of a right of compensation under the statute. * * * The compensation act provides social insurance in the common interest as well as [in] the interest of the injured workman. Indemnity for the risks of service, even without fault, is made to fall upon industry as an incident of the operation and eventually upon the consumer."[73] The contrary view was expressed by the Kansas Supreme Court, as follows, "[w]orkmen are not in any respect under guardianship or other disability; they and their employers are free agents; they may release their employers from liability for injuries on any agreed terms satisfactory to both."[74]

Notwithstanding questions about theoretical propriety, settlement has become a practical reality in modern workers' compensation practice. Most state statutes permit settlement and compromise if approved by the board or commission.[75] Although the scope of permissible compromise varies considerably among jurisdictions, one common restriction prohibits or restricts the release of the employer's liability for future medical expenses.[76] Also, recall from the materials in Chapter 9 that in some states an employee's settlement of his claim may not necessarily bar the claims of survivors for death benefits.

The settlement of workers' compensation claims that involve current or soon-to-be Medicare beneficiaries has become more complex in recent years.[77] Medicare is a federal program enacted in 1965 that provides medical benefits to older Americans. After Medicare's enactment, workers' compensation settlements often were structured so that the employer's responsibility for medical care would end once the claimant became eligible for Medicare. This, of course, effectively shifted the responsibility for providing medical care from the workers' compensation carrier to the federal Medicare program. In order to stem the wholesale shifting of medical costs from workers' compensation to Medicare,

---

73 Nagy v. Ford Motor Co., 6 N.J. 341, 350, 78 A.2d 709 (1951).

74 Dotson v. Proctor & Gamble Mfg. Co., 102 Kan. 248, 250, 169 P. 1136, 1137 (1918).

75 See, 8 A. Larson & L. Larson, Larson's Workers' Compensation Laws § 132.03 (2013).

76 E.g., Brooks v. Arkansas–Best Freight System, Inc., 247 Ark. 61, 444 S.W.2d 246 (1969); Great Bay Distrib. v. Everett, 513 So.2d 187 (Fla.App.1987).

77 This account of the history of the MSPA and its impact on workers' compensation is taken from David B. Torrey, Compromise Settlements Under State Workers' Compensation Acts, 16 Widner L. J. 199, 389–398 (2007). See also, Bradford Peterson, Survey of Illinois Law: Summary of Medicare, Workers' Compensation and Set-Aside Trusts, 26 So. Ill. L. J. 713 (2002).

Congress passed the Medicare Secondary Payer Act (MSPA) in 1981.[78] The general thrust of the MSPA was to declare that Medicare's obligation to pay for medical care was secondary and the obligation of other available insurance, such as workers' compensation, was primary. For the next twenty years, however, little was done to enforce the MSPA. As a consequence of lax enforcement, Medicare continued to pay for medical care that otherwise would have been the obligation of the workers' compensation system. A General Accounting Office study concluded that between 1991 and 1998 $43 billion "was paid in cash by the Federal Government for medical benefits for workers' compensation related claims."[79] Beginning in 2001, the federal agency responsible for administering Medicare, the Centers for Medicare and Medicaid Services (CMS), issued a series of letter memoranda and established protocols designed to put teeth in the enforcement of the MSPA. A key component of these efforts is requiring that settlement agreements of workers' compensation claims of employees who are or soon will be eligible for Medicare benefits be submitted to CMS for approval. A critical requirement for such approval is the inclusion of a Medicare "set-aside" arrangement (MSA) or trust within the workers' compensation settlement agreement. The purpose of the set-aside arrangement or trust is to make sure that funds obtained through the settlement will be available to pay for workers' compensation-related medical expenses even after the worker becomes eligible for Medicare.

Currently, proposed settlements of workers' compensation claims should be submitted to CMS (1) if the claimant is a Medicare beneficiary and the settlement amount is $25,000 or more; and (2) if the claimant has a "reasonable expectation" of enrolling in Medicare within 30 months from the date of the settlement and the "anticipated total settlement amount" is expected to be greater than $250,000. State workers' compensation authorities, aware of the preemptive effect of MSPA, generally will not approve of a settlement of workers' compensation claim without CMS approval. The requirement of CMS approval and the inclusion of set-aside arrangements or trusts often lead to delays and uncertainty in the settlement of this sub-set of workers' compensation claims.[80]

---

78 42 U.S.C. § 1395y(b).

79 Torrey, supra note 77, at 391–92.

80 A group of experienced defense attorneys explained the practical impact of Medicare on the settlement of workers' compensation claims as follows: "In the most serious of workers' compensation cases, and especially those involving catastrophic injuries, MSAs as required by CMS are frequently in the hundreds of thousands of dollars and in many instances are so large as to preclude any financial incentive for the parties to settle. As a result, many claims continue on the periodic payment structure required under the Workers' Compensation Act, inhibiting a claimant's ability to settle and expanding both future risk and reserve obligations for workers' compensation insurers and self-insured employers." H. Michael Bagley, Daniel C. Kniffen, and Katherine D. Dixon, Workers' Compensation, 60 Mercer L. Rev. 433, 452 (2008). Other thoughtful discussions of the impact MSPA on the settlement of workers' compensation claims

Congress passed legislation in 2012 intended to ease the procedures related to Medicare approval of settlements. Strengthening Medicare and Repaying Taxpayers Act of 2012 (SMART Act), Public Law No: 112–242. A preliminary assessment of this law concluded that it "will have very little impact on the settlement of workers' compensation claims. . . . [T]his new legislation does absolutely nothing to address the issue of future medical obligations and that is by far the most costly and problematic component of workers' compensation settlements involving Medicare beneficiaries."[81]

A separate issue is whether to permit lump sum payments (or "washouts") when the parties agree on liability and the extent of benefits. When an award has been made, or the parties agree that an award should be made, the claimant may wish to receive a single lump sum payment instead of weekly payments of income benefits extended into the future. The lump sum thus involves a commutation of benefit payments rather than a compromise of amount.

Critics of lump sum awards point out that periodic (weekly) payment of income benefits advances the important objective of ensuring that workers regularly receive income support for the duration of disability and allows for adjustments if conditions change. Some observers fear that workers will dissipate a single lump sum before the disability ends, leaving the disabled workers with no income support.[82] Other considerations, however, favor awarding lump sum payments. Many claimants prefer having a larger sum of money in hand to the guarantee of smaller periodic payments in the future. This may enable workers to improve their earning capacity by financing retraining or capitalizing a new business. Insurers and employers tend to favor the lump sum option to reduce administrative costs in monitoring individual files, and claimants' attorneys prefer receiving fees in full out of the lump sum to being paid in smaller weekly installments over a period of time.

These arguments have been resolved in most states to permit lump sum awards in appropriate cases. Ordinarily the statutes provide only general standards[83] that charge the administrative agencies with the

---

include Crystal L. Fraser, Note and Commentary, The Complexity of the Mandatory Medicare Section 111 Reporting Rules and Its Practical Effects—Is There a Break in Sight? 17 Conn. Ins. L. J. 445 (2010/2011); Jeffrey R. Kutchel, Comment, Frustrated Settlements: Common Problems and Solutions in Liability Settlements Invoking the Medicare Secondary Payer Statutes, 73 Mont. L. Rev. 395 (2012).

[81] Jennifer C. Jordon, Strengthening Mediacare and Repaying Taxpayers Act (Smart Act), 2013 Emerging Issues 6924 (February 19, 2013).

[82] 8 A. Larson and L. Larson, Larson's Workers' Compensation Law § 132.07 [1](2013) ("Experience has shown that in many cases the lump sum is soon dissipated and the worker is right back where he or she would have been if workers' compensation had never existed.").

[83] E.g., Alaska Stat. § 23.30.012 (authorizing lump sum award when in the "best interest of the employee"); 820 Ill. Comp. Stat. 305/9 (authorizing lump sum payment when it is in the "best interest of the parties"); Mich.Comp.Laws Ann. § 418.835 (authorizing lump sum payment if

paternal responsibility of safeguarding the claimants' long term interests. Much of the litigation on this point concerns the agency's assessment of the purported need for a lump sum payment with the critical factor often being whether a lump sum payment can realistically be expected to improve the claimant's ability to earn a living.[84]

7. REOPENING AND MODIFYING AWARDS

Judgments in personal injury litigation and awards in a workers' compensation claims differ markedly in their finality. The trial of a tort claim is intended to resolve all factual disputes completely and conclusively, including those pertaining to the future consequences of the plaintiff's injuries. Courts do not monitor subsequent developments and will not modify a jury's award simply because the plaintiff's actual injuries turned out to be more or less severe than determined at trial. By contrast, the workers' compensation system is less embued with the notion of ultimate finality. Almost every state has some provision authorizing the administrative body to reopen cases and modify awards.[85] The statutes vary as to the period of time within which modifying action may be taken and the reasons for which modification is permitted.

The reopening period varies from as little as six months to no time limitation at all,[86] but the vast majority of jurisdictions places some fixed limit on the time to reopen an award. Some states calculate the limitation period by reference to the date of the injury, whereas others refer to the date of the original award or the date of the last payment.[87]

"special circumstances" exist). Cf. State ex rel. Kenner Products v. Industrial Comm., 21 Ohio App.3d 232, 486 N.E.2d 1280 (1985) (statute authorized lump sum payment if "special circumstances" existed, but administrative regulations prohibited the award of lump sum payments for the purchase of luxury items such as television sets; Commission award of lump sum payment for purchase of a television set, automobile, and air conditioner reversed).

[84] Compare City of Miami v. Mercer, 513 So.2d 149 (Fla.App.1987) (approving a lump sum award to pay for aviation training) with Ventura v. Palm Springs General Hospital, 463 So.2d 414 (Fla.App.1985) (upholding the denial of a request for lump sum payment to be used to purchase rental property when claimant had no experience in real estate management and investment).

[85] For a brief description of the practices of every state regarding the modification of awards, see 8 A. Larson & L. Larson, Larson's Workers' Compensation Laws § 131.01 (2013).

[86] E.g., Neb.Rev.Stat. § 48–141 (6 months from the date of the award or agreement); Ga.Code Ann. § 34–9–104(b) (two years from the date of the last payment); Md. Code Ann., Lab. & Empl. § 9–736(b) (five years from the date of the last payment); N.D.Cent.Code § 65–05–04 ("any time").

[87] E.g., Colo.Rev.Stat. § 8–43–303 (6 years from the date of the injury); 820 Ill. Comp. Stat. 305/19(h) (30 months from the date of the award); Ga.Code Ann. § 34–9–104(b) (2 years from the date of the last payment).

Many statutes incorporate specific grounds for modifying an award, such as fraud, mistake, or newly discovered evidence.[88] Others authorize modifications in expansive terms, such as for "good cause" or any grounds "as may be justified."[89] Nevertheless, the most common reason for modifying an award is that the claimant's physical condition has changed in a way that affects the existence or extent of disability. Often the employee attempts to establish a worsened physical condition and entitlement to greater benefits. The worsening may be due to aggravation or deterioration of the original injury, discovery of a new and more serious condition, or simply the failure to heal as completely as predicted.[90] States are divided on the question of whether a change in economic conditions alone can justify a modification of an award.[91]

A considerable amount of litigation focuses on whether the worsening of the claimant's physical impairment should be considered a change in condition or a new injury. Consider, for example, the worker who suffers a back injury and receives an award for a 10% impairment to the body as a whole. The worker recuperates and returns to work, but later reinjures the back injury and becomes totally disabled. Is the second disability a change in condition or a new injury? Several important practical consequences flow from how this question is answered. If the injury is determined to be a change in condition, the claim might be untimely, whereas, if determined to be a new injury, it would not be. If the employee has changed jobs or if the employer has changed insurance carriers between the first and second injuries, the characterization will determine which employer or insurance company is responsible for payment of any benefits due.[92]

---

[88] E.g., Ky.Rev.Stat.Ann. § 342.125 (change in condition, mistake, fraud or newly discovered evidence); Colo.Rev.Stat. § 8–43–303 (error, mistake, or change in condition and overpayment).

[89] E.g., Cal. Labor Code § 5803 ("good cause"); Md. Code Ann., Lab. & Empl. § 9–736(b) (such modifications as the committee considers "justified"); N.Y. Work.Comp. Law § 123 (such modifications as "may be just").

[90] E.g., Pascucci v. Industrial Comm., 126 Ariz. 442, 616 P.2d 902 (App.1980) (an award may be increased in light of a previously undiscovered herniated disc caused by the work injury); Zachary v. Bituminous Cas. Corp., 371 So.2d 1249 (La.App.1979) (increasing award when the claimant did not recover from a work-related knee injury as originally predicted); Rightnour v. Kare–Mor, Inc., 236 Mont. 108, 768 P.2d 871 (1989) (previously settled claim may be reopened when subsequent aggravation of back injury produces total disability).

[91] Compare Hartford Accident & Indemnity Co. v. Bristol, 242 Ga. 287, 248 S.E.2d 661 (1978) and Blacksmith v. All–American, Inc., 290 N.W.2d 348 (Iowa 1980) (both cases increasing awards due to economic change in condition) with Petrie v. Industrial Comm., 160 Ill.App.3d 165, 111 Ill.Dec. 858, 513 N.E.2d 104 (1987) (limiting modifications to changes in physical condition).

[92] E.g., Bryan County Emergency Medical Services v. Gill, 187 Ga.App. 125, 369 S.E.2d 495 (1988) (employee suffered a back injury in 1977 for which he received medical treatment paid for by his employer's workers' compensation insurance carrier; the claimant continued to work until 1985 when his back condition deteriorated to the point of requiring surgery; the court found the employee had suffered a "new accident" in 1985 when he became unable to work; the court held that the claim was not barred by the statute of limitations, and the now self-insured employer was responsible for the payment of benefits).

The line separating a change in condition from a new accident is sometimes hard to draw. Courts often invoke a quasi-causation analysis to resolve the issue. The closer the causal connection between the original compensable injury and the second disability, the more likely the second disability will be characterized as a change in condition. For example, the board may modify an award for a change in condition when a subsequent fall was plainly caused by a previously compensated leg disability.[93] By contrast, the more tenuous the causal connection between the two events, or the greater the number of intervening factors, the more likely the second injury will be treated as a new injury. Thus, the second injury may be considered a new accident if it arises from a preexisting condition or an intervening cause not attributable to the claimant's first compensable injury.[94] Nevertheless, in workers' compensation, as in torts, the concept of causation is subject to shifting meanings. The extent to which a second injury may be considered attributable to the first is explored in more detail in Chapter 7.

8. EVALUATING THE ADMINISTRATIVE PROCESS

Some of the observed differences between workers' compensation administration and tort litigation are substantive in nature, such as the standard of liability and the use of schedules to calculate standardized awards, and others are procedural, such as the workers' compensation notice of injury requirements. The "tort crisis" of the mid-1980s prompted a renewed interest in comparing the workers' compensation system and tort. Some critics of tort litigation have looked to workers' compensation as a more efficient mechanism for relieving the economic consequences of injury but have come away with mixed findings. For example, a comprehensive study on personal injury conducted under the auspices of the American Law Institutes drew the following conclusion about the relative administrative efficiencies of workers' compensation, tort litigation and other social insurance programs.

---

[93] E.g., Burt v. Oklahoma National Bank, 632 P.2d 440 (Okl.App.1981).

[94] E.g., Hawthorne v. Industrial Comm., 114 Ariz. 63, 559 P.2d 183 (App.1976) (affirming the denial of worker's petition to reopen a claim when the hearing officer found that the worker's present back condition was not caused by his prior work injuries); Certain v. United States Fidelity & Guaranty Co., 153 Ga.App. 571, 266 S.E.2d 263 (1980) ("ordinarily the distinguishing feature that will characterize the disability as either a 'change of condition' or a 'new accident' is the intervention of *new circumstances.*"); Board of Supervisors v. Martin, 3 Va.App. 139, 348 S.E.2d 540 (1986) (claimant suffered a compensable knee injury and later reinjured the knee when slipping on a wet floor; the second fall was considered a new accident, in part, because the slippery floor and not the earlier injury was deemed to be the cause of the fall).

The American Law Institute Reporters' Study Enterprise Responsibility for Personal Injury[95]

"In addition to these distinctive substantive policies of WC [workers' compensation], another major institutional step was taken in the general design of the program. Responsibility for at least front-line decision making about entitlement and the scope of compensation was taken from courts and juries because of concern about technical formalities that only lawyers could deal with effectively. That role was assigned instead to specialized administrative tribunals which would permit workers and employers to resolve the problems on their own, ideally more informally, expeditiously and economically. Under WC the courts serve essentially as a backstop to insure that the administrative tribunal acts in reasonable accord with its statutory mandate."

"In practice there have been major compromises in the non-legal cast of WC, which is perhaps to be expected in any serious liability system. Nevertheless, at least in aggregate terms WC is an administratively faster and cheaper system than tort litigation. In cases in which entitlement is not contested, benefits begin to be paid on average in three weeks. Even in contested cases, the average disposition time is roughly four months.[96] Abstracting from the business costs incurred by any private insurance system in selling insurance and collecting premiums, WC spends roughly 15 to 20 percent of its total claim costs on administrative expenses (as opposed to benefits), whereas tort litigation spends 50 to 55 percent on administration."[97]

"It is true that the majority of WC claims are made (though less than half of WC dollars are paid) for comparatively minor injuries. In contrast, product liability and medical malpractice litigation tend to screen out most of the smaller claims and to produce more incentive to litigate the sizable claims that remain. Still, this factor is largely controlled for in motor vehicle accident litigation, which spends between 45 and 50 percent of claims dollars on administration. However, in the motor vehicle context as well, the bulk of the claims are made (though not dollars paid) for

---

[95] Copyright 1991 by The American Law Institute reprinted with the permission of the American Law Institute, vol. I, pp. 118–121 (April 15, 1991). (Footnotes in the quoted material have been renumbered to be sequential in this text.)

[96] See R. Conley and J. Noble, *Workers' Compensation and Reform: Challenge for the 80s* 57 (1979).

[97] The figure for WC administrative costs is calculated in the ALI Working Paper by P. Weiler, [Legal Policy for Workplace Injuries (ALI Working Paper, 1986)] at 20, drawing on figures from the insurer and public claims administration costs contained in Price, ["Workers' Compensation: 1976–80 Benchmark Revisions," 47 *Social Security Bulletin 7* (July, 1984)], and on estimates of injured worker expenditures on lawyers presented by M. Bernstein, *Litigation, Representation and Claimant Protection and Workers' Compensation* (1979). The figures for the tort system are calculated in another ALI Background Paper, P. Weiler, *Legal Policy for Medical Injuries* 128–30 (1988), drawing primarily, although not entirely, on the data developed by J. Kakalik and N. Pace, *Costs and Compensation Paid in Tort Litigation* (1986).

smaller cases. The difference between WC and motor vehicle tort litigation provides some sense of the potential administrative payoff attainable by eliminating fault and using standardized benefit formulas."

"Yet WC looks somewhat less attractive along that dimension in comparison with a social insurance program such as SSDI [Social Security Disability Insurance], which has an administrative cost ratio under 5 percent, less than one-third that of WC. Even more important, the administrative burden of WC is attributable disproportionately to the two trouble spots * * * PPD [permanent, partial disability] and occupational disease claims."

"Empirical study of PPD cases found that more than half of these cases (compared with 10 percent in the overall program) were initially contested by the employer or insurer. These percentages were even greater in cases with higher impairment ratings and larger wage losses. Consequently, the victims in such cases had to hire a lawyer and pay significant attorney's fees. This combination of delay and cost has led to a widespread practice of "compromise and release" settlements for lump-sum payments at only a fraction of the already too low levels of non-indexed PPD pensions."[98]

"The picture is even worse for occupational disease claims. A national survey of closed WC claims in the mid-1970s found that fully 90 percent of these cases were contested, three-quarters of them on the issue of cause and entitlement. This meant that 65 percent of these disease claimants had to hire or pay for a lawyer (versus 15 percent for accident victims). They then had to wait a year on average for resolution and payment of their claims (versus two months for accidents), and at the end of that time the average award was valued at $9,000, or only about 10 percent of the earnings lost."[99]

"Thus, systematic research about the performance of WC in these two settings corroborates the intuitive impressions of many observers that this version of the no-fault model has its own significant deficiencies as a solution to the problems in tort litigation."

For more critical assessment of the modern workers' compensation system see Michael J. Graetz and Jerry L. Mashaw, True Security 82–87 (1999). Graetz and Mashaw argue that due to increased litigiousness, escalating medical costs, and legislative limitations on coverage and indemnity benefits, the current workers' compensation system does not provide a sufficient level of income protection and operates at an excessive administrative cost.

---

98 See generally M. Bernstein, supra note 97.

99 The details of this survey are presented and analyzed in the U.S. Department of Labor [Interim Report to Congress On Occupational Diseases 69–71 (1980)], as well as in P. Barth, [and H. Hunt, Workers' Compensation and Work-Related Illnesses and Diseases (1980)].

CHAPTER 11

THE EXCLUSIVE REMEDY DOCTRINE AND THE THIRD-PARTY SUIT

■ ■ ■

One of the cornerstones of the original workers' compensation compromise is the employer's immunity from tort suits by an injured employee. This immunity is reflected in what is commonly called the exclusive remedy doctrine, which provides that workers' compensation is the employee's exclusive remedy vis à vis the employer. While the exclusive remedy doctrine generally bars a tort claim against an injured worker's employer, it does not preclude tort claims against third parties who might be responsible for the injuries. Under the proper set of facts, the injured worker may pursue both remedies simultaneously. That is, the worker may recover workers' compensation benefits from the employer and at the same time sue a third party in tort. The intersection of tort and workers' compensation has been the source of enhanced friction in recent years. Workers and third parties have pressed for greater employer accountability in tort. At the heart of the controversy is the continued vitality of the exclusive remedy doctrine. The materials in this chapter explore the contours of the exclusive remedy doctrine and its impact on third party actions.

1. THE EXCLUSIVE NATURE OF WORKERS' COMPENSATION

N. Y. Workers' Comp. Law § 11 (2009)

> The liability of an employer prescribed by the [workers' compensation act] shall be exclusive and in place of any other liability whatsoever, to such employee, his or her personal representatives, spouse, parents, dependents, or distributees, or any person otherwise entitled to recover damages, contribution or indemnity, at common law or otherwise, on account of such injury or death. . . .

HYETT V. NORTHWESTERN HOSPITAL FOR WOMEN AND CHILDREN

Supreme Court of Minnesota, 1920.
147 Minn. 413, 180 N.W. 552.

BROWN, C.J.

Plaintiff was in the employ of defendant, a Minnesota corporation, in the capacity of fireman in charge of its heating plant. Both were within and subject to the Workmen's Compensation Act (Gen.St.1913, §§ 8195–8230). Plaintiff was injured while engaged in his employment, by reason of which he was disabled for a brief period from the discharge of his duties, in adjustment of which there was paid to him the sum of $44. There were, as we understand the matter, no compensation proceedings, but that is not of special importance. At the time of the accident resulting in the disability stated plaintiff received an additional independent injury, but not amounting to a disability to perform his work, for which the Compensation Act makes no express or other provision for compensation. The additional injury was to his left pubic nerve, totally destroying the functions thereof, rendering him permanently impotent. Finding no remedy under the Compensation Act for the particular injury, plaintiff brought this action at law to recover therefor, alleging that it was caused by the negligence of defendant. Defendant interposed in defense, among other things, that the parties were within the Compensation Act, and that the remedy there provided is exclusive. Plaintiff demurred to that part of the answer, and defendant appealed from an order sustaining the same.

The only question presented is whether an employee, within the Compensation Act, who suffers an injury in the course of his employment which results (1) in a disability, temporary or permanent, for which compensation may be had under the act; and (2) an associate injury not amounting to a disability, either temporary or otherwise and for which no compensation is provided, may maintain an action at law for the latter injury on the ground that it was occasioned by the negligence of the employer. We answer the question in the negative.

The question is of first impression in this state, though it has come before the courts of other jurisdictions. It is important, for a decision thereof will determine whether our Workmen's Compensation Act, as heretofore generally understood, furnishes the exclusive relief of an injured employee, or whether, in addition to the relief thus provided, he may resort to a common-law action for injuries not amounting to a disability. Every personal injury causes pain and suffering, measured in degree by the character of the injury; some result in the disfigurement of the person—the loss of a hand or other member of the body, an eye, scalds and burns upon the hands or face, all of which must be carried through life to the mental distress of the victim. And in given cases, like that at bar an injury, accidental or otherwise, may impair and totally destroy some function of the human body not of a character to incapacitate the employee from his usual employment, or affect his earning capacity, therefore not within the letter of the Compensation Act. Matters of that character are proper elements of damage in the negligence action, but our Compensation Act makes no provision for a consideration thereof in the award to an injured employee, even though they may constitute his major or principal grievance.

In some of the jurisdictions of this country, and in England, situations of the kind are expressly covered by statute. Bradbury, Compensation Acts (3d Ed.) 874. But not by the statute of this state. The whole scheme of our statute is one of reciprocal concessions by employer and employee, from which benefits and protection fall to each which without the law neither could demand or recover; of benefit to the employee for he is thereby given protection for injuries impairing his earning capacity, without regard to the culpability of the employer, when without the statute he would be remediless. In consideration of this insured compensation and protection by the acceptance of the act he by necessary implication relinquishes his common-law remedies, and thus places a limit on his rights to that measured and granted by the Compensation Act. Section 8204, G.S.1913. In return for the required payment of compensation for the accidental injury, for which the common law furnishes the employee no relief, the employer is protected from the suit at law for the negligent injury. Thus we have the reciprocal yielding and giving up of rights existing at common law for the new and enlarged rights and remedies given by the Compensation Act. That this comes about by force of compulsory legislation (section 8204) in no way alters the legal character of the relation of the parties. That the Legislature was within its authority in so enacting, in the interests of the general welfare and in regulation of rights, duties, and obligations between employer and employee as a class has been affirmed by all the courts where compensation acts have been sustained. Matheson v. Minneapolis Street Railway Co., 126 Minn. 286, 148 N.W. 71, L.R.A.1916D, 412; Jensen v. Southern Pacific Railway Co., 215 N.Y. 514, 109 N.E. 600, L.R.A.1916A, 403, Ann.Cas. 1916B, 276.

That the remedy so given and provided is exclusive of all others seems to be the prevailing opinion of the courts where the question has received attention. Shanahan v. Monarch Engineering Co., 219 N.Y. 469, 114 N.E. 795; Gregutis v. Waclark Wire Works, 86 N.J.L. 610, 92 A. 354; Peet v. Mills, 76 Wash. 437, 136 P. 685, L.R.A.1916A, 358, Ann.Cas.1915D, 154; King v. Viscoloid Co., 219 Mass. 420, 106 N.E. 988, Ann.Cas.1916D, 1170. Connors v. Semet–Solvay Co., 94 Misc.Rep. 405, 159 N.Y.S. 431, in which it was said that Shinnick v. Clover Farms Co.,

169 App.Div. 236, 154 N.Y.Supp. 423, holding to the contrary had been overruled by Jensen v. Southern Pacific, supra. If the case was not in effect there overruled, it clearly was so disposed of by the later decision of the Court of Appeals in the Shanahan Case above cited. The case of Boyer v. Crescent Paper Co., 143 La. 368, 78 So. 596, takes the other view of the Louisiana Compensation Act and supports plaintiff in the case at bar. But to follow that rule would in a large measure be destructive of the main purpose and scheme of the statute, and deprive the employer of a right expressly granted him in return for his concession of liability for the nonactionable injury. It would result also in opening wide the door to double litigation in a great majority of the compensation cases. With the opportunity presented the discovery of negligence in some respect contributing to a particular injury would not be difficult, and thus the employer exposed to a second suit in which recovery could be had for pain and suffering, disfigurement of person, in addition to a recovery of compensation for actual disability under the Compensation Act. A personal injury received at the hands of a wrongdoer constitutes but one right of action. It cannot be divided into several parts to accord with the elements of damages recoverable therefor. It presents a single controversy to be settled in a single action. Dunnell's Dig. 5167. That is elementary, and it is manifest that there was no intention on the part of the Legislature to change or abrogate it by the Compensation Act; and no such intention should be presumed by the court. On the other hand, it is clear that the intention of that body was to present to the employers and employees of the state a comprehensive act embracing their exclusive rights and remedies for accidental or other injuries suffered by the employee. Morris v. Muldoon, 190 App.Div. 689, 180 N.Y.S. 319. If the compensation so provided is deemed inadequate, or that the act should be made to include all or any of the common-law elements or ingredients of relief found in the negligence law, the change should come about by legislation and not by rule of court.

For the reasons stated the demurrer to the answer should have been overruled, and the order sustaining it is accordingly reversed.

NOTES

1. Why is the employer's immunity from tort claims by an injured worker considered fundamental to the operation of the workers' compensation system? Is it a matter of fairness, economics, or constitutional necessity?

2. *Hyett* illustrates the general rule that the exclusive remedy doctrine bars a tort suit against the employer when the injury is covered by workers' compensation, even if it is not compensable because it does not impair earning capacity. This general rule has precluded tort actions seeking recovery for noncompensable injuries to reproductive organs, Kline v. Arden H. Verner Co., 307 Pa.Super. 573, 453 A.2d 1035 (1982), aff'd 503 Pa. 251,

469 A.2d 158 (1983), loss of sense of taste and smell, Swilley v. Sun Oil Co., 506 So.2d 1364 (La.App.1987), and mental anguish, Witty v. American Gen. Capital Distrib., 727 S.W.2d 503 (Tex.1987).

Even if the worker is not entitled to receive disability benefits for an injury that does not impair earning capacity, medical or rehabilitation benefits may be available. See, Spyhalsky v. Cross Const., 294 A.D.2d 23, 743 N.Y.S.2d 212 (App.Div.2002) (ordering artificial insemination of injured worker's wife); Regnier v. Indus. Comm'n., 146 Ariz. 535, 707 P.2d 333 (App.1985) (artificial spermatocele implant), Crain Burton Ford Co. v. Rogers, 12 Ark.App. 246, 674 S.W.2d 944 (1984) (penile implant) Mullins v. 7–Eleven, Inc., 5 So.3d 35 (Fl. App. 2009) (breast implant). In some states, injuries that do not produce any demonstrable loss in earning capacity may be compensable under schedules that cover loss of use of any member or part of the body. See, Bess v. Tyson Foods, Inc., 125 N.C.App. 698, 482 S.E.2d 26 (1997) (loss of sense of taste and smell is compensable as a permanent injury to an "important external or internal organ"); Chrysler Corporation v. Chambers, 288 A.2d 450 (Del.Super.), affirmed 299 A.2d 431 (Del.1972) (loss of testicle compensable under schedule for loss of member or part of the body).

3. The exclusive remedy provision of most workers' compensation statutes also bars tort suits against employers brought by family members that arise from a compensable injury to the worker. Thus, claims for loss of spousal consortium are almost always precluded. E.g., LeFiell Mfg. Co. v. Superior Court, 55 Cal.4th 275, 145 Cal.Rptr. 3d 543, 282 P.3d 1242 (2012); Vallery v. Southern Baptist Hosp., 630 So.2d 861 (La.App.1993); Mardian Constr. Co. v. Superior Court, 157 Ariz. 103, 754 P.2d 1378 (App.1988); West v. Plastifax, Inc., 505 So.2d 1026 (Miss.1987); Young v. Prevue Products, Inc., 130 N.H. 84, 534 A.2d 714 (1987) Similarly, an employer is protected from claims by parents for the lost services of their injured or deceased minor children. E.g., Slagle v. Reynolds Metals Co., 344 So.2d 1216 (Ala.1977); Salin v. Pacific Gas & Electric Co., 136 Cal.App.3d 185, 185 Cal.Rptr. 899 (1982). Next of kin and others are barred from bringing a wrongful death action against an employer even if they are not entitled to death benefits under workers' compensation. E.g., Sabb v. Massachusetts CVS, 452 Mass. 564, 896 N.E.2d 615 (2008); Leech v. Georgia–Pacific Corp., 259 Or. 161, 485 P.2d 1195 (1971); Morrill v. J & M Construction Co., 635 P.2d 88 (Utah 1981). What is the quid pro quo for the family member who loses the right to bring a tort action but receives no benefits under workers' compensation?

4. Family members have been permitted to sue employers in tort when the alleged injury does not arise from a personal injury to a worker, but is based on their own personal injury. For example, in Raney v. Walter O. Moss Regional Hosp., 629 So.2d 485 (La.App.1993) a hospital employee was exposed to hepatitis "B" on the job. As a result, her husband and children had to undergo a series of vaccinations. The children's tort suits against the employer for their fear of contracting the disease, medical expenses and pain and suffering were not barred by the exclusive remedy doctrine. Similarly, a

number of courts have allowed children to sue their mothers' employers for injuries inflicted on the children while they were in utero. E.g., Snyder v. Michael's Stores, Inc., 16 Cal.4th 991, 68 Cal.Rptr.2d 476, 945 P.2d 781 (1997) (unborn child exposed to hazardous levels of carbon monoxide); Pizza Hut of America v. Keefe, 900 P.2d 97 (Colo.1995) (death of child born prematurely allegedly caused by employer's insistence that the mother work in violation of her medical work restrictions); Hitachi Chem. Electro–Products v. Gurley, 219 Ga.App. 675, 466 S.E.2d 867 (1995) (employees and minor children allowed to sue employer in tort for birth defects allegedly caused by the parents exposure to hazardous chemicals at the workplace prior to the birth of the children).

2. LIMITATIONS ON THE EXCLUSIVE REMEDY DOCTRINE

TRAVIS V. DREIS AND KRUMP MANUFACTURING COMPANY

Supreme Court of Michigan, 1996.
453 Mich. 149, 551 N.W.2d 132.

BOYDE, J.

These consolidated cases involve the proper construction of the intentional tort exception to the exclusive remedy provision of the Worker's Disability Compensation Act, MCL § 418.131(1); MSA § 17.237(131)(1). The precise issues framed by the parties are (1) whether the facts alleged by the plaintiffs are sufficient as a matter of law to state a question for the jury regarding liability within the intentional tort exception of the WDCA, (2) whether it is a question for the court or the jury whether an intentional tort has been committed by an employer, and (3) the extent to which, if at all, plaintiff Stanislaw Golec may maintain his intentional tort claim against the individual co-employees.

* * *

Facts and Procedural History

* * *

[The first case involved the suit brought by Aimee Sue Travis against her employer, Greenville Wire Products Co. Travis operated a "press brake" equipped with a "die" used to form refrigerator wires. She was instructed by her supervisor (Clarke) to place the wires into the die by hand and then activate the machine by pushing the "palm buttons" with both hands. She would remove the wires by hand after they were formulated by the machine. The machine was designed so that it could not be activated without the operator pushing both palm buttons. This design was intended to prevent the activation of the machine while the operator's hands were in the die. The machine that Travis operated, however, had a history of "double cycling," i.e., cycling two times when the palm buttons were pushed only once. The machine had been double cycling for about a month. The tool room supervisor (King) advised Clarke to shut down the machine so that it could be repaired. Clarke refused to shut down the machine because exterior adjustments temporarily corrected the problem; a shut down "would take too long"; and he felt that the cycle was so slow that "an operator could avoid injury even when it was double cycling. . . . Unfortunately, [Travis'] hands were in the die space when the press double cycled, and she was unable to remove her hands before the die came down. [Travis] suffered severe injuries to her hand, including the amputation of both of her fifth fingers."]

[The second case involved a suit brought by Stanislaw Golec against his employer, Metal Exchange Corporation. Golec used a tractor to load scrap metal into a furnace for smelting. Although the tractors were usually equipped with a plexiglass splash guard, Golec's tractor was not so equipped. Nor was Golec provided any protective clothing other than a helmet. Golec's employer allegedly was aware that wet scrap or scrap that contains closed aerosol cans could explode when placed in the furnace. The parties disputed whether Golec had been instructed to separate closed aerosol cans before loading scrap into the furnace. On the night in question, a minor explosion occurred in the furnace, splashing Golec with molten aluminum. Golec reported the incident to his shift leader (Mazur) saying that he thought the explosion was due to either wet scrap or the presence of closed aerosol cans in the pile of scrap. The shift leader notified his supervisor (Rziemkowski) who allegedly instructed Golec to return to work. Later that night there was a "huge explosion" resulting in severe burns to thirty percent of Golec's body.]

[Both Travis and Golec filed tort claims against their respective employers. The trial courts in both cases granted the employers' motions for summary judgment on the ground that the claims were barred by the exclusive remedy doctrine. The court of appeals reversed both cases reasoning that the facts alleged, if accepted as true, supported claims for intentional torts.]

Analysis

I

Introduction

The present version of subsection 131(1) of the WDCA was enacted in 1987 PA 28. It indicates that an employee's exclusive remedy for a personal injury or occupational disease is the recovery permitted under the Worker's Disability Compensation Act. The one exception to this recovery scheme is when an employer commits an intentional tort. Subsection 131(1) provides:

> The right to the recovery of benefits as provided in this act shall be the employee's exclusive remedy against the employer for a personal injury or occupational disease. The only exception to this exclusive remedy is an intentional tort. *An intentional tort shall exist only when an employee is injured as a result of a deliberate act of the employer and the employer specifically intended an injury. An employer shall be deemed to have intended to injure if the employer had actual knowledge that an injury was certain to occur and willfully disregarded that knowledge.* The issue of whether an act was an intentional tort shall be a question of law for the court. This subsection shall not enlarge or reduce rights under law. [MCL § 418.131(1); MSA § 17.237(131)(1) (emphasis added).]

The Court's primary task in this case is the proper construction of the intentional tort exception as set forth in 1987 PA 28.

II

Background of the Intentional Tort Exception

Before its amendment by 1987 PA 28, subsection 131(1) was silent regarding whether an employee could sue in tort for an intentional tort suffered at the hands of his employer. This Court construed the prior version of subsection 131(1) in Beauchamp v. Dow Chemical Co., 427 Mich. 1; 398 N.W.2d 882 (1986).

In *Beauchamp*, the plaintiff was exposed at work to the chemical "agent orange" and, as a result, suffered physical and mental injuries. He sued his employer, alleging in part that his employer intentionally misrepresented and fraudulently concealed potential danger, intentionally assaulted him, and committed the tort of intentional infliction of emotional distress. The first issue before the Court was whether intentional torts should be excluded from coverage under the WDCA. The Court determined that intentional conduct by an employer was not within the act's exclusivity provision. It reasoned, "because the Legislature intended to limit and diffuse liability for accidental injury by no means suggests the Legislature intended to limit and diffuse liability for intentional torts. Accidents are an inevitable part of industrial production; intentional torts by employers are not."

The *Beauchamp* Court's next task, then, was to construe the parameters of the newly created "intentional tort exception." The version of the WDCA before the Court was silent with regard to whether intentional torts were covered by its provisions. The Court reviewed other jurisdictions and recognized two lines of cases. Some jurisdictions required an actual intent to injure in order for conduct to fall outside the parameters of the worker's compensation system. Other jurisdictions defined intentional tort more broadly. The latter line of cases did not limit recovery to cases in which the consequences were intended, but rather allowed tort recovery where the employer knew that the consequences of his actions were certain, or substantially certain, to occur. The Court explained that under this latter line of cases, the employer may be deemed to possess the intent to injure if it is substantially certain that the injury will occur as a consequence of its actions.

Beauchamp adopted the "substantial certainty" standard, reasoning:

> The problem with the true intentional tort test appears to be that it allows employers to injure and even kill employees and suffer only workers' compensation damages so long as the employer did not specifically intend to hurt the worker.... Prohibiting a civil action in such a case "would allow a corporation to 'cost-out' an investment decision to kill workers."

Under *Beauchamp*, the substantial certainty standard is defined as:

> If the actor knows that the consequences are certain, or substantially certain, to result from his act, and still goes ahead, he is treated by the law as if he had in fact desired to produce the result. It does not matter whether the employer wishes the injury would not occur or does not care whether it occurs. If the injury is substantially certain to occur as a consequence of actions the employer intended, the employer is deemed to have intended the injuries as well.

Beauchamp held that the plaintiff's complaint had pleaded a prima facie case of the intentional tort exception to the WDCA, reversed the decision of the Court of Appeals, and remanded for further proceedings.

* * *

III

Legislative History of 1987 PA 28

Of relevance to these cases is the amendment of subsection 131(1), which occurred less than five months after *Beauchamp* was released. The parties in these cases do not dispute that the amendment is a legislative reaction to *Beauchamp*, and an attempt to clarify the intentional tort exception to the act's exclusive remedy provision....

* * *

[The court examined competing drafts of the legislation noting that a Senate version used the phrase "deliberately intended," while a House version would have defined intent in terms of actual knowledge that an injury was "likely" to occur. The court also quoted several Senators who had different understandings of the language ultimately adopted. Senator Dillingham, for example, understood the statute "to restore the integrity of the exclusive remedy provision and avoid a new window of litigation that would threaten the financial stability of Michigan business and government." Senator Cherry, on the other hand, commented that the "change in the standard although narrowing the substantial certainty test does not preclude the specific cases which the Supreme Court indicated were actionable under the *Beauchamp* decision."]

We interpret the statute's history as indicating that the language of the final bill was a compromise. Senator Cherry's comments indicate that although *Beauchamp* needed to be tightened, there was still room for tort recovery in this area. Senator Dillingham advocated a much more rigorous standard. The legislation finally adopted did not restrict recovery to "true" intentional torts. Our task is therefore to discover what compromise the Legislature struck.

IV

Construing the Statute Consistently With Legislative Intent

At issue are two sentences of subsection 131(1). . . .

The first sentence reads, "An intentional tort shall exist only when an employee is injured as a result of a deliberate act of the employer and the employer specifically intended an injury." MCL § 418.131(1); MSA § 17.237(131)(1). The two phrases in this first sentence we must construe are: "deliberate act" and "specifically intended an injury."

The Legislature's use of the phrase "deliberate act" may indicate either that the employer must have deliberated about the act[7] or that the act must be one of commission rather than omission. Although not free from doubt, we construe the phrase "deliberate act," to encompass both commissions and omissions. . . . The legislative history indicates that employer omissions may constitute the "act" necessary to establish an intentional tort. Senator Cherry cited several cases that indicate that events other than a traditional battery may fulfill the "deliberate act" requirement. . . . The interpretation is also supported by the second sentence in which the employer is deemed to have the requisite intent from the failure to act in certain circumstances. Therefore, we construe the phrase "deliberate act" to include a situation in which an employer consciously fails to act.

The more difficult issue is what the Legislature intended by the phrase "specifically intended an injury." The commonly accepted meaning of the word "intent" includes a state of mind in which the actor is substantially certain that his act will produce a certain result. . . .

* * *

[7] For example, if an employer punches his employee, the punch could be considered deliberate; yet if the employer suffers an involuntary muscle spasm that causes his arm to make contact with his employee, the spasm cannot be considered deliberate.

[The court observed that the substantial certainty test is endorsed by both Prosser & Keeton, Torts § 8 (5th ed. 1984) and 1 Restatement (Torts) 2d § 8A]

It would be an absurd construction, however, to conclude that the Legislature meant to define "intended" to include when the actor was "substantially certain" of the consequences of his acts. That the Legislature intended a meaning other than the "substantially certain" language of Prosser and the Restatement is clear from the fact that the amendment was intended to reject *Beauchamp* and from the use of the word "certain," not "substantially certain," in the second sentence. Whatever else the Legislature intended, we are confident it intended to prohibit tort liability if an employer is only substantially certain that injury will result from his acts. Therefore, we conclude that the phrase "specifically intended an injury" means that the employer must have had in mind a purpose to bring about given consequences.

* * *

Construing the entire first sentence according to the Legislature's intent, to state a claim against an employer for an intentional tort, the employer must deliberately act or fail to act with the purpose of inflicting an injury upon the employee.

The most difficult problem of interpretation is ascertaining the intent of the Legislature under the second sentence defining the intentional tort exception. That sentence reads: "An employer shall be deemed to have intended to injure if the employer had actual knowledge that an injury was certain to occur and willfully disregarded that knowledge." MCL § 418.131(1); MSA § 17.237(131)(1).... [T]he second sentence will be employed when there is no direct evidence of intent to injure, and intent must be proved with circumstantial evidence. It is a substitute means of proving the intent to injure element of the first sentence. The three phrases in this sentence that we must construe are: "actual knowledge," "certain to occur," and "willfully disregarded."

A

Actual Knowledge

Because the Legislature was careful to use the term "actual knowledge," and not the less specific word "knowledge," we determine that the Legislature meant that constructive, implied, or imputed knowledge is not enough. Nor is it sufficient to allege that the employer should have known, or had reason to believe, that injury was certain to occur.... A plaintiff may establish a corporate employer's actual knowledge by showing that a supervisory or managerial employee had actual knowledge that an injury would follow from what the employer deliberately did or did not do.

B

Injury Certain to Occur

Once we conclude that the employer must have actual knowledge that an injury would occur, the question becomes when does a dangerous condition rise to the level of "certain to occur"? . . . When an injury is "certain" to occur, no doubt exists with regard to whether it will occur. Thus, the laws of probability, which set forth the odds that something will occur, play no part in determining the certainty of injury. Consequently, scientific proof that, for example, one out of ten persons will be injured if exposed to a particular risk, is insufficient to prove certainty. Along similar lines, just because something has happened before on occasion does not mean that it is certain to occur again. Likewise, just because something has never happened before is not proof that it is not certain to occur.

Moreover, conclusory statements by experts are insufficient to allege the certainty of injury contemplated by the Legislature. . . . Under the Michigan statute, . . . even if the expert opined that the injury was "certain to occur," and not merely "substantially certain to occur," this affidavit would be insufficient. It merely parrots the language of the legal test and gives no scientific or factual support for its conclusion. . . .

One case which is directly on point is Gulden v. Crown Zellerbach Corp., 890 F.2d 195 (C.A.9, 1989). In *Gulden*, the defendant's plant was contaminated with toxic levels of polychlorinated biphenyls (PCBs). After hazardous waste specialists were unsuccessful in reducing the level of PCBs on the plant floor, the defendant ordered the plaintiffs to scrub the floor on their hands and knees, with no protective clothing. This assignment continued for five days, during which time the plaintiffs' clothing was soaked with PCBs. The court held that under Oregon's narrow intentional tort exception,[10] the plaintiffs' complaint withstood summary judgment. The court found that the injury in question was the exposure to the PCBs itself, because the level of toxicity was sufficient to produce a body level of PCBs of six to ten times higher than normal and to trigger serious health concerns. The court then held that the injury was certain to occur. It reasoned that the defendant was aware that contact with the PCBs would injure the plaintiffs, yet deliberately ordered them to perform their task "in a manner requiring them to initiate and maintain contact with the PCBs." These facts would constitute allegations of certainty of injury under the Michigan statute.

A further question under the certainty requirement, closely related to the actual-knowledge requirement, is the level of awareness an employer

[10] Oregon's statute permits a civil tort claim to be filed "if injury or death results to a worker from the deliberate intention of the employer of the worker to produce such injury or death. . . ." [Or. Rev. Stat. 656.156(2).]

must possess: is it enough that the employer know that a dangerous condition exists, or must the employer be aware that injury is certain to occur from what the actor does? We find the latter interpretation the proper one. . . .

Despite the very high threshold required to deem an injury "certain to occur," some situations constitute examples of certain injury. For example, Professor Larson, in his treatise on worker's compensation, agrees that the *Film Recovery* case discussed in *Beauchamp*, constitutes an intentional tort.[12] He explains:

> The fumes . . . were continuously operative, and the employer knew it. . . . The exposure to fumes did in fact occur. The only possible "unknown" might have been the effect of inhaling the fumes, but this unknown was removed by the plain warning on the package. The hiring of only workers who could not read warning labels confirms that the employer wanted those employees to continue to inhale these and suffer these known consequences. A court could well say that this amounted to intending the injury. [2A Larson, Workmen's Compensation, § 68.15(e), pp 13–105 to 13–106.]

We agree with Professor Larson's reasoning. When an employer subjects an employee to a continuously operative dangerous condition that it knows will cause an injury, yet refrains from informing the employee about the dangerous condition so that he is unable to take steps to keep from being injured, a factfinder may conclude that the employer had knowledge that an injury is certain to occur.

C

Willfully Disregards

Finally, the term "willfully disregards" must be construed. . . . Because the purpose of the entire second sentence is to establish the employer's intent, we find that the use of the term "willfully" in the second sentence is intended to underscore that the employer's act or failure to act must be more than mere negligence, that is, a failure to act to protect a person who might foreseeably be injured from an appreciable

---

[12] The facts of the case, as set forth by Beauchamp, are as follows,

> Film Recovery Systems went into the business of recovering silver from film negatives. This was done by placing the negatives into vats of cyanide. Hydrogen cyanide gas would bubble up from the vats and there was inadequate ventilation. The employer knew about the dangers. The labels on the chemicals being used contained adequate warnings; as a result, the employer hired only employees who could not speak or read English. The workers complained about the fumes daily. In 1981, an inspector had warned that the operation had outgrown the plant. The employer's response was to move the executive offices while tripling the size of the operations. Eventually one worker died and several others were seriously injured because of hydrogen cyanide poisoning. The corporate officers were convicted of involuntary manslaughter.

risk of harm. An employer is deemed to have possessed the requisite state of mind when it disregards actual knowledge that an injury is certain to occur.

D

Inference of Intent

In short, under the second sentence, the Legislature has permitted the employer's state of mind to be inferred from its actions when there is no direct evidence of the employer's intent to injure. . . .

If we read both sentences of the intentional tort exception together, it becomes evident that an employer must have made a conscious choice to injure an employee and have deliberately acted or failed to act in furtherance of that intent. The second sentence then allows the employer's intent to injure to be inferred if the employer had actual knowledge that an injury was certain to occur, under circumstances indicating deliberate disregard of that knowledge. The applications that follow are our attempt to give effect to the expressions of legislative intent contained in the statute: an intent to create a rigorous threshold for a claim of intentional tort, and an intent that the threshold created not be so rigorous as to preclude all claims of intentional torts.

Application

* * *

Conclusion

We would reverse the opinion of the Court of Appeals in Travis, and reinstate the trial court's order granting summary disposition for defendant. We would affirm the Court of Appeals opinion in Golec with regard to defendants Metal Exchange and Rziemkowski, and would remand to the trial court for further proceedings consistent with this opinion.

[concurring and dissenting opinions are omitted]

NOTES

1. Should either Travis' or Golec's claim survive a summary judgment motion under the standards adopted by the court? A majority affirmed summary judgment against Travis. The majority concluded that evidence was insufficient as a matter of law to prove that the injury was certain to occur. "Although Clarke had actual knowledge that the press was malfunctioning, he did not have knowledge that an injury was certain to occur. . . . [I]n this case, unlike *Film Recovery*, supra, plaintiff was not required to confront a continually operating dangerous condition. The press double cycled only intermittently." A majority reversed the employer's summary judgment against Golec. "If the facts as alleged by plaintiff are established at trial, then

plaintiff has proved the existence of a continually operative dangerous condition. Accordingly, we conclude that a genuine issue of material fact is presented regarding whether the injury was certain to occur."

Three justices agreed with the test adopted by the majority, but concluded that summary judgment was appropriate in both cases. In their view, there was insufficient evidence that Golec's employer had "actual knowledge that an injury was certain to occur." Two justices concluded that summary judgment was not authorized in either case. In their view, the majority placed too much importance on whether there was "a continuously operative dangerous condition that [the employer] knows will cause injury." They would draw from prior decisions in which the intended injury exception applied to "isolated but extremely dangerous activities."

2. Either by express statutory provision or judicial construction, every state allows employees to sue their employers in tort for intended injuries. See 6 A. Larson and L. Larson, Larson's Workers' Compensation Law § 103.01 (2013) for a compilation of cases. *Beauchamp*, quoted in the principal case, articulates the traditional doctrinal explanation for this exception to the exclusive remedy rule: intended injuries are not "accidental" within the meaning of workers' compensation coverage. Consider the following policy justification offered by the North Dakota Supreme Court:

> Other strong public policy considerations support permitting an intentional tort cause of action. An underlying objective of workers' compensation is to promote a safe work environment. Affording employers immunity for intentional acts does not promote that objective. . . . Employers would not be held individually responsible for their intentional actions. In effect, it would allow an employer to buy the right to hit an employee. . . . Furthermore, . . . [p]roviding immunity to employers for intentional torts is inconsistent with [state] insurance law that generally denies coverage for willful acts.

Zimmerman v. Valdak Corp., 570 N.W.2d 204, 207 (N.D.1997). To what extent is exposure to tort liability needed to "promote a safe workplace"? Do employers have incentives to minimize occupational injury and disease other than liability concerns?

3. The early cases applying the intended injury exception to the exclusive remedy doctrine involved fist fights and similar traditional assaults and batteries. E.g., Heskett v. Fisher Laundry & Cleaners Co., 217 Ark. 350, 230 S.W.2d 28 (1950). Many recent cases like *Travis* explore the application of this exception to business decisions that consciously and systematically increase the employee's exposure to risk. This new line of cases force courts to come to grips with the meaning of "intent."

Many states, perhaps a majority, limit the intended injury exception to instances where the employer subjectively desires to injure the employee. Few claims other than those involving fist fights can satisfy this exacting standard. See, Fenner v. Municipality of Anchorage, 53 P.3d 573 (Alaska

2002) (expressly rejecting the substantial certainty test and adopting a specific intent to injure standard); Davis v. United States Employers Council, Inc., 147 Or. App. 164, 934 P.2d 1142 (1997) (employer did not provide adequate safety equipment despite knowledge that workers were suffering harm as a result of excessive exposure to toxic fumes; no "deliberate intention" since employer did not subjectively desire to injure employees); Zimmerman v. Valdak, Corp., 570 N.W.2d 204 (N.D.1997) (employer knew that a safety device was inoperable and was warned that an injury was "substantially certain" to occur if the machine was not repaired; employer deliberately chose not to shut down the machine for repair; no intent to injure); Miller v. Ensco, Inc., 286 Ark. 458, 692 S.W.2d 615 (1985) (knowingly exposing employee to polychlorinated byphenyls (PCB's) without adequate protection is not an intended injury); Kearney v. Denker, 114 Idaho 755, 760 P.2d 1171 (1988) (employer's failure to install safety guards and cut off switch was not "willful or unprovoked physical aggression" that would allow injured employee to maintain a common law tort action); Noonan v. Spring Creek Forest Products, 216 Mont. 221, 700 P.2d 623 (1985) (employer's failure to repair equipment known to violate OSHA safety standards does not constitute an intent to injure); Mullins v. Biglane Operating Co., 778 F.2d 277 (5th Cir.1985) (employer who deliberately withheld safety equipment did not actually intend to injure employee).

Many other states, however, look beyond subjective intent and allow employees to sue their employers in tort when the employer knew the injury was "substantially certain" to occur. E.g., Turner v. PCR, Inc., 754 So.2d 683 (Fla.2000) (injuries resulting from chemical plant explosion were actionable in tort when the evidence could support a finding that the explosion was substantially certain to occur); Woodson v. Rowland, 329 N.C. 330, 407 S.E.2d 222 (1991) (wrongful death action based on fatal trench cave-in; plaintiff's expert gave an affidavit attesting that given the height and slope of the trench, the cave-in was substantially certain to occur; jury issue as to intent); Mayer v. Valentine Sugars, Inc., 444 So.2d 618 (La.1984) (allegations that the employer knew to a substantial certainty that violations of safety regulations would produce an explosion are sufficient to state a cause of action for an intended injury). Delgado v. Phelps Dodge Chino, Inc., 131 N.M. 272, 34 P.3d 1148 (2001) (death resulting from explosion at smelting plant is actionable in tort when employer knew that its conduct was substantially certain to result in serious injury or death; actual intent standard expressly rejected); Parret v. UNICCO Service Co., 127 P.3d 572 (Okla. 2005) (substantial certainty test strikes the proper balance between the employer's interest in limited liability and the employee's interest in protection from employer misconduct). As a general proposition, employees are more likely to successfully assert tort claims against their employers under the substantial certainty standard of intent than they would under the subjective intent to injure test. Even in the former jurisdictions, however, courts will summarily dispose of tort claims if evidence of the likelihood of injury does not rise to the level of substantial certainty. E.g., Monge v. RG Petro-Machinery Co. Ltd., 701 F.3d 598 (10th Cir. 2012) (evidence sufficient to establish that the employer knew there was a substantial *likelihood* of an injury does not establish that the employer knew that the injury was substantially *certain* to occur; applying Oklahoma law); Nichols v. Horseshoe Casino, 999 So.2d 1255 (La. App. 2009) (asthmatic employee died on his first day of work; 'rumor' that the employee's supervisor was aware that the employee was experiencing breathing difficulty yet denied the employee's request to go home or get treatment was insufficient evidence of intent to bring the case outside of workers' compensation); Rose v. Isenhour Brick & Tile Co., 344 N.C. 153, 472 S.E.2d 774 (1996) (employer had actual knowledge that employees routinely by-passed safety guards on machines; no serious injuries or deaths had occurred in six years prior to fatal incident; summary judgment for employer, affirmed); Millison v. E.I. du Pont de Nemours & Co., 101 N.J. 161, 501 A.2d 505 (1985) (evidence that employer deliberately concealed from employees the risk of exposure to asbestos did not establish knowledge that injury was substantially certain to occur; summary judgment for the employer, affirmed).

4. The substantial certainty standard is endorsed by the Restatement (Third) Torts § 1 (Proposed Final Draft 2005) and is used in most states in the context of non-workplace intentional torts. Yet, as the Restatement itself acknowledges, a large number of states reject this standard in the context of an exception to the exclusive remedy doctrine. See comment a. Why would a state allow a non-workplace battery claim to proceed on the strength of evidence that the defendant knew to a substantial certainty that a harmful contact would occur, but require a worker to prove that her employer subjectively intended to injure her? What are the perceived stakes in selecting a subjective intent to injure or a substantial certainty standard?

5. The Utah Supreme Court recently spoke to the issue of when an employer's conduct will trigger the "intentional injury exception" to the exclusive remedy doctrine. Helf v. Chevron USA, Inc., 203 P.3d 962 (Utah 2009). A tort suit was brought by an employee against her employer after she was injured by exposure to toxic fumes. She alleged that she was told to work in an "open-air pit" designed to neutralize toxic sludge despite the fact that during a previous shift earlier that same day that process had produced a toxic cloud that injured several other employees and set off safety alarms. The court cautioned that care must be taken to clearly distinguish between motive intent.

> The distinction between intent and motive is particularly important in applying the 'intent to injure' standard because an intentional injury may arise in instances where the employer intentionally placed an employee in harms way, but the employer's motive was to increase profits, not to inflict injury.

203 P.3d at 972. This passage suggests that a "subjective desire to injure" standard of intent is too narrow. That is, employers should be subject to tort liability under certain circumstances even if it was not their subjective desire to injure the employee.

At the same time, the court expressed concern that the "substantial certainty" approach conflates probability with intent, suggesting that intent may be imputed where a high probability of injury exists because the employer knew that harm was substantially likely to occur sometime to some employee.

203 P.3d at 973.

The court then articulated its standard as follows:

> We therefore hold that the 'intent to injure' standard requires a specific mental state in which the actor knew or expected that injure would be the consequence of his action. To demonstrate intent, a plaintiff may show that the actor desired the consequence of his actions, or that the actor believed the consequences were *virtually certain* to occur . . . For a workplace injury to qualify as an intentional injury under the Act, the employer or supervisor must know or expect that the assigned task will injure the particular employee that undertakes it. In other words, the employer must know or expect that a specific employee will be injured doing a specific task.

203 P.3d at 974 (emphasis added).

Is the standard articulated by the Utah court in *Helf* substantively different from that provided in *Travis*, the Restatement, or the approaches reflected in the note 6 below?

6. Michigan is not the only state to attempt to statutorily define the scope of the intentional tort exception to the exclusive remedy doctrine. A West Virginia statute limits tort actions to cases where the employer acts with a specific intent to injure the employee, or if all of the following facts are proven:

> (A) That a specific unsafe working condition existed in the workplace which presented a high degree of risk and a strong probability of serious injury or death;
>
> (B) That the employer, prior to the injury, had actual knowledge of the existence of the specific unsafe working condition and of the high degree of risk and the strong probability of serious injury or death presented by the specific unsafe working condition;
>
> (C) That the specific unsafe working condition was a violation of a state or federal safety statute, rule or regulation, . . . or of a commonly accepted and well-known safety standard within the industry . . . ;
>
> (D) That notwithstanding the existence of the facts set forth in subparagraphs (A) through (C) inclusive of this paragraph, the employer nevertheless thereafter intentionally exposed an employee to such specific unsafe working condition intentionally; and

(E) That the employee exposed suffered serious compensable injury or compensable death . . . as a direct and proximate result of the specific unsafe working condition.

W.Va. Code § 23–4–2(d)(2)(ii). In Blake v. Skidmore Truck Stop, Inc., 201 W.Va. 126, 493 S.E.2d 887 (1997) an employee sued her employer in tort after she was robbed, stabbed, and beaten by a third party robber. In support of her claim, the employee presented the following evidence:

> Among other things, Mrs. Blake testified that: (1) there were no limitations on the amount of money she should keep in the cash register; (2) customers could stand directly behind her when she using [sic] the cash register; (4) she could not see out any windows when she was standing at the cash register; (5) there was no "drop safe" in the Store; (6) the area was not well lit after dark; and (7) she did not recall being instructed by the manager of the Store that she was to hand over the money in the cash register in the event of the robbery.
>
> Appellants also presented evidence from Ira Somerson, an expert witness . . . [who] testified that it is standard security practice in the convenience store industry to have "a cash control or a cash management policy" . . . That it is important to keep the cash register visible from the outside (by positioning it in front of a window and having proper lighting so those passing by the store can see it) and to train employees about what to do in case of a robbery. Mr. Somerson also commented that putting a barrier or counter between a cashier and a customer is "so automatic . . . that's like cars have wheels."

493 S.E.2d at 895–96. Mrs. Blake's employer contended that, as a matter of law injuries, resulting from the criminal acts of a third party could never rise to a claim under W.Va. Code § 23–4–2 and, in any event, the evidence presented by the plaintiff did not satisfy the five-part test of § 23–4–2(c)(2)(ii). Should Blake's case be submitted to a jury? See also, Smith v. Apex Pipeline Services, Inc., 741 S.E.2d 845 (W.Va. 2013) (employee failed to present evidence sufficient to meet the "high threshold" of proving that his employer had "actual knowledge" of a "specific unsafe working condition;" summary judgment for the employer, affirmed).

The Ohio experience reflects a tug-of-war between the courts and the legislature. In the early 1980s, several cases expanded employer exposure to tort liability. In response to these decisions, the Ohio legislature enacted a statute that purported to limit the intentional tort exception to instances where the employer acts with the "deliberate intent to cause . . . injury." A rebuttable presumption of such intent would arise if the employer deliberately removed safety guards from machinery or deliberately misrepresented toxic or hazardous substances. Ohio Rev. Code Ann. § 41.21.80. This statute also eliminated the right to a trial by jury, recognized certain defenses, and created a fund to pay for damages. This statute was declared unconstitutional in Brady v. Safety–Kleen Corp., 61 Ohio St.3d 624, 576 N.E.2d 722 (1991). The legislature passed another statute in 1995 that states that the only suit an employee may bring against an employer is one for an "employment intentional tort" which is defined as "an act committed by an employer in which the employer deliberately and intentionally injures . . . an employee." Ohio Rev. Code Ann. § 2745.01 (D)(1). The statute imposed a clear and convincing evidence standard of proof. Ohio Rev. Code Ann. § 2745.01 (C)(1). The explicit purpose of this statute was to supersede standards created in prior court decisions and replace them with a more limited cause of action. The Ohio Supreme Court held that this statute unconstitutionally deprived workers of equal protection by imposing on them different and more difficult standards for pursuing intentional tort claims. Johnson v. BP Chemicals, Inc., 85 Ohio St.3d 298, 707 N.E.2d 1107 (1999). The legislature reenacted Ohio Rev. Code Ann. § 2745.01 in 2005 and the Ohio Supreme Court upheld the law over a number of constitutional challenges. Kaminiski v. Metal & Wire Products Co., 125 Ohio St.3d 250, 927 N.E.2d 1066 (2010). Thus, an Ohio employer is protected by the exclusive remedy doctrine unless it acts with the deliberate intent to injure an employee. E.g., Houdek v. Thyssenkrupp Materials NA, 134 Ohio St. 3d 491, 983 N.E.2d 1253 (2012). For a history of the tug of war between the Ohio legislature and courts over the scope of the intended injury exception to the exclusive remedy doctrine, seeAamir Mahboob, The Judicial-Legislative War: Employer Intentional Torts in Ohio, 42 U. Toledo L. Rev. 525 (2011).

In California, workers may recover tort damages from their employers for injuries caused by the "knowing removal of, or knowing failure to install, a point of operation guard on a power press." Cal.Labor Code § 4558. Cf. Lefiell Mfg. Co. v. Superior Court, 55 Cal.4th 275, 145 Cal.Rptr.3d 543, 282 P.3d 1242 (2012) (the statutory "power press" exception to the exclusive remedy doctrine authorizes claims for loss of consortium only in cases of death). It should be noted, however, that violations of safety statutes or regulations do not generally trigger the intended injury exception to the exclusive remedy doctrine. E.g., Sullivan v. Lake Compounce Theme Park, 277 Conn. 113, 889 A.2d 810 (2006); Wise v. CNH America, LLC., 333 Mont. 181, 142 P.3d 774 (2006).

What are the differences among these various statutes? Are statutory formulations of exceptions to the exclusive remedy doctrine preferable to judicially crafted rules? How would you articulate a standard for determining when an employee must accept workers' compensation benefits as her exclusive remedy and when she can sue her employer in tort? What standard would provide the best mix of societal objectives to create incentives to reduce occupational injuries, preserve the quid pro quo of the workers' compensation bargain, and achieve fairness for the parties?

7. Employees sometimes couch their tort claims against their employers in terms of fraud. Several courts distinguish between fraudulent concealment of the risks of employment and the fraudulent concealment of an already-contracted disease or injury. The former is not actionable as a tort

because it is said to "merge" with the subsequent compensable injury or disease for which workers' compensation provides the exclusive remedy. See e.g., Wilkins v. West Point–Pepperell, Inc., 397 So.2d 115 (Ala.1981) (alleged fraudulent concealment of risk of "brown lung" disease in a textile plant); Johnson v. Kerr–McGee Oil Ind., Inc., 129 Ariz. 393, 631 P.2d 548 (App.1981) (failure to warn of hazards of working in a uranium mine); Johnson v. Hames Contracting Inc., 208 Ga.App. 664, 431 S.E.2d 455 (1993) (alleged intentional failure to warn of asbestos exposure). The fraudulent concealment of diseases already developed is considered a separate wrong that lies outside the scope of the exclusive remedy doctrine. See, e.g., Potts v. UAP–GA. AG. CHEM., Inc., 270 Ga. 14, 506 S.E.2d 101 (1998); Millison v. E.I. du Pont de Nemours & Co., 101 N.J. 161, 501 A.2d 505 (1985); Johns–Manville Prods. Corp. v. Contra Costa Superior Court, 27 Cal.3d 465, 165 Cal.Rptr. 858, 612 P.2d 948 (1980) (subsequently codified in Cal.Labor Code § 3602(b)(2)). In terms of the moral culpability of the employer or the nature of the injury, how convincing is the distinction between the fraudulent concealment of the initial workplace risk and the fraudulent concealment of an already-contracted disease? Which party should bear the burden of determining how much harm occurred after the fraudulent concealment? See Cal.Labor Code Ann. § 3602(b)(2) (the burden of proof respecting apportionment of damages rests upon the employer). The plaintiffs in *Millison* were ultimately successful in proving that the defendants had deliberately concealed the plaintiffs' asbestos-related diseases. See, Millison v. E.I. du Pont de Nemours & Co., 226 N.J.Super. 572, 545 A.2d 213 (1988), affirmed 115 N.J. 252, 558 A.2d 461 (1989).

8. An alternative strategy for reducing risks posed by exposure to hazardous substances is reflected in what are commonly called right-to-know laws. On the federal level, the Occupational Safety and Health Administration (OSHA), adopted regulations that require employers in the manufacturing sector to implement a "hazard communication" program encompassing labeling, material safety data sheets, and employee training. See, 29 C.F.R. § 1910.1200 et. seq. Additionally, close to half the states have enacted right-to-know laws that mandate the identification of hazardous substances to which employees are exposed in the course of employment. Furthermore, right to know laws generally obligate employers to inform their employees of the potential health risks posed by such exposure. These laws vary in their degree of comprehensiveness. Some legislation simply requires the maintenance of lists of hazardous substances, while other statutes incorporate strict training procedures. For a listing of specific statutes, see O'Reilly, Driving a Soft Bargain: Unions, Toxic Material, and Right to Know Legislation, 9 Harv.Envtl.L.Rev. 307, 309 n. 13 (1985). For an insightful discussion of the difficulties in communicating information pertaining to risk, see Nordenstam and DiMento, Right to Know: Implications of Risk Communication Research for Regulatory Policy, 23 U.Cal.Davis L.Rev. 333 (1990). How might administratively regulated disclosure of information affect the level of risk in the workplace? What role should workers' compensation and tort play in such a scheme?

BYRD V. RICHARDSON–GREENSHIELDS SECURITIES, INC.

Supreme Court of Florida, 1989.
552 So.2d 1099.

BARKETT, JUSTICE.

We have for review *Byrd v. Richardson–Greenshields Securities, Inc.*, 527 So.2d 899, 902 (Fla. 2d DCA 1988), which certified "the contention in this case concerning the exclusivity of worker's compensation benefits." The case presents the following question of law:

> WHETHER THE WORKERS' COMPENSATION STATUTE PROVIDES THE EXCLUSIVE REMEDY FOR A CLAIM BASED ON SEXUAL HARASSMENT IN THE WORKPLACE.

We have jurisdiction. We answer in the negative and quash the opinion below.

The plaintiffs, all female employees, brought claims for assault and battery, intentional infliction of emotional distress, and negligent hiring and retention of employees. These claims were based on incidents in which male employees repeatedly touched the women and made verbal sexual advances on them in the workplace during work hours. In their suit, the women claimed this resulted in emotional anguish and stress.

The trial court dismissed the complaint on grounds that the workers' compensation statute provided the exclusive remedy for the women. On appeal, the Second District affirmed.

Our analysis must begin with the premise, now well established in our law, that workers' compensation generally is the sole tort remedy available to a worker injured in a manner that falls within the broad scope and policies of the workers' compensation statute. Indeed, section 440.11, Florida Statutes, provides that workers' compensation is the exclusive remedy and is "in place of all other liability of such employer . . . on account of such injury or death." This statute expresses a plain legislative intent that any potential liability arising from "injury or death" is abolished in favor of the exclusive remedy available under workers' compensation. However, if the liability arises from something other than "injury or death," the other potential bases of liability remain viable.

Thus, the definition of the word "injury" is crucial to the determination of this case. That definition is provided in the statute itself. Section 440.02(14), Florida Statutes, states that "injury" means "*personal injury . . . by accident* arising out of and in the course of employment, and such diseases or infection as naturally or unavoidably result from such injury" (emphasis added). Moreover, section 440.02(1), Florida Statutes, defines "accident" as "only an unexpected or unusual event or result, happening suddenly."

It is apparent, however, that the term "accident arising out of . . . employment" has been construed well beyond the more limited definition suggested by the statutory language. This judicial extension of the statutory language is in keeping with the liberal construction accorded the workers' compensation statute . . . and has affected both the terms "accident" and "arising out of."

As far back as the case of *Czepial v. Krohne Roofing Co.*, 93 So.2d 84, 85–86 (Fla.1957), for instance, the Court recognized that an injury was compensable under the statute even though caused by the gradual accumulation of otherwise insignificant injuries arising from repeated exposure to somewhat noxious substances at the workplace. This is true even though, strictly speaking, a cumulative injury of this type is not an "accident" within the dictionary definition of the word.[3]

In a similar manner, the Court has accepted that even a suicide precipitated by serious workplace injuries can be compensable. We have qualified this statement only by requiring that the suicide must arise from a mental disturbance directly attributable to an actual workplace injury.

An analogous line of cases has held that severe emotional disorders also may be compensable where caused by actual physical injury at the workplace. This is not true, however, where no physical injury has occurred, since the statute by its own terms excludes such matters. Indeed, the statute expressly prohibits a workers' compensation award for "[a] mental or nervous injury due to fright or excitement only." § 440.02(1), Fla.Stat.

Similarly, Florida courts have extended the definition of "accident arising out of . . . employment" to encompass a wide variety of injuries caused by intentional torts, provided there is a sufficient nexus with the activities of the workplace itself. This is true where workplace tensions lead one employee to assault another, where jealousy over a lovers' triangle causes one worker to attack another with a workplace tool, where an employee is robbed at the workplace by an armed gunman, and where a worker is robbed at home by persons seeking workplace cash register receipts.[5]

In a recent extension from this prior line of cases, the First District has held that sexual harassment claims are governed by the same general principles. Thus, in *Brown v. Winn–Dixie Montgomery, Inc.*, 469 So.2d

[3] Webster's Third New International Dictionary 11 (1981), for instance, defines "accident" as "a usu. sudden event or change occurring without intent or volition through carelessness, unawareness, ignorance, or a combination of causes and producing an unfortunate result."

[5] However, an injury intentionally inflicted by the employer himself or his or her alter egos does not fall within these principles, since workers' compensation was not established to excuse misconduct of this type. *See* Schwartz v. Zippy Mart, Inc., 470 So.2d 720, 724 (Fla. 1st DCA 1985).

155, 159 (Fla. 1st DCA 1985), the district court concluded that the workers' compensation statute barred a claim for battery and intentional infliction of emotional distress based on an incident in which a male supervisor grabbed the breast of a female employee.

The *Brown* decision in turn rested on the First District's prior analysis in *Schwartz v. Zippy Mart, Inc.*, 470 So.2d 720, 724 (Fla. 1st DCA 1985). *Schwartz* had held that sexual harassment falls outside the rule that, under workers' compensation, an employer remains liable in tort for his or her own intentional misconduct. The First District buttressed this rationale with the following quote from a treatise on the subject:

> "When the person who intentionally injures the employee is not the employer in person nor a person who is realistically the alter ego of the corporation, but merely a foreman, supervisor or manager, both the legal and the moral reasons for permitting a common-law suit against the employer collapse, and a substantial majority of modern cases bar a damage suit against the employer."

Id. at 724 (quoting 2A *Larson's Workmen's Compensation Law* § 68.21, 13–28 (1982)). Under this rationale, the First District held that claims for assault and battery were barred as a result of an incident in which two female workers had been subjected to pinching, grabbing, and other gestures of a sexual nature. *Id.* at 724–25.

We acknowledge and reaffirm the strong policies regarding workers' compensation that form the foundation of the decisions discussed above. As the Court often has noted, our obligation is to honor the obvious legislative intent and policy behind an enactment, even where that intent requires an interpretation that exceeds the literal language of the statute.

In this context, we cannot find that acts constituting sexual harassment were ever meant to fall under workers' compensation. Moreover, we have an equal obligation to honor the intent and policy of other enactments and, accordingly, may not apply the exclusivity rule in a manner that effectively abrogates the policies of other law. In this instance, we find that the First District in *Brown* and *Schwartz*, and the Second District in the instant case, have ignored an equally important expression of public policy emanating from both federal and state enactments.

There can be no doubt at this point in time that both the state of Florida and the federal government have committed themselves strongly to outlawing and eliminating sexual discrimination in the workplace, including the related evil of sexual harassment. The statutes, case law, and administrative regulations uniformly and without exception condemn sexual harassment in the strongest possible terms. We find that the present case strongly implicates these sexual harassment policies and, accordingly, may not be decided by a blind adherence to the exclusivity rule of the workers' compensation statute alone. Our clear obligation is to construe both the workers' compensation statute and the enactments dealing with sexual harassment so that the policies of both are preserved to the greatest extent possible.

Thus, we must examine the scope of the public policies regarding sexual harassment. The primary source of these policies, both historically and under the supremacy clause of the United States Constitution, article VI, clause 2, is a portion of Title VII of the Civil Rights Act of 1964, which provides in pertinent part:

> It shall be an unlawful employment practice for an employer . . . to discriminate against any individual with respect to his compensation, terms, conditions, or privileges of employment, because of such individual's . . . sex. . . .

42 U.S.C. § 2000e–2(a)(1) (1982). This federal provision was the model of Florida's Human Rights Act of 1977, sections 760.–01–.10, Florida Statutes (1987), which uses virtually the same language in prohibiting the same practices. The Human Rights Act provides in pertinent part:

> "It is an unlawful employment practice for an employer . . . to discriminate against any individual with respect to compensation, terms, conditions, or privileges of employment, because of such individual's . . . sex. . . ."

§ 760.10(1)(a), Fla.Stat.

In interpreting Title VII, the federal courts have stated unequivocally that any sort of workplace sexual harassment is unlawful under Title VII and contrary to public policy. So strong is this policy that the United States Supreme Court has stated that,

> [w]ithout question, when a supervisor sexually harasses a subordinate because of the subordinate's sex, that supervisor "discriminate[s]" on the basis of sex. . . . The phrase "terms, conditions, or privileges of employment" evinces a congressional intent " 'to strike at the entire spectrum of disparate treatment of men and women' " in employment.

Meritor Sav. Bank v. Vinson, 477 U.S. 57, 64, 106 S.Ct. 2399, 2404, 91 L.Ed.2d 49 (1986). Indeed, in *Meritor* the Supreme Court expressly rejected the notion that Title VII addresses only "economic discrimination." *Id.* The *Meritor* Court quoted with approval a statement by the Eleventh Circuit Court of Appeals that

> "Sexual harassment which creates a hostile or offensive environment for members of one sex is every bit the arbitrary

> barrier to sexual equality at the workplace that racial harassment is to racial equality. Surely, a requirement that a man or woman run a gauntlet of sexual abuse in return for the privilege of being allowed to work and make a living can be as demeaning and disconcerting as the harshest of racial epithets."

Id. at 67, 106 S.Ct. at 2405 (quoting *Henson v. City of Dundee*, 682 F.2d 897, 902 (11th Cir.1982)).

In light of this overwhelming public policy, we cannot say that the exclusivity rule of the workers' compensation statute should exist to shield an employer from all tort liability based on incidents of sexual harassment. The clear public policy emanating from federal and Florida law holds that an employer is charged with maintaining a workplace free from sexual harassment. Applying the exclusivity rule of workers' compensation to preclude any and all tort liability effectively would abrogate this policy, undermine the Florida Human Rights Act, and flout Title VII of the Civil Rights Act of 1964.

This, we cannot condone. Public policy now requires that employers be held accountable in tort for the sexually harassing environments they permit to exist, whether the tort claim is premised on a remedial statute or on the common law.

We find this conclusion harmonizes with the policies and scope of workers' compensation. As often has been noted, workers' compensation is directed essentially at compensating a worker for lost resources and earnings. This is a vastly different concern than is addressed by the sexual harassment laws. While workplace injuries rob a person of resources, sexual harassment robs the person of dignity and self esteem. Workers' compensation addresses purely economic injury; sexual harassment laws are concerned with a much more intangible injury to personal rights. To the extent these injuries are separable, we believe that they both should be, and can be, enforced separately.

Certainly, whenever a claim is based on the Human Rights Act, Title VII of the Civil Rights Act of 1964, the Educational Equity Act, or any other statute prohibiting sexual discrimination or harassment, that claim cannot in logic or fairness be barred by the exclusivity rule. Doing so would improperly nullify a statute by judicial fiat and, in the case of the Civil Rights Act of 1964, would defy the Constitution.

Similarly, to the extent that the claim alleges assault, intentional infliction of emotional distress arising from sexual harassment or the specific type of battery involved in this case,[8] the exclusivity rule also will

[8] Because the battery involved in cases of this type differs significantly from that addressed in our prior case law, we distinguish this case factually from our opinions in W.T.

not bar them. This is so because these causes of action address the very essence of the policies against sexual harassment—an injury to intangible personal rights.

For the foregoing reasons, we quash the opinion of the district court below and remand for further proceedings consistent with the views herein. We express no opinion as to whether petitioners in this case have alleged sufficient facts to state a cause of action under the common law, an issue we do not reach. To the extent they conflict with this opinion, we disapprove *Schwartz v. Zippy Mart, Inc.*, 470 So.2d 720, 724 (Fla. 1st DCA 1985), and *Brown v. Winn–Dixie Montgomery, Inc.*, 469 So.2d 155, 159 (Fla. 1st DCA 1985). We answer the certified question in the negative.

It is so ordered.

MCDONALD, SHAW and KOGAN, JJ., concur.

EHRLICH, C.J., concurs in result.

OVERTON, J., dissents.

GRIMES, JUSTICE, concurring.

If the plaintiffs had suffered physical and emotional injuries as a result of sexual batteries perpetrated by the two employees whose conduct is complained of in this action, they would have a compensable workers' compensation claim and their lawsuit against the employer would be barred by virtue of the exclusiveness of the workers' compensation remedy. Here, because the plaintiffs incurred no physical injury, are they barred from recovery because the touching in a technical sense constituted a battery? Professor Larson suggests that the determination of the applicability of the workers' compensation law depends upon the nature of both the tort and the injury:

> To test . . . the conclusion that the element of damage must be considered along with the legal components of the tort, we may adduce the tort of assault. Here, we are fortunate in having an actual decided case that makes the point. In *Ritter v. Allied Chemical Corporation*, [295 F.Supp. 1360 (D.S.C.1968), *aff'd*, 407 F.2d 403 (4th Cir.1969)] plaintiff brought suit against her employer for an assault by one of her superiors. She stated that the only result of the assault was a scratch on her hand and some soreness, and did not claim any disability or other elements

---

Edwards Hospital v. Rakestraw, 114 So.2d 802, 803 (Fla.App.1959); Tampa Maid Seafood Products v. Porter, 415 So.2d 883, 885 (Fla.App.1982); Prahl Brothers, Inc. v. Phillips, 429 So. 2d 386, 387 (Fla. 1st DCA 1983); and Strother, 383 So. 2d at 623. That is, we do not perceive the battery alleged in this instance as involving wage loss or workplace injury, but an unlawful intrusion upon personal rights protected by remedial legislation such as the Florida Human Rights Act.

which might have provided compensation under the workmen's compensation laws of South Carolina. Because the injuries for which plaintiff was suing were not those which were covered by the compensation act, the court held that, on defendant's motion for judgment on the pleadings, the tort action against the employer was not barred.

> This case is a reminder of the fact that, as every law student should know by his third week, the tort of assault does not require physical injury or even touching. Its minimal essence is putting the victim in fear of bodily harm. If bodily harm accompanies assault, as it usually does, the exclusiveness bar comes into play. If bodily harm does not accompany assault, the exclusiveness bar does not come into play. The conclusion must be that the test is not just the legal ingredients of assault, but also the results—specifically whether physical injury of the kind dealt with by the compensation act is produced.
>
> To summarize: If the essence of the tort, in law, is non-physical, and if the injuries are of the usual non-physical sort, with physical injury being at most added to the list of injuries as a make-weight, the suit should not be barred. But if the essence of the action is recovery for physical injury or death, the action should be barred even if it can be cast in the form of a normally non-physical tort.

2A A. Larson, *The Law of Workmen's Compensation* § 68.34(a) at 13–116 to 117 (1989) (footnotes omitted).

Measured by the foregoing criteria, I concur that the plaintiffs' suit is not barred by the exclusive remedy of workers' compensation. Whether the amended complaint states a cause of action against the employer remains a question for the district court of appeal to decide.

NOTES

1. Most courts have allowed workers to pursue common law tort or statutory civil rights claims under circumstances similar to those presented in *Byrd*. See, See e.g., Busby v. Truswal Systems Corp., 551 So.2d 322 (Ala.1989) (claim for intentional infliction of emotional distress is not barred by the exclusive remedy doctrine for emotional injuries caused by sexual harassment); Ford v. Revlon, 153 Ariz. 38, 734 P.2d 580 (1987) (claim for intentional infliction of emotional distress is not barred by the exclusive remedy doctrine for emotional injuries caused by sexual harassment); Horodyskyj v. Karanian, 32 P.3d 470 (Colo.2001) (Common law tort claims to redress sexual harassment are not barred by the exclusive remedy doctrine) Byers v. Labor and Industry Review Comm'n., 208 Wis.2d 388, 561 N.W.2d 678 (1997) (claim under state Fair Employment Act for sexual harassment is

not barred by the exclusive remedy doctrine); Cox v. Brazo, 165 Ga.App. 888, 303 S.E.2d 71 (1983), affirmed 251 Ga. 491, 307 S.E.2d 474 (1983) (negligent supervision of sexually abusive supervisor); Boscaglia v. Michigan Bell Telephone Co., 420 Mich. 308, 362 N.W.2d 642 (1984) (sexual harassment violated state civil rights and fair employment practices acts); Kerans v. Porter Paint Co., 61 Ohio St.3d 486, 575 N.E.2d 428 (1991) (sexual harassment as a non-physical injury tort). Nelson v. University of Hawaii, 97 Hawai'i 376, 38 P.3d 95 (2001) (statutory exception to the exclusive remedy doctrine for tort claims stemming from sexual harassment).

A number of jurisdictions have ruled that workers' compensation is the employee's exclusive remedy in a sexual harassment context. E.g., Konstantopoulos v. Westvaco, Corp., 690 A.2d 936 (Del.Supr.1996) (common law tort claims barred by the exclusive remedy doctrine); Green v. Wyman–Gordon Co., 422 Mass. 551, 664 N.E.2d 808 (1996) (common law tort claims barred by the exclusive remedy doctrine); Knox v. Combined Ins. Co., 542 A.2d 363 (Me.1988) (assault, battery and intentional infliction of emotional distress claims barred); Loges v. Mack Trucks, Inc., 308 S.C. 134, 417 S.E.2d 538 (1992) (assault, battery and intentional infliction of emotional distress claims barred, but claim for slander was actionable); Baker v. Wendy's of Montana, Inc., 687 P.2d 885 (Wyo.1984) (assault, battery and intentional infliction of emotional distress claims barred).

For a collection of cases see Linda A. Sharp, Workers' Compensation as Precluding Employee's Suit Against Employer for Sexual Harassment in the Workplace, 51 A.L.R. 5th 163 (1998).

2. A variety of explanations have been offered to explain why statutory and common law tort claims can be asserted by employees against employers for sexual harassment. Among the arguments that appear in the cases are: sexual harassment is not an "accident"; dignitary interests injured by sexual harassment are not covered by workers' compensation; the risk of sexual harassment is not incidental to the character of employment; acts of sexual harassment are directed at employees for reasons personal to the employee; and public policy as reflected in state and federal civil rights laws support allowing such claims. Reasons given in support of the conclusion that workers' compensation is the exclusive remedy in the sexual harassment context include: workplace assaults are now commonly viewed to arise out of employment; insulating employers from tort liability is a central component of the workers' compensation principle; and exceptions to the exclusive remedy doctrine should come explicitly from the legislature.

Which of these arguments are most persuasive? Which are least persuasive? Is there a conflict between *Hyett*'s conclusion that the exclusive remedy doctrine bars a tort claim against an employer whose negligence causes noncompensable impotence and *Byrd*'s conclusion that an employer may be sued in tort for sexual harassment? How does one distinguish between assaults by co-workers that are compensable under workers' compensation and those for which workers' compensation is not the exclusive remedy?

3. Note that a majority of jurisdictions give a narrow scope to the intended injury exception to the exclusive remedy doctrine but allow tort suits against employers for sexual harassment. Why should workers' compensation be the exclusive remedy for the worker injured when his employer knowingly exposed him to asbestos, but the employee subject to sexual harassment is allowed to pursue a claim in tort? Consider the comments of Professor McCluskey:

> The reasoning in these cases points to a central issue underlying controversies over the bounds of the intentional tort exception. To distinguish "intentional" from "accidental" work injuries, we must decide the political and moral question of how much and what kinds of harm workers should have to assume as part of the standard work relationship (subject to limited compensation), and how much and what kinds of harm employers should be obligated to avoid (subject to more costly tort remedies). The willingness of many jurisdictions to exempt sexual harassment tort claims from exclusive remedy provisions reflects a change toward the value judgment that sexual harassment is neither necessary nor appropriate to a normal, productive economy. The unwillingness of most jurisdictions to exempt tort claims [from the exclusive remedy doctrine] for knowing exposure to occupational diseases (such as asbestos dust) reflects the persistence of the value judgment that such illnesses and injuries are a necessary part of productive workplaces.
>
> These judgments about the normal production process do not merely describe an economic fact about modern employment, nor do they merely reflect social norms about employment. Instead, they also implicitly prescribe what the normal conditions of employment should be. These courts insist that sexual harassment (unlike asbestos exposure) is a harm not reasonably connected to the production process. In theory, however, some employers might be able to increase profits or production (at least in the short run) by overlooking or condoning sexual harassment in the workplace . . . The decision by some courts to view sexual harassment as outside the bounds of workers' compensation rests on an implicit determination that employers *should not* be allowed to profit from sexual harassment in the workplace, even if they could. In contrast, the perception that asbestos exposure has a productive purpose is the result of political decisions to allow employers to treat workers' exposure to toxic materials as a cost of doing business. Unlike sexual harassment, then, employers can overlook or tolerate asbestos exposure in the pursuit of profit.

Martha T. McCluskey, The Illusion of Efficiency in Workers' Compensation "Reform," 50 Rutgers L. Rev. 657, 911–12 (1998) (footnotes omitted; emphasis in original).

4. In 1991 Congress enacted legislation that authorizes a limited damage remedy against employers who engage in or tolerate sexual harassment. See 42 U.S.C.A. § 1981A. Should the availability of a damage remedy under federal law affect whether the exclusive remedy doctrine precludes a tort action under state law? For a discussion of Title VII remedies see Mark Hager, Harassment as a Tort: Why Title VII Hostile Environment Liability Should Be Curtailed, 30 Conn. L. Rev. 375 (1998).

5. Justice Grimes' concurring opinion in *Byrd* refers to Professor Larson's distinction between physical injury and non-physical injury torts. Relying on this distinction, courts have held that workers' compensation is not the exclusive remedy for such torts as false imprisonment, libel, malicious prosecution, and intentional infliction of emotional distress. E.g., Fermino v. Fedco, Inc., 7 Cal.4th 701, 30 Cal.Rptr.2d 18, 872 P.2d 559 (1994) (false imprisonment claim is not barred by the exclusive remedy doctrine); Dietz v. Finlay Fine Jewelry Corp., 754 N.E.2d 958 (Ind.App.2001) (a law suit stemming from loss of a job; common law tort claims for defamation, false imprisonment and, intentional infliction of emotional distress are not barred by the exclusive remedy doctrine); Miraliakbari v. Pennicooke, 254 Ga.App. 156, 561 S.E.2d 483 (2002) (employee's suit for false imprisonment and intentional infliction of emotional distress was not barred by the exclusive remedy doctrine; dispute stemmed from employer's alleged refusal to allow employee to leave or make a phone call to care for her 6 year old son who suffered a broken bone at school); Operating Engineers Local 3 v. Johnson, 110 Cal.App.4th 180, 1 Cal.Rptr.3d 552 (2003) (workers' compensation is not the exclusive remedy for the breach of employee's constitutional right of privacy). Snead v. Harbaugh, 241 Va. 524, 404 S.E.2d 53 (1991) (law professor's suit against the dean and other members of the faculty for alleged defamation is not precluded by the exclusive remedy doctrine); Schusse v. Pace Suburban Bus Div., 334 Ill.App.3d 960, 268 Ill.Dec. 645, 779 N.E.2d 259 (2002) (suit for spoliation of evidence is not barred by the exclusive remedy doctrine). Cf. Williams v. Caruso, 966 F.Supp. 287 (D.Del.1997) (claims for tortious interference with contract are not barred by the exclusive remedy doctrine). For a collection of cases see, 6 A. Larson and L. Larson, Larson's Workers' Compensation Law § 104.01 (2013). Is an exception to the exclusive remedy doctrine grounded in the type of injury any easier to justify or apply than one based on the employer's state of mind? See Love, Actions for Nonphysical Harm: The Relationship Between the Tort System and No-Fault Compensation (With an Emphasis on Workers' Compensation), 73 Cal.L.Rev. 857 (1985).

SMOTHERS V. GRESHAM TRANSFER, INC.

Supreme Court of Oregon, 2001.
332 Or. 83, 23 P.3d 333.

LEESON, J.

Plaintiff filed this negligence action against defendant, his employer, after an administrative law judge (ALJ) of the Workers' Compensation Board upheld the insurer's denial of plaintiff's workers' compensation claim. The ALJ found that plaintiff's exposure to sulfuric, hydrochloric, and hydrofluoric acid mist and fumes at work was not the "major contributing cause" of plaintiff's respiratory condition and other ailments and, therefore, that plaintiff had not suffered a "compensable injury" under the workers' compensation statutes. Nonetheless, plaintiff believed that he had suffered an injury at work. Accordingly, he brought this action against his employer for negligence. The trial court dismissed plaintiff's complaint for failure to state a claim, reasoning that *ORS 656.018* (1995) makes workers' compensation law the "exclusive remedy" for work-related injuries, whether or not a claim is compensable. The Court of Appeals affirmed. This court allowed review to address plaintiff's contention that he has been denied a remedy for the injuries that he suffered at work, in violation of the remedy clause in Article I, section 10, of the Oregon Constitution. For the reasons that follow, we hold that, if a workers' compensation claim alleging an injury to a right that is protected by the remedy clause is denied for failure to prove that the work-related incident giving rise to the claim was the major contributing cause of the injury or condition for which the worker seeks compensation, then the exclusive remedy provisions of *ORS 656.018* (1995) are unconstitutional under the remedy clause. Applying that holding to the facts of this case, we reverse the decision of the Court of Appeals and the judgment of the trial court and remand the case to the trial court for further proceedings.

I. Background

A. Facts

Plaintiff's job as a lube technician for defendant's trucking company required him to work in a pit more than four feet deep in a mechanics' shop where trucks were serviced. A truck-washing area was located outside the shop. Defendant's employees cleaned the exteriors of trucks by spraying them with a chemical mixture of diluted sulfuric acid and small amounts of hydrochloric and hydrofluoric acids. When the doors to the shop were open, acid mist and fumes from the truck-washing area drifted into the shop and down into the pit where plaintiff worked. For many months, plaintiff experienced headaches, as well as itching, burning, and watering eyes.

In January 1993, plaintiff contracted an upper respiratory infection that developed into pneumonia. He was hospitalized for five days, and he was unable to work for a month. Plaintiff returned to work, but he suffered another episode of pneumonia in February 1993. In November 1993, his physician diagnosed him with bronchitis. In December 1993, plaintiff's coworkers found him so ill that he was lying on the lunchroom floor. He was sent home, where he was bedridden with bacterial bronchitis for most of the holiday season.

Plaintiff returned to work in January 1994, but his physician expressed concern about his slow rate of recovery. Plaintiff called in sick several times between March and mid-June 1994. In June 1994, claimant stopped working for defendant because of his illness.

Thereafter, plaintiff filed a workers' compensation claim for his lung condition. Defendant's insurer denied plaintiff's claim. At a hearing before an ALJ, the issue was whether plaintiff had a compensable occupational disease. After the hearing, the ALJ upheld the insurer's denial, because plaintiff had failed to prove that his work exposure was the major contributing cause of his lung disorder. *See ORS 656.802(2)(a)* ("The worker must prove that employment conditions were the major contributing cause of the disease.").

B. Legal Context for Plaintiff's Negligence Action

In *Errand v. Cascade Steel Rolling Mills, Inc.*, 320 Or. 509, 525, 888 P.2d 544 (1995), this court held that the exclusive remedy provisions in *ORS 656.018* (1993) did not preclude workers whose workers' compensation claims had been denied from bringing civil actions against their employers in an effort to recover damages for their work-related injuries. In this case, after the ALJ had upheld the denial of plaintiff's workers' compensation claim, plaintiff, relying on *Errand*, filed this action against defendant. His complaint alleged that defendant's negligence in subjecting him to the acid mist and fumes at work had caused permanent injury to his lungs; skin blisters, pain and swelling in the joints of his hands, elbows and knees; degeneration of his toenails, fingernails, and teeth; and other physical ailments.

Meanwhile, in response to this court's decision in *Errand*, the 1995 Legislature amended *ORS 656.018* and added subsection (6) to provide that workers' compensation is the exclusive remedy for work-related injuries, even if a claim is not compensable. Ore. Laws 1995, ch 332, § 5. As amended, *ORS 656.018* (1995) provides, in part:

* * *

"(6) *The exclusive remedy provisions* and limitation on liability provisions of this chapter *apply to all injuries and to diseases, symptom complexes or similar conditions of subject workers arising out of and in the course of employment whether or not they are determined to be compensable under this chapter*." (Emphasis added.)

Those amendments took effect on June 7, 1995, after plaintiff had filed his complaint, and they apply to "all claims or causes of action existing or arising on or after the effective date of this Act, regardless of the date of injury or the date a claim is presented[.]"

* * *

C. Parties' Arguments

Before this court, plaintiff repeats his contention that, under the mandate of the remedy clause of Article I, section 10, the legislature may not deprive a person of a remedy for an injury to person, property, or reputation that was recognized at common law, unless the legislature makes available an equivalent remedy. Defendant's response to plaintiff's constitutional argument is twofold. First, defendant contends that the legislature has plenary authority to define what constitutes a cognizable injury to person, property, or reputation. Second, defendant contends that the remedy clause does not limit the legislature's power to modify any common-law or statutory remedy.

* * *

II. Remedy Clause

* * *

[A lengthy an detailed discussion of the Oregon Remedy Clause is omitted. The court examines the text of the provision, the historical context in which it arose, the structure and language of similar provisions in other state constitutions, the Oregon constitutional convention, and case law from Oregon and other states.]

Summary

Having analyzed the remedy clause, we reach the following conclusions. As one of the provisions of the Oregon Bill of Rights, the remedy clause of Article I, section 10, protects rights respecting person, property, and reputation that, in 1857, the common law regarded as "absolute," that is, that derive from nature or reason rather than solely from membership in civil society. By the seventeenth century, the remedial side of the common law had developed to protect those rights in the event of injury by any other subject of the English realm. The function of common-law causes of action was to restore "justice" or "right" following injury. "Injury" at common law meant any harm or wrong to absolute rights for which a cause of action existed.

Drafters of remedy clauses in state constitutions sought to protect absolute common-law rights by mandating that a remedy always would be available for injury to those rights. The drafters of the Oregon remedy clause identified absolute rights respecting person, property, and reputation as meriting constitutional protection under the remedy clause. As to those rights, the remedy clause provides, in mandatory terms, that remedy by due course of law shall be available to every person in the event of injury. The word "remedy" refers both to a remedial process for seeking redress for injury and to what is required to restore a right that has been injured. Injury, in turn, is a wrong or harm for which a cause of action existed when the drafters wrote the Oregon Constitution in 1857. A common-law cause of action is a constitutionally adequate remedy for seeking redress for injury to protected rights. However, the remedy clause does not freeze in place common-law causes of action that existed when the drafters wrote the Oregon Constitution in 1857. The legislature may abolish a common-law cause of action, so long as it provides a substitute remedial process in the event of injury to the absolute rights that the remedy clause protects. At a minimum, to be remedy by due course of law, the statutory remedy must be available for the same wrongs or harms for which the common-law cause of action existed in 1857. That is, if the common law provided a cause of action for an injury to one of the rights that the remedy clause protects, then a legislatively substituted remedial process must be available for that injury.

It follows from the foregoing that, in analyzing a claim under the remedy clause, the first question is whether the plaintiff has alleged an injury to one of the absolute rights that Article I, section 10 protects. Stated differently, when the drafters wrote the Oregon Constitution in 1857, did the common law of Oregon recognize a cause of action for the alleged injury? If the answer to that question is yes, and if the legislature has abolished the common-law cause of action for injury to rights that are protected by the remedy clause, then the second question is whether it has provided a constitutionally adequate substitute remedy for the common-law cause of action for that injury.

E. Analysis of This Case

In light of the foregoing principles for analyzing claims under Article I, section 10, we turn to the specific issue to be decided in this case. At the outset, we emphasize that the issue is a narrow one. Plaintiff does not challenge the constitutionality of the workers' compensation system as a whole. Neither does he contend that the "exclusive remedy" provisions of *ORS 656.018* (1995) per se are unconstitutional. [P]laintiff here does not assert that substituting the workers' compensation remedial process for the common-law cause of action by an employee against an employer for negligence violates Article I, section 10. Moreover, and as context for the discussion that follows, we note that, since Evanhoff [v. State Industrial Accident Comm'n] in 1915, this court implicitly has recognized the legislature's constitutional authority to substitute workers' compensation for the common-law negligence cause of action for work-related injuries. Nothing in this case challenges those precepts. The constitutionality of the overall workers' compensation statutory program is not in question.

The narrow issue in this case is whether the exclusive remedy provisions of *ORS 656.018* (1995) are unconstitutional under the remedy clause to the extent that there now is a category of workers who have been injured at work but receive no compensation benefits, because they cannot prove that the work-related incident was the *major* contributing cause of their injury or disease. From the perspective of the workers' compensation system, such workers are deemed to have suffered no injury and therefore are not entitled to compensation benefits. At common law, by contrast, injury was understood to be any wrong or harm to person, rights, reputation, or property.

We turn to the facts of this case. Plaintiff contends that he was injured at work, that is, that he suffered a harm to his person in the form of severe and progressive respiratory problems, as well as other physical ailments, after he inhaled sulfuric, hydrochloric, and hydrofluoric acid mist and fumes while working in the pit in defendant's shop. Before his exposure, plaintiff had not experienced any of his symptoms. Because plaintiff was unable to prove that his work exposure was the major contributing cause of his disabling lung condition, however, he did not have a compensable injury under present workers' compensation law. Moreover, as we have explained, under *ORS 656.018* (1995), workers' compensation purports to be the exclusive remedy for work-related injuries, whether or not a claim is a compensable claim. Thus, under present workers' compensation law, plaintiff was left with no means for seeking redress for the injuries that he alleges that he suffered at work and for which a common-law cause of action would have been available before the advent of the workers' compensation system.

After the ALJ had denied plaintiff's workers' compensation claim, plaintiff filed this negligence action. Defendant moved to dismiss for failure to state a claim. ORCP 21 A(8). Although defendant did not dispute that plaintiff might have suffered an injury at work, it argued that plaintiff had not suffered a compensable injury, as that term presently is defined in workers' compensation law, and that *ORS 656.018* (1995) makes workers' compensation the exclusive remedy for work-related injuries, whether or not a claim is compensable. In response to defendant's motion to dismiss, plaintiff argued, among other things, that the exclusive remedy provisions of *ORS 656.018* (1995) violated the remedy clause of Article I, section 10. Plaintiff contended that the remedy clause guarantees the availability of a process for seeking redress for injuries that were recognized at common law and that *ORS 656.018* (1995) impermissibly eliminated the existence of a remedy for the injuries that he believes he suffered at work. The trial court granted defendant's motion to dismiss for failure to state a claim. [The Court of Appeals affirmed].

* * *

The Court of Appeals ... relied on *Kilminster v. Day Management Corp.*, 323 Ore. 618, 919 P.2d 474 (1996), in holding that plaintiff in this case had no "right" that would support the argument that he had been deprived of a remedy. In *Kilminster*, a worker died when he fell from a radio tower that his employer had ordered him to climb without providing adequate fall-protection equipment. The decedent's parents brought an action for wrongful death under *ORS 30.020(1)*. That statute gives a plaintiff a right to bring a wrongful death action only " 'if the decedent might have maintained an action, had the decedent lived.' " In other words, *ORS 30.020(1)* gives a plaintiff only a derivative right. If the decedent in *Kilminster* had lived, then the "exclusive remedy" provisions of *ORS 656.018* would have barred him from pursuing a common-law action against his employer.

The plaintiffs in *Kilminster* argued that the "exclusive remedy" bar deprived them of their right to pursue a claim for the wrongful death of their son. This court rejected that argument. It reasoned:

> "Because the legislature has chosen not to provide decedent's parents with a wrongful death action based on a theory of negligence, and because Oregon has no common law action for wrongful death [citations omitted], they have suffered no legally cognizable injury to their person, property, or reputation."

Unlike the plaintiffs in *Kilminster*, plaintiff's right to remedy for injury in this case does not derive from a statute. Rather, plaintiff's right is grounded in the common law of negligence. Although Oregon has no common-law action for wrongful death, it does have a common-law action for negligence. The Court of Appeals erred in relying on *Kilminster* to affirm the trial court's dismissal of plaintiff's complaint in this case.

* * *

[W]e turn to an application of the methodology discussed earlier in this opinion for analyzing claims under the remedy clause. The first question is whether plaintiff has alleged an injury to one of the rights for which the remedy clause mandates that a remedy be available by due course of law. Plaintiff's complaint alleges that he suffered permanent injury to his lungs and that he suffers other physical ailments, because defendant negligently permitted mist and fumes from sulfuric, hydrochloric, and hydrofluoric acid to drift into the shop area and pit where plaintiff worked, was aware that exposure to them could cause harm to plaintiff, failed to provide plaintiff with proper safety instructions or protection from the chemicals, and failed to warn plaintiff that he would be exposed to the chemicals. To answer the first question, we must decide whether, when the drafters wrote the Oregon Constitution, the common-law of Oregon would have recognized an action for negligence under the circumstances of this case. We conclude that it would.

The territorial law of Oregon of June 27, 1844, provided, in part:

> "The Common Law of England and principles of equity, not modified by the statutes of Iowa or of this government, not incompatible with its principles, shall constitute a part of the law of this land."

This court has held that, in their reference to the common law, the drafters of the Oregon Constitution "must have had reference to that law as it existed, modified and amended by the English statutes passed prior to the Revolution."

It is undisputed that, at the time of the American Revolution, the common law recognized a cause of action for negligence. This court's case law is replete with cases involving that tort.

Our next, more specific, inquiry is whether at common law in Oregon in 1857, an employee would have had a cause of action against an employer for failure to provide a safe workplace and failure to warn of dangerous working conditions to which the employee would be exposed. That is, and unlike most other exercises in constitutional construction, the substantive content of the constitutional right can be established only by identifying the content of the common law in 1857. Although no Oregon cases addressed the common-law rights of employees to bring such negligence actions against their employers in the years immediately surrounding the creation of the Oregon Constitution, the content of the common law in 1857 may be divined from a wide range of sources. Cases from other jurisdictions, as well as Oregon cases decided within a relatively short period after 1857, are instructive.

* * *

[A discussion of cases from other jurisdictions is omitted]

This court's first opportunity to address the question of an employer's common-law liability to an employee for negligence was in 1888. In *Anderson v. Bennett*, 16 Ore. 515, 19 P. 765 (1888), the plaintiff, a laborer who had been hired to help construct a tunnel for the Northern Pacific Railroad Company, was blinded when his supervisor negligently ordered him to drill a hole in some rock and the drilling caused an explosion. The plaintiff's employer sought to avoid liability on the grounds that the plaintiff had assumed the risk and that a master was not liable for injuries caused by the negligence of a fellow servant. This court rejected both arguments, drawing on common-law rules that had developed in other jurisdictions. . . .

* * *

This court held that an employer, and the employer's representatives, have a duty "to use reasonable care and diligence and [to] make reasonable provision for the servant's safety," and that failure to do so subjected the employer to liability. Although *Anderson* was decided some 30 years after the drafters wrote the Oregon Constitution, nothing in the court's opinion in that case suggested that the holding was novel or that the decision marked a departure from any previous decisions or jurisprudence on the subject. We conclude that, in 1857, the common law of Oregon would have recognized that a worker had a cause of action for negligence against his employer for failing to provide a safe workplace and failing to warn of the dangerous conditions to which the worker would be exposed at work.

The next question is whether there is a remedial process available to plaintiff for seeking redress for the injuries that he alleges that he suffered to his lungs and other parts of his body when he was exposed to acid mist and fumes at work. As we have explained, when the drafters wrote the Oregon Constitution, plaintiff would have had a negligence cause of action against his employer for his alleged injuries. However, in 1913, the Oregon Legislature adopted the "Workmen's Compensation Act". . . .

* * *

Earlier, this court had observed that the twofold purposes of workers' compensation statutes were to afford protection to workers in the form of compensation for work-related injuries and to protect employers from expensive litigation. The Workmen's Compensation Act achieved those purposes by providing compensation to injured workers in lieu of the common-law remedy, and by making workers' compensation the exclusive remedy for work-related injuries, unless provided otherwise by statute. In keeping with the purposes of the act, this court long has held that an award of compensation is the full and complete measure of a worker's recovery for work-related injuries, including all consequences of the injury, such as aggravation.

When the workers' compensation program was adopted, and for almost 70 years thereafter, the statutory scheme provided that a work-related injury was a "compensable injury" if the worker could show, as a plaintiff had been required to show at common law, that the work-related incident was a contributing cause of the injury. Moreover, this court held that the word "injury" in the workers' compensation statutes was to be given "broad and liberal construction in view of the remedial and humanitarian purposes of the [Workers'] Compensation Law."

Under current workers' compensation law, an occupational disease generally is considered to be an injury. However, as we have explained, workers' compensation law now provides that occupational diseases and some injuries are "compensable" injuries only if the worker can prove that the work-related incident was the major contributing cause of the disease or injury. The major contributing cause standard means a cause, or combination of causes, that contributes more to the injury for which the worker seeks compensation than all other causes combined, or most of the cause. The major contributing cause standard did not exist at common law. Thus, for those workers' compensation claims that are subject to the major contributing cause standard, workers' compensation law does not provide compensation for a work-related incident that was only a contributing cause of the worker's injury. Therefore, workers' compensation law no longer provides a remedy for some wrongs or harms occurring in the workplace for which a common-law negligence cause of action had existed when the drafters wrote the Oregon Constitution in 1857. Nevertheless, under *ORS 656.018* (1995), workers' compensation law purports to be the exclusive remedy for work-related injuries, whether or not a claim is compensable.

In *Errand*, this court examined the legislature's intent when it enacted the "exclusive remedy" provisions of *ORS 656.018* (1993). The court concluded that the legislature had not intended to prevent a worker whose workers' compensation claim had been denied for failure to meet the major contributing cause standard from pursuing civil negligence claims against the employer in the effort to receive at least some damages for work-related injuries. Because this court decided *Errand* based on its analysis of the legislature's intent when it enacted *ORS 656.018* (1993), the court did not reach the argument that the exclusive remedy provisions of the statute violated the remedy clause.

As we have explained, in response to *Errand*, the 1995 Legislature amended *ORS 656.018* to make workers' compensation the "exclusive remedy" for work-related injuries, whether or not a claim is compensable. That is, the legislature made clear that, in enacting the 1995 amendments, it *did* intend what this court had assumed it had *not* intended in *Errand*. The question of the constitutionality of the exclusive remedy provisions in *ORS 656.018* that the court was not required to address in *Errand* therefore is presented squarely in this case.

Based on our analysis of the remedy clause of Article I, section 10, we conclude that determining whether the exclusive remedy provisions of *ORS 656.018* (1995) violate that clause involves a case-by-case analysis. The first inquiry is whether a workers' compensation claim alleges an injury to an "absolute" common-law right that the remedy clause protects. If it does, and the claim is accepted and the worker receives the benefits provided by the workers' compensation statutes, then the worker cannot complain that he or she has been deprived of a remedial process for seeking redress for injury to a right that the remedy clause protects. Neither can the worker complain that he or she has been deprived of a remedial process if a compensation claim is denied because the worker is unable to prove that the work-related incident was a contributing cause of the alleged injury, which is what a plaintiff would have had to prove in a common-law cause of action for negligence. However, if a workers' compensation claim for an alleged injury to a right that is protected by the remedy clause is denied because the worker has failed to prove that the work-related incident was the major, rather than merely a contributing, cause of the injury, then the exclusive remedy provisions of *ORS 656.018* (1995) are unconstitutional under the remedy clause, because they leave the worker with no process through which to seek redress for an injury for which a cause of action existed at common law.

[P]laintiff alleges that he suffered injuries to his lungs and other ailments when he was exposed to sulfuric, hydrochloric, and hydrofluoric acid mist and fumes at work. [F]or those injuries, he would have had a common-law cause of action when the drafters wrote the Oregon Constitution in 1857. However, plaintiff followed the procedures prescribed by Oregon statutes and first filed a workers' compensation claim. The ALJ held that plaintiff had not suffered a compensable injury because, although the work exposure might have contributed to his injuries, plaintiff could not prove that the work exposure was the major contributing cause of his injuries.

[P]laintiff believed that he had suffered *an* injury at work, albeit not a *compensable* injury as defined under present workers' compensation law. Therefore, after his workers' compensation claim was denied, plaintiff filed this action to seek redress for his injuries. For the reasons that we have explained, the remedy clause mandates that a remedy be available to all persons—including workers—for injuries to "absolute" common-law rights for which a cause of action existed when the drafters wrote the Oregon Constitution in 1857. Having alleged an injury of the kind that the remedy clause protects, and having demonstrated that there was no remedial process available under present workers' compensation laws, plaintiff should have been allowed to proceed with his negligence action. The Court of Appeals erred in affirming the trial court's dismissal of plaintiff's complaint on the ground that the exclusive remedy provisions of *ORS 656.018* (1995) barred his claim.

The decision of the Court of Appeals is reversed. The judgment of the circuit court is reversed, and the case is remanded to that court for further proceedings.

NOTES

1. What explains the different results in *Hyett* and *Smothers*? Both Hyett and Smothers suffered on-the-job injuries for which they received no benefits under workers' compensation and attempted to sue their employers in tort. Hyett's tort claim was barred by the exclusive remedy doctrine and Smothers' tort claim was not barred. Larson offers the following explanation:

> A distinction must be drawn, of course, between an injury which does not come within the fundamental coverage provisions of the [workers' compensation] act, and an injury which is in itself covered but for which, under the facts of the particular case, no compensation is payable.

6 A. Larson and L. Larson, Larson's Law of Workers' Compensation § 100.04 (2013). Can you articulate why *Smothers* falls in the former category and *Hyett* in the latter? This distinction was applied in McClendon v. Mid–City Discount Drugs, Inc., 876 S.W.2d 657 (Mo.App.1994) to allow a wrongful death suit to proceed against an employer when its employee died following a fall down a flight of stairs. McClendon's death was not covered by workers' compensation because he was intoxicated at the time of the fall and the workers' compensation statute expressly excluded injuries to intoxicated workers from coverage.

2. Paralleling developments in the "tort reform" movement, several states in addition to Oregon enacted legislation designed to restrict workers' compensation coverage during the 1990s. See Martha T. McCluskey, The Illusion of Efficiency in Workers' Compensation "Reform," 50 Rutgers L. Rev. 657 (1998). The ironic effect of cases like *Smothers* is that legislation intended to limit an employer's liability exposure under workers' compensation actually expands its exposure to liability in tort. The rationale underlying *Smothers* has been applied in a variety of settings. Thus,

(A) legislation restricting coverage of mental or psychological disability claims has led to employer tort liability in some states. E.g. Onstad v. Payless Shoesource, 301 Mont. 259, 9 P.3d 38 (2000); Bunger v. Lawson Co., 82 Ohio St. 3d 463, 696 N.E. 2d 1029 (1998) (both cases involving post-traumatic stress disorder of employees following sexual assaults by third parties); Bullin v. Correctional Medical Services, Inc., 908 So. 2d 269 (Ala. App. 2004) (health care employee held hostage at knife point by inmate can sue employer in tort when state workers' compensation law excluded "pure psychological" disabilities from coverage). Cf., Coates v. Wal-Mart Stores, Inc., 127 N.M. 47, 976 P. 2d 999 (1999) (statutory restrictions on coverage of mental disability claims cited as a reason why tort claim against employer for sexual harassment by supervisor was not barred by the exclusive remedy doctrine).

(B) employers have been held subject to tort suit where restrictive occupational disease provisions remove the alleged injury from coverage. E.g., O'Regan v. Preferred Enterprises, Inc., 758 So.2d 124 (La.2000) (workers' compensation occupational disease claim for aplastic anemia allegedly caused by occupational exposure to hazardous chemicals was defeated by statutory presumption that a disease is non-occupational if the employee has been on the job less than twelve months; employee can sue in tort); McCarthy v. Dept. of Social and Health Services, 110 Wash.2d 812, 759 P.2d 351 (1988) (employee's tort suit against employer stemming from occupational exposure to second hand cigarette smoke is not barred by the exclusive remedy doctrine when the alleged injury is not covered by workers' compensation act due to restrictive occupational disease provisions). Cf., Adams v. Alliant Techsystems, Inc., 261 Va. 594, 544 S.E.2d 354 (2001) (employee can sue employer in tort for hearing loss when such injury was not covered by the workers' compensation act); Automated Conveyor Systems v. Hill, 362 Ark. 215, 208 S.W.3d 136 (2005) (employee whose neck injury was brought about gradually was denied compensation benefits; state law required cumulative trauma injuries to be the result of motion that was both rapid and repetitive; since injury is excluded from coverage, employee's tort claim is not barred by the exclusive remedy doctrine).

Some decisions, however, hold that tort suits against employers are barred by the exclusive remedy doctrine even when the injury is excluded from workers' compensation coverage by reason of some restrictive statutory provision. E.g. Synalloy Corp. v. Newton, 254 Ga. 174, 326 S.E.2d 470 (1985) (employee's tort claim against employer for injuries resulting from exposure to carcinogen was barred by the exclusive remedy doctrine even though it was not compensable under a restrictive definition of occupational disease); Shamrock Coal Co. v. Maricle, 5 S.W.3d 130 (Ky.1999) (employees' tort claim against employer for respiratory impairments resulting from exposure to coal dust were barred by the exclusive remedy doctrine even though a statutory amendment made such impairments of less than twenty percent not compensable under workers' compensation laws); Bias v. Eastern Associated Coal Corp., 220 W.Va. 190, 640 S.E.2d 540 (2006) (employee's tort suit against employer for "pure mental" injuries is barred by the exclusive remedy doctrine even though it was not compensable under workers' compensation). For a general discussion of these cases see Eston W. Orr, Note, The Bargain is No Longer Equal: State Legislative Efforts to Reduce Workers' Compensation Costs Have Impermissibly Shifted the Balance of the Quid Pro Quo In Favor of Employers, 37 Ga. L. Rev. 325 (2002).

3. Note that in Errand v. Cascade Steel Rolling Mills, Inc., 320 Or. 509, 888 P.2d 544 (1995) the Court concluded that the legislature did not intend for tort suits for injuries not covered by the workers' compensation act to be barred by the exclusive remedy doctrine. Thus, *Errand* and most of the

cases cited in the preceding note have been resolved as a matter of statutory construction. The constitutional issue became ripe in *Smothers* only when the legislature clarified its intent to exclude the injury from workers' compensation coverage and bar the tort claim. The redacted portions of *Smothers* provide an instructive discussion of the substantive aspects of a state constitutional "right to a remedy." Should a state legislature be permitted to eliminate both the workers' compensation and tort remedy for some work-related injuries and diseases? If such action does not violate the state constitution, would it violate federal constitutional protections? Would the Oregon statute survive a federal constitutional challenge under New York Central R.R. Co. v. White, 243 U.S. 188, 37 S.Ct. 247, 61 L.Ed. 667 (1917) reprinted in Chapter 2?

4. Other circumstances occasionally arise in which the exclusive remedy doctrine will not apply. For example, employees may bring common law tort actions against their employers if their relationship is not covered by workers' compensation at the time of the injury. Thus, farm laborers may bring tort suits against their employers in states that exclude such employment from workers' compensation coverage. E.g., Eastway v. Eisenga, 420 Mich. 410, 362 N.W.2d 684 (1984); Baskin v. Worker's Compensation Division, 722 P.2d 151 (Wyo.1986). A worker who is not in the course of employment when injured may sue the employer in tort. E.g., Dixie Road Builders, Inc. v. Sallet, 318 Ga. App. 228, 733 S.E.2d 511 (2012) (disputed issue of fact regarding whether the work day had ended (i.e., whether employee was in the course of employment) at the time he was shot at an employer run convenience store precluded summary judgment in employee's tort suit against employer); Beckham v. Estate of Brown, 100 N.M. 1, 664 P.2d 1014 (App.1983) (salesman died in plane crash on his way to attend a basketball game; trip was a prize for sales contest at work; widow allowed to proceed with wrongful death claim); Estate of Milos v. Quality Asphalt Paving, Inc., 145 P.3d 533 (Alaska 2006) (error to grant summary judgment to employer when evidence could support a finding that employee was "off shift" at time of his death). In many states an employee may maintain a tort action against an employer who fails to secure workers' compensation insurance. E.g., Ehredt v. DeHavilland Aircraft Co., 705 P.2d 913 (Alaska 1985) (uninsured employer held liable for death of employee in air crash). The uninsured employer is typically stripped of traditional tort defenses such as assumption of risk and comparative negligence. E.g., Grothe v. Olafson, 659 P.2d 602 (Alaska 1983) (employee's 20% comparative negligence would not reduce tort recovery against uninsured employer); Arvas v. Feather's Jewelers, 92 N.M. 89, 582 P.2d 1302 (App.1978) (common law defenses not available to uninsured employer sued by an employee who fell through unprotected opening in attic).

5. If it is unclear whether an injury is covered by workers' compensation or is actionable in tort under an exception to the exclusive remedy doctrine, must the employee "elect" one or the other remedy? The New Jersey Supreme Court spoke to this issue as follows:

> Our view is that in light of the Compensation Act's purpose of assisting disabled workers, the best approach is to allow a plaintiff to process his workers' compensation claim without forfeiting the opportunity to establish that he was injured as a result of conduct that amounted to an intentional wrong, entitling him to seek damages beyond those available in workers' compensation. If, however, a plaintiff should prevail in his suit based on intentional wrong, he would not be entitled to keep the entire amount of his compensation award as well as his civil suit remedy. . . . [I]f the trier-of-fact determines that du Pont and/or its doctors have been guilty of an intentional wrong as a result of their alleged fraudulent concealment of existing occupational diseases, du Pont or its insurance carrier will be able to offset compensation benefits previously paid to the extent that the civil damage award would serve as a double recovery.

Millison v. E.I. du Pont de Nemours & Co., 101 N.J. 161, 501 A.2d 505, 519 (1985). Accord, Smith v. Desautels, 183 Vt. 255, 953 A.2d 620 (2008). Not all courts agree with *Millison* on this point. See Zurowska v. Berlin Indus., 282 Ill.App.3d 540, 217 Ill.Dec. 499, 667 N.E.2d 588 (1996) (acceptance of compensation benefits barred claim for intentional tort); Werner v. State, 53 N.Y.2d 346, 441 N.Y.S.2d 654, 424 N.E.2d 541 (1981) (acceptance of workers' compensation benefits forecloses suit against employer for alleged intentional tort); Barrino v. Radiator Specialty Co., 315 N.C. 500, 340 S.E.2d 295 (1986) (employee who recovered workers' compensation benefits made a "binding election" of remedies that precluded tort claim against employer for alleged assault). See 6 A. Larson and L. Larson, Larson's Workers' Compensation Law § 102.03 (2013).

6. The exclusive remedy doctrine may be preempted by federal legislation. See, Adams Fruit Co., Inc. v. Barrett, 494 U.S. 638, 110 S.Ct. 1384, 108 L.Ed.2d 585 (1990) (Florida exclusive remedy provision preempted by the Migrant and Seasonal Agricultural Worker Protection Act, 29 U.S.C.A. 1801 et seq.); McClary v. O'Hare, 786 F.2d 83 (2d Cir.1986) (civil rights claim brought under 42 U.S.C.A. 1983 is not barred by state exclusive remedy doctrine). Cf., Jackson v. Sedgwick Claims Management Services, Inc., F.3d 731 F. 3d 556 (6th Cir. 2013) (federal Racketeer Influenced and Corrupt Organizations Act (RICO) does not pre-empt state workers' compensation law; civil RICO claim against workers' compensation claims administrator is barred by Michigan exclusive remedy doctrine). How does a preemption analysis differ from that used by the court in *Byrd*? See Paul J. Zech, Federal Pre-emption and State Exclusive Remedy Issues in Employment Litigation, 72 N. D. L. Rev. 325 (1996).

7. In 1972 the National Commission on State Workmen's Compensation Laws identified the encouragement of safety conditions as one of the objectives of a workers' compensation system. To what extent do the cases in this section reflect a concern that the limited recovery under workers' compensation and the exclusive remedy doctrine too greatly dilute

the employer's economic incentives to reduce accident costs? What factors other than compensation costs might affect an employer's investment in workplace safety? What strategies might a lawmaker consider to regulate risk in the workplace?

3. THIRD-PARTY ACTIONS: WHO IS A THIRD PARTY?

Cal.Labor Code Ann. § 3852

> The claim of an employee . . . for compensation does not affect his or her claim or right of action for all damages proximately resulting from the injury or death against any person other than the employer.

WRIGHT ASSOCIATES, INC. V. RIEDER

Supreme Court of Georgia, 1981.
247 Ga. 496, 277 S.E.2d 41.

HILL, PRESIDING JUSTICE.

The Georgia Education Authority contracted with Wright Associates, Inc., for the construction of an academic building at Macon Junior College. Wright Associates, as the general or prime contractor, then contracted with Eastern Steel Erectors, Inc., an independent subcontractor, for certain on-site work. Thomas Rieder, an Eastern employee, was injured in an on-site accident and recovered worker's compensation benefits from Eastern. He then sued Wright Associates in April, 1978, alleging that his injury was caused by the negligence of a Wright employee. Nearly two years after answering, Wright moved for summary judgment on the ground, raised for the first time in its motion, that Rieder's tort action was barred by Code Ann. [§§ 34–9–11, 34–9–8]. The trial court denied the motion for summary judgment but certified the question for immediate review. After the Court of Appeals denied the application for interlocutory review, Wright Associates petitioned for writ of certiorari, which was granted.

Code Ann. [§ 34–9–8] . . . provides that "A principal, intermediate, or subcontractor shall be liable for compensation to any employee injured while in the employ of any of his subcontractors engaged upon the subject-matter of the contract, to the same extent as the immediate employer. . . ."

By this Code Section the principal or intermediate contractor is made the "statutory employer" of the subcontractor's employee.

Under the facts of this case [the] issue [is] whether an employee of an independent subcontractor can recover in tort against the principal contractor.

In *Blair v. Smith*, 201 Ga. 747, 41 S.E.2d 133 (1947), this court cited Code Ann. [§ 34–9–8], but held without discussion of it that the employee of an independent contractor who recovered worker's compensation benefits from his immediate employer could maintain an action in tort against the principal contractor. Subsequently the Court of Appeals reluctantly followed *Blair*.

In 1979, this court decided *Haygood v. Home Transportation Co.*, 244 Ga. 165, 259 S.E.2d 429 (1979), in which we held that a principal contractor is the statutory employer of the employee of a subcontractor who is an independent contractor.... Since Home Transportation Company was the statutory employer of Mrs. Haygood's deceased husband, Home was liable for worker's compensation benefits to Mrs. Haygood. In that case, Home did in fact pay benefits to Mrs. Haygood. This court held that as a statutory employer who had paid compensation benefits, Home was immune from suit in tort under Code Ann. [§ 34–9–8]. In a concurring opinion, Justice Jordan (now Chief Justice) contended that *Haygood* overruled *Blair v. Smith.*

In the case before us, we have the same facts as in *Haygood, supra*, except that here the employee recovered worker's compensation benefits not from the statutory employer, Wright Associates, but from his immediate employer, Eastern Steel Erectors. Wright Associates argues that as a statutory employer liable to pay worker's compensation benefits under Code Ann. [§ 34–9–8], it should receive the correlative benefit of tort immunity under Code Ann. [§§ 34–9–11, 34–9–8]. We agree and so hold. As one commentator has pointed out in his discussion of statutory employers, "Since the general contractor is thereby, in effect, made the employer for the purposes of the compensation statute, it is obvious that he should enjoy the regular immunity of an employer from third-party suit when the facts are such that he could be made liable for compensation; and the great majority of cases have so held." 2A Larson, The Law of Workmen's Compensation, § 72.31 at p. 14–47.

Rieder contends that even if a statutory employer is normally insulated from tort liability despite the fact that he has not paid worker's compensation benefits, he should not be where, as here, he has a contract with the subcontractor which provides that the subcontractor shall carry worker's compensation insurance and in the event that the statutory employer is held liable for worker's compensation benefits, he will be indemnified by the subcontractor. Because Code Ann. [§ 34–9–8] gives a right of indemnification absent a contract, this amounts to an argument that because of the statutory right of indemnification as to compensation benefits, a statutory employer should not be immune from tort liability. We cannot agree. The purpose of Code Ann. [§ 34–9–8] is to ensure that employees in construction and other industries are covered by worker's compensation. In order to do so, it places an increased burden, in the form of potential liability for worker's compensation benefits, on the statutory employer. This encourages the statutory employer to require subcontractors to carry worker's compensation insurance. The fact that the statutory employer reacts to the statute in the manner intended by the legislature should not result in a penalty on the statutory employer. Conversely, if the statutory employer does not require subcontractors to provide compensation benefits (as intended by the statute), the statutory employer may acquire tort immunity. See, *Haygood v. Home Transportation Co., supra*. The quid pro quo for the statutory employer's potential liability is immunity from tort liability. The fact that the statutory employer has a right to indemnification, statutory or contractual, does not strip him of his tort immunity. See 2A Larson, The Law of Workmen's Compensation, § 72.31, p. 14–55, 56, § 72.32, p. 14–66 n. 72.

Judgement reversed.

All the Justices concur, except UNDERCOFLER, J., who dissents.

UNDERCOFLER, JUSTICE, dissenting.

The majority here finds that since the general contractor is a statutory employer and has a potential liability for workers' compensation to the independent sub-contractor's employee, the general contractor is immune from tort liability to that employee. The majority reasons: "The quid pro quo for the statutory employer's potential liability is immunity from tort liability." In my view, it is not potential liability for workers' compensation which insulates a statutory employer from tort liability but actual liability. *Blair v. Smith*, 201 Ga. 747, 41 S.E.2d 133 (1947); *Haygood v. Home Transportation Co.*, 244 Ga. 165, 259 S.E.2d 429 (1979). Unless the general contractor is required to pay workers' compensation as a statutory employer there is no quid pro quo and he remains liable in tort for his wrong. Here the general contractor had no actual liability. The sub-contractor paid the workers' compensation. Thus the majority opinion has gratuitously relieved the general contractor of liability for his tort.

I would not overrule *Blair v. Smith, supra.* Its judgment is correct that a general contractor who has not been held liable for workers' compensation may be sued in tort. *Blair* has stood for thirty-three years unchanged by the legislature and stare decisis compels that we adhere to it.

Haygood v. Home Transportation Co., Inc., supra is not support for the majority opinion. In that case the general contractor scheduled Haygood as his employee with his compensation carrier which paid the benefits due.

NOTES

1. *Wright* illustrates the prevailing view that statutory employers enjoy the protection of the exclusive remedy doctrine even if the immediate employer pays workers' compensation benefits. E.g., Edwards v. Price, 191 Colo. 46, 550 P.2d 856 (1976); Fireman's Fund Ins. v. Sherman & Fletcher, 705 S.W.2d 459 (Ky.1986); Parker v. Williams and Madjanik, Inc., 275 S.C. 65, 267 S.E.2d 524 (1980); Crowe v. Brasfield & Gorrie Contractor, Inc., 688 So.2d 752 (Miss.1996). A few jurisdictions treat statutory employers as third parties subject to suit unless they actually provide the workers' compensation insurance. E.g., Boettner v. Twin City Constr. Co., 214 N.W.2d 635 (N.D.1974); Bence v. Pacific Power and Light Co., 631 P.2d 13 (Wyo.1981). Some statutes have been construed to allow injured workers to bring suit against their statutory employer even when the statutory employer has paid compensation benefits. E.g., Webb v. Montana Masonry Constr. Co., 233 Mont. 198, 761 P.2d 343 (1988). See 6 A. Larson and L. Larson, Larson's Workers' Compensation Laws § 111.04 (2013).

2. A similar problem is posed by the borrowed servant line of cases considered in Chapter 3. Workers' compensation is the exclusive remedy for the "borrowed servant" against his "special employer". E.g., Capps v. N.L. Baroid–NL Industries, Inc., 784 F.2d 615 (5th Cir.1986) (applying Longshore and Harbor Workers' Compensation Act); Santa Cruz Poultry v. Superior Court (Stier), 194 Cal.App.3d 575, 239 Cal.Rptr. 578 (1987); Six Flags Over Georgia v. Hill, 247 Ga. 375, 276 S.E.2d 572 (1981); Kidder v. Miller–Davis Co., 455 Mich. 25, 564 N.W.2d 872 (1997); Vigil v. Digital Equipment Corp., 122 N.M. 417, 925 P.2d 883 (App.1996); Schwager v. VHS Acquisition Corp., 213 Ariz. 414, 142 P.3d 1227 (App. 2006). Defendants sued in tort by injured workers usually raise the exclusive remedy defense by motion for summary judgment. If the defendant's status as special employer turns on disputed issues of material fact, the defense cannot be summarily established and the case is submitted to the jury. E.g., Whittington v. New Jersey Zinc Co., 775 F.2d 698 (6th Cir.1985); Barajas v. USA Petroleum Corp., 184 Cal.App.3d 974, 229 Cal.Rptr. 513 (1986); Food Giant, Inc. v. Davison, 184 Ga.App. 742, 362 S.E.2d 447 (1987). In a few jurisdictions, the special employer may be subject to suit as a third party if the general employer actually paid the

compensation benefits to the injured worker. E.g., Lang v. Edward J. Lamothe Co., Inc., 20 Mass.App.Ct. 231, 479 N.E.2d 208 (1985).

A growing number of states address this issue in specific statutes. Most of these statutes confer immunity on the special employer. E.g., Colo. Rev. Stat. § 8–41–303; Conn. Gen. Stat. Ann. § 31–292; Wis. Stat. Ann. § 102.29. See Brian C. Baugh, Comment, Workers' Compensation: Temporary Employees and the Exclusiveness-of-Remedy Provision, 86 Ky. L.J. 163 (1997–98).

3. Another frequently raised issue is whether workers' compensation insurers are protected by the exclusive remedy doctrine. This issue often arises in claims stemming from alleged bad faith or other mishandling of workers' compensation claims. Many courts have held that such suits are barred by the exclusive remedy doctrine. E.g., DeOliveira v. Liberty Mutual Ins. Co., 273 Conn. 487, 870 A.2d 1066 (2005) (collecting cases); Travelers Indemnity Co. v. Reker, 100 S.W.3d 756 (Ky.2003); Doss v. Food Lion, Inc., 267 Ga. 312, 477 S.E.2d 577 (1996); Liberty Mutual Ins. Co. v. Coleman, 313 Ark. 212, 852 S.W.2d 816 (1993). Other courts, however, allow such actions. E.g., Sizemore v. Continental Casualty Co., 142 P.3d 47 (Okla. 2006); Vaughan v. McMinn, 945 P.2d 404 (Colo.1997); Leathers v. Aetna Cas. & Sur. Co., 500 So.2d 451 (Miss.1986). Cf., Hawkes v. Commercial Union Ins. Co., 764 A.2d 258 (Me.2001) (exclusive remedy does not protect insurance company from tort suit for trespass, invasion of privacy, and intentional infliction of emotional distress stemming from investigation of claim). Two important factors in deciding whether insurance companies are protected by the exclusive remedy doctrine are whether the statutory definition of "employer" expressly includes its insurer and whether there are explicit remedies or penalties within the compensation statute for the alleged misconduct. In several states, judicial decisions allowing tort suits against insurers triggered legislation restricting or barring such claims. E.g., Madera v. State Industrial Ins. System, 114 Nev. 253, 956 P.2d 117 (1998); Brown v. Labor and Industry Review Comm'n., 267 Wis.2d 31, 671 N.W.2d 279 (2003). Following the judicial recognition of a tort claim against a compensation carrier for alleged improper denial of compensation benefits, the Indiana legislature enacted a law that vested exclusive jurisdiction in the Workers' Compensation Board to consider such claims. This legislation has withstood constitutional attack. Sims v. United States Fidelity & Guaranty Co., 782 N.E.2d 345 (Ind.2003). See generally, Robert. R. Potter and Joan T.A. Gabel, The Emerging Bad Faith Cause of Action Takes on the Exclusive Remedy Doctrine, 48 Mercer L. Rev. 63 (1996).

The Sixth Circuit Court of Appeals recently held that employees could not maintain a federal civil claim under the Racketeer Influenced and Corrupt Organizations Act (RICO) against their employer and a claims administrator allegedly engaged in a fraudulent scheme involving the mail to avoid paying workers' compensation benefits to injured employees. Jackson v. Sedgwick Claims Management Services, Inc., 731 F.3d 556, (6th Cir. 2013). The court noted that personal injuries and any pecuniary losses resulting from personal injuries are not recoverable under RICO. Rather, a RICO claim must be based on an injury to "business or property." The plaintiffs argued that the defendants' racketeering activities injured their "property" right to collect workers' compensation benefits. The Court rejected that argument, reasoned that the right to recover workers' compensation benefits under state law is not "property" under federal RICO law and that Congress, in enacting RICO, did not intend to "recalibrate state and federal power in an area [workers' compensation] that has traditionally been the province of the state government. . . ."

4. Insurance carriers have also been sued by injured workers for alleged negligence in conducting inspections. The common allegation is that the insurance company undertook to inspect the work premises and failed to discover, warn of, or remedy the dangerous condition that caused the worker's injury. Insurance companies maintain that they should be afforded the same immunity from suit as the employer. The great majority of courts that have addressed this issue have concluded under varying rationales that the compensation carrier is immune from tort liability to the injured worker. In some states, the insurance carrier enjoys an express statutory immunity from such claims. E.g., Mich.Comp.Laws Ann. § 418.827. Other states confer the protection of the exclusive remedy doctrine on "employers" who are statutorily defined to include the compensation carrier. E.g., Ga.Code Ann. § 34–9–1(3); Pa.Stat.Ann., tit. 77, § 501. A few courts discern from the overall structure of the workers' compensation act a legislative intent to immunize insurance carriers from such claims. E.g., Kifer v. Liberty Mutual Ins. Co., 777 F.2d 1325 (8th Cir.1985) (construing Arkansas law). Several jurisdictions, however, permit employees to sue workers' compensation insurers for negligent safety inspections. Silva v. Hodge, 583 So.2d 231 (Ala.1991); Thompson v. Bohlken, 312 N.W.2d 501 (Iowa 1981); Derosia v. Duro Metal Products Co., 147 Vt. 410, 519 A.2d 601 (1986). A few states distinguish between safety inspections conducted by workers' compensation carriers and those conducted by general liability insurers. Tort suits against the compensation insurer are barred, but general liability carriers are treated as third parties subject to suit. E.g., Latour v. Commercial Union Ins. Co., 528 F.Supp. 231 (D.R.I.1981) (applying Rhode Island law); Wilson v. Rebsamen Ins., Inc., 330 Ark. 687, 957 S.W.2d 678 (1997); Sims v. American Casualty Co., 131 Ga.App. 461, 206 S.E.2d 121 (1974), affirmed sub nom. Providence Washington Ins. Co. v. Sims, 232 Ga. 787, 209 S.E.2d 61 (1974). Cf., Coker v. Deep South Surplus of Georgia, Inc., 258 Ga.App. 755, 574 S.E.2d 815 (2002) (third party hired by the workers' compensation carrier to conduct a safety inspection is not protected by the exclusive remedy doctrine). Aside from legislative language, what policy considerations are relevant to deciding whether an insurance carrier should be subject to suit for an alleged negligent safety inspection?

5. Uninsured/Underinsured Motorist Insurance (UM) may provide compensation to a person injured in an automobile accident if the person at fault either is uninsured or does not have sufficient insurance to cover the

liability. As we have seen throughout the book, automobile accidents give rise to a large number of workers' compensation claims. The question often arises whether an employee injured in a work-related automobile accident can recover workers' compensation benefits and assert a claim under an UM policy. Is the uninsured motorist a third party not protected by the exclusive remedy doctrine? Should the answers to these questions depend on whether the injured employee or her employer purchased the UM policy? Or whether the uninsured motorist was the employer, a co-employee, or a genuine third party? See Otterberg v. Farm Bureau Mut. Ins. Co., 696 N.W.2d 24 (Iowa 2005) ("the great weight of authority holds" that an injured employee cannot recover UM benefits if the uninsured motorist is a co-employee protected by the exclusive remedy doctrine); Barfield v. Barfield, 742 P.2d 1107 (Okl. 1987) (permitting the spouse of a worker killed in an automobile accident in a car driven by a co-employee and who had recovered death benefits under workers' compensation, to recover UM benefits; recovery under a UM policy is a matter of *contract* law and hence is not precluded co-employee the *tort* immunity conferred by the exclusive remedy doctrine); Matter of Elrac, Inc. v. Exum, 18 N.Y.3d 325, 961 N.E.2d 643, 938 N.Y.S.2d 252 (2011) (employee injured in work-related automobile accident in a car owned by his employer can recover workers' compensation and UM benefits under employer's UM policy when the uninsured motorist was a third party). For a thorough discussion of the coordination of uninsured motorist insurance and workers' compensation, see 6 A. Larson & L. Larson, Larson's Workers' Compensation § 110.05 (2013).

6. Is the parent company of a wholly-owned subsidiary a "third party?" See, Boggs v. Blue Diamond Coal Co., 590 F.2d 655 (6th Cir.1979) (the survivors of miners killed in a mining disaster allowed to sue the parent company of their husbands' employer); Boswell v. May Centers, Inc., 669 S.W.2d 585 (Mo.App.1984) (employee of parent company allowed to sue wholly-owned subsidiary for its negligence in maintaining a parking lot). Howsden v. Roer's Real Estate Co., 282 Neb. 666, 805 N.W.2d 640 (2011) (premises liability claim brought by employee against a holding company of the employer is not barred by the exclusive remedy doctrine; holding company is a third party). But cf. Poch v. Bayshore Concrete Products, 747 S.E.2d 757 (S.C. 2013) (evidence supported the finding that the subsidiary was the alter ego of the parent company; both are protected by the exclusive remedy doctrine); Beck v. Flint Construction Co., 154 Ga.App. 490, 268 S.E.2d 739 (1980) (parent company that so dominated the affairs of its wholly-owned subsidiary so as to be considered its "alter-ego" would be entitled to the subsidiary's immunity from tort suit). Of course, even if the parent company is a legally distinct third party subject to suit, the claim will fail if the injured workers fails to establish wrong doing by the parent. See e.g., Minton v. Ralston Purina Co., 146 Wash.2d 385, 47 P.3d 556 (2002).

7. In the absence of a special provision in the compensation statute, co-workers are generally considered third parties subject to suit by an injured employee. E.g., Vittum v. New Hampshire Ins. Co., 117 N.H. 1, 369 A.2d 184

(1977). A great majority of states, however, have extended the exclusive remedy doctrine to also preclude tort actions against co-employees. E.g., Alaska Stat. § 23.30.055; Cal.Labor Code § 3601(a); Conn.Gen.Stat.Ann. § 31–293a. Does the injured worker receive any quid pro quo in exchange for losing his right to sue a co-employee? Can it be argued that tort immunity is an additional benefit conferred upon the worker? Is a quid pro quo necessary to uphold the constitutionality of co-employee immunity? Compare Estabrook v. American Hoist & Derrick, Inc., 127 N.H. 162, 498 A.2d 741 (1985) (striking down a statute creating co-employee immunity, in part, on the absence of an off-setting quid pro quo) with Young v. Prevue Products, Inc., 130 N.H. 84, 534 A.2d 714 (1987) (quid pro quo is not required to uphold the constitutionality of bar on suit for loss of consortium). In view of the fact that an employer is universally entitled to indemnity against a "third party" who wrongfully injured the worker, would tort liability of a co-employee result eventually in relieving the employer's enterprise of the compensation cost and shifting this onto the shoulders of one of the workers? See, Steffen, The Employer's Indemnity Action, 25 U.Chi.L.Rev. 465 (1958). As is the case with employers, the co-employee's immunity does not preclude tort suits based on intended injury. See Torres v. Parkhouse Tire Service, Inc., 26 Cal.4th 995, 30 P.3d 57, 111 Cal.Rptr.2d 564 (2001), or if the co-employee is not in the course of employment at the time of the accident. Smith v. Ellis, 291 Ga. 566, 731 S.E.2d 731 (2012).

Some states allow a worker to bring a medical malpractice claim against a company physician who might otherwise be considered a co-employee. E.g., Davis v. Stover, 258 Ga. 156, 366 S.E.2d 670 (1988). The underlying rationale is that the relationship between the company physician and the employee is professional in nature. "[I]t is the [company physician's] professional standing that creates a trusting relationship that cannot be breached with impunity." 258 Ga. at 157. Courts have been reluctant to apply this rationale beyond physicians. See e.g., McLeod v. Blase, 290 Ga.App. 337, 659 S.E.2d 727 (2008); Stringer v. Minnesota Vikings Football Club, LLC, 705 N.W.2d 746 (Minn. 2005) (both holding that certified athletic trainers were co-employees of professional athletes; tort claims barred by the exclusive remedy doctrine). While the company physician may be subject to suit, the employer remains protected by the exclusive remedy doctrine. E.g., Rheem Mfg. Co. v. Butts, 292 Ga.App. 523, 664 S.E.2d 878 (2008) (tort claim against employer for alleged negligence of company physician is barred by the exclusive remedy doctrine).

8. The "dual capacity doctrine" illustrates an attempt to characterize the employer as a third party. The leading early case applying this approach was Duprey v. Shane, 39 Cal.2d 781, 249 P.2d 8 (1952). The plaintiff in *Duprey* was a nurse who was injured on the job. Her chiropractor-employer further injured her in the course of treating her compensable injury. The court upheld the employee's right to sue her employer for malpractice since his negligence was performed in his "capacity" as a doctor, rather than in his capacity as her employer.

In the late 1970s and early 1980s, some courts expanded the concept of dual capacity. Employers who manufactured or modified equipment used on the job were held suable in tort in their capacity as product manufacturers. E.g., Bell v. Industrial Vangas, Inc., 30 Cal.3d 268, 179 Cal.Rptr. 30, 637 P.2d 266 (1981) (employer liable in capacity of manufacturer when employee was injured while delivering the gas that his employer had manufactured); Mercer v. Uniroyal, Inc., 49 Ohio App.2d 279, 361 N.E.2d 492 (1976) (truckdriver-employee could recover from his employer, Uniroyal, when injured in an on-the-job automobile accident caused by a defective Uniroyal tire). The dual capacity doctrine came under considerable attack. With only slight imagination, negligent employers could be cast in some other capacity, such as product manufacturer or premises owner. Critics maintained that the dual capacity doctrine threatened the basic structure of the quid pro quo compromise that underlies workers' compensation. See, 6A A. Larson and L. Larson, Larson's Workers' Compensation Law § 113.01[4] (2013). Jurisdictions that once warmly embraced the expansion of the dual capacity doctrine began to substantially limit its application. E.g., Bakonyi v. Ralston Purina Co., 17 Ohio St.3d 154, 478 N.E.2d 241 (1985) (employer who sold fertilizer to the public and used it in the workplace was not subject to liability for employee's injury under the dual capacity doctrine). California legislatively abolished this exception to the exclusive remedy doctrine. Cal.Labor Code § 3602(a).

Today, efforts to sue employers on the basis of their alleged dual capacities are overwhelming unsuccessful. Employers and co-employees are protected by the exclusive remedy doctrine even when the alleged negligence pertains to the provision of medical treatment, the very context that gave rise to the original doctrine. E.g., Suburban Hospital, Inc. v. Kirson, 362 Md. 140, 763 A.2d 185 (2000) (collecting cases); Hawksby v. DePietro, 165 N.J. 58, 754 A.2d 1168 (2000); Tatum v. Medical University of South Carolina, 346 S.C. 194, 552 S.E.2d 18 (2001); Payne v. Galen Hospital Corp., 28 S.W.3d 15 (Tex.2000). Suits against employers in their capacity of "product manufacturer" have likewise failed. E.g., Bowen v. Goodyear Tire & Rubber Co., 516 So.2d 570 (Ala.1987); Stewart v. CMI Corp., 740 P.2d 1340 (Utah 1987). See also, Van Bebber & Assoc., Inc. v. Cook, 870 So. 2d 150 (Fla. App. 2004). ("We decline to adopt the 'dual capacity' doctrine because it would circumvent the legislative plan and purpose [of the Florida workers' compensations statutes.]")

9. A similar concept, called dual persona, remains a viable doctrinal basis for avoiding the exclusive remedy doctrine in certain instances. In contrast to dual capacity, the concept of dual persona involves an employer who also has a distinctly different legal identity. This distinct legal identity may be considered a "third party" for purposes of the exclusive remedy doctrine. An example of the successful use of the dual persona idea lies in the corporate merger area. An employee injured by defective equipment manufactured by X Corporation has been allowed to sue the merged corporate employer in tort when the original employer's business merged

with X Corporation after the sale of the product. E.g., Percy v. Falcon Fabricators, 584 So.2d 17 (Fla.App.1991); Kimzey v. Interpace Corp., 10 Kan.App.2d 165, 694 P.2d 907 (1985); Billy v. Consolidated Machine Tool Corp., 51 N.Y.2d 152, 432 N.Y.S.2d 879, 412 N.E.2d 934 (1980); Schweiner v. Hartford Acc. & Indem. Co., 120 Wis.2d 344, 354 N.W.2d 767 (App.1984). Cf. Tatum v. Medical University of South Carolina, 346 S.C. 194, 552 S.E.2d 18 (2001) (rejecting the application of the dual persona principle on the facts; collecting recent cases). The defendant is subject to tort liability in such cases not because it is the plaintiff's employer, but because it is the successor in interest to the third party manufacturer. Through the law governing corporate mergers, the employer has taken on the additional legal identity as successor in interest to the merged manufacturer. Part of that identity includes acceptance of the former corporation's liabilities. Should it make any difference whether the former corporation manufactured the defective equipment only for use in its workplace? Compare Billy v. Consolidated Machine Tool Corp., 51 N.Y.2d 152, 432 N.Y.S.2d 879, 412 N.E.2d 934 (1980) (employer held liable) with Corr v. Willamette Indust., Inc., 105 Wash.2d 217, 713 P.2d 92 (1986) and Herbolsheimer v. SMS Holding Co., 239 Mich.App. 236, 608 N.W.2d 487 (2000) (no liability).

4. THE RIGHTS OF EMPLOYER AND EMPLOYEE IN THIRD-PARTY ACTIONS

CASTLEMAN v. ROSS ENGINEERING, INC.

Supreme Court of Tennessee, 1997.
958 S.W.2d 720.

REID, J.

* * *

I

On November 3, 1989, the plaintiff, Billy Castleman, an employee of a subcontractor, Jack Castleman d/b/a J.E.C. Electric Company, sustained a compensable injury under the workers' compensation law, for which the general contractor's workers' compensation insurance carrier, Hartford Accident and Indemnity Company, paid the plaintiff benefits in the approximate amount of $100,000.

A tort action for personal injuries was filed by the plaintiff against a third party, Ross Engineering, Inc., on April 3, 1990. Hartford filed an intervening petition, asserting a subrogation right and a lien pursuant to Tenn. Code Ann. § 50–6–112(c)(1) (1991) on any recovery by the plaintiff from Ross Engineering.

The case was tried on March 4, 1993, 10 months after the release of the decision in *McIntyre v. Balentine*, 833 S.W.2d 52 (Tenn.1992).[1] The case was submitted to the jury on instructions that fault could be apportioned among the plaintiff, Castleman, the defendant, Ross Engineering, and the employer, J.E.C. Electric. The jury found damages of $1,500,000, and attributed 68 percent of the fault to the defendant, 16 percent of the fault to the plaintiff, and 16 percent of the fault to the employer. The court entered judgment against Ross Engineering for $1,020,000, 68 percent of the $1,500,000. The plaintiff did not appeal from the judgment on the jury verdict.

On May 26, 1993, the plaintiff acknowledged full satisfaction of the judgment, and the plaintiff received from Ross Engineering full payment of the amount of the judgment less $100,000, which was retained by consent pending resolution of Hartford's subrogation claim. By order entered on July 7, 1995, Hartford was awarded the $100,000 claimed, less attorneys fees and expenses incurred in pursuing the third-party claim, a net amount of $68,489.

On appeal to the Court of Appeals, the plaintiff contested the subrogation award to Hartford, insisting that Hartford's right to subrogation was conditioned on the plaintiff's recovery of the damages for fault attributed to the employer as well as fault attributed to Ross Engineering. The Court of Appeals rejected the plaintiff's contention and affirmed the trial court's decision.

II

The plaintiff does not deny that Hartford has a subrogation claim against the third party judgment for the total amount of workers' compensation benefits paid to the plaintiff Section 50–6–112 (1991) provides that when the injury compensated under the Workers' Compensation Law was caused by the negligence of a third party, the injured employee may pursue an action against the third party. Subsection (c)(1) provides as follows:

> In [the] event of such recovery against such third person by the worker, or by those to whom such worker's right of action survives, by judgment, settlement or otherwise, and the employer's maximum liability for workers' compensation under this chapter has been fully or partially paid and discharged, the employer shall have a subrogation lien therefor against such recovery, and the employer may intervene in any action to protect and enforce such lien.

[1] In McIntyre v. Balentine, 833 S.W.2d 52 (Tenn.1992), the "all-or-nothing rule of contributory negligence" was replaced with principles of comparative fault so that "so long as a plaintiff's negligence remains less than the defendant's negligence the plaintiff may recover; in such a case, plaintiff's damages are to be reduced in proportion to the percentage of the total negligence attributable to the plaintiff." Id. at 57.

The plaintiff insists, however, that the enforcement of that right is conditioned upon the employee, as the subrogor, being "made whole." The plaintiff defines "made whole" as being able to recover for all damages found by the jury except damages representing fault attributed to him. In this case, recovery making the plaintiff whole would include the approximately [$240,000] for damages attributed to the fault of the employer, J.E.C. Electric.

* * *

In the case of *Ridings v. Ralph M. Parsons Co.*, the tort defendants sought to assert as an affirmative defense that the employer contributed to the employee's injuries. The defendants argued that under *McIntyre*, "fault can be attributed to the employer, and the liability of the defendants [could] be decreased accordingly, without the imposition of liability upon the employer." *Ridings v. Ralph M. Parsons Co.*, 914 S.W.2d at 81. Though *Ridings* was a transitional case, the Court found that "application of comparative fault principles to this case requires no transitional procedure [because] the acts and omissions of an employer covered by the worker's compensation law neither enlarge nor limit the rights or liabilities of any party to a tort action by an employee governed by the doctrine of comparative fault." Id. at 80–81. The Court concluded that "fault may be attributed only to those persons against whom the plaintiff has a cause of action in tort." Id. at 81.

* * *

Under *Ridings*, the trial court erred in instructing the jury that fault could be attributed to the employer, and the plaintiff would have been entitled to relief from that error on appeal. However, the plaintiff did not appeal, but instead accepted payment of the judgment awarded against Ross Engineering as satisfaction in full for his cause of action. Of course, this Court cannot provide relief for errors that are not preserved on appeal.

The decisions governing the application of comparative fault principles have sought to achieve fairness to the parties within the constraints of statutory law providing immunity in particular situations:

> Limiting the parties to whom fault may be attributed to those subject to liability, accomplishes the policy objectives of fairness and efficiency. Since liability is several and is in direct proportion to legal fault, each defendant will be liable only for the percentage of the damages caused by it. Since fault is limited to the plaintiff and those against whom the plaintiff has a cause of action, the plaintiff is not denied the right to recover those damages to which it is entitled. However, the plaintiff will bear

the loss for any liability that it fails or is unable to assert and any judgment that cannot be enforced.

Ridings v. Ralph M. Parsons Co., 914 S.W.2d at 83.

The plaintiff's rights as they existed prior to the release of the decision in *McIntyre* have not been adversely affected by the adoption of the principles of comparative fault; consequently, this is not a transitional case entitled to special consideration.

This conclusion also resolves the plaintiff's primary contention, that the insurer is not entitled to enforce its right of subrogation because the plaintiff has not been "made whole." The plaintiff acknowledges that Hartford has a subrogation claim for benefits paid under the workers' compensation law but, asserting principles of equitable subrogation, insists that the subrogation claim is not enforceable unless the employee has recovered the full amount of the damages not attributed to his own fault.

The statute creating the subrogation claim does not by its terms condition the claim upon the employee obtaining a full recovery of damages sustained. The subrogation lien attaches to "the net recovery collected" and secures the amount "paid" by the employer or the amount of the employer's "future liability, as it accrues."[6] It appears that, under the statute, the subrogation lien attaches to any recovery from the tort-feasor "by judgment, settlement or otherwise." Id. Consequently, even if under equitable principles of subrogation the employer was not entitled to assert the subrogation lien, the statute specifically creates that right.

The record does not support the premise on which the plaintiff bases his argument, that he has not been made whole. Further, the plaintiff has

---

[6] Tenn Code Ann. § 50–6–112(c) provides:

1. In [the] event of a recovery against the third person by the worker, or by those to whom the worker's right of action survives, by judgment, settlement or otherwise, and the employer's maximum liability for workers' compensation under this chapter has been fully or partially paid and discharged, the employer shall have a subrogation lien against the recovery, and the employer may intervene in any action to protect and enforce the lien.
2. In the event the net recovery by the worker, or by those to whom the worker's right of action survives, exceeds the amount paid by the employer, and the employer has not, at the time, paid and discharged the employer's full maximum liability for workers' compensation under this chapter, the employer shall be entitled to a credit on the employer's future liability, as it accrues, to the extent the net recovery collected exceeds the amount paid by the employer.
3. In the event the worker, or those to whom the worker's right of action survives, effects a recovery, and collection of that recovery, from the other person, by judgment, settlement or otherwise, without intervention by the employer, the employer shall nevertheless be entitled to a credit on the employer's future liability for workers' compensation, as it accrues under this chapter, to the extent of the net recovery.

asserted no basis on which the subrogation claim created by statute should be denied.

The judgment of the Court of Appeals is affirmed.

NOTES

1. All states recognize an employer's right to be reimbursed for compensation benefits from the proceeds from an employee's tort claim against a third party. There are several general legislative approaches to this area of the law. A few states unconditionally assign the employee's cause of action to the payor of compensation benefits. E.g., 85 Okla. St. § 348. This approach gives the employer or its workers' compensation insurance carrier control over the tort claim against the third party tortfeasor. Other states allow both the worker and the employer to pursue claims against the third party tortfeasor simultaneously, with provision for joinder of the two claims. E.g., Rana v. Ritacco, 236 Conn. 330, 672 A.2d 946 (1996); Hartford Casualty Ins. Co. v. Albertsons Grocery, 931 S.W.2d 729 (Tex.App.1996). The most common statutory scheme establishes a priority as to who may initiate the third party action. Priority is most often given to the employee as the party with the greater interest in the litigation. E.g., Ariz.Rev.Stat.Ann. § 23–1023; Haw.Rev.Stat. § 386–8; N.Y.Work.Comp.Law § 29. If the party having the first right to initiate the third party action fails to do so within a specified period of time, the other becomes authorized to do so. E.g., Fla.Stat.Ann. § 440.39. For a thorough discussion of the various forms of subrogation, see 6 A. Larson and L. Larson, Larson's Workers' Compensation Law § 116.01 (2013).

2. The amount of the employer's lien often is stated in terms of compensation benefits "paid or payable." Calculating the precise amount of the lien is complicated by two factors. The first is that the extent of the employer's liability for future compensation benefits often is unknown. Some states calculate the lien by computing the present value of the probable future compensation benefits. E.g., N.Y.Work.Comp.Laws § 29. Most states, however, merely treat the excess of a third party recovery over past compensation actually paid as a credit against future compensation liability. E.g., Moore v. General Foods, 459 A.2d 126 (Del.1983); Mastin v. Liberal Markets, 674 S.W.2d 7 (Ky.1984); Buco Bldg. Constructors, Inc. v. Myrick, 863 So.2d 1130 (Ala App. 2003). For a discussion of whether courts or the administrative agency should determine the effect of future compensation benefits on the employer's lien, see Johnson v. Southern Industrial Constructors, Inc., 347 N.C. 530, 495 S.E.2d 356 (1998) (agency is "better equipped . . . to make the determinations and dispensations" contemplated by the statute).

The second complicating factor is allocating the expenses of the third party claim between the employer and employee. In many cases, it is the worker who incurs most of the expenses in maintaining the third party action. The employer or its insurer merely enforces its lien against any resulting judgment or settlement. Since the employer benefits financially from the employee's efforts, as in *Castleman* most states require the employer to bear a portion of the expenses of litigation, including attorney's fees. One equitable approach to this problem is to base the employer's share of litigation expenses on the ratio of compensation benefits to the third party recovery. In Fitzgerald v. Challenge Cook Bros., 80 Mich.App. 524, 264 N.W.2d 348 (1978), for example, the employer's insurance carrier paid the worker \$8,533.95 in compensation benefits. The worker then secured a judgment against a third party for \$57,000. The expenses of securing that judgment, including attorney fees was \$21,383. The court apportioned the expenses of the third party action according to the following formula:

$$\frac{\text{Benefits paid}}{\text{Judgment}} = \frac{\$8{,}533.95}{\$57{,}000} = 14.84\%$$

Thus the employer's share of the litigation expenses was 14.84% of \$21,383. Any sums actually expended by the employer in the third party action would be included in determining both the total expenses and the employer's proportionate share of those expenses. See Hodder v. Goodyear Tire & Rubber Co., 426 N.W.2d 826 (Minn.1988); Kindt v. Otis Elevator Co., 32 Cal.App.4th 452, 38 Cal.Rptr.2d 121 (1995) (burden on lienholder to prove it had actively participated in the lawsuit).

3. The Tennessee Supreme Court in *Castleman* rejected the employee's argument that subrogation was conditioned on the employee being "made whole." Some statutes contain such a limitation. E.g., Ga. Code Ann. § 34–9–11.1(b) ("the employer's or insurer's [subrogation lien] . . . shall only be recoverable if the injured employee has been fully and completely compensated . . . for all economic and noneconomic losses incurred as a result of the injury"). Why would a legislature place such a limit on the right of subrogation? How much of a limitation does it create? In Bartow County Board of Education v. Ray, 229 Ga.App. 333, 494 S.E.2d 29 (1997) a bus driver (Ray) was injured in a work-related motor vehicle collision. She received almost \$40,000 in compensation benefits and sued the driver of the other vehicle in tort. The jury returned a general verdict for Ray for \$175,000. Her employer sought to enforce its right of subrogation. The court held that the general verdict made it impossible to determine "what portion of the award applied to economic loss and what portion applied to noneconomic losses." 494 S.E.2d at 31. The third party defendant claimed that some of the plaintiff's damages were attributable to injuries sustained in a previous accident. The court concluded that the subrogation lien was properly denied, reasoning that "[g]iven that circumstance, reference to the general verdict alone . . . cannot rule out the possibility that the jury reduced its award based on that defense." Id. What should an employer or its insurer do to better protect its right of subrogation? See Sun Trust Bank v. Travelers Property and Casualty Co., 321 Ga. App. 538, 740 S.E.2d 824 (2013) (Insurance company is entitled to a hearing to attempt to prove that the employee was "made whole" by a settlement with a third-party tortfeasor despite statement

in the settlement agreement that the employee was not fully and completely compensated; insurance company did not take part in the settlement negotiations).

4. Should the employers' lien attach to items of damages not covered by workers' compensation? Suppose the judgment or settlement of the third party action segregates items of recovery, such as pain and suffering. The prevailing view, based largely on the language of the subrogation statute, holds that the lien attaches to the entire judgment or settlement, regardless of how it is structured. E.g., United States v. Lorenzetti, 467 U.S. 167, 104 S.Ct. 2284, 81 L.Ed.2d 134 (1984) (lien under Federal Employees Compensation Act attaches to sums recovered in third party action limited to noneconomic damages); Barth v. Liberty Mut. Ins. Co., 212 Ark. 942, 208 S.W.2d 455 (1948) (third party suit limited to pain and suffering; subrogation lien attaches); Page v. Hibbard, 119 Ill.2d 41, 115 Ill.Dec. 544, 518 N.E.2d 69 (1987) (lien attaches to pain and suffering). Is the issue any different when the damages are earmarked for the employee's spouse's claim for lost consortium? See Page v. Hibbard, 119 Ill.2d 41, 115 Ill.Dec. 544, 518 N.E.2d 69 (1987) (lien does not attach to wife's recovery for loss of consortium); Rascop v. Nationwide Carriers, 281 N.W.2d 170 (Minn.1979) (subrogation does not extend to so much of a settlement as was earmarked for the wife's loss of consortium). How might this affect the structure of settlements? See Thompson v. Workers' Comp. Appeal Bd., 566 Pa. 420, 781 A.2d 1146 (2001) (Court should review settlement to see if it was structured in a way that was intended to unlawfully defeat the employer's subrogation rights); Hodges v. Indiana Mills & Mfg. Inc., 451 Fed. Appx. 452 (11th Cir. 2011) (affirming district court's allocation of $1.16 million out of a total settlement of $5.8 million to wife's lost consortium claim); Dearing v. Perry, 499 N.E.2d 268 (Ind.App.1986) (injured worker and spouse cannot negotiate settlement with third party that allocates substantial sums to loss of consortium without participation of insurer); Nichols v. Cantara & Sons, 659 A.2d 258 (Me.1995) (although lien does not attach to portion of settlement earmarked for spouses' loss of consortium, such division must be clear in the settlement agreement). Courts have also split on whether the lien should attach to an award of punitive damages. Compare Mississippi Power Co. v. Jones, 369 So.2d 1381 (Miss.1979) (employer's lien attaches to "net proceeds" of third party action, including punitive damages) with Hodder v. Goodyear Tire & Rubber Co., 426 N.W.2d 826 (Minn.1988) (employer's right of subrogation does not reach amounts awarded as punitive damages in third party action). See also Colorado Compensation Ins. Authority v. Jorgensen, 992 P.2d 1156 (Colo.2000) (insurer is not entitled to subrogation for any non-economic damages or loss of consortium).

5. Should a jury be permitted to apportion a percentage of fault against an employer in a tort suit brought by an employee against a third party? This question is of tremendous practical significance in those jurisdictions that have abrogated the rule of joint and several liability. For example, in Unzicker v. Kraft Food Ingredients Corp., 203 Ill.2d 64, 270

Ill.Dec. 724, 783 N.E.2d 1024 (2002) the plaintiff was seriously injured while working at Kraft's plant. The plaintiff sued Kraft under a premises liability theory. A jury found that the plaintiff's total damages were $879,400, of which $788,000 was for non-medical damages (e.g., lost earnings and pain and suffering) and $91,400 was for past and future medical expenses. The jury apportioned 1% of the fault to Kraft and 99% to the plaintiff's employer. Under Illinois law, a defendant who is less than 25% at fault is jointly and severally liable for only medical damages. The combination of the employer's immunity, the jury's allocation of fault, and the abrogation of joint and several liability resulted in Unzicker recovering only $7,880 of the $788,000 for his non-medical damages.

Castleman, in reaffirming Ridings v. Ralph M. Parsons, Co., 914 S.W.2d 79 (Tenn.1996), reflects the view of a substantial number of states that juries should not apportion fault to the immune employer. E.g., Durniak v. August Winter and Sons, Inc., 222 Conn. 775, 610 A.2d 1277 (1992); Varela v. American Petrofina Co., 658 S.W.2d 561 (Tex.1983); Seattle–First National Bank v. Shoreline Concrete Co., 91 Wash.2d 230, 588 P.2d 1308 (1978). Several states have allowed juries to calculate the percentage of fault of the employer. E.g., Unzicker v. Kraft Food Ingredients Corp., 203 Ill.2d 64, 270 Ill.Dec. 724, 783 N.E.2d 1024 (2002); Dietz v. General Electric Co., 169 Ariz. 505, 821 P.2d 166 (1991); Williams v. White Mountain Const. Co., 749 P.2d 423 (Colo.1988); Powers v. Kansas Power & Light Co., 234 Kan. 89, 671 P.2d 491 (1983). In these jurisdictions, should the employer's fault also effect its subrogation lien? See Brabander v. Western Cooperative Electric, 248 Kan. 914, 811 P.2d 1216 (1991) (subrogation claim reduced by employer's comparative percentage of responsibility multiplied by the amount of the subrogation claim).

6. Most tort suits are resolved by settlement. Ideally, settlement of employee tort suits against third parties would address subrogation issues thereby avoiding disputes. Such is not always the case, however. Sometimes the employee's tort suit is settled without the knowledge or approval of the employer. In such instances, the employee may jeopardize his right to future workers' compensation benefits. E.g., Pannell–Pringle v. District of Columbia Dept. of Employment Services, 806 A.2d 209 (D.C.App.2002) (unauthorized settlement does not automatically preclude compensation award, but may do so if the employer can demonstrate prejudice). See also, Bohn v. Industrial Comm'n, 196 Ariz. 424, 999 P.2d 180 (2000) (burden of proof rests with employee to show that unapproved settlement was reasonable). Even when the employer participates in the settlement in some fashion, problems may arise. For example, in Buco Bldg. Constructors, Inc. v. Myrick, 863 So.2d 1130 (Ala. App. 2003) the employee argued that the employer had agreed to accept half its expenditure for the employee's medical care in satisfaction of its subrogation claim. The court held that the employee did not prove that the employer agreed to accept this amount as full payment and the employer could apply the settlement recovery as a credit against future medical expenses. As discussed in Note 3, some states condition the subrogation lien

on the employee having been "made whole" or having received "full and complete" compensation for his injury. A settlement agreement may affect this issue as well. Compare Georgia Electric Membership Corp. v. Hi–Ranger, 275 Ga. 197, 563 S.E.2d 841 (2002) (settlement and release of manufacturer acts as a waiver of the employee's right to insist that the employer prove that he has been fully and completely compensated) with Travelers Ins. Co. v. O'Hara, 350 Ark. 6, 84 S.W.3d 419 (2002) (where settlement agreement did not make the employee whole, subrogation lien did not arise).

We will return to the question of how to allocate responsibility among employees, employers and third parties in the next section. But first, consider how another common tort reform measure, modification of the collateral source rule, might affect an employer's right of subrogation.

SCHONBERGER V. ROBERTS

Supreme Court of Iowa, 1990.
456 N.W.2d 201.

HARRIS, JUSTICE. . . .

On July 22, 1987, the plaintiff, Rodney Schonberger, was driving west on U.S. Highway 30 in Carroll, Iowa. He had picked up his employer's mail and was headed to work when an accident occurred. Schonberger was preparing to turn into his employer's parking lot when he was struck by the defendant, Carroll John Roberts, who was driving a truck owned by defendant Buck Hummer Trucking, Inc.

As a result of the accident Schonberger was unable to return to work for three and one-half weeks. He suffered injuries to his neck, back, and knee. His medical bills totaled $7,625.40 at the time of trial. These expenses, as well as future medical expenses, are being reimbursed as part of the workers' compensation benefits Schonberger is receiving. Schonberger's injuries were permanent, and he will continue to incur medical expenses as a result of the accident.

Schonberger then brought this tort suit for his injuries which resulted in a jury verdict in his favor. The jury assessed eighty percent of the negligence to Roberts and twenty percent to Schonberger. It determined past damages were $18,000 and that future damages were $115,000. The jury also found that Schonberger was not wearing a seat belt and determined the award should be reduced an additional two percent.

Although defendants assert the damage awards were excessive—a matter we later address—the preeminent issue in the case is defendants' challenge to a trial court ruling refusing to admit evidence. Defendants sought to introduce evidence regarding the payment of medical bills and other workers' compensation benefits to Schonberger. The trial court ruled the evidence inadmissible. This ruling is defendants' first assignment of error on appeal.

Since 1913 an Iowa statute, now Iowa Code section 85.22 (1989), has provided a right of indemnity to workers' compensation employers (or their insurers) for amounts paid under the Act from recoveries realized by the worker in tort actions for the same injuries. Without doubt Schonberger's workers' compensation insurer is entitled to be compensated from his recovery in this suit for any amounts paid to or for him on account of this injury. See, e.g., *Liberty Mut. Ins. Co. v. Winter*, 385 N.W.2d 529, 531–32 (Iowa 1986).

In 1987 the General Assembly amended the comparative fault Act, to include a special provision, Iowa Code at 668.14, also aimed at prohibiting an injured worker to recover twice for the same industrial injury. Both section 85.22 (in a limited situation) and section 668.14 (in a broader sense) are limitations on the collateral source rule, a principle long recognized as a part of our common law. Under the collateral source rule a tortfeasor's obligation to make restitution for an injury he or she caused is undiminished by any compensation received by the injured party from a collateral source. *Clark v. Berry Seed Co.*, 225 Iowa 262, 271, 280 N.W. 505, 510 (1938).

The trial court's rejection of the proffered evidence was in reaction to the obvious inconsistency between compelling the injured worker to pay back his benefits from his recovery and at the same time have the jury reduce his recovery because of them. To remedy this inconsistency the trial court rested its exclusion of evidence of workers' compensation benefits on Iowa Rule of Evidence 402 (all irrelevant evidence is inadmissible). Schonberger argues in support of the ruling in part by contending that the workers' compensation Act is, because of its design and regulated status, a state program. State programs are expressly exempted from the sweep of section 668.14.

> I. There are well-recognized limits to the extent to which courts will slavishly ascribe literal meanings to the words of a statute. Because legislative intent is the polestar of statutory interpretation it is clear that if the literal import of the text of an act is inconsistent with the legislative meaning or intent, or if such interpretation leads to absurd results, the words of the statute will be modified to agree with the intention of the legislature.

2A Sutherland, Statutory Construction at 46.07 (Sands 4th Ed. 1984) (citing *Graham v. Worthington*, 259 Iowa 845, 854, 146 N.W.2d 626, 633 (1966)).

In construing various statutes we have often applied this rule by refusing to attribute to the General Assembly an intention to produce an absurd result. *Harden v. State*, 434 N.W.2d 881, 884 (Iowa 1989).

A literal application of section 668.14 under the present circumstances would also lead to an absurd result. Under section 85.22 Schonberger must repay from his recovery his workers' compensation insurer any benefits he has received. The only conceivable purpose of informing the jury of those benefits is to invite the jury to reduce his recovery because of them. But, to any extent the jury does reduce the damage award because of the benefits, Schonberger is in effect paying, not once, but twice. We are convinced the legislature did not intend to call for this double reduction.

To avoid this unintended result we interpret the statute so as to deem its requirements satisfied when the requirements of section 85.22 are complied with. The case is remanded to district court for a proceeding in which it must be established that the proceeds of any recovery received by Schonberger are pledged to reimburse his workers' compensation insurer in accordance with Iowa Code section 85.22. Upon such a showing the judgment of the trial court shall stand as affirmed.

Affirmed and remanded.

All Justices concur except MCGIVERIN, C.J., and NEUMAN, and ANDREASEN, JJ., who dissent.

MCGIVERIN, C.J. (dissenting).

I respectfully dissent.

The majority opinion substantially sets aside the clear terms of Iowa Code section 668.14 and, as a practical matter, fully reinstates the judicially created collateral source rule by use of Iowa Rule of Evidence 402, at least in cases where collateral benefits are paid subject to a statutory right of subrogation.

Unlike the majority, I believe that the terms of section 668.14 can be respected without visiting inequity on Schonberger and others in his position.

Under the collateral source rule, damages awarded to a successful tort plaintiff against a tort defendant are not reduced by any sums which the plaintiff has received, or will receive, from another source (a "collateral source") on account of the plaintiff's injury. See *Groesbeck v.*

Napier, 275 N.W.2d 388, 391–92 (Iowa 1979); 22 Am.Jur.2d Damages at 566 (1988). Typically these sources are insurance benefits of one form or another, such as the workers' compensation benefits in this case. As a common law rule of evidence, the collateral source rule bars evidence of such "collateral benefits." See, e.g., *Stewart v. Madison*, 278 N.W.2d 284, 293–94 (Iowa 1979). As a common law rule of damages, the rule provides that a damages award against a tort defendant will not be reduced by reason of such collateral benefits. See, e.g., *Rigby v. Eastman*, 217 N.W.2d 604, 609 (Iowa 1974).

One effect of the common law collateral source rule is that in cases where the plaintiff receives collateral benefits which are not paid subject to a right of subrogation in the payor, and also is compensated for the same injuries from a tort suit against the defendant, the plaintiff receives duplicate damages to the extent that the collateral benefits and tort recovery overlap. 22 Am.Jur.2d Damages at 566 (1988). This is commonly known as "double dipping" and is thought by tort defendants to unfairly overcompensate the plaintiff. Carlson, Fairness in Litigation or "Equity for All," 36 Drake L.Rev. 713, 719 (1987). The counter-argument is that to allow collateral benefits to reduce the tort recovery would relieve the defendant of the consequences of tortious conduct. *Clark v. Berry Seed Co.*, 225 Iowa 262, 271, 280 N.W. 505, 510 (1938). As between the plaintiff and the tortfeasor, the common law deems it more just that the plaintiff profit from collateral benefits. See id.; 22 Am.Jur.2d Damages at 566 (1988).

On the other hand, in cases where collateral benefits are paid subject to a right of subrogation, the plaintiff is not double dipping because the subrogee will recover the collateral benefits out of the plaintiff's tort recovery from the defendant. Schonberger's case is a prime example of this situation because under Iowa Code section 85.22, the workers' compensation benefits he received will have to be repaid out of his tort recovery.

The majority of the study commission recommended that the legislature enact a statute which would allow the factfinder in a tort suit to hear evidence and argument on certain collateral benefits in cases where the plaintiff's losses were "replaced" or "indemnified" by a collateral source. Liability Report at 134. In those cases the factfinder would be allowed but not required to reduce the plaintiff's tort recovery by the amount of collateral benefits, presumably avoiding a double dipping situation whenever the factfinder took the collateral benefits into account. See id.; cf. Iowa Code at 147.136 ("damages awarded [in a medical malpractice action] shall not include actual economic losses . . . to the extent that those losses are replaced or are indemnified [by certain collateral sources].")

II. The legislature apparently approved of this recommendation and enacted a statute—Iowa Code section 668.14—very similar to that recommended by the majority of the study commission. Iowa Code section 668.14 provides:

> 1. In an action brought pursuant to this chapter seeking damages for personal injury, the court shall permit evidence and argument as to the previous payment or future right of payment of actual economic losses incurred or to be incurred as a result of the personal injury for necessary medical care, rehabilitation services, and custodial care except to the extent that the previous payment or future right of payment is pursuant to a state or federal program or from assets of the claimant or the members of the claimant's immediate family.
>
> 2. If the evidence and argument regarding previous payments or future rights of payment is permitted pursuant to subsection 1, the court shall also permit evidence and argument as to the costs to the claimant of procuring the previous payments or future rights of payment and as to any existing rights of indemnification or subrogation relating to the previous payments or future rights of payment.
>
> 3. If evidence or argument is permitted pursuant to subsection 1 or 2, the court shall, unless otherwise agreed to by all parties, instruct the jury to answer special interrogatories or, if there is no jury, shall make findings indicating the effect of such evidence or argument on the verdict.
>
> 4. This section does not apply to actions governed by section 147.136. (Emphasis added.) For purposes of this opinion I will assume that workers' compensation benefits are not paid "pursuant to state or federal program" within the meaning of Iowa Code subsection 668.14(1).

Under subsection (1) of this statute, evidence of certain collateral benefits paid the plaintiff is clearly admissible. The statute says "the court shall permit" such evidence. Subsection (2) allows the plaintiff to counter this evidence by introducing evidence of the cost of obtaining the collateral benefits and evidence of any rights of subrogation relating to the benefits. The language could not be more clear. The evidence excluded by the trial court here should have been admitted.

By enacting section 668.14, the legislature intended to change the evidentiary portion of the judicially created collateral source rule. The statute allows the factfinder to consider all the facts concerning payment of the plaintiff's losses. Under the common law collateral source rule, the factfinder is not given all those facts.

III. I do not believe, however, that the legislature intended that a plaintiff in Schonberger's position should have his tort recovery reduced by the amount of collateral benefits and also have to repay the collateral benefits out of his remaining tort recovery. In this respect, I agree with the majority. In my view, however, the obvious inequity produced by such an application of section 668.14 is to be avoided in a jury case by appropriate jury instructions and interrogatories.

Under section 668.14 evidence of collateral benefits should be admitted pursuant to subsections (1) and (2). Then, pursuant to subsection (3), the jury should be instructed that if it finds liability it must find whether any of the plaintiff's claimed damages were or will be paid by collateral sources and, if so, how much. The jury should also be instructed to find whether any of those collateral sources are subrogated to the plaintiff's recovery from the tort defendant. Next, the jury should be instructed that if it finds that such rights of subrogation do exist, the plaintiff's recovery from the defendant may not be reduced by the amount of those collateral benefits. Finally, the jury should be asked to state the amount of economic losses of the plaintiff that were or will be paid by collateral sources and which are also included in its jury award to the plaintiff.

The result of this approach would be to prevent double dipping—which only occurs in cases where the plaintiff receives collateral benefits which are not subject to subrogation—but avoid the inequity correctly perceived by the majority. At the same time, the evidence called for by the legislature in section 668.14 would be admitted. Where the collateral benefits are not paid subject to rights of subrogation, it is left to the jury to prevent or allow double dipping.

The majority indicates that an absurd result, not intended by the legislature, would be reached by a literal application of section 668.14. When evidence made admissible in subsections 668.14(1) and 668.14(2) is accompanied by appropriate instructions pursuant to subsection 668.14(3), an absurd result is avoided and the entire statute is given effect.

V. I would reverse the trial court judgment and remand for a new trial on the issue of damages. The parties should be allowed to introduce evidence before the jury pursuant to Iowa Code section 668.14. Then the jury should be instructed appropriately and allowed to state the effect of such evidence on its verdict.

The court should work within the intent and language of section 668.14 rather than against it. Section 668.14 was the result of a studied decision by the legislature to abrogate the collateral source rule as a common law rule of evidence, and to prevent double dipping. The majority effectively refuses to acknowledge that fact. Therefore, I dissent.

NEUMAN and ANDREASEN, JJ., join this dissent.

NOTES

1. Many states abolished or modified the collateral source rule as a component of an overall package of tort reform. See 4 Harper, James & Gray, The Law of Torts § 25.22 n. 7 (3d ed. 2007) for citations to and a discussion of this legislation. *Schonberger* illustrates the problem of reconciling a modification of the collateral source rule with the employer's right of subrogation. Both the right of subrogation and the abrogation of the collateral source rule have as a goal the prevention of a double recovery by the worker-plaintiff. There is widespread agreement, however, that both rules should not apply simultaneously. That is, the employee should not have a tort recovery reduced by the amount of workers' compensation received (modified collateral source rule) and then repay the employer for those benefits (subrogation) out of the reduced tort judgment. To prevent a double reduction of recovery, either the modified collateral source rule legislation or the employer's right of subrogation must yield to the other. Several jurisdictions do not apply the modified collateral source rule statute when the employer retains a right of subrogation. E.g., American Mut. Ins. Co. v. Decker, 518 So.2d 315 (Fla.App.1987); Western National Mutual Ins. Co. v. Casper, 549 N.W.2d 914 (Minn.1996); Nance v. Westside Hospital, 750 S.W.2d 740 (Tenn.1988).

2. Some tort reform statutes have been interpreted to disallow the employer's subrogation lien. In Toomey v. Surgical Services, P.C., 558 N.W.2d 166 (Iowa 1997) the employee's third party action was against a doctor for alleged malpractice committed in the course of treating a work related injury. Under an Iowa malpractice reform statute, damage awards in malpractice cases "shall not include" economic loss covered by workers' compensation. Under these circumstances, the court held that the employer's subrogation lien could not be enforced. Is *Toomey* consistent with *Schonberger*? See also Graham v. W.C.A.B., 210 Cal.App.3d 499, 258 Cal.Rptr. 376 (1989) (pursuant to a medical malpractice reform statute, an employer's subrogation lien is eliminated when evidence of compensation benefits is admitted in the malpractice action).

From a policy standpoint, is it better to reduce the tort award against the third party by amounts recovered in workers' compensation, or to not reduce the tort award and reimburse the employer or its insurer from the tort recovery?

3. Recall from the notes following *Smothers* that some states require an employee to elect between seeking compensation benefits and suing his employer in tort. Should an employee have to elect between seeking compensation benefits from his employer and bringing a tort claim against a third party? In a majority of states, an employee may seek remedies against

the employer under workers' compensation and against a third party in tort. Historically, a few states required that an employee elect between claiming workers' compensation benefits and pursuing a tort claim against a third party. Under a "strict election," a worker who guessed wrongly about which was the appropriate remedy could end up with neither. E.g., Ott v. St. Paul Union Stockyards, 178 Minn. 313, 227 N.W. 47 (1929) (unsuccessful workers' compensation claim precluded later third party action). The few states that require an election today have adopted doctrine that allows employees who are unsuccessful in pursuing one remedy to seek the other. For a general discussion of these issues, see A. Larson and L. Larson, Larson's Workers' Compensation Law § 115.01 (2013).

5. ADJUSTMENT OF RIGHTS OF THIRD PARTIES AND NEGLIGENT EMPLOYERS

LAMBERTSON V. CINCINNATI CORP.

Supreme Court of Minnesota, 1977.
312 Minn. 114, 257 N.W.2d 679.

SHERAN, CHIEF JUSTICE.

Cincinnati Corporation, defendant and third-party plaintiff in a personal injury/product liability action, appeals from a judgment of the district court which awarded a worker $34,000 in damages but denied defendant manufacturer contribution from an employer which was partly at fault for the accident. We reverse in part and remand with instructions.

Cincinnati is the manufacturer of a press brake, a large machine used for bending metal. The brake has a large vertical ram which moves up and down. Dies are placed on the ram and on the bed of the machine, and metal to be bent is placed between the ram and the bed. When the ram comes down onto the metal, a bend, or brake, is made in the metal at the point where the die on the ram matches the die in the bed. The movement of the ram is controlled by the operator by means of a single foot pedal at the base of the machine.

Cincinnati sold a press brake to Hutchinson Manufacturing and Sales, Inc., plaintiff's employer. On April 25, 1972, plaintiff was assisting a co-employee in the operation of the press brake. The co-employee was controlling the foot pedal, and plaintiff was placing long metal strips between the ram and the bed and removing them after they had been bent. As the ram was being raised after one cycle, a piece of metal which had been bent fell to the side of the bed opposite to the side where plaintiff was working. Plaintiff reached through the jaws of the machine to retrieve the piece of metal, but his co-employee had kept his foot on the pedal, thus permitting the ram to descend again, crushing plaintiff's arm between the ram and the bed.

After recovering workers' compensation from Hutchinson, plaintiff brought this action against Cincinnati. Plaintiff testified that he had never operated the press brake before and did not know it was capable of double cycling, i.e., continuing through another cycle without the ram's stopping at the top. He testified that he knew he should not have put his arm between the jaws, but that he did not know that his co-employee still had his foot on the pedal or that the ram would descend again before he could retrieve the piece of metal.

Plaintiff introduced expert testimony and safety rules and regulations from which the jury could have found that certain safety devices and features could have been installed on the press brake at the time of its manufacture and sale to Hutchinson in 1967, and that such devices would have prevented the accident. Sufficiency of this evidence to support a finding of negligence on the part of Cincinnati is not contested on this appeal. Cincinnati does, however, ask for indemnity from Hutchinson based on events occurring after 1967.

In 1969, after representatives of Cincinnati viewed the particular uses to which the press brake was put at Hutchinson, Cincinnati offered to Hutchinson (at Hutchinson's expense) two changes in the machine: (1) Operation by two or more palm buttons or foot switches; (2) automatic stoppage of the ram at the top of the cycle—i.e., no double cycling. These changes apparently were declined. In 1971, Cincinnati sent out a sales pamphlet to all owners of its press brakes describing a Waveguard safety device, an electronic sensing device designed to deter foreign matter in the press and stop the press if such matter were present. Hutchinson did not order or install such a device. There was testimony by plaintiff's expert from which one could conclude that the absence of two of these offered features—the automatic stop and the electronic sensor—constituted defects in the machine that were causally related to this accident.

When plaintiff's left forearm was crushed in the press brake, both bones were broken in such a way that the lower part of the arm was at a 90-degree angle to the upper part. It took 5 to 6 minutes to reverse the press and extricate his arm. He reported considerable pain. The fractures were surgically set and he was hospitalized initially for 10 days. During the succeeding 2 months his cast had to be removed and replaced 5 times so that the wound could be cleaned and X-rays taken. The fractures did not unite properly, and subsequent surgery was necessary. The bones were reset, using steel plates and screws. Plaintiff remained in a cast until February 1973, received medical for pain, and underwent physical therapy to regain the use of his arm. He was unable to work for a year after the accident and sustained an approximately $6,000 wage loss plus $2,600 in medical expenses.

The case was submitted to the jury on special verdict on a theory of negligence. The jury found all parties causally negligent and apportioned their comparative negligence as follows: Plaintiff—15 percent; Cincinnati—25 percent; Hutchinson—60 percent. The jury found damages of $40,000. The trial court ordered judgment against Cincinnati for $34,000, the full amount of the verdict less 15 percent for plaintiff's negligence, and denied Cincinnati's claim for contribution or indemnity from Hutchinson.

* * *

4. The final and most important issue in this case concerns the claim of Cincinnati, a third-party tortfeasor, for indemnity or contribution from Hutchinson, plaintiff's employer. This issue is a troublesome one and has generated a substantial amount of debate in the bench and bar of this and other states. Arthur Larson, a leading commentator on workmen's compensation law, has called the controversy surrounding indemnity and contribution against employers in third-party actions "[p]erhaps the most evenly-balanced controversy in all of compensation law." 2A Larson, Workmen's Compensation Law, § 76.10. The essence of the controversy is this: If contribution or indemnity is allowed, the employer may be forced to pay his employee—through the conduit of the third-party tortfeasor—an amount in excess of his statutory workers' compensation liability. This arguably thwarts the central concept behind workers' compensation, i.e., that the employer and employee receive the benefits of a guaranteed, fixed-schedule, nonfault recovery system, which then constitutes the exclusive liability of the employer to his employee. See, Minn.St. 176.031. If contribution or indemnity is not allowed, a third-party stranger to the workers' compensation system is made to bear the burden of a full common-law judgment despite possibly greater fault on the part of the employer. This obvious inequity is further exacerbated by the right of the employer to recover directly or indirectly from the third party the amount he had paid in compensation regardless of the employer's own negligence. Minn.St. 176.061, subds. 5, 6(d). See, *Nyquist v. Batcher*, 235 Minn. 491, 51 N.W.2d 566 (1952). Thus, the third party is forced to subsidize a workers' compensation system in a proportion greater than his own fault and at a financial level far in excess of the workers' compensation schedule.

The even balance in this controversy results from conflicts among the policies underlying workers' compensation, contribution/indemnity, and comparative negligence and the fault concept of tort recovery. . . .

[T]he interests of the respective parties in the workers' compensation system are therefore as follows: The employer has a primary interest in limiting his payment for employee injury to the workers' compensation schedule and a secondary interest in receiving reimbursement when a third party has caused him to incur obligations to his employee. See, *Nyquist v. Batcher, supra.* The employee has a primary interest in receiving full workers' compensation benefits and, to the extent a third party has caused him injury, a common-law recovery from that third party.

In contrast, the third party's interest is that of any other co-tortfeasor—to limit its liability to no more than its established fault. This interest is vindicated through contribution or indemnity. Contribution and indemnity are variant common-law remedies used to secure restitution and fair apportionment of loss among those whose activities combine to produce injury. As this court stated in *Hendrickson v. Minnesota Power & Light Co.*, 258 Minn. 368, 370, 104 N.W.2d 843, 846 (1960):

> "Contribution is the remedy securing the right of one who has discharged more than his fair share of a common liability or burden to recover from another who is also liable the proportionate share which the other should pay or bear. Contribution rests upon principles of equity. Indemnity is the remedy securing the right of a person to recover reimbursement from another for the discharge of a liability which, as between himself and the other, should have been discharged by the other. Indemnity is generally said to rest upon contract, either express or implied. However, there are numerous exceptions and situations in which a contract is implied by law, and contract, therefore, seems to furnish too narrow a basis. In the modern view, principles of equity furnish a more satisfactory basis for indemnity.
>
> "Contribution and indemnity are variant remedies used when required by judicial ideas of fairness to secure restitution. Although similar in nature and origin and having a common basis in equitable principles, they differ in the kind and measure of relief provided. Contribution requires the parties to share the liability or burden, whereas indemnity requires one party to reimburse the other entirely. Differing thus in their effect, these remedies are properly applicable in different situations. Contribution is appropriate where there is a common liability among the parties, whereas indemnity is appropriate where one party has a primary or greater liability or duty which justly requires him to bear the whole of the burden as between the parties."

When one tortfeasor has paid or is about to pay more than his equitable share of damages to an injured party, he has an interest in obtaining indemnity or contribution from his fellow tortfeasors.

Comparative negligence, which is embodied in Minn.St. 604.01 and was substantially borrowed from our sister state of Wisconsin in 1969, introduces yet another dimension to the third-party tortfeasor's predicament. By abolishing the defense of contributory negligence in cases where plaintiff's percentage of total causal negligence is less than defendant's, it permits an injured workman to recover against the third party more frequently. In addition, Minn.St. 604.01, subd. 1, specifies a rule for contribution:

> " . . . When there are two or more persons who are jointly liable, contributions to awards shall be in proportion to the percentage of negligence attributable to each, provided, however, that each shall remain jointly and severally liable for the whole award."

Thus, a jointly liable tortfeasor has an interest, at least where the other tortfeasors are solvent and otherwise available for contribution, in contributing no more to the plaintiff's recovery than the percentage of negligence attributable to him.

In *Hendrickson v. Minnesota Power & Light Co.*, 258 Minn. 368, 104 N.W.2d 843 (1960), this court denied recovery to a third-party tortfeasor seeking contribution or indemnity from a negligent employer. The court held: (1) There was no right of contribution because there was no common liability to the employee, i.e., the employer was not liable in tort to the employee because of the exclusive-remedy provision of our workers' compensation law; (2) there was no right of indemnity because the facts did not fall within one of the exceptional situations in which indemnity is allowed, unlike the facts in *Lunderberg*.

In the years following *Hendrickson*, this court also upheld an award of indemnity against an employer who had breached contractual duties to observe safety rules and an express contract of indemnity. In *Keefer v. Al Johnson Construction Co.*, 292 Minn. 91, 100, 193 N.W.2d 305, 310 (1971), we commented that the negligence of the third party was imputed or vicarious as compared with the active negligence of the employer. But we reaffirmed, in *Froysland v. Leef Bros., Inc.*, 293 Minn. 201, 197 N.W.2d 656 (1972), the rule of *Nyquist v. Batcher*, 235 Minn. 491, 51 N.W.2d 566 (1952), and held that the employer's contributory negligence was not available to the third party as a defense, since the rights of the employee in the third-party action were primary. *Froysland* did not involve any claim of indemnity.

Cincinnati initially seeks indemnity from Hutchinson chiefly on the ground that it offered safety devices to Hutchinson which, if installed on the press brake, could have prevented the accident. The difficulty with this argument lies in the jury's unchallenged finding that Cincinnati was 25-percent negligent in the first instance, when it placed its press brake in the stream of commerce without certain kinds of safety devices. Since the independent acts of negligent manufacture and sale by Cincinnati and refusal of safety devices by Hutchinson combined to produce plaintiff's injury, liability should be apportioned between them, not shifted entirely to one or the other. Therefore, if Cincinnati is entitled to any remedy, that remedy is contribution.

Cincinnati's claim for contribution, however, confronts two further problems: (1) Our holding in *Hendrickson v. Minnesota Power & Light Co.*, 258 Minn. 368, 104 N.W.2d 843 (1960), that contribution is not available because of the absence of a common liability; and (2) the policy interest of the employer in paying no more than his workers' compensation liability because of an employee injury and the other conflicting policies and statute discussed earlier in this opinion.

Considering the first of these problems, we cannot find any continuing persuasive force in the reasoning of the court in *Hendrickson*. . . . While there is no common liability to the employee in *tort*, both the employer and the third party are nonetheless liable to the employee for his injuries; the employer through the fixed no-fault workers' compensation system and the third party through the variable recovery available in a common law tort action. Contribution is a flexible, equitable remedy designed to accomplish a fair allocation of loss among parties. Such a remedy should be utilized to achieve fairness on particular facts, unfettered by outworn technical concepts like common liability.

The second problem confronting Cincinnati's claim is a more formidable one. The equitable merit in Cincinnati's claim is plain: It has been forced to bear the entire burden of plaintiff's recovery despite the fact that it was only 25-percent negligent and has a 60-percent employer joined in the action and available for contribution. In contrast, granting contribution would result in substantial employer participation in its employee's common-law recovery despite the exclusive-remedy clause. This problem is, in large part, a legislative one which demands a comprehensive solution in statutory form.

* * *

While the opinions of other jurisdictions must be read with caution on this issue because of different statutes and concepts of recovery in negligence cases, we have found direction in the approach taken by the Pennsylvania Supreme Court. That court has allowed contribution from the employer up to the amount of the workers' compensation benefits. *Maio v. Fahs*, 339 Pa. 180, 14 A.2d 105 (1940); *Brown v. Dickey*, 397 Pa. 454, 155 A.2d 836 (1959). See, also, *Stark v. Posh Construction Co.*, 192 Pa.Super. 409, 162 A.2d 9 (1960). This approach allows the third party to obtain limited contribution, but substantially preserves the employer's interest in not paying more than workers' compensation liability. While this approach may not allow full contribution recovery to the third party in all cases, it is the solution we consider most consistent with fairness and the various statutory schemes before us. If further reform is to be accomplished, it must be effected by legislative changes in workers' compensation third-party law.

For the reasons expressed above, the judgment is reversed and the case is remanded with instructions to grant contribution against Hutchinson in an amount proportional to its percentage of negligence, but not to exceed its total workers' compensation liability to plaintiff.

Affirmed in part, reversed in part and remanded with instructions.

NOTES

1. *Lambertson* addresses the allocation of financial responsibility for workplace injuries between the tort and workers' compensation systems. This issue is germane to all types of third party tort actions, but is most acute in the products liability field. Consider the following commentary:

> [S]ystemic differences [between workers' compensation and tort create] an incentive structure that explains why workplace product liability claims tend to be "high stakes" litigation. As explained by Professor Viscusi:
>
>> From the worker's standpoint there is little incentive to pursue a third-party suit unless these stakes are substantial. Collateral source rules prevent the courts from lowering a tort award because the injured worker has received workers' compensation benefits. The worker, however, cannot obtain a double recovery since in such contexts the employer or the insurer who paid the claim is generally subrogated to the worker's tort claim, up to the amount of workers' compensation benefit. . . . Thus, the injured party's financial incentive to file a product liability claim will be diminished by the extent of the workers' compensation benefits that have been already received. As a result, the cases for which litigation is worthwhile will tend to be only those with larger losses. [W. Kip Viscusi, *The Interaction Between Product Liability and Workers'*

Compensation as Ex Post Remedies for Workplace Injuries, 5 J.L. Econ. & Org. 185, 187 (1989).]

This profile is supported by the limited available data. A frequently cited study from the 1970s estimates that while approximately 11% of all product liability suits are filed by injured workers, these cases account for more than 40% of total product liability payments. A 1980s study found that workplace product liability claims account for 60% of all payments exceeding $100,000. Workplace product liability claims are four times as likely to involve fatalities and twice as likely to go to trial than are other types of product liability claims.

Product-related injuries also appear to be "high stakes" from a workers' compensation perspective. This conclusion may be drawn inferentially from the limited available data regarding costs of claims. Employers in all states may obtain reimbursement of workers' compensation benefits paid to injured employees from tort damages the employee recovers from third parties, such as product manufacturers. This reimbursement procedure is generally referred to as a right of subrogation. Product-related injures for which subrogation is sought constitute a small percentage of all workers' compensation claims, but are the second largest category of claim in which subrogation rights are asserted. The average total cost for claims with subrogation is more than twice that of claims without subrogation.

Thomas A. Eaton, Revisiting the Intersection of Workers' Compensation and Product Liability: An Assessment of a Proposed Federal Solution to an Old Problem, 64 Tenn. L. Rev., 881, 884–86 (1997) (footnotes omitted).

With this background in mind, consider what adjustments should be made to achieve a "proper" allocation of injury costs between the workers' compensation and tort systems.

For other discussions of this topic see, William A. Dreier, Injuries to Production Workers: Reform of the Workers' Compensation Product Liability Interface, 48 Rutgers L. Rev. 813 (1996); Weiler, Workers' Compensation and Product Liability: The Interaction of a Tort and a Non-Tort Regime, 50 Ohio State L.J. 825 (1989); Weisgall, Product Liability in the Workplace: The Effect of Workers' Compensation on the Rights and Liabilities of Third Parties, 1977 Wis.L.Rev. 1035.

2. Contrary to the result reached in *Lambertson*, most courts hold that a third party tortfeasor is not entitled to contribution from a negligent employer. E.g., Satilla Community Service Bd. v. Satilla Health Services, Inc., 275 Ga. 805, 573 S.E.2d 31 (2002); Thompson v. Stearns Chemical Corp., 345 N.W.2d 131 (Iowa 1984); Diamond Int'l. Corp. v. Sullivan and Merritt, Inc., 493 A.2d 1043 (Me.1985); Downie v. Kent Products, Inc., 420 Mich. 197, 362 N.W.2d 605 (1984), clarified 421 Mich. 1202, 367 N.W.2d 831 (1985);

Glass v. Stahl Specialty Co., 97 Wash.2d 880, 652 P.2d 948 (1982). See Nicholas B. Clifford, Jr., Kotecki v. Cyclops Welding Corp.: The Efficacy of a Limited Contribution Rule and Its Effect on Good Faith Settlement, 68 U.Chi.—Kent L. Rev. 479, 492 n. 84 (1992) (citing cases from 45 jurisdictions); Edward J. Kionka, Recent Developments in the Law of Joint and Several Liability and the Impact of Plaintiff's Employer's Fault, 54 La. L. Rev. 1619, 1630–35 (1994) (state by state summary). The primary justification for this result is that the exclusive remedy doctrine immunizes employers from tort liability to their employees. Since the employer is not a tortfeasor vis a vis the injured worker, it shares no common liability with the third party upon which to base a claim for contribution. This traditional "no contribution" rule combined with the employers' right of subrogation effectively allocates all the costs of workplace injuries to the third party tortfeasor, even when the employer is more culpable. E.g., Stephenson v. R.A. Jones & Co., Inc., 103 N.J. 194, 510 A.2d 1161 (1986) (manufacturer who was held to be 5% negligent could not recover contribution from employer who was 95% at fault).

Is a third party entitled to contribution when the employer intended to injure the employee? Compare Harsh International v. Monfort Industries, 266 Neb. 82, 662 N.W.2d 574 (2003) (employer is not subject to contribution claim even if the employer is alleged to be an intentional tortfeasor) with Conley v. Brown, 82 Ohio St.3d 470, 696 N.E.2d 1035 (1998) (a claim against an employer for an intentional workplace injury "may be maintained by the employee or his or her legal representative, an assignee of the right of action against the employer, or any other person or entity with a statutory or common-law right against the employer, including a third party tortfeasor with a statutory or common-law claim for contribution or for indemnification, or the subrogee of the third party tortfeasor's rights or claims.").

3. New York and Illinois formerly permitted tortfeasors to bring a third party claim against the negligent employer for contribution based on the proportionate fault of the parties. See, Skinner v. Reed–Prentice Division Package Machinery Co., 70 Ill.2d 1, 15 Ill.Dec. 829, 374 N.E.2d 437 (1977); Dole v. Dow Chemical Co., 30 N.Y.2d 143, 282 N.E.2d 288, 331 N.Y.S.2d 382 (1972). Unlimited contribution exposes an employer to damages that greatly exceed its liability under workers' compensation. Does the Dole–Skinner approach give appropriate weight to the employer's interest in limited liability reflected in the exclusive remedy doctrine?

Illinois subsequently adopted a rule akin to *Lambertson* under which the right of contribution against the employer is limited to the amount of compensation paid. Kotecki v. Cyclops Welding Corp., 146 Ill.2d 155, 166 Ill.Dec. 1, 585 N.E.2d 1023 (1991). In 1995, the Illinois legislature adopted a system of direct reduction discussed in note 5 below. Under these rules, the plaintiff's tort recovery is reduced by the amount of compensation benefits and the employer's subrogation lien is reduced by the same amount. 740 Ill. Comp. Stat. Ann. § 100/3.5, 820 Ill. Comp. Stat. Ann. § 305/5. Unzicker v. Kraft Food Ingredients Corp., 203 Ill.2d 64, 270 Ill.Dec. 724, 783 N.E.2d 1024

(2002) offers an interesting application of the Illinois law. The injured worker recovered compensation benefits from his employer and sued a third party (Kraft) in tort. A jury allocated 1% of fault to Kraft and 99% to the employer. Under Illinois law, Kraft and the employer were jointly and severally liable for the medical damages and Kraft could obtain contribution up to the amount of workers' compensation paid. The court held that the employer was liable to Kraft for $90,486 in contribution, which represented 99% of the medical damages. For a history of the Illinois law see Michael A. Bilandic, Workers' Compensation, Strict Liability, and Contribution in Illinois: A Century of Legal Progress?, 83 Ill. B.J. 292 (1995).

In 1996, New York amended its statute to limit the *Dole* rule to cases involving "grave injuries" defined in terms of death, loss of certain extremities, and other specific conditions. N.Y. Work. Comp. Law § 11. For background on the New York legislation, see Martha T. McCluskey, The Illusion of Efficiency in Workers' Compensation "Reform," 50 Rutgers L. Rev. 657, 902–908 (1998).

4. Sometime the contribution issue may involve a co-employee. In Isabella v. Hallock, 733 F. 3d 384 (2d Cir. 2013), an employee (Isabella) was injured in a work-related automobile accident. He was a passenger in a car driven by his co-worker (Oldenborg) and was owned by the driver's husband (Koubek). Isabella brought a tort suit against the driver of the other vehicle (Hallock). Hallock could not seek contribution from Oldenborg because, as a co-employee, Oldenborg was immune from tort liability under the exclusive remedy doctrine. Instead, Hallock sought contribution from Koubek, invoking a New York statute that renders the owner of a car liable for injuries caused by the negligence of a person driving the vehicle with the owner's consent. The parties stipulated that Isabella's damages to be $800,000 and that Hallock would be responsible for the entire amount if not permitted to assert a contribution or indemnity claim against Koubek. The district court denied Koubek's motion for summary judgment ruling, in effect, that Hollock could secure contribution from Koubek. The case was submitted to a jury which apportioned 90% of the fault to Oldenborg/Koubek and 10% to Hallock. Isabella appealed arguing that the lower court erred in allowing the jury to apportion fault to the owner of the car when the driver was a co-employee. The Second Circuit Court of Appeals found that lower state court opinions addressing this issue were not in harmony and certified the following question to the New York Court of Appeals, the highest court of the state:

> "Whether a defendant may pursue a third-party contribution claim under . . . [the New York statute imposing vicarious liability upon the owner of a car] where the vehicle's driver's negligence was a substantial factor in causing the plaintiff's injuries, but the driver is protected from suit by the exclusive remedy provisions of New York's workers' compensation laws. . . ."

Should the third-party be permitted to secure contribution from a party who is not protected by the exclusive remedy doctrine, but whose liability is derivative of a party who is so protected?

5. Note that the combination of contribution and subrogation leads to money changing hands several times, and thus high transaction costs. Some jurisdictions address this inefficiency by directly reducing the tort recovery against the third party by the amount of compensation benefits paid by the negligent employer. E.g., Witt v. Jackson, 57 Cal.2d 57, 17 Cal.Rptr. 369, 366 P.2d 641 (1961); Barnett v. Eagle Helicopters, Inc., 123 Idaho 361, 848 P.2d 419 (1993); Runcorn v. Shearer Lumber Products, 107 Idaho 389, 690 P.2d 324 (1984); Hunsucker v. High Point Bending & Chair Co., 237 N.C. 559, 75 S.E.2d 768 (1953). Note that this approach still requires an adjudication of employer negligence. Some commentators have proposed a system that would reduce the plaintiff's tort recovery against the third party by the amount of the workers' compensation award in all cases, while at the same time eliminating the employer's right of subrogation. See 2 American Law Institute, Reporters' Study on Enterprise Liability 197–98 (1991); Thomas A. Eaton, Revisiting the Intersection of Workers' Compensation and Product Liability: An Assessment of a Proposed Federal Solution to an Old Problem, 64 Tenn. L. Rev. 881, 908–911 (1997); Model Uniform Product Liability Act § 114, 44 Fed.Reg. 62,714 (1979). The direct reduction of the third party tort recovery would leave the worker fully compensated and reduce the transaction costs associated with contribution and subrogation. Is it fair to deny the non-negligent employer a right of subrogation? Is this fairness objection blunted by the no-fault nature of the employer's basic obligation under workers' compensation? What effect would such a system have on safety incentives for employers and third parties?

6. The manufacturer in *Lambertson* also sought indemnity from the employer. Indemnity, in contrast with contribution, shifts the entire loss to one party. A successful claim for indemnity by a third party would render the employer ultimately liable for both compensation benefits and tort damages. Also, in contrast with contribution, a claim for indemnity is not based on the concept of a common liability. An indemnity claim against an employer is grounded on the employer's breach of some duty owed directly to the third party, rather than the employer's breach of duty owed to the injured worker. The exclusive remedy doctrine is less of a conceptual obstacle to indemnity since the third party's claim against the employer rests upon an independent duty. The employer's separate obligation to indemnify the third party may be express or implied. Virtually all courts allow third parties to enforce unambiguous express contractual rights of indemnity against employers. E.g., Goodyear Tire & Rubber Co. v. J.M. Tull Metals Co., 629 So.2d 633 (Ala.1993); General Tel. Co. of the Southeast v. Trimm, 252 Ga. 95, 311 S.E.2d 460 (1984); Union Pacific R.R. v. Kaiser Agricultural Chem. Co., 229 Neb. 160, 425 N.W.2d 872 (1988); Barsness v. General Diesel & Equip. Co., 422 N.W.2d 819 (N.D.1988); Redford v. City of Seattle, 94 Wash.2d 198, 615 P.2d 1285 (1980).

Claims for implied indemnity are generally less successful, however. Several opinions emphasize that one who is at fault is not entitled to indemnity for its own acts. E.g., Woodruff Constr. Co. v. Barrick Roofers, 406 N.W.2d 783 (Iowa 1987); Ramos v. Browning Ferris Indust., 103 N.J. 177, 510 A.2d 1152 (1986); Mulder v. Acme–Cleveland Corp., 95 Wis.2d 173, 290 N.W.2d 276 (1980). In other cases the relationship between the employer and the third party has not been deemed sufficiently "special" to give rise to an implied obligation of indemnity. In particular, courts have ruled that the purchaser-employer does not owe the manufacturer a duty of care in use of its products. E.g., Harsh International v. Monfort Industries, 266 Neb. 82, 662 N.W.2d 574 (2003) (relationship of vendor and vendee would not support a claim for implied indemnification); Decker v. Black & Decker Mfg. Co., 389 Mass. 35, 449 N.E.2d 641 (1983) (refusing to imply a duty of care that "flows upstream from the purchaser [of a product] to the manufacturer"); Steinmetz v. Bradbury Co., Inc., 618 F.2d 21 (8th Cir.1980) (no implied obligation under Iowa law for purchaser-employer to indemnify the manufacturer for the purchaser's failure to instruct his employee in the safe operation of the machine). Cf. Satilla Community Service Bd. v. Satilla Health Services, 275 Ga. 805, 573 S.E.2d 31 (2002) (contract called for third party to indemnify employer; this does not create an "identical reciprocal implied contractual indemnification [right of indemnity]" from employer to third party). For a critique of this general approach, see Comment, Indemnity Under Workers' Compensation: Recognizing a Special Legal Relationship Between Manufacturer and Employer, 1987 Duke L.J. 1095. If the third party and the employer are found to stand in a special legal relationship, however, the third party may be entitled to implied indemnity from the employer. E.g., Tucson Elec. v. Swengel–Robbins Constr., 153 Ariz. 486, 737 P.2d 1385 (App.1987) (special relationship created by statute); Lunderberg v. Bierman, 241 Minn. 349, 63 N.W.2d 355 (1954) (owner of car who was liable for employee's injury under financial responsibility statute was entitled to implied indemnity from negligent employer; bailor-bailee relationship).

7. Over the years there have been several efforts to enact federal product liability legislation. One of these bills would bring about significant change in existing state practices. As discussed in note 2 above, in the vast majority of states workplace product manufacturers cannot recover contribution from negligent employers, but employers have a subrogation lien against employee's product liability recovery against the manufacturer. The combination of these rules channels money from the tort system into the workers' compensation system. The proposed federal law would reverse this flow of money. It would reduce the product manufacturer's tort liability by the amount of compensation benefits paid to the worker in cases where there is clear and convincing evidence that the injury was caused by the fault of either the employer or a co-employee. It would also reduce the employer's subrogation lien by the same amount. Common Sense Product Liability Reform Act of 1996, H.R. 956, 104th Cong. § 111 (1996). The combination of these rules would result in compensation benefits reducing tort liability. Is a federal solution to the question of how to adjust the interests of product

manufacturers, employers and employees appropriate? Is this proposed federal solution an improvement over the existing state practices? Why would the proposed federal solution differ from the one adopted by the vast majority of states? For commentary on this proposed legislation see Thomas A. Eaton, Revisiting the Intersection of Workers' Compensation and Product Liability: An Assessment of a Proposed Federal Solution to an Old Problem, 64 Tenn. L. Rev. 881 (1997).

8. Commentators have proposed a variety of solutions to the problems created by the intersection of the tort and workers' compensation systems. On the one extreme are proposals to eliminate third party actions entirely. Workers' compensation would become the employee's sole remedy. See, Don Dewees et al., Exploring the Domain of Accident Law 432 (1996); Oliver, Once is Enough: A Proposed Bar of the Injured Employee's Cause of Action Against a Third Party, 58 Ford.L.Rev. 117 (1990); O'Connell, Supplementing Workers' Compensation Benefits in Return for an Assignment of Third-Party Tort Claims—Without an Enabling Statute, 56 Tex.L.Rev. 537 (1978); Berstein, Third Party Claims in Workers' Compensation: A Proposal To Do More With Less, 1977 Wash.U.L.Q. 543. On the other extreme are proposals to substantially eliminate the exclusive remedy doctrine thus subjecting the employer to tort claims by employees and third parties. Haas, On Reintegrating Workers' Compensation and Employers' Liability, 21 Ga.L.Rev. 843 (1987); Lynch, The Clash Between Products Liability and the Workers' Compensation Exclusivity Rule: The Negligent Employer and the Third-Party Manufacturer, 50 Ins.Couns.J. 35 (1983). Other commentators appear to accept the exclusive remedy doctrine and third party suit as givens and explore ways to reduce the friction at the intersection of the two systems. See, Larson, Third Party Action over Against Workers' Compensation Employer, 1982 Duke L.J. 483; Epstein, Coordination of Workers' Compensation Benefits With Tort Damages, 13 Forum 464 (1977); Davis, Third-Party Tortfeasors' Rights Where Compensation-Covered Employers Are Negligent—Where Do Dole and Suspan Lead?, 4 Hofstra L.Rev. 571 (1976). Having considered the interests of the various parties, what is your ideal allocation of workplace injury costs?

CHAPTER 12

CONFLICT OF LAWS

■ ■ ■

1. INTRODUCTION TO THIS CHAPTER

Prior to the advent of workers' compensation laws, personal injury claims by employees against employers typically "sounded" in tort, and courts using traditional choice of law conventions applied the law of the place of injury (*lex loci delicti*). Soon after the states began enacting workers' compensation laws, cases arose that presented questions as to whether the law of one state or that of another was to be applied. Such a case might involve an injury that occurred outside the state of the forum, the issue being whether to apply the statute of the forum or that of the state where the injury took place. It might involve an injury that occurred within the forum state, but for some reason the claim was made that the law of a state other than the forum should be applied.

The emergence of such questions was inevitable in view of the freedom with which American industry crosses state lines. Not infrequently, an employee is hired in one state to perform work in one or more other states where he may suffer injury. There may be additional "foreign elements" in the case; e.g., the residence of the employee may be in a third state, the principal place of business of the employer in a fourth, or the parties may have agreed in the original contract of employment that the law of a specified state should govern.

Through the use of textual material, this chapter will survey many of the conflict of laws problems which arise in the workers' compensation context. But before proceeding to the text, let's first take a look at a case which reveals some of the complexities that may be encountered. While the *Williams* case addresses the issue of "subject matter jurisdiction," determination on that point typically coincides with the conflict of laws question, namely, "which state's workers' compensation statute applies?" *See* 9–140 Larson's Workers' Compensation Law, Matthew Bender, Section 140.02 (2013).

WILLIAMS V. PORT AUTHORITY OF NEW YORK AND NEW JERSEY

Supreme Court of New Jersey, 2003.
175 N.J. 82, 813 A.2d 531.

COLEMAN, J.

In this workers' compensation case, the petitioner has filed a claim alleging that he has sustained an occupational pulmonary disease that is causally related to his twenty-eight years of employment with the Port Authority of New York and New Jersey (Port Authority). The sole issue before us is whether the New Jersey Division of Workers' Compensation (Division) should have exercised subject-matter jurisdiction based on four months of exposure in New Jersey that predated twenty-one years of subsequent exposure in New York. The Division and a majority in the Appellate Division held that the four-month exposure was sufficiently substantial to constitute injury, thereby conferring jurisdiction. We disagree and reverse.

I.

Petitioner was employed by the Port Authority from 1969 until the time of his age retirement in 1997. The employment contract was made in New York where petitioner resided throughout his employment. Prior to February 1973, petitioner worked as an elevator operator in New York. Thereafter, he was assigned to perform maintenance work. He worked from February 4, 1973, until June 11, 1973, a period of approximately four months, on the New Jersey side of the George Washington Bridge cleaning tollbooths and tiled walls of the tunnels associated with the bridge. He used strong chemicals as cleaning and degreasing agents. In addition, he was exposed to exhaust fumes from vehicles crossing the bridge. At no time during that four-month interval did petitioner complain of symptoms or a disability related to his work. At the end of the four months, petitioner was assigned to perform work at LaGuardia Airport, using the same chemicals and degreasing agents, where he remained for approximately eight years. He was then assigned to perform the same work at Kennedy. Although the Port Authority raised the defense of lack of subject-matter jurisdiction in its answer, the Judge of Compensation reserved decision on the jurisdictional issue until the conclusion of the trial. At the conclusion of the trial, the judge found that the Division should exercise jurisdiction and awarded petitioner a partial permanent disability of twenty percent for chronic bronchitis. The Port Authority appealed, contending that the Division should not have exercised extraterritorial jurisdiction. A divided panel in the Appellate Division in a published opinion, *Williams v. Port Authority,* 345 *N.J.Super.* 549, 552–53, 786 *A.*2d 114 (2001), relied on this Court's opinion in *Boyle v. G. & K. Trucking Co.,* 37 *N.J.* 104, 112, 179 *A.*2d 514

(1962), and affirmed. The majority concluded that petitioner sustained an injury in New Jersey during the four months of exposure in this State. The court reasoned that because petitioner had a gradually progressive occupational disease from the cumulative exposure, our decisional law regarding apportionment of occupational disease disability among successive employers, *Bond v. Rose Ribbon & Carbon Mfg. Co.*, 42 *N.J.* 308, 311, 200 *A.*2d 322 (1964), and case law related to the computation of the statute of limitations in occupational disease cases, *Earl v. Johnson & Johnson*, 158 *N.J.* 155, 161, 728 *A.*2d 820 (1999), should be followed in determining whether petitioner's four-month employment exposure in New Jersey was sufficient to permit the Division to exercise jurisdiction. The majority concluded that petitioner's exposure in New Jersey "was not a casual, brief or insubstantial period of exposure." Finally, the majority concluded that because it cannot be determined at what point during the twenty-one year exposure the pulmonary-disease process commenced, it should be deemed to have commenced simultaneously with the beginning of the exposure on February 4, 1973 in New Jersey. The dissenting member of the panel [Judge Wefing] concluded that the majority's reliance on *Bond*, *Earl*, and *Peck v. Newark Morning Ledger Co.*, 344 *N.J.Super.* 169, 781 *A.*2d 58 (App.Div.2001), was misplaced. That member asserted that the issue before the court was one of jurisdiction and not one involving the statute of limitations, liability for exposure, or waiver of workers' compensation benefits. Judge Wefing concluded that petitioner's four months of work in New Jersey, which predated the termination of his last exposure by more than twenty-one years, were insufficient to warrant New Jersey exercising jurisdiction. This appeal is before us based on that dissent.

II.

Petitioner invoked the jurisdiction of the Division based on the assertion that he was injured in this State. He took that position because the four-month work exposure is his only nexus to New Jersey. The Port Authority contends that New Jersey has no legitimate interest in accepting jurisdiction based on petitioner's assertion that an injury occurred here given that all but four months of petitioner's twenty-eight-year career with the Port Authority was spent in New York. The Port Authority argues that the work in New Jersey was for such a short time and so long ago that petitioner is unable to demonstrate that he was injured here.

A.

Initially, we must determine what should be the appropriate standard for resolving whether an occupational exposure in this State sufficiently caused an injury in this State to permit the invocation of the Division's jurisdiction. We begin our analysis with *Boyle v. G. & K.*

Trucking Co., supra, 37 *N.J.* at 112, 179 *A.*2d 514, where the Court held that the Division has jurisdiction to entertain a claim filed by a resident employed by an out-of-state business when "he was accidentally injured here while performing his duties here on a work assignment from his employer." *Boyle* involved traumatic injuries caused by an automobile accident and did not purport to establish a standard with respect to occupational disease claims. It did, however, cite with approval Professor Arthur Larson's list of practical factors that should be considered when determining whether a state should exercise its jurisdiction to hear a "claim by a workman hired elsewhere but injured within its borders." *Id.* at 109, 179 A.2d 514. Those factors are:

> 1. Place where the injury occurred;
> 2. Place of making the contract;
> 3. Place where the employment relation exists or is carried out;
> 4. Place where the industry is localized;
> 5. Place where the employee resides; or
> 6. Place whose statute the parties expressly adopted by contract.
>
> [9 *Larson's Workers' Compensation Law* § 142.01 at 142–2 (2000).]

Professor Larson also provides guidance with respect to which state's law should control if jurisdiction is exercised. He states:

> "When one of these [factors] falls within the local state, and some or all of the others occur in another state, the question arises whether the local state can apply its statute without being accused of denying full faith and credit to the statute of the other. As matters now stand, it is clear that the state which was the *locus* of any one of the first three items—contract, injury or employment—and probably also of the next two—employee residence and business localization—can constitutionally apply its statute if it wants to." [*Ibid.*]

Although the New Jersey Workers' Compensation Act (Act), *N.J.S.A.* 34:15–1 to –128, does not address the issue of extraterritoriality, *Connolly v. Port Authority,* 317 *N.J.Super.* 315, 318, 722 *A.*2d 110 (App.Div.1998), all of the cases cited in *Boyle* involve accidents occurring in New Jersey as opposed to periods of occupational exposure within New Jersey. The fact that the employer is a bi-state agency has not heretofore been recognized as a basis to assume jurisdiction. *Connolly, supra,* 317 *N.J.Super.* at 320–21, 722 *A.*2d 110. Indeed, the majority in this case recognized as much. *Williams, supra,* 345 *N.J.Super.* at 553, 786 *A.*2d 114. The traumatic accidents involved in *Boyle* and cases cited therein that caused injury in New Jersey, thereby satisfying Professor Larson's place of injury extraterritoriality requirement, involved claims that allegedly satisfied the Act's requirements for a compensable accident, *N.J.S.A.* 34:15–7. There is a substantial difference between an accidental injury and an occupational injury. A compensable accident, although not defined in the Act, has been defined judicially as an "'unlooked for mishap or an untoward event which is not expected or designed.'" *Ciuba v. Irvington Varnish & Insulator Co.,* 27 *N.J.* 127, 134, 141 *A.*2d 761 (1958); *Joy v. Florence Pipe Foundry Co.,* 64 *N.J.Super.* 13, 20, 165 *A.*2d 191 (App.Div.1960) (quoting *Bryant v. Fissell,* 84 *N.J.L.* 72, 76, 86 *A.* 458 (N.J.Sup.Ct.1913)), *certif. denied,* 34 *N.J.* 67, 167 *A.*2d 55 (1961). Thus, the concept of injury is simple when the injury has been caused by a traumatic accident, such as occurred in *Boyle,* because the injuries are evident almost immediately. For extraterritorial-jurisdictional purposes, a single traumatic event forms the sole basis for compensation sought for the injuries caused by the event. Therefore, the single accidental injury involved in the *Boyle*-type case provides a substantial nexus to New Jersey.

In contrast, an occupational injury based on an occupational exposure at work over a period of time is much more complex. Yet, when a petitioner seeks to invoke the subject-matter jurisdiction of the Division based on the assertion of an occupational injury, meaning an occupational case in which the injury was caused or occurred in New Jersey, a standard must be established that is comparable to the *Boyle* standard used in accident cases. Such a standard is required because the Act directs that claims for accidental injuries and death, and claims for occupational injuries and death, generally should be treated the same. *N.J.S.A.* 34:15–35. However, unlike most accidental-traumatic injuries, many occupational diseases generally remain unknown or undisclosed throughout a long history of continued work exposure. But that fact alone is an insufficient basis to hold that *any* exposure in New Jersey, even for a few days or weeks that may minimally contribute to the development of an occupational disease, should permit the Division to exercise jurisdiction.

Because there are critical differences between accidental and occupational injuries, the appropriate starting point in the formulation of a standard for deciding when to exercise extraterritorial jurisdiction in occupational injury cases is the occupational disease section of the Act itself, *N.J.S.A.* 34:15–31(a). That subsection defines "compensable occupational disease[s]" as those diseases established by a preponderance of the credible evidence to have arisen "out of and in the course of employment, which are due in a *material degree* to causes and conditions which are or were characteristic of or peculiar to a particular trade, occupation, process or place of employment." *Ibid.* (emphasis added). "Material degree" means "'degree substantially greater than *de minimis*.'" *Fiore v. Consol. Freightways,* 140 *N.J.* 452, 467, 659 *A.*2d 436

(1995) (quoting *Dwyer v. Ford Motor Co.,* 36 *N.J.* 487, 493–94, 178 *A.*2d 161 (1962)); *see also N.J.S.A.* 34:15–7.2 (defining material degree as "an appreciable degree or a degree substantially greater than de minimis").

Being guided by the principle that New Jersey generally will take jurisdiction and apply its Act when the State has a substantial interest, such as when an injury has occurred in this State, we adopt the following benchmark for determining when there is jurisdiction in New Jersey in an occupational disease case. The three-part test that we adopt reflects in part the standard this Court adopted for determining when to apportion liability among successive insurers in such cases. We hold that, in this case, exposure for the relatively short period at issue cannot satisfy the injury requirement. The exposure was not to highly toxic materials known to cause disease even with minimal contact, i.e., asbestos and polychlorinated biphenyls (PCBs). In other words, in order to invoke the jurisdiction of the Division in extraterritorial occupational disease cases based on the occurrence of injury in New Jersey, the petitioner must demonstrate either that (1) there was a period of work exposure in this State that was not insubstantial under the totality of circumstances and given the nature of the injury; (2) the period of exposure was not substantial but the materials were highly toxic; or (3) the disease for which compensation is sought was obvious or disclosed "by medical examination, work incapacity, or manifest loss of physical function," while working in New Jersey. *Bond, supra,* 42 *N.J.* at 311, 200 *A.*2d 322; *see Akef v. BASF Corp.,* 140 *N.J.* 408, 415, 658 *A.*2d 1252 (1995); *Giagnacovo v. Beggs Bros.,* 64 *N.J.* 32, 37–38, 311 *A.*2d 745 (1973). That test is consistent with the Act's requirement that a partial-permanent disability, whether caused by an accident or an occupational disease, must be "based upon demonstrable objective medical evidence, which restricts the function of the body or of its members or organs," *N.J.S.A.* 34:15–36, or that the exposure was substantial enough to infer that injury occurred even in the absence of any manifestation of the disease.

We recognize the need for a more flexible standard for those occupational exposures that cause more seriously disabling diseases. When the occupational exposure in this State has been to highly toxic materials, chemicals or substances such as asbestos or PCBs, for jurisdictional purposes, injury will be presumed to have occurred beginning with the early exposure and continued throughout the exposure even though manifestation of a disease may not occur until the exposure had ended. When exposures are highly toxic, it is presumed that injury occurred even during the latency period. *See Owens-Illinois, Inc. v. United Ins. Co.,* 138 *N.J.*437, 451–54, 650 *A.*2d 974 (1994). In those cases, it is not merely the exposure that permits the Division to exercise jurisdiction, but a combination of exposure and the early infliction of permanent injury. In that class of cases, this Court has recognized that

> "[t]he medical evidence is uncontroverted that 'bodily injury' in the form of tissue damage takes place at or shortly after the initial inhalation of asbestos fibers. . . .
>
> "[T]he courts which have endorsed the 'exposure' theory in the asbestosis cases have not said that mere exposure to a substance is bodily injury.
>
> "Rather, those courts have concluded from medical testimony that the inhalation of asbestos causes immediate tissue damage, although the effects of that damage do not immediately manifest themselves. . . ."
>
> [Hartford Acc. & Indem. Co. v. Aetna Life & Cas. Ins. Co., 98 N.J. 18, 28, 483 A.2d 402 (1984) (quoting unpublished opinion of Skillman, J.S.C.) (quoting Insurance Co. of N. America v. Forty-Eight Insulations, 633 F.2d 1212, 1222 (6th Cir.1980), certif. denied, 454 U.S. 1109, 102 S.Ct. 686, 70 L.Ed.2d 650 (1981)).]

The three-part jurisdictional standard we have articulated is more analogous to the processing of occupational claims against the first employer in a chain of employers involving the same or similar work exposure over many years than to statute of limitations issues posed under *N.J.S.A.* 34:15–34. Here, petitioner can file a claim in New York where approximately 98.4% of his exposure occurred. Cases addressing statute of limitations issues under *N.J.S.A.* 34:15–34 have reasoned that unless the claim can proceed in New Jersey, the petitioner would forever be foreclosed from having his or her claim heard. That rationale simply does not apply in extraterritorial-jurisdictional cases. We nevertheless adjure the Division in the first instance to apply the standard we adopt flexibly on a case-by-case basis bearing in mind the multiple combinations of exposure.

B.

Applying the standard we adopt to the facts of this case leads us to conclude that the Division mistakenly exercised jurisdiction. The period of exposure in New Jersey was *de minimis* by any standard. Petitioner worked here for four months which was 1.6% of his total exposure. Based on that brief period of exposure in New Jersey, it cannot be said that such an exposure contributed, to a *material* degree, to the development of chronic bronchitis that was not diagnosed until twenty years after his New Jersey exposure had ended. In addition to that lack of medical examination, there was no manifest loss of physical function until many years after the work in New Jersey had ended. Just as there would be no apportionment of disability if petitioner had been performing the same work for a different employer during the same four months, the Division should not have exercised jurisdiction simply because petitioner worked for the same employer the entire time.

Finally, even assuming that each of the four months of exposure in New Jersey cumulatively contributed to the twenty-percent pulmonary disability attributable to petitioner's total exposure of 252 months, proration based on the total exposure would mean that the four-month exposure caused less than a third of one percent of his disability. Clearly, that is the kind of nuisance or minor injury or disability the 1979 amendments to the Act were designed to preclude. *Perez v. Pantasote, Inc.,* 95 *N.J.* 105, 111–15, 469 *A.*2d 22 (1984) (quoting Senate Labor, Indus. and Professions Comm., Joint Statement to Substitute for S.802 & A.840 at 1 Nov. 13, 1979). Further, petitioner was not exposed to the type of highly toxic materials to which we have adverted in developing the standard to be applied in these cases. Thus, any injury suffered by petitioner while working in New Jersey, "was so minor that [it] was not compensable." *Perez, supra,* 95 *N.J.* at 115, 469 *A.*2d 22.

III.

The judgment of the Appellate Division is reversed. The matter is remanded to the Division to dismiss the claim petition. The Port Authority has agreed to waive any statute of limitations defense to petitioner filing a claim in New York within a reasonable time.

LONG, J., dissenting.

I would affirm substantially for the reasons expressed by the Appellate Division in the thorough and thoughtful opinion penned by Judge Pressler. *Williams v. Port Authority,* 345 *N.J.Super.* 549, 786 *A.*2d 114 (2001). In my view, that decision stands on well-settled legal principles governing jurisdiction.

I.

It is not at all unusual for more than one state to have an interest in a single compensation claim or for there to be a marked difference in the benefits available under the statutes of different states. *Wilson v. Faull,* 27 *N.J.* 105, 116–17, 141 *A.*2d 768 (1958) (recognizing that variety of circumstances could operate to provide more than one state with interest in redress of work-connected injury and application by either forum of its compensation law); *see also* Lex K. Larson & Arthur Larson, *Workers' Compensation Law: Cases, Materials, and Text* § 32.03 (3d ed. 2000). So long as a state has more than a "casual" connection to the employment, it may apply its compensation law to the worker's claim. *Wenzel v. Zantop Air Transp., Inc.,* 94 *N.J.Super.* 326, 330–31, 228 *A.*2d 104 (Union County Ct.) (observing that, given liberal interpretation to coverage under workers' compensation statute and expanded jurisdictional concepts of due process, when more than casual employment services were performed in New Jersey, it is appropriate forum for compensation action). When an employee has a choice of forum, he or she is entitled to invoke the jurisdiction of the state providing "the highest available amount of compensation, . . . consonant with the high-minded remedial purposes underlying compensation enactments." *Boyle v. G. & K. Trucking Co.,* 37 *N.J.* 104, 112, 179 *A.*2d 514 (1962). The state chosen need only be *one* appropriate forum, not the "only" one or even the "best" one. The sole inquiry is whether the state has more than a casual connection to the employment. Among the considerations we traditionally have recognized as relevant in determining whether a state's interest is more than casual are those identified by Professor Larson as nearly universally accepted by our sister jurisdictions: the place of injury; the place of contract execution; the place where the employment relation is carried out; the place where the industry is localized; the place of the employee's residence; and the law of the place on which the parties agreed. 9 *Larson's Workers' Compensation Law* § 142.01 at 142–2 (2000), *cited with approval in Boyle, supra,* 37 *N.J.* at 109, 179 *A.*2d 514. Of those indicators, Larson has said, "As matters now stand, it is clear that the state which was the *locus* of any one of the first three items—contract, injury or employment—and probably also of the next two—employee residence and business localization—can constitutionally apply its statute if it wants to."

Our case law essentially tracks the Larson principles:

> Traditionally, an injury in New Jersey will trigger jurisdiction in the New Jersey compensation court. *Boyle* [*supra,* 37 *N.J.* at 108, 179 *A.*2d 514]. So too where New Jersey is the place of the employment contract or hiring. *Gotkin v. Weinberg,* 2 *N.J.* 305, 307, 66 *A.*2d 438 (1949); *Rivera v. Green Giant Co.,* 93 *N.J.Super.* 6, 11, 224 *A.*2d 505 (App.Div.1966). The employee's New Jersey residency appears, as well, to be sufficient, *Bunk v. Port Authority of New York and New Jersey,* 144 *N.J.* 176, 180–81, 676 *A.*2d 118 (1996), at least where there are also some employment contacts in New Jersey, *Parks v. Johnson Motor Lines,* 156 *N.J.Super.* 177, 180–81, 383 *A.*2d 734 (App.Div.1978); *Beeny v. Teleconsult, Inc.,* [160 *N.J.Super.*22, 27–28, 388 *A.*2d 1269 (App.Div.1978)]. [*Connolly v. Port Auth.,* 317 *N.J.Super.*315, 320, 722 *A.*2d 110 (App.Div.1998).]

Connolly went on to address Professor Larson's "industry localization" factor and held that, although that factor "is not sufficient *ipso facto* to establish jurisdiction," it "can be *one* of several considerations. . . ." *Id.* at 321. Indeed, localization was specifically considered in *Phillips v. Oneida Motor Freight, Inc.,* 163 *N.J.Super.* 297, 303, 394 *A.*2d 891 (App.Div.1978), where Judge Conford, writing for the court, held that jurisdiction can be exercised even when the injury, the execution of the contract, and the residence of the employee are elsewhere if the "composite employment incidents present a[n] . . . identification of the employment relationship with this State." In *Phillips,* the employer's localization in New Jersey was one of the composite employment incidents justifying the exercise of jurisdiction. That is the backdrop for our inquiry.

II.

In light of those standards, it is clear that the Workers' Compensation judge and the Appellate Division correctly assessed New Jersey's interest in Williams's employment as more than casual. The Appellate Division began its analysis by noting that the Port Authority is a bi-state agency of New York and New Jersey. As such, it is at least in part "localized" here. *Lieberman v. Port Auth.,* 132 *N.J.* 76, 84, 622 *A.*2d 1295 (1993).

On the issue of place of injury, the Appellate Division stated:

> "Because it cannot be determined when during the period of exposure as a continuum, including the exposure on the bridge and at the New York airports, the pulmonary disease process commenced, we see no reason not to apply the rule we applied in *Peck [v. Newark Morning Ledger, Co.,]* 344 *N.J.Super.* 169, 781 *A.*2d 58 [(App.Div.2001)] . . . namely that for all practical purposes, the commencement of a continuous period of exposure and the commencement of the disease process are simultaneous. [*Williams, supra,* 345 *N.J.Super.*at 557, 786 *A.*2d 114.]"

That principle is well established. *See Owens–Illinois, Inc. v. United Ins. Co.,* 138 *N.J.* 437, 451, 650 *A.*2d 974 (1994) (commenting that in environmental contamination insurance coverage cases, injury is considered as simultaneous with exposure); *Bond v. Rose Ribbon & Carbon Mfg. Co.,* 42 *N.J.* 308, 311, 200 *A.*2d 322 (1964) (holding liable employer or compensation insurance carrier during whose employment or coverage progressive occupational disease was disclosed when triggering or inception date of disease is unknown and undisclosed). The experienced Workers' Compensation judge and all the judges of the Appellate Division (including the dissenter) accepted the notion that, for practical reasons, the onset of progressive occupational disease and exposure must be considered "equatable." *Williams, supra,* 345 *N.J.Super.* at 557, 786 *A.*2d 114. Once that is accepted, it follows, as a matter of law, that at least some of Williams's injury occurred in New Jersey.

The Appellate Division elaborated on the point, noting that, as a matter of fact, the period of exposure was not "casual, brief or insubstantial":

> We are persuaded that petitioner's four-month exposure on a daily basis was sufficiently substantial to constitute an injury. During that time period, as he described his job, he was, on a daily basis and for eight hours each day, cleaning toll booths inside and out, "sweeping, degreasing with chemicals which cut the grease from the cement and also cleaning windows on the booths where people breeze through." He used the degreasing chemicals both in cleaning toll booths and in "washing down the tiles in the tunnel where the bridge meets coming out." With respect to the tunnel tiles, he explained that "they have what they call a flush truck and you would get on the truck and you would wash the walls down with cleaning chemical and like a mop." He further explained that "Yeah, [I was] exposed to like smoke and stuff from the cars because you're inside this tunnel and they don't close the whole tunnel. They don't close down like one lane and you're dealing with the smoke and smog coming from the traffic and fumes from the traffic going back and forth out. And also there's accumulation from the smell. From the cleaning agent is a smoke, I mean a chemical that you will smell too. It is not, you know, very healthy."

Certainly Port Authority recognized that the hazard was sufficient to require respirator masks although, according to petitioner, they were not provided on a daily basis. In our view this was not a casual, brief or insubstantial period of exposure. [*Id.* at 556–57, 786 *A.*2d 114.] Moreover, the employment relationship between Port Authority and Williams was carried out, in part, in New Jersey. As the Workers' Compensation judge emphasized:

> "Whether subject matter or in personam, the Port Authority lost its jurisdiction argument when it assigned Mr. Williams to work in New Jersey. It is quite clear that had Mr. Williams sustained an accident while working in New Jersey, he could file a claim in New Jersey without objection by the respondent. He should also be able to file in New Jersey when his occupational exposure was, at least in part, incurred in New Jersey. This is especially so when it was the respondent alone who controlled and determined whether the petitioner would work in New Jersey. The respondent Port Authority put Mr. Williams in New Jersey as well as New York; by assigning the petitioner to work in New Jersey—four months of degreasing tunnels and toll lanes—the respondent itself created this significant purposeful contact with New Jersey. The Port Authority could have prevented this contact with New Jersey and could have ensured that any workers' compensation claim by Mr. Williams would be cognizable only in New York had it assigned Mr. Williams to jobs

only in New York. It did not do so, and it is unseemly for the respondent Port Authority, who created the situation, to contend now that it is being unfairly or improperly brought into New Jersey to defend Mr. Williams's case."

In sum, the Port Authority, a bi-state agency with a major presence in New Jersey, purposefully assigned Williams to work here and in so doing exposed him to noxious substances. It was here that, as a matter of law, some of Williams's injury is deemed to have occurred. Plainly, the composite employment incidents reveal that New Jersey's interest is more than fleeting and casual.

Had New York been chosen as a forum by Williams, that state also would have been empowered to exercise jurisdiction over the claim based on service in that venue along with "localization" of the Port Authority and place of injury. In other words, Williams was presented with a choice between two jurisdictions, each of which had more than a casual interest in his claim. In exercising that choice, he was entitled to invoke the jurisdiction of the state whose laws would provide the highest available amount of compensation from his employer. In this case, that was New Jersey.

III.

The majority has set forth the requirement that: "[I]n order to invoke the jurisdiction of the [Workers' Compensation] Division in extraterritorial occupational disease cases based on the occurrence of injury in New Jersey, the petitioner must demonstrate either that (1) there was a period of work exposure in this State that was not insubstantial under the totality of circumstances and given the nature of the injury; (2) the period of exposure was not substantial but the materials were highly toxic; or (3) the disease for which compensation is sought was obvious or disclosed 'by medical examination, work incapacity, or manifest loss of physical function,' while working in New Jersey." There are several problems with that articulation. First, it confuses jurisdictional principles with those underlying liability and apportionment. Indeed, that confusion is underscored by the authority the majority cites as supporting its standard. *Bond, supra,* 42 *N.J.* at 311, 200 *A.*2d 322 (establishing standard for apportioning compensation liability for occupational exposure disease between successive employments or insurance coverages); *Akef v. BASF Corp.,* 140 *N.J.* 408, 658 *A.*2d 1252 (1995) (determining which, among successive employers, was to be held liable for worker's occupational disease); *Giagnacovo v. Beggs Bros.,* 64 *N.J.* 32, 311 *A.*2d 745 (1973) (deciding whether exposure of petitioner during last period of employment, though short, contributed to his occupational disease). It may make sense to set forth detailed standards to determine liability and apportionment in an occupational disease case between sequential employers and insurers to assure parity between risk exposure and the actual payment of a compensation award. However, such details, and the trial that will be required to resolve them, have no place whatsoever in a jurisdictional analysis involving the question of which state will adjudicate a worker's claim against a single employer. More importantly, the majority opinion effectively singles out one class of workers, those who by happenstance have been exposed to noxious substances both within and outside our borders, for a different jurisdictional burden than all other workers. There is simply no warrant for such a move. All workers' compensation cases should be subject to the same jurisdictional threshold and to the analysis by which we have classically abided. As a judicial system, we have absolutely no interest that will be vindicated by closing our doors to workers like Williams.

For those reasons I dissent.

JUSTICE ZAZZALI joins in this opinion.

NOTES AND COMMENTARY

1. Another, perhaps, more typical illustration of the type of fact pattern which can be seen in these "conflict" cases is found in Carroll v. Industrial Commission of Illinois, 205 Ill.App.3d 885, 150 Ill.Dec. 763, 563 N.E.2d 890 (1990). Thomas Carrol was hired in 1966 as an over-the-road truck driver at the Chicago terminal of Consolidated Freightways. At the time of hiring, Carroll was a resident of Illinois. Carroll moved to Michigan in 1969 but continued to commute to work at the Chicago terminal. In 1970, petitioner was assigned to the North Platte, Nebraska terminal where he remained for seven years. In 1978, he was transferred to the Idaho terminal. On March 8, 1988, Carroll was injured in Kent, Washington while trying to unhook a dolly from a trailer. Consolidated began payments to Carroll pursuant to the terms of the Idaho workers' compensation law. Carroll then filed a claim under the more favorable terms of the Illinois Workers' Compensation Act claiming that Illinois jurisdiction was proper because his contract of hire was executed in Illinois. An arbitrator and the Industrial Commission determined that Illinois jurisdiction was proper and awarded benefits under that act. The Circuit Court reversed and the Appellate Court of Illinois affirmed and dismissed the claim holding that Illinois jurisdiction did not exist. Several cases involving similar conflict issues have arisen in the context of claims brought by professional athletes. See e.g. Pro-Football Inc. v. McCants, 428 Md. 270, 51 A.3d 586 (2012) (claimant, a wide receiver for Washington, suffered multiple injuries several of which occurred in states other than Maryland; half of the team's games were played at Washington's home field in Landover, Maryland, half at the opposing teams' stadiums in other states; team practices were held at the team's corporate headquarters practice facility in Ashburn, Virginia; claimant brought claims for all injuries before the Maryland Workers' Compensation Commission; Commission denied all out-of-state injury claims; held, Commission reversed; claimant

was regularly employed by Washington in Maryland and therefore Maryland workers' compensation law applied with respect to all injuries sustained); See also Pro-Football v. Tupa, 428 Md. 198, 51 A.3d 544 (2012); and Atlanta Falcons Football Club LLC v. National Football League Players Ass'n, 906 F.Supp.2d 1278 (N.D.Ga. 2012); and, see the administrative decision of the California Workers' Compensation Appeals Board in McKinley v. Arizona Cardinals, 2013 WL 183945 (Cal. W.C.A.B. 2013).

2. It is not difficult to envision some of the legal and practical possibilities created by such cases. In the early days of workers' compensation, one of the states involved might have had a compensation act while the other state might have had an employer's liability act or, perhaps, was still dealing with work injuries on the basis of the common law of master and servant. Now that all states have adopted workers' compensation acts, there may be significant differences in the statutory provisions or case law governing types of employment covered, conditions of compensability, amount and character of benefits, requirements for notice, or periods of limitation. There is almost certain to be some difference in the procedure for enforcement of the obligation to pay compensation. As a result of these differences, the decision as to which law is to be applied in a given case may result in considerable advantage or disadvantage to one party or the other. If the law of more than one state is applied, the possibility of multiple recoveries for the employee and multiple liabilities for the employer arises; such multiple recoveries and liabilities may be under two or more workers' compensation acts or may be a combination of a compensation award and common law damages. If the law of *neither* state is applied, there is danger that the employee will receive no compensation at all for a work injury for which each of the states involved would normally provide compensation.

3. At the time workers' compensation acts came into existence, "choice of law" problems were not new to the jurisprudence of the United States. From the beginning, the federal system of separate states in this country had caused the American judiciary to be confronted with cases involving this kind of question. Solutions had been found usually by resorting to that rather vague and flexible body of ideas that had evolved over the centuries on the Continent and in England, usually classified under the heading "conflict of laws." When workers' compensation cases involving similar questions came under consideration, it was natural for the courts to turn to conflicts doctrines with which they were familiar, and the early cases reflect this approach. As time went on, however, difficulties appeared and substantial differences of opinion developed. One reason was that in making the primary characterization, different courts made different assumptions as to the juridical nature of the liability created by the workers' compensation laws. Some regarded it as a species of tort liability and applied conflict rules taken from tort cases. Others treated compensation liability as having its basis in contract and applied the conflict rule normally used in contract cases. Neither assumption was necessarily well founded and the results that followed were sometimes unsatisfactory. Furthermore, it became apparent that more than

the purely private rights of the parties had to be taken into account. In a workers' compensation case, the general interest of society in the well-being of its members is, perhaps, more prominently involved than it is in most other types of controversy. Hence, established choice of law doctrines growing out of conventional private litigation might be quite unsuited to the workers' compensation context.

4. These and other considerations prompted many legislatures to intervene with special statutory provisions to supersede court-made rules or to forestall court action and thus implement desired state policy in this area. As a result, in all but a few states, the shape of the law on this issue is determined by a statute or by an intermixture of statutory provisions and judicial decisions. From a national viewpoint, the pattern that originally emerged was far from harmonious. The theories and terms of the statutes differed substantially and the decisions applying them did not provide much uniformity. But the area achieved much greater uniformity following the promulgation in 1972 of Recommendation No. 2.11 by the National Commission on State Workmen's Compensation Laws. That provision provides as follows:

> "We recommend that an employee or his survivor be given a choice of filing a workmen's claim in the state where the injury or death occurred, or where the employment was principally localized, or where the employee was hired."

And see 9–143 Larson's Workers' Compensation Law, Matthew Bender, Section 143.01 (2013).

5. It goes without saying that in order to apply the law of the forum it is essential that the employer be subject to service of process in the forum state so that personal jurisdiction can be acquired by the local court or administrative agency.

6. As demonstrated in the principal case, if it is concluded that the workers' compensation law of another state is applicable and that the law of the forum is not, the employee's claim is usually dismissed and jurisdiction will not be exercised by the local court or tribunal to enforce the rights that may have accrued under the workers' compensation law of another state. The reason for this policy is obvious: almost all workers' compensation laws provide special administrative machinery and procedure for enforcing rights of employees under the act. There may be no right at all until this administrative remedy has been pursued, but even if the right could be said to exist, it is ordinarily considered impracticable for the courts or tribunals of one state to enforce the provisions of the workers' compensation law of another state. Logan v. Missouri Valley Bridge & Iron Co., 157 Ark. 528, 249 S.W. 21 (1923); 9–140 Larson's Workers' Compensation Law, Matthew Bender, Sections 140.02 (1)–(7) (2013). Also, pursuant to the 1958 amendment to 28 U.S.C.A. Section 1445(c), federal courts may not entertain removal of claims which arise under state workers' compensation laws. This statutory restriction applies regardless of whether there is diversity of

citizenship, and regardless of whether the non-removable claim is combined with claims otherwise removable. McCormack v. R.R. Donnelley & Sons, 436 F. Supp. 2d 857 (E.D.Ky. 2006). And, see Sheckles v. Ralcorp Frozen Bakery Products, Inc., 2011 WL 873507 (W.D. Ky. 2011) (cause of action for retaliatory discharge arose under Kentucky's workers' compensation act and such action could not be removed to federal court). The result may be different if the foreign statute is designed to be administered by the courts. Texas Pipe Line Co. v. Ware, 15 F.2d 171 (8th Cir.1926); Watkins v. Jim Walter Homes, Inc., 666 F.Supp. 102 (S.D.Miss. 1987) (" . . . where the workers' compensation law in question provides for its enforcement in the courts of that state, the liability created is enforceable in the courts of another state."). And see Ferguson v. Ram Enterprises, Inc., 900 S.W.2d 19, at 22 (Tenn.1995).

In a few states, the workers' compensation law provides that an employee who is hired outside the state may enforce rights acquired under the law of the state of hire before the forum state's commission or courts, provided that the rights are capable of being reasonably determined and dealt with by the local bodies. See, e.g. Hawaii Revised Stats. § 386–6 (2013); and 21 Vermont Stat. Ann. § 620 (2013).

7. Of course, if proceedings have been had under the workers' compensation law of one state and have resulted in an enforceable award in that state, such award may be sued upon and enforced in another state on much the same basis that applies in the case of a suit on a judgment of a foreign state. In re Phillips, 206 A.D. 314, 200 N.Y.S. 639 (1923); Chicago R. I. & P. Ry. Co. v. Schendel, 270 U.S. 611, 46 S.Ct. 420, 70 L.Ed. 757 (1926); Dennison v. Payne, 293 F. 333 (2d Cir.1923); Hagens v. United Fruit Co., 135 F.2d 842 (2d Cir.1943). But cf. Kindle v. Cudd Pressure Control, 792 F.2d 507 (5th Cir.1986).

8. In the United States, another aspect of the conflict of laws issue in workers' compensation cases is created by the provision that appears in Article IV, Section 1 of the Constitution of the United States stating that "Full faith and credit shall be given in each state to the public acts * * * of every other state." The statutes of a state, such as its workers' compensation statute, are "public acts" within the meaning of this provision. Consequently, in a specific case, a question may exist as to whether or not a particular choice of law rule, whether statutory or common law, is valid in the light of this Constitutional requirement. This matter will be explored in Section 5 *infra*.

9. With respect to maritime and waterfront employees, certain special issues exist because of federal jurisdiction of admiralty and maritime affairs. Also, employees of interstate rail carriers are covered by federal law. The relationship between state workers' compensation acts and federal statutes as they intersect often raise difficult conflict issues. These areas will be considered in Sections 7, 8 and 9, *infra*.

10. The following textual material is intended to acquaint you with a variety conflict of laws issues which have arisen in the workers' compensation arena.

2. APPLICATION OF FORUM STATE'S LAW TO OUT-OF-STATE INJURIES

Claimant is employed by a State A employer to solicit orders in State B. While working in State B, claimant is killed in a street accident that meets all requirements for compensability. Are claimant's survivors entitled to an award of compensation under the law of State A?

A. JUDICIAL THEORIES

The early reaction of many American courts confronted with this kind of problem was to invoke the "tort theory" which assumed that workers' compensation was merely a statutory substitute for the common law remedy of the employee for the employer's negligence. On this assumption, the conventional conflicts approach was that the law of the place of injury governed, and accordingly State A's workers' compensation law was deemed inapplicable to injuries occurring outside the boundaries of the state. In these early decisions, the courts were very concerned with the implications that the extraterritorial application of workers' compensation statutes would pose for federalism and for the sovereignty of the individual states.

Cases denying coverage for out-of-state injuries focused on geographical boundaries and the equal treatment of all who were within them. They also expressed great concern for the autonomy of individual states. In so doing, the courts discussed the ability of the states to govern affairs within their borders and to embody their chosen public policy within their statutes. See, e.g., In re Gould, 215 Mass. 480, 102 N.E. 693 (1913) ("If employees and employers from different states carry their domiciliary personal injury law with them into other jurisdictions, confusion would ensue in the administration of the law, and at least the appearance of inequality among those working under similar conditions."); North Alaska Salmon Co. v. Pillsbury, 174 Cal. 1, 162 P. 93 (1916) ("It will not be supposed that the legislature of this state undertook to pass a law which would trench upon the sovereign powers of any other jurisdiction. But the Workmen's Compensation Act would embody such attempt if it were construed in such manner as to create, to the exclusion of any other liability, a liability to pay for injuries received in another jurisdiction."); and Union Bridge and Construction Co. v. Industrial Commission, 287 Ill. 396, 122 N.E. 609 (1919) ("No law of this state has any effect as a law, by its own force, beyond the territorial limits of the state . . . but a law effective in this state as such may create rights and liabilities arising from acts occurring outside of the state . . .

There have been decisions in other states that compensation is to be awarded for injuries occurring beyond the territorial limits of the state, but they have been based upon provisions of the acts showing such a legislative intention.").

The courts which found State A's workers' compensation statutes did apply to out-of-state accidents approached the questions of state sovereignty and control over internal public policy from the vantage point of the contract of employment. The courts employing this "contract theory" examined the expectations of the employer and the employee that were contained within that agreement. As in the "tort theory" cases which denied State A's workers' compensation coverage to out-of-state injuries, the courts in these "contract theory" decisions devoted considerable attention to the issue of predictability of results. Kennerson v. Thames Towboat Co., 89 Conn. 367, 94 A. 372 (1915) ("The parties to each contract [of employment] had accepted the provisions of . . . our Workmen's Compensation Act. As a consequence, the Act became a part of these contracts. . . . [Our Act] intended that the employer should know his liability in this regard. . . . If our Act intends its contracts of employment to include compensation for injuries occurring only within our jurisdiction, it manifestly defeats its own ends."); Industrial Commission of Colorado v. Aetna Life Insurance Co., 64 Colo. 480, 174 P. 589 (1918) (" . . . if we are to determine, in the absence of any provision of the statute to the contrary, that the doctrine of lex loci contractus does not govern, it will be to destroy the very spirit and purpose of the law as it affects the employer, the employee, and the public welfare. . . . Thus, the employer, the employee, his dependents and the public all have been deceived and cheated, because forsooth the accident occurred beyond the imaginary line that marks the boundary of the Commonwealth, though it happened within the line of employment.").

While this line of judicial reasoning achieves the desired result in most cases, it embodies a considerable element of fiction and does not always stand careful analysis. The early workers' compensation law in many states was elective but in others compulsory. Today the reverse is true. Where the law is compulsory it is unrealistic to say that the parties to the employment contract "agree" to come under it. Even when many laws were elective, the choice, as the Arizona court said, was comparable to the choice given to one who is told "your money or your life." Ocean Accident & Guarantee Corp. v. Industrial Comm., 32 Ariz. 275, 279, 257 P. 644 (1927).

Another judicial theory for dealing with this question is the "business localization test" enunciated in early Minnesota decisions. See, e.g., Chambers v. District Court of Hennepin County, 139 Minn. 205, 166 N.W. 185 (1918). In that case, the Supreme Court of Minnesota said:

> "A basic thought underlying the compensation act is that the business or industry shall in the first instance pay for accidental injuries as a business expense or a part of the cost of production. It may absorb it or it may put it partly or wholly on the consumer if it can. The economic tendency is to push it along just as it is to shift the burden of unrestrained personal injury litigation. When a business is localized in a state there is nothing inconsistent with the principle of the compensation act in requiring the employer to compensate for injuries in a service incident to its conduct sustained beyond the borders of the state. The question of policy is with the legislature. It may enact an elective compensation act bringing such result if it chooses. In the case before us, the business of the employer was localized in the state. What the employee did, if done in Minnesota, was a contribution to the business involving an expense and presumably resulting in a profit. It was not different because done across the border in North Dakota. It was referable to the business centralized in Minnesota."

Under this test, neither the place of contract nor the place of injury was controlling; the worker may have been hired in Iowa and injured in Wisconsin, but if the business was localized in Minnesota, the workers' compensation law of the latter was to be applied. Severson v. Hanford Tri–State Airlines, 105 F.2d 622 (8th Cir.1939). Conversely, if the business was localized in another state, the Minnesota court would not have applied Minnesota law. See, e.g., De Rosier v. Jay W. Craig Co., 217 Minn. 296, 14 N.W.2d 286 (1944) ("The business of constructing the airport was entirely localized in South Dakota. The contract of employment was made there, and the injury occurred in that state. . . .").

The common law test which is probably most suitable to the purpose of the workers' compensation system commonly goes under the name of the "place of employment" test. It relates the applicability of local law to the question of whether the status of employer-employee existed within the state. Various factors are taken into account: the place of contract, the residence of the worker, any changes of residence made to accommodate work, and whether there is a fixed or transitory location at which the work is performed, all play a part in the ultimate result. The approach was well stated by the New York Court of Appeals in Cameron v. Ellis Constr. Co., 252 N.Y. 394, 169 N.E. 622 (1930). The employer was a Massachusetts corporation engaged in building a highway in New York. For this purpose it operated a sand pit in Canada just across the border. The worker was a resident of Canada and was employed to work at the sand pit where he was injured in the course of his employment. The New York court said:

"Nothing in the statute suggests that the State of New York has attempted to stretch forth its arm to draw within the scope of its own regulations the relations of employer and employee in work conducted beyond its borders. Hazardous employment here is regulated by the Workmen's Compensation Law; hazardous employment elsewhere, though connected with a business conducted here, does not come within its scope. Even where the contract of employment is made within the State, we have said that the State 'does not attempt to regulate the duty of foreign employers in the conduct of their business within foreign jurisdictions.' * * * The principle is not, however, limited to foreign employers. The statute imposes upon every employer, foreign or domestic, the duty to secure to his workmen compensation for injuries, wherever sustained, arising out of and in the course of employment located here. Absence of a workman from the State in the course of such employment does not interrupt that duty where the duty has been imposed upon the employer under the statute. It has not been imposed upon the employer in connection with employment located outside the State. The test in all cases is the place where the employment is located.

"When the course of employment requires the workman to perform work beyond the borders of the State, a close question may at times be presented as to whether the employment itself is located here. Determination of that question may at times depend upon the relative weight to be given under all the circumstances to opposing considerations. The facts in each case, rather than juristic concepts, will govern such determination. Occasional transitory work beyond the State may reasonably be said to be work performed in the course of employment here; employment confined to work at a fixed place in another State is not employment within the State, for this State is concerned only remotely, if at all, with the conditions of such employment. Such illustrations may indicate the manner in which the test should be applied, we do not now attempt a more definite classification intended to cover all the varying circumstances that may enter into the question in other cases."

See also Ala. Code Section 25–5–35(b) (2013); Todacheene v. G & S Masonry, 116 N.M. 478, 863 P.2d 1099 (1993); and Conwood Corp. v. Guinn, 201 Ga.App. 43, 410 S.E.2d 315 (1991) (Corporation was located in Tennessee and claimant had office in his Georgia home. " . . . in addition to storing samples and damaged goods in his home office, claimant conducted company business from his home office . . . [and] deducted the cost of his home office on his federal income tax return. . . . [Employer] shipped goods to claimant's home office [and] claimant began and ended each workday from his home office. . . . Claimant generally covered his entire 13 county area in a six-week period, spending approximately 14 to 15 1/2 days in Tennessee stores and 13 to 14 1/2 days in Georgia stores." Held, even though claimant was injured in Tennessee, "we cannot conclude that the ALJ's determination that Georgia was the principal locality of the employment relationship was erroneous.").

The contract of employment may provide that the law of a particular state is to be applied to work injuries. In a number of states, the statutes expressly authorize this type of agreement. The Missouri statute, V.A.M.S. Sec. 287.110 (2) (2013), was applied in Woodward v. J. J. Grier Co., 270 S.W.2d 155 (Mo.App.1954).[1] In the absence of a statute authorizing such a contract the courts have been inclined to disregard such provisions when it appears either that an existing jurisdiction was sought to be displaced,[2] or when the effect of the contract would have been to create a jurisdiction in a state where it did not otherwise exist. Daniels v. Trailer Transport Co., 327 Mich. 525, 42 N.W.2d 828 (1950) (". . . the legislature has established the boundary, and limits the jurisdiction, of the Commission for out-of-state injuries . . . the responsibilities and benefits provided under the act cannot be enlarged or diminished by agreement of the parties. It follows that the jurisdiction of the Commission cannot be extended by agreement.").

B. STATUTORY PROVISIONS

Most of the states have statutes that deal in one way or another with the question of whether the workers' compensation law is to be applicable to out-of-state injuries. The provisions of these laws may differ widely, but a modicum of uniformity was achieved following the publication of the recommendations of the 1972 National Commission on State Workmen's Compensation Laws. See in this regard 9–143 Larson's Workers' Compensation Law, Matthew Bender, Section 143.01 (2013). The promulgation of the "model act" by the Council of State Governments (see Appendix A *infra*) further facilitated uniformity among the dozen or so states that adopted it wholly or in a modified form as did the American Law Institute's promulgation of Restatement of the Law, Second, Conflict of Laws §§ 181–185, *infra*.

One type of statute does no more than state in general terms that the local law is applicable to out-of-state injuries, leaving it to the courts to

---

[1] Compare this to Alaska Packers, *infra*, where the U.S. Supreme Court found that California did not "exceed its constitutional power by prohibiting any stipulation exempting the employer from liability for the compensation prescribed by the California statute."

[2] See, e.g., Gotkin v. Weinberg, 2 N.J. 305, 66 A.2d 438 (1949) ("Neither the implied intention of the parties respecting the law which was to govern their contract . . . nor any express intention . . . can vitiate the statute laws and declared public policy of this state.").

work out any restrictions that may be necessary or advisable. See, e.g., Mass. Gen. Laws Ann. 152 § 26 (2013).

Most statutes, however, designate specifically the circumstances under which it is intended that the law will be applied to an out-of-state injury. An examination of these laws reveals that in formulating them, the legislatures have drawn heavily on the basic theories and tests that the courts originally worked out, although they frequently combine two or more theories or tests in a fashion that brings a result quite different from the original judge-made law of that state.

Another type of state statute embodies the "contract theory." Under such a statute, the single fact that the contract of employment was made in that state is enough to make the local law applicable to an out-of-state injury, sometimes with the limitation that the contract may provide otherwise. See, e.g., 85 Okla. Stats. Ann. Section 310 (2013); and, for examples of cases applying a "place of contract" statute, see Potter v. Patterson UTI Drilling Co., 148 N.M. 270, 234 P.3d 104 (2010) (under "place of contract" or "place of hiring" theory as embodied in NMSA § 52–1–64 in determining whether New Mexico has jurisdiction to award workers' compensation benefits when work injury occurs outside the state, the place where the employment contract was made is determinative and requires an analysis of the technical requirements for contract formation; held New Mexico had jurisdiction under facts of this case); and, Hopel v. Liberty Mutual, 40 So.3d 1078 (La.App. 5 Cir. 2010) (evidence was sufficient to support office of workers' compensation determination that no contract for hire was entered into in Louisiana as is required to trigger jurisdiction under LSA-R.S. 23:1035.1).

The statutes of a number of states are oriented basically towards the place of contract approach, but some additional fact or facts must appear to warrant application of the local law to an out-of-state injury. For example, in California, it must also appear that the injured employee's residence was in California. See West's Ann. Cal. Labor Code, § 5305 (2013). See also, Janzen v. WCAB, 61 Cal.App.4th 109, 71 Cal.Rptr.2d 260 (1997) (contract made over the telephone between employer located in Wyoming and employee located in California for work to be done exclusively in Wyoming; held, contract was formed where offeree, employee, was located; and because employee was a California resident at time contract was formed, California's workers' compensation law applied to industrial accident that occurred in Wyoming). In 2009, the Michigan statute, Mich. Comp. Laws Ann. Section 418.485, was amended to provide that its workers' compensation agency has jurisdiction over extra-territorial injuries if either the employee is a resident of the state at the time of the injury or the contract of hire was made in Michigan. Prior to the 2009 amendment, the statute required both Michigan residency and that the contract had been made in Michigan. A series of pre-2009 cases had read this dual requirement out of the statute. See, Roberts v. I. X. L. Glass Corp., 259 Mich. 644, 244 N.W. 188 (1932); Wearner v. West Michigan Conference of Seventh Day Adventists, 260 Mich. 540, 245 N.W. 802 (1932); and Boyd v. W.G. Wade Shows, 443 Mich. 515, 505 N.W.2d 544 (1993); but, see Karaczewski v. Farbman Stein & Co., 478 Mich. 28, 732 N.W.2d 56 (2007) insisting on the dual requirement; and Bezeau v. Palace Sports & Entertainment, Inc., 487 Mich. 455, 795 N.W.2d 797 (2010) limiting Karaczewski to prospective application. It would appear that the 2009 statutory amendment reinstated the position established in the pre-Karaczewski line of cases.

In Georgia, O.C.G.A. Section 34–9–242 (2013) not only requires that the employment contract have been made within the state, but also that either the employer's place of business or the injured employee's residence be within the state and that the employment was for services not to be performed exclusively outside the state. See Guinn v. Conwood Corp., 185 Ga.App. 41, 363 S.E.2d 271 (1987) (first inquiry is whether the employment was principally located in Georgia; if so, the worker is not employed "elsewhere than in this state" and the statutory section does not apply; only if the employment is located primarily outside of Georgia does the issue of where the contract was signed arise.).

Some states have statutes which provide that if the employee has been hired within the state (or is regularly employed there), the local law shall apply to an out-of-state injury provided that the accident occurs within six months after leaving the state, unless the employer has filed a notice electing to extend the coverage for a greater period of time. See, e.g., Colo. Rev. Stats., Section 8–41–204 (2013); and see Utah Code Ann. Section 34A–2–405 (2013). Virginia's statute, West's V.C.A. § 65.2–508(A) (2013), provides that its workers' compensation commission has jurisdiction to hear claims for out-of-state injuries so long as the contract of employment was not expressly for service exclusively outside of Virginia. See Anagua v. Sosa, 59 Va. App. 506, 721 S.E.2d 14 (2012) (held, claimant's contract of employment was expressly for service exclusively in Delaware and commission lacked jurisdiction).

Another type of statute makes the place of regular employment the basic element in determining the applicability of the local law to out-of-state injuries, sometimes as an alternative to the requirement concerning the place of the employment contract. See Ariz. Rev. Stats. § 23–904 (2013); Minn. St. Ann.Section 176.041 Subds. 2 and 3 (2013).

Lastly, over a dozen states have patterned their statutes on the Workmen's Compensation and Rehabilitation Law as promulgated by the Council on State Governments ("Model Act"). See Appendix A, Sec. 7, *infra*; and see, e.g., Alaska Stat. Section 23.30.011 (2013); and 77 Purdon's Pa. Stat. Ann. Section 411.2 (2013). And, as noted above, courts often look for guidance to the American Law Institute's promulgation of the Restatement of the Law, Second, Conflict of Laws §§ 181, *et seq.*

RESTATEMENT OF THE LAW SECOND—CONFLICTS

§ 181. Permissible Range of Territorial Application

A State of the United States may consistently with the requirements of due process award relief to a person under its workmen's compensation statute, if

(a) the person is injured in the State, or

(b) the employment is principally located in the State, or

(c) the employer supervised the employee's activities from a place of business in the State, or

(d) the State is that of most significant relationship to the contract of employment with respect to the issue of workmen's compensation under the rule in §§ 187–188 and 196, or

(e) the parties have agreed in the contract of employment or otherwise that their rights would be determined under the workmen's compensation act of the State, or

(f) the State has some other reasonable relationship to the occurrence, the parties and the employment.

For two cases applying § 181, see Knapp v. Hamm & Phillips Service Company, Inc., 2012 S.D. 82, 824 N.W.2d 785 (2012) (though any one factor is not dispositive, the court considers factors such as those listed in the Restatement Second, Conflict of Laws § 181 in evaluating whether South Dakota is the location of the employment relationship as is required for jurisdiction over a workers' compensation claim; held, South Dakota was not the place of employment relationship and did not have jurisdiction where: the worker was a South Dakota resident who worked 60% of time in North Dakota and 35% in South Dakota, the injury occurred in North Dakota, the employer's office was located in North Dakota, the employer did not have an office or other facilities in South Dakota and the contract for employment was formed in North Dakota); and see Martin v. American Colloid Co., 2011 S.D. 57, 804 N.W.2d 65 (2011) (claimant sought workers' compensation benefits in South Dakota for injuries suffered in Wyoming while working for a Delaware employer which was headquartered in Illinois; held, citing case law, treatises, and § 181, South Dakota was not the place of the employment relationship because claimant's only connection to South Dakota was that she resided there; Wyoming was the place where the claimant was hired, worked exclusively and was injured).

3. APPLICATION OF FORUM STATE'S LAW TO INJURIES OCCURRING WITHIN THE FORUM STATE

Claimant is employed in State A by a State A employer to make freight deliveries throughout the United States. While passing through State B, in the course of employment, claimant was seriously injured in a traffic accident that meets all requirements for compensability. May claimant recover under State B's workers' compensation law?

A. JUDICIAL THEORIES

The workers' compensation law of the state in which the injury occurred will be applicable to the vast majority of work injuries occurring within the boundaries of the forum state, but there may be cases from time to time in which a plausible argument is possible that the law of some other state ought to govern. If the state of the forum is one that has no statute expressly dealing with this question, its court is likely to resolve the issue in accordance with its earlier judge-made conflicts rule. Perhaps, the state's statute dealing with out-of-state injuries may reflect a basic conflict of laws policy that will serve as a guide.

In a jurisdiction where the general approach was to resolve this issue by the "contract theory," the logical result would be that the law of the state of injury would not apply if the contract of employment was made outside that state. A number of early decisions have reached this conclusion. Hall v. Industrial Comm., 77 Colo. 338, 235 P. 1073 (1925); Hopkins v. Matchless Metal Polish Co., 99 Conn. 457, 121 A. 828 (1923); but see Cleveland v. U.S. Printing Ink, 218 Conn. 181, 588 A.2d 194 (1991) (Court noted that while early Connecticut cases followed the "contract theory," they would extend that theory when necessary to promote the interests of employers and employees. The court noted that Connecticut ultimately jettisoned this approach in favor of one suggested by the Restatement (Second) Conflict of Laws § 181 and the 1972 recommendations of the National Commission on State Workmen's Compensation Laws.). The *Cleveland* case was effectively reversed by Conn. St. Ann. Section 31–275(9)(B)(vi) (2013); and see Kluttz v. Howard, 228 Conn. 401, 636 A.2d 816 (1994), where the court discusses the effect of the 1993 legislative change upon cases such as *Cleveland*. See also Proper v. Polley, 259 N.Y. 516, 182 N.E. 161 (1932). If the basic approach of the jurisdiction had been the "tort theory," the logical result is that the local law, being the law of the place of injury, is applied. Bagnel v. Springfield Sand & Tile Co., 144 F.2d 65 (1st Cir.1944) (Workers' Compensation Act of Massachusetts held applicable to injury occurring in that state even though contract of employment made in New York; court relied heavily on Gould's case 215 Mass. 480, 102 N.E. 693 (1913), generally regarded as the leading case for the "tort theory.").

Most courts, in reaching a decision on this issue (whether on the basis of a common law or statutory conflicts rule), take cognizance of the extraterritorial effect of the law of any other states having a significant interest in the case, and of the possibility or likelihood that by nonapplication of the law of the state of injury the worker may be denied any compensation, or may be seriously hampered in recovering the compensation due. If it appears that either of these consequences may ensue, courts feel free to apply the local law despite possible logical difficulties. Hopkins v. Matchless Metal Polish Co., 99 Conn. 457, 121 A. 828 (1923); Weaver v. Missouri Comp. Comm., 339 Mo. 150, 95 S.W.2d 641 (1936); and United States Cas. Co. v. Hoage, 77 F.2d 542 (D.C.Cir.1935). See also Cleveland v. U.S. Printing Ink, *supra*, and 9–143 Larson's Workers' Compensation Law, Matthew Bender, Section 143.02[5] (2013). A notable example to the contrary is found in House v. State Industrial Accident Commission, 167 Or. 257, 117 P.2d 611 (1941). In that case, the employer had its main automobile dealership in southern Oregon just north of the California border. It had a branch business in California about six miles south of the Oregon border. Decedent, a resident of California, was employed for about four months as a used car salesman at the Oregon site and was then made manager of the California branch. He resided in California. Sometime later while decedent was on his way to Portland to attend a salesman's meeting, he was killed in an accident that occurred in Oregon. The widow filed a claim first in California, but that state rejected jurisdiction because it required the place of contract to be in California. When she brought proceedings in Oregon, that state's Supreme Court held that Oregon's statute did not apply to the accident because Oregon then required the place of regular employment to be in Oregon. Thus claimant was left without any remedy. The *House* case was unique in its apparent disregard of consequences for the sake of a somewhat slavish adherence to its own conflicts doctrines. The Oregon statute has been amended since the date of the House decision. See O.R.S. Section 656.126 (2013). Whether or not the amended statute would provide coverage under the facts of *House* is unclear.

The court in Toebe v. Employers Mut. of Wausau, 114 N.J.Super. 39, 274 A.2d 820 (1971) resolved a difficult issue in a novel manner. Claimant was an employee of a Minnesota trucking concern and was injured in New Jersey. He claimed compensation in New Jersey and received an award, but the employer never paid it. Claimant then sued the employer's insurance carrier in New Jersey. The carrier defended on the ground that its policy limited its liability to awards arising under Minnesota law. The Minnesota statute of limitations had expired, and under its law the right ceased to exist. The Superior Court ordered the New Jersey compensation authorities to fashion an award which would reflect what the claimant would have recovered under Minnesota law for which the carrier would then be held liable. The Supreme Court of New Jersey ordered that under the doctrine of *forum non conveniens* "the amount of plaintiff's claim was to be determined under Minnesota law in a proceeding in the State of Minnesota under terms insuring a judgment on the merits in that state." When advised that the terms of the order had been carried out, the Supreme Court reversed the judgment of the Superior Court, 63 N.J. 198, 306 A.2d 66 (1973). Contrast, Philyaw v. Arthur H. Fulton, Inc., 569 So.2d 787 (Fla.App.1990) where the court found, "There is no provision in [Florida's workers' compensation statute] Chapter 440 in the nature of a *forum non conveniens* statute that would permit a judge of compensation claims otherwise having jurisdiction to dismiss the claim in deference to the more substantial contacts the claimant and the employer may have with another state."

B. STATUTORY PROVISIONS

The question of whether the local workers' compensation law is to be applied to cases involving injuries occurring within the state is expressly answered in the affirmative in some states by the statute itself. The Missouri Act, for example, provides in material part as follows: "This chapter shall apply to all injuries received and occupational diseases contracted in this state, regardless of where the contract of employment was made. . . ." Vernon's Ann. Mo. Stat. Section 287.110 (2013). The Hawaii statute provides, "The provisions of this chapter shall be applicable to all work injuries sustained by employees within the territorial boundaries of this state." Hawaii Rev. Stat. Ann. § 386–6 (2013). In some other states, coverage of an injury within the state is excluded if specified conditions exist. Montana has rather elaborate provisions for such an exclusion if it appears that the employee when injured was only temporarily in Montana doing work for a nonresident employer; that the employee and employer are bound by the workers' compensation act or similar act of the other state; that act applies to them when they are in Montana; and there is reciprocity of recognition of extraterritorial provisions and coverage between that state and Montana. Additional provisions were added in the 2013 legislative session regarding, among other things, required coverage of out of state construction workers. Montana Code Ann. Sec. 39–71–402(1)(b), *et seq.* (2013); and see West's Ann. Cal. Labor Code Section 3600.5(b) (2013). The Ohio statute provides that if the employee is a non-resident and is protected by the workers' compensation law or similar law of another state, the law of that other state shall cover him for injuries suffered while he is temporarily in Ohio and the Ohio law shall not be applicable. Baldwin's Ohio Rev. Code Ann. § 4123.54(H)(3) (2013); and see Hardy v. Proctor & Gamble Co., 2011 WL 5022918 (Ohio App. 2011) (employee receiving workers' compensation benefits under Colorado law for injury incurred while attending two-day seminar in Ohio, was "temporarily" in Ohio, thus precluding her from seeking Ohio benefits). States which have adopted the "Model Act" provisions regarding extraterritorial coverage often adopt that Act's terms regarding injuries which occur within the state in employment by an employee who is domiciled in another state. For example, Washington's statute begins as follows: "If a worker or beneficiary is entitled to compensation under this title by reason of an injury sustained in this state. . . ." This language does not seem to mandate coverage of injuries simply because they occur within the state, but such an interpretation is plausible. See "Model Act," Appendix A, Section 7(c), *infra*; and see, e.g., Idaho Code § 72–219 (2013); 19 Del. Code § 2303(c) (2013); and West's Rev. Code of Wash. Ann. § 51.12.120(4) (2013).

4. EFFECT OF FOREIGN WORKERS' COMPENSATION LAW ON LOCAL COMMON LAW ACTION

Today all states have workers' compensation laws. As Chapter 11, *supra*, demonstrates, each state's act contains an exclusive remedy provision granting the employer immunity from common law tort actions filed by injured employees. This immunity was a cornerstone of the original workers' compensation compromise as the U.S. Supreme Court recognized in its 1917 decision in New York Central v. White, *supra,* Chapter 2. It remains a cornerstone today. It is, therefore, somewhat of a rarity to see employees suing their employers in common law tort actions.

There are, however, exceptions to the general immunity rule which are recognized to one degree or another in the various jurisdictions. These exceptions take different shape and form in the states, sometimes because of variations in the statutory immunity provisions, and sometimes because of judicial interpretations of them.

Areas where exceptions to the general immunity of the employer have developed are addressed in Chapter 11, *supra*. These include situations where the employer has intentionally harmed the employee, or where, perhaps, statutory employers are accorded different immunity than immediate employers. Also, states may create tort remedies by statute despite the existence of workers' compensation coverage. See, e.g., West's Cal. Labor Code Section 4558 (2013) (tort liability imposed for knowing removal of safety device from power press). In the early days of workers' compensation when a significant number of state acts were elective, employers or employees could opt out of coverage of the workers' compensation system. When that occurred, the employer was subject to a common law tort action even though the compensation law of another state may have been applicable. See, e.g., Davis v. Morrison–Knudsen Co. Inc., 289 F.Supp. 835 (D.C.Or.1968) (To have decided otherwise would have been to contradict Oregon public policy which gives employers the choice of whether or not to be bound by the workers' compensation act). *Davis* was cited with approval in Garcia v. American Airlines, 12 F.3d 308 (1st Cir.1993). Today, states in specific instances allow an employer or employee to elect exemption from coverage. See, e.g., O.C.G.A. 34–9–2.1 (2013) (corporate officers may exempt themselves from coverage).

These state to state variations create the possibility that conflict of laws issues will arise. This prospect is enhanced by virtue of employers conducting their businesses across state lines and across international boundaries. For example, in Spelar v. American Overseas Airlines, Inc., 80 F.Supp. 344 (S.D.N.Y.1947), a flight engineer who was a resident of New York was killed in Newfoundland on an international flight in the crash of an airplane operated by a Delaware corporation that had its principal place of business in New York. It was held that the case was governed by the New York workers' compensation law rather than by the wrongful death statute of Newfoundland.

As a general rule, when employees sue employers in tort in one jurisdiction, that jurisdiction will not override the workers' compensation exclusive remedy provisions of the laws of another state. See, e.g., Barnhart v. American Concrete Steel Co., 227 N.Y. 531, 125 N.E. 675 (1920) (both employee and employer were residents of New Jersey and both had chosen to come under New Jersey's elective workers' compensation law; employee's estate sued employer in New York; in denying the claim for wrongful death, the court focused on the voluntary selection made by the parties; "The plaintiff's intestate, having the right to accept or reject the statutory scheme of compensation, exercised the option to accept it and contracted accordingly with the defendant. Such contract became binding upon him and, like any other valid contract, enforceable in the State of New York, unless [contrary] to its public policy."); Mitchell v. J. A. Tobin Constr. Co., 236 Mo.App. 910, 159 S.W.2d 709 (1942). See also 9–144 Larson's Workers' Compensation Law, Matthew Bender, Section 144.01 [2][3] (2013).

Two typical examples of cases involving a conflict of laws issue in the context of the statutory employer setting are Busby v. Perini Corp., 110 R.I. 49, 290 A.2d 210 (1972) and Anderson v. Commercial Const. Services, Inc., 531 F.3d 1190 (2008). In Busby, the claimant, a resident of Massachusetts, was an employee of a subcontractor, a Massachusetts corporation, and was injured at work on a construction project in Rhode

Island of which defendant was general contractor. The employment contract was made in Massachusetts. Massachusetts law barred tort actions against general contractors; Rhode Island law did not. Recognizing that it was not circumscribed by the Federal Full Faith and Credit Clause (see Section 5 *infra*) the court affirmed summary judgment in defendant's favor. After pointing out that various courts have used different legal routes to the same result, the court expressed approval of the Restatement of the Law, Second, Conflict of Laws, § 184 which is set forth below. In the Anderson case, *supra*, a Nebraska subcontractor's employee was injured performing work in Kansas. The employee collected workers' compensation benefits from his immediate employer and then filed a tort action against the general contractor in federal court in Kansas. In Nebraska, a general contractor is considered a third party and is subject to tort liability. In Kansas, general contractors receive the same immunity as immediate employers. The federal court discussed, *inter alia*, §§ 184 and 185 of the Restatement of the Law, Second, Conflict of Laws. That court determined that Kansas would apply *the lex loci delicti* choice of law rule. Thus, because the injury occurred in Kansas, that state's law applied to the resolution of the exclusive remedy issue and the employee's tort action was determined to be barred. For an article considering, *inter alia*, statutory employer immunity in the conflict of laws context see, Sedler, Interest Analysis, Party Expectations and Judicial Method in Conflict Torts Cases: Reflections on Cooney v. Osgood Machinery, 59 Brooklyn Law Review 1323 (1994).

RESTATEMENT OF THE LAW SECOND—CONFLICTS

§ 184. Abolition of Right of Action for Tort or Wrongful Death

> Recovery for tort or wrongful death will not be permitted in any state if the defendant is declared immune from such liability by the workmen's compensation statute of a state under which the defendant is required to provide insurance against the particular risk and under which (a) the plaintiff has obtained an award for the injury, or (b) the plaintiff could obtain an award for the injury, if this is the state (1) where the injury occurred, or (2) where employment is principally located, or (3) where the employer supervised the employee's activities from a place of business in the state, or (4) whose local law governs the contract of employment under the rules of §§ 187–188 and 196.

Further examples of cases citing and relying upon § 184 are Burton v. Phoenix Fabricators and Erectors, Inc., 670 S.E.2d 581 (2009) (two employees of an Indiana employer were killed while working on a water tower in North Carolina; their survivors were paid death benefits under the Indiana Workers' Compensation act; spouses of the two workers then, alleging intentional torts against the employer, pursued common law wrongful death actions in North Carolina; citing case precedent and § 184 of the Restatement of the Law, Second, Conflict of Laws, the North Carolina court held, in dismissing the actions, that the Indiana Workers' Compensation law applied and that North Carolina courts lacked subject matter jurisdiction) and Scott v. AMEC Kamtech, Inc., 583 F. Supp.2d 912 (E.D. Tenn. 2008) (employee was a Tennessee resident who was injured while working as a millwright for a Tennessee subcontractor on a construction project in Texas; workers' compensation benefits were paid pursuant to the Tennessee Workers' Compensation Act; employee then sued the general contractor and a fellow employee in tort in Federal District Court for the Eastern District of Tennessee; under Tennessee law the defendants would be immune from tort liability; under Texas law both could be liable; court determined that Tennessee law not Texas law applied; in reaching this conclusion the court determined that Tennessee would follow § 184; this conclusion dictated the granting of the defendants' motions for summary judgment).

But while the principles set forth in the above-quoted § 184 of the Second Restatement are quite consistently applied in cases in which the defendant is claimant's employer, or is a principal contractor in the position of a statutory employer, they will not be applied if the defendant's immunity is obnoxious to the public policy of the forum state. Thus, in Hutzell v. Boyer, 252 Md. 227, 249 A.2d 449 (1969), the injured worker sued his fellow employee in Maryland for an accident that occurred in that state while they were riding in an employer-owned truck in which they went to and from their Maryland homes to a paving job in Virginia. The employer was a Virginia corporation. The Maryland Workmen's Compensation Commission had denied a claim for want of jurisdiction. No claim was filed in Virginia, although it appears likely that a successful claim could have been made there. The Virginia compensation law extended immunity from tort liability to fellow-employees; the Maryland law did not. In affirming a judgment for plaintiff, the Maryland court said it was unable to make a finding that the immunity was not obnoxious to that state's public policy. It disagreed with the decision in Stacy v. Greenberg, 9 N.J. 390, 88 A.2d 619 (1952), in which the opposite result was reached. See also Powell v. Erb, 349 Md. 791, 709 A.2d 1294 (1998).

Where a third-party tortfeasor is subject to a common law suit in the forum state, State A, by an employee who has recovered workers' compensation from the employer in State B, the employer's subrogation rights under State B's workers' compensation act may be affected by State A's different treatment of the substantive and procedural aspects of the subrogation claim. Compare Hile v. Liberty Mutual Ins. Co., 281 Ala. 388, 203 So.2d 110 (1967) (holding workers' compensation insurance carrier was entitled to reimbursement under the terms of the Wisconsin act), and TRA Transp. v. Patterson, ___ So.3d ___, 2013 WL 4873481, (Ala.Civ.App., 2013) with Middle Atlantic Transp. Co. v. New York, 206 Misc. 535, 133 N.Y.S.2d 901 (1954) (refusing to give extraterritorial effect to Michigan law). And see Miller v. Dorr, 262 F. Supp.2d 1233 (D.Kan., 2003) in which the court relied upon § 185 Restatement of the Law, Second, Conflict of Laws to resolve the issue of which state's subrogation law governed. Section 185 as quoted in *Miller* provides:

> "The local law of the state under whose workmen's compensation statute the claimant has received an award for an injury determines what interest the person who paid the award has in the recovery of any cause of action for tort or wrongful death that the employee may have against a third person on account of the same injury."

See also 9–144 Larson's Workers' Compensation Law, Matthew Bender, Section 144.02[3] (2013).

Another problem area may be encountered when employees recover workers' compensation from their employers and then pursue a common law action against a third-party tortfeasor. In such a case, the third-party tortfeasor may seek to implead the employer to recover contribution or indemnity. The employer's immunity or lack thereof with respect to the contribution or indemnity claim may vary from one jurisdiction to another. See, e.g., Lamb v. McDonnell–Douglas, et. al., 712 F.2d 466 (11th Cir.1983), where Lamb was an employee of Delta Airlines based in Chicago, Illinois. The flights on which she served originated from O'Hare Airport in Chicago. During Lamb's tenure with Delta, she underwent periodic training in Atlanta, Georgia. In one such training session, she was engaged in an emergency evacuation simulation using an evacuation slide manufactured by Sargent Industries, a California corporation. While using the slide, she suffered a fall leading to serious injuries. Even though she was eligible to receive workers' compensation benefits from Delta in either Illinois or Georgia, she chose to file her claim in Illinois. She later brought a product liability and negligence claim against Sargent in the U. S. District Court for the Northern District of Georgia based on diversity of citizenship. Sargent filed a third-party complaint against Delta alleging negligence and seeking contribution and indemnity. Under Georgia law, an employer who had paid workers' compensation benefits to an employee was immune from such a third-party claim. In Illinois, however, no immunity was recognized. Sargent argued that because Lamb had filed her workers' compensation claim in Illinois that state's law should control. The district court granted Delta's motion for summary judgment based on Georgia's conflict rule which looked to the law of the place of the injury. The Court of Appeals for the Eleventh Circuit affirmed.

5. FULL FAITH AND CREDIT

The first serious attempt to determine the jurisdictional limitations on state workers' compensation laws imposed by the Full Faith and Credit Clause (Article 4, § 1, U.S. Constitution) was in Bradford Electric Co., Inc. v. Clapper, 286 U.S. 145, 52 S.Ct. 571, 76 L.Ed. 1026 (1932). Clapper, a resident of Vermont, entered into a contract of employment in that state with defendant, a Vermont corporation; he was a lineman for emergency service. Clapper was sent on a temporary basis into New Hampshire to a substation to replace certain fuses. He was killed there while performing his job. Plaintiff, administratrix, was a citizen and resident of New Hampshire. She brought an action for damages under the New Hampshire Employers' Liability and Workmen's Compensation Act which then allowed an election of remedies. The Vermont Workers' Compensation Law prohibited any action for damages for a work injury whether it occurred within or outside of Vermont. Defendant moved to dismiss on the ground that the Federal District Court was bound to apply Vermont law under the Full Faith and Credit Clause. Ultimately, a divided Supreme Court concluded that the Full Faith and Credit Clause compelled dismissal of the action. Justice Stone, in his concurring opinion, would have placed the result on the basis of comity and thus avoided the full faith and credit issue. He wrote:

> * * * "The Full Faith and Credit Clause has not hitherto been thought to do more than compel recognition, outside the state, of the operation and effect of its laws upon persons and events within it." (Citations omitted.)

In four cases during the next 23 years, the Supreme Court revised the *Clapper* doctrine to the point of obliteration. Alaska Packers Ass'n. v. Industrial Acc. Comm., 294 U.S. 532, 55 S.Ct. 518, 79 L.Ed. 1044 (1935), involved a non-resident worker who entered into a contract of employment in San Francisco with an employer doing business in California. He agreed to work in Alaska during the salmon packing season and to be bound by Alaska's workers' compensation law. He was injured in Alaska and after his return to California he received an award of compensation under the workers' compensation law of California. The award was upheld, the Supreme Court centering its attention on the comparative interests of California and Alaska in the case. The interest of California involved consideration of the facts that claimant was an alien 2000 miles from his home in Mexico; that there was little chance of his returning to Alaska to pursue his remedy there; and he was, therefore, a potential public charge in California. That interest was deemed greater than the interest of Alaska where he "was never a resident and to which he may never return."

In Pacific Employers Ins. Co. v. Industrial Acc. Comm., 306 U.S. 493, 59 S.Ct. 629, 83 L.Ed. 940 (1939), the employer was a Massachusetts corporation that had a branch in California and its head office in Massachusetts. One of its employees was temporarily in California and was injured there. The California Commission awarded compensation and a petition was filed by the carrier to set aside the award. The state courts refused to do so, and the United States Supreme Court affirmed. Recognizing that California's policy was to apply its own provisions for compensation to injuries occurring within its borders to the exclusion of all other remedies, Justice Stone quoted with approval the following statement from the opinion of the California Supreme Court: "It would be obnoxious to that policy to deny persons who have been injured in this state the right to apply for compensation when to do so might require physicians and hospitals to go to another state to collect charges for medical care and treatment given to such persons."

Another basis of interest or concern for the exercise of jurisdiction under the workers' compensation statute was recognized in Cardillo v. Liberty Mut. Ins. Co., 330 U.S. 469, 67 S.Ct. 801, 91 L.Ed. 1028 (1947). In that case, the employee lived in the District of Columbia, was hired there and the employer's business was headquartered there. The work was located in Virginia and the fatal injury occurred in Virginia while claimant was driving home at the end of the day. The claim for compensation was filed under the District of Columbia workers' compensation law and an award was entered. The employer and insurance carrier brought an action in federal court to set aside the award; the District Court dismissed the complaint but the Court of Appeals reversed. The United States Supreme Court granted certiorari and reversed the Court of Appeals. It held that in light of the claimant's and the decedent's residence in the District, the fact that the claimant was hired in the District, that he was under orders from the District while working in Virginia, that he was subject to transfer at any time to a project in the District, that his pay was either carried to him from the District or given to him in the District, and that he commuted daily between his home and place of work in Virginia, the jurisdictional objection was without merit.

The demolition of *Clapper* to all intents and purposes was completed in Carroll v. Lanza, 349 U.S. 408, 75 S.Ct. 804, 99 L.Ed. 1183 (1955). Carroll was an employee of a subcontractor, both being residents of Missouri and the employment contract being entered into in that state. The work was to be done in Arkansas where the injury occurred. After receiving 34 weekly payments under the Missouri compensation law, Carroll commenced a tort action in Arkansas against Lanza, the general contractor. The Missouri compensation law provided that the rights and remedies granted by it "shall exclude all other rights and remedies" at common law or otherwise for injury or death. Arkansas law, however, did not extend such immunity to third parties which Lanza was considered to be. The Supreme Court held that the Full Faith and Credit Clause was not an obstacle to Carroll's action. Justice Douglas' opinion, after reviewing *Clapper* and the cases that came after it, concluded:

> "Missouri can make her Compensation Act exclusive, if she chooses, and enforce it as she pleases within her borders. Once that policy is extended into other states, different considerations come into play. Arkansas can adopt Missouri's policy if she likes. Or, as the Pacific Employers' Insurance Co. case teaches, she may supplement it or displace it with another, insofar as remedies for acts occurring within her boundaries are concerned. Were it otherwise, the State where the injury occurred would be powerless to provide any remedies or safeguards to nonresident employees working within its borders. We do not think the Full Faith and Credit Clause demands that subserviency from the State of the injury."

There was a dissent by Justices Burton, Frankfurter and Harlan which urged that the Court should continue to balance the competing interests of the states involved and not base the decisions simply on recognition of one interest of the forum state. They seemed to suggest that *Clapper* was being overruled, saying:

> "and if Clapper is to be overruled, on which I and those who join me express no opinion, it should be done with reasons making manifest why Mr. Justice Brandeis' long-matured, weighty opinion in that case was ill-founded."

Thus it is clear so far as the Full Faith and Credit Clause is concerned, the Supreme Court recognizes a variety of bases for "legitimate interest" or "concern" on which local compensation acts may be applied, including the place of making the contract, the place of the injury, the residence of the injured person and the place where the employment activity is carried on. There may be others. It would seem that the judicial function is not a matter of weighing or comparing the interests involved but only of identifying them. Thus, the exercise of state power in the workers' compensation context is virtually untrammeled. See also, Dailey v. Dallas Carriers Corp., 43 Cal.App.4th 720, 51 Cal.Rptr.2d 48 (1996); Benoit v. Test Systems, Inc., 142 N.H. 47, 694 A.2d 992 (1997); and Hay, Weintraub & Borchers, Conflict of Laws, Cases and Materials, 14th Ed., 350–386, Foundation Press (2013) (overview of the historical and modern approaches to resolving choice of law questions); Hay, Borchers, Symenonides, Conflict of Laws, 5th Ed., § 17.60 (West 2010). And see 9–142 Larson's Workers' Compensation Law, Matthew Bender, Section 142.03(1)-(5) (2013).

6. MULTIPLE AWARDS OF COMPENSATION

Prior to 1943, it was not uncommon for a state to entertain and grant an application for compensation even though a sister state had previously made an award growing out of the same accident provided that its law was properly applicable to the accident and that credit against its award would be given for any payments received under the first award. The decision of the United States Supreme Court in Magnolia Petroleum Co. v. Hunt, 320 U.S. 430, 64 S.Ct. 208, 88 L.Ed. 149 (1943) changed the situation at least for a time.

In the *Magnolia* case the worker was employed in Louisiana and went to Texas in the course of his employment to work on an oil well where he was injured. Awarded compensation under the Texas statute, he then returned to Louisiana and brought an action in the Louisiana courts for compensation under the Louisiana law. Compensation was awarded. The Supreme Court granted certiorari and by a divided vote (5–4) reversed the Louisiana award. The Texas statute provided, *inter alia*, that employees subject to the act "shall have no right of action against their employer . . . but shall look for compensation solely to the association" (the insurer). Relying to some extent on these terms of the statute, the Supreme Court held that the compensation award had to be given the same effect in another state as in the state in which it was rendered, that the injured worker had only one claim which had been fully adjudicated in Texas and, hence, the Full Faith and Credit Clause barred the claim in Louisiana.

Four years later, Industrial Comm. of Wisconsin v. McCartin, 330 U.S. 622, 67 S.Ct. 886, 91 L.Ed. 1140 (1947) was decided. In that case, the worker and employer were both Illinois residents. The job on which claimant was injured was in Wisconsin. Claimant sought and was awarded compensation under Illinois law paid in a lump sum, the settlement contract expressly reserving all rights under Wisconsin law. McCartin's claim for compensation under Wisconsin law was denied on the authority of *Magnolia*. The United States Supreme Court reversed. It distinguished *Magnolia* on the basis that the Texas award in that case purported to be "final" whereas as to the Illinois award "there is nothing in the statute or in the decisions to indicate that it is completely exclusive, that it is designed to preclude any recovery by proceedings brought in another state for injuries received there in the course of an Illinois employment." Only "some unmistakable language by a state legislature or judiciary would warrant" cutting off an employee's right to sue under other legislation passed for his benefit. Wisconsin was therefore free under the Full Faith and Credit Clause to grant an award of compensation in accord with its own laws.

In the years that have followed *McCartin*, very few courts have held that a second award is prohibited by the Full Faith and Credit Clause. One that did so was the Arizona Court of Appeals in a case that it considered "squarely in point" with *Magnolia*. Claimant, a resident of Texas who was employed in Texas by a Texas employer, received an injury while working in Arizona. He accepted compensation payments made to him in compliance with Texas law for approximately 4 months. He then filed a claim for compensation in Arizona. The administrators held the claim non-compensable and the Court of Appeals affirmed, considering itself constrained by *Magnolia*, although it found that case to be "a questionable interpretation of the Texas statute." Cofer v. Industrial Comm., 24 Ariz.App. 357, 538 P.2d 1158 (1975). The District of Columbia Court of Appeals, applying what it conceived to be Maryland law, denied a second award in Gasch v. Britton, 92 U.S.App.D.C. 64, 202 F.2d 356 (1953), holding that award of compensation under the Maryland law barred recovery of additional benefits allowed under the District of Columbia law. But the Court of Appeals of Maryland reached the opposite result in Wood v. Aetna Cas. & Sur. Co., 260 Md. 651, 273 A.2d 125 (1971). See also, M & G Convoy, Inc. v. Mauk, 85 Md.App. 394, 584 A.2d 101 (1991) (court discussed and agreed with *Wood* holding that "the court [in Wood] held the right to recover [a supplemental award in another state] depends upon the workers' compensation act of the state where the claimant first elected. . . . That has been and remains the law of Maryland.") The court in reaching this conclusion also considered the U.S. Supreme Court's opinion in Thomas v. Washington Gas Light Co., *infra*. Most cases since *McCartin* have reached a similar conclusion finding that the first award was not intended as final and hence the *Magnolia* rule was not applicable. Stanley v. Hinchliffe and Kenner, 395 Mich. 645, 238 N.W.2d 13 (1976); Houle v. Stearns–Rogers Mfg. Co., 279 Minn. 345, 157 N.W.2d 362 (1968); Chapman v. John St. John Drilling Co., 73 N.M. 261, 387 P.2d 462 (1963); Spietz v. Industrial Comm., 251 Wis. 168, 28 N.W.2d 354 (1947); Cook v. Minneapolis Bridge Constr. Co., 231 Minn. 433, 43 N.W.2d 792 (1950); and Lavoie's Case, 334 Mass. 403, 135 N.E.2d 750 (1956).

In 1980, the U.S. Supreme Court revisited the issues in Thomas v. Washington Gas Light Co., 448 U.S. 261, 100 S.Ct. 2647, 65 L.Ed.2d 757 (1980). There, the employee was hired in the District of Columbia and was injured while working in Virginia. Although a workers' compensation claim could have been filed either in D.C. or Virginia, the employee first entered into a settlement and received an award therefrom for disability benefits in Virginia. He then filed a claim and received a subsequent supplemental award under the District of Columbia act. The employer argued that because the Virginia act precluded subsequent awards, the District of Columbia was compelled to give the Virginia act full faith and credit and thereby was prohibited from awarding supplemental benefits to the employee. The District of Columbia ALJ determined that the Virginia act did not preclude supplemental awards by other states. The Benefits Review Board upheld the ALJ's decision; but the U.S. Court of Appeals for the Fourth Circuit reversed. The U.S. Supreme Court reversed, holding that the Virginia act did not by "unmistakable language" preclude a compensation award in another state. The plurality of four justices would have overruled *Magnolia* reasoning as follows:

> ". . . the Full Faith and Credit Clause does not require a state to subordinate its own compensation policies to those of another state," and that "it follows inescapably that the McCartin 'unmistakable language' rule represents an unwarranted delegation to the states of this Court's responsibility for the final arbitration of full faith and credit questions. . . . To vest the power of determining the extraterritorial effect of a state's own laws and judgments in the state itself risks the very kind of parochial entrenchment on the interests of other states that it was the purpose of the Full Faith and Credit Clause . . . to prevent."

The opinion of the three concurring justices would not overrule either *Magnolia* or *McCartin*. The two dissenting justices concluded that the Full Faith and Credit Clause did not allot to the Supreme Court the task of balancing of interests. Thus, neither *Magnolia* nor *McCartin* was overruled. See Felix and Whitten, American Conflicts Law, 6th Ed., § 48, Carolina Academic Press (2011); Hay, Borchers & Symeonides, Conflict of Laws, 5th Ed., Section 24.26, West Group (2010); and Leflar, et. al., American Conflicts Law, 5th Ed., § 162, The Michie Co. (2001).

In the *McCartin* opinion, the Illinois settlement approval was treated as a final award of compensation rather than as a voluntary payment. As to the effect of prior voluntary payments of compensation under the law of one state as a bar to a claim or ground for reduction of a claim of compensation in another state, see Cline v. Byrne Doors, Inc., 324 Mich. 540, 37 N.W.2d 630 (1949), holding that voluntary compensation payments under the Florida statute did not bar a proceeding for compensation under the Michigan statute. And see 9–141 Larson's Workers' Compensation Law, Matthew Bender, Section 141.05 (2013).

There are a few cases in which the employee recovers the entire second award without having to allow credit for payments received under the first award; in effect getting a double recovery. These are usually cases in which the employee appears to have been employed by two employers at the time of the accident and procures an award against one employer in the first state and the other employer in the second state. See, for example, Adams v. Emery Transp. Co., 15 Mich.App. 593, 167

N.W.2d 110 (1969), in which the court expresses great unhappiness that such a result could occur.

7. LONGSHORE AND HARBOR WORKERS' COMPENSATION ACT

The Constitution of the United States vests jurisdiction over admiralty and maritime affairs in the Federal Government (Article III, Section 2; Article I, Section 8). In the exercise of this power, Congress has made provision for the masters and members of the crew of vessels through an employer's liability statute, the "Jones Act," discussed in Section 8, *infra*. Waterfront workers who are not masters or members of crews of vessels may be covered by the Longshore and Harbor Workers' Compensation Act, 33 U.S.C.A. § 901 *et seq.*, that was modeled on the New York state workers' compensation law. The problems associated with compensating waterfront workers for injuries sustained in their employment have presented legal complications for more than 90 years. This section consists of a brief history of the difficulties and a summary of some aspects of the current situation. The record may be divided into 3 parts: the decade between 1917 and 1927; the 45-year period between 1927 and 1972; and the post-1972 era.

In Southern Pacific Co. v. Jensen, 244 U.S. 205, 37 S.Ct. 524, 61 L.Ed. 1086 (1917), the Supreme Court held that the New York workers' compensation law could not be applied to an injury sustained by a stevedore unloading a vessel on navigable waters, because to do so would impair the uniformity of the general maritime law. The decision deprived thousands of waterfront workers of a compensation remedy. Thereafter, Congress twice attempted to deal with the situation by legislation expressly allowing state compensation statutes to operate. The U.S. Supreme Court, however, struck down both acts. Knickerbocker Ice Co. v. Stewart, 253 U.S. 149, 40 S.Ct. 438, 64 L.Ed. 834 (1920); and State of Washington v. W. C. Dawson & Co., 264 U.S. 219, 44 S.Ct. 302, 68 L.Ed. 646 (1924). Finally in 1927, Congress enacted the Longshoremen's and Harbor Workers' Compensation Act 33 U.S.C.A. § 901 *et seq.* The 1984 amendment to the Act substituted "Longshore" for "Longshoremen's." See Sept. 28, 1984, Pub. L. 98–426, Section 27(d)(1), 98 Stat. 1654.

The 1927 enactment was a no-fault compensation statute applicable to disability or death of an employee "but only if the disability or death results from an injury occurring upon the navigable waters of the United States (including any dry dock) and if recovery for the disability or death through workmen's compensation proceedings may not validly be provided by State law." 33 U.S.C.A. Sec. 901.

It was apparent that the limiting language quoted above was an attempt by Congress to keep the Act within the constitutional limits theretofore identified by the Supreme Court. In the interim between *Jensen* and the 1927 enactment, however, the Supreme Court had expressed views and reached decisions that modified the effect of *Jensen*. The Court developed a concept of employment and employment activities that were "local in character though maritime in nature" in which state compensation laws could be applied if injury or death ensued. One kind of case held to be in this category was that of a worker engaged in the construction of a new vessel which, while uncompleted, was afloat in navigable waters. Grant Smith–Porter Ship Co. v. Rohde, 257 U.S. 469, 42 S.Ct. 157, 66 L.Ed. 321, 25 A.L.R. 1008 (1922). Another kind of case held not to be in the "local in character though maritime in nature" category was La Casse v. Great Lakes Engineering Works, 242 Mich. 454, 219 N.W. 730 (1928) (carpenter working on a raft alongside a vessel in process of being repaired (not newly constructed) while floating in Detroit River; state act held inapplicable; good discussion of cases). But, the borderline was hazy between those cases in which state law was applicable and those in which the Longshore Act was applicable. In an effort to solve the difficulty the Court developed the "twilight zone" concept in Davis v. Department of Labor and Industries, 317 U.S. 249, 63 S.Ct. 225, 87 L.Ed. 246 (1942). In that case, claimant was the widow of a worker drowned in a navigable river while dismantling a drawbridge. The Court noted that longshore and harbor workers were clearly protected by the federal act but that "employees such as decedent here, occupy that shadowy area within which, at some undefined and undefinable point, state laws can validly provide compensation." and that both the federal act and the state compensation statute "show clearly that neither was intended to encroach on the field occupied by the other." Since this "jurisdictional, dilemma" made it difficult for an injured worker to determine on which side of the line his particular case fell, the result in some cases had been that the worker obtained no compensation at all. In this "twilight zone" where the facts of a given case might place an injured worker on either side of the line, the Court held that it would give great weight to the administrative findings in cases brought under the federal act, and to the presumption of constitutionality in cases arising under state statutes. Because of this presumption of constitutionality the claimant in *Davis* was allowed her state remedy.

The practical effect of the decision in *Davis* was that in "twilight zone" cases the claimant might claim under either law, depending on which might be most advantageous. The difficulty that it left in its wake was that of deciding which cases fell within the twilight zone and which were in the full light on either side. See Moores' Case, 323 Mass. 162, 80 N.E.2d 478 (1948) in which the state court called this a "most important question" and complained that no test had been suggested.

In 1962, the U.S. Supreme Court decided Calbeck v. Travelers Ins. Co., 370 U.S. 114, 82 S.Ct. 1196, 8 L.Ed.2d 368. In that case, claimants were workers injured while engaged in completing the construction of a vessel afloat on navigable waters. This was an established category of "maritime but local" cases in which state law could be applied validly. Awards were made under the Longshore Act over the carrier's objection that the act was not applicable by its terms since it covered injuries only if "occurring upon the navigable waters of the United States . . . and if recovery . . . through workmen's compensation proceedings may not validly be provided by State law." The Court upheld the awards. After reviewing the legislative history of the Longshore Act, Mr. Justice Brennan wrote:

> "There emerges from the complete legislative history a congressional desire for a statute which would provide federal compensation for all injuries to employees on navigable waters; in every case, that is, where Jensen might have seemed to preclude state-compensation. The statute's framers adopted this scheme in the Act because they meant to assure the existence of a compensation remedy for every such injury, without leaving employees at the mercy of the uncertainty, expense, and delay of fighting out in litigation whether their particular cases fell within or without state acts under the 'local concern' doctrine."
>
> * * *
>
> "We conclude that Congress used the phrase 'if recovery . . . may not validly be provided by State law' in a sense consistent with the delineation of coverage as reaching injuries occurring on navigable waters. By that language Congress reiterated that the Act reached all those cases of injury to employees on navigable waters as to which Jensen, Knickerbocker and Dawson had rendered questionable the availability of a state compensation remedy. Congress brought under the coverage of the Act all such injuries whether or not a particular one was also within the constitutional reach of a state workmen's compensation law."

The dissenting opinion by Mr. Justice Stewart, in which Justice Harlan joined, pointed out that the effect of the majority's decision was to eliminate the language relating to permissible state compensation. Referring to the *Davis* case *supra*, the dissenters wrote:

> "Whatever else may be said of the *Davis* decision, it thus clearly rested on a construction of the statute precisely opposite to that adopted by the Court today. Indeed, if today's decision is correct, then there was no reason for a 'twilight zone' doctrine worked out with such travail in Davis. For the Court now holds

that the problem which led to the *Davis* decision never really existed. Yet as recently as 1959 the Court began a *per curiam* opinion with this topic sentence: 'By its terms, the Longshoremen's and Harbor Workers' Compensation Act does not apply if recovery for the disability or death through workmen's compensation proceedings *may validly be provided by State* law.' Hahn v. Ross Island Sand & Gravel Co., 358 U.S. 272, 79 S.Ct. 266, 3 L.Ed.2d 292. Today the Court simply removes these 'terms' from the Act."

There remained, of course, the requirement that in order for the Longshore Act to be operative, the injury or death must occur on navigable waters of the United States. In Nacirema Operating Co., Inc. v. Johnson, 396 U.S. 212, 90 S.Ct. 347, 24 L.Ed.2d 371 (1969), the Court held the Act inapplicable to employees who were "slingers" attaching cargo from railroad cars located on piers to ships' cranes for removal to the ships. One was killed and the other injured when the cargo swung unexpectedly. The majority held that the piers were land and not navigable waters, and that the language of the Act clearly limited it so that it did not apply to land injuries even though the injured person was a longshoreman. The three dissenters argued that the Act should apply to an injured person who was a longshoreman simply because of that status.

In the majority's opinion the following language appears:

> "Congress might have extended coverage to all longshoremen by exercising its power over maritime contracts. But the language of the Act is to the contrary and the background of the statute leaves little doubt that Congress' concern in providing compensation was a narrower one." 396 U.S. 215–216, 90 S.Ct. 349.

Within three years, Congress reacted to the constitutional implications of the *Calbeck* and *Nacirema* opinions. In the 1972 amendments to the Act (in which there were many amendments to the substantive provisions of the law) there was a substantial change in the language relating to coverage. Two sections of the Act are pertinent for this overview:

> 902. Definitions
>
> (3) The term "employee" means any person engaged in maritime employment, including any longshoreman or other person engaged in longshoring operations, and any harborworker including a ship repairman, shipbuilder, and ship-breaker, but such term does not include a master or member of a crew of any

vessel or any person engaged by the master to load or unload or repair any small vessel under eighteen tons net.[3]

903. Coverage

(a) Compensation shall be payable under this chapter in respect of disability or death of an employee, but only if the disability or death results from an injury occurring upon the navigable waters of the United States (including any adjoining pier, wharf, dry dock, terminal, building way, marine railway, or other adjoining area customarily used by an employer in loading, unloading, repairing, or building a vessel).

* * *

It is apparent, as Judge Gibbons of the Third Circuit Court of Appeals observed, that "the draftsmanship of the 1972 amendments leaves something to be desired." Sea–Land Service Inc. v. Director, 540 F.2d 629, 638 (3d Cir.1976). Its deficiencies have bred litigation concerning coverage and led to sharp differences of opinion among the Federal Circuits.

There are two requirements that must be satisfied for the worker to come within the coverage of the Act. The worker must be working at a place within the statutory definition of "navigable waters," (Section 903) sometimes called the "situs" requirement, and must be "engaged in maritime employment," (Section 902) sometimes called the "status" requirement. Both requirements have divided the courts. The following references are intended only as illustrative.

As to the "situs" requirement, the 1972 amendment to Section 903 expanded coverage beyond navigable waters to "adjoining . . . area[s] . . . ." This language is susceptible to either broad or narrow judicial interpretation. Examples of cases on both ends of the interpretation spectrum are *Sea–Land Service, supra*, and Jacksonville Shipyards, Inc. v. Perdue, 539 F.2d 533 (5th Cir.1976). The Third Circuit in *Sea–Land Services* held the Act applicable to a worker injured on a public street in a "sprawling marine terminal area" in Port Elizabeth, New Jersey. The U.S. Supreme Court, in Northeast Marine Terminal Co., Inc. v. Caputo, 432 U.S. 249, 97 S.Ct. 2348, 53 L.Ed.2d 320, fn. 40 (1977), observed that the 3rd Circuit in *Sea–Land Service* had essentially discarded the "situs" requirement. In contrast, the Fifth Circuit in *Jacksonville Shipyards* denied compensation to a shipfitter who left work on an aircraft carrier berthed at a naval station and was injured on his way to "punch out" at a

[3] In 1984, the two exclusions were designated as subparagraphs "G" and "H" and six additional subparagraphs, "A" to "F," were added designating additional exclusions from the term "employee." And, as part of the American Recovery and Reinvestment Act of 2009, Pub.L.111–5, 2009 HR1, 123 Stat. 187, the definition of employee was contracted further to exclude individuals employed to build, repair or dismantle any recreational vessels.

time clock located on the station about a mile from the ship. The court rejected "the argument that the new Act covers every point in a large marine facility where a ship repairman might go at his employer's direction." Texports Stevedore Co. v. Winchester, 632 F.2d 504 (C.A.5, 1980) later overruled the more narrow approach of *Jacksonville Shipyards*; but, as the saga continued, New Orleans Depot Services, Inc. v. Director, Offices of Workers' Compensation Programs, 718 F.3d 384 (C.A.5, 2013) seems to have moved back to a more narrow construction of "situs" as it criticized and overruled *Texports* and its progeny. The *New Orleans Depot* case includes a good review of the treatment of the "situs" requirement by its "sister circuits".

The "status" requirement of Section 902 has forced the courts to contend with its references to "maritime employment." In one case, for example, it was held by the Fourth Circuit that the concept of "maritime employment" did not extend beyond the "point of rest," which meant coverage was limited to workers who unload inbound cargo from the ship to the first point of rest at the terminal, or load outbound cargo on the ship from the last point of rest at the terminal. I. T. O. Corp. of Baltimore v. Benefits Review Bd., 529 F.2d 1080 (4th Cir.1975). The "point of rest" concept was rejected by the United States Supreme Court in *Northeast Marine Terminal Co. supra.* 432 U.S. 249, 275, 97 S.Ct. 2348, 2363, 53 L.Ed.2d 320, 340 (1977). Subsequently it vacated the *I.T.O. Corp.* judgment and remanded the case for further consideration. 433 U.S. 904, 97 S.Ct. 2967, 53 L.Ed.2d 1088 (1977).

The Third Circuit has adopted a test based on whether the worker's job bears a "functional relationship" to the activities mentioned in the statutory definition of "employee." Dravo Corp. v. Maxin, 545 F.2d 374 (3d Cir.1976) held that the job of a worker in a steel structural shop "burning" steel plates that would ultimately become bottoms and decks of barges was an integral part of shipbuilding (as described in the 1967 Encyclopedia Britannica) and therefore satisfied the functional relationship test. In Alabama Dry Dock and Shipbuilding Co. v. Kininess, 554 F.2d 176 (5th Cir.1977), it was held that a worker who was injured while sandblasting a disassembled crane which would later be used for building ships was "directly involved" in shipbuilding and covered by the Act. The U.S. Supreme Court, in Director, Office of Workers' Compensation Programs v. Perini North River Assocs., 459 U.S. 297, 103 S.Ct. 634, 74 L.Ed.2d 465 (1983), suggested that any worker who had been covered prior to 1972 would continue to be covered under the 1972 amendment despite the newly added "status" test in Section 902. For a discussion of the opinion and its somewhat ambiguous meaning see 9–145 Larson's Workers' Compensation Law, Matthew Bender, § 145.02[8][d] (2013). Two years later, the Court in Herb's Welding, Inc. v. Gray, 470 U.S. 414, 105 S.Ct. 1421, 84 L.Ed.2d 406 (1985), distinguished and explained the *Perini* case: "We point out that [Perini] was carefully limited to coverage of an employee 'injured while performing his job on actual navigable waters. . . .' [Perini] says nothing about the contours of the status requirement as applied to a worker like Gray, who was not injured on navigable waters." The Court further stated: "As we have said, the maritime employment requirement is an occupational test that focuses on loading and unloading." The Court noted that the amendments were not meant "to cover employees who are not engaged in loading, unloading, repairing, or building a vessel, just because they are injured in an area adjoining navigable waters used for such activity." In a case in which the worker who was described as a data processor was allowed recovery, the Second Circuit held that while both situs and status are requirements of the Act, certain kinds of situs (e.g. physical presence on navigable waters) would fulfil the status requirement so long as the worker is not otherwise excluded from coverage. Lockheed Martin Corp. v. Marganti, 412 F.3d 407 (C.A.2, 2005).

The "twilight zone" continues to exist under the 1972 amendments. In Poche v. Avondale Shipyards, Inc., 339 So.2d 1212 (La.1976), decedents were engaged in new ship construction in a shipyard area located entirely over land when they were injured. The court held that the survivors could elect either a proceeding under the state workers' compensation act or under the Longshore Act. In Johnson v. Texas Employers Ins. Ass'n, 558 S.W.2d 47 (Tex.Civ.App.1977), plaintiff was an assistant crane operator in a fabrication shop at employer's shipyard about 75 to 100 feet from navigable water when he was injured. The court held that plaintiff was covered and eligible for benefits under the Longshore Act and also under the Texas compensation law and that an award could be had under both statutes with appropriate credit. In Parfait v. Deroche, 356 So.2d 1051 (La.App.1977), claimant was working as a fitter's helper and sustained an injury when he slipped on a synchrolift (a submerged apparatus designed to lift a vessel from the water). The court found that claimant was within the twilight zone and could elect to seek compensation under the Longshore Act or under the Louisiana compensation act. The U.S. Supreme Court, in Sun Ship, Inc. v. Pennsylvania, 447 U.S. 715, 100 S.Ct. 2432, 65 L.Ed.2d 458 (1980), confirmed these decisions holding: "Given that the pre-1972 Longshoremen's Act ran concurrently with state remedies in the 'maritime but local' zone, it follows that the post-1972 expansion of the Act landward would be concurrent as well. For state regulation of worker injuries is even more clearly appropriate ashore than it is upon navigable waters." See also, Bourgeois v. Puerto Rican Marine Management, Inc., 589 So.2d 1226 (La.App. 4th Cir.1991) (where stevedore's death occurred on land side of waterfront cargo facility, survivors could choose between state workers' compensation coverage or Longshore Act).

There are many more issues and problems associated with the 1972 amendments than it is possible to cover in this limited space. Excellent discussion is found in Larson, *The Conflicts Problem Between the Longshoremen's Act and State Workmen's Compensation Acts Under the 1972 Amendments,* 14 Houston L.Rev. 287 (1977); and, for general treatments of the area, see the following: Schoenbaum, Admiralty and Maritime Law, 5th Ed., §§ 5[1]-[14], West (2012); *"Maritime Employment" Coverage Under Longshoremen's and Harbor Workers' Compensation Act,* 41 A.L.R. Fed. 685 (2011); and, 9–145 Larson's Workers' Compensation Law, Matthew Bender, §§ 145.01 through 145.07[5] (2013).

8. JONES ACT

The Jones Act (Merchant Marine Act), 46 U.S.C.A. Section 30104 (formerly 46 U.S.C.A. Section 688, as amended in 2006 and 2008) provides as follows:

> "A seaman injured in the course of employment or, if the seaman dies from the injury, the personal representative of the seaman may elect to bring a civil action at law, with the right of trial by jury, against the employer. Laws of the United States regulating recovery for personal injury to, or death of, a railway employee apply to an action under this section."

The Act by its terms makes the Federal Employers' Liability Act (See Section 9, *infra*, and Chapter 1, Section 3, *supra*, and Appendix B, *infra*) applicable to cases involving the personal injury or death of a seaman.

Cases often arise in which the issue is whether the claimant's remedy, if any, is under the Jones Act, a state workers' compensation act, or the Longshore Act. The crucial inquiry in many of these cases is whether or not the claimant is a "seaman" within the meaning of the Jones Act. For example, in Wilkes v. Mississippi River Sand & Gravel Co., 202 F.2d 383 (6th Cir.1953), the injured employee worked on dredges in the Mississippi River loading barges with gravel as it was pumped from the riverbed. The Federal District Court held that the employee was not a "seaman" but was covered by the Longshore Act. A divided Court of Appeals reversed, holding that the employees who lived on board the dredge at their own option to take advantage of the free board and lodging, were sufficiently connected with the dangers of marine service to require a finding that they were seamen and could sue under the Jones Act. The *Wilkes* court also stated a three part test for determining "seaman" status developed in earlier cases: (1) the vessel must be in navigation; (2) the worker must be more or less permanently connected with the vessel; and (3) the worker must be aboard primarily to aid in navigation.

One of the most influential federal circuit court opinions defining "seaman" status was Offshore Company v. Robison, 266 F.2d 769 (5th Cir.1959). *Robison* noted the three-part test as referenced in *Wilkes* and recast the definition of "seaman" as follows:

> " . . . there is an evidentiary basis for a Jones Act case to go to the jury: (1) if there is evidence that the injured workman was assigned permanently to a vessel (including special purpose structures not usually employed as a means of transport by water but designed to float on water) or performed a substantial part of his work on the vessel; and (2) if the capacity in which he was employed or the duties which he performed contributed to the function of the vessel or the accomplishment of its mission, or to the operation or welfare of the vessel in terms of its maintenance during its movement or during anchorage for its future trips."

This opinion was followed in most federal courts over the next 32 years with the exception of the Seventh Circuit Court of Appeals. That court continued to apply the "aid in navigation" requirement. The U.S. Supreme Court, in McDermott v. Wilander, 498 U.S. 337, 111 S.Ct. 807, 112 L.Ed.2d 866 (1991), agreed with the *Robison* approach holding that the "aid in navigation" test should be jettisoned. That opinion reasoned that one need not aid in the navigation of a vessel or perform transportation related functions in order to qualify as a seaman; a foreman on a paint boat who directed the substantial work of sandblasting and painting off-shore drilling platforms was not precluded from having "seaman status" under the Jones Act.

Later Supreme Court decisions further refined the test of seaman status. See e.g. Chandris, Inc. v. Latsis, 515 U.S. 347, 115 S.Ct. 2172, 132 L.Ed.2d 314 (1995) (the test for seaman status has two essential elements: (1) the worker's duties must contribute to the function of the vessel or the accomplishment of its mission; and (2) the worker must have a connection to a vessel in navigation (or an identifiable group of vessels) that is substantial in both its duration and its nature). See also, Harbor Tug and Barge Co. v. Papai, 520 U.S. 548, 117 S.Ct. 1535, 137 L.Ed.2d 800 (1997) (agreeing with and explaining the *Chandris* language "substantial connection to a vessel or fleet of vessels").

Another requirement of the Jones Act is that the seaman must suffer personal injury or death while "in the course of his employment." Those who have seaman status do not automatically lose that status while on shore. They may recover under the Jones Act wherever they are injured in the course of their employment regardless of whether the injury occurs on or off the ship. See, e.g., O'Donnell v. Great Lakes Dredge & Dock Co., 318 U.S. 36, 63 S.Ct. 488, 87 L.Ed. 596 (1943); and Braen v. Pfeifer Oil

Transp. Co., 361 U.S. 129, 80 S.Ct. 247, 4 L.Ed.2d 191 (1959) (if the seaman is performing a task "pursuant to his employer's orders" he is in the course of his employment and covered by the Jones Act).

This can work to the disadvantage of the seaman where there is little or no chance of showing negligence on the part of the employer, a requirement of the Jones Act. In Rudolph v. Industrial Marine Service, 187 Tenn. 119, 213 S.W.2d 30 (1948) decedent was a member of the crew of a vessel that was docked and his employer ordered him to go into the city to purchase a faucet for the boat. While so engaged, he was hit by a train and killed. It was held that the Tennessee workers' compensation law was not applicable and that the exclusive remedy of the widow was under the Jones Act.

A seaman on shore leave is often considered to be in the course of employment. See, e.g., Daughenbaugh v. Bethlehem Steel Corp., Great Lakes S.S. Div., 891 F.2d 1199 (6th Cir.1989) (intoxicated seaman returning from shore leave was in course of employment); but see Colon v. Apex Marine Corp., 832 F.Supp. 508 (D.R.I.1993) (seaman on shore leave injured while attempting to break up a fight in a bar between two shipmates; held seaman was pursuing his own private interests and was not injured in the course of his employment).

The seaman's commute from a shore-based home to work on the vessel is addressed under the going and coming concept and the results vary. See, e.g., Daughdrill v. Diamond M. Drilling Co., 447 F.2d 781 (5th Cir.1971) (seaman was not on shore leave nor within the course of employment when killed in automobile accident while traveling from home to work after several days off duty); but see Williamson v. Western Pacific Dredging Corp., 441 F.2d 65 (9th Cir.1971) (allowing recovery for death sustained while commuting from home to dredge).

Because the Jones Act, when it is applicable, preempts the field involving injury or death suffered by seamen, claims under state workers' compensation acts are almost always precluded. Even though under the Jones Act the seamen or their dependents must prove employer negligence and the employer may assert the defense of pure comparative negligence, the more lucrative tort-type damages recoverable are usually thought to be preferable to the less generous benefits provided by state workers' compensation laws.

But, if there is no ability to prove employer negligence and thus no recovery available under the Jones Act (excluding the potential for the seaman to receive "maintenance and cure," a subject beyond the scope of this discussion) is it possible to apply state workers' compensation law to the claim? If not, the seaman and dependents may be left without remedy and those who provided medical, hospital and other care, services and subsistence may go unreimbursed.

In Maryland Casualty Co. v. Toups, 172 F.2d 542 (5th Cir.1949), all of this played a part in the court's decision. Decedent was a pilot of a boat that ferried pilots to seagoing vessels. On a day when his boat was undergoing repairs, he sat on the dock making fenders (cushions to soften the impact when docking the boat). While doing so, he fell into the water and drowned. Pointing out that there was no possibility of proving negligence under the Jones Act, the court held that the Texas workers' compensation law was applicable. (Citing Millers' Indemnity Underwriters v. Braud, 270 U.S. 59, 46 S.Ct. 194, 70 L.Ed. 470 (1926); Grant Smith–Porter Ship Co. v. Rohde, 257 U.S. 469, 42 S.Ct. 157, 66 L.Ed. 321 (1922); and Davis v. Dept. of Labor and Industries of Washington, 317 U.S. 249, 63 S.Ct. 225, 87 L.Ed. 246 (1942) (applying the "twilight zone" concept in context of Longshore and Harbor Workers Act; see Section 7, *supra*)).

On the other hand, the Mississippi court, in a case in which the decedent was clearly a seaman and died of a heart attack while on the vessel, refused to apply the Mississippi Workers' Compensation Act even though an action under the Jones Act held no promise for recovery. Valley Towing Co. v. Allen, 236 Miss. 51, 109 So.2d 538 (1959). See also, Indiana & Michigan Electric Co. v. Workers' Compensation Commissioner, 184 W.Va. 673, 403 S.E.2d 416 (1991) (Jones Act seaman injured while working on vessel in maritime waters precluded from filing claim under West Virginia's workers' compensation law; good discussion of "twilight zone" concept under Longshore Act as compared to Jones Act). Compare Cordova Fish & Cold Storage Co. v. Estes, 370 P.2d 180 (Alaska 1962) applying state workers' compensation act to fisherman injured while moving crab pots on deck of a boat tied to a dock and recognizing the "twilight zone" doctrine as applicable to Jones Act cases. See also, Anderson v. Alaska Packers Assn., 635 P.2d 1182 (Alaska 1981); Garrisey v. Westshore Marina Associates, 2 Wash.App. 718, 469 P.2d 590 (1970); and 9–146 Larson's Workers' Compensation Law, Matthew Bender, Sections 146.04[1]–[2] (2013). For a general treatment of the Jones Act, see Schoenbaum, Admiralty and Maritime Law, 5th Ed., §§ 4[20]-[24], West (2012).

9. FEDERAL EMPLOYERS' LIABILITY ACT

The Federal Employers' Liability Act (FELA), 45 U.S.C.A. sec. 51, et seq. (See Chapter 1, Section 3, *supra*, and Appendix B, *infra*) was first enacted by Congress in 1906, but declared unconstitutional by the United States Supreme Court as an invalid attempt to regulate intrastate commerce. See Employers Liability Cases, 207 U.S. 463, 28 S.Ct. 141, 52 L.Ed. 297 (1908). It was reenacted in 1908 in a form which carefully applied the Act only to interstate railroading activities. The 1908 enactment provided in part as follows: "every common carrier by railroad while engaging in commerce between any of the several states . . . shall be liable in damages to any person suffering injury while he is employed by such carrier in such commerce. . . ." The courts in applying this language used what was sometimes referred to as the "on the spot" or "pin-point" test. That test required a careful analysis to determine whether at the moment of the worker's injury, the worker was then and there engaged in interstate transportation or in work so closely related to it as to be practically a part of it. See, e.g., Shanks v. Delaware, L. & W.R. Co., 239 U.S. 556, 36 S.Ct. 188, 60 L.Ed. 436 (1916).

If the "on the spot" test did not bring the employee within coverage of the FELA, the worker would be left to pursue a state remedy. As the states began to enact workers' compensation legislation, the likelihood of conflict between the newly enacted workers' compensation acts and the FELA was significant because of the fact-sensitive nature of the "on the spot" test.

As commerce clause jurisprudence was evolving, Congress in 1939 amended the FELA substantially expanding its reach by covering "any employee of a[n] [interstate rail] carrier, any part of whose duties . . . shall be the furtherance of interstate or foreign commerce; or shall in any way directly or closely and substantially affect such commerce. . . ."

The U.S. Supreme Court interpreted this language expansively in Reed v. Pennsylvania Railroad Co., 351 U.S. 502, 76 S.Ct. 958, 100 L.Ed. 1366 (1956), holding that a clerical employee for the Pennsylvania Railroad was covered by the FELA. The Court reasoned that the 1939 amendment " . . . evinces a purpose to expand coverage substantially as well as to avoid narrow distinctions in deciding questions of coverage. Under the amendment, it is the 'duties' of the employee that must further or affect commerce, and it is enough if 'any part' of those duties has the requisite effect."

After *Reed*, it is plausible to argue that virtually every worker employed by an interstate rail carrier is covered by the FELA. See 9–147 Larson's Workers' Compensation Law, Matthew Bender, § 147.06 (2013).

Because the FELA preempts the field involving injury or death of a covered railway worker, it will be much less likely, following the *Reed* case, that employees of interstate rail carriers will be able to maintain claims under state workers' compensation laws. Thus the likelihood of a conflict of laws issue arising is much reduced. Again, as was pointed out in Section 8, *supra*, this can work to the disadvantage of injured workers or their dependents because under the FELA employer negligence must be proven and the employer may assert the defense of pure comparative negligence.

Lastly, there is a potential for conflict between the Longshore Act and the FELA. For a discussion of that issue, see 9–147 Larson's Workers' Compensation Law, Matthew Bender, § 147.01[2] (2013).

APPENDIX A

WORKMEN'S COMPENSATION AND REHABILITATION LAW

■ ■ ■

(Revised)

THE COUNCIL OF STATE GOVERNMENTS

Lexington, Kentucky

Analysis

WORKMEN'S COMPENSATION AND REHABILITATION LAW

PART I. COVERAGE AND LIABILITY

Section

1. Liability for Compensation.
2. Definitions.
3. Coverage of Employers.
4. Coverage of Employees.
5. Exemptions.
6. Voluntary Coverage.
7. Extraterritorial Coverage.
8. Inmates of Public Institutions. (omitted)
9. Presumption.
10. Exclusiveness of Liability.
11. Third Party Liability.

PART II. MEDICAL, REHABILITATION AND BURIAL SERVICES

Section

12. Medical Services, Appliances and Supplies.

PART III. INCOME BENEFITS

Section

PART IV. PROCEDURES

Section

PART V. INSURANCE

Section

PART VI. ADMINISTRATION

Section

Suggested Legislation

(Title, enacting clause, etc.)

PART I. COVERAGE AND LIABILITY

Section 1. [*Liability for Compensation.*]

(a) Every employer subject to this act shall be liable for compensation for injury or death without regard to fault as a cause of the injury or death.

(b) A contractor who subcontracts all or any part of a contract and his carrier shall be liable for the payment of compensation to the employees of the subcontractor unless the subcontractor primarily liable for the payment of such compensation has secured the payment of compensation as provided for in this act. Any contractor or his carrier who shall become liable for such compensation may recover the amount of such compensation paid and necessary expenses from the subcontractor primarily liable therefor. A person who contracts with another (1) to have work performed consisting of (a) the removal, excavation or drilling of soil, rock or minerals, or (b) the cutting or removal of timber from land, or (2) to have work performed of a kind which is a regular or recurrent part of the work of the trade, business, occupation or profession of such person, shall for the purposes of this section be deemed a contractor, and such other person a subcontractor. This subsection shall not apply to the owner or lessee of land principally used for agriculture who contracts for removal of timber from such land.

(c) Liability for compensation shall not apply where injury to the employee was occasioned solely by his intoxication or by his willful intention to injure or kill himself or another.

Section 2. [*Definitions.*]

As used in this act unless the context otherwise requires:

(a) "Injury" means any harmful change in the human organism arising out of and in the course of employment, including damage to or loss of a prosthetic appliance, but does not include any communicable disease unless the risk of contracting such disease is increased by the nature of the employment.[1]

(b) "Death" means death resulting from an injury.

(c) "Carrier" means any insurer, or legal representative thereof, authorized to insure the liabilities of employers under this act and includes a self-insurer.

(d) "Self-insurer" is an employer who has been authorized under the provisions of this act to carry his own liability to his employees covered by this act.

(e) "Agency" means the [name of state administrative agency].

(f) "Director" means the director of the [name of state administrative agency].

(g) "Board" means the [Workmen's Compensation Appeals Board].

(h) "Disability" means, except for purposes of Section 16(c) relating to schedule losses, a decrease of wage-earning capacity due to injury. Wage-earning capacity prior to injury shall be the average weekly wage as calculated under Section 19. Wage-earning capacity after the injury shall be presumed to be actual earnings after the injury. This presumption may be overcome by showing that these earnings after injury do not fairly and reasonably represent wage-earning capacity, and in such cases, wage-earning capacity shall be determined in the light of all factors and circumstances in the case which may affect the injured worker's capacity to earn wages.

(i) "Income benefits" means payments made under the provisions of this act to the injured worker or his dependents in case of death, excluding medical and related benefits.

(j) "Medical and related benefits" means payments made for medical, hospital, burial and other services as provided in this act other than income benefits.

(k) "Compensation" means all payments made under the provisions of this act, representing the sum of income benefits and medical and related benefits.

---

[1] Section 2(a) complies with the recommendations of the National Commission on State Workmen's Compensation Laws pertaining to coverage of work-related injuries and diseases. There is, however, a difference between the terminology used by the Report of the National Commission and the terminology used in Section 2(a), and the purpose of this note is to clarify the difference.

The Report defines "injury" as "damage to the body resulting from an acute traumatic episode" and "disease" as "damage to the body resulting from a cause other than an injury." Section 2(a) defines "injury" broadly so that the term encompasses both "injury" and "disease" as those terms are defined in the Report. The consequence is that the coverage of injuries and diseases prescribed by the Report and the coverage prescribed by Section 2(a) are equivalent.

(l) "Medical services" means medical, surgical, dental, hospital, nursing and medical rehabilitation services.

(m) "Person" means any individual, partnership, firm, association, trust, corporation, [state compensation insurance fund], or legal representative thereof.

(n) "Wages" means, in addition to money payments for services rendered, the reasonable value of board, rent, housing, lodging, fuel or similar advantage received from the employer, and gratuities received in the course of employment from others than the employer.

(o) "Agriculture" means the operation of farm premises, including the planting, cultivating, producing, growing and harvesting of agricultural or horticultural commodities thereon, the raising of livestock and poultry thereon, and any work performed as an incident to or in conjunction with such farm operations. It shall not include the processing, packing, drying, storing, or canning of such commodities for market, or making cheese or butter or other dairy products for market.

(p) "United States," when used in a geographic sense, means the several States, the District of Columbia, the Commonwealth of Puerto Rico, the Canal Zone and the Territories of the United States.

(q) "Alien" means a person who is not a citizen, a national or a resident of the United States or Canada. Any person not a citizen or national of the United States who relinquishes or is about to relinquish his residence in the United States shall be regarded as an alien.

(r) "Beneficiary" means any person who is entitled to income benefits or medical and related benefits under this act.

(s) "Actually dependent" means dependent in fact upon the employee, and refers only to a person who received more than half of his support from the employee and whose dependency is not the result of failure to make reasonable efforts to secure suitable employment. When used as a noun, the word "dependent" means any person entitled to death benefits under Section 18, or any person for whom added benefits for disability are provided under Section 16.

(t) As used in Sections 16 and 18:

(1) "Wife" or "Widow" means only the employee's wife living with or actually dependent upon him at the time of his injury or

death, or living apart for justifiable cause or by reason of his desertion.

(2) "Widower" means only the deceased employee's husband living with and actually dependent upon her.

(3) "Child" means a child under 18 years of age; or a child 18 years of age or over and physically or mentally incapable of self-support; or any child 18 years of age or over who is actually dependent; or any child between 18 and 25 years of age who is enrolled as a full-time student in any accredited educational institution. The term "child" includes a post-humous child, a child legally adopted or for whom adoption proceedings are pending at the time of death, an actually dependent child in relation to whom the deceased employee stood in the place of a parent for at least one year prior to the time of death, an actually dependent stepchild or an actually dependent acknowledged illegitimate child. "Child" does not include a married child unless receiving substantially entire support from the employee. "Grandchild" means a child, as above defined, of a child as above defined, except that as to the latter child, the limitations as to age in the above definition do not apply.

(4) "Brother" or "sister" means a brother or sister under 18 years of age, or 18 years of age or over and physically or mentally incapable of self-support, or 18 years of age or over and actually dependent. The terms "brother" and "sister" include stepbrothers and stepsisters, half brothers and half sisters, and brothers and sisters by adoption; but the terms do not include married brothers or married sisters unless receiving substantially entire support from the employee.

(5) "Parent" means a mother or father, a stepparent, a parent by adoption, a parent-in-law, and any person who for more than one year immediately prior to the death of the employee stood in the place of a parent to him, if actually dependent in each case.

(6) All questions of relationship and dependency shall initially be determined as of the time of injury for purposes of income benefits for injury, and as of the time of death for purposes of income benefits for death.

Section 3. [*Coverage of Employers.*]

The following shall constitute employers subject to the provisions of this act:

(a) Every person that has in the State one or more employees subject to this act.

(b) The State, any agency thereof, and each county, city, town, township, incorporated village, school district, sewer district, drainage district, public or quasi-public corporation, or any other political subdivision of the State that has one or more employees subject to this act.

Section 4. [*Coverage of Employees.*]

The following shall constitute employees subject to the provisions of this act, except as exempted under Section 5:

(a) Every person, including a minor, whether lawfully or unlawfully employed, in the service of an employer under any contract of hire or apprenticeship, express or implied, and all helpers and assistants of employees whether paid by the employer or employee, if employed with the knowledge, actual or constructive, of the employer.

(b) Every executive officer of a corporation.

(c) Every person in the service of the State or of any political subdivision or agency thereof, under any contract of hire, express or implied, and every official or officer thereof, whether elected or appointed, while performing his official duties. Every person who is a member of a volunteer fire or police department shall be deemed, for the purpose of this act, to be in the employment of the political subdivision of the State where the department is organized. Every person who is a regularly enrolled volunteer member or trainee of the civil defense corps of this State as established under the [State Civil Defense Act] shall be deemed, for the purpose of this act, to be in the employment of the State.

(d) Every person performing service in the course of the trade, business, profession or occupation of an employer at the time of the injury, provided such person in relation to this service does not maintain a separate business, does not hold himself out to and render service to the public, and is not himself an employer subject to this act.

(e) Subject to the proviso in subsection (d) of this section, every person regularly selling or distributing newspapers on the street or to customers at their homes or places of business. For the purposes of this act such a person shall be deemed an employee of any independent news agency for whom he is selling or distributing newspapers or, in the absence of such independent agency, of each publisher whose newspapers he sells or distributes.

Section 5. [*Exemptions.*]

The following employees are exempt from the coverage of this act:

(a) Any person employed in agriculture by an employer who has an annual payroll that in total is less than $1,000. This exemption shall terminate on July 1, 1975.

(b) Any person employed as a household worker in a private home or household who earns less than $50 in cash in any three-month period from a single private home or household and any person employed as a casual worker in a private home or household who earns less than $50 in cash in any three-month period from a single private home or household.

Section 6. [*Voluntary Coverage.*]

(a) An employer who has in his employment any employee exempted under Section 5 may elect to be subject to this act. Such election on the part of the employer shall be made by the employer's securing the payment of compensation to such exempted employees in accordance with Section 46. Any employee, otherwise exempted under Section 5, of such employer shall be deemed to have elected to come under this act if, at the time of the injury for which liability is claimed, such employer has in force an election to be subject to this act with respect to the employment in which such employee was injured and such employee has not, either upon entering into the employment or within five days after the filing of an election by the employer, given to such employer and to the Director notice in writing that he elects not to be subject to this act.

(b) Such employer, within five days after securing the payment of compensation in accordance with Section 46, shall give the Director written notice of his election to be subject to this act. Such employer shall post and keep posted on the premises, where any employee or employees otherwise exempted under Section 5 works, printed notices furnished by the Director stating his acceptance of this act. Failure to give the notices required by this paragraph shall not void or impair the employer's election to be subject to or relieve him of any liability under this act.

(c) Any employer who has complied with subsection (b) of this section may withdraw his acceptance of this act by filing written notice with the Director of the withdrawal of his acceptance. Such withdrawal shall become effective 60 days after the filing of such notice or on the date of the termination of the security for payment of compensation, whichever last occurs. The employer shall theretofore post notice of such withdrawal where the affected employee or employees work or shall otherwise notify such employees of such withdrawal.

Section 7. [*Extraterritorial Coverage.*]

(a) If an employee, while working outside the territorial limits of this State, suffers an injury on account of which he, or in the event of his death, his dependents, would have been entitled to the benefits provided by this act had such injury occurred within this State, such employee, or in the event of his death resulting from such injury, his dependents, shall be entitled to the benefits provided by this act, provided that at the time of such injury

(1) his employment is principally localized in this State, or

(2) he is working under a contract of hire made in this State in employment not principally localized in any State, or

(3) he is working under a contract of hire made in this State in employment principally localized in another State whose workmen's compensation law is not applicable to his employer, or

(4) he is working under a contract of hire made in this State for employment outside the United States and Canada.

(b) The payment or award of benefits under the workmen's compensation law of another State, territory, province, or foreign nation to an employee or his dependents otherwise entitled on account of such injury or death to the benefits of this act shall not be a bar to a claim for benefits under this act; provided that claim under this act is filed within the time limits set forth in Section 26. If compensation is paid or awarded under this act:

(1) The medical and related benefits furnished or paid for by the employer under such other workmen's compensation law on account of such injury or death shall be credited against the medical and related benefits to which the employee would have been entitled under this act had claim been made solely under this act;

(2) The total amount of all income benefits paid or awarded the employee under such other workmen's compensation law shall be credited against the total amount of income benefits which would have been due the employee under this act, had claim been made solely under this act;

(3) The total amount of death benefits paid or awarded under such other workmen's compensation law shall be credited against the total amount of death benefits due under this act.

(c) If an employee is entitled to the benefits of this act by reason of an injury sustained in this State in employment by an employer who is domiciled in another State and who has not secured the payment of compensation as required by this act, the employer or his carrier may file with the Director a certificate, issued by the commission or agency of such other State having jurisdiction over workmen's compensation claims, certifying that such employer has secured the payment of compensation under the workmen's compensation law of such other State and that with respect to said injury such employee is entitled to the benefits provided under such law. In such event:

(1) The filing of such certificate shall constitute an appointment by such employer or his carrier of the Director as his agent for acceptance of the service of process in any proceeding brought by such employee or his dependents to enforce his or their rights under this act on account of such injury;

(2) The Director shall send to such employer or carrier, by registered or certified mail to the address shown on such certificate, a true copy of any notice of claim or other process served on the Director by the employee or his dependents in any proceeding brought to enforce his or their rights under this act;

(3) (i) If such employer is a qualified self-insurer under the workmen's compensation law of such other State, such employer shall, upon submission of evidence, satisfactory to the Director, of his ability to meet his liability to such employee under this act, be deemed to be a qualified self-insurer under this act;

(ii) If such employer's liability under the workmen's compensation law of such other State is insured, such employer's carrier, as to such employee or his dependents only, shall be deemed to be an insurer authorized to write insurance under and be subject to this act; provided, however, that unless its contract with said employer requires it to pay an amount equivalent to the compensation benefits provided by this act, its liability for income benefits or medical and related benefits shall not exceed the amounts of such benefits for which such insurer would have been liable under the workmen's compensation law of such other State;

(4) If the total amount for which such employer's insurance is liable under (3) above is less than the total of the compensation benefits to which such employee is entitled under this act, the Director may, if he deems it necessary,

require the employer to file security, satisfactory to the Director, to secure the payment of benefits due such employee or his dependents under this act; and

(5) Upon compliance with the preceding requirements of this subsection (c), such employer, as to such employee only, shall be deemed to have secured the payment of compensation under this act.

(d) As used in this section:

(1) "United States" includes only the States of the United States and the District of Columbia;

(2) "State" includes any State of the United States, the District of Columbia, or any Province of Canada;

(3) "Carrier" includes any insurance company licensed to write workmen's compensation insurance in any State of the United States or any State or provincial fund which insures employers against their liabilities under a workmen's compensation law;

(4) A person's employment is principally localized in this or another State when (1) his employer has a place of business in this or such other State and he regularly works at or from such place of business, or (2) if clause (1) foregoing is not applicable, he is domiciled and spends a substantial part of his working time in the service of his employer in this or such other State;

(5) An employee whose duties require him to travel regularly in the service of his employer in this and one or more other States may, by written agreement with his employer, provide that his employment is principally localized in this or another such State, and, unless such other State refuses jurisdiction, such agreement shall be given effect under this act;

(6) "Workmen's compensation law" includes "occupational disease law."

Section 8. [*Inmates of Public Institutions.*] (omitted)

Section 9. [*Presumption.*]

In any claim for compensation, where the employee has been killed, or is physically or mentally unable to testify, and where there is unrebutted prima facie evidence that indicates that the injury arose in the course of employment, it shall be presumed, in the absence of substantial evidence to the contrary, that the injury arose out of the employment, that sufficient notice of the injury has been given, and that the injury or death was not occasioned solely by the employee's intoxication or by his willful intention to injure or kill himself or another.

Section 10. [*Exclusiveness of Liability.*]

(a) If an employer secures payment of compensation as required by this act, the liability of such employer under this act shall be exclusive and in place of all other liability of such employer to the employee, his legal representative, husband or wife, parents, dependents, next of kin, and anyone otherwise entitled to recover damages from such employer at law or in admiralty on account of such injury or death. For purposes of this section, the term "employer" shall include a "contractor" covered by Section 1(b), whether or not the subcontractor has, in fact, secured the payment of compensation. The liability of an employer to another person who may be liable for or who has paid damages on account of injury or death of an employee of such employer arising out of and in the course of employment and caused by a breach of any duty or obligation owed by such employer to such other shall be limited to the amount of compensation and other benefits for which such employer is liable under this act on account of such injury or death, unless such other and the employer by written contract have agreed to share liability in a different manner. The exemption from liability given an employer by this section shall also extend to such employer's carrier and to all employees, officers or directors of such employer or carrier, provided the exemption from liability given an employee, officer or director of an employer or carrier shall not apply in any case where the injury or death is proximately caused by the willful and unprovoked physical aggression of such employee, officer or director.

(b) If an employer fails to secure payment of compensation as required by this act, an injured employee, or his legal representative in case death results from the injury, may claim compensation under this act and in addition may maintain an action at law or in admiralty for damages on account of such injury or death, provided that the amount of compensation shall be credited against the amount received in such action, and provided that, if the amount of compensation is larger than the amount of damages received, the amount of damages less the employee's legal fees and expenses shall be credited against the amount of compensation. In such action the defendant may not plead as a defense that the injury was caused by the negligence of a fellow servant, that the employee assumed the risks of his employment, or that the injury was due to the contributory negligence of the employee.

Section 11. [*Third Party Liability.*]

(a) The right to income and other benefits under this act, whether for disability or death, shall not be affected by the fact that the injury or death is caused under circumstances creating a legal liability in some person (other than the employer or another person exempt from liability under Section 10 of this act) to pay damages therefor, such person so liable being hereinafter referred to as the third party. The respective rights and interests of the injured employee, or, in case of his death, his dependents and [any person entitled to sue therefor], and of the employer or person, association, corporation or carrier liable for the payment of compensation benefits under this act, hereinafter called "the carrier," in respect to the cause of action and the damages recovered shall be as provided by this section.

(b) The injured employee, or, in event of his death, his dependents, shall be entitled to receive the income and other benefits provided by this act and to enforce by appropriate proceedings his or their rights against the third party, provided that action against the third party must be commenced not later than [six months]**2** after the carrier accepts liability for the payment of compensation or makes such payment pursuant to an award under this act, except as hereinafter provided. In such case the carrier shall have a lien on the proceeds of any recovery from the third party whether by judgment, settlement or otherwise, after the deduction of reasonable and necessary expenditures, including attorneys' fees, incurred in effecting such recovery, to the extent of the total amount of compensation paid, and to such extent such recovery shall be deemed to be for the benefit of the carrier. Any balance remaining after payment of necessary expenses and satisfaction of the carrier's lien shall be applied as a credit against future compensation benefits for the same injury or death and shall be distributed as provided in subsection (g) of this section. Notice of the commencement of such action shall be given within 30 days thereafter to the Director, the employer and carrier upon a form prescribed by the Director.

(c) If, prior to the expiration of the six months period referred to in subsection (b), or within 90 days prior to the expiration of the time in which such action may be brought, whichever occurs first, the injured employee, or, in event of his death, [the person entitled to sue therefor] shall not have commenced action against or settled with the third party, the right of action of the injured employee,

[2] The language in this section should in each State be modified to fit (1) in reference to an action for injury, the state statute of limitations applicable thereto and (2) in reference to an action for death, the death statute, including limitations, of that State.

or, in event of his death, [the person entitled to sue therefor] shall pass by assignment to the carrier; provided, that such assignment shall not occur less than 20 days after the carrier has notified the injured employee or, in the event of his death, [the person entitled to sue therefor] in writing, by personal service or by registered or certified mail that failure to commence such action will operate as an assignment of the cause of action to the carrier. Prior to the expiration of 90 days after such assignment, the carrier shall give the Director, the injured employee, or, in event of his death, his dependents and [the person entitled to sue therefor] notice, upon a form prescribed by the Director, that action has been or will be commenced against the third party. Failure to give such notice, or to commence such action at least 30 days prior to the expiration of the time within which such action may be brought, as fixed by [state statute of limitations], shall operate as a reassignment of such right of action to the injured employee or, in event of his death, [to the person entitled to sue therefor], and the rights and obligations of the parties shall be as provided by subsection (b) of this section.

If the carrier as such assignee recovers in an action (1) for injury, an amount in excess of the sum of the total of compensation paid or provided the injured employee and the reasonable expenses, including attorneys' fees, incurred in making such recovery, or (2) for death, an amount on behalf of the dependents of the employee in excess of the sum of the income benefits paid such dependents, and the reasonable expenses, including attorneys' fees, incurred in making such recovery, such excess shall be applied as a credit against future compensation benefits for the same injury or death and shall be distributed in accordance with subsection (g) of this section.

(d) If the persons entitled to share in the proceeds of an action brought under subsection (b) or (c) for death of the employee include any person who was not a dependent of the deceased employee, such person's share of any recovery made in such action, less a rateable share of the reasonable expenses incurred in making such recovery, shall be paid to such person or to the personal representative of the deceased.

(e) The injured employee, or, in event of his death, his dependents, and the carrier may, by agreement approved by the Director, or in event of a settlement made during actual trial of the action against the third party, approved by the judge presiding at such trial, provide for a distribution of the proceeds of any recovery in such action different from that prescribed by subsection (b) or (c) of this section.

(f) If the third party, with notice or knowledge of the carrier's lien, and the employee, or, in the event of his death, [the person entitled to sue therefor], make a compromise settlement without the written consent of the carrier for an amount less than the total of the compensation to which he or they are entitled under this act because of such injury or death, such settlement shall be invalid as against the carrier, which shall be entitled to maintain an action against the third party to recover the amount of compensation for which the carrier is liable under this act, less the amount actually inuring to the benefit of the carrier from the proceeds of such settlement.

At the trial of such action the fact of such settlement shall be prima facie evidence that the injury was proximately caused by a breach of duty owed to the employee or a warranty given by the third party.

The carrier shall not unreasonably refuse to approve a proposed compromise settlement with the third party. The injured employee or his dependents may make written application to the Director for a finding that a proposed compromise settlement with the third party is reasonable and fair to all parties. If the Director, after such inquiry as he deems necessary, and after hearing if demanded by either the carrier, the injured employee or his dependents, finds the proposed settlement reasonable and fair, it shall be deemed to have been approved by the carrier.

(g) When there remains a balance of $5,000 or more of the amount recovered from a third party by the beneficiary or carrier after payment of necessary expenses, and satisfaction of the carrier's lien and payment of the share of any person not a beneficiary under the act which is applicable as a credit against future compensation benefits for the same injury or death under either subsection (b) or subsection (c) of this section, the entire balance shall in the first instance be paid to the carrier by the third party. The present value of all amounts estimated by the Director to be thereafter payable as compensation, such present value to be computed in accordance with a schedule prepared by the Director, shall be held by the carrier as a fund to pay such future compensation as it becomes due, and to pay any sum finally remaining in excess thereof to the beneficiaries.

As soon as the Director has fixed the amount to be held by the carrier in such fund, or determined that no future compensation will be due, any excess of the third party recovery over the total amount necessary for payment of necessary expenses, satisfaction of the carrier's lien, and payment of the share of any person not a beneficiary under this act and creation of such fund, if any, shall be paid forthwith to the beneficiary, but shall continue to constitute a credit against future compensation benefits for the same injury or death as to any compensation liability that may exist after such fund has been exhausted.

(h) If death results from the injury and if the employee leaves no dependents entitled to benefits under this act, the carrier shall have a right of action against the third party for any amounts paid into the Special Fund established by Section 55, for reasonable funeral expenses and medical benefits actually paid by the carrier, and such cause of action shall be in addition to any cause of action of the legal representative of the deceased. Such right may be enforced in action at law brought against the third party within two years after the death of the employee.

PART II. MEDICAL, REHABILITATION AND BURIAL SERVICES

Section 12. [*Medical Services, Appliances and Supplies.*]

(a) For any injury covered by this act, the employee shall be entitled, without limitation as to time or dollar amount, to all medical services, appliances and supplies which are required by the nature of his injury and which will relieve pain and promote and hasten his restoration to health and employment. The employer shall furnish such services, appliances and supplies and necessary replacements or repairs of such appliances unless the need for such replacements or repairs is due to lack of proper care by the employee. In addition to the income benefits otherwise payable, the employee, who is entitled to income benefits, shall be paid an additional sum as for a medical benefit of not more than $50 weekly, as may be deemed necessary, when the service of an attendant is necessary constantly to be used by reason of the employee's being totally blind or having lost both hands or both feet or the use thereof or being paralyzed and unable to walk, or by reason of other disability resulting from the injury actually rendering him so helpless as to require constant attendance. The Director shall have authority to determine the necessity, character and sufficiency of any medical services furnished or to be furnished and shall have authority to order a change of physician, hospital or rehabilitation facility when in his judgment such change is desirable or necessary.

Alternative 1 for Section 12(b)

[(b) (1) Subject to the approval of the Director, the employer shall maintain a list of physicians (to be known as the Panel of

Physicians) who are reasonably accessible to the employees. The employer shall post this list in a place or places easily accessible to his employees.

(2) The employee shall have the right to accept the services of a physician selected by his employer or to select a physician from the Panel of Physicians. The employee shall have the right to make an alternative choice of physician from such Panel if he is not satisfied with the physician first selected. If due to the nature of the injury or its occurrence away from the employer's place of business, the employer or the employee is unable to make a selection as outlined above, the selection requirements of this paragraph shall not apply as long as the inability to make a selection persists. The physician selected under this paragraph may arrange for any consultation, referral, extraordinary or other specialized medical services as the nature of the injury shall require. The employer shall not be responsible for the charges for medical services furnished or ordered by any physician or other person selected by the employee in disregard of the provisions of this paragraph or for compensation for any aggravation of the employee's injury attributable to improper treatment by such physician or other person.

(3) The Director may order necessary changes in a Panel of Physicians if he finds that it fails to contain a sufficient number of physicians who are conveniently available to or in the community in which the medical service is required and who are qualified to perform services necessary to meet the particular needs of employees of the employer. The Director may suspend or remove a physician from a Panel of Physicians under rules and regulations adopted by the Director.

(4) If the employer has knowledge of an injury to an employee and the necessity for treatment and shall fail to maintain the Panel of Physicians, or permit an employee to make choice of his physician from such Panel, the injured employee may select a physician to render service at the expense of the employer. No claim for such medical treatment shall be valid and enforceable against such employer, unless within 10 days following the first treatment the physician giving such treatment furnish the employer and the Director a report of such injury and treatment on a form prescribed by the Director. The Director may, however, excuse the failure to furnish such report within 10 days when he finds it to be in the interest of justice to do so, and may, upon application by a party in interest, make an award for the reasonable value of such medical treatment so obtained by the employee.]

Alternative 2 for Section 12(b)

[(b) (1) The employee shall have the right to make the initial selection of his physician from a Panel of Physicians selected by the workmen's compensation agency.

(2) The Director shall select a list of physicians (to be known as the Panel of Physicians) who are reasonably accessible to the employees and shall furnish this list to the employer who shall post it in a place or places easily accessible to his employees.

(3) The employee shall have the right to make an alternative choice of physician from such Panel if he is not satisfied with the physician first selected. If due to the nature of the injury or its occurrence away from the employer's place of business, the employee is unable to make a selection as outlined above, the selection requirements of this paragraph shall not apply as long as the inability to make a selection persists. The physician selected under this paragraph may arrange for any consultation, referral, extraordinary or other specialized medical services as the nature of the injury shall require.

(4) The employer shall not be responsible for the charges for medical services furnished or ordered by any physician or other person selected by the employee in disregard of the provisions of this subsection or for compensation for any aggravation of the employee's injury attributable to improper treatment by such physician or other person.

(5) The Director may make necessary changes in a Panel of Physicians if he finds that it fails to contain a sufficient number of physicians who are conveniently available to or in the community in which the medical service is required and who are qualified to perform services necessary to meet the particular needs of employees of the employer. The Director may suspend or remove a physician from a Panel of Physicians under rules and regulations adopted by the Director.]

Alternative 3 for Section 12(b)

[(b) (1) The employee shall have the right to make the initial selection of his physician from among all licensed physicians in the State.

(2) The employee shall have the right to make an alternative choice of physician if he is not satisfied with the physician first selected. If due to the nature of the injury or its occurrence away from the employer's place of business the employee is unable to make a selection, the selection requirements of this paragraph shall not apply as long as the inability to make a selection

persists. The physician selected under this paragraph may arrange for any consultation, referral, extraordinary or other specialized medical services as the nature of the injury shall require.

(3) The employer shall not be responsible for the charges for medical services furnished or ordered by any physician or other person selected by the employee in disregard of the provisions of this subsection or for compensation for any aggravation of the employee's injury attributable to improper treatment by such physician or other person.]

Section 13. [*Rehabilitation.*]

(a) One of the primary purposes of this act shall be restoration of the injured employee to gainful employment. To this end there is hereby created a Rehabilitation Unit within the Agency which shall be composed of specialists in medical and vocational rehabilitation to be appointed by the Director.

(b) The Unit shall continuously study the problems of rehabilitation, both physical and vocational, and shall investigate and maintain a directory of all rehabilitation facilities, both private and public. The Director, in consultation with the Unit, shall approve as qualified such facilities, institutions and physicians as are capable of rendering competent rehabilitation service to seriously injured employees. No facility or institution shall be considered as qualified unless it is specifically equipped to provide rehabilitation services for persons suffering either from some specialized type of disability or general type of disability within the field of occupational injury and is staffed with trained and qualified personnel, and with respect to physical rehabilitation, unless it is supervised by a physician qualified to render such service. No physician shall be considered qualified unless he has had the experience and training specified by the Director.

(c) An employee who has suffered an injury covered by this act shall be entitled to prompt medical rehabilitation services. When as a result of the injury he is unable to perform work for which he has previous training or experience, he shall be entitled to such vocational rehabilitation services, including retraining and job placement, as may be reasonably necessary to restore him to suitable employment. If such services are not voluntarily offered and accepted, the Director on his own motion, or upon application of the employee or carrier, after affording the parties an opportunity to be heard, may refer the employee to a qualified physician or facility for evaluation of the practicability of, need for, and kind of service, treatment or training necessary and appropriate to render him fit for a remunerative occupation. Upon receipt of such report, and after affording the parties an opportunity to be heard, the Director, in consultation with the Unit, may order that the services and treatment recommended in the report, or such other rehabilitation treatment or service he may deem necessary, be provided at the expense of the employer.

(d) Where rehabilitation requires residence at or near the facility or institution away from the employee's customary residence, reasonable cost of his board, lodging or travel shall be paid for by the employer.

(e) Refusal to accept rehabilitation pursuant to an order of the Director shall result in loss of compensation for each week of the period of refusal.

(f) The Director and the Rehabilitation Unit shall cooperate on a reciprocal basis with the vocational rehabilitation section of the [Department of Education] and the employment service of the [Division of Employment Security].

Section 14. [*Burial Expense.*]

If death results from the injury, the employer shall pay the cost of burying in an amount not to exceed [$___] to any person who performed such service or incurred the liability for the service, whether or not the employee leaves dependents within the meaning of this act. Any such person is hereby authorized to file a petition with the Director for the fixing of the amount of the service and for an order requiring the employer to pay the cost of the service. If death occurs while the employee is away from his usual place of business or residence, the employer will be liable for the reasonable cost of transportation of the body to the employee's place of residence within the United States or Canada.

PART III. INCOME BENEFITS

Section 15. [*Waiting Period.*]

No income benefits shall be allowed for the first three days of the disability; provided, however, that in case the injury results in disability of 14 or more days, income benefits shall be allowed from the date of the disability. The day on which the injury occurred shall be included in computing this waiting period unless the employee has been paid full wages for that day.

Section 16. [*Income Benefits for Disability.*]

Income benefits for disability shall be paid to the employee as follows, subject to the maximum and minimum limits specified in Section 17.

(a) Total Disability: For total disability, $66\frac{2}{3}$ percent of his average weekly wage during such disability.

(b) Partial Disability: For partial disability, $66\frac{2}{3}$ percent of his decrease in wage-earning capacity during the continuance thereof.

(c) Scheduled Income Benefits:[3] For total permanent bodily loss or losses herein scheduled, after and in addition to the income benefits payable during the period of recovery, scheduled income benefits in the amount of 55 percent of the average weekly wage as follows:

	Bodily Loss	Weeks of Disability[4]
(1)	Arm	[240–360]
(2)	Leg	[160–240]
(3)	Hand	[216–324]
(4)	Foot	[112–168]
(5)	Thumb	[86–130]
(6)	Index Finger	[54–81]
(7)	Middle Finger	[43–65]
(8)	Ring Finger	[22–32]
(9)	Little Finger	[11–16]
(10)	Great Toe	[20–30]
(11)	Second Toe	[10–20]
(12)	Third Toe	[5–15]
(13)	Fourth Toe	[5– 8]
(14)	Fifth Toe	[5]
(15)	Total loss of binaural hearing	[156–208]
(16)	Total loss of vision of one eye	[100–150]

[3] The Report of the National Commission on State Workmen's Compensation Laws did not make a recommendation with respect to the 55 percent figure in this subsection and, therefore, this Committee made no change in the suggested language. However, a State may wish to raise this figure to $66\frac{2}{3}$ percent so as to be consistent with subsections (a) and (b).

[4] The number of weeks in which scheduled income benefits are payable are based on 400 and 600 weeks respectively for the whole man and the American Medical Association's evaluation of the relationship of total loss or impairment of the particular member to the whole man. See the American Medical Association's Guides to the Evaluation of Permanent Impairment.

(17) Total loss of bilateral vision [520–750]

(18) Total loss, or total loss of use, of both hands, both arms, both feet or both legs [520–750]

(19) Phalanges: For loss of distal phalanx, one half of the income benefits for loss of the entire digit. For loss of more than the distal phalanx of a digit, the same as loss of the entire digit.

(20) Amputated arm or leg: For an arm or leg amputated to a point no greater than one-third the distance from the wrist to the elbow joint or from the ankle to the knee joint scheduled income benefits shall be the same as those for the loss of the hand or foot.

(21) Two or more digits: For loss of two or more digits, or one or more phalanges of two or more digits, of a hand or foot, scheduled income benefits may be proportioned to the loss of use of the hand or foot occasioned thereby, but shall not exceed the scheduled income benefits for loss of a hand or foot.

(22) Total loss of use: Scheduled income benefits for permanent total loss of use of a member shall be the same as for loss of the member.

(23) Partial loss or partial loss of use: Scheduled income benefits for permanent partial loss of use of a member shall be for a period proportionate to the period benefits are payable for total loss or total loss of use of the member as such partial loss bears to total loss.

(24) Loss of hearing or partial loss of bilateral vision: Scheduled income benefits for partial loss of vision in one or both eyes, or total loss of hearing in one ear, or partial loss of hearing in one or both ears shall be for a period proportionate to the period benefits are payable for total bilateral loss of vision or total binaural loss of hearing as such partial loss bears to total loss. The provisions of paragraphs (4) through (8) inclusive of subsection (f) of this section shall apply to scheduled losses of hearing.

(25) In any case in which there shall be a loss or loss of use of more than one member or parts of more than one member set forth in paragraphs (1) to (24) of this subsection, scheduled income benefits shall be for the

loss or loss of use of each such member or part thereof, with the periods of benefits to run consecutively, except that where the injury affects only two or more digits of the same hand or foot, paragraph (20) of this subsection shall apply.

(26) Other losses: Proper and equitable scheduled income benefits shall be paid for serious permanent disfigurement of face, head, neck or other area normally exposed and for loss or loss of function of a major member or organ when such disfigurement or loss is of a kind likely to handicap the employee in securing or holding employment, not to exceed 100 weeks, in addition to other scheduled income benefits payable under this section. However where scheduled income benefits are paid or payable for a particular member or organ, no additional benefits shall be made under this paragraph.

(27) In any case of total or partial loss of use of a member or organ, of hearing or vision, or in any case of disfigurement, determination of the period for which scheduled income benefits are payable shall not be made until the maximum of healing and of restoration of function has been attained.

(d) Scheduled Income Benefits: Scheduled income losses for bodily loss or losses, or loss of use, partial or total, shall be exclusive and in lieu of all income benefits payable after and in addition to the income benefits payable during the period of recovery except as otherwise provided in subsection (e) of this section.

(e) Major Member Losses: For total loss, or total and permanent loss of use, of an arm, hand, leg, both feet, or total loss of vision of both eyes, whether or not the injury also involves other impairments of the body, income benefits for such major member loss shall be for the period specified for such loss or loss of use in subsection (c), and with respect to any subsequent period of actual disability, income benefits shall be payable as provided in subsection (a) or (b) of this section, as long as the major member loss continues as a total loss and as long as actual disability as defined in Section 2(h) continues.

(f) Scheduled Income Benefits for Occupational Deafness: Occupational deafness means permanent partial or permanent total loss of hearing of one or both ears caused by prolonged exposure to harmful noise in employment. The following provisions shall apply exclusively to loss of hearing compensable under this subsection:

(1) No claim for scheduled income benefits shall be filed until the lapse of six full consecutive calendar months after the termination of exposure to harmful noise in employment. The time limitation for the filing of claims for occupational deafness shall not begin to run earlier than the day following the termination date of such six months' period. The time for filing claim as provided under this paragraph shall be applicable not only in respect of the last employer, but also in respect of any prior employer who may have liability to pay compensation for the occupational deafness.

(2) No employer shall be liable for the payment of scheduled income benefits for occupational deafness unless the employee claiming benefits shall have worked for such employer in employment exposing the employee to harmful noise for a total period of at least 90 days.

(3) An employer, otherwise liable under this subsection, whose employment has contributed to any extent to an employee's occupational deafness shall be liable for the full extent of the deafness of the employee, unless such employer shall establish by competent evidence (including the results of a professionally controlled hearing test) the extent of the employee's deafness as it existed prior to exposure to harmful noise in the employer's employment. Upon such showing the employer shall be liable to the employee only for the proportion of the deafness attributable to employment by him. An employer liable to the employee for the full extent of the employee's occupational deafness may implead, in a compensation proceeding on the employee's claim, any prior employer or employers in whose employment the employee had been exposed to harmful noise, and if it should be found that the impleaded employer would have been liable to the employee under this subsection, had the employee proceeded against him, under the claim being adjudicated, the employer held liable shall be entitled to an award against the impleaded employer. The impleading of an employer shall be accomplished by notice on a form prescribed by the Director. Such notice shall be sent to the impleaded employer and to the Director. An award may be made in favor of the employer liable to the employee, and against

the impleaded employer or employers, which award may be enforced in the same manner as awards to employees. The impleaded employer or employers shall bear equal shares with the employer of the employer's liability to the employee, unless the evidence warrants a different apportionment.

(4) Losses of hearing due to industrial noise for compensation purposes shall be confined to the frequencies of 500, 1000, and 2000 cycles per second. Loss of hearing ability for frequency tones above 2000 cycles per second are not to be considered as constituting disability for hearing.

(5) The percent of hearing loss, for purposes of the determination of compensation claims for occupational deafness, shall be calculated as the average, in decibels, of the thresholds of hearing for the frequencies of 500, 1000, and 2000 cycles per second. Hearing threshold levels which average 25 decibels**5** or less in these frequencies involve no impairment and shall not constitute any compensable hearing disability. If the losses of hearing average 25 decibels or less in the three frequencies, such losses of hearing shall not then constitute any compensable hearing disability. If the losses of hearing average 92 decibels or more in the three frequencies, then the same shall constitute and be a total or 100 percent compensable hearing loss.

(6) In measuring hearing impairment, the lowest measured losses in each of the three frequencies shall be added together and divided by three to determine the average decibel loss. For every decibel of loss exceeding 25 decibels an allowance of 1½ percent shall be made up to the maximum of 100 percent which is reached at 92 decibels.

(7) In determining the binaural percentage of loss, the percentage of impairment in the better ear shall be multiplied by five. The resulting figure shall be added to the percentage of impairment in the poorer ear and the sum of the two divided by six. The final percentage shall represent the binaural hearing impairment.

---

[5] The hearing threshold (decibel) levels specified refer to readings on audiometers calibrated according to American National Standard Specifications for Audiometers, S3.6—1969, American National Standards Institute, Inc., 1430 Broadway, New York, New York 10018. To be equivalent, readings on audiometers calibrated according to American Standard Z24.5, previously applicable, should be increased by 10 decibels for each frequency.

(8) Before determining the percentage of hearing impairment, in order to allow for the average amount of hearing loss from nonoccupational causes found in the population at any given age, there shall be deducted from the total average decibel loss, one-half decibel for each year of the employee's age over 40 at the time of last exposure to industrial noise.

(9) No consideration shall be given to the question of whether or not the ability of an employee to understand speech is improved by the use of a hearing aid.

(g) The period of any scheduled income benefits payable under this section on account of any injury shall be reduced by the period of income benefits paid or payable under such schedule on account of a prior injury if scheduled income benefits in both cases are for disability of the same member or function, or different parts of the same member or function, and the scheduled income benefits payable on account of the subsequent disability in whole or in part would duplicate the scheduled income benefits payable on account of the pre-existing disability.

(h) When an employee, who has sustained disability compensable under subsection (c), and who has filed a valid claim in his lifetime, dies from causes other than the injury before the expiration of the compensable period specified, the income benefits specified and unpaid at the individual's death, whether or not accrued or due at his death, shall be paid, under an award made before or after such death, for the period specified in this subsection, to and for the benefit of the persons within the classes at the time of death and in the proportions and upon the conditions specified in this subsection and in the order named.

(1) To the widow or wholly actually dependent widower, if there is no child under the age of 18 or incapable of self-support; or

(2) If there are both such a widow or widower and such a child or children one-half to such widow or widower and the other half to such child or children; or

(3) If there is no such widow or widower but such a child or children, then to such child or children; or

(4) If there is no survivor in the above classes, then the parent or parents wholly or partly actually dependent for support upon the decedent, or to other wholly or partly actually dependent relatives listed in Section 18(a)(7) or

to both, in such proportions as the Director may provide by regulation.

Section 17. [*Weekly Maximum and Minimum Income Benefits for Disability.*]

(a) The minimum weekly income benefits for total disability shall not be less than 20 percent (computed to the next higher multiple of $1.00) and the maximum weekly income benefit for disability shall be 66⅔ percent (computed to the next higher multiple of $1.00) of the average weekly wage of the State as defined herein; provided, that the maximum weekly benefit amount, rounded to the nearest dollar, shall be increased so that it shall be 100 percent as of July 1, 1975, 133⅓ percent as of July 1, 1977, 166⅔ percent as of July 1, 1979, and 200 percent as of July 1, 1981, of the State's average weekly wage as determined in subsection (b). In any event, income benefits shall not exceed the average weekly wage of the injured employee, except as provided in Section 21, nor shall the benefits be reduced by the amount of any payments from a welfare program or other program based upon need.

(b) For the purpose of this act the average weekly wage in the State shall be determined by the Director as follows: On or before October 1 of each year, the total wages reported on contribution reports to the [agency administering Employment Security Act or Unemployment Compensation Insurance Act] for the preceding calendar year shall be divided by the average monthly number of insured workers (determined by dividing the total insured workers reported for the preceding year by 12). The average annual wage thus obtained shall be divided by 52 and the average weekly wage thus determined rounded to the nearest cent. The average weekly wage as so determined shall be applicable for the 12-month period commencing July 1 following the October 1 determination.

(c) The minimum and maximum income benefits as so determined in Section 17(a) that are in effect on the date of injury, or in effect on the date of disablement in the case of disease, shall be applicable for the full period during which income benefits for disability are payable, except as provided in Section 21.

(d) The minimum or the maximum weekly income benefits shall not be changed unless the computation herein provided results in an increase or decrease of $2.00 or more, raised to the next even dollar in the level of the minimum or the maximum weekly income benefits.

Section 18. [*Income Benefits for Death.*]

If the injury causes death, income benefits shall be payable in the amount and to or for the benefit of the persons following, subject to the maximum limits specified in Section 18(c):

(a) Benefit Amounts for Particular Classes of Dependents.

(1) If there is a widow or widower and no children of the deceased, as defined in Section 2, to such widow or widower 66⅔ percent of the average weekly wage of the deceased, during widowhood or widowerhood.

(2) To the widow or widower, if there is a child or children living with the widow or widower, 45 percent of the average weekly wage of the deceased, or 40 percent, if such child is not or all such children are not living with a widow or widower, and in addition thereto, benefits for the child or children which shall make the total benefits for the widow or widower and child or children 66⅔ percent of the average weekly wage of the deceased. When there are two or more children, the indemnity benefits payable on account of such children shall be divided among such children, share and share alike.

(3) Two years indemnity benefits in one lump sum shall be payable to a widow or widower upon remarriage.

(4) To the child or children if there is no widow or widower, 66⅔ percent of such wage divided among such children, share and share alike.

(5) The income benefits payable on account of any child under this section shall cease when he dies, marries, or reaches the age of 18, or when a child over such age ceases to be physically or mentally incapable of self-support, or if actually dependent ceases to be actually dependent, or, if enrolled as a full-time student in any accredited educational institution, ceases to be so enrolled or reaches the age of 25. A child who originally qualified as a dependent by virtue of being less than 18 years of age may, upon reaching age 18, continue to qualify if he satisfies the tests of being physically or mentally incapable of self-support, actual dependency, or enrollment in an educational institution.

(6) To each parent, if actually dependent, 25 percent.

(7) To the brothers, sisters, grandparents, and grandchildren, if actually dependent, 25 percent to each such dependent. If there should be more than one of such dependents, the total

income benefits payable on account of such dependents shall be divided, share and share alike.

(8) The income benefits of each beneficiary under paragraphs (6) and (7) above shall be paid until he, if a parent or grandparent, dies, marries, or ceases to be actually dependent, or, if a brother, sister, or grandchild, dies, marries, or reaches the age of 18 or if over that age ceases to be physically or mentally incapable of self-support, or ceases to be actually dependent.

(9) A person ceases to be actually dependent when his income from all sources exclusive of workmen's compensation income benefits is such that, if it had existed at the time as of which the original determination of actual dependency was made, it would not have supported a finding of dependency. In any event, if the present annual income of an actual dependent person including workmen's compensation income benefits at any time exceeds the total annual support received by the person from the deceased employee, the workmen's compensation benefits shall be reduced so that the total annual income is no greater than such amount of annual support received from the deceased employee. In all cases, a person found to be actually dependent shall be presumed to be no longer actually dependent three years after such time as of which the person was found to be actually dependent. This presumption may be overcome by proof of continued actual dependency as defined in this subsection and Section 2(s).

(7) Change in Dependents. Upon the cessation of income benefits under this section to or on account of any person, the income benefits of the remaining persons entitled to income benefits for the unexpired part of the period during which their income benefits are payable shall be that which such persons would have received if they had been the only persons entitled to income benefits at the time of the decedent's death.

(8) Maximum and Minimum Total Payments. The maximum weekly income benefits payable for all beneficiaries in case of death shall not exceed $66^2/_3$ percent of the average weekly wage of the deceased as calculated under Section 19, subject to the maximum limits in Section 17, with a minimum of 50 percent (computed to the next higher multiple of $1.00) of the average weekly wage of the State as defined in Section 17(b). The maximum aggregate limitation shall not operate in case of payment of two years' income benefits to the widow or

widower upon remarriage, as provided under subsection (a)(3) of this section, to prevent the immediate recalculation and payments of benefits to the remaining beneficiaries as provided under subsection (b) of this section. The classes of beneficiaries specified in paragraphs (1) and (4) of subsection (a) shall have priority over all other beneficiaries in the apportionment of income benefits. If the provisions of this subsection should prevent payment to other beneficiaries of the income benefits to the full extent otherwise provided for by this section, the gross remaining amount of income benefits payable to such other beneficiaries shall be apportioned by class, proportionate to the interest of each class in the remaining amount. Parents shall be considered to be in one class and those specified in paragraph (7) in another class.

(9) Social Security Offset. The income benefits provided for in this section shall be reduced by the amount of survivor benefits paid under the Old Age Survivors Disability and Health Insurance Act.

(10) The minimum and maximum income benefits as so determined in Section 18(c) that are in effect on the date of injury shall be applicable for the full period during which income benefits for death are payable, except as provided in Section 21.

Section 19. [*Determination of Average Weekly Wage.*]

Except as otherwise provided in this act, the average weekly wage of the injured employee at the time of the injury shall be taken as the basis upon which to compute compensation and shall be determined as follows:

(a) If at the time of the injury the wages are fixed by the week, the amount so fixed shall be the average weekly wage;

(b) If at the time of the injury the wages are fixed by the month, the average weekly wage shall be the monthly wage so fixed multiplied by 12 and divided by 52;

(c) If at the time of the injury the wages are fixed by the year, the average weekly wage shall be the yearly wage so fixed divided by 52;

(d) (1) If at the time of the injury the wages are fixed by the day, hour, or by the output of the employee, the average weekly wage shall be the wage most favorable to the employee computed by dividing by 13 the wages (not including overtime or premium pay) of said employee earned in the employ of the employer in the first, second, third, or fourth period of 13 consecutive calendar weeks in the 52 weeks immediately preceding the injury.

(2) If the employee has been in the employ of the employer less than 13 calendar weeks immediately preceding the injury, his average weekly wage shall be computed under the foregoing paragraph, taking the wages (not including overtime or premium pay) for such purpose to be the amount he would have earned had he been so employed by the employer the full 13 calendar weeks immediately preceding the injury and had worked, when work was available to other employees in a similar occupation.

(e) If at the time of the injury the hourly wage has not been fixed or can not be ascertained, the wage for the purpose of calculating compensation shall be taken to be the usual wage for similar services where such services are rendered by paid employees.

(f) In occupations which are exclusively seasonal and therefore cannot be carried on throughout the year, the average weekly wage shall be taken to be one-fiftieth of the total wages which the employee has earned from all occupations during the 12 calendar months immediately preceding the injury.

(g) In the case of volunteer firemen, police, and civil defense members or trainees, the income benefits shall be based on the average weekly wage in their regular employment.

(h) If the employee was a minor, apprentice or trainee when injured, and it is established that under normal conditions his wages should be expected to increase during the period of disability, that fact may be considered in computing his average weekly wage.

(i) When the employee is working under concurrent contracts with two or more employers and the defendant employer has knowledge of such employment prior to the injury, his wages from all such employers shall be considered as if earned from the employer liable for compensation.

Section 20. [*Payment for Second Injuries From Special Fund.*][6]

(a) If an employee who has a permanent impairment from any cause or origin incurs a subsequent impairment by injury arising out of and in the course of his employment resulting in compensation liability for disability that is substantially greater by reason of the combined effects of the preexisting impairment and subsequent injury or by reason of the aggravation of the preexisting impairment than that which would have resulted from the subsequent injury alone, the employer or his insurance carrier

[6] The Special Fund referred to here is the second or subsequent injury fund that virtually all States have established.

shall in the first instance pay all awards of compensation provided by this act, but such employer or his insurance carrier shall be reimbursed from the Special Fund created by Section 55 for all compensation payments subsequent to those payable for the first 104 weeks of disability.

(b) If the subsequent injury of such an employee shall result in the death of the employee and it shall be determined that the death would not have occurred except for such preexisting permanent impairment, the employer or his insurance carrier shall in the first instance pay the compensation prescribed by this act, but he or his insurance carrier shall be reimbursed from the Special Fund created by Section 55 for all compensation payable in excess of 104 weeks.

(c) In order to qualify under this section for reimbursement from the Special Fund, the employer must establish by written records that the employer had knowledge of the permanent impairment at the time that the employee was hired, or at the time the employee was retained in employment after the employer acquired such knowledge.

(d) As used in this section, "permanent impairment" means any permanent condition, whether congenital or due to injury or disease, of such seriousness as to constitute a hindrance or obstacle to obtaining employment or to obtaining reemployment if the employee should become unemployed. No condition shall be considered a "permanent impairment" unless it is one of the following conditions:

(1) Epilepsy

(2) Diabetes

(3) Cardiac disease

(4) Arthritis

(5) Amputated foot, leg, arm or hand

(6) Loss of sight of one or both eyes or a partial loss of uncorrected vision of more than 75 percent bilaterally

(7) Residual disability from poliomyelitis

(8) Cerebral palsy

(9) Multiple sclerosis

(10) Parkinson's disease

(11) Cerebral vascular accident

(12) Tuberculosis

(13) Silicosis

(14) Psychoneurotic disability following treatment in a recognized medical or mental institution

(15) Hemophilia

(16) Chronic osteomyelitis

(17) Ankylosis of joints

(18) Hyperinsulism

(19) Muscular dystrophies

(20) Arteriosclerosis

(21) Thrombophlebitis

(22) Varicose veins

(23) Heavy metal poisoning

(24) Ionizing radiation injury

(25) Compressed air sequelae

(26) Ruptured intervertebral disk

or unless it would support a rating of disability of 200 weeks or more if evaluated according to standards applied in compensation claims.

(e) The Special Fund shall not be bound as to any question of law or fact by reason of an award or an adjudication to which it was not a party or in relation to which it was not notified at least three weeks prior to the award or adjudication, that it might be subject to liability for the injury or death.

(f) An employer or carrier shall notify the Director and the Director of the Special Fund of any possible claim against the Special Fund as soon as practicable, but in no event later than 100 weeks after the injury or death.

Section 21. [*Benefit Adjustment.*] (omitted)

PART IV. PROCEDURES

Section 22. [*Record of Injury or Death.*]

Every employer shall keep a record of each injury to any of his employees as reported to him or of which he otherwise has knowledge. Such record shall include a description of the injury, a statement of any time during which the injured person was unable to work because of the injury, a description of the manner in which the injury occurred, and such other information relating to the injury or its occurrence as the Director may by regulation require. These records shall be available for inspection by the Director or by any governmental agency at such reasonable times and under such conditions as the Director may prescribe. Upon willful failure or refusal of the employer to keep the record required under this section, the Director may assess against such employer a civil penalty not exceeding [$500], which penalty shall be paid into the Special Fund established under Section 55.

Section 23. [*Report of Injury or Death.*]

(a) Within 15 days after the employer has notice or knowledge of the occurrence of a death or any injury which constitutes a permanent impairment, or which renders the injured person unable to perform a regularly established job at his place of employment during any portion of his regular shift on any calendar day subsequent to the day of injury, a report thereof shall be made in writing by the employer to the Director, upon a form approved by the Director for that purpose, setting forth (1) the name, address, and business of the employer; (2) the name, address, and occupation of the employee; (3) the nature of the injury and a description of the manner in which it occurred; (4) the year, month, day and hour when, and the particular locality where injury or death occurred; and (5) such other information as the Director may prescribe by regulation. In addition, within the same period, except where claim has been filed under Section 26(e), if the case involves death or more than three days' disability, the employer shall notify the Director in writing whether payment shall be made without an award or controverted. If the right to compensation is controverted, the grounds shall be stated, but the stating of such grounds shall not prevent the later assertion of other defenses. For other injuries not resulting in disability but which require medical treatment by a physician beyond ordinary first-aid, monthly summary reports may be required on a form prescribed by the Director. The form, as adopted by the Director to report an injury or death, shall include the information required by the Occupational Safety and Health Act of 1970, as amended.

(b) The mailing to the Director of any such written report as required in subsection (a) of this section within the time prescribed, shall be a compliance with this section.

(c) Whenever an employer willfully fails to file or refuses to file report of injury or death as required in subsection (a) of this section, the Director may assess a penalty not exceeding [$500], which penalty shall be paid into the Special Fund, established under Section 55.

(d) Where the employer has knowledge of any injury or death and willfully fails or refuses to file the report of injury as required in subsection (a) of this section, the limitations prescribed in Section 26 shall not begin to run against the claim of any person entitled to compensation until such report shall have been furnished as required by this section.

(e) All reports submitted to the Director under this section shall be confidential and not admissible in evidence in any administrative or judicial proceedings. Such reports may be made available to other state or federal agencies for study and informational purposes under such limitations as may be prescribed by the Director, but they shall not be used as evidence of any admission against interest for purposes of adjudication, litigation or determination of claims, whether administrative or judicial.

Section 24. [*Method and Time of Payment of Compensation.*]

(a) Compensation under this act shall be paid promptly, and directly to the person entitled thereto, without an award, except where the right to compensation is controverted by the employer.

(b) The first installment of income benefits shall become due on the fifteenth day after the employer has notice or knowledge of the employee's disability or death due to injury, on which date all income benefits then due shall be paid. Thereafter, income benefits shall be paid in biweekly installments, except where the Director determines that payment in installments should be made at some other period.

(c) Upon making the first payment of income benefits, and upon stopping or changing of such benefits for any cause other than final payment under Section 27(c), the employer shall immediately notify the Director, in accordance with a form prescribed by the Director, that the payment of income benefits has begun or has been stopped or changed.

(d) If payments have been made without an award, and the employer then elects to controvert, the notice of controversy shall be filed with the Director within 15 days of the due date of the first omitted payment under this election.

(e) If, after the payment of compensation without an award, the employer elects to controvert the right to compensation, the payment of compensation shall not be considered a binding determination of the obligations of the employer as to future compensation payments. The acceptance of compensation by the employee or his dependents shall not be considered a binding determination of their rights under this act.

(f) The Director (1) may, upon his own initiative at any time in a case in which payments are being made without an award, and (2) shall, upon receipt of information from any person claiming to be entitled to compensation, from the employer, or otherwise that the right to compensation is controverted, or that payment of compensation has been opposed, stopped, or changed, whether or not claim has been filed, promptly make such inquiry as circumstances require, cause such medical examinations to be made, hold such hearings, make such determinations or awards, and take such further action as he considers will properly protect the rights of all parties.

Section 25. [*Notice of Injury or Death.*]

(a) Notice of injury or death shall be given to the employer within 30 days after the date of such injury or death, or within 30 days after the employee or his dependents know the nature of the injury and its relationship to the employment.

(b) Such notice shall be in writing, shall contain the name and address of the employee and a statement of the time, place, nature and cause of the injury or death, and shall be signed by the employee or by some person on his behalf, or, in case of death by any person claiming to be entitled to compensation for such death, or by a person on his behalf.

(c) Notice shall be given to the employer by delivering it to him or his representative or by sending it by mail addressed to him or such agent at the last known place of business of either. Such notice may be given to the employer, partner, superior, foreman, agent, or officer of the employer.

(d) Failure to give such notice shall not bar any claim under this act (1) if the employer (or his representative as identified in subsection (c) above) or the carrier had knowledge of the injury or death, or (2) if the Director excuses such failure on the ground that for some satisfactory reason such notice could not be given or that the employer or carrier has not been prejudiced by failure to receive such notice, or (3) unless objection to such failure is raised in the answer as filed with the Director in accordance with Section 26(e).

Section 26. [*Time Limitation for Filing of Claims.*]

(a) The right to compensation for disability shall be barred unless a claim therefor is filed within three years after the injury or last payment of compensation. The right to income benefits for death shall be barred unless a claim therefor is filed within three years after the death or within three years after the dependents know or by exercise of reasonable diligence should know the possible relationship of the death to the employment. However, in cases in which the nature of the injury or disease or its relationship to the employment is not known to the employee the time for filing claim shall not begin to run until (1) the employee knows or by exercise of reasonable diligence should know of the existence of the injury and its possible relationship to his employment and (2) sustains disability or incurs a scheduled physical loss under Section 16(c) (except paragraph (24)).

(b) Notwithstanding the provisions of subsection (a), failure to file a claim within the period prescribed in such subsection shall not be a bar to such right unless objection to such failure is raised in the answer to the claim filed under subsection (e) of this section.

(c) If a person who is entitled to compensation under this act is incompetent or a minor, the time for filing claim under subsection (a) shall not begin to run so long as such person has no guardian or other authorized representative, but shall run from the date of appointment of such guardian or other representative, or in the case of a minor, if no guardian is appointed before he becomes 21 years of age, from the date he becomes 21 years of age.

(d) Where recovery is denied to any person, in a suit brought at law or in admiralty to recover damages in respect of injury or death, on the ground that such person was an employee and that the defendant was an employer within the meaning of this act, the limitation of time prescribed in subsection (a) of this section shall not begin to run earlier than from the date of final termination of such action.

(e) Upon the filing with him of a claim, demand, or application of any kind by a person seeking determination of his rights under this act, the Director shall transmit a copy thereof to the other party with notice to respond thereto by answer. The Director shall prepare an appropriate form or forms by which to enable the other party to answer. The other party shall respond by answer (in duplicate) within 20 days after receiving such notices or within such extension of that time as the Director may allow. If answer is not filed, the Director or his hearing officer shall proceed to determine the rights following the procedure in Section 24(f).

Section 27. [*Payment of Compensation.*]

(a) If the right to compensation has not been controverted and any amount of compensation payable to the beneficiary without an award is not paid within 14 days after it becomes due, as provided in Section 24(b), there shall be added to such unpaid compensation an amount equal to [10] percent thereof, which shall be paid to the beneficiary at the same time as, but in addition to, such amount due, and without regard to any limitation otherwise applicable upon the amount of the compensation, unless such nonpayment is excused by the Director after a showing by the employer that owing to conditions over which he had no control such compensation could not be paid within the period prescribed for the payment.

(b) If any amount of compensation payable under the terms of an award is not paid within 30 days after it shall become payable under the terms of the award, there shall be added to such unpaid amount an amount equal to [20] percent thereof, which shall be paid to the beneficiary at the same time as, but in addition to, such compensation unless review of the order making such award be had, as provided in Section 31, or unless such nonpayment is excused by the Director after a showing by the employer that owing to conditions over which he had no control such compensation could not be paid within the period prescribed for the payment. If review is had, interest at the rate of [5] percent shall be added to the award from the date of the original award of the Director or hearing officer.

(c) Within 16 days after the final payment of income benefits has been made, the employer shall send to the Director a notice, in accordance with a form prescribed by the Director, stating that such final payment has been made, the total amount of income benefits paid, the name of the employee, and of any other person to whom income benefits have been paid, the date of the injury or death, the dates on which income benefits have been paid, and the period covered by the payment. If the employer fails to notify the Director within such time, the Director may assess against such employer a penalty in an amount not to exceed [$500] which shall be paid into the Special Fund, established under Section 55.

(d) Whenever the Director deems it advisable or necessary to protect a beneficiary, he may require an employer who has not secured the payment of compensation to his employees as required by this act to make a deposit of money with the [State Treasurer] to secure the prompt and convenient payment of compensation payable under an award or modified award. Payments therefrom upon any such award shall be made upon order of the Director.

(e) Whenever the Director determines after a hearing that it is in the interest of the rehabilitation of the injured worker in accordance with regulations established by the Director, and it is recommended by the Rehabilitation Unit, the liability for income benefits under this act, or any part thereof, may be discharged by the payment of a lump sum equal to the present value of future income benefits commuted, computed at [3] percent true discount compounded annually. The probability of the beneficiary's death before the expiration of the period during which he is entitled to income benefits shall be determined in accordance with the United States Life Table, and the probability of the remarriage of a widow shall be determined in accordance with the American Re-Marriage Table. The probability of the happening of any other contingency affecting the amount of duration of the income benefits shall be disregarded.

(f) Unless otherwise intended or agreed upon when the employer pays wages in whole or part during an injured employee's disability, he shall be entitled to a credit not to exceed the amount of income benefits due for the same period when such wages are paid except for scheduled benefits paid under Section 16(c) to which this subsection shall not apply.

Section 28. [*Minors or Incompetents.*] (omitted)

Section 29. [*Recording and Reporting of Payments.*]

Every carrier shall keep a record of all payments of compensation made under the provisions of this act, and of the time and manner of making such payments.

Section 30. [*Invalid Agreements.*]

(a) No agreement by an employee to pay any portion of premium paid by his employer or to contribute to a benefit fund or department maintained by such employer for the purpose of providing compensation as required by this act shall be valid, and any employer who makes a deduction for such purpose from the pay of any employee entitled to the benefits of this act shall be guilty of a [misdemeanor] and upon conviction thereof shall be punished by a fine of not more than [$1,000].

(b) No agreement by an employee to waive his right to compensation under this act shall be valid.

Section 31. [*Assignment and Exemption From Claims of Creditors.*]

No assignment, release, or commutation of income benefits due or payable under this act, except as provided by this act, shall be valid, and such income benefits shall be exempt from all claims of creditors, or other debts and from levy, execution, and attachment or other remedy for recovery or collection of a debt, which exemption may not be waived.

Section 32. [*Compensation a Lien Against Assets.*]

In case of insolvency or bankruptcy, every liability for compensation under this act shall constitute a first lien upon all the property of the employer liable therefor, paramount to all other claims or liens except for wages and taxes, and such liens shall be enforced by order of the court.

Section 33. [*Hearing Procedure.*]

(a) Upon application of a party in interest, or when ordered by the Director [or] his hearing officer, and when issues in a case cannot be resolved by pre-hearing conferences or otherwise, a hearing shall be held for determining the questions at issue. All parties in interest shall be given at least 10 days notice of the hearing and of the issues to be heard, served personally or by mail. Following the presentation of the evidence, the Director or his hearing officer shall determine the questions at issue and file the decision thereon in the office of the [appropriate state agency] within 30 days unless the time for filing the decision is extended by the Director. At the time of such filing, a certified copy of the decision shall be sent by certified mail to all interested parties at the last known address of each. The decision of the Director or his hearing officer shall be made in the form of a compensation order, appropriately titled to show its purpose and containing a report of the case, findings of fact, and conclusions of law, and other explanation of the action taken. A compensation order shall be final unless a timely appeal to the Workmen's Compensation Appeals Board is filed by a party in interest under Section 34.

(b) The Director must adopt rules and regulations of practice and procedure consistent with this act for the hearing, disposition and adjudication of cases, the text of which shall be published and readily available. Such rules shall include provision for procedures in the nature of conferences in order to dispose of cases informally, or to expedite claim adjudication, narrow issues, and simplify the methods of proof at hearings.

(c) In making an inquiry or conducting a hearing the Director or his hearing officer shall not be bound by common law or statutory rules of evidence or by technical or formal rules of procedures, except as provided by this act, but may make such inquiry or conduct such hearing in such manner as best to ascertain the rights of the parties.

(d) All hearings before the Director or his hearing officer shall be open to the public. The Director shall by regulation provide for the preparation of a record of each hearing.

(e) All powers, authority, and duties of the Director in respect to adjudications and hearings shall apply to a hearing officer.

(f) The authority of the Director or hearing officer or their duly authorized representatives to determine controverted claims for compensation shall include the right to enter premises at any reasonable time where an injury or death has occurred, and to make such examination of any tool, appliance, process, machinery, or environmental or other condition as may be relevant to a determination of the cause and circumstances of such injury or death.

Section 34. [*Appeals to the Board.*]

A party in interest may appeal a compensation order to the Workmen's Compensation Appeals Board within 20 days from the date of mailing of the compensation order. If the Board, after a request by any party, determines that a hearing is necessary, it shall schedule a hearing and give at least 10 days notice to all interested parties of the date of such hearing and the issues to be heard. The Board shall have power to review the findings of fact, conclusions of law and exercise of discretion by the Director or his hearing officer in hearing, determining or otherwise handling of any compensation case and may affirm, reverse or modify any compensation case upon review or remand such a case to the Director for further proceedings and action.

The proceedings before the Board shall be on the record made before the Director or his hearing officer and no new or additional evidence shall be received in respect of the appeal. If the Board determines that the case has been improperly, incompletely, or otherwise insufficiently developed on hearing by the Director or his hearing officer, the case may be remanded for proceedings and appropriate action with or without the Board's relinquishing jurisdiction of the case.

The Board shall make a decision disposing of the issues presented by the appeal and file a decision in its office within [60] days of completion of submission of the case to the Board. Upon such filing, the Board shall send a certified copy of the decision by certified mail to all interested parties at the last known address of each. The decision of the Board shall be made in the form of an order, supported by a written opinion or statement setting forth the reasons for the action taken and including necessary findings of fact and conclusions of law.

The decision of the Board shall be final and conclusive as to all matters adjudicated by the Board upon the expiration of the thirtieth day after copy of the decision has been mailed to the parties, unless prior to that day (1) the Board on its own motion or that of a party in interest, and after notice to all parties in interest, shall signify that it will reconsider the decision, or (2) a party in interest shall seek judicial review of the decision authorized under Section 37.

The decision of the Board upon reconsideration of the case shall become final as to all matters considered, upon expiration of the thirtieth day after copy of decision has been mailed to the interested parties unless prior to that day a party in interest shall seek judicial review authorized under Section 37.

Section 35. [*Application for Modification.*]

The Director may review any compensation case and make a determination upon his own initiative or upon application of any party in interest in accordance with the procedure in respect of hearings, which may terminate, continue, reinstate, increase, decrease, or otherwise properly affect the compensation benefits provided by this act, or in any other respect consistent with this act, modify any previous decision, award, or action including the making of an award of compensation if the claim had been rejected in whole or in part.

A review may be had upon application of a party in interest filed with the Director at any time but not later than within two years after the date of the last payment or furnishing of compensation upon the following grounds:

(1) Mistake in determination of fact or failure to make material findings of fact; (2) mistake of law; (3) clerical error or mistake in mathematical calculations; or (4) newly discovered evidence.

A review may be had upon application of a party in interest filed with the Director at any time but not later than within five years after the date of the last payment or furnishing of compensation upon the following grounds:

(1) Change in the nature or extent of the employee's injury, wage-earning capacity, or status of the claimant; or (2) fraud. The Director may review a case at any time in order to correct a manifest injustice. In unusual cases in which the nature of the injury, disease, or its relationship to the employment is not known to the employee, the time for filing an application for review shall not begin to run until (1) the employee knows, or by exercise of reasonable diligence should know, of the existence of the injury and its possible relationship to his employment; (2) the employee sustains disability or incurs a scheduled physical loss under Section 16(c) (except paragraph (24)).

Section 36. [*Authority of the Director and Board for Conducting Hearings.*]

(i) The hearings by the Director or his hearing officer and the hearings by the Board, unless otherwise provided by law, shall be held at such places as the Director and the Board may find most convenient for the parties and most appropriate for ascertaining the rights of the parties.

(j) The Director and any member of the Board shall have the power to preserve and enforce order during hearings; to issue subpoenas for, to administer oaths, and to compel the attendance and testimony of a witness, or the production of books, papers, documents, and other evidence, or the taking of depositions before any designated individual competent to administer oaths; to examine witnesses; and to do all things conformable to law which may be necessary to enable them effectively to discharge the duties of their office.

(k) If any person in proceedings before the Director or Board disobeys or resists any lawful order or process, or misbehaves during a hearing or so near the place thereof as to obstruct the same, neglects to produce, after having been ordered to do so, any pertinent book, paper, or document, or refuses to appear after having been subpoenaed, or upon appearing refuses to take the oath or affirmation as a witness, or after taking the oath or affirmation refuses to be examined according to law, the Director or Board shall certify the facts to the [____ court] where the offense is committed and the court shall, if the evidence so warrants, punish such person in the same manner and to the same extent as for contempt committed before the court, or commit such person upon the same conditions as if the doing of the forbidden act had occurred with reference to the process of or in the presence of the court.

Section 37. [*Judicial Review of Decision by Board.*]

(a) Any party in interest may, within the time limit specified in Section 34, file application for judicial review of such decision with the [intermediate or final appellate court].

(b) The court shall have power and jurisdiction to review decisions filed by the Board under this act on matters of law only and to perform such other judicial functions and to hear such other matters as are provided for by this act. The court may affirm, suspend, remand, modify or set aside, in whole or in part, a decision of the Board or compel administrative action unlawfully withheld or denied. [Appeals from such court may be had as in other civil actions.]

(c) Proceedings to set aside a compensation order or decision shall not be instituted otherwise than as provided for by this act.

(d) Except as hereinafter provided in this subsection, the taking of an appeal shall operate as a supersedeas as to payment of compensation under the award. In proceedings brought to review administrative action in which an award by the hearing officer or Director has been affirmed by the Appeals Board the court may after at least three days' notice to all parties in interest hear an application by the employee for the payment of compensation required under a compensation order or decision pending the outcome of the appeal. If after summary hearing of the parties the court finds that failure to make payments may jeopardize the health or physical well being of the employee or his dependents, the court may in its discretion order payment in whole or in part. Such proceedings shall be given priority over all other cases and such orders shall not be reviewable.

Section 38. [*Enforcement of Payment in Default and Penalties.*] (omitted)

Section 39. [*Witnesses and Their Fees.*] (omitted)

Section 40. [*Costs in Taking Appeal.*] (omitted)

Section 41. [*Costs in Proceeding Brought Without Reasonable Ground.*]

If the hearing authority having jurisdiction of any proceeding under this act, administrative or judicial, determines that such proceeding has been instituted or continued without reasonable ground, the costs of such proceeding including a reasonable attorney's fee for necessary services rendered shall be assessed against the party who has so instituted or continued such proceeding.

Section 42. [Payment by Employer of Fees for Claimant's Legal Services and Witnesses.][7]

(a) If the employer or carrier declines to pay any compensation on or before the thirtieth day after receiving written notice of demand or claim for compensation, on the ground that there is no liability for compensation within the provisions of this act, and the person seeking benefits shall thereafter have utilized the services of an attorney at law in the successful prosecution of his right, claim, or demand before the Director or hearing officer, there shall be awarded, in addition to the award for compensation, a reasonable attorney's fee against the employer or carrier in an amount approved by the Director or hearing officer which shall be paid directly by the employer to the attorney for the claimant in a lump sum after final decision. If the employer or carrier pays or tenders payment of compensation, but controversy relates to the amount of compensation due, and if the award is greater than the amount

[7] This section was drafted only with considerable difficulty and difference of opinion among the drafting group and the Committee on Suggested State Legislation. It is offered with some misgiving because it appears to fly in the face of the tradition that each party to an action is responsible for paying his own legal fees. The section, however, seeks to ensure that a claimant will receive in its entirety an award to which he is entitled by statute—a statute which requires that he give up his common law right to sue his employer for all injuries covered by its provisions. It is recognized that certain safeguards must be included to prevent the section's becoming an invitation to litigation. Fees are subject to approval. If only the amount of the award is controverted, the size of the fee awarded must be related to the difference between the amount of compensation and the amount awarded. Further protection is offered an employer or carrier by his being able to submit the case to impartial medical opinion. Of course, payment of a claimant's legal fees by an employer or carrier presupposes the successful prosecution of his claim by the claimant.

paid or tendered by the employer or carrier, a reasonable attorney's fee based solely upon the difference between the amount awarded and the amount tendered or paid shall be awarded in addition to the amount of compensation; provided, however, that this sentence shall not apply if the controversy relates to degree or length of disability, and if the employer or carrier offers to submit the case for evaluation by impartial medical opinion as provided in Section 12(c)(3) and offers to tender an amount of compensation based upon the degree or length of disability found by the independent medical report at such time as an evaluation of disability can be made. If the claimant is successful in review proceedings before the Board or court in any such case an award may be made in favor of the claimant and against the employer or carrier for a reasonable attorney's fee for claimant's counsel in accord with the above provisions. In all cases, fees for attorneys representing the claimant shall be approved in the manner herein provided. If any proceedings are had before the Board or any court for review of any action, award, order or decision, the Board or court may approve an attorney's fee for the work done before it by the attorney for the claimant. An approved attorney's fee, in cases in which the obligation to pay the fee is upon the claimant, may be made a lien upon the compensation due under an award; and the Director, hearing officer, Board, or court shall fix in the award approving the fee, such lien and manner of payment. The amounts awarded against an employer or carrier as attorney's fee shall not in any respect affect or diminish the compensation payable under this act.

(b) In every case, any fees for attorneys representing the claimant, employer, or insurer shall be reported to the Agency. The Director shall regulate the attorneys' fees for legal services provided prior to any review by any court. If any proceedings are had before any court for review of any action, award, order, or decision, the court shall regulate the attorneys' fees for the work done before the court.

(c) In cases where an attorney's fee is awarded against an employer or carrier there may be further assessed against such employer or carrier as costs, fees and mileages for necessary witnesses attending the hearing at the instance of claimant. Both the necessity for the witness and the reasonableness of the fees must be approved by the Director or hearing officer.

(d) Any person who receives any fees, other consideration, or any gratuity on account of services rendered as a representative of claimant, unless such consideration or gratuity is approved by the Director, hearing officer, Board, or court, or who makes it a business to solicit employment for a lawyer or for himself in respect of any claim or award for compensation, shall be guilty of a [misdemeanor], and upon conviction thereof, for each offense shall be punished by a fine of not more than [$1,000] or by imprisonment for not more than [one year], or by both such fine and imprisonment.

Section 43. [*Penalty for Misrepresentation.*]

Any person who willfully makes any false or misleading statement or representation for the purpose of obtaining or defeating any benefit, fee, or allowance under this act shall be guilty of a [misdemeanor] and on conviction thereof shall be punished by a fine of not to exceed [$1,000] or by imprisonment for not more than [one year], or by both such fine and imprisonment.

Section 44. [*Enforcement of Penalties, Deposits and Assessments.*] (omitted)

Section 45. [*Aliens.*] (omitted)

PART V. INSURANCE

Section 46. [*Security for Payment of Compensation.*][8]

Every employer shall secure the payment of compensation under this act:

(a) By insuring and keeping insured the payment of such benefits with any organization authorized to insure workmen's compensation in this State, or

(b) By furnishing satisfactory proof to the Director of his financial and administrative ability to meet his obligations under this act and by receiving an authorization from the Director to pay such compensation directly.

(1) The Director shall, as a condition to such authorization, require such employer to file with the [appropriate state agency] a bond of a surety company authorized to do business in this State or to deposit in a depository designated by the Director, negotiable securities, at the option of the employer, of a kind and in an amount determined by the Director, to secure the performance by the employer of all obligations imposed upon him under this act, for injuries occurring to his employees during the period of self-insurance and subject to such conditions as the Director may by regulation prescribe, provided that in no case shall the amount of bond or security required be less than [$100,000] for any one employer.

[8] In States having a State Fund, appropriate provisions should be inserted at this point.

(2) Authorization of self-insurance shall be evidenced by a "Certificate of Authorization." Such authorization shall be granted for a period of not more than one year. The Director may, for good cause shown, including failure to provide adequate safety and loss prevention services, and after notice and opportunity of hearing, terminate the authorization of any self-insurer. Failure by a self-insurer to comply with any provision of this act, or of the lawful regulations issued by the Director, or with any lawful order of the Director or a hearing officer, or the failure or insolvency of the surety on his indemnity bond or impairment of financial responsibility of such self-insurer shall be considered good cause for such termination. No termination shall affect the liability of any self-insurer already incurred.

(3) The surety on a bond filed by a self-insurer pursuant to paragraph (1) of this subsection may terminate its liability thereon by giving the Director written notice stating when, not less than 30 days thereafter, such termination shall be effective. In case of such termination, the surety shall remain liable, in accordance with the terms of the bond, with respect to injuries to employees of the self-insurer prior to the termination of the surety's liability. If the bond is terminated for any reason other than the employer's terminating his status as a self-insurer, the employer shall, prior to the date of termination of the surety's liability, comply with the requirements of paragraph (1) of this subsection.

The liability of a surety on a bond filed pursuant to this section shall be released and extinguished and the bond returned to the employer or surety provided (a) such liability is secured by another bond filed or negotiable securities deposited as required by paragraph (1) of this subsection or (b) the employer files with the Director the policy of insurance specified in paragraph (4) of this subsection.

Securities deposited by an employer pursuant to paragraph (1) of this subsection shall be returned to him upon his written request provided the employer (a) files the bond required by paragraph (1) of this subsection or (b) files with the Director the policy of insurance specified in paragraph (4) of this subsection.

(4) Any employer may at any time terminate his status as a self-insurer by giving the Director written notice stating when not less than 30 days thereafter such termination shall be effective provided such termination shall not be effective until the employer shall have complied with the requirements of subsection (a) of this section.

If an employer who ceases to be a self-insurer files with the Director a policy of insurance in a form approved by the [Insurance Commissioner] and issued by an organization authorized to insure workmen's compensation in this State, and covering the entire liability of such employer for injuries to his employees which occurred during the period of self-insurance, the bond, bonds or securities securing such liability and filed or deposited by the employer pursuant to paragraph (1) of subsection (b) of this section shall forthwith be returned to him. The policy of insurance shall be non-cancellable for any cause during the continuance of the liability secured and so covered.

(5) The Director may in cases of default by the self-insurer after sending him notice by certified mail of his intention to do so, bring suit upon such bond or collect the interest and principal of any of the securities as they may become due or sell the securities or any of them as may be required to pay compensation and discharge the obligation of the self-insurer under this act and apply the proceeds to the payment of compensation under this act.

Section 47. [*Posting of Notices.*]

The Director may by regulation require that every employer subject to the provisions of this act shall post and keep posted in a conspicuous place or places in and about the place or places of business a typewritten or printed notice, in accordance with a form prescribed by the Director, stating that such employer has secured the payment of compensation in accordance with the provisions of this act. Such notice shall contain the name and address of the insurance organization, if any, with whom the employer has secured payment of compensation.

Section 48. [*Certificate of Compliance.*] (omitted)

Section 49. [*Insurance Policies.*]

(a) Every policy or contract for the insurance of compensation herein provided for shall be deemed to be made subject to the provisions of this act and provision thereof inconsistent with the act shall be deemed to be reformed to conform with the provisions of this act.

(b) An insurer insuring the liability of an employer under this act shall be deemed to be the insurer for all employees of the employer within the protection of this act. However, if specifically authorized by the Director, a separate insurance policy may be issued for a specified plant or work location if the liability of such employer under this act to all his other employees is otherwise secured.

Section 50. [*Claims Services and Medical Supervision.*] (omitted)

Section 51. [*Assigned Risk.*]

The [Insurance Commissioner], after consultation with carriers authorized to issue workmen's compensation policies in this State, shall put into effect a reasonable system for the equitable apportionment among such carriers of applicants for such policies who are in good faith entitled to but are unable to procure such policies through ordinary methods. Such system shall be so drawn as to guarantee that such an applicant, if not in default on workmen's compensation premiums, shall, following his application to the assigned risk system and tender of required premium, be covered by workmen's compensation insurance. When any such system has been approved, all such carriers shall subscribe thereto and participate therein. Assignment shall be in such manner that, as far as practicable, no carrier shall be assigned a larger proportion of compensation premiums under assigned policies during any calendar year than that which the total of compensation premiums written in the State by such carrier during the preceding year bears to the total compensation premiums written in the State by all such carriers during the preceding calendar year.

Section 52. [*Performance of Insurance Organization.*] (omitted)

Section 53. [*Payment Pending Determination of Policy Coverage.*]

Whenever any claim is presented and the claimant's right to compensation is not in issue, but the issue of liability is raised as between an employer and a carrier or between two or more employers or carriers, the Director shall order payment of compensation to be made immediately by one or more of such employers or carriers. The Director may order any such employer or carrier to deposit the amount of the award or to give such security therefor as he may deem satisfactory. When the issue is finally resolved, an employer or carrier held not liable shall be reimbursed for any such payments by the employer or carrier held liable and any deposit or security so made shall be returned.

Section 54. [*Penalty for Failure to Secure Compensation.*]

(a) Any employer required to secure the payment of compensation under this act who willfully fails to secure the payment of such compensation shall be guilty of a [misdemeanor] and upon conviction thereof shall be punished by a fine of not more than [$1,000], or by imprisonment for not more than [one year], or by both such fine and imprisonment; and in any case where the employer is a corporation any officer or employee of the corporation who had authority to secure payment of compensation on behalf of the corporation and willfully failed to do so shall be individually liable to a similar fine and imprisonment; and such officer or employee shall be personally liable jointly and severally with such corporation for any compensation which may accrue under this act in respect to any injury which may occur to any employee of such corporation while it shall so fail to secure the payment of compensation as required by Section 46 of this act. [The fines shall be paid directly by the court to the Director for deposit in the Uninsured Employers' Fund provided in Section 56.]

(b) Any employer who knowingly transfers, sells, encumbers, assigns, or in any manner disposes of, conceals, secretes, or destroys any property or records belonging to such employer, after one of his employees has been injured within the purview of this act, and with intent to avoid the payment of compensation under this act to such employee or his dependents, shall be guilty of a [misdemeanor] and, upon conviction thereof, shall be punished by a fine of not more than [$1,000] or by imprisonment for not more than [one year], or by both such fine and imprisonment; and in any case where such employer is a corporation, any officer or employee thereof, if knowingly participating or acquiescing in the act, shall be also individually liable to such penalty of imprisonment as well as joint and severally liable with such corporation for such fine.

(c) An employer who has failed to secure payment of compensation for more than 20 days shall pay into the Uninsured Employers' Fund provided in Section 56 as a civil penalty for such failure an amount equal to 1 per centum of his payroll of employees covered by this act for the time during which such failure continued but for not more than three consecutive years. The assessment shall be made by the Director for the year or years immediately preceding the date on which such assessment is made against the employer. The assessment may be collected as a civil penalty in an action brought by the Director against the employer for and on behalf of the Uninsured Employers' Fund. All such assessments shall be deposited in the Uninsured Employers' Fund.

(d) This section shall not affect any other liability of the employer under this act.

Section 55. [*Special Fund.*]

(a) There is hereby established in the [State Treasury] a Special Fund for the sole purpose of making payments in accordance with the provisions of Section 20, Section 21 and this section. The Fund shall be administered by the Director. The [State Treasurer] shall be the custodian of the Fund and all moneys and securities in the Fund shall be held in trust by the [State Treasurer] and shall not be money or property of the State.

(b) The [State Treasurer] is authorized to disburse moneys from the Fund only upon written order of the Director. He shall be required to give bond in an amount to be fixed and with securities approved by the Director conditioned upon the faithful performance of his duty as custodian of the Fund. The premium of the bond shall be paid out of the Fund.

(c) Each carrier shall under regulations prescribed by the Director make payments to the Fund in an amount equal to that proportion of [175] percent of the total disbursement made from the Fund during the preceding calendar year less the amount of the net assets in the Fund as of December 31 of the preceding calendar year, which the total income benefits paid by such carrier bore to the total income benefits paid by all carriers during the fiscal year which ended within the preceding calendar year. An employer who has ceased to be a self-insurer shall continue to be liable for any assessments into the Fund on account of any income benefits paid by him during such fiscal year.

(d) Where there has been default in the payment of compensation due to the insolvency of an insured employer and his carrier or a self-insured employer, payment of any compensation remaining unpaid shall be made from the Special Fund.[9] Such employer and carrier, or self-insured employer and his surety, if any, shall be liable for payment into the Fund of the amounts paid therefrom by the Director under the authority of this subsection, and for the purposes of enforcing this liability, the Director, for the benefit of the Fund, shall be subrogated to all the rights of the person receiving such compensation.

(e) The Director shall be charged with the conservation of the assets of the Fund. In furtherance of this purpose, the Attorney General shall appoint a member of his staff to represent the Fund in all proceedings brought to enforce claims against the Fund.

Alternative (omitted)

Section 56. [*Uninsured Employers' Fund.*]

(a) There is hereby authorized in the [State Treasury] an Uninsured Employers' Fund for the purpose of making payments in accordance with the provisions of subsection (d) of this section. The Fund shall be administered by the Director. The [State Treasurer] shall be the custodian of the Fund and all moneys and securities in the Fund shall be held in trust by the [State Treasurer] and shall not be money or property of the State.

[9] This provision would have to be modified in the many States which already have a security or guarantee fund for insurance companies. A separate security fund for self-insurers would have to be created in those States.

(b) The [State Treasurer] is authorized to disburse moneys from the Fund only upon written order of the Director. He shall be required to give bond in an amount to be fixed and with securities approved by the Director conditioned upon the faithful performance of his duty as custodian of the Fund. The premium of the bond shall be paid out of the Fund.

(c) (c) All amounts collected as fines and penalties under this act except those collected under Section 42(a) and (b) shall be paid into the Uninsured Employers' Fund. The Fund shall become operative when the amount in the Fund reaches [$___].

(d) Once the Uninsured Employers' Fund has become operative, compensation thereafter shall be paid from it when there has been default in the payment of compensation due to the failure of an employer to secure payment of compensation as provided by this act. Such employer shall be liable for payment into the Fund of the amounts authorized to be paid therefrom under the authority of this subsection and for the purposes of enforcing this liability the Director, for the benefit of the Fund, shall be subrogated to all the rights of the person receiving such compensation.

(e) The Director shall be charged with the conservation of the assets of the Fund. In furtherance of this purpose, the Attorney General shall appoint a member of his staff to represent the Fund in all proceedings brought to enforce claims against or on behalf of the Fund.

PART VI. ADMINISTRATION

Section 57. [Agency to Administer the Act.]

(a) This act shall be administered by the Director of the [state administrative agency][10] who shall devote his entire time to the duties of his office. The Governor shall appoint the Director[, by and with the advice and consent of the Senate,] on the basis of administrative ability, education and training, and experience relevant to the duties of the Director under this act. Upon the expiration of his term the Director shall continue to serve until his successor shall have been appointed and qualified. [Before entering upon his duties the Director shall take and subscribe to an oath or affirmation to support the Constitution of the United States and of this State and to faithfully discharge the duties of his office.] Because cumulative experience and continuity in office are essential to the proper administration of a workmen's compensation and rehabilitation law, it is hereby declared to be in

[10] Provision is made for identifying the administration agency in Section 2. [*Definitions.*]

the public interest to continue the Director in office during good behavior and as long as efficiency is demonstrated. The Director may be removed by the Governor for cause, prior to the expiration of his term, but shall be furnished a written copy of the charges against him and shall be accorded a public hearing if he requests it. [He shall be paid a salary at the rate of [$___] per year.][11]

(b) The Director shall appoint such hearing officers and other employees, other than employees and assistants of the Workmen's Compensation Appeals Board, and may establish such branch offices, divisions, sections and advisory committees as he deems necessary to administer the Workmen's Compensation and Rehabilitation Law, and such other offices and committees as are provided for by this act. All employees engaged in the administration of the act shall devote their entire time to their duties. [They shall take and subscribe to an oath or affirmation to support the Constitution of the United States and of this State, and to discharge faithfully the duties of office or employment.] All hearing officers and other employees shall be employed under the [state merit and classification system.]

(c) Hearing officers appointed after the effective date of this act must be lawyers licensed to practice in this State. They shall devote full time to their duties and shall not engage in the private practice of law.

Section 58. [Appeals Board.][12]

(a) There is hereby created a Workmen's Compensation Appeals Board composed of three[13] members appointed by the Governor [by and with the advice and consent of the Senate] for terms of nine years each, except that the terms of members first appointed shall be for three, six, and nine years respectively as designated by the Governor at the time of appointments. A member of the Board must be a lawyer licensed to practice in this State. The Governor shall designate the chairman of the Board. Each member shall hold office until his successor is appointed and qualified. Because cumulative experience and continuity in office are essential to the proper handling of appeals under a workmen's compensation and rehabilitation law, it is hereby declared to be in the public interest to continue Board members in office as long as

---

[11] In States having a general pay act, the Director's salary should be fixed therein.

[12] This full-time Board is recommended for States where the volume of cases is sufficient to justify it. In States where the workload would not warrant a full-time Board, it may be possible for members of the Board to be utilized by the State in similar capacities.

[13] In larger States the Board should have five or more members with rotating terms, and other relevant subsections should be adjusted accordingly, including the use of panels where desired.

efficiency is demonstrated. The members shall devote full time to their duties as members of the Board and shall not engage in the private practice of law. The Governor may at any time remove any member for cause after furnishing him with a written copy of the charges against him and giving him a public hearing if he requests it. Each member of the Board shall be paid a salary at the rate of not less than the minimum salary of [a judge of a state court of general jurisdiction].

(b) The Board shall have power to decide appeals from compensation orders of the Director or his hearing officers and it shall have authority to consider and decide all matters of fact and questions of law properly cognizable under this act.

(c) A decision concurred in by any two members shall constitute a decision of the Board.

(d) A vacancy in the Board, if there remain two members of it, shall not impair the authority of two members to act.

(e) The chairman of the Board shall employ such employees as may be required to carry out the Board's duties under this act, shall assign the work of the Board to the members thereof and its employees, and shall serve as administrative officer of the Board.

(f) The Board shall be within the [state administrative agency] for budgetary and administrative purposes only.

Section 59. [*Authority to Adopt Rules and Regulations.*]

The Director and the Board each shall have authority to adopt reasonable rules and regulations within their respective areas of responsibility, after notice and public hearing, if requested, for effecting the purposes of this act. All rules and regulations, upon adoption, shall be published and be made available to the public, and, if not inconsistent with law, shall be binding in the administration of this act.

Section 60. [*Location of Office.*] (omitted)

Section 61. [*Seal.*] (omitted)

Section 62. [*Operating Expenses.*] (omitted)

Section 63. [*Administration Fund.*] (omitted)

Section 64. [*Reports.*]

(a) Each year the Director shall make a report to the Governor and through him to the [State Legislature] on the operation of this act, including suggestions and recommendations as to improvements in the law and administration thereof, a detailed statement of receipts and expenditures, and a statistical analysis of industrial injury experience and compensation costs.

(b) The Director shall prepare and publish such other statistical and informational reports and analyses based upon the reports and records available which, in his opinion, will be useful in increasing public understanding of the purposes, effectiveness, costs, coverage, and administrative procedures of workmen's compensation and rehabilitation in the State; and in providing basic information regarding the occurrence and sources of work injuries for the use of public and private agencies engaged in industrial injury prevention activities.

Section 65. [*Cooperation With Other Agencies.*] (omitted)

Section 66. [*Severability.*] (omitted)

Section 67. [*Laws Repealed.*] (omitted)

Section 68. [*Effective Date.*]

[Insert effective date.]

APPENDIX B

FEDERAL EMPLOYERS' LIABILITY ACT

■ ■ ■

53 STAT. 1404 (1908) AS AMENDED, 45 U.S.C.A. § 51.

§ 51. Liability of common carriers by railroad, in interstate or foreign commerce, for injuries to employees from negligence; definition of employees

Every common carrier by railroad while engaging in commerce between any of the several States or Territories, or between any of the States and Territories, or between the District of Columbia and any of the States or Territories, or between the District of Columbia or any of the States or Territories and any foreign nation or nations, shall be liable in damages to any person suffering injury while he is employed by such carrier in such commerce, or, in case of the death of such employee, to his or her personal representative, for the benefit of the surviving widow or husband and children of such employee; and, if none, then of such employee's parents; and, if none, then of the next of kin dependent upon such employee, for such injury or death resulting in whole or in part from the negligence of any of the officers, agents, or employees of such carrier, or by reason of any defect or insufficiency, due to its negligence, in its cars, engines, appliances, machinery, track, roadbed, works, boats, wharves, or other equipment.

Any employee of a carrier, any part of whose duties as such employee shall be the furtherance of interstate or foreign commerce; or shall, in any way directly or closely and substantially affect such commerce as above set forth shall, for the purposes of this chapter, be considered as being employed by such carrier in such commerce and shall be considered as entitled to the benefits of this chapter.

§ 52. (Makes Act applicable to railroads in Territories and other Possessions of the United States.)

§ 53. Contributory negligence; diminution of damages

In all actions on and after April 22, 1908 brought against any such common carrier by railroad under or by virtue of any of the provisions of this chapter to recover damages for personal injuries to an employee, or where such injuries have resulted in his death, the fact that the employee may have been guilty of contributory negligence shall not bar a recovery, but the damages shall be diminished by the jury in proportion to the amount of negligence attributable to such employee: *Provided,* That no such employee who may be injured or killed shall be held to have been guilty of contributory negligence in any case where the violation by such common carrier of any statute enacted for the safety of employees contributed to the injury or death of such employee.

§ 54. Assumption of risks of employment

In any action brought against any common carrier under or by virtue of any of the provisions of this chapter to recover damages for injuries to, or the death of, any of its employees, such employee shall not be held to have assumed the risks of his employment in any case where such injury or death resulted in whole or in part from the negligence of any of the officers, agents, or employees of such carrier; and no employee shall be held to have assumed the risks of his employment in any case where the violation by such common carrier of any statute enacted for the safety of employees contributed to the injury or death of such employee.

* * *

§ 56. Actions; limitation; concurrent jurisdiction of courts

No action shall be maintained under this chapter unless commenced within three years from the date the cause of action accrued.

Under this chapter an action may be brought in a district court of the United States, in the district of the residence of the defendant, or in which the cause of action arose, or in which the defendant shall be doing business at the time of commencing such action. The jurisdiction of the courts of the United States under this chapter shall be concurrent with that of the courts of the several States.

INDEX

References are to Pages